MANAGERIAL ACCOUNTING

AN INTRODUCTION TO CONCEPTS, METHODS, AND USES

■

FOURTH EDITION

The HBJ Accounting Series

MANAGERIAL ACCOUNTING

AN INTRODUCTION TO CONCEPTS, METHODS, AND USES

■

FOURTH EDITION

MICHAEL W. MAHER, Ph.D., CPA
University of California—Davis

CLYDE P. STICKNEY, D.B.A., CPA
Dartmouth College

ROMAN L. WEIL, Ph.D., CPA, CMA
University of Chicago

SIDNEY DAVIDSON, Ph.D., CPA
University of Chicago

THE DRYDEN PRESS
HARCOURT BRACE COLLEGE PUBLISHERS
Fort Worth Philadelphia San Diego
New York Orlando Austin San Antonio
Toronto Montreal London Sydney Tokyo

ISBN: 0-15-554768-2

Library of Congress Catalog Card Number: 88-80622

Printed in the United States of America

For our students, with thanks.

Whatever be the detail with which you cram your students, the chance of their meeting in after-life exactly that detail is almost infinitesimal; and if they do meet it, they will probably have forgotten what you taught them about it. The really useful training yields a comprehension of a few general principles with a thorough grounding in the way they apply to a variety of concrete details. In subsequent practice the students will have forgotten your particular details; but they will remember by an unconscious common sense how to apply principles to immediate circumstances.

Alfred North Whitehead
The Aims of Education and Other Essays

Preface

This book provides an introduction to managerial accounting that (1) is logically organized around the major uses of managerial accounting; (2) comprehensively covers managerial accounting topics; and (3) treats managerial accounting as a subject in its own right, not as a subset of financial accounting, economics, or operations research. Introductory undergraduate, graduate, or executive programs can use this book. We have included a variety of end-of-chapter materials, including straightforward exercises, thought-provoking problems, and decision-making cases.

Major Features of the Book

This book contains many features that differentiate it from other textbooks in the field.

Organization

We have logically organized chapters into major parts to provide a cohesive theme. Managerial accounting textbooks often give the appearance that the subject comprises many diverse and unrelated topics. Students respond negatively to this apparent lack of structure. We have organized this book into parts that provide a logical connection among chapters. For example, Part Two contains three chapters dealing with cost methods and systems and Part Three contains five chapters dealing with the use of accounting information for managerial decision making.

Although we have organized the chapters logically into major parts, we allow ample flexibility in sequencing and omitting chapters, as discussed below in "Organization and Use of This Book."

User Orientation

This book stresses the use of financial information for managerial purposes on the job. The text examples and end-of-chapter materials focus on interpretation and application of accounting information.

Students' motivation to learn concepts and methods relates directly to their belief that they can apply the topic in the real world. Most chapters contain short inserts called "Managerial Applications," which describe managerial issues involving accounting choices. Several Managerial Applications discuss the impact of high technology on accounting systems, for example, we feature Hewlett-Packard, ITT, United Airlines, Los Angeles Kings, and American National Bank.

Nonmanufacturing Applications

We have included numerous examples and applications to nonmanufacturing settings. Nearly half of the text examples and assignment materials are nonmanufacturing. Traditionally, accountants have considered certain topics, like cost accumulation and variance analysis, to be the domain of manufacturing, but our chapters on these topics show how to use the concepts in nonmanufacturing organizations.

Extensive Assignment Materials

Extensive assignment materials cover a wide range of questions, exercises, problems, and cases. We have divided the assignment material into four groups:

1. *Questions* review important concepts and terms in the chapter.
2. *Exercises* deal with single concepts or techniques in the chapter.
3. *Problems* challenge students more than exercises and cover more than one concept in the chapter.
4. *Integrative problems and cases* require students to make decisions using accounting information. They integrate materials from several chapters.

Self-Study Materials

Self-study problems comprise a vital part of this text. Many chapters have three or four self-study problems. In addition to self-study problems, we have included "Suggested Solutions to Even-Numbered Exercises" at the end of every chapter with exercises. These materials give students ample opportunity for feedback on their understanding of the text.

Synthesis Chapter

Chapter 16 uniquely synthesizes materials from previous chapters. This chapter also discusses situations where management inappropriately uses data designed for one purpose for a different purpose. The discussion incorporates many examples and cases that present complex issues and require students to draw on previous chapters to address the issues. Graduate and executive classes find this chapter particularly useful.

Conceptual Approach

We present managerial accounting concepts to prepare students to focus on relevant issues in new and different situations. This preparation is more important than ever with the increased emphasis on developing critical thinking skills in current curricula. The Accounting Education Change Commission argues for a more conceptual approach to accounting education. We agree, and provide it in this book. Methods follow concepts, so students start with the big picture before they learn specific procedures. The book supports this conceptual approach with numerous examples and many short exercises.

For example, our presentation of variances in Chapters 12, 13, and 14 starts with a "big picture" comparison of budgeted and achieved results, then presents variance calculations as a finer division of the budget versus achieved comparison. This approach has two advantages. First, it keeps the "big picture" and the purpose of variance calculations in students' minds; they do not lose sight of their overall objectives as they analyze detailed variances. Second, students find the approach intuitive. They may forget how to compute particular variances, but they will remember the overall model, which will enable them to "invent" variance analysis later.

Organization and Use of This Book

We divided the book into five major parts, as follows: Part One, Fundamental Concepts, Chapters 1–2; Part Two, Cost Methods and Systems, Chapters 3–5; Part Three, Managerial Decision Making, Chapters 6–10; Part Four, Managerial Planning and Performance Evaluation, Chapters 11–15; and Part Five, Special Topics, Chapters 16–18.

Part One   covers fundamental concepts and provides an overview of managerial accounting. Instructors may cover the other parts in any sequence, or omit them, after Part One, as the diagram below shows:

Part One ─── → Part Two → Part Three → Part Four
             → Part Three → Part Two → Part Four
             → Part Two → Part Four → Part Three
             → ...

Part Two   describes cost methods and systems companies use. Chapter 3 discusses alternative methods of measuring product costs. Chapter 4 shows how cost flows appear in the accounting systems companies commonly use, including service organizations. Chapter 5 discusses cost allocation.

Part Three   discusses concepts and methods useful for managerial decision making. Chapter 6 discusses methods of estimating cost behavior. Chapters 7 and 8 discuss the use of accounting data in short-run decision making, where capacity is held constant. Chapters 9 and 10 discuss the use of accounting in long-run decision making involving capital budgeting.

Part Four discusses managerial planning, control, and internal performance evaluation. Chapter 11 provides an overview of the planning and control process and discusses economic and behavioral issues in performance evaluation. Chapter 12 considers the development of budgets as tools for planning and control. Chapters 13 and 14 deal with cost variances. Chapter 13 presents the fundamental cost variance model that applies to any type of manufacturing or nonmanufacturing cost. Chapter 14 extends the analysis to cases in which firms use standard costs to measure inventory costs. Chapter 15 focuses on the use of accounting in performance monitoring in decentralized operations.

Part Five deals with special topics. Chapter 16 both synthesizes materials in previous chapters and compares managerial decision making with the way firms report managerial actions. This chapter describes situations where managers may have incentives to take actions that do not serve the best interests of the firm but that make them look good to reviewers of accounting reports. The assignment material includes cases on financial fraud. Chapters 17 and 18 present an overview of financial accounting. For readers familiar with financial accounting, these chapters will serve as a review. Readers who have not studied financial accounting can use these chapters as an introduction to financial accounting concepts, methods, and uses. These chapters are independent of the rest of the book and students may read them at any time.

The appendix to the book discusses compound interest calculations used in discounted cash flow analysis. This appendix is also independent of the rest of the book. The glossary defines comprehensively the concepts and terms used in managerial accounting.

Instructors can cover any of the above chapters out of sequence or omit them, with two exceptions: Chapter 10 should follow Chapter 9 and Chapter 14 should follow Chapter 13.

Related Materials Accompanying the Text

Instructor's Manual and Test Bank

The manual includes sample course structures and class assignments, chapter overviews and outlines, more new examination questions and solutions, and additional resources for the instructor. For example, the manual contains a master list of Check Figures that instructors may duplicate in class quantities.

Solutions Manual

This manual contains responses to questions and solutions to all exercises, problems, and cases. We have thoroughly checked these solutions to eliminate errors.

Study Guide

Professor Anne J. Rich has prepared a student study guide to accompany this text. For each chapter and the appendix, it includes

1. An outline of the chapter with emphasis on key points.
2. A set of matching (term and definition) questions and answers for students' self-help.
3. Several exercises and problems for students' self-help with answers or suggested solutions.
4. A study plan designed to help students solve the problems in the text.
5. Instructions on how to use the student software (see the following for more details).

Student Software

Professors Anne J. Rich and Biagio G. Coppolella have prepared this supplement to give students experience in solving management accounting problems using electronic spreadsheets. This supplement enables students to solve selected problems from this text using the templates provided. Professor Rich provides notes and comments on using the software for students in the *Study Guide* and for the instructor in the *Instructor's Manual*.

Computerized Test Bank

For the first time the test bank is now available in SOPH-TEST® computerized format for most DOS-based and Macintosh personal computers.

Transparencies

New to this edition, a set of acetate transparencies duplicates many of the exhibits in the textbook and solutions to most of the end-of-chapter problems.

Acknowledgments

We gratefully acknowledge the helpful criticisms and suggestions from the following people who reviewed the manuscript at various stages: Paul K. Chaney, Vanderbilt University; Stephen V. Senge, Western Washington University; Philip H. Vorherr, University of Cincinnati; and Roland M. Wright, Belmont College. We further acknowledge the reviewers of the third edition, whose comments guided some of our efforts in this edition as well: Jane L. Butt, Duke University; Fred J. Croop, Wilkes College; Dennis C. Daly, University of Minnesota; Michael Haselkorn, Bentley College; Ilene Kleinsorge, Oregon State University; Larry Lewis, Gonzaga University; Eric W. Noreen, University of Washington; Denis Raihall, Drexel University; Michael F. van Breda, Southern Methodist University; and S. Mark Young, University of Colorado.

Thomas Horton and Daughters, Inc., has given us permission to reproduce material from *Accounting: The Language of Business*. The following have consented to let us use problems or cases they prepared: Case Clearing House, David O. Green, David Solomons, George Sorter, James Reece, James Patell, Gordon Shillinglaw, Jean Lim, David Croll, Robert Colson, and Edward Deakin. Material from the Uniform CPA Examinations and Unofficial Answers, copyright by the American Institute of Certified Public Accountants, Inc., is adapted with permission. Permission has been received from the Institute of Certified Management Accountants of the National Association of Accountants to use questions and/or unofficial answers from past CMA examinations.

We thank the following people for their help in preparing this book: Martin Chew, Betsy MacLean, and Katherine Xenophon-Rybowiak. Cherie Weil prepared the index. Rick Antle, Yale University; Robert H. Colson, Case Western University; Peter Easton, Macquarie University; Timothy Farmer, University of Missouri—St. Louis; Robert Lipe, University of Michigan; M. Laurentius Marais, Mark Penno, and Katherine Schipper, all of University of Chicago, have all provided particularly thought-provoking comments.

Finally, we thank Bill Teague, Paul Raymond, Cheryl Hauser, Leslie Leland, Suzanne Montazer, Avery Hallowell, and Jacqui Parker of Harcourt Brace Jovanovich for their assistance in the preparation of this book.

M.W.M.

C.P.S.

R.L.W.

S.D.

Contents

...PART ONE...

Fundamental Concepts

...

This part contains two chapters that lay the foundation for subsequent chapters. Chapter 1 provides an overview of managerial accounting, shows how decision makers use it, and contrasts it with financial accounting. Chapter 2 discusses cost behavior and the major cost concepts that we use in this book.

... CHAPTER 1 ...

The Management Process and Accounting Information

Chapter Outline

- Uses of Accounting Information
- Organizational Environment
- Professional Environment
- Costs and Benefits of Accounting
- Organization of the Book
- Appendix 1.1: The Value of Information

Accounting affects virtually everyone working in businesses, nonprofit organizations, governmental units, and other organized activities. Accounting helps us make decisions: Should we expand or contract our business? Should we close a particular store? Should we open an organ transplant unit in the hospital? We also use accounting in numerous planning and performance evaluation contexts, including forecasting, budgeting, and employee performance evaluation.

Accounting affects even employees who do not use it directly. Workers in fast-food restaurants may not use accounting themselves, for example, but their superiors use accounting information in ascertaining whether a particular restaurant should remain open and whether to increase or decrease employees' hours.

About 80 percent of small businesses do not survive for more than 5 years. Often they fail because they have inadequate accounting information to help control costs, forecast cash needs, and plan for growth. Organizations with poor accounting systems have difficulty obtaining financing from banks and shareholders. Cost overruns on electrical utility construction projects and defense contracts, small business failures, and rising health care costs are only a few examples of problems resulting from inadequate knowledge about costs.

Accounting touches our lives more than we may think. If you have observed store or mill openings or closings, airline fare discounting, clothing store merchandise sales, or employee hirings to help with seasonal increases in activity at ski resorts or department stores, you have seen the results of decisions that use accounting information.

Exhibit 1.1 shows that accounting is part of an organization's information system, which includes both financial and nonfinancial data. Accounting commonly divides into financial accounting and managerial accounting. **Financial accounting** concerns preparing general purpose reports for persons outside an organization to use. Such users include shareholders (owners) of a corporation, creditors (those who lend money to a business), financial analysts, labor unions, government regulators, and the like. External users wish primarily to review and evaluate the operations and financial status of the business as a whole.

Managerial accounting, on the other hand, concerns providing information that managers inside the organization will use. For example, a production manager wants a report on the number of units of product various workers manufacture in order to evaluate their performance. A sales manager wants a report showing the relative profitability of two products in order to focus selling efforts.

Exhibit 1.1

Accounting as Part of the Information System

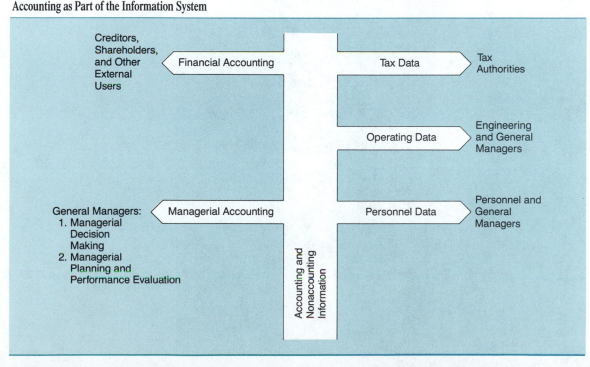

Exhibit 1.2

Managerial Processes and Accounting Information

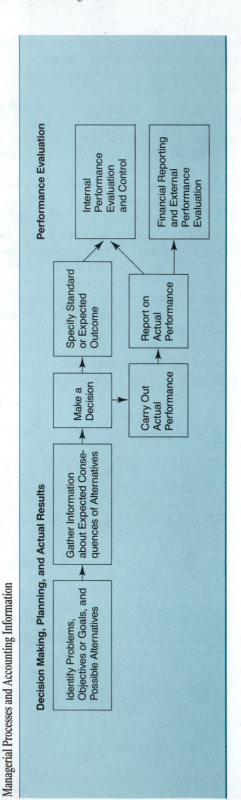

Decision Making, Planning, and Actual Results

Identify Problems, Objectives or Goals, and Possible Alternatives

Gather Information about Expected Consequences of Alternatives

Make a Decision

Specify Standard or Expected Outcome

Carry Out Actual Performance

Report on Actual Performance

Performance Evaluation

Internal Performance Evaluation and Control

Financial Reporting and External Performance Evaluation

Financial accounting reports that publicly held companies prepare are readily available in libraries or from the companies themselves. Firms do not distribute managerial accounting reports widely outside of companies, however, because they often contain confidential information. Consequently, we have relied on research and consulting experience to develop actual managerial accounting examples for this book.

This book focuses on managerial accounting. We consider how accounting aids management in making decisions and in planning and controlling operations. We assume that all of the readers of this book will use accounting data in their careers, though some readers will also be accounting professionals. Consequently, we take a user's perspective of accounting—we want you to understand accounting systems so you can effectively use the data they generate.

Uses of Accounting Information

Accounting provides information for three general uses, as Exhibit 1.2 shows: (1) managerial decision making; (2) managerial planning, control, and internal performance evaluation; and (3) financial reporting and external performance evaluation by shareholders and creditors. This book concentrates on the first two uses. Financial accounting books and courses focus on the third use.

Relations among Three Uses of Accounting

Exhibit 1.2 illustrates the relations among the three principal uses of accounting information discussed in this section. Note the close relation between the managerial decision-making process and the managerial planning and control process. In making a decision, management forms expectations about hypothetical performance if everything goes according to plan. The results of the internal performance evaluation in one period become inputs into the planning and decision-making process of the next period.

Managerial Decision Making

The decision-making process includes the following steps, as the first three boxes in Exhibit 1.2 show:

1. Identify a problem requiring managerial action.
2. Specify the objective or goal to be achieved (for example, maximize return on investment).
3. List the possible alternative courses of action.
4. Gather information about the consequences of each alternative.
5. Make a decision by selecting one of the alternatives.

Managerial accounting plays a critical role in step **4** of the decision-making process.

Example   A health maintenance organization is considering adding dental care to the services it provides. Management wishes to predict the expected costs of operating the proposed dental care service. The managerial accountant must obtain cost data from the records of costs incurred in the past for providing similar types of services. Management and the accountants would then use these data to help project the costs they expect to incur from the proposed dental care service.

Managerial Planning, Control, and Internal Performance Evaluation

The planning and control process includes the following steps or components:

1. Decide on a criterion (standard or budget) specifying what actual performance should be.
2. Measure the results of actual performance.
3. Compare actual performance with the criterion. This evaluation helps management assess actions already taken and decide which courses of action it should take in the future.

Managerial accounting plays an important role in the planning and control process. The information generated in the decision-making process helps establish expectations of performance. In addition, it provides actual results to compare with expectations.

Example   Assume the health maintenance organization in the previous example decided to add the dental care service. An important input to that decision was that management expected the first year's operating costs to be $5 million. This $5 million cost projection could serve as the budget or standard for evaluating the performance of the dental service managers.

If the costs varied significantly from $5 million, management would make an effort to ascertain the cause of the difference, or *variance,* as accounting calls it, between anticipated and actual costs. If factors or conditions that the dental service managers could not control caused the variance, management probably would not hold them responsible for it. For example, a dental technicians' strike might cause a labor shortage, thereby resulting in a loss in sales that managers could not control. Similarly, management might not hold the dental service managers responsible for an unanticipated increase in the cost of materials used for dental work.

Financial Accounting: External Financial Reporting and Performance Evaluation

In contrast to managerial accounting reports prepared for internal use, the financial reports prepared for users external to publicly held firms must follow certain specified formats and measurement rules. For example, a publicly held firm must present its statement of financial position (or balance sheet), statement of net income, and statement of cash flows each year in accordance with generally accepted accounting principles.

Misuse of Accounting Information

Different purposes require different types of accounting data. These purposes include external reporting, tax return preparation, and report preparation for regulatory authorities and for managerial purposes. Firms often mistakenly use data for one purpose that were intended for another. For example, many companies use the

LIFO (last-in, first-out) inventory cost flow assumption and accelerated depreciation for tax purposes; however, these data are not necessarily appropriate for internal, managerial uses.

Further, most managerial decisions require more detailed data than external financial reports provide. For instance, in General Electric's external financial statements, the balance sheet shows single amounts for inventory valuations and the income statement shows single amounts for cost of goods sold expense summarized for all product lines. For managerial purposes, however, management would prefer detailed data about the cost of each of several hundred products. The company's external financial statements provide some revenue and profit data for each major business segment, but managerial purposes would require more detailed information about the cost of operating each plant, department, and division.

Managerial accounting should follow the needs of the user. Managers should identify the problems, goals, and alternatives first, then obtain the information appropriate for decision making.

Managers sometimes assume that they must use the same accounting data that they report to shareholders or in tax returns in their decision making, planning, and other managerial activities. That is simply not true. If the firm thoughtfully designs its basic transaction recording and processing system, accountants can adapt the data to meet multiple needs.

Accountants currently face the challenge of designing systems with sufficient flexibility to provide data for multiple purposes. And managers face the challenge of understanding accounting well enough to know what information to request and to expect from accountants.

Differences between Financial and Managerial Accounting

Managerial and financial accounting differ fundamentally. These differences include the following:

Financial Accounting	Managerial Accounting
Users	
External users of information—usually shareholders, financial analysts, and creditors.	Internal users of information—usually managers.
Generally Accepted Accounting Principles	
Compliance with generally accepted accounting principles.	Need not comply with generally accepted accounting principles.
Future versus Past	
Uses historical data in evaluating performance of the firm and its managers by outsiders.	Uses estimates of the future for decision making and historical data for internal performance evaluation.
Reporting Requirements	
Regulations often specify how much information is enough.	Internal cost/benefit evaluation dictates how much information is enough.
Detail Presented	
Presents summary data.	Requires more detailed data about product costs, revenues, and profits.

Exhibit 1.3

Organization Chart
E.I. du Pont de Nemours & Company

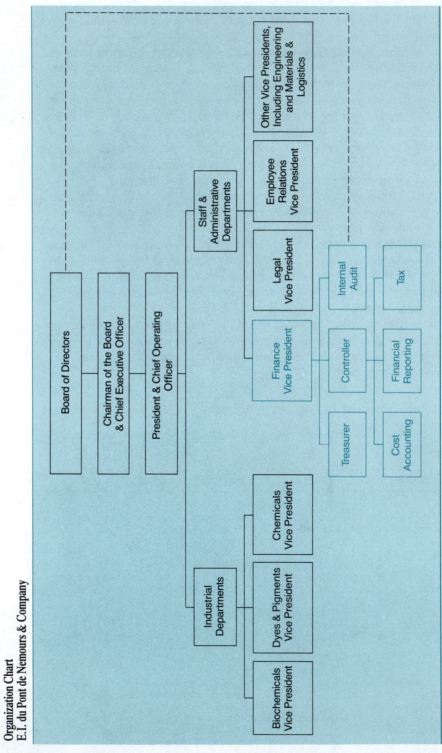

Organizational Environment

Who manages the accounting function in organizations? In most corporate organizations, the **controller** is the chief accounting officer. Recognizing the importance of this function, many organizations place the controller in the same organization rank as the other corporate vice presidents. In other organizations, the controller and the treasurer may both report a financial vice president, who is responsible for both the accounting and financial affairs of the corporation. (The activity that we call "managerial accounting" is known as "finance" in many organizations.) Exhibit 1.3 shows how the finance and accounting functions fit into a typical organization chart, in this case, an abbreviated version of du Pont's organization chart.

Controller

As the chief accounting officer, the controller usually exercises authority both for accounting within the organization and for external reporting. Internally, the controller oversees the supplying of accounting data to operating management. The controller also usually oversees the company's internal control system. External reports include reports to taxing authorities and regulatory bodies such as the Securities and Exchange Commission, as well as the financial statements for shareholders. The controller generally is in charge of all accounting records, including those for inventories; receivables and payables; and property, plant, and equipment. The controller sometimes supervises data processing operations, but frequently data processing is an independent department.

Internal Audit

The **internal audit** department provides a variety of auditing and consulting services in many organizations, including auditing internal controls, auditing data reported inside the company, and assisting external auditors in their audit of an organization's external financial reports. In some organizations, internal auditors are internal consultants who provide an independent perspective on problems operating managers face. Such auditors are usually called "operational auditors." Many auditors in the federal government are operational auditors.

The internal audit manager sometimes reports directly to the controller. Some companies recognize the possibility for conflicts between the controller's record-keeping role and the audit function, however, so they have the internal audit supervisor report directly to the controller's superior. Top management usually gives the internal audit director authority to communicate directly to the audit committee of the board of directors.

Treasurer

The corporate **treasurer** is the manager in charge of raising cash for operations and managing cash and near-cash assets. The treasurer handles credit reviews and sets policy for collecting receivables. The treasurer normally handles relations with banks and other lending or financing sources, including public issues of shares or debt.

Professional Environment

Accountants are not only part of the management team, they are also professionals. Their professional environment influences the types of reports and data bases developed in companies.

Accounting Authorities

Throughout this book we refer to the **generally accepted accounting principles (GAAP)** that govern financial accounting. Firms use these accounting principles in preparing their external financial statements. Although generally accepted accounting principles or other rules and guidelines (such as the income tax laws) do not constrain managerial accounting, the fact that the accounting system must produce reports conforming with those regulations has implications for managerial accounting. Some companies design their accounting systems primarily to comply with such rules and only secondarily to meet managerial needs. The following organizations are important regulatory agencies that contribute to generally accepted principles of accounting.

Securities and Exchange Commission   The U.S. Congress has granted the **Securities and Exchange Commission (SEC)** the legal authority to prescribe accounting principles that most corporations must follow. The SEC has used its power sparingly, however.

Financial Accounting Standards Board   Since 1973, the **Financial Accounting Standards Board (FASB)** has been the highest nongovernmental authority on generally accepted accounting principles. The FASB issues *Statements of Financial Accounting Standards* (and *Interpretations* of these statements) from time to time, establishing or clarifying generally accepted accounting principles.

American Institute of Certified Public Accountants   The American Institute of Certified Public Accountants (AICPA) is the national organization of certified public accountants. Its publications and committees influence the development of accounting principles and auditing practices. It actively promulgates standards of ethics and reviews conduct within the profession.

Internal Revenue Service   Income tax legislation and administration have influenced the practice of accounting, although income tax requirements in themselves do not establish principles and practices for external or internal reporting. The *Internal Revenue Code* (passed by Congress), the *Regulations* and *Rulings* (of the Internal Revenue Service), and the opinions of the U.S. Tax Court form the basis for income tax reporting rules.

Cost Accounting Standards Board   In 1970 the U.S. Congress established the **Cost Accounting Standards Board (CASB)** to set accounting standards for computing costs in cost-based contracts (for example, cost plus a profit) by defense contractors. The diversity in cost accounting systems defense contractors use makes it difficult for the U.S. government to evaluate proposals and to ascertain the payments due contractors. The CASB attempts to set standards to achieve uniformity and consistency in contract proposals and cost reporting. Most of the work of the CASB does not directly affect the form of financial statements, but its requirements carry considerable weight in many areas of practice, especially those dealing with cost allocation. Accountants apply its standards to many transactions between defense contractors and the U.S. government.

Certifications

Certified Public Accountant   The designation **certified public accountant (CPA)** indicates that an individual has qualified to be registered or licensed as a certified public accountant by passing a written examination and satisfying audit experience requirements. The CPA examination includes questions on managerial accounting. We have included several questions from prior CPA examinations in this book.

Certified Management Accountant   Since 1972, the **certified management accountant (CMA)** program recognizes educational achievement and professional competence in management accounting. The examination, educational requirements, and experience requirements are similar to those for the CPA examinations, but they aim at the professional in management and cost accounting. We have included many problems from prior CMA examinations in this book.

Canadian Certifications   Two Canadian organizations provide designations similar to the CPA designation in the United States. The Canadian Institute of Chartered Accountants provides the chartered accountant (CA) designation, and the Certified General Accountants Association of Canada gives the certified general accountant (CGA) designation. The Society of Management Accountants in Canada gives a certified management accountant (CMA) designation similar to the CMA in the United States.

Ethical Issues

Firms generally hold managers accountable for achieving financial performance targets; failure to achieve these targets can have serious negative consequences for managers. If a division or company is having trouble achieving financial performance targets, managers may be tempted to manipulate the accounting numbers, even to commit fraud.

For example, some companies have recorded sales before they earned the revenue. This early revenue recognition would occur just before the end of the reporting period, say, in late December for a company using a December 31 year-end. Management might rationalize the early revenue recognition because the firm would probably make the sale in January anyway; this practice just moved next year's sale (and profits) into this year. Nevertheless, this would be an example of fraudulent financial reporting.

In its Standards of Ethical Conduct for Management Accountants, the National Association of Accountants (NAA) states that management accountants have an obligation to uphold the highest levels of ethical conduct by upholding professional competency, refraining from disclosing confidential information, and maintaining integrity and objectivity in their work.[1] The standards recommend that people faced with ethical conflicts first follow the company's established policies that deal with such conflicts. If the policies do not resolve the conflict, accountants should consider discussing the matter with superiors, potentially as high as the audit committee or the board of directors. In extreme cases, the accountant may have no alternative but to resign.

Managerial Accounting in High-Tech Companies

Many companies have recently installed computer-assisted methods of manufacturing, merchandising, or providing services. These new technologies have changed managerial accounting. For example, where robots and computer-assisted manufacturing methods have replaced people, labor costs have shrunk from 20-40 percent of product costs to less than 5 percent. Accounting in traditional settings required more work to keep track of labor costs than do current systems. On the other hand, in highly automated environments, accountants have had to become more sophisticated in finding causes of costs because labor no longer drives many cost transactions.

The development of **just-in-time (JIT)** production and purchasing methods also affects cost accounting systems. Firms using just-in-time methods keep inventories to a minimum. If inventories are low, accountants can spend less time on inventory valuation for external reporting. For example, a Hewlett-Packard plant eliminated 100,000 journal entries per month after installing just-in-time production methods and adapting the cost accounting system to this new production method, which freed additional accounting and finance people to provide better managerial accounting information for managers.[2]

Costs and Benefits of Accounting

A hospital recently installed an accounting system that cost several million dollars. How did the hospital administrators justify such an expenditure? They believed that better management of information about patient care costs would result in improved cost control and efficiency that would save the hospital enough to justify the cost of the system.

Managers should answer the question "How much information is enough?" for their purposes on a cost/benefit basis, much like the questions "How much advertising is enough?" or "Should we install a computerized inventory system?" Only if the benefits of the information exceed its costs should a firm generate accounting information for managerial purposes.

---

[1]See *Standards of Ethical Conduct for Management Accountants* (Montvale, N.J.: National Association of Accountants, June 1, 1983.)

[2]Rick Hunt, Linda Garrett, and C. Mike Merz, "Direct Labor Cost Not Always Relevant at H-P," *Management Accounting*, February 1985, pp. 58–62.

Managerial Application

The Increasing Importance of Cost Analysis

Note to Readers: We have included "managerial applications" of managerial accounting issues and practices in actual business settings in this and many later chapters. These applications are based on research into actual practice or on articles by practitioners who describe their experiences. We hope you will find these applications useful in thinking about real-world managerial accounting issues.

Engineers for Ford and other automobile companies in the United States believe that Japanese manufacturers can build cars for considerably less than their U.S. counterparts. Domino's Pizza nearly went bankrupt until the owner discovered that the company was losing money on 6-inch pizzas. The company dropped the product line and went on to become a multimillion-dollar company. Many hospitals that thrived when insurers fully reimbursed health care costs are facing large deficits in the face of a new environment with increased price competition and lower dollar limits on payment for particular procedures.

What do all of these situations have in common? They all represent situations in which a better understanding and management of product costs is important for the success of the organization. In general, an organization's ability to manage its costs becomes more important as the environment becomes more competitive. Hospitals, manufacturing companies, airlines, and many other organizations face increasingly stiff competition in the 1990s. As a result, they are seeking new and improved ways of measuring productivity and product costs, which creates many new opportunities for experts in managerial accounting.[a]

[a]For more extensive reading, see R. Kaplan, "Yesterday's Accounting Undermines Production," *Harvard Business Review* (July–August 1984); R. Hayes, "Why Japanese Factories Work," *Harvard Business Review* (July–August 1981); and P. Drucker, "The Emerging Theory of Manufacturing," *Harvard Business Review* (May–June 1990).

In practice, measuring the costs and benefits of accounting is difficult. The analysis of costs and benefits requires considerable communication and cooperation between users and accountants. Users are more familiar with the benefits of information, whereas accountants are more familiar with its costs. As Exhibit 1.4 shows,

Exhibit 1.4

Supply and Demand for Accounting Information

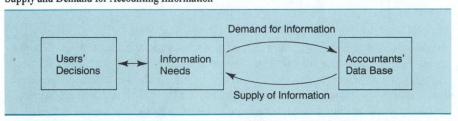

users identify their needs based on the decisions they make and request data from accountants, who develop systems to supply information when a **cost-benefit criterion** justifies it. If accountants and users interact, they eventually settle on a cost-benefit-justified supply of accounting data that meets users' needs.

The Value of Information for Particular Decisions

Deriving the value of information for answering particular questions is important in many managerial settings besides accounting. For example, should the firm undertake an additional marketing study that involves expanded sampling of a new product by consumers? Should the company discontinue its marketing tests and proceed directly to full-scale production? Should a doctor order laboratory tests before taking action in an emergency situation? Should a production manager stop production to test a sample of products for defects, or allow production to continue? Managers solve such problems conceptually by comparing the cost of information with the improvement in the value of actions that results from the information.

Scholars in economics, accounting, and decision theory are working on ways to deal with the difficult problem of measuring the value of information. Appendix 1.1 presents a formal analytical model for evaluating the economics of information.

Both users and accountants recognize that information is not free. Management must take into account the costs and benefits of information in deciding how much accounting is sufficient.

Organization of the Book

Part One of this book (Chapters 1 and 2) provides background concepts for later use. Part Two (Chapters 3 through 5) provides an overview of cost systems to help users of accounting understand how accounting systems are designed. This understanding will help users communicate their information needs to accountants. Parts Three and Four cover the two major uses of managerial accounting information; Part Three (Chapters 6 through 10) discusses the use of accounting for managerial decision making, and Part Four (Chapters 11 through 15) discusses the use of accounting for managerial planning and performance evaluation. Part Five (Chapters 16 through 18) presents special topics.

■ Summary ■

Accounting comprises financial accounting and managerial accounting. Financial accounting refers to the preparation of general-purpose reports for external users; managerial accounting refers to the provision of information to managers inside the organization. This book concentrates primarily on the use of accounting for managerial decision making and planning and performance evaluation.

Whereas externally imposed restrictions and rules constrain financial accounting, they do not constrain managerial accounting. Managerial accounting focuses on providing information for managerial decision making and other managerial activities rather than on satisfying rules. Therefore, managerial accounting reports can differ considerably from organization to organization. Further, managerial accounting comprises many special-purpose reporting activities.

Although external regulations do not constrain managerial accounting directly, those regulations do affect managerial accounting. Generally accepted accounting principles, tax laws, and other regulations affect the design of accounting systems; hence, they affect the data that accounting systems routinely produce. Information that regulations require can also be used for managerial purposes at very low cost—perhaps only for the cost of an additional computer printout. This information, however, is not necessarily relevant or useful for managerial purposes. Accountants must continually ensure that managers do not use information designed for one purpose improperly for another purpose.

Managerial accounting is user-oriented. In the ideal setting, users know what type of accounting data accountants can feasibly provide and whether obtaining the data is worthwhile. Users must understand accounting well enough to communicate effectively with accountants. By doing so, they can obtain the data they want for decision making, and they can influence the design of accounting systems to meet their needs.

Appendix 1.1:
The Value of Information

(*Note:* This appendix assumes that students have some background in elementary probability theory.)

Managers usually make the decision about "how much information is enough" judgmentally. In this appendix, we show how you can apply formal decision theory models to the issue. These models require data that many organizations may not have readily available; hence, you should view this approach more as a systematic method of thinking about the problem than as a tool that managers can easily implement and routinely apply. Analysts have applied the methods described in this appendix to numerous practical problems, however, including obtaining information for drilling oil wells.

To make the analysis concrete, we consider the case of an owner-manager of a small company who is trying to decide whether to accept a special order from a customer. This is a one-time order. Rejection of the order results in no present or future impact on profits. If the firm accepts the order, the increased cash flows from the customer to the company will be $1 million. The owner-manager does not know with certainty the costs of making the products for the special order, but accounting estimates them to be either $800,000 or $1,200,000, depending on how much time their manufacture requires. Hence, acceptance of the order would result in a net gain of $200,000 *or* a net loss of $200,000, whereas rejection will produce neither gain nor loss.

Exhibit 1.5

Decision Tree for Computing the Value of Perfect Information

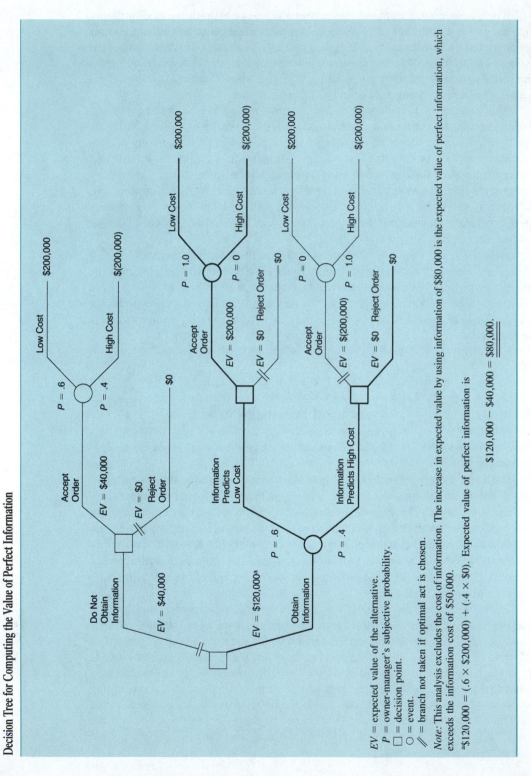

EV = expected value of the alternative.
P = owner-manager's subjective probability.
☐ = decision point.
○ = event.
⫽ = branch not taken if optimal act is chosen.

Note: This analysis excludes the cost of information. The increase in expected value by using information of $80,000 is the expected value of perfect information, which exceeds the information cost of $50,000.

[a]$120,000 = (.6 × $200,000) + (.4 × $0). Expected value of perfect information is

$$120,000 - $40,000 = $80,000.$$

The owner-manager regards the two production cost events as having the following probabilities: (1) a .6 probability that production costs will equal $800,000 and that the firm would make a $200,000 profit on the order; (2) a .4 probability that production costs will equal $1,200,000 and that the firm will incur a $200,000 *loss* if the firm accepts the order. Consequently, accounting computes the expected value of accepting the order as follows:[3]

$$EV = \sum_i P_i V_i$$

$$= (.6 \times \$200,000) + [.4 \times (-\$200,000)]$$

$$= \underline{\$40,000},$$

where

EV = the expected value of the outcomes

P_i = the probability of each outcome occurring

V_i = the value of each outcome.

Value of Information

Note that the owner-manager has enough information to estimate a revenue outcome and two cost outcomes. If the manager knew nothing more than this, the manager would accept the order and expect to earn $40,000.

Suppose that *before* deciding whether to accept or reject the order, the owner-manager has the option of obtaining more information, namely, the cost of a set of special orders already in production. The accountant estimates the costs of setting up the necessary accounting records and analyzing these data to be $50,000. Note that the manager decides whether to obtain this information before deciding whether to accept the special order. The manager would not obtain the information, obviously, unless its benefits exceeded $50,000.

Suppose that the information would tell the owner-manager for certain whether production costs would be $800,000 or $1,200,000; that is, the information is perfect. What is the value of the information to the owner-manager? Exhibit 1.5 diagrams the analysis in a decision tree.

If the owner-manager obtains information, the sequence of events follows:

1. Obtain information at a cost of $50,000.

2a. Information accurately predicts low production costs of $800,000, so accept the order to make a profit of $200,000; or

2b. Information accurately predicts high production costs of $1,200,000, so reject the order to avoid losing $200,000.

---

[3]To avoid complicating the issue, we assume that the owner-manager is risk-neutral. For applications to the risk-averse case, see Joel S. Demski, *Information Analysis* (Reading, Mass.: Addison-Wesley, 1980) and Robert P. Magee, *Advanced Managerial Accounting* (New York: Harper and Row, 1986), particularly Chapters 2 and 3.

Note that the owner-manager's probability estimates of the information signal are the same as the estimates of the event—that is, .6 for low costs and .4 for high costs. If information is perfect, the probability estimates of what information will predict about events are the same as the probability estimates about the events themselves.

What does the owner-manager gain by obtaining information? If the information accurately predicts that production costs will be $800,000, the owner-manager gains nothing from the information. (We assume that the information costs $50,000—and there are no refunds.) The value of the information is that it tells the owner-manager when to avoid the loss from accepting an order and *then* learning that production costs are high. This information could save the owner-manager $200,000. This savings has a .4 probability of occurring; hence, the **expected value of perfect information** is $80,000 (= .4 × $200,000). Taking the difference in the expected values of the "obtain information" and "do not obtain information" alternatives in Exhibit 1.5 also shows the expected value of perfect information:

$$
\begin{array}{ccccc}
\text{Expected Value} & & \text{Expected Value} & & \text{Expected Value} \\
\text{of Perfect} & = & \text{of Alternative} & - & \text{of Alternative} \\
\text{Information} & & \text{with Information} & & \text{without Information} \\
\\
& = & \$120{,}000 & - & \$40{,}000 \\
\\
& = & \underline{\underline{\$\ 80{,}000.}} & &
\end{array}
$$

The rational owner-manager would acquire the information because its expected benefits of $80,000 exceed its cost of $50,000.

Most information is not perfect, of course. The expected value of *perfect* information is a ceiling on the amount that should be paid for information. Cost and advanced managerial accounting textbooks and textbooks on decision making under uncertainty discuss the case of *imperfect* information.[4]

Problem 1 for Self-Study

Overview of the Use of Information for Decision Making, Performance Evaluation, and External Reporting

Cheers Warbuck, Incorporated, is a large, publicly held corporation that operates a chain of retain department stores throughout the United States. It currently faces the decision of whether to build a new "super store" in a rapidly growing regional shopping center in Phoenix.

a.   What type of financial information would top management need in making this decision?

---

[4]For example, see N. Dopuch, J. G. Birnberg, and J. S. Demski, *Cost Accounting,* 3rd ed. (New York: Harcourt Brace Jovanovich, 1982), Chapter 1; E. B. Deakin and M. W. Maher, *Cost Accounting,* 3rd ed. (Homewood, Ill.: Irwin, 1991); or R. S. Kaplan and A. Atkinson, *Advanced Management Accounting,* 2nd ed. (Englewood Cliffs, N.J.: Prentice-Hall, 1989).

b. Assume that top management decided to open the new store. Identify the types of information that top management would need to evaluate the performance of the Phoenix store each year.

c. Identify the types of information that shareholders and potential investors would need for evaluating Cheers Warbuck's decision to open the store. How, if at all, would the information shareholders and potential investors need differ from that top management needs for internal performance evaluation?

d. Discuss similarities and differences in the uses of accounting data identified in parts **a, b,** and **c.**

Suggested Solution

a. The appropriate basis for decisions would be an analysis of the cash inflows and outflows that would result from the decision to open the store in Phoenix.[5] Part Three of this book discusses methods of estimating these cash flows and making such decisions.

b. Top management would need some basis for evaluating the performance of the Phoenix store. Return on investment, profits, and net cash flows are commonly used for this purpose. Part Four of this book discusses the use of financial performance measures.

c. First, the firm must prepare the reports to shareholders in accordance with generally accepted accounting principles, whereas the measures top management uses for performance evaluation can follow whatever method management believes will provide the most helpful information. Second, financial reports to shareholders are highly aggregated. Management usually wants much more detailed information than do shareholders.

d. The following chart summarizes similarities and differences among different uses of accounting data:

Item	Managerial Decision Making	Internal Performance Evaluation	External Performance Evaluation
Time Dimension	Future	Past	Past
Frequency	As Needed	More Frequent, Usually Monthly	Less Frequent
Degree of Aggregation	Detailed	Detailed	More Aggregated
Flexibility in Content	Flexible	Flexible	Relatively Inflexible; Must Follow GAAP
Range of Focus	Cash Flows	Division Profits, Revenues, Costs, and Return on Investment	Net Income, Cash Flows, Return on Shareholders' Equity

[5]Readers familiar with discounted cash flow methods will recognize that these cash flows should be discounted to their present value using a risk-adjusted discount rate. We discuss discounted cash flow methods in Chapter 9.

Problem 2 for Self-Study (*Appendix*)

Soong's Soybean Products (*Contributed by J. Lim*)

After several years of supplying tofu to several supermarket chains, the Soong family decided that it was time to diversify its operations in the light of increasing competition from other tofu manufacturers.

At a recent family conference, several members came up with new product ideas as possible alternatives to tofu. The family considered a dehydrated soybean protein as too low-margin. The family rejected soybean yogurt, despite popularity with some communities, because it was highly perishable and appealed to a small market segment.

Laura Soong, a recent biochemistry graduate, then suggested that the family exploit the growing diet and health food market by introducing a soybean ice cream. "I've perfected it in the lab," she said. "It is low in cholesterol and has only one-quarter the calories of regular ice cream. But more important, it tastes almost like the real thing!" She then provided her estimates of costs for the project.

Based on Laura's figures, David Soong, the family accountant, estimates that if sales are high, the product will increase the company's profits by $150,000 per year. If sales are low, the product will reduce company profits by $100,000 per year. David assigns a prior probability of .5 for high sales and .5 for low sales.

The company can conduct a survey of various health food outlets to obtain information about the true demand for the new product. The costs of such a survey are $20,000.

a. Construct a decision tree like the one in Exhibit 1.5 to show the action the Soong family will take without the survey. What is the expected value of one year's increase or decrease in profits without information?

b. How much would the Soong family be willing to pay for perfect information?

Suggested Solution

a.

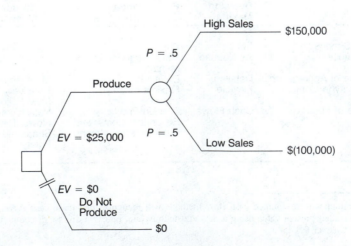

The expected value without information is

$$(.5 \times \$150,000) + [.5 \times (-\$100,000)] = \$25,000.$$

Decision: Produce.

b. See the following diagram.

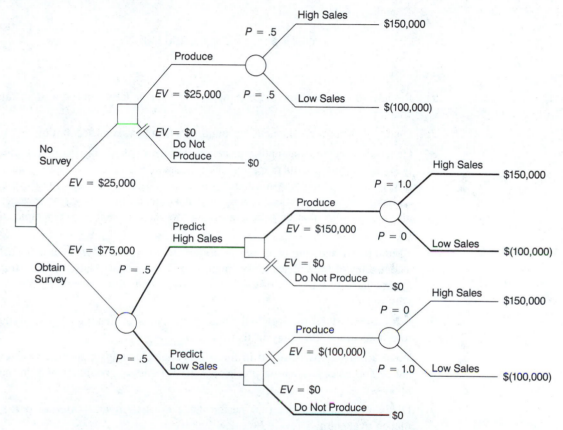

The expected value of perfect information = $75,000 − $25,000 = $50,000. The expected value of perfect information, $50,000, exceeds the cost of the information, $20,000; hence, the information should be acquired.

Key Terms and Concepts

Financial accounting
Managerial accounting
Controller
Internal audit
Treasurer
Generally accepted accounting
  principles (GAAP)

Securities and Exchange
  Commission (SEC)
Financial Accounting Standards
  Board (FASB)
Cost Accounting Standards
  Board (CASB)

continued on page 22

Certified Public Accountant   Just-in-time (JIT)
  (CPA)   Cost-benefit criterion
Certified Management   Expected value of perfect
  Accountant (CMA)   information (Appendix 1.1)

Questions, Problems, and Cases

Questions

1. Review the meaning of the following concepts or terms introduced in this chapter.

2. Distinguish between financial accounting and managerial accounting.

3. Generally accepted accounting principles are the methods of accounting publicly held firms use in preparing their financial statements. A principle in physics, such as the law of gravity, serves as a basis for developing theories and explaining the relations among physical objects. In what ways are generally accepted accounting principles similar to and different from principles in physics?

4. "Managerial accounting is not important in nonprofit organizations, such as agencies of the federal government and nonprofit hospitals, because they do not have to earn a profit." Do you agree with this statement? Why or why not?

5. What are the steps involved in the managerial decision-making process? What role does accounting play in that process?

6. What are the steps involved in the managerial planning, control, and internal performance evaluation process? What role does accounting play in that process?

7. Distinguish between internal performance evaluation and external performance evaluation.

8. Why is it important that financial reports to shareholders not misrepresent managers' actions?

9. "It is important for managerial accountants to understand the uses of accounting data and for users of data to understand accounting. Only in this way can accountants provide the appropriate accounting data for the correct uses." Do you agree with this statement? Why or why not?

10. A student planning a career in management wondered why it was important to learn about accounting. How would you respond?

11. "The best management accounting system provides managers with all of the information they would like to have." Do you agree with this statement? Why or why not?

12. What are the two major uses of managerial accounting information?

13. (Appendix 1.1) What is the expected value of information?

Problems and Cases

14. *Value of information—nonbusiness setting.* Consider the following value of information in a medical context.

    Suppose that a patient visits a doctor's office and that the doctor decides on the basis of the signs that the patient's appendix should be removed immediately. Meanwhile the doctor orders a white blood cell count. The doctor decides that the appendix must be removed no matter what the blood count happens to be.

    a. What is the value to the doctor of the information (in the cost-benefit sense discussed in this chapter) about the blood cell count?

    b. Why might the doctor order the test anyway?

15. *Objectives and uses of financial statements (*adapted from CMA exam*).* Financial statements are an important means that firms use to communicate economic information to interested parties. The objectives of financial reporting have received the attention of the accounting profession, the business community, the government, and the general public at various times and in varying degrees for many years.

    During the past 5 years concern and intensive study of financial reporting objectives has increased. The objectives recommended range from ''the statements are the management's report on its stewardship of the investors' capital'' to ''the statements provide information to investors for predicting, comparing, and evaluating the economic activities of an enterprise.''

    The objectives established for financial reporting will depend on whether management or some other party prepares the reports, what the firm intends the reports to represent (results of past activities or predictions of future actions), for whom the firm intends the statements, and how those parties will use the statements.

    a. Discuss management's responsibilities for the business entity's financial reporting.

    b. Does management prepare financial reports to reflect past performance of the business entity or to help predict the future performance of the entity? Discuss briefly.

    c. Discuss briefly how investors can use financial reports in making investment decisions.

16. *Decision making and financial reporting.* Harry Chapin, a taxi driver, recently considered whether to sell his old Dodge and purchase a newer car. The old car is completely depreciated for accounting (book) purposes and has zero net book value. However, Harry has a buyer who would pay him $300 cash for it. The newer car would cost $7,000 to acquire, and Harry believes that he could keep it for 5 years, after which it would be worth $500. If Harry keeps the old car for the next 5 years instead of buying the newer one, he expects to incur large maintenance costs. In fact, keeping the old Dodge would cost $1,200 more per year for operating costs than would the newer car. Revenues or costs other than those noted previously would not differ. Depreciation is on a straight-line basis.

Show the impact on operating profit (which equals revenues minus cash operating costs minus depreciation for this problem) and cash flows for each of the 5 years, assuming that (a) Harry keeps the old Dodge for 5 years and (b) Harry sells the old Dodge and purchases the newer car. What would you recommend to Harry? Ignore income taxes and the time value of money. Compared to keeping the old car, would buying the newer car make Harry's reported operating profit better or worse each year? The following format may help you address the problem:

	Year 1	Year 2	Year 3	Year 4	Year 5
Operating Profit:					
Keep Old Car:					
Buy Newer Car:					
Cash Flow:					
Keep Old Car:					
Buy Newer Car					

17. *Decision making under uncertainty and the value of information* (appendix; adapted from CMA exam). Vendo Company operates the concession stands at the university football stadium. Records of past sales indicate that there are basically four kinds of football weather, that sales of hot dogs depend on the weather, and that the percentage of football games played in each kind of weather is as follows:

Weather	Percentage of Game Days	Hot Dogs Sold
Snow...	10%	10,000
Rain	20	20,000
Clear/Warm	40	30,000
Clear/Cold	30	40,000

Hot dogs cost Vendo Company $1.00 each, and Vendo sells them for $1.50, resulting in a contribution margin of $.50 per hot dog sold. Hot dogs unsold at the end of each game are worthless. Ignore income taxes.

a. Prepare a table with four rows and four columns showing the contribution margin from each of the four purchasing strategies of buying 10,000, 20,000, 30,000, or 40,000 hot dogs and the four weather conditions of snow, rain, clear/warm, and clear/cold.

b. Assuming that the chances of snow, rain, clear/warm, and clear/cold are 10, 20, 40, and 30 percent, respectively, compute the expected contribution margin from each of the following purchasing strategies:

(i) Buy 10,000 hot dogs.
(ii) Buy 20,000 hot dogs.
(iii) Buy 30,000 hot dogs.
(iv) Buy 40,000 hot dogs.

c. What is the optimal purchasing strategy in the absence of a weather forecast, and what is the expected contribution margin from following this strategy? (This answer will be the largest of the four expected payoffs computed in part **b.**)

d.   If Vendo had a perfect weather forecast for each game, it would buy 10,000 hot dogs when snow is predicted, 20,000 when rain is predicted, 30,000 when clear/warm is predicted, and 40,000 when clear/cold is predicted. What is the expected average contribution margin per football game assuming that a perfect weather forecast is available and that the four kinds of weather will occur with frequencies of 10, 20, 40, and 30 percent?

e.   What is the expected dollar value to Vendo Company of a perfect weather forecast per football game; that is, what is the expected dollar value of the information from a perfect weather forecast?

18.   *Decision making under uncertainty and the value of information* (appendix). If a mother with Rh negative blood bears a child whose father's blood is Rh positive, there may be complications (the medical name is *erythroblastosis fetalis*) in subsequent pregnancies unless the mother receives a shot of D antigen immune globulin soon after the first child is born. Assume that 87 percent of all people have Rh positive blood, that 13 percent have Rh negative blood, and that matings occur randomly among blood types. Assume that the complications occur in 5 percent of the matings where the mother's blood is negative and the father's is positive and that the cost of complications is $12,000.

a.   In what percentage of matings will the complication arise?

b.   What is the expected cost per mating from the complication if doctors do not give the D antigen immune globulin shot to any mothers?

c.   What is the cost per mating if doctors give every mother the shot, which costs $50?

d.   Comparing your answers to parts **b** and **c,** what is the optimal action in the absence of information about blood types, and what is the expected cost per mating from following that action?

e.   Suppose that information on blood types is known. What is the expected cost per mating if the shot is given only in matings with Rh negative mothers and Rh positive fathers?

19.   *Value of information* (appendix; contributed by J. Lim). Carl Valentine, chief executive of CVC Hi-Tech, a high-technology company, is thinking of signing a contract to provide personal computer software. The contract lasts for only 1 year, and Carl does not believe that it would be renewed. CVC Hi-Tech's sales of the software would be a function of the demand for the personal computer using the software.

    Carl estimates that a high volume of sales would earn CVC Hi-Tech $500,000 in profits, a medium volume would give CVC Hi-Tech zero profits, and a low volume of sales would cause CVC Hi-Tech to incur a loss of $300,000. Valentine considers all three events to be equally likely.

a.   What should Carl Valentine decide at this point? Assume that he is risk-neutral and a wealth maximizer.

b.   Suppose that Carl Valentine can hire the services of a market research company for a fee of $30,000. Should he use the company's services if it can give him perfect information?

... CHAPTER 2 ...

Cost Concepts and Behavior

Chapter Outline

- Fundamental Cost Concepts
- General Cost Structure
- Cost Concepts for Managerial Decision Making
- Cost-Volume-Profit Relations
- Cost Concepts for Planning and Performance Evaluation
- Costs Reported on Income Statements

Chapter 1 indicated that managerial accounting deals with the information managers need for making decisions and for planning and performance evaluation. Managers primarily need information about the *costs* of carrying out the organization's activities. Questions that managers ask include the following: "What does product #101X cost?" "What is the cost of the assembly department in our Des Moines plant?" "What are the costs of caring for a patient for one day in the hospital?" Managers also use cost information to value inventory and measure expenses in external financial reports. In this chapter, we introduce important cost concepts that you will use throughout this book and in practice.[1]

---

[1] A glossary of accounting terms and concepts appears at the back of this book to facilitate finding definitions. See especially the compendium of cost definitions under *cost terminology*.

Fundamental Cost Concepts

In principle, a cost is a sacrifice of resources. For example, if you purchased an automobile for a cash payment of $12,000, the cost to purchase the automobile would be $12,000. Accounting would treat a promise to pay $12,000 the same as a cash payment for purposes of measuring costs.

Although this concept is simple, it can be difficult to apply. For example, what does a student sacrifice to obtain a college education? A student sacrifices cash to pay for tuition and books. What about cash paid for living costs? If the student would incur these costs whether or not the student attended college, the student should not consider them to be costs of getting a college education.

Students not only sacrifice cash. They also sacrifice their time. Placing a value on that time is difficult; it depends on the best forgone alternative use of the time. For students who sacrifice high-paying jobs to attend college, the total cost of college may be much larger than the cash sacrificed. Other students may not sacrifice as much in terms of forgone alternatives, so their college costs would be lower. In each case, costs are sacrifices of resources. The most important resources sacrificed to attend college are time and money.

The term *cost* is meaningful only if it is used in some particular context. To say "the cost of this building is $1 million" is ambiguous unless the context of the cost is identified. Does cost mean the original price the current owner paid, the price that the owner would pay to replace it new, or the price to replace it today in its current condition? Is it the annual rental fee paid to occupy the building? Is it the cash forgone from not selling it? Is it the original price paid minus accumulated depreciation? You need to know the context in which the term *cost* is used to reduce its ambiguity. We devote much of this chapter to describing how different contexts affect the meaning of costs.

Opportunity Costs

The definition of a cost as a "sacrifice" leads directly to the **opportunity cost** concept. If a firm uses an asset for one purpose, the opportunity cost of using it for that purpose is the return forgone from its best alternative use.

The opportunity cost of a college education includes forgone earnings. Some other illustrations of the meaning of opportunity cost follow:

1. The opportunity cost of funds invested in a government bond is the interest that an investor could earn on a bank certificate of deposit (adjusted for differences in risk).[2]

2. The opportunity cost of using a plant to produce a particular product is the sacrifice of profits that the firm would make by producing other products (adjusted for differences in risk).

---

[2]A principle in finance is that investors and creditors are compensated for taking risk. For example, U.S. Treasury notes are usually considered to be less risky than commercial notes; hence, commercial notes pay interest at a higher rate.

3. Proprietors of small businesses often take a nominal salary. But the opportunity cost of their time may be much higher than the nominal salary recorded on the books. A proprietor can work for someone else and earn a wage. The highest such wage (adjusting for differences in risk and nonpecuniary costs or benefits of being a proprietor) is the opportunity cost of being a proprietor.

Costs and Expenses

You must distinguish *cost,* as used in managerial accounting, from *expense,* as used in financial accounting. Whereas a cost is a sacrifice of resources, an expense is the historical cost of the goods or services a firm uses in a particular accounting period.

Managerial accounting deals primarily with costs, not expenses. Generally accepted accounting principles and regulations such as the income tax laws specify when the firm can or must treat costs as expenses to be deducted from revenues. We shall reserve the term *expense* to refer to expenses for external reporting as defined by generally accepted accounting principles.

General Cost Structure

Direct and Indirect Costs

Accountants make a distinction between direct and indirect costs. Costs that relate directly to a cost object are **direct costs.** Those that do not, are **indirect costs.** A **cost object** is any item for which the manager wishes to measure cost. Departments, stores, divisions, product lines, or units produced are typical cost objects. The cost object establishes the context for labeling a cost as direct or indirect.

Example Electron, Inc., produces calculators. It buys the components from outside suppliers, assembles the components, and inspects the product for defects in workmanship. The company rents its factory facilities. If the cost object is a calculator, the materials and labor that the firm traces directly to the production of each calculator are direct. Electron considers the components to be direct materials, and workers' time to assemble and inspect the calculator to be direct labor.

In this example, when the cost object is a calculator, the factory rent is indirect. Now suppose that the purpose of calculating costs is to evaluate the performance of the factory manager. In that case, the cost object is the entire factory, not a unit produced, so factory rent would be a direct cost. Factory rent is direct to the factory but indirect to a calculator produced. The distinction between direct and indirect costs is meaningful only with respect to a particular cost object.

Common Costs Indirect costs are common to, or shared by, two or more cost objects, so accountants also call them **common costs.** A common cost results from the common use of facilities (for example, building or equipment) or services (for example, data processing or the legal staff) by several products, departments, or processes.

Examples of common costs include the following:

1. The factory rent Electron, Inc., pays is common to departments within the factory.
2. The cost of buildings that house a business school are usually common to each of the departments (accounting, finance, marketing, and so forth) within the school.
3. The cost of a computer is common to its various uses, such as payroll, accounts payable, and production scheduling.

The allocation of common costs involves assigning these costs to cost objects. Cost allocation pervades both internal and external accounting reports. The subject of cost allocation will come up in numerous places in this text, where we discuss it in the context of managerial decision making and performance evaluation. We also discuss it at length in Chapter 5.

Manufacturing Costs

The type of organization and the nature of its activities affects costs. The most complex organization, in terms of costs, is the manufacturing firm. Its activities include acquisition, production, marketing, administration, and service. An understanding of the cost structure of a manufacturing organization can help you to understand the cost structure of all types of organizations.

Manufacturing involves the transformation of materials into finished goods using labor and capital invested in machines and production facilities. **Manufacturing costs** comprise three elements: direct materials, direct labor, and manufacturing overhead.

Direct materials (also called *raw materials*) are those that the firm can trace directly to a unit of output. They can range from natural materials, such as iron ore to make steel and logs to make lumber, to more synthetic materials, such as electronic chips used in making calculators and plastics used in making toys.

The adjective *direct* is important for classifying materials in this category. Accountants cannot associate many manufacturing materials with particular units of output. Examples of these **indirect materials** include lubricants for machines, lightbulbs, welding rods, cleaning materials, and the like. Accounting classifies indirect materials as part of overhead, which we describe below.

Direct labor represents the wages of workers who transform raw materials into finished products. Examples of direct labor costs are the wages of assembly-line workers who make automobiles, construction workers who build houses, and others whose labor the firm can trace directly to particular units of a product.

Labor costs that the firm cannot trace directly to the creation of products, yet the production process requires, are known as **indirect labor.** Examples include wages of maintenance personnel, supervisors, materials handlers, and inventory storekeepers. Like indirect materials, accounting classifies indirect labor costs as overhead. The sum of direct material and direct labor is **prime cost.**

The third major category of manufacturing costs—**manufacturing overhead**—includes all manufacturing costs that the firm cannot trace to particular units of product as either direct material or direct labor. These costs give the firm the capacity to produce, such as indirect materials and indirect labor, as previously noted, and the cost of utilities, property taxes, depreciation, insurance, rent, and other costs of operating the manufacturing facilities. Manufacturing overhead and direct labor are the costs of converting raw materials into final products. Thus accountants call them **conversion costs.** Exhibit 2.1 diagrams the relation between the full cost of manufacturing a good and the materials, labor, and manufacturing overhead required to produce it.

How indirect can a cost be to the manufacturing activity and still be part of manufacturing overhead? For example, are the costs of operating a factory employee cafeteria, or the plant manager's salary, or the cost of employing the plant's accounting staff part of manufacturing costs? In practice it is difficult to distinguish between such manufacturing and nonmanufacturing costs, so firms typically set their own guidelines and follow them consistently from period to period.

Exhibit 2.1

Components of Manufactured Product Costs

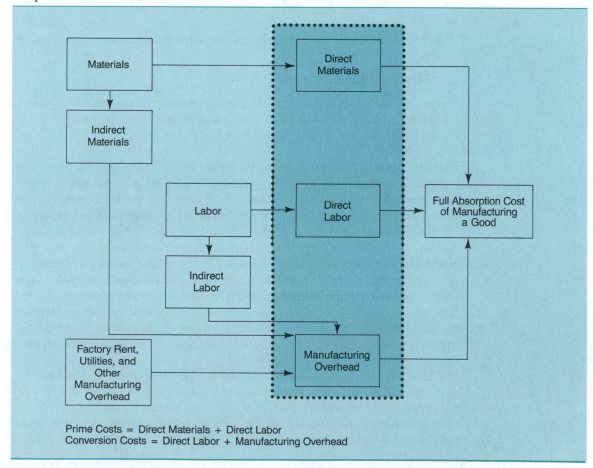

Prime Costs = Direct Materials + Direct Labor
Conversion Costs = Direct Labor + Manufacturing Overhead

Although we use the term *manufacturing overhead*, accountants use many synonyms in practice, including *overhead, burden, factory burden, factory overhead,* and *factory expense*. The term *manufacturing overhead*, as we use it, refers only to manufacturing costs, not to nonmanufacturing marketing and administrative costs.

Nonmanufacturing Costs

Nonmanufacturing costs comprise two elements: marketing costs and administrative costs. **Marketing costs** are those the firm requires to obtain customer orders and to provide the customer with the finished product. These include advertising, sales commissions, shipping, and building occupancy costs, among others. (These costs are also known as *marketing and distribution costs*. We refer to these costs as simply marketing costs.) **Administrative costs** are those the firm requires to manage the organization, including executive and clerical salaries, and to provide staff support, such as legal, data processing, and accounting services.

Cost Concepts for Managerial Decision Making

In this section, we discuss concepts important for managerial decision making.

Cost Behavior: Fixed and Variable Costs

Perhaps the most useful way of classifying costs for managerial decision making is by cost behavior. Do total costs vary with activity (for example, production volume)? If so, they are **variable costs.** If not, they are **fixed.**

Example   Electron, Inc., has received a special order for 10,000 calculators. The company must decide whether to accept or reject the order. Past experience enables management to predict that each calculator made to fill the special order will require $6.00 of direct materials, $1.00 of direct labor, and $1.00 of variable manufacturing overhead. (In some manufacturing settings the firm includes the direct labor costs in overhead. The accounting system at Electron separates direct labor from overhead.) In this example variable manufacturing overhead includes indirect materials, power to run machines, and indirect labor required to handle materials. These are the only variable costs in manufacturing each calculator. In addition, each calculator requires $1.00 variable marketing cost. Hence, the total variable cost per unit to make and sell each calculator is $9.00. Knowing which costs vary permits Electron to estimate the amount of costs incurred if it accepts the special order, which is 10,000 units times $9.00 or $90,000.

Electron, Inc., rents its factory facilities for $10,000 per month. The rental fee is the same regardless of activity level—it is a fixed cost. Knowing that rent behaves in a fixed cost pattern for any level of activity permits Electron to exclude rent from the analysis of which costs will be affected by the special order. Whether or not Electron accepts the order it will pay $10,000 per month in rent. Other examples of fixed costs at Electron are property taxes, utilities to heat and light buildings, and marketing and administrative personnel costs (excluding commissions). In total fixed costs are $110,000 per month composed of $50,000 manufacturing and $60,000 marketing and administrative costs.

The breakdown of the costs for Electron, Inc., into fixed and variable components appears in Exhibit 2.2. For a volume of up to 40,000 calculators per month, accounting assumes fixed costs will remain constant. Accounting assumes total variable costs will increase at the constant rate of $9.00 per calculator made and sold, which is the slope of the variable cost line. Note that the slope of the total cost line is $9.00—the variable cost per unit—whereas the intercept of the total cost line (that is, where it intersects the vertical axis) is $110,000—the fixed cost per month. This equation is expressed as follows:

$$TC = F + VX$$

where TC refers to total cost for a particular period of time, F refers to the fixed costs for the period, V refers to the variable cost per unit, and X refers to the volume for the period in units. For Electron Inc.

$$TC = \$110,000 + \$9.00X.$$

If the volume was 30,000 for a month, the total cost would be

$$TC = \$110,000 + (\$9.00 \times 30,000 \text{ units}) = \$380,000.$$

Cost-Volume-Profit Relations

If we include the average sales price (P) per calculator in the equation, we can derive the profit equation. Assume the price is $25 per calculator.

$$\frac{\text{Operating}}{\text{Profit}} = \frac{\text{Total}}{\text{Revenue}} - \frac{\text{Total Variable}}{\text{Costs}} - \frac{\text{Fixed}}{\text{Costs}}$$

$$\pi = PX - VX - F$$

$$\pi = \$25X - \$9X - \$110,000$$

If the volume was 30,000 units, the profit would be

$$\pi = (\$25 \times 30,000) - (\$9 \times 30,000) - \$110,000$$

$$\pi = \$750,000 - \$270,000 - \$110,000$$

$$\pi = \$370,000.$$

Exhibit 2.3 shows these relationships. The **breakeven point** is the point at which the total cost and total revenue lines intersect. At volumes below this point, total cost exceeds total revenue; at volumes above this point, total revenue exceeds total cost. You can find the breakeven point by setting π in the profit equation equal to zero and solving for the breakeven volume, as follows:

$$\pi = PX - VX - F$$

$$0 = \$25X - \$9X - \$110,000$$

Exhibit 2.2

ELECTRON, INC.
Fixed and Variable Costs

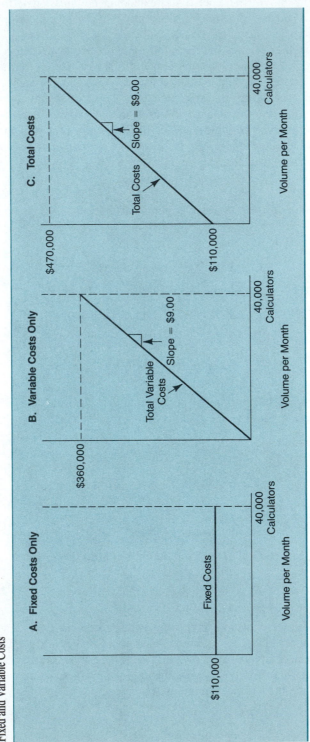

Exhibit 2.3

Cost-Volume-Profit Relations

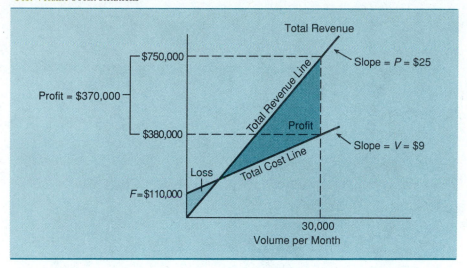

$$X = \frac{\$110,000}{\$16}$$

$$X = 6,875 \text{ units.}$$

(You can prove this result by computing total revenue and total cost at a volume of 6,875 units. You will find that total revenue and total costs both equal $171,875.)

Contribution Margin   The unit **contribution margin** is the excess of the unit selling price over the unit variable cost; that is, $P - V$. The contribution margin is the amount each unit contributes toward covering fixed costs and earning a profit. For Electron, Inc., the contribution margin is $16 (= $25 − $9). Many managerial decision models use the unit contribution margin. For example, linear programming models use it to compute optimal product mix. The contribution margin is such an important concept that it appears throughout this book in many contexts.

Change in Fixed Costs   Fixed costs will not necessarily remain at the same level, even with no inflation. For example, suppose Electron, Inc., can produce a maximum of 40,000 calculators per month with its present facilities. Assume that management wants to increase production and sales volume beyond 40,000 units per month. Now, the firm will have to acquire additional facilities, will incur additional utilities costs, and will have to hire more administrative and marketing personnel. Assume that adding facilities to expand capacity by 35,000 calculators per month would add $40,000 per month to fixed costs. Thus, for an additional capacity of 35,000 calculators, fixed costs would increase from $110,000 per month to $150,000 per month. Exhibit 2.4 illustrates this cost behavior.

In a sense, the marginal cost of the 40,001st calculator is $40,009.00 (that is, $40,000 additional fixed cost for the additional capacity plus $9.00 variable cost for

Exhibit 2.4

ELECTRON, INC.
Fixed and Variable Costs, Additional Capacity

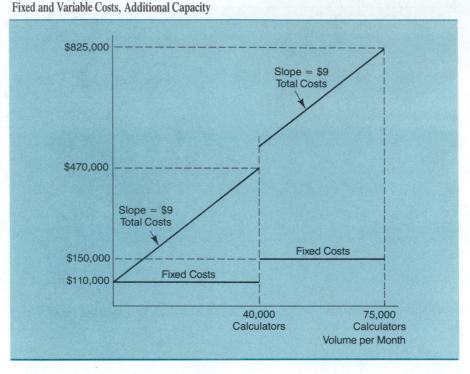

the calculator). Of course, accounting would not charge such a cost to that particular calculator. Instead, the firm considers the $40,000 to be a *capacity cost,* that is, a cost of providing the additional capacity to produce and sell up to 75,000 calculators. If capacity is less than 40,000 calculators per month, fixed costs are $110,000 per month. If capacity increases to a maximum of 75,000 calculators per month, fixed costs are $150,000 per month.

Long-Run Nature of Fixed Costs   Decisions to increase or decrease capacity are usually long-term decisions. Firms decide to increase capacity assuming they will need additional capacity for a long time, say, several years. The length of the commitment to a particular level of capacity varies. An airplane manufacturer might commit for decades. A consulting firm might commit to the shortest lease available for office space.

Fixed costs are not fixed forever; they can change when capacity changes. In fact, we define fixed costs as those that remain the same for a given level of capacity. This definition is consistent with that used by economists, who say that fixed costs do not vary in the short run and that the short run is the period over which capacity remains unchanged. For practical purposes, we usually define the short run to be about 1 year.

Comparison of Direct Costs with Variable Costs   We often use the terms *direct* and *variable* interchangeably in the business world, because many costs that firms can directly trace to a unit are variable. Costs of direct materials are usually variable costs, for example. Variable manufacturing overhead costs, however, are *variable but not direct* if the implied cost object is a unit produced. A comparison of variable/fixed and direct/indirect costs for Electron's manufacturing costs appears in Exhibit 2.5. (This example assumes that the company has not added additional capacity.)

Differential Costs

In making decisions, managers often want to know how taking a certain action would affect costs. These costs are **differential costs;** that is, the costs that *differ* because of an action. We also call them *incremental costs*. Differential costs include both incremental costs (cost increases) and decremental costs (cost decreases).

If the contemplated action increases or decreases volume with no change in capacity, differential costs will be variable costs. In the Electron example, recall that management was considering filling a special order of 10,000 calculators. It assumed only variable costs would be affected. To be specific, an increase in costs of $90,000 (that is, 10,000 calculators times $9.00 per unit variable cost) was expected. These are the differential costs of the special order.

Differential costs need not all be variable costs, however. If an action affects fixed costs, then those costs are differential. Virtually any long-run action involving changes in capacity causes fixed costs to differ. Consider the case in which Electron increased capacity. The additional fixed costs (of $40,000) would be differential costs of the additional capacity.

The differential concept is important in using accounting information for managerial decision making. A question uppermost in the minds of decision makers is "How are costs affected by the actions we are contemplating?" An understanding of how to use accounting data to estimate these differential costs is such an important part of decision making that we devote much of Chapters 6 through 9 to it.

Differential cost analysis implicitly refers to all costs and revenues affected by decisions. As a practical matter, we hold constant other variables that decision

Exhibit 2.5

ELECTRON, INC.
Comparison of Direct Costs with Variable Costs

	Direct versus Indirect Cost		Assumed Cost Behavior	
	Direct[a]	Indirect	Variable	Fixed
Manufacturing Costs:				
Direct Materials	X		X	
Direct Labor	X		X	
Variable Manufacturing Overhead **(e.g., indirect materials, power to** **operate machines)**		X	X	
Fixed Manufacturing Overhead (e.g., factory rent, property taxes)		X		X

[a]By "direct" we mean traceable directly to the production of a unit, in this case.

Managerial Application

Cost and Profit Concepts in a Dispute over the Value of a Patent*

In 1990, a court found Ford Motor Company guilty of infringing a patent issued to Robert Kearns, who had invented a special circuit to operate intermittent wind-shield wipers (IWW). Kearns argued that he was entitled to receive a share of Ford's profits on the IWW options it installed in cars. Kearns pointed to some Ford documents showing contribution margin (revenues less variable material, labor, and marketing costs), which Ford called ''economic profit'' and profit margin (''economic profit'' less certain fixed costs and allocated portions of administrative costs), which Ford called ''accounted profit.'' Kearns asked for royalties amount-ing to about one-third of Ford's internally reported ''economic profit,'' an amount equal to about $300 million.

   Ford argued that even ''accounted profit'' did not accurately reflect the profits on IWW options because that measure fails to account for interest and income taxes. Moreover, Ford argued, if Kearns should receive a share of its profits, then the profits on an IWW option considered alone are irrelevant. Ford can't sell an IWW option without selling a car, and Ford can't sell an individual car without satisfying federal standards for fuel efficiency of the entire fleet that it sells. Ford argued that it prices its car fleets and the options on the cars to meet competition and to satisfy the federal requirements. Therefore the relevant profit figure would be the profit rate on the entire fleet of cars it sells.

   More importantly Ford argued, Kearns should not be entitled to recover any of Ford's profits, but only a portion of Ford's opportunity costs in using the Kearns patent. Because Ford could install IWW options using electrical circuits other than Kearns' invention, Ford should pay no more than the extra cost of the alternative circuit. Ford suggested that a competitor, the Amos circuit, cost only $.10 more each to produce than the Kearns circuit. Ford argued that if it gave Kearns the full $.10 per IWW produced, it should pay only $2 million.

   The court ordered Ford to pay Kearns about $6 million in damages.

*Based on the authors' research.

makers may also consider important (for example, the impact of an action on em-ployee morale or public relations). This is because managerial accountants have a comparative advantage in estimating differential costs but not the other variables. Accounting usually includes differential revenues in the analysis for completeness, but marketing personnel most often estimate them.

Period and Product Costs

All costs firms incur, they eventually expense. If a firm does not expense a cost immediately, but adds it to an inventory account on the balance sheet until it sells the goods, that cost is said to be ''inventoriable.'' We call inventoriable costs **product costs.** We call those that are not inventoriable **period costs,** because the firm expenses them in the period incurred.

Generally accepted accounting principles and income tax regulations require that firms treat all manufacturing costs as product costs for external financial reporting using full absorption costing (sometimes called absorption costing).[3] Using **full absorption costing,** the firm assigns each unit of a good produced the unit's variable manufacturing cost plus a share of fixed manufacturing costs for inventory valuation. Thus the total of units produced "fully absorbs" manufacturing costs.

By contrast, the **variable costing** method of inventory valuation includes only each unit's variable manufacturing cost; firms using variable costing treat fixed manufacturing costs as period costs they expense in the period in which they incur the cost. Firms treat all nonmanufacturing costs as period costs and therefore the costs are noninventoriable under both methods.

Components of Full Costs

By now you realize cost definitions and concepts are numerous. The diagram in Exhibit 2.6 illustrates components of a unit cost. We used the facts for the Electron, Inc., example to make the comparisons concrete. We can compute unit fixed costs only if we specify a particular volume. For this example, we assume a volume of 10,000 for the month.

The diagram shows several important distinctions. First, note the difference between the full cost of making and selling the product and the full absorption cost inventory value. The full cost of making and selling the product includes marketing and administrative costs, but the full absorption cost inventory value does not. Managers who ask accountants for unit costs sometimes find to their surprise that the accountants have provided full absorption inventory costs when the managers wanted full costs.

Second, note the difference between unit variable costs, which include variable marketing and administrative costs, and variable manufacturing costs, which do not. Neither full absorption nor variable costing inventory values include marketing and administrative costs.

Exhibits 2.7 and 2.8 illustrate gross margin, contribution margin, and profit margin computations. Recall that the unit selling price for Electron, Inc., is $25.00. The cost numbers were presented in Exhibit 2.6. Exhibits 2.7 and 2.8 show

$$\text{Unit } \textbf{Profit Margin} = \frac{\text{Unit Selling}}{\text{Price}} - \frac{\text{Full Cost per Unit of Making}}{\text{and Selling the Product.}}$$

For Electron, Inc., the unit profit margin is $5 = $25 − $20.

$$\text{Unit } \textbf{Gross Margin} = \frac{\text{Unit Selling}}{\text{Price}} - \frac{\text{Unit Full Absorption Cost of}}{\text{Making the Product.}}$$

For Electron, Inc., the unit gross margin is $12 = $25 − $13.

$$\text{Unit } \textbf{Contribution Margin} = \frac{\text{Unit Selling}}{\text{Price}} - \frac{\text{Unit Variable Cost of Making}}{\text{and Selling the Product.}}$$

For Electron, Inc., the unit contribution margin is $16 = $25 − $9.

---

[3]These principles and regulations are not precise in differentiating between manufacturing costs and nonmanufacturing costs.

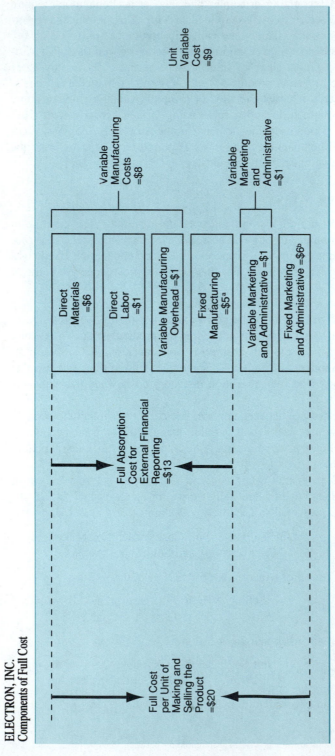

Exhibit 2.6

ELECTRON, INC.
Components of Full Cost

[a]Unitized Fixed Manufacturing Cost = $50,000/10,000.
[b]Unitized Fixed Marketing and Administrative Cost = $60,000/10,000.

Exhibit 2.7

ELECTRON, INC.
Gross Margin

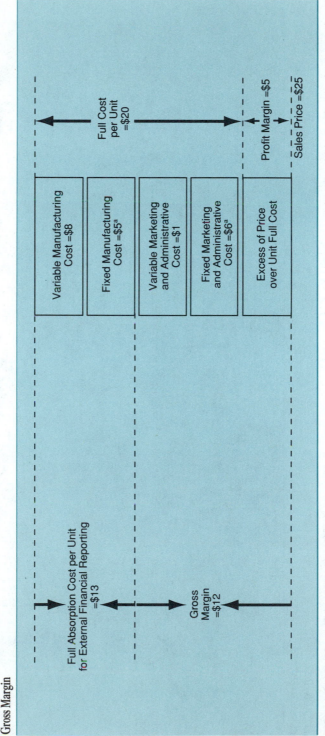

[a]Unit fixed costs based on volume of 10,000 units.

Exhibit 2.8

ELECTRON, INC.
Contribution Margin

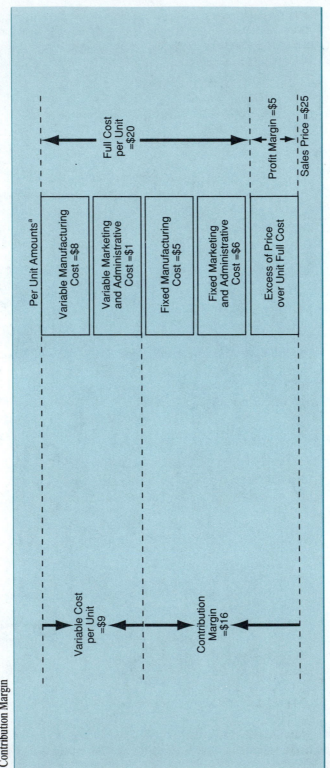

[a]Unit fixed costs based on volume of 10,000 units.

Although gross margin and contribution margin sound similar, and the amounts may be close, they are different concepts. Managers need to distinguish between them because firms routinely report total gross margin on external financial statements, but find contribution margin generally more useful for managerial decisions.

Sunk Costs

Sunk costs result from past expenditures. Decisions do not affect them, because the firm incurred sunk costs in the past, whereas decisions made now affect the future. Many decision makers have difficulty understanding this concept. Some managers, in an effort to overcome the results of unwise decisions in the past, will attempt to "recover their investment" and include sunk costs in their analyses. Such behavior often leads to incorrect decisions, as the following example demonstrates.

Example The buyer for a sporting goods store purchased 200 pairs, at $20 per pair, of a new type of sandal called jog sandals (sandals used for jogging). "These are the coming thing!" claimed the buyer. Unfortunately, in a year the store sold only 2 pairs at the retail price of $40 per pair and 3 pairs more at a reduced price of $25 per pair.

When the store manager suggested selling all the jog sandals at $10 per pair at a local running club, "just to get rid of the things," the store's merchandise buyer questioned, "How can we make a profit when we buy at $20 and sell at $10?" The store manager believed the buyer's argument and held the price at $25 per pair. After another year without a single sale, the manager threw away the shoes, stating, "It's unfortunate that these jog sandals didn't sell better, but at least we didn't sell them at a loss." Thus the manager missed an opportunity to recover $1,950 (= 195 pairs at $10 each).

Past expenditures are generally sunk costs and are irrelevant for decisions. Common examples of sunk costs include the past cost of inventory, whether bought or produced, the past cost of long-term assets (including residential homes), nonrefundable tuition paid for college, and the cost of a large dinner. (Moral: Don't feel obligated to eat all of your dinner just because you paid for it.)

The fact that past expenditures are sunk costs does not mean that information about past amounts spent is totally irrelevant. Managers can use information about the past to help predict differential costs of future actions. Further, managers often compare past expenditures with current expenditures for performance evaluation.

Cost Concepts for Planning and Performance Evaluation

Many of the concepts we already discussed are important for planning and performance evaluation. For example, knowing which costs will vary with changes in activity levels (variable costs) helps managers plan. We have not yet discussed controllability, a particularly important concept for performance evaluation.

Controllable and Noncontrollable Costs

The notion of controllability is important when managers use accounting data for performance evaluation. Knowing which costs employees can control allows managers to set priorities in performing one of their most important missions—cost

Exhibit 2.9

Relation of Cost Control to Organization Level

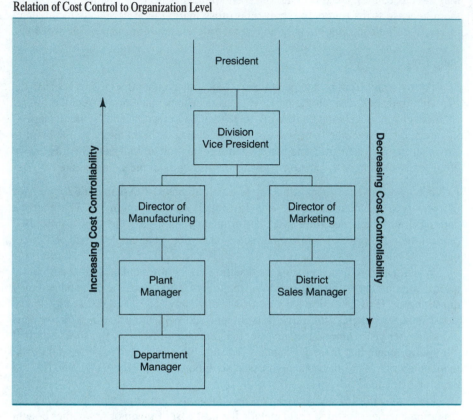

control. Knowing that, in the short run, factory rent is a **noncontrollable cost,**[4] whereas direct labor hours worked are **controllable,** enables managers to focus their attention on costs that they can more easily manage.

Recognizing the relative nature of controllable and noncontrollable costs is important. First, costs that managers cannot control in the short run are likely to become controllable in the long run at some level in the organization. For example, a district manager of a merchandise company that had outlets in shopping centers was taken to task because he never reevaluated the costs of store leases in the territory. "But the accounting reports label these rental costs as noncontrollable," was the district manager's response. Because of its failure to act on these "noncontrollable" costs, the company lost opportunities for better locations at cheaper prices within the shopping centers.

Second, as one moves up the organization to higher levels of management, more and more costs become controllable (see Exhibit 2.9). We consider a cost to

---

[4]The term *noncontrollable* does not mean that costs are out of control. Instead it means that once a commitment has been made (for example, signing a lease), the level of spending cannot be changed by a particular manager.

be controllable at the level in the organization where the management at that level has the power to authorize the cost. If top management but not district sales managers can authorize the advertising budget, top management but not the district sales managers controls advertising costs. Identifying controllable costs is particularly important in high-technology companies in which improvements in production processes reduce both fixed and variable costs.

We can apply the controllable cost concept in a variety of ways. Some companies considered the fuel price increases of the 1970s outside the control of *anyone* in the company. Other companies argued that top management had the authority to change (or close) operations and thus affect fuel usage, so management could control even this cost. In short, management must use its discretion to classify costs as controllable or noncontrollable.

Costs Reported on Income Statements

This section compares the way accounting would present costs for three types of income statements: (1) external financial reporting, (2) managerial decision making, and (3) managerial performance evaluation.

Exhibit 2.10 shows the assumed facts for Electron, Inc., for the month of February.

Income Statement for External Reporting

The income statement for external reporting appears in Exhibit 2.11. To comply with income tax regulations and generally accepted accounting principles using full absorption costing, Electron allocates fixed manufacturing costs to each unit produced, as appears on the following page:

Exhibit 2.10

ELECTRON, INC.
Facts

Units Produced and Sold in February	10,000 Units
Sales Price per Unit	$25 per Unit
Variable Manufacturing Cost per Unit:	
Direct Materials	$6 per Unit
Direct Labor	$1 per Unit
Variable Manufacturing Overhead	$1 per Unit
Fixed Manufacturing Costs:	
Fixed Manufacturing Overhead:	
Rent	$10,000 per Month
Other Manufacturing Overhead	$40,000 per Month
Marketing and Administrative:	
Fixed Costs	$60,000 per Month
Variable Costs	$1 per Unit

$$\text{Fixed Manufacturing Cost per Unit} = \frac{\text{Fixed Manufacturing Costs}}{\text{Units Produced}}$$

$$= \frac{\$50,000}{\$10,000}$$

$$= \$5 \text{ per Unit.}$$

Adding this $5 per unit to the $8 variable manufacturing cost per unit makes the full absorption cost of manufacturing a unit $13. Hence, the cost of goods sold is $130,000 (= $13 × 10,000 units).

Income Statement for Managerial Decision Making

The income statement for external reporting does not show actual manufacturing cost behavior because it "unitizes" fixed manufacturing costs to assign a share of these costs to each unit produced. The income statement in Exhibit 2.12 as prepared for managerial use will help management do its job because it presents cost behavior.

Note the difference between the *gross margin* and the *contribution margin,* as shown in Exhibits 2.11 and 2.12. The gross margin is the difference between revenue and cost of goods sold, whereas the contribution margin is the difference between revenue and variable costs, including variable marketing and administrative costs. We use the term *operating profit* at the bottom of income statements prepared for managerial use to distinguish it from net income used in external reporting.

Income statements such as the one shown in Exhibit 2.12 use variable costing. Recall that, using variable costing, accounting assigns each unit of a good produced the unit's variable manufacturing cost for inventory valuation. Accounting treats fixed manufacturing costs as period costs: the firm does not assign them to units for inventory valuation. (The firm does not assign nonmanufacturing costs to units for

Exhibit 2.11

ELECTRON, INC.
Income Statement for External Financial Reporting
for the Month Ending February 28

Sales Revenue	$250,000[a]
Less Cost of Goods Sold	130,000[b]
Gross Margin	$120,000
Less Marketing and Administrative Expenses	70,000[c]
Net Income before Taxes	$ 50,000

[a]$250,000 = $25 × 10,000 Units.

[b]$130,000 = ($8 Variable Manufacturing Cost × 10,000 Units) + 50,000 Fixed Manufacturing Cost.

[c]$70,000 = ($1 Variable Marketing and Administrative Cost × 10,000 Units) + $60,000 Fixed Marketing and Administrative Costs.

Exhibit 2.12

Income Statement for Managerial Decision Making		
Sales Revenue		$250,000
Less Variable Costs:		
Variable Cost of Goods Sold	$80,000[a]	
Variable Marketing and Administrative Costs	10,000[b]	
Total Variable Costs		90,000
Contribution Margin		$160,000
Less Fixed Costs:		
Fixed Manufacturing Costs	$50,000	
Fixed Marketing and Administrative Costs	60,000	
Total Fixed Costs		110,000
Operating Profit..		$ 50,000

[a]$80,000 = 10,000 \text{ Units} \times \$8 \text{ Variable Cost.}$

[b]$10,000 = 10,000 \text{ Units} \times \$1 \text{ Variable Cost.}$

inventory valuation under either variable or full absorption costing.) Firms often use variable costing for internal reporting because it reflects cost behavior better than full absorption costing does.

Income Statement for Performance Evaluation

Income statements that managers prepare for performance evaluation usually have two characteristics that distinguish them from the previous income statements. First, they partition costs (and perhaps revenues) into amounts that the managers being evaluated can control and those they cannot. Second, they assign costs and revenues to responsibility centers. A **responsibility center** is any part of the organization for which a manager has responsibility. Department managers, for example, are responsible for the revenues and costs in their departments.

    Assume the following facts for the Wizard Bank, which has two branches: Anacortes and Bellingham. Each branch had the following costs and revenues for August:

	Anacortes Branch	Bellingham Branch
Revenues..............................	$100,000	$150,000
Variable Costs (mostly interest costs)	70,000	115,000

In addition, the bank had $60,000 in fixed costs, of which the Anacortes branch controlled $20,000 and the Bellingham branch controlled $30,000.

Exhibit 2.13

Income Statement for Performance Evaluation				
	Controllable by Branches			
	Anacortes Branch	Bellingham Branch	Noncontrollable by Branches	Total for Bank
Revenues..............	$100,000	$150,000		$250,000
Variable Costs..........	(70,000)	(115,000)		(185,000)
Contribution Margin	$ 30,000	$ 35,000		$ 65,000
Fixed Costs Assigned to Branches..........	(20,000)	(30,000)		(50,000)
Other Fixed Costs.......			$(10,000)	(10,000)
Operating Profit.........	$ 10,000	$ 5,000	$(10,000)	$ 5,000

Exhibit 2.13 presents an income statement showing costs and revenues controllable by branches. For performance evaluation, managers would compare the actual amounts shown for each branch with predetermined budgeted controllable costs and revenues.

■ Summary ■

Knowledge of cost concepts is important for external reporting, managerial decision making, and planning and performance evaluation. In concept, a cost is a sacrifice of resources. An opportunity cost is the best alternative use of resources forgone because of some action.

Distinguishing between costs and expenses is important. Whereas costs are a sacrifice of resources, expenses are costs that the firm uses up (and matches against revenues) in a particular accounting period for external reporting purposes.

Manufacturing costs consist of direct materials, direct labor, and manufacturing overhead. Accounting attributes direct materials and direct labor (which are sometimes called prime costs) directly to each unit produced, whereas it does not attribute manufacturing overhead directly to units. Accounting usually classifies nonmanufacturing costs as either administrative or marketing.

Firms use a number of cost classifications in practice. The most common are product versus period; direct versus indirect; controllable versus noncontrollable; and fixed versus variable. Manufacturing costs that firms inventory are product costs, whereas those they cannot are classified as period expenses for external reporting purposes. Firms can attribute direct costs directly to a particular cost object; but cannot attribute indirect costs. This classification is meaningful only within some context; that is, the firm must specify the cost object. The same holds for costs classified as controllable and noncontrollable. Top management can control virtually all costs, but at lower levels of the organization, managers do not have the authority to control as many costs. The time interval is also important for classifying costs as controllable or noncontrollable, because the longer the time interval, the more controllable costs become.

For decision making, cost behavior classifications become important. Activity levels affect variable costs but not fixed costs. This classification is meaningful only over a specified range of activity levels for a specified time interval. Other important cost concepts for decision making are differential costs and sunk costs. Differential costs differ because of an action. Sunk costs are past expenditures irrelevant for future decisions.

We have introduced many concepts and terms in this chapter that you will use throughout the book. You should find it helpful to refer back to these concepts and terms, particularly to Exhibit 2.14, as you proceed through the book.

Exhibit 2.14

Summary of Definitions

Concept	Definition
Nature of Cost	
Cost	A sacrifice of resources.
Opportunity cost	The return that a firm could realize from the best forgone alternative use of a resource.
Expense	The cost charged against revenue in a particular accounting period. We use the term *expense* only when speaking of external financial reports.
Cost Concepts for Cost Accounting Systems	
Product costs	Costs that firms can more easily attribute to products; costs that are part of inventory.
Period costs	Costs that firms can more easily attribute to time intervals.
Full absorption costing method	A method of inventory valuation in which firms use all manufacturing costs—both fixed and variable—in valuing inventory and deriving cost of goods sold.
Variable costing method	A method of inventory valuation in which firms use only variable manufacturing costs in valuing inventory and deriving cost of goods sold.
Cost object	Any item for which the manager wishes to measure cost (e.g., product, department).
Direct costs	Costs directly related to a cost object.
Indirect costs	Costs not directly related to a cost object.
Common costs	Costs two or more cost objects share.
Additional Cost Concepts Used in Decision Making	
Variable costs	Costs that vary with the volume of activity.
Fixed costs	Costs that do not vary with volume of activity in a specified time span.
Differential costs	Costs that change in response to a particular course of action.
Sunk costs	Costs that result from an expenditure made in the past and that present or future decisions cannot change.
Additional Cost Concepts Used for Performance Evaluation	
Controllable costs	Costs influenced or affected by a particular individual.
Noncontrollable costs	Costs not influenced or affected by a particular individual.

Problem 1 for Self-Study

A product manager uses the following cost and price diagram to help relate prices to costs and contribution margins.

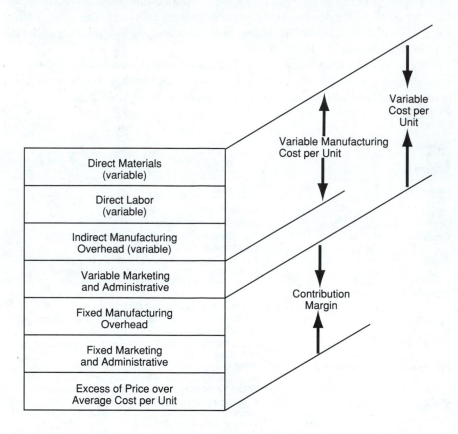

The manager has asked you to complete the diagram, given the following data:

Price per Unit	$ 100
Contribution Margin per Unit	18
Gross Margin for 1,000 Units	21,000
Variable Manufacturing Costs per Unit	70
Direct Materials per Unit	40
Direct Labor per Unit	20
Fixed Marketing and Administrative Cost per Unit	6

You are also asked to indicate the inventory value of each unit under variable costing and full absorption costing.

Suggested Solution

Inventory Values:

Variable Costing . . . . $70 per Unit
Variable
Manufacturing
Cost

Full Absorption Costing = $100 − $\dfrac{\$21{,}000}{1{,}000 \text{ Units}}$ . . . . $79 per Unit

Direct Materials . . . . $40 per Unit
Direct Labor . . . . $20 per Unit
Variable Manufacturing Overhead = $70 − ($40 + $20) = ... $10 per Unit
Variable Costs per Unit = Price − Unit Contribution Margin
  = $100 − $18 = ... $82 per Unit
Variable Marketing and Administrative Costs = $82 − $40 − $20 − $10 = . . $12 per Unit
Fixed Manufacturing Costs per Unit = Manufacturing Costs per Unit
  − Variable Manufacturing Costs per Unit = (Price
  − Gross Margin per Unit) − Variable Manufacturing Costs per Unit
  = $\left(\$100 - \dfrac{\$21{,}000}{1{,}000 \text{ Units}}\right)$ − $70 = ... $9 per Unit
Fixed Marketing and Administrative Cost per Unit = ... $6 per Unit
Excess of Price over Average Cost of Each Unit
  = $100 − ($40 + $20 + $10 + $12 + $9 + $6) = ... $3 per Unit

---

Problem 2 for Self-Study

Klogs, Inc.

After the death of his Uncle Sven early this year, Peter Sorensen left his $40,000-a-year job at an electronics company to assume control of Klogs, Inc., a manufacturer of quality clogs. His $28,000 salary at Klogs was substantially less than what he had earned in his previous job as a sales manager, but a sense of family duty persuaded him to head the ailing company. Besides, this job was a chance for him to test his managerial skills.

Klogs, Inc., a Sorensen family concern for three generations, had been under the conservative leadership of Sven Sorensen for almost half a century. While maintaining a reputation for high-quality craftsmanship, Klogs was never particularly innovative in the styles it put out. In fact, during the last 5 years, Klogs experienced a steady decline in sales due to a shrinking consumer demand for Klogs' clogs.

Reduced to only one product line, Klogs produced 70,000 pairs of clogs last year. At capacity, Klogs could put out 100,000 pairs of clogs. Klogs also has an old inventory of 3,000 pairs of clogs from a discontinued line. The inventory was still valued at $30,000—the manufacturing cost from 3 years ago.

On Peter Sorensen's first visit to the Klogs factory, Hansen, the young manager, gave him a tour of the place. Peter made extensive notes on the tour and obtained the following breakdown of last year's costs.

Item		
(a)	Sandpaper..	$ 200
(b)	Nails...	500
(c)	Leather..	140,000
(d)	Factory Rent—10 Years Remaining on Lease	12,000
(e)	Labor—Cutting..	210,000
(f)	Supervisor's Salary	15,000
(g)	Maintenance—Equipment (fixed)	1,000
(h)	Utilities—Factory (fixed)..	6,000
(i)	Varnish..	7,700
(j)	Sven's Salary	28,000
(k)	Labor—Assembling...	175,000
(l)	Sales Commission to Dealers ($.15 per unit)	9,750
(m)	Shipping Costs ($.10 per unit)	6,500
(n)	Administrative Manager's Salary	20,000
(o)	Office Supplies..	100
(p)	Secretary's Salary	10,000
(q)	Depreciation—Equipment	1,000
(r)	Wood	70,000
(s)	Advertising (fixed)	1,000

Klogs sold 65,000 pairs of clogs last year.

In his conversation with Hansen, Peter discovered that Klogs had conducted very favorable marketing tests on a new clog. But plans for the introduction of this new product line in the spring of last year were shelved because Sven had insisted that the firm dispose of the old inventory at no less than its book value before it undertook any new ventures. Hansen believed that Klogs could introduce this new product line this spring, and predicted that Klogs could expect to sell 40,000 pairs of this new product line. Peter recognized the sales potential in this new clog, which differed radically from the traditional Klogs' clog. It was trendy without sacrificing the quality and comfort of a Klogs' clog. Hansen had done his homework and supplied Peter with the following facts and figures:

Cost of Producing 40,000 New Klogs	
Leather...	$100,000
Wood	48,000
Nails, Varnish, and Sandpaper	1,000
Labor—Cutting	140,000
Labor—Assembling	120,000
Shipping Costs	4,000
Sales Commission to Dealers	6,000

Assuming that Klogs continues to produce 70,000 pairs of traditional Klogs, the Klogs factory will have to operate on Saturdays to meet the additional capacity requirements. The additional costs of operating on Saturday follow:

Supervisor's Overtime Salary	$4,000
Utilities	1,200

So far, Klogs has spent $3,000 in the development of New Klogs and $2,000 in a survey of retail outlets.

Armed with these figures, Peter realized that he needed to analyze current operations and come up with a strategy to reverse the Sorensen fortunes.

a. Ignoring any noneconomic value of self-employment, what is Peter Sorensen's opportunity cost of working for Klogs?

b. Identify the following costs, using last year's figures.
   (1) Unit direct materials costs.
   (2) Unit direct labor costs.
   (3) Unit variable manufacturing overhead, composed of indirect materials.
   (4) Fixed manufacturing overhead.
   (5) Unit variable marketing costs.
   (6) Fixed marketing costs.
   (7) Administrative costs.

c. What was the average unit value of last year's inventory under full absorption costing?

d. Identify the costs that Peter would consider noncontrollable for the next year.

e. How should Peter treat the cost of the unsalable old inventory in any Klogs decision? In analyzing the New Klogs project, identify the costs that require similar treatment.

f. If Klogs wishes to produce an additional 40,000 new clogs, list the differential costs.

g. In Peter's list of last year's costs, what costs would Peter treat as product costs and what costs are period costs for full absorption costing?

h. With two product lines, some costs will be common to both lines. Identify them.

Suggested Solution

Note: Answers may vary somewhat in practice. This solution is one of several that could be correct, depending on particular details about the company's production methods.

a. Opportunity cost = $40,000.

b. **(1)** Items (c) and (r):

$$\frac{\$140,000 + \$70,000}{70,000 \text{ Units}} = \$3.00.$$

   (2) Items (e) and (k):

$$\frac{\$210,000 + \$175,000}{70,000 \text{ Units}} = \$5.50.$$

(3) Items (a), (b), and (i) are probably indirect:

$$\frac{\$200 + \$500 + \$7,700}{70,000 \text{ Units}} = \$.12.$$

(4) Items (d), (f), (g), (h), and (q):

$$\$12,000 + \$15,000 + \$1,000 + \$6,000 + \$1,000 = \$35,000.$$

(5) Items (l) and (m):

$$\frac{\$9,750 + \$6,500}{65,000 \text{ Units}} = \$.25.$$

(6) Item (s): $1,000.

(7) Items (j), (n), (o), and (p):

$$\$28,000 + \$20,000 + \$100 + \$10,000 = \$58,100.$$

c. $$\$3.00 + \$5.50 + \$0.12 + \frac{\$35,000}{70,000 \text{ Units}} = \$9.12.$$

d. Peter would consider factory rent noncontrollable. In addition, he might consider some depreciation and utilities noncontrollable.

e. Klogs should treat the unsalable old inventory as a sunk cost. Other sunk costs (regarding the New Klogs project) are the development costs (= $3,000) and marketing survey costs (= $2,000).

f. Differential costs:

Direct Materials ($100,000 + $48,000)	$148,000
Direct Labor ($140,000 + $120,000)	260,000
Variable Manufacturing Overhead	1,000
Variable Marketing ($4,000 + $6,000)	10,000
Supervisor's Overtime	4,000
Utilities	1,200
Total	$424,200

g. Peter treats all manufacturing costs as product costs and treats all nonmanufacturing costs as period costs.

h. Common costs would probably include fixed manufacturing overhead and fixed marketing and administrative costs.

Key Terms and Concepts

Opportunity cost
Direct versus indirect costs
Cost object
Common costs
Manufacturing costs

Direct versus indirect materials
Direct versus indirect labor
Prime cost
Manufacturing overhead
Conversion costs

Nonmanufacturing costs

Marketing costs

Administrative costs

Variable versus fixed costs

Breakeven point

Contribution margin

Differential costs

Differential cost analysis

Product versus period costs

Full absorption costing

Variable costing

Profit margin and gross margin

Contribution margin

Sunk costs

Noncontrollable versus
controllable costs

Responsibility center

Questions, Exercises, Problems, and Cases

Questions

1. Review the meaning of the concepts or terms given above in Key Terms and Concepts.

2. "The cost of my trip to Hawaii was $3,000." Using the concept of cost developed in this chapter, explain why this statement is ambiguous.

3. Zappa, a mechanic, left his $25,000 a year job at Joe's Garage to start his own body shop. Zappa drew an annual salary of $15,000. Identify his opportunity costs.

4. People often use expenses and costs interchangeably, yet the terms do not always mean the same thing. Distinguish between the two terms.

5. Identify and describe the three elements that make up manufacturing costs.

6. Compare and contrast prime costs and conversion costs.

7. Firms usually classify nonmanufacturing costs as either marketing costs or administrative costs. How do these two types of costs differ?

8. "Since fixed manufacturing overhead costs such as factory rent or property taxes are independent of the number of units produced, we should treat them as period costs rather than product costs." Comment.

9. In financial accounting, accountants always treat manufacturing costs as product costs, and nonmanufacturing costs as period costs. Is this a hard-and-fast rule in accounting in general? Explain.

10. Can costs that we normally considered fixed be variable? Conversely, can normally variable costs be fixed?

11. "All differential costs are variable costs." Comment.

12. Mark Burchinshaw, a member of the Shaughnessy Heights Country Club, paid $400 for unlimited tennis court time for the entire summer because he anticipated spending many hours improving his game. In early June, Mark slipped on a wet floor at work, severely wrenching his ankle. Mark's ankle was put in a cast for 8 weeks. With 3 weeks left on his summer tennis deal, Mark was back on the courts the moment his cast came off, despite his doctor's advice to avoid strenuous exercise for a month. "This summer's tennis court time cost me $400," Mark said. "I have to get my money's worth." Given your understanding of cost concepts, comment.

13. "This is an excellent feasibility study of our new product, Hughes. But why haven't you included the cost of the test marketing we carried out last month in the analysis?" How should Hughes reply?

14. What do managerial accountants mean when they speak of cost behavior? Why is it important in managerial decision making?

15. What is a cost object? How are the concepts of direct and indirect costs related to it? Can direct costs be indirect, or vice versa?

16. Why is the idea of controllability important when managers use accounting data for performance evaluation and decision making?

17. "Fixed costs are really variable. The more you produce, the smaller the unit cost of production." Is that statement correct? Why or why not?

18. *(Adapted from CPA exam.)* You are to match each of the listed items that follow with one of the numbered terms that *most specifically* identifies the cost concept indicated parenthetically. The same term may be used more than once.

Terms

(1) Common cost.
(2) Controllable cost.
(3) Direct cost.
(4) Estimated cost.
(5) Fixed cost.
(6) Historical cost.
(7) Differential cost.
(8) Indirect cost.
(9) Opportunity cost.
(10) Original cost.
(11) Prime cost.
(12) Replacement cost.
(13) Sunk cost.
(14) Full absorption costing.
(15) Variable costing.

Items

a. The management of a corporation is considering replacing a machine that operates satisfactorily with a more efficient new model. Depreciation on the cost of the existing machine is omitted from the data used in judging the proposal, because it has little or no significance with respect to such a decision. *(The omitted cost.)*

b. One of the problems encountered by a bank in attempting to establish the cost of a commercial deposit account is the fact that many revenue-producing activities share many facilities and services. *(Costs of the shared facilities and services.)*

c. A company declined an offer to rent one of its warehouses and elected to use the warehouse for storage of extra raw materials to ensure uninterrupted production. Accounting has charged storage cost with *the monthly amount of the rental offered.* *(This cost is known as?)*

d. A manufacturing company excludes all "fixed" costs from its valuation of inventories, assigning to inventory only applicable portions of costs that vary with changes in volume. *(The term accounting employs for this costing procedure.)*

e. The sales department urges an increase in production of a product and, as part of the data presented in support of its proposal, indicates the total additional cost involved for the volume level it proposes. *(The increase in total cost.)*

f. The "direct" production cost of a unit includes those portions of *labor* and *materials* obviously traceable directly to the unit. *(The term used to specify the sum of the two named components.)*

19. Assuming no income taxes, how should management use each of the following costs in a decision to replace old equipment?
a. Book value of old equipment.
b. Disposal value of old equipment.
c. Cost of new equipment.

20. Classify each of the following costs as variable or fixed or a combination of the two. For each fixed cost, attempt to judge the time period over which the cost is fixed.
    a. Depreciation of an office building.
    b. Costs of raw materials used in producing a firm's products.
    c. Leasing costs of a delivery truck, which is $950 per month and $.38 per mile.
    d. Costs of internal programs for teaching recent business school graduates about the operating procedures and policies of the firm.
    e. Local property taxes on land and buildings.
    f. Compensation of sales staff on straight commission.
    g. Compensation of sales staff on salary plus commission.
    h. Fees paid to an independent firm of CPAs for auditing and attesting to financial statements.

21. A medical doctor (pathologist) and several laboratory technicians staff the pathology laboratory at Presbyterian University Hospital. The lab contains equipment of two basic kinds: microscopes and the like for doing individual tests and sophisticated testing equipment for doing 12 tests simultaneously on batches of specimens from several patients. A list of costs follows.
    a. Salary of the pathologist.
    b. Hourly wages of the lab technicians.
    c. Depreciation of a microscope.
    d. Leasing costs of sophisticated testing equipment. The lab leases the equipment for $2,000 per month plus a charge of $1 per batch of specimens run plus a charge of $.10 per specimen in each batch.
    e. Supplies for tests.
    f. Fees paid to a local university professor of accounting who has been helping the hospital director understand the causes of total costs shown for each month.
    (1) In your judgment, are these costs variable, fixed, or a combination of these?
    (2) For each cost with a fixed component (all but strictly variable), attempt to judge the time period over which the cost is fixed.

Exercises

22. *Opportunity cost analysis.* Geoff Parkhurst operates a covered parking structure that can accommodate up to 300 cars. Geoff charges $1 per hour for parking, and on normal days, including Saturdays and Sundays, the structure is 80 percent full. Parking attendants are paid $4.00 an hour to staff the cashier's booth at Parkhurst Parking. Utilities and other fixed costs average $500 per month. Recently, the manager of a nearby hotel approached Geoff concerning the reservation of 50 spots over an upcoming weekend for a small convention party for a lump sum of $300. Normally, Geoff welcomed such opportunities, but this particular weekend was a football weekend. Because of the structure's proximity to the football stadium, all spots would be taken 2 hours before game time on football Saturdays if the 50 spots were not reserved

for the hotel, and the structure would stay full until the end of the game 6 hours later. What is the opportunity cost of accepting the offer?

23. *Manufacturing cost concepts.* Bubba Brothers, a toy manufacturer, produces a variety of inflatable plastic toys. One day, the owner (Bubbles, as he is affectionately known to his employees) decided to take a look at the manufacturing costs of Squeaky Duck, a product the company introduced 2 years ago. Squeaky Duck is an inflatable plastic duck with a whistle attached to its beak. During the last 6 months, Bubba Brothers produced 10,000 Squeaky Ducks and incurred the following costs:

Plastic	$2,000
Labor—Cutting	1,000
Labor—Assembling	5,000
Whistle	3,000
Paint (nontoxic)	500
Machine Cost (Variable Overhead)[a]	2,000
Fixed Manufacturing Overhead[b]	2,500

[a]Allocated factory machine cost (for example, power and maintenance) based on machine-hours used by product.

[b]Allocated to the product based on machine-hours the product used.

a. Calculate unit prime costs and total conversion costs.
b. Identify the common costs.

24. *Manufacturing costs.* Whizz Incorporated produced 3,000 Kiddy Kars in May. Their plant incurred the following costs for that month:

Variable Costs:					
Cutting		**Fabrication**		**Assembly**	
Wood	$3,000	Labor	$6,000	Paint	$ 1,000
Labor	4,500	Nails	500	Labor	7,500
		Sandpaper	100	Wheels	12,000
				Axles	6,000

Fixed Costs:	
Plant Supervisor's Salary	$1,200
Utilities (independent of units)	200
Depreciation—Machinery	300
Plant Rent	500

For each Kiddy Kar, calculate the following:
a. Direct materials cost.
b. Direct labor cost.
c. Variable manufacturing overhead.
d. Fixed manufacturing overhead.

25. *Nonmanufacturing costs.* Trailblaster, a sleeping bag manufacturer, sold 10,000 sleeping bags in Year 6 and filed the following year-end income statement:

Sales Revenue		$500,000
Less Cost of Goods Sold		300,000
Gross Margin		$200,000
Less:		
Advertising (fixed costs)	$1,000	
Sales Commissions to Dealers	5,000	
Office Rent	4,800	
Office Supplies	200	
Depreciation—Office Equipment	100	
Sales Promotion (fixed cost)	2,000	13,100
Operating Profit		$186,900

   a. Calculate variable marketing costs.
   b. Calculate fixed marketing costs.
   c. Calculate administrative costs.

26. *Product and period costs.* Refer to Trailblaster in Exercise 25. Suppose that the cost of goods sold could be broken down into the following costs:

Direct Materials	$ 50,000
Direct Labor	100,000
Variable Overhead	80,000
Fixed Overhead	70,000

   a. What would the product costs and period costs be according to generally accepted accounting principles using full absorption costing?
   b. If management wants to make an internal decision to treat only variable manufacturing costs as product costs (that is, variable costing), what would the product costs and period costs be?

27. *Differential cost analysis.* Healthy Foods, Inc., is considering a contract to supply a government agency with 10,000 meals per year for senior citizens. Each meal has a variable cost of $4 and Healthy Foods would sell it to the government agency for $6. An opponent of this contract has stated that Healthy Foods should not accept the contract because the cost per meal would be $7, including fixed costs of $30,000 per year allocated to the meals. The total fixed costs in the company would be $1,000,000 whether or not it accepts this contract.

     What is the differential cost per year to Healthy Foods if the contract is accepted? Assuming $6 per meal is the highest price the government agency will pay, should Healthy Foods accept the contract?

28. *Differential costs*. Vito Enterprises, Inc., has a plant capacity that can produce 2,500 units annually. Its predicted operations for the year follow:

Sales (2,000 units at $40 each)	$80,000
Manufacturing Costs:	
Variable	$24 per Unit
Fixed..	$17,000
Marketing and Administrative Costs:	
Variable (sales commissions)	$2.50 per Unit
Fixed..	$2,500

Should the company accept a special order for 400 units at a selling price of $32 each? Assume these units are subject to half the usual sales commission rate per unit, and assume no effect on regular sales at regular prices. How will the decision affect the company's operating profit?

29. *Components of full costs*. Using the following data, put amounts beside each label in Exhibit 2.6 in the text.

Price per Unit	$100
Fixed Costs:	
Marketing and Administrative	$12,000 per Period
Manufacturing Overhead	$20,000 per Period
Variable Marketing and Administrative Costs...............	$5 per Unit
Direct Materials	$30 per Unit
Direct Labor	$15 per Unit
Variable Manufacturing Overhead	$10 per Unit
Units Produced and Sold	1,000 per Period

30. *Cost and margin relations*. Refer to the data in Exercise 29. Put amounts beside each label in Exhibit 2.7 in the text.

31. *Cost and margin relations*. Several exhibits in the text show basic relations among costs and margins. Given the following facts, complete the requirements in parts **a, b,** and **c.**

Sales Price	$200 per Unit
Fixed Costs:	
Marketing and Administrative	$24,000 per Period
Manufacturing Overhead	$30,000 per Period
Variable Costs:	
Marketing and Administrative	$6 per Unit
Manufacturing Overhead	$9 per Unit
Direct Labor	$30 per Unit
Direct Materials	$60 per Unit
Units Produced and Sold	1,200 per Period

    a. How much are each of the following unit costs (see Exhibit 2.6)?
        (1) Variable manufacturing cost.
        (2) Variable cost.
        (3) Full absorption cost.
        (4) Full cost.
    b. How much *per unit* are each of the following margins (see Exhibit 2.7)?
        (1) Profit margin.
        (2) Gross margin.
        (3) Contribution margin.
    c. How much *per unit* are each of the following costs (see Exhibit 2.1)?
        (1) Prime costs.
        (2) Conversion costs.

32. *Product and period costs.* Under full absorption costing, all costs of manufacturing the product are product costs (that is, they are inventoriable). Using the data from Exercise 31, what are the following?
    a. Product cost *per unit,* using full absorption costing.
    b. Period costs for the *period,* using full absorption costing.

33. *Cost-volume-profit relations.* Given the data in Exercise 31:
    a. Graph total revenue and total cost lines (as in Exhibit 2.3).
    b. Compute the breakeven point.

Problems and Cases

34. *Alternative concepts of cost: George Jackson* (adapted from CMA exam). George Jackson operates a small machine shop. He manufactures one standard product available from many other similar businesses and he also manufactures products to customer order. His accountant prepared the following annual income statement:

	Custom Sales	Standard Sales	Total
Sales........................	$50,000	$25,000	$75,000
Material	$10,000	$ 8,000	$18,000
Labor	20,000	9,000	29,000
Depreciation	6,300	3,600	9,900
Power.......................	700	400	1,100
Rent	6,000	1,000	7,000
Heat and Light	600	100	700
Other.......................	400	900	1,300
Total Costs	$44,000	$23,000	$67,000
Operating Profit	$ 6,000	$ 2,000	$ 8,000

    The depreciation charges are for machines used in the respective product lines. The rent is for the building space, which Mr. Jackson has leased for 10 years at $7,000 per year. The accountant apportions the rent and the heat and light to the product lines based on amount of floor space occupied. Material, labor, power, and other costs are variable costs that are direct costs of the product line causing them.

A valued custom parts customer has asked Mr. Jackson to manufacture 5,000 special units. Mr. Jackson is working at capacity and would have to give up some other business in order to take this business. He can't renege on custom orders already agreed to, but he could reduce the output of his standard product by about one-half for 1 year and use the free standard product machine time to produce the specially requested custom part. The customer is willing to pay $7.00 for each part. The material cost will be about $2.00 per unit and the labor will be $3.60 per unit. Mr. Jackson will have to spend $2,000 for a special device that he will discard when the job is done. The new job will also require power costing $300.

a. Calculate and present the following costs related to the 5,000-unit custom order:

(1) The differential cash cost of filling the order.

(2) The opportunity cost of taking the order.

(3) The sunk costs related to the order.

b. Should Mr. Jackson accept the order? Explain your answer.

35. *Differential analysis: Justa Corporation* (adapted from CMA exam). The Justa Corporation produces and sells three products. The company sells the three products, A, B, and C, in a local market and in a regional market. At the end of the first quarter of the current year, Justa has prepared the following income statement:

	Total	Local	Regional
Sales.....................................	$1,300,000	$1,000,000	$300,000
Cost of Goods Sold....................	1,010,000	775,000	235,000
Gross Margin	$ 290,000	$ 225,000	$ 65,000
Marketing Costs	$ 105,000	$ 60,000	$ 45,000
Administrative Costs	52,000	40,000	12,000
Total Marketing and Administrative Costs	$ 157,000	$ 100,000	$ 57,000
Operating Profit	$ 133,000	$ 125,000	$ 8,000

Management has expressed special concern with the regional market because of the extremely poor return on sales. Justa entered this market a year ago because of excess capacity. The firm originally believed that the return on sales would improve with time, but after a year Justa sees no noticeable improvement from the results as reported in the quarterly statement.

In attempting to decide whether to eliminate the regional market, management has gathered the following information:

	Products		
	A	B	C
Sales......................................	$500,000	$400,000	$400,000
Variable Manufacturing Costs as a Percentage of Sales	60%	70%	60%
Variable Marketing Costs as a Percentage of Sales	3%	2%	2%

continued

continued from page 62

Product	Sales by Markets	
	Local	Regional
A	$400,000	$100,000
B	300,000	100,000
C	300,000	100,000

All administrative costs and fixed manufacturing costs are common to the three products and the two markets, and are fixed for the period. Remaining marketing costs are fixed for the period and separable by market. All fixed costs are based on a prorated yearly amount.

a. Prepare the quarterly income statement showing contribution margins by markets.

b. Assuming that Justa has no alternative uses for its present capacity, would you recommend dropping the regional market? Why or why not?

c. Prepare the quarterly income statement showing contribution margins by products.

d. Management believes that it can have a new product ready for sale next year if it decides to continue the research. Justa can produce the new product simply by converting equipment presently used in producing product C. This conversion will increase fixed costs by $10,000 per quarter. What must be the minimum contribution margin per quarter for the new product to make the changeover financially feasible?

36. *Fixed and variable cost analysis* (adapted from a problem by D.O. Green). The sales representatives of the Piney Paper Company have secured two special orders, *either* of which, in addition to regular orders, will keep the plant operating at capacity through the slack season. Hence, the company can accept one order or the other, or neither. One order is for 20 million printed placemats and the other is for 30 million sheets of engraved office stationery. The proposed prices are $.0070 per mat for the placemats and $.0062 per sheet for the stationery. Cost estimates follow:

	Mats (cost per 100 mats)	Stationery (cost per 100 sheets)
Direct Materials	$0.3550	$0.2775
Labor Costs:		
Variable	0.1100	0.0993
Fixed..	0.0300	0.0089
Manufacturing Overhead Costs:		
Variable	0.0430	0.0330
Fixed..	0.0370	0.0523
Variable Marketing and Administrative Cost (already incurred to procure order)	0.0900	0.0912
Fixed Marketing and Administrative Cost (already incurred to procure order)	0.0950	0.0878
Total Cost per 100 items	$0.7600	$0.6500
Selling Price per 100 items	$0.7000	$0.6200

After reviewing these figures, management decides to reject the orders on the basis that "we cannot make much money if it costs more than we can sell it for."

Is management correct? Based on the data in the table, prepare a schedule to show which alternative Piney Paper should accept, if either.

37. *Estimating cash flows for decision making—sensitivity analysis.* An automobile dealer sells its Excalibre model in two versions—one with a gasoline engine and one with a diesel engine. It sells the gasoline version for $12,500 and the diesel version for $13,900. Assume for the purposes of this problem that the dealer actually charges the list prices in purchase transactions. According to federal EPA mileage tests, the gasoline version gets, on average, 23 miles per gallon of gasoline, which costs $1.50 per gallon. The diesel version gets, on average, 30 miles per gallon of diesel fuel, which costs $1.40 per gallon. Assume that a purchaser had decided to acquire one of these two cars and that other operating costs of the two models of cars are identical. The purchaser expects to drive 12,000 miles a year for 5 years before disposing of the car. Experts expect the gasoline version to have a resale value 5 years hence of $2,500, and the diesel a resale value of $2,600.

Assume that analysts expect costs per gallon of gasoline and diesel fuel to remain constant over the 5 years.

a. What cash flows for each year should the purchaser consider who wants to decide which of the two models of Excalibre to buy?

b. Assume that the customer can purchase each of the cars for a 10 percent discount from list price. Repeat the instructions in part **a**.

c. Assume that fuel costs increase at the rate of 10 percent per year and that the customer pays the full list price. Repeat part **a**.

38. *Cost data for multiple purposes: Omega Auto Supplies* (contributed by J. Lim). Omega Auto Supplies manufactures an automobile safety seat for children that it sells through several retail chains. Omega makes its sales exclusively within its five-state region in the Midwest. The cost of manufacturing and marketing children's automobile safety seats at the company's normal volume of 15,000 units per month follows:

Variable Materials	$300,000	
Variable Labor	150,000	
Variable Overhead	30,000	
Fixed Overhead	180,200	
Total Manufacturing Costs		$660,200
Variable Nonmanufacturing Costs	$ 75,000	
Fixed Nonmanufacturing Costs	105,000	
Total Nonmanufacturing Costs		180,000
Total Costs		$840,200

The following questions refer only to the data given here. Unless otherwise stated, assume that the situations described in the questions are not connected; treat each independently. Unless otherwise stated, assume a regular selling price of $70 per unit. Ignore income taxes and other costs that we do not mention in the data or in a question itself.

a. In any normal month, what would be the inventory value per completed unit according to generally accepted accounting principles?

b. On April 1, a nonprofit charitable organization offers Omega Auto Supplies a special-order contract to supply 2,000 units to several orphanages for delivery by April 30. Production for April was initially planned for 15,000 units, and Omega can easily accommodate this special order without any additional capacity costs. (Thus Omega would produce a total of 17,000 units.) The special-order contract will reimburse Omega for all manufacturing costs plus a fixed fee of $25,000. (Omega would incur no variable marketing costs on the special order.) Should Omega accept the special order?

Suggested Solutions to Even-Numbered Exercises

22. *Opportunity cost analysis.* On normal days,

$$\text{Excess Capacity} = 20\% \times 300 \text{ Spots for Cars}$$

$$= 60 \text{ Spots for Cars.}$$

Therefore, Parkhurst's structure can accept the offer on normal business days at an opportunity cost of zero.

On football Saturdays, however, the opportunity cost is

$$50 \text{ Spots for Cars} \times 6 \text{ Hours} \times \$1 = \underline{\$300}.$$

24. *Manufacturing costs*
   a. Direct materials cost:

Wood	$ 3,000
Wheels	12,000
Axles	6,000
	$21,000

Unit direct materials cost = $7.00.

   b. Direct labor cost:

Labor—Cutting	$ 4,500
Labor—Fabrication	6,000
Labor—Assembly	7,500
	$18,000

Unit direct labor cost = $6.00.

c.   Variable manufacturing overhead:

Nails	$ 500
Sandpaper	100
Paint	1,000
	$ 1,600

Unit variable overhead = $0.53.

d.   Fixed manufacturing overhead:

Plant Supervisor's Salary	$ 1,200
Utilities	200
Depreciation	300
Plant Rent	500
	$ 2,200

26.   *Product and period costs*

a.   Product costs are all manufacturing costs using full absorption costing. Therefore,

$$\text{Product Costs} = \$300,000.$$

Period costs are all nonmanufacturing costs. Therefore,

$$\text{Period Costs} = \$13,100$$

b.   Only *variable* manufacturing costs are treated as product costs using variable costing. Therefore,

$$\text{Product Costs} = \$50,000 + \$100,000 + \$80,000$$

$$= \$230,000.$$

All nonmanufacturing costs and fixed manufacturing costs are treated as period costs. Therefore,

$$\text{Period Costs} = \$70,000 + \$13,000$$

$$= \$83,100.$$

28.   *Differential costs*. Yes.

Special-Order Sales (400 × $32)		$12,800
Less Variable Costs:		
Manufacturing (400 × $24)	$(9,600)	
Sales Commissions (400 × $1.25)	(500)	(10,100)
Addition to Company Profit		$ 2,700

30. *Cost and margin relations*

$$\text{Profit Margin} = \text{Price} - \text{Full Cost}$$
$$= \$100 - \$92$$
$$= \$8.$$

$$\text{Gross Margin} = \text{Price} - \text{Full Absorption Cost}$$
$$= \$100 - \$75$$
$$= \$25.$$

$$\text{Contribution Margin} = \text{Price} - \text{Variable Cost}$$
$$= \$100 - \$60$$
$$= \$40.$$

32. *Product and period costs*

a. Product cost per unit:

$$\$60 + \$30 + \$9 + (\$30,000/1,200) = \underline{\underline{\$124}}.$$

b. Period costs:

$$\$24,000 + (\$6 \times 1,200) = \underline{\underline{\$31,200}}.$$

... PART TWO ...

Cost Methods and Systems

...

Each organization has a unique accounting system. Users of accounting information need to understand differences in accounting systems for two reasons. First, various accounting systems measure costs differently; without knowing the type of system that generated the cost, decision makers do not know whether they have the cost number suited to their purpose. Second, decision makers need to know how different accounting systems work to have input into designing them.

Chapter 3 presents alternative methods of computing product costs, including a discussion of a recent development known as activity-based costing. Chapter 4 describes different accounting systems used in various types of organizations: service, manufacturing, and merchandising, as well as accounting in just-in-time production environments. It also shows how cost systems in organizations that focus on jobs, such as construction and consulting, differ from those in organizations with a process orientation, such as producers of steel, cereals, and most consumer products. Chapter 5 discusses cost allocation to products, departments, and divisions, including the rationale for cost allocation, cost allocation methods, and pitfalls of misusing cost allocation in decision making. This chapter expands our discussion of activity-based costing and shows how organizations apply it using the two-stage cost allocation method.

... CHAPTER 3 ...

Product Costing Methods

Chapter Outline

- Product Costing for Managerial Purposes versus Product Costing for External Financial Reporting
- Overview of the Alternatives
- Cost Inclusion: Variable versus Full Absorption Costing
- Cost Measure: Actual or Normal Costing
- Cost Measure: Standard Costing
- Comparison of Product Costs
- Alternative Activity Bases for Applying Overhead
- Overhead Application in High-Technology Companies
- Activity-Based Costing
- Are Some Accounting Methods Systematically Better Than Others?

Chapter 2 emphasized that no single measure of cost is correct for all contexts or relevant for all decisions. Different types of costs are relevant for different purposes. For example, if we are deciding whether to increase the volume of manufacturing activity, we need to know which costs are fixed and which are variable. If we are preparing financial statements for reporting to shareholders, we need full absorption costing for inventory costs and cost of goods sold. The theme of "different costs for different purposes" appears throughout this book.

In the current competitive environment, managers of hospitals look for ways to reduce costs per patient day, partners in CPA firms seek methods of reducing audit costs, and managers in manufacturing firms examine ways to reduce their product costs to meet foreign and domestic competition. These managers, and others in competitive environments, must have a particular interest in understanding product costs if their organizations are to remain in business.

Chapter 2 introduced product costing using the actual costing method. This chapter describes alternatives to actual costing, namely, normal costing and standard costing. The chapter shows how different methods of measuring product costs can have a substantial impact on computations of operating profit and actions taken by managers who use these costs for decision making. Users of accounting data should understand these differences to be certain that they have the right data for their purposes.

Product Costing for Managerial Purposes versus Product Costing for External Financial Reporting

Organizations measure the costs of producing a good in many different ways. The cost of a unit in inventory includes, under generally accepted accounting principles, unit variable manufacturing costs and a share of fixed manufacturing costs. When the firm uses the product's cost for managerial decision making, it might include only the unit's variable manufacturing costs or it might include a share of marketing and administrative costs. The firm often evaluates performance by measuring unit costs using both standard variable costs and actual variable costs. In short, accounting can measure unit costs in different ways for different purposes.

Users of accounting information should know the alternative ways of measuring unit costs to avoid inappropriately using unit costs for one purpose that accountants intended for another purpose. Users of accounting can also put their knowledge of alternative product costing methods to good use by providing meaningful input to the design of accounting systems.

An example of a former student in an MBA class emphasizes the importance of understanding product costing methods. The student, who worked as an industrial engineer for a large automobile company, told of an assignment to operate a computerized model to ascertain the optimal product mix for the company.[1] This model required as input, among other things, the *variable cost* of each product produced. When the firm first implemented the model, the former student asked plant managers and their accountants for the unit cost of each product produced in each plant.

The plant managers and accountants did not realize that the model specifically required *variable* unit costs. They provided data on the unit costs used for finished goods inventory valuation, which were *full absorption* costs. (Recall from Chapter 2 that full absorption unit costs include unit variable manufacturing costs *plus* a

---

[1]Readers familiar with production and management science techniques will recognize this as a linear programming problem, which we discuss in Chapter 8.

Exhibit 3.1

Alternative Cost Measures

	Cost Measure		
Cost Inclusion	Actual Costing	Normal Costing	Standard Costing
Variable Costing	X	X	X
Full Absorption Costing	X	X	X

share of fixed manufacturing costs.) In addition, the costs provided were the actual (historical) costs incurred, not the future costs estimated for the period in which the engineers were to compute the product mix.

Without realizing that the unit costs provided were inappropriate for the model, the company's industrial engineers computed the product mix. It should come as no surprise that the results were suboptimal. Management eventually tracked down and corrected the problem, but not without some lost profits and embarrassment to those involved.

Cases like this one commonly occur in practice. They lead us to emphasize the importance of better communication between the users and suppliers of accounting information.

Overview of the Alternatives

The 2 × 3 matrix in Exhibit 3.1 shows the six fundamentally different ways to measure a product's unit cost.

The choice of product costing method results essentially from answers to the following questions:

1. *Cost inclusion.* What costs will the firm include in per-unit manufacturing costs? The choices are *variable costing* and *full absorption costing.*

2. *Cost measure.* How will the firm measure costs? The choices are *actual costing, normal costing,* and *standard costing.*

For now, we limit our discussion to the cost of producing the product and exclude marketing and administrative costs.

Cost Inclusion: Variable versus Full Absorption Costing

Variable Costing

Chapter 2 introduced the difference between variable costing and full absorption costing. Using a **variable costing** system, the unit manufacturing costs for inventory valuation are the variable manufacturing costs. We assume that direct materials, direct labor, and variable manufacturing overhead are variable costs unless we state otherwise. Of course, firms may fix some or all of the direct labor in the short run. If so, the firm would treat these fixed costs just as we treat fixed manufacturing overhead in our examples.

Full Absorption Costing

When an organization uses **full absorption costing,** the product "fully absorbs" all manufacturing costs, including both variable and fixed manufacturing costs. External financial reporting holds these costs in inventory on the balance sheet until the firm sells the units and then matches the costs against revenue as an expense on the income statement.

Since fixed manufacturing costs are total costs, not unit costs, accounting uses the following formula to convert them to unit costs:

$$\text{Unit Fixed Manufacturing Cost} = \frac{\text{Total Fixed Manufacturing Costs for the Period}}{\text{Activity for the Period}}.$$

Note how full absorption costing "unitizes" fixed costs. Accounting converts a total cost that the firm fixed over a range of activity levels to a "unit" cost by allocating the total cost equally to the units produced.

Because accountants measure and report full absorption unit costs, decision makers sometimes mistake them for relevant variable costs. We discuss this problem, which occurs repeatedly in companies, in numerous contexts throughout this book. Follow this rule of thumb for decision-making purposes: "Do not use data for decision making that contain unitized fixed costs."

Full absorption unit costing information is readily available in companies, because external financial reporting requires these data under generally accepted accounting principles and income tax regulations. Firms easily misuse this information for managerial decisions. Firms may not have variable costs per unit as readily available, however, because accounting often does not break costs down into fixed and variable components.

Profit Effects of Variable Versus Full Absorption Costing

In this section we examine the profit effects when an organization uses variable or full absorption costing for inventory evaluation. Assume the following facts for Electron, Inc., for one month (based on the example in Chapter 2):

1. Electron produced 10,000 units.
2. Variable manufacturing costs are $8 per unit produced, made up of $6 for materials, $1 for direct labor, and $1 for variable overhead. Fixed manufacturing overhead is $50,000 per month, and $5 per unit (= $50,000 cost at 10,000

units). Unit full absorption cost at 10,000 units is $13 (= $8 variable plus $5 fixed).

3. Selling price is $25 per unit.

4. Variable marketing costs are $1 per unit sold.

5. Fixed marketing and administrative costs are $60,000 per month.

Comparison of Variable and Full Absorption Costing: Production Is Greater Than Sales

We first examine the reported profit effects when production exceeds sales and inventories increase. Assume Electron, Inc., had 1,000 calculators in beginning finished goods inventory. Accounting valued these calculators under each method as follows:

	Total (1,000 units)	Per Unit
Variable Costing...	$ 8,000	$ 8.00
Full Absorption Costing	$13,000	$13.00

During the month, Electron produced 10,000 units, incurring the manufacturing costs noted above, and sold 9,000 units. Ending finished goods inventory comprised 2,000 units (= 1,000 units + 10,000 units produced − 9,000 units sold) valued as follows:

	Total (2,000 units)	Per Unit
Variable Costing...	$16,000	$ 8.00
Full Absorption Costing	$26,000	$13.00

Sales revenue was $225,000 (= 9,000 units sold × $25), and variable marketing costs were $9,000 (= 9,000 units sold × $1.00).

Exhibit 3.2 shows the comparative income statements with an increase in inventory. Profits differ under each method because of the different treatment of fixed manufacturing overhead.[2] Under variable costing, Electron expenses all of the fixed manufacturing overhead, $50,000 for the month. Under full absorption costing, some of the period's fixed manufacturing overhead remains in ending inventory. To

---

[2]We use the term *operating profits* to describe the bottom line of the income statement. We use that term whenever a firm prepares the income statement for internal use. We also distinguish operating profits from an economic notion of profits. Economic profits are sales revenue minus the sum of operating costs recorded in the accounting records *and* implicit opportunity costs, which are not recorded in the accounting records. Operating profits are sales revenue minus only the operating costs recorded in the accounting records.

Exhibit 3.2

**Variable and Full Absorption Costing:
Comparative Income Statements with Production (10,000 units) Greater
Than Sales (9,000 units)**

Variable Costing

Sales Revenue (9,000 units sold @ $25.00)		$225,000
Variable Cost of Goods Sold:		
Beginning Inventory (1,000 units @ $8.00)	$ 8,000	
Add Current Month's Production (10,000 units @ $8.00)	80,000	
	$ 88,000	
Subtract Ending Inventory (2,000 units @ $8.00)	16,000	
Variable Cost of Goods Sold		72,000
Variable Marketing Costs		9,000ᵃ
Contribution Margin		$144,000
Fixed Manufacturing Costs		50,000
Fixed Marketing and Administrative Costs		60,000
Operating Profit		$ 34,000

Full Absorption Costing

Sales Revenue (9,000 units sold @ $25.00)		$225,000
Cost of Goods Sold:		
Beginning Inventory (1,000 units @ $13.00)	$ 13,000	
Add Current Month's Production (10,000 units @ $13.00)	130,000	
	$143,000	
Subtract Ending Inventory (2,000 units @ $13.00)	26,000	
Cost of Goods Sold		117,000
Gross Margin		$108,000
Fixed Marketing and Administrative Costs		60,000
Variable Marketing and Administrative Costs		9,000ᵃ
Operating Profit		$ 39,000

ᵃ$1 × 9,000 units.

be precise, Electron expenses only $45,000 of fixed manufacturing overhead, computed as follows:

1.	Electron sold the first 1,000 units from beginning inventory. Fixed Manufacturing Overhead in First 1,000 Units (1,000 × $5.00 fixed overhead per unit)	$ 5,000
2.	Electron produced the next 8,000 units sold this period. Fixed Manufacturing Overhead in Next 8,000 Units (8,000 × $5.00)	40,000
	Total Fixed Manufacturing Overhead Expensed under Full Absorption Costing	$45,000

Under full absorption costing, fixed manufacturing overhead costs expensed are $5,000 lower, and therefore profits are $5,000 higher, as the following computations show:

Difference in Fixed Manufacturing Overhead Expensed = $50,000 (variable costing) − $45,000 (full absorption costing) $5,000

Difference in Profits = $39,000 Profit under Full Absorption Costing − $34,000 Profit under Variable Costing... $5,000

Comparison of Variable and Full Absorption Costing: Production Is Less Than Sales

In the previous example, the company had a beginning inventory of 1,000 units, produced 10,000 units, and sold 9,000 units, leaving an ending inventory of 2,000 units. Now assume that it is the next month, with the following change in facts.

Electron, Inc., had 2,000 units in beginning inventory, valued as follows (this is the previous month's ending inventory):

	Total (2,000 units)	Per Unit
Variable Costing..	$16,000	$ 8.00
Full Absorption Costing	$26,000	$13.00

During the month, Electron produced 10,000 units, incurring the production costs noted in the previous examples, and sold 11,000 units. Ending inventory comprised 1,000 units (= 2,000 units + 10,000 produced − 11,000 units sold), valued as follows:

	Total (1,000 units)	Per Unit
Variable Costing..	$ 8,000	$ 8.00
Full Absorption Costing	$13,000	$13.00

Sales revenue was $275,000 (= 11,000 units sold × $25), and variable marketing costs were $11,000 (= 11,000 units sold × $1.00).

Exhibit 3.3 shows comparative income statements with a decrease in inventory. Full absorption costing shows a lower profit than variable costing. Using variable costing, Electron expenses only the $50,000 fixed manufacturing overhead cost incurred during the period. Using full absorption costing, Electron expenses more than $50,000 fixed manufacturing overhead, computed as follows:

1. Electron sold the first 2,000 units from beginning inventory.
   Fixed manufacturing overhead in the first 2,000 units
   (2,000 × $5.00 fixed overhead per unit) $10,000
2. Electron produced the next 9,000 units sold this period.
   Fixed manufacturing overhead in the next 9,000 units
   (9,000 × $5.00 fixed overhead per unit) $45,000

   Total fixed manufacturing overhead expensed under full absorption
     costing.. $55,000

Exhibit 3.3

Variable and Full Absorption Costing:
Comparative Income Statements with Production Less Than Sales

Variable Costing

Sales Revenue (11,000 units sold @ $25.00)		$275,000
Variable Cost of Goods Sold:		
Beginning Inventory (2,000 units @ $8.00)	$ 16,000	
Add Current Month's Production (10,000 units @ $8.00)	80,000	
	$ 96,000	
Subtract Ending Inventory (1,000 units @ $8.00)	8,000	
Variable Cost of Goods Sold		88,000
Variable Marketing Costs		11,000[a]
Contribution Margin		$176,000
Fixed Manufacturing Costs		50,000
Fixed Marketing and Administrative Costs		60,000
Operating Profit.		$ 66,000

Full Absorption Costing

Sales Revenue (11,000 units sold @ $25.00)		$275,000
Cost of Goods Sold:		
Beginning Inventory (2,000 units @ $13.00)	$ 26,000	
Add Current Month's Production (10,000 units @ $13.00)	130,000	
	$156,000	
Subtract Ending Inventory (1,000 units @ $13.00)	13,000	
Cost of Goods Sold		143,000
Gross Margin		$132,000
Fixed Marketing and Administrative Costs		60,000
Variable Marketing and Administrative Costs		11,000[a]
Operating Profit.		$ 61,000

[a]$1 × 11,000 units.

The amount of fixed manufacturing overhead expensed under variable costing is $50,000. The difference in the amount of costs expensed, $5,000 (= $55,000 − $50,000), is the difference in profits ($5,000 = $66,000 − $61,000) between variable and full absorption costing shown in Exhibit 3.3.

We recap manufacturing overhead expensed and operating profit for the two months from Exhibits 3.2 and 3.3 in Exhibit 3.4. It presents some interesting comparisons. First, the operating profit for the two month period is the same under either method—$100,000. That is because the total fixed manufacturing costs expensed for the two months, $100,000 are the same under both methods.

Second, operating profits are higher under full absorption costing in the first month because units produced exceed units sold (so some fixed costs that Electron expensed under variable costing are not expensed under full absorption costing). The reverse is true in the second month.

Third, the difference in monthly operating profits between the two costing methods equals the *difference in inventory change* between the two methods. In

Exhibit 3.4

Profit Effects of Variable versus Full Absorption Costing

	First Month	Second Month	Total
Variable Costing Income Statement			
Operating Profit.............................	$34,000	$66,000	$100,000
Fixed Manufacturing Cost:			
Incurred	$50,000	$50,000	$100,000
Expensed..............................	50,000	50,000	$100,000
Full Absorption Costing Income Statement			
Operating Profit.............................	$39,000	$61,000	$100,000
Fixed Manufacturing Cost:			
Incurred	$50,000	$50,000	$100,000
Expensed..............................	45,000	55,000	$100,000

general, we can trace differences in profits that arise when firms use alternative product costing methods to differences in inventories.

Fourth, the difference in monthly operating profits equals the difference in fixed manufacturing costs expensed under the two systems. When the amount of fixed manufacturing costs in the beginning inventory under full absorption costing equals the amount in ending inventory for a period, the fixed manufacturing costs expensed and operating profits are equal under both methods. A good rule of thumb is that *when the cost of inventory for manufactured goods does not change from the beginning of the period to the end of the period,* operating profits are *identical using either costing method.*

Our example assumes that the only fixed manufacturing cost is a portion of manufacturing overhead. If other manufacturing costs, such as direct labor, are fixed, accounting treats them as *product* costs under full absorption and *period* costs under variable costing, just like manufacturing overhead in our example.

The difference between full absorption profits and variable costing profits results from the different treatment of *fixed manufacturing costs,* which are the only costs inventoried. It does *not* result from any portion of marketing and administrative costs. These costs are period costs and therefore the firm cannot inventory them as product costs under either variable or full absorption costing.

Summary: Variable versus Full Absorption Costing

The variable costing method measures unit costs using only variable manufacturing costs. The variable costing method treats variable costs as *unit* costs and fixed costs as *period* costs. Managers usually find the variable costing method more useful than the full absorption costing method for managerial decision making, planning, and performance evaluation.

Full absorption costing adds fixed manufacturing costs to variable manufacturing costs to arrive at a unit product cost. Thus, units fully absorb all manufacturing costs. External financial reporting requires using the full absorption method. Virtually all manufacturing companies use full absorption costing for external reporting, but many also use variable costing for management purposes. This classic case shows that accounting information used for one purpose may not be useful (or may even be harmful) for another.

Cost Measure: Actual or Normal Costing

Normal Costing

Our previous comparison of variable and full absorption costing methods assumed that firms measure costs as actual costs incurred. We call this **actual costing.** This section describes a commonly used alternative to actual costing, known as **normal costing.** Normal costing uses *actual* direct material and direct labor costs, plus an amount representing "normal" manufacturing overhead. Under normal costing, a firm derives a rate for applying overhead to units produced before the production period. The firm uses this rate in applying overhead to each unit as the firm produces it. We first discuss the rationale for using normal manufacturing overhead costs; then we show how normal costing works.

Normal overhead costs have advantages over actual costs. First, actual total manufacturing overhead costs may fluctuate because of seasonality (the cost of utilities, for example), recording adjustments (compare actual with accrued property taxes, for example), or other reasons that are not related directly to activity levels. Also, if production is seasonal and overhead costs remain unchanged, the per-unit costs in low-volume months will exceed the per-unit costs in high-volume months, as the following example shows:

	Production	Total Monthly Variable and Fixed Manufacturing Overhead	Per-Unit Overhead Cost
January	1,000 Units	$20,000	$20
July	6,000 Units	30,000	5

Normal costs enable companies to smooth, or normalize, these fluctuations. The *per-unit* overhead cost would be the same throughout the year, regardless of month-to-month fluctuations in actual costs and activity levels.

Accounting systems can supply actual direct material and direct labor costs within a day after the firm incurs the costs in firms that use perpetual inventory systems and a computerized payroll system into which it enters labor time daily. In contrast, a firm may take a month or more to learn about the actual overhead costs for the same units. For example, often 2 weeks to a month (or longer) will elapse after the end of an accounting period before the firm receives invoices for utilities. The firm will not know the cost of supplies used until the end of a quarter or year when it takes an inventory of supplies. Thus firms frequently use a **predetermined overhead rate** to estimate the actual cost in advance of recording the actual cost. (We use the terms *predetermined* rate and *normal* rate interchangeably.).

Applying Overhead Costs to Production

Apply overhead costs to production using these four steps:

1. Select an activity base (for example, machine hours) for applying overhead to production.

2. Estimate the amount of overhead and the level of activity for the period (for example, 1 year).

3. Compute the predetermined (that is, normal) overhead rate from the following formula:

$$\text{Predetermined Manufacturing Overhead Rate} = \frac{\text{Estimated Manufacturing Overhead}}{\text{Normal (or Estimated) Activity Level}}.$$

4. Apply overhead to production by multiplying the predetermined rate computed in step **3** times the actual activity (for example, the actual direct labor hours worked to produce a product).

The first three steps take place before the beginning of the period. For example, a firm could complete these steps in November of Year 1 if it plans to use the predetermined rate for Year 2. Step **4** is done during Year 2.

Next we discuss these steps in more detail and show how a firm would apply them in the Electron example.

Example   In the previous year, Electron's total variable manufacturing overhead cost was $95,000 and the activity level was 50,000 machine hours. The company expects the same level of activity for this year and that variable manufacturing costs will increase to $100,000 because of inflation. Therefore

$$\text{Predetermined Variable Manufacturing Overhead Rate} = \frac{\$100,000}{50,000 \text{ Machine Hours}} = \$2.00 \text{ per Machine Hour.}$$

We compute the fixed manufacturing overhead rate in a similar fashion. Electron estimates manufacturing overhead cost to be $600,000 for this year and the activity level to be 50,000 hours, giving the following rate:

$$\text{Predetermined Fixed Manufacturing Overhead Rate} = \frac{\$600,000}{50,000 \text{ Machine Hours}} = \$12.00 \text{ per Machine Hour.}$$

The predetermined overhead rates mean that for each hour a machine operates, accounting charges the product with $2.00 for variable manufacturing overhead cost and $12.00 for fixed manufacturing overhead.

Assume that Electron actually used 4,500 machine hours for the month. Electron applied the following overhead to production:

Variable Manufacturing Overhead: 4,500 Hours at $2.00 . . . . $ 9,000
Fixed Manufacturing Overhead: 4,500 Hours at $12.00   54,000

We now demonstrate how the overhead would appear on the month's income statement. We use the example for Electron in which production exceeded sales volume. (See Exhibit 3.2 for actual variable and full absorption costing.) The facts are the same except we now assume Electron uses normal costing. We restate the facts here for your convenience.

	Total	Per Unit
Beginning Finished Goods Inventory:		
Variable Costing...	$ 8,000	$ 8.00
Full Absorption Costing	13,000	13.00
(For purposes of this example assume the same value for the beginning inventory whether Electron uses normal or actual costing.)		
Actual costs:		
Materials	$ 60,000	
Direct Labor	10,000	
Variable Overhead.......................................	10,000	
Fixed Overhead...	50,000	
Variable Marketing Costs.................................	9,000	
Fixed Marketing and Administrative Costs.....................	60,000	
Total..	$199,000	
Sales Revenue for 9,000 Units Sold.......................	225,000	

Flows of manufacturing costs through T-accounts using full absorption, normal costing and variable, normal costing appear in Exhibits 3.5 and 3.6. The debits to Work-in-Process Inventory assign costs to production. Electron computes overhead by multiplying the predetermined rate times the actual machine hours worked and applies it to production as work is done. The firm accumulates actual overhead with a debit to the Overhead accounts and credits to accounts such as Accounts Payable for the cost of utilities or Accumulated Depreciation for depreciation of manufacturing equipment.

As goods are finished, accounting credits the actual materials and labor costs and the applied overhead to Work-in-Process Inventory and debits them to Finished Goods Inventory. Accounting bases the credit to Finished Goods Inventory and debit to Cost of Goods Sold on the first-in, first-out cost flow assumption. Note that actual overhead costs do not flow through the inventory accounts if the firm uses normal costing. The firm accumulates them in the Overhead accounts as information becomes available. After the end of the accounting period, when the firm knows the actual costs, accounting closes the Overhead account and debits or credits an amount to the Overhead Adjustment account. Compute the overhead adjustment as follows:

Overhead Adjustment = Actual Overhead − Applied Overhead.

For Electron, Inc.:

$$\frac{\text{Variable Overhead}}{\text{Adjustment}} = \$10,000 - \$9,000 = \$1,000 \text{ (underapplied)}.$$

Exhibit 3.5

ELECTRON, INC.
Cost Flows: Full Absorption, Normal Costing

	Work-in-Process Inventory		Finished Goods Inventory		Cost of Goods Sold

Beginning Balance 0   Beginning Balance 13,000 | 13,000 ──┐
                                                  (1,000 units) │

Materials   60,000

Labor   10,000 | 133,000 ──────────────► 133,000 | 106,400 ──┘──────► 119,400
                                                          (8,000 units)

Variable
Overhead **(1)** 9,000
Fixed
Overhead **(2)** 54,000

Ending
Balance   0   26,600ᵃ

Variable Manufacturing Overhead

Actual	Applied
	$2 × 4,500 Actual
	Machine Hours
10,000	= $9,000 **(1)**
	1,000ᵇ **(3)**

Variable Overhead Adjustment

(3) 1,000ᵇ

Fixed Manufacturing Overhead

	$12.00 × 4,500
	Actual Machine Hours
50,000	= $54,000 **(2)**
(4) 4,000ᶜ	

Fixed Overhead Adjustment

4,000ᶜ **(4)**

ᵃUnit cost = $133,000/10,000 units = $13.30. Total inventory value = 2,000 units × $13.30 = $26,600.

ᵇEntry to close variable overhead cost account and set up variable overhead adjustment account.

ᶜEntry to close fixed overhead cost account and set up fixed overhead adjustment account.

The accounting system can debit or credit this overhead adjustment directly to the Cost of Goods Sold account instead of the Overhead Adjustment account. We use the Overhead Adjustment account in this book to keep track of the amount. Although we have shown the overhead adjustment at the end of the month for demonstration purposes, in practice a firm typically makes the adjustment after the end of the fiscal year. During the year, interim financial statements could show the

Exhibit 3.6

ELECTRON, INC.
Cost Flows: Variable, Normal Costing

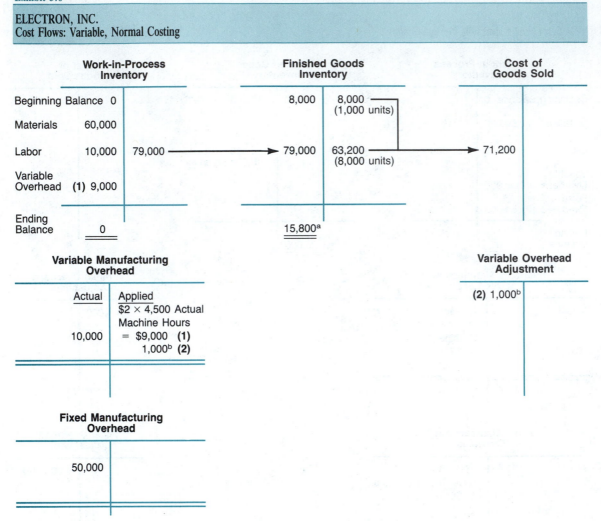

^{a}Unit cost = $79,000/10,000 units. Total inventory value = 2,000 units $\times$ $7.90 = $15,800.

^{b}Entry to close variable overhead account and set up variable overhead adjustment account.

actual materials and direct labor costs and applied overhead costs in Work-in-Process and Finished Goods Inventories and Cost of Goods Sold accounts.

Although a firm could allocate or prorate the overhead adjustment to units in inventory and to those sold, in practice firms typically expense it as a period cost, just as if it were part of the Cost of Goods Sold account. You could easily allocate the overhead adjustment in our simple example, but in practice this can be difficult. Firms typically accumulate actual overhead for a department that works on numerous different products, not for each product. Further, some overhead costs are inherently common to several product lines (for example, the department manager's salary). Because of this problem in assigning actual costs to product lines alone, it is difficult, if not impossible, to know which product line is responsible for differences between actual and applied overhead costs.

Exhibit 3.7 shows the income statements for variable, normal costing and full absorption, normal costing and compares them to corresponding actual costing statements. Note that under variable, normal costing, firms expense the actual fixed manufacturing overhead (just as they do in variable, actual costing).

Comparative Income Statements   Management potentially has more use for the variable costing reports shown in parts B and D of Exhibit 3.7 than the corresponding

Exhibit 3.7

ELECTRON, INC.
Comparative Income Statements for the Month

A. Actual/Full Absorption Costing

Sales Revenue	$225,000
Less Cost of Goods Sold	117,000
Gross Margin	$108,000
Less Marketing and Administrative Costs	69,000
Operating Profits	**$ 39,000**

B. Actual/Variable Costing

Sales Revenue	$225,000
Less:	
Variable Cost of Goods Sold	72,000
Variable Marketing and Administrative Costs	9,000
Contribution Margin	$144,000
Less Fixed Manufacturing Costs	50,000
Less Fixed Marketing and Administrative Costs	60,000
Operating Profits	**$ 34,000**

C. Normal/Full Absorption Costing

Sales Revenue	$225,000
Less Cost of Goods Sold (normal)	119,400
Add Overapplied Overhead	3,000
Gross Margin	$108,600
Less Marketing and Administrative Costs	69,000
Operating Profits	**$ 39,600**

D. Normal/Variable Costing

Sales Revenue	$225,000
Less:	
Variable Cost of Goods Sold (normal)	71,200
Underapplied Overhead	1,000
Variable Marketing and Administrative Costs	9,000
Contribution Margin	$143,800
Less Fixed Manufacturing Costs	50,000
Less Fixed Marketing and Administrative Costs	60,000
Operating Profits	**$ 33,800**

full absorption statements in parts A and C, because the variable costing statements present more information about cost behavior. Firms must use one of the full absorption statements, A or C, for external reporting, however.

Cost Measure: Standard Costing

Using **standard costing,** firms develop a standard or predetermined cost for each unit. In most cases, management establishes these costs as the norm. In that sense, they are the costs that the firm ''should'' incur to produce each unit. Firms develop standards for each input—for example, direct materials, direct labor, and manufacturing overhead in manufacturing companies; and direct labor and overhead in service organizations.

Why Do Companies Use Standard Costs?

- Standards are ''norms'': They are benchmarks for performance. By comparing the actual costs against the standards, companies can measure how well they control costs.

- Planning and decision making require estimates of what costs would be if a firm takes a proposed action. The firm can use standard costs as those estimates.

- Firms also use standard costs in inventory valuation for financial reporting. Firms can reduce much of the clerical work needed to accumulate costs and allocate them to each unit produced if they use standard costing systems.

    In short, firms can use standard costs for all three purposes of accounting information: managerial decision making, planning and performance evaluation, and external reporting.

Standard Costing Methods

Next we describe how we developed and used standard costs for the Electron, Inc., example. We describe an approach similar to one that many companies follow.

Example   Electron, Inc., computed the standard cost of each calculator as follows. (Like many companies, Electron, Inc., revises its standards yearly.)

Direct Materials   Based on engineering studies of the amount of direct materials required to make a calculator and the estimated costs of those materials, Electron set the standard as follows:

Direct Materials . . . . $6.50 per Calculator

Direct Labor   Based on studies of the time required to make a calculator and inevitable idle time, Electron set the standard direct labor time at 0.06 hour per calculator. Electron estimated labor costs, including fringe benefits and employer-paid payroll taxes, to be $20.00 per hour. The direct labor cost follows:

Direct Labor (0.06 hour at $20.00) .... $1.20 per Calculator

---

Variable Manufacturing Overhead   The standard variable overhead *rate* is the same as the predetermined rate under normal costing. Accounting multiplies that rate ($2.00 per machine hour) by standard machine hours per unit, which Electron set at 0.5 hour per unit, to give the standard variable manufacturing overhead cost per unit:

Variable Manufacturing Overhead Cost (0.5 hour at $2.00) .... $1.00 per Calculator

---

Fixed Manufacturing Overhead   The standard fixed overhead *rate* is also the same as the predetermined rate for normal costing. The account system multiplies that rate ($12.00 per machine hour) by the standard machine hours per unit to give the standard fixed manufacturing overhead cost per unit:

Fixed Manufacturing Overhead Cost (0.5 hour at $12.00) .... $6.00 per Calculator

---

Exhibit 3.8 shows the standard cost per calculator.

The flow of standard costs through T-accounts requires an understanding of variances between actual and standard costs. We cover these variances in Chapter 14. The Appendix to Chapter 14 presents the flow of standard costs through accounts.

Exhibit 3.8

ELECTRON, INC.
Standard Costs

Direct Materials..	$ 6.50
Direct Labor (0.06 labor hours × $20.00).....................................	1.20
Variable Manufacturing Overhead (0.5 machine hours × $2.00)	1.00
Total Standard Variable Unit Cost	$ 8.70
Fixed Manufacturing Overhead (0.5 machine hours × $12.00)	6.00
Total Standard Full Absorption Unit Cost	$14.70

Comparison of Product Costs

Exhibit 3.9 summarizes the six combinations of product costing methods we have discussed to this point and warrants special study. Note that full absorption unit costs systematically exceed variable costing unit costs because variable costing excludes fixed manufacturing overhead from product costs. This relation holds as long as fixed manufacturing overhead costs are greater than zero.

Managers use this relation for decision making. Recall that firms use full absorption unit costs in inventory valuation for external financial reporting, whereas they use variable costs for many internal decisions. If decision makers mistakenly use full absorption costs when they think they are using variable costs, they will systematically overstate unit cost estimates and incorrect decisions may result.

Exhibit 3.9

ELECTRON, INC.
Comparison of Product Costs

	Cost Measure		
Cost Inclusion	Actual Costing[a]	Normal Costing[a]	Standard Costing[b]
Variable Costing:			
Direct Materials	Actual = $6.00	Actual = $6.00	Standard = $6.50
Direct Labor	Actual = $1.00	Actual = $1.00	Standard = $1.20
Variable Manufacturing Overhead	Actual = $1.00	Normal = $ .90	Standard = $1.00
Fixed Manufacturing Overhead	—	—	—
Total Product Cost	$8.00	$7.90	$8.70
Full Absorption Costing:			
Direct Materials	Actual = $6.00	Actual = $6.00	Standard = $6.50
Direct Labor	Actual = $1.00	Actual = $1.00	Standard = $1.20
Variable Manufacturing Overhead	Actual = $1.00	Normal = $ .90	Standard = $1.00
Fixed Manufacturing Overhead	Actual = $5.00	Normal = $5.40	Standard = $6.00
Total Product Cost	$13.00	$13.30	$14.70

[a]We give materials and labor costs in the text. Overhead costs are computed as follows:

Actual Costing	Normal Costing

Actual Costing

Variable Manufacturing Overhead:

$$\frac{\$10{,}000 \text{ Actual Costs}}{10{,}000 \text{ Units Produced}} = \$1.00 \text{ per Unit}$$

Fixed Manufacturing Overhead:

$$\frac{\$50{,}000 \text{ Actual Costs}}{10{,}000 \text{ Units Produced}} = \$5.00 \text{ per Unit}$$

Normal Costing

Variable Manufacturing Overhead:

$$\frac{\$2 \times 4{,}500 \text{ Hours}}{10{,}000 \text{ Units Produced}} = \frac{\$9{,}000 \text{ Applied}}{10{,}000 \text{ Units Produced}}$$

$$= \$.90 \text{ per Unit.}$$

Fixed Manufacturing Overhead:

$$\frac{\$12 \times 4{,}500 \text{ Hours}}{10{,}000 \text{ Units Produced}} = \frac{\$54{,}000 \text{ Applied}}{10{,}000 \text{ Units Produced}}$$

$$= \$5.40 \text{ per Unit.}$$

[b]From Exhibit 3.8.

Example   Electron receives a special order for 100 calculators. Filling this order will affect only variable manufacturing costs. Revenue from the order would be $1,000, that is, $10 per calculator. The company's best estimate of the unit cost for this order is the normal cost.

A manager at Electron argues: ''We cannot accept this order. Each unit costs $13.30 (using full absorption, normal cost), and the per-unit price is only $10.''

The manager's error, of course, is that the appropriate per-unit cost is only $7.90 (using variable, normal cost), not $13.30. The full absorption unit cost includes some fixed costs that Electron has allocated to units based on an expected activity level. But this order would not affect fixed costs. In short, the confusion between full absorption and variable unit costs can lead to systematic errors in cost estimation and wrong decisions.

Managerial Application

Variable versus Full Costs in Banking[a]

American National Bank in Chicago offered a check processing service for smaller banks in the Chicago area. Small banks accumulated and sent their checks to American National, which presented them to the banks on which the checks were drawn. The major direct costs of this service were the costs of processing checks and the costs of outside vendor charges, such as the use of the Federal Reserve clearinghouse. In addition, indirect costs are added to the direct costs of each product line. The sum of the direct and indirect costs were the full costs that covered all costs of running the bank, including general and administrative costs.

Several other financial institutions in Chicago also offered this service. Although American National relied on its excellent reputation for quality service to justify charging a higher price than its competitors, it nevertheless had dropped its prices in recent years to remain competitive. At one point its prices were less than 80 percent of the full cost per unit. It appeared that the bank could not justify continuing to offer the service based on a comparison of prices and full costs.

Several executives believed the full cost numbers developed for monthly financial reporting purposes were not appropriate for the decision to drop this service, however. Their analysis indicated that the bank would save few, if any, of the indirect costs allocated to the product lines if it dropped this service. Further, some of the processing costs included depreciation and other costs that would not save cash if the bank discontinued the service. Their differential analysis indicated that the bank could lose several million dollars in contribution margin if it dropped the service. Based on their analysis, the bank decided against dropping the check processing service.

[a]Based on M. W. Maher, ''Economic Effects of Accounting Choice: A Case Study,'' unpublished manuscript, Graduate School of Management, University of California, Davis, 1990.

Alternative Activity Bases for Applying Overhead

Some common bases for applying overhead to products follow:

Activity Base	Predetermined Rate
Direct Labor Hours	Dollars per Direct Labor Hour
Machine Hours	Dollars per Machine Hour
Pounds of Direct Materials Used	Dollars per Pound
Direct Labor Dollars	Percentage of Direct Labor Dollars
Units of Output	Dollars per Unit of Output

(Problem 2 for Self-Study at the end of this chapter shows how to apply overhead using various bases.)

The easiest base to use is units of output produced. Companies with only one product generally apply overhead on that basis. Output is difficult to measure, however, in companies with multiple products. Consider a company such as General Motors which manufactures numerous types of automobiles, engines, auto parts, and other products. With multiple products, companies look for a common denominator to measure their activity. Companies typically use some input measure as a common denominator, such as direct labor hours or direct labor dollars. Companies can easily use direct labor hours and direct labor dollars because information about the amount of labor used on jobs and in departments is readily available from payroll records.

Nonmanufacturing Applications

Firms can adapt these bases to nonmanufacturing applications. For example, a hospital could use hours of nurse time as an activity base or a CPA firm could use hours of audit staff time. Passenger miles (or simply miles) may serve as an application of machine hours for transportation firms such as airlines, commuter railroads, or taxicab companies.

Overhead Application in High-Technology Companies

The activity base management chooses for applying overhead is developing into an important issue for managerial accounting, particularly for manufacturing companies that are changing their production technologies. Experts consider accounting systems that have not adapted to this changing technology outmoded.[3] Before the introduction of machine-intensive manufacturing methods, direct labor costs usu-

---

[3]See Robert S. Kaplan, ''Yesterday's Accounting Undermines Production,'' *Harvard Business Review* (July–August 1984), pp. 95–101 and John Holusha, ''Cost Accounting's Blindspot,'' *New York Times*, October 14, 1986, pp. 1, 54.

ally made up about 30 to 40 percent of the cost of making a product, overhead represented about 10 to 30 percent, and material costs made up the rest. After introducing more machine-intensive methods, many companies have found that their direct labor costs now comprise 10 percent or less of manufacturing costs, whereas overhead has increased to 40 percent or more. As a result, predetermined overhead rates in excess of $100 per labor hour (which itself costs only $10 to $30 per hour) are not unusual, yet overhead may be virtually unrelated to direct labor.

Suppose management selects direct labor hours as the activity base and computes a predetermined rate per direct labor hour. The accounting system charges every direct labor hour that is worked on a job not only with an amount for wages but also with an amount for overhead. Recall that overhead costs are indirect costs by definition, so any activity base that management selects is a somewhat arbitrary allocator for overhead. Suppose overhead actually represents machine-related costs such as machine repairs and power to operate machines. Using direct labor hours as the activity base makes the cost of using direct labor hours appear to be higher than it really is. When an hour is worked on a job, the accounting system appropriately charges that job with one amount for wages plus an additional amount for overhead applied to the job. In this case, the overhead application overstates the cost of direct labor hours and understates the cost of machine hours worked on the job. Thus a manager who wants to reduce the costs of production may mistakenly look for ways to reduce labor time instead of machine time spent on the job.

Multiple Overhead Allocation Bases

Management should use multiple bases for applying overhead, depending on the nature of the overhead cost and the cause of the cost. For example, management may apply the following costs using the corresponding activity bases:

Activity Base	Overhead Costs
Labor Hours or Dollars	Labor-related overhead costs, such as indirect labor, supervision, and personnel services
Machine Hours	Machine-related overhead costs, such as repairs and maintenance, energy costs to operate machines, and depreciation on a unit-of-activity basis
Quantity of Materials	Materials-related costs, such as handling, storage, and purchasing

The amount of effort that should go into the selection of an activity base is subject to cost-benefit analysis. A simplistic method of applying overhead to products may be inaccurate, but that alone does not justify a costly effort to improve the application method. For example, if a company applies overhead to production only to derive an inventory value for tax and external reporting purposes, and if inventories are small relative to other assets, a simple but reasonable method may meet the cost-benefit test.

Next we discuss activity-based costing which extends the use of multiple activity bases for overhead allocation.

Activity-Based Costing

Conventional product costing methods assume that volume is the only cost determinant, other than capacity decisions that affect fixed costs. In fact, many activities affect costs.

For example, consider two construction contractors: one builds standardized houses and one builds customized houses. Assume the average size and materials for the customized houses is the same as that for the standard houses, and that each builder constructs 100 houses. Would you expect the total cost of 100 houses to be the same for both contractors?

The standardized houses would probably cost less than the custom houses. Standardized houses would need only one set of plans. Labor would become more efficient through learning and practice. The contractor could supervise workers more easily because they would follow the same routine from house to house. The contractor could communicate more easily with subcontractors and monitor their work more easily. The contractor could obtain other efficiencies as well. Although the *volume* of customized and standard houses is equal, other activities, such as preparing plans and instructing workers, also cause costs. If the contractor needed more of these other activities to build customized houses, then customized houses would be more expensive.

Many companies have implemented activity-based costing to provide more information about the causes of costs than conventional product costing methods provide. **Activity-based costing** (also called transactions-based costing) is a method of assigning costs to goods and services that assumes all costs vary with the activities used to produce goods and services.

Activity-based costing provides more insight into the causes of costs than conventional costing methods do. Conventional costing methods divide the total costs by the number of units to compute a unit cost. In contrast, activity-based costing starts with the detailed activities required to produce a good or service and computes a product's cost using the following three steps.

1. Identify the activities or transactions that incur costs. We call these activities cost drivers. **Cost drivers** incur costs.

2. Assign a cost to each cost driver.

3. Sum the costs of the cost drivers that make up the product.

For example, Hewlett-Packard recently installed activity-based costing in its Roseville, California, Networks Division.[4] To compute a cost for personal computer circuit boards, for example, the accountants identified the following cost drivers: number of parts in the product, number of times labor inserted components in the circuit boards, hours of testing, and several others. The accountants assigned a cost to each cost driver as shown in Exhibit 3.10, summed these costs, and added the total to direct materials costs to compute the product's costs. (This division puts direct labor into overhead, like many high-tech companies, because direct labor

---

[4]D. Berlant, R. Browning, and G. Foster, "How Hewlett-Packard Gets Numbers It Trusts," *Harvard Business Review,* January–February, 1990, pp. 178–183.

Exhibit 3.10

HEWLETT-PACKARD[a]
Activity-Based Costing for a Circuit Board

Overhead Costs			
Activities (cost drivers)	Cost per Cost Driver	Number of Cost Drivers per Circuit Board	Cost per Circuit Board
Different Parts Purchased (affects cost of purchasing)	$0.10 per Part	× 94 Parts =	$9.40
Manual Insertions of Components	$0.35 per Insertion	× 13 Insertions =	$4.55
Hours of Testing	$70.00 per Hour	× .20 Hours per Circuit Board =	$14.00

Other items have been omitted to simplify this exhibit.
They totaled $19.52 per circuit board $19.52

Total Overhead (includes labor) $47.47

Total Direct Materials $75.17

Total Cost to Make One Circuit Board $122.64

[a]*Source:* D. Berlant, R. Browning, and G. Foster, ''How Hewlett-Packard Gets Numbers It Trusts,'' *Harvard Business Review,* January–February, 1990, pp. 178–183.

costs are too small for the firm to account for separately.) Activity-based costing has enabled Hewlett-Packard managers to identify which cost drivers have significantly affected product costs. From this information they have redesigned certain products to reduce costs.

Activity-based costing is a simple idea that can be costly to implement. Organizations that have complex production methods may find that conventional costing methods, which identify only volume as a cost driver, are inadequate for managerial use. Activity-based costing potentially provides benefits that exceed its costs in these cases.

Are Some Accounting Methods Systematically Better Than Others?

Managers frequently ask, ''What is the best accounting system?'' The answer is usually, ''It depends.'' It depends on the intended use of the accounting system.

In rare cases, however, firms can rank accounting systems for managerial purposes. For example, if two accounting systems are equally costly, the system that is ''finer'' (more detailed) is more desirable than the ''coarser'' system.[5] Suppose that

[5]Readers interested in a more technical, comprehensive discussion should consult J. Demski and G. Feltham, *Cost Determination* (Ames, Ia.: Iowa State University Press, 1976), p. 26; and J. Demski, ''Basic Ideas in the Economic Analysis of Information,'' in G. Lobo and M. Maher, eds., *Information Economics and Accounting Research* (Ann Arbor: School of Business, University of Michigan, 1980), pp. 11–13.

Exhibit 3.11

Summary Comparison of Full Absorption and Variable Costing in Manufacturing Companies

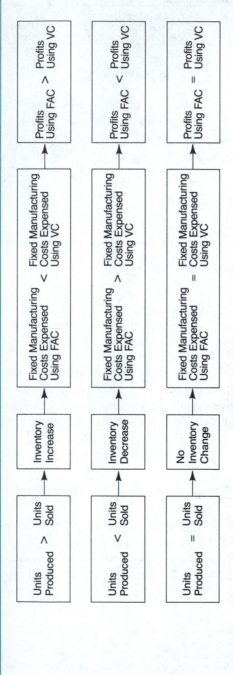

Note: These relations assume that unit costs of inventory do not change from period to period.

FAC = full absorption costing
VC = variable costing
$>$ = "are greater than"
$<$ = "are less than."

data from System 1 contain all of the data that System 2 contains and more. We would consider System 1 finer. For example, suppose that we compare cost data about a product from two accounting methods: one that separates fixed and variable manufacturing costs (System 1) and one that does not (System 2):

	System 1	System 2
Direct Materials	$ 4.00	$ 4.00
Direct Labor	3.00	3.00
Variable Manufacturing Overhead	1.00	
Unit Variable Cost	$ 8.00	
Total Manufacturing Overhead		3.00
Fixed Manufacturing Overhead Allocated to Each Unit ..	2.00	
Total Unit Cost	$10.00	$10.00

We would consider System 1 finer in this case, because it divides manufacturing overhead into variable and fixed elements, whereas System 2 shows only the sum. In a sense, System 1 breaks down the data more finely; thus System 1 contains at least as much information as System 2 and possibly more. We would prefer System 1 to System 2 if the systems were equally expensive to develop and operate.

This example shows another economic analysis of accounting information. Accounting, like any other factor of producing and marketing products, is subject to cost-benefit tests.

▪ Summary ▪

This chapter analyzes alternative product costing methods manufacturing companies typically use. You should understand these costing methods in order to know which cost to use in decision making, particularly when choosing between unit costs under full absorption and variable costing. Decision makers frequently use full absorption unit costs when variable costing unit costs would be appropriate for the decision.

Full absorption and variable costing differ significantly in their treatment of fixed manufacturing costs—full absorption costing "unitizes" them and allocates them to products; variable costing treats them as period expenses. This difference implies that operating profits will differ under each method if units produced and sold differ, as Exhibit 3.11 shows.

Under *normal* costing, accounting charges direct materials and direct labor to products at actual costs, but uses a *predetermined rate* for variable and fixed manufacturing overhead. The total variable and total fixed overhead charged to products for the period is the predetermined rate times a measure of *actual* activity (for example, direct labor hours). The unit variable and unit fixed overhead is the total normal cost divided by the actual number of units produced.

Note that the direct materials and direct labor costs charged to production departments are identical for each method. The choice of product costing method does not affect revenues, marketing costs, or administrative costs. The treatment of manufacturing overhead explains the entire difference in product costs among the four methods.

Problem 1 for Self-Study

Comparison of Variable to Full Absorption Costing: Chelwood Corporation

Chelwood Corporation manufactures a single product with the following costs:

Selling Price	$8.00 per Unit
Variable Manufacturing Costs (direct materials and direct labor) . . .	$4.80 per Unit
Fixed Manufacturing Overhead (all manufacturing overhead is fixed)	$160,000 per Month
Marketing and Administrative Costs (all fixed)	$80,000 per Month
Beginning Inventory:	
Variable Manufacturing Costs	$4.80 per Unit
Fixed Manufacturing Costs	$1.60 per Unit
Total	$6.40 per Unit

Chelwood has no work-in-process inventories and uses FIFO inventory cost flow assumption.

The president of Chelwood wants to analyze the effects of six different variations in sales and production units. To help you, accounting has included the following charts. Comment on the differences in operating profits.

Units[a]	(1)	(2)	(3)	(4)	(5)	(6)
	Sales = Production		Sales > Production		Sales < Production	
Sales	100	80	115	90	90	75
Production	100	80	100	80	100	80
Beginning Inventory	0	0	15	10	0	0
Ending Inventory	0	0	0	0	10	5

[a]All numbers in thousands.

Full Absorption Costing	(1)	(2)	(3)	(4)	(5)	(6)
Revenue						
Cost of Goods Sold						
Gross Margin						
Marketing and Administrative						
Operating Profit						
Beginning Inventory						
Ending Inventory						

Variable Costing

Variable Costing	(1)	(2)	(3)	(4)	(5)	(6)
Revenue						
Variable Cost of Goods Sold						
Contribution Margin						
Fixed Manufacturing Costs						
Fixed Marketing and Administrative						
Operating Profit						
Beginning Inventory						
Ending Inventory						

Suggested Solution

Current Period Unit Costs

Current Period Unit Costs	(1)	(2)	(3)	(4)	(5)	(6)
Full Absorption Unit Manufacturing Cost[a]	$6.40	$6.80	$6.40	$6.80	$6.40	$6.80
Variable Costing Unit Manufacturing Cost	4.80	4.80	4.80	4.80	4.80	4.80

[a]Full absorption unit manufacturing cost is

$$\$4.80 + \frac{\$160,000}{\text{Units Produced}}.$$

Therefore, $\$4.80 + \dfrac{\$160,000}{100,000} = \$6.40, \ \$4.80 + \dfrac{\$160,000}{80,000} = \$6.80.$

Full Absorption Costing[a]

Full Absorption Costing[a]	(1)	(2)	(3)	(4)	(5)	(6)
Revenue (at $8 per unit)	$800	$640	$920	$720	$720	$600
Cost of Goods Sold[b]	640	544	736	608	576	510
Gross Margin	160	96	184	112	144	90
Marketing and Administrative	80	80	80	80	80	80
Operating Profit	80	16	104	32	64	10
Beginning Inventory	0	0	96	64	0	0
Ending Inventory	0	0	0	0	64	34

[a]All dollar amounts in thousands.

[b]Cost of Goods Sold = Full Absorption Cost of Beginning Inventory + Full Absorption Cost of Current Month's Production − Full Absorption Cost of Ending Inventory.

Examples:

	Sales = 100 Production = 100	Sales = 90 Production = 80
Beginning Inventory	$ 0	10 units @ $6.40 = $ 64
+ Current Production	100 units @ $6.40 = $640	80 units @ $6.80 = $544
− Ending Inventory	$ 0	$ 0
= Total Cost of Goods Sold	$640	$608

Variable Costing[a]

	(1)	(2)	(3)	(4)	(5)	(6)
Revenue	$800	$640	$920	$720	$720	$600
Variable Cost of Goods Sold[b]	480	384	552	432	432	360
Contribution Margin	320	256	368	288	288	240
Fixed Manufacturing Costs	160	160	160	160	160	160
Fixed Marketing and Administrative	80	80	80	80	80	80
Operating Profit	80	16	128	48	48	0
Beginning Inventory	0	0	72	48	0	0
Ending Inventory	0	0	0	0	48	24

[a]All dollar amounts in thousands.

[b]Variable cost of goods sold equals variable costing unit cost times number of units sold: $4.80 × 100,000 = $480,000; $4.80 × 80,000 = $384,000; and so forth.

When units produced equal units sold, operating profits are the same under both variable costing and full absorption costing. When units sold exceed units produced, operating profits reported are higher under variable costing. Conversely, when units produced exceed units sold, operating profits are higher under full absorption costing. This difference in operating profits reported under the two product costing methods when units sold do not equal units produced results from the fact that accounting carries fixed manufacturing costs in inventory under full absorption costing, whereas it expenses fixed manufacturing costs as period costs under variable costing.

Problem 2 for Self-Study

Use of Alternative Overhead Bases in Normal Costing

Compute predetermined overhead rates and unit product costs for Pizza Makers using full absorption, normal costing and the following bases for applying overhead to products:

a. Direct labor hours.

b. Percentage of direct labor dollars.

c. Dollars per unit of output (that is, pizza).

Assume that Pizza Makers made the following estimates for the entire year before the accounting period in which it was to use the predetermined rates:

(1) Estimated Variable Overhead	$108,000
(2) Estimated Fixed Overhead	$120,000
(3) Estimated Labor Hours	12,000 Hours
(4) Estimated Labor Dollars per Hour	$20
(5) Estimated Output	120,000 Pizzas

Actual values for the month of March follow:

(1)	Actual Direct Labor Hours..	1,100 Hours
(2)	Actual Number of Units Produced..............................	10,000 Pizzas
(3)	Actual Labor Dollars per Hour	$21
(4)	Actual Direct Labor Cost per Pizza..............................	$2.31
(5)	Actual Direct Materials Cost per Pizza..........................	$1.10

Suggested Solution

Compute the predetermined overhead rates as follows:

	Base	Variable Overhead	Fixed Overhead
a.	Direct Labor Hours............	$\text{Rate} = \dfrac{\$108,000}{12,000 \text{ Hours}}$ $= \$9 \text{ per Hour.}$	$\text{Rate} = \dfrac{\$120,000}{12,000 \text{ Hours}}$ $= \$10 \text{ per Hour.}$
b.	Direct Labor Dollars...........	$\text{Rate} = \dfrac{\$108,000}{\$20 \times 12,000 \text{ Hours}}$ $= \dfrac{\$108,000}{\$240,000}$ $= 45 \text{ Percent of Labor Dollars.}$	$\text{Rate} = \dfrac{\$120,000}{\$20 \times 12,000 \text{ Hours}}$ $= \dfrac{\$120,000}{\$240,000}$ $= 50 \text{ Percent of Labor Dollars.}$
c.	Units of Output	$\text{Rate} = \dfrac{\$108,000}{120,000 \text{ Pizzas}}$ $= \$.90 \text{ per Pizza.}$	$\text{Rate} = \dfrac{\$120,000}{120,000 \text{ Pizzas}}$ $= \$1.00 \text{ per Pizza.}$

Compute the overhead costs per pizza as follows:

	Base	Variable Manufacturing Overhead	Fixed Manufacturing Overhead
a.	Direct Labor Hours....	$\dfrac{\$9 \times 1,100 \text{ Hours}}{10,000 \text{ Pizzas}}$ $= \$.99 \text{ per Pizza.}$	$\dfrac{\$10 \times 1,100 \text{ Hours}}{10,000 \text{ Pizzas}}$ $= \$1.10 \text{ per Pizza.}$
b.	Direct Labor Dollars ...	$\dfrac{45 \text{ Percent of Actual Direct Labor Costs}}{10,000 \text{ Pizzas}}$ $= \dfrac{.45 \times \$23,100}{10,000 \text{ Pizzas}}$ $= \$1.0395 \text{ per Pizza.}$	$\dfrac{50 \text{ Percent of Actual Direct Labor Costs}}{10,000 \text{ Pizzas}}$ $= \dfrac{.50 \times \$23,100}{10,000 \text{ Pizzas}}$ $= \$1.155 \text{ per Pizza.}$
c.	Units of Output (computed when predetermined rates were computed)	$\$.90 \text{ per Pizza.}$	$\$1.00 \text{ per Pizza.}$

Note that the overhead cost per pizza differs for each base because the expected relations among labor hours, labor dollars, and units of output did not hold. For example, Pizza Makers expected the hourly labor rate to be $20, but the actual rate was $21. Hence, the *direct labor dollar* base gives a higher cost per pizza than does the *direct labor hour* base. The following exhibit shows a comparison of units costs for each of the three bases. Note that the normal overhead cost differs for each base.

Actual Costs			Normal Overhead Costs Using Alternative Bases			Normal Costing: Total
Direct Materials	+ Direct Labor	+	Variable Overhead	+ Fixed Overhead	=	Unit Cost per Pizza
			Base			
			Direct Labor Hours $ .99	+ $1.10	=	$5.50
$1.10	+ $2.31	+	Direct Labor Dollars $1.0395	+ $1.155	=	$5.6045
			Units of Output $ .90	+ $1.00	=	$5.31

Key Terms and Concepts

Variable costing
Full absorption costing
Actual costing
Normal costing

Predetermined overhead rate
Standard costing
Activity-based costing
Cost driver

Questions, Exercises, Problems, and Cases

Questions

1. Review the meaning of the concepts or terms given above in Key Terms and Concepts.

2. Distinguish between full absorption costing and variable costing. Which method of costing would a firm use to evaluate the effects of decreasing production by 5 percent if it is currently producing at close to capacity?

3. How does accounting treat marketing and administrative costs under variable costing? Under full absorption costing?

4. Under what circumstances do operating profits under variable costing equal full absorption costing profits? When are variable costing profits smaller? When are they greater?

5. How can a company using full absorption costing manipulate profits without changing sales?

6. Describe comparative inventory changes under both variable costing and full absorption costing when
   a. Sales volume exceeds production volume.
   b. Production volume exceeds sales volume.

7. Does variable costing imply that inventory cost reflects every variable cost associated with a product?

8. "A 15-percent price increase to cover rising costs!" fumed an angry customer. "I know for a fact that materials cost has not increased, and the company has not increased its workers' pay. I bet the owner is lining his pockets!" Suppose that the company uses actual costs to measure book value of its products. Give possible explanations for the increase in costs.

9. How does normal costing differ from actual costing? Explain how accounting data obtained from one system may differ from the other.

10. How does standard costing differ from normal costing?

11. Refer to Exhibit 3.9 that compares the six alternative product costs. Explain the differences in (i) full absorption and variable costs, (ii) normal and actual costs, and (iii) normal and standard costs.

12. How does activity-based costing differ from conventional accounting methods?

Exercises

13. *Computing product costs for variable and full absorption costing.* The Happy Health Center performed 60,000 tests for a particular disease. The center incurred the following testing costs:

Direct Materials Used in Tests	$ 750,000
Direct Labor for Physician, Nurse, and Technician Time	900,000
Variable Overhead for Miscellaneous Supplies	50,000
Fixed Overhead	550,000
Total	$2,250,000

   a. Calculate the unit variable cost per test.
   b. Calculate the unit full absorption cost per test.

14. *Computing inventory value using variable costing and full absorption costing.* The following data pertain to operations of the Sikes Company in Year 1 and Year 5.

	Year 1	Year 5
Beginning Inventory in Units	0	6,000
Units Produced	50,000	48,000
Units Sold	48,000	50,000
Fixed Overhead Production Costs	$12,000	$12,000
Variable Overhead Production Costs	12,000	14,000
Fixed Marketing Costs	10,000	10,000
Direct Labor	36,000	40,000
Direct Materials	48,000	50,000

Sikes has no work-in-process inventories, and uses a FIFO inventory cost flow assumption.

a. Compute the dollar value of ending finished goods inventory in Year 1 under actual full absorption costing.

b. Compute the dollar value of ending finished goods inventory in Year 1 under actual variable costing, assuming that Sikes would incur all fixed overhead production costs even if production equaled zero.

c. Which method, full absorption or variable costing, implies larger reported operating profit for Year 1?

15. *Computing inventory value using variable costing and full absorption costing.* Refer to the data in the preceding problem for Sikes Company.

a. Compute the dollar value of ending finished goods inventory in Year 5 under actual full absorption costing.

b. Compute the dollar value of ending finished goods inventory in Year 5 under actual variable costing, assuming that Sikes would incur all fixed overhead production costs even if production equaled zero.

c. Which method, full absorption or variable costing, implies larger reported operating profit for Year 5?

16. *Computing allocated overhead and finished goods value.* The Speedway Boat Company allocates factory overhead to jobs on a direct labor hour basis at the rate of $3 per hour.

a. Job 745 for four sailboats required $8,400 of direct materials and $10,000 of direct labor at an average rate of $4 per hour. What was the total cost shown for job 745?

b. Job 305 for a small trawler required $6,300 of direct materials and $20,000 of direct labor at an average rate of $5 per hour. Job 305 sold for $40,000. What was the gross margin on this sale? (Gross margin is revenue less total manufacturing costs for the goods sold.)

17. *Applied overhead in a bank.* Megabank uses machine time as the basis for allocating overhead to its check processing activities. On January 1, Megabank estimated that production for the coming year would equal 800 million units. It also estimated that total overhead for the same year would equal $2,000,000 and that estimated machine time would equal 40,000 hours. The actual overhead, units produced, and machine time for the four quarters follow:

Quarter	Actual Units Production (in millions)	Actual Machine Time
1st	300 Checks	16,000 Hours
2nd	300 Checks	15,000 Hours
3rd	200 Checks	9,000 Hours
4th	100 Checks	6,000 Hours

a. Compute the predetermined overhead rate for applying overhead on the basis of machine hours.

    b. Compute the amount of overhead applied under normal costing for each quarter.

    c. Compute the unit cost for each quarter using normal costing.

18. *Comparison of full absorption and variable costing in income statement formats.* Consider the following facts:

	Year 1	Year 2
Sales Volume	70,000 Units	130,000 Units
Production Volume..........................	100,000 Units	100,000 Units
Selling Price	$20 per Unit	$20 per Unit
Variable Manufacturing	$13 per Unit	$13 per Unit
Fixed Manufacturing	$340,000	$340,000
Nonmanufacturing Costs (all fixed)	$150,000	$150,000

Prepare comparative income statements under variable costing and full absorption costing.

19. *Activity-based costing.* Refer to Exhibit 3.10 in the text. Assume engineering and production people at Hewlett-Packard provided the following new information. They have redesigned the circuit board to use only 90 parts and reduced the hours of testing to .15 hours per circuit board. From the accounting staff you learn that the cost of purchasing per part has increased from $.10 to $.12 and the cost per hour of testing has increased from $70 to $80.

    Recompute the cost of the circuit board described in Exhibit 3.10 assuming all other facts remain the same.

20. *Actual costs and normal costs under variable and full absorption costing.* Wyman Company uses a predetermined rate for applying overhead to production. The rates for Year 1 follow: variable, $2 per labor dollar; fixed, $3 per labor dollar. Actual overhead costs incurred follow: variable, $40,000; fixed, $50,000. Actual direct materials costs were $10,000, and actual direct labor costs were $18,000. Wyman produced 20,000 units that year.

    a. Calculate actual unit costs using variable costing and full absorption costing.

    b. Calculate normal unit costs using variable costing and full absorption costing.

21. *Comparison of standard costing to actual and normal costing.* Refer to Exercise 20. Assume unit standard costs are materials, $.40; labor $1.00; and variable overhead and fixed overhead use the rates indicated in Exercise 20 times the standard labor cost per unit. Prepare an exhibit like Exhibit 3.9 in the text.

Problems

22. *Computing applied manufacturing overhead from two different activity bases.* The Tall Texas Company makes a single product: Lone Star belt buckles. You have the following information available about this product for January of Year 2:

Belt Buckles

Actual Volume:	Units	4,200 Buckles
	Direct Labor Hours..............	3,300 Hours
Normal (estimated) Volume: Units		4,000 Buckles
	Direct Labor Hours..............	3,000 Hours
Predetermined Average Wage Rate.......................		$20 per Hour
Actual Average Wage Rate		$19 per Hour
Actual Manufacturing Overhead		$92,000
Actual Direct Materials Cost per Unit		$5 per Buckle
Normal (estimated) Manufacturing Overhead:		
Fixed Portion..		$66,000
Variable Portion		$8 per Labor Hour

---

(Round all calculations to the nearest cent.)

a. Compute unit manufacturing costs for belt buckles under (1) variable, normal and (2) full absorption, normal costing. Assume that Tall Texas applies fixed and variable manufacturing overhead using actual direct labor hours as the basis and that the predetermined manufacturing overhead rates are per direct labor hour.

b. Repeat part **a**, except assume that Tall Texas applies manufacturing overhead as a predetermined percentage of direct labor cost. You will need to derive the predetermined percentage.

23. *Computing product costs using direct labor dollars and labor hours for manufacturing overhead application.* The Kool Kentuckian Company makes a single product: leather cowboy hats. You have the following information available about this product for January of Year 3:

Cowboy Hats

Actual Volume:	Units	2,100 Hats
	Direct Labor Hours	1,100 Hours
Estimated Volume: Units		2,000 Hats
	Direct Labor Hours	1,000 Hours
Predetermined Average Wage Rate........................		$20 per Hour
Actual Average Wage Rate		$19 per Hour
Actual Manufacturing Overhead		$33,000
Actual Direct Materials Cost per Unit		$15 per Hat
Estimated Manufacturing Overhead:		
Fixed Portion..		$25,000
Variable Portion		$8 per Labor Hour

---

(Round all calculations to the nearest cent.)

a. Compute unit manufacturing costs for cowboy hats under (1) variable, normal and (2) full absorption, normal costing. Assume that Kool Kentuckian applies fixed and variable manufacturing overhead using direct labor hours as the basis and that the predetermined manufacturing overhead rates are per direct labor hour.

b. Repeat part **a**, except assume that Kool Kentuckian applies manufacturing overhead as a predetermined percentage of direct labor cost. You will need to derive the predetermined percentage.

24. *Computing overhead using normal costing (contributed by Robert H. Colson).* Mayhew Production Corporation uses machine time as the basis for allocating manufacturing overhead to products. On January 1, Year 2, Mayhew's production superintendent estimated that Mayhew would produce 900,000 units in Year 2, requiring 45,000 hours of machine time. The controller estimated that total manufacturing overhead cost for Year 2 would equal $2,500,000.

Mayhew collected the following records of the actual overhead costs, units produced, and machine time on a quarterly basis in Year 2:

Quarter	Actual Overhead Costs	Actual Units Produced	Actual Machine Time
1st	$800,000	333,333	17,000 Hours
2nd	900,000	333,333	18,000 Hours
3rd	500,000	222,223	11,000 Hours
4th	500,000	111,111	5,000 Hours

Compute the amount of overhead under normal costing for each quarter (round to two decimal places).

25. *Preparing income statements using variable and full absorption costing.* The Semi-Fixed Costs Company operates for two months: Month 1 and Month 2. It produces 20,000 tons in Month 1 and none in Month 2. It sells 10,000 tons of product each month at a selling price of $30 per ton. Its manufacturing costs are $7 per ton plus $210,000 per month. The fixed costs of $210,000 per month occur whether or not the plant produces any tons of product. Selling and administrative costs are $40,000 per month.

a. Prepare income statements for each of the 2 months, using full absorption costing.

b. Prepare income statements for each of the 2 months, using variable costing.

c. Which costing method is management likely to prefer? Why?

26. *Computing unit costs using normal costing.* Fine Homes Construction Company, uses a predetermined overhead rate based on direct labor hours to apply overhead to products. The accountants prepared an estimate of overhead costs for Year 7 as follows:

Direct Labor Hours	100,000	120,000	140,000
Variable Overhead Costs	$325,000	$390,000	$455,000
Fixed Overhead Costs	216,000	216,000	216,000
Total Overhead	$541,000	$606,000	$671,000

Although the annual ideal capacity is 150,000 direct labor hours, company officials have estimated 120,000 direct labor hours to be normal capacity for the year.

The following information is for August of Year 7, Jobs 7-50 and 7-51 were completed during August.

Inventories, August 1, Year 7

Direct Materials and Supplies	$ 10,500
Work in Process (job 7-50)	54,000
Finished Goods	112,500

Purchases of Direct Materials and Supplies

Direct Materials...	$135,000
Supplies	15,000

Materials and Supplies Requisitioned for Production

Job 7-50..	$ 45,000
Job 7-51..	37,500
Job 7-52..	25,500
Supplies	12,000
	$120,000

Direct Labor Hours (DLH)

Job 7-50..	3,500 DLH
Job 7-51..	3,000 DLH
Job 7-52..	2,000 DLH

Labor Costs

Direct Labor Wages	$ 51,000
Indirect Labor Wages (4,000 hours)..........................	15,000
Supervisor Salaries	6,000
	$ 72,000

Building Occupancy Costs (heat, light, depreciation, etc.)

Facilities to Support Construction Work	6,500
Sales Offices...	1,500
Administrative Offices	1,000
	$ 9,000

Administrative Costs

Depreciation on Office Equipment	$ 1,500
Other..	6,500
	$ 8,000

a. Calculate the predetermined overhead rates the company should use to apply variable and fixed manufacturing overhead to individual jobs during Year 7.

b. Compute the total cost of job 7-50.

c. Compute the total manufacturing overhead costs applied to job 7-52 during August.

d. Compute the total amount of overhead (fixed and variable) applied to jobs during August.

e.   Compute actual manufacturing overhead incurred during August.

f.   Compare the amounts computed in parts **d** and **e**. Which is greater?

27.   *Department versus plant-wide overhead rates.* Empire Industries, Inc., had a contract to produce a machine for the R2D2 Company. Departments A, B, and C would produce the machine. The three departments incurred the following costs:

	Dept. A	Dept. B	Dept. C
Materials Used	$6,200	$7,000	0
Direct Labor Cost...................	3,500	6,000	$8,000
Direct Labor Hours	1,000	1,500	2,000
Machine Hours	100	50	500
Overhead Allocation	$8 per Direct Labor Hour	150 Percent of Direct Labor Cost	$14 per Machine Hour

The complexities of this allocation method and the impact of different cost allocations on the computed job costs concerned management. The estimated total overhead in each department and the estimated total overhead bases for this year follow:

	Dept. A	Dept. B	Dept. C
Estimated Overhead	$640,000	$330,000	$140,000
Direct Labor Cost.......................	280,000	220,000	120,000
Direct Labor Hours	80,000	55,000	30,000
Machine Hours	10,000	1,500	10,000

One member of management suggested that Empire establish a plant-wide overhead rate based on direct labor cost. Another stated that plant-wide rates are not very useful.

a.   Compute plant-wide rates and rates by department based on
  (1)   Direct labor cost.
  (2)   Direct labor hours.
  (3)   Machine hours.
b.   Calculate the costs of the R2D2 job using
  (1)   Overhead as initially allocated.
  (2)   Overhead based on plant-wide direct labor costs.
  (3)   Overhead based on plant-wide direct labor hours.
  (4)   Overhead based on plant-wide machine hours.
  (5)   Overhead based on department direct labor costs.
  (6)   Overhead based on department direct labor hours.
  (7)   Overhead based on department machine hours.

28.   *Activity-based costing.* River Adventures specializes in river rafting trips. Last year, the company provided 300 trips, 100 in each of the following three

categories: 3-day float trips, 3-day white-water trips, and 6-day white-water excursions. Each "trip" comprised a raft carrying 6 customers. The costs to provide these trips totaled $468,000, excluding the company's administrative costs, while the revenues from these trips generated only $465,000. Management preferred not to raise prices for these trips that were already at least as high as the company's competitors' prices. Considering that costs exceeded revenues before including administrative costs, management began to investigate ways to make the company profitable.

Management wondered: Were some categories of trips unprofitable? If so, which ones? The company's cost system provided only aggregate costs for all 3 categories. Management knew the average cost per trip was $1,560 (= $468,000/300 trips), but nobody knew the cost of float trips versus the cost of white-water trips versus the cost of white-water excursions. Furthermore, management did not know what activities caused costs, making it impossible to know where to cut costs.

To address management's concerns, the company's accountants applied activity-based costing methods to the trips. First, they identified the activities or cost drivers that caused costs. These activities were

- Advertising the trip
- Obtaining the permit to use the river
- Using equipment
- Insurance
- Employ guides
- Feeding customers

Second, they assigned costs to each cost driver as Exhibit 3.12 shows. Assume the price per customer is float trips, $150; white-water trips, $225; and white-water excursions, $400. Compute the cost per "trip" (that is, one raft carrying 6 customers). Which trips are profitable? How might the company improve its profits?

Exhibit 3.12

RIVER ADVENTURES
Activity-Based Costing

Assign Costs to Activities

	Float Trips	Whitewater Trips	Whitewater Excursions
Advertise Trips	$200 per Trip	$200 per Trip	$200 per Trip
Permit to Use the River	30 per Trip	50 per Trip	50 per Trip
Equipment Use	20 per Trip Plus $5 per Customer	40 per Trip Plus $10 per Customer	60 per Trip Plus $15 per Customer
Insurance	80 per Trip	150 per Trip	180 per Trip
Pay Guides	300 per Trip	400 per Trip	800 per Trip
Food	70 per Customer	70 per Customer	150 per Customer

29. *Activity-based costing.* The Eye Shop is a small optometry practice that has one optometrist, one receptionist, and one assistant.

The receptionist schedules appointments, checks in patients, and handles the billing. The average time per patient for scheduling of an appointment is 2 minutes and the average time per check-in and seating is also 2 minutes. Average time spent per billing is 5 minutes. The receptionist earns $10 per hour.

The assistant conducts the preliminary eye test, shows styles of frames available, and fits frames to the customer. The average time for preliminary tests is 15 minutes, the average time for showing and fitting frames is 20 minutes. The assistant earns $20 per hour.

The optometrist fits new prescriptions, both regular lenses and contacts. The normal checkup includes a glaucoma test, a test to ensure that the current prescription is correct, and an interview with each patient to discuss any specific problems the patient may be experiencing. Fitting for a new prescription for glasses averages 30 minutes. Fitting for contacts requires 1 hour on the initial visit plus two follow-up visits, each lasting 30 minutes. Glaucoma tests take 5 minutes. The test to ensure the current prescription is correct averages 15 minutes, and the individual interview averages 10 minutes. The optometrist charges $50 per hour for his time. Average costs for materials follow: frames, $15; lenses, $25; contacts lenses, including startup kit, $20.

 a. Identify the cost drivers and assign costs to each one.
 b. How much would it cost the Eye Shop to conduct a normal checkup?
 c. How much does it cost the Eye Shop to conduct a preliminary examination and prescribe and fit new glasses? Contacts?

30. *Activity-based costing.* Refer to Problem 29. Calculate the costs for the following situations.

 a. After a preliminary examination, a customer finds she needs vision correction and chooses glasses.
 b. A regular customer comes in, tells the doctor everything is fine, but that she is leaving the country for 6 months and requests a glaucoma test and a second pair of glasses for the trip.
 c. A new customer comes in and has his contact lens prescription with him, but needs a new pair of lenses.

Integrative Problems and Cases

31. *Applying overhead under normal costing using multiple bases* (adapted from CMA exam). The Herbert Manufacturing Company manufactures custom-designed restaurant and kitchen furniture. The company applies the actual overhead costs incurred during the month to the products on the basis of actual direct labor hours required to produce the products. The overhead consists primarily of supervision, employee benefits, maintenance costs, property taxes, and depreciation.

Herbert Manufacturing recently won a contract to manufacture the furniture for a new fast-food chain that is expanding rapidly in the area. In general, this furniture is durable but of a lower quality than Herbert Manufacturing normally manufactures. To produce this new line, Herbert Manufacturing must purchase more molded plastic parts for the furniture than for its current line. The firm's innovative industrial engineering department has developed an efficient manufacturing process for this new furniture that requires only a minimal capital investment. Management is optimistic about the profit improvement the new product line will bring.

At the end of October, the start-up month for the new line, the controller prepared a separate income statement for the new product line. On a consoli-

Exhibit 3.13

HERBERT MANUFACTURING COMPANY
(all dollar amounts in thousands)

	Fast-Food Furniture	Custom Furniture	Consolidated
Nine Months Year-to-Date			
Sales..................................	—	$8,100	$8,100
Direct Material.......................	—	$2,025	$2,025
Direct Labor:			
Forming	—	758	758
Finishing.........................	—	1,314	1,314
Assembly	—	558	558
Manufacturing Overhead.............	—	1,779	1,779
Cost of Sales.......................	—	$6,434	$6,434
Operating Profit.....................	—	$1,666	$1,666
Operating Profit Percentage	—	20.6%	20.6%
October			
Sales..................................	$400	$ 900	$1,300
Direct Material.......................	$200	$ 225	$ 425
Direct Labor:			
Forming	17	82	99
Finishing.........................	40	142	182
Assembly	33	60	93
Manufacturing Overhead.............	60	180	240
Cost of Sales.......................	$350	$ 689	$1,039
Operating Profit.....................	$ 50	$ 211	$ 261
Operating Profit Percentage	12.5%	23.4%	20.1%
November			
Sales..................................	$800	$ 800	$1,600
Direct Material.......................	$400	$ 200	$ 600
Direct Labor:			
Forming	31	72	103
Finishing.........................	70	125	195
Assembly	58	53	111
Manufacturing Overhead.............	98	147	245
Cost of Sales.......................	$657	$ 597	$1,254
Operating Profit.....................	$143	$ 203	$ 346
Operating Profit Percentage	17.9%	25.4%	21.6%

dated basis the gross profit percentage was normal; however, the profitability for the new line was less than expected.

At the end of November, the results improved somewhat. Consolidated profits were good, but the reported profitability for the new product line was less than expected. John Herbert, president of the corporation, is concerned that knowledgeable shareholders will criticize his decision to add this lower-quality product line at a time when profitability appeared to be increasing with the standard product line.

The results as published for the first 9 months, for October, and for November are presented in Exhibit 3.13.

Mr. Jameson, cost accounting manager, has stated that the overhead allocation based on only direct labor hours is no longer appropriate. On the basis of a recently completed study of the overhead accounts, Mr. Jameson believes that the company should allocate only supervision and employee benefits on the basis of direct labor hours and the balance of the overhead on a machine hour basis. In his judgment, the increase in the profitability of the custom-designed furniture results from a misallocation of overhead in the present system.

The following exhibit shows the actual direct labor hours and machine hours for the past 2 months.

	Fast-Food Furniture	Custom Furniture
Machine Hours		
October:		
Forming	660	10,700
Finishing	660	7,780
Assembly	—	—
	1,320	18,480
November:		
Forming	1,280	9,640
Finishing	1,280	7,400
Assembly	—	—
	2,560	17,040
Direct Labor Hours		
October:		
Forming	1,900	9,300
Finishing	3,350	12,000
Assembly	4,750	8,700
	10,000	30,000
November:		
Forming	3,400	8,250
Finishing	5,800	10,400
Assembly	8,300	7,600
	17,500	26,250

The actual overhead costs for the past 2 months follow:

	October	November
Supervision	$ 13,000	$ 13,000
Employee Benefits	95,000	109,500
Maintenance	50,000	48,000
Depreciation	42,000	42,000
Property Taxes	8,000	8,000
All Other	32,000	24,500
Total	$240,000	$245,000

a. Based on Mr. Jameson's recommendation, reallocate the overhead for October and November using direct labor hours as the allocation base for supervision and employee benefits. Use machine hours as the base for the remaining overhead costs.

b. Support or criticize Mr. Jameson's conclusion that the increase in profitability of custom-designed furniture results from misallocation of overhead. Use the data developed in part **a** to support your analysis.

c. Mr. Jameson has also recommended that the company consider using predetermined overhead absorption rates calculated on an annual basis rather than allocating actual cost over actual volume each month. He stated that this is particularly applicable now that the company has two distinct product lines. Discuss the advantages of using annual predetermined overhead rates.

32. *Effect of changes in production and costing method on operating profit: "I enjoy challenges."* Kelly Company uses an actual cost system to apply all production costs to the units produced. Although production has a maximum production capacity of 40 million units, Kelly produced and sold only 10 million units during Year 5. It had no beginning or ending inventories.

KELLY COMPANY
Income Statement for the Year Ending December 31, Year 5

Sales (10,000,000 units each $3.00)		$ 30,000,000
Less Cost of Goods Sold:		
Variable (10,000,000 each $1)	$(10,000,000)	
Fixed	(24,000,000)	(34,000,000)
Gross Margin		$ (4,000,000)
Less Marketing and Administrative Costs		
(all fixed)		(5,000,000)
Operating Profit (Loss)		$ (9,000,000)

This loss concerns the board of directors. A consultant approached the board with the following offer: "I agree to become president for no fixed salary. But I insist on a year-end bonus of 10 percent of operating profit (before considering the bonus)." The board of directors agreed to these terms and hired the consultant.

The new president promptly stepped up production to an annual rate of 30,000,000 units. Sales for Year 6 remained at 10,000,000 units.

The resulting Kelly Company income statement for Year 6 follows:

KELLY COMPANY
Income Statement for the Year Ending December 31, Year 6

Sales (10,000,000 units each $3.00)		$ 30,000,000
Less Cost of Goods Sold:		
Cost of Goods Manufactured:		
Variable (30,000,000 each $1)	$(30,000,000)	
Fixed	(24,000,000)	
Total Cost of Goods Manufactured	$(54,000,000)	
Ending Inventory:		
Variable (20,000,000 each $1)	$ 20,000,000	
Fixed ($\frac{20}{30}$ × 24,000,000)	16,000,000	
Total Inventory	$ 36,000,000	
Cost of Goods Sold		(18,000,000)
Gross Margin		$ 12,000,000
Less Marketing and Administrative Costs		
(all fixed)		(5,000,000)
Operating Profit before Bonus		$ 7,000,000
Less Bonus		(700,000)
Operating Profit after Bonus		$ 6,300,000

The day after the statement was verified, the president took his check for $700,000 and resigned to take a job with another corporation. He remarked, "I enjoy challenges. Now that Kelly Company is in the black, I'd prefer tackling another challenging situation." (His contract with his new employer is similar to the one he had with Kelly Company.)

a. As a member of the board of directors, comment on the Year 6 income statement.

b. Using variable costing, what would operating profit be for Year 5? For Year 6? What are the inventory values at the end of Year 6?

c. Assuming production was 30,000,000 units, at what sales level would the president be indifferent to the product costing approach used to calculate his bonus? Why?

33. *"I enjoy challenges" using normal costing.* Recompute the operating profit before bonus for Year 6 in Problem 32, based on the following assumptions:

(1) All manufacturing overhead is fixed.

(2) Kelly applied overhead based on units of output.

(3) The predetermined overhead rate for Year 6 is $2.40 (= $24,000,000/ 10,000,000 estimated units).

Why are operating profits computed here different than those computed for Year 6 in Problem 32?

34. *Problems in deriving product costs for multiple products.* The Fleetwood Mac Manufacturing Company makes three products: X1, X2, and X3. The predetermined overhead rates are $36 per labor hour or 180 percent of direct labor costs.

Activity measures for January, Year 3, follow:

	X1	X2	X3
Normal (estimated) Volume per Month, in Units	1,000 Units	1,000 Units	2,000 Units
Normal (estimated) Volume per Month, in Direct Labor Hours ...	1,000 Hours	1,500 Hours	4,000 Hours
Actual Volume for January, Year 3, in Units..............	800 Units	1,200 Units	1,500 Units
Actual Volume for January, Year 3, in Direct Labor Hours ...	900 Hours	1,700 Hours	3,200 Hours

The company has not kept past records of manufacturing overhead for each product, nor has it broken down manufacturing overhead into fixed and variable components. The available data about actual costs in January, Year 3, follow:

Actual Direct Materials Costs:	
X1	$17,600
X2	28,800
X3	46,500
Actual Manufacturing Overhead	$232,000
All Other Costs (marketing and administrative)	$100,000
Actual labor rates averaged $21 per hour.	

The company is experimenting with normal costing, using the following two methods of applying manufacturing overhead:

(1) Predetermined rate times actual direct labor hours.

(2) Predetermined percentage times actual direct labor costs.

a. Calculate the normal product cost for each of the three products for January, Year 3, using both methods of applying manufacturing overhead.

b. Given the data provided, can you compare the January, Year 3 actual product cost for Product X3 with the normal product cost for Product X3? If so, compare the two. If not, state why you cannot compare the two.

c. Your superior wants to know how much the variable costs of producing Product X2 were in January, Year 3. What would you say?

35. *Interpreting product cost numbers*. The Marais Company, which started business on January 1, Year 1, manufactures a single product. The company management experimented with the use of three costing systems, including full absorption, normal costing with a predetermined overhead rate (for both fixed and variable overhead) based on labor hours; variable, actual costing; and full absorption, actual costing. You know the following information about the Marais Company:

- The number of units produced exceeded the numbers of units sold.
- Marais applies overhead on the basis of direct labor hours if it uses normal costing. Estimated direct labor hours for Year 1 were 100,000 hours. Actual direct labor hours worked were 120,000 hours.
- Marais had no beginning inventories and no ending Work-in-Process Inventory for Year 1. It had an ending Finished Goods Inventory on December 31, Year 1.

The following data are available for the results of the experiment.

| | Actual Costing | | Normal Costing |
	Variable Costing	Full Absorption Costing	Full Absorption Costing
Sales.................	$2,250,000	$2,250,000	$2,250,000
Operating Profit (before taxes)	438,000	461,000	466,200
Underapplied (Overapplied) Overhead			(52,000)
Actual Materials and Labor Costs Incurred in Production............	1,280,000	1,280,000	1,280,000
Marketing and Administrative Costs (all fixed)	295,000	295,000	295,000
Number of Units Sold	180,000	180,000	180,000
Ending Finished Goods Inventory (cost per unit)	$7.15	$8.30	$8.56

a. Prepare income statements for each of the three product costing methods.
b. How many units are in ending finished goods inventory?
c. How much overhead is in the ending finished goods inventory (per unit) for each product costing method?
d. What is the overhead application rate per labor hour under full absorption costing?
e. What is the actual total variable overhead incurred in Year 1?
f. How much overhead did Marais expense on the income statement for each of the three product costing methods?
g. Why does using full absorption, actual costing result in $23,000 more profit than using variable, actual costing?
h. Why does using full absorption, normal costing result in $5,200 more profit than using full absorption, actual costing?

Suggested Solutions to Even-Numbered Exercises

14. *Computing inventory value using variable costing and full absorption costing*

	a Full Absorption Costing	b Variable Costing
Direct Materials.................................	$ 48,000	$48,000
Direct Labor......................................	36,000	36,000
Variable Overhead	12,000	12,000
Fixed Overhead	12,000	—
Total Production Costs	$108,000	$96,000

$$\text{Ending Inventory Costs} = \frac{2,000}{50,000} \text{ of Costs of Units Produced.}$$

$$\frac{2,000}{50,000} \times \$108,000 = \$4,320 \text{ Full Absorption Costing Ending Inventory.}$$

$$\frac{2,000}{50,000} \times \$96,000 = \$3,840 \text{ Variable Costing Ending Inventory.}$$

c. Inventory increased, so under full absorption costing a portion of the fixed costs is included in ending inventory. Total expenses, therefore, will be less under full absorption costing and income will be larger.

16. *Computing allocated overhead and finished goods value*
   a. Job 745:

Direct Materials	$ 8,400
Direct Labor	10,000
Overhead (10,000/4 × $3)	7,500
Total Manufacturing Costs	$25,900

   b. Job 305:

Revenue		$ 40,000
Less: Direct Materials	$ (6,300)	
Direct Labor	(20,000)	
Overhead (20,000/5 × $3)	(12,000)	(38,300)
Gross Margin		$ 1,700

18. *Comparison of full absorption and variable costing in income statement formats*

Variable Costing: Contribution Margin Format (all dollar amounts in thousands)

	Year 1	Year 2	Total
Sales.....................................	$ 1,400	$ 2,600	$ 4,000
Variable Cost of Goods Sold:			
Beginning Inventory........................	$ 0	$ (390)	$ 0
Current Period Manufacturing Costs........	(1,300)	(1,300)	(2,600)
Less Ending Inventory	390	(0)	(0)
Variable Cost of Goods Sold.................	$ (910)	$(1,690)	$(2,600)
Total Contribution Margin	$ 490	$ 910	$ 1,400
Fixed Manufacturing Costs	(340)	(340)	(680)
Nonmanufacturing Costs	(150)	(150)	(300)
Operating Profits	$ 0	$ 420	$ 420

Full Absorption Costing: Traditional Income Statement Format (all dollar amounts in thousands)

	Year 1	Year 2	Total
Sales.....................................	$ 1,400	$ 2,600	$ 4,000
Full Absorption Cost of Goods Sold:			
Beginning Inventory........................	$ 0	$ (492)	$ 0
Current Period Manufacturing Costs........	(1,640)	(1,640)	(3,280)
Less Ending Inventory	492	0	0
Full Absorption Cost of Goods Sold	$(1,148)	$(2,132)	$(3,280)
Gross Margin	$ 252	$ 468	$ 720
Nonmanufacturing Costs	(150)	(150)	(300)
Operating Profits	$ 102	$ 318	$ 420

20. *Computing actual unit costs and normal unit costs under both variable and full absorption costing*

		Variable	Full Absorption
a.	**Actual Costing**		
	Direct Materials............................	$0.50	$0.50
	Direct Labor..............................	0.90	0.90
	Variable Manufacturing Overhead............	2.00	2.00
	Fixed Manufacturing Overhead	—	2.50
	Total Unit Cost	$3.40	$5.90
b.	**Normal Costing**		
	Direct Materials............................	$0.50	$0.50
	Direct Labor..............................	0.90	0.90
	Variable Manufacturing Overhead............	1.80	1.80
	Fixed Manufacturing Overhead	—	2.70
	Total Unit Cost	$3.20	$5.90

... CHAPTER 4 ...

Accounting for Resource Flows:
Cost Accumulation

Chapter Outline

- Two Stages of Product Costing: Cost Accumulation by Department and Allocation to Products
- Fundamental Accounting Model of Cost Flows
- Production Methods and Accounting Systems
- Job and Process Costing Systems
- Just-in-Time Inventory
- Merchandise Organizations
- Service Organizations
- Appendix 4.1: Computing Equivalent Production

This chapter shows how the accounting system records and reports the flow of resources in organizations. The accounting system accumulates costs to help answer questions such as these:

- What is the cost of a job in a print shop or in a CPA firm?
- How do the costs of Department A compare with the department's budget?
- What is the manufacturing cost of a unit? How does that cost compare to standards?

These and other questions managers ask require an understanding of how the accounting system works. Such an understanding allows managers to have better input into designing and redesigning the system to provide the needed data.

Although this chapter contains less technical accounting detail than a text on cost accounting, it provides a user perspective of the way accounting systems record and report the flow of resources.

Two Stages of Product Costing: Cost Accumulation by Department and Allocation to Products

As earlier chapters discussed, experts must design a managerial accounting system to serve several purposes. For purposes of planning and performance evaluation, departments or other *responsibility centers* accumulate costs. A responsibility center is simply an organizational unit. One or more managers are responsible for the activities in each responsibility center in a company. Examples of responsibility centers include divisions, territories, plants, product lines, and departments.

Exhibit 4.1 shows the relation between **cost accumulation** and **cost allocation** for a typical firm with two manufacturing departments, Assembly and Finishing. Management has designed the accounting system so that, for performance evaluation, the departments initially accumulate costs. The accounting system accumulates the costs of direct materials, direct labor, and manufacturing overhead incurred in production in separate accounts for the manufacturing departments, Assembly and Finishing. Management then compares these costs with the standard or budgeted amounts and investigates significant variances, as we will discuss later in

Exhibit 4.1

Relation between Cost Accumulation and Cost Allocation

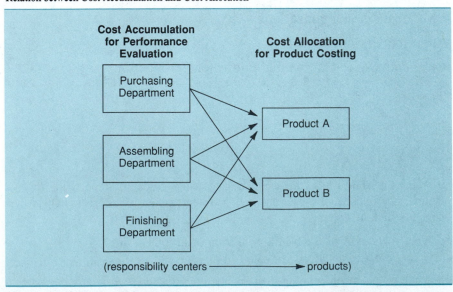

Chapters 12 through 14. Thus the accounting system has served its function of providing data for performance evaluation and control. The accounting system then assigns costs to products for managerial decision making and to derive inventory costs for external reporting.

Nonmanufacturing Applications

You will find this relation between cost accumulation by departments and cost allocation to products also in nonmanufacturing settings. For example, accounting accumulates the costs of performing surgery on a liver transplant patient by department (for example, anesthesia), then allocates them to the liver transplant program, and finally to the particular patient. In general, for the accounting system to provide product cost information, it must assign cost to products from responsibility centers.

Fundamental Accounting Model of Cost Flows

Exhibit 4.2 shows how firms transform materials into finished goods. Note that Work-in-Process is the account that both *describes* the transformation of inputs into outputs in a company and *accounts for* the costs incurred in the process. (Later in this chapter we add the accounts that show the sources of inputs.)

In most companies, each department controls its costs (for example, the Assembly Department or the Finishing Department). Thus each department has a separate Work-in-Process account, as Exhibit 4.2 shows, which accumulates its costs. Management holds department managers accountable for the costs accumulated in their departments.

Companies that operate in competitive markets have little direct control over prices paid for materials or prices received for finished goods. Thus a key factor in a company's success is how well it controls the conversion costs (that is, direct labor and overhead). Companies closely monitor those costs in the Work-in-Process Inventory account.

In short, the accounting system serves two purposes in manufacturing: (1) to accumulate costs by responsibility center (department) for performance evaluation and cost control and (2) to allocate manufacturing costs to units produced for product costing. The next section presents an overview of the process.

Basic Cost Flow Equation

Accounting systems are based on the following **basic cost flow equation:**

$$\text{Beginning Balance} + \text{Transfers In} = \text{Transfers Out} + \text{Ending Balance.}$$

Or in symbols:

$$\text{BB} \quad + \quad \text{TI} \quad = \quad \text{TO} \quad + \quad \text{EB.}$$

This equation is a fundamental equality in accounting. It can help you solve for unknown data as Problem 1 for Self-Study at the end of this chapter demonstrates.

Exhibit 4.2

Flow of Costs through the Accounts and Departments

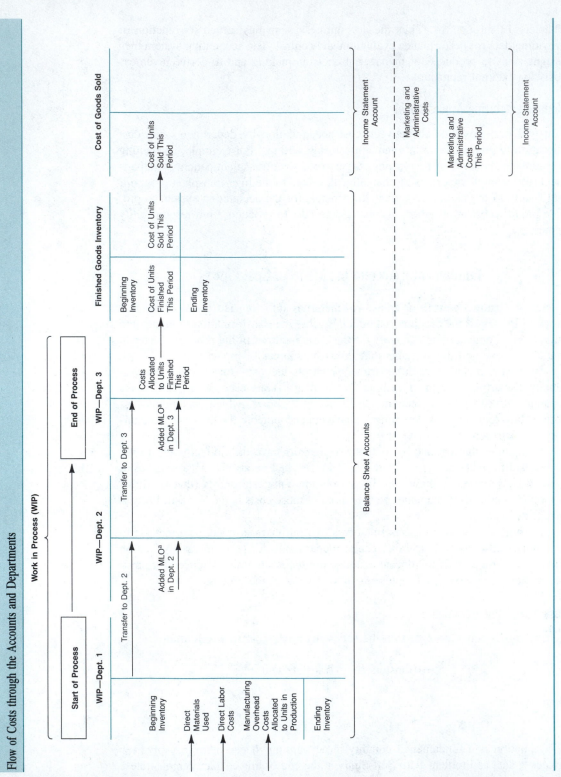

aMLO = Direct Materials, Direct Labor, and Manufacturing Overhead.

Relation of the Flow of Costs to the Cost of Goods Manufactured and Sold Statement

The presence of inventories complicates the statements of cost of goods manufactured and sold. In general, these statements summarize the flow of costs in T-accounts as shown in Exhibit 4.3. On the left side of the exhibit is the basic accounting equation restated from $BB + TI = TO + EB$ to $TI + BB - EB = TO$; the middle presents the descriptions used in the statements; the right side shows the activity in the manufacturing costs accounts. You might not remember the format for these statements, but if you remember the basic cost flow equation, you will know all of the elements in these statements.

Production Methods and Accounting Systems

Exhibit 4.4 shows how production methods vary across organizations, depending on the type of product. Print shops, custom home builders, defense contractors, and custom machine manufacturers are job shops. These organizations use job costing to account for the cost of each job. Certain service organizations such as public

Exhibit 4.3

Relation between the Flow of Costs and Cost of Goods Manufactured and Sold

Accounting Equation	Statement Description	Activity in Account
Work-in-Process Inventory		
BB	Beginning Work-in-Process Inventory	Beginning Balance
+ TI	+ Manufacturing Costs Incurred during the Period	Materials, Labor, and Overhead Debited to Work-in-Process during the Period
− EB	− Ending Work-in-Process Inventory	Ending Balance
= TO	= Cost of Goods Manufactured during the Period[a]	Amount Credited to Work-in-Process and Debited to Finished Goods during the Period
Finished Goods Inventory		
BB	Beginning Finished Goods Inventory	Beginning Balance
+ TI	+ Cost of Goods Manufactured during the Period	Same as Work-in-Process Transfer Out
− EB	− Ending Finished Goods Inventory	Ending Balance
= TO	= Cost of Goods Sold during the Period	Amount Credited to Finished Goods and Debited to Cost of Goods Sold

[a]Cost of goods manufactured could also be called "cost of goods *finished* during the period."

Exhibit 4.4

Production Methods and Accounting Systems

Type of Production	Accounting System	Type of Product	Length of Production Runs
Job Shop (hospital, custom home builder)	Job Costing	Customized	Short, Possibly Only One Product per Run
Batch Production (furniture manufacturer, winery)	Hybrid (for example **batch**)	Several Different Products	Relatively Short
Repetitive Manufacturing (computer terminals, automobiles)	Hybrid (for example **operation**)	Few New Products	Relatively Long
Continuous Flow Processing (oil refinery, chemicals)	Process Costing	Standardized	Long Runs

accounting firms and consulting firms also use job costing to accumulate the cost of each job performed for a client. In addition, hospitals use job costing to accumulate the cost of care for each patient.

Some companies process large orders of identical units as a group through the same production sequence. We call each of these orders a batch. In **batch production** the firm allocates costs to each batch. Whenever production requires a change in the production line to continue, it creates a new batch. A furniture manufacturer may produce a batch of chairs, then a batch of tables, then a batch of chests, and so forth. Generally, management uses job costing concepts to account for batch production and to treat each batch as a job for costing purposes.

Repetitive manufacturing often uses automated equipment that minimizes the amount of manual material handling. Automobile assembly plants, food processing plants, and computer terminal assembly plants are examples of repetitive manufacturing.

Continuous flow processing is at the opposite end of the spectrum from job shops. Process systems generally mass-produce a single, homogeneous product in a continuing process. Chemical manufacturers, flour grinders, and oil refineries use process systems.

Firms use process costing when they produce identical units through an *ongoing series of uniform production steps*. Many organizations use job systems for some work and process systems for others. A home builder might use process costing for standardized homes with a particular floor plan. The same builder might use job costing when building a custom-designed house for a single customer. Honeywell, Inc., a high-tech company, uses process costing for most of its furnace thermostats and job costing for specialized defense and space contracting work. Some organizations use hybrid systems that incorporate both job costing and process costing concepts.

Next we discuss the two major types of accounting systems: job and process costing. In practice, a firm uniquely tailors its accounting system to its production methods and the needs of its managers. All systems use elements of job costing, process costing, or both, however.

Job and Process Costing Systems

This section provides an overview of product cost accounting for the two major types of production operations: job operations and process operations.

In **job costing,** firms collect costs for each "unit" produced. Often each department collects costs for evaluating the performance of departmental personnel.

Example Unique Builders makes a customized product. In April, it started and completed three jobs (no beginning inventories). The manufacturing cost of each job follows:

Job No. 1001	$8,000
Job No. 1002	6,000
Job No. 1003	7,000

Unique Builders sold Job No. 1001. The flow of costs for this company appears in the top panel of Exhibit 4.5.

In **process costing,** firms accumulate costs in a department or production process during an accounting period (for example, a month), then spread those costs evenly over the units produced that month. The formula follows:

$$\text{Unit Cost} = \frac{\text{Total Manufacturing Costs}}{\text{Total Units Produced}}.$$

Firms use process costing when it produces relatively uniform units. Industries that use process costing include repetitive manufacturers like computers and automobile manufacturing and continuous process industries like oil refining.

Example Standard Builders started and completed three homogeneous units in April (no beginning or ending inventories). Total manufacturing costs were $21,000, so Standard Builders assigned each unit a cost of $7,000. It sold one unit. This flow of costs appears in the bottom panel of Exhibit 4.5. Note how much more detail job costing would require for a large number (say, 10,000) of jobs or units.

We have presented an overview of costing in companies with job or process operations. Next, we examine managerial issues in choosing between job and process costing.

Exhibit 4.5

Flow of Costs, Job and Process Costing

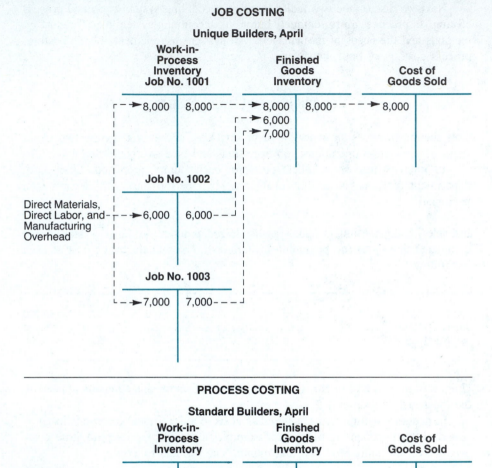

Job versus Process Costing: Cost-Benefit Considerations

Why do firms prefer one accounting system to another? Cost-benefit analysis provides the answer. In general, the costs of record keeping under job costing systems exceed those under process costing. Consider a house builder. Under job costing, the house builder must accumulate costs for each house. If a truck delivers lumber to several houses, it is not sufficient to record the total issued. The driver must keep records of the amount delivered to, and subsequently returned from, each house. If laborers work on several houses, they must keep track of the time spent on *each* house. Process costing, however, simply requires recording the total cost. For the house builder, process costing would report the average cost of all houses built. (In practice, house builders generally use job costing for custom-built houses and process costing for houses having a particular model type or floor plan.)

Under process costing, a firm does not report the direct cost incurred for a particular unit. If all units are homogeneous, this loss of information is probably minimal. Is it important for Kellogg's to know whether the cost of the 1,001st box of Raisin Bran differs from the 1,002nd's cost? Not likely. Cost control and performance evaluation will take place by department or activity, not by unit produced. Thus the additional benefits of job costing would not justify the additional record-keeping costs.

Chapter 3 indicates that a *finer* information system is superior to a *coarser* one if the cost of the two is the same. A job costing system is usually finer than a process costing system, because it contains all of the information found in process costing (that is, total manufacturing costs and total units) and more. The additional information in job costing is the cost of *each unit*. In process costing, that information is not available—only the *aggregate* of costs is available. This aggregate is spread over units to give an *average* unit cost.

Although job costing is finer than process costing, it usually costs more. Thus management and accountants must examine the costs and benefits of information and pick the method that best fits the organization's production operations.

Example   In this example, a custom house builder explains the benefits of job costing for companies that make heterogeneous products.

> We estimate the costs of each house for pricing purposes. Unless we know the actual costs of each house, we cannot evaluate our estimation methods. We use the information for performance evaluation and cost control, too. We assign a manager to each house who is responsible for seeing that actual costs don't exceed the estimate. If we come in less than 10 percent over estimate, the manager gets a bonus.
>
> We need a job system to help us charge customers for any cost overruns, too. Usually, customers make changes as we build. If the changes have a small impact on costs, we absorb them. But if these changes add costs, we like to go to the customer with our tally of estimated and actual costs, and get an adjustment in the price of the house. Sometimes, we build on a cost-plus basis, in which case we *must* know and document costs for each house so we can collect from the customer.

In summary, management usually evaluates the comparative costs and benefits of job and process costing as follows:

Nature of Production Operations	Costing System Used
Heterogeneous Units, Each Unit Large......................	Job Costing
Homogeneous Units, Continuous Process, Many Small Units....	Process Costing

Managerial Application

The Impact of New Technology on Cost Accumulation[a]

After installing a new production process, a Hewlett-Packard plant that makes printed circuit boards found that (1) inventory levels were almost zero, (2) direct labor was only 3 to 5 percent of total product costs, and (3) most labor and overhead costs were fixed. These findings dramatically affected the plant's cost accumulation methods. First, direct labor formed such a small part of total product cost that the firm no longer accounted for it as a separate category; instead, accounting lumped it together with overhead.

Second, lower inventory levels and reduced time between production and delivery of finished product meant that accounting expensed virtually all of the overhead and direct labor incurred in the month in which it was incurred.

> Tracking overhead through work-in-process and finished goods inventory (for each job) provided no useful information. Management decided, therefore, to treat manufacturing overhead as an expense charged directly to cost of goods sold. Overhead remaining in work-in-process and finished goods is maintained with end-of-month adjusting entries.[b]

The accompanying diagram on page 129 compares the new method at the Hewlett-Packard plant with a traditional system. Accounting records only materials in inventory accounts; it expenses labor and overhead when incurred. Hewlett-Packard eliminated an estimated 100,000 journal entries per month by simplifying the accounting system because the new system no longer allocated labor and overhead to each job.

> The net result of these changes is that Hewlett-Packard realized significant savings in staff time and costs without any significant changes in costs reported in their financial statements, or costs used in planning and controlling production, or costs analyzed for pricing and make-or-buy decisions. Production line managers can now understand the simpler reports provided by the accounting department and actually use the information in those reports. Accountants can now "focus on solving tomorrow's problems instead of unraveling yesterday's errors," one of the goals of H-P's accounting staff.[c]

Just-in-Time Inventory (JIT)

Management uses **just-in-time (JIT) inventory** to obtain materials just in time for production and to provide finished goods just in time for sale. This practice reduces, or potentially eliminates, inventories and the cost of carrying them. Just-in-time inventory requires that a firm immediately correct a process making defective units because it has no inventory where it can send defective units to await reworking or scrapping. Managers find that just-in-time production helps eliminate inventories that hide production problems. Using just-in-time system, production does not

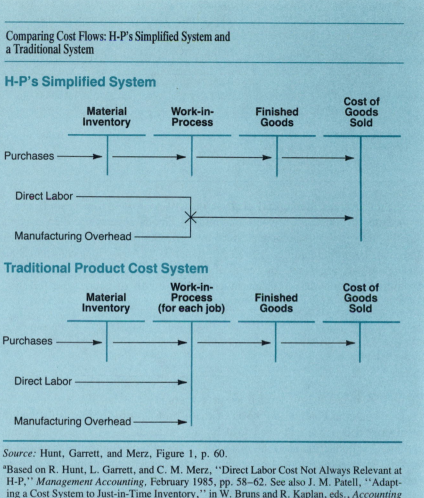

Comparing Cost Flows: H-P's Simplified System and a Traditional System

H-P's Simplified System

Traditional Product Cost System

Source: Hunt, Garrett, and Merz, Figure 1, p. 60.

[a]Based on R. Hunt, L. Garrett, and C. M. Merz, "Direct Labor Cost Not Always Relevant at H-P," *Management Accounting,* February 1985, pp. 58–62. See also J. M. Patell, "Adapting a Cost System to Just-in-Time Inventory," in W. Bruns and R. Kaplan, eds., *Accounting and Management in Organizations: A Field Study Perspective* (Harvard Business School, 1987).

[b]Hunt, Garrett, and Merz, p. 61.

[c]Hunt, Garrett, and Merz, p. 61.

begin on an item until it receives an order. Upon receipt of an order for a finished product, production orders raw materials and begins the production cycle. As soon as production fills the order, production ends. In theory, a JIT system eliminates the need for inventories because no production takes place until the firm knows that it will sell the item. As a practical matter, companies using just-in-time inventory backlog orders to assure continued production.

Since just-in-time production responds to an order receipt, JIT accounting charges all costs directly to cost of goods sold. When it needs to report inventories in the financial statements, accounting "backs out" the inventory amounts from the cost of goods sold account and charges them to inventory accounts.

For example, Biotech Corporation uses JIT. Direct materials cost $1.50 per unit and other manufacturing costs are $.80 per unit. The company received an order for 10,000 units. Biotech incurred materials costs of $15,000 and $8,000 other manufacturing costs on account. The journal entries to record these events follow:

Cost of Goods Sold...	15,000	
Accounts Payable		15,000
To record materials.		
Cost of Goods Sold...	8,000	
Wages and Accounts Payable		8,000
To record the other manufacturing costs.		

Accounting charges (debits) all of these directly to cost of goods sold.

Assume 1,000 units are left in Finished Goods Inventory when accounting prepares the financial statements. Accounting backs out 1,000 units from cost of goods sold based on a unit cost of $2.30, which is $1.50 for materials and $.80 for other manufacturing costs, for a total of $2,300 (= 1,000 units × $2.30 per unit). The journal entry to back out the inventory from cost of goods sold follows:

Finished Goods Inventory	2,300	
Cost of Goods Sold...		2,300
To record inventory.		

Exhibit 4.6 shows these transactions in T-accounts.

If accounting charged the costs of these units to production using traditional costing methods, it would need to debit the materials costs to a direct materials account. As production used the materials, accounting would transfer their costs to Work-in-Process Inventory. Accounting would charge other manufacturing costs to Work-in-Process. As production completed goods, accounting would transfer their costs into Finished Goods and finally into Cost of Goods Sold.

Exhibit 4.6

Just-in-Time Cost Flows

Exhibit 4.7

Flow of Costs: Merchandising

Balance Sheet Account		Income Statement Accounts	
Merchandise Inventory		**Cost of Goods Sold**	

Beginning Inventory Purchases	Cost of Units Sold this Period	Cost of Units Sold this Period	
Ending Inventory			

Marketing and Administrative Costs—Dept. 1

Marketing and Administrative Costs this Period	

Marketing and Administrative Costs—Dept. 2

Marketing and Administrative Costs this Period	

JIT simplifies the accounting system. The firm can save a substantial amount of time given the large volume of accounting entries required in complex operations. For example, JIT saved a Hewlett-Packard plant an estimated 100,000 journal entries per month as we discuss in this chapter's Managerial Application.[1]

Companies have found that they can use JIT if they can obtain materials rapidly from reliable suppliers and receive predictable orders from customers. Many companies do not have literally "just-in-time" production, but have significantly reduced work-in-process inventories.

Merchandise Organizations

Think of merchandising activity as starting where manufacturing leaves off, that is, at Finished Goods Inventory. Merchandising companies purchase goods already manufactured. Merchandising firms have no Direct Material, Direct Labor, Manufacturing Overhead, or Work-in-Process accounts. They simply call Finished Goods Inventory "Merchandise Inventory."

Exhibit 4.7 shows the flow of costs through the accounts. Note that the top accounts in Exhibit 4.7 deal with the purchase and sale of inventory. The purchase

---

[1]R. Hunt, L. Garrett, and C. M. Merz, "Direct Labor Cost Not Always Relevant at H.P.," *Management Accounting,* February 1985, pp. 58–62.

operation in merchandising parallels that in manufacturing. The inventory account displays the costs for which buyers are responsible. One way firms measure buyers' performance is comparing the actual costs charged or debited to inventory and the budgeted costs allowed for the goods purchased.

The accounting system transfers the cost of the units sold during the period to Cost of Goods Sold, just as in manufacturing.

The two lower accounts in Exhibit 4.7 show the costs required to run the company and market the product. Think of these costs as the "value added" in merchandising. Unlike the value added in manufacturing, however, accounting does not add these costs to the value of inventory.

Product costing is easier in merchandising than in manufacturing. The choice of product costing method—for example, full absorption versus variable costing, actual versus normal costing—does not arise in merchandising. In merchandising, a product's cost is generally its purchase price plus costs of transporting the merchandise.[2]

Example   The Campus Bookstore buys calculators from Electron, Inc., and sells them in its retail store. In August, Campus Bookstore purchased 500 Einstein Calculators at $25 each plus $1 each for freight-in and sold 300 of them for $40 each. Campus had 50 calculators on hand on August 1 at $24 each. Direct marketing and administrative costs were $3,000. All transactions were on account. The company uses FIFO (first-in, first-out). The following entries would record these transactions:

(1) Merchandise Inventory..	13,000	
Accounts Payable: Electron, Inc............................		12,500
Accounts Payable: Freight-in		500
To record the purchase of 500 calculators at $25 each plus freight-in at $1 per calculator.		
(2) Accounts Receivable	12,000	
Sales...		12,000
Cost of Goods Sold	7,700	
Merchandise Inventory..................................		7,700
To record the sale of 300 calculators at $40. The first 50 calculators were assigned a cost of $24 each. The next 250 were assigned $26 (= $25 + $1) each.		
(3) Marketing and Administrative Costs	3,000	
Accounts Payable......................................		3,000
To record marketing and administrative costs for August.		

Exhibit 4.8 shows the flow of costs, and Exhibit 4.9 shows the income statement for this example. The merchandising inventory accounting system is simpler than the manufacturing accounting system. Merchandising does not require the extensive product costing apparatus that manufacturing does. Performance evaluation and

---

[2]We do not mean to minimize important financial reporting issues involving inventory such as cost flow assumptions (for example, first-in, first-out or last-in, first-out) or cost basis (current value versus historical cost) assumptions. These issues come up in both merchandising and manufacturing.

Exhibit 4.8

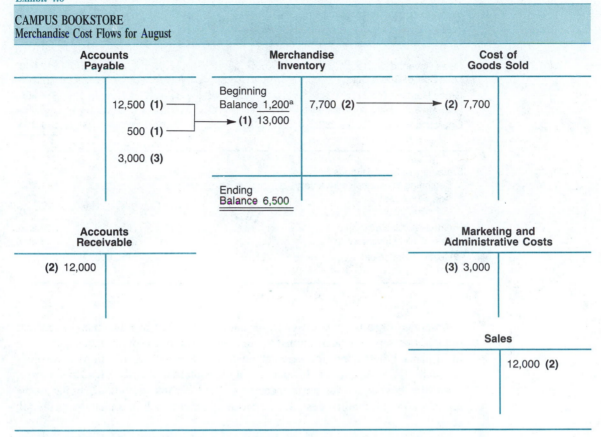

CAMPUS BOOKSTORE
Merchandise Cost Flows for August

Accounts Payable	Merchandise Inventory	Cost of Goods Sold
12,500 **(1)**	Beginning Balance 1,200[a] 7,700 **(2)**	**(2)** 7,700
500 **(1)**	**(1)** 13,000	
3,000 **(3)**		
	Ending Balance 6,500	

Accounts Receivable		Marketing and Administrative Costs
(2) 12,000		**(3)** 3,000

		Sales
		12,000 **(2)**

[a]$1,200 = 50 calculators × $24.00.

Note: Numbers in parentheses correspond to journal entries in the text.

cost control in merchandising focus on marketing and administrative costs, which a firm usually accounts for by product line and department. For example, a retail store would collect and report costs for each major product line and department—sportswear, housewares, furniture, and so on.

Service Organizations

The flow of costs in service organizations is similar to that of manufacturing. Input costs include labor and overhead that are part of the service provided. In multidepartment organizations, the organization often collects costs by departments for performance evaluation. In consulting, public accounting, and similar service organizations, the firm also collects costs by job or client. The accounting method is analogous to that used in manufacturing job shops. As in manufacturing, the firm collects costs by job for performance evaluation, to provide information for cost control, and to compare actual with estimated costs for pricing of future jobs.

Exhibit 4.9

CAMPUS BOOKSTORE Income Statement for the Month Ending August 31	

Sales Revenue	$12,000
Less Cost of Goods Sold	(7,700)
Gross Margin	$ 4,300
Less Marketing and Administrative Costs	(3,000)
Operating Profit	$ 1,300
Statement of Cost of Goods Sold:	
Beginning Merchandise Inventory	$ 1,200
Add: Purchases	12,500
Freight-in	500
Goods Available for Sale	$14,200
Less Ending Inventory	(6,500)
Cost of Goods Sold	$ 7,700

Service organizations differ from manufacturing or merchandising organizations in that service organizations do not show inventories (other than supplies) on the financial statements for external reporting. Service organizations sometimes maintain "Work-in-Process Inventory" in their internal records. This "inventory" shows the cost of service performed for a client but not yet billed, similar to the accumulation of unbilled costs for a special contract or job in a manufacturing job shop.

Example   For the month of July, Conehead Consulting Group (CCG) has the following activity:

- Client A: 400 hours.
- Client B: 600 hours.
- Billing rate to client: $100 per hour.
- Labor costs (all consulting staff): $40 per hour.
- Total consulting hours worked in July: 1,200 hours. (Conehead could not charge 200 hours to a client that it calls "direct labor—unbillable.")
- Actual overhead costs for July: $24,000. (Overhead includes travel, secretarial services, telephone, copying, supplies, and postage.)
- Accounting charges overhead to jobs based on hours worked:

$$\text{Rate per Hour} = \frac{\text{Actual Overhead Costs}}{\text{Actual Labor Hours}}$$

$$= \frac{\$24,000}{1,000 \text{ Hours}} = \$24 \text{ per Hour.}$$

- Marketing and administrative costs: $12,000.
- All transactions are on account.

Entries to record these transactions follow:

(1) Direct Labor—Client A....................................	16,000	
Direct Labor—Client B....................................	24,000	
Direct Labor—Unbillable	8,000	
Wages Payable..		48,000
To record labor costs for July and to assign direct labor costs to Client A (400 hours @ $40 = $16,000) and Client B (600 hours @ $40 = $24,000).		
(2) Overhead—Client A......................................	9,600	
Overhead—Client B......................................	14,400	
Various Payables		24,000
To record overhead costs for July and to assign overhead costs to Client A (400 hours @ $24 = $9,600), to Client B (600 hours @ $24 = $14,400).		
(3) Marketing and Administrative Costs	12,000	
Payables..		12,000
To record marketing and administrative expense for July.		
(4) Accounts Receivable	100,000	
Revenue—Client A.......................................		40,000
Revenue—Client B.......................................		60,000
To record billing for services in July to Client A (400 hours @ $100 = $40,000) and to Client B (600 hours @ $100 = $60,000).		

Exhibits 4.10 and 4.11 show the flow of costs and the income statement.

■ Summary ■

This chapter discusses accounting methods of recording and reporting cost flows for transforming inputs into output. Part of the accounting function for both external reporting and managerial purposes is to trace the flow of resources and to account for them through this process.

The basic cost flow equation,

$$\frac{\text{Beginning}}{\text{Balance}} + \frac{\text{Transfers}}{\text{In}} = \frac{\text{Transfers}}{\text{Out}} + \frac{\text{Ending}}{\text{Balance}}$$

$$\text{BB} + \text{TI} = \text{TO} + \text{EB},$$

relates the flow of costs through the accounts to beginning and ending inventory balances. This equation will help you find unknown balances and cost flows.

In manufacturing, accounting accumulates costs of inputs in work-in-process departments as production occurs. Because these work-in-process departments are the basic responsibility centers in manufacturing, the costs collected in these departments provide important information for performance evaluation and cost control. Firms also need the information for product costing for the purposes of external financial reporting and managerial decision making. Thus in manufacturing organizations accounting focuses on Work-in-Process Inventory accounts.

Exhibit 4.10

CONEHEAD CONSULTING GROUP
Flow of Costs in a Service Organization for July

	Client A	
Payables	**Direct Labor**	**Overhead**
48,000 (1)	(1) 16,000	(2) 9,600
24,000 (2)	**Client B**	
	Direct Labor	**Overhead**
12,000 (3)	(1) 24,000	(2) 14,400

	Unassigned Costs	
	Direct Labor—Unbillable	**Marketing and Administrative Costs**
	(1) 8,000	(3) 12,000

Note: Numbers in parentheses correspond to journal entries in text.

Firms use job costing systems when they have designed manufacturing operations for special jobs or customer orders. Firms use process systems when they have designed manufacturing operations for production of standardized products that pass through several production processes. In job costing, accounting accumulates costs for each unit or job produced; in process costing, it accumulates costs for an entire operation or department and averages them over the units produced.

Exhibit 4.11

CONEHEAD CONSULTING GROUP
Income Statement for the Month Ending July 31

Revenue from Services for Clients	$100,000
Less Costs of Services to Clients:	
Labor	(40,000)
Overhead	(24,000)
Gross Margin...	$ 36,000
Less Other Costs:	
Labor	(8,000)
Marketing and Administrative	(12,000)
Operating Profit...	$ 16,000

Chapters 3 and 4 have presented a 2×3 matrix of alternative costing methods. In addition, firms can use two different costing systems, job and process costing. Thus choice of product costs involves a $2 \times 3 \times 2$ decision, as shown below:

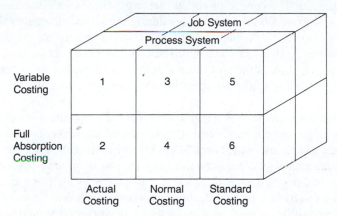

Firms can use *any* of the six product cost methods in process systems or *any* in job systems. Process systems tend to use standard costing because accounting can more easily assign standard costs to the homogeneous units of a process manufacturing system than to the heterogeneous units of a job system. Job systems tend to use actual (or normal) costing. Firms often use actual costs for pricing and performance evaluation of jobs.

Management uses just-in-time inventory to obtain materials just in time for production, to complete each step of the production process just in time for the next step, and to complete products just in time for shipping to customers. This practice reduces inventories and simplifies accounting for cost flows.

Merchandising starts where manufacturing ends. Product costing is easier in merchandising than in manufacturing. Product costs are simply the purchase price plus direct costs of obtaining the product (for example, freight-in). Thus product costing for external financial reporting is not as complicated in merchandising as in manufacturing. For managerial purposes, the firm should design its accounting system to assign costs to merchandising responsibility centers—primarily product lines and departments.

Service organizations have costing systems similar to manufacturing, with one important difference—service organizations usually have no inventories (except for supplies) for external reporting purposes. Many service organizations, such as consulting firms, use job costing. Some service organizations, notably banks, use standard costing. In short, service organizations can, with a few modifications, apply knowledge of how costing is done in manufacturing companies.

Appendix 4.1:
Computing Equivalent Production

This appendix describes product costing methods when a firm has only partially completed work on a product at the beginning or end of a period. For example, assume Davis Contractors, a house builder, is presently building several houses of a particular model. Davis had three partially built houses at the beginning of the second quarter of the year (April 1). Davis started four houses and completed five houses during the second quarter, and had two partially built houses at the end of the quarter (June 30). The contractor knows that expenditures for construction materials, labor, and overhead for these houses during the second quarter total $795,000 and that the cost of the beginning work-in-process inventory for the three houses partially built on April 1 totals $42,000. The contractor does not know several other things, however, such as the cost of each house constructed in the second quarter, the cost of the ending work-in-process inventory, and the cost of the houses completed.

The contractor has several potential uses for the information about the cost of each house. First, the contractor had set prices based on market conditions and the estimate that each house would cost $145,000 to build. If the estimates are incorrect, the contractor would consider changing the prices on the houses or possibly would stop building this type of house if costs were so high that the contractor would make insufficient profits. Second, the contractor holds construction job supervisors responsible for managing and scheduling workers, for minimizing waste, and for other activities that affect construction costs. Product costs can provide feedback about their performance. Third, Davis Contractors prepares the external financial statements for its creditors that require ending inventory valuation and the cost of finished houses sold.

Procedure for Applying Costs to Units Produced

This section describes the five steps required to compute product costs, the cost of ending work-in-process inventory, and the cost of finished goods. Exhibit 4.12 presents the data required to do the analysis for the Davis Contractors example. Exhibit 4.13 summarizes the five steps in the process and presents the analysis for Davis Contractors. Exhibit 4.12 shows that the contractor considered each of the three houses in the beginning work-in-process inventory to be 10-percent complete, on average, and the two houses in the ending work-in-process inventory each to be 30 percent complete, on average. Assume the first-in, first-out (FIFO) cost flow assumption for inventory, for now. (Later, we discuss the effects of using the weighted-average method.)

Step 1: Summarize the Flow of Physical Units   This appears in the top of the production cost report in Exhibit 4.13.

Step 2: Compute Equivalent Units   Since the firm has some partially completed units at the beginning and end of the period, accounting must convert the work into equivalent (finished) units produced. **Equivalent units (E.U.)** represent the translation of partially complete work into equivalent whole units. For example, two units, each 50 percent complete, represent one equivalent unit. Three categories of work done require equivalent unit computations to derive the equivalent work done in a period:

1. **Equivalent units to complete beginning work-in-process inventory.** For Davis Contractors, the three houses in beginning work-in-process (WIP) inven-

Exhibit 4.12

	Units[a]	Product Costs	Percent of Processing Completed
DAVIS CONTRACTORS			
Cost of Houses Produced			
Data for Second Quarter, April 1 through June 30			
Beginning Work-in-Process Inventory, April 1	3	$ 42,000	10
Costs Incurred in Second Quarter	—	795,000	—
Completed and Transferred Out to Finished Goods Inventory	5	?	100
Ending Work-in-Process Inventory	2	?	30

Diagram of Unit Flows

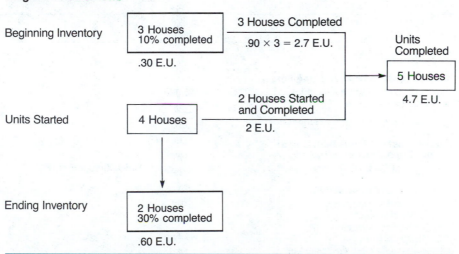

[a]Some of these units are only partially completed.

tory were 10 percent complete when the period started. Since Davis completed them during this period, as the bottom of Exhibit 4.12 shows, Davis did 90 percent of the work on these houses during the second quarter. Therefore, accounting required 2.7 equivalent units (= 3 houses × 90%) to complete the beginning inventory, as Exhibit 4.13 shows.

2. **Equivalent units for work started and completed during the period.** Exhibit 4.12 shows that Davis started and completed two houses during the period, representing two equivalent units produced, as shown in Exhibit 4.13.

3. **Units still in ending WIP inventory.** The ending WIP inventory represents the equivalent work done on units not completed and transferred out during the period. Two houses that Davis had 30 percent complete at the end of the period fit into this category, representing .6 equivalent units (= 2 houses × 30%).

The equivalent units produced for the second quarter are 5.3 units (= 2.7 + 2.0 + .6), as shown in Step 2 in Exhibit 4.13.

Exhibit 4.13

	(Step 1) Physical Units	(Step 2) Compute Equivalent Units (E.U.)
Accounting for Units:		
Units to Account For:		
Beginning Work-in-Process (WIP) Inventory	3	
Units Started This Period.	4	
Total Units to Account For	7	
Units Accounted For:		
Units Completed and Transferred Out:		
From Beginning Inventory	3	2.7[a] (90%)[b]
Started and Completed, Currently	2	2.0
Units in Ending WIP Inventory	2	0.6 (30%)[c]
Total Units Accounted For	7	5.3

	Total Costs	Unit Costs
Accounting for Costs:		
(Step 3) Costs to Be Accounted For:		
Costs in Beginning WIP Inventory	$ 42,000	
Current Period Costs	795,000	
Total Costs to Be Accounted For	$837,000	
(Step 4) Cost per Equivalent Unit of Work Done This Period:		
$795,000/5.3 E.U. . . . . =		$150,000 per E.U.
(Step 5) Costs Accounted For:		
Costs Assigned to Units Transferred Out:		
Costs from Beginning WIP Inventory	$ 42,000	
Current Costs Added to Complete Beginning WIP Inventory:		
2.7 E.U. × $150,000 . . . . =	405,000	
Current Costs of Units Started and Completed:		
2.0 E.U. × $150,000 . . . . =	300,000	
Total Costs Transferred Out	$747,000	$149,400 per Unit (= $747,000/5 Units Transferred Out)
Costs Assigned to Ending WIP Inventory:		
0.6 E.U. × $150,000 . . . . =	90,000	$150,000
Total Costs Accounted For	$837,000	$149,464 [= $837,000/(5 Units Transferred Out + 0.6 Units in Ending WIP Inventory)]

[a]Equivalent units required to complete beginning inventory. For example, 90 percent of 3 units must be added to the beginning inventory to complete it. Therefore, 2.7 (= 90% × 3) equivalent units are required to complete beginning inventory.

[b]Percent required to complete beginning inventory.

[c]Stage of completion of ending inventory.

We base equivalent unit computations on the basic accounting equation. If you know the equivalent work done in beginning and ending work-in-process inventories and the units transferred, you can derive the equivalent units produced during the period as follows:

$$\begin{matrix} \text{Equivalent Units} \\ \text{in the Beginning} \\ \text{Inventory} \end{matrix} + \begin{matrix} \text{Equivalent Units} \\ \text{of Work Done} \\ \text{This Period} \end{matrix} = \begin{matrix} \text{Equivalent Units} \\ \text{Transferred Out} \end{matrix} + \begin{matrix} \text{Equivalent Units} \\ \text{in Ending} \\ \text{Inventory} \end{matrix}$$

In our example, to find the work done this period, use the following formula:

$$\begin{matrix} \text{Equivalent Units} \\ \text{of Work Done} \\ \text{This Period} \end{matrix} = \begin{matrix} \text{Equivalent Units} \\ \text{Transferred Out} \end{matrix} + \begin{matrix} \text{Equivalent Units} \\ \text{in Ending} \\ \text{Inventory} \end{matrix} - \begin{matrix} \text{Equivalent Units} \\ \text{in Beginning} \\ \text{Inventory} \end{matrix}$$

$$= 5.0 + .6 - (3.0 \times 10\%)$$

$$= 5.3 \text{ Equivalent Units of Work Done.}$$

Step 3: Summarize Costs to Be Accounted For   This step merely records the costs in beginning work-in-process inventory and the costs incurred during the period, as Step 3 of Exhibit 4.13 shows.

Step 4: Compute Unit Costs for the Current Period   Exhibit 4.13 shows that the cost per equivalent unit produced this period is $150,000. Note that this cost represents work done during this period only; it does not include costs in beginning inventory. Davis would use this unit cost to evaluate performance in controlling costs, and it would provide information to management about the cost of building houses that Davis can use to assess prices and the profitability of continuing to build this type of house.

Step 5: Compute the Cost of Goods Completed and Transferred Out of Work-in-Process and the Cost of Ending Work-in-Process Inventory   Exhibit 4.13 shows the cost of units transferred out, including the $42,000 from beginning inventory and the cost of the goods still in ending inventory, which accounting assigns a cost of $150,000 per equivalent unit.

Flow of Costs through Accounts   Exhibit 4.14 presents the flow of costs through T-accounts.

Weighted-Average Method

The previous computations assumed FIFO, which means that accounting transferred out the cost of beginning inventory first and that the costs pertinent to ending inventory were the costs of goods produced during the current period.[3] If Davis used the weighted-average method instead of FIFO, accounting would assign the cost of goods transferred out and the cost of goods in ending inventory a weighted-average

---

[3]This statement assumes that the firm completed the units in beginning WIP inventory during the period. If some of the units in beginning inventory were still in WIP inventory at the end of the period, the firm would carry some beginning inventory costs to the ending inventory.

Exhibit 4.14

DAVIS CONTRACTORS
Cost Flow through T-Accounts (FIFO)
Second Quarter

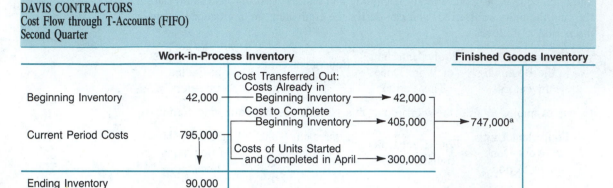

ªTotal costs transferred out of Work-in-Process Inventory

cost that considers both the current period cost and the beginning inventory cost. As the bottom of Exhibit 4.13 shows, the weighted-average cost is $149,464 per unit, which equals the total costs Davis must account for, $837,000, divided by the total equivalent units, 5.6. The 5.6 equivalent units equals 5.3 equivalent units for the period plus .3 in beginning inventory. The 5.6 equivalent units also equals the 5.0 units transferred out plus .6 equivalent units in ending inventory. This result must be true because

$$BB + TI = TO + EB,$$

so

$$.3 + 5.3 = 5.0 + .6,$$

where TI is defined to be the equivalent units produced this period.

Spoilage

Accounting typically includes the cost of normal waste in the cost of work done this period. If Davis Contractors incurs some normal wastage of lumber on a job, accounting would typically include that cost of materials in the cost of work done for the period. If the waste is not normal, accounting would remove it from the costs included in these computations and debit it to an account called "Abnormal Spoilage."

Companies concerned about waste do not treat waste or spoiled goods as normal. Instead they remove costs for such goods from product costs that do not represent waste or spoilage to avoid having waste costs buried in product costs. Some companies have been surprised to discover that, when they removed their waste and spoilage costs from other product costs, these costs were 20 to 30 percent of their total product costs.

Problem 1 for Self-Study

Finding Unknown Costs

The management of Wheeler Industrial Equipment Company wishes to compute various unknown balances and has asked you for assistance. You have the following data:

Account Balances	January 1, Year 1	December 31, Year 1
Materials Inventory	$205,000	$?
Work-in-Process Inventory	68,550	?
Finished Goods Inventory	31,000	65,000
Accounts Payable (all for direct and indirect materials) ..	16,000	24,000
Cost of Goods Sold for Year.........................	0	769,650

The work-in-process balances are for jobs in process at the balance sheet dates. On January 1, Year 1, Wheeler had two jobs in process, as follows:

Date Started	Job Number	Direct Materials	Direct Labor
10/15/Year 0	101	$14,200	$ 8,400
12/17/Year 0	103	6,500	9,000
		$20,700	$17,400

On December 31, Year 1, Wheeler had only one job in process, number 204. However, the only available information about the job was the accumulated direct labor costs of $12,000 and direct materials of $21,900. The company uses full absorption, normal costing. Accounting applies overhead to jobs as a percentage of direct labor costs.

You have the following additional information available for Year 1:

Payments Made to Suppliers of Materials in Year 1	$342,000
Indirect Materials Issued from Inventory	14,000
Direct Labor Costs Incurred..	140,000
Direct Materials Costs Transferred to Finished Goods Inventory	403,800
Current Period Applied Overhead in Finished Goods Inventory on December 31, Year 1	30,000
Actual Manufacturing Overhead Costs Incurred (fixed and variable are combined)	247,000

(*Hint:* Set up T-accounts with the amounts given in the problem entered.)
    Find the following unknown balances and transaction cost flows.

a. Materials purchased in Year 1.

b. Direct materials issued to production (Work-in-Process Inventory) in Year 1.

c.   Materials Inventory, December 31, Year 1.

d.   Rate at which overhead is applied to Work-in-Process.

e.   Overhead applied to Work-in-Process.

f.   Under- or overapplied overhead.

g.   Cost of goods manufactured (that is, transferred to Finished Goods Inventory).

h.   Work-in-Process Inventory, December 31, Year 1.

i.   Applied overhead in ending Work-in-Process Inventory, December 31, Year 1.

Suggested Solution

You can use the basic cost flow equation, $BB + TI = TO + EB$, to solve for the unknowns. (We show cost flows through T-accounts at the end of this solution.)

a.   *Accounts Payable Account*

$$TI \quad = \quad TO \quad + \quad EB \quad - \quad BB$$

$$\begin{array}{c} \text{Materials} \\ \text{Purchased} \end{array} = \begin{array}{c} \text{Payments to} \\ \text{Suppliers} \end{array} + \begin{array}{c} \text{Accounts Payable} \\ \text{Balance—12/31/01} \end{array} - \begin{array}{c} \text{Accounts Payable} \\ \text{Balance—1/1/01} \end{array}$$

$$= \$342,000 \quad + \quad \$24,000 \quad - \quad \$16,000$$

$$= \underline{\$350,000}.$$

b.   *Work-in-Process Account*

$$TI \quad = \quad TO \quad + \quad EB \quad - \quad BB$$

$$\begin{array}{c} \text{Direct} \\ \text{Materials} \\ \text{Issued} \end{array} = \begin{array}{c} \text{Direct} \\ \text{Materials} \\ \text{Costs} \\ \text{Transferred} \\ \text{to Finished} \\ \text{Goods (given)} \end{array} + \begin{array}{c} \text{Direct} \\ \text{Materials} \\ \text{in Ending} \\ \text{Work-in-Process} \\ \text{Inventory—} \\ \text{12/31/01} \\ \text{(given)} \end{array} - \begin{array}{c} \text{Direct} \\ \text{Materials} \\ \text{in Beginning} \\ \text{Work-in-Process} \\ \text{Inventory—} \\ \text{1/1/01} \\ \text{(given)} \end{array}$$

$$= \$403,800 \quad + \quad \$21,900 \quad - \quad \$20,700$$

$$= \underline{\$405,000}.$$

c.   *Materials Inventory Account*

$$EB \quad = \quad BB \quad + \quad TI \quad - \quad TO$$

$$\begin{array}{c} \text{Ending} \\ \text{Materials} \\ \text{Inventory—} \\ \text{12/31/01} \end{array} = \begin{array}{c} \text{Beginning} \\ \text{Materials} \\ \text{Inventory—} \\ \text{1/1/01} \end{array} + \text{Purchases} - \left(\begin{array}{cc} \text{Direct} & \text{Indirect} \\ \text{Materials} + \text{Materials} \\ \text{Issued} & \text{Issued} \end{array} \right)$$

$$= \$205,000 \quad + \$350,000 \quad - \quad (\$405,000 + \$14,000)$$

$$= \underline{\$136,000}.$$

d. *Overhead Application Rate*

    (i) First find the overhead application rate:

$$\begin{array}{l} \text{Overhead} \\ \text{Application} \\ \text{Rate} \end{array} = \frac{\text{Overhead Applied to Jobs in Beginning Inventory}}{\text{Direct Labor Costs of Jobs in Beginning Inventory}}$$

$$= \frac{\text{Overhead Applied to Jobs—1/1/01}}{\$17,400}.$$

    (ii) Next, find the overhead applied to the jobs in beginning Work-in-Process Inventory:

$$\begin{array}{l} \text{Overhead} \\ \text{Applied to} \\ \text{Jobs—} \\ \text{1/1/01} \end{array} = \$68,550 - \$20,700 - \$17,400$$

$$= \$30,450.$$

    (iii) So the rate is

$$\begin{array}{l} \text{Overhead} \\ \text{Application} \\ \text{Rate} \end{array} = \frac{\$30,450}{\$17,400}$$

$$= 175\%.$$

e. *Overhead Applied to Work-in-Process*

$$\begin{array}{l} \text{Amount} \\ \text{Applied} \end{array} = \text{Rate} \times \text{Base (direct labor costs)}$$

$$= 175\% \times \$140,000$$

$$= \$245,000.$$

f. *Under- or Overapplied Overhead*

$$\begin{array}{l} \text{Underapplied} \\ \text{Overhead} \end{array} = \begin{array}{l} \text{Actual} \\ \text{Overhead} \end{array} - \begin{array}{l} \text{Overhead} \\ \text{Applied} \end{array}$$

$$= \$247,000 - \$245,000$$

$$= \$2,000 \ (\text{underapplied}).$$

g. *Finished Goods Inventory Account*

$$\text{TI} \quad = \quad \text{TO} \quad + \quad \text{EB} \quad - \quad \text{BB}$$

$$\begin{array}{l} \text{Costs of Goods} \\ \text{Manufactured} \end{array} = \begin{array}{l} \text{Cost of} \\ \text{Goods Sold} \end{array} + \begin{array}{l} \text{Ending Finished} \\ \text{Goods—12/31/01} \end{array} - \begin{array}{l} \text{Beginning Inventory} \\ \text{Goods—1/1/01} \end{array}$$

$$= \$769,650 \ + \quad \$65,000 \quad - \quad \$31,000$$

$$= \$803,650.$$

h. *Work-in-Process Inventory Account*

$$EB \quad = \quad BB \quad + \quad TI \quad - \quad TO$$

| Ending Work-in-Process Inventory— 12/31/01 | = | Beginning Work-in-Process Inventory—1/1/01 | + | Direct Materials, Direct Labor, and Manufacturing Overhead Charged to the Account during Year 1 | − | Cost of Goods Manufactured |

$$= \quad \$68{,}550 \quad + \quad \begin{pmatrix} \$405{,}000 + \\ \$140{,}000 + \\ \$245{,}000 \end{pmatrix} \quad - \quad \$803{,}650$$

$$= \quad \underline{\$54{,}900}.$$

i. *Applied Overhead in Ending Work-in-Process Inventory*

$$\frac{\text{Applied}}{\text{Overhead}} = \frac{\text{Overhead}}{\text{Rate}} \times \text{Base (that is, direct labor costs)}$$

$$= \quad 175\% \quad \times \quad \$12{,}000 \text{ (given)}$$

$$= \quad \underline{\$21{,}000}.$$

WHEELER INDUSTRIAL EQUIPMENT COMPANY
Manufacturing Cost Flows

Accounts Payable

TO = 342,000[a]	BB = 16,000[a]
	TI = 350,000 **(a)**
	EB = 24,000[a]

Materials Inventory

BB = 205,000[a]	
TI = 350,000 **(a)**	TO = { 14,000[a]
EB = 136,000 **(c)**	405,000 **(b)**

Manufacturing Overhead

(Actual)	(Applied)
247,000[a]	245,000 **(e)**

Work-in-Process Inventory

BB =	68,550[a]	
TI = { Materials	405,000 **(b)**	TO = 803,650 **(g)**
Labor	140,000[a]	
Overhead	245,000 **(e)**	
EB =	54,900 **(h)**	

Finished Goods Inventory

BB = 31,000[a]	
TI = 803,650 **(g)**	TO = 769,650[a]
EB = 65,000[a]	

Cost of Goods Sold

TI = 769,650[a]	

BB = beginning balance.   EB = ending balance.   TI = transfers in.   TO = transfers out.

[a]We gave the amount in the problem.

Letter in parentheses indicates the part of the solution in which the amount was derived.

Problem 2 for Self-Study

Comprehensive Cost Flow Problem for Jobs
(Contributed by J. Lim)

One morning, Patrick O'Leary and James Hughes sat in the office adjacent to their jointly owned factory. They had spent a day trying to devise a better way of pricing their job orders. Last year had been a busy year, but Donegal Woolens posted a loss. "Jim, we ought to go to a management consulting firm before things get worse," O'Leary said. "I guess you're right," Hughes agreed, "but we can hardly afford to spend any more money."

   Both Pat and Jim were recent graduates of a well-known fashion design school. The pair had attracted the attention of several fashion designers. Their company, Donegal Woolens, supplied custom-ordered, hand-knit woolens for a few exclusive stores. They specialized in classic Irish knits, but occasionally created avant-garde designs. Donegal Woolens employed 20 full-time knitters at $5 per hour. Pat and Jim assembled and packed the knitted pieces themselves, and each took a salary of $1,500 per month. Since beginning operations last year, they had priced the various jobs by applying a markup of 20 percent on direct labor and direct material costs. However, despite operating at capacity, last year's performance disappointed them. In total, they accepted and completed ten jobs, incurring the following costs:

Jobs	Raw Materials	Direct Labor Costs
101	$ 7,650	$ 30,740
102	3,230	14,050
103	6,840	23,190
104	4,100	15,260
105	5,900	21,560
106	4,580	18,810
107	7,240	25,950
108	2,060	10,650
109	2,870	12,440
110	7,300	27,350
	$51,770	$200,000
Manufacturing Overhead Costs		$52,000

Donegal considered 30 percent of the $52,000 manufacturing overhead variable overhead and 70 percent fixed.

   This year Donegal Woolens expected to operate at the same activity level as last year and did not expect overhead costs and the wage rate to change.

   For the first quarter of this year, Donegal Woolens had just completed two jobs and was beginning on the third. Donegal incurred the costs that appear on the following page:

Jobs	Raw Materials	Direct Labor Costs
111	$6,860	$24,500
112	4,650	15,620
113	4,700	9,880
Total Factory Overhead		$13,560
Total Marketing and Administrative Costs		5,600

You are a consultant associated with Vesting Concerns Management Consultants, the firm Donegal Woolens has approached. The senior partner of your firm has examined Donegal Woolens' books and has decided to divide actual factory overhead by job into fixed and variable portions as follows:[4]

Jobs	Actual Factory Overhead	
	Variable	Fixed
111	$1,495	$ 5,200
112	1,375	4,410
113	230	850
	$3,100	$10,460

In the first quarter of this year, 40 percent of marketing and administrative costs were variable and 60 percent were fixed.

The senior partner has asked you to do the following for Donegal Woolens:

a. Present in T-accounts the full absorption, actual manufacturing cost flows for the three jobs in the first quarter of this year.

b. Using last year's overhead costs and direct labor hours, calculate a predetermined overhead rate per direct labor hour for variable and fixed overhead.

c. Present in T-accounts the full absorption, normal manufacturing cost flows for the three jobs in the first quarter of this year. Use the overhead rates derived in part b.

d. Prepare income statements for the first quarter of this year under the following costing systems:
   (1) Full absorption, actual.
   (2) Full absorption, normal.
   (3) Variable, actual.
   (4) Variable, normal.

Donegal tells you that it sold Jobs 111 and 112 for $42,500 and $27,500, respectively. Accounting has expensed all over- or underapplied overhead for the quarter on the income statement.

---

[4]Accounting must allocate actual manufacturing costs that firms cannot trace directly to specific jobs. For example, accounting may allocate depreciation on the basis of machine hours, and factory rent on the basis of area used. The allocation can be arbitrary.

Suggested Solution

a.

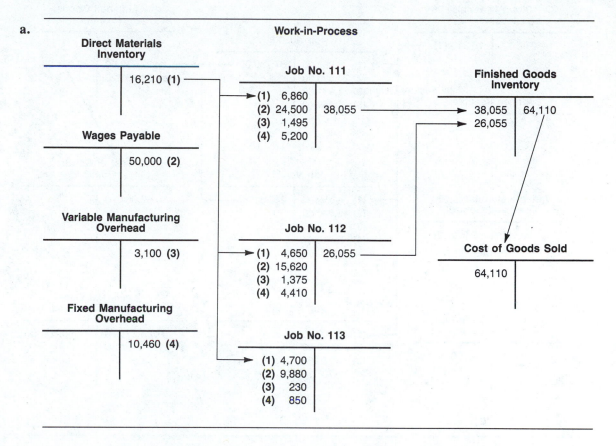

b.

$$\text{Total Direct Labor Costs} = \$200{,}000.$$

$$\text{Total Direct Labor Hours} = \frac{\$200{,}000}{\$5 \text{ per Hour}} = 40{,}000.$$

$$\text{Variable Manufacturing Overhead} = 0.30 \times \$52{,}000$$

$$= \$15{,}600.$$

$$\text{Predetermined Variable Overhead Rate} = \frac{\$15{,}600}{40{,}000}$$

$$= \$0.39 \text{ per Direct Labor Hour.}$$

$$\text{Fixed Manufacturing Overhead} = 0.70 \times \$52{,}000$$

$$= \$36{,}400.$$

$$\text{Predetermined Fixed Overhead Rate} = \frac{\$36{,}400}{40{,}000}$$

$$= \$0.91 \text{ per Direct Labor Hour.}$$

c.

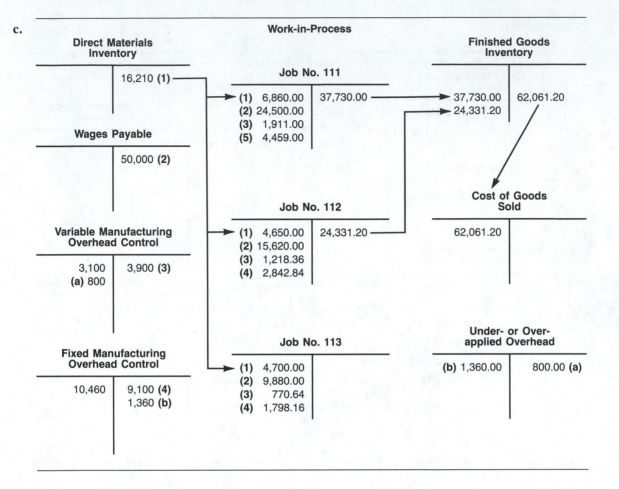

Direct Materials Inventory

| 16,210 (1) | |

Work-in-Process

Job No. 111

(1) 6,860.00	37,730.00
(2) 24,500.00	
(3) 1,911.00	
(5) 4,459.00	

Finished Goods Inventory

| 37,730.00 | 62,061.20 |
| 24,331.20 | |

Wages Payable

| | 50,000 (2) |

Variable Manufacturing Overhead Control

| 3,100 | 3,900 (3) |
| (a) 800 | |

Job No. 112

(1) 4,650.00	24,331.20
(2) 15,620.00	
(3) 1,218.36	
(4) 2,842.84	

Cost of Goods Sold

| 62,061.20 | |

Fixed Manufacturing Overhead Control

| 10,460 | 9,100 (4) |
| | 1,360 (b) |

Job No. 113

(1) 4,700.00	
(2) 9,880.00	
(3) 770.64	
(4) 1,798.16	

Under- or Over-applied Overhead

| (b) 1,360.00 | 800.00 (a) |

d.

	Actual	Normal
Full Absorption Costing		
Sales Revenue	$70,000	$70,000.00
Less Cost of Goods Sold	(64,110)	(62,061.20)
Gross Margin	$ 5,890	$ 7,938.80
Less:		
(Under-) Overapplied Overhead	—	(560.00)
Marketing and Administrative Costs	(5,600)	(5,600.00)
Operating Profit (Loss)	$ 290	$ 1,778.80
Variable Costing		
Sales Revenue	$70,000	$70,000.00
Less:		
Variable Manufacturing Costs	(54,500)	(54,759.36)
Variable Marketing and Administrative Costs	(2,240)	(2,240.00)
Contribution Margin	$13,260	$13,000.64

continued

continued from page 150

Less:

Fixed Manufacturing Costs...........................	(10,460)	(10,460.00)
(Under-) Overapplied Overhead	—	800.00
Fixed Marketing and Administrative Costs	(3,360)	(3,360.00)
Operating Profit (Loss)	$ (560)	$ (19.36)

Problem 3 for Self-Study

Cost Flows in a Service Organization

For the month of September, Touche Andersen & Company worked 200 hours for Client A and 700 hours for Client B. Touche Andersen bills clients at the rate of $80 per hour, whereas the audit staff costs $30 per hour. The audit staff worked 1,000 total hours in September (100 hours were not billable to clients), and overhead costs were $10,000. (Examples of unbillable hours are hours spent in professional training and meetings unrelated to particular clients.) Accounting assigns overhead to clients based proportionally on direct labor hours, so it assigned Client A $2,000, Client B $7,000, and left $1,000 unassigned. In addition, Touche Andersen & Company spent $5,000 in marketing and administrative costs. All transactions are on account.

a. Using T-accounts, trace manufacturing costs and revenue flows.

b. Prepare a full absorption income statement for the company for September.

Suggested Solution

a. TOUCHE ANDERSEN & COMPANY
September

Accounts Receivable	Revenue—Client A	Revenue—Client B	Unassigned Costs
(4) 72,000	16,000 (4)	56,000 (4)	

Wages and Accounts Payable	Direct Labor—Client A	Direct Labor—Client B	Direct Labor—Unbillable
30,000 (1)	(1) 6,000	(1) 21,000	(1) 3,000

	Overhead—Client A	Overhead—Client B	Unassigned Overhead
10,000 (2)	(2) 2,000	(2) 7,000	(2) 1,000

			Marketing and Administrative Costs
5,000 (3)			(3) 5,000

b.   TOUCHE ANDERSEN & COMPANY
Income Statement for the Month Ended September 30

Revenue from Service for Clients		$72,000
Less Costs of Services to Clients:		
Labor	$(27,000)	
Overhead	(9,000)	
Total Costs of Services to Clients		(36,000)
Gross Margin		36,000
Less Other Costs:		
Labor	(3,000)	
Overhead	(1,000)	
Marketing and Administrative Costs	(5,000)	
Total Other Costs		(9,000)
Operating Profit		$27,000

Key Terms and Concepts

Cost accumulation
Cost allocation
Basic cost flow equation
Batch production
Repetitive manufacturing

Continuous flow processing
Job costing
Process costing
Just-in-time (JIT) inventory
Equivalent units (appendix)

Questions, Exercises, Problems, and Cases

Questions

1. Review the meaning of the concepts or terms given above in Key Terms and Concepts.

2. Compare and contrast job costing and process costing systems.

3. Management of a company that manufactures small appliances is trying to decide whether to install a job or process costing system. The manufacturing vice president has stated that job costing gives the best control because it allows assigning costs to specific lots of goods. The controller, however, has stated that job costing would require too much record keeping. Would another costing system meet the manufacturing vice president's control objectives? Explain.

4. Why don't service organizations have inventories?

5. A merchandiser comments: "I perform services that add to the value of the products that I sell. My marketing staff facilitates economic efficiency by purchasing the right product, informing the consuming public of its availability, and distributing it in an efficient manner. Why shouldn't I be allowed to

include my marketing and administrative costs as part of the value of my inventory?'' Reply to this comment.

6. What are the two stages of product costing?

7. What types of savings can firms achieve with just-in-time inventory?

8. Explain the differences in accounting for the flow of costs using just-in-time inventory and traditional accounting when accounting charges costs first to inventory accounts.

9. What operating conditions of companies make just-in-time inventory feasible?

10. Why must firms have reliable suppliers when using just-in-time inventory?

Exercises

11. *Tracing cost flows in a job costing system.* The Mega-Audits Accounting Firm uses a job costing system. For Year 6, the firm estimated total overhead to be $80,000 and the number of direct labor hours to be 20,000. In the last quarter, the firm completed the following audit jobs:

Job	No. 242	No. 301
Supplies	$200	$600
Direct Labor Costs.................................	11,000	14,000
Direct Labor Hours	220 Hours	280 Hours

a. Based on this information, what overhead rate might the firm use?
b. Using T-accounts, trace the cost flows for the two jobs.

12. *Computing manufacturing costs of a job.* The Susan Johnson Products Company uses a job costing system. For Year 4, the firm estimated total overhead to be $40,000 and the number of direct labor hours to be 10,000.
a. Based on this information, what overhead rate might the firm use?
b. Job 247 is a special order for 100 special design tables. The Work-in-Process Inventory account for this job shows raw material costs of $4,600 and direct labor costs of $7,600. The firm has charged 1,200 direct labor hours to the job. What is the total cost of Job 247? What is the unit cost of each table on that job?

13. *Computing over- or underapplied overhead.* The Ortega Manufacturing Company distributes its factory overhead over its jobs as a percentage of direct labor cost. Ortega set the rate for the third quarter of the year at 150 percent, based on an estimated total overhead of $75,000 and an estimated total direct labor cost of $50,000.

Indicate the amount of *overapplied* or *underapplied* overhead for the quarter under each of the following assumptions:
a. Actual overhead, $70,000; actual direct labor, $48,000.
b. Actual overhead, $79,000; actual direct labor, $52,000.
c. Actual overhead, $80,000; actual direct labor, $50,000.

d. Actual overhead, $84,000; actual direct labor, $56,000.

e. Actual overhead, $68,000; actual direct labor, $44,000.

f. Actual overhead, $76,000; actual direct labor, $49,000.

14. *Cost flows in a merchandising organization.* Mohammed's Pharmacy carries three product lines: drugs, cosmetics, and toiletries. Two days after taking the store's month-end inventory, the owner received the following figures:

Product Line	Beginning Inventory	Ending Inventory	Purchases
Drugs	$30,500	$31,600	$40,200
Cosmetics	20,150	21,900	28,400
Toiletries..........................	24,360	23,240	30,600
Marketing Costs			10,000
General and Administrative Costs			8,000

   Use T-accounts to describe these cost flows. Assume Mohammed's incurred all costs on account.

15. *Cost flows in a service company.* Quick Sell, an advertising consulting firm, charges clients $80 per hour for its services. Direct labor costs are $30 per hour, and the predetermined overhead rate is $10 per labor hour. In August, Quick Sell began and completed the following jobs:

   - Job A: 150 hours.

   - Job B: 200 hours.

   - Job C: 400 hours.

   Actual overhead costs were $8,000, and marketing and administrative costs (all fixed) were $5,000.

   a. Using T-accounts, trace the cost flows for the month of August.

   b. Assuming that 40 percent of the overhead is variable, prepare a variable-cost income statement for August.

   c. How would Quick Sell deal with the discrepancy between actual and applied overhead?

16. *Tracing manufacturing cost flows using T-accounts.* Set up T-accounts for Materials Inventory, Work-in-Process Inventory, Finished Goods Inventory, Cost of Goods Sold, and Manufacturing Overhead for Niebok Shoes. Enter the following items in the T-accounts as appropriate for the month of June:

   (1) Beginning inventory accounts follow: Materials Inventory, $40,000; Work-in-Process Inventory, $150,000; Finished Goods Inventory, $120,000.

   (2) Materials purchased during June were $300,000.

   (3) Materials used during June totaled $270,000.

   (4) Direct labor costs incurred during the month were $400,000.

   (5) Manufacturing overhead costs incurred during June totaled $130,000.

   (6) Manufacturing overhead costs applied to units produced totaled $120,000.

(7) The cost of units completed during June was $910,000.

(8) The cost of goods sold during June was $850,000.

17. *Computing the cost of jobs.* Records of the McKinley Machine Company on May 31, before recording the application of factory overhead to products and before recording the transfer of completed units to Finished Goods Inventory, follow:

Work-in-Process Inventory	$16,842
Factory Overhead	3,100

Job costing records show the following data:

	Job 576	Job 577	Job 578	Job 579	Job 580
Work in Process, May 1					
Material	$ 953	$ 824			
Direct Labor	1,250	1,507			
Factory Overhead	1,075	945			
Direct Costs Incurred in May					
Material	$ 170	$ 520	$1,240	$ 950	$1,312
Direct Labor	1,260	842	2,500	1,302	192

Accounting applies manufacturing overhead at the rate of 50 percent of direct labor cost. McKinley completed Jobs 576, 577, and 578 during May. It has Jobs 579 and 580 still in process at the end of May.

a. Compute the total costs allocated to Job 576, to Job 577, and to Job 578.

b. Compute the total costs allocated to Job 579 and to Job 580.

18. *Preparing an income statement for a merchandiser.* Sellout Corporation experienced the following events during a current year:

(1) Incurred marketing costs of $197,000 on account.

(2) Purchased $971,000 of merchandise.

(3) Paid $26,000 in transportation-in costs.

(4) Incurred $400,000 of administrative costs.

(5) Took an inventory on December 31 and learned that it had goods with a cost of $297,000 on hand. It compared this figure with a beginning inventory of $314,000 on January 1.

(6) Sales revenue during the year was $1,850,000.

Prepare an income statement based on these data.

19. *Tracing cost flows under job costing.* Spoljaric Construction Company uses a job costing system. It applies overhead to jobs on a direct labor cost basis at a rate of 50 percent of direct labor cost. It uses an Overhead account to accumulate actual overhead costs.

At August 1, the balance in the Work-in-Process Inventory account was $34,524. It had the following jobs in process at August 1:

Job No.	Materials	Direct Labor	Overhead	Total
478 (irrigation project)	$ 5,100	$ 9,620	$4,810	$19,530
479 (parking lot construction)	3,470	3,960	1,980	9,410
480 (street repair)	4,120	976	488	5,584
Total	$12,690	$14,556	$7,278	$34,524

Selected transactions for the month of August follow:

(1) Materials issued: Job 480, $449; Job 481, $3,570; Job 482, $2,100; indirect materials, $390; total, $6,509.

(2) It assigned labor costs as follows: Job 478, $334; Job 479, $2,650; Job 480, $7,800; Job 481, $5,890; Job 482, $1,726; indirect labor, $853; total, $19,253.

(3) The employer's share of payroll taxes is 8 percent of wages earned. It treats all payroll taxes as overhead costs.

(4) Depreciation of equipment for the month is $3,200.

(5) Building depreciation for the month is $1,200.

(6) Other overhead costs for the month include power, $730; repairs, $520; utility services, $450; fire insurance, $183; property taxes, $317.

(7) It applies overhead for the month to jobs.

(8) It completed and transferred Jobs 478 and 479 to the Finished Goods Inventory account in September.

Set up T-accounts for Direct Materials Inventory, Work-in-Process Inventory, Finished Goods Inventory, and Overhead. Set up the T-account for Work-in-Process Inventory to accumulate the costs of each of the jobs separately. Enter the August 1 amounts plus each of the eight transactions in the T-accounts.

20. *Just-in-time inventory.* Austin Tech uses a just-in-time inventory system. To produce 1,200 units for an order, Austin purchased and used materials costing $10,000 and incurred other manufacturing costs of $11,000, of which $4,000 was labor. All costs were on account.

After Austin completed production and shipped 1,000 units, management needed the Finished Goods Inventory balance for the 200 units and $3,500 remaining in inventory for financial statement preparation.

Prepare journal entries and T-accounts for these entries.

21. *Just-in-time inventory.* Boston Biotech, Inc., uses a just-in-time inventory system. To produce 2,000 units for an order, it purchased and used materials costing $20,000, and incurred other manufacturing costs of $15,000, of which $5,000 was labor. All costs were on account.

After Boston Biotech completed production and shipped 1,600 units, management needed the Finished Goods Inventory balance for the 400 units remaining in inventory for financial statement preparation. The firm incurred costs evenly across all products.

Prepare journal entries and T-accounts for these entries.

22. *Computing equivalent units* (appendix). The Assembly Department had 30,000 units 60 percent complete in Work-in-Process Inventory at the beginning of May. During May, the department started and completed 80,000 units. The department started another 20,000 units and completed 30 percent as of the end of May. Compute the equivalent whole units of work performed during May using FIFO. Assume the department incurred production costs evenly throughout processing.

23. *Computing product costs with incomplete products* (appendix). Refer to the data in Exercise 22. Assume that the cost assigned to beginning inventory on May 1 was $18,000 and that the department incurred $196,000 of production costs during May. Prepare a production cost report like the one shown in Exhibit 4.13.

Problems

24. *Tracing cost flows in a service organization* (contributed by K. McGarvey). White and Brite Dry Cleaners operates with five employees and the president, Hexter Strength. Hexter and one of the five employees attend to all the marketing and administrative duties. The remaining four employees work throughout the operation. White and Brite has four service departments: dry cleaning, coin washing and drying, special cleaning, and sewing repairs and altering. White and Brite marks timecards and keeps records to monitor the time each employee spends working in each department. When business is slow or when all is under control, workers are idle and must also mark the idle time on the timecard. (Note: White and Brite needs some idle time because it promises 60-minute service and must have available direct labor hours to accommodate fluctuating peak demand periods throughout the day and the week.)

A summary of November operating data follows:

	Idle Time	Dry Cleaning	Coin Washing and Drying	Special Cleaning	Sewing Repairs and Altering
Sales Revenue		$2,625	$5,260	$2,000	$625
Direct Labor (in hours)	25	320	80	125	90
Direct Overhead:					
Cleaning Compounds ...		500	250	400	0
Supplies		325	700	265	150
Electricity Usage........		250	625	100	25

Other data follow:
(1) The four employees working in the service departments all make $4 per hour.

(2) The person in charge of marketing earns $1,000 per month, and Hexter earns $1,500 per month.

(3) Indirect overhead amounted to $512 and White and Brite assigns it to departments based on direct labor hours used. Because of idle hours, White and Brite will not assign some overhead to a department.

(4) In addition to salaries paid, marketing costs for such items as Yellow Pages advertising, radio advertising, and special promotions totaled $400.

(5) In addition to Hexter's salary, administrative costs amount to $150.

(6) All revenue transactions are for cash, and all others are on account.

a. Using T-accounts, show the flow of costs.

b. Prepare an income statement for White and Brite for the month of November. White and Brite kept no inventories.

25. *Tracing costs in a job company.* On June 1, Springer Landscaping Company had two jobs in process. Details of the jobs follow:

Job No.	Direct Materials	Direct Labor
A-15	$87	$32
A-38	16	42

Materials inventory (for example, plants and shrubs) on June 1 totaled $460, and Springer purchased $58 in materials during the month. Springer withdrew indirect materials of $8 from materials inventory. On June 1, Finished Goods Inventory comprised of two jobs, Job No. A-07 costing $196 and Job No. A-21 with a cost of $79. Springer transferred both of these jobs to Cost of Goods Sold during the month.

Also during June, Springer completed Jobs No. A-15 and A-38. Completing Job No. A-15 required an additional $34 in direct labor. The completion costs for Job No. A-38 included $54 in direct materials and $100 in direct labor.

Springer started Job No. A-40 during the period but did not finish it. The firm used a total of $157 of direct materials (excluding the $8 indirect materials) during the period, and total direct labor costs during the month amounted to $204. Springer has estimated overhead at 150 percent of direct labor costs, and this relation has been the same for the past few years.

Compute costs of Jobs No. A-15 and A-38 and balances in the June 30 inventory accounts.

26. *Tracing costs in a job company.* The following transactions occurred at Super Dynamics, Inc., a defense contractor that uses job costing:

(1) Purchased $40,000 in materials.

(2) Issued $2,000 in supplies from the materials inventory.

(3) Received materials with a cost of $31,600 at the storeroom.

(4) Paid for the materials purchased in **(1)**.

(5) Issued $34,000 in materials to the production department.

(6) Incurred wage costs of $56,000, which it debited to a temporary account called Payroll. Of this amount, it withheld $18,000 for payroll taxes and other similar liabilities. It paid the remainder in cash to the employees. [See transactions **(7)** and **(8)** for additional information about Payroll.]

(7) Recognized $28,000 in fringe benefit costs, which it incurred as a result of the wages paid in **(6)**. It debited this $28,000 to the temporary account called Payroll.

(8) Analyzed the Payroll account and calculated that 60 percent was direct labor, 30 percent was indirect manufacturing labor, and 10 percent represented administrative and marketing costs.

(9) Paid for utilities, power, equipment maintenance, and other miscellaneous items for the manufacturing plant. The total amount was $43,200.

(10) Paid $53,500 for new equipment.

(11) Applied overhead on the basis of 175 percent of *direct* labor costs, including fringe benefits recorded in **(6)** and **(7)** above.

(12) Recognized depreciation on manufacturing property, plant, and equipment of $21,000.

a. Prepare journal entries to record these transactions.

b. The following balances appeared in the accounts of Super Dynamics, Inc.:

	Beginning	Ending
Materials Inventory.................................	$74,100	—
Work-in-Process Inventory	16,500	—
Finished Goods Inventory	83,000	$ 66,400
Cost of Goods Sold.................................	—	131,700

Prepare T-accounts to show the flow of costs during the period.

27. *Reconstructing product costs from missing data.* Disaster struck the only manufacturing plant of the Great Northern Timber Corporation on December 1. An earthquake destroyed all of the work-in-process inventory. Employees salvaged a few records from the wreckage and from a set of records located at the company's headquarters office. Great Northern Timber is fully insured against the loss if it can supply adequate documentation to the insurance company. The insurance company has also stated that it will pay the "normal" cost of the lost inventory, because company policy states firms should apportion seasonal and other nondirect costs to inventories on an annualized basis. Hence, the cost of work-in-process inventory comprises direct materials, direct labor, and applied overhead.

The following information about the plant appears on the October 31 financial statements at the company's headquarters.

Materials Inventory, October 31	$ 49,000
Work-in-Process Inventory, October 31............................	86,200
Finished Goods Inventory, October 31	32,000
Cost of Goods Sold through October 31	348,000
Accounts Payable, Materials Suppliers, on October 31...............	21,600
Manufacturing Overhead through October 31	184,900
Payroll Payable on October 31	0
Withholding and Other Payroll Liabilities on October 31	9,700
Overhead Applied through October 31	179,600

A count of the inventories on hand on December 1 shows the following:

Materials Inventory...	$43,000
Work-in-Process Inventory	0
Finished Goods Inventory	37,500

Anne Milan, the controller, tells you that Great Northern has outstanding bills to suppliers of $50,100 and has made cash payments of $37,900 during the month to these suppliers.

The payroll clerk informs you that the payroll costs last month included $82,400 for the manufacturing section and that $14,700 of this figure was indirect.

At the end of November, the main office had the following balances available:

Manufacturing Overhead Applied through November 30...............	$217,000
Cost of Goods Sold through November 30	396,600

You recall that each month the firm has only one requisition for indirect materials. Among the ashes you find the requisition for $2,086.

You also learn that during the month the firm overapplied overhead by $1,200.

Compute the "normal" cost of the work-in-process inventory lost in the disaster.

28. *Evaluating full absorption and variable costing using normal costs* (adapted from CMA exam). The vice president for sales of Huber Corporation has received the income statement for November. Accounting has prepared the

statement on the variable costing basis and we reproduce it here. The firm has just adopted a variable costing system for internal reporting purposes.

HUBER CORPORATION
Income Statement for the Month of November
(all dollar amounts in thousands)

Sales Revenue	$2,400
Less Variable Cost of Goods Sold	(1,200)
Manufacturing Contribution Margin	$1,200
Less Fixed Manufacturing Costs	(600)
Gross Margin	$ 600
Less Nonmanufacturing Costs (all fixed)	(400)
Operating Profit	$ 200

The controller attached the following notes to the statements:
(1) The unit sales price for November averaged $24.
(2) Actual fixed manufacturing costs equaled the amount budgeted.
(3) The normal unit manufacturing costs for the month follow:

Variable Cost	$12
Fixed Cost	4
Total Cost	$16

---

(4) Huber predetermines the unit rate for fixed manufacturing costs based on a normal monthly production of 150,000 units.
(5) Production for November exceeded sales by 45,000 units.
(6) The inventory on November 30 consisted of 80,000 units.
a. The vice president for sales is uncomfortable with the variable cost basis and wonders what the operating profit would have been under the previous full absorption cost basis.
  (i) Present the November income statement on a full absorption cost basis.
  (ii) Reconcile and explain the difference between the variable costing and the full absorption costing operating profit figures.
b. Explain the features associated with variable cost income measurement that should appeal to the vice president for sales.

29. *Completing missing data.* After a dispute concerning wages, Ernest Arson tossed an incendiary device into the Flash Company's record vault. Within moments, only a few readable charred fragments remained from the company's factory ledger, as follows:

Direct Materials Inventory		Manufacturing Overhead	
Bal. 4/1 12,000		Actual Costs for April 14,800	

Work-in-Process Inventory		Accounts Payable	
Bal. 4/1 4,500			Bal. 4/30 8,000

Finished Goods Inventory		Cost of Goods Sold	
Bal. 4/30 16,000			

Sifting through the ashes and interviewing selected employees generated the following additional information:

(1)   The controller remembers clearly that the firm based the predetermined overhead rate on an estimated 60,000 direct labor hours to be worked over the year and an estimated $180,000 in manufacturing overhead costs.

(2)   The production superintendent's cost sheets showed only one job in process on April 30. The firm had added materials of $2,600 to the job and expended 300 direct labor hours at $6 per hour.

(3)   The accounts payable are for direct materials purchases only, according to the accounts payable clerk. He clearly remembers that the balance in the account was $6,000 on April 1. An analysis of canceled checks (kept in the treasurer's office) shows that Flash made payments of $40,000 to suppliers during the month.

(4)   A charred piece of the payroll ledger shows that the firm recorded 5,200 direct labor hours for the month. The employment department has verified that pay rates did not vary among employees (this infuriated Ernest, who thought that Flash underpaid him).

(5)   Records maintained in the finished goods warehouse indicate that the finished goods inventory totaled $11,000 on April 1.

(6)   From another charred piece in the vault you discern that the cost of goods manufactured for April was $89,000.

Determine the following amounts:

a.   Work-in-process inventory, April 30.
b.   Direct materials purchased during April.
c.   Overhead applied to work in process.
d.   Cost of goods sold for April.
e.   Over- or underapplied overhead for April.

    f.   Direct materials usage during April.

    g.   Direct materials inventory, April 30.

30. *Incomplete records.* On December 31, Year 3, a fire destroyed the bulk of the accounting records of Houdini Company, a small, one-product manufacturing firm. In addition, the chief accountant mysteriously disappeared. You must reconstruct the records for Year 3. The general manager has said that the accountant had been experimenting with both full absorption costing and variable costing on an actual costing basis.

    The records are a mess, but you have gathered the following data for Year 3:

(1) Sales Revenue	$585,000
(2) Actual Fixed Manufacturing Costs Incurred	85,800
(3) Actual Variable Manufacturing Costs per Unit for Year 3 and for Units in Inventory on January 1, Year 3	3.90
(4) Operating Profit, Full Absorption Costing Basis	78,000
(5) Notes Receivable from Chief Accountant	18,200
(6) Contribution Margin	234,000
(7) Direct Material Purchases	227,500
(8) Actual Marketing and Administrative Costs (all fixed)	27,300
(9) Gross Margin	105,300

    You also learn that full absorption costs per unit in beginning Finished Goods Inventory equal the Year 3 full absorption production cost per unit.

    a.   Prepare a comparative income statement on a full absorption and variable costing basis.

    b.   Calculate the number of units sold.

    c.   Calculate the full absorption cost per unit.

    d.   Calculate the number of units produced.

    e.   Reconcile the operating profit under variable costing with that under full costing, showing the exact source of the difference.

31. *Compare just-in-time to a traditional accounting system.* Illinois Precision Instruments produces heat measurement meters. The company received an order for 8,000 meters. The company purchased and used $240,000 of materials—purchased on account—for this order. The company incurred labor costs of $100,000 and other nonlabor manufacturing costs of $400,000.

    The accounting period ended before the company completed the order. The firm had 5 percent of the materials costs incurred still in Materials Inventory, 10 percent of the total costs incurred still in Work-in-Process Inventory, and 20 percent of the total costs incurred still in Finished Goods Inventory.

    a.   Use T-accounts to show the flow of costs using a just-in-time system.

    b.   Use T-accounts to show the flow of costs using a traditional costing system.

32. *Compare just-in-time to a traditional accounting system.* Vanessa's Video Productions received an order for 10,000 units. The company purchased and used $2,000,000 of materials—purchased on account—for this order. The company incurred labor costs of $900,000 and other nonlabor manufacturing costs of $1,500,000.

The accounting period ended before the company completed the order. The firm had 10 percent of the materials costs incurred still in Materials Inventory, 5 percent of the total costs incurred still in Work-in-Process Inventory, and 20 percent of the total costs incurred still in Finished Goods Inventory.

a. Use T-accounts to show the flow of costs using a just-in-time system.
b. Use T-accounts to show the flow of costs using a traditional costing system.

33. *Computing equivalent units and cost flows under process costing* (appendix). Wilson Manufacturing Corporation uses a process cost accounting system. The firm added materials at the start of processing and incurred direct labor and manufacturing overhead costs evenly over processing. On January 1, Wilson had 5,000 units in process, 80 percent completed, with the following accumulated costs:

Direct Material	$50,000
Direct Labor	40,000
Manufacturing Overhead	10,000

During January, Wilson started 45,000 units in process and incurred the following costs:

Direct Material	$450,000
Direct Labor	420,000
Manufacturing Overhead	105,000

During January, Wilson completed 40,000 units. The units in ending inventory were, on average, 60 percent complete.

Prepare a production cost report such as the one in Exhibit 4.13 using FIFO.

34. *Computing equivalent units and cost flows under process costing* (appendix). Denver Products Company has a process cost accounting system. Denver incurred material, direct labor, and manufacturing overhead costs evenly during processing. On September 1, the firm had 20,000 units in process, 40 percent complete, with the following accumulated costs:

Material	$78,000
Direct Labor	40,000
Manufacturing Overhead	30,000

During September, Denver started 110,000 units in process and incurred the following costs:

Material	$622,000
Direct Labor	490,000
Manufacturing Overhead	367,500

During September, Denver completed 90,000 units. The units in ending inventory were, on average, 40 percent complete.

Prepare a production cost report such as the one in Exhibit 4.13 using FIFO.

35. *Equivalent units—solving for unknowns* (appendix). For each of the following independent cases, calculate the information requested, using FIFO costing.
   a. Beginning inventory amounted to 1,000 units. The firm started and completed 4,500 units during this period. At the end of the period, the firm had 3,000 units in inventory that were 30 percent complete. Using FIFO costing, the equivalent production for the period was 5,600 units. What was the percentage of completion of the beginning inventory?
   b. The ending inventory included $8,700 for conversion costs. During the period, the firm required 4,200 equivalent units to complete the beginning inventory and started and completed 6,000 units. The ending inventory represented 1,000 equivalent units of work this period. What was the total conversion cost incurred during this period?

Integrative Problems and Cases

36. *Comprehensive job costing problem with equivalent units* (adapted from CPA exam). The Custer Corporation, which uses a job costing system, produces various plastic parts for the aircraft industry. On October 9, Year 4, Custer started production on Job No. 487 for 100 front bubbles (windshields) for commercial helicopters.

   Production of the bubbles begins in the fabricating department, where fabricators melt down sheets of plastic (purchased as raw material) and pour the liquid into molds. The employees then place the molds in a special temperature and humidity room to harden the plastic. The fabricators remove the hardened plastic bubbles from the molds and handwork them to remove imperfections.

   After fabrication, employees transfer the bubbles to the testing department, where each bubble must meet rigid specifications. Custer scraps bubbles that fail the tests with no salvage value.

   Employees transfer bubbles that pass the tests to the assembly department, where other employees insert them into metal frames. The frames, purchased from vendors, require no work before installing the bubbles.

   The assembly department then transfers the assembled unit to the shipping department for crating and shipment. Crating material is relatively expensive, and employees do most of the work by hand.

Management has the following information concerning Job No. 487 as of December 31, Year 4 (the information is correct as stated):

(1) Direct materials charged to the job:

    (a) Accounting charged 1,000 square feet of plastic at $12.75 per square foot to the fabricating department. This amount was to meet all plastic material requirements of the job at 10 square feet per bubble, assuming no spoilage.

    (b) Accounting charged 74 metal frames at $408.52 each to the assembly department.

    (c) Accounting charged packing material for 40 units at $75 per unit to the shipping department.

(2) Direct labor charges through December 31 follow:

	Total	Per Unit
Fabricating Department	$1,424	$16
Testing Department	444	6
Assembly Department	612	12
Shipping Department	256	8
	$2,736	

(3) Differences between actual and applied manufacturing overhead for the year ended December 31, Year 4, were immaterial. Accounting charges manufacturing overhead to the four production departments by various allocation methods, all of which you approve.

Accounting allocates manufacturing overhead charged to the fabricating department to jobs based on heat-room hours; the other production departments allocate manufacturing overhead to jobs on the basis of direct labor dollars charged to each job within the department. The following reflects the manufacturing overhead rates for the year ended December 31, Year 4.

	Rate per Unit
Fabricating Department	$.45 per Hour
Testing Department	.68 per Direct Labor Dollar
Assembly Department	.38 per Direct Labor Dollar
Shipping Department	.25 per Direct Labor Dollar

(4) Job No. 487 used 855 heat-room hours during the year ended December 31.

(5) Following is a schedule of equivalent units in production by department for Job No. 487 as of December 31.

CUSTER CORPORATION
Schedule of Physical Activity in Production for Job No. 487
December 31

| | Fabricating Department | | | |
| | Plastic (sq. ft.) | Bubbles (units) | | |
		Materials	Labor	Overhead
Transferred In from Direct Materials Inventory	1,000	—	—	—
Production to Date	(950)[a]	95[a]	89	95
Transferred Out to Other Departments	—	(83)	(83)	(83)
Spoilage	—	—	—	—
Balance at December 31	50	12	6	12

| | Testing Department (units) | | |
| | Bubbles | | |
	Transferred In	Labor	Overhead
Transferred In from Other Departments . . .	83	—	—
Production to Date	—	74	74
Transferred Out to Other Departments	(61)	(61)	(61)
Spoilage	(15)	(6)	(6)
Balance at December 31	7	7	7

| | Assembly Department (units) | | | |
	Transferred In	Frames	Labor	Overhead
Transferred In from Direct Materials Inventory	—	74	—	—
Transferred In from Other Departments	61	—	—	—
Production to Date	—	—	51	51
Transferred Out to Other Departments	(43)	(43)	(43)	(43)
Balance at December 31	18	31	8	8

| | Shipping Department (units) | | | |
	Transferred In	Packing Material	Labor	Overhead
Transferred In from Direct Materials Inventory	—	40	—	—
Transferred In from Other Departments	43	—	—	—
Production to Date	—	—	32	32
Shipped	(23)	(23)	(23)	(23)
Spoilage	(1)	(1)	(1)	(1)
Balance at December 31	19	16	8	8

[a]Custer produced 95 equivalent units requiring 950 square feet of plastic.

Prepare a schedule for Job No. 487 of ending inventory costs for work in process by department, and for cost of goods shipped. The firm charges all spoilage costs to cost of goods shipped.

37. *Comprehensive problem.* After a dispute with the company president, the controller of Vancouver Company resigned in January, Year 5. At that time, her office was converting the internal reporting system from full absorption to variable costing. The Vancouver Company has called you in to prepare financial reports for the previous year. Your investigation reveals that much of the data are missing, but you piece together the following information.

(1) From the production department, you learn that the company manufactures fishing rods that pass through one department.

(2) From the sales department you learn that the firm sold 95,000 units at a price of $35 each during Year 4.

(3) From various sources you learn that actual variable manufacturing overhead was $396,000, and actual fixed manufacturing overhead was $252,000 for Year 4. Nonmanufacturing costs (all fixed) were $336,000.

(4) In one of the desk drawers of the former controller, you discover the draft of a report with the following information:

  (a) "To improve our present accounting system we will adopt the normal costing approach for both internal and external reporting in Year 4. We will expense over- or underapplied overhead in Year 4 rather than allocate it to inventories."

  (b) "Unit costs in Year 4 are $4.80 per unit for materials cost and $2.40 per unit for direct labor. We will apply variable overhead at a rate of 180 percent of direct labor dollars, and fixed overhead at 120 percent of direct labor dollars."

  (c) "We transferred 132,000 units from work-in-process inventory to finished goods inventory. We purchased enough material for 144,000 units of finished product."

  (d) "Beginning finished goods inventory is $14 per unit using either actual or normal, full absorption costing, and $11 per unit using either actual or normal, variable costing. Materials cost in beginning inventory is $4."

Inventory Summary (in units)

	January 1, Year 4	December 31, Year 4
Work-in-Process Inventory	0	0
Finished Goods Inventory	No Records	38,000
Direct Materials Inventory	0	12,000

a. Describe the flow of units, including units started in Work-in-Process Inventory, transferred to Finished Goods, and sold. Be sure to include both beginning and ending inventories. (Assume FIFO.)

b. Show the flow of manufacturing costs during the year, including beginning and ending inventories, and prepare the income statements using:

    (1) Full absorption, actual costing.

    (2) Full absorption, normal costing.

    (3) Variable, actual costing.

    (4) Variable, normal costing.

38. *Midwest Insurance Company: evaluating cost systems used in financial services companies.* John Frank, controller of Midwest Insurance Company, recently returned from a management education program where he had talked to Peter Montgomery, his counterpart at Northern Insurance Company. Both companies had mortgage departments, but whereas Midwest gave loans only to businesses, Northern gave only home mortgage loans.

Peter Montgomery had described the use of standard costs at Northern as follows:

> We have collected data over several years that give us a pretty good idea how much each batch of loans costs to process. We receive loans in three main categories: (1) FHA and VA mortgages, (2) conventional home mortgages, and (3) development loans. Banks and other financial institutions make these loans initially and banks then package the loans and offered them to us as a package. The Mortgage Division is responsible for establishing terms for ascertaining whether we accept the mortgaged property and the mortgagor and for legal work on the loan. We assume that each loan in a category costs about the same. To calculate how much processing loans costs, we periodically have people in the Mortgage Division keep track of their time on each package of loans. Our overhead is about 130 percent of direct labor costs, so we assign overhead accordingly to each package of loans. We don't keep track of the actual costs of processing each package of loans. What we lose in knowing the actual cost of processing each loan, we make up by saving clerical costs that we would incur to keep track of the time spent on each package of loans.

A cost statement for a recent month appears in Exhibit 4.15.

Exhibit 4.15

NORTHERN INSURANCE COMPANY
Mortgage Division
Loan Processing Costs
Month of October

Category of Loans	Labor	Overhead	Number of Loans Processed
Standard Costs			
FHA and VA......................	$ 4,200	$ 5,460	14
Conventional	31,160	40,508	82
Development......................	20,440	26,572	73
Total	$55,800	$72,540	
Actual Costs	$58,172	$74,626	
Variance	$ 2,372	2,086	
	Unfavorable	Unfavorable	

Exhibit 4.16

MIDWEST INSURANCE COMPANY
Mortgage Division
Loan Processing Costs
Month of July

Loan No.	Labor	Telephone	Travel	Outside Services Appraisal	Legal	Other
A48-10136	$ 1,184	$ 113	$ 415	$ 1,500	—	—
A48-11237	3,631	42	—	2,300	—	—
B42-19361	814	78	—	—	1,500	150
C39-21341	4,191	240	$ 110	—	2,200	—
•	•	•	•	•	•	•
•	•	•	•	•	•	•
•	•	•	•	•	•	•
Total	$47,291	$4,843	$2,739	$11,800	$9,950	$1,470

Montgomery's comment about saving clerical costs struck a respondent chord with John Frank. Midwest's accounting costs had reached alarming levels, according to the company president, and Frank was looking for ways to reduce costs. Midwest kept track of the following costs for each loan: labor; telephone costs; travel; and outside services, such as appraisals, legal fees, and the cost of consultants. The costs of processing these loans often amounted to several thousand dollars. A sample of these loans and their processing costs appear in Exhibit 4.16.

When Frank told the Mortgage Division manager about the methods Northern used, the manager responded: "That sounds fine for them because each package of loans in a category has about the same processing costs. The processing costs of each loan in our company vary considerably. I believe it would be invalid to establish standards for our loans."

Frank thought the Mortgage Division manager's comments were reasonable, but he wanted to find some way to save clerical costs by not recording the costs of processing each loan. At the same time, he knew the firm would potentially benefit from having a standard against which to compare actual costs.

a.   What would you advise Mr. Frank to do? Compare the advantages and disadvantages of the system each company uses.

b.   Diagram the flow of costs for each company using the data available in Exhibits 4.15 and 4.16. Treat each loan or category of loans as a separate product in your diagram.

39.   *E-Z Printing: job costing for pricing and performance evaluation.*[5] Deborah Carr, founder and president of E-Z Printing Company, was worried. The company was doing more business than ever before—sales were at an annual

---

[5]© 1968 by l'Institut pour l'Étude des Méthodes de Direction de l'Entreprise (IMEDE), Lausanne, Switzerland, under the title Tipografia Stanca S.P.A. This case was revised and updated in 1984.

rate of about $625,000 a year—but operating profits had declined slightly during recent months, and the ratio of income to sales had dropped sharply. Ms. Carr wondered what had gone wrong and what she could do about it. She called in her chief (and only) accountant, Gene Hockman, and asked him to find out what was happening.

E-Z Printing did a general printing business on a customer-order basis. Ms. Carr set the price E-Z Printing charged for each job. When possible, she waited until the firm completed the job and then quoted a price equal to 140 percent of the cost of the paper stock used, plus $25 for each labor hour. Straight-time wage rates in the past, adjusted for recent wage rate increases, had averaged about $8 per hour, and this formula seemed to provide an adequate margin to cover overhead costs and provide a good profit. Ms. Carr did not modify these prices for seasonality, even though business usually slowed in the winter months and increased in the spring and fall.

E-Z Printing did most of its work on the basis of predetermined contract prices. In bidding on these jobs, Ms. Carr applied her standard pricing formula to her own estimates of the amount of labor and paper stock the job would require. She prided herself on her ability to make these estimates, but she sometimes quoted a price that was higher or lower than the formula price, depending on her judgment of the market situation.

The company's production procedures were simple. When the firm received a customer's order, a clerk assigned it a production order number and issued a production order. The clerk then gave the material to be printed, known as the customer's copy, to a copy editor, who indicated on the copy the sizes and styles of type that the printer should use. The editor sometimes made changes in the copy, usually after telephoning the customer to discuss the changes.

The copy editor sent the customer's material to the composing room, where a typesetter set it in type. The typesetter printed a proof copy by hand and returned it to the copy editor, who checked the printed copy against the original. The copy editor indicated any errors in the proof in the margin and sent the marked proof to the customer for approval. At this point, the customer might decide to make changes in the copy, and the typesetters made these changes, as well as corrections of typesetting errors, as soon as the editor returned the corrected proof to the composing room.

In some cases the editor sent a second proof to the customer for his or her approval, but E-Z Printing sent most orders to the pressroom as soon as the typesetter had made the customer's corrections and the copy editor had approved the second proof.

At this point, the order was ready for production on one of the presses in the pressroom. The production order contained printing instructions, including the particular press to be used; the number of copies to be printed; the color, size, style, weight, and finish of the stock or paper to be used; and similar details. E-Z Printing then printed, bound, and packaged copies for delivery to the customer.

An order could take as little as 1 day in the copyediting and composing room stages or as long as several weeks. Printing, binding, and packaging seldom took more than 2 days except on very large production runs of multi-page booklets.

E-Z Printing's before-tax profit had fluctuated between 13 and 15 percent of net sales. The interim profit report for the first half of Year 4 came as a shock to Ms. Carr. Although volume slightly exceeded that of the first half of Year 3, profit was down to 8.8 percent of sales, an all-time low. The comparison, with all figures expressed as percentages of net sales, follows:

	June 30, Year 4	June 30, Year 3
Net Sales	100.0%	100.0%
Production Costs	77.6	72.3
Selling and Administrative Costs	13.6	13.9
Profit	8.8	13.8

Mr. Hockman knew that the company's problem must be either low prices or excessive costs. Unfortunately, the cost data already available told him little about the cost/price relation for individual jobs. E-Z routinely classified its operating costs into 20 categories, such as salaries, pressroom wages, production materials, depreciation, and so forth. It did not use individual job cost sheets and estimated the cost of goods in process only once a year, at the end of the fiscal year.

He could only obtain detailed data on only two kinds of items: paper stock issued and labor time. When a clerk issued stock, he or she filled out a requisition form, showing the kind of stock issued, the quantity, the unit cost, and the production order number. The clerk reported similar details when unused stock was returned to the stockroom.

As for labor, each employee engaged directly in working on production orders filled in a time sheet each day, on which the employee recorded the time spent on a specific production order and the order number. The payroll clerk also recorded the employee's department number and pay grade on the time sheet.

Mr. Hockman first established some overall cost relations. Employees, for example, fell into three different pay grades, with the following regular hourly wage rates:

Grade	Rate
1	$12
2	8
3	6

These rates applied to a regular work week of 40 hours a week. For work in excess of this number of hours, E-Z paid employees an overtime premium of 50 percent of their hourly wage. Overtime premiums were negligible when the workload was light, but in a normal year they averaged about 5 percent of the total amount of hourly wages computed at the regular hourly wage rate. In a normal year, this amount was approximately $.40 per direct labor hour.

In addition to their wages, the employees also received various kinds of benefits, including vacation pay, health insurance, and retirement pensions. The cost of these benefits to E-Z Printing amounted to about 70 percent of direct labor cost, measured at regular straight-time hourly rates. The overtime premiums did not affect the amount of fringe benefits paid or accrued.

Mr. Hockman estimated that all other shop overhead costs, that is, all copy department, composing room, and pressroom costs other than direct materials, direct labor, overtime premiums, and employee benefits on direct labor payrolls, would average $4 a direct labor hour in a normal year.

Armed with these estimates of general relationships, Mr. Hockman proceeded to measure the costs of several recent production orders. One of these was Job No. A-467. E-Z received this job for copyediting on Monday, April 3, and delivered it to the customer on Friday, April 7. Ms. Carr had quoted a price of $1,800 on this job in advance, on the basis of an estimate of $480 for paper stock costs and 45 direct labor hours. All actual requisitions and time records relating to Job No. A-467 are included in the lists in Exhibits 4.17 and 4.18. (To save space, we have omitted some of the details shown on the requisitions and time tickets from these exhibits.)

a. Diagram or explain to your own satisfaction the flow of actual material, labor, and overhead costs to Job No. A-467.

b. Develop a costing rate or rates for labor costs, E-Z can use to charge a job cost sheet or Factory Overhead account for an hour of labor time. You must decide whether to use a single rate for all pay grades or a separate rate for each. You must also decide whether to include various kinds of fringe benefit costs in the labor costing rates or to regard these as overhead.

c. Prepare a price quote for Job No. A-467 and enter the costs that would be assigned to this job, using the costing rates you developed in the answer

Exhibit 4.17

Partial List of Material Requisitions for the Week of April 3 through 7		
Requisition Number	Job No.	Amount[a]
4058	A-467	$300
R162	A-469	(20)
4059	A-467	60
4060	A-467	36
R165	A-465	(12)
4062	A-467	96
4065	A-458	22
R166	A-467	(32)
4066	A-481	176

[a]Amounts in parentheses are returned materials.

Exhibit 4.18

**Partial Summary of Labor Time Sheets
for the Week of April 3 through 7**

Employee Number	Pay Grade	Department	Job No.[a]	Hours
14	2	Copy	A-467	1.4
15	1	Copy	A-467	3.3
15	1	Copy	—	2.7
15	1	Copy	A-467	8.8
18	3	Press	A-467	4.0
22	1	Composing	A-467	8.4[b]
22	1	Composing	—	1.5
23	2	Press	A-458	3.4
23	2	Press	A-467	4.7[b]
23	2	Press	—	1.1
28	1	Press	A-467	7.0
28	1	Press	A-458	1.0
31	3	Press	—	8.0
33	1	Composing	A-471	7.6
40	2	Press	A-467	4.9
40	2	Press	—	0.2
43	1	Press	A-467	3.5
43	1	Press	A-481	5.8

[a]A dash indicates time spent on general work in the department and not on any one job.

[b]Employee No. 22 worked 6 hours of overtime during the week, none of them on Job No. A-467, while Employee No. 23 worked 8 hours of overtime, including 4 hours on Job No. A-467.

to part **b.** Use estimated labor hours: Grade 1, 30 hours; Grade 2, 11 hours; Grade 3, 4 hours.

d.   What could be the advantages of developing costs for each job? Do you think these advantages would be great enough to persuade Ms. Carr to hire an additional clerk for this purpose at an annual cost of about $20,000?

Suggested Solutions to Even-Numbered Exercises

12.   *Computing manufacturing costs of a job*
   a. $4 per direct labor hour. $40,000/10,000 hours.

   b.

Raw Materials	$ 4,600
Direct Labor	7,600
Overhead (1,200 × $4)	4,800
Total Cost	$17,000
Cost per Unit	$ 170

14. *Cost flows in a merchandising organization*

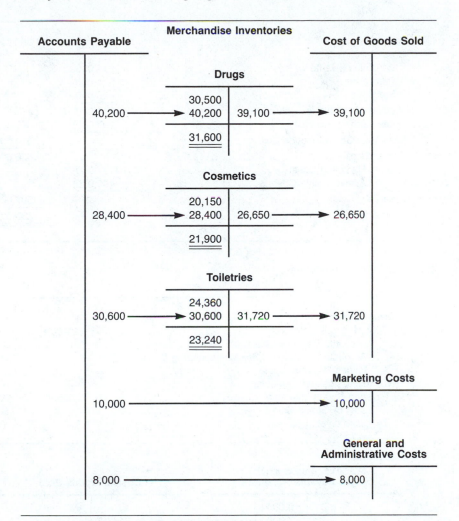

16. *Tracing manufacturing cost flows using T-accounts*

Materials Inventory		Work-in-Process Inventory		Finished Goods Inventory	
(1) 40,000		**(1)** 150,000		**(1)** 120,000	
(2) 300,000	270,000 **(3)**	**(3)** 270,000	910,000 **(7)**	**(7)** 910,000	850,000 **(8)**
		(4) 400,000			
		(6) 120,000			

Manufacturing Overhead		Cost of Goods Sold	
(5) 130,000	120,000 **(6)**	**(8)** 850,000	

18. *Preparing income statement for a merchandiser*

Revenues...		$ 1,850,000
Cost of Goods Sold:		
Beginning Inventory............................	$ 314,000	
Purchases	971,000	
Freight-in	26,000	
Goods Available for Sale	$1,311,000	
Less Ending Inventory	(297,000)	
Less Total Cost of Goods Sold....................		(1,014,000)
Gross Margin		$ 836,000
Less: Marketing Costs	$ (197,000)	
Administrative Costs....................	(400,000)	
Less Total Costs		(597,000)
Operating Profit		$ 239,000

20. *Just-in-time inventory*

Journal Entries:

(1) Cost of Goods Sold	21,000	
Accounts Payable—Materials......................		10,000
Accounts Payable—Other Manufacturing Costs		7,000
Wages Payable		4,000
To record costs of production.		
(2) Finished Goods Inventory	3,500	
Cost of Goods Sold		3,500
To record inventory.		

T-accounts:

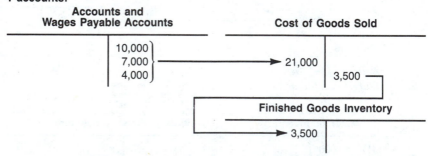

22. *Computing equivalent units* (appendix)

To Complete Beginning Inventory: [(1.0 − .60) × 30,000]............	12,000 E.U.
Started and Completed...	80,000 E.U.
In Ending Inventory: .30 × 20,000	6,000 E.U.
Total	98,000 E.U.

... CHAPTER 5 ...

Cost Allocation

Chapter Outline

- The Nature of Common Costs
- Purpose of Common Cost Allocations
- General Principles of Cost Allocation
- Activity-Based Cost Allocation
- Joint Products and By-Products
- Marketing and Administrative Expenses
- Appendix 5.1: Reciprocal Method for Allocation of Service Department Costs

This chapter discusses concepts and methods of assigning costs to departments, products, and other cost objects. We call such cost assignment *cost allocation*. Critics suggest that cost allocations made in preparing accounting reports cause more misleading and incorrect interpretations of data than any other single factor. Why do accountants make cost allocations? How can they cause misleading or incorrect interpretations? Are some cost allocation methods better than others? This chapter attempts to answer these questions.

The Nature of Common Costs

Accounting distinguishes between a **direct cost** and a **common cost.** (We also call common costs *indirect costs*.) A direct cost is one that firms can identify specifically with, or trace directly to, a particular product, department, or process. For example, direct materials and direct labor costs are direct with respect to products manufactured. A department manager's salary is a direct cost of the department, but common to the units the department produces.

A common cost, in contrast, results from the joint use of a facility (for example, plant or machines) or a service (for example, fire insurance) by several products, departments, or processes. A firm has no natural way to disaggregate this common, or shared, cost and to attribute its parts directly to particular products, departments, or processes. For some reporting purposes, however, firms must disaggregate common costs. In these cases firms need to develop some reasonably systematic basis for allocating common costs.

Common costs pervade accounting to a much greater extent than you may initially suppose. In financial accounting, many costs are common, or joint, to more than one reporting period. For example, firms must allocate the cost of a depreciable asset through depreciation to the years of the asset's useful life.

In addition, many costs are common to different products manufactured. To develop product cost information, firms must allocate these common costs. Examples include the following:

1. A factory or department allocates fixed manufacturing overhead costs to each of the products produced to obtain a value for inventory and to calculate cost of goods sold for use in external financial statements.

2. Firms allocate the costs of operating service departments (for example, computer services, maintenance department) to individual manufacturing departments for several purposes, discussed later in the chapter. We call this practice **service department cost allocation.**

3. Accounting allocates the costs incurred in a manufacturing process that jointly produces several different products simultaneously (for example, beef and hides obtained from cattle) to each of the products for inventory valuation. We call this practice **joint cost allocation.**

Other examples of common costs include central corporate expenses common to each of the corporate divisions and costs incurred in paying property taxes on land, building, and inventory that firms must allocate to the individual assets under certain circumstances.

These examples emphasize the extent to which common cost allocations pervade accounting reports, both internal and external. To understand accounting reports and make appropriate interpretations, you must be familiar with the alternative allocation methods used and their effects on the resulting reports.

Purpose of Common Cost Allocations

Common cost allocations allocate costs to units of production for external financial reporting and tax purposes. Also, many contracts require cost allocations.

Allocations in Contract Disputes

Example   Two companies entered into a partnership and agreed to split the costs fifty-fifty. The partnership was to reimburse each partner for that partner's own costs and to give each partner an equal share of the profits. The first partner submitted an itemized list of costs chargeable to the partnership that included an allocation of $500,000 for corporate headquarters' costs. The second partner argued that the first partner should not charge these costs to the partnership. The first partner asserted that without corporate headquarters the company would not exist and, hence, they needed the costs of the headquarters for the operation of the partnership.

Should the partnership pay for a share of one partner's headquarters' costs? If so, what method should the partnership use to allocate those costs? Settling disputes such as these is seldom simple or straightforward. Indeed, the settlement process may involve costly litigation.

Cost Accounting Standards Board   Sometimes companies in the defense industry contract with the U.S. government on a cost-plus-profit basis. These contracts require the companies to allocate costs between government and commercial work. A particular company may need further allocations among several contracts. Such disputes are frequent enough that the Cost Accounting Standards Board (CASB) formed in 1971 to establish standards for cost allocation to government contracts.

Misleading Cost Allocations

A particular purpose, such as product costing for external financial reporting or satisfying contract requirements, may require cost allocations. They can mislead management, however, as the following examples demonstrate.

Example 1   Technotronics Corporation manufactures a diverse line of electronic equipment. One product, a signal detection device, has a unit production cost (direct material, labor, and manufacturing overhead) of $40, of which $10 is fixed manufacturing overhead allocated to each unit. Another firm has asked Technotronics to accept a special order for 500 signal detection devices for $35 each. Technotronics can produce the devices with currently unused capacity. This order would not affect fixed manufacturing costs, or marketing and administrative costs. Accepting the order would not affect the regular market for this product.

Management should base the decision to accept or to reject the order on an assessment of the differential costs of accepting the order. As long as the differential costs to produce the product (that is, the variable costs) are less than $35, Technotronics should accept the order. Using the $40 unit cost, which includes an allocation of fixed manufacturing overhead cost, could lead to an incorrect decision. Other things being equal, Technotronics should use the $30 unit variable cost before allocation of fixed costs to the product to decide whether to accept the order.

Example 2   Wharton Products Corporation allocates the cost of operating service departments (for example, the maintenance department) to each of the manufacturing departments for purposes of product costing. The accounting department includes these costs in manufacturing overhead. Division A of Wharton Products Corporation is attempting to estimate its overhead cost for the coming year. To develop estimates of fixed and variable overhead costs, it has analyzed past overhead cost behavior using statistical regression and has developed the following budget equation: Total Costs = $100,000 + $5 per Unit Produced. It used these estimates in planning for the coming year.

In the past, the accounting department had allocated maintenance department costs to manufacturing divisions on the basis of square footage each division occupied. This year, corporate management decided to use maintenance hours worked in each division as the basis for allocating maintenance costs in the future. Because the costs allocated under the new rule will differ significantly from those under the old allocation base, using past cost data to construct a budget for total costs could lead to inaccurate plans for the coming year.

Example 3   Diversified Industries, Inc., is organized into 40 autonomous operating divisions. Corporate management uses the divisional rate of return on investment for evaluating the performance of the division managers. In calculating divisional net income, the accountants deduct an allocated share of central corporate expenses. The firm allocates expenses to divisions based on divisional sales. Division B increased its sales by 25 percent during the current year. Because of an increase in total central corporate expenses and an increase in the relative share of these expenses allocated to Division B, the 25 percent increase in sales resulted in only a 5 percent increase in Division B's operating profits.

Including a share of central corporate expenses in Division B's performance report can give a misleading picture of its operations. Allocation of these costs based on sales could lead division managers to reduce sales efforts, to the detriment of the company as a whole.

The message of this section should be fairly clear. Management must interpret carefully accounting data that include common cost allocations.

Use of Cost Allocation for Managerial Purposes

Although we have emphasized the need to be wary of using allocated costs, sometimes cost allocation suits managerial purposes. A firm may use full product costs as inputs to pricing and planning decisions. Such questions as "Will the price received for product A cover all of its costs in the long run?" require knowledge of full product costs, including common or joint costs allocated to the product. We discuss other managerial reasons for allocating costs in the following sections.

Charging the Cost of Service Departments to Users   Virtually every organization has departments whose main job is to service other departments. These departments include the laundry in a hospital, the computer center in a university, maintenance in a factory, security in a retail store, and so forth. Because the firm does not sell the output of these departments to customers outside the organization, it must cover their costs by the contribution margins of revenue-generating departments. Thus organizations often allocate the costs of departments that do not generate revenue (which we call **service departments**) to revenue-generating departments as an attention-getting device.[1] The allocation makes managers of user departments aware that covering just the direct department costs for the organization as a whole is not enough to break even or make a profit; the firm must cover indirect costs as well.

Example   Memorial Hospital did not allocate the costs of its computer department to user departments. In 1990, top management noted that computer department costs exceeded the costs in 1985 by 400 percent. Although top management acknowledged an increasing need for computer services, an increase of this magnitude far exceeded expectations. Top management learned upon investigation that accounting did not charge user departments for using the computer or computer department staff, so they treated the computer and computer staff as if they were free.

To deal with this problem, Memorial Hospital started allocating computer department costs to user departments using a rate per unit of the computer's time and space and a rate per unit of computer personnel time. As a result, user departments reduced their demand for the computer and related services to only those uses for which the department manager believed the benefits to the user department exceeded the cost charged to the user. When computer personnel assisted a user department, the user department's manager monitored the computer personnel's work habits to avoid being charged for time inefficiently spent.

Preventing Users from Treating Services as Free   The previous example demonstrates how cost allocation gives users incentives to control the costs of services. In theory, the user should use a service as long as the marginal benefit of a unit of service exceeds its marginal cost. Thus the firm should charge the marginal cost of supplying a unit of service to the user to induce the user to make the correct (economic) decision about how much of the service to use. Marginal costs are difficult to measure, however, so firms often use variable costs or other surrogates for marginal costs.

Cost allocation also encourages interdepartment monitoring. If the firm allocates the costs of a service department to user departments, managers of user departments have incentives to monitor the service department's costs. Presumably, the more efficient the service department is, the lower the costs that it will pass on to the user departments.

Problems with Allocating Fixed Service Department Costs

The allocation of fixed costs can have unintended effects, as the following example demonstrates.

Example[2]   The top administrators of Southwest University observed that faculty and staff used the University's WATS (Wide Area Telephone Service) so much that the

---

[1]A study of corporate cost allocation found that 84 percent of companies participating in the survey reported allocating some indirect costs. The study indicated that firms primarily used cost allocation for managerial purposes as an attention-getting device to remind responsibility center managers that common costs exist and responsibility center profits must recover them. See J. M. Fremgen and S. S. Liao, *The Allocation of Corporate Indirect Costs* (New York: National Association of Accountants, 1981).

[2]This example is based on one given by Jerold L. Zimmerman, "The Costs and Benefits of Cost Allocations," *The Accounting Review* (July 1979), pp. 510–511.

lines were seldom free during the day. WATS allowed the university unlimited toll-free service within the United States. The fixed cost of WATS was $10,000 per month; variable cost per call was zero.

The top administrators learned that the average usage was 50,000 minutes per month on the WATS line, so they initially allocated the $10,000 monthly charge to callers (that is, departments) at a rate of $.20 per minute (= $10,000/50,000 minutes). Now that they paid for phone calls, faculty and staff reduced their usage of WATS. Hence, the number of minutes used on WATS dropped to 25,000 per month, which increased the rate charged to $.40 per minute (= $10,000/25,000 minutes). The increase led to further reductions in usage until the internal cost allocation per minute exceeded the normal long-distance rates, and the use of WATS dropped almost to zero. Southwest University's total telephone bill increased dramatically.[3]

The top administrators subsequently compromised by charging a nominal fee of $.10 per minute. According to the university's chief financial officer, "The $.10 per minute charge made us aware that the WATS service has a cost, although it is a fixed cost. The charge was sufficiently low, however, so as not to discourage bona fide use of WATS."

Cost Allocation: A Note of Caution

Organizations commonly use cost allocations. Although they often have a purpose, they can easily mislead users of accounting information because users often do not appreciate how arbitrarily firms allocate most costs. We caution the reader to use allocated costs carefully.

Cost allocation is so prevalent that we often take it for granted. Companies must continually challenge the need for cost allocation and ask "Why allocate?" The absence of a sound reason for the cost allocation signals that it is not needed. If you have a reason for cost allocation, be sure you do not misuse the costs allocated for a particular purpose.

Given this word of caution, we now discuss methods of allocating costs.

General Principles of Cost Allocation

The cost allocation process involves three principal steps:

1. Accumulating the costs that relate to the product, department, or division (for example, manufacturing overhead, service department costs, central corporate expenses).

2. Identifying the recipient of the allocated costs (this recipient may be a product, department, or division).

---

[3]According to Zimmerman, the correct price to charge users is "the cost imposed by forcing others who want to use the WATS line to either wait or place a regular toll call . . . this cost varies between zero (if no one is delayed) to, at most, the cost of a regular toll call if a user cannot use the WATS line" (p. 510). The necessary procedure to implement such a pricing system would be difficult and costly. Zimmerman suggests that fixed allocations could be a simplified way of approximating the results of the more complicated, though theoretically correct, pricing system.

Managerial Application

Cost Allocation Practices[a]

Professors Fremgen and Liao studied cost allocation practices in 123 companies to see which indirect cost allocations businesses are actually making and why.

These companies clearly distinguished between two basic types of indirect costs: (1) corporate service costs for the benefit of production departments (e.g., data processing, purchasing, accounting, and legal), and (2) corporate administrative costs (e.g., top management's salaries, the treasurer's functions, and public relations). Corporate service costs relate closely to particular production units, so firms can easily defend their allocation and can make them over quite specific allocation bases. Allocations of corporate administrative costs, on the other hand, are more arbitrary and firms tend to make them over allocation bases reflecting simply the sizes of the various profit centers.

"Despite the many theoretical injunctions against indirect cost allocations, 84 percent of the companies participating in this survey reported that they do allocate at least some corporate indirect costs for some purposes."[b]

Survey respondents were asked why they did or did not allocate indirect corporate costs. For financial reporting, allocation policies generally reflected the requirements of the Financial Accounting Standards Board for segment reporting.

The most widely cited reason for allocations for purposes of performance evaluation was "simply to remind profit center managers that the indirect costs exist and had to be recovered by the profit centers' earnings. . . .the real reason for the allocation is to influence managers' behavior in some positive way, not to measure some amount that will be regarded as uniquely 'correct.' Hence, the allocation may be regarded as good if it works, if it really has the intended effect, even though it is wholly arbitrary."[c]

[a]Based on J. M. Fremgen and S. S. Liao, *The Allocation of Corporate Indirect Costs* (Montvale, N.J.: National Association of Accountants, 1981).

[b]J. M. Fremgen and S. S. Liao, "The Allocation of Indirect Costs," *Management Accounting* (September 1981), p. 66.

[c]Fremgen and Liao, "The Allocation of Indirect Costs," p. 67.

3. Selecting a method or basis for relating the costs in step 1 with the recipient in step 2.

This third step is the most difficult, because you cannot associate common costs directly with a single product, department, or division. You need to find an indirect relation that can serve as a meaningful **allocation base.** Follow some of these guidelines in selecting an allocation base:

1. Does an analysis of past cost behavior suggest a relation between the incurrence of the cost and an allocation base (for example, manufacturing overhead cost and the number of units produced)?

2. Does knowledge of operations suggest a logical relationship between the incurrence of cost and an allocation base (for example, the relationship between

manufacturing overhead and either the number of labor hours worked or the dollar investment in depreciable assets)?

3. If management cannot select an allocation base on empirical or logical grounds, can the parties affected generally accept that the allocations must be arbitrary? If not, perhaps the organization should not allocate the common costs at all or, if allocated, those affected should reach a consensus on the most acceptable base.

Activity-Based Cost Allocation

In the sections that follow, we illustrate allocation procedures for overhead and service department costs, joint product costs, and marketing and administrative expenses.

Allocating Overhead and Service Department Costs

The illustration that follows indicates the types of problems involved in allocating overhead costs. Management could generally apply the method to both manufacturing and nonmanufacturing settings.

We allocate these costs following the principles of activity-based costing discussed in Chapter 3. We assign all costs to cost objects based on the particular activities that cause particular costs.

A division of Berdan Products Company comprises four departments. Departments A and B are production departments. Departments M (maintenance) and S (storeroom) are service departments (that is, they exist to provide support to the production departments). Berdan keeps records of the direct material and direct labor costs incurred in both production departments. Berdan considers all other manufacturing costs to be overhead and accumulates them initially at the division level, not by department. Exhibit 5.1 summarizes these relations.

Berdan accumulates overhead costs at the division level for control purposes. For product costing purposes, Berdan assigns these costs in two stages: Stage 1 allocates costs from service departments to production departments, and stage 2 allocates costs from production departments to products. We outline the allocation procedure next.

Stage 1: cost allocation to production departments.

- The firm allocates first any overhead costs directly attributable to a service or production department (for example, salary of a manager in one of the production departments).

- The firm allocates the remaining manufacturing overhead costs to the service and production departments, using cost drivers or allocation bases selected because of an empirical or logical relation between the cost and the department.

- Next, the firm reallocates the costs allocated in steps 1 and 2 from one service department to another to the two production departments.

Exhibit 5.1

BERDAN PRODUCTS COMPANY
Organization Chart

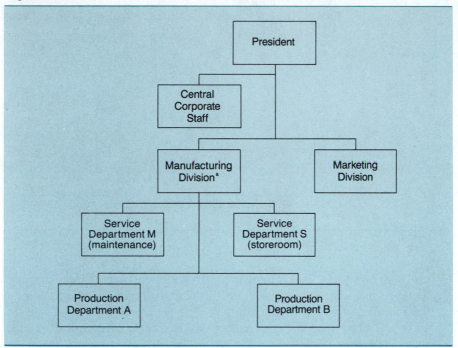

[a]All manufacturing costs other than direct material and direct labor used in the production departments are initially accumulated at the divisional level.

Stage 2: cost allocation from production departments to products.

■ The firm allocates the costs of direct material, direct labor, and share of manufacturing overhead allocated to each production department to the units produced during the period.

Stage 1: Cost Allocation to Production Departments

Column (1) of Exhibit 5.2 shows a listing of the manufacturing overhead costs incurred during the month of March for Berdan Products Company.

1. The firm first allocates overhead costs that Berdan can attribute directly to one of the four departments. Costs in this category include salaries and labor, supplies used, and depreciation. Exhibit 5.2 shows these costs in the appropriate departmental columns. Technically, with respect to the departments, these costs are direct rather than common.

2. Next the firm allocates manufacturing overhead costs that Berdan cannot attribute directly to one of the departments. These costs appear in column (6) of Exhibit 5.2 and include the payment to an outside security agency, property

Exhibit 5.2

BERDAN PRODUCTS COMPANY
Manufacturing Overhead Costs for March

	Total (1)	Dept. A (2)	Dept. B (3)	Dept. S (4)	Dept. M (5)	Indirect Costs (6)
ªManager's Salary for each Department....	$ 7,850	$2,100	$1,950	$1,700	$2,100	
ªMaintenance Labor—Dept. M	6,000				6,000	
ªStoreroom Labor—Dept. S	700			700		
Payment for Security....................	500					$ 500
ªSupplies Used........................	2,750	600	900	800	450	
Property Taxes	1,200					1,200
Payroll Taxes	5,000					5,000
Rent—Factory Building..................	720					720
Utilities:						
Electricity, Gas, and Water	600					600
Miscellaneous	600					600
Total	$25,920	$2,700	$2,850	$3,200	$8,550	$8,620

ªBerdan can assign each of these items directly to a department.

taxes, payroll taxes, rent, electricity, gas, water, and miscellaneous factory costs. At this stage Berdan must select an allocation base. Exhibit 5.3 shows the allocation of each of these costs to the four departments. Note the types of additional information that management must have to make these distributions, as shown below:

Cost	Cost Driver	Allocation Appears in Exhibit 5.3 Section ( )
(1) Security	Number of Visits Made to Each Department	Section (1)
(2) Property Taxes	Book Value of Equipment and Inventory in Each Department	Section (2)
(3) Payroll Taxes	Departmental Labor Costs: Dept. A $29,500 Dept. B 40,000 Dept. S 2,400 Dept. M 8,100 (*Note:* Exhibit 5.2 does not include all labor costs.)	Section (3)
(4) Rent—Factory Building	Floor Space Each Department Occupies	Section (4)
5) Utilities— Electricity, Gas, and Water	Study of Percent Utilities Each Department Uses	Section (5)
(6) Miscellaneous factory costs are distributed equally over the four production and service departments because the firm has no other logical basis for an allocation.		

Exhibit 5.4 shows the results of these allocations of overhead costs.

Exhibit 5.3

BERDAN PRODUCTS COMPANY
Distribution of Various Overhead Costs for March

(1) Security Cost

Dept.	No. Visits	Percent[a]	Distribution of Security Cost to Department[b]
A	12	30	$150
B	12	30	150
S	16	40	200
M	0	—	—
Totals	40	100	$500

(2) Property Taxes

Dept.	Book Value of Assets	Percent	Distribution of Property Taxes to Department
A	$100,000	50	$ 600
B	70,000	35	420
S	26,000	13	156
M	4,000	2	24
Totals	$200,000	100	$1,200

(3) Payroll Taxes

Dept.	Dept. Labor	Percent	Distribution of Payroll Taxes to Department
A	$29,500	36.9	$1,845
B	40,000	50.0	2,500
S	2,400	3.0	150
M	8,100	10.1	505
Totals	$80,000	100.0	$5,000

(4) Rent—Factory Building

Dept.	Square Feet of Floor Space	Percent	Distribution of Rent to Department
A	15,000	37.50	$270
B	15,000	37.50	270
S	6,000	15.00	108
M	4,000	10.00	72
Totals	40,000	100.00	$720

(5) Utilities: Electricity, Gas, and Water

Dept.	Utility Services (Percent)	Distribution of Utilities to Department
A	50	$300
B	45	270
S	3	18
M	2	12
Totals	100	$600

[a]Percent equals number of visits to each department divided by the total visits in a typical night. For Dept. A, 30% = 12 visits/40 total visits.

[b]Distribution to department equals percent times total cost. For example, for Dept. A, $150 = 30% × $500.

Exhibit 5.4

BERDAN PRODUCTS COMPANY
Allocation of Overhead by Step Allocation Procedure
Overhead Allocation Schedule for Month Ending March 31

	Total	Dept. A	Dept. B	Dept. S Storeroom	Dept. M Maintenance	Reference[a]
Dept. Managers' Salaries............	$ 7,850	$2,100	$1,950	$1,700	$2,100	⋆
Maintenance Labor	6,000	—	—	—	6,000	⋆
Storeroom Labor	700	—	—	700	—	⋆
Security	500	150	150	200	—	(1)
Supplies Used	2,750	600	900	800	450	⋆
Property Taxes	1,200	600	420	156	24	(2)
Payroll Taxes	5,000	1,845	2,500	150	505	(3)
Rent—Factory Building..............	720	270	270	108	72	(4)
Utilities: Electricity, Gas, and Water	600	300	270	18	12	(5)
Miscellaneous Factory Costs.........	600	150	150	150	150	(6)
Totals	$25,920	$6,015	$6,610	$3,982	$9,313	

[a]Berdan allocates each item marked with an asterisk directly to a department. The number in parentheses refers to a section of Exhibit 5.3 or to a discussion reference in the text.

[b]See discussion in text under the heading "Redistribution of Service Department Costs to Production Departments."

Redistribution of Service Department Costs to Production Departments

When the firm has completed the initial distribution of the overhead accounts to the various departments, it must distribute the totals of the service departments to the production departments. One logical method, where two or more service departments serve each other as well as the production departments, is the **reciprocal method.** The reciprocal method, which we discuss in Appendix 5.1, requires the use of matrix algebra when more than two service or production departments allocate costs simultaneously from each service department to the other service departments and to production departments.

A less exact but simpler solution follows: Start with the service department that receives the smallest dollar amount of service from the other service departments and distribute its costs to the other service and production departments; then, in the same manner, distribute the total costs of the service department receiving the next smallest amount of service from other service departments, and so on until you have allocated all service department costs to the production departments. Once you have allocated a given service department's costs to other departments, you do not allocate any further costs to that given service department. We call this a **step allocation** method.

Assume Department M, the maintenance department, receives little or no service from Department S, the storeroom department. Therefore, allocate Department M first. Assume the cost driver for maintenance costs is the number of maintenance hours required in each department. These hours and the resulting allocation appear below.

Department	Maintenance Hours	Percent	Distribution of Dept. M Costs
A	400 Hours	50	$4,657
B	200	25	2,328
S	200	25	2,328
Totals	800 Hours	100	$9,313

Assume the cost driver for the storeroom department's costs is the quantity of materials and supplies that Departments A and B requisition. Department A requisitioned 60 percent of the total materials and supplies and Department B the other 40 percent, the firm so allocates these departments 60 and 40 percent, respectively, of storeroom department costs.

Exhibit 5.5 shows the redistribution of maintenance and storeroom costs to the production departments.

Summary of Stage 1 Allocation   Firms allocate three types of costs: (1) allocation of costs directly to departments for costs that are directly traceable to departments (managers' salaries at Berdan Products), (2) allocation of costs not directly traceable to departments using a reasonable method (security costs at Berdan Products),

Exhibit 5.5

BERDAN PRODUCTS COMPANY
Redistribution of Service Department Costs

	Total	Dept. A	Dept. B	Dept. S	Dept. M
Total before Redistribution	$25,920	$ 6,015	$ 6,610	$ 3,982	$ 9,313
		50%	25%	25%	
		↓	↓	↓	
Redistribution of Dept. M to Dept. A, B, and S	—	4,657	2,328	2,328	(9,313)
	$25,920	$10,672	$ 8,938	$ 6,310	
		40%	60%		
		↓	↓		
Redistribution of Dept. S to Dept. A and B	—	2,524	3,786	(6,310)	
Total Production Department Costs	$25,920	$13,196	$12,724		

and (3) allocation of service department costs to the production departments using arbitrary methods. Thus Berdan allocated the total manufacturing overhead of $25,920 as $13,196 to Department A and $12,724 to Department B.

Stage 2: Cost Allocation from Production Departments to Products

Berdan next allocates these amounts to the products manufactured in the two production departments. A firm usually bases this allocation on the number of units produced, machine hours, direct labor hours, direct labor cost, and/or some other activity base, as we discussed in Chapters 3 and 4.

Using a simple example, if a total of 10,000 machine hours were worked in Department A and 20,000 machine hours were worked in Department B during the month, the overhead rates per hour would be as follows:

$$\text{Department A: } \$1.3196 \text{ per Hour} = \frac{\$13,196}{10,000 \text{ Hours}}.$$

$$\text{Department B: } \$ .6362 \text{ per Hour} = \frac{\$12,724}{20,000 \text{ Hours}}.$$

If a particular job required 200 machine hours of work in Department A and 300 machine hours of work in Department B, the firm then would assign $454.78 of overhead to the job, computed as follows:

$$\$454.78 = 200 \text{ Hours in Department A} \times \$1.3196$$
$$+ 300 \text{ Hours in Department B} \times \$.6362.$$

This approach assumes only one cost driver, namely, machine hours. Many companies would use multiple cost drivers reflecting the various activities that cause product costs, as we discussed in Chapter 3. This is known as **activity-based costing.**

Activity-based costing.   If you use multiple cost drivers, then you must pool costs into categories, one category, or "cost pool," for each cost driver.

For example, consider allocating Department A's overhead of $13,196 using three cost drivers, instead of one as in the example above. (In practice, companies using multiple cost drivers often use many more than three cost drivers, but the principles are the same whether companies use three or three hundred cost drivers. We shall use three to make the point without burdening you with details.)

Assume Berdan Company's accountants find the following cost drivers affect Department A's overhead costs.

Cost Driver	Cost Category or "Pool"
Number of Different Parts in the Product	Cost to Purchase, Inspect, Handle and Store the Parts
Machine Hours	Cost to Maintain Machines, Energy Costs to Operate Machines, Machine Depreciation, Wages of Machine Operators
Hours to Set Up a Job	Costs of Changing the Machines to Make Them Appropriate for a New Job, Including Wages of Production Workers, Engineers, and Computer Technicians

Assume the accountants divided Department A's overhead of $13,196 into these three categories, measured the number of units of activity for each cost driver for the period, and derived the following overhead rates per activity unit for each cost driver:

Cost Driver (1)	Overhead in Each Category (Total = $13,196) (2)	Units of Activity for Each Cost Driver for All Jobs (3)	Overhead Rate (2)/(3) (4)
Number of Different Parts in All Products	$1,846	200 Parts	$\frac{\$1,846}{200 \text{ parts}} = \$9.23$ per Part in the product
Machine Hours Worked on All Jobs	$6,150	10,000 Machine Hours	$\frac{\$6,150}{10,000 \text{ hours}} = \$.615$ per Machine Hour Used to Make the Product
Hours Required to Set Up All Jobs	$5,200	200 Setup Hours	$\frac{\$5,200}{200 \text{ hours}} = \$26.00$ per Setup Hour Used to Set Up the Job

This information refers to all products manufactured during the period. Now assume Berdan's production managers inform the accountants that a particular job uses the following amounts of these activities in Department A:

1. Twenty different parts in the job's product,

2. Two hundred machine hours, and

3. Ten hours to set up the job by changing machinery settings to make the equipment suitable for the job's products.

Using the overhead rates for all products and this information for a particular job, the accountants allocated Department A's overhead costs to the job as follows:

(20 parts × $9.23 per part) + (200 machine hours × $.615 per machine hour) + (10 setup hours × $26 per setup hour) = $567.60.

This procedure allocates Department A's overhead, only. The accountants would use similar steps to compute overhead rates for Department B and to allocate Department B's overhead costs to this job.

You can imagine how complex and time consuming this process can be if a company has numerous production departments, and if the accountants use many different overhead rates. Proponents of activity-based costing argue that it increases the accuracy of product costs which improves the quality of information available to management and, therefore, improves the quality of their decisions. Each company must ascertain how much benefit, if any, it obtains from activity-based costing and compare that benefit with the additional costs of developing and using a more complex and time-consuming cost allocation method.

Joint Products and By-Products

A cost allocation problem arises when more than one product emerges from a single production process. The numerous products of meat-packaging plants, the variety of metals often found and extracted together in mining operations, the inevitable production of various grades of finished lumber in the operation of a lumber mill, and the several products made from the original material in the dairy and petroleum industries are common examples of jointly produced goods.

The problems of joint production arise in industries other than manufacturing and mining. For instance, in real estate a similar problem exists in the development of a subdivision. The total cost of developing the tract represents a joint cost for all of the lots that the developer will sell. The developer who wants to calculate a cost and profit for each lot must find some reasonable method of allocating this total figure among the lots.

Understanding the problems of joint cost allocations requires familiarity with some special terminology. Exhibit 5.6 presents the following information graphically. The firm initially introduces direct materials into processing. After the incurrence of some direct labor and manufacturing overhead costs, two identifiable products, product A and product B, emerge from the production process. The firm processes Product A further, but sells Product B immediately. We call the point at which the indentifiable products emerge the **splitoff point.** Costs incurred up to the splitoff point are the **joint costs.** We call costs incurred after the splitoff point **additional processing costs.**

Allocation of Joint Production Costs

Firms can usually compute total cost with a satisfactory degree of accuracy, but have no theoretically correct or objective method of spreading the total cost over the various joint products. We can only describe the methods used as feasible, reasonable, or expedient. In spite of this apparently insurmountable barrier, firms attempt

Exhibit 5.6

Joint Production Process

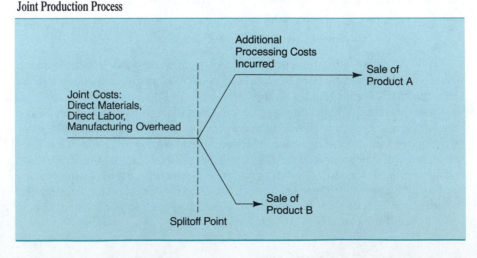

nevertheless to allocate joint costs, primarily to provide figures that they can use for cost of goods sold and inventory purposes.

Firms use one of two methods to allocate joint costs: the **net realizable value method** (also known as the relative sales value method) or the **physical units method.** We describe both in the following illustration based on a real estate development. Sorter Homes Development Company purchases a 2-acre tract of land adjoining a lake for $38,000 and spends $2,000 in legal fees to have the land subdivided into five lots. The company builds a house on each of the lots. Exhibit 5.7 shows the various costs and price data.

The different prices for the half-acre and quarter-acre lots result from differing proximity to the lake. The joint cost problem in this context is to allocate the $40,000 cost of the land to each of the five lots.

Net Realizable Value Method

Suppose that once Sorter legally subdivides the land it has a ready market for the lots without houses and that the market prices for the five lots are shown in column **(3)** of Exhibit 5.7. If such information is available, Sorter Homes allocates the $40,000 of joint cost to the lots in proportion to their relative current market values. Because the cost is 50 percent of the sum of the current market values ($40,000/ $80,000), Sorter Homes would assign each lot a cost of 50 percent of its current market value. Sorter Homes would allocate the cost of $8,000 to lot 1. It would allocate the following costs to the other lots: lots 2 and 3, $12,500 each; lot 4, $2,000; and lot 5, $5,000. Under this method, then, Sorter Homes assigns each lot a portion of the joint cost so that it yields a profit equal to 50 percent of selling price.

Approximate Net Realizable Value Method

To alter the illustration, suppose that the legal agreement allowing subdivision prohibits Sorter Homes from reselling the lots without houses or that for some other reason the information in column **(3)** of Exhibit 5.7 is not available.

Exhibit 5.7

SORTER HOMES DEVELOPMENT COMPANY Data for Joint Cost Allocations					
Lot Number (1)	Size (in acres) (2)	Resale Price after Subdivision (3)	Selling Price for House and Lot (4)	Cost to Build House (5)	Approximate Sales Value of Land at Splitoff (6)
1	½	$16,000	$ 75,000	$ 50,000	$ 25,000
2	½	25,000	80,000	50,000	30,000
3	½	25,000	80,000	50,000	30,000
4	¼	4,000	35,000	30,000	5,000
5	¼	10,000	40,000	30,000	10,000
	2	$80,000	$310,000	$210,000	$100,000

(3) market prices given.

(6) = (4) − (5).

The only information Sorter Homes has is that in columns (4) and (5) from which we calculate column (6). Sorter Homes would not logically assign the land's cost on the basis of the information in column (4), because those prices include the value of the house as well as the land. For example, the selling price of lot-house combination 4 is $35,000, which is about 11 percent of the total selling price of $310,000. We can see from the information in column (3) that lot 4 represents only 5 percent (= $4,000/$80,000) of the value of the total land package. Using final selling prices of lot-house combinations from column (4) to allocate land costs would intermingle land and house prices and would assign 11 percent of the land costs to lot 4, whereas 5 percent of the cost would be more appropriate. The **approximate net realizable value method** should achieve an allocation much like the one obtained from column (3) when the information about the sales value at the splitoff point is unavailable.

The diagram in Exhibit 5.8 may help you understand the nature of the problem. Such a diagram will usually help in analyzing joint cost allocation problems. The splitoff point comes just before the firm incurs the costs of the individual houses. To use the approximate net realizable value method, the firm must derive the relative sales values at the splitoff, as column (6) of Exhibit 5.7 shows.

We define the approximate net realizable value of a lot (joint product) as the selling price of the lot-house combination (final product) less the cost to complete the lot-house combination. Here, the cost to complete is the cost of building the house. The approximate net realizable value of lot 1 is $25,000, or the price of the lot-house combination, $75,000, less the cost of the house, $50,000. The sum of the approximate net realizable values of the lots at the splitoff point is $100,000. Because the cost of the land ($40,000) is 40 percent of the sum of the approximate net realizable values, Sorter Homes would assign each lot a cost of 40 percent (= $40,000/$100,000) of its approximate sales value. Sorter Homes would allocate Lot 1, for example, $10,000 (= .4 × $25,000). Allocations for the other lots appear in column (2) of Exhibit 5.9.

Exhibit 5.8

Splitoff Point in Allocating Joint Costs

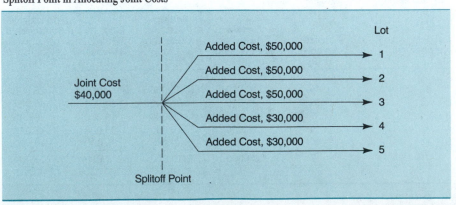

Exhibit 5.9

| | SORTER HOMES DEVELOPMENT COMPANY
Joint Cost Allocation under Various Methods with and without By-Products | | | | | |

| | Joint Product Cost = $40,000 | | | By-Product Cost = $2,000
Joint Product Cost = $38,000 | | |
| | Basis of Allocation | | | Basis of Allocation | | |
Lot Number	Net Realizable Values (1)[a]	Approximate Net Realizable Values (2)[b]	Physical Units (3)[c]	Net Realizable Values (4)[d]	Approximate Net Realizable Values (5)[e]	Physical Units (6)[f]
1	$ 8,000	$10,000	$10,000	$ 7,600	$ 9,500	$ 9,500
2	12,500	12,000	10,000	11,875	11,400	9,500
3	12,500	12,000	10,000	11,875	11,400	9,500
4	2,000	2,000	5,000	1,900	1,900	4,750
5	5,000	4,000	5,000	4,750	3,800	4,750
Total	$40,000	$40,000	$40,000	$38,000	$38,000	$38,000

[a](1) = column (3) of Exhibit 5.7 × 40/80.

[b](2) = column (6) of Exhibit 5.7 × 40/100.

[c](3) = $40,000 × [column (2) of Exhibit 5.7/2].

[d](4) = (1) × 38/40 = column (3) of Exhibit 5.7 × 38/80.

[e](5) = (2) × 38/40 = column (6) of Exhibit 5.7 × 38/100.

[f](6) = (3) × 38/40.

Physical Units Method

We do not base the physical units method on dollar costs but on some obvious physical measure. Here, the obvious measure is area in acres. In other contexts the obvious physical measure may be weight or volume. Because lots 1, 2, and 3 each contain ½ acre out of 2 acres, Sorter Homes would allocate each (.5/2) × $40,000, or $10,000. Sorter Homes would allocate each ¼-acre lot (.25/2) × $40,000, or $5,000.

Firms may easily apply the physical units method, but its results may not make good sense. For example, if a firm applies the physical units method using pounds of salable product to allocate the cost of beef cattle to cuts of meat, tenderloin will carry the same cost per pound as liver. Then the sales of tenderloin will appear extraordinarily profitable, whereas it will show liver to sell at a loss. The net realizable value method will allocate more of the joint costs of beef cattle to a pound of tenderloin than to a pound of liver.

Accounting for By-Products

In accounting for jointly produced products, firms customarily distinguish between by-products and joint products. A firm produces a **by-product** as the inevitable result of the production of a main product and it is of relatively small value. For example, steel shavings in a machine shop and scraps of lumber in a furniture factory are typical instances of by-products. A **joint product** is one that firms treat as equally significant with other products that emerge from a process. The different grades of lumber in a lumber mill, milk and butter in dairy operations, and subdivision lots are examples of joint products. By-products and joint products differ in degree only; the dividing line is not distinct. For instance, a power plant that produces both electricity and steam may consider one or the other as a by-product or may treat them both as joint products.

In accounting for by-products, just as for joint products, firms assign no processing cost to the by-product until production separates it from the joint process. The distinctive feature of by-product accounting is that when production separates the by-product from the joint process, the firm then assigns it a cost equal to its net realizable (or sales) value, which is its estimated selling price minus any costs the firm will incur for further processing, handling, and disposal. The firm then deducts the cost assigned to by-products from the total accumulated joint costs, and the remaining joint costs become the cost of the main product or products. Firms assign by-products a cost so that the expected gain or loss on their sale is zero. The cost assigned to the by-products reduces the cost of the main product or products and thereby increases the main product's profits.

To illustrate the accounting for by-products, reconsider the Sorter Homes example. Suppose that at the time Sorter Homes arranged for legal subdivision of the land purchase, it also sold to the city the rights for the public to use the lake for $2,000. The firm should view the rights to the lake probably as a by-product in this case, so it would treat the rights as a reduction in the cost of the land. The firm would allocate only $38,000 to the joint costs of the five lots. The right-hand panel of Exhibit 5.9 summarizes the allocation of the joint costs.

An alternative method treats the income from the by-product as other income and assigns all by-product costs to the main product.

Marketing and Administrative Expenses

Management often applies techniques similar to those employed in manufacturing cost analysis in allocating marketing and administrative costs. A department store, for example, may wish to have its operating costs and cost of goods sold allocated, as far as possible, by departments; a wholesaler may wish to obtain information concerning the profitability of different territories and types of customers; or a manufacturer may be interested in the cost of handling and selling various products.

Merchandising Analysis

The calculation of departmental operating costs in a merchandising operation is much the same as the allocation of departmental overhead in a manufacturing plant. Merchandising operations can assign some items, such as salaries and commissions of salespeople, directly to departments. These organizations must allocate others, such as rent, insurance, and supervision, after a preliminary accumulation in an overhead control account. Such organizations will adopt appropriate bases for the allocation of these costs. For example, a firm may use floor space as the basis for spreading building service costs, usually on a weighted basis. The different weights applied to the area different departments occupy allows for the greater value of certain sections of the store. For example, a department store would weight more heavily first-floor space of a given size than the same amount of space on an upper floor.

A manufacturing plant must completely allocate all manufacturing costs so that it can assign costs to units produced and so that it can derive unit costs for inventories for external financial reporting. By contrast, management does not include the operating costs of a department store in cost of goods sold or inventory valuations. The department store uses the results of allocations of operating costs only for managerial purposes. Management will better serve such purposes if it limits the allocations to those that it can assign on some reasonably logical basis. Attempts to allocate the more general costs such as office salaries, executives' salaries, general store advertising, and warehouse costs will usually be arbitrary.

Exhibit 5.10 shows some of the bases of allocation that firms have suggested for marketing and administrative costs. One striking aspect of the problem of such cost analysis is that firms must accumulate extensive data in addition to the regular accounting information. Firms can accumulate some of the data regularly. Firms will make other items, because of the cost of obtaining the information, the subject of occasional studies to establish or to correct normal or standard costs of the operation.

■ Summary ■

Common cost allocations permeate accounting reports, both financial and managerial. Managers should read and interpret accounting reports carefully, taking into consideration the effects of common cost allocations. For most decision making,

Exhibit 5.10

Allocation Bases

For Allocation Of	Basis
1. Insurance	Average Value of Finished Goods
2. Storage and Building Costs	Floor Space
3. Cost of Sending Monthly Statements, Credit Investigations, Etc.	Number of Customers
4. Various Joint Costs such as Advertising and Supervision of Selling Activities	Sales, Classified by Dealers, Territories, or Products
5. Credit Investigation, Postage, Stationery, and Other Such Expenses	Number of Orders Received
6. Handling Costs	Tonnage Handled
7. Salespersons' Expenses	Number of Salespersons' Calls
8. Order Writing and Filling	Number of Items on an Order
9. Stenographic Expense	Number of Letters Written
10. Automobile Operation, Delivery Expense, Etc.	Number of Miles Operated

planning, and control purposes, accountants should base their reports on a minimum of cost allocations.

Transactions with outsiders generate costs that accountants allocate to various cost objects. The cost allocation process involves (1) accumulating costs to be allocated, (2) identifying cost objects, and (3) selecting a basis for relating costs to cost objects.

External reporting standards (for example, to value inventory on external financial reports) require cost allocations. Cost-plus contracts and cost-based rate regulations require allocations of common costs. Firms allocate service department costs for managerial purposes to charge users for the cost of services and to encourage users to monitor service department costs.

Appendix 5.1: Reciprocal Method for Allocation of Service Department Costs

How can accountants allocate service department costs to production departments when service departments *serve each other* in addition to servicing production departments? The text mentioned the **reciprocal method** for allocating service departments' costs to production departments, which algebraically solves the problem. This method normally uses matrix algebra, although you do not need matrix algebra if the firm has only two production and two service departments, as Problem 4 for Self-Study demonstrates.

Students unfamiliar with matrix algebra may skip this appendix without losing continuity with the rest of the book.[4]

The data you need to use the **reciprocal method** for Berdan Products Company appear in Exhibit 5.11. The maintenance and storeroom service departments provide service to each other as well as to production departments A and B.

The service department costs requiring allocation are $9,313 in maintenance and $3,982 in the storeroom. The simplified procedure explained in the text in Exhibit 5.5 assumed that the storeroom directly serviced the two production departments. A more realistic treatment allocates the costs in proportion to the cost of factory supplies the storeroom issues to each department. The firm used $2,750 of factory supplies. Maintenance consumed $450, or 16.4 percent of that total. Exhibit 5.11 shows the fractions of storeroom services consumed by the four departments. The storeroom column contains the figure .164 to indicate the maintenance department's consumption. The other entries in the storeroom column, including self-service in the storeroom ($800/$2,750 = .291), result from dividing the factory supplies used in that department by the total factory supplies used, or $2,750. The basis for distributing maintenance department costs remains the same as the step procedure explained in the text because the maintenance department itself required no maintenance.

---

[4]Readers comfortable with matrix algebra who wish to pursue this problem further should refer to Robert S. Kaplan, ''Variable and Self-Service Costs in Reciprocal Allocation Models,'' *The Accounting Review* 48 (October 1973), pp. 738–748.

Exhibit 5.11

BERDAN PRODUCTS COMPANY
Fractions of Service Departments' Outputs Used by Service and Production
Departments for March

	Services Performed By	
	Maintenance *(M)*	Storeroom *(R)*
Services Used By		
Service Departments		
Maintenance	0	.164 Matrix **S**
Storeroom	.25	.291
Production Departments		
A	.50	.218 Matrix **P**
B	.25	.327
	1.00	1.000
Costs to Be Allocated	$9,313	$3,982

Notice that each column in the schedule adds exactly to one. All departments together consume all of a service department's output. The top portion of the schedule shows the service department's use of service department outputs. Matrix **S** denotes that section of the schedule. Matrix element s_{ij} represents the fraction of service department j's output used by service department i. For example, $s_{MR} = .164$, or the maintenance department (M) uses 16.4 percent of the storeroom's (R) output. (We refer to the storeroom as R so you will not confuse it with **S,** which stands for the entire service department matrix.)

The bottom portion of the schedule shows the production department usage. Matrix **P** denotes that section of the schedule. Matrix element p_{ij} represents the fraction of service department j's output that production department i uses. To allocate the service department costs to production departments, we need an allocation matrix such as the one in Exhibit 5.12. In matrix **A,** a_{ij} represents the fraction of service department j's cost allocable to production department i after we take ac-

Exhibit 5.12

BERDAN PRODUCTS COMPANY
Allocation Matrix for March

	Services Performed By	
	Maintenance *(M)*	Storeroom *(R)*
Service Costs Allocated To		
Production Departments		
A	.61	.45 Matrix **A**
B	.39	.55
	1.00	1.00

count of the use of the service department output by the service departments themselves.

The matrix $\mathbf{A}$ results from the matrix equation $\mathbf{A} = \mathbf{P}(\mathbf{I} - \mathbf{S})^{-1}$, where $\mathbf{I}$ is the identity matrix and $(\mathbf{I} - \mathbf{S})^{-1}$ means the inverse of the matrix $(\mathbf{I} - \mathbf{S})$. We can derive the equation for $\mathbf{A}$. For example, a_{AM} represents the fraction of the maintenance department's *(M)* output allocable to product Department A. That fraction is

$$a_{AM} = p_{AM} + a_{AM}s_{MM} + a_{AR}s_{RM}$$

$$= .50 + a_{AM} \times 0 + a_{AR} \times .25,$$

or the direct use of maintenance by Department A *(p_{AM})* plus the fraction of maintenance costs used by maintenance allocable to Department A *(a_{AM}s_{MM})* plus the fraction of maintenance costs used by the storeroom—that is, allocable to Department A *(a_{AR}s_{RM})*. Notice that the equation for a_{AM} shows both a_{AM} and other a_{ij} on the right hand side, so that a system of simultaneous equations for the a_{ij} results.

Consider another example, a_{BR}:

$$a_{BR} = p_{BR} + a_{BM}s_{MR} + a_{BR}s_{RR}$$

$$= .327 + a_{BM} \times .164 + a_{BR} \times .291.$$

The fraction of storeroom costs allocable to Department B equals the sum of the direct use of the storeroom by Department B *(p_{BR})* plus the fraction of storeroom costs maintenance used allocable to Department B *(a_{BM}s_{MR})* plus the fraction of storeroom costs the storeroom used allocable to Department B *(a_{BR}s_{RR})*.

Writing out a similar equation for each a_{ij}, where i represents production department A or B, and j represents service department M or R, yields a matrix equation for the entire system:

$$a_{ij} = p_{ij} + \sum_{k=M,R} a_{ik}s_{kj}$$

or

$$A = P + AS.$$

Rearranging terms yields

$$A - AS = P$$

or

$$A(I - S) = P.$$

Postmultiply both sides by $(\mathbf{I} - \mathbf{S})^{-1}$ to get[5]

$$A = P(I - S)^{-1}$$

---

[5]If the inverse of $(\mathbf{I} - \mathbf{S})$ does not exist, then a subset of the service departments completely uses the entire output themselves without providing any service to the other service departments or to production departments. If you eliminate the subset of service departments that mutually consume each other's output, then you can carry out the procedure.

Exhibit 5.13

BERDAN PRODUCTS COMPANY				
Allocation of Service Department Costs to Production Departments, March				

	Service Departments			
	Matrix Method			Step Approximation Method
Production Department	Maintenance	Storeroom	Total	
A	$5,681	$1,792	$ 7,473	$ 7,181
B	3,632	2,190	5,822	6,114
	$9,313	$3,982	$13,295	$13,295

Once you compute the matrix **A,** to allocate service department costs to production departments is straightforward. The allocation appears in Exhibit 5.13, along with the allocation that the easier, but approximate, step procedure demonstrated earlier provides.

Observe that the matrix method gives different answers than the approximation method. The matrix method is cumbersome to carry out by hand when it involves more than two service departments and two production departments. The solution to the set of simultaneous equations (or the matrix inversion) is tedious and, except for small problems, you should do the calculations on a computer. If all entries in the **S** matrix are zero (that is, when all service departments service only production departments) the matrix procedure and the approximate step procedure will give the same answer.

Problem 1 for Self-Study

The partially completed overhead distribution schedule for Merriam Company appears in Exhibit 5.14. Merriam Company distributes its costs on the following bases:

(1) Janitor's wages and rent of building on the basis of floor space.

(2) Fire insurance and property taxes on the basis of book value of assets in each department.

(3) Worker's compensation insurance and payroll taxes on the basis of proportions of total labor costs, including allocated portion of janitor's wages.

(4) Electricity, gas, and water and miscellaneous factory costs on the basis of percentages given.

(5) Maintenance costs on the basis of chargeable maintenance hours.

(6) Storeroom costs on the basis of proportions of number of requisitions drawn.

Prepare a schedule of allocated costs and use the step method to distribute service department costs. Round all percentages to one decimal place.

Exhibit 5.14

MERRIAM COMPANY
Overhead Distribution Schedule for February

	Total	Dept. A	Dept. B	Dept. C	Dept. S Storeroom	Dept. M Maintenance
Foremen's Salaries...........	$ 2,550.00	$ 600.00	$ 675.00	$ 637.50		$ 637.50
Maintenance Wages..........	1,870.00					1,870.00
Storeroom Wages............	530.00				$ 530.00	
(1) Janitor's Wages..............	350.00					
Supplies Used	1,350.00	200.00	300.00	100.00	600.00	150.00
(2) Fire Insurance	150.00					
(3) Worker's Compensation Insurance	260.00					
(3) Payroll Taxes	1,320.00					
(2) Property Taxes	300.00					
(1) Rent—Factory Building	550.00					
Depreciation of Machinery and Equipment	450.00	202.50	144.00	45.00	36.00	22.50
(4) Electricity, Gas and Water.....	200.00					
(4) Miscellaneous Factory Costs ..	1,270.00					
Total.....................	$ 11,150.00					

	Total	Dept. A	Dept. B	Dept. C	Storeroom	Maintenance
Direct Labor Costs...............	$ 44,700.00	$14,000.00	$15,800.00	$14,900.00	—	—
Book Value of Assets	$100,000.00	$45,000.00	$32,000.00	$10,000.00	$8,000.00	$5,000.00
Floor Space (square feet)	50,000	16,000	12,000	20,000	1,600	400
Chargeable Maintenance Hours ...	500	160	200	120	20	—
Requisitions Drawn	200	140	50	10	—	—
Other Distribution Data:						
Electricity, Gas, and Water	100%	40%	30%	20%	6%	4%
Miscellaneous Factory Costs......	100%	30%	25%	25%	10%	10%

Suggested Solution

MERRIAM COMPANY
Overhead Distribution Schedule for February

	Total	Dept. A	Dept. B	Dept. C	Dept. S Storeroom	Dept. M Maintenance
Foremen's Salaries	$ 2,550.00	$ 600.00	$ 675.00	$ 637.50	$ —	$ 637.50
Maintenance Wages	1,870.00	—	—	—	—	1,870.00
Storeroom Wages	530.00	—	—	—	530.00	—
Janitor's Wages	350.00	112.00	84.00	140.00	11.20	2.80
Supplies Used	1,350.00	200.00	300.00	100.00	600.00	150.00
Fire Insurance........................	150.00	67.50	48.00	15.00	12.00	7.50
Worker's Compensation Insurance......	260.00	76.44	86.06	81.64	2.86	13.00
Payroll Taxes	1,320.00	388.08	436.92	414.48	14.52	66.00
Property Taxes	300.00	135.00	96.00	30.00	24.00	15.00
Rent—Factory Building................	550.00	176.00	132.00	220.00	17.60	4.40

continued

continued from page 202

Depreciation of Machinery and Equipment	450.00	202.50	144.00	45.00	36.00	22.50
Electricity, Gas, and Water	200.00	80.00	60.00	40.00	12.00	8.00
Miscellaneous Factory Costs...........	1,270.00	381.00	317.50	317.50	127.00	127.00
Totals	$11,150.00	$2,418.52	$2,379.48	$2,041.12	$1,387.18	$2,923.70
Redistribution—Dept. M	—	935.58	1,169.48	701.69	116.95	(2,923.70)
	$11,150.00	$3,354.10	$3,548.96	$2,742.81	$1,504.13	
Redistribution—Dept. S	—	1,052.89	376.03	75.21	(1,504.13)	
Total Productive Department Overhead Costs	$11,150.00	$4,406.99	$3,924.99	$2,818.02		

Total Labor Costs

	Direct Labor	Janitor's Wages	Other Labor	Total
Dept. A...	$14,000.00	$112.00	$ 600.00	$14,712.00
Dept. B...	15,800.00	84.00	675.00	16,559.00
Dept. C...	14,900.00	140.00	637.50	15,677.50
Dept. S...	—	11.20	530.00	541.20
Dept. M	—	2.80	2,507.50	2,510.30
Total	$44,700.00	$350.00	$4,950.00	$50,000.00

Allocation Percentages

	Floor Space	Value of Assets	Labor Costs	Maintenance	Requisitions
Dept. A....................................	32.0%	45%	29.4%	32%	70%
Dept. B....................................	24.0	32	33.1	40	25
Dept. C....................................	40.0	10	31.4	24	5
Dept. S.	3.2	8	1.1	4	—
Dept. M	0.8	5	5.0	—	—
Total	100.0%	100%	100.0%	100%	100%

Problem 2 for Self-Study

Up to the point of separation of joint products X, Y, and Z, total production costs amount to $51,500. The firm produced the following quantities.

- Product X: 3,000 units with an estimated sales value of $3 per unit.

- Product Y: 4,500 units with an estimated sales value of $4 per unit.

- Product Z: 9,700 units with an estimated sales value of $5 per unit.

a. Prepare a schedule showing the allocation of production costs to the three joint products and the unit cost of each product, using the net realizable value method.

b. Repeat part a assuming that the firm treats product X as a by-product.

Suggested Solution

a.

	Units	Unit Price	Total Sales Value	Percent of Value	Cost Allocation	Unit Cost
Product X	3,000	$3	$ 9,000	11.92	$ 6,139	$2.046
Product Y	4,500	4	18,000	23.84	12,278	2.728
Product Z	9,700	5	48,500	64.24	33,083	3.411
Total			$75,500	100.00	$51,500	

b.

Total Cost...	$51,500
Value of Product X...	9,000
Costs to Be Allocated to Y and Z.....................................	$42,500

$$\text{Product Y} = \frac{\$18,000}{\$66,500} \times \$42,500$$

$$= .2707 \times \$42,500 = \$11,505.$$

Unit cost = $2.56.

$$\text{Product Z} = \frac{\$48,500}{\$66,500} \times \$42,500$$

$$= .7293 \times \$42,500 = \$30,995.$$

Unit cost = $3.20.

Problem 3 for Self-Study

At the conclusion of process 4, the total cost of processing 25,000 gallons of chemical product K is $362,000. At this point, 5,000 gallons of by-product Y emerge and the processing department transfers the remaining 20,000 gallons of K to process 5 for further work. The Y material will require further processing at an estimated cost of $1 per gallon, and then the firm can sell it for $3 per gallon. Calculate the cost per gallon of chemical product K transferred to process 5.

Suggested Solution

The by-product has a net realizable value of $10,000 [= 5,000 × ($3 − $1)]. Subtract this amount from the joint cost of $362,000. Allocate the remaining $352,000 to Product K. The cost per gallon, therefore, is $352,000/20,000 gallons = $17.60 per gallon.

Problem 4 for Self-Study (Appendix 5.1)

The following data describe services that the four departments of the Oak Bank produced and consumed during October. Using these data, write the system of simultaneous equations describing the proper allocation of service department costs to the production departments. Solve for the final allocation of costs with simultaneous equations or the matrix method explained in Appendix 5.1.

OAK BANK
Fractions of Service Departments' Output Used by Service and Production
Department for October

	Services Performed By	
	Personnel (P)	Administration (A)
Services Used By		
Service Departments		
Personnel (P)	—	.30
Administration (A)	.10	—
Production Departments		
Services (S)................................	.60	.20
Loans (L)	.30	.50
Costs to Be Allocated........................	$40,000	$60,000

Suggested Solution

Using Simultaneous Equations

1. Set up equations to reflect service department usage and costs for each department.

    Production Departments Usage:

    $$(1)\ S\ (\text{Services}) = .6P\ (\text{Personnel}) + .2A\ (\text{Administration})$$

    $$(2)\ L\ (\text{Loans})\quad = .3P + .5A.$$

    Service Departments Usage and Costs:

    $$(3)\ P = .3A + \$40,000$$

    $$(4)\ A = .1P + \$60,000.$$

2. Solve for P in terms of A by substituting equation (4) into equation (3).

    $$(3)\ P = .3A + \$40,000$$

    $$= .3(.1P + \$60,000) + \$40,000$$

    $$= .03P + \$18,000 + \$40,000$$

    $$P - .03P = \$58,000$$

    $$.97P = \$58,000$$

    $$P = \frac{\$58,000}{.97} = \$59,794.$$

3. Now substitute $P = \$59{,}794$ into equation (4).

$$(4) \; A = .1P + \$60{,}000$$
$$= .1(\$59{,}794) + \$60{,}000$$
$$= \$65{,}979.$$

4. Finally, substitute values for A and P into the production department equations and solve to derive the service department cost allocations.

$$S = .6P + .2A$$
$$= .6(\$59{,}794) + .2(\$65{,}979)$$
$$= \$49{,}072.$$

$$L = .3P + .5A$$
$$= .3(\$59{,}794) + .5(\$65{,}979)$$
$$= \$50{,}928.$$

Using Matrix Algebra

▪ Let a_{ij} represent the percentage of service department j's cost allocable to production department i, after accounting for service department usage of its own output.

▪ Let p_{ij} represent the direct use of department j by department i.

▪ Let s_{ij} represent the use of department j by department i, when i and j are both service departments. (See computation below.)

$$a_{sp} = p_{sp} + a_{sa}s_{ap} + a_{sp}s_{pp} = .63918$$
$$a_{sa} = p_{sa} + a_{sa}s_{aa} + a_{sp}s_{pa} = .39175$$
$$a_{lp} = p_{lp} + a_{la}s_{ap} + a_{lp}s_{pp} = .36082$$
$$a_{la} = p_{la} + a_{lp}s_{pa} + a_{la}s_{aa} = .60825.$$

Using the same notation as in the appendix, we find that

$$\mathbf{S} = \begin{bmatrix} 0 & .3 \\ .10 & 0 \end{bmatrix} \quad \mathbf{P} = \begin{bmatrix} .60 & .20 \\ .30 & .50 \end{bmatrix}.$$

Now,

$$(\mathbf{I} - \mathbf{S}) = \begin{bmatrix} 1 & -.3 \\ -.1 & 1 \end{bmatrix},$$

where $\mathbf{I}$ is an identity matrix. The inverse matrix of $(\mathbf{I} - \mathbf{S})$, $(\mathbf{I} - \mathbf{S})^{-1}$, is

$$\begin{bmatrix} 1.03093 & 0.30928 \\ 0.10309 & 1.03093 \end{bmatrix}.$$

Thus

$$A = P(I - S)^{-1} = \begin{bmatrix} .63918 & .39175 \\ .36082 & .60825 \end{bmatrix}.$$

The allocation of service department costs to production departments follows:

	From	
To	Personnel	Administration
Services	.63918 × $40,000 = $25,567	.39175 × $60,000 = $23,505
Loans	.36082 × $40,000 = $14,433	.60825 × $60,000 = $36,495

Total allocation:

Services: $25,567 + $23,505 = $49,072.
Loans: $14,433 + $36,495 = $50,928.

Key Terms and Concepts

Direct cost
Common cost
Service department cost allocation
Joint cost allocation
Service departments
Allocation base
Step allocation method
Activity-based costing
Splitoff point
Joint costs

Additional processing costs
Net realizable value method
Physical units method
Approximate net realizable
  value method
By-product
Joint product
Reciprocal (matrix allocation)
  method (appendix)

Questions, Exercises, Problems, and Cases

Questions

1. Review the meaning of the concepts or terms given above in Key Terms and Concepts.

2. When firms allocate service department costs to production departments, why do they first accumulate these costs at the service department level rather than assigning them directly to production departments?

3. Distinguish between a production department and a service department.

4. What reasoning supports the opinion that, in merchandising (as opposed to manufacturing) enterprises, firms should allocate only those costs that they can assign on some obviously logical basis?

5. Comment on this statement: "The purpose of cost accounting is to compute the cost of producing a unit of product so that the firm can use this production cost to derive a sales price that yields the desired gross profit margin."

6. Why do firms allocate service department costs to production departments?

7. Distinguish between a joint product and a by-product.

8. Comment on the following statement: "The net realizable value method is the best method to use in decisions concerning whether a firm should sell a joint product at splitoff or process it further."

9. Name some of the costs and benefits of cost allocation.

10. A critic of cost allocation noted, "You can avoid arbitrary cost allocations by not allocating any costs." Comment.

11. Give the steps in the cost allocation process.

12. For each of the types of common cost in the first column, select the most appropriate allocation base from the second column:

Common Cost	Allocation Base
Building Utilities	Value of Equipment and Inventories
Payroll Accounting	Number of Units Produced
Property Taxes on Personal Property	Number of Employees
Equipment Repair	Space Occupied
Quality Control Inspection	Number of Service Calls

Exercises

13. *Allocating overhead to departments and jobs.* The accountants of Roberts Films made the following estimates for a year:

	Filming Department	Editing Department	Printing Department
Estimated Overhead	$36,000	$50,000	$56,000
Estimated Direct Labor Cost . . .	$60,000	$50,000	$70,000
Estimated Direct Labor Time	12,000 Hours	12,500 Hours	14,000 Hours

   a. Compute the departmental overhead allocation rates using (1) direct labor cost and (2) direct labor hours as a basis.

   b. Apply the results obtained in part **a** to the data given in the following table for film no. 407. Show the total cost of the job for each basis of overhead allocation.

	Filming Department	Editing Department	Printing Department
Direct Material	$600	—	$80
Direct Labor Cost...............	$1,500	$2,000	$200
Direct Labor Time	250 Hours	400 Hours	38 Hours

14. *Allocating overhead.* The Hamilton Company has two production departments and a maintenance department. In addition, the company keeps other costs for the entire plant in a separate account. The estimated cost data for Year 1 follows:

Cost	Production Dept. 1	Production Dept. 2	Maintenance	General Plant
Direct Labor	$50,000	$30,000	—	—
Indirect Labor	28,000	14,000	$22,500	$20,000
Indirect Materials ...	9,000	7,000	900	8,000
Miscellaneous	3,000	5,000	1,600	5,000
	$90,000	$56,000	$25,000	$33,000
Maintenance	7,000 Hours	13,000 Hours	—	—

The general plant services the three departments in the following proportions: 50 percent (Department 1); 30 percent (Department 2); 20 percent (Maintenance). Allocate maintenance costs based on maintenance hours.

Compute the overhead rate per direct labor dollar for Departments 1 and 2, after allocating maintenance department and general plant costs to production departments.

15. *Allocating overhead to jobs.* The Burns Company uses a job system of cost accounting. The data presented here relate to operations in its plant during January.

Burns has two production departments and one service department. The actual factory overhead costs during the month are $4,000. At the end of the month Burns allocates overhead costs as follows: Department A, $2,100; Department B, $1,600; Department C, $300. Burns redistributes the service department (Department C) overhead as follows: two-thirds to Department A, one-third to Department B.

Burns applies factory overhead to jobs at the predetermined rates of 60 percent of direct labor costs in Department A and 80 percent in Department B. The firm delivers the jobs upon completion. The firm completed job nos. 789, 790, and 791 in January. Job 788 is still in process on January 31.

a. Complete the job production record in the following table by filling in the appropriate amounts. Be sure to show supporting calculations.

b. Compute the over- or underapplied overhead for each department.

Job Production Record

Job Order No.	Jobs in Process, Jan. 1	Direct Labor		Direct Matl.		Applied Overhead		Total Costs	Jobs in Process, Jan. 31	Completed Jobs
		Dept. A	Dept. B	Dept. A	Dept. B	Dept. A	Dept. B			
788	$1,200	$ 300	$ 150	$ 250	$ 150	$	$	$	$	$
789	850	600	300	450	300					
790		800	450	550	350					
791		1,000	600	600	450					
792		1,200	650	900	400					
Totals	$2,050	$3,900	$2,150	$2,750	$1,650	$	$	$	$	$

16. *Allocating service department costs using the step method.* Meridian Box Company has two service departments (maintenance and general factory administration) and two operating departments (cutting and assembly). Management has decided to allocate maintenance costs on the basis of the area in each department and general factory administration costs on the basis of labor hours the employees worked in each of their respective departments.

The following data appear in the company records for the current period:

	General Factory Administration	Maintenance	Cutting	Assembly
Area Occupied (square feet)	1,000	—	1,000	3,000
Labor Hours	—	100	100	400
Direct Labor Costs (operating departments only)			$1,500	$4,000
Service Cost Center Direct Costs	$1,200	$2,400		

Use the step method to allocate these service department costs to the operating departments, starting with maintenance.

17. *Using multiple cost drivers to allocate costs.* Assume Stealth Products uses three allocation bases to allocate overhead costs from departments to jobs: number of different parts, number of machine hours, and number of job setup hours. The information needed to compute the allocation rates follows.

	Department A		Department B	
	Costs	Units of Activity	Costs	Units of Activity
1. Number of Different Parts	$2,000	50 Parts	$400	10 Parts
2. Number of Machine Hours Worked	$100,000	16,000 Hours	$30,000	2,000 Hours
3. Number of Hours to Setup Jobs	$12,000	400 Hours	$4,000	100 Hours

Job 300ZX required the following activities:

Department A: 10 parts, 1,000 machine hours, 20 setup hours.
Department B: 2 parts, 200 machine hours, 10 setup hours.

Allocate overhead cost to Job 300ZX using the two stages described in the chapter.

18. *Allocating service department costs directly to operating departments.* Greene's Good Burgers has a commissary with two operating departments: P1, food inventory control, and P2, paper goods inventory control. It has two service departments: S1, computer services, and S2, administration, maintenance, and all other. Each department's direct costs are as follows:

P1	$90,000
P2	60,000
S1	20,000
S2	30,000

Greene's uses S1's services as follows:

P1	10 Percent
P2	10 Percent
S2	80 Percent

Greene's uses S2's services as follows:

P1	50 Percent
P2	30 Percent
S1	20 Percent

Compute the allocation of service center costs to operating departments. Allocate directly to operating departments. Do not allocate costs from one service center to another.

19. *Allocating service department costs using the step method.* Using the data for Exercise 18, allocate service department costs using the step allocation method, in which the firm allocates service center costs to other service centers as well as to operating departments.

20. *Joint cost allocations—net realizable value method.* A company processes Chemical XX-12 to produce two outputs, D and T. The monthly costs of

processing XX-12 amount to $45,000 for materials and $160,000 for conversion costs. This processing results in outputs that sell for a total of $455,000. The sales revenue from D amounts to $273,000 of the total.

Compute the costs the firm will assign to D and T in a typical month using the net realizable value method.

21. *Joint cost allocations—approximate net realizable value method.* A batch of ore yields three refined products: lead, copper, and manganese. The costs of processing the ore up to the splitoff point, including ore costs, are $55,000 per batch. Selling prices and additional processing costs after splitoff follow (per batch):

Product	Additional Processing Cost	Sales Price
Lead	$8,000	$20,000
Copper	1,000	40,000
Manganese	6,000	30,000

Use the approximate net realizable value method to allocate joint costs to the three refined products.

22. *Joint cost allocations using the physical quantities method—by-products.* The following diagram presents the facts for a group of products:

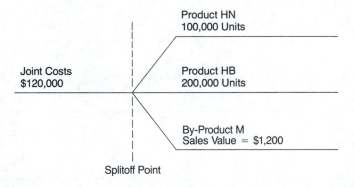

The firm uses by-product sales value to reduce joint product costs before allocation. The $120,000 is the joint cost before reduction for by-product sales value. Allocate joint costs.

23. *Joint costing—solving for unknowns* (adapted from CPA exam). O'Connor Company manufactures Product J and Product K from a joint process. O'Connor produced 4,000 units of Product J with a sales value at the splitoff point of $15,000. If O'Connor processed Product J further, the additional costs would equal $3,000 and the sales value would equal $20,000. O'Connor produced 2,000 units of Product K with a sales value at splitoff of $10,000. If O'Connor processed Product K further, the additional costs would equal $1,000 and the

sales value would equal $12,000. Using the net realizable value at splitoff approach, the firm allocated $9,000 to the portion of the total joint product costs for Product J.

Compute the total joint product costs.

24. *Joint costing—finding missing values.* Demski Enterprises makes stuffed animals, known as "Ralph" toys. From a joint process, Demski produces three toys, anteaters (A), bears (B), and camels (C). The company allocates joint costs based on relative sales value at splitoff. Additional data follows:

| | Product | | | |
	A	B	C	Total
Units Produced................	8,000	4,000	2,000	14,000
Joint Costs	$ 72,000	a	b	$120,000
Sales Value at Splitoff.........	c	d	$30,000	200,000
Additional Costs to Process Further	14,000	$10,000	6,000	30,000
Sales Value If Processed Further	140,000	60,000	40,000	240,000

Derive the values for the lettered items.

Problems

25. *Allocating overhead.* The APCO Company applies manufacturing overhead to all departments by means of allocation ratios. The two departments are Melting and Molding.

From the following data, prepare an overhead distribution schedule showing in detail the manufacturing overhead chargeable to each department. Round all decimals to three places and all dollars to whole dollars.

APCO COMPANY
Manufacturing Overhead Costs during the Month

Indirect Labor:	
Melting	$ 6,600
Molding...	3,600
Supplies Used:	
Melting	1,500
Molding...	900
Taxes (machinery and equipment, $72; building, $144)	216
Compensation Insurance	906
Power	300
Heat and Light..	480
Depreciation: Building	384
Machinery and Equipment	360
Total	$15,246

APCO COMPANY
Other Operating Data

	Floor Space (square feet)	Cost of Machinery and Equipment	Direct Labor per Month	Horsepower Rating
Department:				
Melting	2,000	$35,000	$ 2,000	120
Molding............	6,000	25,000	10,000	180
Total	8,000	$60,000	$12,000	300

26. *Allocating unassigned costs to retail store departments.* The Kellermeyer Specialty Shop has two departments, Clothing and Accessories. The operating expenses for the year ending December 31 follow.

a. Prepare a three-column statement of operating expenses with column headings: Clothing, Accessories, Total. Begin with direct departmental expenses and show a subtotal. Then continue with the allocated expenses, assigning each item to the various departments. Round all values to the nearest dollar and all percentages to one decimal place.

b. Prepare a condensed income statement with columns for Clothing, Accessories, Total. Show the total operating expenses calculated in part **a** as a single deduction from gross margin.

KELLERMEYER SPECIALTY SHOP

	Clothing	Accessories	Unassigned	Total
Salaries:				
Clerks	$78,240	$69,360	—	$147,600
Others..................			$48,000	48,000
Supplies Used	3,800	3,200	1,400	8,400
Depreciation of				
Equipment	1,600	4,800	—	6,400
Advertising................	3,726	8,586	3,888	16,200
Building Rent..............			19,000	19,000
Payroll Taxes..............			12,300	12,300
Worker's Compensation				
Insurance			2,080	2,080
Fire Insurance			1,000	1,000
Delivery Expense			1,800	1,800
Miscellaneous				
Expenses	1,000	800	600	2,400

KELLERMEYER SPECIALTY SHOP

	Clothing	Accessories	Total
Sales................................	$600,000	$400,000	$1,000,000
Cost of Goods Sold	$440,000	$240,000	$680,000

continued

continued from page 214

Equipment	$10,080	$24,960	$35,040
Inventory (average)	$100,800	$139,200	$240,000
Floor Space (square feet)	2,400	3,600	6,000
Number of Employees	10	15	25

KELLERMEYER SPECIALTY SHOP

Expense	Basis of Allocation
Salaries—Other	Gross Margin
Supplies Used (unassigned)	Sales
Advertising (unassigned)	Sales
Building Rent	Floor Space
Payroll Taxes..........................	Salaries (including both direct and other allocated salaries)
Worker's Compensation Insurance	Salaries (including both direct and other allocated salaries)
Fire Insurance	Cost of Equipment and Inventory
Delivery Expense	Sales
Miscellaneous Expenses (unassigned).....	Number of Employees

27. *Allocating service department costs.* The Schneider Spaghetti Company has two production departments, Tubing and Packing, and two service departments, Quality Control and Maintenance. In June, the Quality Control department provided 2,000 hours of service—995 hours to Tubing, 255 hours to Maintenance, and 750 hours to Packing. In the same month, Maintenance provided 2,700 hours to Tubing, 1,800 hours to Packing, and 500 hours to Quality Control. Quality Control incurred costs of $50,000, and Maintenance incurred costs of $105,000.

Use the step method to allocate service department costs sequentially. Start with Maintenance and then allocate Quality Control. Check your solution by making certain that the firm finally allocates $155,000 to the production departments.

28. *Allocating service department costs.* The Horton Hose Factory engages in the manufacture and sale of garden hoses. The firm has two production departments, Slicing and Nozzles. The Personnel and Administration departments serve these departments. In January, the Slicing department consumed 750 hours from Personnel and 300 hours from Administration. Nozzles consumed 450 hours from Personnel and 300 hours from Administration. In addition, Personnel supplied Administration with 150 hours and consumed 200 hours from Administration. Costs for the Personnel department were $60,000 and for Administration were $50,000.

Allocate all service department costs using the step procedure, starting with Personnel, then Administration. Round answers to the nearest dollar and decimals to three places.

29. *Joint cost allocations.* The Roving Eye Cosmetics Company buys bulk flowers and processes them into perfumes. Seduction, their highest-grade perfume, and a residue that the firm processes into a medium-grade perfume called Romance, come from a certain mix of petals. In July, the company used 25,000 pounds of petals. Costs involved in Process A, reducing the petals to Seduction and the residue, follow:

- $200,000 direct materials
- $110,000 direct labor
- $90,000 overhead and other costs.

The additional costs of producing Romance in Process B follow:

- $22,000 direct materials
- $50,000 direct labor
- $40,000 overhead and other costs.

At the end of the month, total completed production equaled 5,000 ounces of Seduction and 28,000 ounces of Romance. In addition, 2,500 ounces of Seduction and 12,500 ounces of Romance had just completed Process A (a continuous process). The firm has no beginning inventory on July 1 and no uncompleted units in Process B.

Packaging costs incurred for each product as completed were $40,000 for Seduction and $161,000 for Romance. Seduction sells for $90 an ounce; Romance sells for $31.50 per ounce.

a. Allocate joint costs using the approximate net realizable value method.

b. Allocate the joint costs using the physical units method. Round all percentages to one decimal place.

c. Will using the physical units method present any problems in this case?

d. Assume that Roving Eye can sell the squeezed petals from Process A to greenhouses for use as fertilizer. In July, the firm had 12,000 pounds of squeezed petals left over that sold for $.75 per pound. The squeezed petals are a by-product of Process A. With this new information, answer parts **a** and **b**.

30. *Joint cost allocations.* The Tru-Life Mannequin Company manufactures female, male, and infant mannequins. The process consists of melting, molding, shaping, sanding, assembling, and painting the mannequins and producing wigs and painted hair.

In October, Tru-Life Mannequin incurred the following types of costs and assigned them to the classes of products as follows:

- Unassigned process costs (other than related to wigs and painted hair): 250,000 pounds of plaster, costing $.10 per pound; labor costs, $90,000; other costs, $35,000.

- Assigned processing costs (other than related to wigs and painted hair): female, $8 each; male, $9 each; infant, $2 each.

- Wigs for female mannequins: material, $1 each; labor, $10,000; overhead, $7,500.

- Painted hair for male and infant mannequins: material, males, $.15 each; material, infants, $.05 each; labor, $18,000; other, $12,000.

Production for October (with no beginning or ending work-in-process inventories) amounted to 50,000 female mannequins, 60,000 male mannequins, and 30,000 infant mannequins. Female mannequins sell for $15 each, male mannequins for $11 each, and infant mannequins for $8 each.

a. Allocate joint costs using the approximate net realizable value method.
b. Allocate joint costs using the physical units method.

31. *Sell or process further.* A joint production process results in the splitoff of three products, A, B, and C. Joint costs incurred total $100,000. At splitoff, 10,000 units of Product A, 10,000 units of Product B, and 20,000 units of Product C emerge.

a. The firm can sell the units at splitoff at the following prices: Product A. $3 each; Product B, $6 each; Product C, $4.50 each. Using the net realizable value method, calculate the net income of each product if the firm sells it at splitoff.

b. By incurring additional processing costs of $1 per unit, the firm can sell Product A for $5 a unit. By incurring additional processing costs of $3 a unit, it can sell Product C for $8 a unit. Using the approximate net realizable value at splitoff method, calculate the net income of each product if additional processing takes place.

c. Which products should the firm sell at splitoff and which products should it process further? Explain.

32. *Joint cost allocations* (adapted from CPA exam). Harrison Corporation produces three products, Alpha, Beta, and Gamma. Alpha and Gamma are main products, whereas Beta is a by-product of Alpha. Information on the past month's production processes follows:

(1) Department I processes 110,000 units of raw material Rho at a total cost of $120,000. After processing, Department I transfers 60 percent of the units to Department II and 40 percent of the units (now unprocessed Gamma) to Department III.

(2) Department II processes the materials received from Department I at a total additional cost of $38,000. Seventy percent of the units become Alpha and Department II transfers them to Department IV. The remaining 30 percent emerge as Beta and the firm sells them at $2.10 per unit. The selling costs for the Beta amount to $8,100.

(3) Department III processes Gamma at an additional cost of $165,000. A normal loss of units of Gamma occurs in this department. The loss equals 10 percent of the units of good output. The firm sells the remaining good output for $12 per unit.

(4) Department IV processes Alpha at an additional cost of $23,660. After this processing, the firm sells Alpha for $5 per unit.

Prepare a schedule showing the allocation of the $120,000 joint cost between Alpha and Gamma using the net realizable value approach. Credit revenue from sales of by-products to the manufacturing costs of the related main product.

33. *Allocation for economic decisions and motivation* (adapted from CMA exam). Bonn Company recently reorganized its computer and data processing system.

Bonn has replaced the individual installations located within the accounting departments at its plants and subsidiaries with a single data processing department at corporate headquarters responsible for the operations of a newly acquired large-scale computer system. The new department has been operating for 2 years and regularly producing reliable and timely data for the past 12 months.

Because the department has focused its activities on converting applications to the new system and producing reports for the plant and subsidiary managements, it has devoted little attention to the costs of the department. Now that the department's activities are operating relatively smoothly, company management has requested that the departmental manager recommend a cost accumulation system to facilitate cost control and the development of suitable rates to charge users for service.

For the past 2 years, the department has recorded costs in one account. The department has then allocated the costs to user departments on the basis of computer time used. The following schedule reports the costs and charging rate for Year 4.

Data Processing Department
Costs for the Year Ended December 31, Year 4

(1) Salaries and Benefits	$ 622,600
(2) Supplies	40,000
(3) Equipment Maintenance Contract	15,000
(4) Insurance	25,000
(5) Heat and Air Conditioning	36,000
(6) Electricity	50,000
(7) Equipment and Furniture Depreciation	285,400
(8) Building Improvements Depreciation	10,000
(9) Building Occupancy and Security	39,300
(10) Corporate Administrative Charges	52,700
Total Costs	$1,176,000
Computer Hours for User Processing[a]	2,750
Hourly Rate ($1,176,000/2,750)	$428

[a]Use of available computer hours:

Testing and Debugging Programs	250
Setup of Jobs	500
Processing Jobs	2,750
Downtime for Maintenance	750
Idle Time	742
	4,992

The department manager recommends that the five activity centers within the department accumulate the department costs. The five activity centers are systems analysis, programming, data preparation, computer operations (processing), and administration. She then suggests that the firm allocate the costs of the administration activity to the other four activity centers before developing a separate rate for charging users for each of the first four activities.

After reviewing the details of the accounts, the manager made the following observations regarding the charges to the several subsidiary accounts within the department:

(1) Salaries and benefits—records the salary and benefit costs of all employees in the department.

(2) Supplies—records punch-card costs, paper costs for printers, and a small amount for other miscellaneous costs.

(3) Equipment maintenance contracts—records charges for maintenance contracts; maintenance contracts cover all equipment.

(4) Insurance—records cost of insurance covering the equipment and the furniture.

(5) Heat and air conditioning—records a charge from the corporate heating and air conditioning department estimated to be the incremental costs to meet the special needs of the computer department.

(6) Electricity—records the charge for electricity based on a separate meter within the department.

(7) Equipment and furniture depreciation—records the depreciation charges for all equipment and furniture owned within the department.

(8) Building improvements—records the amortization charges for the building changes required to provide proper environmental control and electrical service for the computer equipment.

(9) Building occupancy and security—records the computer department's share of the depreciation, maintenance, heat, and security costs of the building; the firm allocates these costs to the department on the basis of square feet occupied.

(10) Corporate administrative charges—records the computer department's share of the corporate administrative costs. The firm allocates them to the department on the basis of number of employees in the department.

a. For each of the ten cost items, state whether or not the firm should distribute it to the five activity centers; and for each cost item that the firm should distribute, recommend the basis on which it should distribute it. Justify your conclusion in each case.

b. Assume that the costs of the computer operations (processing) activity will be charged to the user departments on the basis of computer hours. Using the analysis of computer utilization shown as a footnote to the department cost schedule presented in the problem, determine the total number of hours that should be employed to determine the charging rate for computer operations (processing). Justify your answer.

34. *Cost allocation and decision making* (adapted from CMA exam). The promotion department of the Doxolby Company is responsible for the design and development of all promotional materials for the corporation. This responsibility includes all promotional campaigns and related literature, pamphlets, and brochures. Top management is reviewing the effectiveness of the promotion department to ascertain if an outside promotion agency could manage its activities better and more economically. As a part of this review, top management has asked the promotion department to summarize its costs for the most recent year. The promotion department supplied the following cost summary:

Promotion Department Costs for the Year	
Direct Department Costs	$257,500
Charges from Other Departments	44,700
Allocated Share of General Administrative Overhead	22,250
Total Costs	$324,450

The direct department costs consist of those costs that management can trace directly to the activities of the promotion department, such as staff and clerical salaries, including related employee benefits, supplies, and so on. The charges from other departments represent the costs of services that Doxolby's other departments provide at the request of the promotion department. The company has developed a charging system for such interdepartmental uses of services. For instance, the in-house printing department charges the promotion department for the promotional literature printed. "Charges from Other Departments" includes all services other departments of Doxolby provide to the promotion department. General administrative overhead comprises such costs as top management salaries and benefits, depreciation, heat, insurance, property taxes, and so on. Doxolby allocates these costs to all departments in proportion to the number of employees in each department.

Discuss the usefulness of the cost figures presented here for Doxolby Company's promotion department as a basis for a comparison with a bid from an outside agency to provide the same type of services as Doxolby's own promotion department.

35. *Allocating service department costs* (adapted from CPA exam). The Parker Manufacturing Company has three service departments (general factory administration, factory maintenance, and factory cafeteria) and two production departments (fabrication and assembly). A summary of costs and other data for each department prior to allocation of service department costs for the year ended June 30, Year 1, follow:

	General Factory Administration	Factory Maintenance	Factory Cafeteria	Fabrication	Assembly
Direct Material Costs	0	$65,000	$91,000	$3,130,000	$ 950,000
Direct Labor Costs	$90,000	82,100	87,000	1,950,000	2,050,000
Manufacturing Overhead Costs . . .	70,000	56,100	62,000	1,650,000	1,850,000
Direct Labor Hours	31,000	27,000	42,000	562,500	437,500
Number of Employees	12	8	20	280	200
Square Footage Occupied	1,750	2,000	4,800	88,000	72,000

Parker allocates the costs of the general factory administration department, factory maintenance department, and factory cafeteria on the basis of direct labor hours, square footage occupied, and number of employees, respectively. Round all final calculations to the nearest dollar.

a. Assuming that Parker elects to distribute service department costs directly to production departments without interservice department cost allocation, what amount of factory maintenance department costs would Parker allocate to the fabrication department?

b. Assuming the same method of allocation as in part **a,** what amount of general factory administration department costs would Parker allocate to the assembly department?

c. Assuming that Parker elects to distribute service department costs to other service departments (starting with the service department with the greatest total costs) as well as the production departments, what amounts of factory cafeteria department costs would Parker allocate to the factory maintenance department? (Note: Once the firm has allocated a service department's costs, no subsequent service department costs are allocated back to it.)

d. Assuming the same method of allocation as in part **c,** what amount of factory maintenance department costs would Parker allocate to the factory cafeteria?

36. *Allocating service department costs using simultaneous solution of equations* (adapted from CMA exam). (Note: You do not need matrix algebra for this problem. You may set up an algebraic equation for the costs of each of the two service departments and solve by substitution. See the solution to Problem 4 for Self-Study for an example.)

Barrylou Corporation is developing departmental overhead rates based on direct labor hours for its two production departments, molding and assembly. The molding department employs 20 people, and the assembly department employs 80 people. Each person in these two departments works 2,000 hours per year. Barrylou budgeted $200,000 for the production-related overhead costs for the molding department and $320,000 for the assembly department costs. Two service departments, repair and power, directly support the two production departments and the firm has budgeted $48,000 and $250,000, respectively, for costs. The firm cannot set the production department's overhead rates until it properly allocates the service department's costs. The following schedule reflects the use of the repair department's and power department's output by the various departments.

	Department			
	Repair	**Power**	**Molding**	**Assembly**
Repair Hours....................	0	1,000	1,000	8,000
Kilowatt-Hours...................	240,000	0	840,000	120,000

a. Calculate the overhead rates per direct labor hour for the molding department and the assembly department, allocating service department costs directly to production departments, without interservice department cost allocation.

b. Calculate the overhead rates per direct labor hour for the molding department and the assembly department, using the simultaneous solution method to charge service department costs to each other and to the production department.

37. *Using matrix algebra for cost allocations* (appendix). Refer to the problem data for Schneider Spaghetti Company, Problem 27.

a. Following the method outlined in Appendix 5.1, set up the full matrices of services output, **S,** and usage, **P,** based on the data given in Problem 27.

b. Express algebraically the fraction of the Maintenance department's output allocable to Tubing. Use the notation described in Appendix 5.1 for the Berdan Products example.

c. Express algebraically the fraction of the Quality Control department's output allocable to Packing. Use the notation described in Appendix 5.1 for the Berdan Products example.

d. Use matrices **S** and **P** to solve for matrix **A,** the allocation matrix.

e. Use the results of matrix **A** to allocate the service department costs.

38. *Using matrix algebra for cost allocation* (appendix). Refer to the problem data for Horton Hose Factory, Problem 28.

a. Set up matrices **S** and **P** as described in Appendix 5.1. Round entries to two decimal places but make sure that all columns sum to one by allocating any rounding error.

b. Using the notation explained in Appendix 5.1 for the Berdan Products example, express algebraically the following:

(1) Fraction of Administrative output allocable to Slicing.

(2) Fraction of Personnel output allocable to Nozzles; to Slicing.

Use matrices **S** and **P** to solve for matrix **A,** the allocation matrix.

c. Use the results of matrix **A** to allocate the service department costs.

39. *Cost allocations with matrices given* (appendix). The Twin City Manufacturing Company derived the following allocation matrices (**A**) for April, May, and June:

TWIN CITY MANUFACTURING COMPANY
Allocation Matrices

	Services Performed By	
	Repairs (R)	**Administration (A)**
Services Used in April By		
Production Departments		
Cleaning (C)	.435	.343
Mixing (M)	.215	.358
Pouring (P)	.350	.299
	1.000	1.000
Costs to Be Allocated.......................	$50,000	$60,000

continued

continued from page 222

| | Services Performed By | |
	Repairs (R)	Administration (A)
Services Used in May By		
Production Departments		
Cleaning (C)	.40	.30
Mixing (M)	.40	.20
Pouring (P)	.20	.50
	1.00	1.00
Costs to Be Allocated......................	$52,000	$58,000

| | Services Performed By | |
	Repairs (R)	Administration (A)
Services Used in June By		
Production Departments		
Cleaning (C)	.45	.35
Mixing (M)	.25	.40
Pouring (P)	.30	.25
	1.00	1.00
Costs to Be Allocated......................	$55,000	$64,000

Use the allocation matrices to calculate how much Twin City should charge each production department for service costs for

a. April.
b. May.
c. June.

Integrative Problems and Cases

40. *Relating allocation methods to organizational characteristics for a retailer* (adapted from CMA exam). Columbia Company is a regional office supply chain with 26 independent stores. The firm holds each store responsible for its own credit and collections. The firm assigns the assistant manager in each store the responsibility for credit activities, including the collection of delinquent accounts, because the stores do not need a full-time employee assigned to credit activities. The company has experienced a sharp rise in uncollectibles the last 2 years. Corporate management has decided to establish a collections department in the home office that takes over the collection function companywide. The home office of Columbia Company will hire the necessary full-time personnel. The firm will base the size of this department on the historical credit activity of all the stores.

Top management discussed the new centralized collections department at a recent management meeting. Management has had difficulty deciding on a method to assign the costs of the new department to the stores because this type of home office service is unusual. Top management is reviewing alternative methods.

The controller favored using a predetermined rate for charging the costs to the stores. The firm would base the predetermined rate on budgeted costs. The vice president for sales preferred an actual cost charging system.

In addition, management also discussed the basis for the collection charges to the stores. The controller identified the four following measures of services (allocation bases) that the firm could use:

(1) Total dollar sales.

(2) Average number of past-due accounts.

(3) Number of uncollectible accounts written off.

(4) One twenty-sixth of the cost to each of the stores.

The executive vice president stated that he would like the accounting department to prepare a detailed analysis of the two charging methods and the four service measures (allocation bases).

a.   Evaluate the two methods identified—predetermined rate versus actual cost—that the firm could use to charge the individual stores the costs of Columbia Company's new collections department in terms of

   (1)   Practicality of application and ease of use.

   (2)   Cost control.

   Also indicate whether a centralized or decentralized organization structure would be more conducive for each charging method.

b.   For each of the four measures of services (allocation bases) the controller of Columbia Company identified:

   (1)   Discuss whether using the service measure (allocation base) is appropriate in this situation.

   (2)   Identify the behavioral problems, if any, that could arise as a consequence of adopting the service measure (allocation base).

41.   *Allocation of fixed manufacturing overhead and decision making* (adapted from CMA exam). Jenco, Inc., manufactures a combination fertilizer-weed killer under the name Fertikil. Jenco produces only this product at the present time. Jenco sells Fertikil nationwide through normal marketing channels to retail nurseries and garden stores.

Taylor Nursery plans to sell a similar fertilizer-weed killer compound through its regional nursery chain under its own private label. Taylor has asked Jenco to submit a bid for a 25,000-pound order of the private-brand compound. Although the chemical composition of the Taylor compound differs from that of Fertikil, the manufacturing process is very similar.

Jenco would produce the Taylor compound in 1,000-pound lots. Each lot would require 60 direct labor hours and the following chemicals:

Chemicals	Quantity in Pounds
CW-3	400
JX-6	300
MZ-8	200
BE-7	100

Jenco already uses the first three chemicals (CW-3, JX-6, MZ-8) in the production of Fertikil. Jenco formerly used BE-7 in a compound that it discontinued. Jenco did not sell or discard this chemical because it does not deteriorate and Jenco had adequate storage facilities. Jenco could sell BE-7 at the prevailing market price but would incur $.10 per pound for selling and handling expenses.

Jenco also has on hand a chemical called CN-5, which it manufactured for use in another product that Jenco no longer produces. Jenco can substitute CN-5, which it cannot use in Fertikil, for CW-3 on a one-for-one basis without affecting the quality of the Taylor compound. The quantity of CN-5 in inventory has a salvage value of $500.

Inventory and cost data for the chemicals that Jenco can use to produce the Taylor compound follow:

Raw Material	Pounds in Inventory	Actual Price per Pound When Purchased	Current Market Price per Pound
CW-3	22,000	$ .80	$ .90
JX-6	5,000	.55	.60
MZ-8	8,000	1.40	1.60
BE-7	4,000	.60	.65
CN-5	5,500	.75	(none)

The current direct labor rate is $7.00 per hour. Jenco establishes the manufacturing overhead rate at the beginning of the year and applies it consistently throughout the year, using direct labor hours (DLH) as the base. Jenco's predetermined overhead rate for the current year, based on a two-shift capacity of 400,000 total DLH with no overtime follows:

Variable Manufacturing Overhead	$2.25 per DLH
Fixed Manufacturing Overhead	3.75 per DLH
Combined Rate	$6.00 per DLH

Jenco's production manager reports that the present equipment and facilities can adequately manufacture the Taylor compound. However, Jenco is within 800 hours of its two-shift capacity this month before it must schedule overtime. If necessary, Jenco could produce the Taylor compound on regular time by shifting a portion of Fertikil production to overtime. Jenco's rate for overtime hours is one-and-one-half times the regular pay rate, or $10.50 per hour. The manufacturing overhead rate does not allow for any overtime premium.

Jenco's standard markup policy for new products is 25 percent of full manufacturing cost.

a. Assume that Jenco, Inc., has decided to submit a bid for a 25,000-pound order of Taylor's new compound. Jenco must deliver the order by the end of the current month. Taylor has indicated that this is a one-time order that it will not repeat.

Calculate the lowest price that Jenco should bid for the order and not reduce its operating profit.

b. Without prejudice to your answer to part **a,** assume that Taylor Nursery plans to place regular orders for 25,000-pounds lots of the new compound during the coming year. Jenco expects the demand for Fertikil to remain strong again in the coming year. Therefore, the recurring orders from Taylor will put Jenco over its two-shift capacity. However, Jenco can schedule production so that it can complete 60 percent of each Taylor order during regular hours, or shift Fertikil production temporarily to overtime so that it could produce the Taylor orders on regular time. Jenco's production manager has estimated that the prices of all chemicals will stabilize at the current market rates for the coming year and expects that all other manufacturing costs to maintain the same rates or amounts.

Calculate the price that Jenco, Inc., should quote Taylor Nursery for each 25,000-pound lot of the new compound, assuming that Taylor will make recurring orders during the coming year.

42. *Differential cost analysis with joint products and by-products* (contributed by M. L. Marais). KLEEN Chemical Company conducts comprehensive annual profit planning to estimate unit costs, to calculate pricing, and to plan production. One product group that KLEEN analyzes separately each year involves two joint products and two by-products.

The two joint products, specialty chemicals X and Y, emerge at the end of processing in Department A. KLEEN can sell both chemicals at this splitoff point: X for $25 per kilogram (kg) and Y for $20 per kg. By-product MUTIN-X also emerges at the splitoff point in Department A and KLEEN can sell it without further processing for $1.50 per kg.

In the past, KLEEN has sold chemical Y without further processing, but has transferred X to Department B for additional processing into a refined rodent-control chemical called RAT-BUST. Department B adds no additional raw materials. KLEEN sells RAT-BUST for $30 per kg. The additional processing in Department B creates the by-product MUTIN-Y and KLEEN sells it for $3 per kg.

Exhibit 5.15 presents a portion of the Year 2 budget established in September, Year 1. Shortly after the company compiled this information, it learned that another company was planning to introduce a chemical that would compete with RAT-BUST. The marketing department has estimated that for KLEEN to sell RAT-BUST in present quantities, it would have to permanently reduce prices to $27 per kg.

The introduction of this new chemical will not affect the market for chemical X. Consequently, the quantities of X that KLEEN usually processed into RAT-BUST can sell at the regular price of $25 per kg. Marketing estimates costs of $105,000 to market X. If KLEEN terminates the processing, it will have to dismantle Department B and will eliminate all costs except $115,000 of the company's administrative costs allocated to Department B.

Exhibit 5.15

KLEEN CHEMICALS Year 2 Profit Plan		

	Production and Sales Schedule (kilograms)	
	Chemical Y	Chemical X or RAT-BUST
Estimated Sales and Production Units	60,000	40,000
By-Product Output:		
MUTIN-X		20,000
MUTIN-Y	10,000	

Budgeted Production Costs	Department A	Department B
Raw Materials	$1,300,000	$ —
Costs Transferred from Department A	(577,300)	577,300
Direct Labor......................................	195,000	75,000
Variable Overhead	182,000	70,000
Fixed Overhead (includes corporate administrative costs allocated to departments)	250,000	190,000
	$1,349,700	$912,300

	Chemical Y	RAT-BUST
Budgeted Marketing Costs	$196,000	$105,000

a. What alternative actions can KLEEN Chemical's executives take? How will profits differ among these alternatives? What do you recommend?

b. During discussion of the possibility of dropping RAT-BUST, one person noted that the gross margin for chemical X would be more than 40 percent, whereas the gross margin for chemical Y would be negative. Firms normally mark up by 20 percent products sold in the market with X. For the Y portion of the line, firms normally mark up 25 percent. The person argued that the company's unit costs must be incorrect, because the margins differ from the typical rates. Briefly explain why the margins for KLEEN Chemical's products differ from the normal rates.

43. *Issues in cost allocations: what price progress?*[6] In discussing the costs incident to various types of operations, someone made an analogy of a restaurant that adds a rack of peanuts to the counter, intending to pick up a little additional profit in the usual course of business. Others have attacked this analogy as an oversimplification. However, you will see the accuracy of the analogy when you consider the actual problem the restaurateur (Joe) faces as revealed by his accountant–efficiency expert.

---

[6]This piece appeared as a reprint in a publication by Coopers and Lybrand.

Expert: Joe, you said you put in these peanuts because some people ask for them, but do you realize what this rack of peanuts is *costing* you?

Joe: It's not going to cost! It's going to be a profit. Sure, I had to pay $125 for a fancy rack to hold the bags, but the peanuts cost 30¢ a bag and I sell 'em for 50¢. Suppose I sell 50 bags a week to start. It'll take 12½ weeks to cover the cost of the rack. After that I have a clear profit of 20¢ a bag. The more I sell, the more I make.

Expert: That is an antiquated and completely unrealistic approach, Joe. Fortunately, modern accounting procedures permit a more accurate picture that reveals the complexities involved.

Joe: Huh?

Expert: To be precise, you must integrate those peanuts into your entire operation and allocate to them their appropriate share of business overhead. They must share a proportionate part of your expenditures for rent, heat, light, equipment depreciation, decorating, salaries for your waitresses, cook, . . .

Joe: The *cook?* What's he got to do with the peanuts? He doesn't even know I have them.

Expert: Look, Joe, the cook is in the kitchen, the kitchen prepares the food, the food is what brings people in here, and the people ask to buy peanuts. *That's* why you must charge a portion of the cook's wages, as well as a part of your own salary, to peanut sales. This sheet contains a carefully calculated cost analysis that indicates the peanut operation should pay exactly $6,320 per year toward these general overhead costs.

Joe: The peanuts? $6,320 a year for overhead? Nuts?

Expert: It's really a little more than that. You also spend money each week to have the windows washed, to have the place swept out in the mornings, keep soap in the washroom, and provide free Cokes to the police. That raises the total to $6,565 per year.

Joe: (Thoughtfully) But the peanut salesperson said I'd make money—put 'em on the end of the counter, he said—and get 20¢ a bag profit . . .

Expert: (With a sniff) He's not an accountant. Do you actually know what the portion of the counter that the peanut rack occupies is worth to you?

Joe: Nothing. No stool there—just a dead spot at the end.

Expert: The modern cost picture permits no dead spots. Your counter contains 60 square feet and your counter business grosses $75,000 a year. Consequently, the square foot of space the peanut rack occupies is worth $1,250 per year. Since you have taken that area away from general counter use, you must charge the value of the space to the occupant.

Joe: You mean I have to add *$1,250 a year more to the peanuts?*

Expert: Right. That raises their share of the general operating costs to a grand total of $7,815 per year. Now then, if you sell 50 bags of peanuts per week, these allocated costs will amount to $3 per bag.

Joe: WHAT?

Expert: Obviously, you must add to that your purchase price of 30¢ per bag, which brings the total to $3.30. So you see, by selling peanuts at 50¢ per bag you are losing $2.80 on every sale.

Joe: Something's crazy!

Expert: Not at all! Here are the *figures*. They *prove* your peanut operation cannot stand on its own feet.

Joe: (Brightening) Suppose I sell *lots* of peanuts—thousand bags a week instead of fifty?

Expert: (Tolerantly) Joe, you don't understand the problem. If the volume of peanut sales increases, your operating costs will go up—you'll have to handle more bags, with more time, more depreciation, more everything. The basic principle of accounting is firm on that subject: *"The bigger the operation, the more general overhead costs you must allocate."* No, increasing the volume of sales won't help.

Joe: Okay. You're so smart, *you* tell *me* what I have to do!

Expert: (Condescendingly) Well—you could first reduce operating expenses.

Joe: How?

Expert: Move to a building with cheaper rent. Cut salaries. Wash the windows bi-weekly. Sweep the floors only on Thursday. Remove the soap from the washrooms. Decrease the square-foot value of your counter. For example, if you can cut your expenses 50 percent, that will reduce the amount allocated to peanuts from $7,815 down to $3,907.50 per year, reducing the cost to $1.80 per bag.

Joe: (Slowly) That's better?

Expert: Much, much better. However, even then you would lose $1.30 per bag if you charge only 50¢. Therefore, you must also raise your selling price. If you want a net profit of 20¢ per bag you would have to charge $2.

Joe: (Flabbergasted) You mean even after I cut operating costs 50 percent I still have to charge $2 for a 50¢ bag of peanuts? Nobody's that nuts about nuts! Who'd buy them?

Expert: That's a secondary consideration. The point is, at $2 you'd be selling at a price based on a true and proper evaluation of your then reduced costs.

Joe: (Eagerly) Look! I have a better idea. Why don't I just throw the nuts out—put them in a trash can?

Expert: Can you afford it?

Joe: Sure. All I have is about 50 bags of peanuts—cost about fifteen bucks—so I lose $125 on the rack, but I'm out of this nutsy business and no more grief.

Expert: (Shaking head) Joe, it isn't quite that simple. You are *in* the peanut business! The minute you throw those peanuts out you are adding $6,565 of annual overhead to the *rest* of your operation. Joe—be realistic—*can you afford to do that?*

Joe: (Completely crushed) It's unbelievable! Last week I was making money. Now I'm in trouble—just because I think peanuts on a counter are going to bring me some extra profit—just because I believe 50 bags of peanuts a week is easy.

Expert: (With raised eyebrow) That is the object of modern cost studies, Joe—to dispel those false illusions.

What should Joe do?

44. *Cost-based reimbursement for hospitals.*[7] The annual costs of hospital care under the Medicare program amount to $20 billion per year. In the Medicare legislation, Congress mandated that Medicare would limit reimbursement to hospitals to the costs of treating Medicare patients. Ideally, neither the patients nor the hospitals would bear the costs of the Medicare patients nor would the government bear costs of nonmedicare patients. Given the large sums involved, cost reimbursement specialists, computer programs, publications, and other products and services have arisen to provide hospital administrators with the assistance needed to obtain an appropriate reimbursement for medicare patient services.

Accountants would divide hospital departments into two categories, revenue-producing departments and nonrevenue-producing departments. Accountants use this classification because the traditional accounting concepts associated with service department cost allocation, although appropriate to this context, lead to confusion in terminology. This confusion results because most people consider all of the hospital's departments to render services.

Accountants charge costs of revenue-producing departments to Medicare and nonmedicare patients on the basis of actual usage of the departments. Accountants can apportion these costs relatively simply. Accountants have more difficulty apportioning the costs of nonrevenue-producing departments. The approach to finding the appropriate distribution of these costs begins with the establishment of a reasonable basis for allocating nonrevenue-producing department costs to revenue-producing departments. Accountants must ascertain statistical measures of the relationships between departments. Medicare regulations have established the cost allocation bases listed in Exhibit 5.16 as acceptable for cost reimbursement purposes. Accountants must use the regulated order of allocation for medicare reimbursement even though the general rule may call for another order.

A hospital may then use the step method to allocate costs. If the hospital uses the step method, it allocates costs to the departments in the same order as listed in Exhibit 5.14. Thus it allocates depreciation of buildings before depreciation of movable equipment. It must establish cost centers for each of these nonrevenue-producing costs that are relevant to a particular hospital's operations.

---

[7]Copyright © 1982 by CIPT, Inc.

Exhibit 5.16

Bases for Allocating Nonrevenue Department Costs to Revenue-Producing Departments

Nonrevenue Cost Center	Basis for Allocation
Depreciation—Buildings	Square Feet in Each Department
Depreciation—Movable Equipment	Dollar Value of Equipment in Each Department
Employee Health and Welfare	Gross Salaries in Each Department
Administrative and General	Accumulated Costs by Department
Maintenance and Repairs	Square Feet in Each Department
Operation of Plant	Square Feet in Each Department
Laundry and Linen Service	Pounds Used in Each Department
Housekeeping	Hours of Service to Each Department
Dietary	Meals Served in Each Department
Maintenance of Personnel	Number of Departmental Employees Housed
Nursing Administration	Hours of Supervision in Each Department
Central Supply	Costs of Requisitions Processed
Pharmacy	Costs of Drug Orders Processed
Medical Records	Hours Worked for Each Department
Social Service	Hours Worked for Each Department
Nursing School	Assigned Time by Department
Intern/Resident Service	Assigned Time by Department

In the past year, the hospital reported the following departmental costs:

Nonrevenue-Producing:	
Laundry and Linen	$ 250,000
Depreciation—Buildings	830,000
Employee Health and Welfare	375,000
Maintenance of Personnel	210,000
Central Supply	745,000
Revenue-Producing:	
Operating Room	$1,450,000
Radiology	160,000
Laboratory	125,000
Patient Rooms	2,800,000

Percentage usage of services by one department from another department were as follows:

From	Laundry and Linen	Depreci-ation—Buildings	Employee Health and Welfare	Maintenance of Personnel	Central Supply
Laundry and Linen		.05	.10	0	0
Depreciation—Buildings	.10		0	.10	0
Employee Health and Welfare	.15	0		.05	.03
Maintenance of Personnel	0	0	0		.12
Central Supply	.10	0	0	.08	

continued

continued from page 231

	Operating Rooms	Radiology	Laboratory	Patient Rooms
Laundry and Linen............	.30	.10	.05	.40
Depreciation—Buildings	.05	.02	.02	.71
Employee Health and Welfare..	.25	.05	.04	.43
Maintenance of Personnel.....	.36	.10	.08	.34
Central Supply	.09	.04	.03	.66

The proportional usage of revenue-producing department services by medicare and other patients was as follows:

	Medicare	Other
Operating Rooms..	25%	75%
Radiology..	20	80
Laboratory...	28	72
Patient Rooms	36	64

Ascertain the amount of the reimbursement claim for medicare services using the step method of allocation.

Suggested Solutions to Even-Numbered Exercises

14. *Allocating overhead*

	Department			
	No. 1	No. 2	Maintenance	General Plant
Charged Directly to Department:				
Indirect Labor	$28,000	$14,000	$22,500	$20,000
Indirect Material	9,000	7,000	900	8,000
Miscellaneous	3,000	5,000	1,600	5,000
	$40,000	$26,000	$25,000	$33,000
Allocations:				
General Plant	16,500	9,900	6,600	(33,000)
Maintenance[a]	11,060	20,540	(31,600)	
Total Overhead[b]	$67,560	$56,440	0	0
Direct Labor Cost.........	$50,000	$30,000		
Overhead Allocation Rate	135.12%	188.13%		

[a]Total costs to be allocated: $25,000 + $6,600 = $31,600. Allocate on the basis of maintenance hours.

[b]$67,560 + $56,440 = $40,000 + $26,000 + $25,000 + $33,000.

16. *Allocating service department costs using the step method*

	General Factory Administration	Maintenance	Cutting	Assembly
Service Department Costs	$1,200	$2,400	NA	NA
Maintenance Allocation	480(⅕)	(2,400)	$480(⅕)	$1,400(⅗)
General Factory Administration Allocation	(1,680)		336(⅕)	1,344(⅘)
Total Costs Allocated			$816	$2,784

18. *Allocating service department costs directly to operating departments*

	To	
From	P1	P2
S1	$10,000[a]	$10,000[a]
S2	18,750[b]	11,250[b]
	$28,750	$21,250

[a]$10,000 = .10 \times \dfrac{\$20,000}{.10 + .10}$. (Eighty percent of S1's costs used by S2 are ignored.)

[b]$18,750 = .50 \times \dfrac{\$30,000}{.50 + .30}$.

$11,250 = .30 \times \dfrac{\$30,000}{.50 + .30}$.

20. *Joint cost allocations—net realizable value method.* Total joint costs are $205,000 (based on the $45,000 materials plus $160,000 conversion). The firm allocates these costs as follows:

$$\text{To Output D:} \quad \frac{\$273,000}{\$455,000} \times \$205,000 = \underline{\underline{\$123,000}}.$$

$$\text{To Output T:} \quad \frac{\$455,000 - \$273,000}{\$455,000} \times \$205,000 = \underline{\underline{\$82,000}}.$$

22. *Joint cost allocations using the physical quantities method—by-products.* Deduct the net realizable value of M ($1,200) from the total processing costs ($120,000) to obtain the net processing costs to be allocated ($118,800). Compute the allocation as follows:

$$\text{To HN:} \quad \frac{100,000 \text{ Units}}{100,000 \text{ Units} + 200,000 \text{ Units}} \times \$118,800 = \underline{\underline{\$39,600}}.$$

$$\text{To HB:} \quad \frac{200,000 \text{ Units}}{100,000 \text{ Units} + 200,000 \text{ Units}} \times \$118,800 = \underline{\underline{\$79,200}}.$$

24. *Joint costing—finding missing values.* Since the firm allocates joint costs on the basis of relative sales value, we know that the fraction

$$\frac{\text{Joint Cost}}{\text{Sales Value at Splitoff}}$$

will be the same for all three products and for the total.

For total costs, the ratio is

$$\frac{\$120,000}{\$200,000} = .6.$$

For Product A, since we know the allocated costs, we can express the relation between allocated costs and sales value at splitoff as

$$.6X = \$72,000$$

$$X = \frac{\$72,000}{.6}$$

$$= \underline{\$120,000}   \quad (\text{Answer } \mathbf{c}).$$

For Product C, we do not know allocated joint costs. Since the costs equal .6 of the net realizable value at splitoff, the costs we allocate to C are

$$X = \$30,000 \times .6$$

$$= \underline{\$18,000} \ (\text{Answer } \mathbf{b}).$$

Having found the costs and net realizable values for A and C, we subtract them from the total to find the missing values of Product B.

Total Net Realizable Value.........................	$200,000	
Less:		
Value of A	(120,000)	
Value of C	(30,000)	
Value of B	$ 50,000	(Answer **d**).

Since allocated joint costs are .6 of relative sales value,

$$\$50,000 \times .6 = \underline{\$30,000}   \quad (\text{Answer } \mathbf{a}).$$

Proof:

$$\text{Total Allocated Costs} = \$120,000$$

$$\$72,000 + \$30,000 + \$18,000 = \$120,000.$$

... PART THREE ...

Managerial Decision Making

...

At the beginning of this book, we described two major uses of managerial accounting information: managerial decision making and managerial planning, control, and internal performance evaluation. This part of the book, Chapters 6 through 10, deals with the first use, *managerial decision making*. This use of accounting information emphasizes financial analysis of alternative courses of action to answer questions such as the following:

- What costs will we save if we reduce production volume?
- What is the minimum price that we should charge for our services?
- Should a hospital build a new wing?
- Is it cheaper to perform services internally or to acquire them from external sources?

These examples are only a few of the many economic decisions managers make that require accounting information. All of these decisions have one thing in common—they are future-oriented, which means that managers attempt to estimate the future costs and benefits of alternative operations. The data in the accounting records are, of course, data about the past. These data provide a potentially good source of information about the future when you use them wisely.

Chapter 6 presents methods of estimating cost behavior. We focus on *costs* because cost differences among options are particularly important and challenging to estimate. Chapter 7 shows the interrelations among selling prices, volume, costs, and profits. Chapters 8, 9, and 10 present applications of differential analysis to many important business decisions. Chapter 8 deals with short-term decisions, whereas Chapters 9 and 10 focus on long-term capacity decisions and on capital budgeting.

... CHAPTER 6 ...

Estimating Cost Behavior

Chapter Outline

- The Nature of Fixed and Variable Costs
- Types of Fixed Costs
- Other Cost Behavior Patterns
- Cost Estimation Methods
- Strengths and Weaknesses of Cost Estimation Methods
- Appendix 6.1: Derivation of Learning Curves

Chapter 2 discussed the fundamental distinction between fixed and variable costs. This chapter discusses methods of *estimating* or deriving the breakdown of costs into fixed and variable components. Some costs, such as rent, usually have only a fixed portion, whereas others, such as direct materials, usually have only a variable portion. Many costs, however, have both fixed and variable components.

We can express the total costs of an item as follows:

$$\begin{matrix} \text{Total} \\ \text{Cost} \\ \text{during} \\ \text{Period} \end{matrix} = \begin{matrix} \text{Fixed} \\ \text{Cost} \\ \text{during} \\ \text{Period} \end{matrix} + \begin{pmatrix} \text{Variable} & \text{Units of} \\ \text{Cost per} & \text{Activity} \\ \text{Unit of} & \times & \text{during} \\ \text{Activity} & \text{Period} \end{pmatrix}$$

or, using briefer notation:[1]

$$TC = F + VX.$$

where TC refers to the total cost for a time period. F refers to the total fixed cost for a particular time period, V refers to the variable cost per unit, and X refers to the number of units of activity for the time period. Nearly all managerial decisions deal with choices among different activity levels; hence the manager must estimate which costs will vary with the activity and by how much.

The process of cost estimation works as follows: Suppose management expects a temporary reduction in customers at a particular restaurant during the summer. Some costs will not decline, while others will. Management would estimate the relation between costs and meals served to ascertain which costs would vary. The average unit variable cost, V, multiplied by the number of meals, X, provides the cost of savings, VX. This process estimates future costs because the decision involves reducing production in the future.

Because many costs do not fall neatly into fixed and variable categories, managers use statistics and other techniques for estimating **cost behavior.** These techniques break down costs to identify underlying cost behavior patterns.

The Nature of Fixed and Variable Costs

Short Run versus Long Run

Variable costs change as the level of activity changes, whereas **fixed costs** do not change with changes in activity levels. During short time periods, say 1 year, the firm operates with a relatively fixed sales force, managerial staff, and set of production facilities. Consequently, many of its costs are fixed. Over long time spans— many years perhaps—no costs are fixed.

This fact provides the basis for the distinction drawn in economics between the long run and the short run and in accounting between fixed costs and variable costs. To the economist, the **short run** is a time period long enough to allow management to change the level of production or other activity within the constraints of current total productive capacity. Management can change total productive capacity only in the **long run.**

To the manager, costs that vary with activity levels in the short run are variable costs: costs that will not vary in the short run no matter what the level of activity are fixed costs. The accounting concepts of variable and fixed costs are, then, short-run concepts. They apply to a particular period of time and relate to a particular level of productive capacity.

Consider, for example, the total costs (both variable and fixed) for a firm appearing in Exhibit 6.1. The graph on the left shows the total costs in the long run.

---

[1]A specific form of the general functional relation follows:

$$Y = a + bX,$$

where Y is the dependent variable, a is the intercept, b is the slope, and X is the independent variable. This is the equation for a straight line.

Exhibit 6.1

Long-Run versus Short-Run Nature of Costs

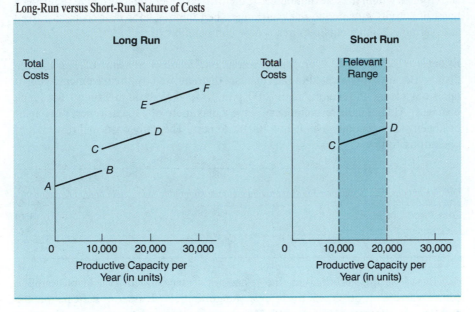

If the productive capacity of the firm is 10,000 units per year, total costs will vary as on line *AB*. If the firm acquires new production facilities to increase capacity to 20,000 units, total costs will be as on line *CD*. An increase in capacity to 30,000 units will increase the total costs as on line *EF*. These shifts in capacity represent long-run commitments. Of course some overlap will occur; production of 10,000 units per year could be at the high-volume end of the *AB* line or at the low-volume end of the *CD* line.

In the short run, a firm has only one capacity level; namely, the capacity of the existing plant. The total costs in the short run appear at the right side of the graph in Exhibit 6.1, on the assumption that the capacity of the existing plant is 20,000 units per year. Note that line *CD* represents costs for the production level of approximately 10,000 units to 20,000 units only. Production levels outside of this range require a different plant capacity, and the total costs line will shift up or down.

Relevant Range

Managers frequently use the notion of relevant range in estimating cost behavior. The **relevant range** is the range of activity over which the firm expects a set of cost behaviors to hold. For example, if the relevant range of activity shown in Exhibit 6.1 is between 10,000 and 20,000 units, the firm assumes that certain costs are fixed while others are variable within that range. The firm would not necessarily assume that costs fixed within the relevant range will stay fixed outside the relevant range. As Exhibit 6.1 shows, for example, costs step up from point D to point E when production increases from the right side of the 10,000 to 20,000 range, to the left side of the 20,000 to 30,000 range.

Estimates of variable and fixed costs apply only if the contemplated level of activity lies within the relevant range. If the firm considers an alternative requiring a level of activity outside the relevant range, then the breakdown of costs into fixed and variable components requires a new computation.

Example   Exotic Eats, a profitable restaurant, features a menu of Far Eastern dishes. Because it is located in the financial district of a city, management keeps it open only from 11:00 a.m. until 2:00 p.m., Monday through Friday, for lunch business. Although the restaurant can serve a maximum of 210 customers per day, it has been serving a daily average of 200 customers. The daily costs and revenues of operations follow:

Revenues...	$1,000
Less Variable Costs	(400)
Less Fixed Costs...	(350)
Operating Profits	$ 250

Based on this information, the restaurant's management considers doubling capacity, which is outside of the relevant range. Initial calculations indicate that the number of customers would double. Management wants to know whether operating profits would double. A simple extrapolation indicates that the operating profits would *more* than double, as Exhibit 6.2 shows, because total revenues would double whereas total costs would not.

Exhibit 6.2

EXOTIC EATS
Analysis Ignoring Increase in Fixed Costs (which is incorrect)

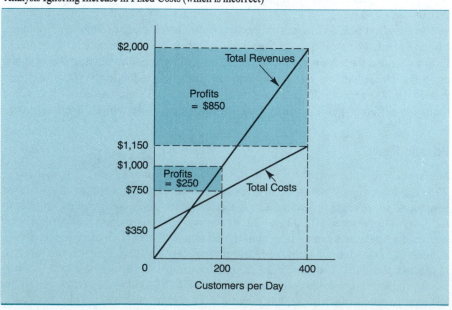

This simple extrapolation assumes ·that the total revenues and total variable costs double to $2,000 and $800, respectively, whereas fixed costs remain constant at $350. When capacity changes, fixed costs will not likely remain constant. The management of Exotic Eats realizes that with additional capacity and increased customers, it must hire additional cooks, occupancy costs (for example, space rental) would increase, and other fixed costs would increase. The projected new volume is outside the relevant range of volume over which the originally assumed costs behavior pattern would hold. The original cost behavior pattern would be invalid.

A revised, more realistic analysis of the cost behavior pattern estimates the unit variable cost of $2 per customer to be the same as before, but estimates fixed costs to increase from $350 to $550 per day. The revised cost behavior pattern appears in Exhibit 6.3. Exhibit 6.4 compares profits at the original activity level, 200 customers per day, with the projected increase to 400 per day. Management would use these cost estimates to decide about increasing capacity. These decisions usually require discounted cash flow analysis in addition to the estimated change in cash flow discussed here. (Discounted cash flow analysis is discussed in Chapter 9.)

Types of Fixed Costs

In practice, where the short run stops and the long run starts is fuzzy. The accountant divides fixed cost into subclassifications to explain the relation between particular types of fixed costs and current capacity.

Exhibit 6.3

EXOTIC EATS
Increase in Fixed Costs Accompanying Expansion

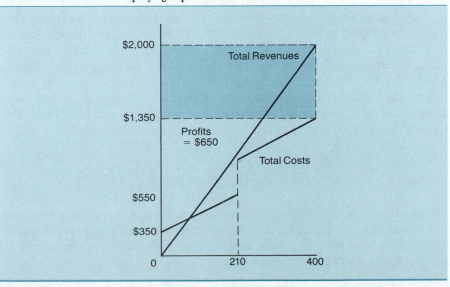

Exhibit 6.4

EXOTIC EATS			
Comparison of Profits at Original and Projected Activity Levels			
		Alternative: 400 Customers per Day	
	Status Quo: 200 Customers per Day	Incorrect Assumption That Fixed Costs Are Constant	Correct Assumption That Fixed Costs Will Change
Revenues...................	$1,000	$2,000	$2,000
Less Variable Costs	(400)	(800)	(800)
Total Contribution Margin	$ 600	$1,200	$1,200
Less Fixed Costs	(350)	(350)	(550)
Operating Profits...........	$ 250	$ 850	$ 650

Capacity Costs

Certain fixed costs, called **capacity costs,** provide a firm with the capacity to produce or sell or both. A firm incurs some capacity costs even if it temporarily shuts
down operations. Examples include property taxes and some executive salaries.

Other capacity costs cease if the firm's operations shut down, but continue in
fixed amounts if the firm carries out operations at any level. A firm can lay off a
security force if production ceases, but once employed, the security force guards the
plant no matter how little or how much activity goes on inside.

Discretionary Costs

Productive or selling capacity requires fixed capacity costs, but not other fixed **discretionary costs.** These costs are also called **programmed costs** or **managed costs.**
They include research, development, and advertising to generate new business.

These costs are discretionary because the firm need not incur them in the short
run to operate the business. They are, however, usually essential for achieving
long-run goals. Imagine the long-run impact on Proctor & Gamble of eliminating
media advertising. Or consider the effects if Hewlett-Packard were to drop research
and development. Although these companies would survive for a time, after a while
they would become different, and likely less profitable, companies. Discretionary
costs reflect top management's policies and commitments to activities. Once management makes such commitments, discretionary costs remain fixed.

Other Cost Behavior Patterns

We have made the following distinction between fixed and variable costs: Total
fixed costs remain constant for a period of time (the short run) over a range of
activity level (the relevant range); total variable costs change as the volume of
activity changes within the relevant range.

Curved Variable Costs

The straightforward linear fixed and variable cost behavior patterns, shown in Exhibits 6.2 and 6.3, do not always arise in practice. Total variable cost behavior may be curved, or curvilinear as Exhibit 6.5 shows with three different examples of variable cost behavior. **Curvilinear variable cost functions** indicate that the costs vary with the volume of activity, but not in constant proportion. For example, as volume increases, the unit prices of some inputs, such as materials and power, may decrease. Another example of curved cost behavior occurs when employees become more efficient with experience, as discussed below.

Learning Curves

Systematic learning from experience often occurs. As employees' experience increases, productivity improves and costs per unit decrease. This phenomenon frequently occurs when a firm initiates new products or processes or hires a group of new employees.

The effect of learning is often expressed as a **learning curve** (also known as an **experience curve**). The learning curve function shows how the amount of time required to perform a task goes down, per unit, as the number of units increases.

Accountants model the nature of the learning phenomenon as a constant percentage reduction in the *average* direct labor input time required per unit as the *cumulative output* doubles. For example, assume a time reduction rate of 20 percent (that is, an 80 percent cumulative learning curve). Assume also that the first unit

Exhibit 6.5

Examples of Curvilinear Total Variable Cost Behavior

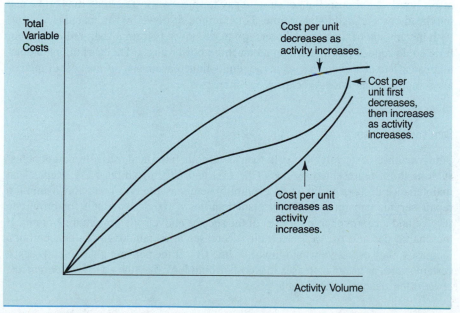

takes 125 hours. The *average* for two units should be 100 hours per unit (.80 × 125 hours), a total of 200 hours for both units. Four units would take an average of 80 hours each (= .80 × 100 hours), or a total of 320 hours. Appendix 6.1 presents the mathematical formula for the learning curve.

The results in this example follow:

| | Quantity | Time in Hours | |
Unit	Cumulative Units	Cumulative	Average per Unit
First............................	1	125	125
Second...........................	2	200	100 (= .80 × 125)
Third and Fourth	4	320	80 (= .80 × 100)
Fifth through Eighth...............	8	512	64 (= .80 × 80)

Exhibit 6.6 shows the relation between volume and *average* labor hours in graph A, between volume and *total* labor hours in graph B, and between volume and total labor costs in graph C. The labor costs is $20 per hour.

The possible consequences of learning on costs can affect decision making and performance evaluation. Suppose that you are trying to decide whether to make a new product that would be subject to the 80 percent cumulative learning curve. Using the data in Exhibit 6.6, if you assumed that the product would require labor costs of $2,500 per unit for the first eight units made, you would seriously overstate the costs for the eight units. If you used the $2,500 per unit as a standard for judging actual cost performance, you would set too loose a standard for all but the first unit.

To what costs do learning curves apply? The learning phenomenon results in savings of time; any costs that vary over time could be affected. Learning may affect hourly labor costs but not straight pay for piecework. Learning may affect any overhead costs related to labor time. For example, if power to run machinery varies with the amount of time that laborers run machines to peform a task, reducing labor time could reduce machine time and machine power costs. The learning phenomenon can affect material costs, as in the semiconductor industry, if the cost of materials scrapped goes down as experience increases.

Semivariable Costs

Semivariable costs refer to costs that have both fixed and variable components, such as those represented by lines *CD, CE,* and *CF* in Exhibit 6.7A. Repair and maintenance costs or utility costs exemplify semivariable cost behavior. Minimum repair service capability within a plant requires a fixed cost (*OC*) for providing service and an extra charge for uses of the service above some minimum amount. If the charge per unit of, say, electricity decreases at certain stages as consumption increases, the cost curve would look like line *CF*. If the per-unit charge increases at certain stages as usage increases, the costs would look like line *CD*. The term *mixed costs* often denotes semivariable costs.

Exhibit 6.6

Impact of Learning Curves on Time and Cost Behavior

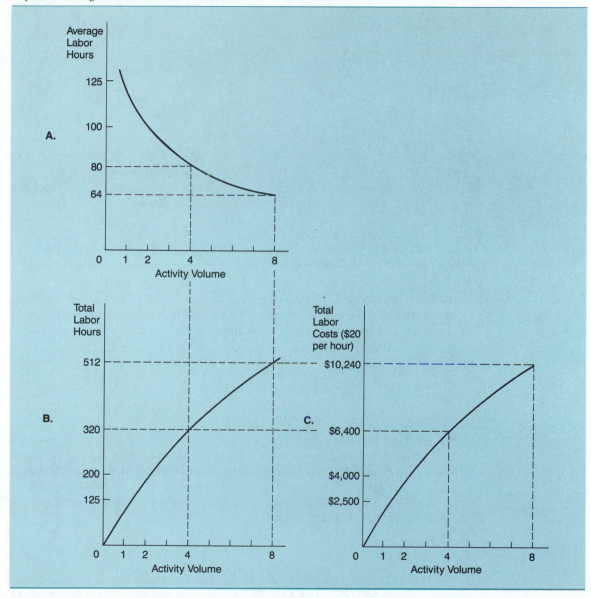

Exhibit 6.7

Patterns of Cost Behavior: Semivariable and Semifixed Costs

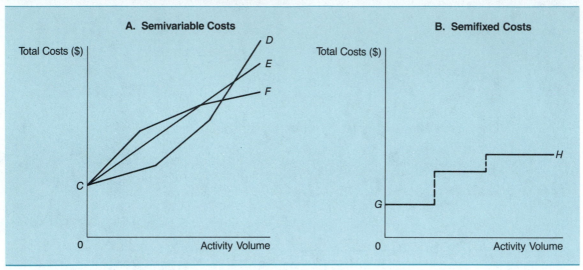

Example Mykrochip Corporation has an automated plant. The hours of electricity used varies directly with the number of units produced. Past experience suggests that electricity costs behave in a semivariable pattern as follows:

Up to 5,000 Units..	$300
Next 2,000 Units	$.06/Unit
Next 2,000 Units	$.05/Unit

Myckrochip Corporation expects to produce 6,500 units if it refuses an order for 1,000 units. The expected cash outflow for electricity is $390 [= $300 + (1,500 × $.06)]. If it accepts the order for 1,000 units, production will increase to 7,500 units (= 6,500 + 1,000). Electricity costs will therefore be $445 [= $300 + (2,000 × $.06) + (500 × $.05)]. The incremental cash outflow for electricity from accepting this order is $55 (= $445 − $390).

Semifixed Costs

The term **semifixed costs** refers to costs that increase in steps, such as those shown by the broken line *GH* in Exhibit 6.7B. Accountants sometimes describe semifixed costs as *step costs*. If a quality-control inspector can examine 1,000 units per day, inspection costs will be semifixed, with a break for every 1,000 units per day.

Example Radio House hires one quality-control inspector for each 25,000 toy robots produced per month. The annual salary is $30,000 per inspector. Production has been 65,000 units, so the company has three inspectors. If a special order increases volume from 65,000 to 75,000 units the firm need hire no additional inspectors. If the special order increases production to a level greater than 75,000 units (say, to 85,000 units), the firm must hire a fourth inspector.

The distinction between fixed and semifixed costs is subtle. A change in fixed costs (other than for inflation or other price changes) usually involves a change in long-term assets, whereas a change in semifixed costs often does not.

Summary

Costs vary with the volume of activity in several ways. Some costs do not vary in the short run over a relevant range—they are *fixed*. Others vary with volume—that is, they are *variable*. Some costs, neither strictly fixed nor strictly variable, contain both components.

To simplify the analysis of cost behavior decision makers usually assume that costs are either strictly fixed or linearly variable. The reason is that the incremental cost of analyzing the more complex data often exceeds the incremental benefits of doing so.[2] The assumed simple linear variable-fixed cost behavior, though unrealistic, usually sufficiently approximates reality for decision-making purposes. Many cases require estimates and analysis of cost behavior with greater precision.

Cost Estimation Methods

An important step in **cost estimation** is to break down total costs (TC) into fixed and variable components:

$$TC = F + VX,$$

F is total fixed costs during the period, V is variable cost per unit of activity, and X is the number of units of activity. For example, assume that analysis finds the total cost of utilities per month to be \$400 plus \$.05 per kilowatt-hour used. If the firm expects to use 100,000 kilowatt-hours next month, it estimates utilities cost to be \$5,400 [= \$400 + (\$.05 per kilowatt-hour × 100,000 kilowatt-hours)].

The activity represented by X is often called the **independent variable** and the amount of total costs is the **dependent variable.** In some analyses, more than one activity or independent variable influences total cost. If so, such a relation may be expressed as

$$TC = F + V_1X_1 + V_2X_2 + \cdots + V_nX_n$$

F is total fixed cost per period. V_1 is the variable cost per unit of activity X_1 carried out. V_2 is the variable cost per unit of activity X_2 carried out, and so on. X_1 might be

---

[2]Simplification of complex cost behavior patterns into strictly fixed and variable costs is analogous to our discussion of the costs and benefits of information in Chapter 1. The basic concept of "simplification" is that by simplifying we lose some information but we reduce the costs of information and analysis. Any time we simplify we sacrifice understanding the full complexities of cost causation, depreciation measurement, revenue recognition, and so forth. We are simplifying, presumably because the costs of more complex analysis exceed the benefits.

For an expanded discussion of simplification, see Joel S. Demski, *Information Analysis* (Reading, Mass.: Addison-Wesley, 1980), pp. 44–61.

number of automobiles produced and X_2 might be the number of trucks produced, for example.

The following explains the major methods of estimating cost behavior. Each method attempts to estimate the equation $TC = F + VX$ for the particular cost item under study.

Engineering Method of Estimating Costs

Engineering estimates indicate what costs *should be*. The **engineering method of cost estimation** probably got its name because managers first used it in estimating manufacturing costs from engineers' specifications of the inputs required to manufacture a unit of output. The method is not, however, confined to manufacturing. Banks, fast-food companies, governmental units, hospitals, and other nonmanufacturing enterprises use time-and-motion studies and similar engineering methods to estimate what costs ''should be'' to perform a particular service.

Virtually all business activities attempt to produce output from various labor, material, and equipment inputs. The engineering cost estimates result from study of the physical relation between the quantities of these inputs and each unit of output. (Economists call this a *production function*.) The accountant assigns costs to each of the physical inputs (wages, material prices, insurance charges, etc.) to estimate the cost of the outputs.

Using the engineering method to estimate costs presents several difficulties. The cost estimate can be inaccurate if the actual amounts of inputs used vary over time during the production process because of waste, spoilage, or labor inefficiencies. Also, estimating the indirect costs of production—the cost of utilities, supervision, maintenance, security—with the engineering method is difficult. The method is more reliable when costs vary directly with output (for example, direct labor and direct materials). Finally, the engineering method is surprisingly costly to use. Analysis of time, motion, materials, operating characteristics of equipment, and the abilities of workers with varying skills, requires experts, and expert engineers are costly.

In short, the engineering method of estimating costs is most useful when input/output relations are well defined and fairly stable over time. For a company that does not change its production function over time, the engineering method results in good estimates for the amount of direct materials, direct labor, and some overhead required to make a product.

Account Analysis

In contrast to the engineering method, other methods of estimating cost behavior use actual accounting data. The **account analysis method** reviews each cost account and classifies it according to cost behavior. People familiar with the activities of the firm, and the way the firm's activities affect costs, do the classification.

Example   The administrators of the Chicago Hospital want to classify operating room overhead costs into fixed and variable components. They will use the information to estimate the effects of increases or decreases in the number of operations performed on operating room overhead costs.

Exhibit 6.8

CHICAGO HOSPITAL
Cost Behavior
Account Analysis

Account	Account Codes Itemª	Behaviorᵇ
Supplies Directly Assigned to Particular Operations	101	V
Labor (physicians and nurses)	102	V
Operating Room Overhead:		
Indirect Supplies	103	V
Indirect Labor (janitorial, supply room, personnel)	104	V
Utilities (heat, lights)	105	F
Insurance	106	F

ªEach account is assigned a different number.

ᵇV = variable cost; F = fixed cost.

Note: Additional codes can be used to assign costs to departments or other responsibility centers.

Exhibit 6.8 shows operating room costs coded according to cost behavior. Virtually all organizations have a chart of accounts that presents the numerical codes assigned to accounts. Exhibit 6.8 codes variable costs as V and fixed costs as F. If management wants a more complex classification of cost behavior, such as classification into semivariable costs or discretionary fixed costs, the coding system can have additional symbols added.

The accountant assigned a code to each operating room overhead account for Chicago Hospital to indicate whether it was fixed or variable. The following table shows the sum of the amounts in the respective fixed and variable categories for a year. During the year the operating room was in service for 5,700 hours of surgery.

Code	Cost Behavior	Amount
V	Variable	$3,990,000
F	Fixed	1,491,000
		$5,481,000

Dividing the fixed costs by 12 gives a monthly average of $124,250. Dividing the variable costs by the 5,700 operating room hours gives a variable cost rate per hour of operating room use: $700 per operating room hour. The following monthly estimated cost equation results:

$$TC = \$124,250 + (\$700 \times \text{Operating Room Hours Used during Month})$$

Account analysis requires detailed examination of the data, presumably by accountants and managers who are familiar with it. Their expert judgments can uncover cost behavior patterns that other methods may overlook. Because account analysis is judgmental, different analysts are likely to provide different estimates of cost behavior.

Estimation of Costs Using Historical Data

When a firm has been carrying out activities for some time and expects future activities to be similar to those of the past, the firm can analyze the historical data to estimate the variable and fixed components of total cost and to estimate likely future costs. The procedure for analyzing historical cost data requires two steps:

1. Make an estimate of the past relation for $TC = F + VX$.
2. Update this estimate so that it is appropriate for the present or future period for which management wants the estimate. This step requires adjusting costs for inflation and for changes that have occurred in the relation between costs and activity. For example, if a firm expects the production process to be more capital intensive in the future, the accountant should reduce variable costs and increase fixed costs.

Accountants use several methods to estimate costs from historical data; these range from simple "eyeball estimates" to sophisticated statistical methods. Before relying on cost estimates, whatever the method based on historical data, the manager should take some preliminary steps.

Preliminary Steps in Analyzing Historical Cost Data

Data analysts use the acronym GIGO, "garbage-in, garbage-out." GIGO means that the results of an analysis cannot be better than the input data. Before using cost estimates, the analyst should be confident that the estimates make sense and result from valid assumptions.

Keep in mind that we are trying to find fixed costs per period, F, and variable cost per unit, V, of some activity variable, X, in the relation

$$TC = F + VX.$$

The historical data comprise several observations. An observation is the total cost amount for a period and the level of activity carried out during that period. Thus we may have total labor costs by months (the dependent variable) and the number of units produced during each of the months, or the number of direct labor hours worked during each of the months (the independent variable). Exhibit 6.9 shows 12 observations, one for each month, for Chicago Hospital.

We do not provide here an exhaustive list of all the steps to take in analyzing historical data, but the following are important.

1. **Review Alternative Activity Bases (Independent Variable)** An activity base ideally measures the activity that *causes* costs. The activity bases, if not the sole cause of costs, should directly influence cost incurrence. Operating room hours is an example of an activity base in a hospital; machine hours is an example in a manufacturing firm; labor hours is an example in a service firm.
2. **Plot the Data** One simple procedure often omitted by lazy analysts involves plotting each of the observations of total costs against activity levels. Such plots can highlight an outlier observation—one unlike the others. Such outliers may indicate faulty data collection, incorrect arithmetic, or merely a time period when production was out of control. Ignoring the outlier observation in

Exhibit 6.9

CHICAGO HOSPITAL Operating Room Overhead Cost Data by Month		
Month	**Total Overhead Costs Incurred during Month**	**Operating Room Hours[a]**
January	$ 558,000	600
February	433,000	550
March	408,000	350
April	283,000	300
May	245,500	250
June	308,000	200
July	358,000	400
August	445,500	450
September	533,000	500
October	658,000	650
November	558,000	700
December	693,000	750
	$5,481,000	5,700

[a]An operating room hour is one hour that one operating room is being used for surgery.

estimating the average relations among total, fixed, and variable costs may be sensible. Moreover, plotting the data may make it clear that no relation or only a nonlinear relation exists between the activity base and actual costs.[3]

3. **Examine the Data and Method of Accumulation** Do the time periods for the cost data and the activity correspond? Occasionally, accounting systems will record costs actually incurred late on a given day as occurring on the following day. Deducing valid relations is difficult when the accounts compile data for the dependent variable (total costs, in this case) for a different period from data for the independent variable (activity base, in this case).

    Are the time periods covered by each observation of total costs and the activity base long enough to be meaningful? Are they short enough to allow for variations in activity levels? On the one hand, observations collected by the hour can highlight variations in the relation between the dependent and independent variables. Workers may be more efficient in the morning and less so in the late afternoon. On the other hand, observations collected by the month may smooth over meaningful variations of activity level and cost that would appear if the accountant collected data based on weekly observations.

    Be aware that a number of common recording procedures can make data appear to exhibit incorrect cost behavior patterns. As in Chapters 3 and 4, accounting systems often charge fixed manufacturing overhead to production on the basis of some activity measure, such as direct labor hours. This unitizing of fixed manufacturing costs makes these costs appear to be variable.

---

[3]The cost estimation methods discussed in this chapter assume that a linear relation exists between the dependent and independent variables. Nonlinear relations require more sophisticated estimation methods.

Therefore, the manufacturing overhead cost observations should be *actual total costs,* not the *applied unit cost.*

Sometimes an inverse relation seems to appear between activity and particular costs—when activity is high, these costs are low; when activity is low, these costs are high. An excellent example is maintenance, which firms sometimes purposefully do only when activity is slow. High maintenance levels often occur during plant shutdowns for automobile model changes, for example. The analyst would be naive to infer that low activity levels cause high maintenance costs.

These examples are a few of the data-recording methods that could lead the analyst astray. In general, the accountant should investigate cost allocations, accruals, correcting and reversing entries, and relations between costs and activity levels to ensure that costs match activities in the appropriate time period for estimating costs.[4] Invalid relations between activity and costs will invalidate the analysis.

Methods of Cost Estimation Using Historical Data

Having taken the preliminary steps to analyze the historical data, the accountant can use several methods to estimate the historical relations between total costs and activity levels, this is, to estimate $TC = F + VX$.

This section discusses the estimation of variable and fixed overhead for the Chicago Hospital operating room. After analysts compute this estimate from past data, they can adjust the estimate for known changes in costs (for example, inflation) and the relation between costs and the activity base (for example, a change in surgical procedures). Keep in mind that the concepts apply to any type of organization.

Total operating room overhead costs of the Chicago Hospital for each month during the previous year appear in Exhibit 6.9. Exhibit 6.10 plots them. The task is to estimate the relation between total overhead costs and activity.[5] We expect that, of the possible activity bases, the number of operating room hours during the month primarily causes total overhead costs. Exhibit 6.9 shows total overhead costs and operating room hours each month.

The cost relation we will estimate is

$$\begin{array}{ccc} \text{Total Overhead} & & \text{Fixed} \\ \text{Costs per} & = & \text{Costs} \\ \text{Month} & & \text{per Month} \end{array} + \left(\begin{array}{ccc} \text{Variable Overhead} & & \text{Operating Room} \\ \text{Cost per} & & \text{Hours} \\ \text{Operating} & \times & \text{Used during} \\ \text{Room Hour} & & \text{Month} \end{array} \right)$$

$$TC = F + VX.$$

Before estimating the cost relation, we plot the data, as in Exhibit 6.10. No outliers are apparent for the 12 observation pairs in Exhibit 6.9. Two outliers appear on the

---

[4]For an extension of these remarks, see G. Benston, "Multiple Regression Analysis of Cost Behavior," *Accounting Review,* 41, (October 1966), pp. 657–672. W. E. Wecker and R. L. Weil, "Statistical Estimation of Incremental Costs from Accounting Data," Chapter 30 in P. Frank, et al., editor *Litigation Series Handbook,* New York: John Wiley & Sons, 1990.

[5]Alternatively, we could study the behavior of each of these overhead costs individually and aggregate the fixed and variable cost components to obtain an estimate of total overhead costs. These alternative approaches normally yield approximately the same results.

Exhibit 6.10

CHICAGO HOSPITAL
Scatter Plot of Total Monthly Overhead Costs
and Operating Room Hours Used during Month

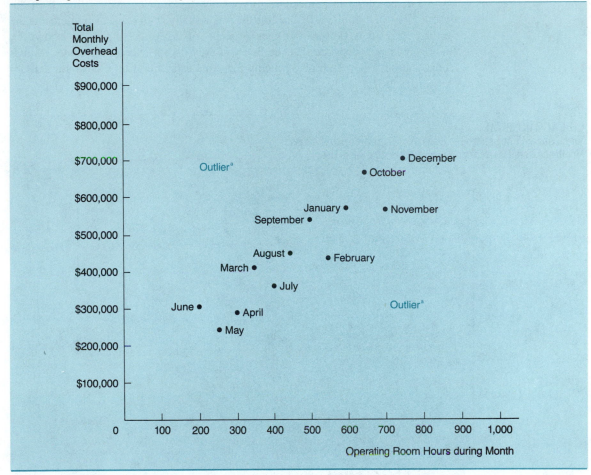

[a]Outliers are assumed and plotted for purposes of illustration. They do not appear in the data in Exhibit 6.9.

plot so that you can see what we mean by an outlier.[6] If only one or two months had outliers such as those shown, we would investigate those months and once we understood their cause, possibly discard the observations.

Next, we illustrate two common methods of estimating the cost relationship, that is, identifying F and V in the preceding equation.

_____

[6]One of the outliers, the one corresponding roughly to 750 hours and $300,000 of total costs, has total costs much less than one's intuition says they should be. We suspect that the cause here is faulty data recording; but if not, we would want to know what happened that month. Investigation of outliers illustrates the concept called "management by exception." Understanding the cause of outliers is particularly important for managerial control, as we discuss in the topic of variance analysis in Chapter 13.

Visual Curve-Fitting Method   One method of estimating costs from data such as those in Exhibit 6.10 is visual curve fitting. In the **visual curve-fitting method** we draw a straight line through the data points that seems to fit well. By ''fit,'' we mean a straight line that goes through the middle of the data points as closely as possible.

To demonstrate the procedure to yourself, try drawing such a line to fit the observations in Exhibit 6.10. The line that we visually fit to these data intercepts the vertical axis of $100,000 and has a slope of $750 per hour, as shown in Exhibit 6.11. Chances are that the line you drew is not exactly the same as ours. Yours and ours may each give roughly the same estimate of total costs for activity

Exhibit 6.11

CHICAGO HOSPITAL
Visual Curve-Fitting Method of Estimating Fixed Overhead Costs per Month and Variable Overhead Costs per Operating Room Hour

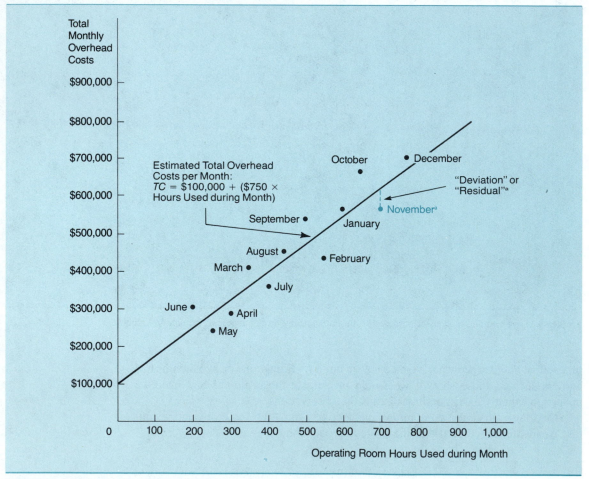

Note: This exhibit is based on data in Exhibit 6.9.

[a]The graph shows vertical distance between the line and the observation, called a *deviation or residual,* for November. Because the November data point is below the line, the residual is negative.

ranging from 300 to 600 operating room hours per month, but would probably give significantly different estimates of total costs for 100 or 1,000 hour per month. You can understand the shortcoming of this method by noting the difference between your visually fit line and ours. The visually fit line is subjective, and different analysts may reach different conclusions from the same data.

Once you have drawn a line to fit the data, you have estimated the fixed cost component. F as the total cost for a zero level of activity—the amount at the point where the line crosses the vertical axis.[7] The estimate of the variable cost per unit of activity is the slope of the line. You can derive it numerically by reading the numbers for any two points *on the line*. The relation is as follows, where subscripts 1 and 2 refer to the two points:

$$\begin{array}{c}\text{Variable Cost}\\\text{per Unit of}\\\text{Base Activity}\end{array} = V = \frac{TC_1 - TC_2}{X_1 - X_2}$$

$$= \frac{\text{Change in Costs between Two Points}}{\text{Change in Activity between the Two Points}} = \text{Slope of Total Cost Line.}$$

In our case, we use the following points:

- Point 1: 800 hours; $700,000 total costs.
- Point 2: 0 hours; $100,000 total costs.

Using the preceding formula, we find that

$$V = \frac{\$700,000 - \$100,000}{800 \text{ Hours} - 0 \text{ Hours}} = \frac{\$600,000}{800 \text{ Hours}} = \$750 \text{ per Hour.}$$

Thus we have estimated the total overhead cost relation as

$$\begin{array}{c}\text{Total Overhead}\\\text{Costs per Month}\end{array} = \$100,000 + \$750 \text{ per Operating Room Hour.}$$

Your estimate of the fixed and variable overhead costs will differ if the line you drew differs from ours.

A variation of the visual curve-fitting approach is the *high-low method,* in which you fit a curve to the highest and lowest total cost observations.

Regression Analysis   With a computer available, you will find that the most cost-effective and accurate method for estimating cost relations is the statistical method known as **regression analysis.** Rather than estimating the cost relation by the visual curve-fitting method, the regression analysis "fits" a line to the data by the method of least squares. The method fits a line to the observations to minimize the sum of the squares of the vertical distance of the observation points from the point on the regression line. (See November in Exhibit 6.11 for an illustration of the vertical distance.) The statistical regression locates the line that best goes through the data points using the least-squares criterion.

---

[7]This estimate of F is outside of the range of observations, so it should be viewed with some skepticism.

Managerial Application

United Airlines Uses Regression to Estimate Profit of Apollo[a]

In the 1970s United Air Lines (UAL) developed Apollo, a computer reservation system costing several hundred million dollars. UAL sold the right to install Apollo computers and communications equipment to travel agencies. These systems allow an agency to communicate directly with UAL and other airlines about reservations. In the late 1980s, UAL decided to sell part of its ownership interest in Apollo. In deciding on a sales price, UAL analyzed the profitability of Apollo. UAL suspected that one benefit of having Apollo is that some passengers who might not otherwise fly on UAL would do so. The travel agent, with an Apollo reservations system, may prefer making a reservation for its customers on a United flight, rather than some other airline's flight. The question arose, what are UAL's incremental profits, if any, from the passengers who would otherwise use another airline?

Thus, UAL analysts undertook to ascertain the incremental costs of flying incremental revenue passenger miles. The analysts had quarterly data on UAL costs, classified into several hundred accounts, revenue passenger miles, and revenues. The UAL analysts decided to attempt to extract the needed information from the data with regression analysis. Air travel is seasonal. Thus, the simple regression of total costs (transformed into dollars of constant purchasing power) on revenue passenger miles and takeoffs showed high correlation in the time series of residuals from the fitted regression (that is, autocorrelation). UAL analysts respecified the regression model by regressing the *change* in total costs each period against the *changes* in revenue passenger miles and system-wide takeoffs. Analysis of the residuals from this regression showed no correlation in the residuals, and the other regression diagnostics indicated a satisfactory specification. The analysts concluded that about 70 percent of UAL's costs varied with passenger traffic and takeoffs.

This result surprised other analysts who thought that UAL's costs must be mostly fixed. These skeptics observed that UAL averages 35 percent empty seats on its flights. They thought that when UAL carried a few extra passengers, these passengers would sit in the otherwise empty seats. Then, the only incremental costs would be about 25 percent of revenues for extra fuel, and food, check-in agents, and baggage handling. The skeptics assumed UAL would not buy new airplanes and other major assets to handle the incremental passenger traffic.

The analysts who developed the regression estimates derived a model of an airline facing demand characterized by statistical uncertainty. This model showed that, optimally, the airline responds to an increase in demand for seats by expanding its total airline capacity, not just planning to put the extra passengers in otherwise empty seats.

UAL sold about half the ownership interest in Apollo and related systems in 1989 for approximately $500 million.

[a]Based on the authors' research.

In our example, an observed actual value of total overhead cost is TC, and the line we fit by the least squares regression will be of the form

$$\hat{TC} = \hat{F} + \hat{V}X,$$

where the $\hat{}$ on $\hat{TC}$ indicates that we have estimated the value of TC. The right-hand side of the equation should already be familiar to you. Standard terminology designates the vertical distance between the actual and the fitted values, $TC - \hat{TC}$, as the *residual*. The method of least squares fits a line to the data to minimize the sum of all the squared residuals.

This text merely introduces the methods of regression analysis, but virtually every computer system and spreadsheet software package for personal computers can execute regression analysis. Furthermore, pocket calculators available for less than $50 will perform many of these calculations. Here we illustrate statistical methods and explain how to interpret the results. You should be aware that entire books explain these methods and their uses.

Running the data for TC and X in Exhibit 6.9 through a computer least-squares regression program gives the following results, which we explain later.

Estimated
Total
Overhead $= \$100,168 + \left(\$751 \times \begin{array}{l}\text{Operating Room Hours} \\ \text{Worked during Month}\end{array} \right)$
Costs $\quad\quad\ \ (\$47,005) \quad\ (\$93)$
per Month

$\qquad R_2 \quad = \quad 0.85.$

Exhibit 6.12 presents the line implied by this equation.

By now, you should be able to interpret the $100,168 and $751 amounts. The first is the intercept, which estimates the fixed overhead cost per month, and the second estimates the variable overhead cost per unit of base activity, operating room hours worked during the month. The two numbers, $100,168 (for fixed costs) and $751 (for variable costs), are the *coefficients* of the regression equation, sometimes called the regression coefficients.

The previous discussion dealt only with one independent variable. *Multiple regression* has more than one independent variable.

Standard Errors of the Coefficients   The numbers shown in parentheses below the regression coefficients are the **standard errors of the coefficients.** The standard errors of the coefficients measure their variation and give an idea of the confidence we can have in the fixed and variable cost coefficients. The smaller the standard error relative to its coefficient, the more precise the estimate. (Such computational precision does not necessarily indicate that the estimating procedure is *theoretically correct*, however.)

For example, the standard error of the fixed overhead cost per month is $47,005; the estimate of fixed costs of $100,168 is 2.13 ($= \$100,168/\$47,005$) times as large as the standard error. The ratio between an estimated regression coefficient and its standard error is known as the *t*-value or *t*-statistic. If the *t*-statistic is approximately 2 or larger, we can be relatively confident that the actual

Exhibit 6.12

CHICAGO HOSPITAL
Statistical (Least-Squares Regression) Method of Estimating
Fixed Overhead Costs per Month and Variable
Overhead Costs per Operating Room Hour

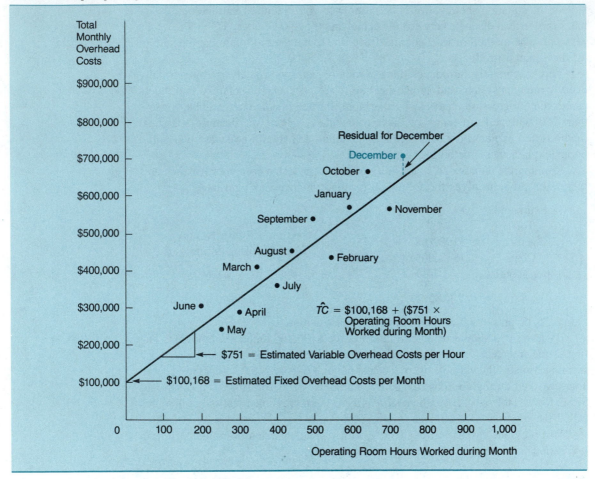

Note: This illustration is based on data in Exhibit 6.9.

coefficient differs from zero.[8] The estimated variable cost coefficient is relatively large compared to the standard error of the variable cost coefficient in this example; the *t*-statistic is relatively large: $751/$93 = 8.08. We conclude, therefore, that a statistically significant relationship exists between changes in total overhead costs and changes in operating room hours: Larger amounts of operating room hours worked per month imply larger amounts of overhead costs.

In cases where the standard error of the cost coefficient is large relative to the coefficient (small *t*-statistic), the cost coefficient does not differ significantly from zero. If a variable cost coefficient has a small *t*-statistic, we may conclude that little,

---

[8]Statistics books provide *t*-tables that make the analysis of *t*-statistics more precise.

Exhibit 6.13

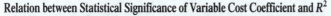

Relation between Statistical Significance of Variable Cost Coefficient and R^2

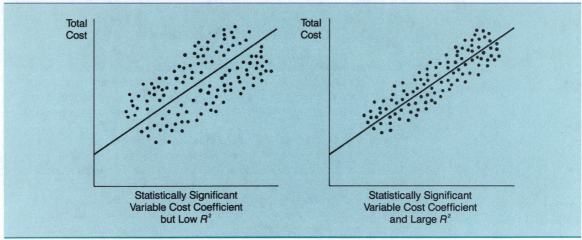

if any, relation exists between this particular activity (or independent variable) and changes in costs. If a fixed cost coefficient has a small t-statistic, we may conclude that these costs have little, if any, fixed cost component (which we would expect for operating room supplies or direct materials in manufacturing, for example).

R^2 The **R^2** attempts to measure how well the line fits the data (that is, how closely the data points cluster about the fitted line). If all the data points were on the same straight line, the R^2 would be 1.00—a perfect fit. If the data points formed a circle or disk, the adjusted R^2 would be zero, indicating that no line passing through the center of the circle or disk fits the data better than any other.[9] Technically, R^2 is a measure of the fraction of the total variance of the dependent variable about its mean that the fitted line explains.[10] An R^2 of 1 means that the regression explains all of the variance; and R^2 of zero means that it explains none of the variance. R^2 is sometimes known as the "coefficient of determination."

Many users of statistical regression analysis believe that low R^2s indicate a weak relation between total costs (dependent variable) and the activity base (independent variable). A low standard error (or high t-statistic) for the estimated variable cost coefficient signals whether or not the activity base performs well as an explanatory variable for total costs. With a large number of data observations, both low R^2 and significant regression coefficients can occur. Exhibit 6.13 illustrates this possibility.

---

[9]Other situations can also lead to an R^2 of zero.

[10]Many books and computer outputs report both an adjusted and an unadjusted R^2. The adjustment takes into account the number of coefficients fit to the data—two in a linear regression of the kind illustrated here: one for the constant (fixed costs in our applications) and one for the coefficient of the activity variable. An adjusted R^2 measures better than an unadjusted R^2 because the mathematics penalizes the adjusted R^2 for the use of more independent variables. (If you used as many independent variables as you have observations, you would always get an unadjusted R^2 of 1.00.) The unadjusted R^2 for a simple linear regression is the square of the correlation coefficient between the independent and dependent variables.

Managerial Application

Estimating Cost Behavior

The health-care industry has been faced with increasing pressure to control costs. Health care costs have increased more rapidly than general inflation rates. At the same time, health care facilities face price competition for services because insurance companies and government-funded health programs are limiting opportunities for cost reimbursement.

To control costs, one must first relate the costs of providing services to the volume of activity. For example, Robert Kaplan reported in a study done for a hospital that the accounting data could not provide an answer to this question: Did high nursing costs result from inefficiency or because the volume of activity was high?[a] Consequently, the first step was to estimate a cost model, TC = F + VX, where X refers to the volume of activity. Examples of activity bases included patient days (to estimate nurse staff costs) and number of procedures (to estimate costs in a radiology department).

Although it may appear simple to estimate the relation $TC = F + VX$, Kaplan found no good data to make the estimates. For example, the cost of medical supplies shown in the accounting records was the cost of purchases, not the cost of supplies *used*. Consequently, large purchases in one month followed by no purchases in the next month made these costs appear to behave in unrealistic ways. Recent pressures on health-care facilities to reduce costs, however, have increased the incentives for administrators and doctors to improve recordkeeping to enable them to estimate and control costs.

[a] R. S. Kaplan, "Management Accounting in Hospitals: A Case Study," *Accounting for Social Goals* (New York: Harper & Row, 1974), pp. 131–148.

Using the Regression to Estimate Costs   The least-squares regression equation,

$$TC = \$100,168 + (\$751 \times \text{Operating Room Hours}),$$

appears as a heavy straight line in Exhibit 6.14 with the observations identified by month. The dashed line graphed on Exhibit 6.14 shows that these same data observations may result from a nonlinear relation between costs and activity that appears to be linear in the range of observations.

We should be wary of predicting total costs for operating room hours worked less than about 200 per month or more than about 800 per month. We should be wary of our estimate of fixed costs, because it is outside the relevant range. We can check the regression estimate of fixed costs with the account analysis or other methods to be sure that it makes sense. If we made this check here, we might find that the dashed line in Exhibit 6.14, not the assumed straight line, represents the true relation between costs and activity.

Warning   Computers easily perform statistical estimating techniques but often do not provide the necessary warnings. We conclude this section by providing three

Exhibit 6.14

CHICAGO HOSPITAL
Comparison of Regression Estimate to Possible Nonlinear Relation

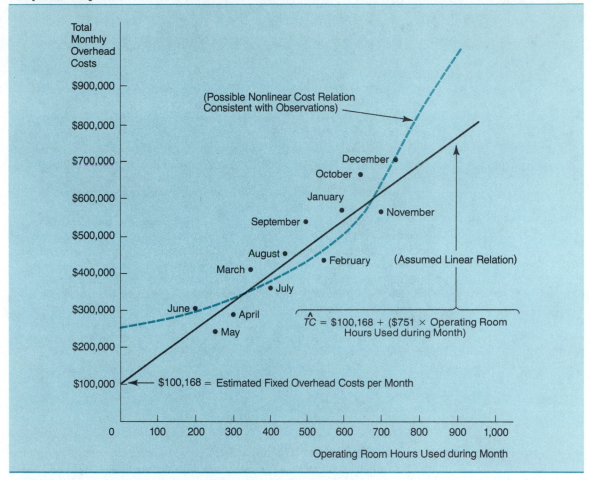

Note: This illustration is based on data in Exhibit 6.9.

warnings. First, a relation achieved in a regression analysis does not imply a causal relation; that is, a correlation between two variables does not imply that changes in one will cause changes in the other. An assertion of causality must be based on either *a priori* knowledge or some analysis other than a regression analysis.

Second, users of regression analysis should be wary of drawing too many inferences from the results unless they are familiar with such statistical estimation problems as *multicollinearity, autocorrelation,* and *heteroscedasticity* and how to deal with them. Statistics books deal with these statistical estimation problems.

Briefly, *multicollinearity* refers to the problem caused in multiple linear regression (more than one independent variable) when the independent variables are not independent of each other but are correlated. When severe multicollinearity occurs, the regression coefficients are unreliable. For example, direct labor hours worked

Managerial Application

Multicollinearity Defeats an Attempt to Estimate Incremental Costs

Hughes Tool Company produces a variety of equipment used in drilling for oil. Hughes owns a patent on a seal used to keep drilling mud out of the mechanism on bits used in drilling. A competitor, Smith International, wanted to license the patent to produce its own drill bits. Hughes needed to know how much incremental profit it earned on its drill bits so it could know what it would lose if Smith produced and sold the bits. Hughes engaged a consultant from its auditing firm, one of the largest accounting firms. The consultant did a regression analysis on Hughes' costs, as reflected in its internal accounting records, to estimate the incremental costs of producing drill bits. Hughes planned to deduct the resulting cost estimate from the price of a drill bit to estimate potentially lost profit.

The oil drilling business is cyclical and the demand for various oil drilling equipment is highly correlated. That is, in a period when Hughes manufactures and sells many drill bits, it also manufactures and sells much drill pipe. Conversely, in periods when Hughes manufactures and sells few drill bits, it manufactures and sells little drill pipe. Hughes' accounting data did not separate the costs of producing drill bits from the costs of producing the other oil drilling equipment. Consequently, the consultant doing the regression analysis faced multicollinearity in the data. He estimated the incremental costs associated with an extra dollar of sales revenue, but he was unable to separate the incremental costs of drill bits from the incremental costs of the other oil drilling equipment.

Ultimately, Hughes relied on account analysis to estimate the incremental costs of drill bits.

during a month are likely to be highly correlated with direct labor costs during the month, even when wage rates change over time. If both direct labor hours and direct labor costs are used in a multiple linear regression, we would expect to have a problem of multicollinearity.

When activity bases are multicollinear, the regression equation can have high adjusted R^2, but the regression coefficient will have low t-values.

Autocorrelation refers to the phenomenon that occurs when, for example, a linear regression is fit to data where a nonlinear relation exists between the dependent and independent variables. In such a case, the deviation of one observation from the fitted line can be predicted from the deviation of the prior observation(s). For example, if demand for a product is seasonal and production is also seasonal, a month of large total costs will more likely follow another month of large total costs than a month of small total costs. In such a case, we would have autocorrelation in the deviations of the data points from a fitted straight line.

Autocorrelation problems can arise only when the data represent observations over time. Most cost data are observations over time. Although statisticians have provided several tests for autocorrelation, most computer spreadsheet programs do not incorporate them.

Heteroscedasticity refers to the phenomenon that occurs when the average deviation of the dependent variable from the best-fitting linear relation is systematically larger in one part of the range of independent variable(s) than in others. For example, if the firm uses less reliable equipment and less skilled labor in months of large total production, variation in total costs during months of large total production is likely to be greater than in months of small total production.

Third, users of regression analysis should be aware of problems in the data base. This awareness comes from a thorough study of the activities that give rise to the data. For example, one should estimate operating room overhead costs only after studying the activities in the operating room that cause overhead costs to be incurred. Activity-based costing, which is discussed in Chapters 3 and 5, is a useful method to identify the activities that cause costs.

Strengths and Weaknesses of Cost Estimation Methods

Each of the methods discussed has advantages and disadvantages. Probably the most informative estimate of cost behavior results from using several of the methods discussed, because each method has the potential to provide information not provided by the others. When deciding which to use in practice, compare the cost of each method with its benefits. Exhibit 6.15 summarizes the strengths and weaknesses of these methods.

Exhibit 6.15

Strengths and Weaknesses of Cost Estimation Methods

Method	Strengths	Weaknesses
Engineering Method	Based on studies of what future costs should be rather than what past costs have been.	Not particularly useful when the physical relation between inputs and outputs is indirect. Can be costly to use.
Account Analysis	Provides a detailed expert analysis of the cost behavior in each account.	Subjective.
Visual Curve-Fitting Method	Uses all the observations of cost data. Relatively easy to understand and apply.	The fitting of the line to the observations is subjective. Difficult to do where several activity bases cause costs.
Regression Method	Uses all of the observations of cost data. The line is statistically fit to the observations. Provides a measure of the goodness of fit of the line to the observations. Relatively easy to use with computers and sophisticated calculators.	The regression model requires that several relatively strict assumptions be satisfied for the results to be valid.

■ Summary ■

Managers need estimates of cost behavior to apply manufacturing overhead to products, to estimate how decisions will affect costs, to plan, and to develop budgets.

For these purposes, categorizing costs into fixed and variable components is useful. Variable costs change with the level of activity, whereas fixed costs remain constant. These categories remain valid within some assumed time period (usually called the short run) and range of activity (the relevant range).

Many fixed costs are capacity costs: they will remain constant (in the absence of inflation) as long as the firm does not change capacity. Other fixed costs are discretionary costs. These costs include such things as advertising and research and development, which may not be absolutely essential for operating the business but are essential for achieving long-run goals.

Many costs are not simply fixed nor variable. Variable costs may be curvilinear (curved) as well as linear. Curvilinear variable costs may occur in cases where learning reduces labor and labor-related costs per unit as workers gain experience with a new product or process.

Costs also may be *semivariable,* having both fixed and variable components. *Semifixed* costs are those that increase in steps.

There are numerous methods for estimating cost behavior. Each method attempts to estimate *TC, F,* and *V* in the equation

$$TC = F + VX,$$

where *TC* is the total cost during the period. *F* is the fixed cost during the period, *V* is the variable cost per unit of activity, and *X* is the number of units of activity during the period.

The *engineering method* involves a study of the physical inputs required to produce each unit of output. This method forms the basis for estimating the costs of each unit of output. The *account analysis method* analyzes each cost account and classifies the account according to cost behavior—usually either fixed or variable.

Two methods, *visual curve fitting* and *regression analysis,* rely on historical data in the accounting records. Keeping in mind the adage "garbage-in, garbage-out," we recommend the following steps in analyzing these data:

1. Select an activity base (that is, the independent variable) whose variation closely associates with the cost item being estimated.

2. Plot the data.

3. Examine the data and cost accumulation methods. Be sure that the costs (dependent variable) match the activity expected to create the costs (independent variable) by time period.

4. Examine the constancy of the production process to ensure that data represent periods when no major changes occurred in the production process.

The visual curve-fitting method estimates the relation between costs and activity from a line drawn to provide the best visual fit of the data. Regression analysis fits a line to the data to minimize the sum of the squares of the vertical distance of each observation point from the regression line.

The results of computerized regression analyses provide more than fixed and variable cost estimates. *Standard errors of the coefficients* of the regression equation give an idea of the confidence we have in the coefficients—the smaller the standard error relative to its coefficient, the better. The R^2 attempts to measure how well the regression line fits the data. To use regression to estimate costs, (1) find a logical relation between the costs and the activity base, (2) examine the data base for problems induced by the accounting system, and (3) consider and deal with statistical estimation problems signalled by the regression outputs.

Appendix 6.1:
Derivation of Learning Curves[11]

Mathematically, the learning curve effect is

$$Y = aX^b,$$

where

Y = average number of labor hours required per unit for X units
a = number of labor hours required for the first unit
X = cumulative number of units produced
b = index of learning equal to the log of the learning rate divided by the log of 2.

For the learning curve example in the text, $b = -.322$, which we derive as follows.

If the first unit takes a hours, then the average for 2 units is $.8a$ hours according to the model. Because $X = 2$, the equation gives $.8a = a2^b$. Taking logs,

$$\log 0.8 + \log a = \log a + b \log 2.$$

Simplifying,

$$b = \log 0.8/\log 2 = -.322.$$

Thus we can derive the average number of labor hours from the example in the text as follows:

X	Y	
1	125	
2	100	$Y = 125 \times (2^{-.322}) = 100$
3	88	$Y = 125 \times (3^{-.322}) = 88$
4	80	$Y = 125 \times (4^{-.322}) = 80$
.	.	
.	.	
.	.	
8	64	$Y = 125 \times (8^{-.322}) = 64$

---

[11]The learning curve derivation in this appendix is known as the cumulative-average-time learning model.

The function

$$Y = aX^b$$

is curvilinear, as shown in the text. The function is linear when expressed in logs, because

$$\log Y = \log a + b \log X,$$

so the function is linear when plotted on log-log paper, as the following exhibit shows.

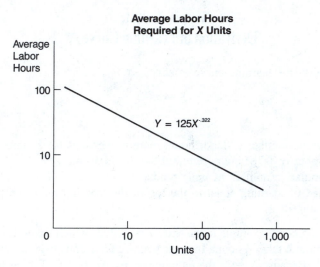

Average Labor Hours Required for X Units

Operations management textbooks provide expanded discussions.[12]

Problem 1 for Self-Study

Sketch appropriate cost graphs for each of the following situations.

a. Costs of direct materials used in producing a firm's products.

b. Wages of delivery truck drivers. The firm requires one driver, on average, for each $1 million of sales.

c. Leasing costs of a delivery truck, which is $250 per month and $.18 per mile.

d. Fixed fee paid to an independent firm of CPAs for auditing and attesting to financial statements.

---

[12]For accounting application of learning curves, see F. P. Kollaritsch and R. B. Jordan, "The Learning Curve: Concepts and Application," in H. A. Black and J. D. Edwards, eds., *The Managerial and Cost Accountant's Handbook* (Homewood, Ill.: Dow Jones–Irwin, 1979), pp. 971–1017; W. J. Morse, "Reporting Production Costs That Follow the Learning Curve Phenomenon," *The Accounting Review* 47 (October 1972), pp. 761–773; J. Chen and R. Manes, "Distinguishing the Two Forms of the Constant Percentage Learning Curve Model," *Contemporary Accounting Research,* Spring 1985, pp. 242–252; and A. Belkaoui, *The Learning Curve: A Management Accounting Tool* (Westport, Conn.: Quorum Books, 1986).

e. Compensation of sales staff with salary of $10,000 plus commission rates that increase as sales increase: 4 percent of the first $100,000 of annual sales, 6 percent of all sales from $100,000 to $200,000, and 8 percent for sales in excess of $200,000.

f. Cost of electricity, where the electric utility charges a flat rate of $50 the first 5,000 units, $.005 per unit for the next 45,000 units, and $.004 per unit for all units in excess of the first 50,000 units.

Suggested Solution

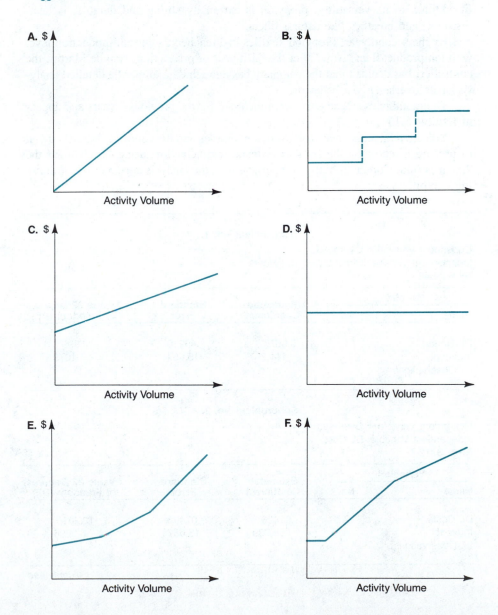

Problem 2 for Self-Study

Propylon Textiles (*Contributed by J. Lim*)

Propylon, the wonder fabric of the 1980s, was the brainchild of Henry Carr, scion of an old banking family. Pursuing his special interest in polymers as a chemistry graduate student, Carr created a synthetic compound whose polymer threads were far superior to any of the synthetics used by the textile industry. The fabric was crease-resistant, wrinkle-free, and had both the appearance and feel of natural-fiber fabrics. Propylon took the world by storm when production began 3 years ago. In addition to its versatility, propylon is extremely strong and durable, is heat-resistant, and breathes like natural fibers.

By the second year, Propylon Textiles had reached its current production level with ten product lines. Now, after the third year of production, Natalie Martin, the controller, has decided that the company has enough data to merit a detailed analysis of its overhead cost behavior.

The monthly overhead costs were recorded for the previous 2 years and appear in Exhibit 6.16.

You are a financial analyst at Propylon Textiles and the controller has asked you to prepare a report on the firm's overhead cost behavior, using the data for the 2-year period. Computer output to help you with the analysis appears in the following exhibit.

Subproblem No. 1:

Dependent Variable = Overhead
Independent Variable: Direct Labor (DL) Hours
R^2 = .8848

Variable Name	No.	Estimated Coefficient	Standard Error	t-value 22 Degrees of Freedom (DF)
DL Hours	1	5.9676	.45910	12.999
Intercept		−111,267	15,654	−7.1079
24 Observations				

Subproblem No. 2:

Dependent Variable = Overhead
Independent Variable: DL Cost
R^2 = .8712

Variable Name	No.	Estimated Coefficient	Standard Error	t-value 22 Degrees of Freedom (DF)
DL Costs	2	.91426	.07493	12.201
Intercept		−98,789	15,657	−6.3096
24 Observations				

---

continued

continued from page 268

Subproblem No. 3:

Dependent Variable = Overhead
Independent Variable: Machine Hours
$R^2 = .8630$

Variable		Estimated	Standard	t-value 22 Degrees
Name	No.	Coefficient	Error	of Freedom (DF)
Machine Hours	3	4.9015	.41645	11.770
Intercept		−117,279	17,796	−6.5902
24 Observations				

Subproblem No. 4:

Dependent Variable = Overhead
Independent Variable: Units Produced
$R^2 = .8700$

Variable		Estimated	Standard	t-value 22 Degrees
Name	No.	Coefficient	Error	of Freedom (DF)
Units Produced	4	23.799	1.9610	12.136
Intercept		−109,217	16,597	−6.5805
24 Observations				

---

a. Using the account analysis method, calculate the monthly average for fixed costs and the variable cost rate per

(1) Direct labor hour.

(2) Machine hour.

(3) Unit of output.

Write the cost equation for each of the three activity bases. To help you, the controller has classified the various accounts as follows:

Account	Cost Behavior
Indirect Materials	Variable
Indirect Labor	Variable
Lease	Fixed
Utilities	Fixed
Power	Variable
Insurance	Fixed
Maintenance	Fixed
Depreciation	Fixed
Research and Development	Fixed

Exhibit 6.16

PROPYLON TEXTILES
Cost Data
(all dollar amounts in thousands)

Month, First Year

	J	F	M	A	M	J	J	A	S	O	N	D
Indirect Materials	$22	$20	$23	$24	$22	$21	$20	$19	$19	$18	$18	$20
Indirect Labor	40	30	40	40	40	30	20	10	10	10	10	20
Lease	12	12	12	12	12	12	12	12	12	12	12	12
Utilities	9	9	8	8	12	7	8	7	8	8	9	9
Power	5	4	5	6	6	5	3	3	3	2	2	4
Insurance	1	1	1	1	1	1	1	1	1	1	1	1
Maintenance	20	6	6	6	6	6	20	6	6	6	6	6
Depreciation	2	2	2	2	2	2	2	2	2	2	2	2
Research and Development	7	8	10	9	8	10	6	6	7	4	5	8
Total Overhead	$118	$92	$107	$108	$105	$94	$92	$66	$68	$63	$65	$82
Direct Labor Hours	36.0	34.2	37.4	37.8	36.4	35.0	33.2	30.8	30.9	29.4	30.0	33.4
Direct Labor Costs ($)	216.0	205.2	224.4	226.8	218.4	210.0	199.2	184.8	185.4	176.4	180.0	200.4
Machine Hours	45.0	42.6	45.0	47.0	45.2	43.6	41.2	40.0	39.4	37.2	36.5	42.0
Units Produced	8.9	8.6	9.2	9.5	8.9	8.6	8.0	7.8	7.6	7.4	7.2	8.1

Month, Second Year

	J	F	M	A	M	J	J	A	S	O	N	D	2-Year Totals
Indirect Materials	$21	$21	$23	$24	$24	$21	$22	$20	$19	$19	$21	$22	$ 503
Indirect Labor	20	30	40	50	30	30	30	20	10	10	30	30	630
Lease	12	12	12	12	12	12	12	12	12	12	12	12	288
Utilities	10	10	9	9	8	8	8	8	9	9	10	10	206
Power	5	5	6	7	6	4	5	4	2	2	5	5	104
Insurance	1	1	1	1	1	1	1	1	1	1	1	1	24
Maintenance	20	6	6	6	6	6	20	6	6	6	6	6	200
Depreciation	4	4	4	4	4	4	4	4	4	4	4	4	72
Research and Development	6	8	1	9	8	8	7	7	7	5	8	9	171
Total Overhead	$99	$97	$102	$122	$99	$94	$109	$82	$70	$68	$97	$99	$2,198
Direct Labor Hours	33.2	34.2	36.9	39.6	35.2	34.0	35.2	32.4	30.2	30.4	34.2	35.8	815.8 Hours
Direct Labor Costs ($)	207.5	213.7	230.6	247.5	220.0	212.5	220.0	202.5	188.7	190.0	213.7	223.7	$4,997.4
Machine Hours	43.4	43.2	46.4	50.0	44.2	42.6	43.2	41.2	38.2	37.6	43.8	44.2	1,022.7 Hours
Units Produced	8.4	8.6	9.1	9.8	8.9	8.4	8.7	8.1	7.7	7.5	8.6	8.9	202.5 Units

b. Plot direct labor costs against total overhead. Are there any outliers? If so, ascertain possible causes.

c. Subproblems 1 through 4 in the preceding computer output are simple linear regressions with overhead as the dependent variable and direct labor hours, direct labor costs, machine hours, and units of output, respectively, as the independent variables. Select the most appropriate activity base for overhead cost and explain your choice.

d. Plot indirect labor costs against direct labor hours. What cost behavior pattern do you observe?

e. Using direct labor hours as the activity base, sketch the overhead cost function. What does this overhead cost function tell you about the relation between current production levels and capacity?

Suggested Solution

a.	Indirect Materials.	$ 503,000
	Indirect Labor.	630,000
	Power	104,000
	Total Variable Costs	$1,237,000
	Lease	$ 288,000
	Utilities	206,000
	Insurance	24,000
	Maintenance	200,000
	Depreciation	72,000
	Research and Development	171,000
	Total Fixed Costs	$ 961,000

$$\text{Monthly Fixed Costs} = \frac{\$961,000}{24} = \$40,042.$$

$$\text{Variable Cost per Direct Labor Hour} = \frac{\$1,237,000}{815,800} = \$1.516.$$

$$TC = \$40,042 + (\$1.516 \times \text{Direct Labor Hours}).$$

$$\text{Variable Cost per Machine Hour} = \frac{\$1,237,000}{1,022,700} = \$1.210.$$

$$TC = \$40,042 + (\$1.210 \times \text{Machine Hours}).$$

$$\text{Variable Cost per Unit Produced} = \frac{\$1,237,000}{202,500} = \$6.109.$$

$$TC = \$40,042 + (\$6.109 \times \text{Units Produced}).$$

b.

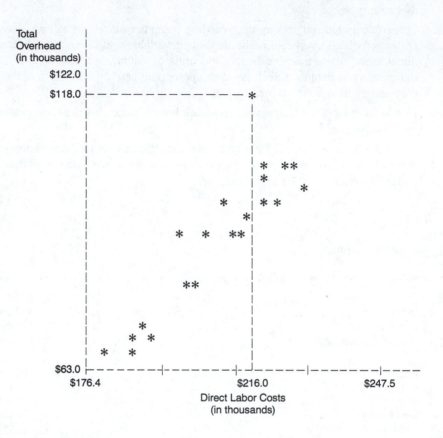

The first observation ($216,000, $118,000) appears to be an outlier. The most probable cause for the higher overhead cost is the relatively higher amount spent on maintenance that month.

c. Based on the R^2 and t-values, the four regressions are about the same. Management should search for a logical relation between overhead and the most appropriate activity base. Machine hours may be appropriate if machine processes for the various product lines do not differ radically. Direct labor cost is not a good measure if wage rates vary and do not relate to overhead. Units of output may not be a good activity base because there are ten different product lines. Direct labor hours is a good alternative for overhead costs related to labor activity.

d. The costs are semifixed or step costs.

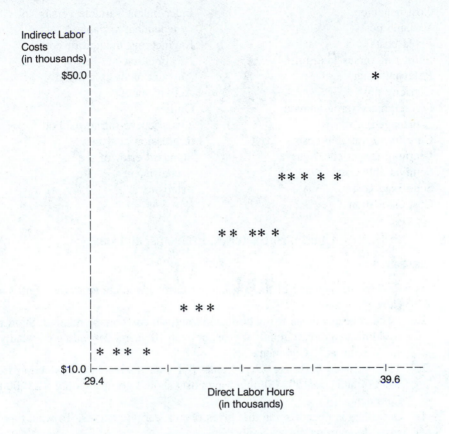

e. The steepness of the overhead function within the relevant range seems to imply that the firm is currently operating at capacity and is facing increasing marginal costs. In the long run, the company should seriously consider capacity expansion.

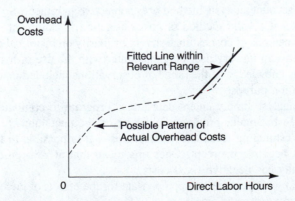

Key Terms and Concepts

Cost behavior
Variable costs
Fixed costs
Short run versus long run
Relevant range
Capacity costs
Discretionary (programmed,
  managed) costs
Curvilinear variable costs
Learning (experience) curves
Semivariable costs
Semifixed costs
Cost estimation

Independent variable versus
  dependent variable
Engineering method of cost
  estimation
Account analysis method
Activity base
Outlier
Visual curve-fitting method
Regression analysis
Standard error of the
  coefficient
t-statistic
R^2

Questions, Exercises, Problems, and Cases

Questions

1. Review the meaning of the concepts or terms given above in Key Terms and Concepts.

2. "The concepts of short-run costs and long-run costs are so relative: Short run could mean a day, a month, a year, or even 10 years, depending on what you are looking at." Comment.

3. "My variable costs are $2 per unit. If I want to increase production from 100,000 units to 150,000 units, my costs should go up by only $100,000." Comment.

4. Describe the phenomenon that gives rise to learning curves. To what type of costs do learning curves apply?

5. "Simplification of all costs into just fixed and variable costs distorts the actual cost behavior pattern of a firm. Yet businesses rely on this method of cost classification." Comment.

6. Which method of cost estimation does not rely primarily on historical cost data? What are the drawbacks of this method?

7. "The account analysis method uses subjective judgment. So we cannot really consider it a valid method of cost estimation." Comment.

8. What methods of cost estimation rely primarily on historical data? Discuss the problems an unwary user may encounter with the use of historical cost data.

9. Why is knowledge of the range of observations included in a data set for cost estimation purposes?

10. If an analyst simply enters data into a program to compute regression estimates, what major problems might he or she encounter?

11. When estimating fixed and variable costs, it is possible to have an equation with a negative intercept. Does this mean that at zero production level the company has negative fixed costs?

12. Suggest ways that one can compensate for the effects of price instability when preparing cost estimates.

Exercises

13. *Graphs of cost relations*. Sketch cost graphs for the following situations:
    a. A 20 percent increase in fixed costs will enable Twickenham Products to produce up to 50 percent more. Variable costs will remain unchanged.
    b. Refer to part **a**. What if Twickenham Products' variable costs double for the additional units it intends to produce?
    c. Aerodyne's variable marketing costs per unit decline as more units are sold.
    d. Richmond Paper pays a flat fixed charge per month for electricity plus an additional rate of $.10 per unit for all consumption over the first 1,000 units.
    e. Indirect labor costs at National Bank consist only of supervisors' salaries. The bank needs one supervisor for every ten clerks.
    f. Petersham Plastics currently operates close to capacity. A short-run increase in production would result in increasing unit costs for every additional unit produced.

14. *Cost behavior in event of capacity change*. Muller's Gasthaus, a lodge located in a fast-growing ski resort, is planning to open its new wing this coming winter, increasing the number of beds by 40 percent. Although variable costs per guest-day will remain unchanged, fixed costs will increase by 25 percent. Last year's costs follow:

Variable Costs	$50,000
Fixed Costs	$30,000

The occupancy rate percentage is expected to stay the same as last year.
    a. Sketch the cost function.
    b. Calculate the additional operating costs that Muller's Gasthaus will incur next year.

15. *Cost behavior when costs are semivariable*. Data from the shipping department of Penno Company for the last 2 months follow:

	Number of Packages Shipped	Shipping Department Costs
November	3,000	$4,500
December	4,500	6,000

    a. Sketch a line describing these costs as a function of the number of packages shipped.
    b. The line should indicate that these shipping costs are semivariable. What is the apparent fixed cost per month of running the shipping department during November and December?
    c. What is the apparent variable cost per package shipped?

16. *Cost behavior when costs are semivariable*. Data from the shipping department of Pete's Coffee for the last 3 months follow:

	Number of Packages Shipped	Shipping Department Costs
June	2,000	$3,500
July	2,500	4,500
August	1,500	3,000

What is the apparent relation between shipping department costs and the number of packages shipped?

17. *Cost estimation using visual curve fitting*. The Anwell Accounting Company prepares tax returns for small businesses. Data on the company's total costs and output for the past 6 months appear in the table that follows.
   a. Estimate fixed costs per month and variable cost per tax return prepared from the data in the table, using a straight line visually fit to a plot of the data.
   b. Estimate total monthly costs for a month when 250 tax returns are prepared, using the estimates of fixed and variable costs from part a.

ANWELL ACCOUNTING COMPANY

Month	Tax Returns Prepared	Total Costs
January	200	$160,000
February..	280	192,000
March	300	198,000
April...	260	190,000
May..	260	186,000
June	240	164,000

18. *Learning curve*. R&D Co. makes technical products for mysterious customers. To make Product RPE, the company recently recorded the following costs, which decline subject to a 75-percent cumulative learning.

Cumulative Number of Units Produced	Average Manufacturing Costs per Unit
1	$1,333
2	1,000
4	?
8	?
16	?

Complete the chart by filling in the cost amounts for volumes of 4, 8, and 16 units.

19. *Average cost calculations*. Soma Beds has the following cost equation:

$$\text{Total Costs} = \$13,266 + \$150n,$$

where n = units of output.

a. Calculate Soma's average fixed cost per unit when output is 500 units.
b. Calculate the average variable cost per unit when output is 500 units.
c. Calculate the average cost per unit when output is 500 units.

20. *Repair cost behavior*. The Baiman Company analyzed repair costs by month using linear regression analysis. The equation fit took the following form:

$$\begin{matrix} \text{Total} \\ \text{Repair} \\ \text{Costs} \end{matrix} = \begin{matrix} \text{Fixed} \\ \text{Costs} \end{matrix} + \left(\begin{matrix} \text{Variable Repair Costs} \\ \text{per Machine Hour Used} \\ \text{during Month} \end{matrix} \times \begin{matrix} \text{Machine Hours} \\ \text{Actually Used} \\ \text{during Month} \end{matrix} \right)$$

$$TRC = a + bx.$$

The results were (standard error of coefficients appear in parentheses)

$$TRC = \$20,000 - \$.75x$$
$$(\$7,000) \quad (\$.25)$$

The R^2 was 0.90.

Average monthly repair costs have been $18,800, and machine hours used have averaged 1,600 hours per month. Management worries about the ability of the analyst who carried out this work because of the *negative* coefficient for variable cost.

What is your evaluation of these results?

21. *Interpreting regression results*. The output of a regression of overhead costs on direct labor costs per month follows:

Regression Results:

Equation:

Intercept..	$16,400
Slope	2.15

Statistical Data:

Correlation Coefficient..	.92
R^2	.85

The company plans to operate at a level that would call for direct labor costs of $14,000 per month for the coming year.

a. Use the regression output to write the overhead cost equation.
b. Based on the cost equation, compute the estimated overhead cost per month for the coming year.
c. Comment on the regression.

22. *Interpreting regression data*. A marketing manager of a company used a pocket calculator to estimate the relation between sales dollars for the past

3 years and monthly advertising expenditures (the independent variable). The regression results indicated the following equation:

$$\text{Sales Dollars} = \$97,000 - (145 \times \text{Advertising Dollars})$$
$$\text{Correlation Coefficient} = -.814.$$

Do these results imply that advertising hurts sales? Why would there appear to be a negative relation between advertising expenditures and sales?

23. *Cost estimation using visual curve fitting*. Okanagan Beverages has observed the following overhead costs for the past 12 months:

Month	Overhead Costs	Gallons of Output
January	$45,600	18,000
February	62,400	44,000
March	67,200	48,000
April	48,000	22,000
May	56,400	36,000
June	62,400	42,000
July	52,800	30,000
August	49,200	20,000
September	62,400	46,000
October	51,600	24,000
November	57,600	34,000
December	60,000	40,000

a. Prepare a scatter plot of the data.
b. By visual inspection, fit a line through the plotted points and calculate the approximate monthly fixed cost and unit variable cost.

Problems

24. *Interpreting multiple regression results*. To select the most appropriate activity base for allocating overhead, Mercury Gas, an oil refinery, ran a multiple regression of several independent variables against its nonmaintenance overhead cost. The results were as follows for 24 observations:

Variable Name	Coefficient	Standard Error	t-Statistic
Direct Labor Hours	.876	2.686	.326
Units of Output	10.218	5.378	1.900
Maintenance Costs	$(12.786)	$1.113	(11.488)
Cost of Utilities	.766	.079	9.696
Intercept	12.768	6.359	2.008
R^2 for the Multiple Regression = 0.90			

Discuss the appropriateness of each of these variables for use as an activity base. Which would you recommend selecting? Why?

25. *Interpreting regression results* [adapted from an example by G. Benston, *The Accounting Review* 41 (October 1966), pp. 657–672]. The Benston Company

manufactures widgets and digits. Benston assembles the widgets in batches, but makes digits one at a time. Benston believes that the cost of producing widgets is independent of the number of digits produced in a week. The firm gathered cost data for 156 weeks. The following notation is used:

C = Total manufacturing costs per week
N = Number of widgets produced during a week
B = Average number of widgets in a batch during the week
D = Number of digits produced during the week

A multiple linear regression fit to the observations gave the following results (standard errors of estimated coefficients are shown in parentheses under the coefficients):

$$C = \$265.80 + \$8.21N - \$7.83B + \$12.32D.$$
$$(\$110.80) \quad (\$.53) \quad (\$1.69) \quad (\$2.10)$$

The adjusted R^2 was .89.

a. According to the regression results, how much are weekly costs expected to increase if the number of widgets increases by 1?

b. What are the expected costs for the week if Benston produces 500 widgets in batches of 20 each and produces 300 digits during the week?

c. Interpret the negative coefficient $\$(7.83)$ estimated for the variable B.

26. *Regression analysis, multiple choice.* Armer Company estimated the behavior pattern of maintenance costs. Data regarding maintenance hours and costs for the previous year and the results of the regression analysis follow:

	Hours of Activity	Maintenance Costs
January	480	$ 4,200
February	320	3,000
March	400	3,600
April	300	2,820
May	500	4,350
June	310	2,960
July	320	3,030
August	520	4,470
September	490	4,260
October	470	4,050
November	350	3,300
December	340	3,160
Sum	4,800	43,200
Average	400	3,600

$$TC = \quad F \quad + \quad VX$$
$$= 684.65 + 7.2884X$$
$$(49.515) \quad (.121)$$

Intercept	684.65
V Coefficient	7.2884
Standard Error of the Intercept	49.515
Standard Error of the V Coefficient	.121
R^2	.997
t-Statistic for the Intercept	13.827
t-Statistic for the V Coefficient	60.105

a. In the equation $TC = F + VX$, the best description of the letter V is as the
  (1) Independent variable.
  (2) Dependent variable.
  (3) Coefficient for the intercept.
  (4) Variable cost coefficient.

b. The best description of TC in the preceding equation is as the
  (1) Independent variable.
  (2) Dependent variable.
  (3) Constant coefficient.
  (4) Variable coefficient.

c. The best description of the letter X in the preceding regression equation is as the
  (1) Independent variable.
  (2) Dependent variable.
  (3) Coefficient for the intercept.
  (4) Variable cost coefficient.

d. Based on the data derived from the regression analysis, 420 maintenance hours in a month mean that the maintenance costs would be estimated at
  (1) $3,780.
  (2) $3,461.
  (3) $3,797.
  (4) $3,746.
  (5) Some other amount.

e. The percentage of the total variance that the regression equation explains equals
  (1) 99.7%.
  (2) 69.6%.
  (3) 80.9%.
  (4) 99.8%.
  (5) Some other amount.

27. *Graphing costs and interpreting regression output* (adapted from CMA exam). Management of Monahan's Pizza wants to estimate overhead costs accurately to plan the company's operations and its financial needs. A trade association publication reports that certain overhead costs tend to vary with pizzas made. Management gathered monthly data on pizzas and overhead costs for the past 2 years for 12 pizza restaurants. No major changes in operations were made over this time period. The data follow:

Month No.	Pizzas	Overhead Costs
1	20,000	$84,000
2	25,000	99,000
3	22,000	89,500
4	23,000	90,000
5	20,000	81,500
6	19,000	75,500

continued

continued from page 280

7	14,000	70,500
8	10,000	64,500
9	12,000	69,000
10	17,000	75,000
11	16,000	71,500
12	19,000	78,000
13	21,000	86,000
14	24,000	93,000
15	23,000	93,000
16	22,000	87,000
17	20,000	80,000
18	18,000	76,500
19	12,000	67,500
20	13,000	71,000
21	15,000	73,500
22	17,000	72,500
23	15,000	71,000
24	18,000	75,000

An analyst entered these data into a computer regression program and obtained the following output:

Coefficient of Correlation	.9544
R^2	.9109
Coefficients of the Equation:	
Intercept	39,859
Independent Variable (slope)	2.1549
Standard Error of the Independent Variable	.1437

a. Prepare a graph showing the overhead costs plotted against pizzas.

b. Use the results of the regression analysis to prepare the cost estimation equation and to prepare a cost estimate for 22,500 pizzas for one month.

c. Evaluate how well the regression estimates overhead cost behavior.

28. *Regression analysis in a process* (adapted from CMA exam). The Johnstar Company makes an expensive chemical product. The costs average about $1,000 per unit of weight, and the material sells for $2,500 per unit of weight. Materials storage is extremely hazardous; therefore, the firm makes a batch each day to fill customer orders for the day. Failure to deliver the required quantity results in a shutdown for the customer with a corresponding cost penalty assessed against Johnstar. However, Johnstar must dispose of excess chemical on hand at the end of the day in costly, secure facilities.

The chemical increases in weight during processing, but the exact increase varies depending on temperature and pressure conditions as well as on the impurities present in the input materials. The company needs to know the final weight from any batch as soon as possible so that it can start a new batch if the expected final weight falls short of customer needs.

Johnstar hired a consultant to advise the company on how to estimate the final weight of the product. The consultant recommended that an engineer weigh the product after 3 hours and that a model be used to predict the weight at the end of processing from 20 processed batches. The weight after 3 hours provided the following observations:

Batch No.	Weight at 3 Hours	Final Weight	Batch No.	Weight at 3 Hours	Final Weight
1	55	90	11	60	80
2	45	75	12	35	60
3	40	80	13	35	80
4	60	80	14	55	60
5	40	45	15	35	75
6	60	80	16	50	90
7	50	80	17	30	60
8	55	95	18	60	105
9	50	100	19	50	60
10	35	75	20	20	30

Data obtained from the regression analysis included the following:

R^2	.41
Coefficients of the Regression:	
Constant..	28.64
Slope	1.01
Standard Error of Slope Coefficient	.28
t-Statistic for Slope	3.61

a. Use the results of the regression to estimate the final weight of today's batch, which at the end of 3 hours weighs 42 units.

b. Customer orders for today total 68 units. The smallest batch that the firm can start must weigh at least 20 units at the end of 3 hours. What factors should the firm consider in deciding whether to start a new batch?

29. *Effect of learning on cost behavior.* Zipper Incorporated manufactures aircraft parts for various commercial airlines. One particular contract, including the design and manufacture of special containers, resulted in the following costs:

Cumulative Number of Units Produced, X	Average Manufacturing Costs (in real dollars), Y
1	$1,333
2	1,000
3	845
4	750

continued

continued from page 282

5	684
6	634
7	594
8	562

a. Sketch the relation between X and Y.

b. If there is a learning phenomenon, estimate the constant percentage reduction in manufacturing costs.

30. *Learning curves* (adapted from CMA exam). The Kelly Company plans to manufacture a product called Electrocal, which requires a substantial amount of direct labor on each unit. Based on the company's experience with other products that required similar amounts of direct labor, management believes that learning affects the production process used to manufacture Electrocal.

Each unit of Electrocal requires 50 square feet of direct material at a cost of $30 per square foot for a total material cost of $1,500. The standard direct labor rate is $25 per direct labor hour. The accounting system assigns variable manufacturing overhead to products at a rate of $40 per direct labor hour. The company adds a markup of 30 percent to variable manufacturing cost in setting an initial bid price for all products.

Data on the production of the first two lots (16 units) of Electrocal follow:

(1) The first lot of 8 units required a total of 3,200 direct labor hours.

(2) The second lot of 8 units required a total of 2,240 direct labor hours. Based on prior production experience, Kelly anticipates that production time will not improve significantly after the first 32 units. Therefore, a standard for direct labor hours will be established based on the average hours per unit for units 17 through 32.

a. What is the basic premise of the learning curve?

b. Based on the data presented for the first 16 units, what learning rate appears to apply to the direct labor required to produce Electrocal? Support your answer with appropriate calculations.

c. Calculate the standard for direct labor hours that Kelly Company should establish for each unit of Electrocal.

d. After Kelly had manufactured the first 32 units, the customer asked Kelly to submit a bid for an additional 96 units. What price should Kelly bid on this order of 96 units? Explain your answer.

e. Knowledge of the learning curve phenomenon can be a valuable management tool. Explain how management can apply the learning curve in planning and controlling business operations.

Integrative Problems and Cases

31. *Comprehensive problem in estimating costs for historical data.* The accounting department at Ling National Bank has available the data shown in the accompanying table: observations by month on total overhead costs for the month, on direct labor hours worked for the month, and on direct labor costs for the month in dollars for the last 3 years. The problem is to estimate the fixed overhead costs per month and the variable overhead costs per unit of base activity. Analysis of the overhead costs indicates that direct labor hours required and direct labor costs both closely vary with variable overhead costs. The procedures and questions that follow mirror the steps taken by the accountants at Ling National Bank in estimating fixed and variable overhead costs.

a.   Before estimating costs, what questions should the analyst raise and answer about how data shown in the accompanying table pass through the accounting system? Assume that these questions have satisfactory answers before the analyst takes the following steps.

b.   Prepare a graph with total overhead costs on the vertical axis and direct labor *hours* on the horizontal axis. Plot the 36 monthly observations.

c.   Prepare a graph with total overhead costs on the vertical axis and direct labor *costs* in dollars on the horizontal axis. Plot the 36 monthly observations.

d.   Visually fit a linear cost relation to the graphs drawn in parts **b** and **c**, and estimate the fixed cost and variable cost coefficients from your visually fit lines.

e.   The analyst used a computer regression program. The first regression specified total overhead costs as the dependent variable and direct labor hours as the independent variable. The results follow:

	Coefficient	Standard Error	t-Statistic
Fixed Costs................................	$9,553	$558.08	17.1
Direct Labor Hours	$.03527	$.00226	15.6
R^2 = .88			

A second regression specified total overhead costs as the dependent variable and direct labor costs in dollars as the independent variable. The results follow:

	Coefficient	Standard Error	t-Statistic
Fixed Costs................................	$5,707	542.47	10.5
Direct Labor Costs.....................	$.00723	.00031	23.0
R^2 = .94			

Interpret the results of these regressions. Which appears to be the most useful? What cost estimates can you make?

LING NATIONAL BANK
Observations of Total Overhead Costs, Direct Labor
Hours, and Direct Labor Costs by Month

	Direct Labor Hours Worked during Month	Direct Labor Costs Incurred during Month	Total Overhead Costs for Month
Year 1			
January	300,000	$1,920,000	$19,200
February..............	300,000	1,920,000	20,000
March	315,000	2,016,000	20,000
April.................	285,000	1,824,000	19,200
May..................	315,000	2,016,000	19,600
June	330,000	2,112,000	20,000
July	330,000	2,112,000	20,800
August	345,000	2,208,000	22,000
September	360,000	2,304,000	22,000
October	345,000	2,208,000	21,600
November	300,000	1,920,000	22,000
December	315,000	2,268,000	22,400
Year 2			
January	285,000	$2,052,000	$20,000
February..............	225,000	1,620,000	18,000
March	240,000	1,728,000	18,400
April.................	210,000	1,512,000	16,800
May..................	225,000	1,620,000	17,200
June	210,000	1,512,000	16,400
July	225,000	1,620,000	17,600
August	225,000	1,620,000	16,800
September	150,000	1,080,000	12,800
October	195,000	1,404,000	15,200
November	180,000	1,296,000	15,200
December	180,000	1,440,000	15,600
Year 3			
January	165,000	1,320,000	15,200
February..............	150,000	1,200,000	14,800
March	180,000	1,440,000	16,400
April.................	180,000	1,440,000	16,000
May..................	195,000	1,572,000	16,800
June	195,000	1,572,000	17,200
July	210,000	1,692,000	18,000
August	210,000	1,692,000	18,400
September	150,000	1,200,000	14,400
October	180,000	1,452,000	16,800
November	195,000	1,572,000	17,600
December	210,000	1,704,000	17,200

32. *Learning curves, managerial decisions* (adapted from CMA exam). The Xyon Company purchases 80,000 pumps annually from Kobec, Inc. The price has increased each year and reached $68 per unit last year. Because the purchase price has increased significantly, Xyon management has asked its analyst to estimate the cost to manufacture the pump in its own facilities. Xyon's products consist of stampings and castings. The company has little experience with products requiring assembly.

The engineering, manufacturing, and accounting departments have prepared a report for management that includes the following estimate for an assembly run of 10,000 units. The firm would hire additional production employees to manufacture the subassembly. It would not need extra equipment, space, or supervision.

The report estimates total costs for 10,000 units at $957,000, or $95.70 a unit. The current purchase price is $68 a unit, so the report recommends continued purchase of the product.

Components (outside purchases)...........	$120,000
Assembly Labor[a]	300,000
Factory Overhead[b]	450,000
General and Administrative Overhead[c]......	87,000
Total Costs	$957,000

Fixed Overhead	50 Percent of Direct Labor Dollars
Variable Overhead.......................	100 Percent of Direct Labor Dollars
Factory Overhead Rate	150 Percent of Direct Labor Dollars

[a]Assembly labor consists of hourly production workers.

[b]Factory overhead is applied to products on a direct labor dollar basis. Variable overhead costs vary closely with direct labor dollars.

[c]General and administrative overhead is applied at 10 percent of the total cost of material (or components), assembly labor, and factory overhead.

a. Was the analysis prepared by the engineering, manufacturing, and accounting departments of Xyon Company and the recommendation to continue purchasing the pumps that followed from the analysis correct? Explain your answer and include any supportive calculations you consider necessary.

b. Assume Xyon Company could experience labor cost improvements on the pump assembly consistent with an 80 percent learning curve. An assembly run of 10,000 units represents the initial lot or batch for measurement purposes. Should Xyon produce the 80,000 pumps in this situation? Explain your answer.

Suggested Solutions to Even-Numbered Exercises

14. *Cost behavior in event of capacity change*

   a.

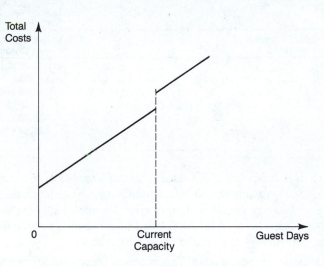

   b.   Additional Operating Costs = 0.40(50,000) + 0.25(30,000)
$$= \underline{\underline{\$27,500}}.$$

16. *Cost behavior when costs are semivariable*

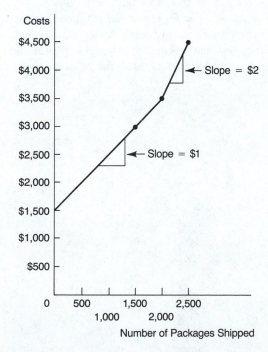

Costs are semivariable. The fixed-cost component estimate is $1,500, and the variable cost component is $1 per package up to 2,000 packages. With only three data points, you should view these estimates skeptically.

18. *Learning curve*

Cumulative Number of Units Produced	Average Manufacturing Costs per Unit
1	$1,333
2	1,000 ($1,333 × 75%)
4	750 ($1,000 × 75%)
8	562.50 ($750 × 75%)
16	421.88 ($562.50 × 75%)

20. *Repair cost behavior.* The t-statistic of the variable cost coefficient is -3 $(= -.75/.25)$, which should help convince management that the variable cost coefficient differs significantly from zero. The most likely explanation for the inverse relation between production and repair costs is that the firm schedules repair work during slow, rather than busy, times.

22. *Interpreting regression data.* This problem frequently arises when applying analytical techniques to certain costs. Quite often the advertising expenditures result in sales being generated in the following month or later. In addition, many companies increase their advertising when sales are declining and cut back on advertising when manufacturing is at capacity. A better model might relate this month's sales to last month's advertising.

Similar problems exist for repair and maintenance costs, because routine repairs and maintenance usually occur during slow periods. An inverse relation often exists between salespersons' travel expenses and sales, if the sales staff spends more time traveling when the sales are more difficult to make.

... CHAPTER 7 ...

Cost-Volume-Profit Analysis

Chapter Outline

- The Cost-Volume-Profit Model
- Applications of the Cost-Volume-Profit Model
- Using Sales Dollars as a Measure of Volume
- Income Taxes
- Multiproduct Cost-Volume-Profit
- Simplifications and Assumptions

Successful management requires understanding the relations among revenues, costs, volume, and profits. The cost-volume-profit model represents the firm's activities because virtually all decisions affect costs, volume, or profits. Managers can use it as a macro model to describe a firm's financial activities. For example, an automotive company executive stated that the company did not show a quarterly profit because, "Given the prices we can charge and the costs we incur, we simply did not have enough volume to break even last quarter."

In addition, managers can use cost-volume-profit analysis as a micro tool to answer questions such as "How many patients do we need for the new medical clinic to break even?" "What is the expected profit from Product S-29 if we increase advertising by $2 million?"

The analysis relies on concepts of fixed and variable cost behavior that Chapter 2 discussed. This chapter presents the cost-volume-profit model and demonstrates how managers can use (or misuse) it in a number of decision-making situations. The chapter focuses on short-run operating decisions, those which do not involve a change in capacity.

After reading this chapter, you should understand the nature of the cost-volume-profit model, applications of the model, and the model's limitations and assumptions.

The Cost-Volume-Profit Model

The **cost-volume-profit model** specifies a relation among selling prices, unit costs, volume sold, and profits. It starts with the basic equation relating profits to revenues less costs:

$$\pi = TR - TC,$$

where π = operating profit for the period, TR = total revenues for the period, and TC = total costs for the period.

The cost-volume-profit equation in more detail is

$$\begin{aligned}\pi &= TR - TC \\ &= PX - (F + VX),\end{aligned}$$

where P = unit selling price, X = number of units sold in the period, F = fixed operating costs for the period, and V = unit variable costs.

Profits in managerial models or on internal reports differ from net income for external financial reporting under generally accepted accounting principles (GAAP). For example, costs in the managerial model may include as "depreciation" an estimate of the decline in economic value of an asset because of its use over a period of time. This contrasts with depreciation for external reporting, which allocates over time the price paid for the asset. Also, the cost-volume-profit model treats fixed manufacturing overhead as a cost of the period (that is, the variable costing method), not as a unit cost as required for external reporting under GAAP (the full absorption method). The cost-volume-profit model typically omits financing costs such as interest expense on long-term debt.

Example   We base much of our discussion in this chapter on illustrative data for Baltimore Company, which makes a particular type of computer software known as BC-1234. These data appear in the top panel of Exhibit 7.1. The cost-volume-profit equation for Baltimore Company is

$$\begin{aligned}\pi &= PX - (F + VX) \\ &= \$30X - (\$4,800 + \$22X).\end{aligned}$$

The bottom panel of Exhibit 7.1 presents two linear relations: total revenue, $TR = PX = \$30X$; and total cost as a function of units sold,[1] $TC = \$4,800 + \$22X$.

---

[1]We assume the firm produced and sold units in the same time period to keep the analysis from becoming unnecessarily complex.

Exhibit 7.1

BALTIMORE COMPANY
Cost-Volume-Profit Data

Selling Price per Unit $30

Cost Classification	Variable Cost (per unit)	Fixed Cost (per month)
Manufacturing Costs	$17	$3,060
Marketing and Administrative Costs	5	1,740
Total Costs.	$22	$4,800

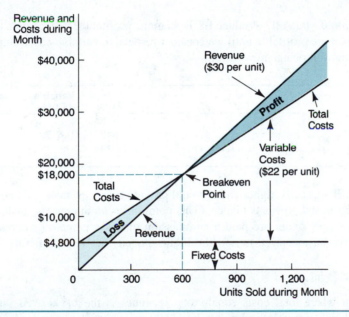

Because the fixed costs are $4,800 per month, the total cost line goes through the vertical axis at $4,800. Because variable costs are $22 per unit, the total cost line increases $22 for each increase in units produced and sold during the month.

The Contribution Concept

Each unit sold contributes to fixed costs and the earning of profit. The **contribution margin per unit** is the excess of unit selling price over unit variable cost.[2]

$$\text{Contribution Margin per Unit} = P - V.$$

---

[2]Both the concepts of "sales revenue less total variable cost" and "sales revenue per unit less variable cost per unit" are often known as *contribution margin*. The former is actually *total contribution margin*, whereas the latter is *contribution margin per unit*. We, and others, often use the term *contribution margin* to mean one or the other, depending on the context.

For the Baltimore Company, the contribution margin is

$8 = $30 Selling Price per Unit − $22 Variable Cost per Unit.

The contribution margin has important applications in product choice decisions. Suppose that you have the opportunity to produce and sell equal quantities of one of the following products to a customer (not both):

	Price
Product A	$12
Product B	15

Which would you sell? Product B? Is it more profitable? We cannot tell which product is more profitable until we consider respective variable costs. Suppose that we find the following information:

	Price	Variable Cost	Contribution Margin
Product A.....................................	$12	$ 7	$5
Product B.....................................	15	11	4

Although B's price is higher and it would provide more revenues, A's contribution to fixed costs and profits is higher. (This point raises an interesting incentive problem if sales personnel are paid a commission that is a percent of revenue. They would have an incentive to sell the higher-priced, but less-profitable, product.)

Breakeven Point

The point where total costs equals total revenues is the **breakeven point**.[3] The monthly breakeven point in Exhibit 7.1 is 600 units. At sales volumes less than 600 units per month, the firm incurs a loss equal to the vertical distance between the total cost line and the revenue line. For example, verify that at a sales volume of 300 units, the loss is $2,400 [$TR = \$30 \times 300$ units $= \$9,000$; $TC = \$4,800 + (\$22 \times 300) = \$11,400$.]

The breakeven point derives from the equation

$$\pi = PX - (F + VX).$$

At the breakeven point, profit, π, must be zero. In our example, we know that $P = \$30$, $F = \$4,800$, and $V = \$22$. Thus the breakeven sales volume, which is represented by X_b in the equation, is found as follows:

$$0 = \$30X_b - (\$4,800 + \$22X_b),$$

---

[3]Cost-volume-profit analysis is sometimes called *breakeven analysis*. Finding the breakeven point, however, is only one application of cost-volume-profit analysis.

or

$$0 = \$8X_b - \$4{,}800$$
$$\$8X_b = \$4{,}800$$
$$X_b = \frac{\$4{,}800}{\$8}$$
$$= 600 \text{ Units.}$$

In general, the breakeven equation is

$$\text{Breakeven Point in Units} = \frac{\text{Fixed Costs per Period}}{\text{Contribution Margin per Unit}},$$

or, in symbols,

$$X_b = \frac{F}{P - V}.$$

Finding Target Profits

Managers frequently use the preceding equations to find the volume required for a target profit. For example, if Baltimore Company wants to know the amount of sales required in a month to achieve a profit of $5,000, it can solve the following:

$$\$5{,}000 = \$30X - (\$4{,}800 + \$22X)$$
$$\$5{,}000 = \$8X - \$4{,}800$$
$$\$8X = \$9{,}800$$
$$X = 1{,}225 \text{ Units per Month.}$$

The Profit-Volume Model

The **cost-volume-profit graph** in Exhibit 7.1 shows the breakeven point or provides a rough idea of profit or loss at various sales levels. However, because the profit or loss appears as the vertical distance between two lines, neither of which is horizontal, the graph does not conveniently depict the profit or loss as a function of sales volume. Consequently, accountants often express the relation between profit and volume with the profit-volume graph as in Exhibit 7.2.

The profit-volume relation derives from the cost-volume-profit equation. Start with the cost-volume-profit equation:

$$\pi = PX - (F + VX).$$

Rearrange terms to get

$$\pi = PX - F - VX,$$

and

$$\pi = -F + (P - V)X,$$

which is the **profit-volume equation.**

The vertical axis of the profit-volume graph shows the amount of profit or loss for the period—1 month in our example. At zero sales, the loss equals the fixed

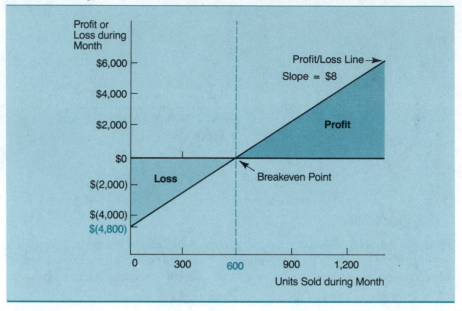

Exhibit 7.2

BALTIMORE COMPANY
Profit-Volume Graph

costs, F, of \$4,800. At the breakeven point, 600 units in our example, the profit is
zero. The slope of the profit line is equal to $P - V$ (the contribution margin per unit
sold) = \$30 − \$22 = \$8.

Applications of the Cost-Volume-Profit Model

In this section, we illustrate several uses of the cost-volume-profit model.

Example 1: Required Selling Price   The manager of Baltimore Company wants to
know the price it must charge if sales are 800 units per month and the target profit is
\$4,000 per month. Fixed costs per month are \$4,800 and unit variable costs are \$22.
We can solve for the required selling price as follows:

$$\text{Profit} = \text{Revenues} - \text{Costs}$$
$$\$4,000 = 800P - [\$4,800 + (800 \times \$22)]$$
$$800P = \$17,600 + \$4,800 + \$4,000$$
$$800P = \$26,400$$
$$P = \$33 \text{ Required Selling Price per Unit.}$$

Example 2: New Breakeven Point with an Increase in Fixed Costs   The manager of Baltimore Company wants to know how many units it must sell each month to break
even under the following conditions: fixed costs increase to \$5,600 per month, but

variable costs remain at $22 per unit and selling price remains at $30 per unit. Solving for X, which represents the number of units produced and sold, we have

$$\text{Profit} = \text{Revenues} - \text{Costs}$$
$$\$0 = \$30X - (\$5,600 + \$22X)$$
$$\$8X = \$5,600$$
$$X = 700 \text{ Units Required to Break Even.}$$

Example 3: Sensitivity Analysis One useful application of cost-volume-profit analysis, particularly for planning, is sensitivity analysis. **Sensitivity analysis** explores the impact of changes or variations in estimates of prices, costs, and volumes. It asks "what-if" questions and receives "if-then" answers. For example, the manager of Baltimore Company wants to know the impact of changing costs, prices, and volume on profits. Specifically, consider the following alternative cases ("what-ifs"):

- Costs:
  (1) No change
  (2) 10 percent increase.

- Price and volume:
  (1) No change
  (2) 10 percent price increase and 5 percent volume decrease.

The following matrix shows the results (that is, the "if-thens") from applying the cost-volume-profit equation:

$$\text{Profit} = \text{Revenues} - \text{Costs}$$
$$\pi = PX - (F + VX).$$

The status quo (starting point) is

$$\$1,600 = (\$30 \times 800) - [\$4,800 + (\$22 \times 800)].$$

Profit as a Function of Cost, Volume, and Price

		Costs	
		No Change	10 Percent Increase
Price and Volume	No Change	Profit = ($30 × 800) − [$4,800 + ($22 × 800)] = **$1,600**	Profit = ($30 × 800) − [$5,280 + ($24.20 × 800)] = **$(640)**
	10 Percent Price Increase 5 Percent Volume Decrease	Profit = ($33 × 760) − [$4,800 + ($22 × 760)] = **$3,560**	Profit = ($33 × 760) − [$5,280 + ($24.20 × 760)] = **$1,408**

Exhibit 7.3

Comparison of Variable Company and Fixed Company

	Variable Company (1,000,000 units)	Fixed Company (1,000,000 units)
Sales.................................	$1,200,000	$1,200,000
Variable Costs........................	750,000	250,000
Contribution Margin...................	$ 450,000	$ 950,000
Fixed Costs...........................	250,000 — Total Costs = $1,000,000	750,000 — Total Costs = $1,000,000
Operating Profit......................	$ 200,000	$ 200,000
Breakeven Point.......................	$X_b = \dfrac{F}{P-V}$ $= \dfrac{\$250{,}000}{\$1.20 - .75}$ $= 555{,}556$ Units	$X_b = \dfrac{F}{P-V}$ $= \dfrac{\$750{,}000}{\$1.20 - .25}$ $= 789{,}474$ Units
Margin of Safety (units)..............	Sales Volume − Breakeven Volume = 1,000,000 − 555,556 = 444,444 Units	Sales Volume − Breakeven Volume = 1,000,000 − 789,474 = 210,526 Units
Margin of Safety as a Percentage of Forecast Sales Volume..............	$\dfrac{444{,}444}{1{,}000{,}000} = 44$ Percent	$\dfrac{210{,}526}{1{,}000{,}000} = 21$ Percent

These results show the manager that a 10 percent cost increase, with no change in selling price or volume, produces a loss for the company. The results also show that if costs do not increase, but prices increase by 10 percent, causing volume to drop by 5 percent, profits more than double. You can easily perform a sensitivity analysis like this with a personal computer.

Example 4: Comparison of Alternatives   The manager of Baltimore Company is considering an alternative production method. With the current method, variable costs are $22 per unit and fixed costs are $4,800. The alternative would substitute machines for labor; variable costs would drop to $18 per unit, but the annual lease of the machines and machine maintenance would increase fixed costs to $6,000 per month. The alternative requires no new investment in the machines. Under both alternatives, the selling price will be $30 per unit and the company will sell 800 units each month. The expected profit under the status quo is

$$\begin{aligned}
\text{Profit} &= \text{Revenues} - \text{Costs} \\
&= (\$30 \times 800) - [\$4,800 + (\$22 \times 800)] \\
&= \$24,000 - \$22,400 \\
&= \$1,600.
\end{aligned}$$

The expected profit under the proposed alternative is

$$\begin{aligned}
\text{Profit} &= \text{Revenues} - \text{Costs} \\
&= (\$30 \times 800) - [\$6,000 + (\$18 \times 800)] \\
&= \$24,000 - \$20,400 \\
&= \$3,600.
\end{aligned}$$

The analysis indicates that the alternative will increase expected profits.

Margin of Safety

The **margin of safety** is the excess of projected (or actual) sales units over the breakeven unit sales level. The formula for margin of safety is

$$\text{Sales Units} - \text{Breakeven Sales Units} = \text{Margin of Safety}.$$

In our example, the level of activity is 800 units, whereas the breakeven point is 600 units. Therefore, the margin of safety is 200 units. Sales volume can drop 25 percent before the firm incurs a loss, other things held constant.

Companies that become more capital intensive, substituting fixed costs for variable costs, often find that their margin of safety declines. Consider two companies that are alike in every respect, except that 75 percent of Variable Company's total costs are variable, whereas 75 percent of Fixed Company's total costs are fixed at current volume levels. (See Exhibit 7.3.)

Fixed Company has a lower margin of safety. It will incur losses sooner than Variable Company if sales volume decreases. Companies in capital-intensive industries such as automobiles and computers that have relatively high fixed costs have found that small decreases in sales volume can result in losses.

Using Sales Dollars as a Measure of Volume

Firms selling services not easily measured in units can measure volume in sales dollars. For example, how do you define units of output in a consulting firm? Such firms often use sales dollars to measure the volume of activity.

With this measure, the cost-volume-profit equation remains the same as before, except that PX is total revenue, not "price times quantity," and VX is total variable costs, not "unit variable cost times quantity." We substitute PX for X when solving for volume of activity. For example, the breakeven volume in units for Baltimore Company is

$$X_b = \frac{F}{P - V}$$
$$= \frac{\$4,800}{(\$30 - \$22)}$$
$$= 600 \text{ Units.}$$

With volume defined as PX, we multiply both sides of the breakeven formula by P to express volume in sales dollars:

$$PX_b = \left(\frac{F}{P - V}\right)P$$
$$= \frac{F}{(P - V)/P}$$
$$= \frac{\$4,800}{(\$30 - \$22)/\$30}$$
$$= \frac{\$4,800}{.26667}$$
$$= \$18,000.$$

Thus the breakeven volume expressed in sales *dollars* is \$18,000. (You can verify that this result is the same as 600 units sold at \$30 per unit.)

The term $(P - V)/P$ in the denominator of the breakeven equation is the **contribution margin ratio,** that is, the ratio of the unit contribution margin to unit price. Hence, the formula in words is

$$\text{Breakeven Sales Dollars} = \frac{\text{Fixed Costs}}{\text{Contribution Margin Ratio}}.$$

In the example, this ratio states that each dollar of sales generates \$.26667 of contribution.

Income Taxes

You can include income taxes in the cost-volume-profit model as follows:

$$\text{After-Tax Profit} = \text{Before-Tax Profit} \times (1 - \text{Tax Rate}).$$

This means that the after-tax profit equals the before-tax profit minus taxes, where taxes equal the tax rate times the before-tax profit. If π_{at} designates after-tax profits, π_{bt} designates before-tax profits, and t designates the tax rate, we have

$$\pi_{at} = \pi_{bt}(1 - t)$$
$$= [(P - V)X - F](1 - t).$$

Example The management of Baltimore Company wants to know the volume of sales required to provide $1,920 profit *after taxes* in April. $P = \$30$, $V = \$22$, $F = \$4,800$, and $t = .40$ (that is, an average tax rate for April of 40 percent). We find the volume that provides an after-tax profit of $1,920 as follows:

$$\pi_{at} = \pi_{bt}(1 - t)$$
$$\$1,920 = [(P - V)X - F](1 - t)$$
$$= [(\$30 - \$22)X - \$4,800](1 - .40)$$
$$= [(\$8X - \$4,800)(.60)]$$
$$= \$4.8X - \$2,880$$
$$\$4,800 = \$4.8X$$
$$\frac{\$4,800}{\$4.8} = X$$
$$X = 1,000 \text{ Units.}$$

Multiproduct Cost-Volume-Profit

Most companies produce or sell many products. Multiple products make using cost-volume-profit analysis more complex, as the following example shows.

Example Sport Autos, a sports car dealership, sells two models, Sleek and Powerful. The relevant prices and costs of each appear in Exhibit 7.4.

Average monthly fixed costs of the new car department are $100,000.

We expand the cost-volume-profit equation presented earlier to consider the contribution of each product:

$$\pi = (P_s - V_s)X_s + (P_p - V_p)X_p - F,$$

Exhibit 7.4

SPORT AUTOS
Price and Cost Data

	Sleek		Powerful	
Average Selling Price per Car................		$20,000		$30,000
Less Average Variable Costs:				
Cost of Car..............................	$(11,000)		$(15,000)	
Cost of Preparing Car for Sale	(3,000)		(3,000)	
Sales Commissions	(1,000)	(15,000)	(2,000)	(20,000)
Average Contribution Margin per Car		$ 5,000		$10,000

where the subscript s designates the Sleek model, and the subscript p designates the Powerful model. Based on the information for Sport Autos, the company's profit equation is

$$\pi = (\$20,000 - \$15,000)X_s + (\$30,000 - \$20,000)X_p - \$100,000$$
$$= \quad \$5,000X_s \quad + \quad \$10,000X_p \quad - \$100,000.$$

The complexity of analysis increases when the firm has more than one product, particularly when managers attempt to derive breakeven points or target volumes. For example, the chief executive of Sport Autos has been listening to a debate between two of the salespeople about the breakeven point for the company. According to one, "We have to sell 20 cars a month to break even." But the other one claims that 10 cars a month would be sufficient. The chief executive wonders how these two salespeople could hold such different views.

The breakeven volume is the volume that provides a contribution that just covers all fixed costs. For Sport Autos, that is

$$\$5,000X_s + \$10,000X_p = \$100,000.$$

The claim that 20 cars must be sold to break even is correct if the firm sells *only* the Sleek model, whereas the claim that only 10 cars need to be sold is correct if the firm sells *only* the Powerful model. In fact, Sport Autos has many possible product mix combinations at which it would break even.

Managerial Application

Cost Analysis for Chrysler Corporation[a]

Cost-volume-profit analysis showed how much Chrysler had to improve just to break even in 1979. In that year, the breakeven point was 2.2 million units, but the company was selling considerably fewer than 2 million units. Faced with a severe recession in the automobile industry, Chrysler had virtually no chance to increase sales enough to break even. Meanwhile, the company had received loan guarantees from the U.S. government, which evoked considerable criticism that the federal government was supporting a "failing" company.

By 1982, Chrysler reduced its breakeven point to 1.1 million units, and the company reported a profit for the first time in several years. The headlines read, "'We're in black,' Iacocca chortles."[b] The turnaround came despite continued low sales in the automobile industry; it resulted primarily from severe cost cutting, which reduced fixed costs in constant dollars from $4.5 billion in 1979 to $3.1 billion in 1982. In addition, the company made improvements in its production methods, which enabled it to maintain its volume of output despite the reduction in fixed costs.

[a]See R. S. Miller, "The Chrysler Story," *Management Accounting* (August 1983), pp. 22–27.
[b]*Detroit Free Press*, June 6, 1982.

Exhibit 7.5 lists all possible breakeven points for Sport Autos. Exhibit 7.6 presents graphically the possible breakeven volumes for the company. The breakeven line in Exhibit 7.6 is one of a family of lines known as isoprofit lines (*iso* means *equal*). Profits are the same for any combination of product volumes on the isoprofit line. (To see this, find a couple of breakeven points from Exhibit 7.5 on the breakeven line in Exhibit 7.6.) Any combination of product volumes to the right of the line provides a profit; any to the left results in a loss.

This simple example demonstrates how complex multiproduct cost-volume-profit analysis can become. In a company with many products, billions of combinations of product volumes can provide a specific target profit. To deal with this problem, managers and accountants can (1) assume that all products have the same contribution margin, (2) assume that a particular product mix does not change, (3) assume a weighted-average contribution margin, or (4) treat each product line as a separate entity. In addition to these simplifications, firms can conduct multiproduct analyses with a mathematical method known as *linear programming,* discussed in Chapter 8. We now look at each of these alternatives.

1. Assume the Same Contribution Margin   The analyst can often group products so that they have equal or nearly equal contribution margins. It does not matter whether the firm sells a unit of Product A or a unit of Product B if both have the same contribution margin. (This approach won't work for Sport Autos, because Sleeks and Powerfuls have different contribution margins.)

2. Assume a Fixed Product Mix   Suppose the experience at Sport Autos is that Sleeks outsell Powerfuls at a rate of 2 to 1. Define a "package sale," X^*, to be the sale of two Sleeks and one Powerful. The contribution from this package is

$$
\begin{array}{lrr}
\text{Sleek:} & 2 \times \$5,000 = & \$10,000 \\
\text{Powerful:} & 1 \times \$10,000 = & \underline{10,000} \\
\text{Total Package:} & & \underline{\$20,000}
\end{array}
$$

Exhibit 7.5

SPORT AUTOS
Combinations of Breakeven Quantities

Sleek Model		Powerful Model		Total Contribution	Fixed Costs	Profit
Quantity	Contribution	Quantity	Contribution			
20	$100,000	0	$ 0	$100,000	$100,000	$0
18	90,000	1	10,000	100,000	100,000	0
16	80,000	2	20,000	100,000	100,000	0
•	•	•	•	•	•	•
•	•	•	•	•	•	•
•	•	•	•	•	•	•
4	20,000	8	80,000	100,000	100,000	0
2	10,000	9	90,000	100,000	100,000	0
0	0	10	100,000	100,000	100,000	0

Exhibit 7.6

SPORT AUTOS
Possible Breakeven Volumes

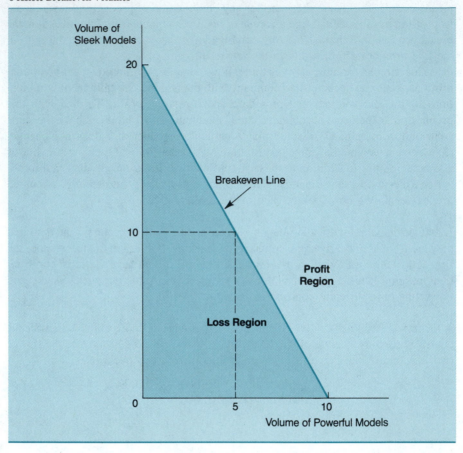

The breakeven point is

$$X_b^* = \frac{\$100,000}{\$20,000}$$
$$= 5.$$

This equation shows that the sale of five packages, each comprising two Sleeks and a Powerful, contribute enough to break even. In other words, the breakeven volume for the month is 15 units—10 Sleeks and 5 Powerfuls.

3. Assume a Weighted-Average Contribution Margin   Another way of applying the assumed product mix is to use a weighted-average contribution margin. If we assume the product mix to be two Sleeks for every Powerful, the per-unit weighted-average contribution margin is

Sleeks   *Powerfuls*
$(\tfrac{2}{3} \times \$5,000) + (\tfrac{1}{3} \times \$10,000) = \$6,667.$

The breakeven point is

$$X_b = \frac{\$100,000}{\$6,667}$$
$$= 15 \text{ Cars,}$$

of which 10 are Sleeks and 5 are Powerfuls, according to the product mix assumption required to derive the weighted-average unit contribution margin.

What is the effect of incorrect assumptions in this analysis about product mix? If the actual mix is richer than assumed (more Powerfuls, in our example), the firm requires fewer units than predicted to break even. The firm requires more units than predicted to break even if the mix is poorer than assumed. (See, for example, the data in Exhibits 7.5 and 7.6.)

4. Treat Each Product Line as a Separate Entity This method requires allocating fixed costs to product lines. To illustrate, we must allocate part of the Sport Autos' $100,000 monthly fixed costs that the two products share to Sleek automobiles and the rest to Powerfuls. The problem is to find a reasonable method of allocating costs. Often the product lines share these costs, so any allocation method is arbitrary. In such situations, companies often resort to allocating on the basis of relative sales dollars or on the basis of quantities of the product lines. Other allocation bases used include relative total contributions, relative direct costs, relative number of employees per product line (particularly to allocate labor-related costs), or relative square feet of space used by each product line (particularly to allocate space-related costs).

Suppose that of the $100,000 common costs, Sport Autos arbitrarily allocates 40 percent to Sleeks and 60 percent to Powerfuls. We can then do breakeven analysis and other cost-volume-profit analyses by product line, as follows:

For Sleeks:

$$\pi = (P - V)X - F$$
$$= (\$20,000 - \$15,000)X - \$40,000$$
$$X_b = \frac{\$40,000}{\$5,000}$$
$$= 8 \text{ Units.}$$

For Powerfuls:

$$\pi = (P - V)X - F$$
$$= (\$30,000 - \$20,000)X - \$60,000$$
$$X_b = \frac{\$60,000}{\$10,000}$$
$$= 6 \text{ Units.}$$

Allocating fixed costs to product lines facilitates product line cost-volume-profit analysis. But decision makers should be wary of any analysis that relies on arbitrary cost allocations. It would be a mistake to believe that Sleeks cause fixed costs of $40,000 and Powerfuls cause fixed costs of $60,000. The two product lines *combined* cause fixed costs of $100,000; the breakdown of those costs is arbitrary. Further, note that a change in the arbitrary allocation method changes the breakeven volumes. (For example, if we allocated the $100,000 as $20,000 to Sleeks and $80,000 to Powerfuls, breakeven requires the sale of 4 Sleeks [= $20,000/$5,000 per unit] and 8 Powerfuls [= $80,000/$10,000 per unit].)

Simplifications and Assumptions

The cost-volume-profit model simplifies costs, revenues, and volume to make the analysis easier. A more complete description of the economic relations than the model gives is possible but costly. The careful user of cost-volume-profit analysis should be aware of the following common assumptions and be prepared to perform sensitivity analysis to see how the assumptions affect the model's results.

Comparison with Economists' Profit Maximization Model

Textbooks in economics usually present nonlinear cost and revenue curves, as in Exhibit 7.7. Total revenue increases at a decreasing rate if the firm faces a downward-sloping demand curve. Total costs increase at an increasing rate as volume approaches capacity. In Exhibit 7.7, the economists' cost curve includes the opportunity cost of owners' invested capital, whereas the linear approximation from the

Exhibit 7.7

Comparison of Economics and Accounting Assumptions
about Cost and Revenue Behavior

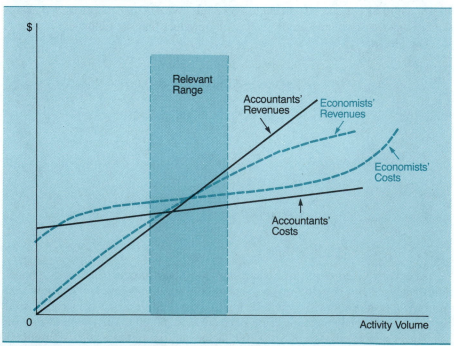

accounting records typically does not. Neither the economists' nor the accountants' cost and revenue curves are correct in an absolute sense. Both approximate actual cost and revenue behavior.

Basic Assumption Required to Make the Model Work: Total Cost Breakdown into Fixed and Variable Components

You can use the cost-volume-profit model most powerfully by analyzing how various alternatives affect operations. This analysis works because the model captures most of the important operating relations of the firm in a single equation. We can analyze the effects of changes in any of the following variables on the remaining variables: selling price, number of units sold, variable cost, fixed cost, sales mix, and production mix. The model requires the major assumption that *total costs have only fixed and variable components*.

Our illustrations in this chapter assume a linear relation between revenues and volume and between costs and volume. You can, however, apply the model with nonlinear revenue and cost functions. Practice usually assumes cost and revenue curves to be linear over some **relevant range** of activity, as discussed in Chapter 6. Exhibit 7.7 presents an example where cost and revenue curves are reasonably linear within the relevant range limits, even though the curves are nonlinear outside the relevant range.

We also implicitly assumed that the analyst can predict the variables in the model with certainty. You can relax this assumption. Accountants have developed techniques for applying the cost-volume-profit model under conditions of uncertainty.[4]

Assumptions Required to Derive Breakeven Point

If we use the cost-volume-profit (CVP) model to derive a unique breakeven point, we require two more assumptions:

1. Selling price per unit, total fixed costs, and variable costs per unit will not change as the level of activity changes. This assumption implies that prices paid and charged are constant, and workers' productivity does not change during the period.

2. The production mix and sales mix will not change as the level of activity changes.

Income Statements: Contribution Format versus Traditional Format

We can use the cost-volume-profit model to predict the effect of changes in prices, costs, or volumes on the net income reported to readers of external financial statements. If so, revenues and costs computed for the cost-volume-profit model must equal the revenues and expenses computed for external reporting purposes. The

---

[4]Cost accounting textbooks discuss these techniques. See E. B. Deakin and M. W. Maher, *Cost Accounting,* 3rd ed. (Homewood, Ill.: Irwin, 1991), Chapter 24, for example.

Exhibit 7.8

BALTIMORE COMPANY
Comparative Income Statements

Contribution Format[a]			Traditional Format[b]	
Revenue..............		$18,000[c]	Revenue	$18,000[c]
Less Variable Costs:			Less Cost of	
Variable Manufacturing			Goods Sold	(12,495)[f]
Costs	($10,200)[d]		Gross Margin	$ 5,505
Variable Marketing			Less Marketing	
and Administrative			and Administrative	
Costs	(3,000)[e]	(13,200)	Costs	(4,740)[g]
Total Contribution			Operating Profit	$ 765
Margin		$ 4,800		
Less Fixed Costs:				
Fixed Manufacturing				
Costs	$(3,060)			
Fixed Marketing				
and Administrative				
Costs	(1,740)	4,800		
Operating Profit..........		$ 0		

[a]The contribution format uses the *variable costing* method of product costing.

[b]The traditional format uses the *full absorption* product costing method.

[c]30×600 Units Sold = $18,000.

[d]17×600 Units = $10,200. 800 units produced but only 600 units sold.

[e]5×600 Units = $3,000.

[f]Variable portion of cost of goods sold = $10,200 from footnote d. Fixed portion of cost of goods sold = $2,295 = 600 Units Sold $\times \dfrac{\$3,060}{800 \text{ Units Produced}}$ = 600 $\times$ $3.825 per Unit. Total cost of goods sold = $12,495 = $10,200 + $2,295.

[g]$4,740 = ($5 \times 600$ Units Sold) + $1,740 = $3,000 + $1.740.

cost-volume-profit model assumes that fixed manufacturing costs become expenses in the period incurred (in accordance with variable costing). External reporting allocates fixed manufacturing costs to units produced and does not expense these costs until the period when the firm sells the units (in accordance with full absorption costing).

If the firm sells all units produced each period, as we assume in our example, the fixed manufacturing costs become expenses in the period incurred, even under full absorption costing.[5] Suppose, however, that fixed manufacturing costs were $3,060 in March and that the firm produced 800 units but sold only 600 (assume no beginning inventory). External reporting, using full absorption, actual costing, would expense only 75 percent, or $2,295, of the fixed manufacturing cost, which is part of the $12,495 cost of goods sold shown in the traditional format in Exhibit 7.8. The other $765 would remain in inventory until the firm sells those units. The

[5]This is also known as the ''no change in inventory'' assumption.

contribution format in Exhibit 7.8 shows the **variable costing approach,** in which all $3,060 would be expensed.

Summary of Assumptions

The following summarizes the previous assumptions:

1. Total costs divide into fixed and variable components.

2. Cost and revenue behavior is linear throughout the relevant range of activity. This assumption implies the following:
    a. Total fixed costs do not change throughout the relevant range of activity.
    b. Variable costs *per unit* remain constant throughout the relevant range of activity.
    c. Selling price per unit remains constant throughout the relevant range of activity.

3. Product mix remains constant throughout the relevant range of activity.

4. Inventory does not change. Without this assumption, we must reconcile the treatment of fixed manufacturing costs under CVP (that is, as period costs) with their treatment for external financial reporting purposes (that is, as product costs expensed only when the firm sells the units).

Assumptions of the cost-volume-profit model make it easy to use, but they also make it unrealistic. Before criticizing the model for being unrealistic, however, you need to consider the costs and benefits of relaxing those assumptions to create more realism. Often the cost of more realism exceeds the benefits from improved decision making.

One method of dealing with the assumptions is to perform some sensitivity or "what-if" analyses. For example, the mean or expected value of Baltimore Company's variable costs per unit is $22. But suppose that a reasonable range of values is from $15 to $29; that is, management estimates a very small probability that variable costs are less than $15 or greater than $29. Managers would probably want a sensitivity analysis performed to ascertain whether decisions would change if variable costs were (say) $15 or $29 instead of $22 per unit.

■ Summary ■

The cost-volume-profit model shows relations among revenues, costs, volume, and profits. The manager can use it as an economic model to describe a firm's activities, or as an analytical model to derive, for example, a product line breakeven point, target profits for a store, or the impact of a change in volume on profits.

In equation form, the model is

$$\pi = TR - TC$$
$$= PX - (VX + F)$$
$$= (P - V)X - F,$$

where

$$\pi = \text{Operating Profit}$$
$$TR = \text{Total Revenues}$$
$$TC = \text{Total Costs}$$
$$P = \text{Selling Price per Unit}$$
$$V = \text{Variable Cost per Unit}$$
$$F = \text{Fixed Costs per Period}$$
$$X = \text{Volume per Period}$$
$$(P - V) = \text{Contribution Margin per Unit.}$$

Sensitivity analysis is one of the most useful applications of the cost-volume-profit model, particularly for planning. It enables managers to respond to "what-if" questions such as "If costs are 10 percent higher than expected, or if volume is 5 percent higher than expected, what will be the impact on profits?"

The contribution format for income statements in Exhibit 7.8 uses cost behavior as the primary classification method. Thus the contribution format derives from the cost-volume-profit model.

The simple cost-volume-profit model assumes a single product. Many organizations, however, have multiple products. This does not affect the usefulness of the model as a tool for descriptive work or sensitivity analysis, but makes deriving breakeven points more difficult. Some ways of dealing with this multiproduct problem follow:

(1)   Assume that all products have the same contribution margin so that product mix does not affect the breakeven point.

(2)   Assume a particular product mix.

(3)   Assume a weighted-average contribution margin based on an assumed product mix.

(4)   Treat each product as a product line, which usually requires an arbitrary allocation of common costs.

The careful user of the cost-volume-profit model will recognize that it is merely a model, not a complete description of reality. The simpler the model, the greater its potential applications but the less realistic it is. Making the model more realistic is costly. For example, you can use a more realistic nonlinear model of cost behavior if the benefits of better decision making exceed the additional costs of building nonlinear relations into the model.

Problem 1 for Self-Study

For each of the following segments on the graph in Exhibit 7.9, identify the concept from the list on the right that corresponds to the line segment.

Line Segment	Concept
a. $0A$.	**(1)** Variable Cost per Unit.
b. IG.	**(2)** Fixed Cost per Period.
c. $0D$.	**(3)** Revenue.
d. $B0$.	**(4)** Contribution Margin per Unit.
e. $0H - 0D$.	**(5)** Margin of Safety in Units.
f. $B0/0D$.	**(6)** Breakeven Sales in Units.
g. $HF + HG$.	**(7)** None of the Above.

Refer to the graph in Exhibit 7.9. Answer each of the following as True or False.

h. If revenue is CD, the margin of safety is zero.

i. If revenue is HE, the margin of safety is $D0$.

Exhibit 7.9

Graph for Problem 1 for Self-Study

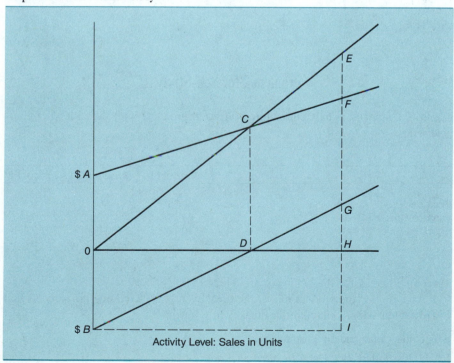

j. Total profit could never be larger than total expense.

k. If selling price increases, breakeven sales in units would decrease.

l. If selling price increases, *HF* would increase.

m. $FE = HG$.

Suggested Solution

a. 0*A*.

(2) Fixed Cost per Period.

b. *IG*.

(7) Total Contribution Margin.

c. 0*D*.

(6) Breakeven Sales in Units.

d. *B*0.

(2) Fixed Cost per Period; also, Operating Loss When Sales Are Zero.

e. 0*H* − 0*D*.

(5) Margin of Safety in Units.

f. *B*0 − 0*D*.

(4) Contribution Margin per Unit.

g. *HF* + *HG*.

(3) Revenue.

h. True.

i. False; if revenue is *HE*, the margin of safety is *DH*.

j. False.

k. True.

l. False.

m. True.

Problem 2 for Self-Study

Triple X Company manufactures three different products with the following characteristics:

	Product I	Product II	Product III
Price per Unit	$5	$6	$7
Variable Cost per Unit	$3	$2	$4
Expected Sales (units)	100,000	150,000	250,000

Total fixed costs for the company are $1,240,000.

Assume that the product mix at the breakeven point would be the same as that for expected sales. Compute the breakeven point in

a. Units (total and by product line).

b. Sales dollars (total and by product line).

a. Compute weighted-average contribution margin:

	Product I	**Product II**	**Product III**
Product Mix	$\dfrac{100{,}000\ \text{Units}}{500{,}000\ \text{Units}}$ $= .20$	$\dfrac{150{,}000}{500{,}000}$ $= .30$	$\dfrac{250{,}000}{500{,}000}$ $= .50$
Weighted-Average Contribution Margin ($P^* - V^*$)	.20($2)	+ .30($4) + $= \$3.10$	.50($3)

Or

$$\frac{(100{,}000\ \text{Units})(\$2) + (150{,}000)(\$4) + (250{,}000)(\$3)}{500{,}000} = \$3.10$$

$$X = \frac{\$1{,}240{,}000}{\$3.10}$$

$$X = 400{,}000\ \text{Units}.$$

b. To compute breakeven sales dollars, find the weighted-average price and variable costs:

$$P^* = (.20)(\$5) + (.30)(\$6) + (.50)(\$7)$$
$$P^* = \$6.30$$
$$V^* = (.20)(\$3) + (.30)(\$2) + (.50)(\$4)$$
$$V^* = \$3.20$$

$$\text{Breakeven } PX = \frac{F}{\dfrac{P-V}{P}} = \frac{\$1{,}240{,}000}{\$3.10/\$6.30}$$

$$= \frac{\$1{,}240{,}000}{.492\ (\text{rounded})}$$

$$= \$2{,}520{,}000.$$

(Check: 400,000 units × $6.30 = 2,520,000.)
    Product line amounts:

	Total (100%)	**Product I (20%)**	**Product II (30%)**	**Product III (50%)**
Units	400,000	80,000	120,000	200,000
Unit Price	$6.30	$5	$6	$7
Sales Dollars	$2,520,000	$400,000	$720,000	$1,400,000

Key Terms and Concepts

Cost-volume-profit model
Contribution margin per unit
Breakeven point
Cost-volume-profit graph
  (compared to profit-volume graph)
Profit-volume equation

Sensitivity analysis
Margin of safety
Contribution margin ratio
Relevant range
Variable costing approach (compared
  to full absorption costing)

Questions, Exercises, Problems, and Cases

Questions

1. Review the meaning of the following terms or concepts given above in Key Terms and Concepts.

2. Define the profit equation.

3. Define the term *contribution margin*.

4. How does the total contribution margin differ from the gross margin often seen on companies' financial statements?

5. Compare cost-volume-profit analysis with profit-volume analysis. How do they differ?

6. Is a company really breaking even if it produces and sells at the breakeven point? What costs may not be covered?

7. What is usually the difference between cost-volume-profit analysis on a cash basis and that analysis on an accrual accounting basis? For a company having depreciable assets, would you expect the accrual breakeven point to be higher, lower, or the same as the cash breakeven point?

8. How does the profit equation change when the analyst uses the multiproduct cost-volume-profit model?

9. Why does multiproduct cost-volume-profit analysis often assume a constant product mix?

10. When would the sum of the breakeven quantities for each of a company's products not be the breakeven point for the company as a whole?

11. Distinguish between economic *profits* and accounting *net income* or *operating profit*.

12. Name three common assumptions of a linear cost-volume-profit analysis.

13. Why does the operating profit calculated by cost-volume-profit analysis differ from the net income reported in financial statements for purposes of external reporting?

14. Fixed costs are often defined as "fixed over the short run." Does this mean that they are not fixed over the long run? Why or why not?

15. Why do accountants use a linear representation of cost and revenue behavior in cost-volume-profit analysis? Justify this use.

16. What effect could the following changes, occurring independently, have on (1) the breakeven point, (2) the contribution margin, and (3) the expected profit?
   a. An increase in fixed costs.
   b. A decrease in wage rates applicable to direct, strictly variable labor.
   c. An increase in the selling price of the product.
   d. An increase in production volume.
   e. An increase in insurance rates.

17. Assume the linear cost relation of the cost-volume-profit model for a single-product firm and use the following answer key:
   (1) More than double.
   (2) Double.
   (3) Increase, but less than double.
   (4) Remain the same.
   (5) Decrease.
   Complete each of the following statements, assuming that all other quantities remain constant.
   a. If price doubles, revenue will _____.
   b. If price doubles, the total contribution margin (contribution margin per unit times number of units) will _____.
   c. If price doubles, profit will _____.
   d. If contribution margin per unit doubles, profit will _____.
   e. If fixed costs double, the total contribution margin will _____.
   f. If fixed costs double, profit will _____.
   g. If fixed costs double, the breakeven point of units sold will _____.
   h. If total sales of units double, profit will _____.
   i. If total sales dollars double, the breakeven point will _____.
   j. If the contribution margin per unit doubles, the breakeven point will _____.
   k. If both variable costs per unit and selling price per unit double, profit will _____.

Exercises

18. *Breakeven and target profits.* Analysis of the operations of the Super Ski Wax Company shows the fixed costs to be $100,000 and the variable costs to be $4 per unit. Selling price is $8 per unit.

a. Derive the breakeven point expressed in units.
b. How many units must the firm sell to earn a profit of $140,000?
c. What would profits be if revenue from sales was $1,000,000?

19. *Cost-volume-profit; volume defined in sales dollars.* An excerpt from the income statement of the Wooster and Valley Company follows.

WOOSTER AND VALLEY COMPANY
Income Statement
Year Ended December 31, Year 1

Sales...		$2,000,000
Operating Expenses:		
Cost of Goods Sold	$950,000	
Selling Costs	300,000	
Administrative Costs	150,000	
Total Operating Costs		1,400,000
Profit...		$ 600,000

Estimated fixed costs in Year 1 are $440,000.
a. What percentage of sales revenue is variable cost?
b. What is the breakeven point in sales dollars for Wooster and Valley Company?
c. Prepare a cost-profit-volume graph for Wooster and Valley Company.
d. If sales revenue falls to $1,800,000, what will be the estimated amount of profit?
e. What volume of sales produces a profit of $1,120,000?

20. *Cost-volume-profit graph.* Identify each item on the following graph:
a. The total cost line.
b. The total revenue line.
c. The total variable costs.
d. Variable cost per unit.
e. The total fixed costs.
f. The breakeven point.
g. The profit area (or volume).
h. The loss area (or volume).

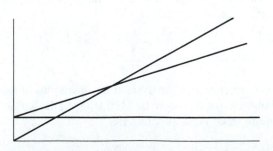

21. *Profit-volume graph*. Identify the places on the profit-volume graph indicated by the letters:

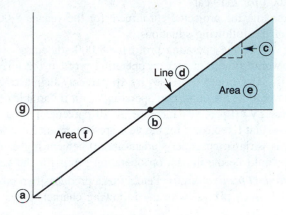

22. *Cost-volume-profit analysis*. Surf's Up Company produces one type of sunglasses with the following costs and revenues for the year:

Total Revenues	$5,000,000
Total Fixed Costs	$1,000,000
Total Variable Costs	$3,000,000
Total Quantity Produced and Sold	1,000,000 Units

   a. What is the selling price per unit?
   b. What is the variable cost per unit?
   c. What is the contribution margin per unit?
   d. What is the breakeven point?
   e. What quantity of units is required for Surf's Up Company to make an operating profit of $2,000,000 for the year?

23. *Breakeven and target profits; volume defined in sales dollars*. The manager of Tarmin Company estimates operating costs for the year will total $300,000 for fixed costs and that variable costs will be $2 per unit.
   a. Find the breakeven point in sales dollars at a selling price of $3 per unit, using the contribution margin ratio.
   b. Find the breakeven point in sales dollars at a selling price of $4 per unit.
   c. How many units must be sold at a price of $5 per unit to generate a profit of $150,000?

24. *CVP—sensitivity analysis*. Giovanni Kitchen Creations is considering introducing a new gourmet cooking seminar with the following price and cost characteristics:

Tuition	$100 per Student
Variable Cost (supplies, food, etc.)	$60 per Student
Fixed Costs (advertising, instructor's salary, insurance, etc.)...	$200,000 per Year

a. What enrollment enables Giovanni to break even?
b. How many students will enable Giovanni to make an operating profit of $100,000 for the year?
c. Assume that the projected enrollment for the year is 8,000 students for each of the following situations:
(1) What will be the operating profit for 8,000 students?
(2) What would be the impact on operating profit if the tuition per student (that is, sales price) decreases by 10 percent? Increases by 20 percent?
(3) What would be the impact on operating profit if variable costs per student decrease by 10 percent? Increase by 20 percent?
(4) Suppose that fixed costs for the year are 10 percent lower than projected, whereas variable costs per student are 10 percent higher than projected. What would be the impact on operating profit for the year?

25. *Multiple product profit analysis*. Pete's Pizza produces two products, 12-inch pizzas and 16-inch pizzas, with the following characteristics:

	12-Inch Pizza	16-Inch Pizza
Selling Price per Unit	$5	$6
Variable Cost per Unit........................	$3	$2
Expected Sales (Units)	100,000	150,000

The total fixed costs for the company are $700,000.
a. What is the anticipated level of profits for the expected sales volumes?
b. Assuming that the product mix would be the same at the breakeven point, compute the breakeven point in terms of each of the products.
c. If the product sales mix were to change to four 12-inch pizzas for each 16-inch pizza, what would be the new breakeven volume for each of the products?

26. *Multiple product profit analysis*. The Multiproduct Company produces and sells three different products. Operating data for the three products follow.

	Selling Price per Unit	Variable Cost per Unit	Fixed Cost per Month
Product P..................................	$3	$2	—
Product Q	5	3	—
Product R	8	5	—
Entire Company	—	—	$48,000

Define a unit as the sum of one unit of product R sold, two units of product Q sold, and three units of product P sold.
a. Draw a cost-volume-profit graph for the Multiproduct Company.
b. At what sales revenue does the Multiproduct Company break even?
c. If the Company sells two units of product P for every two units of product Q and one unit of product R, at what sales revenue does it break even?

Problems

27. *Explaining sales and cost changes*. You have acquired the following data for Years 1 and 2 for Metropolitan Art Institute:

	Year 1		Year 2		Dollar Increase
Revenue from Admissions ..	$750,000	100%	$840,000	100%	$90,000
Variable Costs of Operating the Institute	495,000	66	560,000	66⅔	65,000
Contribution Margin	$255,000	34%	$280,000	33⅓%	$25,000
Admission Price per Person	$10		$12		

Explain the increase in sales and cost of goods sold between Year 1 and Year 2.

28. *CVP—missing data*. Management of Ferdinand's Frozen Foods has performed cost studies and projected the following annual costs based on 40,000 units of production and sales:

	Total Annual Costs	Percent of Total Annual Cost That Is Variable
Direct Material	$400,000	100%
Direct Labor	360,000	75
Manufacturing Overhead	300,000	40
Selling, General, and Administrative	200,000	25

a. Compute Ferdinand's unit selling price that will yield a projected profit of 10 percent of sales dollars, given sales of 40,000 units.

b. Assume that management selects a selling price of $30 per unit (40,000 units). Compute Ferdinand's dollar sales that will yield a projected 10 percent profit on sales, assuming that the previously shown variable-fixed cost relations are valid.

29. *CVP—sensitivity analysis*. In the last year, the sales revenue of the Hernandez Hair Salon was $1,200,000, fixed costs were $400,000, and variable costs were $600,000.

a. At what level of sales revenue will the salon break even?

b. If sales revenue increases by 15 percent but unit prices, unit variable costs, and total annual fixed costs do not change, by how much will profit increase?

c. If fixed costs decrease by 10 percent, by how much will profit increase?

d. If variable costs decrease by 10 percent, by how much will profit increase?

30. *Solving for unknowns* (Problems 30 through 33 adapted from problems by D. O. Green). When Britain's auto business slumped in 1921, William R.

Morris (the ''Henry Ford of Britain'') gambled on cost saving from his new assembly lines and cut prices to a point where his expected loss per car in 1922 would be $240 if sales were the same as in 1921, or 1,500 cars. However, sales in 1922 rose to 60,000 cars, and profits for the year were $810,000. For 1922, calculate:

a. Contribution margin per car.
b. Total fixed costs.
c. Breakeven point in cars.

31. *Solving for unknowns.* During the third quarter of a recent year, a division of an automobile company sold 45,000 cars for $250 million and realized a loss for the quarter of $24 million. The breakeven point was 60,000 cars. Calculate for the quarter:

a. Contribution margin per car.
b. Total fixed costs.
c. Profits had sales been twice as large.

32. *Solving for unknowns. Time* magazine reported that the future of the American Motor Company seemed so shaky that its creditors, a consortium of banks headed by Chase Manhattan, examined the books every 10 days. The new management trimmed fixed costs by $20 million to cut the breakeven point from 350,000 cars in one year to 250,000 cars for the next year. From this information, calculate:

a. Contribution margin per car (assumed constant for both years).
b. Fixed costs for both years.
c. Losses in the first year, assuming sales of 300,000 cars.
d. Profits in the second year, assuming sales of 400,000 cars.

33. *Solving for unknowns.* Reporting on Chrysler Corporation's performance, *The Wall Street Journal* once pointed out that Chrysler had boosted its market share from 10 percent six years before to 18 percent at that time. The next year, however, countermeasures by Ford and General Motors, coupled with a 10 percent decline, or 1 million cars, in U.S. industry sales, created problems for Chrysler. Chrysler cut prices, increased advertising, and reduced fixed costs.

Refer to these as Years 1 and 2. Assume the contribution margin per car was $100 less in Year 2 than in Year 1, and that fixed costs were 20 percent lower in Year 2 than in Year 1. Despite the changes, Chrysler's profits in Year 2 were only $80 million on sales of 1.4 million autos, whereas Year 1's profits had been $300 million. From this information, calculate:

a. Industry sales (in autos) for Years 1 and 2.
b. Chrysler's total fixed costs for Years 1 and 2.
c. Chrysler's contribution margin per car in Years 1 and 2.

34. *Solving for unknowns.* The Unitec Corporation had Year 0 revenues of $400,000 and profit equal to $4 per unit sold. Early in Year 1, the president of Unitec learned that a rival firm had contracted for a nationwide advertising program of extraordinary proportions to launch a competing product. Thereupon, the president of Unitec Corporation ordered a price cut for Unitec's single product. At the start of Year 1, the president ordered an increase of

$48,000 in advertising expenditures to publicize the price cut. The price cut and increased advertising produced Year 1 sales in units double the Year 0 sales in units, but left profit unchanged in Year 1 compared to Year 0.

Had the new, Year 1 price been in effect during Year 0, revenues on its actual Year 0 sales volume would have been $96,000 less than actual Year 0 revenues, and the loss would have been equal to $2 per unit sold.

Compute each of the following quantities for Year 1:

a. Sales volume in units.
b. Revenues.
c. Profit.
d. Contribution margin per unit.
e. Fixed costs.

35. *Solving for unknowns*. Lecarla Company increased its market share from 12 percent in Year 0 to 36 percent in Year 5. By Year 6, however, competitors' actions and a 10 percent decline of 1,000 units in total industry sales from their Year 5 level created severe problems for Lecarla Company. In an unsuccessful effort to maintain its market share, the company reduced selling prices during Year 6, resulting in a decrease in contribution margin of $10 per unit compared to Year 5. Cutbacks in administrative activities reduced total fixed costs by 20 percent in Year 6. Operating profit in Year 6 was only $12,000 on sales of 2,800 units, whereas Year 5 operating profit had been $54,000.

Compute each of the following:

a. Fixed costs during Year 5.
b. Fixed costs during Year 6.
c. Contribution margin per unit during Year 5.
d. Contribution margin per unit during Year 6.
e. Breakeven sales in units during Year 5.
f. Breakeven sales in units during Year 6.

36. *CVP—missing data; assumptions*. Despite an increase in sales revenue from $4,704,000 in Year 8 to $4,725,000 in Year 9, the Western Agriculture Company recently reported a decline in net income of $129,500 from Year 8 to an amount equal to 2 percent of sales revenue in Year 9. The average total cost per bushel increased from $2.200 in Year 8 to $2.205 in Year 9.

a. Compute the changes, if any, in average selling price and sales in bushels from Year 8 to Year 9.
b. Can you compute the total fixed costs and variable cost per bushel during Year 9? If so, do so. If not, illustrate why with a graph and discuss any important assumptions of the cost-volume-profit model that this application violates.

37. *Alternatives to reduce breakeven sales*. The Sunnyside Fruit Farms operated near the breakeven point of $1,125,000 during Year 1, while incurring fixed costs of $450,000. Management is considering two alternatives to reduce the breakeven level. Alternative A trims fixed costs by $100,000 annually; doing so, however, will reduce the quality of the product and result in a 10 percent decrease in selling price, but no change in the number of bushels sold. Alternative B substitutes mechanical fruit-picking equipment for certain operations

now performed manually. Alternative B will result in an annual increase of $150,000 in fixed costs, but a 5 percent decrease in variable costs per bushel produced, with no change in product quality, selling price, or sales volume.

a. What was the total contribution margin (contribution margin per unit times number of units sold) during Year 1?

b. What is the breakeven sales in dollars under alternative A?

c. What is the breakeven sales in dollars under alternative B?

d. What should the company do?

38. *Solving for cost-based selling price*. United Instruments Corporation follows a cost-based approach to pricing. Prices are 120 percent of cost. The annual cost of producing one of its products follows:

Variable Manufacturing Costs	$40 per Unit
Fixed Manufacturing Costs	$100,000 per Year
Variable Selling and Administrative Costs	$10 per Unit
Fixed Selling and Administrative Costs.....................	$60,000 per Year

a. Assume that United produces and sells 10,000 units. Calculate the selling price per unit.

b. Assume that United produces and sells 20,000 units. Calculate the selling price per unit.

39. *Solving for cost-based selling price*. Western Health Clinic follows a cost-based approach to pricing. It sets prices equal to 110 percent of cost. The clinic has annual fixed costs of $600,000. The variable costs of the clinic's services follow:

Treatment Type	Variable Cost per Procedure
A	$10
B	20
C	30

The clinic expects to provide 1,000 type A treatments, 4,000 type B treatments, and 1,000 type C treatments.

a. Compute the price of each treatment if the clinic allocates fixed costs to services on the basis of the number of treatments.

b. Compute the selling price of each treatment if the clinic allocates fixed costs to treatments on the basis of total variable costs.

40. *CVP analysis with semifixed (step) costs*. Mountaineer Co. has one product: dehydrated meals for backpacking. The sales price of $10 remains constant per unit regardless of volume, as does the variable cost of $6 per unit. The company is considering operating at one of the following three monthly levels of operations:

	Volume Range (production and sales)	Total Fixed Costs	Increase in Fixed Costs from Previous Level
Level 1	0–16,000	$40,000	—
Level 2	16,001–28,000	72,000	$32,000
Level 3	28,001–38,000	94,000	22,000

    a. Calculate the breakeven point(s).

    b. If the company can sell everything it makes, should it operate at level 1, level 2, or level 3? Support your answer.

41. *CVP analysis with semifixed costs and changing unit variable costs.* The Eades Company manufactures and sells one product. The sales price, $50 per unit, remains constant regardless of volume. Last year's sales were 15,000 units and operating profits were $200,000. Fixed costs depend on production levels, as the following table shows. Variable costs per unit are 40 percent *higher* for level 2 (two shifts) than for level 1 (day shift only). The additional labor costs result primarily from higher wages required to employ workers for the night shift.

	Annual Production Range (in units)	Annual Total Fixed Costs
Level 1 (day shift)	0–20,000	$100,000
Level 2 (day and night shifts)	20,001–36,000	164,000

Eades expects last years' cost structure and selling price not to change this year. Maximum plant capacity is 36,000. The company sells everything it produces.

    a. Compute the contribution margin per unit for last year for each of the two production levels.

    b. Compute the breakeven points for last year for each of the two production levels.

    c. Compute the volume in units that will maximize operating profits. Defend your choice.

42. *CVP analysis with semifixed costs.* Beverly Miller, director and owner of the Discovery Day Care Center, has a master's degree in elementary education. In the 7 years she has been running the Discovery Center, her salary has ranged from nothing to $20,000 per year. "The second year," she says, "I made 62 cents an hour." (Her salary is what's left over after meeting all other expenses.)

    Could she run a more profitable center? She thinks perhaps she could if she increased the student-teacher ratio, which is currently five students to one teacher. (Government standards for a center such as this set a maximum of 10 students per teacher.) She refuses to increase the ratio to more than six-to-one. "If you increase the ratio to more than 6:1, the children don't get enough attention. In addition, the demands on the teacher are far too great." She does not hire part-time teachers.

Beverly rents the space for her center in the basement of a church for $900 per month, including utilities. She estimates that supplies, snacks, and other nonpersonnel costs are $80 per student per month. She charges $380 per month per student. Teachers receive $1,200 per month, including fringe benefits. She has no other operating costs. At present, she cares for 30 students and employs six teachers.

a. What is the present operating profit per month of the Discovery Day Care Center before Ms. Miller's salary?

b. What is (are) the breakeven point(s), before Ms. Miller's salary, assuming a student-teacher ratio of 6:1?

c. What would be the breakeven point(s), before Ms. Miller's salary, if the student-teacher ratio increased to 10:1?

d. Ms. Miller has an opportunity to increase the student body by six students. She must take all six or none. Should she accept the six students, if she wants to maintain a maximum student-teacher ratio of 6:1?

e. (Continuation of part **d.**) Suppose that Ms. Miller accepts the six children. Now she has the opportunity to accept one more, which requires hiring one more teacher. What would happen to profit, before her salary, if she accepts one more student?

43. *CVP with taxes* (adapted from CMA exam). R. A. Ro and Company, maker of quality, handmade pipes, has experienced a steady growth in sales for the past 5 years. However, increased competition has led Mr. Ro, the president, to believe that to maintain the company's present growth requires an aggressive advertising campaign next year. To prepare the next year's advertising campaign, the company's accountant has prepared and presented Mr. Ro with the following data for the current year, Year 1.

Cost Schedule

Variable Costs:	
Direct Labor	$ 8.00 per Pipe
Direct Materials	3.25
Variable Overhead	2.50
Total Variable Costs	$13.75 per Pipe
Fixed Costs:	
Manufacturing	$ 25,000
Selling	40,000
Administrative	70,000
Total Fixed Costs	$135,000
Selling Price, per Pipe	$25.00
Expected Sales, Year 1 (20,000 pipes)	$500,000.00
Tax Rate: 40 Percent	

Mr. Ro has set the sales target for Year 2 at a level of $550,000 (or 22,000 pipes).

a. What is the projected after-tax operating profit for Year 1?

b. What is the breakeven point in units for Year 1?

c. Mr. Ro believes that to attain the sales target requires an additional selling expense of $11,250 for advertising in Year 2, with all other costs remaining constant. What will be the after-tax operating profit for Year 2 if the firm spends the additional $11,250?

d. What will be the breakeven point in dollar sales for Year 2 if the firm spends the additional $11,250 for advertising?

e. If the firm spends the additional $11,250 for advertising in Year 2, what is the sales level in dollars required to equal Year 1 after-tax operating profit?

f. At a sales level of 22,000 units, what is the maximum amount that the firm can spend on advertising to earn an after-tax operating profit of $60,000?

Integrative Problems and Cases

44. *CVP—partial data; special order*. Partial income statements of Ford Food Service for the first two quarters of Year 2 follow.

FORD FOOD SERVICE
Partial Income Statements for First and Second Quarters of Year 2

	First Quarter	Second Quarter
Sales at $3.60 per Meal (unit)	$ 36,000	$ 63,000
Total Costs.....................................	49,000	67,000
(Loss)	$(13,000)	$ (4,000)

Each dollar of variable cost per meal comprises 50 percent direct labor, 25 percent direct materials, and 25 percent variable overhead costs. Ford expects sales units, price per unit, variable cost per unit, and total fixed costs to remain at the same level during the third quarter as during the second quarter. Ford sold 17,500 meals in the second quarter.

a. What is the breakeven point in meals (units)?

b. The company has just received a special order from a government agency that provides meals for senior citizens for 7,500 meals at a price of $3.20 per meal (unit). If the company accepts the order, it will not affect the regular market for 17,500 meals in the third quarter. The company can produce the additional meals with existing capacity, but direct labor costs per meal will increase by 10 percent for *all* meals produced because of the need to hire and use new labor. Fixed costs will increase $3,000 per quarter if the company accepts the new order. Should it accept the government order?

c.   Assume that the company accepts the order in part **b.** What level of sales to nongovernment customers provides third-quarter profit of $6,800? (The third quarter would be just like the second quarter if the company does not accept the government order.)

45.   *CVP under uncertainty* (this problem should be assigned only to students with some statistics and access to tables for the normal distribution). The Brown Corporation provides the following estimates of quantities relating to its business operations:

Selling Price	$2.00 per Unit
Variable Costs	$1.50 per Unit
Fixed Costs	$5,000 per Month
Expected (Mean) Level of Sales, Which Are Normally Distributed	16,000 Units per Month
Standard Deviation of Monthly Sales	4,000 Units

a.   What is the breakeven level of sales units?
b.   What is the profit at the expected level of sales?
c.   Ascertain the probability of the company's at least breaking even in a given month.
d.   Ascertain the probability of profit being at least $5,000 for a given month.

46.   *Comprehensive CVP case.*[6] Bill French picked up the phone and called his boss, Wes Davidson, controller of Duo-Products Corporation. "Say, Wes, I'm all set for the meeting this afternoon. I've put together a set of breakeven statements from my new graphics software package that should really make folks sit up and take notice—and I think they'll be able to understand them, too." After a brief conversation about other matters, the call ended and French turned to his charts for one last check-out before the meeting.

French had begun work 6 months earlier as a staff accountant. He was directly responsible to Davidson and, up to the time of this case, had been doing routine types of analysis work. French graduated from a liberal arts college and attended a graduate business school, and associates considered him capable and conscientious. His conscientiousness had apparently caused him to "rub some of the workers the wrong way," as one of his co-workers put it. French was aware of his capabilities and took advantage of every opportunity to educate those around him. Wes Davidson's invitation for French to attend an informal manager's meeting had come as some surprise to others in the accounting group. When French requested permission to make a presentation of some breakeven data, Wes Davidson acquiesced. The Duo-

[6]Copyright © 1959, 1987 by the President and Fellows of Harvard College. Harvard Business School case 104-039. R. G. Hill prepared this case under the direction of Neil E. Harlan as the basis for class discussion rather than to illustrate either effective or ineffective handling of an administrative situation. Reprinted by permission of the Harvard Business School.

Products Corporation had not been using this type of analysis in its review or planning programs.

Basically, French had computed the level at which the company must operate to break even. As he phrased it:

> The company must be able to at least sell a sufficient volume of goods so that it will cover all the variable costs of producing and selling the goods; further, it will not make a profit unless it covers the fixed, or nonvariable, costs as well. The level of operation that just covers total costs (that is, variable plus nonvariable) is the breakeven volume. This volume should be the lower limit in all our planning.

The accounting records provided the following information that French used in constructing his chart:

- Plant capacity—2 million units.
- Past year's level of operations—1.5 million units.
- Average unit selling price—$1.20.
- Total fixed costs—$520,000.
- Average variable unit cost—$.75.

From this information, French observed that each unit contributed $.45 to fixed overhead after covering the variable costs. Given total fixed costs of $520,000, he calculated that the firm must sell 1,155,556 units in order to break even. He verified this conclusion by calculating the dollar sales volume required to break even. Because the variable costs per unit were 62.5 percent of the selling price, French reasoned that 37.5 percent of every sales dollar was left available to cover fixed costs. Thus, fixed costs of $520,000 require sales of $1,386,667 in order to break even.

He constructed a breakeven chart to present the information graphically and to verify his conclusions. The chart also made clear that the firm was operating at a fair margin over the breakeven requirements, and that the profits accruing (at the rate of 37.5 percent of every sales dollar over breakeven) increased rapidly as volume increased (see Exhibit 7.10).

Shortly after lunch, French and Davidson left for the meeting. Several representatives of the manufacturing departments attended, as well as the general sales manager, two assistant sales managers, the purchasing officer, and two people from the product engineering office. Davidson introduced French to the few people he had not already met, and then the meeting got under way.

French had prepared enough copies of his chart and supporting calculations for everyone at the meeting. He described his work and explained that if the volume of sales activity remains at past levels the next year would be profitable. Some of the participants had known in advance French's planned discussion; they came prepared to challenge him and soon took control of the meeting. The following exchange ensued (see Exhibit 7.11 for a checklist of participants with their titles):

Exhibit 7.10

Bill French Breakeven Chart

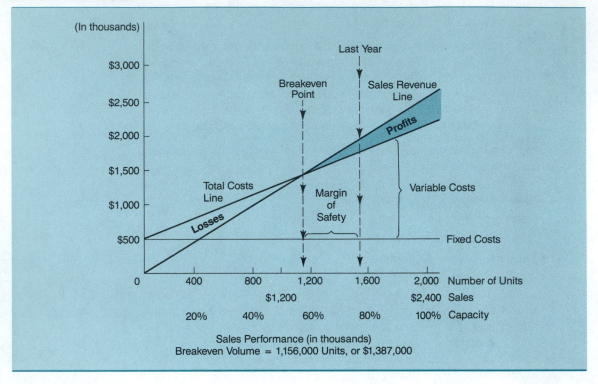

Sales Performance (in thousands)
Breakeven Volume = 1,156,000 Units, or $1,387,000

Cooper (production control): You know, Bill, I'm really concerned that you haven't allowed for our planned changes in volume next year. It seems to me that you should have allowed for the sales department's guess that we'll boost sales by 20 percent, unitwise. We'll be pushing 90 percent of what we call capacity then. It sure seems that this would make quite a difference in your figuring.

Exhibit 7.11

List of Participants in the Meeting

Bill French	Staff Accountant
Wes Davidson	Controller
John Cooper	Production Control
Fred Williams	Manufacturing
Ray Bradshaw	Assistant Sales Manager
Lucy Chivez	General Sales Manager
Anne Fraser	Administrative Assistant to the President

French: That might be true, but as you can see, all you have to do is read the cost and profit relationship right off the chart for the new volume. Let's see—at a million-eight units we'd . . .

Williams (manufacturing): Wait a minute, now!!! If you're going to talk in terms of 90 percent of capacity, and it looks like that's what it will be, you had better note that we'll be shelling out some more for the plant. We've already got okays on investment money that will boost your fixed costs by $10,000 a month, easy. And that may not be all. We may call it 90 percent of plant capacity, but there are a lot of places where we're just full up and we can't put things up any tighter.

Cooper: See, Bill? Fred Williams is right, but I'm not finished on this bit about volume changes. According to the information that I've got here—and it came from your office—I'm not sure that we can use your breakeven chart even if there will be no changes next year. Looks to me like you've got average figures that don't allow for the fact that we're dealing with three basic products. Your report here (see Exhibit 7.12) on costs, according to product lines, for last year makes it pretty clear that the "average" is way out of line. How would the breakeven point look if we took this on an individual product basis?

French: Well, I'm not sure. Seems to me that the firm has only one breakeven point. Whether we take it product by product or in total, we've got to hit that point. I'll be glad to check for you if you want, but . . .

Bradshaw (assistant sales manager): Guess I may as well get in on this one, Bill. If you're going to do anything with individual products, you ought to know that we're looking for a big swing in our product mix. Might even

Exhibit 7.12

Product Class Cost Analysis (Normal Year)				
	Aggregate	A	B	C
Sales at Full Capacity (units)	2,000,000			
Actual Sales Volume (units)	1,500,000	600,000	400,000	500,000
Unit Sales Price	$1.20	$1.67	$1.50	$.40
Total Sales Revenue	$1,800,000	$1,000,000	$600,000	$200,000
Variable Cost per Unit	$.75	$1.25	$.625	$.25
Total Variable Cost	$1,125,000	$750,000	$250,000	$125,000
Fixed Costs	$520,000	$170,000	$275,000	$75,000
Net Profit	$155,000	$80,000	$75,000	—
Ratios:				
Variable Costs to Sales	.63	.75	.42	.63
Variable Income to Sales	.37	.25	.58	.37
Utilization of Capacity	75.0%	30.0%	20.0%	25.0%

start before we get into the new season. The A line is really losing out and I imagine that we'll be lucky to hold two-thirds of the volume there next year. Wouldn't you buy that, Lucy? [Agreement from the general sales manager.] That's not too bad, though, because we expect that we should pick up the 200,000 that we lose, and about a quarter million units more, over in C production. We don't see anything that shows much of a change in B. That's been solid for years and shouldn't change much now.

Chivez (general sales manager): Bradshaw's called it about as we figure it, but there's something else here too. We've talked about our pricing on C enough, and now I'm really going to push our side of it. Ray's estimate of maybe half a million—450,000 I guess it was—up on C for next year is on the basis of doubling the price with no change in cost. We've been priced so low on this item that it's been a crime—we've got to raise the price, for two reasons. First, for our reputation; the price is out of line classwise and is completely inconsistent with our quality reputation. Second, if we don't raise the price, we'll be swamped and we can't handle it. You heard what Williams said about capacity. The way the whole C field is exploding, we'll have to answer to another half-million units in unsatisfied orders if we don't increase the price. We can't afford to expand that much for this product.

At this point, Anne Fraser (administrative assistant to the president) walked up toward the front of the room from where she had been standing near the rear door. The discussion broke for a minute, and she took advantage of the lull to interject a few comments.

Fraser: This has certainly been enlightening. Looks like you folks are pretty well up on this whole operation. As long as you're going to try to get all the things together that you ought to pin down for next year, let's see what I can add to help you.

Number One: Let's remember that everything that shows in the profit area here on Bill's chart is pretax and taxes take about half of pretax profits. Now, for last year we can read pretax profit of about $150,000. Well, that's right. But we kept only half of that, and then paid our dividends of $50,000 to the stockholders. Since we've got an anniversary year coming up, we'd like to put out a special dividend of about 50 percent extra. We ought to hold $25,000 in for the business, too. This means that we'd like to hit $100,000 *after* taxes.

Number Two: From where I sit, it looks like we're going to have a talk with the union again, and this time it's liable to cost us. All the indications are—and this isn't public—that we may have to meet demands that will boost our production costs—what do you call them here, Bill—variable costs—by 10 percent across the board. This may kill the bonus-dividend plans, but we've got to hold the line on past profits. This means that we can give that much to the union only if we can make it in added revenues. I guess you'd say that that raises your breakeven point, Bill—and for that one I'd consider the company's profit to be a fixed cost.

Number Three: Maybe this is the time to think about switching our product emphasis. Lucy Chivez may know better than I which of the products is more profitable. You check me out on this, Lucy, and it might be a good idea for you and Bill French to get together on this one, too. These figures that I have (Exhibit 7.12) make it look like the percentage contribution on line A is the lowest of the bunch. If we're losing volume there as rapidly as you sales folks say, and if we're as hard-pressed for space as Fred Williams has indicated, maybe we'd be better off grabbing some of that big demand for C by shifting some of the facilities over there from A. That's all I've got to say. Looks to me like you've all got plenty to think about.

Davidson: Thanks, Anne. I sort of figured that we'd get wound up here as soon as Bill brought out his charts. This is an approach that we've barely touched, but, as you can see, you've all got ideas that have got to be made to fit here somewhere. I'll tell you what let's do. Bill, suppose you rework your chart and try to bring into it some of the points that were made here today. I'll see if I can summarize what everyone seems to be looking for.

First of all, I have the idea buzzing around in the back of my mind that your presentation requires important assumptions. Most of the questions these folks raised were really about those assumptions; it might help us all if you try to set the assumptions down in black and white so that we can see just how they influence the analysis.

Then, I think that Cooper would like to see you consider the unit sales increase. He'd also like to see whether there's any difference if you base the calculations on an analysis of individual product lines. Also, as Bradshaw suggested, since the product mix is bound to change, why not see how things look if the shift materializes as sales has forecast?

Lucy Chivez would like to see the influence of a price increase in the C line; Fred Williams looks toward an increase in fixed manufacturing costs of $10,000 a month. Anne Fraser has suggested that we should consider taxes, dividends, expected union demands, and the question of product emphasis. I think that ties it all together. Let's hold off on our next meeting, fellows, until Bill has time to work this all into shape.

With that, the participants broke off into small groups and the meeting disbanded. French and Wes Davidson headed back to their offices and French, in a tone of concern, asked Davidson, "Why didn't you warn me about the hornet's nest I was walking into?"

"Bill, you didn't ask."

a. What did French assume in computing his firm's breakeven point?

b. On the basis of French's revised information, what does next year look like?

   (1) What is the breakeven point?

   (2) What level of operations must the firm achieve to meet the union demands, ignoring bonus dividends, but continuing to earn $150,000 in pretax profit?

   (3) What level of operations must the firm achieve to meet both bonus dividends and expected union requirements?

c. Can cost-volume-profit analysis help the company decide whether to alter the existing product emphasis? Could it help the company decide how much to invest for additional C capacity?

d. For what can cost-volume-profit analysis best be used?

Suggested Solutions to Even-Numbered Exercises

18. *Breakeven and target profits*

a. $\text{Contribution Margin (per unit)} = \text{Unit Selling Price} - \text{Unit Variable Cost}$

$= \$8 - \$4$

$= \$4$

$\text{Profit} = (\text{Contribution Margin per Unit} \times \text{Units}) - \text{Fixed Costs}$

$0 = (\$4 \times \text{Units}) - \$100,000$

$\text{Units} = 25,000.$

b. $\$140,000 = (\$4 \times \text{Units}) - \$100,000$

$\$240,000 = \$4 \times \text{Units}$

$60,000 = \text{Units}.$

c. $\text{Contribution Margin Percentage} = \dfrac{\text{Unit Selling Price} - \text{Unit Variable Cost}}{\text{Unit Selling Price}}$

$= \dfrac{\$8 - \$4}{\$8} = \dfrac{\$4}{\$8} = 50\%.$

$\text{Profit} = (.5 \times \$1,000,000) - \$100,000$

$= \$400,000.$

20. *Cost-volume-profit graph*

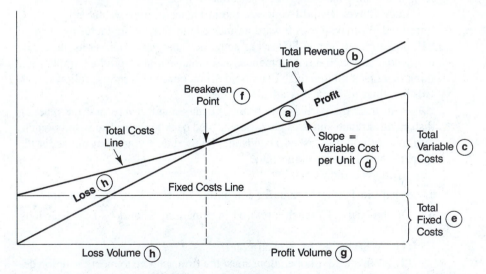

22. *Cost-volume-profit analysis*

a. $\$5,000,000/1,000,000 \text{ Units} = \$5 \text{ per Unit.}$

b. $\$3,000,000/1,000,000 \text{ Units} = \$3 \text{ per Unit.}$

c. $\$5 - \$3 = \$2 \text{ per Unit.}$

d. $\pi = (\$5 - \$3)X - \$1,000,000.$

$\text{Let } \pi = 0.$

$0 = (\$5 - \$3)X - \$1,000,000.$

$X = \dfrac{\$1,000,000}{(\$5 - \$3)} = 500,000 \text{ Units.}$

e.
$$\text{Let } \pi = \$2,000,000.$$
$$\$2,000,000 = (\$5 - \$3)X - \$1,000,000.$$
$$X = \frac{\$3,000,000}{(\$5 - \$3)} = 1,500,000 \text{ Units.}$$

24. *CVP—sensitivity analysis*

a.
$$\pi = (P - V)X - F$$
$$0 = (\$100 - \$60)X - \$200,000$$
$$X = \frac{\$200,000}{(\$100 - \$60)} = 5,000 \text{ Students.}$$

b.
$$\$100,000 = (\$100 - \$60)X - \$200,000$$
$$X = \frac{\$300,000}{(\$100 - \$60)} = 7,500 \text{ Students.}$$

c. **(1)**
$$\pi = (\$100 - \$60)8,000 - \$200,000$$
$$= \$120,000.$$

(2) *10 percent price decrease. Now P = \$90.*
$$\pi = (\$90 - \$60)8,000 - \$200,000$$
$$= \$40,000.$$

π decreases by \$80,000 (67 percent).
20 percent price increase. Now P = \$120.
$$\pi = (\$120 - \$60)8,000 - \$200,000$$
$$= \$280,000.$$

π increases by \$160,000 (133 percent).

(3) *10 percent variable cost decrease. Now V = \$54.*
$$\pi = (\$100 - \$54)8,000 - \$200,000$$
$$= \$168,000.$$

π increases by \$48,000 (40 percent).
20 percent variable cost increase. Now V = \$72.
$$\pi = (\$100 - \$72)8,000 - \$200,000$$
$$= \$24,000.$$

π decreases by \$96,000 (80 percent).

(4)
$$\pi = (\$100 - \$66)8,000 - \$180,000$$
$$= \$92,000.$$

π decreases by \$28,000 (23 percent).

26. *Multiple product profit analysis*

a.

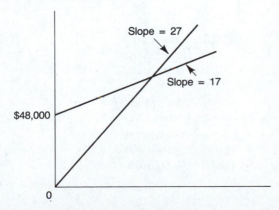

Slope = 27

Slope = 17

\$48,000

0

$$A \text{ unit} = \text{production of one product R, two product Qs,}$$
$$\text{and three product Ps.}$$

$$\frac{\text{Variable Cost}}{\text{per Unit}} = (3 \times \$2) + (2 \times \$3) + (1 \times \$5) = \$17$$

$$\frac{\text{Revenue}}{\text{per Unit}} = (3 \times \$3) + (2 \times \$5) + (1 \times \$8) = \$27.$$

b.
$$0 = \text{Total Revenue} - \text{Total Cost}$$
$$0 = \$27X - (\$17X + \$48,000)$$
$$\$10X = \$48,000$$
$$X = 4,800 \text{ Units.}$$

Production at breakeven point is

Product P $= 3 \times 4,800 = 14,400$

Product Q $= 2 \times 4,800 = 9,600$

Product R $= 1 \times 4,800 = 4,800.$

$$\frac{\text{Total Revenue at}}{\text{Breakeven Level}} = 4,800 \text{ Units} \times \$27 = \$129,600.$$

c.
$$A \text{ unit} = \text{two product Ps, two product Qs,}$$
$$\text{and one product R.}$$

$$\frac{\text{Variable Cost}}{\text{per Unit}} = (2 \times \$2) + (2 \times \$3) + (1 \times \$5) = \$15$$

$$\frac{\text{Revenue}}{\text{per Unit}} = (2 \times \$3) + (2 \times \$5) + (1 \times \$8) = \$24$$

$$0 = \text{Total Revenue} - \text{Total Cost}$$
$$0 = \$24X - (\$15X + \$48,000)$$
$$\$9X = \$48,000$$
$$X = 5,333.3 \text{ Units.}$$

Sales at breakeven point are

Product P $= 2 \times 5,333.3 = 10,667$

Product Q $= 2 \times 5,333.3 = 10,667$

Product R $= 1 \times 5,333.3 = 5,333.$

$$\frac{\text{Total Revenue}}{\text{at Breakeven}} = 5,333.3 \text{ Units} \times \$24$$
$$= \$128,000.$$

... CHAPTER 8 ...

Short-Run Decisions and Differential Analysis

Chapter Outline

- The Differential Principle
- Problems in Identifying Costs
- Pricing Decisions
- Make-or-Buy Decisions
- Adding and Dropping Parts of Operations
- Product Choice Decisions
- Inventory Management Decisions
- Appendix 8.1: Linear Programming
- Appendix 8.2: Economic Order Quantity Model

This chapter continues our discussion of the use of accounting information for managerial decision making. It deals with the use of accounting information in making such managerial decisions as pricing, accepting special orders, making versus buying products, and choosing the optimal mix of products.

These short-run decisions span the period during which the manager assumes capacity is fixed. Chapter 9 deals with long-run decisions that involve changes in capacity.

Exhibit 8.1

Differential Analysis Model[a]

	Alternative	−	Status Quo	=	Difference
Revenue......................................	P_1X_1	−	P_0X_0	=	ΔPX
Less Variable Costs	V_1X_1	−	V_0X_0	=	ΔVX
Total Contribution Margin	$(P_1 − V_1)X_1$	−	$(P_0 − V_0)X_0$	=	$\Delta(P − V)X$
Less Fixed Costs	F_1	−	F_0	=	ΔF
Operating Profit............................	π_1	−	π_0	=	$\Delta \pi$

[a]P = price per unit; X = volume per period; V = variable cost per unit; $P − V$ = contribution margin per unit; F = fixed costs per period; π = operating profit per period; Δ = amount of difference.

This chapter deals with several applications of one principle—**differential analysis**—the analysis of differences among particular alternative actions.[1] Owners typically judge management's performance on the basis of a firm's profitability. Thus managers want to know the differential effect of various alternative actions on profits. As you go through each application of differential analysis, we encourage you to keep the following questions in mind: What differs among the alternatives? By how much?

The Differential Principle

Managerial decision making is the process of making choices. If a manager must choose among alternatives, the alternatives must differ. The differential analysis model, shown in Exhibit 8.1, extends the cost-volume-profit model discussed in Chapter 7. The first column represents the alternative being considered. The second column presents the **status quo,** or baseline. The third column shows the difference between the status quo and the alternative. If the difference is such that $\pi_1 > \pi_0$, the alternative is more profitable than the status quo. If $\pi_0 > \pi_1$, the status quo is more profitable. A *differential cost* is a cost that changes (differs) as a result of taking some action.

The following example illustrates differential analysis. To provide continuity, we use the facts from this example throughout the chapter. We use a manufacturing firm in this illustration because it is the most comprehensive and complex of any type of organization. The concepts apply as well to service, financial, merchandising, and other organizations.

Example   Assume the following status quo data for Baltimore Company, a high-tech company that makes a particular type of computer software known as BC-1234.

---

[1]Differential analysis is also known as *incremental analysis* or *marginal analysis*.

Units Made and Sold	800 Units Per Month
Maximum Production and Sales Capacity	1,200 Units per Month
Selling Price	$30

Cost Classification	Variable Cost (per unit)	Fixed Cost (per month)
Manufacturing Costs	$17	$3,060
Marketing and Administrative Costs	5	1,740
Total Costs	$22	$4,800

The management of the Baltimore Company believes that it can increase volume from 800 units to 900 units per month by decreasing the selling price from $30 to $28 per unit. Would the price reduction be profitable? The result of differential analysis for this problem, appearing in Exhibit 8.2, indicates that the alternative would not increase profits.

Relevant Costs

Note in Exhibit 8.2 that this particular decision does not affect all costs. Specifically, fixed costs in this example do not change. Thus only revenues and *total* variable costs are relevant to the analysis; fixed costs are not. We sometimes call differential analysis **relevant cost analysis** as it identifies the costs (or revenues) relevant to the decision. A cost or revenue is *relevant* if an amount appears in the Difference column; all others are irrelevant. Thus we could ignore fixed costs in this

Exhibit 8.2

BALTIMORE COMPANY
Differential Analysis of a Price Reduction[a]

	Alternative P = $28 X = 900	− Status Quo P = $30 X = 800	= Difference
Revenue	$25,200[b]	− $24,000[d]	= $ 1,200
Less Variable Costs	(19,800)[c]	− (17,600)[e]	= (2,200)
Total Contribution Margin	$ 5,400	− $ 6,400	= $(1,000)
Less Fixed Costs	(4,800)	− (4,800)	= 0
Operating Profit	$ 600	− $ 1,600	= $(1,000)

[a]Numbers within parentheses are costs or losses; numbers with minus signs are the result of row operations.
[b]$25,200 = $28 × 900 Units.
[c]$19,800 = $22 × 900 Units.
[d]$24,000 = $30 × 800 Units.
[e]$17,600 = $22 × 800 Units.

example. (This is not true in general. Fixed costs nearly always differ in long-run decisions involving changes in capacity, and they sometimes differ in short-run operating decisions, as we shall see later in this chapter.)

As you become familiar with differential analysis, you will find shortcuts by ignoring irrelevant costs (and revenues) from the outset of your work. For instance, you needed to work only with revenues and total variable costs in the previous example to get the answer.

Problems in Identifying Costs

Focus on Cash Flows

The most difficult part of decision making is estimating the benefits and costs of each alternative. Although benefits and costs have several dimensions, the most important dimensions for business decisions are the amounts and timing of **cash flows.** (Chapter 9 provides analytical methods of dealing with the *timing* of cash flows; this chapter deals only with the *amount* of cash flows.) The emphasis on cash flows is fundamental for two reasons:

1. Cash is the medium of exchange. The firm can use cash immediately to pay debts or dividends or to purchase equipment. The firm can eventually convert noncash assets into cash, but this step takes time and perhaps some additional costs.

2. Cash serves as a common, objective measure of the benefit and costs of alternatives. If the analysis states one alternative in terms of units of inventory to be produced and another in terms of the number of machines to be acquired, it is not expressing the alternatives in a common measuring unit. Before the manager can compare these alternatives, the analysis must reexpress their benefits and costs in a common measuring unit. Cash flows are the common measuring unit because they represent the most objective and quantifiable measure of benefits and costs.

Consequently, differential analysis focuses mostly on differential cash flows. The previous example assumed both differential revenues and costs to be cash flows or near-cash flows (for example, it assumed that revenues and costs on account are cash flows). Managers who focus on cash flows alone, however, may overlook two additional costs: opportunity costs and economic depreciation.

Economic Depreciation

Depreciation may create confusion in differential analysis. In financial accounting, depreciation allocates part of an asset's cost to time periods or to units of production. Differential analysis involves the change in the economic value of an asset because of its use. This change in value is **economic depreciation.** Differential analysis focuses on cash flows. The cash outflow to acquire an asset less the cash inflow when the firm sells is a differential cost. Differential analysis, therefore, takes into account economic depreciation, which is the decline in value of an asset.

Example   Management of a rental car company is deciding between purchasing a fleet of Oldsmobile or Buick automobiles. All operating costs for both models are equal. However, economic depreciation differs. The Buicks cost $15,000 each and have a salvage value of $11,000 if sold after 6 months. The Oldsmobiles cost $15,000 each and have a salvage value of $12,000 if sold after 6 months. The following table shows that the Oldsmobiles have a lower economic depreciation in this case. (We have excluded the time value of money to simplify the illustration.) Regardless of the depreciation recorded in the accounting records, the cash flows show the economic depreciation.

	Alternative 1: Buick	_	Alternative 2: Oldsmobile	=	Difference (1 − 2)
Cost of Car (cash outflow)	$(15,000)	−	$(15,000)	=	$ 0
Salvage Value after 6 months (cash inflow)	11,000	−	12,000	=	(1,000)
Economic Depreciation (decline in value)	$ (4,000)	−	$ (3,000)	=	$ 1,000

Uncertainty and Differential Analysis

Cost and revenue estimates for the status quo are usually more certain than estimates for alternatives. The status quo represents something known, whereas estimates for alternatives may be little more than educated guesses. Analysts may easily omit some critical aspect of the alternative.

Most managers are averse to risk and uncertainty unless they receive additional compensation to bear risk. They prefer the known to the unknown, all other things being equal. Consequently, we sometimes see managers rejecting, because of uncertainty, an alternative expected to be more profitable than the status quo. Managers often deal with uncertainty and differential analysis by setting high standards for the alternative. (For example, "The alternative must increase profits by 25 percent before we will accept it.")

Pricing Decisions

Decisions regarding the prices a firm charges for its products are complex, involving factors such as competitors' actions and market conditions. In many cases a firm will not be in a position to set prices. The more highly competitive the market, the more likely the firm must accept the market price as given. In some situations, however, firms do have some control over prices they charge. For example, many firms sell to government agencies or other buyers with cost-plus-fixed-fee contracts. In this section, we consider pricing decisions to show that correct pricing decisions involve the principles of differential analysis.

Cost-Based Approach to Pricing

One approach to setting prices is to add a markup to the firm's costs.[2] Suppose that the management of the Baltimore Company has set a goal of reporting profits of $2,000 per month. If it estimated the volume to be 800 units per month, it would calculate the per-unit price as follows:

$$\pi = PX - (VX + F)$$

$$\$2,000 = (P \times 800) - [(\$22 \times 800) + \$4,800]$$

$$= (P \times 800) - \$22,400$$

$$\$24,400 = P \times 800$$

$$P = \frac{\$24,400}{800}$$

$$= \$30.50.$$

So it would set the unit price at $30.50.

If a firm is to remain in business in the long run, it must recover all of its accounting costs and provide an adequate return to its owners.[3] It is desirable, then, that long-run average prices approximate the amount derived from a cost-based approach to pricing. Basing prices on costs, however, has four shortcomings.

First   Basing prices on costs ignores the relation between P (price) and X (quantity sold) in the market. If the Baltimore Company faces a downward-sloping demand curve, it may not be able to sell 800 units at a price of $30.50.

---

[2]Economics provides a justification for basing prices on costs. Managerial economics and microeconomics texts point out that marginal revenue, MR, is a function of both price, P, and the price elasticity of demand (percentage change in quantity divided by percentage change in price), η:

$$MR = P(1 + 1/\eta).$$

In profit-maximizing equilibrium, a firm sets marginal revenue equal to marginal costs, MC. Substituting MC for MR in the above equation and solving for P yields

$$P = MC[1/(1 - 1/\eta)].$$

Thus a firm should base its prices on markup over costs, properly measured as marginal costs (or incremental costs). The optimizing markup relates inversely to the elasticity of demand. The less elastic the demand, the larger the markup. So, for example, department stores have small markups on basic underwear, for which the elasticity of demand is large, while setting large markups on furniture, for which the elasticity of demand is small. See, for example, E. Mansfield, *Managerial Economics,* New York: W. W. Norton & Company, 1990, pp. 83–84 and 415–422.

[3]Accountants and economists realize that "an adequate return for owners" is an economic (opportunity) cost, but not an accounting cost (appearing in the financial statements).

Second   Cost-plus pricing is often simplistic, such as, "Add $2.50 to the total cost of producing and selling each unit to get the price." Basing prices on costs creates a circularity. The number of units produced critically affects the per-unit cost of a product. As the number of units increases, the amount of fixed cost allocated to each unit decreases. Thus the per-unit cost of a product if Baltimore Company produced 800 units is

$$\$22 + \frac{\$4,800}{800} = \$28.$$

If the company produces 1,000 units, the per-unit cost is

$$\$22 + \frac{\$4,800}{1,000} = \$26.80.$$

In the former case,

$$P = \$2.50 + \$28$$

$$= \$30.50,$$

whereas in the latter case,

$$P = \$2.50 + \$26.80$$

$$= \$29.30.$$

If management priced in this manner, it might drop prices when demand was stronger and raise them when it was weaker.

Moral: If managers base prices on per-unit total costs and per-unit total costs change with volume and volume depends on prices, then prices are highest when volume is lowest and vice versa.

Third   Accounting practices and conventions not appropriate for the decision may affect the costs attributable to a particular product. For example, the acquisition cost of using a plant and machinery determines the accounting cost of these assets. Accounting gives no recognition to the opportunity cost of using the plant and machinery in manufacturing the product. Also, the depreciable life and depreciation method used affect the portion of the acquisition cost of these assets allocated to each period. The allocation of various costs to specific products becomes particularly questionable as the cost of items becomes more indirect with respect to the product. Consider, for example, the allocation of the president's salary to each of a firm's products. Accounting practices for such costs raise questions about the validity of product cost amounts for decision-making purposes.

Fourth   Cost-based pricing can lead to incorrect decisions, particularly in the short run. For example, assume that the Baltimore Company has received a special order for 100 units for $25 per unit. This order will not affect the firm's regular market, and the company can fill the order with existing capacity. If the company uses a cost-based approach to pricing, it will probably reject this special order because the $25 price is less than the $28 per-unit full cost ($28 = $22 + $4,800/800). Some might advocate spreading the fixed costs over 900 units. That would give a per-unit

Exhibit 8.3

BALTIMORE COMPANY						
Differential Analysis of a Special Order						
		Alternative	**−**	**Status Quo**	**=**	**Difference**
Revenue...................................		$26,500[a]	−	$24,000	=	$2,500
Less Variable Costs		(19,800)[b]	−	(17,600)	=	(2,200)
Total Contribution		$ 6,700	−	$ 6,400	=	$ 300
Less Fixed Costs		(4,800)	−	(4,800)	=	0
Operating Profit...........................		$ 1,900	−	$ 1,600	=	$ 300

[a]$26,500 = $24,000 + ($25 × 100 Units).
[b]$19,800 = $17,600 + ($22 × 100 Units).

full cost of $22 + $4,800/900 = $27.33, which exceeds the special-order price. Exhibit 8.3 demonstrates that rejecting this order is incorrect. Applying the differential approach to pricing results in the correct decision.

Differential Approach to Pricing

The differential approach to pricing presumes that the price must at least equal the **differential cost** of producing and selling the product. In the short run, this practice will result in a positive contribution to covering fixed costs and generating profit. In the long run, this practice will require covering all costs, because *both fixed and variable costs become differential costs in the long run*.

    The differential approach particularly helps in making special-order decisions. Consider the special order discussed previously. Exhibit 8.3 presents an analysis of the effects of not accepting and of accepting the special order, assuming that the regular market is 800 units sold at a price of $30 a unit. Exhibit 8.3 demonstrates that Baltimore should accept the special order at $25 per unit, because that price permits the firm to cover the differential costs of $22 per unit and provide a contribution of $3 per unit toward covering fixed costs and earning profit. (A shortcut computes the per-unit contribution margin on the special order, $3, and multiplies it by the number of units, 100. This computation gives the additional total contribution from the special order, $300.)

    The differential approach to pricing works well for special orders but some criticize it for pricing a firm's regular products. Critics suggest that following the differential approach in the short run (that is, setting prices equal to variable cost) will lead to underpricing in the long run, because the contribution to covering fixed costs or generating profits will be inadequate.

    Others respond in two ways to this criticism. First, the differential approach does lead to correct short-run pricing decisions. Once the firm has set plant capacity and incurred fixed costs, the fixed costs become irrelevant to the short-run pricing decision. The firm must attempt to set a price at least equal to the differential, or variable, costs. Second, in both the short and long run, the differential approach provides only an indicator of the *minimum* acceptable price. The firm can always

Exhibit 8.4

BALTIMORE COMPANY Data for Pricing		
Short-Run Differential Costs (variable costs)	$22	= Short-Run Minimum Price
Fixed Cost	6[a]	
Long-Run Incremental Costs	$28	= Long-Run Minimum price
Expected Profits	2	
Target Selling Price	$30	= Long-Run Desired Price

[a]$6 = $4,800/800. This assumes a long-run volume of 800 units.

charge some higher amount, taking into consideration market demand, competitor's actions, and similar factors.

Consider the data for the Baltimore Company in Exhibit 8.4. The minimum acceptable price in the short run is the differential cost of $22 per unit. In the long run, the minimum acceptable price is $28 per unit, because the firm must cover both variable and fixed costs. A more desirable long-run price is $30, which includes a profit. Between the $22 short-run minimum price and the (say) $30 long-run desired price lies the range of price flexibility for the firm. The firm may set a price slightly higher than the variable cost for a special order as long as excess capacity exists and doing so will not affect the firm's regular market.

If Baltimore Company faces a competing market for its regular product, it can set a price slightly higher than the $22 minimum. The firm hopes to underprice competitors and to capture a larger share of the market. The increase in quantity sold may more than offset the reduction in the contribution margin per unit from a lower selling price, resulting in a larger *total* contribution margin.[4]

If a firm is the only supplier of this product, it can charge a price higher than $28. If the firm sets the price too high, however, it will earn high profits which may induce other firms to sell the product, thereby splitting the market. Thus, the pricing decision should include an analysis of short-run and long-run differential costs, market conditions, and competitors' actions.

Make-or-Buy Decisions

When a firm must decide whether to meet its needs internally or to acquire goods or services from external sources, it faces a **make-or-buy decision.** A restaurant that serves its meals from frozen entrees "buys," whereas one that uses fresh ingredients "makes." A steel company that mines its own iron ore and coal and processes it through to final product "makes" the pig iron, whereas one that purchases these raw materials "buys." Housing contractors who do their own site preparation and foundation work "make," whereas those who hire subcontractors "buy."

---

[4]This result assumes an elastic demand curve such that the negative effects on total contribution margin of percentage decreases in the contribution margin per unit are more than offset by the positive effects of percentage increases in quantity. Managers must be careful, for antitrust reasons, not to sell below cost. Most courts have held that as long as prices cover average variable costs, the prices are not illegally low; however, courts have not been clear about the meaning of "average variable cost."

Whether to make or to buy depends on cost factors and on nonquantitative factors such as dependability of suppliers and quality control of purchased materials. The decision may appear to be a one-time choice between making or buying, but managers usually make such decisions in the context of the firm's strategy to become more or less self-reliant.

Example   The Baltimore Company has an opportunity to buy part of its product for $12 per unit. This purchase would affect prices, volume, and costs as follows:

	Alternative: Buy	Status Quo: Make
Unit Selling Price	$30	$30
Volume	800 per Month	800 per Month
Unit Variable Manufacturing Costs	$6	$17
Purchased Parts, per Unit	$12	$0
Unit Variable Marketing and Administrative Costs	$5	$5
Fixed Manufacturing Costs	$2,100	$3,060
Fixed Marketing and Administrative Costs	$1,740	$1,740

Exhibit 8.5 shows that the alternative to buy is more profitable.

Adding and Dropping Parts of Operations

Managers must decide when to add or drop products from the product line and when to open or abandon sales territories. These can be either long-run decisions involving a change in capacity or short-run decisions in which capacity does not change. This chapter deals with these as short-run decisions.

Exhibit 8.5

BALTIMORE COMPANY
Differential Analysis of Make-or-Buy Decision

	Alternative: Buy	−	Status Quo: Make	= Difference
Revenue..................................	$24,000	−	$24,000	= —
Less:				
Variable Costs to Produce and Sell	(8,800)[a]	−	(17,600)	= $8,800
Variable Costs of Goods Bought	(9,600)[b]	−	—	= (9,600)
Total Contribution Margin	$ 5,600	−	$ 6,400	= $ (800)
Less Fixed Costs	(3,840)[c]	−	(4,800)	= 960
Operating Profit............................	$ 1,760	−	$ 1,600	= $ 160

[a]$8,800 = ($6 + $5) × 800 Units.

[b]$9,600 = $12 × 800 Units.

[c]$3,840 = $2,100 + $1,740.

The differential principle implies the following analysis. If the differential revenue from the sale of a product exceeds the differential costs required to provide the sales, the product generates profits and the firm should continue its production. This decision is correct even though the product may show a loss in financial statements because of overhead costs allocated to it. If the product more than covers its differential costs, and if no other alternative use of the production and sales facilities exists, the firm should retain the product.

Example Suppose that the Baltimore Company had three products, not just the one in the previous examples, and used common facilities to produce and sell all three. Neither product affects sales of the others. The relevant data for these three products follow:

| | Product | | | |
	A	B	C	Total
Sales Volume per Month	800	1,000	600	—
Unit Sales Price	$30	$20	$40	—
Sales Revenue	$24,000	$20,000	$24,000	$68,000
Unit Variable Cost	$22	$14	$35	—
Fixed Cost per Month	—	—	—	$13,600

Management has asked the accounting department to allocate fixed costs to each product so that it can evaluate how well each product is doing. Total fixed costs were 20 percent of total dollar sales, so the accountant charged fixed costs to each product at 20 percent of the product's sales. For example, Product C received $4,800 (= .20 × $24,000 sales) of fixed costs.

As the product-line income statements on the top panel of Exhibit 8.6 show, the report demonstrated an apparent loss of $1,800 for Product C. One of Baltimore's managers argued, "We should drop Product C. It is losing $1,800 per month." A second manager suggested performing a differential analysis on dropping Product C to see the costs saved and the revenues lost. The bottom panel of Exhibit 8.6, the differential analysis, shows dropping Product C makes the company less profitable.

The first manager incorrectly assumed that dropping the product would save fixed costs. The firm should investigate more profitable uses of the facilities for producing and selling Product C, because its contribution margin appears to be the weakest of the three products. Until such alternatives emerge, however, producing and selling Product C is profitable.

Product Choice Decisions

Managers ask, "Which products should we sell?" Most firms can supply a number of goods and services to the market, but manufacturing or distribution constraints limit what firms can do. A small CPA firm may have to choose between performing work for Client A or for Client B because of a shortage of personnel. Students have

Exhibit 8.6

BALTIMORE COMPANY
Differential Analysis of Dropping a Product

Income Statement Analysis

| | Product | | | |
	A	B	C	Total
Sales.........................	$24,000	$20,000	$24,000	$68,000
Less Variable Costs	(17,600)	(14,000)	(21,000)	(52,600)
Total Contribution Margin	$ 6,400	$ 6,000	$ 3,000	$15,400
Less Fixed Costs Allocated to Each Product.......................	(4,800)[a]	(4,000)[a]	(4,800)[a]	(13,600)
Operating Profit (Loss)............	$ 1,600	$ 2,000	$ (1,800)	$ 1,800

Differential Analysis

	Alternative: Drop Product C	−	Status Quo	= Difference
Sales.....................................	$44,000	−	$68,000	= $(24,000)
Less Variable Costs	(31,600)	−	(52,600)	= 21,000
Total Contribution Margin	$12,400	−	$15,400	= $ (3,000)
Less Fixed Costs	(13,600)	−	(13,600)	= 0
Operating Profit (Loss).....................	$ (1,200)	−	$ 1,800	= $ (3,000)

[a]Fixed costs of $13,600 allocated in proportion to sales; 20 percent of sales dollars charged to each product as fixed costs.

to choose how to allocate their study time between accounting and finance, or their time between Question 1 and Question 2 on a final exam. An automobile manufacturer with limited production facilities must decide whether to produce subcompacts, compacts, or some other model.

We normally think of these product-choice problems as short-run decisions. The automobile manufacturer may be able to produce both subcompacts and compacts in the *long run* by increasing capacity. The CPA firm could serve both Client A and Client B in the *long run* by hiring more professional staff. With enough time, students can study for *both* accounting and finance. In the short run, however, capacity limitations require choices among options.

Example   The Baltimore Company has just purchased one machine that can make Products L, M, and N. The market for these products will absorb all of them, or any combination. Management wants to pick the most profitable product, or combination of products, to produce. The firm has only 400 hours of time available on the machine each month.

The time requirements for each of the three products, their selling prices, and their variable costs appear in Exhibit 8.7. For this example, assume that all market-

Exhibit 8.7

Rationing Scarce Capacity (Machine is available only 400 hours per month.)			

	Product		
	L	**M**	**N**
Time Required on the Machine per Unit Produced	0.5 Hour	2.0 Hours	4.0 Hours
Selling Price per Unit	$5.00	$12.00	$16.00
Less Variable Costs to Produce One Unit	(3.00)	(5.00)	(6.00)
Contribution Margin per Unit	$2.00	$ 7.00	$10.00
Contribution Margin per Hour on the Machine (contribution margin per unit/time requirement in hours)	$4.00 per Hour[a]	$3.50 per Hour[b]	$2.50 per Hour[c]
Total Contribution from Using 400 Hours on the Machine	$1,600	$1,400	$1,000

[a]$4.00 per Hour = $2.00/0.5 Hour.
[b]$3.50 per Hour = $7.00/2.0 Hours.
[c]$2.50 per Hour = $10.00/4.0 Hours.

ing and administrative costs are fixed. Also assume that fixed manufacturing, marketing, and administrative costs are the same (that is, are not differential) whichever product or combination of products the firm produces.

Even though Product N has a per-unit contribution of $10.00, whereas Product L has a per-unit contribution of only $2.00, Product L is still the best product to produce given the capacity constraint on the machine. Product L contributes $4.00 per hour (= $2.00 per unit/.5 hour per unit) of time on the machine, whereas Product N contributes only $2.50 per hour ($10.00 per unit/4 hours per unit) of time on the machine. Differential analysis indicates that the total contribution margin from using the machine to produce Product L is $1,600, whereas the contribution from producing Product M is $1,400 and that from producing Product N is $1,000.

If the machine time were unlimited, the Baltimore Company should produce and sell all three products in the short run because all have a positive contribution margin. But with constrained machinery time, the most profitable product is *the one that contributes the most per unit of time*. As a general rule, use a scarce resource to contribute the most per unit of the resource consumed. (If you face time constraints on an examination and must choose between Question 1 and Question 2, and if working on Question 1 provides 1 point per minute and Question 2 provides 2 points per minute, then work on Question 2.)

When there is only one scarce resource, as in this example where the scarce resource is time on the machine, the decision is easy to make: Choose the product that gives the largest contribution per unit of the scarce resource used. When each product uses different proportions of several scarce resources, the computational problem becomes more difficult. Appendix 8.1 describes linear programming, a

Managerial Application

Differential Analysis for Superstars[a]

When the Los Angeles Kings acquired Wayne Gretzky from the Edmonton Oilers for $15 million and other considerations, many hockey executives and analysts said it was a good deal for both sides. The different business situations for the two teams affected their differential cost analyses.

The Edmonton Oilers were an established NHL powerhouse with a captive sports audience. While fans initially criticized the trade of the national hero, attendance declined little.

The Oilers benefitted substantially. In addition to the fifteen million dollar receipt, the Oilers laid the foundation for the future by acquiring a young star and three number one draft picks over the next five years. If the competition for the Edmonton sports dollar became more intense, the Oilers would be able to maintain their fan loyalty by fielding a consistently outstanding team. Finally, the Oilers would be reducing their payroll. For the Oilers, potential differential revenues lost in the short-run were less than the differential cost savings.

The differential analysis for the Los Angeles Kings was more complicated. The Kings needed a big draw to compete in a highly competitive sports market that included several professional teams with stars like Magic Johnson and Orel Hershiser as well as two major college sports powers. The Kings management hoped that Gretzky would provide star quality and provide the foundation for a winning franchise. Before making the deal the Kings estimated differential revenues and costs from increased concessions, television and radio rights, and ticket sales, and estimated additional revenues from ticket sales. Based on their analysis, they estimated an increased annual revenue of $10.5 million, increased additional payroll costs of $2 million per year, plus interest on the money borrowed to acquire Gretzky. The Kings concluded that they would recover their $15-million investment in less than three years.

[a]Based on Joshua Mills, "Gretzky: Deal with Dividends," *New York Times* (August 20, 1988), 17, 29.

mathematical tool for solving such multiple constrained decision problems. Textbooks on operations research and quantitative methods describe these techniques in more detail.

Incorrect Use of Accounting Data   Many accounting systems routinely provide unit cost information that includes an *allocation* of fixed costs to each unit. This is the full absorption method of product costing. We assume the variable costing method so far in this chapter. Full absorption unit costs for short-run decision making will lead to incorrect decisions as the following example demonstrates.

Example   We have seen that production of Product L is optimal because its total monthly contribution is the highest of the three products. (Refer to Exhibit 8.7.)

Exhibit 8.8

Rationing Scarce Capacity by Incorrectly Using Full Absorption Unit Costs

	Product		
	L	**M**	**N**
(1) Time Required on the Machine per Unit Produced	0.5 Hour	2.0 Hours	4.0 Hours
(2) Selling Price per Unit.........................	$5.00	$12.00	$16.00
Variable Costs to Produce One Unit:			
(3) Direct Materials	$1.00	$2.00	$2.50
(4) Direct Labor	1.50	2.00	2.50
(5) Variable Manufacturing Overhead	.50	1.00	1.00
(6) Total Variable Costs per Unit	$3.00	$5.00	$6.00
(7) Allocation of Fixed Costs at 100 Percent of Direct Labor	1.50	2.00	2.50
(8) Full Absorption Cost per Unit.................	$4.50	$7.00	$8.50
(9) Gross Margin per Unit [line (2) minus line (8)]	$ .50	$5.00	$7.50
(10) Gross Margin per Hour......................	$1.00 per Hour	$2.50 per Hour	$1.875 per Hour

Suppose that each product carries fixed manufacturing costs at a rate of 100 percent of direct labor costs, using the full absorption, normal costing method Chapter 3 describes.[5] The unit cost for each product under full absorption, normal costing appears on line (8) of Exhibit 8.8. Users of accounting data would typically see only the unit costs on line (8) of Exhibit 8.8, so the margin-per-hour calculation would use the **gross margin** (that is, selling price minus full absorption unit cost) instead of **contribution margin.** As line (10) of Exhibit 8.8 shows, full absorption cost may lead to an incorrect assessment that Product M is most profitable and Product L is least profitable per machine hour.

The point: if fixed costs do not vary with units produced, do not unitize fixed costs. Unitizing fixed costs makes them appear to vary with units when they do not.

---

[5]The full absorption costing system derives unit costs by adding an allocation of fixed manufacturing costs to variable costs. Thus the two methods generate different unit margins, as follows:

Variable Costing:

$$\frac{\text{Selling Price}}{\text{per Unit}} - \frac{\text{Variable Manufacturing}}{\text{Cost per Unit}} = \frac{\text{Contribution}}{\text{Margin per Unit.}}$$

Full Absorption Costing:

$$\frac{\text{Selling}}{\text{Price}} - \left(\frac{\text{Variable}}{\text{Manufacturing}} + \frac{\text{Allocation}}{\text{of Fixed}} \right) = \frac{\text{Gross}}{\text{Margin}}$$
$$\begin{array}{c} \text{Price} \\ \text{per} \\ \text{Unit} \end{array} \quad \begin{array}{c} \text{Cost per} \\ \text{Unit} \end{array} \quad \begin{array}{c} \text{Cost to Each} \\ \text{Unit} \end{array} \quad \begin{array}{c} \text{per} \\ \text{Unit} \end{array}$$

Under *normal* costing, the allocation of fixed manufacturing cost results from a predetermined normal rate. Any differences between actual fixed manufacturing costs and the amount allocated to units produced are written off as a period cost.

This example shows how the use of accounting data intended for one purpose may not be useful for other purposes. External reporting requires full absorption unit cost data. Most managerial decision models, on the other hand, assume *variable* unit costs.

Unsophisticated users of accounting data often incorrectly assume that any calculated unit cost is a variable cost. You should not *assume* that the unit cost reported by an accounting system is a variable cost. Those unit costs often contain unitized fixed costs.

Inventory Management Decisions

Inventory management affects profits in merchandising, manufacturing, and other organizations with inventories. Having the correct type and amount of inventory can prevent a production shutdown in manufacturing. In merchandising, having the correct type of merchandise inventory may mean making a sale. Inventories are costly to maintain, however. The costs include storage costs, insurance, losses from damage and theft, property taxes, and the opportunity cost of funds tied up in inventory. Key inventory management questions include the following:

1. How many units of inventory should be on hand and available for use or sale?
2. How often should the firm order a particular item? What is the optimal size of the order?

Differential Costs for Inventory Management

Inventory management decisions involve two types of opposing costs. The firm incurs differential costs each time it places an order or makes a production run (for example, the cost of processing each purchase order or the cost of preparing machinery for each production run). These are **setup or order costs.** The firm could minimize them by minimizing the number of orders or production runs.

By ordering or producing less frequently, however, each order or production run must be for a larger number of units. The firm will carry a larger average inventory. Larger inventories imply larger **carrying costs** for these inventories (for example, the cost of maintaining warehouse facilities).

Management would like to find the optimal trade-off between these two types of opposing costs, carrying costs and order costs. Refer to Exhibit 8.9, based on the example below. (We refer to both order costs and setup costs as *order costs* for the rest of our discussion.) The problem is to calculate the optimal number of orders or production runs each year and the optimal number of units to order or produce. The optimal number of units to order or produce is the **economic order quantity (EOQ).**

Example   California Merchandising sells 6,000 units of a product per year, spread evenly throughout the year. Each unit costs $2 to purchase. The differential cost of preparing and following up on an order is $100 per order. The cost of carrying a unit in inventory is 30 percent of the unit's cost. Thus, if the firm places one order for the year, it will purchase 6,000 units and have, *on average,* 3,000 units ($3,000) in inventory during the year. The carrying cost would be $900 (= $3,000 × .30) for

Exhibit 8.9

Inventory Costs

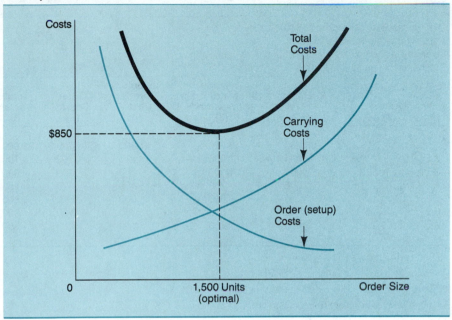

the year. Exhibit 8.10 presents the inventory carrying costs, order costs, and total costs of the inventory. Note the trade-off between carrying costs and order costs: As one decreases, the other increases. The optimal number of orders per year is four, which has the lowest total costs [see column (6) in Exhibit 8.10].

A formal model (called the EOQ model) for deriving the optimal number of orders (or setups of production runs) and the optimal number of items in an order (or in a production run) appears in Appendix 8.2.

Estimating the Costs of Maintaining Inventory

Managers, industrial engineers, analysts, and others who attempt to derive optimal solutions to inventory management problems typically use costs the accounting system provides. An important but difficult task for management accountants is estimating inventory order costs and carrying costs. Keep in mind that only *differential* costs matter. For example, suppose that the firm uses one purchasing agent whether customers place one order or twelve orders per year, and the number of orders made does not affect the agent's salary. Assume that the opportunity cost of the agent's time equals zero. Therefore, the agent's salary does not differ, and it would not be part of the order costs.

Order Costs   To estimate differential order costs, consider whether any salaries or wages differ because of the number of orders and whether there are opportunity costs of lost time. Production setups, in particular, usually result in lost time for production employees. Order costs should include differential costs of receiving and inspecting orders, costs of processing invoices from suppliers, and freight costs.

Exhibit 8.10

CALIFORNIA MERCHANDISING
Economic Order Quantity Calculation

Differential costs per order are $100.
Annual requirement is 6,000 units.
Inventory carrying costs are 30 percent per year.
Purchase cost per unit is $2.00.

Orders (1)	Order Size[a] (2)	Average Number of Units in Inventory[b] (3)	Inventory Carrying Costs[c] (4)	Order Costs[d] (5)	Total Costs[e] (6)
1	6,000	3,000	$1,800	$ 100	$1,900
2	3,000	1,500	900	200	1,100
3	2,000	1,000	600	300	900
4	1,500	750	450	400	850[f]
5	1,200	600	360	500	860
6	1,000	500	300	600	900
12	500	250	150	1,200	1,350

[a]6,000 units/number of orders from column (1).

[b]Number of units in an order from column (2)/2.

[c]Amount in column (3) $\times$ $2 cost per unit $\times$ .30.

[d]$100 $\times$ number of orders from column (1).

[e]Amount in column (4) + amount in column (5).

[f]Lowest total cost. Optimal number of orders is four per year.

Example   If freight costs are a constant amount (say $.10) per unit, they do not differ as the number of orders varies. If the firm pays freight charges per *shipment,* however (say, $50 per shipment), costs increase as the number of shipments increases. In this case, freight is a differential cost.

Carrying Costs   Differential carrying costs include insurance, inventory taxes, the opportunity cost of funds invested in inventory, and other costs that differ with the number of units held in inventory. If the firm pays additional wages or leases additional warehouse space because inventory quantity increases, these costs are differential carrying costs. Carrying costs should not include an allocated portion of warehouse depreciation or rent if these costs do not vary with the number of units in inventory. Such depreciation and rent are not differential carrying costs.

Example   Consider the following data obtained from the accounting records of EOQ Incorporated:

Orders Handled per Year on Average.....................	40 Orders
Average Order Size.......................................	1,000 Units
Total Units Purchased per Year	40,000 Units
Purchase Price of Merchandise	$12,000 per Unit
Freight-in	$.50 per Unit

continued

continued from page 350

Costs to Place an Order:

Fixed Cost (per year)	$2,000
Variable Cost (per order)	$11
Cost to Unload a Shipment (fixed labor costs of $4,000 per year/40 shipments per year + variable costs of $30 per shipment)	$130 per Shipment
Inventory Taxes	10 Percent of Inventory Value
Salary of Supervisor	$18,000 per Year
Insurance on Inventory	4 Percent of Inventory Value
Warehouse Rental (fixed rental of $2,000 per year; average inventory level is 500 units)	$4.00 per Unit
Costs to Inspect and Count Inventory	$1.10 per Unit
Cost of Capital	20 Percent

In the past, the company had an average of 40 orders per year and an average inventory level of 500 units. Management suspects those figures are not optimal. Which costs should management include in computing the optimal order size computation?

Differential carrying costs per unit include the following:

(1) Inventory Taxes: 10 Percent × $12.50 (inventory value is assumed to include freight-in)	$1.25 per Unit
(2) Inventory Insurance: 4 Percent × $12.50	.50 per Unit
(3) Costs to Inspect and Count Inventory	1.10 per Unit
(4) Cost of Capital: 20 Percent × $12.50	2.50 per Unit
Total per Unit	$5.35

Note that the purchase price and freight-in are not differential, because the number of orders placed or the average level of inventory do not affect the total number of units purchased for a year. Warehouse rental is a fixed cost, even though the data schedule shows it as a unit cost. (Seldom does any benefit flow from unitizing fixed costs.) EOQ Incorporated's carrying cost per year would be $2,675 (= 500 × $5.35), excluding fixed costs.

Differential order costs include the following:

(1) Cost of Placing an Order (variable portion only)	$11.00
(2) Cost of Unloading (variable portion only)	30.00
Total per Order	$41.00

The salary of the supervisor is fixed, and the accounting system excludes the fixed portions of ordering costs and unloading costs. EOQ Incorporated's order cost per year would be $1,640 (= 40 × $41).

The optimal order size turns out to be 784 (rounded) units per order, giving an average inventory level of 392 units. The optimal number of orders per year is 51 (= 40,000 units per year/784 units per order). (We round all numbers to the nearest whole number.) We derived these amounts using an economic order quantity model

Exhibit 8.11

Differential Cost Analysis for Inventory Management						
	Alternative	**−**	**Status Quo**		**= Difference**	
Differential Carrying Costs.........	$2,097 (= $5.35 × 392 units)	−	$2,675 (= $5.35 × 500 units)	=	$(578)	
Differential Order Costs	2,091 (= $41 × 51 orders)	−	1,640 (= $41 × 40 orders)	=	451	
Total Differential Costs	$4,188	−	$4,315	=	$(127)	
Nondifferential Costs:						
Fixed Cost of Placing an Order	2,000	−	2,000	=	0	
Fixed Cost to Unload a Shipment	4,000	−	4,000	=	0	
Fixed Salary of Supervisor.......	18,000	−	18,000	=	0	
Fixed Warehouse Rental	2,000	−	2,000	=	0	
Total Costs	$30,188	−	$30,315	=	$(127)	

described in Appendix 8.2. Problem 3 for Self-Study at the end of this chapter computes the minimum total cost using the format shown in Exhibit 8.10. Exhibit 8.11 shows that the company could save $127 per year with the proposed order size and inventory level.

Costs of Not Carrying Sufficient Inventory

Order costs and carrying costs are not the only inventory related costs. Management must consider the costs of not carrying sufficient inventory. These costs include production shutdowns or customer ill will if inventory is unavailable for production or sale, as well as added freight and handling charges to expedite special handling. To manage inventory, management must consider this third category of cost.

Safety stocks are buffers against running out of inventory. Our EOQ Incorporated example assumed that the optimal pattern of ordering and inventory depletion was as follows:

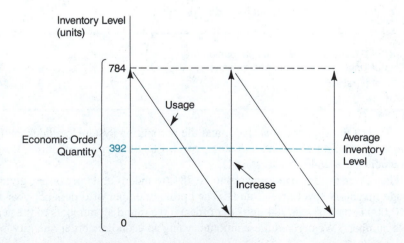

The model assumes replenishment just as inventory levels reach zero. Many events could result in a stock-out—a delivery truck delay, for example. The firm may have to stop production or sales to await the delivery of inventory. To prevent such a stock-out, management will provide a safety stock, as the following figure shows:

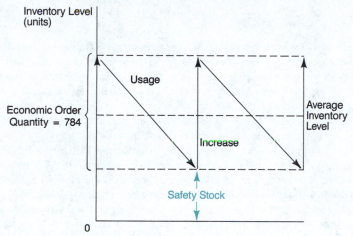

What is the optimal level of safety stock? The level depends on the trade-off between **stock-out costs** and holding costs. The higher the stock-out costs, the higher the safety stock, whereas the higher the holding costs, the lower the safety stock.

Just-in-Time Inventory

Managers attempt to reduce inventory levels. Many organizations, including hospital supply rooms, merchandising firms, wholesalers, and manufacturing companies, have improved their ability to forecast demand so that they can reduce inventories. **Just-in-time inventory** is a method of managing purchasing, production, and sales, where the firm attempts to produce each item only as needed for the next step in the production process, or where the firm attempts to time purchases so that items arrive just in time. This practice can reduce inventory levels virtually to zero.

Just-in-time inventory requires that production correct a process resulting in defective units immediately because the plan does not include accumulating defective units while they await reworking or scrapping. This turns out to be a major advantage of just-in-time. EOQ models that omit this benefit overstate the optimal level of inventory. Manufacturing managers find that eliminating inventories can prevent the hiding of production problems.

Japanese manufacturing companies have been successful in reducing inventories.[6] American manufacturers have also reduced inventory levels. Firestone Tire and Rubber Company, finding that it had $300,000,000 in excess inventory, overhauled its inventory system.[7] If inventory carrying costs were 20 percent of the

---

[6]See Robert H. Hayes, ''Why Japanese Factories Work,'' *Harvard Business Review* (July–August 1981).

[7]*The Wall Street Journal*, August 15, 1980, p. 15.

Managerial Application

Recent Innovations in Inventory Management and Flexible Manufacturing

Recent innovations in production could revolutionize both the production process and the accounting in manufacturing companies.[a] The use of just-in-time inventory enables accountants to spend less time on inventory valuation for external reporting purposes and more time obtaining data for managerial decisions such as those discussed in this chapter.

Another innovation has the potential to reduce both setup costs and inventory levels. As this chapter discusses, reducing inventory levels means increasing the number of setups. Consider an automobile manufacturer that makes fenders for several models of cars. When the time comes to change from left fenders to right fenders, or from fenders for cars to fenders for trucks, the production line stops while workers modify the machines to make the new fenders. Making only a few fenders of each type during a single production run requires many separate setups. Many companies are experimenting with flexible manufacturing methods that use computer-assisted machines to make these changeovers quickly, thereby reducing the cost of downtime in production.

The use of flexible manufacturing practices to reduce setup costs enhances companies' abilities to use just-in-time inventory. If setup costs are low, each production run can be small—perhaps just one unit. These innovations are likely to decrease the need for detailed record keeping for inventory valuation and to increase accountants' time spent on managerial activities.

[a]For example, see D. Berlant, R. Browing, and G. Foster, ''How Hewlett-Packard Gets Numbers It Can Trust,'' *Harvard Business Review*, January/February, 1990, pp. 178–183.

inventory value, Firestone could save $60 million per year by reducing excess inventory. A Buick plant reduced its inventory of one part by 80 percent by changing delivery times from alternate-day rail deliveries to three-times-daily truck deliveries.[8]

■ Summary ■

This chapter considers *differential analysis:* that is, ascertaining *what* would differ and by *how much* if the firm takes an alternative action, rather than status quo. Differential analysis compares alternatives to the status quo, or present situation, as follows (where the terms have the same definitions as earlier):

[8]Reported in Robert S. Kaplan, ''Measuring Manufacturing Performance: A New Challenge for Management Accounting Research,'' *Accounting Review* 58 (October 1983).

	Alternative – Status Quo = Difference		
Revenue.....................................	P_1X_1 –	P_0X_0 =	ΔPX
Less Variable Costs	V_1X_1 –	V_0X_0 =	ΔVX
Total Contribution Margin	$(P_1 - V_1)X_1$ –	$(P_0 - V_0)X_0$ =	$\Delta(P - V)X$
Less Fixed Costs	F_1 –	F_0 =	ΔF
Operating Profit	π_1 –	π_0 =	$\Delta \pi$

We applied differential analysis to several short-run operating decisions, and we focused on identifying and measuring *differential costs*. These costs will differ because of an action. Identifying relevant costs is important for decision making. Costs that do not differ are not relevant for ascertaining the financial consequences of a contemplated action. Differential costs comprise differential cash flows.

Prices sometimes result from cost analysis as well as from market factors. Firms enter into special cost-based contracts, such as those between government agencies and defense contractors. For any organization, prices must at least cover differential costs if the organization is to maximize its profit position. In the short run, this practice will result in a positive contribution toward covering fixed costs and generating a profit. In the long run, this practice will cover all costs, because both fixed and variable costs become differential in the long run.

In addition to pricing, differential analysis aids decisions to make-or-buy products, decisions to accept special orders, and decisions to add products or close parts of operations. Routine accounting reports rarely provide the relevant costs for these decisions. Special analysis of cost behavior is nearly always necessary. Choice of the optimal product mix when capacity limitations exist requires not only estimating differential cost (that is, variable cost) per unit but also differential cost per unit of scarce resource each product consumes.

Inventory management decisions require an estimate of differential order costs and differential inventory carrying costs. Part of the inventory management problem is finding the optimal trade-off between number of orders (or production runs) and the level of inventory so that total costs are minimized. In recent years, companies have emphasized reducing inventory levels. Just-in-time inventory refers to the management of inventory so that the firm produces or purchases inventory "just-in-time," as needed.

Appendix 8.1:
Linear Programming

Factors such as factory capacity, personnel time, floor space, and so forth constrain most managerial decisions. If the firm has enough time before implementing a decision, it can relax constraints by increasing capacity. In the short run, however, decision makers face a constrained amount of resources available to them. **Linear programming** solves problems of this type. We refer to linear programming as a *constrained optimization* technique, because it solves for the optimal use of scarce (that is, constrained) resources.

Two simple examples demonstrate how linear programming works. We solve these using graphs and simple algebra. More complex problems require some systematic procedure like the *simplex method,* described in textbooks on operations research and quantitative methods. Most linear programming problem solutions result from computer implementation of the simplex method or variations of it.

Profit Maximization

Example   Moline Company produces two products, 1 and 2. The contribution margins per unit of the two products follow:

Product	Contribution Margin per Unit
1	$3
2	4

Fixed costs are the same regardless of the combination of products 1 and 2 the firm produces; therefore, the firm wants to maximize the total contribution per period of these two products.

Both products have a positive contribution margin. If Moline Company faced no constraints, it should make (and sell) both products, eliminating our problem. When production of a unit of each product consumes the same quantity of a scarce resource, managers solve the problem by making and selling only the highest contribution item. For our example, if Product 1 and Product 2 each require one hour of machine time, and the quantity of machine hours is finite, Moline would choose Product 2, all else being equal. Products usually do not consume equal amounts of scarce resources, however. So the problem is to find the optimal mix of products given the amount of a scarce resource each product consumes.

Moline Company uses two scarce resources to make the two products, labor time and machine time. Twenty-four hours of labor time and 20 hours of machine time are available each day. The amount of time required to make each product follows:

	Product	
	1	2
Labor Time	1 Hour per Unit	2 Hours per Unit
Machine Time	1 Hour per Unit	1 Hour per Unit

This problem formulation follows. (X_1 and X_2 refer to the quantity of Products 1 and 2 produced and sold.)

(1)   Maximize: $\$3X_1 + \$4X_2 = $ Total Contribution

(2)   Subject to: $X_1 + 2X_2 \leq 24$ Labor Hours

(3) $X_1 + X_2 \leq 20$ Machine Hours.

The first line, the **objective function,** states the objective of our problem as a linear equation. Here the objective is to maximize total contribution where each unit of Product 1 contributes $3 and each unit of Product 2 contributes $4. The lines that follow specify the parameters of the constraints. Line (2) is the labor time constraint, which states that each unit of Product 1 requires 1 labor hour and each unit of Product 2 requires 2 labor hours. Total labor hours cannot exceed 24 per period (that is, one day). Line (3) is the machine time constraint, which states that Product 1 and Product 2 each use 1 machine hour per unit, and total machine hours cannot exceed 20.

Exhibit 8.12 graphs the constraints. The shaded area shows feasible production; production does not use up more scarce resources than are available. The lowercase letters show the *corner points*. We find the optimal solution by deriving the total contribution margin at each point, using the following steps.

Step 1   Find the production level of Product 1 and Product 2 at each point. Points a and c are straightforward. At a, $X_1 = 20$ and $X_2 = 0$; at c, $X_2 = 12$ and $X_1 = 0$. Point b requires solving for two unknowns using the two constraint formulas:

$$\text{Labor Time:} \qquad X_1 + 2X_2 = 24$$

$$\text{Machine Time:} \qquad X_1 + X_2 = 20.$$

Exhibit 8.12

**Linear Programming, Graphic Solution
Comparison of Corner and Noncorner Points**

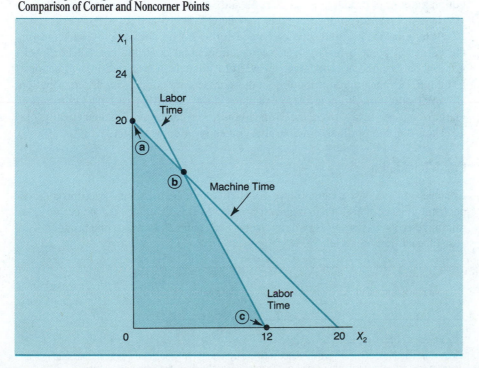

Exhibit 8.13

Optimal Product Mix

	Production		Contribution		
Point	X_1	X_2	1	2	Total
a	20	0	$60	$ 0	$60
b	16	4	48	16	64
c	0	12	0	48	48

Setting these two equations equal, we have

$$X_1 = 24 - 2X_2$$
$$X_1 = 20 - X_2,$$
$$24 - 2X_2 = 20 - X_2$$
$$4 = X_2.$$

If $X_2 = 4$, then

$$X_1 = 20 - X_2$$
$$= 20 - 4$$
$$= 16.$$

At point b, Moline produces 16 units of Product 1 and 4 units of Product 2.

Step 2   Find the total contribution margin at each point. (Recall that the unit contribution margins of products 1 and 2 are $3 and $4.) Exhibit 8.13 shows the solution.

It is optimal to produce at point b, where $X_1 = 16$ and $X_2 = 4$.

Why must the optimal solution be at a corner? If production moves away from the corner at point b in any feasible direction, total contribution will be lower. Exhibit 8.14 shows a movement away from point b in four feasible directions. Exhibit 8.15 compares contributions at those noncorner points with the contribution at corner point b. Although these examples show intuitively that the contribution margin declines away from the corner point, we can prove mathematically our assertion that the optimal solution always lies on a corner point.[9]

Cost Minimization

Example   In our last example, we found the product mix that maximized total contribution and therefore maximized profits. In this example, the objective is to minimize costs. A firm uses two raw materials, A and B, to make one product. The cost of each raw material follows:

A	$4 per Pound
B	$3 per Pound

[9]Sometimes multiple corners have the same total contributions. Any point on a straight line joining these corners has a total contribution equal to the total contribution at the adjoining corners.

Exhibit 8.14

Linear Programming, Graphic Solution
Comparison of Corner and Noncorner Points

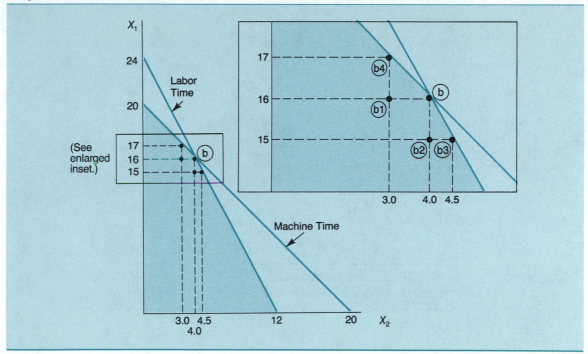

Exhibit 8.15

Comparison of Corner Point with Noncorner Points

Point	Production		Contribution		
	X_1	X_2	1	2	Total
b	16	4	\$48	\$16	\$64
b1	16	3	48	12	60
b2	15	4	45	16	61
b3[a]	15	4.5	45	18	63
b4[b]	17	3	51	12	63

[a]Let $X_1 = 15$ and find X_2 as follows:

$$X_1 = 24 - 2X_2$$
$$15 = 24 - 2X_2$$
$$2X_2 = 9$$
$$X_2 = 4.5.$$

[b]Let $X_2 = 3$ and find X_1 as follows:

$$X_1 = 20 - X_2$$
$$= 20 - 3$$
$$= 17.$$

Exhibit 8.16

Minimization Problem

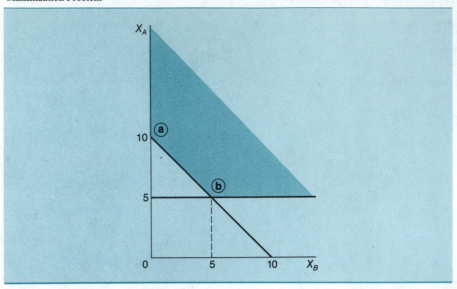

Note: Shaded area is the feasible region.

[a]To find the amount of B used when $X_A = 5$, let

$$X_A = 10 - X_B$$
$$5 = 10 - X_B$$
$$X_B = 5.$$

At least 5 pounds of A must be used and at least 10 pounds of A plus B must be used. You would formulate the problem as follows:

$$\text{Minimize:} \quad \$4X_A + \$3X_B$$

$$\text{Subject to:} \quad X_A \quad\quad \geq 5$$

$$\quad\quad\quad\quad X_A + X_B \geq 10.$$

The objective is to find the combination of X_A and X_B that minimizes the cost of producing a unit of output. Exhibit 8.16 shows that the optimal (that is, least costly) use of raw materials is 5 units of A and 5 units of B.

Sensitivity Analysis

The contribution margins and costs in the objective functions are estimates, subject to error. Decision makers frequently need to know how much the estimates can change before the decision changes. Knowing the range of error helps ascertain how much effort making the cost and revenue estimates deserves.

To demonstrate our point, we use our earlier profit-maximization problem for Moline Company, which we formulated as appears on the following page:

$$\text{Maximize:} \quad \$3X_1 + \$4X_2 = \text{Total Contribution}$$

$$\text{Subject to:} \quad X_1 + 2X_2 \leq 24 \text{ Labor Hours}$$

$$X_1 + X_2 \leq 20 \text{ Machine Hours.}$$

Suppose that the variable cost estimate for Product 2 was $.50 per unit too low, so Product 2's unit contribution margin should have been $3.50 instead of $4.00. What effect would this have? We have calculated the new contributions in Exhibit 8.17. If you compare Exhibit 8.17 with Exhibit 8.13, you will see that the contribution for Product 2 changes; thus the total contribution changes. The optimal decision to produce 16 units of Product 1 and 4 units of Product 2 does not change, however. In spite of the change in costs and thus in contributions, the *decision* does not change. In this example, the unit contribution margin of Product 2 would have to drop to less than $3 per unit before the optimal decision would change, assuming that all other things remained constant.

Most linear programming computer programs can provide this type of sensitivity analysis. With it, managers and accountants can ascertain how much a cost or contribution margin can change before the optimal decision will change.

Opportunity Costs

Any constrained resource has an opportunity cost, which is the profit forgone by not having an additional unit of the resource. For example, suppose that Moline Company in our previous example could obtain one additional hour of machine time. With one more hour of machine time, the machine constraint would move out, as shown in Exhibit 8.18. We find the new production level at point b as follows:

$$X_1 = 24 - 2X_2$$

$$X_1 = 21 - X_2$$

$$24 - 2X_2 = 21 - X_2$$

$$X_2 = 3$$

$$X_1 = 18.$$

Exhibit 8.17

Optimal Product Mix: Revised Cost Estimates

	Production		Contribution		
Point[a]	X_1	X_2	1	2	Total
a	20	0	$60	$ 0	$60
b	16	4	48	14[b]	62
c	0	12	0	42	42

[a]The graph in Exhibit 8.13 presents these points.
[b]Four units × $3.50 per unit.

Exhibit 8.18

Linear Programming, Graphic Solution
Increase in Machine Time from 20 to 21 Hours

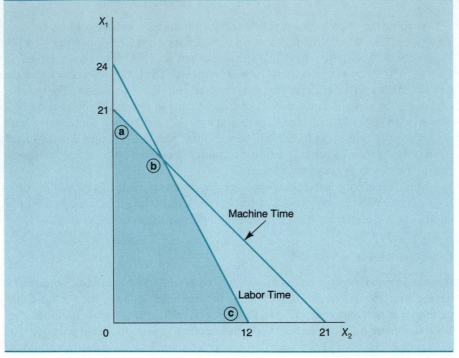

$^{a}X_1 = 24 - 2X_2$ and $X_1 = 21 - X_2$, so

$$24 - 2X_2 = 21 - X_2$$
$$X_2 = 3$$
$$X_1 = 21 - X_2$$
$$= 21 - 3$$
$$= 18.$$

The new total contribution at point b would be $\$3(18) + \$4(3) = \$66$, compared to
$64 when machine time was constrained to 20 hours per day, as shown for point b in
Exhibit 8.14. Thus the opportunity cost of not having an extra hour of machine time
is $2 (= $66 − $64).

Linear programming computer programs regularly provide opportunity costs,
called **shadow prices** (or values of the dual variables). Opportunity cost data indicate the benefits of acquiring more units of a scarce resource. For example, if
Moline Company could rent one more machine hour for less than $2 per hour, the
company would profit by doing so, all other things being equal.

Appendix 8.2:
Economic Order Quantity Model

You can derive the optimal number of orders or production runs per period from the following formula:

$$N = \frac{D}{Q},$$

where

$$Q = \sqrt{\frac{2K_0D}{K_c}}$$

N = the optimal number of orders or production runs for the period

Q = the economic order quantity, or the optimal number of items in an order or production run

D = the period demand in units

K_0 = the order or setup cost

K_c = the cost of carrying one unit in inventory for the period.

The formula $Q = \sqrt{2K_0D/K_c}$ results from using calculus to minimize total cost with respect to Q. The total cost (TC) formula is

$$\frac{\text{Total Cost}}{\text{per Period}} = \frac{\text{Carrying Costs}}{\text{per Period}} + \frac{\text{Order Costs}}{\text{per Period}}$$

$$TC = K_c\frac{Q}{2} + K_0\frac{D}{Q}.$$

Take the first derivative of TC with respect to Q, set it equal to zero, and solve for Q:

$$\frac{dTC}{dQ} = \frac{d}{dQ}\left(K_c\frac{Q}{2} + K_0\frac{D}{Q}\right)$$

$$= \frac{K_c}{2} - \frac{K_0D}{Q^2} = 0.$$

$$Q = \sqrt{\frac{2K_0D}{K_c}}.$$

Example The following facts for the California Merchandising example appeared in the text:

D = period demand = 6,000 units per year

K_0 = order cost = $100 per order

K_c = carrying cost = 30 percent of the cost of inventory or
$.60 per unit ($.60 = 30 percent $\times$ $2.00 per unit).

Solving for Q (the optimal number of items in an order), we have

$$Q = \sqrt{\frac{2K_0 D}{K_c}}$$

$$= \sqrt{\frac{2 \times \$100 \times 6{,}000 \text{ Units}}{\$.60}}$$

$$= \sqrt{2{,}000{,}000 \text{ Units}}$$

$$= 1{,}414 \text{ Units per Order.}$$

$$N = \frac{D}{Q}$$

$$= \frac{6{,}000 \text{ Units}}{1{,}414 \text{ Units}}$$

$$= 4.2 \text{ Orders per Year.}$$

From these equations, we derived the optimal order size, 1,414 units, and the optimal number of orders per year, 4.2. This result is approximately the same one we derived by trial and error earlier. Using the economic order quantity model is usually more efficient for finding the least costly size and number of orders (or productions).

This is known as **economic order quantity (EOQ) model.** Textbooks on operations research and quantitative methods present many variations and applications of this model.

Problem 1 for Self-Study

Skedaddle Snowblasters (*Contributed by J. Lim*)

Memories of dogsled travel during his childhood in Alaska prompted Scott Cameron to start Skedaddle Snowblasters 5 years ago. An experienced engineer with an entrepreneurial streak, Cameron had left his research and development job with a major auto company to exploit what he perceived to be a growing market in snowmobiles.

Currently Skedaddle Snowblasters produces two lines of snowmobiles, the Standard Snowblaster and the Deluxe Snowblaster. Operating at capacity, the company ran into bottlenecks in both its body fabrication department and engine production department. Last month, Skedaddle Snowblasters put out 15,000 Standard Snowblasters and 6,250 Deluxe Snowblasters. The unit costs incurred follow:

	Standard	Deluxe
Body Fabrication		
Materials	$210	$290
Direct Labor	75	120
Variable Overhead	20	25
Fixed Overhead[a]	85	115
Total Costs	$390	$550

continued

continued from page 364

	Standard	Deluxe
Engine Production		
Materials	$450	$ 520
Direct Labor	150	280
Variable Overhead	30	20
Fixed Overhead[a]	260	490
Total	$890	$1,310
Assembly		
Materials	$ 40	$ 35
Direct Labor	60	95
Variable Overhead	30	15
Fixed Overhead[a]	80	120
Total	$210	$265
Marketing and Administrative Costs (all fixed[a])	$10	$15
Selling Price	$1,800	$2,500

[a]All fixed costs are allocated.

Beginning and ending inventories in all departments were zero.

Cameron has several decisions facing him this coming month, and he believes that he should consider each alternative in isolation. Analyze each of the following alternatives independently, using last month's data as the status quo.

a. An outside supplier has offered to supply Deluxe bodies for $600 each. This alternative would allow production of 15,000 Standard Snowblasters and 10,000 Deluxe Snowblasters. Should Cameron accept the offer to buy 3,750 Deluxe bodies?

b. The Canadian government has offered to buy 1,000 modified Deluxe Snowblasters for $2,600 each. These modifications will require extra time in the fabrication department, incurring additional labor costs of $20 per unit and reducing standard production by 100 units. Should Skedaddle Snowblasters accept the contract?

c. *(Appendix 8.1)* At capacity, the engine production department can produce either 30,000 Standards or 20,000 Deluxes. The body fabrication department can produce 20,000 Standards or 25,000 Deluxes. Given these constraints, what is Skedaddle Snowblasters' optimal product mix?

Suggested Solution

a.

	Alternative	− Status Quo	= Difference
Sales Revenue	$52,000,000[a]	− $42,625,000[d]	= $9,375,000
Less Variable Costs	(30,593,750)[b]	− (24,725,000)[e]	= (5,868,750)
Contribution Margin	$21,406,250	− $17,900,000	= $3,506,250
			continued

continued from page 365

Less Fixed Costs	$(11,150,000)^c - (11,150,000) = \underline{\qquad 0}$
Operating Profit..................	$\underline{\$10,256,250} \quad - \underline{\$ 6,750,000} \quad = \underline{\$3,506,250}$

[a]$1,800(15,000) + \$2,500(10,000)$.
[b]$24,725,000 + \$1,565(3,750)$.
[c]$435(15,000) + \$740(6,250)$.
[d]$1,800(15,000) + \$2,500(6,250)$.
[e]$1,065(15,000) + \$1,400(6,250)$.

Skedaddle Snowblasters should *accept* the supplier's offer.

b.

	Alternative	− Status Quo	= Difference
Sales Revenue	$42,545,000[a]	− $42,625,000	= $(80,000)
Less Variable Costs	(24,638,500)[b]	− (24,725,000)	= 86,500
Contribution Margin	$17,906,500	− $17,900,000	= $ 6,500
Less Fixed Costs	(11,150,000)	− (11,150,000)	= 0
Net Operating Profit................	$ 6,756,500	− $ 6,750,000	= $ 6,500

[a]$1,800(14,900) + \$2,500(5,250) + \$2,600(1,000)$.
[b]$1,065(14,900) + \$1,400(5,250) + \$1,420(1,000)$.

Skedaddle Snowblasters should *accept* the contract offer.

c. Let X_S and X_D refer to the volume of Standard and Deluxe. The contribution margin per unit is $735 for X_S and $1,100 for X_D.

Maximize: $735X_S + 1,100X_D$

Subject to:

$$5X_S + \quad 4X_D \le 100,000 \quad \text{(Body)}.$$

$$2X_S + \quad 3X_D \le 60,000 \quad \text{(Engine)}.$$

Points (X_S, X_D)	Total Contribution
(a) 20,000; 0.....................	$735(20,000) = \$14,700,000$
(b) 8,570; 14,290................	$735(8,570) + \$1,100(14,290) = \$22,017,950^a$
(c) 0; 20,000.....................	$1,100(20,000) = \$22,000,000$

[a]Optimal mix. Additional computations follow.

Additional computations for point b:

$$5\left(\frac{60,000 - 3X_D}{2}\right) + 4X_D = 100,000;$$

$X_S = 8,570$ and $X_D = 14,290$, rounded to the next 10.

Problem 2 for Self-Study

Jackson Technologies (*Contributed by Robert H. Colson*)

Jackson Technologies, Inc. produces a valve used in electric turbine systems. The costs of the valve at the company's normal volume of 5,000 units per month appear in Exhibit 8.19.

The following questions refer only to the data in Exhibit 8.19. Unless stated otherwise, treat each question independently. Unless specified otherwise, the regular selling price per unit is $1,750. Ignore income taxes and other costs not shown in Exhibit 8.19 unless the question specifically provides data.

a.   Market research estimates that a price increase to $1,900 per unit would decrease monthly volume to 4,500 units. The accounting department estimates that the only costs affected by such a price change would be fixed manufacturing costs, which would increase to $165 per unit. Would you recommend that the firm take this action? What would be the impact on monthly revenues, costs, and profits?

b.   Refer to part **a.** Given the information available, what is the opportunity cost of keeping the price of valves at $1,750?

c.   An outside contractor proposes to make and ship 1,000 valves per month directly to Jackson Technologies' customers as Jackson's sales force receives orders. This proposal would not affect Jackson's fixed nonmanufacturing costs, but its variable nonmanufacturing costs would decline by 25 percent for the 1,000 units the contractor produced. Jackson's plant would operate at 80 percent of its normal level, and total fixed manufacturing costs would decline by 15 percent. What in-house unit cost should the firm use to compare with the price quotation received from the contractor?

d.   Assume the same facts as in part **c,** except that the firm would use the idle facilities to produce 600 modified regulator valves for nuclear reactors. The firm can sell these modified valves for $2,500 each. The variable costs of

Exhibit 8.19

Cost Data for Jackson Technologies

Unit Manufacturing Costs:		
Variable Materials...	$250	
Variable Labor..	175	
Variable Overhead	75	
Fixed Overhead	150	
Total Unit Manufacturing Costs		$ 650
Unit Nonmanufacturing Costs:		
Variable	200	
Fixed..	175	
Total Unit Nonmanufacturing Costs		375
Total Unit Costs...		$1,025

manufacturing these units would be $700, and variable nonmanufacturing costs would be $225 per unit. In addition, Jackson Technologies must satisfy a government regulation that all nuclear reactor valve manufacturers meet certain minimum safety standards. To satisfy these safety standards, Jackson Technologies would have to incur a 20 percent increase in normal fixed manufacturing costs and $25,000 increase in fixed nonmanufacturing costs. What is the maximum purchase price per unit that Jackson should be willing to pay?

Suggested Solution

a.

	Alternative	− Status Quo	= Difference
Price	$1,900	$1,750	
Volume	4,500	5,000	
Revenue	$8,550,000	− $8,750,000	= $(200,000)
Variable Costs	(3,150,000)	− (3,500,000)	= 350,000
Contribution Margin	5,400,000	− 5,250,000	= $ 150,000
Fixed Costs	(1,617,500)[a]	− (1,625,000)	= 7,500
Operating Profit......................	$3,782,500	− $3,625,000	= $ 157,500

[a](4,500 × $165) + ($175 × 5,000) = $1,617,500.

Jackson Technologies should raise its prices to $1,900.

b. $3,782,500 − $3,625,000 = $157,500.

c.

	Alternative: Contract for 1,000 Units	− Status Quo: All Production In-House	= Difference
Revenue	$8,750,000	− $8,750,000	= $ 0
Variable Manufacturing Costs....	(2,000,000)	− (2,500,000)	= 500,000
Variable Nonmanufacturing Costs	(950,000)	− (1,000,000)	= 50,000
Contribution Margin	$5,800,000	− $5,250,000	= $ 550,000
Fixed Manufacturing Costs	(637,500)	− (750,000)	= 112,500
Fixed Nonmanufacturing Costs ..	(875,000)	− (875,000)	= 0
Payment to Contractor..........	(X)	− 0	= (X)
Operating Profit	$4,287,500 − X$	− $3,625,000	= $662,500 − X$

$$X = \$4,287,500 - \$3,625,000$$

$$= \$662,500 \text{ for 1,000 Units,}$$

or

$$\frac{\$662,500}{1,000} = \$662.50 \text{ per Unit.}$$

d. *Differential analysis table (all dollar amounts in thousands):*

	Alternative				Status Quo		
	Contract 1,000 Regular Valves, Produce 4,000 Regular and 600 Modified						
	Regular (in)	Regular (out)	Modified	Total	5,000 Regular Valves In-House		Difference
Revenue.....................	$7,000	$1,750	$1,500	$10,250 –	$8,750	=	$1,500
Variable Manufacturing Costs	(2,000)	—	(420)	(2,420) –	(2,500)	=	80
Variable Nonmanufacturing Costs	(800)	(150)	(135)	(1,085) –	(1,000)	=	(85)
Contribution Margin	$4,200	$1,600	$ 945	$ 6,745 –	$5,250	=	$1,495
Fixed Manufacturing Costs				(900) –	(750)	=	(150)
Fixed Nonmanufacturing Costs				(900) –	(875)	=	(25)
Contractor Payment...........				(X) –	0	=	(X)
Operating Profit				$4,945 – X –	$3,625	=	$1,320 – X

X = $4,945 thousand – $3,625 thousand = $1,320 thousand for the order or $1,320 per unit.

Alternative method of analysis:

X = Increase in Revenue – Increase in Costs

= $1,500 + 80 – 85 – 150 – 25 = $1,320 (in thousands).

Problem 3 for Self-Study

EOQ Incorporated

Compute the minimum total costs for EOQ Incorporated, given the following summary facts, presented in more detail in the text:

Differential Costs per Order..	$41
Total Units Purchased per Year	40,000 Units
Differential Carrying Costs per Unit of Inventory.......................	$5.35 per Unit

Find the minimum total costs of ordering and holding the inventory:

a. Using a trial and error method.

b. Using the economic order quantity model (Appendix 8.2).

Suggested Solution

a. The trial and error method finds total costs as appears on the next page:

Annual Orders	Order Size[a]	Average Number of Units in Inventory	Inventory Carrying Costs[b]	Order Costs[c]	Total Costs
40	1,000	500	$2,675	$1,640	$4,315
.					
.					
.					
50	800	400	2,140	2,050	4,190
51	784	392	2,097	2,091	4,188
52	769	384.5	2,057	2,132	4,189
53	755	377.5	2,020	2,173	4,193
.					
.					
60	667	333.5	1,784	2,460	4,244

[a]40,000 units/number of orders.

[b]Average units in inventory × $5.35.

[c]Number of orders × $41.

Minimum total costs are $4,188 at 51 orders per year.

b. We can find the optimal number of orders from the formula presented in Appendix 8.2.

$$N = \frac{D}{Q}$$

where

$$Q = \sqrt{\frac{2K_0 D}{K_c}}$$

N = optimal number of orders or production runs for the period

Q = economic order quantity, or optimal number of items in an order or production run

D = period demand in units = 40,000 units per year

K_0 = order or setup cost = $41 per order

K_c = cost of carrying one unit in inventory for the period = $5.35 per unit.

Thus

$$Q = \sqrt{\frac{2 \times \$41 \times 40{,}000 \text{ Units}}{\$5.35}}$$

$$= \sqrt{613{,}084}$$

$$= \underline{\underline{783}}$$

$$N = \frac{D}{Q} = \frac{40{,}000}{783} = \underline{\underline{51.086}} \text{ Orders.}$$

We have rounded to whole numbers so that there are 51 orders per year, 784 units per order, and 392 average inventory balance.

Key Terms and Concepts

Differential analysis

Status quo

Relevant cost analysis

Cash flows

Economic depreciation

Differential cost

Make-or-buy decision

Gross margin versus contribution
  margin

Setup or order costs

Carrying costs

Economic order quantity (EOQ)

Safety stocks

Stock-out costs

Just-in-time (JIT) inventory

Linear programming (Appendix 8.1)

Objective function (Appendix 8.1)

Shadow prices (Appendix 8.1)

Economic order quantity (EOQ)
  model (Appendix 8.2)

Questions, Exercises, Problems, and Cases

Questions

1. Review the meaning of the terms and concepts given above in Key Terms and Concepts.

2. "Users of differential analysis should use revenues and expenses of a particular period rather than cash flows, because they better represent a firm's performance during a given period." Comment.

3. "A proper evaluation of any project using differential analysis requires the consideration of all relevant costs—past, present, and future." Comment.

4. Assume that there are no income taxes. How should each of the following costs enter into a decision to replace old equipment?
   a. Book value of old equipment.
   b. Disposal value of old equipment.
   c. Cost of new equipment.

5. How significant are opportunity costs and economic depreciation in differential analysis? When will you use or not use these costs?

6. State and explain the shortcomings of using a cost-based approach to product pricing.

7. What is a common criticism made against the differential approach to product pricing? How can you refute this criticism?

8. When a firm faces one or several scarce resources, how does it make optimal use of its resources? Describe one technique a firm could use to solve such a constrained decision problem.

9. You are asked to supply profit figures for a linear program your firm wishes to run. Do you give the gross margin per unit or contribution margin per unit? Why?

10. Inventory management problems usually involve two types of opposing costs. Describe them and sketch a graph depicting their behavior with order size.

Exercises

11. *Special order*. Surf 'n' Turf Products has the capacity to produce 4,000 swimsuits (units) per year. Its predicted operations for the year follow:

Sales (3,000 units @ $70).....................................	$210,000
Manufacturing Costs:	
Variable	$48 per Unit
Fixed..	$22,000
Marketing and Administrative Costs:	
Variable	$4 per Unit
Fixed..	$6,000

     Should the company accept a special order for 500 units at a selling price of $60? Variable marketing and administrative costs for this order will be zero, and regular sales will not change. How will the decision affect the company's operating profit?

12. *Product choice*. Yuppie Enterprises renovated an old train station into warehouse space, office space, restaurants, and specialty shops. If used all for warehouse space, the estimated revenue and variable costs per year to Yuppie would be $960,000 and $40,000, respectively. If used all for office space, the revenue and variable cost per year would be $982,800 and $70,000. If used all for restaurants and specialty shops, the revenue and variable costs would be $1,101,100 and $95,000, respectively. Fixed costs per year would be $600,000 regardless of the alternative chosen.
     What should Yuppie Enterprises do?

13. *Special order*. Anticipating unusually high sales for May, Mr. Twinkles, a breakfast cereal company, plans to produce 40,000 pounds of cereal, using all available capacity. Mr. Twinkles anticipates production and marketing costs for May as follows:

Unit Manufacturing Costs per Pound:		
Variable Direct Materials Cost................................	$0.15	
Variable Labor	0.02	
Variable Overhead...	0.03	
Fixed Overhead	0.10	
Total Manufacturing Costs		$0.30
Unit Marketing Costs per Pound:		
Variable	$0.03	
Fixed..	0.20	
Total Marketing Costs		0.23
Total Unit Costs		$0.53
Selling Price per Pound		$0.80

     On April 30, Mr. Twinkles received a contract offer from Feed the Hungry (FTH), a government agency, to supply 5,000 pounds of cereal for delivery by May 31. The FTH offer would reimburse Mr. Twinkles' share of manufacturing costs plus a fixed fee of $2,000. Variable marketing costs will be zero for this order; fixed costs will not change. Should Mr. Twinkles accept the offer? Why or why not?

14. *Make or buy*. Reliant Enterprises, a sailboat manufacturer, is currently operating at 70 percent capacity and producing about 10,000 units a year. To use more capacity, the manager has been considering the research and development department's suggestion that Reliant Enterprises manufacture its own sails. Currently Reliant purchases sails from a supplier at a unit price of $28. Estimates show that Reliant Enterprises can manufacture its own sails at $10 per unit direct materials cost and $8 direct labor cost. The factory overhead is $2 per direct labor dollar, of which 20 percent is variable.

    a.   Should Reliant Enterprises make or buy the sails?

    b.   Suppose that Reliant Enterprises could rent out the currently unused part of the factory for $1,000 a month. How would this affect the decision in part **a**?

15. *Dropping a product line*. British Columbia Wood Products currently operates at 75 percent capacity. Worried about the company's performance, Blondell, the general manager, segmented the company's income statement product by product and obtained the following picture:

	Product		
	A	**B**	**C**
Sales.....	$32,600	$42,800	$51,200
Less Variable Costs	(22,000)	(38,000)	(40,100)
Total Contribution Margin	$10,600	$ 4,800	$11,100
Less Allocated Fixed Costs	(4,700)	(5,600)	(7,100)
Net Operating Profit (Loss)	$ 5,900	$ (800)	$ 4,000

Should British Columbia Wood Products drop Product B, if that would reduce total fixed costs by 20 percent?

16. *Product mix decisions*. Timeless Products, a clock manufacturer, operates at capacity. Constrained by machine time, the company decides to drop the most unprofitable of its three product lines. The accounting department came up with the following data from last year's operations.

	Manual	**Electric**	**Quartz**
Machine Time per Unit	0.4 Hour	2.5 Hours	5.0 Hours
Selling Price per Unit	$20	$30	$50
Less Variable Costs per Unit	(10)	(14)	(28)
Contribution Margin	$10	$16	$22

Which line should Timeless Products drop?

17. *Product choice using linear programming* (Appendix 8.1). Fortuna Corporation manufactures two products whose contribution margins follow:

Product	Contribution Margin
A	$ 9
B	15

Each month Fortuna Corporation has only 6,000 hours of machine time and 7,200 hours of labor time available. The amount of time required to make Products A and B follows:

	Product A	Product B
Labor Time	2 Hours per Unit	4 Hours per Unit
Machine Time	3 Hours per Unit	2 Hours per Unit

The firm sells all units produced.

   Set the problem up in the linear programming format and solve for the optimal production mix.

18. *Economic order quantity.* (You can work this exercise using either trial and error or the model in Appendix 8.2.) The Magee Foundry regularly uses 1,000 bolts per day, 250 days per year. It can purchase bolts in lots of 1,000 for $10 per lot or in lots of 10,000 for $96.10 per lot. Ordering costs are $10 per order, and the holding costs of items in inventory are 20 percent of cost per year.

   a. What is the economic order quantity and annual ordering costs, assuming that only lots of 1,000 items are available?

   b. What is the economic order quantity and annual ordering costs, assuming that only lots of 10,000 items are available?

   c. Compare the costs of the two preceding answers and state the optimal ordering policy for these bolts, assuming that lots of 1,000 or 10,000 can be ordered.

19. *Economic order quantity.* (You can work this exercise using either trial and error or the model in Appendix 8.2.) The purchasing agent responsible for ordering cotton underwear estimates that Soares Retail Stores sells 10,000 packages of cotton underwear evenly throughout each year, that each order costs $24 to place, and that holding a package of underwear in inventory for a year costs $.12 per package.

   a. How many packages of underwear should Soares request in each order?

   b. How many times per year should Soares order underwear?

20. *Product mix decisions* (Appendix 8.1; adapted from CPA exam). The Random Company manufactures two products, Zeta and Beta. Each product must pass through two processing operations. All materials enter production at the start of Process No. 1. Random has no work-in-process inventories. Random may

produce either one product exclusively or various combinations of both products, subject to the following constraints:

	Process No. 1	Process No. 2	Contribution Margin per Unit
Hours Required to Produce One Unit of:			
Zeta..............................	1	1	$4.00
Beta	2	3	5.25
Total Capacity per Day in Hours	1,000	1,275	

A shortage of technical labor has limited Beta production to 400 units per day. The firm has *no* constraints on the production of Zeta other than the hour constraints in the preceding schedule. Assume that all relations between capacity and production are linear.

What is the total contribution from the optimal product mix?

21. *Product mix decisions* (Appendix 8.1). Use the information for the Random Company in Exercise 20 and assume that the present Process No. 1 cost for each unit of Zeta is $2.35. What is the maximum price that Random would be willing to pay for an additional hour of Process No. 1 time?

22. *Finding most profitable price-quantity combination.* The Culler Company is introducing a new product and must decide what price should be set. An estimated demand schedule for the product follows:

Price	Quantity Demanded (in units)
$10	40,000
12	36,000
14	28,000
16	24,000
18	18,000
20	15,000

Estimated costs follow:

Variable Manufacturing Costs	$4 per Unit
Fixed Manufacturing Costs	$40,000 per Year
Variable Selling and Administrative Costs	$2 per Unit
Fixed Selling and Administrative Costs......................	$10,000 per Year

a. Prepare a schedule showing the total revenue, total cost, and total profit or loss for each selling price.
b. Which price should Culler select? Explain.

Problems

23. *Special order.* North Carolina Furniture Company has a capacity of 100,000 tables per year. The company is currently producing and selling 80,000 tables per year at a selling price of $200 per table. The cost of producing and selling one table at the 80,000-unit level of activity follows:

Variable Manufacturing Costs	$ 80
Fixed Manufacturing Costs	20
Variable Selling and Administrative Costs	40
Fixed Selling and Administrative Costs	10
Total Costs	$150

The company has received a special order for 10,000 tables at a price of $130. Because it need not pay sales commission on the special order, the variable selling and administrative costs would be only $25 per table. The company has rejected the offer based on the following computations:

Selling Price per Table	$130
Variable Manufacturing Costs	(80)
Fixed Manufacturing Costs	(20)
Variable Selling and Administrative Costs	(25)
Fixed Selling and Administrative Costs	(10)
Net Loss per Table	$ (5)

Should North Carolina Furniture Company have accepted the special order? Show your computations.

24. *Using fixed costs in analyzing alternatives.* MacInnes Electronics Corporation manufactures citizens' band (CB) radios. In 1976 it invested $20 million in manufacturing facilities that could produce 23-channel CB radios. Data for 1976 follow:

Number of Radios Produced and Sold	40,000
Variable Cost per Radio	$30
Fixed Cost per Radio	25
Selling Price per Radio	80

In 1977, the federal government increased the number of channels permitted from 23 to 40. Market demand for 23-channel radios decreased significantly, and market price dropped to $50 a radio. Management has decided to close down its production facilities. The president stated: ''We are hurt no matter what we do. We cannot adapt our current production facilities to manufacture

40-channel radios. However, if we continue manufacturing 23-channel radios, we will lose $5 on each unit produced and sold. We are, therefore, better off just to close down.''

a. Show how the president calculated the $5 loss on each 23-channel radio.

b. Do you agree with the president's decision? If not, explain why and show your computations.

25. *Special order*. Whitley Electronics Company produces precision instruments for airplanes. It currently operates at capacity. It has received an invitation to bid on a government contract for 1,000 specially designed precision instruments. The company has estimated its costs for the contract to be as follows:

Variable Manufacturing Costs	$20,000
Allocated Fixed Manufacturing Costs	15,000
Special Design and Production Setup Costs	10,000
Shipping Costs	5,000
Special Administrative Costs	5,000
Total Costs	$55,000
Cost per Precision Instrument ($55,000/1,000)	$ 55

If Whitley accepts the government contract, it will have to forgo regular sales of 1,000 units. These 1,000 units would have a selling price of $80 each, variable costs of $40 each, and fixed costs of $20 each.

a. What is the lowest per-unit price that Whitley can bid on this contract without sacrificing profits?

b. Whitley has learned that it will receive the contract if it bids $78 or less per unit. What action should Whitley take?

26. *Economic order quantity*. (You can work this problem using trial and error or the model in Appendix 8.2.) The Lewis Company sells 3,000 medium-priced stereo sets per year in addition to many other items. The medium-priced stereo sets cost Lewis Company $100 each. Total costs of holding inventory for a year are 16 percent of an item's cost. A single purchasing department processes all purchase orders. Data on purchasing department costs for each of the last several years follow:

LEWIS COMPANY
Total Orders Placed and Costs Incurred in Purchasing Department

Year	Orders Placed	Total Ordering Costs
1	5	$3,997
2	75	4,000
3	98	4,002
4	130	4,595
5	200	6,010
6	250	6,995

The purchasing department will be placing about 130 orders during the next year for items other than medium-priced stereo sets.

a. What is the apparent relation between orders placed and total order costs? What is the incremental cost of placing an order for medium-priced stereo sets?

b. What is the optimal number of medium-priced stereo sets to order at a time?

c. What is the optimal number of orders to place each year for medium-priced stereo sets?

27. *Dropping a machine from service*. The Brunson Grain Company has four large milling machines of approximately equal capacity. Each was run at close to its full capacity during Year 5. Each machine is depreciated separately using an accelerated method. Data for each machine follow:

	No. 1	No. 2	No. 3	No. 4
Date Acquired	1/1/X0	1/1/X1	1/1/X3	1/1/X4
Cost	$50,000	$60,000	$75,000	$80,000
Operating Costs, Year 5:				
Labor	$20,000	$18,000	$22,000	$21,500
Materials	5,000	6,000	4,500	3,000
Maintenance	1,000	1,000	700	550
Depreciation	3,363	5,454	10,910	13,091
Total	$29,363	$30,454	$38,110	$38,141

Brunson expects activity in Year 6 to be less than in Year 5, so it will drop one machine from service. Management proposes that Brunson drop No. 4 on the grounds that it has the highest operating costs. Do you agree or disagree with this proposal? Why or why not?

28. *Make or buy*. Austin Computers produces computer boards of which part no. 301 is a subassembly. Austin Computers currently produces part no. 301 in its own shop. The Silicon Chips Company offers to supply it at a cost of $200 per 500 units. An analysis of the costs of Austin Computers' producing part no. 301 reveals the following information:

	Cost per 500 Units
Direct (Variable) Material	$ 65
Direct (Variable) Labor	90
Other Variable Costs	22
Fixed Costs[a]	110
Total	$287

[a]Fixed overhead comprises largely depreciation on general-purpose equipment and factory buildings.

    a.   Should Austin Computers accept the offer from Silicon Chips if Austin's plant is operating well below capacity?

    b.   Should the offer be accepted if Silicon Chips reduces the price to $165 per 500 units?

    c.   If Austin can find other profitable uses for the facilities it now uses in turning out part no. 301, what maximum purchase price should it accept?

29. *Bidding on a contract*. The T. Boone Company is considering making a bid on a contract to supply the Defense Department with 500,000 gallons of chemicals. The capacity of the plant is 10,000,000 gallons a year, and T. Boone is currently producing and selling at the rate of 8,500,000 gallons a year. The fixed costs of the plant total $5,400,000 per year regardless of the level of operations. The variable costs of chemicals of this type is approximately $2 per gallon. The sales manager says that a bid of no more than $1,200,000 would probably enable the company to get the contract.

    a.   Should T. Boone make a bid of $1,200,000? Explain.

    b.   Assume that T. Boone sells the present production at an average price of $3 per gallon and average variable costs equal $2 per gallon. Compute the operating profit (1) if T. Boone loses the government contract and (2) if T. Boone lands the government contract at a bid of $1,200,000.

30. *Accepting or rejecting an order*. The Milky Way Company produces a precision part for use in rockets, missiles, and a variety of other products. In the first half of the year, it operated at 80 percent of capacity and produced 160,000 units. Manufacturing costs in that period follow:

Direct Material	$430,000
Direct Labor	770,000
Other Variable Costs	150,000
Fixed Costs	450,000

    The company sold all the parts at a price of $14 per unit.

    The AMF Aircraft Company offers to buy as many units of the part as the Milky Way Company can supply at a price of $10 per unit. Milky Way estimates that to increase operations to a 100 percent capacity level would increase office and administrative costs by $50,000 for a 6-month period. Management believes that sales to AMF at this price will not affect the company's ability to reach the previous level of sales at the regular price. There are no legal restrictions on selling at the lower price.

    Present a schedule indicating whether Milky Way should accept the AMF offer. (Show your calculations.)

31. *Machine replacement*. On the last day of last year Oliver bought a new, special-purpose machine for $150,000 to use during a project that will last for 3 years. One week after Oliver purchased the machine, a salesperson from another company showed Oliver a different machine that costs $180,000. The latter machine is technically superior. Neither machine will have any salvage or disposal value in 3 years. As compared to the "old machine," the new machine will save $55,000 per year in operating costs—raw materials and labor. The old machine can be sold now for only $50,000.

Oliver is confident that the new machine would save $55,000 each year for 3 years, but he hesitates to recognize a loss on the old machine by selling it now. "I will use the old machine for 3 years and I will have no loss; by using the machine for 3 years, I'll get my money out of it."

Annual cash operating costs for the old machine are $80,000; this amount does not include any charge for depreciation. Sales, all for cash, will be $1 million each year. All other expenses will amount to $700,000 each year and Oliver will pay them in cash. The amount of all other cash expenses is independent of the machine used. The machine in question is the only long-term asset that Oliver uses. Ignore income taxes and compound interest considerations.

a. Prepare a statement of cash receipts and disbursements for each of 3 years assuming that the old machine is kept.

b. Repeat part **a** assuming that the new machine is acquired.

c. What is the total net difference between cash flows of the alternatives over the 3 years? Which alternative has the higher cash flows?

d. Calculate the operating profit for each of the 3 years assuming that the old machine is kept and straight-line depreciation is used.

e. Repeat part **d** assuming that the new machine is acquired and straight-line depreciation is used.

f. What is the total net difference between operating profits of the two alternatives over the 3 years, and which alternative has the larger total operating profit?

g. How would the answers to parts **c** and **f** differ if the old machine had cost $200,000 instead of $150,000? $300,000 instead of $150,000?

h. What is the name for the kind of cost represented by the $150,000 cost of the old machine just after its purchase?

32. *Cost estimate for bidding: consulting firm.* Clear Computer Consultants (CCC) operates a computer consulting firm. It has just received an inquiry from a prospective client about its prices for educational seminars for the prospective client's employees. The prospective client wants bids for three alternative activity levels: (1) one seminar with 20 participants, (2) four seminars with 20 participants each (80 participants total), or (3) eight seminars with 150 participants in total. The consulting firm's accountants have provided the following differential cost estimates:

Startup Costs for the Entire Job	$ 500
Materials Costs per Participant (brochures, handouts, etc.)	50
Differential Direct Labor Costs:	
One Seminar	900
Four Seminars	3,600
Eight Seminars	6,750

In addition to the differential costs listed above, CCC allocates fixed costs to jobs on a direct-labor-cost basis, at a rate of 80 percent of direct labor costs (excluding setup costs). For example, if direct labor costs are $100, CCC would also charge the job $80 for fixed costs. CCC seeks to make a profit of 10 percent of the bid price for each job. For this purpose, profit is revenue minus all costs assigned to the job, including allocated fixed costs. CCC has enough excess capacity to handle this job with ease.

a. Assume CCC bases its bid on the average total cost, including fixed costs allocated to the job, plus the 10 percent profit margin. What should CCC bid for each of the three levels of activity?

b. Compute the differential cost (including startup cost) and the contribution to profit for each of the three levels of activity.

c. Assume the prospective client gives three options. It is willing to accept either of CCC's bids for the one-seminar or four-seminar activity levels, but the prospective client will pay only 90 percent of the bid price for the eight-seminar package. CCC's president responds, "Taking the order for 10 percent below our bid would wipe out our profit! Let's take the four-seminar option; we make the most profit on it." Do you agree? What would be the contribution to profit for each of the three options? The differential cost?

33. *Alternative machines*. The Able Bakery now purchases frozen precut cookie dough at a cost of $.03 per cookie. Management is considering purchasing either an automatic or semiautomatic cookie cutter. If it purchases the automatic machine, the annual fixed costs will increase by $8,000. In addition, the variable cost per cookie will be $.010. Use of a semiautomatic machine will increase fixed costs per year by $4,500 plus $.015 variable cost per cookie.

a. At what volume of operations will the total annual costs incurred by using the semiautomatic machine equal outside purchase costs?

b. At what volume of operations will the total annual costs incurred by using the automatic machine equal outside purchase costs?

c. Which of the three alternatives is least costly if annual production volume is 600,000 cookies?

d. Which of the three alternatives is least costly if annual production volume is 800,000 cookies?

e. At which level of production volume are the costs incurred by using the two machines equal?

34. *Product mix decision*. The Vancil Company has one machine on which it can produce either of two products, Y or Z. Sales demand for both products is such that the machine could operate at full capacity on either of the products and Vancil can sell all output at current prices. Product Y requires 2 hours of machine time per unit of output and Product Z requires 4 hours of machine time per unit of output. Vancil charges machine time (depreciation) to products at the rate of $8 per hour.

The following information summarizes the per-unit cash inflows and costs of Products Y and Z.

	Per Unit	
	Product Y	**Product Z**
Selling Price	$60	$110
Materials	$ 9	$ 11
Labor	3	5

continued

continued from page 381

Machine Depreciation[a]	16	32
Allocated Portion of Fixed Factory Costs[b]	12	20
Total Cost of Unit Sold	$40	$ 68
Gross Margin per Unit	$20	$ 42

[a]This item under these circumstances could be referred to as "variable factory costs."

[b]Allocated in proportion to (direct) labor costs.

Selling costs are the same whether Vancil produces Product Y or Z, or both. You may ignore them. Should Vancil Company plan to produce Product Y, Product Z, or some mixture of both? Why?

35. *Department closing.* Prior to 19X0, Kahn Wholesalers Company had not kept departmental income statements. To achieve better management control, the company decided to install department-by-department accounts. At the end of 19X0, the new accounts showed that although the business as a whole was profitable, the Dry Goods Department had shown a substantial loss. The income statement for the Dry Goods Department, shown here, reports on operations for 19X0.

KAHN WHOLESALERS COMPANY
Dry Goods Department
Partial Income Statement for 19X0

Sales..	$500,000	
Cost of Goods Sold	(375,000)	
Gross Margin.....................................		$125,000
Costs:		
Payroll, Direct Labor, and Supervision	$(33,000)	
Commissions of Sales Staff[a]	(30,000)	
Rent[b]	(26,000)	
State Taxes[c]	(3,000)	
Insurance on Inventory	(4,000)	
Depreciation[d]	(7,000)	
Administration and General Office[e]	(22,000)	
Interest for Inventory Carrying Costs[f]	(5,000)	
Total Costs.......................................		(130,000)
Loss before Allocation of Income Taxes		$ (5,000)

Additional computations:

[a]All sales staff are compensated on straight commission, at a uniform 6 percent of all sales.

[b]Rent is charged to departments on a square-foot basis. The company rents an entire building, and the Dry Goods Department occupies 15 percent of the building.

[c]Assessed annually on the basis of average inventory on hand each month.

[d]Eight and one-half percent of cost of departmental equipment.

[e]Allocated on basis of departmental sales as a fraction of total company sales.

[f]Based on average inventory quantity multiplied by the company's borrowing rate for 3-month loans.

Analysis of these results has led management to suggest that it close the Dry Goods Department. Members of the management team agree that keeping the Dry Goods Department is not essential to maintaining good customer relations and supporting the rest of the company's business. In other words, eliminating the Dry Goods Department is not expected to affect the amount of business done by the other departments.

What action do you recommend to management of Kahn Wholesalers Company? Why?

36. *CVP and differential costs* (adapted from CPA exam). Management of the Arcadia Corporation asks you for help in making certain decisions. Arcadia has its home office in Ohio and leases factory buildings in Texas, Montana, and Maine, all of which produce the same product. The management of Arcadia has provided you with a projection of operations for the forthcoming year, as follows:

	Total	Texas	Montana	Maine
Sales Revenue	$4,400,000	$2,200,000	$1,400,000	$800,000
Fixed Costs:				
Factory	$1,100,000	$ 560,000	$ 280,000	$260,000
Administration	350,000	210,000	110,000	30,000
Variable Costs	1,450,000	665,000	425,000	360,000
Allocated Home Office Costs	500,000	225,000	175,000	100,000
Total	$3,400,000	$1,660,000	$ 990,000	$750,000
Profit from Operations	$1,000,000	$ 540,000	$ 410,000	$ 50,000

The sales price per unit is $25.

Because of the poor results of operations of the factory in Maine, Arcadia has decided to close its operations there. Arcadia expects that the proceeds from the sale of Maine's assets would equal termination costs.

However, Arcadia would like to continue serving its customers in that area if it is economically feasible. It considers one of the three following alternatives:

(1) Close the Maine factory and expand the operations of the Montana factory by using space presently idle. This move would result in the following changes in that factory's operations:

	Increase Over Factory's Current Operations
Sales Revenue	50%
Fixed Costs:	
Factory	20
Administration	10

(2)   Close the Maine Factory and enter into a long-term contract with a competitor who will serve that area's customers. This competitor would pay Arcadia a royalty of $4 per unit based on an estimate of 30,000 units being sold.

(3)   Close the Maine factory and neither expand the operations of the Montana factory, nor enter into the contract with the competitor.

To assist the management of Arcadia Corporation in choosing the best alternative, prepare schedules showing Arcadia's estimated profit from total operations that would result from each of the three alternatives stated above.

37.   *Analyzing the differential costs of marketing alternatives* (adapted from CMA exam). The High Impact Corporation has been a major producer and distributor of safety goggles for industrial use. Annual sales have averaged $60,000,000 for the past 4 years.

Late last year the company decided to enter the consumer market by producing snow-ski goggles. Management is considering two marketing alternatives for the product. The first is to add this responsibility to High Impact's current marketing department. The other alternative is to acquire a small, new company named Jasco, Inc., which has not yet started operations.

High Impact has never used independent distributors. Consequently, the management would prefer to acquire a distributor rather than merely enter into a contract for distribution of the product. The founders of Jasco are receptive to such an approach. In fact, High Impact could acquire Jasco complete with personnel for a nominal sum, which High Impact would incorporate into the salaries of Jasco personnel.

The manufacturing costs will be the same for either marketing alternative. The product engineering department has prepared the following estimates of the unit manufacturing costs for the new ski goggles.

Direct Materials	$14.00
Direct Labor	3.50
Manufacturing Overhead	10.00
Total	$27.50

The total overhead rate for all of High Impact's manufacturing activities is $20 per hour. The rate comprises $5 per hour for supplies, employee benefits, power, and so on and $15 per hour for supervision, depreciation, insurance, taxes, and so on.

High Impact's marketing department has used its experience in the sale of industrial products to develop a proposal for the distribution of ski goggles. The marketing department proposes to reorganize so that several positions scheduled for elimination now would handle the new product. The marketing department's forecast of the annual financial results for its proposal to market the new storage units follows.

High Impact Marketing Department Proposal:

Sales Revenue (100,000 units @ $45).............................	$4,500,000
Costs:	
Cost of Units Sold (100,000 units @ $27.50)	$2,750,000
Marketing Costs:	
Positions That Were to Be Eliminated.........................	600,000
Sales Commissions (5 percent of sales)	225,000
Advertising Program	400,000
Promotion Program	200,000
Share of Current Marketing Department's Management Costs	100,000
Total Costs	$4,275,000
Operating Profit	$ 225,000

The Jasco founders also prepared a forecast of the annual financial results based on their experience in marketing consumer products. The following forecast assumes that Jasco would become part of High Impact and would be responsible for marketing the new ski goggles in the consumer market.

Jasco Proposal:

Sales Revenue (120,000 units @ $50)............................	$6,000,000
Costs:	
Cost of Units Sold (120,000 units @ $27.50)	$3,300,000
Marketing Costs:	
Personnel—Sales	560,000
Personnel—Sales Management[a]	300,000
Commissions (10 percent)...................................	600,000
Advertising Program	800,000
Promotion Program	200,000
Office Rental (the annual rental of a long-term lease already	
signed by Jasco)	50,000
Total Costs	$5,810,000
Operating Profit	$ 190,000

---

[a]Includes nominal amount paid to acquire Jasco.

Prepare a schedule of differential costs and revenues to assist management in deciding which marketing alternative to use.

38. *Product choice with constraints* (Appendix 8.1; adapted from CMA exam). Leastan Company manufactures a line of carpeting that includes a commercial carpet and a residential carpet. Both types of carpeting use two grades of fiber—heavy-duty and regular. The mix of the two grades of fiber differs in each type of carpeting, with the commercial grade using a greater amount of heavy-duty fiber.

Leastan will introduce a new line of carpeting in 2 months to replace the current line. The new line cannot use the fiber now in stock. Management wants to exhaust the present stock of regular and heavy-duty fiber during the last month of production.

Data regarding the current line of commercial and residential carpeting follow:

	Commercial	Residential
Selling Price per Roll	$1,000	$800
Production Specifications per Roll of Carpet:		
Heavy-Duty Fiber.............................	80 Pounds	40 Pounds
Regular Fiber	20 Pounds	40 Pounds
Direct Labor Hours	15 Hours	15 Hours
Standard Cost per Roll of Carpet:		
Heavy-Duty Fiber ($3 per pound)................	$240	$120
Regular Fiber ($2 per pound)	40	80
Direct Labor ($10 per direct labor hour)	150	150
Variable Manufacturing Overhead (60 percent of direct labor cost)	90	90
Fixed Manufacturing Overhead (120 percent of direct labor cost)	180	180
Total Standard Cost per Roll..................	$700	$620

Leastan has 42,000 pounds of heavy-duty fiber and 24,000 pounds of regular fiber in stock. Leastan will sell all fiber not used in the manufacture of the present types of carpeting during the last month of production for $.25 a pound.

A maximum of 10,500 direct labor hours are available during the month. The labor force can work on either type of carpeting.

Sufficient demand exists for the present line of carpeting so that the firm can sell all quantities produced.

a.   Calculate the number of rolls of commercial carpet and residential carpet Leastan Company must manufacture during the last month of production to exhaust completely the heavy-duty and regular fiber still in stock.

b.   Can Leastan Company manufacture these quantities of commercial and residential carpeting during the last month of production? Explain your answer.

39.   *Product choice with constraints* (Appendix 8.1; adapted from CMA exam). Excelsion Corporation manufactures and sells two kinds of containers—paperboard and plastic. The company produced and sold 100,000 paperboard containers and 75,000 plastic containers during the month of April. It used a total of 4,000 and 6,000 direct labor hours in producing the paperboard and plastic containers, respectively.

The company has not been able to maintain an inventory of either product because of the high demand and expects this situation to continue in the future. The firm can shift workers from the production of paperboard to plastic containers and vice versa, but additional labor is not available in the com-

Exhibit 8.20

EXCELSION CORPORATION
Income Statement for the Month Ended April 30

	Paperboard Containers	Plastic Containers
Sales Revenue	$220,800	$222,900
Less:		
Returns and Allowances	$ 6,360	$ 7,200
Discounts	2,440	3,450
	$ 8,800	$ 10,650
Net Sales	$212,000	$212,250
Cost of Sales:		
Direct Material Cost	$123,000	$120,750
Direct Labor	26,000	28,500
Indirect Labor (variable with direct labor hours)	4,000	4,500
Depreciation—Machinery	14,000	12,250
Depreciation—Building	10,000	10,000
Cost of Sales	$177,000	$176,000
Gross Profit	$ 35,000	$ 36,250
Nonmanufacturing Expenses:		
Variable	$ 8,000	$ 7,500
Fixed	1,000	1,000
Commissions—Variable	11,000	15,750
Total Operating Expenses	$ 20,000	$ 24,250
Income before Tax	$ 15,000	$ 12,000
Income Taxes (40 percent)	6,000	4,800
Net Income	$ 9,000	$ 7,200

munity. In addition, a labor strike at the facilities of a key supplier will cause a shortage of plastic material used in the manufacture of the plastic container in the coming months. Management has estimated it will have only enough direct material to produce 60,000 plastic containers during June.

Exhibit 8.20 presents the income statement for Excelsion Corporation for the month of April. The company expects the costs presented in the statement, which represent prior periods, to continue at the same rates or levels in the future.

a. What is the contribution per unit of scarce resource?

b. What is the optimal product mix given the constraints in the problem?

40. *Formulating a linear programming problem* (Appendix 8.1; adapted from CMA exam). The Witchell Corporation manufactures and sells three grades, A, B, and C, of a single wood product. Witchell must process each grade through three phases—cutting, fitting, and finishing—before selling it.

Unit information follows:

	A	B	C
Selling Price	$10.00	$15.00	$20.00
Direct Labor	5.00	6.00	9.00
Direct Materials	.70	.70	1.00
Variable Overhead	1.00	1.20	1.80
Fixed Overhead	.60	.72	1.08
Materials Requirements in Board Feet	7	7	10
Labor Requirements in Hours:			
Cutting	$3/6$	$3/6$	$4/6$
Fitting	$1/6$	$1/6$	$2/6$
Finishing	$1/6$	$2/6$	$3/6$

Witchell can purchase only 5,000 board feet of direct materials per week. The cutting department has 180 hours of labor available each week. The fitting and finishing departments each have 120 hours of labor available each week. No overtime is allowed.

Contract commitments require the company to make 50 units of A per week. In addition, company policy is to produce at least 50 additional units of A and 50 units of B and C each week to remain active in each of the three markets. Because of competition, Witchell can sell only 130 units of C each week.

Formulate and label the objective function and the constraints necessary to maximize the contribution margin.

41. *Computing optimal safety-stock levels* (adapted from CMA exam). The Starr Company manufactures several products. One of its main products requires an electric motor. The management of Starr Company used the EOQ model to learn that the optimum number of motors to order is 3,000 per order. Management now wants to decide how much safety stock to keep on hand.

The company uses 30,000 motors annually at the rate of 100 per working day. The motors regularly cost $60 each. The lead time for an order is 5 days. The cost to carry a motor in stock is $10. If a stock-out occurs, management must purchase motors at retail from an alternate supplier. The alternate supplier charges $80 per motor.

Starr Company has analyzed the usage during the past reorder periods by examining inventory records. The records indicate the following usage patterns during past reorder periods:

Usage during Lead Time	Number of Times Quantity Was Used
440	6
460	12
480	16
500	130
520	20
540	10
560	6
	200

Compute the least-cost safety stock level and the total differential costs at that level.

42. *Differential cost analysis in a service organization, with taxes* (contributed by Robert H. Colson). Engineering Services, Inc., provides engineering consulting services for an hourly fee. Major customers include corporate, professional, and government organizations.

   The cost per billable hour of service at the company's normal volume of 8,000 billable hours per month appears in Exhibit 8.21. (A billable hour is one hour billed to a client.)

   Treat each question independently. Unless given otherwise, the regular fee per hour is $220. State and federal income taxes are 40 percent of before-tax income.

   a. How many hours must the firm bill per month to break even?
   b. Market research estimates that a fee increase to $250 per hour would decrease monthly volume to 6,000 hours. The accounting department estimates that fixed overhead costs would be $100 per hour, while variable cost per hour would remain unchanged. How would a fee increase affect profits?
   c. Engineering Services is operating at its normal volume. It has received a special request from one of its longtime customers to provide services on a special-order basis. Because of the long-term nature of the contract (4 months) and the magnitude (1,000 hours per month), the customer believes a fee reduction is in order. Engineering Services has a capacity limitation of 8,500 hours per month. Fixed costs will not change if the firm accepts the special order. What is the lowest fee Engineering Services would be willing to charge?

Integrative Problems and Cases

43. *Inventory costs versus costs for inventory management* (adapted from CMA exam). Pointer Furniture Company manufactures and sells office furniture. To compete effectively in different markets, it produces several brands of office furniture. Pointer has organized the manufacturing operation by item produced,

Exhibit 8.21

ENGINEERING SERVICES, INC.
Cost per Billable Hour of Service

Average Cost per Hour Billed to Client:	
Variable Labor—Consultants	$50
Variable Overhead, Including Supplies and Clerical Support	20
Fixed Overhead, Including Allowance for Unbilled Hours	80
	$150
Marketing and Administrative Costs per Billable Hour (all fixed)	40
Total Hourly Cost	$190

rather than by furniture line. Pointer manufactures desks in batches. For example, it may manufacture 10 high-quality desks during the first 2 weeks in October and 50 units of a lower-quality desk during the last 2 weeks. Because each model has its own unique manufacturing requirement, the change from one model to another requires adjustment to the factory's equipment.

Management of Pointer wants to compute the most economical production run for each of the items in its product lines. Before using the model, Pointer must estimate the setup cost incurred when manufacturing changes to a different furniture model. The accounting department is to estimate the setup cost for the desk (Model JE 40) in its junior executive line as an example.

The equipment maintenance department is responsible for all of the changeover adjustments on production lines, in addition to the preventive and regular maintenance of all the production equipment. The equipment maintenance staff has a 40-hour work week; the size of the staff changes only if a change in the work load expected to persist for an extended period of time occurs. The equipment maintenance department employed 10 people last year, and they each averaged 2,000 hours for the year. They receive wages of $9 an hour, and employee benefits averaged 20 percent of wage costs. The other departmental costs, which include items such as supervision, depreciation, insurance, and so on, total $50,000 per year.

To make the change on the desk line for Model JE 40 requires two workers from the equipment maintenance department. They spend an estimated 5 hours setting up the equipment. Five workers operate the desk production line for manufacturing Model JE 40. During the changeover, these workers assist the maintenance workers when needed and operate the line during the test run. (The test run takes 1 machine hour.) However, they are idle for approximately 40 percent of the time required for the changeover.

The production workers receive a basic wage rate of $7.50 an hour. The firm applies the overhead costs of this production line using two overhead bases, because some of the costs vary in proportion to direct labor hours whereas others vary with machine hours. The overhead rates applicable for the current year follow:

	Based on Direct Labor Hours	Based on Machine Hours
Variable	$2.75	$ 5.00
Fixed...............................	2.25	15.00
	$5.00	$20.00

These department overhead rates result from an expected activity of 10,000 direct labor hours and 1,500 machine hours for the current year. The firm expects this department to operate at less than full capacity because production capability currently exceeds sales potential.

The estimated cost of the direct materials used in the test run totals $200. Salvage material from the test run should total $50.

a. Prepare an estimate of Pointer Furniture Company's setup cost for desk Model JE 40 for use in the economic production run model. For each cost item identified in the problem, justify the amount and the reason for including the cost item in your estimate. Explain the reason for excluding any cost item from your estimate.

b. Identify the cost items that would be included in an estimate of Pointer Furniture Company's cost of carrying the desks in inventory.

44. *Comprehensive differential costing case.* Hospital Supply, Inc., produces hydraulic hoists used by hospitals to move bedridden patients. Exhibit 8.22 shows the costs of manufacturing and marketing hydraulic hoists at the company's normal volume of 3,000 units per month.

Unless otherwise stated, assume that the situations described in the questions are not connected; treat each independently. Unless otherwise stated, assume a regular selling price of $740 per unit.

a. What is the breakeven volume in units? In sales dollars?

b. Market research estimates that volume could be increased to 3,500 units which is well within hoist production capacity limitations, if the firm reduces the price from $740 to $650 per unit. Assume that the cost behavior patterns implied by the data in Exhibit 8.22 are correct. Do you recommend that the firm take this action? What would be the impact on monthly sales, costs, and income?

c. On March 1, Hospital Supply receives a contract offer from the federal government to supply 500 units to Veterans Administration hospitals for delivery by March 31. Because of an unusually large number of rush orders from its regular customers, Hospital Supply plans to produce 4,000 units during March, which will use all available capacity. If it accepts the government order, it will lose to a competitor 500 units normally sold to regular customers. The contract offered by the government would reimburse the government's share of March manufacturing costs, plus pay a fixed fee (profit) of $50,000. (The firm would not incur any

Exhibit 8.22

HOSPITAL SUPPLY
Costs per Unit for Hydraulic Hoists

Unit Manufacturing Costs:		
Variable Materials	$100	
Variable Labor	150	
Variable Overhead	50	
Fixed Overhead	120	
Total Unit Manufacturing Costs		$420
Unit Marketing Costs:		
Variable	$ 50	
Fixed	140	
Total Unit Marketing Costs		190
Total Unit Costs		$610

variable marketing costs on the government's units.) What impact would accepting the government contract have on March income?

d. Hospital Supply can enter a foreign market in which price competition is keen. An attraction of the foreign market is that demand there is greatest when demand in the domestic market is low; thus the firm could use idle production facilities without affecting domestic business.

The firm received an order for 1,000 units at a below-normal price in this market. Shipping costs for this order will be $75 per unit; total costs of obtaining the contract (marketing costs) will be $4,000. This order will not affect domestic business. What is the minimum unit price Hospital Supply should consider for this order of 1,000 units?

e. An inventory of 230 units of an obsolete model of the hoist remains in the stockroom. If the firm does not sell these units through regular channels at reduced prices, the inventory will soon be worthless. What is the minimum acceptable price for selling these units?

f. The firm receives a proposal from an outside contractor who will make and ship 1,000 hydraulic hoist units per month directly to Hospital Supply's customers as Hospital Supply's sales force receives orders. The proposal would not affect Hospital Supply's fixed marketing costs, but its variable marketing costs would decline by 20 percent for these 1,000 units produced by the contractor. Hospital Supply's plant would operate at two-thirds of its normal level. Total fixed manufacturing costs would decline by 30 percent.

What in-house unit cost should the firm use to compare with the quotation received from the supplier? Should the firm accept the proposal for a price (that is, payment to the contractor) of $425 per unit?

g. Assume the same facts as in part **f**, except that the firm will use idle facilities to produce 800 modified hydraulic hoists per month for hospital operating rooms. It can sell these modified hoists for $900 each, while the costs of production would be $550 per unit variable manufacturing expense. Variable marketing costs would be $100 per unit. Fixed marketing and manufacturing costs will not change whether the firm manufactures the original 3,000 regular hoists or the mix of 2,000 regular hoists plus 800 modified hoists. What is the maximum purchase price per unit that Hospital Supply should be willing to pay the outside contractor? Should it accept the proposal for a price of $425 per unit?

45. *Make or buy—Liquid Chemical case.* See Problem 30 at the end of Chapter 9. Identify four alternative actions and the differential cash flows for each alternative.

Suggested Solutions to Even-Numbered Exercises

12. *Product choice*

- Alternative 1: Warehouse.
- Alternative 2: Office space.
- Alternative 3: Restaurants and specialty shops.

	Alternative		
	1	2	3
Revenue................................	$960,000	$982,800	$1,101,100
Less Variable Costs	40,000	70,000	95,000
Total Contribution Margin	$920,000	$912,800	$1,006,100
Less Fixed Costs......................	600,000	600,000	600,000
Operating Profit	$320,000	$312,800	$ 406,100

Yuppie Enterprises should choose alternative 3.

14. *Make or buy*

a.

	Buy	−	Make	= Difference
Raw Materials	$(280,000)	−	$(100,000)	= $(180,000)
Direct Labor	0	−	(80,000)	= 80,000
Variable Overhead	0	−	(32,000)	= 32,000
Total Variable Costs	$(280,000)	−	$(212,000)	= $(68,000)

Reliant Enterprises can save $68,000 by making its own sails.

b. The opportunity cost of utilizing the factory space will be $12,000 per year. The opportunity cost will not alter the decision in part **a**, but will reduce the net benefits to $56,000.

16. *Product mix decisions*

	Manual	Electric	Quartz
Machine Time per Unit	0.4 Hours	2.5 Hours	5.0 Hours
Contribution Margin	$10.00	$16.00	$22.00
Contribution Margin per Machine Hour	$25.00	$6.40	$4.40

Timeless Products should drop the quartz line.

18. *Economic order quantity*

a. $D = 250$ Batches of 1,000 Bolts

$K_0 = \$10$

$K_c = 0.20 \times \$10 = \$2$

$$Q = \sqrt{\frac{2 \times \$10 \times 250}{\$2}} = \underline{\underline{50}}$$

$$N = \frac{D}{Q} = \frac{250}{50} = \underline{\underline{5}}$$

Annual ordering costs $= \underline{\underline{\$50}}$.

b. $D = 25$ Batches of 10,000 Bolts

$K_0 = \$10$

$K_c = 0.20 \times \$96.10 = \$19.22$

$$Q = \sqrt{\frac{2 \times \$10 \times 25}{\$19.22}} = \underline{\underline{5.1}}$$

$$N = \frac{D}{Q} = \frac{25}{5.1} = \underline{\underline{4.9}}.$$

Annual ordering costs = \$49. It would not be possible, however, to order 51,000 bolts at a time, because bolts are only available in 10,000 bolt batches.

c. If both size batches can be ordered, the optimum solution is to make 4.9 orders per year of 51,000 bolt batches (5 lots of 10,000 and one lot of 1,000).

20. *Product mix decisions*

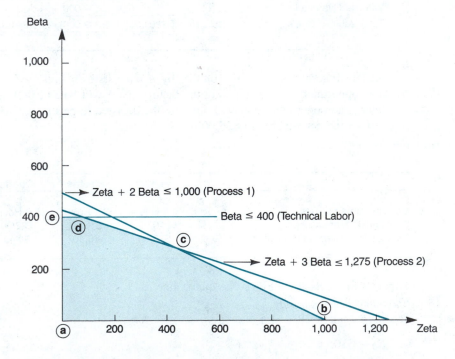

Problem Formulation:

Maximize Total Contribution Margin = 4.00 Zeta + 5.25 Beta.

Subject to:

Process 1 Constraint:	Zeta	+ 2 Beta ≤ 1,000
Process 2 Constraint:	Zeta	+ 3 Beta ≤ 1,275
Technical Labor Constraint:		Beta ≤ 400.

Critical Points	Produce and Sell Zeta	Produce and Sell Beta	Total Contribution Margin[c]
a	0	0	0
b	1,000	0	$4,000.00*
c	450[a]	275[a]	$3,243.75
d	75[b]	400[b]	$2,400.00
e	0	400	$2,100.00

*Optimal solution.

[a]Zeta + 2 Beta = 1,000 (Process 1 Constraint).

Zeta + 3 Beta = 1,275 (Process 2 Constraint).

Solving simultaneously:

$$(1,000 - 2 \text{ Beta}) + 3 \text{ Beta} = 1,275$$
$$\text{Beta} = \underline{\underline{275}}.$$
$$\text{Zeta} + 2(275) = 1,000$$
$$\therefore \text{Zeta} = \underline{\underline{450}}.$$

[b]Zeta + 3 Beta = 1,275

Beta =   400.

Solving simultaneously:

$$\text{Zeta} + 3(400) = 1,275$$
$$\text{Zeta} = \underline{\underline{75}}.$$

[c]Total Contribution Margin = $4.00 Zeta + $5.25 Beta.

22. *Finding most profitable price-quantity combination*

a.

Price (1)	Quantity Demanded (2)	Revenues (3)	Total Variable Manufacturing Costs[a] (4)	Total Variable Selling and Administrative Costs[b] (5)	Total Costs[c] (6)	Total Profit[d] (7)
$10	40,000	$400,000	$160,000	$80,000	$290,000	$110,000
12	36,000	432,000	144,000	72,000	266,000	166,000
14	28,000	392,000	112,000	56,000	218,000	174,000
16	24,000	384,000	96,000	48,000	194,000	190,000
18	18,000	324,000	72,000	36,000	158,000	166,000
20	15,000	300,000	60,000	30,000	140,000	160,000

[a]Quantity demanded × $4.

[b]Quantity demanded × $2.

[c]Columns (4) + (5) + $50,000 (fixed manufacturing + administrative costs).

[d]Column (3) − (6).

b. Select a price of $16, because it results in the most profit.

... CHAPTER 9 ...

Long-Run Decisions: Capital Budgeting and Discounted Cash Flows

Chapter Outline

- Capital Budgeting: Investment and Financing Decisions
- Discounted Cash Flow Methods
- The Cost of Capital—An Opportunity Cost
- Sensitivity of Net Present Value to Estimates
- Complications in Computing Periodic Cash Flows

Earlier chapters applied the differential principle to several kinds of short-run operating decisions. In each case, the firm's capacity was fixed. The manager must decide how best to use that fixed capacity in the short run. For example, how many units should we produce this month? Should a management consulting firm accept a one-time consulting assignment?

This chapter shifts attention to the long run. We focus on decisions to change operating capacity. Should a paper manufacturer build a larger plant? Should a bank open a new branch? Should a retail store expand? Should a consulting firm hire more staff consultants on long-term employment contracts? Should a job shop acquire new machinery to replace older, less efficient machinery? Should an auto parts manufacturer acquire new technology that will perform services currently performed by workers? No decision affects the long-run success of a firm more than deciding which investment projects to undertake.

Short-run operating decisions and long-run capacity decisions both rely on a differential analysis of cash inflows and cash outflows. Long-run capacity decisions involve cash flows over several future periods, whereas typical operating decisions involve only short-range cash flows. When the cash flows extend over several future periods, the analyst must use some technique to make the cash flows comparable, because the value of one dollar received now exceeds that of one dollar received several years from now. Present value analysis, sometimes called discounted cash flow (or DCF) analysis, provides the technique. The appendix at the back of this book further illustrates present value techniques. You should be familiar with its contents before studying this chapter.

Capital Budgeting: Investment and Financing Decisions

Capital budgeting involves making decisions about which long-term investments to undertake and how to finance them. A firm faced with a decision to acquire a new plant or equipment must decide (1) whether to acquire the new asset (the investment decision) and (2) how to raise the funds required to obtain the new asset (the financing decision). The firm may raise funds through borrowing, from curtailing dividends, or by issuing additional capital stock.

One significant contribution to the theory of financial economics in recent years is the principle that a firm should make the **investment decision** independently of the **financing decision.** In other words, the firm should generally make the investment decision first, and only after a project gets the go-ahead should management begin to consider how to finance it.

Separating the investment and financing decisions results from the premise that all of a firm's equities (that is, liabilities plus owners' equity) finance all of a firm's assets. Acquiring a new asset will involve investing funds, but once the firm adds the asset to its portfolio of assets, all of the firm's equities finance that asset. Specific equities generally do not finance specific assets.

The capital budgeting decision involves estimating future cash flows, deciding on an appropriate interest rate for discounting those cash flows, and, once the firm makes a decision to undertake a project, deciding on how to finance that project. This text focuses on the first of these three issues. Although we discuss the last two, we leave their details to corporate finance courses.

Discounted Cash Flow Methods

If you have an opportunity to invest $1 today in return for $2 in the future, your evaluation of the attractiveness of the opportunity depends, in part, on how long you have to wait for the $2. If you must wait only 1 week after making the initial investment, you are much more inclined to accept the offer than if you have to wait

10 years to receive the $2. **Discounted cash flow (DCF) methods** aid in evaluating investments involving cash flows over time where the time elapsing between cash payment and receipt is significant. The two discounted cash flow methods are the net present value (NPV) method and the internal rate of return (IRR) method. This chapter discusses the net present value method. Chapter 10 discusses the internal rate of return method.

The Net Present Value Method

The net present value method involves the following steps:

1. Estimate the amounts of future cash inflows and future cash outflows for each alternative under consideration.

2. Discount the future cash flows to the present using the firm's cost of capital. The **net present value of cash flows** of a project is the value of the cash inflows minus the present value of the cash outflows.

3. Accept or reject the proposed project or select one from a set of mutually exclusive projects.

If the present value of the future cash inflows exceeds the present value of the outflow for a proposal, the firm should accept the alternative. If the net present value of the future cash flows is negative, the firm should reject the alternative. If the firm must choose one from a set of mutually exclusive alternatives, it should select the one with the largest net present value of cash flows.

This three-step procedure summarizes a complex process involving many estimates and projections. Later discussion treats these complexities. For now, however, we examine two illustrations of the net present value method, the first ignoring income taxes and the second considering income taxes.

Illustration Ignoring Income Taxes

The example in this section illustrates the steps of the net present value method. After we introduce the basics here, we make the example more realistic in a later section. Finally, the Problems for Self-Study at the end of the chapter show more complicated examples.

JEP Realty Syndicators, Inc., is contemplating the acquisition of computer hardware that will allow it to bring a new variety of real estate investment partnerships to the market. The hardware and software cost $100,000 and will last 5 years before becoming obsolete. Exhibit 9.1 shows the cash inflows and cash outflows expected from this investment during each of the 5 years of its useful life. At the end of Year 0 (that is, at the start of the project), the firm purchases the computer system for $100,000. The decreasing pattern of cash inflows over the 5 years results from the expected reaction of other real estate syndicators, who will copy the investment instrument and force down the commissions and underwriting fees.

The cash outflows for each of the 5 years are for programmers, sales staff, and supplies. We have assumed that the hardware has zero salvage value at the end of 5 years. Column **(4)** shows the net cash flow for each year.

Exhibit 9.1

JEP REALTY SYNDICATORS, INC.
Cash Flows Associated with New Real Estate Investment Products
(ignoring income taxes)[a]

Cash Flow Analysis

End of Year (1)	Cash Inflows (2)	Cash Outflows (3)	Net Cash Inflow (Outflows) (4)	Present Value Factor at 20 Percent (5)	Present Value of Cash Flows (6)
0	—	$100,000	$(100,000)	1.00000	$(100,000)
1	$120,000	70,000	50,000	0.83333	41,667
2	80,000	40,000	40,000	0.69444	27,778
3	60,000	30,000	30,000	0.57870	17,361
4	50,000	25,000	25,000	0.48225	12,056
5	40,000	25,000	15,000	0.40188	6,028
Total	$350,000	$290,000	$ 60,000		$ 4,890

Accounting Income Data

Year (7)	Revenues – (8)	Other Expenses – (9)	Depreciation = (10)	Net Income (11)
0	—	—	—	—
1	$120,000	$ 70,000	$ 20,000	$30,000
2	80,000	40,000	20,000	20,000
3	60,000	30,000	20,000	10,000
4	50,000	25,000	20,000	5,000
5	40,000	25,000	20,000	(5,000)
Total	$350,000	$190,000	$100,000	$60,000

[a]Amounts in columns are derived as follows:

(2), (3), (8), (9): given.

(4) = (2) − (3).

(5) taken from Table 2 at the back of the book.

(6) = (4) × (5).

(10) = $100,000/5.

(11) = (8) − (9) − (10).

The cash flow related to the computer equipment in column (3) represents the initial outlay for its acquisition. Distinguish cash flow from accounting costs, such as for depreciation. Depreciation appears in the financial statements, as in column (10) in the bottom panel of Exhibit 9.1. Depreciation allocates costs to periods of benefit. Although the acquisition has no immediate impact on income, it does require an expenditure or cash outflow at the time of acquisition. (In practice, a cash inflow can occur upon disposal of the asset at the end of the project's life.)

Cash flow data show the timing of cash flows, not accrual accounting data. Hence, cash flows enable decision makers to compute the time value of money as needed for investment decisions. Use cash flow data, not accrual accounting data, for making investment decisions. In accrual accounting, over long-enough time spans, income equals cash in minus cash out. Thus, the equality of the sums in columns **(4)** and **(11)** is not a coincidence. The timing of accounting income differs from the timing of cash flows. DCF analysis focuses on cash flow, not accounting income.

Because you can invest cash over time to earn interest, cash you receive or pay today has a higher present value than cash you receive or pay at some time in the future. To put the cash flows in column **(4)** on an equivalent basis, we discount them to their present value. This illustration uses a 20 percent discount rate. (We discuss the selection of an appropriate discount rate later.) If the firm can invest cash to earn 20 percent, the right to receive $90,000 at the end of Year 1 is equivalent to receiving $75,000 (= $90,000/1.20) today. Column **(5)** shows the discount factors for the present value of $1 for various periods at 20 percent. (These discount factors appear in the tables following the appendix at the back of the book. Some calculators or computer spreadsheet programs contain functions to provide these factors.) Column **(6)** shows the present value of each cash flow.

This project results in a positive net present value of $4,890; that is, the present value of the net future cash inflows exceeds the initial investment by $4,890. JEP should, therefore, accept this project because its net present value is greater than zero. Accepting positive net present value projects increases the value of the firm when the discount rate is the firm's opportunity cost of capital, as discussed later.

Illustration Considering Income Taxes

Income taxes affect both the *amounts* of cash flows and the *timing* of cash flows, and, consequently, the firm must consider them in making investment decisions.

Reconsider the proposed computer acquisition by JEP Realty. In this case, assume a combined federal and state income tax rate of 40 percent. The discount rate for after-tax cash flows is 12 percent [= .20 × (1 − .40)], because the pretax cost of capital is 20 percent and the tax rate is 40 percent. Also assume that the firm uses straight-line depreciation. The top panel of Exhibit 9.2 shows the calculation of the proposed project's net present value, assuming that the firm depreciates the equipment using the straight-line method for income tax purposes. Although depreciation for tax purposes is not itself a cash flow, it does represent a deductible expense. Hence, **depreciation affects cash flows** by its effect on taxable income and the income taxes paid. Using a 12-percent discount rate, the project has a positive net present value of $2,208 and the firm should accept it.

Accelerated Cost Recovery   One of the most important effects of income tax laws on investment decisions arises from the firm's ability to use accelerated depreciation methods, called the **accelerated cost recovery system** or **ACRS,** in the income tax laws. Because the laws allowing ACRS for tax purposes have changed, some writers refer to MACRS, denoting the modified accelerated cost recovery system.

Exhibit 9.2

JEP REALTY SYNDICATORS, INC.
Cash Flows Associated with New Real Estate Investment Products
(considering income taxes)[a]

End of Year (1)	Cash Inflows (2)	Cash Outflows (3)	Pretax Net Cash Flow (4)	Depreciation Deduction (5)	Taxable Income (6)	Income Tax Payable (7)	Net Cash Inflow (8)	Present Value Factor at 12 Percent (9)	Present Value of Cash Flows (10)
A. Straight-Line Depreciation Method									
0	—	$100,000	$(100,000)	—	—	—	$(100,000)	1.00000	$(100,000)
1	$120,000	70,000	50,000	$ 20,000	$30,000	$12,000	38,000	0.89286	33,929
2	80,000	40,000	40,000	20,000	20,000	8,000	32,000	0.79719	25,510
3	60,000	30,000	30,000	20,000	10,000	4,000	26,000	0.71178	18,506
4	50,000	25,000	25,000	20,000	5,000	2,000	23,000	0.63552	14,617
5	40,000	25,000	15,000	20,000	(5,000)	(2,000)[b]	17,000	0.56743	9,646
Total	$350,000	$290,000	$ 60,000	$100,000	$60,000	$24,000	$ 36,000		$ 2,208
B. Accelerated Cost Recovery Method									
0	—	$100,000	$(100,000)	—	—	—	$(100,000)	1.00000	$(100,000)
1	$120,000	70,000	50,000	$ 20,000	$30,000	$12,000	38,000	0.89286	33,929
2	80,000	40,000	40,000	32,000	8,000	3,200	36,800	0.79719	29,337
3	60,000	30,000	30,000	19,000	11,000	4,400	25,600	0.71178	18,222
4	50,000	25,000	25,000	14,500	10,500	4,200	20,800	0.63552	13,219
5	40,000	25,000	15,000	14,500	500	200	14,800	0.56743	8,398
Total	$350,000	$290,000	$ 60,000	$100,000	$60,000	$24,000	$ 36,000		$ 3,105

[a]Amounts in columns are derived as follows:

(2), (3): given.
(4) = (2) − (3).
(5) Panel A = $100,000/5.
(5) Panel B: $100,000 × .20 = $20,000.
       $100,000 × .32 = $32,000.
       $100,000 × .19 = $19,000.
       $100,000 × .145 = $14,500.
       $100,000 × .145 = $14,500.

(6) = (4) − (5).
(7) = .40 × (6).
(8) = (4) − (7).
(9) Taken from Table 2 of
    the Compound Interest
    and Annuity Tables at
    the back of the book.
(10) = (8) × (9).

[b]Assumes that in Year 5 there is sufficient otherwise-taxable income that the tax loss in Year 5 will reduce income taxes otherwise payable.

ACRS generally shifts depreciation deductions from later to earlier years as compared to the straight-line method. This practice shifts taxable income and tax payments from earlier to later years. Although accelerated cost recovery does not change the total tax liability generated by a project over its life, it does influence the desirability of the project by affecting the timing of cash flows.

The lower panel of Exhibit 9.2 shows the calculation of the net present value of the project assuming that the firm uses ACRS for tax reporting. Assume that tax law requires equipment with a 5-year life, such as the computer JEP Realty acquires, to be depreciated over 5 years for tax purposes under ACRS: 20 percent in the first year, 32 percent in the second, 19 percent in the third, and 14.5 percent in both the

Managerial Application

DCF Analysis in Plant Expansion and Dispute Resolution

Union Carbide decided in the mid-1980s that the market for polycrystalline silicon (polysilicon), a key ingredient in the manufacture of computer chips, was about to expand rapidly. It entered into an agreement with a Japanese manufacturer, Komatsu, under which it would expand its polysilicon plant and manufacture large quantities of polysilicon that Komatsu would purchase. The agreement specified that Carbide and Komatsu would submit to arbitration any disputes arising between them.

Before entering the agreement, Carbide gathered data on plant expansion technologies, the expected cash flows for each, and the size of the projected market. It performed a discounted cash flow analysis both to decide whether the expansion would be profitable and to choose the preferred method of expanding. In carrying out the DCF analysis, Carbide used its cost of capital, estimated at about 23 percent per year. Ultimately, Carbide invested $80 million in expanding its polysilicon manufacturing plant in the state of Washington.

After Carbide completed the plant expansion, Komatsu began building its own plants to produce polysilicon. Carbide viewed Komatsu's doing so as breach of the agreement. Carbide invoked the arbitration clause of the agreement and asked Komatsu for compensation for damages caused by the alleged contract breach. Komatsu argued that any damages Carbide may have suffered resulted from the collapse of the market for computer chips, not from Komatsu's actions. In settling the dispute between Carbide and Komatsu, Carbide produced copies of its earlier DCF analysis to show that it had undertaken the expansion only after careful planning. Carbide and Komatsu settled their dispute prior to formal arbitration, but the terms are confidential.

fourth and fifth years. Note that the total depreciation expense in column **(5)** is $100,000 under both straight-line and ACRS. In the latter case, however, the deductions occur sooner; they are more *accelerated*. The net cash flows in column **(8)** total $36,000 in both cases, but they occur in a different pattern. The net present value of the project is $897 (= $3,105 − $2,208) greater if the firm uses accelerated cost recovery, rather than straight-line, for tax calculations.

Identifying Cash Flows

In practice, analysts consider a variety of cash flows. The following checklist of cash flows is reasonably detailed. Later sections explain and illustrate some of the more difficult steps. The cash flows associated with an investment project divide into those at the inception of the project (the initial cash flows), those occurring during the life of the project (the periodic cash flows), and those occurring at the conclusion of the project (the terminal cash flows). This three-way classification of cash flows includes the list on the following page.

Initial Cash Flows

1. Asset cost—outflow.
2. Freight and installation costs—outflow.
3. Salvage or other disposal value of existing asset—inflow.
4. Income tax effect of gain or loss on disposal of existing asset—outflow (if gain) or inflow (if loss).
5. Investment tax credit, if any, on new asset—inflow.[1]

Periodic Cash Flows

1. Receipts (*not* revenues, which generally precede receipt of cash) from sales—inflow.
2. Lost ''other'' inflows caused by undertaking this particular project, if any—outflow. (For example, the new equipment for JEP Realty allows the company to market a new investment package. If this decreases the sales of other packages, there would be lost ''other'' inflows.)
3. Expenditures for fixed and variable production costs—outflow (at time of incurrence, which generally precedes date of sale.)
4. Savings for fixed and variable production costs, if any—inflow.
5. Selling, general, and administrative expenditures—outflows.
6. Savings in selling, general, and administrative expenditures, if any—inflows.
7. Income tax effects of flows **1** through **6**—which are opposite in sign to the cash flow that generates the tax consequences. For example, extra cash inflow from customers' payments results in extra cash outflows for income taxes. Extra cash outflow for computer programmers results in savings in cash outflows for income taxes. The tax effect may occur in a period different from the preceding items. For example, the tax-reducing effect of deducting cost of goods manufactured and sold occurs for the period of sale, which generally follows the period of cash outflow to purchase raw materials and manufacture the goods.
8. Savings in taxes caused by deductibility of depreciation on tax return (sometimes called ''depreciation tax shield'')—inflow.
9. Loss in tax savings from lost depreciation, if any—outflow. Conversely, any gain in tax savings from additional depreciation deductions on the tax return is an inflow.
10. Do *not* count noncash items such as financial accounting depreciation expense or allocated items of overhead not requiring differential cash expenditures.

Terminal Cash Flows

1. Proceeds of salvage of equipment—inflow.
2. Tax on gain (or loss) on disposal, if any—outflow (or inflow).

---

[1] As this book goes to press, the U. S. income tax rules do not provide for an investment tax credit, but the rules have granted such credit at various times, in varying amounts, over the past several decades.

The Cost of Capital—An Opportunity Cost

Financial economics suggests that the discount rate appropriate for use in evaluating investment projects of average risk is the firm's cost of capital. The cost of capital (or the normal rate of return or the hurdle rate) is the opportunity cost of funds. The **opportunity cost of capital** used for an investment is the income the owner could have earned if the owner invested the funds elsewhere. The term **cost of capital** means the minimum rate of return required by the owner of an asset to justify using it.

Measuring the Cost of Capital

Often, firms measure the cost of capital by computing the cost of all of the liabilities and owners' equity on the balance sheet. All of a corporation's funds raised from various sources finance all its assets. When financial markets are in equilibrium, one can compute the rates of return required on the assets from the cost of raising the funds used to acquire assets. Measuring the cost of capital as the weighted average of the sources of funds is often useful, but it confuses some people into thinking that the average cost of liabilities and owners' equity is the cost of capital. It is not; the cost of capital is the **required rate of return** on the assets themselves.

Cost of capital is a notion about assets; the measurement just described concerns liabilities and other equities. Take an extreme example to cement this concept.[2] Suppose that we have $10,000 cash to invest. Assume that the highest risk-free interest that we can earn from using that cash fixes the required rate of return on that asset. If this rate is 9 percent per year, then the cost of capital for projects of such risk is 9 percent per year. Notice that the derivation of the required rate of return, the cost of capital, does not require knowing how we raised the asset, $10,000 cash. If we earned the $10,000 by hard physical labor, or won it in a lottery, or even found it in the street, its cost of capital is 9 percent. No matter the origin of the funds, the cost of capital—the rate of return required on the asset cash—is 9 percent. Note that the cost of capital does not depend on the source of funds used to acquire those assets. It does depend on the risk characteristics of the alternative investments: the riskier the project, the higher the cost of capital for the assets used to carry out the project.[3]

---

[2]Professor Ezra Solomon of Stanford University, to our knowledge, first suggested this example.

[3]Because we separate the investment and financing decisions, we expect each investment project (with risk equal to the average for the firm) to earn a rate of return equal to at least the *average* cost of capital for the firm.

Assume that the market value of a firm's shares is the present value of the net cash flows to be earned by the firm. Corporate finance texts provide insight into why this assumption is generally valid. See, for example, J. Fred Weston and Eugene F. Brigham, *Essentials of Managerial Finance,* 9th ed. (Hinsdale, Ill.: The Dryden Press, 1990) or J. Fred Weston and Thomas E. Copeland, *Managerial Finance,* 8th ed. (Hinsdale, Ill.: The Dryden Press, 1989). If an investment project earns just the cost of capital (that is, the project has a zero net present value), the market value of the firm's shares will remain unchanged as a result of it. If a project has a positive net present value, the market value of the firm's shares should increase when the firm undertakes that project. The shares increase in value because the firm is able to generate a higher rate of return than the average rate required by the suppliers of capital. Because the returns to creditors and preferred shareholders are fixed, this excess return accrues to the benefit of the common shareholders.

One may choose to *measure* the cost of capital by looking at the cost of liabilities and owners' equity, but one should not confuse that measure of the cost of capital with the actual cost of capital, which is the rate of return required on assets of comparable risk.

Sensitivity of Net Present Value to Estimates

The calculation of the net present value of a proposed project requires three types of projections or estimates:

1. The amount of future cash flows.
2. The timing of future cash flows.
3. The cost of capital rate.

Some error is likely in the amount predicted or estimated for each of these three items. The net present value model exhibits different degrees of sensitivity to such errors.

Amounts of Future Cash Flows

Errors in predicting the amounts of future cash flows will likely have the largest impact of the three items. Exhibit 9.2 indicated that the proposed project for JEP Realty had a net present value (using the straight-line depreciation method) of $2,208 based on the cash flows initially predicted. Suppose that these predictions err by 10 percent and that the estimate of future cash flows (excluding the initial $100,000 outlay) each year should have been 10 percent less than the amounts appearing in column (8) of Exhibit 9.2. The net present value of the proposed project using the same 12 percent discount rate is a negative $8,013.[4] The total error in present value dollars is $10,221 (= $2,208 + $8,013), which is about 10 percent of the initial investment of $100,000. Given the sensitivity of the net present value to errors in the projections of cash flows, the manager will want accurate projections. Statistical techniques have recently been developed for dealing with the uncertainty inherent in predictions of cash flows.[5]

Timing of Future Cash Flows

The degree of sensitivity of the net present value model to shifts in the pattern, but not in the total amount, of cash flows depends on the extent of the shifting. Column (8) of Exhibit 9.2 shows net cash flows for Years 1 through 5 of $38,000, $32,000, $26,000, $23,000, and $17,000, or $136,000 in total, assuming the straight-line depreciation method. Suppose that the pattern of cash flows will be relatively stable, as follows: $28,000, $27,000, $27,000, $27,000, again totaling $136,000.

---

[4]Note that $(100,000) + .90 × [$33,929 + $25,510 + $18,506 + $14,617 + $9,646] = $(8,013).

[5]Interested readers might consult the following book for additional discussion of capital budgeting under uncertainty: Harold Bierman, Jr., and Seymour Smidt, *The Capital Budgeting Decision,* 7th ed. (New York: Macmillan, 1988). See also the computer spreadsheet add-on program, At Risk.

Then, net present value will be *minus* $1,778, as compared to $2,208 in Exhibit 9.2.[6] The error is $3,986 (= $2,208 + $1,778) in present value terms, or about 4 percent of the initial investment. We could construct other examples that would result in a different percentage effect. Errors in predicting the amount of cash flows tend to be more serious than in predicting their pattern.

Calculation of Cost of Capital

A third uncertain factor in the net present value calculation is the cost of capital. The difficulty here lies not in predicting a future cash flow but in estimating returns to alternative uses of capital. Financial economists have not yet developed foolproof techniques for empirically verifying a firm's estimate of its cost of capital rate.

What loss does a firm suffer if it incorrectly calculates its cost of capital? Using the 12 percent aftertax cost of capital for JEP Realty in Exhibit 9.2 results in a net present value of $3,104 for the proposed project using ACRS depreciation. If the after tax cost of capital is 15 percent, the net present value of this project is about minus $3,047. Management miscalculated the cost of capital by one-fourth [= (.15 − .12)/.12]. That large error resulted in a faulty estimate of the net present value by about $6,151 (= $3,104 + $3,047), or about 6 percent of the initial investment. In general, if a project appears marginally desirable for a given cost of capital, it will ordinarily not be grossly undesirable for slightly higher rates. If a project is clearly worthwhile when the cost of capital is 12 percent, for example, it is likely to be worthwhile even when the cost of capital is 15 or 18 percent.

Using Spreadsheet Features to Deal with Uncertain Estimates

Personal computer spreadsheet programs, such as Lotus 1-2-3 and Microsoft Excel, have become the preferred tool for analysts carrying out DCF computations. Refer to rows 1 through 5 of Exhibit 9.2. Note that although the numbers differ from one row to the next, the formulas for each of the numbers in a given column, except column (5), are the same for each row. In fact, the notes at the foot of the exhibit give those formulas. The personal computer spreadsheets allow the analyst to replicate the computations required to derive the periodic cash flows from repetitive computational structures. The analyst will write the formulas once, for row 1, say, and then with a few key strokes, copy the structure of those formulas to rows 2 through 5.

An even more useful feature of the spreadsheet programs helps the user see the effect on the net present value of changes in assumptions and estimates. Thoughtful design of a computer spreadsheet enables the user to change assumptions (such as for growth rates in sales, tax rates, discount rates) with a few key strokes. The net present value changes as the assumptions change and the process takes only a few seconds. This method is the best way to study the sensitivity of DCF analyses to assumptions.

Exhibit 9.7 accompanying Problem 2 for Self-Study at the end of this chapter shows part of a computer spreadsheet for a complex DCF analysis.

---

[6]$(100,000) + [$28,000 × .89286] + [$27,000 × .79719] + [$27,000 × .71178] + [$27,000 × .63552] + [$27,000 × .56743] = $(1,778).

Managerial Application

Investing in Improved Technology

Boston Metal Products, a small manufacturer in Medford, Massachusetts, considered buying a robot. The company controller calculated whether the $200,000 investment made financial sense. The controller found that "[I]t didn't even come close. It was hard to scrape together enough to convince us it was a reasonable risk, let alone a positive investment. There was no way an M.B.A. would have justified it."[a]

The company bought the robot anyway, because the president wanted to inject new technology into the company's manufacturing operations. According to company management, "the robot's prowess in welding has speeded up deliveries, allowing the company's sales of steel shelving for supermarket refrigerators to grow fourfold in three years. The investment has paid off. What standard accounting procedures failed to see were some of the intangibles in such an investment—improved quality, greater flexibility, and lower inventories."[b]

Many apparently worthwhile investments in improved technology do not show a positive net value when an investment analysis is performed. Technological innovations usually have a high investment outlay and a long time period before cash flows are returned from the project. It is not unusual for an investment in automated equipment to take two or three years (or more) before it is fully operational. In companies with high discount rates, cash flows received or cash savings several years in the future have low present values. Further, as noted in the Boston Metal Products example, technological improvements usually provide benefits that are not easily quantified, so they are often omitted from the analysis.

[a]From *The New York Times,* Business Section, Tuesday, October 14, 1986, p. 1.
[b]*New York Times,* October 14, 1986, p. 1.

Complications in Computing Periodic Cash Flows

Previous sections have described and illustrated the steps for using the net present value method. In practice, decision makers sometimes have difficulty computing the periodic after-tax cash flows. Some of the difficulty results from confusion between accounting data and cash flow data. Other difficulty stems from an inability to identify the differential cash flows. This section describes and illustrates a number of such potential difficulties. Problem 2 for Self-Study at the end of the chapter contains a comprehensive example.

New Asset Acquisition: Deriving the Net Proceeds When the Firm Retires Assets

Often, when a firm undertakes a new investment, it already owns a product line which it must, or can, discontinue and already owns assets which it can sell or retire. Treating the proceeds from selling off such assets requires clear thinking. These cases represent **mutually exclusive investments** because selecting any one alternative precludes selecting all others. The best strategy to deal with this potential confusion constructs a series of mutually exclusive investment alternatives, evaluates each, and chooses the best.

Example   A kitchen appliance manufacturer currently makes food blenders. The manufacturer is considering producing a more versatile and complex food processor. If the manufacturer continues to make and sell blenders, the existing product line of blenders will generate net cash flows of $200,000 at the end of each of the next 10 years. The firm can sell today the currently owned blender equipment for $1,000,000. This equipment will last 10 more years; by then it will have no salvage value. New equipment for manufacturing food processors will cost $5,000,000 but will generate net cash flows of $900,000 at the end of each of the next 15 years. After 15 years, it will have no salvage value. Ignore tax considerations. The two cases that follow illustrate the construction of the mutually exclusive alternatives.

Case A   If the firm markets food processors, it will have no further market for blenders. Although you can find the right answer in several ways, you can easily err if you try to combine the cash flow implications of the various strategies. The three mutually exclusive alternatives and their cash flows are as follows:

1.   Sell the existing blender equipment and get out of the business. This implies cash flow $1,000,000 today, a net present value of $1,000,000 at any discount rate.

2.   Stay in the blender business. This implies net cash flows of $200,000 at the end of each of the next 10 years.

3.   Sell the blender equipment and purchase the processor equipment. This implies cash flow of $(4,000,000) [= $(5,000,000) for new + $1,000,000 from selling old] today and $900,000 at the end of each of the next 15 years.

Using the cost of capital, one computes three net present values and chooses the alternative with the largest one. If alternative 1 is not a realistic alternative, ignore it.

Case B   The manufacturer has the alternative of keeping the blender business while adding the processor business. For simplicity, however, we assume that the net cash flow for the first 10 years is $1,050,000 if the firm markets both blenders and processors. In this case, a fourth mutually exclusive project results:

4.   Stay in the blender business and add the processor business. This implies cash flow of ($5,000,000) today, $1,050,000 per year at the end of the next 10 years, and $900,000 per year at the end of the following 5 years.

Disposal of Currently Owned Assets: Sale or Trade-in

Much of the impact on after-tax cash flows results from the effect of income taxes. If a taxpayer sells an asset below its taxable basis (book value for tax purposes), the taxpayer can offset the loss against other taxable income, reducing taxes otherwise payable.

Special rules apply to trade-in transactions. Assume the taxpayer trades in the old equipment on the new. The taxpayer may not deduct from currently taxable income the amount of the loss, but will increase the tax basis of the new asset by the amount of the loss. The increase in tax basis results in higher income tax depreciation deductions over the life of the new asset, reducing taxes payable in those later years. The present value of those future tax deductions is generally less than the present value of taking the loss today.

Example   The firm currently owns blender equipment which the firm can sell for $1,000,000. The equipment has a taxable basis of $3,000,000. The income tax rate is 40 percent of pretax income and the manufacturer has sufficient other taxable income to offset losses or depreciation or both on equipment transactions. The owner can sell the old equipment for $1,000,000 cash or trade it in on the new equipment. The seller has offered a trade-in allowance of $1,200,000 toward the purchase price of $5,000,000.

If the manufacturer sells the equipment for $1,000,000 cash, it will have a tax loss of $2,000,000 (= $3,000,000 basis − $1,000,000 proceeds of sale) to deduct on the current tax return. This loss results in cash savings of $800,000 (= .40 × $2,000,000) from reduced income taxes otherwise payable. Then the manufacturer will have to pay $5,000,000 cash for the equipment, and the depreciable basis for taxes will be $5,000,000. The total cash outflow is $3,200,000 (= $1,000,000 + $800,000 − $5,000,000).

If, on the other hand, the manufacturer trades in the old equipment on the new, the initial cash outflow will be $3,800,000 (= $5,000,000 − $1,200,000). The journal entry to record the new equipment for tax purposes will be as follows:

Equipment—New...	6,800,000	
Equipment—Old (Net)		3,000,000
Cash...		3,800,000

No gain or loss recognized on trade-in; the tax basis of the new asset is equal to the cash paid for it plus the tax basis of the old asset traded in. (The journal entry for financial reporting may differ from this.)

The depreciable basis of the new asset exceeds its $5,000,000 cost by the $1,800,000. That amount represents the loss arising from trading in an asset for $1,200,000 when it has a book value of $3,000,000. In this case, the analyst must consider two mutually exclusive projects:

1. *Sell outright*. Initial cash outlay of $3,200,000 (= $5,000,000 for equipment reduced by $1,000,000 proceeds of sale and $800,000 in tax savings) followed by depreciation charges (reducing income taxes in later years) based on an asset with a tax basis of $5,000,000.

2. *Trade-in*. Initial cash outlay of $3,800,000 followed by depreciation charges (reducing income taxes in later years) based on an asset with a tax basis of $6,800,000.

Another way to view this choice is to ask if one should pay $600,000 (= $3,800,000 − $3,200,000) today in return for an extra $1,800,000 (= $6,800,000 − $5,000,000) in depreciation deductions over the life of the asset. The depreciation deductions of $1,800,000 will total $720,000 (= .40 × $1,800,000) in cash savings for income taxes otherwise payable over the depreciable life of the equipment. A net present value analysis will show whether paying $600,000 now for $720,000 received in the future is worthwhile.

Depreciation and Cash Flow

Depreciation expense reduces income, but does not use cash. The cash effects occur in the year the owner acquires the asset. Depreciation itself does not affect cash flows for net present value analysis. Insofar as depreciation is deductible on the tax return, however, it shields otherwise taxable income from taxation. The analyst must be careful to focus on the tax shield provided by depreciation while recognizing that depreciation itself does not affect cash.

Example   A firm will depreciate an automobile costing $15,000 over 5 years using the straight-line method for financial reporting. On the tax return, the firm will depreciate the automobile over 5 years using ACRS: 20 percent in the first year, 32 percent in the second, 19 percent in the third, 14.5 percent in the fourth, and 14.5 percent in the fifth. The firm's current and expected future combined federal and state income tax rate is 40 percent of taxable income. The company has sufficient other taxable income that the depreciation deductions can reduce taxable income dollar for dollar. The cash flows relevant for a net present value analysis are ($15,000) today followed by $1,200 (= $15,000 × .20 × .40) tax saving at the end of the first year, $1,920 (= $15,000 × .32 × .40) at the end of the second year, $1,140 (= $15,000 × .19 × .40) at the end of the third year, and so on. (Of course, the automobile must produce other positive cash inflows or savings in outflows to be worthwhile.)

Salvage Value of Equipment

When a firm acquires an asset for a specific project, the asset's cost will be a cash outflow at the start of the project. At the end of the project, the firm will scrap or sell the asset or possible convert it to another use. The firm must include in the DCF analysis the cash flow impact of the disposal and any tax implications thereof. Typically, that cash flow occurs in the last period.

Example   The firm expects the food-processing equipment described earlier to have a fair market value of $400,000 at the end of the 15-year period of production of food processors. At that time, the manufacturer plans to sell the equipment to a distributor of spare parts. The DCF analysis should increase the cash flows for the fifteenth year by $400,000. (Tax consequences may affect the calculation.)

Impact on Working Capital

Ordinarily, when a firm starts a new business, it expects to tie up cash in inventories, accounts receivable, and bank accounts. Eventually it sells these inventories for cash, collects the accounts receivable, and uses the cash. Cash flows out in the early periods but flows back in the later periods. The cash spent to acquire inventories, the cash not immediately received from customers who purchase on account, and the ultimate cash flow require no special treatment. The analyst needs to show all cash outlays in the period when they occur and all cash inflows in the period collected, which may differ from the period of sale.[7]

Effects of Inflation on the Cost of Capital and Cash Flows

Cost of Capital   The cost of capital or discount rate used in computing net present values reflects, at least in part, current market interest rates. Recall that the cost of capital is an opportunity cost, and one alternative opportunity available to all investors is the purchase of relatively risk-free bonds issued by the federal government and by some low-risk corporations. Market interest rates, a factor determining the cost of capital, reflect three separate phenomena:

1. A *pure* or *real* rate of interest reflecting the productive capability of capital assets. (Economists debate the results of empirical research, but most would agree that the pure rate of interest generally lies between 0 and 5 percent per year.)

2. A risk factor reflecting the likelihood of default of the particular borrower. (The federal government has the lowest probability of default, so government bonds usually have the lowest risk premiums.)

3. A premium reflecting inflation expected to occur over the life of the loan. (A lender lends out dollars with a particular purchasing power and receives at maturity dollars with a smaller purchasing power if inflation has occurred during the loan term. As the expected rate of inflation increases, the lender will charge a higher interest rate to compensate for the correspondingly larger expected decline in the purchasing power of the dollars lent.)

If the pure rate of interest is p, the risk premium is r, and the expected inflation is e, then the market rate of interest i satisfies the following equations:

$$(1 + i) = (1 + p)(1 + r)(1 + e),$$

or

$$i = (1 + p)(1 + r)(1 + e) - 1.$$

The market rate is sometimes called the *nominal* rate.

---

[7]Some textbooks on managerial finance, in treating the subject of working capital requirements for investments projects, show explicit investments in working capital at the start of the project and a specific recovery of it sometime later. This special treatment of the investment in working capital is more likely to confuse than to help. Why should DCF analysis treat this particular investment differently from any other? We prefer to show all cash inflows and outflows in parallel, not treating any of them differently from the others. The important point is, in constructing a dated schedule of cash flows (for example, for sales), to use the time of collection of cash from a sale, not the time of the sale.

Example   Assume a pure rate of interest of 3 percent, a risk premium for the IBM Corporation of 2 percent, and an expected rate of inflation for the next year of 5 percent. The market rate of interest i for IBM is

$$i = (1.03)(1.02)(1.05) - 1$$

$$\cong .103 \text{ or } 10.3 \text{ percent.}$$

Effect of Inflation on Cash Flows   In times of expected general inflation, interest rates exceed those in times of lower expected general inflation. High costs of capital, other things being equal, reflect high expected inflation.[8] Decision makers using market interest for net present value computations, are reflecting anticipated inflation in the discounting process. Such decision makers would be inconsistent if they did not also reflect the effects of anticipated future inflation on cash flows.

Consider the following points in carrying out a capital budgeting analysis:

1.   If forecasts of future cash flows involve nominal (that is, actual) dollar amounts, discount nominal dollar cash flows at a rate that includes anticipated inflation. If forecasts involve real dollar cash flows, discount using a rate that excludes anticipated inflation.

2.   If you expect general inflation, but no change in relative prices, you need not forecast anticipated inflation. Discounting of real cash flows will provide correct results. If you expect relative prices to change significantly and you can forecast these relative changes, then forecast nominal dollars and discount rate with a nominal cost of capital.

3.   Because you compute the depreciation tax shield from the acquisition cost of the equipment, its amount is fixed, even when you anticipate inflation in the nominal cash flows. The value, but not the amount, of the depreciation shield will fall as anticipated inflation increases.

4.   If you anticipate significant inflation, you may need larger amounts of cash to provide working capital.

Example   An owner of a plot of land zoned for commercial use considers renting the land to the operator of a supermarket. Rental payments to the owner will be based on a percentage of retail sales. Analysis projects that, given the traffic patterns in the area, 4,000 families per week will do their shopping in this store. Because of competing stores in nearby neighborhoods and the lack of room for further real estate development in the market area of the proposed supermarket, the owner is fairly sure that the number of families using the store will not change substantially over time. The owner's after-tax cost of capital is 15 percent per year. The owner can easily estimate the rental payments for the first year.

Given an estimate that the number of families shopping will not increase over time, the analyst might project level cash flows for the 10-year proposed lease term. Assume, for example, that the rental terms propose a payment by the supermarket

---

[8]Compare, for example, the rate of interest and rates of inflation in the early 1980s to those of the late 1980s.

to the lessor of $100,000 at the end of the first year. If the owner projects rental payments of $100,000 each year for 10 years and discounts them at 15 percent per year, the present value of the cash flows is $501,877 (= $100,000 × 5.01877; see Table 4 at the back of the book, 10-period row, 15 percent column). An after-tax cost of capital of 15 percent per year is so high for projects of this risk that the cost of capital appears to anticipate substantial general inflation over the life of the lease. To be consistent, the analysis should anticipate that such inflation will also increase disposable incomes of shoppers and prices of the merchandise they purchase in the store.

Thus, careful analysis will probably project price increases for the items sold in the stores, in the net sales of the store, and in the rental revenues to the owner. If, for example, sales prices increase at the rate of 6 percent per year, the stream of rental payments will be $106,000 (= $100,000 × 1.06) at the end of the first year, $112,360 (= $100,000 × 1.06^2) at the end of the second year, . . . , $179,085 (= $100,000 × 1.06^{10}) at the end of the tenth year. The net present value of that stream of payments discounted at 15 percent per year is $656,411.[9] This figure is almost one-third larger than the net present value assuming no increase in selling price and rentals.

■ Summary ■

In deciding whether to invest cash today in return for cash payoffs in the future, the decision maker should take into account the time value of money using a discounted cash flow (DCF) method.

The net present value method involves making forecasts of future cash inflows and outflows for the proposed project. Making effective investment decisions requires careful analysis of accounting data to derive cash flows, which do not equal revenues less expenses in any given period. The DCF analysis discounts estimated cash flows to present value with a rate equal to the required rate of return on assets. The required rate of return is the cost of capital or the hurdle rate. Analysts often measure the cost of capital by taking a weighted average of the equities that provide a firm's financing, even though the cost of capital reflects the opportunity cost of the assets to be committed to the proposed project.

Problem 1 for Self-Study

Kary Kinnard has an opportunity to open a franchised pizza outlet. He can lease the building, so he needs to invest only in equipment, which he estimates will cost $60,000. He will depreciate the equipment over 6 years using ACRS percentages of

---

[9]Note that

$$\sum_{i=1}^{10} \frac{\$100,000 \times (1.06)^i}{(1.15)^i} = \sum_{i=1}^{10} \frac{\$100,000}{(1.15/1.06)^i}$$

Because 1.15/1.06 − 1 = 8.49 percent (rounded), the computation is equivalent to computing the present value of a level annuity of $100,000 per year discounted at 8.49 percent per year.

20, 32, 19.2, 11.5, 11.5, and 5.8. For financial reporting, he will depreciate the equipment over 6 years using the straight-line method. For purposes of this analysis, assume the equipment will last for 6 years, after which Kinnard will sell it for $6,000. He will pay taxes at 40 percent on the taxable gain on the disposal at the end of Year 6.

Kinnard estimates the following revenues, variable costs, and fixed costs from operations for the 6-year period. He has included expected inflation in these estimates. Assume end-of-year cash flows.

	1	2	3	4	5	6
Revenues.............	$30,000	$36,000	$41,000	$45,000	$48,000	$50,000
Variable Costs	12,000	14,400	16,400	18,000	19,200	20,000
Fixed Costs (includes depreciation of $10,000 per year) ...	15,000	15,200	15,500	15,900	16,400	17,000

Use an after-tax cost of capital of 12 percent per year and an income tax rate of 40 percent for this analysis. The $60,000 outlay for the equipment will be made at the beginning of Year 1.

Should Kinnard make the investment?

Suggested Solution

Depreciation Schedule; ACRS Basis Is $60,000

Year	Rate	Depreciation
1	.200	$12,000
2	.320	19,200
3	.192	11,520
4	.115	6,900
5	.115	6,900
6	.058	3,480
		$60,000

See Exhibit 9.3 (page 416) for cash flow analysis. Kinnard should undertake the project, because it has positive net present value.

Problem 2 for Self-Study

This comprehensive problem illustrates the analysis of accounting data to derive cash flows for an investment decision and the choice among mutually exclusive alternatives. The last section of the answer to this problem presents a computer spreadsheet application.

Exhibit 9.3

Operating Cash Flow Analysis (Problem 1 for Self-Study)						
	1	2	3	4	5	6
Cash Inflows	$30,000	$36,000	$41,000	$45,000	$48,000	$50,000
Less Variable Costs Cash Outflows	12,000	14,400	16,400	18,000	19,200	20,000
Less Fixed Cost Cash Outflows	5,000	5,200	5,500	5,900	6,400	7,000
(1) Cash Flow before Taxes and Depreciation	$13,000	$16,400	$19,100	$21,100	$22,400	$23,000
Depreciation (ACRS)	12,000	19,200	11,520	6,900	6,900	3,480
Taxable Income	$ 1,000	$(2,800)	$ 7,580	$14,200	$15,500	$19,520
(2) Tax (40% rate)	400	(1,120)	3,032	5,680	6,200	7,808
(3) Cash Flows from Operations = (1) − (2)	12,600	17,520	16,068	15,420	16,200	15,192
(4) Present Value Factors (12%)	.89286	.79719	.71178	.63552	.56743	.50663
Present Value .... $63,343 =	$11,250	$13,967	$11,437	$ 9,800	$ 9,192	$ 7,697

	Present Value at Beginning of Year 1
Analysis of All Cash Flows	
Operating Cash Flows	$ 63,343
Cash Outlay for Machinery	(60,000)
Salvage Proceeds from Selling Machinery—Year 6, $6,000 × .50663	3,040
Taxes on Gain of $6,000 (= $6,000 Proceeds − $0 Tax Basis); Year 6, $6,000 × .40 × .50663	(1,216)
Net Present Value	$ 5,167

Problem Data

Magee Company considers undertaking a new product line. If it does so, it must acquire new equipment with a purchase price of $150,000 at the beginning of Year 1. The equipment will last for 5 years and Magee expects to sell it at the end of the fifth year for its salvage value of $2,500 if there is no inflation. Magee forecasts equipment prices, including prices of used equipment of this sort, to rise at an annual rate of 12 percent, so the actual salvage expected to be realized at the end of the fifth year is $4,406 (= $2,500 × 1.12^5). Magee will pay taxes on any gain on disposal at 40 percent at the end of Year 6.

Magee Company owns old manufacturing equipment with a book value of $18,000 that it must retire, independent of whether it acquires the new machine. Magee can sell the old equipment for $25,000 cash or trade it in on the new equipment for a reduction of $28,000 in cash purchase price. If Magee sells the old equipment, it will pay taxes at the rate of 40 percent on the gain of $7,000 (= $25,000 − $18,000) at the end of Year 1. If Magee trades in the old equipment, the "gain," not taxed at trade in, will reduce the depreciable basis of the new asset (and future depreciation charges) both for financial accounting and for tax purposes. If Magee trades in the old equipment, paying cash of $122,000 (= $150,000 − $28,000), the journal entry will be as follows:

New Equipment...	140,000	
Old Equipment (Net)		18,000
Cash		122,000

Book value of new equipment is $140,000 for both tax and financial reporting.

Magee will depreciate any new equipment over 5 years for tax purposes using the following ACRS cost percentages: 20, 32, 19, 14.5, and 14.5.

Salvage value does not affect ACRS deductions for tax purposes but does affect financial reporting purposes. Magee will depreciate the equipment for financial reporting over 5 years using the straight-line method. (These combinations result from the rules of generally accepted accounting principles and the income tax law, not from our wish to make the example complicated.)

Magee makes the following forecasts and projections:

1. Sales volume will be 15,000 units each year.

2. Sales price will be $7.00 per unit during Year 1, but will increase by 10 percent per year, to $7.70 in Year 2, $8.47 in Year 3, and so on.

3. Variable manufacturing costs are $3.00 per unit in Year 1, but will increase by 8 percent per year, to $3.24 in Year 2, and so on.

4. Selling costs are $5,000 per year plus $.50 per unit in Year 1. Variable selling costs per unit will increase by 10 percent per year to $.55 in Year 2, $.61 in Year 3, and so on.

5. Income tax rates will remain at 40 percent of taxable income each year.

6. The after-tax cost of capital is 15 percent per year.

Magee makes the following assumptions about the timing of cash flows:

7. It will pay all variable manufacturing costs in cash at the beginning of each year.

8. It will pay all selling costs, fixed and variable, in cash at the end of each year.

9. It will collect cash from customers at the end of each year.

10. It will pay income taxes for each year's operations at the end of the year.

Magee makes the following assumptions about its operations and accounting:

11. Although it may deduct selling costs on the tax return in the year incurred, it may not deduct manufacturing costs until it sells the goods.

12. It will have sufficient other taxable income that losses on this project in any period will offset that income, saving $.40 in income taxes for every $1.00 of operating loss.

13. It must produce enough each year to meet each year's sales, except that it must product 20,000 units in Year 1 to provide a continuing supply of inventory of 5,000 units. It need produce only 10,000 units in Year 5, so that ending inventory will be zero.

14. It will use a LIFO cost flow assumption for inventories.

15. It will charge all depreciation for a year to the cost of units it produces that year.

a. List the mutually exclusive alternatives that Magee Company faces.

b. Construct a schedule of cash flows for the alternative of trading in the old equipment on the new.

c. Explain why the trade-in alternative in part **b** must dominate the alternative of selling outright the old equipment and purchasing the new.

d. Analyze the alternatives and suggest a decision to management of Magee Company.

e. Prepare income statements for Years 1 through 5, assuming the treatment in part **b**. Explain the causes of the differences between net income and net cash flow for each year.

f. Consider the alternative of trading in the old asset on the new. Compare the sum of the net incomes over the 5 years of the project to the sum of the cash flows over the same 5 years. Note that the sum of the incomes is less than the sum of the cash flows by $18,000, exactly equal to the book value of the old asset traded in on the new. Is this relation a coincidence? Comment.

Suggested Solution

a.   **Alternatives**
   (1)   Sell the old equipment and do not acquire the new.
   (2)   Trade in the old equipment on the new equipment.
   (3)   Sell the old equipment and purchase the new.
   Note that this problem does not have an alternative to retain the old equipment and continue using it, which would be possible in many situations.

b.   **Trade in Old Asset on New Asset**   Exhibits 9.4 and 9.5 consider the case of trading in the old equipment on the new. Exhibit 9.4 derives the operating cash flows, including income tax effects. Exhibit 9.5, discussed later, combines operating and nonoperating cash flows. The calculations for the various lines of Exhibit 9.4 follow:

Line (1)   Magee sells 15,000 units each year and produces those amounts each year except in Year 1, when production is 20,000, or 5,000 units more than sales, and in Year 5, when production is 10,000, or 5,000 units fewer.

Line (2)   Variable cost per unit is $3.00 for Year 1 and $3.24 for Year 2 and increases at the rate of 8 percent per year thereafter to $3.50 in Year 3, $3.78 in Year 4, and $4.08 in Year 5.

Line (3)   Total variable costs result from multiplying line **(1)** by line **(2)**. Magee pays this amount in cash at the beginning of the year, so transfers it to line **(17)** as a cash outflow at the beginning of each year.

Exhibit 9.4

MAGEE COMPANY
Analysis of Cash Flow Data by Year[a]
(Part b of Problem 2 for Self-Study)

		1	2	3	4	5
Production and Selling Costs during Year						
(1)[a]	Number of Units Produced	20,000	15,000	15,000	15,000	10,000
(2)	Variable Manufacturing Cost per Unit......	$ 3.00	$ 3.24	$ 3.50	$ 3.78	$ 4.08
(3)	Total Variable Costs (at the beginning of year) = (1) × (2)....................	$ 60,000	$ 48,600	$ 52,500	$ 56,700	$ 40,800
(4)	Depreciation Charge for Year for Taxes ...	28,000	44,800	26,600	20,300	20,300
(5)	Total Manufacturing Costs for Taxes = (3) + (4)	$ 88,000	$ 93,400	$ 79,100	$ 77,000	$ 61,100
(6)	Manufacturing Cost per Unit for Taxes = (5)/(1)	$ 4.40	$ 6.23	$ 5.27	$ 5.13	$ 6.11
(7)	Variable Selling Cost per Unit	$ .50	$ .55	$ .61	$ .67	$ .73
Revenues, End of Year						
(8)	Number of Units Sold	15,000	15,000	15,000	15,000	15,000
(9)	Selling Price per Unit....................	$ 7.00	$ 7.70	$ 8.47	$ 9.32	$ 10.25
(10)	Total Revenues = (8) × (9)..............	$105,000	$115,500	$127,050	$139,800	$153,750
Tax Return for Year						
(11)	Revenues = (10).........................	$105,000	$115,500	$127,050	$139,800	$153,750
(12)	Less Manufacturing Costs of Sales	66,000	93,400	79,100	77,000	83,100
(13)	Less Selling Expenses	12,500	13,250	14,150	15,050	15,950
(14)	Taxable Income = (11) − (12) − (13)	$ 26,500	$ 8,850	$ 33,800	$ 47,750	$ 54,700
(15)	Income Taxes Payable = .40 × (14).......	$ 10,600	$ 3,540	$ 13,520	$ 19,100	$ 21,880

Cash Flow at:							
End of Year	0	1	2	3	4	5	
Beginning of Year	1	2	3	4	5	6	
(16) Revenues = (10).........................	—	105,000	$115,500	$127,050	$139,800	$153,750	
(17) Less Variable Costs = (3)	$ 60,000	48,600	52,500	56,700	40,800	—	
(18) Less Selling Expenses = (13), Lagged	—	12,500	13,250	14,150	15,050	15,950	
(19) Less Income Taxes for Year = (15), Lagged	—	10,600	3,540	13,520	19,100	21,880	
(20) Net Cash Inflow (Outflow) = (16) − (17) − (18) − (19)	$(60,000)	$ 33,300	$ 46,210	$ 42,680	$ 64,850	$115,920	
(21) Present Value at 15 Percent = $126,672...........................	$(60,000)	$ 28,957	$ 34,941	$ 28,063	$ 37,078	$ 57,633	

[a]See text for discussion of line-by-line derivation.

Exhibit 9.5

MAGEE COMPANY
Analysis of All Cash Flows from Trading in Old Equipment on New Equipment for Project
(Parts b and f of Problem 2 for Self-Study)

	Present Value at Beginning of Year 1	Undiscounted Cash Flows
Operating Cash Flows (Exhibit 9.4)	$126,672	$242,960
Cash Outlay for Equipment at Beginning of Year 1 ($150,000 cost − $28,000 trade-in)	(122,000)	(122,000)
Salvage Proceeds from Selling Equipment at End of Year 5 ($4,406 × .49718).	2,191	4,406
Taxes at 40 Percent on Salvage Proceeds of $4,406 Paid at the End of Year 6 ($4,406 × .40 × .43233)	(762)	(1,762)
Total	$ 6,101	$123,604

Line (4)   Depreciation charge for the year results from multiplying the taxable depreciable basis, $140,000, by the ACRS percentages: 20, 32, 19, 14.5, and 14.5. The financial statement depreciation will be $27,119 [= ($140,000 − $4,406)/5] per year, but this fact is irrelevant for the analysis of cash flows. Tax depreciation is relevant only because of its impact on tax deductible cost of goods sold, which affects taxable income and income tax payments.

Line (5)   Total manufacturing cost is the sum of the preceding two lines.

Line (6)   Manufacturing cost per unit is generally irrelevant for decision making in the absence of taxes. Because, however, inventory builds up in Year 1 for sale in Year 5, and because tax rules require full absorption costing, Magee must compute the full cost of the units put into inventory in Year 1. Any firm must compute such unit costs to derive tax effects whenever production volume differs from sales volume.

Line (7)   Variable selling costs of $.50 per unit per year increase at the rate of 10 percent per year. The figure affects total selling costs later on line **(13)** and cash outflow for selling costs on line **(18).**

Line (8)   Magee has forecast the number of units it will sell.

Line (9)   Selling price per unit increases at the rate of 10 percent per year. (The numbers here result from using this formula: Selling price at the end of Year $t = \$7.00 \times 1.10^{t-1}$. One might multiply each year's price by 1.10 to derive the next year's price. These two procedures do not differ significantly, but because of different rounding conventions, analysts may reach differing numbers by the fifth year.)

Line (10)   Total revenue results from multiplying the preceding two lines. The product appears on line **(11)** for tax purposes and to line **(16)** for cash flow calculations.

Line (11)   See discussion of line **(10).**

Line (12)   Manufacturing cost comes from line **(5)** except for Years 1 and 5. In Year 1, manufacturing cost is the product of manufacturing cost per unit, line **(6)**, times number of units sold, line **(8)**: $4.40 × 15,000 = $66,000. Magee uses a LIFO cost flow assumption. In Year 5, 10,000 units carry Year 5 manufacturing costs and 5,000 units carry Year 1 manufacturing costs: $61,100 + ($4.40 × 5,000) = $83,100.

Line (13)   Selling expenses are variable costs per unit on line **(7)** multiplied by the number of units sold from line **(8)** plus $5,000.

Line (14)   Taxable income is revenues, line **(11)**, minus expenses on lines **(12)** and **(13).**

Line (15)   Income taxes are 40 percent of the amount on line **(14)**. Magee pays the amounts at the end of the year of sale.

Line (16) through (20)   These lines show all cash flows. Be careful to align the timing of the cash flows. Note that the preceding lines show operations for a period. Magee assumes each cash flow occurs at a specific moment. Because the end of one year is also the beginning of the next, we find it convenient to label these moments with both their end-of-year and beginning-of-year designations to aid analysis. Note, for example, how the cash flows for variable manufacturing costs appear in one column, but the revenues from sale of the items produced appear in the next column.

Line (21)   The present values at the beginning of Year 1 result from multiplying the numbers on line **(20)** by the appropriate factor from the 15 percent column in Table 2 at the back of the book. The sum of the numbers on line **(21)** is $126,672.

Analysis of All Cash Flows   Exhibit 9.5 shows all the cash flows, operating and nonoperating, for the trade-in decision with present values at the beginning of Year 1. Magee pays taxes at the end of Year 6 on the salvage proceeds from the end of Year 5. Tax reporting under ACRS ignores salvage value in computing depreciation. The entire depreciable basis of $140,000 becomes deductible through ACRS. Thus, the gain on sale is equal to all the salvage proceeds, $4,406 (= $4,406 − $0).

    The net present value of this project is positive, $6,101. Magee should not undertake it, however, without considering the net present value of its mutually exclusive alternatives.

c.   **Sell Old Equipment and Acquire New for Cash**   The trade-in alternative analyzed in Exhibits 9.4 and 9.5 clearly dominates the alternative of selling the old equipment and acquiring the new equipment for cash. The skeptic would have to construct an analysis such as those found in Exhibits 9.4 and 9.5, with depreciation charges based on $150,000, rather than $140,000 on line **(4)**, plus cash proceeds from selling the equipment outright, offset with taxes (as analyzed in the preceding paragraph). Trade-in is superior, because (1) it leads to immediately reduced cash outflow of $3,000: $28,000 lower cost for the equipment reduced by the $25,000 cash proceeds from selling and (2) Magee must pay immediately the taxes on the gain on sale, but effectively pays the same taxes over the depreciable life of the new equipment.

d. **Selling the Old Equipment**   If Magee sells the old equipment outright, it will receive cash proceeds of $25,000 immediately and realize a taxable gain upon sale of $7,000 (= $25,000 proceeds − $18,000 net book value). It will not pay the taxes of $2,800 (= .40 × $7,000) until the end of Year 1, so the taxes have a net present value of $2,435 (= $2,800 × .86957). Thus the present value of selling the old equipment outright is $22,565 (= $25,000 cash proceeds − $2,435 present value of tax on gain).

The Decision   Selling the old equipment has a net present value of $22,565, whereas trading it on the new has a net present value of only $6,101. The analysis suggests that Magee should sell the old equipment and not acquire the new equipment, but the decision is close. Other factors would probably influence a decision as close as this. Note, for example, that Magee uses an after-tax cost of capital of 15 percent and an income tax rate of 40 percent. Thus the pretax cost of capital is 25 [= .15/(1.00 − .40)] percent. A pretax cost of capital as large as 25 percent incorporates substantial inflation or risk premium, or both, into the analysis.[10] If the undertaking is not particularly risky, the analyst may wonder why inflation on the order of 15 percent is being implicitly assumed for the cost of capital but sales revenues and costs for the project are being forecast to increase at smaller rates.

   If the after-tax cost of capital was sufficiently lower than 15 percent, acquiring the new equipment via trade-in would have an edge over not acquiring it. (Exercise 20 at the end of this chapter requires working through this analysis using an after-tax cost of capital of 12 percent per year to show that the net present value of selling remains about $22,500, whereas that of trading in on the new increases to more than $23,500.)

---

[10]If the pretax costs of capital (interest rate) is 25 percent, the real rate of interest is 3 percent, and the risk premium for a firm is 6 percent, then you can find the implied expected rate of inflation using a transposition of the interest formula discussed in the chapter.
   From

$$1 + i = (1 + p)(1 + r)(1 + e),$$

we derive

$$1 + e = \frac{1 + i}{(1 + p)(1 + r)}$$

or

$$e = \frac{1 + i}{(1 + p)(1 + r)} - 1$$

$$= \frac{1.25}{1.03 \times 1.06} - 1$$

$$= 14.5 \text{ percent.}$$

Because the new equipment does not generate substantial amounts of positive cash flows in the last few years and because the result is not substantially better than selling the old equipment outright, we prefer the outright sale, assuming that is a realistic business alternative. We would not conclude, however, that these data indicate a clear-cut decision either way. Whatever Magee Company does is not likely to be too costly, as compared to the rejected alternative.

e. **Income Statements**   Exhibit 9.6 shows the income statements for each of the 5 years. Lines (22) through (24) derive total manufacturing costs for use in computing costs of goods sold. [Line numbers start with (22) because lines (1) through (21) appear in Exhibit 9.4.]

Line (22)   Variable costs of production appear on line (3) of Exhibit 9.4.

Line (23)   Financial statement depreciation per year, based on the straight-line method, is $140,000 book value less $4,406 estimate of salvage value, divided by 5 years. The last year's amount is $1 smaller to correct for a cumulative rounding error.

Line (24)   Total manufacturing costs are the sum of the preceding two lines.

Line (25)   Revenues appear on line (10) of Exhibit 9.4.

Line (26)   Costs of goods sold comes from line (24) except in Years 1 and 5, when the number of units sold differs from the number produced. In Year 1,

Exhibit 9.6

MAGEE COMPANY Financial Statements[a] (Part e of Problem 2 for Self-Study)					
	1	2	3	4	5
Schedule of Manufacturing Costs for Year					
(22)[a] Variable Costs of Production	$ 60,000	$ 48,600	$ 52,500	$ 56,700	$ 40,800
(23) Depreciation	27,119	27,119	27,119	27,119	27,118
(24) Total Manufacturing Costs = (22) + (23) .	$ 87,119	$ 75,719	$ 79,619	$ 83,819	$ 67,918
Income Statement for Year					
(25) Revenues	$105,000	$115,500	$127,050	$139,800	$153,750
(26) Less Cost of Goods Sold	65,339	75,719	79,619	83,819	89,698
(27) Less Selling Costs	12,500	13,250	14,150	15,050	15,950
(28) Pretax Income = (25) − (26) − (27)	$ 27,161	$ 26,531	$33,281	$ 40,931	$ 48,102
(29) Income Taxes = .40 × (28)	(10,864)	(10,612)	(13,312)	(16,372)	(19,241)
(30) Net Income = (28) − (29)	$ 16,297	$ 15,919	$ 19,969	$ 24,559	$ 28,861

[a]See text for discussion of derivation, line by line. Lines (1) through (21) are in Exhibit 9.4.

costs of goods sold is $87,119 \times 15,000/20,000 = $65,339, because Magee sells only 15,000 of the 20,000 units produced. The remainder of the costs of $21,780 (= $87,119 − $65,339) become inventory (assuming LIFO costs flow) until Year 5. Then, they become manufacturing costs of that year's production to derive costs of goods sold for Year 5: $21,780 + $67,918 = $89,698.

Line (27)   Selling expenses appear on line **(13)** of Exhibit 9.4.

Line (28)   Pretax income is revenues minus cost of goods sold and selling expenses.

Line (29)   This amount differs from income taxes payable because of the financial accounting treatment of timing differences, discussed briefly later and in more detail in financial accounting textbooks.

Line (30)   Net income is pretax income minus income taxes.
    The amounts of income in each year differ from the amounts of cash flow for each year for four reasons:

1.   Expenditures for asset acquisition affects cash flows, whereas depreciation affects financial statement amounts.
2.   The financial statements match revenues and cost of goods sold although the cash expenditure to produce inventory occur in periods different from the collection from its sale.
3.   Income tax expense differs from income taxes payable. Accounting bases financial statement income tax expense on pretax financial statement income, not on taxable income as reported on the tax return. (Whenever the financial statements and the tax return differ in amounts that will eventually reverse, *timing differences* result and accounting bases income tax expense on financial statement pretax income.)
4.   Cash flow from disposal of the asset at the end of its life appears in Exhibit 9.5, but as long as actual salvage value equals estimated salvage value, reported income will not change. If actual salvage value differs from book value at the time of disposal, a gain or loss will occur at that time.

f.   **Net Income**   Net income over the life of the project is the sum of the numbers on line **(30)** of Exhibit 9.6: $16,297 + $15,919 + $19,969 + $24,559 + $28,861 = $105,605. The sum of the cash flows over the life of the project is $123,604, as in the second column of Exhibit 9.5. The difference between these two numbers of $18,000 (= $123,604 − $105,604, rounded) is the $18,000 book value of the old asset traded in on the new. This result is not a coincidence. Over sufficiently long time periods in accounting, income equals cash inflows less cash outflows (except for transactions with owners). Magee had not yet charged $18,000 of cost of the old equipment (its net book value) to income in any period. That cost increased the cost of the new asset, so the sum of depreciation charges for the new asset exceeds by $18,000 the cash expenditure for the new asset. Magee spent $18,000 cash at the time it acquired the old asset. Without the trade-in transactions, the sum of the cash flows would equal the sum of the net incomes.

Personal Computer Spreadsheet Application

The text recommends personal computer spreadsheets such as Lotus 1-2-3 and Microsoft Excel for analyzing DCF problems. The discussion here does not teach spreadsheet use. To learn how to use spreadsheets, you need hands-on experience. We hope this short presentation persuades those who do not already know how to use computer spreadsheets to learn to use them. The exhibit may teach users some new techniques. Exhibit 9.7 shows part of the Lotus 1-2-3 file we used to construct Exhibits 9.4, 9.5, and 9.6. Observe the following:

1. The exhibit shows only part of the spreadsheet for Exhibit 9.4, the assumptions, called parameters, at the top and the calculations at the bottom.

2. Think of a computer spreadsheet as a chess board, a rectangular grid of squares, called cells. Identify a cell with a column letter and a row number. Every item of data or text in a computer spreadsheet appears in a cell. For example, cell D5 contains the number $3.00, and cell B3 contains the caption "Parameter Section."

3. The parameters section gathers in one place all of the assumptions needed for Exhibit 9.4.

4. The calculation section shows the columns for Year 3 and Year 4 in numerical form. We rounded the numbers for Exhibit 9.4.

5. The calculation section shows also a column of formulas. These are the actual formulas appearing in the cells of the spreadsheet. For example, cell C35 contains the formula +C32*C33, not the number $52,488. When the computer multiplies the contents of cell C32 by the contents of cell C33, the number $52,488 results. Cell C35 shows the number. Cell F35 shows the formula as it would appear in column F.

6. The formulas in column F use Lotus 1-2-3 (identical to Excel) notation. We do not explain that notation.

7. The formulas in columns, C, D, and F use the parameter cells. Observe that cell D5 contains the variable manufacturing cost per unit, $3 in our example. If you change cell D5 to $4, then the formula for cells C33 and D33 will automatically use the changed number. To see this, note that the formula in cell F33 shows $D$5, which means that the formula does not use $3 every time the program executes, but uses the contents of cell D5, whatever it may be at the time.

Good spreadsheet technique requires discipline and patience. Someone trying to rush through a solution might, for example, not parameterize cell D5. One could just insert the $3 number for variable manufacturing cost for Year 1 in the formula for cell C33. You can construct the spreadsheet faster this way and it will appear simpler. If you do so, you will be unable to test easily the sensitivity of the final result to the assumption about variable manufacturing cost per unit in Year 1.

Exhibit 9.7

PERSONAL COMPUTER SPREADSHEET EXCERPT
For Exhibit 9.4, Lines (1)–(15): All Parameters and Calculations for Years 3 and 4

	B	C	D	E	F	G
1						
2						
3	Parameter Section					
4						
5	Variable manufacturing cost in Year 1			$3.00	Tax Depreciation	
6	Growth rate in variable manufacturing costs per year			8.0%	Rate by Year	
7	Variable selling cost in Year 1			$0.50		
8	Growth rate in variable selling costs per year			10.0%	Year 1 =	20.0%
9	Fixed selling costs per year			$5,000	Year 2 =	32.0%
10	Selling price per unit in Year 1			$7.00	Year 3 =	19.0%
11	Growth rate in selling price per unit			10.0%	Year 4 =	14.5%
12	Income tax rate			40.0%	Year 5 =	14.5%
13	New asset tax basis (assumes trade in of old asset)			$140,000		
14	Number of units sold each year			15,000		
15	Number of units produced in Year 1			20,000		
16	Number of units produced in Years 2, 3, and 4			15,000		
17	Number of units produced in Year 5			10,000		
18	Discount rate per year			15.0%		
19						
20	Net present value (calculations not shown here)			$126,672		
21						
22						
23						

Note: Body of exhibit is actual output from Lotus 1-2-3 file. This exhibit omits rows for lines (16)–(21) of Exhibit 9.4. The spreadsheet carries all data to several more significant digits than appear here. For example, cell C33 is actually $3.49920 in the computer.

	B	C	D	E	F	G
24						
25	Calculation Section					
26						
27			Calculations		Formulas	
28						
29	Year	3	4		Insert year number as column head	
30						
31	(1) Production and Selling Costs during Year					
32	Number of Units Produced	15,000	15,000		+$D$16	
33	(2) Variable Manufacturing Costs per Unit	$3.50	$3.78		+$D$5*(1+$D$6)^(F29−1)	
34						
35	(3) Total Variable Manufacturing Costs	$52,488	$56,687		+F32*F33	
36	(4) Depreciation Charge for Year for Taxes	26,600	20,300		+$G$9*$D$13	
37						
38	(5) Total Manufacturing Costs for Taxes	$79,088	$76,987		+F35+F36	
39		=======	=======			
40	(6) Manufacturing Costs per Unit for Taxes	$5.27	$5.13		+F38/F32	
41		=======	=======			
42	(7) Variable Selling Costs per Unit	$0.61	$0.67		+$D$7*(1+$D$8)^(F29−1)	
43		=======	=======			
44	Revenues, End of Year					
45	(8) Number of Units Sold	15,000	15,000		+$D$14	
46	(9) Selling Price per Unit	$8.47	$9.32		+$D$10*(1+$D$11)^(F29−1)	
47						
48	(10) Total Revenues	$127,050	$139,755		+F45*F46	
49		=======	=======			
50	Tax Return for Year					
51	(11) Total Revenues	$127,050	$139,755		+F45*F46	
52	(12) Less: Manufacturing Cost of Sales	(79,088)	(76,987)		−F38	
53	(13) Less: Selling Expenses	(14,075)	(14,983)		−$D$9−F32*F42	
54						
55	(14) Taxable Income	$33,887	$47,785		@SUM(F51..F53)	
56						
57	(15) Income Taxes Payable	$13,555	$19,114		+F55*$D$12	
58		=======	=======			

Key Terms and Concepts

Capital budgeting
Investment decision versus
  financing decision
Discounted cash flow (DCF)
  methods
Net present value of cash flows
Effect of depreciation expense on
  cash flows

Accelerated cost recovery system
  (ACRS)
Opportunity cost of capital
Cost of capital
Required rate of return
Mutually exclusive investments

Questions, Exercises, Problems, and Cases

Questions

1. Review the meaning of the concepts or terms given above in Key Terms and Concepts.

2. The capital budgeting process comprises two distinct decisions. Describe these.

3. Assume a margin of error of plus or minus 10 percent in estimating any number required as an input for a capital budgeting decision. Under ordinary conditions, the net present value of a project is most sensitive to the estimate of which of the following?
    (1) Amounts of future cash flows.
    (2) Timing of future cash flows.
    (3) Cost of capital.

4. Financial accounting writers emphasize that "depreciation is not a source of funds." This chapter states that accelerated cost recovery methods result in larger cash flows that does the straight-line depreciation method. Reconcile these two statements.

5. How, if at all, should the amount of inflation incorporated in the cost of capital influence projected future cash flows for a project?

6. In *measuring* the cost of capital, management often measures the cost of the individual equities. A firm has no contractual obligation to pay anything to common shareholders. How can the capital they provide be said to have a cost other than zero?

7. A firm has a choice of three alternative investments:
    (1) Short-term government note promising a return of 8 percent.
    (2) Short-term commercial paper (issued by a blue-chip corporation) promising a return of 10 percent.
    (3) Short-term, lower-grade commercial paper (issued by a less well-established corporation) promising a return of 15 percent.
    How can one define the opportunity cost of capital as the marginal investment available to the firm with at least three such alternatives, each with a different promised rate?

8. Assume no change in marginal income tax rates over the life of new equipment about to be acquired. "So long as the trade-in allowance for an already-owned asset is at least as large as its book value for tax purposes, it will never pay to sell the asset rather than trade it in."

   Comment.

9. Assume no change in marginal income tax rates over the life of new equipment about to be acquired. "Whenever the trade-in allowance for an already-owned asset is smaller than its book value for tax purposes, it will always pay to sell that asset rather than trade it in."

   Comment.

10. "Because the Accelerated Cost Recovery System ignores salvage value for tax purposes in computing depreciation charges and the only effect of depreciation on cash flows is for income taxes, the analyst can safely ignore salvage value in capital budgeting."

    Comment.

11. Describe the factors that influence the market rate of interest a company must pay for borrowed funds.

12. Describe the chain of influence, if any, between the rate of anticipated inflation in an economy and the opportunity cost of capital to a firm in that economy.

13. "But, Mr. Miller, you have said that the opportunity cost of capital is the rate of return on alternative investment projects available to the firm. So long as the firm has debt outstanding, one opportunity for idle funds will be to retire debt. Therefore, the cost of capital cannot be higher than the current cost of debt for any firm with debt outstanding."

    How should Mr. Miller reply?

Exercises

14. *Computing net present value.* Compute the net present value of
    a. An investment of $15,000 that will yield $1,000 for 28 periods at 4 percent per period.
    b. An investment of $100,000 that will yield $250,000 8 years from now at 10 percent compounded semiannually.

15. *Computing net present value.* A firm has an after-tax cost of capital of 10 percent. Compute the net present value of each of the five projects listed in the following exhibit.

Project	After-Tax Cash Flow, End of Year			
	0	1	2	3
A	$(10,000)	$4,000	$4,000	$4,000
B	(10,000)	6,000	4,000	2,000
C	(10,000)	2,000	4,000	6,000
D	(10,000)	4,400	4,400	4,400
E	(10,000)	3,600	3,600	3,600

16. *Computing net present value*. Hammersmith Homes is considering four possible housing development projects, each requiring an initial investment of $5,000,000. The cash inflows from each of the projects follow:

Year	Project A	Project B	Project C	Project D
1	$2,000,000	$4,000,000	0	$1,000,000
2	2,000,000	2,000,000	0	2,500,000
3	2,000,000	2,000,000	0	3,000,000
4	2,000,000	1,000,000	0	2,500,000
5	2,000,000	1,000,000	$10,000,000	1,000,000

a. Ignoring tax effects, compute the net present value of each of the projects. Hammersmith's cost of capital is 15 percent.

b. Hammersmith can take on only one project; which should it choose? Explain why this project is superior to the others.

17. *Computing net present value*. Westminster Products is considering a project that requires an initial investment of $800,000 and that will generate the following cash inflows for the next 6 years:

Year	Cash Inflow at End of Year
1	$100,000
2	200,000
3	300,000
4	400,000
5	300,000
6	200,000

Ignoring tax effects, calculate the net present value of this project if Westminster's cost of capital is

a. 12 percent.

b. 20 percent.

18. *Computing net present value*. Megatech, a computer software developer, is considering a software development project that requires an initial investment of $200,000 and subsequent investments of $150,000 and $100,000 at the end of the first and second years. Megatech expects this project to yield annual after-tax cash inflows for 6 more years: $90,000 for the third through eighth years. Megatech's after-tax cost of capital is 10 percent.

Calculate the net present value of this project.

19. *Deriving cash flows and computing net present value*. The Eastern States Railroad (ESRR) is considering replacing its power jack tamper, used to maintain track and roadbed, with a new automatic-raising power tamper. ESRR spent $36,000 5 years ago for the present power jack tamper and estimated it to have a total life of 12 years. If ESRR keeps the old tamper, it

must overhaul the old tamper 2 years from now at a cost of $10,000. ESRR can sell the old tamper for $5,000 now; the tamper will be worthless 7 years from now.

A new automatic-raising tamper costs $46,000 delivered and has an estimated physical life of 12 years. ESRR anticipates, however, that because of developments in maintenance machines, it should retire the new machine at the end of the seventh year for $10,000. Furthermore, the new machine will require an overhaul costing $14,000 at the end of the fourth year. The new equipment will reduce wages and fringe benefits by $8,000 per year.

Track maintenance work is seasonal, so ESRR normally uses the equipment only from May 1 through October 31 of each year. ESRR transfers track maintenance employees to other work but pays them at the same rate for the rest of the year.

The new machine will require $2,000 per year of maintenance, whereas the old machine requires $2,400 per year. Fuel consumption for the two machines is identical. ESRR's cost of capital is 12 percent per year, and because of operating losses, ESRR pays no income tax.

Should ESRR purchase the new machine?

20. *Observing the effects of using different discount rates.* Refer to the data and analysis developed for the Magee Company in Exhibits 9.4 and 9.5. Evaluate the alternatives using an after-tax cost of capital of 12 percent.

21. *Deriving cash flows and computing net present value.* The Largay Corporation is contemplating selling a new product. Largay can acquire the equipment necessary to distribute and sell the product for $100,000. The equipment has an estimated life of 10 years and has no salvage value. The following schedule shows the expected sales volume, selling price, and variable cost per unit of production:

Year	Sale Volume	Selling Price	Variable Cost of Production
1	10,000 Units	$5.00	$3.00
2	12,000	5.00	3.10
3	13,000	5.50	3.25
4	15,000	5.75	3.25
5	20,000	6.00	3.30
6	25,000	6.00	3.40
7	20,000	6.10	3.50
8	18,000	6.10	3.50
9	15,000	6.25	3.50
10	15,000	6.30	3.75

Production in each year must be sufficient to meet each year's sales. In addition, Largay will purchase 5,000 extra units in Year 1 to provide a continuing inventory of 5,000 units. Thus production in Year 1 will be 15,000 units but in Year 10 will be only 10,000 units, so that at the end of Year 10, ending inventory will be zero. Largay will use a LIFO (last-in, first-out) cost flow assumption. Largay's income tax rate is 40 percent, and its after-tax cost of capital is 10 percent per year. It receives cash at the end of the year when it makes sales and spends cash at the end of the year when it incurs costs. Largay estimates variable selling expenses at $1 per unit sold. Depreciation on the new distribution equipment is not a product cost but is an expense each period. For tax reporting, depreciation will follow the ACRS percentages: 20 percent in the first, 32 percent in the second, 19.2 percent in the third, 11.5 percent in the fourth, 11.5 percent in the fifth, 5.8 percent in the sixth, and zero thereafter. The Largay Corporation generates sufficient cash flows from other operations so that it can use all depreciation deductions to reduce current taxes otherwise payable.

a. Prepare a schedule of cash flows for this project.

b. Verify that the net present value of the project is approximately $7,485.

Problems

22. *Net present value graph and indifference cost of capital.* The after-tax net cash flows associated with two mutually exclusive projects, G and H, are as follows:

Project	Cash Flow, End of Year		
	0	**1**	**2**
G	$(100)	$125	—
H	(100)	50	$84

a. Calculate the net present value for each project using discount rates of 0, .04, .08, .12, .15, .20, and .25.

b. Prepare a graph as follows. Label the vertical axis "Net Present Value in Dollars" and the horizontal axis "Discount Rate in Percent per Year." Plot the net present value amounts calculated in part **a** for project G and project H.

c. State the decision rule for choosing between project G and H as a function of the firm's cost of capital.

d. What generalizations can you draw from this exercise?

23. *Deriving cash flows for asset disposition.* The Wisher Washer Company (WWC) purchased a made-to-order machine tool for grinding washing machine parts. The machine costs $100,000 and WWC installed it yesterday. Today, a vender offers a machine tool that will do exactly the same work but costs only $50,000. Assume that the cost of capital is 12 percent, that both machines will last for 5 years, that WWC will depreciate both machines on a straight-line basis for tax purposes with no salvage value, that the income tax rate is and will continue to be 40 percent, and that WWC earns sufficient income that it can offset any loss from disposing of or depreciating the "old" machine against other taxable income.

How much, at a minimum, must the "old" machine fetch upon resale at this time to make purchasing the new machine worthwhile?

24. *Deriving cash flows for abandonment decision*. The Ingram Company must decide whether to continue selling a line of children's shoes manufactured on a machine that has no other purpose. The machine has a current book value of $12,000 and Ingram can sell it today for $7,000. Ingram depreciates the machine on a straight-line basis for tax purposes assuming no salvage value and could continue to use it for 4 more years. If Ingram keeps the machine in use, it can retire it at the end of 4 years for $600, although this will not affect the depreciation charge for the next 4 years. The variable cost of producing a pair of shoes on the machine is less than the cash received from customers by $13,000 per year. To produce and sell the children's shoes requires cash outlays of $10,000 per year for administrative and overhead expenditures as well. Ingram Company pays taxes at a rate of 40 percent. The rate applies to any gain or loss on disposal of the machine as well as to other income. From its other activities, Ingram Company earns more income than any losses from the line of children's shoes or from disposal of the machine.
    a. Prepare a schedule showing all the cash and cost flows that Ingram Company needs to consider in order to decide whether to keep the machine.
    b. Should Ingram Company keep the machine if its after-tax cost of capital is 12 percent?
    c. Repeat part **b** assuming an after-tax cost of capital of 15 percent.

25. *Net present value analysis of tax advantages of ACRS*. Assume an after-tax cost of capital of 15 percent per year and an income tax rate of 40 percent. Also assume that all cash flows for taxes occur at year-end.
    a. Compute the present values of the tax shield provided by straight-line depreciation over 10 years of an asset costing $10,000.
    b. Compute the present value of the tax shield provided by accelerated cost recovery over 6 years using the following percentages: 20, 32, 19.2, 11.5, 11.5, and 5.8.

26. *Outright sale versus trade-in of existing asset* (adapted from problems by D. O. Green). Brogan Company must buy a crane. It can buy a new one from the factory for $150,000. Cromwell Company, a competitor, bought an identical model last week for $150,000, finds that it needs a larger crane, and offers to sell its crane to Brogan. The new factory crane and the Cromwell crane have economic lives of 5 years with no salvage value.

    Cromwell Company can sell its crane to Brogan or can trade in the crane on the larger model, which also has a 5-year life with no salvage value. The cash price of the larger model is $300,000, and the factory will give Cromwell an allowance of $135,000 if Cromwell trades in the "old" crane. If Cromwell trades in the old crane it may not recognize the loss for tax purposes, but the depreciable cost of the new asset is the book value of the old asset plus any cash paid for the new asset. Cromwell uses accelerated cost recovery for tax purposes with the following percentages of cost claimed in the 5 years: 25, 38, 37, and 0, and 0. It has a cost of capital of 12 percent and pays taxes at a marginal rate of 40 percent. If Cromwell sells to Brogan, Cromwell may deduct any loss from taxable income at the time of sale—that is, immediately. Round dollar calculations to the nearest hundred dollars.

    a. What is the lowest price Cromwell can get from Brogan and be as well off as by trading in?

    b. At what price will the two parties, if they are acting rationally, agree for Cromwell to sell to Brogan?

27. *Deriving cash flows for two mutually exclusive alternatives; no income taxes.* Reinhardt Hospital's director needs a new car. The purchasing agent has narrowed the alternatives to buying one with either a gasoline or diesel engine. The gasoline model costs $18,000, whereas the diesel model costs $22,000. The gasoline model gets 20 miles per gallon of gasoline, whereas the diesel model gets 30 miles per gallon of diesel fuel. Gasoline currently costs $1.40 per gallon. Reinhardt expects gasoline to increase in price at the rate of 12 percent per year. Diesel fuel costs $1.20 per gallon. Reinhardt expects diesel fuel to increase in price at the rate of 8 percent per year. Reinhardt will drive the car for 4 years: 36,000 miles in the first year, 30,000 miles each in the second and third years, and 24,000 miles in the fourth year. The expected salvage value of the gasoline model is $7,000 at the end of the fourth year. Assume that all other operating costs (oil, insurance, and so on) will be the same for the two different kinds of cars.

    Assume that all cash flows occur at the start of the year but that receipt of salvage proceeds occurs at the end of the fourth year. Because Reinhardt Hospital is a tax-exempt, nonprofit institution, it need not consider income taxes. The cost of capital to the hospital is 15 percent per year.

    You have two mutually exclusive alternatives to analyze. You can subtract the cash flows from acquiring the diesel from those of acquiring the gasoline model to derive the cash flows of an investment project called "acquisition of diesel rather than gasoline model."

    Using this shortcut, derive the cash flows of acquiring the diesel rather than the gasoline model, compute the net present value of those cash flows, and decide which model car the hospital should acquire.

28. *Computing present value of operating cost savings and replacement cost of used asset.* The Pepper River Electric Company (PREC) produces electricity. Its current oil-burning plant is several years old and can produce electricity for 20 more years. It can produce 15 million kilowatt-hours of electricity per year by burning oil costing $500,000 per year. If PREC were to rebuild a 20-year oil-burning plant today, the costs would be $10 million. Because of drastic increases in oil prices since PREC built the current plant, PREC would not build an oil-burning plant today. Instead, it would build a coal-burning plant. The coal-burning plant would cost $11 million to build, have a 20-year useful life, and produce 15 million kilowatt-hours of electricity per year by burning coal costing $100,000 per year.

    Assume a cost of capital of 12 percent per year. Assume also that the fuel cost differential stays constant for 20 years and that all fuel costs are incurred at the beginning of each year. Ignore income tax considerations.

    a. What is the present value of the cash savings from lower fuel costs resulting from operating a coal-burning plant rather than an oil-burning plant?

b. What is the current replacement cost of the productive capacity owned by PREC? (The chapter does not give guidance on this question, which we ask so that you will consider issues beyond those discussed.)

29. *Deriving cash flows and performing breakeven analysis; comprehensive sensitivity analysis.* In the mid-1970s, Peugeot offered its automobile Model 504 in two versions—one with a gasoline engine and one with a diesel engine. The gasoline version had a list price of $6,270, and the diesel version had a list price of $6,986. Assume for the purpose of this problem that dealers actually charge the list prices in purchase transactions. According to federal EPA mileage tests and using then-current fuel prices, the operating cost savings for the diesel over the gasoline model amount to $.01108 cent per mile or $133 per year assuming 12,000 miles of use each year. Assume that a purchaser decided to acquire one of these two cars and that the purchaser expected to drive 12,000 miles a year for 5 years before retiring the car. The gasoline version will have a resale value in 5 years of $1,500 and the diesel, a resale value of $1,675.

Assume that the operating cost differential remains constant over the 5 years. Assume also that the automobile purchase and the first year's fuel payments occur on January 1 of each year, and the owner retires the automobile on January 1 of Year 6.

a. If the purchaser uses a discount rate of 12 percent per year, which version should the purchaser acquire, and what is the net present value of the savings from buying this version rather than the other?

b. At what mileage driven each year, assuming equal annual mileage per year for 5 years, constant resale values, and a discount rate of 12 percent, is the purchaser indifferent between the two versions?

c. Assume that the purchaser drives 12,000 miles each year. At what discount rate is the purchaser indifferent between the two versions? (Find the approximate answer, using the tables at the back of the book.)

Integrative Problems and Cases

30. *Make-or-buy—Liquid Chemical Co.*[11] The Liquid Chemical Company manufactures and sells a range of high-grade products. Many of these products require careful packing. The company has a special patented lining made from a material known as GHL, and the firm operates a department to maintain its containers in good condition and to make new ones to replace those beyond repair.

Mr. Walsh, the general manager, has for some time suspected that the firm might save money, and get equally good service, by buying its containers from an outside source. After careful inquiries, he approached a firm specializing in container production, Packages, Inc., and asked for a quotation from it. At the same time, he asked Mr. Dyer, his chief accountant, to let him have an up-to-date statement of the costs of operating the container department.

---

[11] Adapted from a case by Professor David Solomons, Wharton School, University of Pennsylvania.

Within a few days, the quotation from Packages, Inc., arrived. The firm proposed to supply all the new containers required—at that time, running at the rate of 3,000 a year—for $1,250,000 a year, the contract to run for a guaranteed term of 5 years and thereafter to be renewable from year to year. If the number of containers required increased, the contract price would increase proportionally. Also, independent of this contract, Packages, Inc., proposed to carry out purely maintenance work on containers, short of replacement, for a sum of $375,000 a year, on the same contract terms.

Mr. Walsh compared these figures with Mr. Dyer's cost figures, which covered a year's operations of the container department of the Liquid Chemical Company and appear in Exhibit 9.8

Walsh concluded that he should immediately close the department and sign the contracts offered by Packages, Inc. He felt bound, however, to give the manager of the department, Mr. Duffy, an opportunity to question this conclusion before acting on it. Walsh told Duffy that Duffy's own position was not in jeopardy: even if Walsh closed his department, another managerial position was becoming vacant to which Duffy could move without loss of pay or prospects. The manager Duffy would replace also earns $80,000 a year. Moreover, Walsh knew that he was paying $85,000 a year in rent for a warehouse a couple of miles away for other corporate purposes. If he closed Duffy's department, he'd have all the warehouse space he needed without renting.

Duffy gave Walsh a number of considerations to think about before closing the department. "For instance," he said, "what will you do with the machinery? It cost $1,200,000 4 years ago, but you'd be lucky if you got $200,000 for it now, even though it's good for another 5 years. And then there's the stock of GHL (a special chemical) we bought a year ago. That cost us $1,000,000, and at the rate we're using it now, it'll last us another 4 years.

Exhibit 9.8

LIQUID CHEMICAL Container Department		
Materials		$ 700,000
Labor:		
Supervisor		50,000
Workers		450,000
Department Overheads:		
Manager's Salary	$80,000	
Rent on Container Department	45,000	
Depreciation of Machinery	150,000	
Maintenance of Machinery	36,000	
Other Expenses	157,500	
		468,500
		$1,668,500
Proportion of General Administrative Overheads		225,000
Total Cost of Department for Year		$1,893,500

We used up about one-fifth of it last year. Dyer's figure of $700,000 for materials includes $200,000 for GHL. But it'll be tricky stuff to handle if we don't use it up. We bought it for $5,000 a ton, and you couldn't buy it today for less than $6,000. But you'd get over $4,000 a ton if you sold it, after you'd covered all the handling expenses.''

Walsh worried about the workers if he closed the department. ''I don't think we can find room for any of them elsewhere in the firm. I could see whether Packages can take any of them. But some of them are getting on. Walters and Hines, for example, have been with use since they left school 40 years ago. I'd feel bound to give them a pension—$15,000 a year each, say.''

Duffy showed some relief at this. ''But I still don't like Dyer's figures,'' he said. ''What about this $225,000 for general administrative overheads? You surely don't expect to sack anyone in the general office if I'm closed, do you?'' Walsh agreed.

''Well, I think we've thrashed this out pretty fully,'' said Walsh, ''but I've been turning over in my mind the possibility of perhaps keeping on the maintenance work ourselves. What are you views on that, Duffy?''

''I don't know,'' said Duffy, ''but it's worth looking into.We shouldn't need any machinery for that, and I could hand the supervision over to the current supervisor who earns $50,000 per year. You'd need only about one-fifth of the workers, but you could keep on the oldest and save the pension costs. You wouldn't save any space, so I suppose the rent would be the same. I don't think the other expenses would be more than $65,000 a year.''

''What about materials?'' asked Walsh.

''We use 10 percent of the total on maintenance,'' Duffy replied.

''Well, I've told Packages, Inc., that I'd give them my decision within a week,'' said Walsh. ''I'll let you know what I decide to do before I write to them''

Assume the company has an after-tax cost of capital of 10 percent per year and uses an income tax rate of 40 percent for decisions such as these. Liquid Chemical would pay taxes on any gain or loss on the sale of machinery or the GHL at 40 percent. (Depreciation for book and tax purposes is straight-line over 8 years.) The tax basis of the machinery is $600,000.

Assume the company had a 5-year time horizon for this project. Also assume that any GHL needed for Year 5 is purchased during Year 5.

a. What are the four alternatives available to Liquid Chemical?

b. What action should Walsh take? Support your conclusion with a net present value analysis of all the mutually exclusive alternatives.

c. What, it any, additional information do you think Walsh needs to make a sound decision? Why?

31. *Comprehensive review.* Demski Company may venture into a new product line. If it does so, it must acquire new equipment at the beginning of Year 1 for $135,000. The equipment, which requires installation expenditures of $15,000, will last for 10 years and will have salvage value then of $2,000 if there is no inflation. Demski expects equipment prices, including prices of used equipment of this sort, to rise at an annual rate of 6 percent, so the actual

salvage value expected at the end of the tenth year is $3,582 (= $2,000 \times 1.06^{10}$). Demski will pay taxes on any gain on disposal at 40 percent at the end of Year 10.

Demski Company owns old manufacturing equipment with a book value of $18,000 that it must retire. Demski can sell the old equipment for $27,000 cash or trade it in on the new equipment for a reduction of $28,000 in cash purchase price. If Demski sells the old equipment, it will pay taxes on the gain at the rate of 40 percent at the end of Year 1. If Demski trades in the old equipment it will not pay taxes on the "gain" on disposal, but will reduce the depreciable basis of the new asset (and future depreciation charges) both for financial accounting and for tax purposes. If Demski trades in the old asset, paying cash of $122,000 (= $150,000 - $28,000), the journal entry will be as follows:

New Equipment	140,000	
Old Equipment (Net)		18,000
Cash		122,000

Demski will depreciate the new equipment for financial reporting over 10 years using the straight-line method but over 6 years using ACRs for tax purposes. Depreciation deductions on the tax return will equal the following percentages of depreciable basis: 20 percent in the first year, 32 percent in the second, 19.2 percent in the third, 11.5 percent in the fourth, 11.5 percent in the fifth, 5.8 percent in the sixth, and zero thereafter. Recall that Demski does not have to consider salvage value in computing ACRS deductions for tax purposes.

Demski forecasts sales volume, by year, as follows:

Year 1	10,000 Units
Year 2	12,000
Year 3	15,000
Year 4	18,000
Year 5	20,000
Year 6	25,000
Year 7	28,000
Year 8	23,000
Year 9	19,000
Year 10	15,000

Demski makes the following forecasts and projections:

- Sales price will be $5.50 per unit during Year 1, but will increase by 10 percent per year, to $6.05 in Year 2, $6.66 in Year 3, and so on.

- Variable manufacturing costs are $3.00 per unit in Year 1, but will increase by 8 percent per year, to $3.24 in Year 2, and so on.

- Selling costs are $5,000 per year plus $.50 per unit in Year 1. Variable selling costs per unit will increase by 10 percent per year to $.55 in Year 2, $.61 in Year 3, and so on.

- Income tax rates will remain at 40 percent of taxable income each year.

- The after-tax cost of capital is 15 percent per year.

Demski makes the following assumptions about the timing of cash flows:

- It will pay all variable manufacturing costs in cash at the beginning of each year.

- It will pay all selling costs, fixed and variable, in cash at the end of each year.

- It will collect cash from customers at the end of each year.

- It will pay income taxes for each year's operations at the end of the year.

Demski makes the following assumptions about its operations and accounting:

- Although it may deduct selling costs on the tax return in the year incurred, it may not deduct manufacturing costs until it sells the goods.

- It will have sufficient other taxable income that losses on this project in any period will offset that income, saving $.40 in income taxes for every $1.00 of operating loss.

- It must produce enough each year to meet each year's sales, except that it must produce 15,000 units in Year 1 to provide a continuing supply of inventory of 5,000 units. It need produce only 10,000 units in Year 5, so that ending inventory will be zero.

- It will use a LIFO cost flow assumption for inventories.

- It will charge all depreciation for a year to the cost of units it produces that year.

   a. List the mutually exclusive alternatives facing Demski Company.
   b. Construct a schedule of cash flows for the alternative of trading in the old equipment on the new and using the new equipment.
   c. Explain why the alternative in part **b** dominates the alternative of selling the old equipment outright and purchasing the new, rather than trading in.
   d. Analyze the alternatives and suggest a decision to the management of Demski Company.

Suggested Solutions to Even-Numbered Exercises

14. *Computing the net present value*
   a. Net Present Value $= -\$15,000 + \$1,000 \times 16.66306$
                            $= \$1,663.$

   b. Net Present Value $= -\$100,000 + \$250,000 \times 0.45811$
                            $= \$14,528.$

16.   *Computing net present value*

a.

Year	Present Value Factor	Discounted Cash Flows			
		Project A	Project B	Project C	Project D
0	1.00000	$(5,000,000)	$(5,000,000)	$(5,000,000)	$(5,000,000)
1	.86957	1,739,140	3,478,280	0	869,570
2	.75614	1,512,280	1,512,280	0	1,890,350
3	.65752	1,315,040	1,315,040	0	1,972,560
4	.57175	1,143,500	571,750	0	1,429,375
5	.49718	994,360	497,180	4,971,800	497,180
		$ 1,704,320	$ 2,374,530	$ (28,200)	$ 1,659,035

b.   Hammersmith should take Project B, which has the largest net present value. Even though all four projects have similar undiscounted total cash flow streams, that is, $10,000,000, Project B is superior because the bulk of the cash returns come in the earlier years.

18.   *Computing net present value*

Year (1)	Net Cash Flow (2)	10% Present Value Factor (3)	Present Value (4)[a]
0	$(200,000)	1.00000	$(200,000)
1	(150,000)	.90909	(136,364)
2	(100,000)	.82645	(82,645)
3	90,000	.75131	67,618
4	90,000	.68301	61,471
5	90,000	.62092	55,883
6	90,000	.56447	50,803
7	90,000	.51316	46,184
8	90,000	.46651	41,986
			$ (95,064)

[a](4) = (2) × (3).

20.   *Observing the effects of using different discount rates*

MAGEE COMPANY
Operating Cash Flows, End of Year
(cost of capital, 12 percent)

End of Year (1)	Cash Flow (2)	Present Value Factor at 12 Percent (3)	Present Value at 12 Percent = (2) × (3) (4)
0	$(60,000)	1.00000	$(60,000)
1	33,300	.89286	29,732
2	46,210	.79719	36,838

continued

continued from page 440

3	42,680	.71178	30,379
4	64,850	.63552	41,213
5	115,920	.56743	65,776
Total			$143,938

**Present Value of All Cash Flows from Trading in
Old Equipment on New Equipment**

Operating Cash Flow	$143,938
Cash Outlay for Equipment	(122,000)
Salvage Proceeds End of Year 5: $4,406 $\times$ .56743	2,500
Taxes on Salvage End of Year 6: $4,406 $\times$ .40 $\times$ .50663	(893)
Net Present Value	$ 23,545

Present Value of Outright Sale

Sale Proceeds	$ 25,000
Taxes Paid on Gain 1 Year Later: $7,000 $\times$ .40 $\times$ .89286	(2,500)
Net Present Value	$ 22,500

... CHAPTER 10 ...

Capital Budgeting: A Closer Look

Chapter Outline

- Alternative Methods for Evaluating Projects
- Separating Investment and Finance Decisions
- Leasing Is a Form of Financing

Chapter 9 introduced the fundamentals of capital budgeting: separating the investment decision from the financing decision, analyzing cash flows, and summing the cash flows after discounting them at the firm's opportunity cost of capital. This chapter (1) describes other methods for making capital budgeting decisions, (2) evaluates their strengths and weaknesses and (3) explores in greater depth the fact that sound analysis requires separating the investment decision from the financing decision.

Alternative Methods for Evaluating Projects

Managers have used many methods for evaluating projects, but most are inferior to using the net present value (or discounted cash flow) method with a discount rate equal to the cost of capital. Some methods that take the time value of money into account often give the same decision results as the net present value rule. In practice, they prove to be satisfactory. Alternative methods that do not take the time value of money into account are easy to use because they do not involve present value computations. This simplicity is their chief virtue.

The strength of the net present value method for making capital budgeting investment decisions rests on its focus on discounted cash flows. The manager can find the net present value itself, a dollar number with a sign—positive or negative—difficult to compare across alternatives. Some decision makers believe that comparing a project with a net present value of $10,000 to one with a net present value of $100,000 may not be meaningful if the first project requires an initial investment much different from the second's. Decision makers are sometimes uncomfortable with the net present value method because it seems to be independent of the size of the underlying investment. The net present value rule states merely that a positive net present value is good and a negative one is bad.

Practitioners have developed variants of the discounted cash flow method, called internal rate of return analysis and the excess present value index, to take into account the *size* of the projects being considered. We discuss these next, as well as alternative methods often found in practice. We show that these variants can cause other problems and that the net present value method dominates them for decision making.

Internal Rate of Return

The **internal rate of return (IRR),** sometimes called the time-adjusted rate of return, of a series of cash flows is the discount rate that equates the net present value of that series to zero. Stated another way, the IRR is the rate that discounts the future cash flows to a present value just equal to the initial investment. The IRR method is another discounted cash flow (DCF) method.

Calculating the Internal Rate of Return   To illustrate the calculation of the internal rate of return, assume that a proposed project requires an initial investment of $11,059 and promises to yield net cash inflows for the next 4 years as follows: Year 1, $5,000; Year 2, $4,000; Year 3, $3,000; Year 4, $2,000. To calculate the internal rate of return, compute the rate that discounts the net cash *inflows* during years 1 to 4 so that they have a present value of $11,059; that is, the net present value of the inflows and outflows is zero. Mathematically, this step involves solving the following equation for r, the discount rate:

$$\$11,059 = \frac{\$5,000}{(1 + r)^1} + \frac{\$4,000}{(1 + r)^2} + \frac{\$3,000}{(1 + r)^3} + \frac{\$2,000}{(1 + r)^4}.$$

Computers and some pocket calculators can compute this discount rate quickly. Whatever device we use, we must try various discount rates until we find the proper one. Using trial and error, we begin by trying a discount rate of 10 percent. Columns (3) and (4) of Exhibit 10.1 shows that at this discount rate the net present value is positive. This result suggests that the internal rate of return must be larger than 10 percent. So we try 12 percent, Column (6) of Exhibit 10.1 shows that a 12 percent discount rate equates the net present value to zero. Twelve percent therefore is the internal rate of return for this project. (If the net present value for a given trial rate were *negative*, we would try a *smaller* rate at the next trial.) The compound

Exhibit 10.1

Calculation of Internal Rate of Return

End of Year (1)	Cash Inflow (Outflow) (2)	Present Value Factor at 10 Percent (3)	Present Value of Cash Flows at 10 Percent (4)	Present Value Factor at 12 Percent (5)	Present Value of Cash Flows at 12 Percent (6)
0	$(11,059)	1.00000	$(11,059)	1.00000	$(11,059)
1	5,000	.90909	4,545	.89286	4,464
2	4,000	.82645	3,306	.79719	3,189
3	3,000	.75131	2,254	.71178	2,135
4	2,000	.68301	1,366	.63552	1,271
Net Present Value			$ 412		$ 0

interest appendix at the back of this book provides further illustrations of finding the internal rate of return.

Using the Internal Rate of Return When using the internal rate of return to evaluate investment alternatives, one specifies a **cutoff rate,** such as 15 percent for the JEP Realty Syndicators example in the previous chapter. The IRR method accepts a project if its internal rate of return exceeds the cutoff rate and rejects if its internal rate of return is less than the cutoff rate. The cutoff rate is sometimes called the **hurdle rate.**

Advocates of the internal rate of return argue that the method does not require knowing the firm's cost of capital and is therefore easier to use than the net present value rule. This assessment is short-sighted, however. For the internal rate of return rule to give the correct answers, the cutoff rate must be the cost of capital. Otherwise, the IRR method will reject some projects that will increase the value of the firm to its owners or accept some projects that will decrease value. The net present value method requires no more data than the internal rate of return method.

Superiority of Net Present Value Method over Internal Rate of Return Method

Single Ranking Measure The net present value method provides a single net present value amount for each project that the analyst can use to make the accept-reject decision. The internal rate of return method, however, may give more than one internal rate of return for a particular project. This mathematical phenomenon can occur when the pattern of yearly net cash flows contains an intermixing of net cash inflows and outflows. For example, if a project requires cash expenditures at the end of its life to return the plant site to its original condition, then individual cash flows can be negative both at the beginning and at the end of a project's life but positive in between. Projects with intermixing of cash inflows and outflows can have multiple internal rates of return.[1] Examples of multiple internal rates of return

[1] Solving for the internal rate of return involves finding the roots of a polynomial. Descartes's rule of signs tells how to determine the limit to the number of roots of such a polynomial. See the Glossary for an explanation of this rule.

have arisen in practice for coal mining companies that use strip mining to generate cash inflows from coal but who must spend cash at the completion of the mining phase to reclaim the stripped land. Problem **17** at the end of this chapter gives an example.

Better Ranking of Alternatives   Under the net present value (NPV) rule, projects are either acceptable or unacceptable. When projects are mutually exclusive, the decision maker can choose only one of a set of projects. The NPV rule tells us to choose the project with the largest net present value. The internal rate of return rule ranks projects in the same way as the net present value rule only when the scenario meets each of the four following conditions:

1. The cutoff rate used for the internal rate equals the cost of capital.
2. Projects are not mutually exclusive.
3. Projects have the same life in periods.
4. There is only one internal rate of return.

Otherwise, the internal rate of return leads to incorrect decisions about projects, as demonstrated next.

Mutually Exclusive Projects   **Mutually exclusive projects** are a set of alternatives from which the decision maker can choose only one. For example, a firm needing a new truck may prepare a net present value analysis for trucks meeting the firm's specifications from each of four different suppliers. After it selects one of the trucks, it will not consider the other three. The firm needs only one truck. The net present value decision rule for choosing among mutually exclusive projects accepts the project with the largest net present value and rejects the others. The internal rate of return analysis can signal the wrong selection from mutually exclusive projects. Assume that the after-tax cost of capital is 10 percent per year and that a firm can choose only one of the projects, A or B, as shown in Exhibit 10.2. Project A provides a simple illustration for calculating the internal rate of return. The internal rate of return on Proposal A is the rate r such that

$$\$100 = \frac{\$120}{1 + r}.$$

Exhibit 10.2

Data for Projects A and B

Project Name	After-Tax Cash Flows by Year, End of Year 0	1	Internal Rate of Return	Net Present Value at 10 Percent
A	$(100)	$120	20%	$ 9.09
B	(300)	345	15	13.64

Solving gives $r = .20$. The internal rate of return of .15 for Project B is similarly easy to calculate. The internal rate of return rule prefers Project A to Project B, whereas the net present value rule prefers Project B.

To see that Project B is better for the firm, consider what the firm must do with the other $200 it will have to invest if the firm chooses Project A. It must invest that $200, by definition, at the after-tax cost of capital of 10 percent and will receive $220, after taxes, at the end of the first year. So the total flows available at the end of the first year from Project A and from the investment of the other funds at 10 percent will be $120 + $220 = $340. This result is less than the $345 available after taxes from Project B. The firm will prefer the results from choosing Project B as the net present value rule signals. A firm choosing Project B will be $5 wealthier at the end of Year 1 than a firm choosing Project A.

To understand better why the net present value ranking is superior, decide whether you would rather invest $.10 today to get $2 a year from now ($r = 1,900$ percent) or invest $1,000 today to get $2,500 a year from now ($r = 150$ percent). You may not do both. We guess that you, as we, would prefer the second alternative even though the internal rate of return on the first is more than 12 times larger than for the second. The internal rate of return rule, applied to mutually exclusive projects, ignores the amount of funds that the firm can invest at that rate. This shortcoming is sometimes called the **scale effect**.[2]

Projects with Different Lifetimes   When a project has an initial investment (cash inflow) followed by a series of cash outflows, the analysis must take into account how the firm will use the cash inflows until the project is complete. The major failing of the IRR method is that it assumes that the firm can reinvest all cash outflows from the project at the IRR of the project, rather than at the cost of capital. Consider projects C and D shown in Exhibit 10.3. The internal rate of return on Project D is the rate r that satisfies the equation

$$\$100 = \frac{\$50}{(1 + r)} + \frac{\$84}{(1 + r)^2}.$$

Exhibit 10.3

Data for Projects C and D

Project Name	Cash Flows by Year, End of Year			Internal Rate of Return	Net Present Value at 10 Percent
	0	1	2		
C	$(100)	$125	—	25%	$13.64
D	(100)	50	$84	20	14.88

[2]The scale effect problem often arises in using the internal rate of return method to evaluate alternatives to existing projects. Refer to Case A (food blenders and processors) on page 409 of Chapter 9. What is the internal rate of return on alternative 2 described there? It is infinite because there is no initial cash outflow. Whenever you must compare a status quo to alternatives requiring initial cash outflows, the internal rate of return analysis is likely to be difficult.

You can verify that the internal rate of return is 20 percent by using the 20 percent column of Table 2 at the back of the book. The internal rate of return rule ranks Project C as being better than Project D, whereas the net present value rule ranks Project D as being better than Project C.

To see why Project D is better for the firm, consider what the firm must do during Year 2. If it accepts Project C, it must invest $125 in the average investment project available to the firm. The return from such an average project is, by definition, the cost of capital, 10 percent. At the end of Year 2, the firm will have $125 × 1.10 = $137.50. If the firm accepts Project D, it will invest the $50 cash inflow at the end of the first year at 10 percent to grow to $50 × 1.10 = $55 by the end of Year 2. Thus, the total available at the end of the second year is $55 + $84 = $139, which exceeds the $137.50 if the firm accepts Project C. The internal rate of return rule ignores the fact that the firm must invest the idle funds at the cost of capital.[3]

Excess Present Value Index

Compute the **excess present value index** as follows:

$$\text{Excess Present Value Index} = \frac{\text{Present Value of Future Cash Flows}}{\text{Initial Investment}}.$$

This index indicates the number of present value dollars generated per dollar of investment. For example, if the present value of the *future* cash flows is $17,000 and the initial investment is $12,000, the excess present value index is 1.42 (= $17,000/$12,000). The excess present value (EPV) rule says to accept a project with an index greater than 1.0 and reject it if the index is less than 1.0.

In the absence of mutually exclusive projects, the net present value method and the excess present value method result in the same accept-reject decisions.

When projects are mutually exclusive the net present value and excess present value index methods can give conflicting signals. Consider the data in Exhibit 10.4. The rankings of the four projects differ depending on whether the rankings result from net present values or from excess present value indexes. The difference in the rankings arises because of a scale effect. In Exhibit 10.4 the EPV rule prefers the small Project H to the large Project E. Using the net present value rule will maximize the wealth of the firm because the rule focuses on total dollar return, not the rate of return per dollar. The EPV rule can fail for mutually exclusive projects when the firm must invest other funds at the cost of capital.

Payback Period

Another method for evaluating investment projects involves the payback period. The **payback period** is the length of time that elapses before total cumulative after-tax cash inflows from the project equal the initial cash outlay for the project.

---

[3]The firm may invest the idle funds at another rate, which, although different, is equivalent when the analysis takes into account the differential risk.

Exhibit 10.4

Ranking of Projects According to Net Present Value and Excess Present Value Index Methods

Project (1)	Initial Cash Outlay Required (2)	Present Value of Future Cash Inflows (3)	Net Present Value (4)[a]	Ranking by Net Present Value (5)	Excess Present Value Index (6)[b]	Ranking by Excess Present Value Index (7)
E	$120,000	$170,000	$50,000	1	1.42	3
F	110,000	150,000	40,000	2	1.36	4
G	70,000	100,000	30,000	3	1.43	2
H	30,000	55,000	25,000	4	1.83	1

[a]Column (4) = column (3) − column (2).

[b]Column (6) = column (3)/column (2).

Refer to Exhibit 10.1. The proposed project has a payback period of about 2.7 years. By the end of the first year, the firm has recovered $5,000 of the initial investment. By the end of the second year, the cumulative cash inflows total $9,000 (= $5,000 + $4,000). The firm receives the remaining $2,059 (= $11,059 − $9,000) approximately two-thirds of the way through the third year. Hence the payback is 2.7 years. The payback period rule states that the decision maker should accept projects when the payback period is as short as some designated cutoff time period, such as 2 years, and reject them otherwise.

The payback period rule ignores both the time value of money and all cash flows subsequent to the payback date. One project could have a shorter payback period than another but much smaller net present value. The payback period rule focuses concern on the firm's liquidity. The net present value rule takes liquidity into account, because the cost of capital is the rate of return required to justify a firm's employing additional assets in the business should a possibility arise.

A mathematical artifact of the payback method follows: When the analyst considers projects not mutually exclusive, each having the same life and uniform cash inflows over its life, the results of using the payback method will be the same as using the net present value method.[4] This fact, plus the fact that in earlier times computing devices were not as accessible and inexpensive as they are today, led to the education of a generation of managers with the techniques of payback analysis. Be aware that some in the business world still use payback methods; they will not necessarily get wrong answers.

Advocates of the payback period rule argue that the net present value rule, even with its discounting of future cash flows, gives too much weight to cash flows more than 3 or 4 years into the future. They point out that many managers have favorite projects they would like the company to undertake. Managers have learned that they

[4]If the net cash inflows per year from a project are constant and occur for a number of years at least twice as long as the payback period, and when the discount rate is reasonably large—say, 10 percent per year or more—the reciprocal of the payback period is approximately equal to the internal rate of return on the project. Thus the payback period will rank projects in the same way as the internal rate of return and, hence, the net present value method, under the conditions stated.

can make marginal projects look acceptable under the net present value method by setting some of the distant cash inflows unrealistically large. (They might make optimistic projections of future increases in sales revenues or optimistic estimates of the rate at which production costs will decline as workers learn new skills.) Such managers might figure that they will not be on the same job by the time top management learns that the cash inflows projected for, say, 5 years hence had been too optimistic. Such managers may reasonably expect to have been promoted or fired by the time 5 years elapse. Thus they expect not to be held accountable for their distant projections. Analysts who fear being misled by overly optimistic managers insist on using a payback rule to find out the near-term profitability of a project. Advocates of the net present value method caution about accepting cash flow projections without careful study, but maintain that the net present value method is still conceptually superior. They suggest that the analyst use a higher cost of capital rate for distant years, reflecting increased risk of projections for those years. Although none of the examples so far have illustrated this fact, the discount rate need not be identical for each year.

Discounted Payback Period

Given the widespread use of the payback period rule and its inability to yield good decisions for the most general case, some accountants have suggested that firms that want a payback rule should use the discounted payback period.[5] The **discounted payback period** resembles the ordinary payback period, but it is defined as the length of time that elapses before the *present value* of the cumulative cash inflows just exceeds the initial cash outlay. The discount rate used in this calculation is most often the cost of capital. The discounted payback period gives some recognition to the time value of funds that flow before payback occurs. The ordinary payback periods of projects J and K in Exhibit 10.5 are the same, 3 years, but the discounted payback criteria will properly prefer K to J.

Exhibit 10.5

Illustrative Data for Payback Rules, Projects J, K, and L						
Project Name	**Cash Flow at End of Year**					
	0	**1**	**2**	**3**	**4**	**5**
J.....................	$(10,000)	$2,000	$3,000	$5,000	$2,000	—
K...................	(10,000)	5,000	3,000	2,000	2,000	—
L..................	(10,000)	—	—	—	—	$50,000

---

[5]See the results of the following surveys: T. Klammer, "Empirical Evidence of the Adoption of Sophisticated Capital Budgeting Techniques," *Journal of Business* 45 (July 1972), p. 393; L. Schall, G. Sundem, and W. Geijsbeck, "Survey and Analysis of Capital Budgeting Methods," *Journal of Finance* 33 (March 1978), pp. 281–287; and S. H. Kim and E. J. Farragher, "Current Capital Budgeting Practices," *Management Accounting* 62, 12 (June 1981), pp. 26–32.

Either payback rule would improperly prefer both J and K to Project L. Yet analysts sometimes recommend the discounted payback rule to firms that are wary of applying the net present value rule to projects like Project L. As we pointed out previously, the manager who made the original forecast for $50,000 cash inflow for Year 5 may not be around to be accountable when the firm learns that the forecast was too optimistic.

Accounting Rate of Return

The **accounting rate of return,** sometimes called the rate of return on investment or (ROI), for a project is

$$\frac{\text{Average Yearly Income from the Project}}{\text{Average Investment in the Project}}.$$

Assume that a project requiring an investment of $10,000 promises total income of $3,300 over 4 years. The average yearly income is $825. The average investment in the project, assuming straight-line depreciation and no salvage value, is $5,000 [= ($10,000 + $0)/2]. Hence, the accounting rate of return is $825/$5,000 = 16.5 percent. The accounting rate of return pays no attention to the time value of money and uses accounting income, rather than cash flows, data.

Assume that the project results in equal annual after-tax cash flows of $3,325 at the end of each of the 4 years. Net income over the life of the project, then, is $3,300 (= 4 × $3,325 − $10,000). Because the internal rate of return on an investment of $10,000 to yield $3,325 in arrears for 4 years is about 12.5 percent, the net present value of this project will be positive only for discount rates less than 12.5 percent. If the firm has an after-tax cost of capital of 15 percent, this project is not a worthwhile undertaking because it has a negative net present value of about −$500 at that rate. The ROI is 16.5 percent, which may induce the manager making decisions with ROI to think the project is worthwhile.[6]

Because the accounting rate of return ignores the time value of money and uses accounting data rather than cash flow data, it is generally an inferior decision-making tool. To see why analysts often use ROI in spite of this, consider three points. First, ROI is easy to compute. Second, the ROI and the internal rate of return for some projects do not drastically differ, so using ROI for decision making will not always lead to wrong decisions. Third, as later chapters discuss, firms often use ROI in performance measurement. Managers who expect to be evaluated by ROI after they make decisions will not always ignore ROI in making decisions.

Thus we see why companies using ROI for performance measurements will use ROI to make decisions. Chapter 15 shows that a refinement of ROI, residual income, provides better data for performance evaluation, so firms need not use ROI

---

[6]Furthermore, the ROI will be the same, 16.5 percent, even if all the cash flow from the project occurs at the end of the fourth year, whereas the internal rate of return drops to 7.4 percent in this case. To take another extreme case, assume that $12,300 of cash flows occurred at the end of the first year and $1,000 occurred at the end of the fourth. The ROI would remain 16.5 percent, but the internal rate of return would increase dramatically, to more than 26 percent.

for either decision making, before it undertakes plans, or for performance evaluations, after the fact.[7]

Evaluation of Capital Budgeting Decision-Making Tools

The manager must decide whether to undertake some investment project. We have seen that the net present value method applied to cash flow data will lead to maximizing the owners' wealth and that the internal rate of return is almost as good. Sometimes, however, firms use other methods such as payback and ROI, because the computational work may be less burdensome for the analyst. When thousands of dollars are at stake and managers have computer terminals available to them more readily than pencil sharpeners, competent managers will use the computationally more complex discounted cash flow methods. The simple methods can make gross partitions of projects as either (1) clear rejects or (2) those to be considered further with more refined methods.

Separating Investment and Financing Decisions

Make investment decisions independently of financing decisions. If a project can earn a return at least as large as the firm's cost of capital, undertake it. How to raise the specific funds needed for the project is a separate question.

Apparent Net Present Value Benefits to Borrowing

Combining the investment and financing decisions can mislead decision makers into believing that a project financed with debt is worth more than the same project financed with cash on hand. The examples in this section show how the confusion results. Assume that a firm borrows money at the market rate of interest and makes the required debt service payments, both principal and interest, on schedule. Such an undertaking, by itself, can never be worthwhile in the same sense that an investment project with a positive net present value is worthwhile. Such borrowing increases the leverage of the firm, increasing the risk of the owners' equity. Such increased leverage is a gamble, but in a technical sense it is a fair gamble. In this framework, a positive net present value is a favorable gamble, because it promises a rate of return higher than those otherwise available to the firm.

Exhibit 10.6 illustrates the net present values that result from analyzing borrowing activity as though it were an investment project. It assumes a firm with a pretax cost of capital of 25 percent, an income tax rate of 40 percent, and thus an after-tax cost of capital of 15 percent. The firm has sufficient other income that interest expense deducted on the tax return reduces cash outflows for taxes by $.40 for each $1.00 of interest expense.

In Exhibit 10.6, column **(3)** shows the pretax cash flows from borrowing, and column **(5)** shows the cash flows after-tax effects for the deductibility of interest

---

[7]Financial accounting, which often requires evaluations of entire businesses after the fact, often uses various ROI measures. See Chapter 18. To summarize, ROI measures are poor for decision making but may be valid for evaluation.

Exhibit 10.6

Net Present Values from Borrowing at Various Interest Rates, Discounted at 15 Percent Cost of Capital

			Cash Flows		
End of Year (1)	Event (2)	Pretax (3)	From Reduced Income Taxes Caused by Deducting Interest Expense (4)	After-Tax (5)	Present Value at 15 Percent (6)
12 Percent Loan					
0	Borrow	$1,000	—	$1,000	$1,000
1	Interest	(120)	$48	(72)	(63)
2	Interest	(120)	48	(72)	(54)
2	Repayment	(1,000)	—	(1,000)	(756)
	Net Present Value				$ 127
18 Percent Loan					
0	Borrow	$1,000	—	$1,000	$1,000
1	Interest	(180)	$72	(108)	(94)
2	Interest	(180)	72	(108)	(82)
2	Repayment	(1,000)	—	(1,000)	(756)
	Net Present Value				$ 68
25 Percent Loan					
0	Borrow	$1,000	—	$1,000	$1,000
1	Interest	(250)	$100	(150)	(130)
2	Interest	(250)	100	(150)	(114)
2	Repayment	(1,000)	—	(1,000)	(756)
	Net Present Value				$ 0

Column (3): Interest expense determined by terms of loan: 12, 18, or 25 percent.

Column (4): .40 × (3) when column (3) is deductible on tax return.

Column (5): (3) + (4).

Column (6): Amount in column (5) discounted at 15 percent using factors from Table 2.

End of Year 0	1,00000
End of Year 1	.86957
End of Year 2	.75614

expense. Column (6) shows the net present values of the cash flows, positive in the top two panels and zero in the third.

The top two panels of Exhibit 10.6 show apparently positive net present value from an outright borrowing. The first two might indicate to a naive analyst that the borrowing is worthwhile.[8]

---

[8]In the top panel of Exhibit 10.6, the market interest rate—12 percent—is lower than the after-tax cost of capital of 15 percent. The other two panels show interest rates—18 percent and 25 percent—higher than the after-tax cost of capital. Twenty-five percent is the breakeven rate—the borrowing rate at which the net present value of the borrowing goes to zero. One would never expect to see a case where the borrowing rate was as high as the pretax cost of capital. We show this case to illustrate the breakeven point.

A net present value analysis of the cash flows from a loan will show a positive net present value whenever the pretax borrowing rate is less than the pretax cost of capital. In this example, the pretax cost of capital is 25 percent [= .15/(1.00 − .40)]. Put differently, a loan will show positive net present value whenever the after-tax cost of borrowing is less than the cost of capital. In this case, the after-tax cost of borrowing is the interest rate multiplied by .60 (= 1.00 − .40 income tax rate). For example if the borrowing rate is 12 percent, the after-tax cost of borrowing is 7.2 percent.

A loan will, as in Exhibit 10.6, show a positive net present value whenever the after-tax cost of capital exceeds the after-tax borrowing rate. This positive net present value appears even though the loan does not improve the borrower's risk-adjusted expected returns. The fact that the present value is positive and the firm is not better off shows the weakness of embedding the financing arrangement in the net present value analysis. Next, we illustrate such an embedding and the misleading signal it causes.

Leasing Is a Form of Financing

Types of Leases

Leases are of two broad types. **Cancelable leases,** such as for the use of telephones by the month or of cars by the day or week, are generally short-term and either party in the rental transaction can cancel it. These leases do not present any analytic difficulties because they involve no long-term commitments to cash flows.

Noncancelable leases, on the other hand, run for longer periods of time. Under these leases, a firm commits itself to payments over the term of the lease whether or not it continues to use the leased asset. The obligation under a noncancelable lease does not, in an economic sense, differ significantly from a loan from a bank or other creditor. These leasing arrangements are, in effect, installment purchases of the property. The noncancelable lease is a means of financing the acquisition of an asset's service for a specified period of time.

Evaluating Leases

Properly evaluating a leasing proposal separates the investment and financial decisions. First, decide if the firm should acquire the asset's services (the investment decision). To do this, calculate the net present value of the cash flows expected to be generated by the asset, assuming that the firm purchases the asset immediately for cash. Use the cost of capital as the discount rate. If the net present value is positive, consider the form of financing. If the net present value is negative, do not consider the proposal further.[9]

---

[9]In stating the rule this way, we assume that the lessor has not reduced the implicit purchase price in the lease as compared to the outright purchase price.

Illustration of the Lease Evaluation Procedure

Return to the example of JEP Realty Syndicators discussed in Chapter 9. The company considers acquiring computer hardware that will permit it to market a new investment package. To purchase the computer requires an immediate cash payment of $100,000. Alternatively, the manufacturer will lease the asset to JEP Realty for a rental fee of $29,832 a year for 5 years, after which the lessor will scrap the asset.

Investment Decision   First decide if acquiring the asset's services is a good investment, as in Exhibit 9.2. The analysis appears again in the top panel of Exhibit 10.7. The analysis assumes that JEP purchases the asset outright and that it discounts annual cash flows at the cost of capital of 12 percent per year. If JEP purchases the

Exhibit 10.7

Annual Net Cash Flows and Net Present Values of Alternatives Available to JEP Reality Syndicators for Acquiring Use of Asset[a]

End of Year (1)	Pretax Cash Inflows Minus Cash Outflow Expenses (2)	Depreciation (3)	Lease Payments (4)	Pretax Income (5)	Income Tax Expense (6)	Net Cash Inflows (Outflows) (7)	Present Value of Net Cash Flows at 12% (8)
Purchase Asset Outright; No Borrowing (See Exhibits 9.1 and 9.2)							
0	$(100,000)	—	—	—	—	$(100,000)	$(100,000)
1	50,000	$ 20,000	—	$30,000	$12,000	38,000	33,929
2	40,000	20,000	—	20,000	8,000	32,000	25,510
3	30,000	20,000	—	10,000	4,000	26,000	18,506
4	25,000	20,000	—	5,000	2,000	23,000	14,617
5	15,000	20,000	—	(5,000)	(2,000)	17,000	9,646
	$ 60,000	$100,000		$60,000	$24,000	$ 36,000	$ 2,208
Lease Asset; Lease Payment Made at the End of Each Period							
0	—	—	—	—	—	—	—
1	$ 50,000	—	$ 29,832	$20,168	$ 8,067	$ 12,101	$ 10,804
2	40,000	—	29,832	10,168	4,067	6,101	4,864
3	30,000	—	29,832	168	67	101	72
4	25,000	—	29,832	(4,832)	(1,933)	(2,899)	(1,842)
5	15,000	—	29,829	(14,829)	(5,932)	(8,897)	(5,048)
	$160,000		$149,157	$10,843	$ 4,336	$ 6,507	$ 8,850

[a]Discount rate is 12 percent per year; income taxes are 40 percent of pretax income.

Column (2): Refer to Exhibit 9.2. The amounts shown here are the amounts in column (2) minus the amounts shown in column (3) of Exhibit 9.2. The initial outlay is not an expense.

Column (3): Straight-line method; $100,000 cost/5-year life.

Column (5): Amount in column (2) minus amounts in columns (3) and (4).

Column (6): Forty percent of amount in column (5).

Column (7): Amount in column (2) minus amounts in columns (4) and (6).

Column (8): Amount in column (7) multiplied by present value factor for 12 percent discount rate.

asset, the net present value of the investment project is $2,208. Acquiring the asset is, therefore, worthwhile.

Financing Decision   Next we must consider how JEP should finance the investment. We must consider this second question because leasing is a form of financing.

The bottom panel of Exhibit 10.7 shows the calculation of the net present value assuming that JEP acquires the asset by leasing. Instead of a cash outflow of $100,000 at time zero, the cash outflow is $29,832 per year for 4 years for lease payments and $29,829 in the last year. To simplify the illustration, we assume that lease payments occur at the end of each year. Because JEP Realty is leasing the asset, it will not deduct depreciation expense in calculating taxable income but will deduct rent expense. JEP discounts the net after-tax cash flows using the cost of capital of 12 percent. The net present value of acquiring the asset's services through leasing is $8,850. Notice that the net present value of leasing is four times as large as the net present value of outright purchase.

Some managers would note the much larger net present value for the leasing plan and conclude that leasing is surely better for the firm than buying outright. *Comparing the net present values of buying outright versus leasing is invalid.* The analysis has combined the investment decision with the financing decision. A noncancelable lease is a form of borrowing. In the first case, the firm is not borrowing; in the second case, it is borrowing. To evaluate the leasing plan, the manager should analyze alternative financing plans as well. It will apply the methods of corporate finance.

Why Does Leasing Appear More Attractive Than Outright Purchase?

Leasing has a net present value more than four times as large as the net present value of the outright purchase. Why? We can rephrase this question to make the managerial implications clearer. Suppose that the cash flow in Year 1 were only $45,000, not $50,000. The analysis of the outright purchase then shows a negative net present value, indicating that the project is not worthwhile for the company. The analyses of leasing shows a positive net present values, indicating that the project is worthwhile when leased but not when purchased. What should the manager conclude?

The answers to both questions involve the difference between the after-tax interest cost of debt and the cost of capital used in making investment decisions. In the illustration for JEP Realty, the after-tax cost of capital is 12 percent, whereas the borrowing rate is 15 percent. The net present value analysis of the leasing alternative charges the company with interest on borrowings at 15 percent, with an after-tax cost of 9 percent [$= (1.00 - .40) \times 15$ percent], but discounts the cash flows at 12 percent. Any present value analysis of a series of interest payments discounted at a higher rate than the after-tax rate implied by the loan contract will show the present value of the debt service payments to have a lower present value than the face amount of the borrowing. Recall the discussion of financing methods illustrated in Exhibit 10.6.

The phenomenon of **leverage** occurs when the rate of return on total capital increases because the rate typically earned by the company on its projects exceeds the rate paid to borrow. The difference between the net present values of leasing and outright purchase results from showing the expected returns to leverage as a part of the return to the specific project. But, of course, the firm always has the option to borrow at the current market rate of interest. The returns and risks of leverage accrue to the firm's financing policy as a whole. The analysis should not attribute them to any one investment project.[10]

Considering Investment and Financing Decisions Simultaneously Can Be Acceptable

Are there conditions under which the analysis in the second panel of Exhibit 10.7 is correct for making an investment decision? In other words, can it ever be correct to consider the net present value of the combined operating and financing cash flows? Yes.

If the lessor allows the lessee to make debt service (lease) payments solely from the cash flows produced by the leased asset, then correct analysis combines the financing plan and the operating cash flows. This is *not* the same thing as saying that the leased asset is collateral for the loan.

Example   The Burlington Northern (BN) Railroad leases for 12 years from the General Electric Credit Company a new heavy-duty locomotive for hauling coal from the Powder River Basin in Wyoming to San Antonio. BN promises to pay $2,000,000 per year for 12 years. BN must make the payments whatever use (if any) it makes of the locomotive. If the railroad fails to make payments, the Credit Company may seize the locomotive, which it owns.

Case A   The Credit Company expects payments from whatever cash BN has on hand, independent of the business that generated the cash. If BN should go bankrupt, the Credit Company may collect amounts due to it, just as any other creditor. In this case, the decision to acquire the locomotive is independent of the particular financing arrangements offered by the lessor. The railroad ought to make the investment decision on the basis of the cash flows from using the locomotive, assuming that it is purchased for cash.

Case B   The Credit Company is willing to have debt service (lease) payments made solely from the revenues of hauling coal with this particular locomotive. If BN does not use the locomotive for any reason for a given year, BN need not make the

---

[10]The nature of leasing contracts can be somewhat more complicated than indicated here. For example, the lessee may pay in advance, with the initial lease payment being immediately deductible for tax purposes. It is not usually possible to arrange a straight loan with interest payable in advance that is deductible for tax purposes. (In theory, there is no such thing as interest paid in advance. If a borrower makes payments before interest has accrued, theory says that those payments must be a reduction in the principal amount of the loan, not interest.) Another complication arises when the manufacturer offers a "package deal," where the combined interest payments and asset cost are smaller together than they would be separately. (Automobile dealers often are willing to sell at a lower price when the buyer borrows from the dealer than when the buyer makes an outright purchase.) The advanced questions raised by some leasing contracts are beyond the scope of this introductory, but already sophisticated, discussion. The reader interested in a more advanced discussion can consult Chapter 8 of *Handbook of Modern Accounting,* 2nd ed., Sidney Davidson and Roman L. Weil, eds. (New York: McGraw-Hill, 1977) and S. Basu, *Leasing Arrangements: Managerial Decision Making and Financial Reporting Issues* (Hamilton, Ontario: Society of Management Accountants of Canada, 1980).

$2,000,000 payment for the year. In this case BN can consider the financing deci-
sion simultaneously with the investment decision, because BN's acquisition of the
debt in becoming the lessee of the locomotive will not affect its ability to borrow
funds (or issue new equity shares) to finance other parts of its business. This situation would be unusual, but occasionally arises, particularly in some leveraged leases.

■ Summary ■

The optimal method for evaluating investment projects should take the time value of
money into account. All the methods that do take the time value of money into
account require a cutoff rate or discount rate, sometimes called a hurdle rate. If the
firm wants to make correct economic decisions, it must set the cutoff or discount
rate equal to the cost of capital. If the firm is to use the cost of capital rate, the net
present value rule is no more complex than the others. Using the net present value
rule will lead to decisions that will make present value of the firm's wealth equal to
or larger than that from using any of the other rules.

Under many circumstances, the net present value method and the internal rate
of return method give identical answers. In some circumstances, particularly those
involving mutually exclusive projects, the internal rate of return method can give
misleading results. Thus the analyst should use the net present value method in
making the investment decision.

Analysis should separate the investment decision and the financing decision for
investment projects. The use of the present value rule and the differential principle
for making decisions will enable the manager to choose between various methods of
financing only if the contending financing plans involve equal amounts of borrowing for equal amounts of time. Otherwise, the analysis will combine the benefits of
financial leverage with the benefits from a particular investment project.

Problem 1 for Self-Study

Management of the Antle Company considers an investment project that requires an
initial investment of $10,000 and that promises to return $14,641, after taxes, at the
end of 4 years. Because the firm's after-tax cost of capital is 10 percent per year, the
net present value of the investment is zero. An investment banker points out, however, that if the firm borrows the $10,000 via a 4-year annual coupon bond issue,
the annual interest expense (based on 8 percent coupons) will be $800 but will be
only $480 after taxes at a 40 percent rate. The net present value of the project will
increase from zero to $1,648, and the project will be worthwhile. The banker offers
to arrange a $10,000 loan at an 8 percent rate.

a. Verify that the net present value of the project is zero.

b. Reproduce the investment banker's analysis given above; use five-place present
    value factors.

c. Comment on the investment banker's proposal and advise the Antle Company
    as to how it should evaluate the project.

Exhibit 10.8

ANTLE COMPANY
(Problem 1 for Self-Study)

End of Year (1)	Cash Flow If Borrow $10,000 (2)	Present Value Factor at 10 Percent (3)	Amount = (2) × (3) (4)
0	$10,000 − $10,000 = $ 0	1.00000	$ 0
1	(800) × (1 − .40) = (480)	.90909	(436)
2	(800) × (1 − .40) = (480)	.82645	(397)
3	(800) × (1 − .40) = (480)	.75131	(361)
4	(800) × (1 − .40) = (480)	.68301	(328)
4	14,641 − 10,000 = 4,641	.68301	3,170
			$1,648

Suggested Solution

a. Table 2, 4-period row, 10 percent column is .68301; $14,641 × .68301 = $10,000.

b. See Exhibit 10.8.

c. The analysis in Exhibit 10.8 combines the investment and financing decision. Antle should ignore the investment banker's advice unless the only collateral for the loan is the investment project itself *and* the only source of debt service payments for the bond issue is cash flows from the project. (Because the project has cash flows only in the last years, no lender is likely to make such a loan.) Otherwise, this analysis indicates that Antle Company should be indifferent to this project.

Problem 2 for Self-Study

Fabco Manufacturing Company considers the purchase of two different types of machines to manufacture rubber gaskets, one of the many products it produces for industrial markets. The two machines are alike in the following ways: Each requires an initial investment of $750,000; lasts 5 years, after which the salvage value is zero; and has sufficient capacity to meet the projected steady demand. The main difference between the two machines is the timing and amount of operating cash flows. Machine A's operating cash costs would start out high and then decrease in subsequent years. Machine B promises constant operating cash costs. The end-of-year incremental net cash flows (revenues minus operating cash costs) for the two machines follow:

	After-Tax Cash Flow per Year, End of Year					
	0	1	2	3	4	5
Machine A	$(750,000)	$100,000	$200,000	$200,000	$300,000	$550,000
Machine B	(750,000)	250,000	250,000	250,000	250,000	250,000

Fabco needs to decide which, if either, of the two machines to buy to manufacture rubber gaskets. Unsure of which method of evaluation to use, the vice president has asked that calculations be made for the following methods:

(1) Payback period (assume, for this calculation only, that cash flows occur evenly throughout the year).

(2) Accounting rate of return.

(3) Internal rate of return.

(4) Net present value (cost of capital = 10 percent).

(5) Net present value (cost of capital = 12 percent).

a. Perform these calculations for each machine. (Use discount factors rounded to five decimal places.) For each method, state which machine appears to be the better investment.

b. Why does the net present value method yield different decisions at the two different discount rates? Does the internal rate of return method exhibit the same phenomenon?

c. Comment on the usefulness of each of the preceding methods for choosing between the two machines.

Suggested Solution

Exhibit 10.9 provides data used in various parts of the solution.

Exhibit 10.9

FABCO MANUFACTURING COMPANY
(Problem 2 for Self-Study)

	Cash Flow	Discount Factor at 10 Percent	Present Value at 10 Percent	Discount Factor at 12 Percent	Present Value at 12 Percent
Machine A					
Year 0..................	$(750,000)	1.00000	$(750,000)	1.00000	$(750,000)
Year 1..................	100,000	.90909	90,909	.89286	89,286
Year 2..................	200,000	.82645	165,290	.79719	159,438
Year 3..................	200,000	.75131	150,262	.71178	142,356
Year 4..................	300,000	.68301	204,903	.63552	190,656
Year 5..................	550,000	.62092	341,506	.56743	312,087
Net Present Value			$ 202,870		$ 143,823
Machine B					
Year 0..................	$(750,000)	1.00000	$(750,000)	1.00000	$(750,000)
Year 1..................	250,000	.90909	227,273	.89286	223,215
Year 2..................	250,000	.82645	206,613	.79719	199,298
Year 3..................	250,000	.75131	187,828	.71178	177,945
Year 4..................	250,000	.68301	170,753	.63552	158,880
Year 5..................	250,000	.62092	155,230	.56743	141,858
Net Present Value			$ 197,697		$ 151,196

a. **(1)**   Payback period:

Machine A. Cumulative cash inflow at the end of Year 3 = $500,000. Total investment of $750,000 − $500,000 = $250,000 remaining to be recouped in Year 4.

$$\frac{\$250,000}{\$300,000} = .83.$$

Thus payback period = 3.83 years.

Machine B:

$$\text{Payback Period} = \frac{\$750,000}{\$250,000 \text{ per Year}} = 3.0 \text{ Years.}$$

Decision: Purchase Machine B if a payback period of 3 years is acceptable.

(2)   Accounting rate of return (or return on investment):

Machine A:

$$\text{Average Net Income} = \frac{\text{Total Cash Flow} - \text{Total Depreciation}}{5}$$

$$= \frac{\$1,350,000 - \$750,000}{5}$$

$$= \$120,000.$$

$$\text{Average Investment} = \frac{\$750,000}{2}$$

$$= \$375,000.$$

$$\text{ROI} = \frac{\$120,000}{\$375,000} = 32\%.$$

Machine B:

$$\text{Average Net Income} = \frac{\$1,250,000 - \$750,000}{5} = \$100,000.$$

$$\text{Average Investment} = \frac{\$750,000}{2} = \$375,000.$$

$$\text{ROI} = \frac{\$100,000}{\$375,000} = 26.7\%$$

Decision: Purchase Machine A if 32 percent is an acceptable ROI.

(3)   Internal rate of return:

Machine A:

$$\text{At } 12\%, \quad \text{NPV} = \$143,823,$$

At 20%,   NPV = ($46,330),

calculated using five-decimal-place discount factors.
By interpolation, IRR is approximated as follows:

$$\frac{(\$46,330)}{\$143,823 + \$46,330} \times (20\% - 12\%) = -1.95\%$$

$$20\% - 1.95\% = 18.05\% \text{ IRR.}$$

Or, using a pocket calculator, IRR = 17.78 percent.

Machine B:

At 12%,   NPV = $151,195,

At 20%,   NPV = ($2,350),

calculated using five-decimal-place discount factors.
Interpolating:

$$\frac{(\$2,350)}{\$151,195 + \$2,350} \times (20\% - 12\%) = -.12\%$$

$$20\% - .12\% = 19.88\% \text{ IRR.}$$

Or, using a pocket calculator, IRR = 19.86 percent.
Decision: Purchase Machine B if 19.86 percent is considered a sufficiently high IRR.

(4)   Net present value at 10 percent (see Exhibit 10.9):

Machine A: NPV = $202,870.

Machine B: NPV = $197,697.

Decision: Purchase Machine A. Both have a positive NPV, and the NPV for machine A is higher.

(5)   Net present value at 12 percent (see Exhibit 10.9):

Machine A: NPV = $143,823.

Machine B: NPV = $151,196.

Decision: Purchase Machine B. Both have a positive NPV, and Machine B's is higher.

b.   Machine A's cash inflows occur later than those of Machine B. Therefore, at higher discount rates, Machine A looks less attractive than Machine B. But because Machine A's total cash inflows are greater, at a sufficiently low discount rate its NPV is greater than that of Machine B. The crossover point occurs somewhere between the discount rates of 10 percent and 12 percent. The internal rate of return is higher than the discount rate at which Machine B becomes more attractive than Machine A; hence, Machine B dominates Machine A using IRR.

c.   The payback period and ROI methods both ignore the time value of money. As these two machines differ mainly in the timing of their cash inflows, failure to consider the time value of money results in an incomplete comparison of cash flows.

The internal rate of return method considers all the cash flows and the time value of money, but it still does not always lead to the same decision as the net present value method. As discussed in part **b**, the IRR for each machine is a single number to be compared to the hurdle rate, whereas the relative NPVs for the two machines depend on the firm's cost of capital. The most useful method for making the purchase decision is the net present value method, with careful thought about the firm's measure of its cost of capital.

Problem 3 for Self-Study

The purpose of this problem is to expand on the text's discussion of the impact of financing on capital budgeting decisions.

Only in exceptional cases will a specific financing instrument be tied so closely to a specific investment project that the capital cost of the investment is the cost·of the specific financing instrument.

Consider two firms, Company A and Company B. Both companies operate two lines of business of the same size. The first line of business is owning, and leasing to others, railroad oil tank cars. Their second line of business is owning and leasing vacation homes near recreational lakes. In financing the two businesses, Company A and Company B borrow funds from local banks to supplement the funds invested by the owners. For purchases of oil tank cars to be put on lease, First National Bank will lend 80 percent of the purchase price through long-term, fixed-interest-rate loans. For purchases of vacation homes, Second National Bank will lend only 40 percent of the purchase price through long-term, fixed-interest-rate loans. First National Bank finances only tank car loans and Second National Bank finances only vacation home loans.

Company A   First National Bank has agreed that Company A needs to make interest payments on the tank car debt and all tank car debt principal repayments only out of tank car rentals. The only collateral for the loans is the tank cars. Company A need not use the proceeds from vacation home rentals in any way to service the tank car debt to First National Bank. The financing of the vacation homes is similar: Debt service payments to Second National Bank will come only from rentals of vacation homes, and the only collateral for the loan is the home being financed with a given loan.[11]

Company B   Company B, while identical in its assets and operations to Company A, has conventional installment note financing for both its tank car and vacation home purchases. That is, both banks look to all income of the firm—from whatever source—for payment of interest and principal on debt. The banks can receive the

---

[11]These simplified facts highlight the issue. Only in the cases of some leveraged leases and certain loans from the federal Small Business Administration to new businesses have we actually seen financing of this sort.

payments as they come due from the assets Company B has on hand. Thus Company B must pay interest due First National Bank, for example, with earnings from vacation homes if tank car rentals are insufficient. Moreover, if Company B defaults on its loans to the First National Bank, the bank can expect to receive some of the proceeds of disposing of the vacation homes.

Analyze the differences between Company A's and Company B's financings. How do the implications of these differences affect capital budgeting decisions?

Suggested Solution

The risks assumed by the banks in lending to Company A differ from the risks assumed in lending to Company B. Management of Company A would be correct to consider simultaneously the investment and financing decision for a new tank-car debt. The interest rate on the loan is the appropriate cost of funds for management of Company A to consider in making decisions about new tank cars. At Company B, however, a new loan for a new tank-car deal affects the likelihood of repayment of *all* old loans. Thus the impact of new loans on the company's entire business must be considered. Management of Company B must consider more than cost of the new debt used to acquire new assets. Situations like Company A, where specific financings relate to specific assets, are unusual enough that managers who believe they have one ought to be careful to make sure they understand all aspects of the financing.

Key Terms and Concepts

Internal rate of return (IRR)

Cutoff (hurdle) rate

Mutually exclusive projects

Scale effect

Excess present value index

Payback period

Discounted payback period

Accounting rate of return

Cancelable lease contrasted with
   noncancelable lease

Leverage

Questions, Exercises, Problems, and Cases

Questions

1. Review the meaning of the concepts or terms given above in Key Terms and Concepts.

2. **a.** The internal rate of return rule and the net present value rule both take the time value of money into account and usually give the same decision. When may they give different decisions?

   b. "The internal rate of return is more difficult to compute than the net present value of a project. The internal rate of return method can never give a better answer than the net present value method.'' Why, then, do you suppose that so many people use the internal rate of return method?

3. What are the weaknesses of using the payback period as a device for capital budgeting decisions?

4. For mutually exclusive projects, the project with the lowest net present value of cash inflow per dollar of initial cash outlay can be the best alternative for the firm. How can this be?

5. ''Under no conditions should the investment decision be made simultaneously with the financing decision.''

    Comment.

6. Assume that a firm borrows cash at a fair market interest rate less than its opportunity cost of capital. The net present value of the cash flows from this loan is positive when the cash flows are discounted at the firm's cost of capital.

    Why will this loan *not necessarily* increase the wealth of the firm or its owners?

7. Assume that a firm borrows at a fair market interest rate and computes the net present value of the cash flows—proceeds of borrowings and after-tax debt-service payments—using the after-tax cost of capital. Generally, the result will be a positive number, indicating that the borrowing project is a worthwhile undertaking according to the net present value rule.

    Comment on this phenomenon.

Exercises

8. *Net present value and mutually exclusive projects.* The Larson Company must choose between two mutually exclusive projects. The cost of capital is 12 percent. Given the following data, which project should Larson choose, and why?

	After-Tax Cash Flows, End of Year			
Project Label	0	1	2	3
M.........................	$(500,000)	$175,000	$287,500	$400,000
N.........................	(450,000)	477,000	195,000	60,000

9. *Computing internal rate of return.* What is the internal rate of return on the following projects, each of which requires a $10,000 cash outlay now and returns the cash flows indicated?

    a. $5,530.67 at the end of Years 1 and 2.
    b. $1,627.45 at the end of Years 1 through 10.
    c. $1,556.66 at the end of Years 1 through 13.
    d. $2,053.39 at the end of Years 1 through 20.
    e. $2,921.46 at the end of Years 3 through 7.

     f. $2,101.77 at the end of Years 2 through 10.

     g. $24,883.20 at the end of Year 5 only.

10. *Computing payback.* What is the payback period of the projects in Exercise 9, **a** through **g**?

11. *Relation between internal rate of return and payback period.* Compare the internal rate of return on the projects in Exercise 9, **a** through **d**, with the *reciprocal* of the payback period for those projects computed in Exercise 10. Notice that the internal rate of return on **d** is exactly equal to the reciprocal of its payback period, but this relation does not hold for the other projects. Explain.

12. *Computing payback.* What is the payback period of the projects in Exercise 9, **a** through **g**, assuming that cash flows occur uniformly throughout the year?

13. *Working backwards with net present value method.* A manager's favorite project requires an after-tax cash outflow on January 1 of $4,000 and promises to return $1,000 of after-tax cash inflows at the end of each of the next 5 years. The after-tax cost of capital is 10 percent per year.

     a. Use the net present value method to decide whether this favorite project is a good investment.

     b. How much would the projected cash inflow for the end of Year 5 have to increase for the project to be acceptable?

     c. How much would the projected cash inflow for the end of Year 5 have to increase for the project to have a net present value of $100?

14. *Computing internal rate of return.* Carlo Company is considering acquiring a machine that costs $40,000 and that promises to save $8,000 in cash outlays per year, after taxes, at the end of each of the next 12 years. Carlo expects the new machine to have no salvage value at the end of its useful life. (You may compute the actual return on your calculator or use Table 4 at the back of the book and interpolate.)

     a. Compute the internal rate of return for this project.

     b. Compute the internal rate of return, assuming that the cash savings were to last only 6, instead of 12, years.

     c. Compute the internal rate of return, assuming that the cash savings were to last 20, rather than 12, years.

     d. Compute the internal rate of return, assuming that the cash savings would be $6,000 rather than $8,000 per year for 12 years.

15. *Computing net present value of leverage.* Compute the apparent benefits of financial leverage for each of the following annual coupon bond issues. Assume an income tax rate of 40 percent and an after-tax cost of capital of 12 percent.

     a. $100,000 borrowed for 5 years at 12 percent.

     b. $100,000 borrowed for 10 years at 12 percent.

     c. $100,000 borrowed for 5 years at 15 percent.

     d. $100,000 borrowed for 5 years at 20 percent.

Problems

16. *Managerial incentives of performance evaluation based on accounting data.* A firm with an opportunity cost of capital of 20 percent faces two mutually exclusive investment projects:

(1) Acquire goods at the start of the year, ship them to Japan, and sell them at the end of the year. The internal rate of return on this project is 25 percent, and it has positive net present value.

(2) Making certain expenditures today that will cause reported earnings for the year to decline. This will result, however, in large cash flows at the ends of the second and third years. The internal rate of return on this project is 35 percent, and it has even larger net present value than the first project. Management observes that for the current year the second project will result in smaller earnings reported to its shareholders than the first.

How might management's observation influence its choice between the two investment projects?

17. *Multiple IRRs.* Consider an investment in a strip-mining operation where the cash flows are negative at the outset, positive during the intermediate years, and negative at the end because of expenditures to restore the mine site to its premining environment. For simplicity, assume that there are only three periodic cash flows: $100,000 initial investment, $225,000 cash inflow from ore at the end of the first period, and a $126,500 cash outflow for restoration at the end of the second period.

a. Demonstrate that this project has two internal rates of return: 10 percent per period and 15 percent per period. Observe that the internal rate of return methodology for capital budgeting as usually stated (''compute the internal rate of return and accept the project if the rate exceeds the hurdle rate'') fails to give clear guidance in this case.

b. Compute the net present value of this project at discount rates of 5 percent, 12 percent, and 20 percent.

c. Using the net present value method, state a decision rule for accepting or rejecting this project as a function of the cost of capital.

18. *Leverage and decision making.* Management of the Xenophon Company is considering an investment project that requires an initial investment of $100,000 and promises to return $176,234, after taxes, at the end of 5 years. Because the after-tax cost of capital of the firm is 12 percent per year, the net present value of this investment is zero. Management finds itself indifferent to the project. A financial analyst points out, however, that if the firm will borrow the $100,000 via a 5-year annual coupon bond issue, the annual interest expense will be $15,000, or $9,000 after taxes, the net present value of the project will increase from zero to $10,814, and it will become worthwhile.

a. Verify that the net present value of the project is zero.

b. Reproduce the analysis that the financial analyst has in mind.

c. Comment on the suggestion of the financial analyst.

19. *Definition of alternatives to be considered*. Consider two mutually exclusive alternatives facing a manufacturer of food blenders:

    (1) Sell the existing blender equipment and get out of the business, netting $1,000 cash proceeds from sale.

    (2) Stay in the blender business, generating $200 of net cash inflows per year at the end of each of the next 10 years.

    a. Why is there no well-defined internal rate of return on alternative (1)?

    b. Why is there no well-defined internal rate of return on alternative (2)?

    c. Some who favor the internal rate of return methodology would "rescue" that methodology from the difficulty in situations such as this one by defining the *incremental* investment project, which is the algebraic difference between the cash flows of the two alternatives. Consider the incremental project defined as cash flows from alternative (2) minus cash flows from alternative (1), as described previously. Such a project shows an outflow of $1,000 now in return for inflows of $200 at the end of each of the next 10 years. (One may be tempted to say that this incremental project represents the opportunity cost—an investment of $1,000—of staying in business, followed by the actual cash inflows of staying in business—$200 per year. Such intermixing of opportunity costs and actual cash flows can confuse even the experienced analyst.) Demonstrate that such a project has an internal rate of return of about 15 percent and that staying in the blender business is superior to getting out as long as the cost of capital is less than or equal to 15 percent.

    d. Consider a third alternative facing the manufacturer of food blenders:

    (3) Sell the blender equipment and purchase equipment for manufacturing food processors. This alternative implies cash expenditures of $4,000 currently and cash flows of $900 per year in arrears for 15 years.

    How can you compare such an alternative to alternatives (1) and (2) with the internal rate of return methodology?

    e. Consider a fourth alternative facing the manufacturer:

    (4) Stay in the blender business and add the processor business. This alternative implies cash outflow of $5,000 currently, followed by cash inflows of $1,050 at the end of each of the next 10 years and cash inflows of $900 at the end of each of the 5 years thereafter.

    How can you compare such an alternative to (1), (2), and (3) with the internal rate of return methodology?

    f. What do you conclude about "rescuing" the internal rate of return method using the technique of constructing incremental investment projects?

20. *Analyzing a lease*. The Myers Company wonders whether to acquire a computer that has a 3-year life, costs $30,000, and will save $25,000 per year before taxes in cash operating costs as compared to the present data processing system. Myers Company can borrow for 3 years at 12 percent per year. The computer manufacturer is willing to sell the computer for $30,000 or to lease it for 3 years on a noncancelable basis—that is, on the basis that Myers Company must make payments for the 3 years no matter what happens. The annual lease payment will be $12,490 except in the third year, when it is

$12,491. The income tax rate is 40 percent. If Myers purchases the computer, it will depreciate the computer over 3 years, using accelerated cost recovery percentages of 25 percent in the first year, 38 percent in the second, and 37 percent in the third.

Prepare an analysis that will help Myers Company decide what it should do. Round discount factors to two places. The after-tax cost of capital is 10 percent.

Integrative Problems and Cases

21. *Compare lease with borrow/buy.* The Carom Company plans to acquire, as of January 1, 19X0, a computerized cash register system that costs $100,000 and that has a 5-year life and no salvage value. The new computerized system will save $35,000 in cash operating costs per year. The company is considering two plans for acquiring the system:

(1) Outright purchase. To finance the purchase, Carom will issue $100,000 of par value, 5-year, 15-percent annual coupon bonds January 1, 19X0, at par.

(2) Lease. The lease requires five annual payments to be made on December 31, 19X0, 19X1, 19X2, 19X3, and 19X4. The lease payments are to be $29,832 and they have a present value of $100,000 on January 1, 19X0, when discounted at 15 percent per year.

The firm's after-tax cost of capital is 12 percent. Carom will use accelerated cost recovery for tax purposes with the following percentages in each of the 5 years, respectively: 25, 38, 37, 0, and 0. The income tax rate is 40 percent.

a. Construct an exhibit similar to Exhibit 10.7. Round discount factors to two decimal places. Use three panels, one for each of the following alternatives.

(i) Outright purchase for cash.
(ii) Outright purchase with borrowing as explained in (1).
(iii) Lease under terms as explained in (2).

b. Should Carom acquire the services of the asset? How did you reach this conclusion?

c. Which of the financing plans, borrowing via a bond issue or leasing, appears preferable? How can one financing plan with an interest cost of 15 percent per year (bond issue) appear to be preferable to another financing plan with an interest cost of 15 percent per year (lease)? What can you conclude from the answers to these two questions?

d. Now assume that the lease contract calls for payments of $28,500 per year (an implicit interest rate of only 13.1 percent). Construct a fourth panel in the exhibit called for in part a. Which financing plan, leasing at 13.1 percent or borrowing at 15 percent, appears to be preferable? How can one plan of financing with an interest cost of 15 percent per year (bond issue) appear to be preferable to another plan of financing with an interest cost of 13.1 percent per year (lease)? What can you conclude from the answers to these two questions?

e. Should Carom Company lease the asset or purchase it? How can you tell? If you judge that purchase is preferable, what is the minimum after-tax payment that the lessor could offer to make Carom Company indifferent to leasing?

22. *Merits of internal rate of return.* A well-known university sponsors a continuing education program for engineers. One of its programs is called "Evaluating Project Alternatives by Rate of Return." The advertising copy for this program says, in part:

> *Why You Should Attend* Traditionally, a large percentage of business decisions have been based solely on payback. Although the payback method has the advantage of computational simplicity, it is not a true measure of life-cycle cost effectiveness and can lead to erroneous accept-reject decisions.

> *Why Use Rate of Return*

> (1) Takes into account:
>   Cash flows beyond the payback period.
>   Timing of cash flows within the payback period.
> (2) Does not discriminate against long-lived projects.
> (3) Does not ignore the time value of money.
> (4) Differentiates between debt and equity capital.
> (5) Does not require stipulation of an interest rate.
> (6) Provides for:
>   Return of and on debt and equity capital.
>   Income taxes, income tax write-offs.
>   Inflation.
>   Costs that escalate at a rate greater than the rate of inflation.
> (7) Permits an accurate ranking of alternatives.
> (8) Gives correct choice among independent alternatives.
> (9) Maximizes return on investment.

Assume that by "rate of return," this advertising means the "internal rate of return."

Comment on the nine numbered points from the copy. Consider these points as they apply to both the internal rate of return method and the net present value method.

23. *Merits of lessee's benefits of leasing.* A well-known company with a financing subsidiary promotes its leasing activities (as lessor) with material containing the following statements. Evaluate these statements.

> *Retain Favorable Tax Advantages* Many companies in capital intensive industries are not in a position to use accelerated depreciation to full advantage. Yet these companies often need new equipment. Leasing offers a solution to the problem: The lessee can assign tax benefits—benefits it cannot use—to the lessor in exchange for reduced lease payments. No other form of equipment financing provides this important advantage.

Conserve Cash   Normally, leasing affords 100 percent financing. There are no down payments or compensating balances. If a company ties up its cash to purchase equipment, the earning power of the cash itself is lost. But if the same company were to lease equipment, it could still put the cash into other profitable investments. For this reason, in the long run, leasing can help maximize the use of a company's resources. Leasing gives a company the opportunity to use more equipment or to spend less for equipment. Leasing, in fact, can often do both.

Match Income and Expense, and Stay within Capital Budgets   If a company purchases equipment, it immediately pays for the last day of production as well as the first. But leasing allows the payment for equipment to be made from the income generated by its use. Furthermore, lease payments can be tailored to fit even the tightest capital equipment budgets. Combined, these attributes make leasing an effective way for companies to sustain rapid growth.

Reduce the Impact of Inflation   If inflation continues, a company that purchases capital equipment will find in the future that the true value of its depreciation allowance has been reduced. But companies that lease equipment will benefit from a reduction in the true value of future lease payments. For this reason leasing can provide an effective hedge against inflation; and to maximize the advantage, many companies choose to lease depreciating assets such as equipment, while purchasing appreciating assets such as property.

Preserve Other Sources of Financing   Growing companies need many sources of financial assistance. When they lease equipment, companies preserve the flexibility to use alternative credit sources in other ways. If a company leases its income-producing equipment, it can still use its bank lines of credit for short-term needs, or it can hold them open in anticipation of future capital requirements.

Control the Use of Equipment   It is the use—not the ownership—of equipment that generates income. A unit of equipment has the same productive capacity regardless of whether it is leased or owned. When equipment is leased, however, its disposition is much easier. At the end of the lease period, the equipment can be leased again, can be purchased, or can be returned to the lessor. The decision is made on the basis of whether the equipment is still profitable, not whether it is owned.

Obtain Favorable Balance Sheet Treatment   When correctly structured, some leases can qualify as operating leases for the purpose of the lessee's accounting treatment. Operating lease payment obligations are not capitalized on the lessee's balance sheet as a liability.

Suggested Solutions to Even-Numbered Exercises

8. *Net present value and mutually exclusive projects.* Choose Project N. See the following table.

End of Year	Discount Factors at 12 Percent	Cash Flows in Thousands		Present Value of Cash Flows in Thousands	
		M	N	M	N
0	1.00000	$(500)	$(450)	$(500.0)	$(450.0)
1	.89286	175	477	156.3	425.9
2	.79719	287.5	195	229.2	155.5
3	.71178	400	60	284.7	42.7
				$170.2	$174.1

Net present value of cash flows discounted at 12 percent is larger for N.

10. *Computing payback*
In years:　**a.** 2　　**e.** 6
　　　　　　b. 7　　**f.** 6
　　　　　　c. 7　　**g.** 5
　　　　　　d. 5

12. *Computing payback*
In years:　**a.** 1.81　　**e.** 5.42
　　　　　　b. 6.14　　**f.** 5.76
　　　　　　c. 6.42　　**g.** 4.40
　　　　　　d. 4.87

14. *Computing internal rate of return*
Actual internal rate of return:
a. 16.94%　　**b.** 5.47%　　**c.** 19.43%　　**d.** 10.45%
Using Table 4 and interpolating:
a.　　　　　　　　　　$40,000/$8,000 = 5.0
Present Value of Annuity, 12 periods, 12% = 6.19437
Present Value of Annuity, 12 periods, 20% = 4.43922
　　　　　　　　　　　　　　　　　　　　　1.75515

　　　　　　　　6.19437 − 5.0 = 1.19347
　　　　　　1.19437/1.75515 = .68049
　　.68049 × (20% − 12%) = 5.44392%
　　　12% + 5.44392% = 17.44392%.

b.　　　　　　　　　　$40,000/$8,000 = 5.0
Present Value of Annuity, 6 periods, 5% = 5.07569
Present Value of Annuity, 6 periods, 6% = 4.91732
　　　　　　　　　　　　　　　　　　　　0.15837

$$5.07569 - 5.0 = .07569$$
$$.07569/.15837 = .47793$$
$$.47793 \times (6.0\% - 5.0\%) = .47793\%$$
$$5\% + .47793\% = \underline{5.47793\%}.$$

c.
$$\$40,000/\$8,000 = 5.0$$

Present Value of Annuity, 20 periods, 12% = 7.46944

Present Value of Annuity, 20 periods, 20% = $\underline{4.86958}$

$$\underline{\underline{2.59986}}$$

$$7.46944 - 5.0 = 2.46944$$
$$2.46944/2.59986 = .94984$$
$$.94984 \times (20\% - 12\%) = 7.59872\%$$
$$12\% + 7.59872\% = \underline{19.59872\%}.$$

d.
$$\$40,000/\$6,000 = 6.66667$$

Present Value of Annuity, 12 periods, 10% = 6.81369

Present Value of Annuity, 12 periods, 12% = $\underline{6.19437}$

$$\underline{.61932}$$

$$6.81369 - 6.66667 = .14702$$
$$.14702/.61932 = .23739$$
$$.23739 \times (12\% - 10\%) = .47478\%$$
$$10\% + .47478\% = \underline{10.47478\%}.$$

... PART FOUR ...

Managerial Planning and Performance Evaluation

...

This part of the book deals with the use of managerial accounting information for managerial planning, control, and internal performance evaluation. We refer to this idea as *planning and performance evaluation* for short.

Part Three of this book, Chapters 6 through 10, focused on managerial decision making. If management applies the principles of differential analysis, it should make economically sound decisions. Once management has made a decision, its job is only partially complete. It must translate selected alternatives into action; then it must evaluate the actions, once taken, to ensure that performance coincides closely with expectations. These latter tasks make up the planning and performance evaluation process. Managers use accounting information to address planning and performance evaluation questions such as these:

- What is our projected level of profits for the year?
- How much should budgeted costs go down if the volume of service calls drops 10 percent?
- How do we measure the efficiency of production activities?

- How can we measure the performance of decentralized parts of the organization?
- How can we design performance measurement systems to encourage employees to act in the best interests of the organization?

Managerial accounting helps managers deal with these issues. Managers use accounting to assign responsibility for actions, primarily through the use of budgets and standards. The accounting system provides information about actual performance that managers can compare with these budgets and standards.

Chapter 11 overviews the planning and performance evaluation process. We show the big picture before discussing detailed methods and concepts. This process ties together goals for the organization, plans for achieving these goals, decisions and activities, and performance evaluation. All of this becomes an ongoing cycle in the organization.

Chapter 12 focuses on developing profit plans and comparing the results with the objectives. Chapters 13 and 14 give more detail about ways to measure and interpret cost variances from plans.

Chapter 15 considers performance evaluation in decentralized operations that have both investment and profit responsibilities.

CHAPTER 11

Planning, Control, and Incentives

Chapter Outline

- The Planning and Control Process
- Motivating People
- Matching the Planning and Control System to Organizational Characteristics
- Responsibility Centers
- Types of Planning and Control Systems
- Incentive Compensation Plans

This chapter overviews the planning and control process that takes place in organizations. It shows how the planning and control process fits the ongoing cycle of setting goals, providing incentives for managers to take actions consistent with organizational objectives, measuring the results of those actions, and comparing results with objectives. This chapter is more qualitative than quantitative; Chapters 12 through 14 present more extensive quantitative analysis.

The Planning and Control Process

The **planning and control process** helps managers direct a firm's resources, including people, to achieve particular goals. The planning and control process comprises the following phases (see Exhibit 11.1):

Exhibit 11.1

Overview of the Planning and Control Process

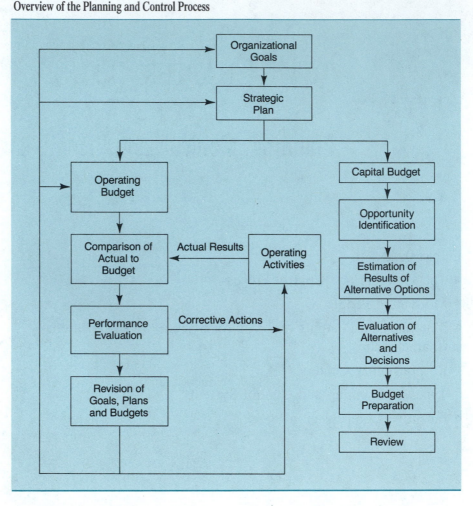

- Setting organizational goals.
- Strategic planning.
- Capital budgeting.
- Operating budgeting.
- Comparison with actual results.
- Performance evaluation and corrective action.
- Revisions of goals, plans, and budgets.

Organizational Goals

Management establishes organizational goals, the set of broad objectives toward which employees work. For example, a *Fortune* 500 company's management recently stated the firm's goals as follows:

Our long range objective is to increase earnings consistently while maintaining our current share of market sales, and maintain an ROI which is within the top one-third of our industry. We plan to achieve these goals while providing our customers with high quality products, and meeting our social responsibilities to our employees and the communities in which they live.[1]

Strategic Plan

The strategic plan states the method or strategy for achieving organizational goals. For example, the previously mentioned firm's strategies include

1. *Cost control.* Optimize contribution from existing product lines by holding product cost increases to less than the rate of inflation. This step will involve installing new machinery proposed in the capital budget, as well as replacing our five least-efficient plants over the next 5 years.

2. *Market share.* Maintain market share by providing a level of service and quality comparable to our top competitor's. This requires improving our quality control so that customer complaints drop from a current level of 4 percent of sales to 1 percent within 2 years.

A **strategic plan** includes long-range (typically 5 years or more) forecasts of sales, including new products, production and capacity requirements, aggregate levels of costs, and financing requirements. The plan also addresses the major capital investments required to maintain present facilities, increase capacity, or diversify to other products. In short, the strategic plan states the long-run strategy for achieving organizational goals. Capital and operating budgets, discussed later, are more specific and detailed. The operating budget, in particular, focuses on near-term time periods.

Planning and Control of Capital Expenditures

Capital investment decisions involve large dollar amounts and commit organizations to long-term plans not easily changed. For example, National Intergroup decided to install a continuous slab caster in a steel plant. This decision committed the company to a particular production process for more than a decade.

Chapters 9 and 10 discussed techniques for making capital investment decisions. Capital budgeting decision making is, however, only one step in planning and controlling capital expenditures. The entire process comprises the five following steps.

1. *Identify opportunities for capital expenditures.* We can classify opportunities for capital expenditures as (a) those dealing with ongoing operations, including replacement, cost-saving methods, and quality improvement methods and (b) those dealing with major changes in operations, including adding or dropping product lines and opportunities for vertical or horizontal integration. Ideas

---

[1]Taken from an internal company document.

about new opportunities for ongoing operations often come from operating personnel—those closest to day-to-day activities. Ideas about major changes in operations usually come from top management and high-level staff positions.

2. *Identify alternative options and estimate results of each.* A firm will drop many opportunities early because they are infeasible or inappropriate. For the remaining opportunities, managers identify alternatives and make estimates of the results that would occur if they implement alternatives. Because of the uncertainty inherent in this process, management should make a range of estimates, "optimistic," "pessimistic," "most likely," and so on. Using computer simulation, analysts can assign probabilities to events and simulate a large number of alternative outcomes.[2]

3. *Evaluate alternatives and make decisions.* In this step, managers select the most appropriate alternative. As Chapters 9 and 10 discuss, managers base choices on a combination of financial factors. These factors include the amount and timing of estimated cash flows, the risk of the project, and nonfinancial factors such as regulatory requirements, employee safety, corporate image, and community responsibility. Although the decisions require judgment, techniques such as discounted cash flow analysis help quantify the financial analysis.

4. *Prepare the capital budget.* The **capital budget** comprises the cash flows for authorized capital projects, such as new computers, machines, and buildings. Management and the board of directors (or legislators in governmental units) approve the requests based on net present value and other analyses. Then the budget becomes an expenditure authorization. Most organizations have controls that preclude expenditures above a predetermined capital budget amount unless approved by top management or the board.

5. *Conduct a follow-up and performance review.* Managers should not omit the follow-up and performance review, which has three purposes: (1) to ascertain if expenditures matched intentions and authorizations; (2) to evaluate the success of the capital project (for example, did expected cost savings occur); and (3) to evaluate the capital budgeting process (for example, did analysts bias cash flow estimates).

This completes the capital budgeting cycle, from identifying opportunities through follow-up and performance review.

Operating Budgets

After selecting the best products, making capital investment decisions, selecting production techniques, and making other decisions, management can develop a formal short-run plan of action known as the **operating budget.** The accountant prepares an operating, or period, budget usually for 1 year at a time. Many firms

---

[2]For example, see the classic paper by David B. Hertz, "Risk Analysis in Capital Investment," *Harvard Business Review* (January–February 1964), pp. 96–108.

prepare detailed budgets for the coming year and less detailed budgets for following years. Some firms prepare these budgets for as many as 10 years into the future.

You can visualize budgets by imagining you are preparing a set of estimated financial statements for each month of the coming year. (You need not prepare these estimates in accordance with generally accepted accounting principles.) Managers find some financial statements more useful than others. Budgets of cash flows are useful for financing decisions, particularly for helping the treasurer's department. The income statement, or **profit plan,** forecasts the results of operations, so general managers find it the most useful.

One of the Integrative Cases at the end of this chapter, Continental Can Company of Canada, Ltd. (Problem **32**), describes the budgeting process at Continental Can in detail. We recommend it for readers interested in a detailed discussion of budget development.

Feedback Phase

The remaining parts of the planning and control process depicted in Exhibit 11.1 make up the **feedback phase**—comparison of actual results to budget, performance evaluation, and revision of goals, plans, and budgets. The feedback phase serves three purposes: (1) to motivate employees, (2) to guide corrective actions, and (3) to help revise goals and plans. By comparing actual performance with the budget and investigating the reasons for any variances, management has a basis for evaluating employees' past performance. For example, a production supervisor may compare the actual number of units produced by various workers with the standard for a period to decide which workers should receive bonuses or promotions. A company president may compare the rate of return on assets of an operating division with a standard to assess the division manager's performance.

Information from the feedback phase alerts management to activities needing attention. Managers cannot personally watch all activities for which they are responsible, so they rely on information from planning and control systems to do a large part of the monitoring. In this way managers can focus on the large variances between actual performance and the budget or standard.[3] Then they can take corrective actions where necessary. Basing action on exceptional variances is often referred to as **management by exception.**

Finally, information about actual performance provides feedback for revising goals and plans.

Variances between actual results and budgets need not result from good or bad performance but can result from unrealistic goals and plans. Sometimes managers carelessly prepare budgets. Also, unforeseen events may occur. For example, a severe winter storm made the activities of one of National Intergroup's plants so inefficient that virtually all unit variable costs were higher than standard. The firm did not hold managers responsible for the unfavorable variances attributable to the storm.

---

[3]Managers and accountants often use the terms *budget* and *standard* interchangeably.

Motivating People

When you evaluate a planning and control system, ask the following two questions:

1.   What types of behavior does the system motivate?

2.   Is this behavior in the best interests of the organization?

These two questions raise the issue of *incentive compatability*.

This section discusses issues in motivating people to perform in the best interests of the organization.

When managers use planning and control systems to evaluate performance, they are expecting people to perform in a particular way. Managers expect that evaluating employees' efforts and rewarding (or penalizing) them for high (or low) efforts will induce higher quality work.

The motivation problem occurs because principals (for example, supervisors) have delegated duties or entrusted responsibilities to their agents (for example, subordinates).[4] We find these principal-agent relationships in many settings, including the following:

Principals	Agents
Shareholders......................................	Board of Directors
Board of Directors	Corporate (Top) Management
Corporate (Top) Management	Divisional Managers
Divisional Managers	Plant Managers
Owner of a Taxi Company............................	Drivers of the Taxicabs
Retail Store Managers	Department Managers
Nursing Supervisor	Staff Nurses

Much of both financial and managerial accounting has developed to monitor agency relationships. Corporate management, for example, provides financial statements to shareholders. Division managers report on their activities to their superiors at corporate headquarters. In general, accounting provides information about subordinates (agents) to superiors (principals) for performance evaluation. These reports allow superiors to make decisions about the subordinates' future employment prospects. (For example, should they be promoted? Fired?) In addition, employment contracts use accounting information. Often an employee receives a bonus based on accounting performance measures.

Thus accounting affects motivation. Subordinates who know managers evaluate them with accounting measures have incentives to make themselves look good with those measures. (Analogously, consider how students have incentives to ma-

---

[4]For comprehensive reviews of analytical research in this area, see L. Peter Jennergen, "On the Design of Incentives in Business Firms—A Survey of Some Research," *Management Science* 25 (February 1980); Joel Demski, *Information Analysis,* 2nd ed. (Reading, Mass.: Addison-Wesley, 1980); Stanley Baiman, "Agency Research in Managerial Accounting: A Survey," *Journal of Accounting Literature* 1 (Spring 1982), pp. 154–213; Gerald Feltham, "Financial Accounting Research: Contributions of Information Economics and Agency Theory," in R. Mattessich, ed., *Modern Accounting Research: History, Survey, and Guide* (Vancouver, B.C.: CGA Research Foundation, 1984); and Daniel B. Thornton, "A Look at Agency Theory for the Novice," *CA Magazine* (November 1984 and January 1985).

nipulate grade-point averages by choosing easy courses, if employers or graduate school admissions offices use grade-point averages without regard to difficulty of courses.)

How Much Information Is Enough?   Like other accounting systems, planning and control systems should be cost-effective. If information were costless to generate and to process, superiors would always prefer more information to less. But information is not free, so the manager must compare the cost of obtaining more information about subordinates to the benefits of evaluating their future employment prospects and motivating them to take desired actions.

Goal Congruence

Goal congruence occurs if members of an organization have incentives to perform in the common interest. Although complete goal congruence is rare, we observe team efforts in many cases. Examples include some military units and athletic teams. Many companies attempt to achieve this esprit de corps by carefully selecting employees whom management believes will be loyal, for example. Observers of Japanese industry report that Japanese managers and owners have created team orientations with considerable goal congruence.

Complete goal congruence is, however, unlikely to occur in most business settings.[5] For example, employees may prefer to work less hard than the firm would like. Consequently, firms design performance evaluation and incentive systems to increase goal congruence by encouraging employees to behave more in the firm's interest.

The classroom setting is a good example. Examinations, written assignments, indeed, the entire grading process, is part of a performance evaluation and incentive system to encourage students to learn. Sometimes the system encourages the wrong type of behavior, because students may select easy courses to improve their grades instead of difficult courses in which they will learn more.

Problems of this type occur in all organizations where employees acting in their own best interests do not take actions that serve the best interests of the organization. Consider the case of a plant manager who believes that a promotion and bonus will follow from high plant operating profits. Undertaking a needed maintenance program will reduce profits in the short run, but the company will benefit in the long run because its product quality will improve. The manager faces a classic trade-off between doing what looks good in the short run and doing what serves the best interests of the company. (This point is analogous to the problem faced by a student in deciding between an easy course that will bolster the grade-point average or a hard course that will have more long-term benefits.)

---

[5]Control systems may induce risk-averse employees to take actions that are suboptimal for the organization. See R. O. Swalm, "Utility Theory—Insight into Risk Taking," *Harvard Business Review* (November–December 1966), pp. 123–136 and J. L. Zimmerman, "Budget Uncertainty and the Allocation Decision in a Nonprofit Organization," *Journal of Accounting Research* 14 (Autumn 1976), pp. 301–319. Also, other evidence suggests that employee performance is directly related to goal congruence. See M. W. Maher, K. V. Ramanathan, and R. B. Peterson, "Preference Congruence, Information Accuracy and Employee Performance: A Field Study," *Journal of Accounting Research* 17 (Autumn 1979), pp. 476–503 and A. Harrell, "The Decision-Making Behavior of Air Force Officers and the Management Control Process," *The Accounting Review* 52 (October 1977), pp. 833–841.

Planning and control systems for compensation that induce employees to act in the best interest of the organization are known as **incentive compatible compensation schemes.** Designing such schemes can be costly. Management must trade off the costs and benefits of planning and control systems. The optimal expenditure on planning and control may still allow employees considerable opportunity for behavior contrary to the best interests of top management.

Matching the Planning and Control System to Organizational Characteristics

Firms should match planning and control systems to the characteristics of the organization. A computer chip manufacturer may find a formal, quantitative system designed to regulate output and control costs to be the most desirable. A company that does research and development for a governmental agency under cost-plus-fixed-fee contracts would not be as concerned about regulating output and controlling costs. It would desire a system that encouraged quality and meeting contract deadlines while accounting for costs by job or contract so that the company could receive payment.

The following examples describe three different kinds of control mechanisms—markets, bureaucracies, and clans—for different types of activities. We base these examples on an article describing planning and control systems for a specific company.[6]

Example 1:
Controlling the Purchasing Agent Using a Market Mechanism

The work of the purchasing agent is largely subject to market mechanisms.

> [The agent] simply puts each part out for competitive bids and permits the competitive process to define a fair price. . . . The work of the manager who supervises these agents is also greatly simplified, because he needs only to check the decisions against the simple criterion of cost minimization rather than observing the steps through which they work. . . .[7]

Example 2:
Controlling the Warehousing Function Using a Bureaucratic Mechanism

> In marked contrast to purchasing, warehousing . . . is subject to a variety of explicit routines of monitoring and directing. . . . The fundamental mechanism of control involves close personal surveillance and direction of subordinates by supervisors.[8]

---

[6]We take the examples from William Ouchi, "A Conceptual Framework for the Design of Organizational Control Mechanisms," *Management Science* 25 (September 1979), pp. 833–848.

[7]Ouchi, pp. 834–835.

[8]Ouchi, p. 835.

This bureaucratic mechanism conforms to the idea of formal planning and control systems in companies. Unlike the market mechanism, in which the market coordinates and controls activities of participants, in a bureaucracy a superior coordinates and controls the activities of subordinates. Superiors control subordinates by setting standards and budgets, or other rules, and compare the subordinate's performance to them.

Example 3:
Informal Controls

The article reported evidence of informal controls that firms could use to control activities. These informal controls help when the firm cannot easily evaluate an individual's work, as in research and development. Other examples include many governmental and health care employees, auditors in public accounting firms, financial analysts, and data processing systems designers. A key informal control in these cases is the process of socialization, where the firm indoctrinates employees with a set of values. (When large groups become socialized, they are often called ''professions.'')

When an organization cannot easily measure individuals' outputs, it will sometimes reduce costs by hiring people with a particular set of values or instill these values rather than use formal control methods. For example, K mart has would-be store managers go through several years of on-the-job training before promotion to store manager. Superiors observe these employees during this period, and, as a company executive told us, ''we weed out those who do not have company loyalty before we trust them with a store of their own.''

In short, different activities and organizations call for different types of planning and control systems. Market mechanisms work when market exchanges require little teamwork, such as for some sales personnel, buyers, and piecework employees. Firms use formal planning and control systems when market exchanges are infeasible but the firm can measure employees' performance. Firms use informal controls (for example, socialization) when they cannot easily measure employees' outputs.

Performance Measures

The measures used for evaluating performance should be relevant to the objectives or purposes of the responsibility centers. If the purpose of a production department is to manufacture products of a particular quality at the lowest cost, then the firm might use manufacturing cost per unit passing quality inspection as the performance measure. If the objective of a secretarial typing pool is to type quality copy at the lowest cost, the evaluation measure might be correct lines typed per dollar of cost in the pool.

An improperly designed performance measure—an incentive incompatible scheme—may misdirect the efforts of employees who attempt to perform so that they succeed relative to the measure. For example, a performance measure for the traveling sales staff that relates revenue generated to the number of calls made to customers (that is, sales divided by calls made) may lead salespeople to *reduce* the number of calls made to improve their performance reports. If the development of a good relationship between the salespeople and the customers is critical and depends on frequent calls by the sales staff, this performance measure could lead to action (reduced numbers of sales calls) not in the best interest of a firm.

Use of Performance Measures When Employee Input Is Not Observable One problem in designing incentive compatible planning and control systems for some activities is that the firm cannot objectively measure performance. In most cases this occurs because management cannot observe the relation between inputs and outputs. For example, consider research and development activity. Assume the desired output is a set of new inventions and developments that will permit a firm to maintain or improve its market position. Management cannot observe the effort of research scientists, which may or may not lead to the desired output. Suppose we observe no new inventions for a long time. Does this mean the scientists are not working or do not have the requisite skills to perform well? Not necessarily.

When the firm cannot observe inputs, the planning and control systems tend to be less formalized and more subjective. As a manager of a research and development department put it:

> We hire people we can trust to work hard even though we cannot measure their output. We encourage peer group pressure and a sense of loyalty to the company. And we have them submit a written annual report of their activities. If we tried to impose quantitative performance measures on our research and development people, we would not only incur system costs, but also we would damage morale such that our people's performance would probably go down, not up.

Informative Performance Measures To be useful, performance measures provide information about an employee's actions. The evaluation can use information about activities that one does not normally consider to be part of the employee's responsibility, however. For example, suppose a division manager, H. Washington, reports division profits 20 percent higher than budgeted for a particular year. Washington's performance looks good compared to the budget. But how did Washington's performance compare with those of other division managers facing similar circumstances? Suppose top management learns that the managers of other divisions in the same industry as Washington's are performing exceptionally well because of a recent increase in demand. Given that information, top management decides Washington's division *should* have performed 40 percent above budget.

The idea that information about the performance of other divisions may be potentially informative about Washington's performance is analogous to the idea of grading on the curve: the instructor uses exam scores to learn about the difficulty of the exam.[9] Thus a score of 40 percent on an examination may appear to be low in absolute terms but may be the best *relative* to the scores of others taking the examination.

---

[9]For research on this topic, see R. Antle and A. Smith, ''An Empirical Investigation of the Relative Performance Evaluation of Corporate Executives,'' *Journal of Accounting Research* 24 (Spring 1986), pp. 1–39; and M. Maher, ''The Use of Relative Performance Evaluation in Organizations,'' in W. J. Bruns, Jr., and R. S. Kaplan, eds., *Accounting and Management: Field Study Perspectives* (Boston: Harvard Business School Press, 1987), pp. 295–315.

Employee Participation in Setting Performance Measures   Although employee participation is costly to the organization because it consumes employee time, it provides data to management that may not be available otherwise. Whether or not employee participation positively motivates employees remains an open question. To appreciate the issues, consider some of the questions that analysts have addressed in the research on this issue.

1. Does participation lead employees to feel that they are a more integral part of an organization and, because of this ego involvement, result in improved performance?

2. Does participation merely lead to greater group cohesiveness among employees, which can then work either to the advantage or disadvantage of the firm, depending on the group's feeling about the benefits of participation?

3. Do the results of participation differ in the following situations?
    a. Employees merely provide inputs to the standard-setting process but have no voice in actual standard setting.
    b. Employees both supply inputs and participate in setting specific standards.

4. Do the results of participation differ depending on the managerial style of supervisors (authoritarian, democratic) and the personality characteristics of employees?

5. Do the results of participation differ depending on the educational backgrounds and technical skills of employees and the nature of the tasks (production versus research and development or legal services)?

6. How does participation relate to the creation of slack in organizations (a term referring to the difference between the resources available to a firm and the amount necessary to maintain the organization coalition of individuals and groups)?

Interested readers may consult the references listed in the footnote to explore these questions more fully.[10]

Tightness of Performance Standards   The firm may set loose standards for performance that employees meet a large percentage of the time or tight standards met only a small percentage of the time. Empirical research suggests that employees underperform when firms set standards too loosely. Introducing a moderate level of tension by way of tighter standards leads to higher employee motivation and, therefore, better performance. The principal question, then, is just how tight management should set the standards. The literature describes two types of standards: ideal standards and normal or currently attainable standards.

Ideal standards are those that employees can meet under the most efficient operating conditions for existing resources (plant, equipment, employees). The firm

---

[10]Andrew C. Stedry, *Budget Control and Cost Behavior* (Englewood Cliffs, N.J.: Prentice-Hall, 1960); Chris Argyris, "Organizational Leadership and Participative Management," *Journal of Business* 27 (January 1955), pp. 1–7; Selwyn Becker and David Green, Jr., "Budgeting and Employee Behavior," *Journal of Business* 35 (October 1962), pp. 392–402; Michael Schiff and Arie Y. Lewin, "The Impact of Budgets on People," *The Accounting Review* 45 (April 1970), pp. 259–268; and Ken Milani, "The Relationship of Participation in Budget-Setting to Industrial Supervisor Performance and Attitudes: A Field Study," *The Accounting Review* 50 (April 1975), pp. 274–284.

uses ideal standards when management believes such standards provide the best incentive to good performance. Generally, however, empirical research shows that standards do not provide an incentive to perform well unless the employee being evaluated perceives the standard to be reasonable and attainable.[11] Ideal standards may cause employees to lose initiative for seeking more efficient performance and may discourage them because they can seldom achieve the standards.

Normal or currently attainable standards are those that employees can meet under reasonably efficient operating conditions with provision for normal spoilage, rest periods, and other time that is lost because of, for example, normal machine breakdowns. By definition, normal standards are loose enough that management can reasonably expect employees to meet them but stringent enough so that workers who achieve them have reason to be satisfied with their performance.

It is difficult to generalize about how tight management should set standards. Standards that are currently attainable but sufficiently tight to motivate employees are probably best.

Timely Feedback

A control system requires timely feedback to be effective. Management needs to be aware of significant variances of actual performance from the standards in time to take corrective action. Employees need to know whether employers judge their performance to be satisfactory or unsatisfactory. Satisfactory performance tends to reinforce employee behavior and leads to greater employee motivation. Unsatisfactory performance may lead to greater employee motivation (if employees still consider standards to be attainable) or to withdrawal (when employees do not consider the standards attainable or the employee no longer feels a part of the management-employee coalition in the firm).

The frequency of feedback differs, depending on the nature of the activity. An automated production line may require feedback within seconds or minutes so that operators can take corrective action quickly. For purposes of evaluating the overall performance of a division of a firm, monthly or quarterly feedback is probably sufficient.

Benefits Exceed Costs

Accounting, like other activities, should be subject to cost-benefit analysis. One of the most important criteria for evaluating a planning and control system is the requirement that the benefits of the system exceed the costs of designing and implementing it. For example, the benefits of a sophisticated system for the acquisition and use of paperclips is not likely to justify the costs incurred.

The costs and benefits of planning and control systems are difficult to measure and quantify. Consequently, managers must judgmentally assess the costs and benefits.[12]

---

[11]Stedry, *Budget Control and Cost Behavior;* also see Gary L. Holstrum, "The Effect of Budget Adaptiveness and Tightness on Managerial Decision Behavior," *Journal of Accounting Research* 9 (Autumn 1971), pp. 268–277.

[12]The method we used to assess the value of information in Appendix 1.1 could, in theory, be applied to cost-benefit decisions about planning and control systems.

Responsibility Centers

An organization develops planning and control systems around responsibility centers. A **responsibility center** is a division or department in a firm responsible for managing a particular group of activities in the organization. A store manager is responsible for the activities in the store, a department head is responsible for the activities in the department, and so forth. Accountants classify responsibility centers according to the activities for which the manager is responsible, as follows:

1. **Cost centers,** where management is responsible for costs. Manufacturing departments are examples, because the managers are responsible for the costs of making products.

2. **Revenue centers,** where management is responsible primarily for revenues. Marketing departments are ''revenue centers'' if the managers are responsible for revenues. If marketing managers have responsibility for marketing costs— for example, sales commissions and advertising—these are sometimes called ''marketing centers.''

3. **Profit centers,** where management is responsible for both revenues and costs.

4. **Investment centers,** where management is responsible for revenues, costs, and assets. Most corporate divisions are profit centers or investment centers.

There are two categories of cost centers, based on the type of costs incurred in the center. Most production costs in both service and manufacturing companies are assumed to be **engineered costs**—in other words, input-output relations are sufficiently well established that a particular set of inputs will provide a predictable and measurable set of outputs. Such cost centers are **engineered cost centers.** Many activities do not have well specified input-output relations, however. Output is relatively unpredictable and difficult to measure for most organizations' staff functions (research, administration, legal, and advertising) and for most activities in governmental units. Responsibility centers in which input-output relations are not well specified are **discretionary cost centers.** Managers of such centers receive from their superiors a cost budget that provides a ceiling on the center's costs. To ascertain the effectiveness of such centers requires managerial judgment. Most administrative, research, and staff activities are discretionary cost centers.

Management by Objectives

Many organizations attempt to plan and control discretionary costs using **management by objectives (MBO).**[13] With MBO, responsibility center managers state their objectives, things they will do to attain those objectives, uncertainties and known impediments, resources they require, and costs they expect to incur. For performance evaluation, managers compare actual performance in terms of objectives achieved, costs incurred, and so forth, with the plan.

---

[13]An organization can use management by objectives for any activity.

Managerial Application

Measuring Division Performance at ITT with Accounting Numbers[a]

ITT is a conglomerate with divisions in a wide variety of businesses, including insurance (Hartford), hotels (Sheraton), and financial services. Top management of ITT has considered annual earnings growth to be a primary measure of corporate performance. Divisional performance measures provide strong incentives for division managers to achieve annual budgeted profit amounts.

Achieving these budgeted profit targets is important to division managers. ITT based division managers' bonuses on achieving profit targets. Also, failure to achieve these targets for 2 years in a row could have a strong negative impact on managers' promotion prospects. Each year is essentially "a new game" for division managers. They have short-run incentives to focus on financial targets. The approach is consistent with the philosophy of Harold Geneen, former ITT chief executive officer, who stated,

> Managing means that once you set your business plan and budget for the year, you *must* achieve the sales, the market share, the earnings, and whatever to which you committed yourself.[b]

Because achieving profit targets is important to division managers, one would expect division managers to have incentives to play games with the "scorekeeping" system from time to time. For example, divisions may be expected to write off as many expenses as possible in years when they can easily achieve the profit target. Division managers have little control over the internal financial reporting system, however. The corporate controller's office specifies methods of accounting for transactions within the division, so division operating managers have little opportunity to make accounting choices that would put their performance in its most favorable light. According to Ray Alleman, the corporate controller,

> We believe that because of the special nature of a controller's responsibilities, the importance of neutrality, objectivity, and integrity—as well as the watchdog function—it is necessary that the prime duty and loyalty (of the division controller) be directly to the total corporation and its shareholders, and not to the individual section of the company or division.[c]

[a]Based on interviews with ITT executives.
[b]Harold Geneen, *Managing* (Garden City, N.Y.: Doubleday, 1984), p. 106.
[c]R. Alleman, "Comptrollership at ITT," *Management Accounting* (May 1985), pp. 24–30.

Zero-Base Budgeting

Many organizations have tried to tie MBO to the accounting system. Many organizations, including Texas Instruments, Xerox, and Control Data, some state and local governmental units, and many parts of the federal government, have used variations of **zero-base budgeting.**[14] In principle, zero-base budgeting requires responsibility center managers to justify every dollar of costs from a zero base. This practice contrasts with *incremental budgeting,* which justifies only additions to previous cost levels. In practice, budgeting from an absolute zero base has often proved to be too costly for the benefits obtained. Nevertheless, many aspects of zero-base budgeting are currently in use, particularly for discretionary cost centers.

Problems in Assigning Responsibility

Firms should measure the performance of a particular manager or group of employees in terms of things for which they are responsible. The following examples illustrate that this principle is not easy to apply.

Example 1: Shared Responsibility   Horton Hospital has a purchasing department responsible for the acquisition of the hospital's supplies. Department supervisors inform the purchasing department of the quantities and qualities of supplies needed at various times. The purchasing department then searches for suppliers that will provide the needed materials at the best price. Top management holds the purchasing department accountable if the prices actually paid vary from the standard prices allowed.

The purchasing department is a responsibility center with respect to the price paid for supplies. Suppose, however, that because of poor planning, the supervisor of the emergency room places a rush order for supplies that must be received within 3 days. The purchasing department employees do not process the purchase order for 2 days. To obtain the supplies on time, the purchasing department has agreed to pay a premium price to expedite the order. As a consequence, the actual price paid exceeds the standard or expected price. Should top management hold the purchasing department accountable for this unfavorable price variance?

Responsibility is often difficult to assign. In the rush-order example, management would probably hold both the emergency room and the purchasing department responsible for the unfavorable price variance, even though the excess price paid would normally be the responsibility of just the purchasing department.

Example 2: Short Run versus Long Run   The division managers of First Bank submit capital budgeting proposals to corporate headquarters. Top management decides which capital investment proposals will be accepted and which will be rejected. In the long run, the division managers who generate capital investment proposals and top management who select particular proposals share the responsibility for fixed-

---

[14]Similar methods have gone by different names over the years. It is often politically useful to develop a new title for an old idea. For an excellent discussion, see Robert N. Anthony, ''Zero-Base Budgeting: Useful Fraud?'' *Government Accountants Journal* (Summer 1977). Although the methods described here are often called zero-base budgeting, the same idea has other names.

capacity costs (for example, property taxes and insurance on the facilities). In the short run, however, neither of these two sets of managers need to have control over certain fixed-capacity costs. For example, suppose property tax rates or insurance premiums increase so that these costs have an unfavorable fixed-cost variance. In this case, the division managers have little control over property taxes and insurance in the short run. Top management will probably not hold them accountable for the cost variances. Showing the variances on the cost report would make the division managers more aware of these costs, however, which they could partially control in the long run.

The identification of responsibility centers within a firm is an important first step in designing planning and control systems. Setting the boundaries of responsibility for a particular center is far from precise. Nonetheless, the firm must make an attempt if the planning and control system is to be effective.

Types of Planning and Control Systems

Organizations have three broad types of planning and control systems: operational, divisional, and organization-wide. To understand the distinction better, refer to the organization chart in Exhibit 11.2.

Operational Planning and Control Systems

The organization chart in Exhibit 11.2 illustrates how firms design **operational planning and control systems** for activities closest to day-to-day manufacturing, marketing, and other activities of the organization. For example, firms would de-

Exhibit 11.2

Types of Planning and Control Systems at Different Organizational Levels

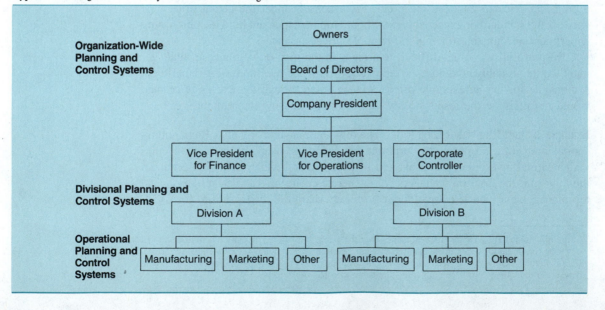

sign operational control systems for such activities as materials acquisition and storage, office typing and record keeping, and activities of the sales personnel to obtain orders.

Cost centers and revenue centers are the responsibility centers typically used for operational planning and control.

Divisional Planning and Control Systems

Firms design **divisional planning and control systems** for the next major level above operational control in the organization chart, where the agency relations are usually between top management (the principal) and division managers (the agents). Divisions combine and coordinate the activities of operating units and, in effect, are organizations within an organization. A company that produces and markets a single product may have no divisions or only one division. Companies with multiple products or with geographically dispersed facilities often have many divisions. Divisional planning and control systems typically focus on the profit performance of the divisions, which may be either a measure of the divisional operating profits or return on the company's investment in the division. Hence, divisions are profit centers or investment centers. Chapter 15 discusses divisional performance measurement and control.

Organization-Wide Planning and Control Systems

Organization-wide planning and control systems involve a periodic review of the organization's activities by the board of directors, by trustees, or, in the case of governmental units, by legislative bodies. They tend to be less formal than those for divisional or operational activities. The comparison of actual results with the expected level of performance may occur quarterly or perhaps only once a year.

In recent years, various regulatory and other trends have increased top managements' accountability for their organizations' actions. For example, the New York Stock Exchange requires **audit committees** of all companies whose stock trades on the exchange. The audit committee nominates independent auditors and reviews significant audit findings with them. The internal audit department in many companies reports to the audit committee. To ensure outside monitoring of top management's activities, the audit committee must comprise people who are not company employees.

One of the audit committee's functions has been to oversee the activities of the firm's external auditors. The audit committee sometimes asks the external auditors to extend the usual audit of the financial statements to search for management fraud or illegal payoffs. As these audit committees have become established, they have increased the scope of their activities. They give greater attention to other aspects of the firm's activities, such as community relations, employee morale, and environmental protection. Management consulting firms have been hired to study various aspects of a company's operations and make recommendations for changes. Analysts expect the scope of activities of corporate audit committees to continue to broaden in the future.

Government regulation of top management's activities is a form of top management control. Many of the securities laws, antitrust regulations, and affirmative action and environmental protection laws attempt to control top management. One such regulation was the Foreign Corrupt Practices Act of 1977, which not only prohibited kickbacks and bribes to foreign government officials but also regulated the adequacy of internal accounting control systems.

Managerial accounting focuses on operational and divisional planning and control, not on organization-wide planning and control. Organization-wide methods involve external financial reporting, external auditing, executive incentive systems, and various government regulations, all designed to make top management accountable to its constituents.

Incentive Compensation Plans

The method of rewarding managers for their performance is an important part of the total planning and control process. Firms design incentive compensation plans to provide incentives for managers to achieve organizational objectives. For top managers, incentive compensation plans usually include rewards both for current performance based on accounting numbers and for increasing stockholder share values. The latter is often in the form of stock options that can be quite lucrative if the value of the company's shares increases substantially over time.[15] For example, most of Chrysler Corporation chairperson Lee Iacocca's compensation from Chrysler has come from exercising stock options.

Some critics point out that rewarding executives for performance reflected in annual accounting numbers gives managers incentives to take actions that improve short-run performance but not actions that benefit organizations in the long run. A classic example would be a firm's failure to develop new production methods and new products that may substantially increase expenses in the short run but provide more value for shareholders in the long run. General Motors, for example, is concerned about this issue. It has recently replaced its bonus plan based on short-run profit growth with a system that focuses more managerial attention on long-run increases in value to stockholders.

Using accounting numbers in performance measurement may give managers incentives to make accounting choices and otherwise manipulate accounting data to put their performance in the most favorable light.[16]

Divisional Incentive Compensation Plans

Effective incentive compensation schemes must induce individual behavior compatible with increasing the firm's wealth. Management can evaluate a company's performance using both accounting numbers and returns to stockholders, the latter reflecting a market assessment of how well the company is doing. Divisions normally do not have their own shares trading in capital markets, and the impact of one division's performance on the total company's share value would typically be small. Consequently, stock market assessments of performance are less useful at the divisional level than at the company level.

---

[15]Stock options give an individual the right to purchase a certain number of shares of the company's stock at a specified price within a certain time period.

[16]See the articles in M. Jensen and J. Zimmerman, eds., ''Symposium on Management Compensation and the Managerial Labor Market,'' *Journal of Accounting and Economics* 7 (April 1985), pp. 3–251.

Managerial Application

Example of Incentive-Incompatible Compensation Scheme[a]

A large, multidivision manufacturer of industrial and consumer electrical products is organized as a series of divisional profit centers. The firm rewards each division manager, at least in part, on the basis of the accounting profits and rate of return on assets that the division earned. Each division has its own controller, who reports directly to the central corporate controller. This direct reporting line, bypassing the division president, gives division controllers a feeling of independence from the division presidents, who would otherwise be their bosses. Central corporate management wants independent scorekeepers providing unbiased reports about ongoing operations.

In spite of this organizational design, the division controllers' compensation results in part from the same formula as that of the division presidents—a function of accounting profits and the rate of return on assets. Thus, division controllers have a financial stake in the reported profits of their divisions, giving them an incentive, at the margin, to boost reported profits.

The division controllers are aware of the potential conflict between their charge from central corporate management and their compensation packages. They feel conflict. At periodic meetings of controllers, they express their dissatisfaction to top management but so far have not been able to persuade top management that the compensation schemes are incentive-incompatible.

[a]This example derives from a study of this company by the authors. We do not reveal the company's name at management's request.

A study of divisional incentive compensation plans found that most of these plans have the following characteristics.[17]

1. Cash bonuses and profit sharing plans reward managers for short-term performance.

2. Deferred compensation, such as stock and stock options, are available to managers several years after they earn the compensation. Deferring receipt of proceeds from stock gives managers incentives to take actions that increase long-run share value.

3. Firms give special awards for particular actions or extraordinary performance. For example, a pharmaceutical company in the study makes a special stock award to employees responsible for developing new products. Top management and the board of directors believe new product development is critical to the future success of the company.

---

[17]See M. Maher and S. Butler, *Management Incentive Compensation Plans* (Montvale, N.J.: National Association of Accountants, 1986).

When designing incentive systems, management must ascertain the behavior the system motivates and the behavior management desires. Although incentive plans universally attempt to motivate good performance, each organization has its own particular set of problems that affect incentive system design. For example, a food products company in the study noted previously acquired a fast-food hamburger chain. Because the acquiring company's managers had little experience in managing fast-food restaurants, the company wanted to provide incentives for the hamburger chain's managers to remain until the acquiring company's managers learned how to manage the restaurants. Consequently, the incentive system provided for lucrative deferred compensation that the hamburger chain managers would forgo if they quit. Each company's top management and board of directors must match its incentive system to its particular set of circumstances in deciding what type of behavior is desired. The goal is to design an incentive-compatible compensation scheme.

■ Summary ■

This chapter introduces the planning and control process and shows the role of accounting in this process. Management formulates strategic plans for achieving an organization's goals. These plans include long-range forecasts of sales, capacity requirements, aggregate levels of costs, and financing arrangements. Capital budgets authorize the expenditure of funds to satisfy the capacity requirements for the strategic plan. Operating budgets, annual short-run plans, provide more detail about how the coming year's operations will carry out the organization's strategic plans.

Operating budgets include pro forma financial statements prepared before the period. Management chiefly uses them for planning, coordinating activities among various people in the organization, and authorizing expenditures. They become benchmarks for performance evaluation.

The feedback phase of budgeting involves comparing actual results to the budget. The purposes of feedback are

1. To evaluate the performance of people and responsibility centers.
2. To guide management in making changes in the organization's activities.
3. To revise goals, plans, and budgets.

Accounting systems exist in large part to report on the activities of agents (for example, subordinates) to their principals (for example, superiors). These systems both motivate agents and inform principals about their agents' performance. Goal congruence occurs when all members of an organization have incentives to perform in the common interest. Planning and control systems that enhance goal congruence encourage employees to work in their own best interest while they are, at the same time, working in the organization's best interest.

A good planning and control system will do the following:

1. Use performance measures that provide information about employees' actions.
2. Evaluate performance using measures relevant to achieving desired objectives.

3. Match the planning and control system to the nature of the organization.

4. Provide timely feedback.

5. Provide benefits that exceed the costs of the planning and control system.

Two behavioral issues affect the setting of performance measures:

1. Should the firm allow employees to participate in budgeting?

2. Should the firm set standards for performance norms loosely or tightly?

Participation is costly, but it may have a positive motivational effect on employees and may provide a source of data not otherwise available to management. The conventional wisdom concerning performance norms is to set standards that are tight but attainable. This wisdom results from observation of practice and some research results, but many exceptions exist.

Operational planning and control deals with day-to-day operations, usually at departmental levels. Divisional systems concern the next level up in the organization. Operating systems usually deal with one aspect of an organization's activities— for example, purchasing or selling or production. Divisional systems, on the other hand, take into account a responsibility center's multiple activities (for example, purchasing *and* production *and* selling). Organization-wide systems deal with broader questions of top management's accountability and the organization's responsibility to various constituents, including shareholders, employees, customers, and government regulators.

Top management intends incentive compensation plans to motivate managers to achieve organizational objectives.

Problem for Self-Study

(*Adapted from CMA exam.*) Springfield Corporation operates on a calendar year basis. It begins the annual budgeting process in late August, when the president establishes targets for the next year's total dollar sales and net income before taxes.

The president gives the sales target to the marketing department, where the marketing manager formulates a sales budget by product line in both units and dollars. From this budget, managers set sales quotas by product line in units and dollars for each of the corporation's sales districts. The marketing manager also estimates the cost of the marketing activities required to support the target sales volume and prepares a tentative marketing expense budget.

The executive vice president uses the sales and profit targets, the sales budget by product line, and the tentative marketing expense budget to calculate the dollar amounts that the firm can devote to manufacturing and corporate office expense. The executive vice president prepares the budget for corporate expenses and then forwards to the production department the product-line sales budget in units and the total dollar amount that it can devote to manufacturing.

The production manager meets with the factory managers to develop a manufacturing plan that will produce the required units when needed within the cost constraints that the executive vice president set. The budgeting process usually comes to a halt at this point because the production department does not consider the financial resources allocated to be adequate.

When this standstill occurs, the vice president of finance, the executive vice president, the marketing manager, and the production manager meet together to set the final budgets for each of the areas. This meeting normally results in a modest increase in the total amount available for manufacturing costs, but cuts in the marketing expense and corporate office expense budgets. The total sales and net income figures that the president proposed rarely change. Although the participants seldom like the compromise, these budgets are final. Each executive then develops a new detailed budget for the operations in his or her area.

None of the areas has achieved its budget in recent years. Sales often run below the target. When sales fall below budget, top management expects each area to cut costs so that the firm can still meet the president's profit target. However, the firm seldom meets the profit target because managers do not cut costs enough. In fact, costs often run above the original budget in all functional areas. Disturbed that Springfield has not been able to meet the sales and profit targets, the president hires a consultant who has considerable experience with companies in Springfield's industry. The consultant reviews the budgets for the past 4 years and concludes that the product-line sales budgets were reasonable and that the cost and expense budgets were adequate for the budgeted sales and production levels.

a. Discuss how the budgeting process contributed to the failure to achieve the president's sales and profit targets.

b. Suggest how Springfield Corporation could revise its budgeting process to correct the problems.

c. Should Springfield expect the functional areas to cut their costs when sales volume falls below budget? Explain your answer.

Suggested Solution

a. The budget at Springfield is an imposed "top down" budget that fails to consider both the need for realistic data and the human interaction essential to an effective budgeting and control process. The president has not given any basis for his goals, so we cannot know whether they are realistic for the company. True participation of company employees in preparation of the budget is minimal and limited to mechanical gathering and manipulation of data. This fact suggests that employees will show little enthusiasm for implementing the budget.

The budget process should merge the requirements of all facets of the company on a basis of sound judgment and equity. Specific instances of poor procedures include the following:

(1) The sales by product line should result from an accurate sales forecast of the potential market. Therefore, the president should have developed the sales by product line first to derive the sales target, rather than the reverse.

(2) Managers could most easily and accurately estimate production costs. Given variable and fixed production costs, managers could estimate the sales volume needed to cover manufacturing costs plus the costs of other aspects of the operation. Having this information before setting budgets for marketing costs and corporate office expenses will help.

(3) The initial meeting between the vice president of finance, executive vice president, marketing manager, and production manager should occur earlier in the cycle.

b. Springfield should consider the adoption of a "bottom up" budget process. "Bottom up" means that the people responsible for performance under the budget would participate in the decisions for establishing the budget. This approach provides information from sales, financial, and production personnel. Although time consuming, the approach should produce a more acceptable, informative, and workable goal-control mechanism.

The sales forecast should consider internal sales forecasts as well as external factors. Analysts should divide costs within departments into fixed and variable, controllable and noncontrollable, discretionary and nondiscretionary categories.

c. Top management should not necessarily expect the functional areas to cut costs when sales volume falls below budget. The time frame of the budget (1 year) is short enough so that many costs are relatively fixed in amount. Division managers have little hope for a reduction in fixed costs as a consequence of short-run changes in volume. However, the functional areas should be able to cut costs when sales volume falls below target so long as

- The firm exercises control over the costs within its function.
- Budgeted costs are more than adequate for the originally targeted sales (i.e., slack is present).
- Budgeted costs vary to some extent with changes in sales.
- The firm can delay or omit discretionary costs with no serious effect on the department.

Key Terms and Concepts

Planning and control process
Strategic plan
Capital budget
Operating budget
Profit plan
Feedback phase
Management by exception
Goal congruence
Incentive compatible compensation
  scheme
Ideal standards
Normal or currently attainable
  standards
Responsibility center
Cost center
Revenue center

Profit center
Investment center
Engineered cost center (engineered
  costs)
Discretionary cost center
  (discretionary costs)
Management by objectives (MBO)
Zero-base budgeting
Operational planning and control
  system
Divisional planning and control
  system
Organization-wide planning and
  control system
Audit committee

Questions, Problems, and Cases

Questions

1. Review the meaning of the concepts or terms given above in Key Terms and Concepts.

2. Explain the difference between the strategic plan and the budget plan.

3. Why would more detail appear in a budget for the coming period than would appear in a longer-range forecast?

4. The chief executive officer of a large company remarked, ''I don't understand why other companies waste so much time in the budgeting process. I set our company goals, and everyone strives to meet them.'' Comment on the executive's budgeting method.

5. What is the danger in relying entirely on lower management estimates of sales, costs, and other data used in budget planning?

6. A company recently established a bonus plan for its employees. An employee receives a bonus if the employee's subunit meets the cost levels specified in the annual budget plan. If the subunit's costs exceed the budget, employees of that subunit earn no bonus. What problems might arise with this bonus plan?

7. What is the difference between a cost center and a profit center? What is the difference between a profit center and an investment center?

8. Why is it difficult to assess the effectiveness of discretionary cost centers?

9. Who, among university administrators, is most likely to be responsible for each of the following?
   a. Quantity of supplies used in executive education classes that the business school conducts.
   b. Electricity for equipment the university's printing operations use.
   c. Charge for classroom maintenance the business school uses.
   d. Finance professors' salaries.

10. Accounting is supposed to be a neutral, relevant, and objective measure of performance. Why would problems arise when applying accounting measures to performance evaluation contexts?

11. A company prepares the master budget by taking each division manager's estimate of revenues and costs for the coming period and entering the data into the budget without adjustment. At the end of the year, division managers receive a bonus if their division profit exceeds the budget. Do you see any problems with this system?

12. When is top management an agent in the principal-agent relationship described in the chapter?

13. When is top management a principal in the principal-agent relationship described in the chapter?

14. Sales personnel in a company receive a bonus based on the number of units sold, regardless of the number of defective units returned. How may that incentive system lead to dysfunctional consequences?

15. What are the major components of executive incentive compensation systems?

Problems

16. *Assigning responsibility for variances.* Neptune Automobile Company is organized into two divisions, Assembling and Finishing. The Assembling Division combines raw materials into a semifinished product. The product then goes to the Finishing Division for painting, polishing, and packing.

During May, the Assembling Division incurred significantly higher raw materials costs than expected because poor-quality raw materials required extensive rework. As a result of the rework, Assembly transferred fewer units than expected to the Finishing Division. The Finishing Division incurred higher labor costs per unit of finished product because workers had substantial idle time.

a. Who should the firm hold responsible for the raw materials variance in the Assembling Department? Explain.

b. Who should the firm hold responsible for the labor (idle time) variance in the Finishing Department? Explain.

17. *Performance evaluation in a CPA firm.* Cameron and MacInnes, Certified Public Accountants, employ 30 staff accountants. The accountants audit the financial statements of the firm's clients. At the completion of each audit assignment, the supervisor evaluates the performance of each staff accountant using a numerical scoring system. The quantitative measures influence promotion and compensation decisions. The scoring system involves assignment of a 0, 1, or 2 for each of the following factors scored:

(1) General physical appearance.

(2) Impression made on client.

(3) Ability to work with other staff accountants.

(4) Meeting, surpassing, or falling short of last year's audit time on each assigned task.

(5) Potential for advancement to partnership.

Evaluate the strengths and weaknesses of this numerical scoring system as a tool for evaluating and controlling performance.

18. *Controls over cash funds.* The Langston Advertising Agency maintains a petty cash fund of $5,000 in its office. The fund is used to make cash payments for postage, freight, business luncheons, and other costs that do not exceed $25 per expenditure. Before the firm will distribute cash, the petty cash custodian must receive an invoice or other evidence. To authorize the payment requires the initials of two people other than the custodian. At the end of each day, a clerk counts the petty cash fund to ensure that the custodian has cash and authorized receipts totaling $5,000. The fund then receives cash equal in amount to the authorized receipts. As a further check on the custodian, internal auditors make surprise counts of the fund during the day approximately twice each week.

Evaluate the strengths and weaknesses of these control procedures for the petty cash fund.

19. *Performance evaluation of airline reservations.* Trans American Airlines is a large domestic airline servicing all major cities throughout the United States. It uses control systems for many of its activities, including airplane maintenance, baggage handling, customer check-in, and others. One such control system, described next, is for telephone reservation services.

The control system's objective is to increase the likelihood that customers will receive prompt, courteous, and efficient service when they phone in for reservations. The standards for performance are stated in terms of a list of quantitative and qualitative attributes regarding the telephone conversation.

(1) Answer the telephone call no later than the third ring.

(2) If a customer is placed on hold because of a backlog of calls, the hold period should be no longer than 1 minute.

(3) The reservation clerk should present a pleasant and helpful disposition to the customer.

(4) In cases where a requested flight is full, the reservation clerk should make an effort to place the customer on another Trans American flight before offering information on flights of other airlines.

(5) After the reservation clerk makes the flight reservations, the clerk should read the flight numbers and times back to the customer.

The company uses two methods of monitoring the telephone reservation service. First, personnel in the controller's department listen to the telephone conversations by way of telephone taps located in central corporate headquarters. They then prepare a written evaluation of the reservation clerk's performance using the previously described standards. Because the clerks are unaware that the firm monitors their conversations, they act naturally. The second monitoring method involves a periodic call to customers to have them evaluate the conversation.

Evaluate the strengths and weaknesses of this control system as a basis for evaluating the performance of the reservation clerks.

20. *Control system to screen employees.* An Atlanta-based textile firm employs 30,000 workers in its local plant. A personnel department handles hiring and some aspects of training. Before hiring a worker, the personnel department checks his or her credit standing, previous job experience references, and any other factors that bear on performance. If the checker is satisfied, the firm hires the applicant immediately or places him or her on a short waiting list.

Ten individuals perform this initial checking in the firm's personnel department. The department supervisor allocates new employment applications to one of the ten checkers and carries out other personnel department activities.

Outline an effective control system for this initial processing activity. Note important strengths and weaknesses as you proceed.

21. *Controls over planning function.* First Federal Bank set up an independent planning department at corporate headquarters. This department is responsible for most aspects of budgeting (revenue and expense forecasting, profit planning, capital investment). Planning department personnel are responsible to the vice president for administration. The resulting budgets are incorporated

into the control system that the controller's department designed and administered.

Outline an effective control system for the planning department's activities (that is, how the firm should evaluate the performance of the planning department).

22. *Controls over research and development.* Consolidated Electronics Corporation conducts its research and development activities in a separate building near the central corporate headquarters. The research staff comprises 20 scientists and engineers and 30 research assistants. The staff spends approximately 60 percent of its time on improvement of existing products and processes. Most of this work results from requests of personnel in the firm's operating divisions. The staff spends the remaining 40 percent of its time on projects of particular interest to the scientists and engineers. In some cases, these efforts result in patents for new products or processes that Consolidated either uses or sells to other companies. In other cases, these research efforts lead to publishable papers in professional journals. In some instances, nothing usable results and the firm discontinues the project.

Design an effective control system for this research and development activity.

23. *Effect of participation and standard setting on budgets.* Stedry (*Budget Control and Cost Behavior*) studied the relations among (1) participation in standard setting, (2) tightness of standards, and (3) performance. The task a group of students performed was solving a series of short numerical problems. Stedry measured performance in terms of the number of correct solutions in a 7-minute period.

Students operated under one of three types of budgeting arrangements:
   (1) Imposed budgets—students knew how many correct solutions the experimenter expected of them in each 7-minute period. The students did not participate in setting the number.
   (2) Pseudoparticipation budgets—the experimenter asked the students to write down the number of solutions they aspired to get correct in each 7-minute period. After doing this, the experimenter gave the students a *preset* budgeted amount. The students were not aware that the experimenter did not consider their input in setting the budget amounts.
   (3) Imposed/aspiration-level budgets—the experimenter told students the number of correct solutions expected of them in each 7-minute period. The experimenter then asked them to write down the number of solutions they aspired to get correct.

Students operated under one of three types of standards with respect to tightness: (1) low, (2) medium, or (3) high. The experimenter set these amounts based on performance during the preceding 7-minute period but adjusted them to reflect the different degrees of tightness. Everyone started with a budget of five correct solutions.

The average number of correct solutions for students in each of the nine combinations of budgeting arrangements and tightness of standards appears in the following table.

	Budgeting Arrangement		
Tightness of Standard	Imposed Budget	Pseudoparticipation Budget	Imposed Aspiration-Level Budget
Low	4.09	4.70	4.56
Medium	4.35	5.45	5.50
High	5.13	4.04	5.85

a. What observations can you make from these results regarding the relation between participation in setting standards and performance?

b. What observations can you make from these results regarding the relation between tightness of standards and performance?

24. *Budget process: behavioral issues* (adapted from CMA exam). RV Industries manufactures and sells recreation vehicles. The company has eight divisions strategically located to be near major markets. Each division has a sales force and two to four manufacturing plants. These divisions operate as autonomous profit centers responsible for purchasing, operations, and sales.

John Collins, the corporate controller, described the divisional performance measurement system as follows:

> We allow the divisions to control the entire operation from the purchase of direct materials to the sale of the product. We, at corporate headquarters, get involved only in strategic decisions, such as developing new product lines. Each division is responsible for meeting its market needs by providing the right products at a low cost on a timely basis. Frankly, the divisions need to focus on cost control, delivery, and services to customers to become more profitable.

> Although we give the divisions considerable autonomy, we watch their monthly income statements closely. We compare each month's actual performance with the budget. If the actual sales or contribution margin is more than 4 or 5 percent below the budget, we immediately jump on the division people. I may add that we don't have much trouble getting their attention. All of the management people at the plant and division level can add appreciably to their annual salaries with bonuses if actual net income exceeds the budget.

The budgeting process begins in August when division sales managers, after consulting with their sales personnel, estimate sales for the next calendar year. These estimates go to plant managers, who use the sales forecasts to prepare production estimates. Operating personnel at the plants develop production statistics, including direct material quantities, labor hours, production schedules, and output quantities. Using the statistics that the operating personnel prepare, the plant accounting staff estimates costs and prepares the plant's budgeted variable cost of goods sold and other plant expenses for each month of the coming calendar year.

In October, each division's accounting staff combines plant budgets with sales estimates and adds additional division expenses. Collins says:

> After the divisional management is satisfied with the budget, I visit each division to go over their budget and make sure it is in line with corporate strategy and projections. I emphasize the sales forecasts because of the volatility in the demand for our product. For many years, we lost sales to our competitors because we didn't project high enough production and sales, and we couldn't meet the market demand. More recently, we were caught with large excess inventory when the bottom dropped out of the market for recreational vehicles.
>
> I generally visit all eight divisions during the first two weeks in November. After that we combine the division budgets and my staff reconciles them, then they are ready for approval by the board of directors in early December. The board seldom questions the budget.
>
> Plant and division managers complain that we penalize them for circumstances beyond their control. For example, they failed to predict the recent sales decline. As a result, they didn't make their budget and, of course, they received no bonuses. However, I point out that they are well rewarded when they exceed their budget. Furthermore, they provide most of the information for the budget, so it's their own fault if the budget is too optimistic.

a. Identify and explain the biases the corporate management of RV Industries should expect in the communication of budget estimates by its division and plant personnel.

b. What sources of information can the top management of RV Industries use to monitor the budget estimates its divisions and plants prepare?

c. What services could top management of RV Industries offer the divisions to help them in their budget development, without appearing to interfere with the division budget decisions?

d. The top management of RV Industries is attempting to decide whether it should get more involved in the budget process. Identify and explain the variables management needs to consider in reaching its decision.

25. *Budgeting research expenditures.* According to an article by Peter F. Drucker, innovative companies have two separate budgets, an operating budget and an innovation budget. The operating budget provides for everything already being done. The innovation budget provides for things to be done differently and different things to be worked on.

In reviewing the different budgets, top management asks different questions. For the operating budget, management asks: What is the optimization point? However, for innovations, top management asks: Is this the right opportunity? If the answer is yes, top management asks: What is the *most* this opportunity can absorb by way of resources at this stage?"

Suppose that the top management of your company wants the budget to encourage innovation. How would the budgeting and performance evaluation methods differ for innovative activities compared to routine operating activities?

26.   *Divisional performance measurement: behavioral issues* (adapted from CMA exam). Divisional managers of SIU Incorporated have been expressing growing dissatisfaction with the methods used to measure divisional performance. Top management evaluates divisional operations every quarter by comparing performance with the budget prepared during the previous year. Divisional managers claim that many factors are completely out of their control but remain in this comparison. This results in an unfair and misleading performance evaluation, they claim.

The managers have been particularly critical of the process used to establish standards and budgets. The annual budget, stated by quarters, is prepared 6 months before the beginning of the operating year. Top management's pressure to reflect increased earnings has often caused divisional managers to overstate revenues or understate expenses. In addition, once the firm has established the budget, SIU required divisions to live with it. Frequently, the budget parameters that top management supplied to the divisions have not adequately recognized external factors such as the state of the economy, changes in consumer preferences, and actions of competitors. The credibility of the performance review is curtailed when the budget cannot be adjusted to incorporate these changes.

Top management, recognizing the current problems, has agreed to establish a committee to review the situation and to make recommendations for a new performance evaluation system. The committee comprises each division manager, the corporate controller, and the executive vice president, who serves as the chair. At the first meeting, one division manager outlined an Achievement of Objectives System (AOS). In this performance evaluation system, divisional managers would be evaluated according to three criteria:

(1)   Doing better than last year. Management would compare various measures to the same measures of the prior year.

(2)   Planning realistically. Management would compare actual performance for the current year to realistic plans and/or goals.

(3)   Managing current assets. Management would evaluate the divisional management's achievements and reactions to changing business and economic conditions using various measures.

A division manager believed this system would overcome many of the inconsistencies of the current system because top management could evaluate divisions from three different viewpoints. In addition, the firm would give managers the opportunity to show how they would react and account for changes in uncontrollable external factors.

A second division manager was also in favor of the proposed AOS. However, the manager cautioned that the success of a new performance evaluation system would be limited unless it had the complete support of top management. Further, management should visibly show this support within all divisions. The manager believed that the committee should recommend some procedures that would enhance the motivational and competitive spirit of the divisions.

a.   Explain whether the proposed AOS would be an improvement over the measure of divisional performance SIU Incorporated now uses.

b. Develop specific performance measures for each of the three criteria in the proposed AOS that top management could use to evaluate divisional managers.

c. Discuss the motivational and behavioral aspects of the proposed performance system. Also, recommend specific programs that top management could institute to promote morale and give incentives to divisional management.

27. *Change to more centralized organization structure: behavioral issues* (adapted from CMA exam). Greengrass Company is an established manufacturer and wholesaler of a broad line of lawn fertilizer and yard maintenance products. Greengrass Company has annual sales of approximately $100 million and has been a wholly owned subsidiary of a large conglomerate, KSU Corporation, for the past 5 years. Before that, it was an independent corporation with the founding and managing family controlling the stock.

Al B. Cardwell, son of the founder, is currently the president of the company, but he is scheduled to retire in May of next year. His nephew, B. C. Cardwell, is currently executive vice president and has been heir apparent to the presidency ever since Al B. Cardwell became president.

Greengrass Company had maintained a pattern of increasing profits for many years. During the past 3 years, however, profits have decreased significantly. Management has attributed this decrease to reduced demand caused by cool, wet summers in the company's primary marketing area, coupled with intense competitive activity.

Following his return from a week-long corporate management planning meeting, Al B. Cardwell called a staff meeting to discuss plans for next year's marketing season. At the close of the meeting, he announced that the KSU Board had named William Thoma to become president of Greengrass Company in May of next year. Cardwell explained that KSU's management was concerned with the subsidiary's slumping profits and had decided to assume a greater degree of control over Greengrass operations. Thoma's appointment was the first step in this direction. In addition, they installed a new system of financial reporting to KSU management.

Mr. Thoma's reputation was well known to the entire staff. He had been executive vice president of two other KSU-owned companies during the previous 3 years. In both cases, the companies had records of declining profits before his appointment. A significant management reorganization occurred in each of those companies within 12 months after his appointment. In each case, he gave some members of senior management early retirement or released them, depending on their ages. Their replacements usually came from other KSU companies with which Thoma had been associated. Although earnings did increase following the reorganizations, he changed the entire "personality" of the companies.

a. Discuss the ways top management can expect the change to a more centralized organization and decision structure to influence the behavior of Greengrass managers.

b. Discuss the impact of William Thoma's selection as the new president on the behavior of Greengrass managers.

28.   *Controlling operations: nonprofit organization* (contributed by D. Croll). On November 1, the navy assigned Captain William Shefford as the commanding officer of the Admiral Mahon Weapons Station. Except during the war years, the billet of commanding officer for Mahon had been seen as a nice, restful final duty station after 30 years in the navy. This time, however, the Bureau of Personnel told Captain Shefford that the situation had changed. The Mahon Weapons Station had some major problems that necessitated the attention of a bright, hard-charging, career-minded captain still in the running for promotion—or at least that's what the Bureau of Personnel told him.

The assigning officer briefed him that "because others have viewed the commanding officer's billet as the final step before full retirement, control had become lax." Captain Jennings, the commanding officer he would replace, presented this picture of the CO's job: "It is mostly ceremonial. The work here is so technical that it is impossible to learn even a rudimentary level in the 3 years the tour lasts." Since the navy assigned personnel to the base in support positions, he, Jennings, limited his involvement with civilian personnel to official functions, and spent his time with the military problems of the naval personnel. The navy assigned a high-level civilian technical director to the base who dealt with the technical problems. The technical director did not handle the actual day-to-day operations, however, but the 13 research directors who reported to him did. The technical director's time was taken up with refereeing "turf fights" among the 13 research directors.

The research directors nominally covered 13 separate areas of research. In practice, the research directors made proposals and contracted for research jobs directly with clients (that is, other naval commands). When they received a contract, the research directors would assemble a team of researchers and other employees to complete the contract. A research director who brings in more contracts receives more resources. When interest in a specific area of research ended, the research director faced the choice of either seeing the allocation of resources and personnel greatly diminish or branching out into more currently popular areas of research. It was no wonder that the technical director spent so much of his time arguing over who should do the research and how to allocate personnel and resources.

On his second day as commanding officer, Bill Shefford called a meeting with the technical director, the research directors, and the heads of all the support activities. He was disappointed to find that even though only one of the research directors called to be excused, only the technical director arrived in person. The remaining 12 research directors sent their number-two people, and the support people sent secretaries. The group could discuss none of the important items on the agenda because none of the people at the meeting, with the exception of the technical director, felt competent to make a decision for his or her area.

Within the next 3 weeks, Captain Bill Shefford averaged two calls a day from other military commanders and technical directors of similar facilities complaining that the Admiral Mahon Weapons Station was bidding on work their operations had done in the past. Although much less frequently, Bill also received calls from commanding officers of "client" commands demanding to know why Mahon had not bid on their projects even though they had bid on similar projects in the past. Bill was further frustrated because without the help of the technical director he was unable to ascertain the research director responsible for each project. The base was at full employment, and everyone seemed overworked and happy but Bill.

To make matters worse for Bill, a legislator, publicly complaining about duplication of effort within the military, received from the staff of a competing naval research station examples of military duplication. Bill was sure he needed to justify certain proposals Mahon made on projects previously done at other stations.

The final straw came when an old classmate from the Naval Academy asked Bill, "What exactly do you people do down there on the bay?" and Bill didn't have an answer.

a.   Outline chronologically what Bill Shefford must do to get control of his command.

b.   What problems will he face as he tries to implement the solution outlined previously?

c.   Why was Bill's meeting so poorly attended?

Integrative Problems and Cases

29.   *Project performance reporting* (adapted from CMA exam). Walton Research does electronics research for business firms and the federal government. Most of the company's work is based on contracts calling for prototypes, or models, of new products. Each project has two phases: a "design phase" and a "build phase." The design phase involves designing the product in accordance with the customer's guidelines. The firm usually prepares several designs before finding one acceptable to the customer.

The build phase of the project involves building the prototype to meet the specifications. After building the prototype, the firm turns over the specifications and the prototype to the customer. Walton Research never mass-produces the project; it prepares specifications and builds only prototypes.

Walton Research's reputation for building quality prototypes on time is extremely important for the company's long-term success. Most of Walton's contracts are "cost-plus" a fixed fee (that is, profit), with shared costs over a specific amount. For example, Walton currently has a contract to make a product called XT-214, which is a navigational device for use on spaceships. The specified cost limit the firm has negotiated with the customer is $800,000. The fixed fee on the contract is $80,000. The customer has agreed to pay for 50 percent of the costs in excess of $800,000. If the project actually costs $760,000, for example, Walton Research will receive $840,000 (equals cost of $760,000 plus fixed fee of $80,000). If the project costs $860,000, Walton will receive $910,000 (equals cost limit of $800,000 plus 50 percent of the $60,000 cost overrun, or $30,000, plus the fixed fee of $80,000).

A recent project performance report provides the following data about the XT-214 project:

Project	Budget	Actual	Remaining	Status
XT-214	$800,000	$750,000	$50,000	95 Percent Complete

Top management of Walton Research meets in the second week of each month to review the performance of the preceding month. One of the managers at the meeting commented that the project manager for the XT-214 project was performing well. "The manager is doing well at holding the line on costs on the XT-214 project," a top manager stated. "I hope we take that into account at promotion time."

Another top manager at the meeting stated, "I disagree. Project XT-214 is a disaster! The 95-percent completion figure comes from the manager, and according to him, this project has been 95 percent complete for 2 months. The preliminary quality control tests indicate that a complete teardown and rework will be necessary. Further, the customer is furious because the project is 2 months behind schedule. I realize the project looks good on the performance report, but I can assure you that the report does not present the full story about Project XT-214."

a. How is the present project performance report inadequate for projects like the XT-214?

b. What improvements would you recommend in the report? Give particular attention to the way the report presents things that are important to Walton Research. Consider the costs and benefits of your recommendations to the extent possible.

30. *Evaluating performance evaluation system* (adapted from CMA exam). ATCO Company purchased Dexter Company 3 years ago. Before the acquisition, Dexter manufactured and sold electronic products to many different customers. Since becoming a division of ATCO, Dexter now manufactures only electronic components for products that ATCO's Macon Division makes.

ATCO's corporate management gives the Dexter Division management a considerable amount of authority in running the division's operations. However, corporate management retains authority for decisions regarding capital investments, price setting of all products, and the quantity of each product that the Dexter Division will produce.

ATCO has a formal performance evaluation program for the management of all of its divisions. The performance evaluation program relies heavily on each division's return on investment. Dexter Division's income statement provides the basis for the evaluation of Dexter's divisional management.

The corporate accounting staff prepares the financial statements for the divisions. The accountants allocate the corporate general services costs on the basis of sales dollars, and apportion the computer department's actual costs among the divisions on the basis of use.

Recent competitive pressures on ATCO have led ATCO's management to reduce the prices ATCO pays to Dexter. This, in turn, has put pressure on Dexter management to cut its costs because its division operating profits were low.

ATCO COMPANY
Dexter Division
Income Statement for the Year Ended October 31
(all dollar amounts in thousands)

Sales Revenue		$3,600
Costs and Expenses:		
Product Costs:		
Direct Materials	$ 500	
Direct Labor	1,100	
Factory Overhead	1,300	
Total	$2,900	
Less increase in inventory	(350)	$2,550
Engineering and Research		120
Shipping and Receiving		240
Division Administration:		
Manager's Office	$ 210	
Cost Accounting	40	
Personnel	82	332
Corporate Costs:		
Computer	$ 48	
General Services	230	278
Total Costs and Expenses		$3,520
Divisional Operating Profit		$ 80

Discuss the financial reporting and performance evaluation methods program of ATCO Company as it relates to the responsibilities of the Dexter Division.

31. *Incentive plans at McDonald's.* McDonald's Corporation is one of the world's largest and most successful food service companies. As in all service companies, the way the service employees perform their jobs affects the success of the company.

The performance of managers of McDonald's company-owned restaurants is critical to the quality and efficiency of service provided at McDonald's. Over the past 2 decades, McDonald's has tried several incentive compensation plans for its company-owned restaurant managers. We describe five of those plans here.

- *Plan 1:* Manager's bonus is a function of the restaurant's sales volume increase over the previous year.

- *Plan 2:* Manager's bonus is based on subjective evaluations by the manager's superiors. Bonuses are not tied explicitly to any quantitative performance measure.

- *Plan 3:* Manager's bonus comprises the following components:
  (1) A bonus of 10 percent of salary is paid if the manager meets the budgeted costs. This budget is based on sales volume and the standard allowed per unit.
  (2) Management visits each restaurant each month and evaluates its performance with regard to quality, cleanliness, and service. Founder Ray Kroc identified these three key success factors for the company. Managers in restaurants receiving an A get a bonus of 10 percent of salary, managers of restaurants receiving a B get a bonus of 5 percent of salary, and managers of restaurants receiving a C receive no bonus for this component of the plan.
  (3) An additional bonus up to 10 percent of salary is earned based on increases in sales volume over the previous year. (The manager can still receive this bonus if volume does not increase because of circumstances beyond the manager's control.)

- *Plan 4:* Superiors evaluate the manager as to the following six performance indicators: quality, service, cleanliness, training ability, volume, and profit. Each indicator is scored 0, 1, or 2. A manager receiving a score of 12 points receives a bonus of 40 percent of salary, a score of 11 points provides a bonus of 35 percent of salary, and so forth.

- *Plan 5:* The manager receives a bonus of 10 percent of the sales volume increase over the previous year plus 20 percent of the restaurant's profit.

Evaluate each of these incentive plans. Are there better alternatives? Be sure to consider the important things a manager and a restaurant should do to contribute to McDonald's overall company success.

32. *Comprehensive planning and control case.*[18] The Continental Can Company of Canada is a manufacturing company with plants located throughout Canada. Mr. David R. Arnold, the company's corporate controller for 15 years, coordinates the efforts of various segments of the company. One such segment, the Metal Division, had successfully used the company's control system, which we describe next.

Background on Products, Technology, and Markets Continental Can Company of Canada operated a number of Canadian plants. The principal products of its Metal Division's St. Laurent plant were Open Top food cans, bottle caps and crowns, steel pails, and general line containers. Of these, Open Top cans constituted the largest group. The firm manufactured these cans for the major packers of vegetable products—peas, beans, corn, and tomatoes—and for the soup manufacturers. Beer and soft drink cans were a growing commodity, and the firm produced large quantities of general line containers of many different

[18]Copyright © 1982 by the President and Fellows of Harvard College. Harvard Business School case 182-197. Cynthia A. Vahlkamp prepared this case under the direction of Richard F. Vancil as the basis for class discussion rather than to illustrate either effective or ineffective handling of an administrative situation. Reprinted by permission of the Harvard Business School.

configurations to hold solvents, paints, lighter fluids, waxes, antifreeze, and so on. The firm also produced several styles of steel pails of up to five-gallon capacity to hold many specialized products.

The firm produced most of the thousands of different products, varying in size, shape, color, and decoration, to order. The firm had typical lead times between the customer's order and shipment from the plant of two to three weeks, having reduced them from five and one half to six weeks a decade before, according to St. Laurent plant executives.

Quality inspection of the can manufacturing operation was critical, as the can maker usually supplied the closing equipment and assisted in or recommended the process the packagers should use in the final packing procedure. In producing Open Top food cans, for example, St. Laurent formed, soldered, and flanged the can body at speeds exceeding 400 cans per minute. After the firm attached the bottom or end unit to the body, each can was air tested to reject poor double seams or poor soldering or plate inclusions that could cause pin holes. Both side seams and double seams underwent periodic destruction testing to ensure that assembly specifications were met. Although the firm used a number of measuring devices in the process, much of the inspection was still visual, involving human inspection and monitoring. The quality of the can also affected the filling and processing procedure: it had to withstand internal pressures from expansion of the product as it was heated, and then it had to sustain a vacuum without collapsing when it was cooled. Costly claims could result if the container failed in the field and manufacturer had to withdraw the product from store shelves.

Almost all of the containers required protective coatings inside and out, and the majority were decorated. The coating and decorating equipment was sophisticated and required sizable investment. This part of the operation was unionized, and the lithographers or press workers were among the highest paid of the various craftsmen in the plant.

The parent organization designed and developed most of the key equipment over many years. The St. Laurent plant spent substantial sums each year to modernize and renovate its equipment. The firm needed to modernize and implement new techniques to increase speed, reduce material costs, and improve quality as volume increased. Over the years, St. Laurent discontinued many of the small-run, handmade boxes and pails and scrapped the equipment. The firm automated other lines and retrained personnel to handle the higher mechanical skills and changeovers required. In spite of these changes, however, according to a general foreman, a production worker who left twenty years ago could return and not feel entirely out of place. Many of the less skilled machine operators were required to handle several tasks on the higher-speed equipment. In general, most of the jobs in the plant were relatively unskilled, highly repetitive, and gave the worker little control over method or pace. The firm considered the die makers who made and repaired the dies, the machine repairmen, and those who made equipment set-up changes between different products to possess the highest level of skill.

All production workers below the rank of assistant foreman were unionized; however, employees had never gone on strike at the plant. Wages were high compared to other similar industries in the Montreal area. The union was not part of the Master Agreement that governed all other plants in Canada and most of the plants in the United States, but management made every effort to apply equality to this plant. Management established output standards for all jobs, but paid no bonus for exceeding standards.

The metal can industry was relatively stable, with little product differentiation. The two or three largest companies in the industry competed on the basis of product quality and customer service rather than price. Nonmetal containers presented perhaps the largest competitive threat.

The Metal Division's various plants to some extent shipped products throughout Canada, although transportation costs limited each plant's market primarily to eastern Canada. While some large customers bought in huge quantities (between 300 and 500 million cans), many customers were relatively small and purchased a more specialized product.

Organization   Continental Can Company of Canada, a diversified company, was organized into several major product divisions of which the Metal Division was one. (See Exhibit 11.3.) A division vice president headed each division. Each division vice president reported directly to the corporate executive vice president, who coordinated the various divisions. Customer service and product research staff supported the division vice president. The general manager of manufacturing and the general manager of marketing each reported to a division vice president. (See Exhibit 11.4 on page 516.)

Five staff groups supported the executive vice president, providing a policy review function: the controller, the treasurer, the chief accountant, the market research department, and the labor relations department. The controller's department comprised Mr. David R. Arnold and the assistant controller, Mr. Edward J. Lynn. All corporate and division management was located in Toronto, Canada.

Exhibit 11.3

CONTINENTAL CAN COMPANY OF CANADA, LTD.
Top Management Group

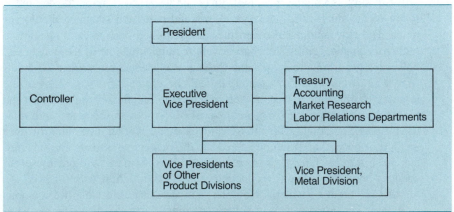

Budgetary Control System   The budgetary control system reflected the managerial philosophy and organizational structure at Continental Can Company of Canada. Operating on a decentralized basis, with divisions performing all functions inherent in any independent company (with the exception of not being responsible for sources of funds and cross-divisional labor relations), the company required a control system to provide an integrative function. Mr. Arnold commented, ''Certainly, in our case, the budget is much more than a narrow statistical accounting device.''

Sales Budget   Preparing the sales budget initiated the budget preparation procedure. As early as May 15 prior to the beginning of the budget year, top management asked the various product division vice presidents to submit preliminary reports. Top management intended these reports to be interpretive statements reflecting the operating executives' practical feelings about their divisions' capital requirements and outlooks for sales and income for the coming budget year. Top management also expected division vice presidents to indicate trends in sales and income, particularly those manifested over the previous two years. Senior management at this stage was not interested in too much detail, and wanted the estimates to be based on forecasts prepared in last year's budget and data in the five-year plan for capital requirements.

Next, the market research staff developed a formal statement detailing the marketing climate for the forthcoming budget year and providing a general assessment for the subsequent two years. These general factors then became the basis for a sales forecast for the company and for each division.

In preparing its report, the market research group projected such factors as the general economic condition, growth of the various markets, weather conditions related to the end uses of the company's products, competitive effort, and labor disturbances. The report stated the underlying assumptions relating to such parameters as price and weather conditions. In forecasting sales data, the marketing research group also considered new product introduction, gains or losses in particular accounts, forward buying, new manufacturing plants, and any changes in the definition or accounting of certain items. The market research group also assessed the probable impact of industry growth trends, inventory carry-overs, and developments in alternative packaging. The group reviewed relevant factors with respect to all product lines, regardless of size and importance.

Once the market research group had completed its analysis, it forwarded the sales forecasts to the appropriate divisions for review, criticism, and adjustments. Corporate staff groups assisted in the forecasting of sales data by assuring uniformity among divisions with regard to basic assumptions on business conditions, pricing, and the treatment of possible emergencies. Also, the market research groups paid attention to assure that the company's overall sales forecast was reasonable and obtainable.

At this point, product division top management requested the district sales managers to prepare independent sales forecasts. Corporate and division staffs offered guidance for the sales managers, although the sales manager was solely responsible for projecting the forecast.

Exhibit 11.4

CONTINENTAL CAN COMPANY OF CANADA, LTD.
Metals Division, Top Management and Staff

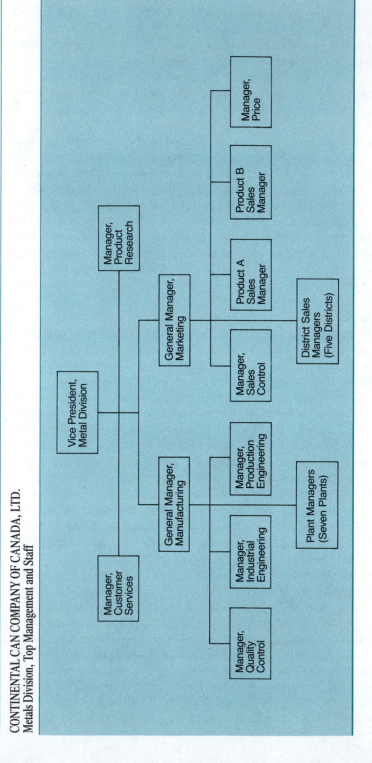

The district sales managers submitted their forecasts to top divisional management, and the division's general manager of marketing consolidated and reviewed them. At this time, the general manager of marketing could suggest that district sales managers revise their budgets. Mr. Arnold described a typical situation in which a revision would be suggested:

> Consolidating the district sales managers' sales estimates may, for example, indicate that an increase of 20 to 25 percent might be expected. Obviously this increase is unreasonable. What has happened is that each district sales manager has been told by the customers that they expect an increase in sales. Summing all of these anticipated individual sales increases produced the unreasonably high expected growth in market. What has not been taken into account are reductions in sales of company A as a result of increases in sales of company B.
>
> Individually, the district sales managers know little of what's happening outside their territory. However, from the headquarters point of view, we can ascertain the size of the whole market and the customer's probable relative market share. That's where the market research group's studies come in handy.

Even when the general manager suggested revisions, the district sales manager's forecast was not changed unless the district manager agreed. Once the budget was approved, only top-management approval could relieve a manager of responsibility to comply with the budget. Also, no one could make arbitrary changes in an approved budget without the concurrence of all those responsible for the budget.

The firm repeated this process of review and revision at the division and headquarters levels until agreement on a sound budget was reached. Then, each level of management took responsibility for its particular portion of the budget. These sales budgets then became fixed objectives.

In reviewing the sales forecasts, Arnold suggested that the divisions had other objectives in addition to formulating a realistic sales budget. Arnold said:

> I would say they have four general objectives in mind: First, a review of the division's competitive position, including plans for improving the position. Second, an evaluation of its efforts to gain either a larger share of the market or offset competitors' activities. Third, a consideration of the need to expand facilities to improve the division's products or introduce new products. Finally, a review and development of plans to improve product quality, delivery methods, and service.

Manufacturing Budgets   Once the vice presidents, executive vice presidents, and company president approved the sales budgets, the process of preparing the manufacturing budgets began. Plants had profit responsibility, and the plant manager prepared a budget for each.

Initially, the plant manager prepared a sales budget for each plant from the division sales budget according to the proportion of finished goods shipped from that plant. The manager then further broke down the annual plant budget on a monthly basis by price, volume, and end-use.

Given a sales volume goal, the plant manager calculated the cost of producing that volume. The plant manager calculated the fixed overhead and variable costs—at standard—that would accrue to meet the demands of the sales budget. Then plants were able to budget their contribution margin, fixed expenses, and income before taxes.[19] Mr. Arnold explained the philosophy underlying this process:

> In some companies I know of, the head office gives each plant manager sales and income figures that the plant has to meet. We don't operate that way. We believe that type of directive misses the benefit of all the field experience of those at the district sales and plant levels. If we gave a profit figure to our plant managers to meet, how could we say it was their responsibility to meet it?
>
> What we say to the plant manager is this: Assuming that you have to produce this much sales volume, how much do you expect to spend for your programs allied to obtaining these current and future sales?
>
> Requiring the plant managers to make their own plans is one of the most valuable aspects of the budget system.

The plant manager divided responsibility for the overall plant budget among the various departments. (See Exhibit 11.5.) Given the sales forecasts, the departments contributed data regarding physical requirements (such as tons of raw materials), which the manager then priced at standard cost. The Plant Industrial Engineering Department developed these standard costs by calculating budget performance standards for each of the plant's operations, cost centers, and departments. The industrial engineer prepared this part of the budget in conjunction with department line supervisors.

Other calculations performed in this phase of the budget included budgeted cost reductions, budgeted unfavorable variances from standard, and budgeted programmed fixed costs in the manufacturing area, such as service labor.

Once the plant budget was complete, a group from head office visited the plants. The group spent approximately a half day at each plant, visiting all plants over a three-week period. In the case of the Metal Division, Mr. Arnold, Mr. Lynn, and representatives of the Metal Division manufacturing staffs visited each of the division's plants. At the plants, this group met with the plant manager and any supervisors that the plant manager invited, and discussed the budget. Also, the group discussed in detail the property replace-

---

[19]Contribution margin was defined as the difference between gross sales, less discounts, and variable manufacturing costs (such as direct labor, direct material, and variable manufacturing overheads). Income was the difference between contribution margin and fixed costs.

Exhibit 11.5

CONTINENTAL CAN COMPANY OF CANADA, LTD.
Typical Plant Organization—Metals Division

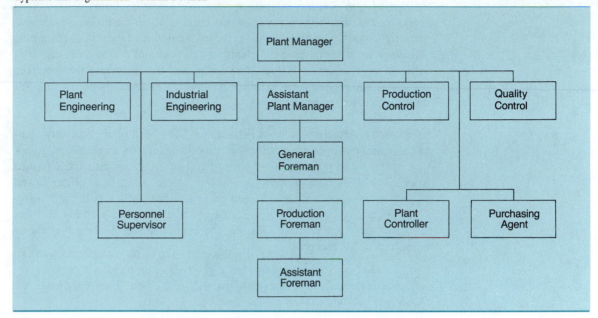

ment and maintenance budget with the plant engineer. Mr. Arnold commented on the purpose of these visits:

> Let me stress this point: We do not go on these trips to pass judgment on the plant's proposed budget. Rather, we go with two purposes in mind.
>
> First, we wish to acquaint ourselves with the thinking behind the figures that each plant manager will send in to Toronto. This is helpful because when we come to review these budgets with the top management (that is, the management above our level), we will have to answer questions about the budgets and we will know the answers.
>
> Second, the review is a way of giving guidance to the plant managers as to whether or not they are in line with what the company needs to make in the way of profits.

During the plant visits, the group from head office explained to the plant managers that, while their budget looked good initially, after all the plants' budgets had been consolidated the managers would have to make changes if projected profit was insufficient.[20]

---

[20]The budgeted plant profit was the difference between the fixed sales-dollar budget and the budgeted variable costs at standard and the fixed overhead budget. The plant managers were responsible to meet the budgeted profit figure even if actual dollar sales dropped below the budgeted level.

In the beginning of September, once the head office group completed the plant tours, managers submitted plant budgets to Toronto for the accounting department to consolidate. Product divisional vice presidents then reviewed their respective division budgets for reasonableness in terms of perceived corporate top-management expectations. If dissatisfied, the division vice president requested the various plants in the division to trim their budget figures.

Once the division vice presidents and the executive vice president were satisfied with the plant budget, they submitted the budget to the company president. The president could accept the division budgets or specify areas for the divisions to reexamine.

Comparison of Actual and Standard Performance   The head office routinely compared actual performance with standard performance on the basis of exception; that is, head office required plant managers to explain only those figures in excess of budgeted amounts. In analyzing gross sales, head office looked closely at price and changes in sales mix. The head office paid particularly close attention to net sales, gross margin, and the plant's ability to meet standard manufacturing cost. Mr. Arnold explained the thinking underlying management by exception:

> We believe this (system) has a good effect on morale. The plant managers don't have to explain everything they do. They only have to explain where they go off base.

The plant managers summarized the cost and revenue information on a standard form, the Profit Planning and Control Report (PPCR) #1, and backed it up with a number of supporting documents (PPCR#2–PPCR#11). See Exhibits 11.6 and 11.7. The plant PPCR#1 and the month-end trial balance showing both actual and budget figures were received in Toronto, at the close of the eighth business day after month-end. The accounting department then consolidated these reports to show operating results by division and by company. The accounting department distributed the consolidated reports the next day.

Head office received performance information in advance of PPCR#1. The head office prepared a monthly variance analysis sheet at the end of the sixth business day after the month-end from information wired to head office from each plant. Within a half hour after receipt of all plant reports, the head office compiled variance analysis sheets for the divisions and plants. On the morning of the seventh business day after month-end, the head office forwarded these reports to appropriate top management. Mr. Arnold commented:

> The variance analysis sheet highlights the variances in what we consider to be critical areas. Receiving this report as soon as we do helps us at head office to take timely action. Let me emphasize, however, we do not accept the excuse that the plant manager had to go to the end of the month to know what happened during the month. He has to be on top of these particular items daily.

In addition to the end-of-month reports, plant managers prepared at the beginning of each month current estimates for the upcoming month and quar-

Exhibit 11.6

CONTINENTAL CAN COMPANY OF CANADA, LTD.
Profit Planning and Control Report No. 1

MONTH					YEAR TO DATE		
Income Gain (+) or Loss (−) From						Income Gain (+) or Loss (−) From	
Prev. Year	Budget	Actual	Ref.		Actual	Budget	Prev. Year
			1	Gross Sales to Customers			
			2	Discounts & Allowances			
			3	Net Sales to Customers			
%	%		4	% Gain (+)/Loss (−)		%	%
				DOLLAR VOLUME GAIN (+)/ LOSS (−) DUE TO:			
			5	Sales Price			
			6	Sales Volume			
			6(a)	Trade Mix			
			7	Std. Variable Cost of Sales			
			8	Contribution Margin			
				CONTRIB. MARGIN GAIN (+)/ LOSS (−) DUE TO:			
			9	Profit Volume Ratio (P/V)*			
			10	Dollar Volume			
%	%	%	11	Profit Volume Ratio (P/V)*		%	%	%
			12	Budgeted Fixed Mfg. Cost			
			13	Fixed Manufacturing Cost-Transfers			
			14	Plant Income (standard)			
%	%	%	15	% of Net Sales		%	%	%
%	%	%	16	% Mfg. Efficiency		%	%	%
			17	Manufacturing Variances			
			18	Methods Improvements			
			19	Other Revisions of Standards			
			20	Material Price Changes			
			21	Division Special Projects			
			22	Company Special Projects			
			23	New Plant Expense			
			24	Other Plant Expenses			
			25	Income on Seconds			
			26				
			27				
			28	Plant Income (actual)			
%	%		29	% Gain (+)/Loss (−)			%	%
%	%	%	30	% of Net Sales		%	%	%
			36A				
				CAPITAL EMPLOYED			
			37	Total Capital Employed			
%	%	%	38	% Return		%	%	%
			39	Turnover Rate			

_____ _____ _____ 19 ____
     Plant   Division   Month

Exhibit 11.7

CONTINENTAL CAN COMPANY OF CANADA, LTD.
Brief Description of PPCR#2 through PPCR#11

Individual Plant Reports

Report	Description
PPCR#2	*Manufacturing expense:* Plant materials, labor, and variable overhead consumed. Detail of actual figures compared with budget and previous years' figures for year-to-date and current month.
PPCR#3	*Plant expense:* Plant fixed expenses incurred. Details of actual figures compared with budget and previous years' figures for year-to-date and current month.
PPCR#4	*Analysis of sales and income:* Plant operating gains and losses due to changes in sales revenue, profit margins, and other sources of income. Details of actual figures compared with budget and previous years' figures for year-to-date and current month.
PPCR#5	*Plant control statement:* Analysis of plant raw material gains and losses, spoilage costs, and cost-reduction programs. Actual figures compared with budget figures for current month and year-to-date.

Division Summary Reports

PPCR#6	*Comparison of sales by principal and product groups:* Plant sales-dollars, profit margin, and P/V ratios broken down by end-product use (soft drinks, beer, etc.). Compares actual figures with budgeted figures for year-to-date and current month.
PPCR#7	*Comparative plant performance, sales, and income:* Gross sales and income figures by plants. Actual figures compared with budget figures for year-to-date and current month.
PPCR#8	*Comparative plant performance, total plant expenses:* Profit margin, total fixed costs, manufacturing efficiency, other plant expenses, and P/V ratios by plants. Actual figures compared with budgeted and previous years' figures for current month and year-to-date.
PPCR#9	*Manufacturing efficiency:* Analysis of gains and losses by plant in areas of materials, spoilage, supplies, and labor. Current month and year-to-date actuals reported in total dollars and as a percentage of budget.

Division Summary Reports

PPCR#10	*Inventory:* Comparison of actual and budget inventory figures by major inventory accounts and plants.
PPCR#11	*Status of capital expenditures:* Analysis of the status of capital expenditures by plants, months, and relative to budget.

ter. The managers presented these estimates on forms similar to the variance analysis sheets. These beginning-of-month estimates had two primary purposes: First, the estimates alerted the head office to possible adverse trends in operations and, second, plant managers were encouraged to run their plants with an eye toward the future. Mr. Arnold explained the value of these reports:

> If we see a sore spot coming up, or if the plant manager draws our attention to a potential trouble area, we may ask for daily reports concerning this item to be sent to the particular division top management involved. In addition, division top management may send a division staff specialist—say, a quality control expert—to the plant concerned. The division staff members can make recommendations,

but it is up to the plant manager to accept or reject these recommendations. Of course, it is well known throughout the company that we expect the plant managers to accept gracefully the help of the head office and division staffs.

Sales-Manufacturing Relations   Mr. Arnold felt that preparing the budget improved the understanding of operations and reduced the risk of potential chaos arising from sudden, unexpected sales declines at year-end. If actual sales volume fell below budgeted sales volume early in the year, and if plant managers convinced head office that the change was permanent, head office would revise the plant budgets to reflect the new circumstances. If, however, the change was unexpected and at year-end, the firm would have insufficient time to change the budget plans. In this case, the head office would ask plant managers to review their budgets with their staffs to identify possible areas to reduce expenses. Specifically, Mr. Arnold suggested that they might ask plant managers to consider what they might eliminate this year or delay until next year. He commented:

> I believe it was Confucius who said: "We make plans so we have plans to discard." Nevertheless, I believe it is wise to make plans, even if you have to discard them. Having plans makes it a lot easier to figure out what to do when sales fall off from the budgeted level. The understanding of operations that comes from preparing the budget takes away a lot of the potential chaos and confusion that might arise if we were under pressure to meet a stated profit goal and sales decline quickly and unexpectedly at year-end, just as they did this year.
>
> Under these circumstances, we don't try to ram anything down the plant managers' throats. We ask them to tell us where they can reasonably expect to cut costs below the budgeted level.

In some cases, a plant manager's costs increased when the sales group insisted on a production schedule change to accommodate an unexpected rush order. In this case, Mr. Arnold said:

> The customer's wants are primary. Our company is a case where sales wags the rest of the dog. Whenever a problem arises at a plant between sales and production, the local people are supposed to solve the problem themselves. Suppose a customer's purchasing agent insists he wants an immediate delivery and this delivery will disrupt the production department's plans. The production group can recommend alternative ways to take care of the problem, but the sales manager is responsible to get the product to the customer. The sales staff is supposed to judge whether the customer really needs the product. If the sales manager says the customer needs the product, that ends the matter.
>
> If the change in the sales program involves a major expense at the plant which is out of line with the budget, then the sales manager passes the matter up to division for decision.

As I said earlier, the sales department has the sole responsibility for the production price, sales mix, and delivery schedules. They do not have direct responsibility for plant operations or profit. That's the plant management's responsibility. However, it is understood that the sales group will cooperate with the plant people wherever possible. We believe the whole budgetary control system works best if we can get cooperation. But, within the framework of cooperation, the sales and production groups have very clear responsibilities.

Motivation   The firm used several devices to motivate plant managers to meet their profit goals. In addition to a monetary incentive program, the firm gave wide publicity to a plant's manufacturing efficiency.[21] Each month the firm put together a bar chart showing, by division and plant, the ranking of the manufacturing units by manufacturing efficiency. Mr. Arnold commented:

The efficiency bar chart and efficiency measure itself are perhaps a little unfair in some respects in comparing plants. Different kinds of products are produced at different plants, requiring different set-ups, etc., that impact the plant's position. However, the efficiency rating is generally a good indicator of the quality of the plant manager and the supervisory staff.

Additionally, some plants ran competitions within the plants, which rewarded department heads or foremen based on their relative standing with respect to certain items.

While profit was the goal, at the plant level managers emphasized quality (defined both by physical quality and such items as meeting delivery schedules). The firm transmitted this message to plant employees:

If the company is to be profitable, it must produce high-quality items at reasonable cost. This ensures the plant's ability to maximize profits for the company under prevailing circumstances.

Said Mr. Arnold, "The plant managers, their staffs, and employees have great pride in their plant."

The Future   Mr. Arnold projected the future of the budgetary control system:

An essential part of the budgetary control system is planning. We have developed a philosophy that we must begin our plans where the work is done—in the line organization and out in the field. Perhaps, in the future, we can avoid or cut back some of the budget preparation steps and start putting our sales budget together later on in the year than May 15. However, I doubt if we will change the basic philosophy.

---

[21]Manufacturing Efficiency $= \dfrac{\text{Total Actual Variable Manufacturing Costs}}{\text{Total Standard Variable Manufacturing Costs}}$.

Frankly, I doubt if the line operators would want any major change in the system—they are very jealous of the management prerogatives the system gives them.

We must manage the budget. We have to be continually on guard against it managing us. Sometimes, the plants lose sight of this fact. Something must make them conscious daily of the necessity of having the sales volume to make a profit. And, when sales fall off and we reduce their plant programs, they do not always appear to see the justification for budget cuts. Although, I do suspect that they see more of the justification for these cuts than they will admit. It is this human side of the budget to which we will have to pay more attention in the future.

a. Describe each step of Continental Can's budget process from its start on May 15 until its final approval. Relate each step to the organization charts in Exhibits 11.4 and 11.5.

b. Evaluate Continental Can's budgeting process. Has it related the budget to organizational goals? Do district sales managers, plant managers, and other participants have incentives to provide biased information?

c. Evaluate the strength and weaknesses of Continental Can's performance evaluation methods and organization structure. Should the plants continue to be profit or investment centers, or should they be cost centers? Why? (This question may be postponed until Chapter 15.)

... CHAPTER 12 ...

Operating Budgets

Chapter Outline

- Use of Operating Budgets
- The Master Budget
- Incentives for Accurate Forecasts
- Using the Budget for Performance Evaluation and Control
- Achieved Results versus Flexible Budget

This chapter focuses on the short-term operating budget. This budget quantitatively states management's plan of action for the coming year. This chapter considers the development of such budgets, their uses, and how managers compare actual results of operations with budgets to derive variances for performance evaluation.

Uses of Operating Budgets

Budgets are useful tools for (1) planning, (2) control, and (3) employee motivation.

Tool for Planning

After management selects the best alternatives for products, prices, levels of output, production techniques, and so on, it translates these choices into a formal, integrated plan of action. This step forces management to take each of the choices made and make sure that it coordinates with other alternatives selected. It also presents management with a comprehensive picture of the expected effects of its decisions on the firm as a whole. Put another way, budgets are estimates of financial statements prepared before the actual transactions occur.

As **tools for planning,** budgets are generally static; that is, the firm develops budgets for a particular expected level of activity, such as sales or production in units. The budgeting process derives a set of estimates for sales, manufacturing costs, selling and administrative expenses, and profit in the **static budget.**

Tool for Control

Budgets provide estimates of expected performance. As such, they serve as standards for evaluating performance. Comparing budgeted and actual amounts provides a basis for evaluating past performance and guiding future action. To be effective as **tools for control,** the firm must initially develop its budgets for individual responsibility centers. The firm develops budgets for production, marketing, purchasing, administration, and so on. Then the firm integrates these separate budgets into a master budget for the firm as a whole. In this way, top management can evaluate the performance of each responsibility center with respect to those activities over which it had control during a particular period.

Flexible Budgets   Budgets used as tools for control are generally flexible. A **flexible budget** states a fixed cost expected to be incurred regardless of the level of activity, and a variable cost per unit of activity that can change *in total* as the level of activity changes. The "flex" in a flexible budget concerns the variable costs (that is, those costs that vary with changes in activity levels). The budget for fixed costs is static.

Example   Studies of past cost behavior indicate that the Testing department of a computer company should incur total fixed costs of $100,000 and variable costs of $10 per unit tested next period. For planning purposes, the company estimates that it will test 50,000 units. The static cost budget for the division used for planning purposes is therefore $600,000 [= $100,000 + ($10 × 50,000)]. Suppose, however, that due to unexpected demand during the period, the Testing department tested 70,000 units. Management will not wish to compare, for control purposes, the actual cost of producing 70,000 units with the expected cost of producing 50,000 units. The underlying levels of activity differ. To evaluate actual performance, accounting must express the budget or standard in terms of what costs should have been to produce 70,000 units. The flexible budget is useful in this situation. It indicates that testing costs should have been $800,000 [= $100,000 + ($10 × 70,000)] during the period. This is the more appropriate standard for control. Note that the estimates of fixed and variable costs form the inputs into both the static budget for planning and the flexible budget for control.

Tool for Employee Motivation

The human factor is important in the planning and control process. Standards or budgets can motivate employees if the firm sets standards at levels that are tight but currently attainable with reasonably efficient performance. The budget of expected costs for planning purposes may differ from the standard costs that will best motivate employees. This instance is another in which budgeting and managerial accounting systems must adapt to serve multiple purposes.

The Master Budget

The **master budget,** sometimes called the *comprehensive budget,* is a complete blueprint of the planned operations of the firm for a period. It emphasizes the relation of the various inputs in all areas of the company to final output and sales.

To prepare it requires recognizing the interrelations among the various units of a firm. For example, to prepare a master budget requires knowing how a projected increase in sales of product A affects the several producing departments; the selling, general, and administrative effort; and the financial position of the company.

Preparing a master budget requires time and effort by management at all levels. Despite this difficulty, or perhaps because of it, management can effectively use the master budget as an instrument for planning and control. Almost all organizations of any size recognize master budget preparation as a vital task of management.

No simple example can effectively convey the complexity of the process, but the illustration on the following pages indicates some of the problems and possible solutions.

Example   We illustrate the budget preparation process for Victoria Corporation for a single period, assumed to be one month. This example continues in our discussion of performance evaluation in this chapter and in Chapters 13 and 14. An organization chart of Victoria Corporation appears in Exhibit 12.1. Each box in the

Exhibit 12.1

VICTORIA CORPORATION
Organization Chart

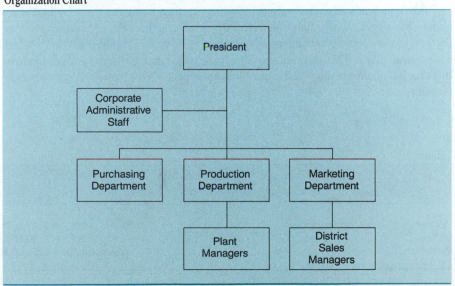

organization chart is a responsibility center. To keep the illustrations simple, we do not show additional details for the production, marketing, and corporate staff departments.

Phase 1: Organizational Goals, Strategic Plans, and the Capital Budget

Operating budgets exist within a larger planning and control framework. Organizational goals and strategies for achieving them have a direct bearing on budgeted operations.

Operating budgets interact with capital budgets as well. Capital investment decisions rely on cash flow forecasts that should be consistent with forecasts for operating budgets. The capital budget establishes capacity and constrains the level of operations for future periods.

Knowing where to start in forecasting activity levels may be a problem, but generally one factor constrains the level of activity. This factor precludes the firm from doing everything management would like. For most firms the critical factor is the volume of anticipated sales. The critical factor could also be the availability of raw materials or the supply of labor or manufacturing capacity. We assume that budgeted sales is the critical factor for Victoria Corporation. We start with the sales budget; the other budgets build on the sales budget, as we shall soon see.

Phase 2: The Sales Forecast

The sales budget appears in Exhibit 12.2. Responsibility for preparing the budget usually belongs to the chief marketing executive of the firm. The marketing executive relies on inputs from the market research group as well as from salespeople or district managers in the field. The discussions among sales groups in budget preparation frequently brings out problems in the firm's selling and advertising programs and broadens the participants' thinking about the firm's place in the market.

Previous sales experience is usually the starting point for sales budget estimates. Managers modify these historical data to recognize relevant factors such as market trends, anticipated changes in general economic conditions, and altered advertising plans. The marketing executive usually makes the final decisions on the precise quantities and dollar amounts to appear in the sales budget for each product.

Exhibit 12.2

VICTORIA CORPORATION
Sales Budget for Period 1

Optimistic	90,000 Units at $7 = $630,000
Median	70,000 Units at $6 = $420,000
Pessimistic	50,000 Units at $5 = $250,000

Example   Victoria Corporation produces one product of which it expects to sell 70,000 units at $6 per unit. Market researchers developed an initial sales forecast. They estimated pessimistic, optimistic, and median forecasts of total product sales in the market and Victoria's market share. The company defined optimistic as "probability of sales this high or higher is .2"; they defined pessimistic as "probability of sales this low or lower is .2." The probability of sales larger (or smaller) than the median was .50. The marketing vice president also had district sales managers prepare optimistic, pessimistic, and median forecasts for their districts.

According to the marketing vice president, who is the chief marketing executive at Victoria Corporation, the data bases that the two groups used differed:

> The market research group uses consumer studies, economic forecasts, and past data about the company. The group provides a good macro-level forecast of economic conditions and consumer preferences for our products, but it explains little about the day-to-day efforts of our sales personnel.
>
> This is where our sales managers' forecasts are most valuable. They know about potential customers, they know which of our present customers we are likely to lose, and they can forecast sales quite accurately for the first few months of the budget year. When I combine the forecasts of the market research group and the sales managers, I have a good idea of both the market conditions affecting the demand for our product and the immediate wishes of our customers.

The marketing vice president, combining the forecasts from the two groups with personal experience and knowledge of the company, prepared the forecasts shown in Exhibit 12.2. Although we show all three forecasts—optimistic, pessimistic, and median—we use only the median in subsequent discussion to keep the example simple.

Production Budget

The sales budget, combined with estimates of beginning inventories and estimates of desired ending inventories, forms the basis of the production budget for the Victoria Corporation shown in the top panel of Exhibit 12.3. The ending inventory is to service customers in the period following the one being budgeted.

We compute the quantity of each product to be produced from a variant of the basic accounting equation:

$$\text{Beginning Balance} + \text{Transfers In} = \text{Transfers Out} + \text{Ending Balance},$$

$$\text{BB} + \text{TI} = \text{TO} + \text{EB}.$$

Expressing the equation in units and relating it to units produced and sold, the basic accounting equation becomes:

$$\text{Units to Be Produced} = \text{Number of Units Sold} + \text{Units in Ending Inventory} - \text{Units in Beginning Inventory}.$$

The costs to be incurred in producing the desired number of units appear in the lower panel of Exhibit 12.3.

Exhibit 12.3

VICTORIA CORPORATION
Production Budget for the Budget Period

Units to Be Produced

Budgeted Sales, in Units (see sales budget)	70,000
Desired Ending Inventory (assumed)	8,000
Total Units Needed	78,000
Less Beginning Inventory (assumed)	(8,000)
Units to Be Produced	70,000

Cost Expected to Be Incurred

Direct Materials (1 pound per unit at $1.00 per pound)	$ 70,000
Direct Labor (⅛ hour per unit at $20 per hour)	175,000
Manufacturing Overhead:	
Indirect Labor ($.10 per unit)	7,000
Supplies ($.04 per unit)	2,800
Power ($1,000 per period plus $.03 per unit)	3,100
Maintenance ($13,840 per period)	13,840
Rent ($6,000 per period)	6,000
Insurance ($1,000 per period)	1,000
Depreciation ($10,360 per period)	10,360
Total Production Costs	$289,100

Direct Materials   Direct materials are raw materials traceable to individual units produced. Direct materials costs are almost always variable. Management estimates that each finished unit at Victoria will require 1 pound of direct materials. The estimates of direct materials requirements result from engineering studies of material usage. The $1.00 cost per pound of the direct materials comes from studies of past cost behavior and projected prices of suppliers. Hence, the budgeted or standard direct materials cost per finished unit is $1.00 × 1 pound per finished unit = $1.00 per finished unit.[1]

Direct Labor   Direct labor represents work traceable directly to particular units of product. Engineering time and motion studies and studies of past labor time usage behavior indicate that a unit requires about 7.5 minutes of labor time. This estimate allows for normal, periodic rest periods. The standard is tight enough to motivate employees to perform efficiently. The standard wage rate, including fringe benefits and payroll taxes (for example, employer's share of Social Security and unemployment taxes) for production workers in Victoria Corporation's plant is $20.00 per hour and results from negotiations with the local labor union.

Manufacturing Overhead   Variable manufacturing costs vary with units produced. Fixed manufacturing overhead costs give a firm the capacity to produce. As Exhibit 12.3 shows, indirect labor and supplies are variable manufacturing overhead costs.

---

[1]Managers and accountants often use the terms *budgets* and *standards* interchangeably.

Power is a semivariable, or mixed, cost, having both variable and fixed components. Maintenance, rent, insurance, and depreciation are fixed manufacturing overhead costs.

These estimates result from past experience and projected changes in costs and production methods. One can apply statistical regression methods to overhead to (1) separate fixed from variable overhead and (2) find the relations between variable overhead and a measure of activity (for example, direct labor hours or output). For Victoria Corporation, the measure of activity is output, and we assume variable manufacturing overhead to be $.17 per unit of output.

Summary of Production Budget The budget in Exhibit 12.3 shows planned production department activity for the period. The production manager must schedule production to manufacture 70,000 units. The production budget can help management evaluate the performance of the production department at the end of the period. If the projected production in units and input costs occurs, the production department should incur costs of $289,100 during the period.

If the level of production differs from the projected amounts, we apply the flexible budget concept to compute the amount of costs that the production department should have incurred. The flexible budget for the production department is

$$\begin{matrix} \text{Total Budgeted} \\ \text{Manufacturing} \\ \text{Costs for} \\ \text{Production} \\ \text{Departments} \end{matrix} = \$32{,}200 + (\$3.67 \times \text{Units Produced}).$$

Expected fixed costs comprise the estimates for power, maintenance, rent, insurance, and depreciation: $32,200 = $1,000 + $13,840 + $6,000 + $1,000 + $10,360. Expected variable costs comprise the estimates for direct materials, direct labor, indirect labor, supplies, and power: $3.67 = $1.00 + $2.50 + $.10 + $.04 + $.03.

Marketing and Administrative Costs The budget for marketing costs for the Victoria Corporation's marketing department appears in Exhibit 12.4. Management expects all of the items except commissions and shipping costs to be fixed. Commissions are 2 percent of sales dollars, or $.12 per unit if the selling price is $6 per unit as budgeted; $.12 = 2% × $6. Shipping costs are $.02 per unit shipped. Hence, the variable marketing cost per unit sold is $.14. Note that variable marketing costs vary with units *sold,* whereas variable manufacturing costs vary with units *produced.*

Management estimates all of the month's central corporate administrative costs in Exhibit 12.5 to be fixed.[2]

Discretionary Fixed Costs Many of the so-called fixed costs in the production, marketing, and administration budgets are discretionary costs. Maintenance, donations,

---

[2]In practice, administrative costs can be fixed or variable.

Exhibit 12.4

VICTORIA CORPORATION Marketing Cost Budget		
Variable Costs		
Commissions (2 percent of sales; see Exhibit 12.2, sales budget)	$ 8,400[a]	
Shipping Costs ($.02 per unit shipped; see Exhibit 12.2, sales budget)	1,400	
Total Variable Marketing Costs		$ 9,800
Fixed Costs		
Salaries ($25,000 per period)	$25,000	
Advertising ($30,000 per period)	30,000	
Sales Office ($8,400 per period)	8,400	
Travel ($2,000 per period)	2,000	
Total Fixed Marketing Costs		65,400
Total Marketing Cost Budget		$75,200

[a]Also, $.12 per unit sold × 70,000 units sold = $8,400.

and advertising are examples. Although management budgets them as fixed costs, managers realize that these costs are not like committed costs (for example, factory rent), which are required to provide the firm's basic capacity to produce and market its product.

When economic conditions make it doubtful that the firm will achieve its budgeted profit goals, management can cut discretionary costs. When managers state that they have reduced their fixed costs, or reduced their breakeven points, they have often cut discretionary costs, not committed costs. Discretionary costs are tempting cost-cutting targets because their reduction does not have serious short-term effects on production and marketing. The long-term consequences could be disastrous, however, if management cuts maintenance and advertising programs.

Exhibit 12.5

VICTORIA CORPORATION Administrative Cost Budget	
President's Salary	$10,000
Salaries of Other Staff Personnel	17,000
Supplies	2,000
Heat and Light	1,400
Rent	4,000
Donations and Contributions	1,000
General Corporate Taxes	8,000
Depreciation—Staff Office Equipment	1,400
Total Administrative Cost Budget	$44,800

Profit Plan (Budgeted Income Statement)   The profit plan, or budgeted income statement, appears in Exhibit 12.6. The top part presents this statement on a variable costing basis for internal, managerial use at Victoria Corporation. The bottom part shows the income statement prepared using full absorption costing, which generally accepted accounting principles require for external financial reporting and income tax regulations require for tax reporting. Earlier chapters indicated that full absorption costing "unitizes" fixed manufacturing costs, which can mislead management in decision making.

Note that although the formats of the two statements differ, the operating profits are the same because *units produced equal units sold*. Later discussions examine the case when the two differ. For the rest of this chapter and the next, we rely on the variable costing profit plan, unless otherwise specified, in discussing the use of accounting for performance evaluation.

After compiling the budget, management projects an operating profit of $10,900. (Recall that this figure is *before taxes* and miscellaneous income and expenses.) If top management is satisfied with this budgeted result and can find adequate cash to carry out the operations, it will approve the master budget. If management considers the budgeted results unsatisfactory, it will consider ways to improve the budgeted results using cost reductions or sales increases.

Exhibit 12.6

VICTORIA CORPORATION
Master Budget Profit Plan (income statement)

Variable Costing Basis

Sales (70,000 units at $6)	$420,000
Less: Variable Manufacturing Cost of Goods Sold (70,000 units at $3.67)	(256,900)
Variable Marketing Costs (70,000 units at $.14)	(9,800)
Contribution Margin	$153,300
Less: Fixed Manufacturing Costs	(32,000)
Fixed Marketing and Administrative Costs	(110,200)
Operating Profits (variable costing)	$ 10,900

Full Absorption Costing Basis

Sales (70,000 units at $6)	$420,000
Less Cost of Goods Sold (70,000 units at $4.13)[a]	(289,100)
Gross Margin	$130,900
Less Marketing and Administrative Costs	(120,000)
Operating Profits (full absorption costing)	$ 10,900

[a]Full Absorption Manufacturing Cost per Unit

$$= \text{Total Manufacturing Costs/Total Units Produced}$$

$$= \$289{,}100/70{,}000 \text{ Units}$$

$$= \$4.13 \text{ per Unit.}$$

Summary of the Master Budget

The master budget profit plan expresses top management's financial plans for achieving a targeted profit performance for the company. Generally, the board of directors reviews the master budget profit plan and considers it to be at least an implied contract with management about management expectations.

The master budget also helps allocate resources to the organization's responsibility centers, and it helps coordinate purchasing, production, sales, financing, personnel hiring, and so forth. Management follows variances from the master budget to ascertain whether the firm should cutback or expand personnel, whether the firm needs more or less financing, whether the firm should curtail or increase material purchases, and whether operating inefficiencies have occurred.

The master budget includes a budgeted balance sheet, a cash flow budget, and other relevant budgets, as well as the profit plan developed in the preceding pages. Appendix 12.1 presents a comprehensive master budget including the profit plan, budgeted balance sheets, and the cash flow budget.

Preparing the master budget usually requires the participation of all managerial groups from lower-level responsibility centers to the top executives of the company. Once adopted, the budget becomes a major planning and control instrument. Further, it becomes the authorization to produce units, to purchase materials, to hire employees, and to carry out other similar actions. In governmental units, the budget becomes the *legal* authorization for expenditure.

Master budgets are almost always static budgets; that is, they consider the likely results of operations at the one level of operations specified in the budget. This may facilitate the planning process, but it weakens the effectiveness of the budget as a control device when the scale of operations deviates from the planned level. Under those circumstances, flexible budgets are necessary. Flexible budgets consider the varying amounts of revenues and costs that are appropriate at various levels of operations, and they will be described later in this chapter.

Incentives for Accurate Forecasts

You can see the importance of the sales forecast to the entire budget process from our Victoria Corporation example. If the sales forecast is too high, for example, and the company produces to meet the forecast, the company will have excess inventory.

If the sales forecast is too low, the firm will likely lose sales opportunities because purchasing and production were planning on lower operating levels. Or, to meet unexpected sales demand, employees will work overtime and receive a premium, emergency purchases of materials and supplies will occur at prices above normal, and other costs will increase because production, purchasing, personnel, and other departments were not prepared to meet the sales demand. Yet sales personnel may look good because favorable sale variances occur.

Rewarding managers only for accurate forecasting could create disincentives for better performance—managers would try merely to meet the forecast, not to beat it. Companies use many different methods of providing incentives for both accurate forecasting *and* performance. These methods include comparing sales fore-

Managerial Application

Budgeting for New Products at 3M[a]

Several articles and books in the business press have heralded 3M for its product innovation and entrepreneurship. At the same time, good financial planning and tight cost control permeate the organization. 3M accomplishes these objectives by using financial targets "to set goals and measure performance rather than to deny expenditures or punish for unmet expectations. For example, an overall corporate goal is to derive 25 percent of total sales each year from products introduced in the last five years."[b]

When the lab develops a new product, and a market is established, the laboratory, manufacturing people, and financial people work out the budgeted costs and revenues. If new equipment is involved, manufacturing, engineering, and finance work out the cost of that equipment and how fast it will run.

"From the lab, we will decide how the product is to be made, where it's going to be made, and we will apply some estimated (overhead) rates and costs to try to come up with a projected cost on that particular product. The marketing people then will be looking at the market and projecting volumes and what they think the selling price will be. We try to look at what the market will bear and look at the cost of the product to try to come up with a good return for 3M. Sometimes the controller must keep other division members on track. For example, if marketers tend to be overly aggressive and year after year, quarter after quarter, miss their forecasts, the controller lets them know."[c]

[a]Based on "The Magic of 3M: Management Accounting Excellence," *Management Accounting* (February 1986), pp. 20–27.

[b]"Magic of 3M," pp. 20–21.

[c]"Magic of 3M," p. 23.

casts from year to year and obtaining forecasts from multiple sources. Probably the most common method of ascertaining the reasonableness of forecasts is for sales managers to know enough about their subordinates' products and territories to have intuitive knowledge of what is reasonable. Accountants have developed formal incentive models; Appendix 12.2 discusses them.

We emphasized the sales forecast in this section. The discussion applies to any type of forecast where the forecaster has incentives to bias the forecast.

Using the Budget for Performance Evaluation and Control

This section shows how accountants compare actual results achieved with budgets to derive **variances** for performance evaluation. We emphasize the use of the budget to control operations; hence, we discuss only the master budget profit plan.

Exhibit 12.7

VICTORIA CORPORATION
Flexible Budget and Profit Plan Volume Variance

	Flexible Budget (based on actual sales volume of 80,000)	Sales Volume Variance	Master Budget (based on a prediction of 70,000 units sold)
Sales............................	$480,000[a]	$60,000 F	$420,000[d]
Less:			
Variable Manufacturing Costs....	293,600[b]	36,700 U	256,900[e]
Variable Marketing Costs	11,200[c]	1,400 U	9,800[f]
Contribution Margin	$175,200	$21,900 F	$153,300
Less:			
Fixed Manufacturing Costs	32,200	—	32,200
Fixed Marketing Costs..........	65,400	—	65,400
Fixed Administration Costs	44,800	—	44,800
Operating Profit.................	$ 32,800	$21,900 F	$ 10,900

[a]80,000 units sold at $6.00.   [e]70,000 units sold at $3.67.
[b]80,000 units sold at $3.67.   [f]70,000 units sold at $.14.
[c]80,000 units sold at $.14.   U denotes unfavorable variance.
[d]70,000 units sold at $6.00.   F denotes favorable variance.

Comparison of Actual Results with the Flexible and Master Budgets

The following discussion compares the master budget with the flexible budget and with actual results. This comparison ties the results of the planning process (which results in the master budget) with flexible budgeting, and forms the basis for analyzing differences between plans and actual results.

Flexible versus Master Budget   Exhibit 12.7 compares the flexible budget with the master budget profit plan for Victoria Corporation. The master budget results from the profit plan shown in Exhibit 12.6. To review, some of the important amounts follow:

Sales Price per Unit	$6.00
Sales Volume per Period	70,000 Units
Variable Manufacturing Costs per Unit	$3.67
Variable Marketing Costs per Unit (2 percent sales commission plus $.02 per unit shipping costs)	$.14
Fixed Manufacturing Costs per Period	$32,200
Fixed Marketing Costs per Period	$65,400
Fixed Administrative Costs per Period	$44,800

We base the flexible budget in this case on the actual sales volume.[3] Variable costs and revenues should change as volume changes. The flexible budget indicates expected budgeted revenues and costs at the actual activity level, which is sales volume in this case. You can think of the flexible budget as the cost equation:

$$TC = F + VX,$$

where TC = total budgeted costs, F = budgeted fixed costs, V = budgeted variable cost per unit, and X = actual volume.

Although management predicted sales volume to be 70,000 units, Victoria sold 80,000 units during the period. The **sales volume variance** is the difference in profits caused by the difference between the master budget sales volume and the actual sales volume. In this case, the difference of $21,900 between operating profits in the master budget and the flexible budget is a sales volume variance. It results from the 10,000 unit difference in sales volume from the sales plan of 70,000 units. We can also compute $21,900 by multiplying the 10,000 unit increase times the budgeted contribution margin per unit of $2.19 (= $6.00 − $3.67 − $.14).

What Is the Meaning of Favorable and Unfavorable?   Note the use of F (favorable) and U (unfavorable) beside each of the variances in Exhibit 12.7. These terms describe the impact of the variance on the budgeted operating profits. A **favorable variance** means that the variance would *increase* operating profits, holding all other things constant. An **unfavorable variance** would *decrease* operating profits, holding all other things constant.

We do not use these terms in a normative sense. A favorable variance is not *necessarily* good, and an unfavorable variance is not *necessarily* bad. Further note the variable cost variances—they are labeled unfavorable. Does this reflect unfavorable conditions in the company? Highly unlikely! These variable costs are *expected* to increase because the actual sales volume is higher than planned. In short, the labels favorable or unfavorable do not automatically connote good or bad conditions. Rather, a favorable variance implies that actual profits are higher than budgeted, all other things (for example, other variances) being ignored; conversely, an unfavorable variance implies that actual profits are lower than budgeted, all other things being ignored. Ultimately, the accounting will credit favorable variances and debit unfavorable variances to income statement accounts.

Information Use   The information presented in Exhibit 12.7 has a number of uses. First, it shows that the increase in operating profits from the master budget results from the increase in sales volume over the level planned. Sales variances are usually the responsibility of the marketing department, so this information may be useful feedback to personnel in that department, and managers may find it informative for

---

[3] The relevant activity variable is *sales* volume because this is a profit plan (that is, an income statement). If the objective were to compare the flexible production budget with the master production budget, the relevant activity variable would be *production* volume. Sales and production volumes are assumed to be equal throughout this example so we can avoid allocating fixed manufacturing costs to inventories. Later in this chapter, we relax this assumption.

Exhibit 12.8

VICTORIA CORPORATION
Profit Variance Analysis: A Comparison of Profits Achieved with the Profit Plan

	Achieved Profits (based on actual sales volume of 80,000 units) (1)	Purchasing and Production Variances (2)	Marketing and Administrative Cost Variances (3)	Sales Price Variance (4)	Flexible Budget (based on actual sales volume of 80,000 units) (5)	Sales Volume Variance (6)	Master Budget (based on a plan of 70,000 units sold) (7)
Sales	$488,000[a]	—	—	$8,000 F	$480,000[f]	$60,000 F	$420,000[i]
Less:							
Variable Manufacturing Costs	305,600[b]	$12,000 U	—	—	293,600[g]	36,700 U	256,900[j]
Variable Marketing Costs	12,800[c]	—	$1,440 U[d]	160 U[e]	11,200[h]	1,400 U	9,800[k]
Contribution Margin	$169,600	$12,000 U	$1,440 U	$7,840 F	$175,200	$21,900 F	$153,300
Less:							
Fixed Manufacturing Costs	34,000	1,800 U	—	—	32,200	—	32,200
Fixed Marketing Costs	64,400	—	1,000 F	—	65,400	—	65,400
Fixed Administrative Costs	44,600	—	200 F	—	44,800	—	44,800
Operating Profits	$ 26,600	$13,800 U	$ 240 U	$7,840 F	$ 32,800	$21,900 F	$ 10,900

Total Profit Variance from Flexible Budget = $6,200 U

Total Profit Variance from Master Budget = $15,700 F

[a] 80,000 units sold at $6.10 per unit.
[b] 80,000 units sold at $3.82 per unit.
[c] 80,000 units sold at $.16 per unit.
[d] $1,440 U = $12,800 − $11,200 − $160.
[e] $160 U = .02 × $8,000 F Sales Price Variance.

[f] 80,000 units sold at $6.00.
[g] 80,000 units sold at $3.67.
[h] 80,000 units sold at $.14.
[i] 70,000 units sold at $6.00.

[j] 70,000 units sold at $3.67.
[k] 70,000 units sold at $.14.
U denotes unfavorable variance.
F denotes favorable variance.

evaluating performance. Second, the resulting flexible budget shows budgeted sales, costs, and operating profits *after* taking into account the volume increase but *before* considering differences in unit selling prices, differences in unit variable costs, and differences in fixed costs from the master budgets.

Achieved Results versus Flexible Budget

Assume that actual results achieved for period 1 follow:

Sales Price per Unit	$6.10
Sales Volume for the Period	80,000 Units
Variable Manufacturing Costs per Unit	$3.82
Variable Marketing Costs per Unit	$.16
Fixed Manufacturing Costs for the Period	$34,000
Fixed Marketing Costs for the Period	$64,400
Fixed Administrative Costs for the Period	$44,600

We can now compare these results with both the flexible budget and the master budget, as in Exhibit 12.8. We carry Columns (5), (6), and (7) forward from Exhibit 12.7. We calculate Column (1) in Exhibit 12.8 from the facts presented previously.

Overview of the Profit Variance

Exhibit 12.8 shows the source of the total variance from the profit plan, which is $15,700 favorable. The analysis of the causes of the total profit variance (that is, the $15,700 difference between the profit budgeted in the master budget and the profit earned for the period) is known as **profit variance analysis.**

Column (2) in Exhibit 12.8 summarizes purchasing and manufacturing variances, which Chapter 13 discusses in more detail. Columns (3) and (4) show marketing and administrative variances. The increased commissions of $160 (= 2% × $8,000) partly offset the favorable sales price variance of $8,000. The remaining $1,440U marketing and administrative cost variance is the residual: $12,800 actual − $11,200 flexible budget − $160 = $1,440.

Performance Appraisal   What is your overall assessment of Victoria Corporation's performance for the period? Clearly the company did better than expected, because sales prices and volume were both higher than expected. However, costs were also higher than expected, even after allowing for the increase in volume. The $12,000 unfavorable variable manufacturing cost variance could be of particular concern. Note that the flexible budget has increased the allowance for variable manufacturing costs from $256,900 in the master budget to $293,600 in the flexible budget. However, the actual costs were even higher—$305,600. This implies either that inefficiencies in manufacturing occurred or that the company paid more than expected for variable manufacturing inputs, such as direct materials, direct labor, or variable manufacturing overhead items.

"Do Not Get Lost in Details"   Variance computations and analysis can become detailed, and users of variances (as well as students) sometimes do not see how such detailed computations fit into the "big picture" comparison of achieved results with the master budget. Exhibit 12.8 presents the big picture. Chapters 13 and 14 go into more detailed computations.

Exhibit 12.9 summarizes these results graphically. Note that the flexible budget line shows expected profits for various activity levels.

Exhibit 12.9

VICTORIA CORPORATION
Flexible Budget Line

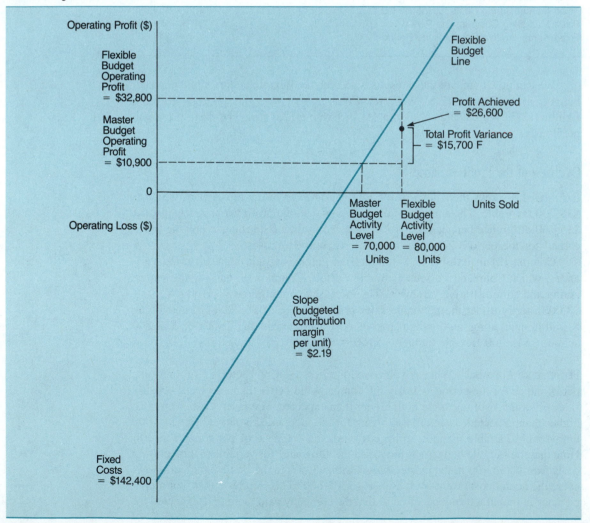

Key Variances

Many top executives receive daily variance reports about a few key items. For example, airline officials receive variance reports on seats sold the previous day; officials in steel companies receive variance reports on the number of tons of steel produced; and officials of merchandising companies receive daily variance reports on sales. As these examples demonstrate, most of these key items deal with *output*. Input variances (that is, cost variances) usually require more detailed data collection. Accounting systems report these weekly or monthly. Accountants prepare reports such as Exhibit 12.8 that tie all the pieces together less frequently, perhaps monthly, quarterly, or yearly.

■ Summary ■

This chapter discusses the operating budget, which managers use for planning, control, and employee motivation. After management makes decisions about products to produce, pricing, levels of output, production techniques, and so forth, accountants translate the choices into a formal plan of action, known as the master budget profit plan. This plan starts with goals and objectives—a plan is not helpful unless it specifies goals.

Forecast first the critical factor that most constrains the firm. Because the marketplace constrains most firms, the sales forecast is usually the place to start. Both sales personnel and market research staff usually provide input for sales forecasts. These groups increasingly provide probabilistic estimates of sales. The budgeted volume is a function of the sales forecast and desired beginning and ending inventory levels.

Budgeted material purchases and labor needs are part of the production budget. Accountants estimate the quantities of direct materials and direct labor required to make a product using engineering studies, blueprints, and product specifications. The cost per unit of input is based on projected materials prices and labor wage rates, fringe benefits, and payroll taxes. Whereas direct materials and direct labor costs are often engineered—that is, traceable directly to a unit of finished product— manufacturing overhead costs are not. Estimates of marketing and administrative costs complete the profit plan. (The profit plan is only one part of the master budget, which also includes the cash budget and budgeted balance sheet. Appendix 12.1 presents the complete master budget.)

The master budget profit plan is fixed; that is, it is based on the *budgeted* sales volume. The flexible budget is based on the *actual* sales volume, however. Whereas the fixed budget shows budgeted costs at the projected sales volume, the flexible budget shows budgeted costs at the *actual* sales volume.

The following diagram summarizes the causes of variances:

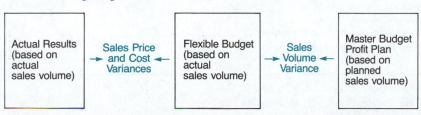

Exhibit 12.10

Sales Budget[a]

70,000 Units at $6	$420,000

Production Budget[b]

Units to Be Produced

Budgeted Sales, in Units (see sales budget)	70,000 Units
Desired Ending Inventory (assumed)	8,000
Total Units Needed	78,000 Units
Beginning Inventory (assumed)	8,000
Units to Be Produced	70,000 Units

Cost Expected to Be Incurred

Direct Materials (1 pound per unit at $1.00 per pound)		$ 70,000
Direct Labor (⅛ hour per unit at $20 per hour)		175,000
Manufacturing Overhead:		
Indirect Labor ($.10 per unit)	$ 7,000	
Supplies ($.04 per unit)	2,800	
Power ($1,000 per period plus $.03 per unit)	3,100	
Maintenance ($13,840 per period)	13,840	
Rent ($6,000 per period)	6,000	
Insurance ($1,000 per period)	1,000	
Depreciation ($10,360 per period)	10,360	44,100
Total Production Costs		$289,100

Marketing Cost Budget[c]

Variable Costs

Commissions (2 percent of sales; see sales budget)	$ 8,400	
Shipping Costs ($.02 per unit shipped; see sales budget)	1,400	
Total Variable Marketing Costs		$ 9,800

Fixed Costs

Salaries ($25,000 per period)	$25,000	
Advertising ($30,000 per period)	30,000	
Sales Office ($8,400 per period)	8,400	
Travel ($2,000 per period)	2,000	
Total Fixed Marketing Costs		65,400
Total Marketing Cost Budget		$ 75,200

Administrative Cost Budget[d]

President's Salary	$ 10,000
Salaries of Other Staff Personnel	17,000
Supplies	2,000
Heat and Light	1,400
Rent	4,000
Donations and Contributions	1,000
General Corporate Taxes	8,000
Depreciation—Staff Office Equipment	1,400
Total Administrative Cost Budget	$ 44,800

[a]*Source:* Exhibit 12.2. [c]*Source:* Exhibit 12.4.
[b]*Source:* Exhibit 12.3. [d]*Source:* Exhibit 12.5.

People who provide forecasts that managers will use to establish budgets for performance evaluation are likely to have incentives to bias those forecasts. For example, sales personnel who know their performance will be evaluated on the basis of whether they beat their forecasts have incentives to bias their forecasts downward, thus making them easily achieved and keeping actual performance results from bettering the forecasts.

Appendix 12.1:
Comprehensive Master Budget—
Victoria Corporation

This appendix presents the comprehensive master budget for Victoria Corporation. First, we summarize the profit plan developed in the chapter. Second, we tie the profit plan into the other budgets, such as the cash budget and the capital budget. Finally, we present the budgeted balance sheet. The master budget ties together the financial activities of the firm for the budget period. Hence, it can aid both planning and coordination. For example, planning for cash needs requires knowing cash flows to and from operating activities and also knowing cash needs for the capital budget.

Exhibit 12.10 summarizes the information from the chapter about projected sales and production volumes, revenues, and costs. Exhibit 12.11 presents the master budget profit plan from the chapter.

Exhibit 12.11

VICTORIA CORPORATION Master Budget Profit Plan	
Variable Costing Basis	
Sales (70,000 units at $6)	$420,000
Less:	
Variable Manufacturing Cost of Goods Sold (70,000 units at $3.67)	(256,900)
Variable Marketing Costs (70,000 units at $.14)	(9,800)
Contribution Margin	$153,300
Less:	
Fixed Manufacturing Costs	(32,200)
Fixed Marketing and Administrative Costs	(110,200)
Operating Profits (variable costing)	$ 10,900
Full Absorption Costing Basis	
Sales (70,000 units at $6)	$420,000
Less:	
Cost of Goods Sold (70,000 units at $4.13)	(289,100)
Gross Margin.	$130,900
Less:	
Marketing and Administrative Costs	(120,000)
Operating Profits (full absorption costing).	$ 10,900

Source: Exhibit 12.6.

Exhibit 12.12

VICTORIA CORPORATION
Materials Purchases Budget

Quantities to Be Purchased (in pounds):

Units to Be Used (see Exhibit 12.10)	70,000 Units
Purchases Required at a Budgeted Cost of $1 per Pound	$70,000

There are no materials inventories.

Materials Purchases Budget

The purchasing department is responsible for purchasing materials in Victoria Corporation. Exhibit 12.12 presents the materials purchases budget. The production budget is the basis for the materials purchases budget. For simplicity in presentation, we assume that payments to suppliers equal purchases each period.

Capital Budget

The capital budget, Exhibit 12.13, shows Victoria Corporation's plan for acquisition of depreciable, long-term assets during the next period. Management plans to purchase major items of equipment, financing part of the cost by issuing notes payable to equipment suppliers in a later period. The capital budget deducts the expected proceeds of the note issuance from the cost of the acquisitions to estimate current cash outlays for equipment. An accepted alternative treatment would have viewed the note issuance as a cash inflow, with the entire cost of the equipment included in cash outflows.

Cash Outlays Budget

Exhibit 12.14 presents a schedule of the planned cash outlays for the budget period. The first items come from the cash outlay lines of earlier exhibits. Each period, the Victoria Corporation pays the income taxes accrued in the previous period. Income

Exhibit 12.13

VICTORIA CORPORATION
Capital Budget

	Period 1
Acquisition of New Factory Machinery	$12,000
Miscellaneous Capital Additions	2,000
Total Capital Budget	$14,000
Borrowings for New Machinery—Long-Term Notes Payable	(6,000)
Current Cash Outlay	$ 8,000

Exhibit 12.14

VICTORIA CORPORATION
Cash Outflows Budget

	Period 1
Materials (Exhibit 12.12)	$ 70,000
Labor (Exhibit 12.10)	175,000
Manufacturing Overhead (Exhibit 12.10)[a]	33,740
Marketing Costs (Exhibit 12.10)	75,200
Administrative Costs (Exhibit 12.10)[b]	43,400
Capital Expenditures (Exhibit 12.13)	8,000
Payments on Short-Term Notes[c]	13,000
Interest[c]	3,000
Income Taxes[d]	6,200
Dividends[c]	5,000
Total Cash Outflows	$432,540

[a]Manufacturing Overhead Costs − Depreciation = $44,100 − $10,360 = $33,740.

[b]Administrative Costs − Depreciation = $44,800 − $1,400 = $43,400.

[c]Assumed for illustration.

[d]The firm pays income taxes on earnings of previous period in current period. We assume the amount in this case.

taxes payable at the start of the budget period appears as $6,200 on the beginning balance sheet (first column of Exhibit 12.18). The firm expects to declare and pay dividends of $5,000 in the budget period.

Receivables and Collections Budget

Victoria collects most of each period's sales in the period of sale, but there is some lag in collections. The budget for cash collections from customers appears in Exhibit 12.15. Collections for sales of a given period normally occur as follows: 85 percent in the period of sale and 15 percent in the next period. We could introduce sales discounts and estimates of uncollectible accounts into the illustration, but we omit them for simplicity. The estimated accounts receivable at the start of the budget period of $71,400 appears on the beginning balance sheet (first column of Exhibit 12.18). The amount represents 15 percent of the previous period's sales of $476,000; $71,400 = .15 × $476,000. In the budget period, the firm expects to collect 85 percent of sales, leaving $63,000 in Accounts Receivable at the end of the budget period ($63,000 = 15 percent of budget period sales of $420,000).

Cash Budget

Cash flow is important. No budget is more important for financial planning than the cash budget, illustrated in Exhibit 12.16. This budget helps management plan to avoid unnecessary idle cash balances or unneeded, expensive borrowing. Almost all firms prepare a cash budget.

Exhibit 12.15

VICTORIA CORPORATION Receivables and Collections Budget	
	Budget Period
Accounts Receivable, Start of Period:	
From the Period Immediately Preceding the Budget Period (15 percent of $476,000)	$ 71,400
Budget Period Sales	420,000
Total Receivables	$ 491,400
Less Collections:	
Current Period (85 percent of $420,000)	$(357,000)
Previous Period (15 percent of $476,000)	(71,400)
Total Collections	$(428,400)
Accounts Receivable, End of Period	$ 63,000

The budgeted amounts for cash outflows and collections from customers come from Exhibits 12.14 and 12.15, respectively. Management estimates the other income, interest and miscellaneous revenues, to be $2,000 for the period.

Budgeted (Pro Forma) Income and Retained Earnings Statement

The budgeted income and retained earnings statement and the budgeted balance sheet pull together all of the previous budget information. Exhibit 12.17 illustrates the budgeted income and retained earnings statement. At this stage in the budgeting

Exhibit 12.16

VICTORIA CORPORATION Cash Budget	
	Budget Period
Cash Receipts:	
Collections from Customers (Exhibit 12.15)	$428,400
Other Income[a]	2,000
Total Receipts	$430,400
Cash Outflows (Exhibit 12.14)	(432,540)
Increase (Decrease) in Cash during Period	$ (2,140)
Cash Balance at Start of Period[a]	79,800
Cash Balance at End of Period...	$ 77,660

[a]Assumed for illustration.

Exhibit 12.17

VICTORIA CORPORATION
Budgeted (pro forma) Income and Retained Earnings Statement

Sales (70,000 units at $6)	$420,000
Less Cost of Goods Sold (70,000 units at $4.13)	(289,100)
Gross Margin	$130,900
Less Marketing Expenses	(75,200)
Less Administrative Expenses	$44,800)
Operating Income (Exhibit 12.11)	$ 10,900[a]
Other Income (Exhibit 12.16)	2,000
	$ 12,900
Less Interest Expense (Exhibit 12.14)	(3,000)
Pretax Income	$ 9,900
Less Income Taxes[b]	(3,861)
Net Income	$ 6,039
Less Dividends (Exhibit 12.14)	(5,000)
Increase in Retained Earnings	$ 1,039
Retained Earnings at Start of Period (Exhibit 12.18)	56,500
Retained Earnings at End of Period (Exhibit 12.18)	$ 57,539

[a]This is the amount called operating profits on the master budget profit plan, Exhibit 12.11.

[b]Income taxes average approximately 39 percent of pretax income. The amount $3,861 is shown as the end-of-period income taxes payable in Exhibit 12.18.

process, management's attention switches from decision making, planning, and control to external reporting to shareholders. In other words, management becomes interested in how the income statement and balance sheet will reflect the results of its decisions. Accordingly, accountants prepare the budgeted income statement and balance sheet in accordance with generally accepted accounting principles. The statement in Exhibit 12.17 is an *income statement,* rather than a profit plan, and we present it using full absorption costing as required for external reporting.

Compilation of all of the data for the period indicates a budgeted income of $6,039. If top management finds this budgeted result satisfactory, and can make available cash adequate to carry out the operations as indicated by Exhibit 12.16, it will approve the master budget. If management does not consider the budgeted results satisfactory, it will consider ways to improve the budgeted results through cost reductions or altered sales plans.

Budgeted Balance Sheet

The final exhibit of this series, Exhibit 12.18, shows the budgeted balance sheets at the start and end of the period. (Accountants prepare the budget before the beginning of the budget period; hence, they must estimate the beginning balance sheet.

Exhibit 12.18

VICTORIA CORPORATION
Budgeted Balance Sheet

	Start of Budget Period	End of Budget Period
Assets		
Current Assets		
Cash (Exhibit 12.16)......................................	$ 79,800	$ 77,660
Accounts Receivable (Exhibit 12.15).......................	71,400	63,000
Finished Goods Inventory	33,040[a]	33,040[a]
Total Current Assets.....................................	$184,240	$173,700
Plant Assets		
Equipment (Exhibit 12.13)..............................	460,000	474,000
Less Accumulated Depreciation.............................	(162,000)[b]	(173,760)[b]
Total Assets..	$482,240	$473,940
Equities		
Current Liabilities		
Accounts Payable.......................................	$ 96,540[b]	$ 96,540[b]
Short-Term Notes and Other Payables......................	41,000[b]	28,000[b]
Income Taxes Payable (Exhibits 12.14 and 12.17)............	6,200	3,861
Total Current Liabilities	$143,740	$128,401
Long-Term Liabilities		
Long-Term Equipment Notes (Exhibit 12.13)	82,000[b]	88,000[b]
Total Liabilities	$225,740	$216,401
Shareholders' Equity		
Capital Stock ($20 par value)	$200,000[b]	$200,000[b]
Retained Earnings (Exhibit 12.17)	56,500[b]	57,539[b]
Total Shareholders' Equity	$256,500	$257,539
Total Equities...	$482,240	$473,940

[a]8,000 units in inventory according to Exhibit 12.10 at $4.13 per unit. $4.13 was given in the chapter as the full absorption manufacturing cost per unit.

[b]Assumed for purposes of illustration.

For example, accountants would prepare a budget for the calendar year during the preceding September through November.)

Here, as in the budgeted income statement, management will have to decide if the budgeted overall results will be acceptable. Will cash balances be satisfactory? Is the receivables turnover up to plan? Will the final capital structure and debt-equity ratio conform to management's desires? If the budgeted balance sheet and income statement are satisfactory, they will become the initial benchmarks against which management will check actual performance in the ensuing period.

Summary of the Master Budget

The master budget summarizes management's plans for the period covered. Preparing the master budget requires the participation of all managerial groups, from local plant and sales managers to the top executives of the firm and the board of directors. Once management adopts the budget, it becomes the major planning and control instrument.

Master budgets are almost always static budgets; that is, they consider the likely results of operations at the one level of operations specified in the budget. If preparing the master budget requires a lot of hand calculation, preparing multiple master budgets can be cumbersome and costly. Computerizing the process makes it less costly to develop multiple master budgets that take into account various uncertainties facing the firm, such as market conditions, material prices, labor difficulties, and government regulations.

Appendix 12.2:
Incentive Model for Truthful Reporting

How does management provide employees with incentives both for truthful reporting and for high performance?

Example   Assume that the Harris Raviv Company solicits sales forecasts from each of its district sales managers. These forecasts become budgets that management compares to actual sales to evaluate performance.

The firm's general manager of marketing wants to provide each district sales manager with a salary and a bonus. Previously sales managers earned a bonus by beating the budget. The sales managers, however, began to "low-ball" the forecasts. Management knew this was happening, but it did not know how high the forecasts *should* have been, because it did not have the information the managers had. The general manager of marketing explained:

> Managers could always counter our arguments with data that we could not audit. Their low estimates wreaked havoc with our production schedules, purchasing, and hiring decisions.
>
> Next we tried to give them incentives for accurate forecasts. We rewarded them if the actual sales were close to the forecasts, and penalized if actual and forecast deviated a lot. With this system, the managers forecast sales at a level that was sufficiently low to be achievable, then they "managed" their sales such that actual was almost right at the forecast. The consequences were that they had disincentives to beat the budget. Also, our internal auditors found numerous cases where managers had delayed sales orders until the following year and even turned down some orders because they did not want the current year's sales to overshoot the forecast.

The incentive plan to deal with this problem has three components.

1. Rewards are positively related to forecasted sales to give managers incentives to forecast high rather than low. Thus, if b_1 is a bonus coefficient that is a

percent of forecasted sales, and forecasted sales are $\hat{Y}$, then this component of the bonus is

$$b_1\hat{Y}.$$

2. The plan provides incentives for the sales manager to increase sales beyond the forecast. If b_2 is the bonus coefficient for the excess of Y, over $\hat{Y}$, forecast sales, then this component of the bonus is

$$b_2(Y - \hat{Y}), \qquad \text{for } Y \geq \hat{Y}.$$

3. When actual sales, Y, are less than the forecast, $\hat{Y}$, the plan penalizes the sales manager. If b_3 is the bonus coefficient for the shortfall, $Y - \hat{Y}$, then this component of the bonus is

$$-b_3(\hat{Y} - Y), \qquad \text{for } \hat{Y} > Y.$$

If B is the dollar bonus paid to the manager, the overall bonus plan is

$$B = \begin{cases} b_1\hat{Y} + b_2(Y - \hat{Y}), & \text{for } Y \geq \hat{Y} \text{ (i.e., when actual sales exceed the forecast);} \\ b_1\hat{Y} - b_3(\hat{Y} - Y), & \text{for } \hat{Y} > Y \text{ (i.e., when the forecast exceeds actual sales).} \end{cases}$$

The coefficients are set such that

$$b_3 > b_1 > b_2 > 0,$$

and a rule of thumb is that b_3 should be at least 30 percent greater than b_1, and b_1 should be at least 30 percent greater than b_2.[4] Management intends for this incentive plan to reward both accurate forecasts and outstanding performance.

Harris Raviv Company established an incentive system using the methods described here. Exhibit 12.19 shows the bonus that would result from various combinations of forecasted sales and actual sales. For example, if the forecast is $1,100,000 and the actual sales are $1,000,000, the district sales manager receives a bonus of $48,000; if both the forecast and actual sales are $1,100,000, the sales manager receives a bonus of $55,000; and so forth.

Implications

What are the implications of this incentive system? If you read down a column in Exhibit 12.19, you will see that after making the forecast, the manager receives a larger reward for more sales even if an increase in sales makes the forecast inaccurate. Reading across the rows reveals that the manager receives the highest bonus when the forecast equals actual sales; hence, the manager has an incentive to make accurate forecasts.

This system provides incentives for accurate forecasting and sales output simultaneously. Although our example has dealt with sales forecasts, the method described applies to virtually any type of forecasting (for example, production levels, costs, productivity). At this point, we have little evidence about implementation difficulties. Whereas the method appears to be a clever innovation, we shall have to

---

[4]See M. Weitzman, "The New Soviet Incentive Model," *Bell Journal of Economics* (Spring 1976), pp. 253–254.

Exhibit 12.19

HARRIS RAVIV COMPANY
Incentives for Accurate Forecasting Bonus Paid to District Sales Managers
(thousands omitted from sales and bonus amounts)

Let b_1 = 5 percent, b_2 = 3 percent, and b_3 = 7 percent

$$B = \begin{cases} .05\hat{Y} + .03(Y - \hat{Y}), & \text{for } Y \geq \hat{Y}; \\ .05\hat{Y} - .07(\hat{Y} - Y), & \text{for } \hat{Y} > Y. \end{cases}$$

		Forecasted Sales, $\hat{Y}$		
		$1,000	**$1,100**	**$1,200**
Actual	**$1,000**	50[a]	48[d]	46[g]
Sales,	**$1,100**	53[b]	55[e]	53[h]
Y	**$1,200**	56[c]	58[f]	60[i]

[a]$50 = .05($1,000).
[b]$53 = .05($1,000) + .03($1,100 − $1,000).
[c]$56 = .05($1,000) + .03($1,200 − $1,000).
[d]$48 = .05($1,100) − .07($1,100 − $1,000).
[e]$55 = .05($1,100).

[f]$58 = .05($1,100) + .03($1,200 − $1,100).
[g]$46 = .05($1,200) − .07($1,200 − $1,000).
[h]$53 = .05($1,200) − .07($1,200 − $1,100).
[i]$60 = .05($1,200).

see it in operation before we pass judgment on it. (Note that top management can adjust the bonus coefficients, b_1, b_2, and b_3, to suit the needs of the particular situation.)

In summary, analysts have developed incentive methods that provide rewards for both accurate forecasts and good performance. Rewards are positively related to forecasted sales to give incentives to forecast high rather than low. Employees receive additional rewards for beating the forecast and penalties for results worse than forecast.

Problem 1 for Self-Study[5]

In April, Computer Supply, Inc., produced and sold 50,000 minicomputer cases at a sales price of $10 each. (Budgeted sales were 45,000 units at $10.15.)

Budget

Standard Variable Costs per Unit This Month, as in Previous Months ..	$4.00
Fixed Manufacturing Overhead Cost: Monthly Budget	$80,000
Marketing and Administrative:	
Variable	$1.00 per Case
Fixed (monthly budget).......................................	$100,000
	continued

---

[5]This self-study problem continues in Chapters 13 and 14.

continued from page 553

Actual

Actual Manufacturing Costs:

Variable Costs per Unit...	$4.88
Fixed Overhead	$83,000

Actual Marketing and Administrative:

Variable (50,000 at $1.04)	$52,000
Fixed...	$96,000

Using a contribution margin format, prepare a profit variance report comparing actual results with the flexible and master budgets for April. (See Suggested Solution on page 555.)

<h1 style="text-align:center">Problem 2 for Self-Study
(Appendix 12.2; Contributed by J. Lim)</h1>

Peter Kirillov started a pastry shop on the Upper West Side of New York more than 15 years ago. His current operation consists of a chain of ten pastry shops scattered around the New York area.

Recently, Kirillov became disturbed by the poor profit performance of some of the chain's branches, which he suspects results from poor production planning. Kirillov expects branch managers to match daily production as closely as possible to daily sales. Branch managers mark down day-old pastries 50 percent. Should a particular type of pastry run out, a branch manager can schedule a rush order at his or her discretion. A rush order, however, may increase production costs by as much as 40 percent above standard.

Kirillov believes that if branch managers forecasted sales more accurately, production planning would improve, resulting in greater profits. About a year ago, Kirillov's childhood friend, Raskolnikov, mentioned a new incentive plan in one of his letters. This plan, Raskolnikov said, was designed to provide an incentive for more accurate forecasting in the Soviet shoe factory he managed. Kirillov believes that such a bonus plan may provide the necessary incentive for his managers to forecast sales more accurately.

a. Suppose that daily sales for a typical pastry store range from $2,000 to $4,000. What bonus would a branch manager receive daily for forecasting daily sales of $2,000, $2,500, $3,000, $3,500, and $4,000 under the following incentive plan?

$$\text{Bonus} = \begin{cases} 0.03\hat{Y} + 0.01(Y - \hat{Y}) & \text{for } Y > \hat{Y}, \\ 0.03\hat{Y} - 0.05(\hat{Y} - Y) & \text{for } \hat{Y} > Y, \end{cases}$$

where

$$\hat{Y} = \text{Forecasted Sales in Dollars}$$

$$Y = \text{Actual Sales in Dollars.}$$

b. Discuss the disincentives to overforecast or underforecast in the bonus plan developed in part a. (See Suggested Solution on page 556.)

Suggested Solution

Profit Variance Analysis:
Comparison of Achieved Profits to Budgeted Profits, April

	Achieved Profits (based on 50,000 units)	Purchasing and Production Variances	Marketing and Administrative Variances	Sales Price Variances	Flexible Budget (based on 50,000 units)	Sales Volume Variance	Master Budget (based on 45,000 units)
Sales Revenue	$500,000	—	—	$7,500 U	$507,500	$50,750 F	$456,750
Less:							
Variable Manufacturing Costs	244,000	$44,000 U	—	—	200,000	20,000 U	180,000
Variable Marketing and Administrative Costs	52,000	—	$2,000[a] U	—	50,000	5,000 U	45,000
Contribution Margins	$204,000	$44,000 U	$2,000 U	$7,500 U	$257,500	$25,750 F	$231,750
Less:							
Fixed Manufacturing Costs	83,000	3,000 U	—	—	80,000	—	80,000
Fixed Marketing and Administrative Costs	96,000	—	4,000 F	—	100,000	—	100,000
Operating Profits	$ 25,000	$47,000 U	$2,000 F	$7,500 U	$ 77,500	$25,750 F	$ 51,750

Total Profit Variance from Flexible Budget = $52,500 U

Total Profit Variance from Master Budget = $26,750 U

[a]$2,000 = $.04 × 50,000 = ($1.04 − 1.00) 50,000 units.

Suggested Solution

a.

Actual Sales, Y	Forecasted Sales, $\hat{Y}$				
	$2,000	$2,500	$3,000	$3,500	$4,000
$2,000	$60[a]	$50[f]	$ 40[k]	$ 30[p]	$ 20[u]
2,500	65[b]	75[g]	65[l]	55[q]	45[v]
3,000	70[c]	80[h]	90[m]	80[r]	70[w]
3,500	75[d]	85[i]	95[n]	105[s]	95[x]
4,000	80[e]	90[j]	100[o]	110[t]	120[y]

[a]$60 = 0.03(\$2,000).

[b]$65 = 0.03(\$2,000) + 0.01(\$2,500 - \$2,000).

[c]$70 = 0.03(\$2,000) + 0.01(\$3,000 - \$2,000).

[d]$75 = 0.03(\$2,000) + 0.01(\$3,500 - \$2,000).

[e]$80 = 0.03(\$2,000) + 0.01(\$4,000 - \$2,000).

[f]$50 = 0.03(\$2,500) - 0.05(\$2,500 - \$2,000).

[g]$75 = 0.03(\$2,500).

[h]$80 = 0.03(\$2,500) + 0.01(\$3,000 - \$2,500).

[i]$85 = 0.03(\$2,500) + 0.01(\$3,500 - \$2,500).

[j]$90 = 0.03(\$2,500) + 0.01(\$4,000 - \$2,500).

[k]$40 = 0.03(\$3,000) - 0.05(\$3,000 - \$2,000).

[l]$65 = 0.03(\$3,000) - 0.05(\$3,000 - \$2,500).

[m]$90 = 0.03(\$3,000).

[n]$95 = 0.03(\$3,000) + 0.01(\$3,500 - \$3,000).

[o]$100 = 0.03(\$3,000) + 0.01(\$4,000 - \$3,000).

[p]$30 = 0.03(\$3,500) - 0.05(\$3,500 - \$2,000).

[q]$55 = 0.03(\$3,500) - 0.05(\$3,500 - \$2,500).

[r]$80 = 0.03(\$3,500) - 0.05(\$3,500 - \$3,000).

[s]$105 = 0.03(\$3,500).

[t]$110 = 0.03(\$3,500) + 0.01(\$4,000 - \$3,500).

[u]$20 = 0.03(\$4,000) - 0.05(\$4,000 - \$2,000).

[v]$45 = 0.03(\$4,000) - 0.05(\$4,000 - \$2,500).

[w]$70 = 0.03(\$4,000) - 0.05(\$4,000 - \$3,000).

[x]$95 = 0.03(\$4,000) - 0.05(\$4,000 - \$3,500).

[y]$120 = 0.03(\$4,000).

b. From the bonus payoff matrix developed in part **a,** we see that the system penalizes overforecasting (5 percent of each forecasted sales dollar in excess of actual sales). On the other hand, underforecasting results in the excess of actual sales over forecasted sales being rewarded at a lower rate. For every level of actual sales, the system pays the highest bonus when the forecast equals actual sales.

Key Terms and Concepts

Budgets as tools for planning
Static budget
Budgets as tools for control
Flexible budget
Master budget

Variances
Sales volume variance
Favorable versus unfavorable
    variance
Profit variance analysis

Questions, Exercises, Problems, and Cases

Questions

1. Review the meaning of the concepts or terms discussed above in Key Terms and Concepts.

2. "Last month we sold more units than planned, yet our performance report shows unfavorable sales volume variances for all variable manufacturing costs. I don't consider an increase in sales to be unfavorable." Please explain.

3. Why is a contribution margin format more useful than a traditional (full absorption) format for performance reporting?

4. A superior criticized a sales manager for selling high-revenue, low-profit items instead of lower-revenue but higher-profit items. The sales manager responded, "My income is based on commissions that are a percent of revenues. Why should I care about profits? I care about revenues!" Comment.

5. "The flexible budget is a poor benchmark. You should develop a budget and stay with it." Comment.

6. Why is the sales forecast so important in developing the master budget?

7. When would the master budget profit equal the flexible budget profit?

8. Managers in some companies claim that they do not use flexible budgeting, yet they compute a sales volume variance that takes into account total variable cost changes. How is that different from flexible budgeting?

9. The sales volume variance is sometimes computed using only the change in revenue. At other times it is computed taking variable costs into account. What is the disadvantage of ignoring changes in variable costs?

Exercises

10. *Solving for materials requirements*. Bala Company expects to sell 84,000 units of finished goods over the next 3-month period. The company currently has 44,000 units of finished goods on hand and wishes to have an inventory of 48,000 units at the end of the 3-month period. To produce 1 unit of finished goods requires 4 units of raw materials. The company currently has 200,000 units of raw materials on hand and wishes to have an inventory of 220,000 units of raw materials on hand at the end of the 3-month period.

    How many units of raw materials must the Bala Company purchase during the 3-month period?

11.   *Solving for budgeted manufacturing costs*. Venus Candy Company expects to sell 100,000 cases of chocolate bars during the current year. Budgeted costs per case are $120 for direct materials, $100 for direct labor, and $50 (all variable) for manufacturing overhead. Venus began the period with 30,000 cases of finished goods on hand and wants to end the period with 10,000 cases of finished goods on hand.

Compute the budgeted manufacturing costs of the Venus Candy Company for the current period. Assume no beginning or ending inventory of work in process.

12.   *Solving for cash collections* (Appendix 12.1). Jones Corporation normally collects cash from credit customers as follows: 50 percent in the month of sale, 30 percent in the first month after sale, 18 percent in the second month after sale, and 2 percent never collected. Jones Corporation expects its sales, all on credit, to be as follows:

January	$500,000
February	600,000
March	400,000
April	500,000

a.   Calculate the amount of cash Jones Corporation expects to receive from customers during March.

b.   Calculate the amount of cash Jones Corporation expects to receive from customers during April.

13.   *Solving for cash payments* (Appendix 12.1). Wallace Corporation purchases raw materials on account from various suppliers. It normally pays for 60 percent of these in the month purchased, 30 percent in the first month after purchase, and the remaining 10 percent in the second month after purchase. Raw materials purchases during the last 5 months of the year follow:

August	$1,400,000
September	1,800,000
October	2,000,000
November	3,500,000
December	1,500,000

Compute the budgeted amount of cash payments to suppliers for the months of October, November, and December.

14.   *Profit variance analysis*. Austin Company prepared a budget last period that called for sales of 7,000 units at a price of $12 each. The costs per unit were estimated to be $5 variable and $3 fixed. During the period, production was exactly equal to actual sales of 7,100 units. The selling price was $12.15 per unit. Variable costs were $5.90 per unit. Fixed costs were $20,000.

Prepare a profit variance report to show the difference between the master budget and the achieved profits.

15. *Analyzing contribution margin changes*. The Oakland Optical Center, which sells eyeglasses, provided the following data for years 1 and 2:

	Year 1	Year 2
Sales Volume	6,000 Pairs of Glasses	5,000 Pairs of Glasses
Sales Revenue	$720,000	$750,000
Variable Costs	(630,000)	(525,000)
Contribution Margin	$ 90,000	$225,000

What impact did the changes in sales volume and in sales price have on the contribution margin?

16. *Graphic comparison of budgeted and actual costs.*

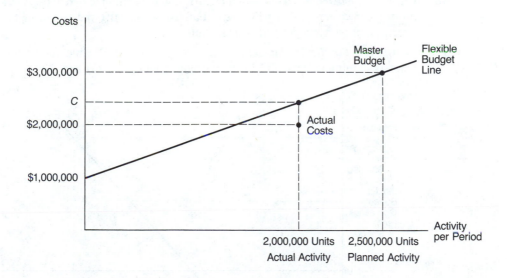

a. Given the data shown in the graph, what is the budgeted variable cost per unit?

b. What is the flexible budget cost for an activity level of 2,000,000 units (C on the graph)?

c. If the actual activity had been 4,000,000 units, what would have been the flexible budget cost amount?

17. *Preparing flexible budgets* (adapted from CPA exam). The exhibit on the following page provides information concerning the operations of the Full Ton Company for the current period. The firm has no inventories. Prepare a flexible budget for the company.

	Actual	Master Budget
Sales Volume	90 Units	100 Units
Sales Revenue	$9,200	$10,000
Manufacturing Cost of Goods Sold:		
Variable	3,440	3,900
Fixed	485	500
Cost of Goods Sold	$3,925	$ 4,400
Gross Profit	$5,275	$ 5,600
Operating Costs:		
Marketing Costs:		
Variable	$1,030	$ 1,100
Fixed	1,040	1,000
Administrative Costs, All Fixed	995	1,000
Total Operating Costs	$3,065	$ 3,100
Operating Profits	$2,210	$ 2,500

18. *Comparing master budget to actual results*. Use the exhibit above to prepare a profit variance report that will enable Full Ton to identify the variances between the master budget and actual results.

19. *Interpreting the flexible budget line*. The graph shows a flexible budget line with some missing data. Fill in the missing amounts for (a) and (b).

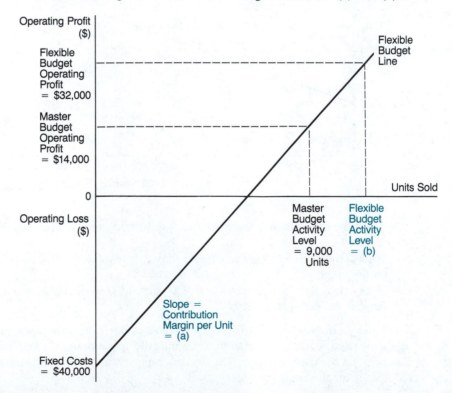

20. *Interpreting the flexible budget line.* Label (a) and (b) on the graph and give the number of units sold for each.

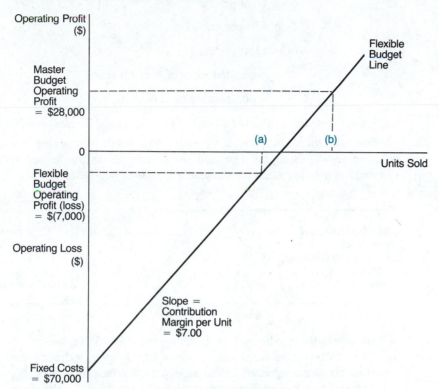

21. *Incentives for accurate forecasting* (Appendix 12.2). Compute the bonus, B, paid to a pizza company's franchise managers using the following formulas:

$$B = b_1\hat{Y} + b_2(Y - \hat{Y}), \qquad \text{for } Y \geq \hat{Y}$$

$$B = b_1\hat{Y} - b_3(\hat{Y} - Y), \qquad \text{for } \hat{Y} > Y$$

where

$$b_1 = 4\%$$

$$b_2 = 2\%$$

$$b_3 = 6\%$$

$$\hat{Y} = \text{forcasted sales revenue}$$

$$Y = \text{actual sales revenue.}$$

Let Y and $\hat{Y}$ each have values of $2,500, $3,000, and $3,500.

22. *Incentives for accurate forecasting* (Appendix 12.2). Compute the monthly bonus, B, paid to an automobile dealership using the following formulas:

$$B = b_1\hat{Y} + b_2(Y - \hat{Y}), \qquad \text{for } Y \geq \hat{Y}$$

$$B = b_1\hat{Y} - b_3(\hat{Y} - Y), \qquad \text{for } \hat{Y} > Y$$

where

$$b_1 = \$100 \text{ per car}$$

$$b_2 = \$70 \text{ per car}$$

$$b_3 = \$150 \text{ per car}$$

$$\hat{Y} = \text{forecasted sales of cars (in units)}$$

$$Y = \text{actual number of cars sold.}$$

Let Y and $\hat{Y}$ each have values of 20 cars, 21 cars, 22 cars, 23 cars, and 24 cars.

23. *Flexible budgeting—manufacturing costs.* As a result of studying past cost behavior and adjusting for expected price increases in the future, Wilson Corporation estimates that its manufacturing costs will be as follows:

Direct Materials	$2.00 per Unit
Direct Labor	$1.50 per Unit
Manufacturing Overhead:	
Variable	$.50 per Unit
Fixed...	$50,000 per Period

Wilson adopts these estimates for planning and control purposes.

a. Wilson Corporation expects to produce 10,000 units during the next period. Prepare a schedule of the expected manufacturing costs.

b. Suppose that Wilson Corporation produces only 8,000 units during the next period. Prepare a flexible budget of manufacturing costs for the 8,000-unit level of activity.

c. Suppose that Wilson Corporation produces 13,000 units during the next period. Prepare a flexible budget of manufacturing costs for the 13,000-unit level of activity.

24. *Marketing cost budget.* Refer to the marketing cost budget of the Victoria Corporation shown in Exhibit 12.4. Prepare a flexible marketing cost budget for the period, assuming the following levels of sales and shipments.

	Case 1	Case 2	Case 3
Units	60,000	75,000	64,000

25. *Administrative cost budget.* Refer to the central corporate administrative budget of the Victoria Corporation in Exhibit 12.5. Prepare a flexible central corporate administrative cost budget for the period, assuming that production and sales were 100,000 units. Is the term *flexible budget* a misnomer in this case? Explain.

26. *Computing sales price variances*. Budgeted sales of Holt Electronics Merchandisers for 19X0 were as follows:

Product X (5,000 units)	$100,000
Product Y (200 units)	20,000
Product Z (50,000 units)	250,000
Total Budgeted Sales	$370,000

Actual sales for the period were as follows:

Product X (5,300 units)	$111,300
Product Y (240 units)	23,040
Product Z (48,000 units)	192,000
Total Actual Sales	$326,340

Calculate the sales price variances for sales of the three products.

27. *Estimating flexible selling expense budget and computing variances*. Reynolds Products, Incorporated, estimates that it will incur the following selling expenses next period:

Salaries (fixed)	$ 20,000
Commissions (.05 of sales revenue)	15,000
Travel (.03 of sales revenue)	9,000
Advertising (fixed)	50,000
Sales Office Costs ($4,000 plus $.05 per unit sold)	7,000
Shipping Cost ($.10 per unit sold)	6,000
Total Selling Expenses	$107,000

a. Estimate the cost equation ($y = a + bx$) for selling expenses.
b. Assume that Reynolds sells 50,000 units during the period at an average price of $6 per unit. Calculate the sales price and volume variance.
c. The actual selling expenses incurred during the period were $110,000. Assuming sales as given in part b, calculate the total selling expense variance.

Problems

28. *Profit variance analysis in a service organization*. Wolfson & Scholes (WS) is a CPA firm that gets a large portion of its revenue from tax services. Last year, WS's billable tax hours were up 20 percent from expected levels, but, as the following data shows, profits from the tax department were lower than anticipated.

	Achieved Results	Master Budget
Billable Hours[a]	60,000 Hours	50,000 Hours
Revenue......................................	$3,300,000	$3,000,000[b]
Production Costs:		
Professional Salaries (all variable)......	1,850,000	1,500,000
Other Variable Costs (e.g., supplies,		
certain computer services)..........	470,000	400,000
General Administrative (all fixed)	580,000	600,000
Tax Department Profit...................	$ 400,000	$ 500,000

[a]These are hours billed to clients. Hours worked exceed this amount because of nonbillable time (e.g., slack periods, time in training sessions) and because WS does not charge all time worked for clients.

Prepare a comparison of the reported income statement results to the master and flexible budgets. Adapt the approach shown in Exhibit 12.8 to this service organization.

29. *Finding missing data.* Find the values of the missing items (a) through (q).

	Achieved Results, 750 Units	Purchasing and Production Variances	Marketing and Administrative Variances	Sales Price Variance	Flexible Budget (a)	Variance	Master Budget 800 Units
Sales Revenue	$1,890			(b)	$2,025	(c)	(d)
Variable Manufacturing Costs	(e)	$60 F			(f)	$38 F	(g)
Variable Marketing and Administrative ...	(h)		(i)		(j)	(k)	$216
Contribution Margin	$1,180	(l)	(m)	(n)	(o)	(p)	(q)

30. *Comprehensive problem.* The Micro Company, which makes computer chips, has the following master budget income statement for the month of May:

	Master Budget (based on 8,000 units)
Sales Revenue (8,000 units at $20)	$160,000
Less:	
Variable Manufacturing Costs	80,000[a]
Variable Marketing and Administrative Costs.................	8,000[b]
Contribution Margin	$ 72,000
Less:	
Fixed Manufacturing Costs	20,000
Fixed Marketing and Administrative Costs	45,000
Operating Profit	$ 7,000

[a]8,000 budgeted units at $10 unit.

[b]8,000 budgeted units at $1 per unit.

The company uses the following estimates to prepare the master budget:

Sales Price	$20 per Unit
Sales and Production Volume	8,000 Units
Variable Manufacturing Costs	$10 per Unit
Variable Marketing and Administrative Costs......................	$1 per Unit
Fixed Manufacturing Costs	$20,000
Fixed Marketing and Administrative Costs	$45,000

Assume that the actual results for May were as follows:

	Actual
Sales Price	$19 per Unit
Sales and Production Volume	10,000 Units
Variable Manufacturing Costs	$105,440
Variable Marketing and Administrative Costs......................	$11,000
Fixed Manufacturing Costs	$21,000
Fixed Marketing and Administrative Costs	$44,000

Compare the master budget, flexible budget, and actual results for the month of May.

31. *Finding missing data.* Find the values of the missing items (a) through (u).

	Achieved Based on Actual Sales Volume	Cost and Sales Price Variances	Flexible Budget Based on Actual Sales Volume	Sales Volume Variance	Master Budget Based on Budgeted Sales Volume
Units	(a)		(b)	2,000 F	10,000
Sales Revenue	(g)	18,000 F	(h)	(l)	$150,000
Less:					
Variable Manufacturing Costs	(n)	9,000 U	$96,000	(j)	$ 80,000
Variable Marketing and Administrative Costs	$21,600	(o)	24,000	4,000 U	(c)
Contribution Margin	(p)	(r)	$60,000	(k)	$ 50,000
Less:					
Fixed Manufacturing Costs	(q)	2,000 F	(m)		(d)
Fixed Marketing and Administrative Costs	$18,000	(t)	15,000		(e)
Operating Profits	(s)	(u)	$20,000	(l)	(f)

32. *Comparing actual to budgeted production costs* (adapted from CMA exam). The Melcher Co. produces farm equipment at several plants. The business is seasonal and cyclical in nature. The company has attempted to use budgeting

for planning and controlling activities, but the fluctuating nature of the business has caused some company officials to be skeptical about budgeting's usefulness to the company. The accountant for the Adrian plant has been using flexible budgeting to help plant management control operations. The accountant presents the following data.

Planned Level of Production for January 19X0 (in units)	4,000
Budgeted Cost Data	
Direct Materials ($9.00 per unit)	$36,000
Direct Labor ($6.00 per unit)	$24,000
Variable Costs (with production):	
Indirect Labor	$ 6,650
Indirect Materials	600
Repairs	750
Total Variable	$ 8,000
Fixed Costs:	
Depreciation	$ 3,250
Supervision	3,000
Total Fixed	$ 6,250
Total Manufacturing Costs	$74,250
Actual Data for January 19X0	
Units Produced	3,800
Costs Incurred:	
Material	$36,000
Direct Labor	25,200
Indirect Labor	6,000
Indirect Materials	600
Repairs	1,800
Depreciation	3,250
Supervision	3,000
Total	$75,850

a. Prepare flexible budgets for January based on planned production levels of 3,800 units and of 4,000 units.

b. Prepare a report for January comparing actual and flexible budget costs based on the actual level of production for the month.

33. *Projected income statements.* The Norwood Corporation has patented a new household product and is now actively marketing it. Its income statement for the first quarter of 19X2 follows.

The $7 per unit manufacturing cost presently comprises material cost, $2; direct labor cost, $4; and overhead costs, $1. The productive capacity of the present plant, working one 8-hour shift per day, is 50,000 units per quarter. The sales manager is certain that the firm could sell additional units if they were available. Top management is reluctant to increase the size of the plant and instead decides to consider the advisability of adding a second, and perhaps a third, shift.

The production manager estimates the following:
(1) Each additional shift would increase output by 50,000 units per quarter.
(2) If the firm adds a second shift, labor costs per unit for that shift's output would increase 10 percent, and total overhead costs would increase 25 percent.
(3) If the firm adds a third shift, labor costs per unit for that shift's output would be 25 percent higher than for one-shift operations, and total overhead would be 75 percent higher than for one-shift operations. With three-shift operations, the firm estimates that it could reduce material costs of all units by 4 percent because of larger quantity purchases.

The sales manager estimates the following:
(1) The firm can sell 100,000 units a quarter at the current price, but to sell 150,000 units each quarter, it must reduce the unit price by 5 percent.
(2) Selling expenses for 100,000 units per quarter will be 50 percent higher and for 150,000 units will be 90 percent higher than for 50,000 units.

Total administrative costs will increase from the 50,000 unit figure by 20 percent for sales of 100,000 units and by 40 percent for sales of 150,000 units.

Prepare projected second-quarter income statements assuming
a. Two-shift operations.
b. Three-shift operations.

THE NORWOOD CORPORATION
Partial Income Statement
January 1 to March 31, 19X2

Sales (50,000 units at $10 per unit)		$500,000
Operating Costs:		
Cost of Goods Sold ($7 per unit)	$350,000	
Selling Costs	45,000	
Administrative Costs	30,000	
Total Costs		425,000
Operating Profit		$ 75,000

---

34. *Flexible budget* (adapted from CMA exam). The University of Burns operates a motor pool with 21 vehicles. The motor pool furnishes gasoline, oil, and other supplies for the cars and hires one mechanic who does routine maintenance and minor repairs. A nearby commercial garage does major repairs. A supervisor manages the operations.

Each year, the supervisor prepares a master budget for the motor pool. The accountant records depreciation on the automobiles in the budget to calculate the costs per mile.

The schedule that follows presents the master budget for the year and for the month of March.

UNIVERSITY MOTOR POOL
Budget Report of March

	Annual Master Budget	One-Month Master Budget	March Actual Costs	Over or (Under)
Gasoline.....................	$ 36,000	$ 3,000	$ 3,800	$800
Oil, Minor Repairs, Parts, and Supplies	3,600	300	380	80
Outside Repairs	2,700	225	50	(175)
Insurance	6,000	500	525	25
Salaries and Benefits	30,000	2,500	2,500	—
Depreciation	26,400	2,200	2,310	110
	$104,700	$ 8,725	$ 9,565	$840
Total Miles	600,000	50,000	63,000	
Cost per Mile	$0.1745	$0.1745	$0.1518	
Number of Automobiles	20	20	20	

The annual budget was based on the following assumptions:
(1)   20 automobiles in the pool.
(2)   30,000 miles per year per automobile.
(3)   15 miles per gallon per automobile.
(4) $0.90 per gallon of gas.
(5) $0.006 per mile for oil, minor repairs, parts, and supplies.
(6) $135 per automobile per year in outside repairs.
      The supervisor claims the report unfairly presents his performance for March. His previous employer used flexible budgeting to compare actual costs to budgeted amounts.
a.   What is the monthly flexible budget for gasoline and the resulting amount over or under budget? (Use miles as the activity base.)
b.   What is the monthly flexible budget for oil, minor repairs, parts, and supplies and the amount over or under budget? (Use miles as the activity base.)
c.   What is the monthly flexible budget for salaries and benefits and the resulting amount over or under budget?
d.   What is the *major* reason for the cost per mile to decrease from $0.1745 budgeted to $0.1518 actual?

35.   *Computing master budget given actual data.* Consulting Enterprises lost the only copy of the master budget for this period. Management wants to evaluate this period's performance but believes it needs the master budget to do so. Actual results for the period follow:

Sales Volume	12,000 Billable Hours
Sales Revenue.....................................	$672,000
Variable Costs	208,600

continued

continued from page 568

Contribution Margin	$463,400
Fixed Costs	318,200
Operating Profit	$145,200

The company planned on 10,800 billable hours at a price of $50 each. At that volume, the contribution margin would have been $380,000. Fixed costs were $272,000 for the period. Management notes, ''We budget an operating profit of $10 per billable hour.''

a. Construct the master budget for the period.

b. Prepare a profit variance report comparing actual sales to the flexible budget and master budget.

36. *Performance evaluation using flexible budgets* (adapted from CMA exam). Persons Restaurant-Deli is planning to expand operations and wants to improve its performance reporting system. The budgeted income statement for its Akron facility, which contains a delicatessen and restaurant operations, follows (all dollar amounts in thousands):

	Delicatessen	Restaurant	Total
Gross Sales	$1,000	$2,500	$3,500
Purchases	$ 600	$1,000	$1,600
Hourly Wages	50	875	925
Franchise Fee	30	75	105
Advertising	100	200	300
Utilities	70	125	195
Depreciation	50	75	125
Lease Cost	30	50	80
Salaries	30	50	80
Total	$ 960	$2,450	$3,410
Operating Profit	$ 40	$ 50	$ 90

The performance report that the company uses for management evaluation follows:

PERSONS RESTAURANT-DELI
Akron, Ohio
Operating Profit for the Year
(all dollar amounts in thousands)

	Actual Results				Over (Under) Budget
	Delicatessen	Restaurant	Total	Budget	
Gross Sales	$1,200	$2,000	$3,200	$3,500	$(300)[a]
Purchases[b]	780	800	1,580	1,600	(20)
Hourly Wages[b]	60	700	760	925	(165)
					continued

continued from page 569

Franchise Fee[b]	36	60	96	105	(9)
Advertising	100	200	300	300	—
Utilities[b]	76	100	176	195	(19)
Depreciation	50	75	125	125	—
Lease Cost	30	50	80	80	—
Salaries	30	50	80	80	—
Total	$1,162	$2,035	$3,197	$3,410	$(213)
Operating Profit......	$ 38	$ (35)	$ 3	$ 90	$ (87)

[a]There is no sales price variance.   [b]Variable costs. All other costs are fixed.

Prepare a profit variance report to indicate the flexible budget and relevant variances for the delicatessen department. (*Hint:* Use gross sales as your measure of volume.)

37. *Production budget, budgeted income statement, and cash forecast* (Appendix 12.1; adapted from CPA exam). Modern Products Corporation, a manufacturer of molded plastic containers, decided in October 19X0 that it needed cash to continue operations. The corporation began negotiating for a 1-month bank loan of $100,000 starting November 1, 19X0. The bank would charge interest at the rate of 1 percent per month and require the company to repay interest and principal on November 30, 19X0. In considering the loan, the bank requested a projected income statement and cash budget for the month of November.

The following information is available:

(1) The company budgeted sales at 120,000 units per month in October 19X0, December 19X0, and January 19X1, and at 90,000 units in November 19X0.

The selling price is $2 per unit. The company bills sales on the fifteenth and last day of each month on terms of 2/10, net 30. (That is, a 2 percent discount is offered for payment within 10 days. Payment is due, in any case, within 30 days.) Experience indicates that sales occur evenly throughout the month and that 50 percent of the customers pay the billed amount within the discount period. The remainder pay at the end of 30 days, except for uncollectible amounts, which average ½ percent of gross sales. On its income statement the corporation deducts the estimated amounts for cash discounts on sales and expected uncollectibles from sales.

(2) The inventory of finished goods on October 1 was 24,000 units. The finished goods inventory at the end of each month is to equal 20 percent of sales anticipated for the following month. There is no work in process.

(3) The inventory of raw materials on October 1 was 22,800 pounds. At the end of each month, the raw materials inventory is to equal not less than 40 percent of production requirements for the following month. The company purchases materials as needed in minimum quantities of 25,000 pounds per shipment. The company pays for raw material purchases for each month in the next succeeding month on terms of net 30 days.

(4) The company pays all salaries and wages on the fifteenth and last day of each month for the period ending on the date of payment.

(5) The company pays all manufacturing overhead and selling and administrative expenses on the tenth of the month following the month incurred. Selling expenses are 10 percent of gross sales. Administrative expenses, which include depreciation of $500 per month on office furniture and fixtures, total $33,000 per month.

(6) The manufacturing budget for molded plastic containers, based on expected production of 100,000 units per month, follows:

Materials (50,000 pounds, $1.00 each).........................	$ 50,000
Labor	40,000
Variable Overhead...	20,000
Fixed Overhead (includes depreciation of $4,000)	10,000
Total	$120,000

(7) The company expects the cash balance on November 1 to be $10,000. Prepare the following for Modern Products Corporation, assuming that the bank grants the loan. Ignore income taxes.

a. Schedules computing inventory budgets by months for
   (i) Finished goods production in units for October, November, and December.
   (ii) Raw material purchases in pounds for October and November.

b. A projected income statement for the month of November. Cost of goods sold should equal the variable manufacturing cost per unit times the number of units sold plus the total fixed manufacturing cost budgeted for the period.

c. A cash forecast for the month of November showing the opening balance, receipts (itemized by dates of collection), disbursements, and balance at the end of month.

38. *Incentives for truthful reporting* (Appendix 12.2). Cellol, Inc., a wholesaler in the record industry, has approached All Purpose Consulting Agency to help it design an incentive system that will motivate its sales account managers to make accurate forecasts for monthly sales. Suppose that you are a consultant with All Purpose Consulting Agency. Show the management of Cellol how the following bonus plan would work with forecasts of $8,000, $10,000, $12,000, $14,000, and $16,000 by preparing an exhibit similar to Exhibit 12.19.

$$\text{Bonus} = \begin{cases} 0.04\hat{Y} + 0.02(Y - \hat{Y}) & \text{for } Y > \hat{Y}, \\ 0.04\hat{Y} - 0.06(\hat{Y} - Y) & \text{for } \hat{Y} > Y, \end{cases}$$

where

$$\hat{Y} = \text{Forecasted Sales}$$

$$Y = \text{Actual Sales}.$$

39. *Incentives for accurate forecasting* (Appendix 12.2; contributed by Jean Lim). Kathy Kelly, the vice president of production operations, was not pleased with the unfavorable sales volume variances that Kelowna's lawn-mower line had been showing over the last four quarters. Kelly suspected that the source of her problem is the marketing department. The production depart-ment had a very good cost control system, but because of very long supplier lead times and a rigid production plan process, the department production had to plan well in advance, based on quarterly sales forecasts. The current bonus system employed by the marketing department paid Kelowna's sales repre-sentatives a sales commission of 2 percent of actual dollar sales. Kelly be-lieved that the present bonus system encouraged overly optimistic forecasting, since a large inventory reduced the risk of a stockout. Wishing to motivate more accurate sales forecasting by the company's sales force, Kelly decided to present to top management an alternative bonus system described in the All Purpose Consulting Agency seminar she attended a month ago. Briefly, Kelly hopes to propose a system whereby:

$$\text{Bonus} = \begin{cases} \$2\hat{Y} + \$1(Y - \hat{Y}) & \text{for } Y \geq \hat{Y}, \\ \$2\hat{Y} - \$3(\hat{Y} - Y) & \text{for } \hat{Y} \geq Y, \end{cases}$$

where

$$\hat{Y} = \text{Forecasted Sales in Units}$$

$$Y = \text{Actual Sales in Units}.$$

a. Suppose that you are Kathy Kelly's assistant. Prepare a bonus payoff matrix for actual and forecasted sales of 8,000 units, 10,000 units, 12,000 units, and 14,000 units to help her illustrate her bonus plan.

b. Suppose that the average manufacturer's sales price per lawnmower is $90. How would the current bonus plan compare to Kelly's proposed alternative?

Integrative Problems and Cases

40. *Cost data for multiple purposes: Omega Auto Supplies.* Omega Auto Sup-plies manufactures an automobile safety seat for children that it sells through several retail chains. Omega makes sales exclusively within its five-state re-gion in the Midwest. The cost of manufacturing and marketing children's automobile safety seats at the company's forecasted volume of 15,000 units per month follows:

Variable Materials	$300,000
Variable Labor	150,000
Variable Overhead	30,000
Fixed Overhead	180,200

continued

continued from page 572

Total Manufacturing Costs	$660,200
Variable Nonmanufacturing Costs	$75,000
Fixed Nonmanufacturing Costs........................	105,000
Total Nonmanufacturing Costs	180,000
Total Costs	$840,200

Unless otherwise stated, you should assume a regular selling price of $70 per unit. Ignore income taxes and other costs the problem does not mention.

Early in July, the senior management of Omega Auto Supplies met to evaluate the firm on performance for the first half of the year. The following exchange ensued.

Bob Wilson (president): ''Our performance for the first half of this year leaves much to be desired. Despite higher unit sales than forecast, our actual profits are $200,000 lower than what we expected.''

Sam Brown (sales manager): ''I suspect production needs to shape up'' (he said smugly). ''We in sales have pursued an aggressive marketing strategy and the three-quarters of a million sales revenue higher than forecast is proof enough of our improved performance.''

Linda Lampman (production manager): ''Wait a minute, now! We managed to bring down unit costs from $44.00 to $43.00—with no help from sales, I must add! What's the use of production plans when sales can change them any time it likes? In February, Sam wanted a rush order for 4,000. In March, it was 8,000 units. Then in April he said to hold off on production; then in June he wanted 6,000. You know what I think . . .''

Wilson: ''Hold on, now! I refuse to let this degenerate into a witch-hunt. We have to examine this problem with more objectivity.'' (He turned to his assistant, who had been quietly taking notes.) ''Do you have any ideas, Smith?''

You also know that planned production and sales for each month of the year is 15,000 units per month. You also know that 108,000 units were produced and sold in the first 6 months of this year, and the income statement was as follows:

Sales Revenue		$7,020,000
Manufacturing Costs:		
Variable Materials	$2,160,000	
Variable Labor	1,134,000	
Variable Overhead.............................	324,000	
Fixed Overhead	1,026,000	(4,644,000)
Gross Margin		$2,376,000
Marketing Costs:		
Variable Marketing.............................	$ 648,000	
Fixed Marketing	650,000	(1,298,000)
Operating Profit		$1,078,000

Suppose that you are in Smith's position: What would you tell the president?

41. *Formulating the analysis; setting up the profit variance analysis for an analysis over time.* Santa Barbara Stables, Inc., owns four horse stables at which it boards horses for their owners. Owners pay a fee per unit: one unit refers to boarding one horse for one month. Lawrence Lookalot is considering investing in Santa Barbara Stables and has asked for your assistance in evaluating the performance of the stables. He had obtained the 3 years of income statements shown in Exhibit 12.20. According to Lawrence, these financial statements show an encouraging trend. "Revenue has remained constant each year, but operating profits are improving. Don't you think the prospects for the future are bright?" he asks.

Prepare a profit analysis comparing the results from each year to those of each other year (that is, Year 1 with Year 2, Year 2 with Year 3, and Year 1 with Year 3 directly). For example, replace the Master Budget, Flexible Budget, and Achieved Profits columns in Exhibit 12.8 with Year 1 results, Year 2 volume at Year 1 prices and costs, and Year 2 results, respectively. Comment on Santa Barbara Stables' performance. For example, why are profits in Year 3 higher than profits in Year 2 when revenue was lower in Year 3?

42. *Adapting budget control concepts to projects in a research organization* (adapted from CMA exam). A report at Argo Labs breaks down each research project into phases, with the completion time and the cost of each phase estimated. The project descriptions and related estimates serve as the basis for development of the annual research department budget.

The following schedule presents the costs for the approved research activities for a recent year. The actual costs incurred by project or overhead cate-

Exhibit 12.20

SANTA BARBARA STABLES, INC.
Income Statements

	Income Statements		
	Year 3	Year 2	Year 1
Revenues....................................	$84,000	$90,000	$80,000
Expenses....................................	76,000	83,000	82,000
Operating Profits.............................	$ 8,000	$ 7,000	$ (2,000)

Other data:

Volume: Year 1, 1,600 units; Year 2, 1,500 units; Year 3, 1,200 units (one unit is one horse boarded for one month).

Prices charged per unit: Year 1, $50; Year 2, $60; Year 3, $70.

Variable costs, including feed and labor to care for animals: Year 1, $32,000; Year 2, $31,000; Year 3, $30,000.

Fixed costs (all cash), including Year 2 maintenance of stables: Year 1, $50,000; Year 2, $52,000; Year 3, $46,000.

Inflation: 5 percent per year.

gory are compared with the approved activity and the variances noted on this same schedule.

The director of research prepared a narrative statement of research performance for the year to accompany the schedule. The director's statement follows:

> The year has been most successful. We finished the two projects scheduled for completion in this year, 4-1 and 8-1. Project 8-2 is progressing satisfactorily and we should complete it next year as scheduled. The fourth phase of project 5-3, with estimated direct research costs of $100,000, and the first phase of project 8-3, both included in the approved activity for the year, could not be started because the principal researcher left our employment. We resubmitted them for approval in next year's activity plan.

From the information given, prepare an alternative schedule that will provide the management of Argo Company with better information than the existing schedule by which to judge the research cost performance for the given year.

ARGO COMPANY
Comparison of Actual with Budgeted Research Costs
(all dollar amounts in thousands)

	Approved Activity for the Year	Actual Costs for the Year	(Over) Under Budget
Projects in Progress at the Beginning of the Year, Including Allocated General Research Overhead Costs from Below:			
4–1	$ 23.2	$ 46.8	$(23.6)
5–3	464.0[a]	514.8	(50.8)
New Projects, Including Allocated General Research Overhead Costs from Below:			
8–1	348.0	351.0	(3.0)
8–2	232.0	257.4	(25.4)
8–3	92.8	—	92.8
Total Research Costs..............	$1,160.0	$1,170.0	$(10.0)
General Research Overhead Costs (allocated to projects in proportion to their direct costs):			
Administration	$ 50.0	$ 52.0	$ (2.0)
Laboratory Facilities	110.0	118.0	(8.0)
Total	$ 160.0	$ 170.0	$(10.0)

---

[a]Phases 3 and 4 only.

43. *Solving for unknowns; cost-volume-profit and budget analysis* (adapted from a problem by D. O. Green). A partial income statement of Baines Corporation for 19X0 follows. The company uses just-in-time inventory, so production each year equals sales. Each dollar of finished product produced in 19X0 contained $.50 of direct materials, $.33⅓ of direct labor, and $.16⅔ of overhead costs. During 19X0, fixed overhead costs were $40,000. No changes in production methods or credit policies are anticipated for 19X1.

BAINES CORPORATION
Partial Income Statement for 19X0

Sales (100,000 units at $10).........................		$1,000,000
Cost of Goods Sold		600,000
Gross Margin.......................................		$ 400,000
Selling Costs	$150,000	
Administrative Costs	100,000	250,000
Operating Profit....................................		$ 150,000

Management has estimated the following changes for 19X1:

- 30 percent increase in number of units sold.
- 20 percent increase in unit cost of materials.
- 15 percent increase in direct labor cost per unit.
- 10 percent increase in variable overhead cost per unit.
- 5 percent increase in fixed overhead costs.
- 8 percent increase in selling costs because of increased volume.
- 6 percent increase in administrative costs arising solely because of increased wages.

  There are no other changes.

a. What must the unit sales price be in 19X1 for Baines Corporation to earn a $200,000 operating profit?

b. What will be the 19X1 operating profit if selling prices are increased as before, but unit sales increase by 10 percent rather than 30 percent? (Selling costs would go up by only one-third of the amount projected previously.)

c. If selling price in 19X1 remains at $10 per unit, how many units must be sold in 19X1 for the operating profit to be $200,000?

44. *Differential analysis and budgeting.* The Monmouth Company is preparing its budget for the year 19X1. If the same selling policies that were in effect in 19X0 are continued in 19X1, the budget officer estimates that the profit plan will appear as shown in the exhibit that follows.

All variable costs vary with the number of units sold. The company could increase its output to 1 million units per year without increasing its fixed manufacturing and administrative costs. In order to increase its income, the company wants to use the presently unused capacity. Two plans have been suggested to improve the income picture.

Plan A. The company estimates that it could increase unit sales by 25 percent if (1) it reduced selling price per unit by 5 percent and (2) it instituted an additional advertising campaign that would increase fixed selling costs by $15,000.

Plan B. The company has an opportunity to obtain a government contract for an additional 200,000 units if it quotes a low enough price. If it gets the government contract, the regular sales of 800,000 units will be unaffected.

a. Assuming that Plan A was adopted and the results are as anticipated, present the profit plan for 19X1.

b. If Plan A functions as planned, what is the lowest price the company should bid on the government contract in Plan B? (Show your computations.)

c. If the company decides that Plan A is not feasible, what is the lowest price the company should bid on the contract? (Show your computations.)

THE MONMOUTH COMPANY
Projected Partial Profit Plan
Year 19X1

Sales (800,000 units at $2 per unit)		$1,600,000
Operating Costs:		
Cost of Goods Sold:		
Variable	$600,000	
Fixed.	300,000	
Total Cost of Goods Sold.		$900,000
Administrative Costs:		
Variable	$ 20,000	
Fixed.	100,000	
Total Administrative Costs.		120,000
Selling Costs:		
Variable	$ 30,000	
Fixed.	120,000	
Total Selling Costs	150,000	
Total Operating Costs		(1,170,000)
Operating Profit.		$ 430,000

Suggested Solutions to Even-Numbered Exercises

10. *Solving for materials requirements*

$$\frac{\text{Finished Units}}{\text{to Be Produced}} = \frac{84{,}000}{\substack{\text{Units} \\ \text{to Be Sold}}} + \frac{48{,}000 \text{ Units}}{\substack{\text{in Ending} \\ \text{Inventory}}} - \frac{44{,}000 \text{ Units}}{\substack{\text{in Beginning} \\ \text{Inventory}}}$$

$$\frac{\text{Units to}}{\text{Be Produced}} = \underline{\underline{88{,}000}}.$$

$$\begin{array}{l}\text{Units of Raw} \\ \text{Materials to} \\ \text{Be Used}\end{array} = \begin{array}{l}\text{4 Units of Raw} \\ \text{Materials per} \\ \text{Finished Unit}\end{array} \times 88{,}000 \text{ Finished Units} = 352{,}000.$$

$$\begin{array}{l}\text{Units of Raw} \\ \text{Materials to} \\ \text{Be Purchased}\end{array} = \begin{array}{l}352{,}000 \text{ Units} \\ \text{to Be Used}\end{array} + \begin{array}{l}220{,}000 \text{ Units} \\ \text{Desired Ending} \\ \text{Inventory}\end{array} - \begin{array}{l}200{,}000 \text{ Units} \\ \text{in Beginning} \\ \text{Inventory}\end{array}$$

$$= \underline{\underline{372{,}000.}}$$

12. *Solving for cash collections* (Appendix 12.1)
   a. Budgeted cash collections in March:

From January Sales (.18 × $500,000)	$ 90,000
From February Sales (.30 × $600,000)	180,000
From March Sales (.50 × $400,000)	200,000
Total Budgeted Collections in March	$470,000

   b. Budgeted cash collections in April:

From February Sales (.18 × $600,000)	$108,000
From March Sales (.30 × $400,000)	120,000
From April Sales (.50 × $500,000)	250,000
Total Budgeted Collections in April	$478,000

14. *Profit variance analysis*

	Achieved (7,100 units)	Cost Variances	Sales Price Variance	Flexible Budget (7,100 units)	Sales Volume Variance	Master Budget (7,000 units)
Sales Revenue	$86,265[a]		$1,065 F	$85,200[c]	$1,200 F	$84,000[d]
Less Variable Costs	41,890[b]	$6,390 U		35,500	500 U	35,000
Contribution Margin	$44,375	$6,390 U	$1,065 F	$49,700	$ 700 F	$49,000
Fixed Costs	20,000	1,000 F	—	21,000	—	21,000[e]
Operating Profits	$24,375	$5,390 U	$1,065 F	$28,700	$ 700 F	$28,000

[a] 7,100 units × $12.15.

[b] 7,100 units × $5.90.

[c] 7,100 units × $12.

[d] 7,000 units × $12.

[e] 7,000 units × $3.

16. *Graphic comparison of budgeted and actual costs*
  a. <u>$.80 per Unit</u>

$$V = (TC - F) \neq X$$

$$= (\$3,000,000 - \$1,000,000) \div 2,500,000$$

$$= \$.80.$$

  b. <u>$2,600,000</u>

$$TC = F + VX$$

$$= \$1,000,000 + (\$.8 \times 2,000,000)$$

$$= \$2,600,000.$$

  c. <u>$4,200,000</u>

$$TC = F + VX$$

$$= \$1,000,000 + (\$.8 \times 4,000,000)$$

$$= \$4,200,000.$$

18. *Comparing master budget to actual results.*

	Actual (90 units)	Manufac- turing Variances	Marketing and Administrative Variances	Sales Price Variance	Flexible Budget (90 units)	Sales Volume Variance	Master Budget (100 units)
Sales Revenue	$9,200			$200 F	$9,000	$1,000 U	$10,000
Variable Costs:							
Manufacturing	3,440	$70 F			3,510	390 F	3,900
Marketing	1,030		$40 U		990	110 F	1,100
Total Variable Costs	$4,470				$4,500		$ 5,000
Contribution Margin	$4,730	$70 F	$40 U	$200 F	$4,500	$ 500 U	$ 5,000
Fixed Costs:							
Manufacturing	485	15 F			500	—	500
Marketing	1,040		40 U		1,000	—	1,000
Administrative	995		5 F		1,000	—	1,000
Operating Profit	$2,210	$85 F	$75 U	$200 F	$2,000	$ 500 U	$ 2,500

20. *Interpreting the flexible budget line*
  a. Actual Units Sold:

$$\text{Profit} = (P - V)X - F$$

$$\$(7,000) = \$7X - \$70,000$$

$$X = \frac{\$63,000}{7}$$

$$= \underline{\underline{9,000 \text{ Units}}}.$$

b.   Budgeted Units to Be Sold:

$$\$28,000 = \$7X - \$70,000$$

$$X = \frac{\$98,000}{7}$$

$$= \underline{\underline{14,000 \text{ Units.}}}$$

22.   *Incentives for accurate forecasting* (Appendix 12.2)

		Forecasted Sales, $\hat{Y}$				
		20	**21**	**22**	**23**	**24**
Actual Sales, Y	**20**	$2,000[a]	$1,950[f]	$1,900[i]	$1,850	$1,800
	21	2,070[b]	2,100[g]	2,050[j]	2,000	1,950
	22	2,140[c]	2,170[h]	2,200	2,150	2,100
	23	2,210[d]	2,240	2,270	2,300	2,250
	24	2,280[e]	2,310	2,340	2,370	2,400

[a]$2,000 = $100 (20).
[b]$2,070 = $2,000 + $70 (21 − 20).
[c]$2,140 = $2,000 + $70 (22 − 20).
[d]$2,210 = $2,000 + $70 (23 − 20).
[e]$2,280 = $2,000 + $70 (24 − 20).

[f]$1,950 = $100 (21) − $150 (21 − 20).
[g]$2,100 = $100 (21).
[h]$2,170 = $2,100 + $70 (22 − 21), etc.
[i]$1,900 = $100 (22) − $150 (22 − 20).
[j]$2,050 = $2,200 − $150 (22 − 21), etc.

24.   *Marketing cost budget*
Fixed Costs:

Salaries	$25,000
Advertising...	30,000
Sales Office Costs...	8,400
Travel	2,000
Total	$65,400

Variable Costs:

Shipping Costs = $.02 per Unit Sold and Shipped.

Commissions = 2 Percent of Sales, or .02 × Units Sold × $\dfrac{\text{Selling Price}}{\text{per Unit.}}$

$$\text{Variable Costs} = \left(\$.02 \times \frac{\text{Units}}{\text{Shipped}}\right) + \left(\$.02 \times \$6 \; \frac{\text{Unit}}{\text{Selling}} \times \frac{\text{Units}}{\text{Sold}}\right).$$

Selling Expense Flexible Budget:

$$\$65,400 + \left(\$.02 \times \frac{\text{Units}}{\text{Shipped}}\right) + \left(\$.12 \times \frac{\text{Units}}{\text{Sold}}\right).$$

Case 1:

$$\$65,400 + (\$.02 \times 60,000) + (\$.12 \times 60,000)$$

$$= \$65,400 + \$1,200 + \$7,200$$

$$= \underline{\$73,800}.$$

Case 2:

$$\$65,400 + (\$.02 \times 75,000) + (\$.12 \times 75,000)$$

$$= \$65,400 + \$1,500 + \$9,000$$

$$= \underline{\$75,900}.$$

Case 3:

$$\$65,400 + (\$.02 \times 64,000) + (\$.12 \times 64,000)$$

$$= \$65,400 + \$1,280 + \$7,680$$

$$= \underline{\$74,360}.$$

26. *Computing sales price variances*

	Actual Sales	Sales Price Variance	Flexible Budget
Product X Sales.....................	$111,300	$ 5,300 F	$106,000[a]
Product Y Sales.....................	23,040	960 U	24,000[b]
Product Z Sales.....................	192,000	48,000 U	240,000[c]
	$326,340	$43,660 U	$370,000

[a] $5,300 \text{ Units} \times \dfrac{\$100,000}{5,000 \text{ Units}} = \$106,000.$

[b] $240 \text{ Units} \times \dfrac{\$20,000}{200 \text{ Units}} = \$24,000.$

[c] $48,000 \text{ Units} \times \dfrac{\$250,000}{50,000 \text{ Units}} = \$240,000.$

... CHAPTER 13 ...

Measuring and Interpreting Variances

Chapter Outline

- Variance Analysis
- Responsibility for Variances
- Separating Variances into Price and Efficiency Components
- Variable Cost Variance Model
- Variable Overhead in Service Organizations
- Use of Variances in Nonmanufacturing Settings
- Variance Analysis in High-Technology Companies

Chapter 11 stated that the feedback phase is an important part of the planning and control process. During the feedback phase, managers compare actual results to budgets, evaluate performance, and revise goals, plans, and budgets. By comparing actual performance with the budget and investigating reasons for variances, management can evaluate past performance, take corrective actions where necessary, penalize or reward employees, and revise goals, plans, and budgets. The use of variances results from the philosophy of **management by exception,** which focuses managerial attention on exceptions, or variances, from the norm.

Chapter 12 presented profit variance analysis, which compares the profits achieved with those budgeted. This chapter presents more detail in analyzing cost variances. As you encounter variance analysis in practice, remember that each

Exhibit 13.1

VICTORIA CORPORATION
Profit Variance Analysis: Comparison of Achieved Profits to Budgeted Profits
(This is Exhibit 12.8, repeated for reader's convenience.)

	Achieved Profits (based on actual sales volume of 80,000 units) (1)	Purchasing and Production Variances (2)	Marketing and Administrative Cost Variances (3)	Sales Price Variance (4)	Flexible Budget (based on actual sales volume of 80,000 units) (5)	Sales Volume Variance (6)	Master Budget (based on a plan of 70,000 units sold) (7)
Sales	$488,000ᵃ	—	—	$8,000 F	$480,000ᶠ	$60,000 F	$420,000ⁱ
Less:							
Variable Manufacturing Costs	305,600ᵇ	$12,000 U	—	—	293,600ᵍ	36,700 U	256,900ʲ
Variable Marketing Costs	12,800ᶜ	—	$1,440 Uᵈ	160 Uᵉ	11,200ʰ	1,400 U	9,800ᵏ
Contribution Margin	$169,600	$12,000 U	$1,440 U	$7,840 F	$175,200	$21,900 F	$153,300
Less:							
Fixed Manufacturing Costs	34,000	1,800 U	—	—	32,200	—	32,200
Fixed Marketing Costs	64,400	—	1,000 F	—	65,400	—	65,400
Fixed Administrative Costs	44,600	—	200 F	—	44,800	—	44,800
Operating Profits	$ 26,600	$13,800 U	$ 240 U	$7,840 F	$ 32,800	$21,900 F	$ 10,900

Total Profit Variance from Flexible Budget = $6,200 U

Total Profit Variance from Master Budget Profit Plan = $15,700 F

ᵃ80,000 units sold at $6.10 per unit.
ᵇ80,000 units sold at $3.82 per unit.
ᶜ80,000 units sold at $.16 per unit.
ᵈ$1,440 U = $12,800 − $11,200 − $160.
ᵉ$160 U = .02 × $8,000 Favorable Price Variance.

ᶠ80,000 units sold at $6.00.
ᵍ80,000 units sold at $3.67.
ʰ80,000 units sold at $.14.
ⁱ70,000 units sold at $6.00.

ʲ70,000 units sold at $3.67.
ᵏ70,000 units sold at $.14.
U denotes unfavorable variance.
F denotes favorable variance.

organization calculates variances in a unique way, based on the nature of the organization and the needs of its decision makers. We present the fundamental variance analysis model that all types of organizations commonly use in one form or another. Organizations differ in their applications, but the basic concepts underlying the applications are generally the same in all organizations.

Variance Analysis

This chapter continues the Victoria Corporation example discussed in Chapter 12. For convenience, Exhibit 13.1 reproduces Exhibit 12.8, which compares actual results with the budget.

Exhibit 13.1 shows the total variance in operating profits from the original plan, $15,700 favorable. The next step investigates and analyzes the variance to find causes, to ascertain whether the firm needs to take corrective steps, and to reward or penalize employees, where appropriate.

Responsibility for Variances

This section describes variance calculations for each of the major groups responsible for variances in organizations: marketing, administration, purchasing, and production. We calculate each responsibility center's variances, *holding all other things constant*. Hence, we separate marketing variances from production, production variances from purchasing, and so forth. After accountants compute variances, managers investigate the causes of variances and take corrective action if needed.

Marketing

Management usually assigns responsibility for sales volume, sales price, and marketing cost variances to marketing. Thus the marketing department at Victoria Corporation would be responsible for the variances shown in Exhibit 13.2.

The $21,900 favorable sales volume variance measures the favorable impact on profits of higher-than-expected sales volume as the exhibit shows. The sales volume

Exhibit 13.2

VICTORIA CORPORATION Marketing Department Variances	
Variable Marketing Cost	$ 1,440 U
Fixed Marketing Cost	1,000 F
Sales Volume	21,900 F
Sales Price (net of commissions)	7,840 F[a]

[a]$8,000 F price variance − $160 higher commissions associated with higher than expected price = $7,840.

variance may be a function of factors outside the marketing department's influence, however, such as unexpected or unpredictable changes in the market. The sales volume variance is a contribution margin variance, which equals the budgeted contribution margin times the difference between budgeted and actual sales volume. Chapter 12 stated that each unit sold generates $6.00 of revenue, each unit has a budgeted (or standard) variable manufacturing cost of $3.67, a budgeted shipping cost of $.02 per unit, and a budgeted sales commission of $.12 (= 2 percent × $6.00). Thus the contribution margin expected from each unit is $2.19 (= $6.00 − $3.67 − $.02 − $.12).

Why is the *standard* variable cost used to compute the contribution margin instead of the *actual* cost? Recall that we are calculating the effect of sales *volume* alone. By using standard variable cost in computing contribution margins, we avoid mixing cost variances with the effect of sales volume.

Marketing also may be responsible for the sales price variance. Note that the increase in sales commission (2 percent of $8,000 = $160), as a result of the higher-than-budgeted selling price, partially offsets the favorable sales price variance of $8,000.

The $1,440 (unfavorable) variable marketing cost variance investigation should start with sales commissions. Did the firm inappropriately pay commissions—for example, on sales that customers returned? Did the commission rate exceed the 2 percent budgeted? Did the sales staff earn commissions in previous periods reported in the current period? Managers would ask similar questions about shipping costs. Did rates increase, for example?

The accounting staff usually ascertains whether variances result from bookkeeping adjustments or errors, whereas marketing managers investigate marketing activities that may have caused the variances.

Fixed marketing costs are often discretionary. A favorable variance does not necessarily mean good performance. For example, the $1,000 favorable variance at Victoria Corporation could mean that the company did less advertising than intended, which could have a negative effect on future sales.

Administration

The accounting process assigns a $200 favorable variance to administration. Administrative variances are often the hardest to manage because they are not *engineered;* that is, no well-defined causal relation exists between administrative input and administrative output.

Management usually budgets administrative costs with discretion, placing a ceiling on costs for a particular set of tasks. For example, suppose an organization's corporate internal audit staff received a budget of $2,000,000 for 40 people's salaries and an additional $400,000 for travel, supplies, and other costs. The internal audit department may not spend more than those limits without obtaining approvals, which would normally come from top executives (for example, the company president) or the board of directors.

Although discretionary budgets can provide a ceiling for expenditure, they do not provide a norm like a flexible manufacturing cost budget. If you cannot measure output, then you cannot measure the input-output relation, which makes ascertaining the "proper" levels of costs difficult. You should take these difficulties into account when you evaluate an administrative cost variance or any other discretionary cost variance.

Purchasing

Purchasing departments are responsible for purchasing the materials to make products and provide services. Monitoring a purchasing department's success in getting a good value for the money is important because materials make up 50 to 60 percent of a product's cost. Materials are not limited to manufacturing. They comprise a substantial portion of the cost of providing services in many nonmanufacturing businesses, for example, surgical, laboratory, medical supplies in hospitals, and food in restaurants.

Managers use the materials price variance to evaluate a purchasing department's performance.[1] This variance measures the difference between the actual and standard prices paid for materials. To demonstrate how accountants compute the materials price variance, assume that Victoria Corporation actually purchased 81,000 pounds of direct materials at $1.05 per pound. Recall that the standard cost was $1.00 per pound. The process would charge purchasing with an unfavorable price variance of $4,050 [= ($1.05 − $1.00) × 81,000 pounds purchased].

Production

The accounting process would charge production departments with the remaining variable manufacturing cost variance that it did not assign to purchasing and with the fixed manufacturing cost variance. For Victoria Corporation, the process would assign variances as follows:

	Total	− Purchasing	= Production
Variable Manufacturing Cost Variance.........	$12,000 U −	$4,050 U	= $7,950 U
Fixed Manufacturing Cost Variance	$1,800 U −	0	= $1,800 U

Separating Variances into Price and Efficiency Components

Accountants generally split variable manufacturing cost variances into *price* and *efficiency* components. The price component is the difference between the budgeted (or standard) price and the actual price paid for each unit of input. The efficiency variance measures the efficiency with which the firm uses inputs to produce outputs. To demonstrate, suppose that Victoria Corporation's $12,000 unfavorable variable manufacturing cost variance comprises the manufacturing cost variances

---

[1] A study of internal control practices in U.S. companies found the purchase price variance to be the most common measure used to evaluate a purchasing department's performance. See R. K. Mautz, et al., *Internal Control in U.S. Corporations* (New York: Financial Executives Research Foundation, 1980).

shown in Exhibit 13.3. For illustrative purposes, assume that Victoria produced 80,000 units.

Note that these total manufacturing variances also appear in column (2) of Exhibit 13.1.

At this point, you should calculate price and efficiency variances without looking ahead. We recommend this exercise because students often make variance calculations by memorizing formulas that they quickly forget. Most organizations incorporate these formulas into computer programs, so you need not memorize formulas.

A **price variance** measures the difference between the price set as the norm—that is, the standard or budgeted price—and the actual price. For direct labor, this amount was $1.10 favorable (= $18.90 actual − $20.00 standard) per hour for Victoria Corporation. The company purchased 10,955 hours of labor, so the favorable labor price variance was $12,050 (= $1.10 × 10,955 hours, rounded down). You could calculate the materials purchase price variance in a similar way, giving an unfavorable price variance of $4,050, as we noted earlier in our discussion of performance evaluation of the purchasing department.

An **efficiency variance** measures the difference between the actual quantity of inputs used and those allowed at standard to make a unit of output. Victoria Corporation allows 1 pound of direct material for each unit produced. If it used 81,000 pounds to produce 80,000 units, an unfavorable efficiency variance of 1,000 pounds in quantity, or $1,000 (= 1,000 pounds × $1 standard price per pound) would result.

Exhibit 13.3

VICTORIA CORPORATION
Manufacturing Variances

	Actual	Standard Allowed Based on Actual Production Output of 80,000 Units	Variance
Variable Costs:			
Direct Materials	81,000 Pounds at $1.05 = $85,050	80,000 Pounds at $1.00 = $80,000	$ 5,050 U
Direct Labor	10,955 Hours at $18.90 = $207,050 (rounded to nearest dollar)	10,000 Hours (= 80,000 Units × ⅛ Hour) at $20 = $200,000	7,050 U
Variable Manufacturing Overhead	$13,500	80,000 Units at $0.17 = $13,600	100 F
Total Variable Manufacturing Costs	$305,600	$293,600	$12,000 U

	Actual	Budget	Variance
Fixed Costs:			
Fixed Manufacturing Overhead	$34,000	$32,200	$ 1,800 U

Variable Cost Variance Model

A general model for variance calculations appears in Exhibit 13.4. We apply that model to the calculation of direct materials, direct labor, and variable manufacturing overhead variances for Victoria Corporation in Exhibit 13.5. We have divided direct materials and direct labor variances into price and efficiency components. We will make an additional analysis of the variable overhead cost variance later in this chapter.

Note that Exhibit 13.5 breaks down the total variable manufacturing cost variance in column (2) of Exhibit 13.1 into more detail. Think of Exhibit 13.1 as the "big picture" and of Exhibit 13.5 as a detailed supporting schedule.

Interpret the computations in column (3) of Exhibit 13.5 carefully. Note that the term SQ refers to the **standard quantity of input allowed to produce the actual output.** SQ is *not* the expected production volume. If each unit of output produced has a standard of $\frac{1}{8}$ hour of direct labor time, and if 80,000 units of output are *actually produced*, then $SQ = 10,000$ hours ($= \frac{1}{8}$ hour $\times$ 80,000 units).

Note that column (3) is also the flexible *production* budget, which you should not confuse with the flexible *sales* budget. Managers use the flexible sales budget to

Exhibit 13.4

General Model for Variance Analysis: Variable Manufacturing Costs

^{a}The terms *price* and *efficiency* variances are general categories. Although terminology varies from company to company, the following specific variance titles are frequently used:

Input	Price Variance Category	Efficiency Variance Category
Direct Materials	Price (or Purchase Price) Variance	Usage or Quantity Variance
Direct Labor	Rate Variance	Efficiency Variance
Variable Overhead	Spending Variance	Efficiency Variance

We shall avoid unnecessary labeling by simply referring to these variances as either *price* or *efficiency* variances.

Exhibit 13.5

VICTORIA CORPORATION
Calculation of Variable Manufacturing Cost Variances

ACTUAL Actual price (AP) times actual quantity (AQ) of input for actual production output (AP × AQ) (1)	INPUTS AT STANDARD Standard price (SP) times actual quantity (AQ) of input for actual production output (SP × AQ) (2)	FLEXIBLE PRODUCTION BUDGET Standard price (SP) times standard quantity (SQ) of input allowed for actual output (that is, 80,000 units produced) (SP × SQ) (3)

Direct Materials

$1.05 × 81,000 Pounds
 = $85,050

$1.00 × 81,000 Pounds
 = $81,000

$1.00 × 80,000 Pounds
 = $80,000

Price Variance:
$4,050 U

Efficiency Variance:
$1,000 U

Shortcut Formulas:
 (AP − SP) × AQ
($1.05 − $1.00) × 81,000 Pounds
 = $4,050 U

SP × (AQ − SQ)
$1.00 × (81,000 Pounds − 80,000 Pounds)
 = $1,000 U

Direct Labor

$18.90 × 10,955 Hours
 = $207,050

$20 × 10,955 Hours
 = $219,100

$20 × 10,000 Hours[a]
 = $200,000

Price Variance:
$12,050 F

Efficiency Variance:
$19,100 U

Shortcut Formulas:
 (AP − SP) × AQ
($18.90 − $20) × 10,955 Hours
 = $12,050 F

SP × (AQ − SQ)
$20 × (10,955 Hours − 10,000 Hours)
 = $19,100 U

**Variable Manufacturing
  Overhead**

$13,500

$.17 × 80,000 Units
 = $13,600

Variable Manufacturing
Overhead Variance:
$100 F

[a]10,000 hours allowed = 80,000 units produced × ⅛ hours per unit allowed.

Note: It is sometimes difficult to see intuitively which variances are favorable (F) and which are unfavorable (U). Keep in mind that for cost variances you are comparing amounts on the left—actual—with those on the right—budget or standard. If the amount on the left (the actual) exceeds the amount on the right (the budget or standard), the variance is *unfavorable* because higher costs than budgeted mean lower profits than budgeted. The reverse is true for favorable variances; the amounts on the left (actuals) are lower than those on the right. *Caution:* We set up all of the cost variance calculations in this book consistently, with actual costs on the left, standard or budget on the right, so the preceding rule works in this book. Other books and company practices do not necessarily consistently follow this practice.

analyze differences between actual and budgeted profits [see column (5) in Exhibit 13.1]. In Exhibits 13.4 and 13.5, the activity of interest is production, so production volume drives the budget. In short, column (3) of Exhibits 13.4 and 13.5 shows the **standard cost allowed to produce the actual output,** whereas column (1) of Exhibits 13.4 and 13.5 show the **actual costs incurred to produce the actual output.** The differences between columns (1) and (3) are the variable manufacturing cost variances, which you can further separate into price and efficiency variances.

This overview of manufacturing variances provides the essential calculations for management use of variances. Most companies carry out this analysis in much greater detail. Most companies report variances for each type of material, for each category of labor, and for major cost components of variable overhead (for example, power to run machines, indirect materials and supplies, indirect labor).

Reasons for Materials and Labor Variances

Variance reports include explanations for the variances. These explanations help managers to ascertain whether they should investigate variances and take corrective action, whether they should reward people responsible for variances, or whether they should take other managerial action. Why do variances occur? First, a variance is simply the difference between a predetermined norm or standard and the actual results. Some difference should be expected simply because one measure is expected and the other is actual. For example, if you and several of your friends were each to flip a coin ten times, not all of you would come up with five heads, even though five heads (= 50 percent of ten coin flips) may be the expected value. In short, even when standards are unbiased expected values, and no *systematic* reasons explain variances, some variances will occur anyway.

Second, the standards themselves may be biased. Sometimes managers set standards intentionally loose or tight. Sometimes they are unintentionally biased, such as when the firm omits expected labor wage increases or an allowance for waste on direct material usage.

Reasons for Materials Variances   **Materials price variances** occur for numerous reasons. They may result from failure to take purchase discounts, from using a better (or worse) grade of raw material than expected so that the price paid was higher (or lower) than expected, or from changes in the market supply or demand for the raw material that affected prices. A number of factors cause **materials efficiency variances.** When management, industrial engineers, and others set standards for the amount of direct materials that a unit of output should use, they usually allow for material defects, inexperienced workers who ruin materials, improperly used materials, and so forth. If the firm uses materials more efficiently than these standards, favorable efficiency variances result; usage worse than these standards results in unfavorable variances. Sometimes purchasing, not production, causes a materials efficiency variance. In an effort to reduce prices (and create a favorable price variance), purchasing departments may have bought inferior materials. Purchasing may also be responsible for ordering the wrong materials.

Reasons for Labor Variances   **Direct labor price** (or wage) **variances** can occur because managers do not correctly anticipate changes in wage rates. Wage rates established by a union contract may differ from the forecasted amount, for example. Also, a wage rate change may occur but the firm will not have adjusted standards to reflect it.

The **direct labor efficiency variance** measures labor productivity. Managers watch this variance because they can usually control it. Many of the things that create variances affect all competitors about the same. Labor wage rates going up dramatically because of a union contract settlement usually affects all companies in an industry, so little competitive advantage or disadvantage results. Labor efficiency is unique to a firm, however, and can lead to competitive advantages or disadvantages.

A financial vice president of a manufacturing company told us:

> Raw materials are 57 percent of our product cost, direct labor is only 22 percent. Yet we carry out the labor efficiency variance to the penny, we break it down by product line, by department, and sometimes by specific operation, while we give the raw materials variances only a passing glance. Why? Because there's not much we can do about some of our other variances, like materials price variances, but there's a lot we can do to keep our labor efficiency in line.

Labor efficiency variances have many causes. The cause may be the workers themselves—poorly motivated or poorly trained workers will be less productive, whereas highly motivated and well-trained workers may generate favorable efficiency variances. Other causes include poor materials, faulty equipment, poor supervision, and scheduling problems.

Although most firms hold production managers responsible for direct labor efficiency variances, they sometimes attribute responsibility to purchasing managers for buying faulty materials. Scheduling problems may result from upstream production departments that have delayed production, from the personnel department that provided the wrong type of worker, or from numerous other sources.

Note that the labor price variance in the Victoria Corporation example was favorable, whereas the labor efficiency variance was unfavorable. A manager would probably ask first: "Did we use workers who were lower paid and not as efficient as expected?" Although firms go to great lengths to break variances down into small components that they can easily understand and trace to particular responsibility centers, managers should not overlook the fact that variances are usually interrelated.

Variable Overhead Price and Efficiency Variances

Separating variable overhead variances into price and efficiency components helps control overhead costs. For example, energy costs in many firms are both sufficiently large and controllable to warrant special attention.

The manager can use the same method to compute price and efficiency variances for variable overhead as for other variable manufacturing costs. The computation requires a measure of overhead input activity not yet presented in the Victoria

Corporation example, however. Suppose the variable overhead at Victoria Corporation consisted of machines' operating costs, such as power and maintenance. The longer the machines ran, the more variable overhead cost is incurred. A **variable overhead price variance** results when the cost per machine hour is either more or less than the standard cost allowed per machine hour. A **variable overhead efficiency variance** results if the machine hours required to make the actual production output exceeds the standard machine hours allowed to make that output. For example, suppose the firm makes a large batch of units that consumed several hundred machine hours. Subsequently, the firm found these units to be defective and destroyed them; thus the accounting system did not count them as part of the actual production output. (Managers implicitly assume only good units are counted as part of the actual production output.)

Assume the standard for machine usage was 40 units per machine hour at a standard cost allowed of $6.80 per hour. (This is equivalent to $.17 per unit of output, because $6.80/40 = $.17.) Also assume the actual production output of 80,000 units required 2,100 machine hours, so the efficiency variance was $680 U, as Exhibit 13.6 shows. The actual costs for variable overhead totaled only $13,500, so the favorable variable overhead price variance was $780 F.

The manager should interpret variable overhead price and efficiency variances with care. The accountant sometimes selects the input activity base (machine hours

Exhibit 13.6

VICTORIA CORPORATION
Variable Manufacturing Overhead Variances

ACTUAL Actual price (*AP*) times actual quantity (*AQ*) of input for actual production output (*AP* × *AQ*) (1)	INPUTS AT STANDARD Standard price (*SP*) times actual quantity (*AQ*) of input for actual production output (*SP* × *AQ*) (2)	FLEXIBLE PRODUCTION BUDGET Standard price (*SP*) times standard quantity (*SQ*) of input allowed for actual output (i.e., 80,000 units produced) (*SP* × *SQ*) (3)
$13,500[a]	$6.80 × 2,100 Mach. Hrs. = $14,280	$6.80 × 2,000 Mach. Hrs. = $.17 × 80,000 Units = $13,600

Price Variance: $780 F   Efficiency Variance: $680 U[b]

Variable Manufacturing Overhead Variance: $100 F

[a]Because the firm does not typically purchase overhead per machine hour or per unit of some other activity base, the total variable overhead does not contain an actual price (*AP*) component.

[b]Shortcut Formula:

$$SP \times (AQ - SQ)$$
$$\$6.80 \times (2,100 \text{ Hours} - 2,000 \text{ Hours})$$
$$= \$6.80 \text{ U.}$$

in our example) without regard for the nature of variable overhead costs. For example, if a company used direct labor hours to apply variable overhead, an unfavorable efficiency variance results when the company inefficiently uses direct labor hours. That variance means nothing if none of the variable overhead costs associates with direct labor costs. This particular problem occurs in capital-intensive companies in which variable overhead mostly relates to machine usage.

In general, managers are wise to establish a detailed breakdown of variable overhead into cost categories that relate logically to the input activity base. For example, the following variable overhead costs could be applied on the following input activity bases:

Cost	Activity Base
Indirect Labor	Direct Labor Hours
Power to Run Machines	Machine Hours
Materials Inventory Carrying Costs	Materials Inventory

Overview of Variances

Exhibit 13.7 presents an overview of variances for Chapters 12 and 13. The top panel reproduces columns (1) through (5) of the profit variance analysis discussed in Chapter 12 and presented in Exhibit 13.1. The bottom panel illustrates the breakdown of variable manufacturing costs into direct materials, direct labor, and variable overhead. This breakdown shows that the cost variance analysis discussed in this chapter simply extends the profit variance analysis discussed in Chapter 12.

Fixed Manufacturing Cost Variances   The only fixed cost variances computed for managerial purposes are the price variances (also called spending or budget variances). Because fixed costs do not vary with the measure of activity (such as units), there are no efficiency variances for fixed costs.[2]

Variable Overhead in Service Organizations

Variable overhead often makes up a large portion of the cost of providing services. Next we apply the overhead analysis model to a service organization.

Example   American Parcel Delivery, a parcel service, competes with the U.S. Postal Service and United Parcel Service. Each driver is responsible for picking up and delivering parcels in a particular geographic area. One major cost is fuel for the

---

[2]In Chapter 14, we discuss the production volume variance, a fixed manufacturing cost variance that results when the firm uses full-absorption costing to value inventory. The production volume variance is not an eficiency variance. In fact, it has little, if any, information content for managerial purposes.

Exhibit 13.7

VICTORIA CORPORATION
Overview of Variance Analysis

Profit Variance Analysis

	Achieved Profit (based on actual sales volume of 80,000 units) (1)	Purchasing and Production Variances (2)	Marketing and Administrative Cost Variances (3)	Sales Price Variance (4)	Flexible Budget (based on actual sales volume of 80,000 units) (5)
Sales..........................	$488,000	—	—	$8,000 F	$480,000
Less:					
Variable Manufacturing Costs ..	305,600	$12,000 U	—	—	293,600
Variable Marketing Costs	12,800	—	$1,440 U	160 U	11,200
Contribution Margin	$169,600	$12,000 U	$1,440 U	$7,840 F	$175,200
Less:					
Fixed Manufacturing Costs	34,000	1,800 U	—	—	32,200
Fixed Marketing Costs	64,400	—	1,000 F	—	65,400
Fixed Administrative Costs	44,600	—	200 F	—	44,800
Operating Profits	$ 26,600	$13,800 U	$ 240 U	$7,840 F	$ 32,800

Total Profit Variance from Flexible
Budget = $6,200 U

Cost Variance Analysis

ACTUAL Actual price (AP) times actual quantity (AQ) of input for actual production output (AP × AQ) (1)	INPUTS AT STANDARD Standard price (SP) times actual quantity (AQ) of input for actual production output (SP × AQ) (2)	FLEXIBLE PRODUCTION BUDGET Standard price (SP) times standard quantity (SQ) of input allowed for actual output (that is, 80,000 units produced) (SP × SQ) (3)

Direct Materials

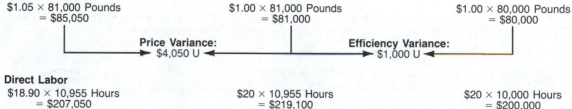

$1.05 × 81,000 Pounds = $85,050

$1.00 × 81,000 Pounds = $81,000

$1.00 × 80,000 Pounds = $80,000

Price Variance: $4,050 U

Efficiency Variance: $1,000 U

Direct Labor

$18.90 × 10,955 Hours = $207,050

$20 × 10,955 Hours = $219,100

$20 × 10,000 Hours = $200,000

Price Variance: $12,050 F

Efficiency Variance: $19,100 U

Variable Manufacturing Overhead

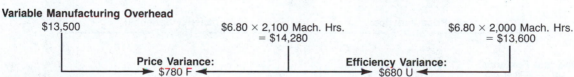

$13,500

$6.80 × 2,100 Mach. Hrs. = $14,280

$6.80 × 2,000 Mach. Hrs. = $13,600

Price Variance: $780 F

Efficiency Variance: $680 U

Totals $305,600	$8,780 F		$20,780 U	$293,600

Total Variances $12,000 U

pick-up and delivery vans. The firm uses a fuel efficiency variance to evaluate the performance of drivers. The firm calculates a standard amount of fuel consumption per parcel, whether delivered or picked up, for each territory. These allowances take the population density of the territory into account—allowing more fuel per parcel for sparsely populated territories, less for densely populated territories. Drivers control this variance primarily by scheduling trips to avoid unnecessary driving.

For a particular territory, the standard was .08 gallon of fuel per parcel. The driver assigned to this territory handled 1,100 parcels during March; hence, the budget allows 88 gallons (= 1,100 parcels × .08 gallons per parcel). In all, the driver actually used 93 gallons of fuel. Exhibit 13.8 shows the efficiency variance. Although the driver was not responsible for the fuel price variance, Exhibit 13.8 presents it to complete the comparison of actual with standard. Note the similarity between these calculations and the direct materials and direct labor calculations presented earlier.

Managers often calculate variances for particularly important, controllable overhead items such as power or fuel costs. Computing price and efficiency variances for variable overhead as a total is more difficult. Sometimes managers perform this computation when variable overhead correlates highly with another pro-

Exhibit 13.8

AMERICAN PARCEL DELIVERY
Example, Variable Overhead Efficiency Variance—Fuel Costs

Facts
Actual:

Output..	1,100 Parcels Picked Up or Delivered
Fuel Required..	93 Gallons
Cost per Gallon..	$1.58 per Gallon

Standard:

Fuel Allowed...	.08 Gallon per Parcel Picked Up or Delivered
Cost per Gallon..	$1.60 per Gallon

Actual (AP × AQ)	Inputs at Standard (SP × AQ)	Flexible Production Budget (SP × SQ)
$1.58 per Gallon × 93 Gallons = $146.94	$1.60 per Gallon × 93 Gallons = $148.80	$1.60 per Gallon × (.08 Gallon × 1,100 Parcels) = $1.60 × 88 Gallons = $140.80

Price Variance:
$1.86 F ◄

Efficiency Variance:
$8.00 U ◄

Shortcut Formulas:

$(AP - SP) \times AQ$
$($1.58 - $1.60) \times 93$ Gallons
$= 1.86 F

$SP \times (AQ - SQ)$
$1.60 \times [93$ Gallons $- (.08$ Gallon $\times 1,100$ Parcels$)]$
$= 1.60×5 Gallons
$= 8.00 U

duction input. For example, suppose that variable overhead correlates highly with direct labor hours. The firm could reasonably hold the manager who is responsible for direct labor efficiency variances also responsible for variable overhead efficiency variances.

Use of Variances in Nonmanufacturing Settings

Manufacturing has the most comprehensive set of variances of any type of organization; you should not infer, however, that manufacturing firms are the only ones to use variances. In fact, retail stores, banks, fast-food restaurants, hospitals, and many other organizations use standard costs and variance analyses.

Service organizations use the labor and overhead variances we have calculated. Fast-food restaurants calculate limits for the actual versus standard amount of food served, as well as labor time incurred for food service, cooking, and other labor activities. Banks compute variances for labor time spent in processing transactions. Governmental units compute variances for labor costs required to make inspections, write parking tickets, and so forth.

Nondollar Variances

Sometimes firms do not compute a dollar value for variances. For example, management sometimes computes variances for response time to emergency calls by fire, police, and medical personnel. Other service organizations, such as banks and government offices, measure performance with variances from standard for length of service time. A retail store might measure performance for its clerks in terms of time, rather than in dollars.

In short, variances are an integral part of performance evaluation and decision making. Any situation for which management can establish a standard, norm, or plan lends itself to variance analysis. In this chapter we presented a comprehensive model of variance analysis that you can generalize to many settings. A thorough understanding of that model will allow you to use variances in virtually any setting.

Variance Analysis in High-Technology Companies

The variance analysis model in Exhibit 13.4 generally applies to all types of organizations; however, high-technology firms apply the model somewhat differently. Most changes toward high technology involve substituting computerized equipment for direct labor. Examples include automatic teller machines in banks, robots in manufacturing plants, and word processors in various organizations. The result is less direct labor and more overhead.

The substitution of computerized equipment implies that the firm should treat labor more appropriately as a fixed cost than as a variable cost. In high-technology manufacturing companies employees monitor and maintain machines rather than produce output. Labor efficiency variances may no longer be meaningful because direct labor is a capacity cost, not a cost expected to vary with output. Variable overhead may associate more with machine usage than labor hours. Some high-technology manufacturing organizations have found that the two largest variable costs involve materials and power to operate machines. If so, the model in Exhibit 13.4 would apply to those costs.

■ Summary ■

Variances between actual results and norms or standards provide a basis for management to take corrective actions where necessary, penalize and reward employees, and revise goals, plans, and budgets. In this chapter we presented fundamental variance analysis models that are the basis for variance calculations in organizations. Variance analysis is rooted in the philosophy of management by exception, which focuses managerial attention on exceptions, or variances, from the norm.

Management generally assigns responsibility for variances as follows:

Departments	Responsible For
Marketing	Sales Price Variances, Sales Volume Variances, Sales Mix Variances, Marketing Cost Variances
Administration	Administrative Cost Variances
Purchasing	Materials Purchase Price Variances
Production	Direct Materials Usage Variances, Direct Materials Mix Variances, Direct Labor Variances, Manufacturing Overhead Variances

The general model for calculating variable cost variances follows:

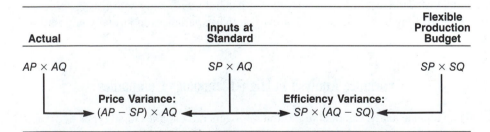

Firms commonly apply this model to direct materials and direct labor costs, but also may apply it to variable marketing costs, variable overhead costs, or any other variable costs.

Why do variances occur? We can classify most reasons for variances as one of the following:

1. Random variation of actual around the standard. Some fluctuation is normal and not worth your concern.

2. Bias in setting the standard (that is, standard is tighter or looser than the expected cost under normal operating conditions). If management intends this bias, it leaves the standard alone; if not, it adjusts the standard to remove the bias.

3. Systematic variance not due to bias in the standard.

Of these three reasons, only the third may require investigation and correction, assuming that the benefits of investigation and correction exceed the costs.

Variable cost variances are often split into price and efficiency components.

1. The price component refers to the difference between the actual price and the standard price allowed per unit. If the accounting system expresses the price variance as a total amount, that total is the price variance per unit times the actual units purchased.

2. The efficiency variance is a measure of productivity. It compares the actual input used to make the actual output with the standard allowed to make the actual output. Note that the accounting system bases the efficiency variance on *actual* output, not budgeted output. If the system calculates manufacturing cost efficiency (for example, efficiency in using labor to manufacture products), the relevant measure of output is production volume.

Exhibit 13.9 diagrams all the variances discussed. It breaks down the $15,700 total favorable variance from Exhibit 13.1 into components and shows their assignment to responsibility centers—marketing, administration, purchasing, and production. Generally, accounting systems report variances in much more detail than we show here. The analysis shows more detailed cost items—by type of direct material, labor, and overhead, for example.

Problem for Self-Study[3]

During the past month, the following events took place at Computer Supply, Inc.:

1. Produced 50,000 and sold 40,000 minicomputer cases at a sales price of $10 each. (Budgeted sales were 45,000 units at $10.15.)

2. Standard variable costs per unit (that is, per case) were as follows:

Direct Materials: 2 Pounds at $1 per Pound	$2.00
Direct Labor: .10 Hours at $15 per Hour	1.50
Variable Manufacturing Overhead: .10 Labor Hours at $5 per Hour	.50
Total	$4.00 per Case

3. Fixed Manufacturing overhead cost was as follows:

Monthly Budget	$80,000

---

[3]This problem continues Problem 1 for Self-Study in Chapter 12.

Exhibit 13.9

VICTORIA CORPORATION
Variance Diagram

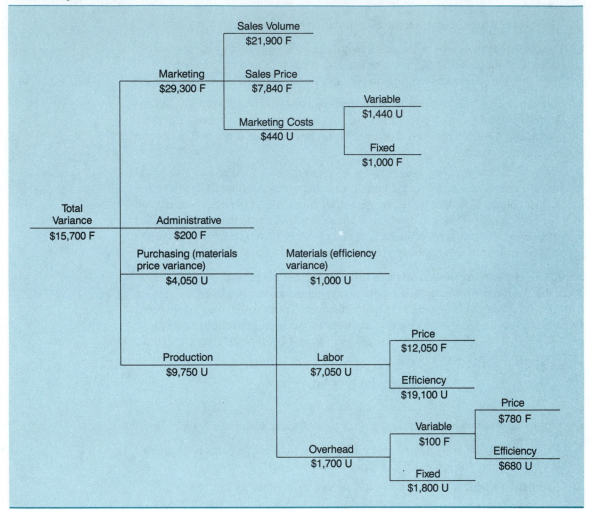

4. Actual production costs were as follows:

Direct Materials Purchased and Used: 110,000 Pounds at $1.20	$132,000
Direct Labor: 6,000 Hours at $14.....................................	84,000
Variable Overhead	28,000
Fixed Overhead	83,000

Compute variable manufacturing cost variances in as much detail as possible.

Suggested Solution

Variable manufacturing cost variances:

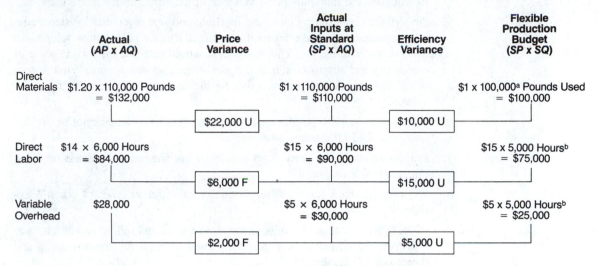

	Actual (AP x AQ)	Price Variance	Actual Inputs at Standard (SP x AQ)	Efficiency Variance	Flexible Production Budget (SP x SQ)
Direct Materials	$1.20 x 110,000 Pounds = $132,000		$1 x 110,000 Pounds = $110,000		$1 x 100,000[a] Pounds Used = $100,000
		$22,000 U		$10,000 U	
Direct Labor	$14 x 6,000 Hours = $84,000		$15 x 6,000 Hours = $90,000		$15 x 5,000 Hours[b] = $75,000
		$6,000 F		$15,000 U	
Variable Overhead	$28,000		$5 x 6,000 Hours = $30,000		$5 x 5,000 Hours[b] = $25,000
		$2,000 F		$5,000 U	

[a]Standard direct materials pounds used in production per unit times units produced (2 pounds × 50,000 units).

[b].10 × 50,000 units produced.

Key Terms and Concepts

Management by exception
Price variance
Efficiency variance
Standard quantity of input allowed to produce actual output
Standard cost allowed to produce actual output
Actual costs incurred to produce actual output

Materials price variance
Materials efficiency variance
Direct labor price variance
Direct labor efficiency variance
Variable overhead price variance
Variable overhead efficiency variance

Questions, Exercises, Problems, and Cases

Questions

1. Review the meaning of the concepts or terms given above in Key Terms and Concepts.

2. Why is a materials efficiency variance typically not calculated for the purchasing activity?

3. Why is a materials price variance typically not calculated for the production activity?

4. Comment on the following statement: "If both materials purchases and materials usage are the responsibility of the production department, it is just as well to calculate the materials price variance at the time materials are used."

5. An airline is considering changing its flight and seat reservation system, enabling customers to make reservations directly using push button telephones and computer terminals. This innovation would increase the airline's use of computers and almost eliminate the use of reservations agents. What impact would this change have on variances for the department responsible for reservations?

6. Why might the total variable manufacturing overhead variance not be divided into price and efficiency components?

7. For control purposes, why is an efficiency variance not calculated for fixed manufacturing overhead?

8. "Timely feedback means different things for different types of costs." Explain.

9. "The control systems for manufacturing overhead and selling and administrative costs are frequently not as sophisticated as those for direct material and direct labor." Explain.

10. How would you compute price and efficiency variances for taxicab drivers where the major variable costs are drivers' wages and automobile costs?

Exercises

11. *Materials and labor variances.* The Rubber Duck Company produces toys. Recently established standard costs are as follows: Materials, 5 pieces per unit at $.20 per piece; Labor, .50 hour per unit at $4.50 per hour. In November, 28,000 pieces of material were purchased for $5,040. Twenty-seven thousand pieces of material were used in producing 5,000 units of finished product. Labor costs were $12,015 for 2,700 hours worked.
    a. Compute the materials price variance.
    b. Compute the materials efficiency variance.
    c. Compute the labor price variance.
    d. Compute the labor efficiency variance.

12. *Materials and labor variances.* The Space Invader Company's budget contains these standards for materials and direct labor for a unit of 10 boxes:

Material—2 Pounds at $.50 per Pound	$1.00
Direct Labor—1 Hour at $4.50	4.50

Although the firm budgeted 100,000 units for September, it produced only 97,810. It purchased two hundred thousand pounds of materials for $105,500. Production used materials weighing 193,880 pounds. Direct labor costs were $396,800 for 99,200 hours:
    a. Compute the materials price variance.
    b. Compute the materials efficiency variance.

    c. Compute the labor price variance.

    d. Compute the labor efficiency variance.

13. *Materials and labor variances.* Crusty Croissants presents the following data for October:

	Standards per Batch	Actual
Materials	2 Pounds at $5 per Pound	195,000 Pounds
Labor	3 Hours at $6 per Hour	280,000 Hours
Units Produced................		96,000 Batches

During the month, the firm purchased 100,000 pounds of materials for $505,500. Wages earned were $1,708,000. Compute all labor and material variances.

14. *Solving for materials quantities and costs.* Crystal Clear Pool Services uses from one to three chemicals to clean swimming pools. Variance data for the month follow (F indicates favorable variance; U indicates unfavorable variance):

	Chemical A	Chemical B	Chemical C
Materials Price Variance..........	$ 42,000 F	$ 25,000 F	$ 21,000 U
Materials Efficiency Variance......	40,000 U	30,000 U	48,000 U
Net Materials Variance	$ 2,000 F	$ 5,000 U	$ 69,000 U
Pools Cleaned Requiring this Chemical	100,000	110,000	125,000

The budget allowed two pounds of each kind of chemical for each pool cleaning requiring that kind of chemical. For chemical A, the average price paid was $.20 per pound less than standard; for chemical B, $.10 less; for chemical C, $.07 greater. The firm purchased and used all chemicals in a given period.

    For each of the three types of chemicals, calculate the following:

    a. Number of pounds of material purchased.

    b. Standard cost per pound of material.

    c. Total standard material cost.

15. *Nonmanufacturing variances.* Direct Marketing Company uses standard costs and variances for controlling costs. As a result of studying past cost data, it has established standards as follows: variable costs, $2 per sales call; 10 sales calls per unit sold. Actual data for January, February, and March follow:

	Sales Calls	Units Sold	Actual Costs
January	320,000	30,000	$650,000
February......................	310,000	40,000	610,000
March	260,000	20,000	570,000

Compute the variable cost price and efficiency variances for each month.

16. *Labor and overhead variances (adapted from CPA exam).* The following data relate to the current month's activities of the Southside Video Productions:

Actual Total Direct Labor	$43,400
Actual Hours Worked	14,000
Standard Hours Allowed for Actual Output (flexible budget)	15,000
Direct Labor Price Variance	$1,400 U
Actual Total Overhead	$32,000
Budgeted Fixed Costs	$9,000
Actual Fixed Overhead Costs	$9,100
Standard Variable Overhead Rate per Direct Labor Hour	$1.50

Compute the following variances:
a. Labor and overhead price variances.
b. Labor and overhead efficiency variances.
c. Fixed overhead price variance.

17. *Materials variances.* Information on Milwaukee Company's direct materials costs is as follows:

Actual Quantities of Direct Materials Used	20,000
Actual Costs of Direct Materials Used	$40,000
Standard Price per Unit of Direct Materials	$2.10
Flexible Budget for Direct Materials	$41,000

a. What was Milwaukee Company's direct materials price variance?
b. What was the company's direct materials efficiency variance?

18. *Overhead variances.* Hyperspace, Inc., which uses standard costing, shows the following overhead information for the current period:

Actual Overhead Incurred	$12,600 of which $3,500 Is Fixed
Budgeted Fixed Overhead	3,300
Variable Overhead Rate per Machine Hour	$3
Standard Hours Allowed for Actual Production	3,500
Actual Machine Hours Used	3,200

What are the variable overhead price and efficiency variances and the fixed overhead price variance?

19. *Solving for labor hours.* Second Interstate Bank reports the following direct labor information for clerical staff in its commercial lending department:

Month: October	
Standard Rate	$6.00 per Hour
Actual Rate Paid	$6.10 per Hour
Standard Hours Allowed for Actual Production	1,500 Hours
Labor Efficiency Variance	$600 U

What are the actual hours worked?

20. *Finding purchase price*. Information on Gretsky Softball Company's direct materials cost is as follows:

Standard Price per Materials Unit	$3.60
Actual Quantity Used	1,600
Standard Quantity Allowed for Production	1,450
Materials Price Variance...	$240 F

What was the actual purchase price per unit, rounded to the nearest cent?

Problems

21. *Hospital supply variances*. Healthy Hospital had the following supplies costs for two products used in its operating room. Standard costs for one surgery: Item A, 10 pieces at $100 each; Item B, 20 pieces at $150 each. During August the following data apply to the hospital:

Surgeries Performed	2,000
Supplies Purchased and Used:	
Item A...	22,000 Pieces at $90
Item B...	39,000 Pieces at $152

Compute materials price and efficiency variances.

22. *Labor variances*. Quicki-Burger has two categories of direct labor: unskilled, which costs $8 per hour; and skilled, which costs $12 per hour. Management had established standards per "equivalent meal," which it has defined as a typical meal consisting of a sandwich, a drink, and a side order. Managers set standards as follows: skilled labor, 4 minutes per equivalent meal; unskilled labor, 10 minutes per equivalent meal. During May, Quicki-Burger sold 30,000 equivalent meals and incurred the following labor costs:

Skilled Labor: 1,600 Hours	$19,000
Unskilled Labor: 4,200 Hours	37,000

Compute labor price and efficiency variances.

23. *Overhead variances*. The manufacturing overhead costs of Windum Industries, Inc., separate into fixed and variable components. The flexible budget for overhead costs follows: fixed costs, $100,000 per period; variable costs, $10 per unit. During the period, 20,000 units were produced. Actual manufacturing overhead costs were $350,000.

   a. Compute the total manufacturing overhead variance.

   b. Assume that, of the $350,000 total overhead costs incurred, $120,000 were fixed costs and $230,000 were variable costs. Compute the total fixed cost variance and the total variable cost variance.

    c.   Assume that each unit of output requires 2 hours of labor and that variable overhead costs vary both with labor hours and units of output. Thus the firm expects variable overhead costs to be $10 per unit or $5 per direct labor hour. During the period, the firm used 42,000 labor hours to produce 20,000 units of output. Split the total variable overhead variance computed in part **b** into a price variance and an efficiency variance.

24. *Labor and overhead variances.* Direct labor and variable overhead standards per finished unit for Columbia Metals Company are as follows: direct labor, 10 hours at $5.00 per hour; variable overhead, 10 hours at $2.00 per hour. During July, the firm produced 5,000 finished units. Direct labor costs were $234,000 (52,000 hours). Actual variable overhead costs were $103,000.

    a.   Compute the price and efficiency variances for direct labor.

    b.   Compute the price and efficiency variances for variable overhead.

    c.   What similar factors cause both the direct labor price variance and the variable overhead price variance?

    d.   What similar factors cause both the direct labor efficiency variance and the variable overhead efficiency variance?

25. *Performance evaluation in a service industry.* National Insurance Company estimates that its overhead costs for policy administration should be $72 for each new policy obtained and $2 per year for each $1,000 face amount of insurance outstanding. The company set a budget of 5,000 new policies for the coming period. In addition, the company estimated that the total face amount of insurance outstanding for the period would equal $10,800,000.

    During the period, actual costs related to new policies amounted to $358,400. A total of 4,800 new policies were obtained.

    The cost of maintaining existing policies was $23,200. Had the firm incurred these costs at the same prices as were in effect when it prepared the budget, the costs would have amounted to $22,900. However, $12,100,000 in policies were outstanding during the period.

    Prepare a schedule to indicate the differences between a master production budget and actual costs for this operation.

26. *Manufacturing variances.* The standard cost of Acme Company's product A comprises the following items: material, 6 pounds at $.75 per pound; labor, 1 hour at $5.00 per hour; and overhead, $2,500 per month plus $2.50 per unit. During January, the firm purchased 30,000 pounds of material at an average cost of $.76 a pound and used 29,000 pounds; the firm used 5,000 direct labor hours at an average rate of $5.05 per hour; and actual overhead costs were $15,500, of which $2,400 was fixed. The firm started and completed 5,000 units during the month.

    Compute the amount of each of the following variances:

    a.   Materials price variance.

    b.   Materials efficiency variance.

    c.   Labor price variance.

    d.   Labor efficiency variance.

    e.   Total overhead variances in as much detail as possible.

27. *Manufacturing variances.* Alger Company manufactures salad bowls. The company makes two types of bowls, A and B, from the same material. The company has no fixed overhead. The following are the standards and production data for November:

	Bowl A	Bowl B
Standard Costs		
Raw Materials.................	$ .25	$ .50
	(.05 pounds at $5.00)	(.10 pounds at $5.00)
Labor	.40	.45
	(6 minutes at $4.00)	(6 minutes at $4.50)
Overhead.....................	1.60 per	1.50 per
	Direct Labor Hour	Direct Labor Hour
Production Data for November		
Units........................	5,000	3,000
Pounds of Raw Materials		
Used........................	250	305
Direct Labor Hours Used	500	299
Labor Costs Incurred	$2,060.00	$1,330.55

Total overhead was $1,236. The firm has decided to allocate this amount proportionately to the total costs of the two products on the basis of standard direct labor hours. The firm purchased one thousand pounds of raw materials for $5,020. The labor efficiency variance for bowl A was zero.
a. Compute the raw materials price variance.
b. Compute the raw materials efficiency variance for bowl A and for bowl B.
c. Compute the direct labor price and efficiency variances for bowl A and for bowl B.
d. Compute the variable overhead price and efficiency variances for bowl A and for bowl B.

28. *Solving for materials and labor.* Under the flexible budget of the Ceramic Tile Company, budgeted variable overhead is $60,000 when the firm uses 60,000 direct labor hours, whereas budgeted direct labor costs are $300,000. All data apply to the month of February.

The following are some of the variances for February (F denotes favorable; U denotes unfavorable):

Variable Overhead Price Variance	$12,000 U
Variable Overhead Efficiency Variance	10,000 U
Materials Price Variance...	15,000 F
Materials Efficiency Variance......................................	8,000 U

During February, the firm incurred $325,500 of direct labor costs. According to the standards, 1 pound of material should cost $2.00. One pound of material is the standard for each unit of product. The firm produced one hundred thousand units in February. The unit materials price variance was $.20 per pound, whereas the average wage rate exceeded the standard average rate by $.25.

Compute the following for February, assuming opening but no closing inventories of materials:

a. Pounds of materials purchased.

b. Pounds of material usage over standard.

c. Standard hourly wage rate.

d. Standard direct labor hours for the total February production.

29. *Manufacturing variances.* The Old Style Company mass-produces children's desks. The standard costs follow:

Wood	25 Pounds at $3.20 per Pound
Trim..	8 Pounds at $5.00 per Pound
Direct Labor	5 Hours at $6.00 per Hour
Variable Overhead............................	$15 per Unit
Fixed Overhead	$62,000 per Period

Transactions during February follow:

(1) The firm purchased 80 tons of wood at $3.25 per pound and issued 155,000 pounds to production.

(2) The firm purchased 25 tons (50,000 pounds) of trim at $4.80 per pound and issued 48,500 pounds to production.

(3) The direct labor payroll was 31,000 hours at $5.75.

(4) Overhead costs were $151,000, of which $60,500 were fixed.

(5) The firm produced 6,000 desks during February.

Calculate all variances to the extent permitted by the data.

30. *Manufacturing cost variances.* The Seasonal Company makes Christmas cards and other greeting cards. The firm budgets fixed overhead at $6,000 per month. The firm expects variable overhead of $9,500 when it uses 10,000 direct labor hours per month.

The following data are available for April (F denotes favorable; U denotes unfavorable):

Materials Purchased	20,000 Units
Direct Labor Costs Incurred......................................	$36,000
Total Direct Labor Variance	$500 F
Average Actual Wage Rate ($.20 less than the standard wage rate) ..	$4.80
Variable Overhead Costs Incurred	$6,675
Materials Price Variance..	$200 F
Materials Efficiency Variance......................................	$610 F
Price of Purchased Materials	$.60 per Unit
Materials Used	15,000 Units
Actual Fixed Overhead	$7,200

Using these data, identify and present computations for all variances.

31. *Manufacturing cost variances.* The standard materials and labor cost per unit for the manufacturing departments of the Davis Company are as follows:

Materials, 2 Pounds of Material A at $3.00	$6.00
Labor, 4 Standard Hours at $2.00 per Hour	8.00

The flexible budget shows the following monthly allowances for manufacturing overhead costs:

	8,000 Units	10,000 Units	12,000 Units
Units Produced..............			
Manufacturing Overhead Costs:			
Fixed......................	$30,000	$30,000	$30,000
Variable	32,000	40,000	48,000
Total Manufacturing Overhead Costs	$62,000	$70,000	$78,000

During the month of December, manufacturing completed 8,000 units at the following costs:

Materials Purchased and Used, 16,200 Pounds at $3.20................	$51,840
Direct Labor, 31,800 Hours at $2.10	66,780
Manufacturing Overhead Costs ($32,000 fixed, $31,000 variable)	63,000

Compute all possible variances.

32. *Controlling labor costs.* Kellogg Hospital has a contract with its full-time nurses that guarantees a minimum of $2,000 per month to each nurse with at least 12 years of service. One hundred employees currently qualify for coverage. All nurses receive $20 per hour.

The direct labor budget for Year 1 anticipates an annual usage of 400,000 hours at $20 per hour, or a total of $8,000,000. Management believes that, of this amount, $200,000 (100 nurses × $2,000) per month (or $2,400,000 for the year) was fixed. Thus the budgeted labor costs for any given month resulted from the formula Budgeted Labor Costs = $200,000 + $14.00 × direct labor hours worked.

Data on performance for the first 3 months of Year 1 follow:

	January	February	March
Nursing Hours Worked	22,000	32,000	42,000
Nursing Costs Budgeted	$508,000	$648,000	$788,000
Nursing Costs Incurred..............	440,000	640,000	840,000
Variance......................	68,000 F	8,000 F	52,000 U

The results, which show favorable variances when hours worked were low and unfavorable variances when hours worked were high, perplex a hospital administrator. This administrator had believed the control over nursing costs was consistently good.

a. Why did the variances arise? Explain and illustrate, using amounts and diagrams as necessary.

b. Does this budget provide a basis for controlling nursing costs? Explain, indicating changes that management may make to improve control over nursing costs and to facilitate performance evaluation of nurses.

33. *Computing nonmanufacturing cost variances.* Rock City Insurance Company estimates that its overhead costs for policy administration should amount to $82 for each new policy obtained and $2 per year for each $1,000 face amount of insurance outstanding. The company set a budget of selling 6,000 new policies during the coming period. In addition, the company estimated that the total face amount of insurance outstanding for the period would equal $12,000,000.

During the period, actual costs related to new policies amounted to $430,000. The firm sold a total of 6,200 new policies.

The cost of maintaining existing policies was $27,000. Had the firm incurred these costs at the same prices as were in effect when it prepared the budget, the costs would have been $26,000. However, some costs changed. Policies worth $13,000,000 were outstanding during the period.

Prepare a schedule to show the variances between the flexible budget and actual costs for this operation.

34. *Computing variances for marketing costs.* High Pressure Sales, Inc., uses telephone solicitation to sell products. The company has set standards that call for $450 of sales per hour of telephone time. Telephone solicitors receive a commission of 10 percent per dollar sales. The firm expects other variable costs, including costs of sales in the operation, to be 45 percent of sales revenue. It budgets fixed costs at $411,500 per month. The firm computes the number of sales hours per month based on the number of days in a month minus an allowance for idle time, scheduling, and other inefficiencies. This month the firm expected 180 hours of telephone calling time for each of 40 callers.

During the month, the firm earned $2,700,000 of revenues. Actual calling hours amounted to 7,050. Marketing and administrative cost data for the period follow:

	Actual	Master Budget
Cost of Sales	$810,000	$972,000
Telephone Time Charges	32,200	32,400
Delivery Services	161,100	194,400
Uncollectible Accounts	121,500	145,800
Other Variable Costs	112,700	113,400
Fixed Costs	409,000	411,500

Using sales dollars as a basis for analysis, compute the marketing cost variances for the period. Include a measure of the efficiency of marketing operations for the month. (*Hint:* Consider sales volume as an output measure and calling hours as an input.)

Integrative Problems and Cases

35. *Revisions of standards (adapted from CMA exam).* The Lenco Company employs a standard cost system as part of its cost control program. It establishes the standard cost per unit at the beginning of each year. It does not revise standards during the year for any changes in material or labor inputs or in the manufacturing processes. It defers any revisions in standards until the beginning of the next fiscal year. However, to recognize such changes in the current year, the company includes planned variances in the monthly budgets prepared after such changes have been introduced.

It set the following labor standard for one of Lenco's products effective July 1, Year 4, the beginning of the fiscal year.

Class I Labor: 4 Hours at $6	$24.00
Class II Labor: 3 Hours at $7.50	22.50
Class V Labor: 1 Hour at $11.50	11.50
Standard Labor Cost per 100 Units	$58.00

Management set the standard based on the quality of material that it had used in prior years and expected for the Year 4 fiscal year. The labor team consists of four persons with class I skills, three persons with class II skills, and one person with class V skills. The combination is the most economical for the company's processing system.

The manufacturing operations occurred as expected during the first 5 months of the year. The standard costs contributed to effective cost control during this period. However, managers had some indications that operations would require some changes in the last half of the year. The company had received a significant increase in orders for delivery in the spring. An inadequate number of skilled workers were available to meet the increased production. As a result, the production teams, beginning in January, would comprise more class I labor and less class II labor than the standard contemplated. The teams would comprise six class I persons, two class II persons, and one class V person. This labor team would be less efficient than the normal team. The reorganized teams work more slowly, producing only 90 units in the same time period that would normally yield 100 units. The firm will lose no direct materials as a result of the change in the labor mix. The firm has never rejected completed units in the final inspection process as a consequence of faulty work; it expects this practice to continue.

In addition, the material supplier notified Lenco that it would supply a lower-quality material after January 1. Each good unit produced normally requires one unit of direct material. Lenco and its supplier estimated that quality standards will reject 5 percent of the units manufactured upon final inspection due to defective material. The firm had lost no units because of defective material.

a. How much of the lower-quality material must the firm put into production to make 42,750 units of good production in January with the new labor teams? Show your calculations.

b. How many hours of each class of labor will the firm need to produce 42,750 good units from the material input? Show your calculations.

c. What amount should the firm include in the January budget for the planned labor variance caused by the labor team and material changes? What amount of this planned labor variance associates with (1) the material change and (2) the team change? Show your calculations.

36. *Finding budget and actual amounts from variances (knowledge of normal costing is required).* Columbus Company manufactures a new electronic game with the trademark "Dandy." The current standard costs per game are as follows:

Direct Materials, 6 Kilograms at $1 per Kilogram	$ 6 per Game
Direct Labor, 1 Hour at $4 per Hour	4 per Game
Overhead	3 per Game
Total Costs	$13 per Game

The following data appeared in the Columbus Company records at the end of the past month:

Actual Production	4,000 Units
Actual Sales	2,500
Purchases (26,000 kilograms)	$27,300
Materials Price Variance	1,300 U
Materials Efficiency Variance	1,000 U
Direct Labor Price Variance	760 U
Direct Labor Efficiency Variance	800 F
Underapplied Overhead (total)	500 U

The firm computes the materials price variance at the time of purchase.

a. Prepare a schedule showing the flexible production budget, price and efficiency variances, and actual costs for direct materials and direct labor.

b. Assume that all manufacturing overhead is fixed and that the $500 underapplied is the only overhead variance that can be computed. What are the actual and applied overhead amounts?

37. *Comprehensive problem: Tondamakers, Inc.* (See Problem **32** in Chapter 14 for an extension of this problem.) Tondamakers produced and sold 1,000 Tonda riding lawnmowers in Year 1, its first year of operation. Actual costs of production appear on the following page:

Actual Results for the Year:
Direct Materials: 11,000 Pounds at $19 . . . . $209,000
Direct Labor: 2,050 Hours at $31.   63,550
Manufacturing Overhead ($205,000 fixed)   245,000
Actual Marketing and Administrative
  Costs ($320,000 fixed)   380,000
Total Revenue: 1,000 Units at $940   940,000
Actual Machine Hours Worked . . . .   550 Hours
Standard Variable Costs:
Materials: 10 Pounds at $20 . . . . $200
Labor: 2 Hours at $30   60
Variable Overhead: .5 Machine Hours
  at $80.   40
Budget Information:
Budgeted Fixed Manufacturing Costs . . . . $200,000 for Year 1
Master Budget Sales Volume . . . .   900 Tondas
Budgeted Marketing and Administrative
  Costs . . . . $350,000 + $50 per Unit Sold
Budgeted Sales Price . . . . $1,000 per Unit

Prepare profit and cost variance analyses such as those in Exhibit 13.7.

Suggested Solutions to Even-Numbered Exercises

12. *Materials and labor variances*

a. Materials Price Variance $= 200,000 \times \left(\dfrac{\$105,500}{200,000} - \$.50 \right) = \$5,500$ U.

b. Materials Efficiency Variance $= (193,880 - 195,620) \times \$.50 = \$870$ F.

c. Labor Price Variance $= 99,200 \times \left(\dfrac{\$396,800}{99,200} - \$4.50 \right) = \$49,600$ F.

d. Labor Efficiency Variance $= (99,200 - 97,810) \times \$4.50 = \$6,255$ U.

14. *Solving for materials quantities and costs*

Chemical A:

a. Price Variance $= \$.20$ F per Pound.
Total Price Variance $= \$42,000$ F.

$$\text{Pounds Purchased and Used} = \frac{\$42,000}{\$.20} = 210,000.$$

b. Standard Pounds Allowed for 100,000 Units $= 200,000$.
Used over Standard $= 210,000 - 200,000 = 10,000$.
Efficiency Variance $= \$40,000$ U.

$$\text{Standard Unit Price} = \frac{\$40,000}{10,000} = \$4.00.$$

c. 200,000 Pounds $\times$ $4.00 per Pound $= \$800,000$.

Chemical B:

a. $\text{Pounds Purchased and Used} = \dfrac{\$25,000}{\$.10} = 250,000.$

b. Standard Unit Price $= \dfrac{\$30,000}{(250,000 - 220,000)} = \dfrac{\$30,000}{30,000} = \$1.00.$

c. $220,0000 \times \$1.00 = \$220,000.$

Chemical C:

a. Pounds Purchased and Used $= \dfrac{\$21,000}{\$.07} = 300,000.$

b. Standard Unit Price $= \dfrac{\$48,000}{(300,000 - 250,000)} = \$.96.$

c. $250,000 \times \$.96 = \$240,000.$

16. *Labor and overhead variances*

	Actual Costs	Price Variance	Inputs at Standard Prices	Efficiency Variance	Flexible Production Budget
Direct Labor	$43,400		$43,400 − $1,400 = $42,000		15,000 × $3.00ᵃ = $45,000
		→ $1,400 U ←		→ $3,000 F ←	
Variable Overhead	$32,000 − $9,100 = $22,900		14,000 × $1.50 = $21,000		15,000 × $1.50 = $22,500
		→ $1,900 U ←		→ $1,500 F ←	
Fixed Overhead	$9,100				$9,000
		→ $100 U ←			

ᵃ$3.00 per Hour $= \dfrac{\$42,000}{14,000 \text{ Hours}}.$

18. *Overhead variances*

	Actual Costs	Price Variance	Inputs at Standard Prices	Efficiency Variance	Flexible Budget
Variable Overhead	$12,600 − $3,500 = $9,100		$3 × 3,200 Hours = $9,600		$3 × 3,500 Hours = $10,500
		→ $500 F ←		→ $900 F ←	
Fixed Overhead	$3,500				$3,300
		→ $200 U ←			

20. *Finding purchase price*

Actual Costs	Price Variance	Inputs at Standard Prices
1,600 × AP		1,600 × $3.60 = $5,760
	→ $240 F ←	
	1,600 × AP = $5,760 − $240	
	AP = $3.45	

... CHAPTER 14 ...

Measuring and Interpreting Variances: Additional Topics

Chapter Outline
- Fixed Manufacturing Cost Variances
- Effect of Difference between Production and Sales Volumes
- Materials Purchased and Used Are Not Equal
- Mix Variances
- Variance Investigation Models
- Appendix 14.1: Standard Costs

Chapters 12 and 13 presented the fundamental conceptual framework for computing variances that applies to most nonmanufacturing and manufacturing costs and revenues. This chapter shows how analysts modify the profit variance analysis (Chapter 12) and cost variance analysis (Chapter 13) to deal with the following situations:

1. Computing the fixed manufacturing cost production volume variance, which occurs when the firm uses predetermined overhead application rates to apply fixed overhead to products and uses full absorption costing to value inventory.

2. Understanding how to interpret the variances that result when units produced do not equal units sold.

3. Understanding how to interpret the materials purchase price variance when materials purchased do not equal materials used.

4. Computing mix variances.

In addition, we discuss statistical models that help decision makers choose which variances to investigate. Appendix 14.1 presents cost flows through accounts and journal entries used in companies that employ standard costing for inventory valuation.

Because this chapter builds on the profit variance analysis and cost variance analysis from Chapters 12 and 13, Exhibit 14.1 presents an overview of the variances computed in those chapters. Exhibit 14.1 repeats Exhibit 13.7, which summarized the variance computations for the Victoria Corporation example. You may use Exhibit 14.1 to review the variances computed so far and to compare the analyses in this chapter with the work previously done.

Fixed Manufacturing Cost Variances

Chapters 12 and 13 treated fixed costs as lump-sum, period costs in comparing budgeted and actual costs. This practice is appropriate for managing fixed cost expenditures for most managerial purposes. Manufacturing companies, however, use full absorption costing to value inventory, which unitizes fixed manufacturing costs and adds them to variable manufacturing costs to compute the cost of inventory produced.

Companies frequently use a predetermined overhead rate to apply fixed overhead to units produced. For example, assume the following facts for Victoria Corporation:

Estimated (budgeted) Fixed Manufacturing Costs	$32,200
Estimated Production Volume	70,000 Units
Actual Production Volume	80,000 Units
Actual Fixed Manufacturing Costs	$34,000

If Victoria Corporation used full absorption, standard costing, it would apply its fixed manufacturing costs to units as follows:

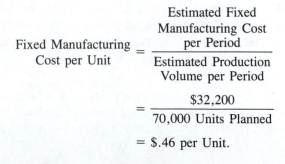

$$\text{Fixed Manufacturing} \atop \text{Cost per Unit} = \frac{\text{Estimated Fixed Manufacturing Cost per Period}}{\text{Estimated Production Volume per Period}}$$

$$= \frac{\$32,200}{70,000 \text{ Units Planned}}$$

$$= \$.46 \text{ per Unit.}$$

Exhibit 14.1

VICTORIA CORPORATION
Overview of Variance Analysis (Exhibit 13.7 is repeated for convenience.)

Profit Variance Analysis

	Achieved Profit (based on actual sales volume of 80,000 units) (1)	Purchasing and Production Variances (2)	Marketing and Administrative Cost Variances (3)	Sales Price Variance (4)	Flexible Budget (based on actual sales volume of 80,000 units) (5)
Sales........................	$488,000	—	—	$8,000 F	$480,000
Less:					
Variable Manufacturing Costs ..	305,600	$12,000 U	—	—	293,600
Variable Marketing Costs	12,800	—	$1,440 U	160 U	11,200
Contribution Margin	$169,600	$12,000 U	$1,440 U	$7,840 F	$175,200
Less:					
Fixed Manufacturing Costs	34,000	1,800 U	—	—	32,200
Fixed Marketing Costs	64,400	—	1,000 F	—	65,400
Fixed Administrative Costs	44,600	—	200 F	—	44,800
Operating Profits	$ 26,600	$13,800 U	$ 240 U	$7,840 F	$ 32,800

Total Profit Variance from Flexible
Budget = $6,200 U

Cost Variance Analysis

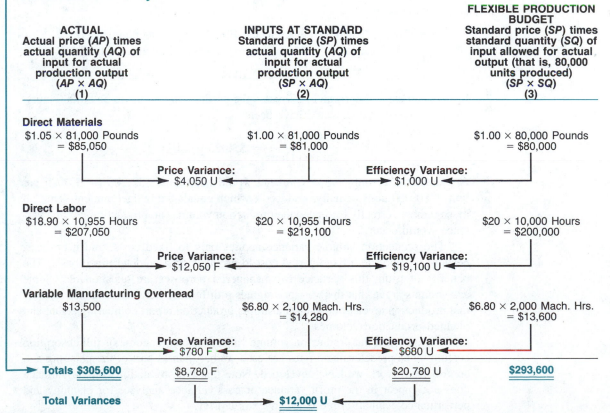

ACTUAL Actual price (AP) times actual quantity (AQ) of input for actual production output (AP × AQ) (1)	INPUTS AT STANDARD Standard price (SP) times actual quantity (AQ) of input for actual production output (SP × AQ) (2)	FLEXIBLE PRODUCTION BUDGET Standard price (SP) times standard quantity (SQ) of input allowed for actual output (that is, 80,000 units produced) (SP × SQ) (3)

Direct Materials

$1.05 × 81,000 Pounds = $85,050 $1.00 × 81,000 Pounds = $81,000 $1.00 × 80,000 Pounds = $80,000

Price Variance: $4,050 U   Efficiency Variance: $1,000 U

Direct Labor

$18.90 × 10,955 Hours = $207,050 $20 × 10,955 Hours = $219,100 $20 × 10,000 Hours = $200,000

Price Variance: $12,050 F   Efficiency Variance: $19,100 U

Variable Manufacturing Overhead

$13,500 $6.80 × 2,100 Mach. Hrs. = $14,280 $6.80 × 2,000 Mach. Hrs. = $13,600

Price Variance: $780 F   Efficiency Variance: $680 U

Totals **$305,600** $8,780 F $20,780 U   **$293,600**

Total Variances   **$12,000 U**

Note that we use production, not sales, volumes to unitize fixed manufacturing costs. If you were to unitize fixed marketing costs, you would divide the cost by sales volume.

During the period, the firm produced 80,000 units, so 80,000 units times $.46 per unit equals $36,800 applied to Work-in-Process Inventory. The amount "applied" is the amount of fixed manufacturing overhead debited to Work-in-Process Inventory. The firm could apply fixed manufacturing costs using an input basis such as machine hours. Assume the standard is 40 units per machine hour, or $\frac{1}{40}$ hour per unit. Then you would compute the rate per hour as follows:

$$\frac{\text{Fixed Manufacturing}}{\text{Cost Rate per Hour}} = \frac{\$32,200}{70,000 \text{ Units} \times \frac{1}{40}} = \frac{\$32,200}{1,750 \text{ Hours}}$$

$$= \$18.40 \text{ per Hour.}$$

The amount applied would still be $36,800 (= $18.40 per Hour $\times \frac{1}{40}$ Hours per Unit $\times$ 80,000 Units = $18.40 per Hour $\times$ 2,000 Hours).

Production Volume Variance

Applied fixed manufacturing overhead would have been $32,200 (= $.4025 per Unit $\times$ 80,000 units actually produced), which equals the budget amount. Thus, if management correctly estimated the production volume, no production volume variance would occur.

$$\frac{\text{Production Volume}}{\text{Variance}} = \frac{\text{Budgeted Fixed}}{\text{Manufacturing Costs}} - \frac{\text{Applied Fixed}}{\text{Manufacturing Costs}}$$

$$\$4,600 \text{ F} \quad = \quad \$32,200 \quad - \quad \$36,800.$$

If management had accurately estimated the production volume to be 80,000 units, the estimated unit cost would have been

$$\frac{\$32,200}{80,000 \text{ Units}} = \$.4025 \text{ per Unit.}$$

Applied fixed manufacturing overhead would have been $32,200 (= $.4025 per unit $\times$ 80,000 units actually produced), which equals the budget amount. Thus, if management correctly estimated the production volume, no production volume variance would occur.

The production volume variance applies only to fixed costs, and it emerges because we allocate a fixed period cost to products on a predetermined basis. The benefits of using this variance for managerial purposes are questionable. Some accountants argue that this variance signals a difference between expected and actual production levels, but so does a simple production report comparing actual and planned production volumes.

We approach the production volume variance as an outcome of full absorption costing when predetermined rates are used, rather than as part of the planning and control framework we have developed. Note that the production volume variance does not appear in the profit variance or cost variance analyses for planning and performance evaluation presented in Exhibit 14.1.

Price (Spending) Variance

Recall from Chapter 13 that the **price variance** (sometimes called the **spending variance**) **for fixed manufacturing costs** is the difference between the actual costs and the budgeted costs. Compute the fixed manufacturing price variance for Victoria Corporation as follows:

$$\begin{array}{c}\text{Price} \\ \text{Variance}\end{array} = \begin{array}{c}\text{Actual Fixed} \\ \text{Manufacturing Costs}\end{array} - \begin{array}{c}\text{Budgeted Fixed} \\ \text{Manufacturing Costs}\end{array}$$

$$\$1,800 \text{ U} = \qquad \$34,000 \qquad - \qquad \$32,200.$$

Although we use manufacturing costs for this example, you can compute the price variance this way for any fixed cost.

The fixed manufacturing cost variance used for management and control of fixed manufacturing costs is the price variance, whereas the **fixed manufacturing cost production volume variance** occurs only when we compute inventory values using full absorption costing and predetermined overhead rates.

Relation of Actual, Budget, and Applied Fixed Manufacturing Costs

Fixed manufacturing cost variances and the relation among actual, budget, and applied fixed manufacturing costs appears in Exhibit 14.2. A graphic presentation appears in Exhibit 14.3.

Effect of Difference between Production and Sales Volumes

Until now, in our variance analysis we assumed that actual production volume equals actual sales volume. Although the conceptual models for variance analysis presented in Chapters 12 and 13 still apply, introducing inventory changes that

Exhibit 14.2

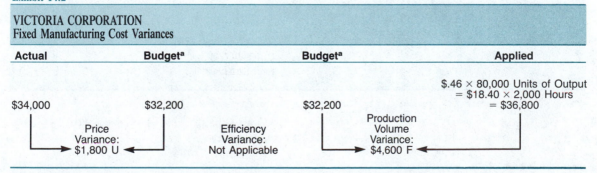

VICTORIA CORPORATION
Fixed Manufacturing Cost Variances

Actual	Budgetᵃ		Budgetᵃ		Applied

$.46 × 80,000 Units of Output
= $18.40 × 2,000 Hours
= $36,800

$34,000 $32,200 $32,200 $36,800

Price Variance: $1,800 U   Efficiency Variance: Not Applicable   Production Volume Variance: $4,600 F

ᵃNote that the master and flexible budgets for fixed costs do not differ here because we assume fixed costs do not vary with volume. If fixed costs differed in the flexible budget from the master budget, you would use the flexible budget fixed costs to compute these variances, because we use the flexible budget for performance evaluation and control purposes.

Exhibit 14.3

VICTORIA CORPORATION
Graphic Presentation of Fixed Overhead Variances

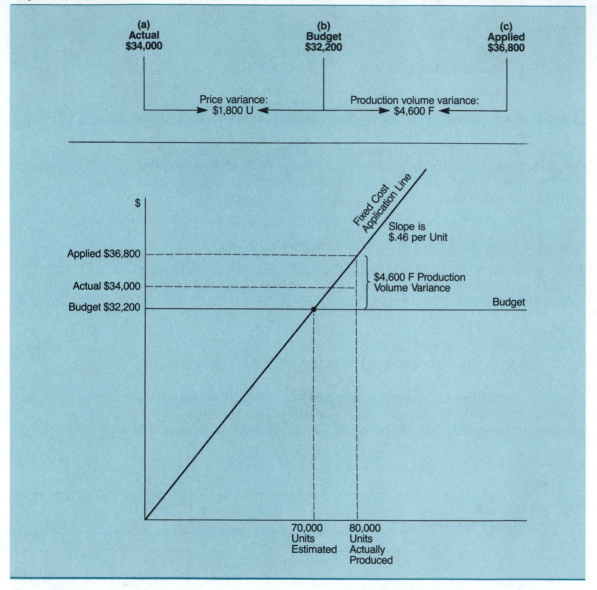

Exhibit 14.4

VICTORIA CORPORATION Modified Example When Production Volume Does Not Equal Sales Volume		
	Actual Costs Incurred to Make 85,000 Units	**Standard Allowed to Produce 85,000 Units**
Variable Manufacturing Costs:		
Direct Materials......................	$1.05 per Pound × 86,063 Pounds = $90,366	$1.00 per Pound × 1 pound per Unit × 85,000 Units Produced = $85,000
Direct Labor........................	$18.90 per Hour × 11,640 Hours = $219,996	$20 per Hour × $\frac{1}{8}$ Hour per Unit × 85,000 Units Produced = $20 × 10,625 Hours = $212,500
Variable Manufacturing Overhead (2,230 actual machine hours)[a].................	$14,338	$6.80 per Mach. Hr.[a] × $\frac{1}{40}$ Mach. Hr. per Unit × 85,000 Units Produced = $6.80 × 2,125 Mach. Hrs. = $14,450
Total Variable Manufacturing Costs	$324,700	$311,950

Note: We round unit amounts to nearest whole cent and totals to the nearest whole dollar.

[a]Victoria uses machine hours to apply variable overhead to units produced. The standard machine hour usage is $\frac{1}{40}$ hour per unit; actual machine hours used for the period totaled 2,230 hours.

occur when production and sales volumes differ creates potential problems for interpreting and using variances.

So far, we have assumed that actual production and sales volume equal 80,000 units for Victoria Corporation. Now we let production and sales be unequal, as follows:

	Actual	**Planned**
Production Volume..	85,000	70,000
Sales Volume	80,000	70,000

Assume no beginning inventories and that ending inventory comprises only finished goods. The revised variable manufacturing cost data reflecting the higher production volume appear in Exhibit 14.4. (Note that both actual and standard variable manufacturing costs are higher than when the volume was 80,000 units. Because the standard results from a flexible budget, it changes as the production volume changes.)

Other facts are the same as in the previous Victoria Corporation example—we repeat them in the table on page 623 for convenience:

Exhibit 14.5

VICTORIA CORPORATION
Comparison of Achieved to Budget When Production and Sales Volumes Are Not Equal
(incomplete report)

	Achieved Using Standard Variable Costing to Value Inventory (actual sales of 80,000 units) (1)	Purchasing and Production Variances (2)	Marketing and Administrative Cost Variances (3)	Sales Price Variance (4)	Flexible Budget Using Standard Variable Costing to Value Inventory (actual sales of 80,000 units) (5)	Sales Volume Variance (6)	Master Budget Using Standard Variable Costing to Value Inventory (based on a plan of 70,000 units sold) (7)
Sales................................	$488,000	—	—	$8,000 F	$480,000	$60,000 F	$420,000
Less:							
Variable Manufacturing Costs Incurred................	?	?			?	36,700 U	256,900
(Ending Inventory)..............	(?)	(?)			(?)	(0)	(0)
Variable Manufacturing Costs Expensed................	?	?			?	36,700 U	256,900
Variable Manufacturing and Administrative Costs......	12,800		1,440 U	160 U	11,200	1,400 U	9,800
Contribution Margin..............	$?	$?	$1,440 U	$7,840 F	$?	$21,900 F	$153,300
Less:							
Fixed Manufacturing Costs.....	34,000	1,800 U	—	—	32,200	—	32,200
Fixed Marketing Costs..........	64,400	—	1,000 F	—	65,400	—	65,400
Fixed Administrative Costs.....	44,600	—	200 F	—	44,800	—	44,800
Operating Profits................	$?	$?	$ 240 U	$7,840 F	$?	$21,900 F	$ 10,900

	Actual	Budget or Standard
Sales Price per Unit	$6.10	$6.00
Sales Volume for the Period	80,000 Units	70,000 Units
Variable Manufacturing Costs per Unit	$3.82	$3.67
Variable Marketing Costs per Unit	$.16	$.14
Fixed Manufacturing Costs for the Period	$34,000	$32,200
Fixed Marketing Costs for the Period	$64,400	$65,400
Fixed Administrative Costs for the Period	$44,600	$44,800

Only *sales* volume affects variable selling and administrative costs.

Exhibit 14.5 presents the amounts that do not change when we relax the assumption that sales and production volumes are equal. For example, all of the marketing and administrative costs are the same in Exhibit 14.5 as in Exhibit 14.1, because they do not vary with production volume. A question mark in Exhibit 14.5 indicates the amounts that may change because sales and production volume differ.

Inventory Valuation Using Variable, Standard Costing

Since Victoria produced 85,000 units but sold only 80,000, finished goods inventory increased by 5,000 units. If Victoria Corporation uses variable, standard costing to value inventory, it would value the inventory as follows:

$$\begin{aligned}\text{Inventory Value}\\\text{Using Variable,} &= 5,000 \text{ Units} \times \$3.67\\\text{Standard Costing}\\&= \qquad \$18,350.\end{aligned}$$

Exhibit 14.4 shows that the total actual variable manufacturing costs incurred are $324,700 for the 85,000 units produced. Victoria only expenses $306,356 for the 80,000 units sold, as follows:

$$\underset{\text{Incurred}}{\text{Costs}} + \underset{\text{Beginning Inventory}}{\text{Costs from}} - \underset{\text{Ending Inventory}}{\text{Costs to}} = \underset{\text{Expensed}}{\text{Costs}}$$

$$\$324,700 + \quad 0 \quad - \quad \$18,350 \quad = \$306,350.$$

The profit variance and cost variance analyses appear in the top and bottom panels of Exhibit 14.6. Line (2) shows the flexible budget and actual variable manufacturing costs based on production of 85,000 units. This line relates the total actual costs to the standard allowed, as well as to the variances at the bottom of the cost variance analysis (see the bottom of Exhibit 14.6).

Line (3) subtracts the inventory value increase that results from adding 5,000 units to inventory. (Using variable, standard costing the amount is $18,350, as noted previously.) Line (4) shows the amount expensed. You should interpret the reported manufacturing variance carefully. The manufacturing variance does not relate to the 80,000 units sold, but to the 85,000 units produced.

Exhibit 14.6

VICTORIA CORPORATION
Variance Analysis

Profit Variance Analysis

	Achieved Using Standard Variable Costing to Value Inventory (actual sales of 80,000 units) (1)	Purchasing and Production Variances (2)	Marketing and Administrative Cost Variances (3)	Sales Price Variance (4)	Flexible Budget Using Standard, Variable Costing to Value Inventory (actual sales of 80,000 units) (5)
(1) Sales....................	$488,000	—	—	$8,000 F	$480,000
(2) Less Variable Manufacturing Costs Incurred	324,700	$12,750 U	—	—	$311,950
(3) (Inventory Increase).......	(18,350)	—	—	—	(18,350)
(4) Variable Manufacturing Costs Expensed	306,350	$12,750 U	—	—	293,600
Variable Marketing Costs ..	12,800	—	$1,440 U	160 U	11,200
Contribution Margin	$168,850	$12,750 U	$1,440 U	$7,840 F	$175,200
Less:					
Fixed Manufacturing Costs	34,000	1,800 U	—	—	32,200
Fixed Marketing Costs ..	64,400	—	1,000 F	—	65,400
Fixed Administrative Costs	44,600	—	200 F	—	44,800
Operating Profits	$ 25,850	$14,550 U	$ 240 U	$7,840 F	$ 32,800

Cost Variance Analysis

Variable Manufacturing Costs

ACTUAL Actual price (AP) times actual quantity (AQ) of input for actual production output (AP × AQ)		INPUTS AT STANDARD Standard price (SP) times actual quantity (AQ) of input for actual production output (SP × AQ)		FLEXIBLE PRODUCTION BUDGET Standard price (SP) times standard quantity (SQ) of input allowed for actual output (that is, 85,000 units produced) (SP × SQ)
Direct Materials $1.05 × 86,063 Pounds = $90,366		$1.00 × 86,063 Pounds = $86,063		$1.00 × 85,000 Pounds = $85,000
	Price Variance: → $4,303 U ←		Efficiency Variance: → $1,063 U ←	
Direct Labor $18.90 × 11,640 Hours = $219,996		$20 × 11,640 Hours = $232,800		$20 × 10,625 Hours = $212,500
	Price Variance: → $12,804 F ←		Efficiency Variance: → $20,300 U ←	
Variable Manufacturing Overhead $14,338		$6.80 × 2,230 Mach. Hrs. = $15,164		$6.80 × 2,125 Mach. Hrs. = $14,450
	Price Variance: → $826 F ←		Efficiency Variance: → $714 U ←	
Actual Totals **$324,700**				**Standard Allowed** **$311,950**

Total Variable Manufacturing Cost Variance → $12,750 U ←

Note that none of the current period manufacturing variance went into inventory; all of it became expense. Thus the manufacturing cost variance reported on the financial statements measures performance for the activity in production and purchasing that occurred during this period, regardless of when the goods are sold. As an alternative, you may prorate variances to inventories, which converts inventories to **actual costs.**

Prorating Variances

Analysts sometimes prorate, or allocate, manufacturing cost variances to inventory. For example, suppose we had allocated the variable manufacturing cost variance of $12,750, 5/85 to inventory and 80/85 to cost of goods sold, as follows:

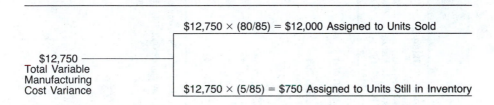

$12,750 × (80/85) = $12,000 Assigned to Units Sold

$12,750
Total Variable
Manufacturing
Cost Variance

$12,750 × (5/85) = $750 Assigned to Units Still in Inventory

In this case, lines (2), (3), and (4) in Exhibit 14.6 would appear as shown in Exhibit 14.7. The 5,000 unit increase in inventory now carries actual, variable costs. The variable manufacturing cost variance now relates to the 80,000 units sold, not the 85,000 units produced.

Exhibit 14.7

VICTORIA CORPORATION
Costs Reported When the Accounting System Prorates Variances
(adaptation of Exhibit 14.6)

	Achieved Using Actual, Variable Costing to Value Inventory[a] (1)	Purchasing and Production Variances (2)	...	Flexible Budget[b] (5)
(2) Variable Manufacturing Costs Incurred	$324,700	$12,750 U	. . .	$311,950
(3) (Inventory Increase)	(19,100)[c]	(750)[d]	. . .	(18,350)
(4) Variable Manufacturing Costs Expensed	$305,600	$12,000 U	. . .	$293,600

[a]Prorating variances converts standard costs in inventory to actual costs.

[b]The inventory value under the flexible budget is at standard, not actual.

[c]$19,100 = $18,350 standard, variable cost + $750 of the total allocated to inventory.

[d]We allocate $750 of the total variance to inventory: $750 = (5,000 units inventory increase/85,000 total units produced) × $12,750 total variable manufacturing cost variance.

Exhibit 14.8

VICTORIA CORPORATION
Reconciling Variable and Full Absorption Costing

	Achieved Using Standard, Full Absorption Costing to Value Inventory (1a)	Full Absorption Inventory Adjustment: Add Fixed Manufacturing Costs to Inventory (1b)	Achieved Using Standard, Variable Cost to Value Inventory (from Exhibit 14.6) (1)
Sales..............................	$488,000	—	$488,000
Less:			
Variable Manufacturing Costs Expensed	306,350	—	306,350
Variable Marketing Costs	12,800	—	12,800
Contribution Margin	$168,850	—	$168,850
Less:			
Fixed Manufacturing Costs Expensed	**31,700**[a]	**2,300**[a]	**34,000**
Fixed Marketing Costs	64,400	—	64,400
Fixed Administrative Costs	44,600	—	44,600
Operating Profits	$ 28,150[b]	$2,300[b]	$ 25,850[b]

[a]Standard, full absorption costing adds $2,300 (= $.46 per unit × 5,000 units) of current period fixed manufacturing costs to inventory.
[b]Operating profits are $2,300 higher using full absorption costing because full absorption costing inventories $2,300 of fixed manufacturing cost that variable costing expenses.

Common Practice Does Not Prorate Variances Companies generally do *not* prorate variances for internal reporting purposes. When prorating minimally affects inventory values and measures of profit, managers consider it a waste of time.

In addition, accountants often do not prorate production variances because managers consider them to be *period* costs. If a variance results from production in a particular period, managers want it reported that period, not in some future period.

What if variances are sufficiently large that failure to prorate would materially misstate fully absorbed cost of inventories and net income for financial reporting to shareholders? In such a case, accountants would prorate variances for external reporting. Even so, they need not prorate variances for internal reporting if prorating them serves no useful purpose. Unless stated otherwise, assume we do not prorate variances; that is, we do not allocate them to inventories.

Inventory Valuation Using Full Absorption, Standard Costs

The variance analyses presented in Exhibit 14.6 aid managerial decision making. Such analyses do not comply with generally accepted accounting principles for external reporting, however, because they do not value inventory using full absorption costing. Manufacturing companies with changes in inventory can reconcile the profits reported in the profit variance analysis with the full absorption amounts shown in Exhibit 14.8. The inventory adjustment column shows the portion of fixed manufacturing cost that full absorption standard costing adds to inventories. The fixed manufacturing cost is $.46 per unit, or $18.40 per machine hour, as computed.

The amount of fixed overhead added to the 5,000 unit inventory increase is $2,300 using full absorption, standard costing, computed as follows:

Units: $.46 $\times$ 5,000 Units $=$ $2,300.
Hours: $18.40 $\times$ (1/40 $\times$ 5,000 Units) $=$ $18.40 $\times$ 125 Hours $=$ $2,300.

Appendix 14.1 presents the flow of costs through T-accounts and journal entries if the firm uses standard, full absorption costing to value inventory.

Materials Purchased and Used Are Not Equal

In the Victoria Corporation example, the direct materials purchased equalled the amount used. What if they are not equal? Are direct materials variances based on *purchases* or *usage?* Accountants generally base the *price* variance on *purchases,* but base the *efficiency* variance on materials *used.*

This practice enables managers to spot price variances at the time the firm purchases materials, rather than waiting until they enter into production. In addition, it emphasizes that the purchasing department has responsibility for purchase price variances at the time of purchase, whereas the manufacturing departments have responsibility for efficiency variances.

For example, if Victoria Corporation had purchased 90,000 pounds of material at $1.05 per pound, used 81,000 pounds, and had a standard of 80,000 pounds, we would modify the cost variance model presented in Exhibit 14.1 as shown in Exhibit 14.9. The purchase price variance would have been $4,500 U [$= 90,000 $\times$ ($1.50 $-$ 1.00)] instead of $4,050 U when the firm purchased only 81,000

Exhibit 14.9

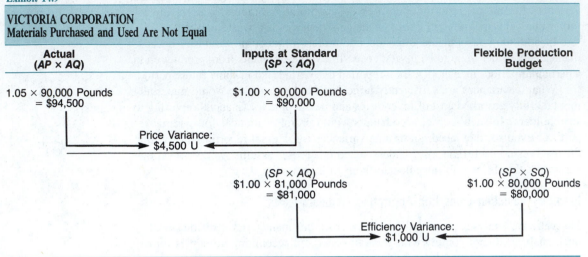

VICTORIA CORPORATION
Materials Purchased and Used Are Not Equal

Actual (AP × AQ)	Inputs at Standard (SP × AQ)	Flexible Production Budget
1.05 × 90,000 Pounds = $94,500	$1.00 × 90,000 Pounds = $90,000	

Price Variance: $4,500 U

| | (SP × AQ) $1.00 × 81,000 Pounds = $81,000 | (SP × SQ) $1.00 × 80,000 Pounds = $80,000 |

Efficiency Variance: $1,000 U

pounds. The efficiency variance would still be $1,000 U [= (81,000 pounds − 80,000 pounds) × $1.00]. Materials inventory would increase by $9,000 [= (90,000 pounds − 81,000 pounds) × $1.00].

Mix Variances

Most organizations use multiple inputs for their output. A hospital uses a combination of registered nurses, licensed practical nurses, and nurse's aides to provide nursing care to patients. A steel company uses a combination of iron ore, coke, and other raw materials to make its product. A **mix variance** shows the impact on profits of using something other than the budgeted mix.

Example   Engineering Associates, a consulting firm, has bid on a particular job assuming 600 hours of partner time at a cost of $80 per hour and 1,400 hours of staff time at $30 per hour. If it gets the job, these hour and cost assumptions become the flexible budget. During the job, scheduling problems arise; the partner spends 1,000 hours because the staff member spends only 1,000 hours. If the cost is actually $80 and $30 for partner and staff time, respectively, no labor price variance occurs. Further, the 2,000 hours required is exactly what was expected. Nevertheless, the job is $20,000 over the flexible budget, as shown in the following calculation:

$$\text{Actual Cost} = (1,000 \text{ Hours} \times \$80) + (1,000 \text{ Hours} \times \$30)$$

$$= \$80,000 + \$30,000$$

$$= \underline{\underline{\$110,000}}.$$

$$\text{Budgeted Cost} = (600 \text{ Hours} \times \$80) + (1,400 \text{ Hours} \times \$30)$$

$$= \$48,000 + \$42,000$$

$$= \underline{\$90,000}.$$

The $20,000 unfavorable variance results from a mix variance: The substitution of 400 hours (= 1,000 hours actual − 600 hours budgeted) of partner time at $80 for 400 hours of staff time at $30. The mix variance is the difference in labor costs per hour of $50 (= $80 − $30) times the 400 hours substituted.

Exhibit 14.10 shows the computation of a mix variance that ties this variance to the previous cost variance analysis. Columns (2) and (3) in the bottom part of Exhibit 14.10 show the mix variance computed from the following difference between actual and budgeted mix:

$$\text{Mix Variance} = \overbrace{\$80 \times |(.5 \times 2{,}000 \text{ Hours}) - (.3 \times 2{,}000 \text{ Hours})|}^{\text{Partner}} -$$

$$\overbrace{\$30 \times |(.5 \times 2{,}000 \text{ Hours}) - (.7 \times 2{,}000 \text{ Hours})|}^{\text{Staff}}$$

$$= (\$80 \times 400 \text{ Hours}) - (\$30 \times 400 \text{ Hours})$$

$$= \underline{\$20{,}000} \text{ Unfavorable.}$$

This example demonstrates the general concept of a mix variance. You should note two factors when considering mix variances. First, consider an assumed *substitutability;* here the manager presumed that partner time was substitutable for staff time. Second, the prices must be different for a mix variance to be nonzero. If the cost per hour were the same for both partner and staff, the substitution of hours would not affect the total cost of the job.

Note that Exhibit 14.10 would have called the mix variance an efficiency variance if we had not calculated a separate mix variance. We call the portion of the efficiency variance that is not a mix variance a **yield variance.** The yield variance measures the input-output relation holding the standard mix of inputs constant.

In this example, we purposely make the yield variance equal to zero to show that the entire variance results from the mix. Problem 2 for Self-Study at the end of this chapter presents a case in which the yield variance is not zero.

Managers use mix variances not only to measure performance when inputs are substitutes, as in the preceding example, but also to measure marketing performance with respect to sales mix. Companies with multiple products assume a particular sales mix in constructing their sales budget. If the actual mix of products sold differs from the budgeted mix, and if the products are substitutes, managers often compute a mix variance to measure the impact of the change in mix from the budget.

Variance Investigation Models

Managers may receive reports that contain hundreds or even thousands of variances. Managerial time is a scarce resource—following up and investigating variances is costly. When confronted with variance reports, managers ask: Which variances should we investigate?

Exhibit 14.10

ENGINEERING ASSOCIATES
Mix Variance

Cost Variances Ignoring Mix Variance

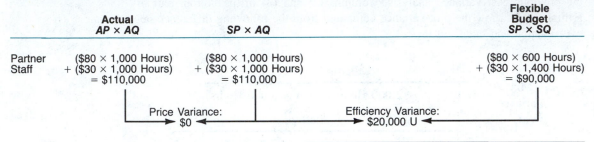

	Actual AP × AQ	SP × AQ		Flexible Budget SP × SQ
Partner Staff	($80 × 1,000 Hours) + ($30 × 1,000 Hours) = $110,000	($80 × 1,000 Hours) + ($30 × 1,000 Hours) = $110,000		($80 × 600 Hours) + ($30 × 1,400 Hours) = $90,000

Price Variance:
→ $0 ←

Efficiency Variance:
→ $20,000 U ←

Cost Variances Considering Mix Variance

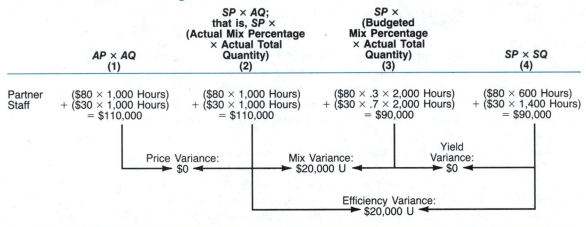

	AP × AQ (1)	SP × AQ; that is, SP × (Actual Mix Percentage × Actual Total Quantity) (2)	SP × (Budgeted Mix Percentage × Actual Total Quantity) (3)	SP × SQ (4)
Partner Staff	($80 × 1,000 Hours) + ($30 × 1,000 Hours) = $110,000	($80 × 1,000 Hours) + ($30 × 1,000 Hours) = $110,000	($80 × .3 × 2,000 Hours) + ($30 × .7 × 2,000 Hours) = $90,000	($80 × 600 Hours) + ($30 × 1,400 Hours) = $90,000

Price Variance:
→ $0 ←

Mix Variance:
→ $20,000 U ←

Yield
Variance:
→ $0 ←

Efficiency Variance:
→ $20,000 U ←

Managers can deal with the decision of whether to investigate a variance like other decisions—on a cost-benefit basis. Hence they should investigate variances if they expect the benefits from investigation to exceed the costs of investigation. These benefits may include improvements from taking corrective action, such as repairing defective machinery, instructing workers who were performing their tasks incorrectly, or changing a standard purchase order so that the firm can purchase cheaper materials. Further, managers generally believe that periodically investigating or auditing employees improves performances. Because measuring the benefits and costs of investigation is often difficult, decisions about the value of investigating variances rely considerably on managerial judgments.

The major cost of **variance investigation** is the opportunity cost of employees' time. Investigators spend time as do those being investigated. Although measuring costs and benefits of variance investigation is difficult, in many cases the benefits are clearly too low or costs are clearly too high to make investigation worthwhile. In other cases variances are so large that obviously something must be done about them.

Managers use a variety of methods to help them ascertain which variances to investigate, including rules of thumb that have worked well in the past (for example, any variance greater than 10 percent of standard cost, any variance that has been unfavorable for 3 months in a row, and so on). Although we emphasize that managerial experience and good judgment are the most important ingredients for variance investigation decisions, accountants have developed some decision aids to assist managers.

Tolerance Limits

Quality control techniques have long relied on the use of tolerance limits. Quality is allowed to fluctuate within predetermined tolerance limits. Applying this concept to variances requires establishing predetermined limits within which variances may fluctuate. These limits may differ for various cost items. For example, managers usually allow greater tolerance for direct materials prices than for labor efficiency, because they have less control over the former because of market fluctuations. Some managers set tighter tolerance limits for unfavorable variances than for favorable variances.

Statistical Significance   Our knowledge about the properties of statistical distributions can help set tolerance limits. Managers can establish tolerance limits based on statistical confidence limits.

Example   The manager of a kitchen that makes meals for a college cafeteria wants to set tolerance limits on labor efficiency variances so that variances fall outside the limits less than 5 percent of the time. This analysis assumes that labor efficiency costs are normally distributed; based on past experience, expected labor time is 58 minutes per meal, and estimated standard deviation is 8 minutes per meal.

Exhibit 14.11 presents a control chart of actual observations reported to the kitchen manager for 5 days. A time series of observations allows the manager to see trends and look for cumulative effects of variances. The manager gets this report at 9:00 a.m. each day for the 5 previous working days. The kitchen manager received the report shown in Exhibit 14.11 at 9:00 a.m. Friday. The manager would have investigated the labor efficiency variance for Monday, presumably on Tuesday, because it fell outside the tolerance limits. In addition, the manager would probably investigate this labor variance after receiving the report on Friday because of the trend indicating a shift away from standard.

Decision Models

Although control charts provide data about variances, they do not incorporate the costs and benefits of variance investigation. The simple decision model in the following example shows how to do this.

Exhibit 14.11

Labor Efficiency Variance Report: Friday through Thursday Control Chart[a]

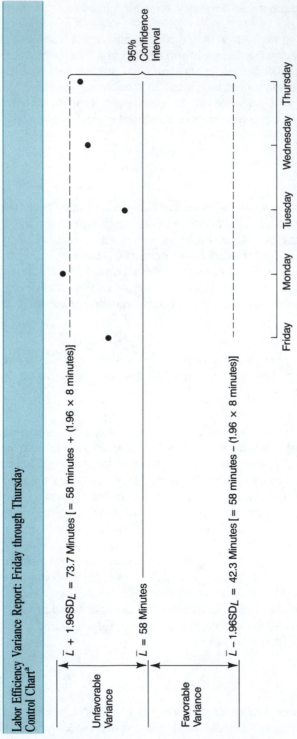

$\bar{L} + 1.96SD_L = 73.7$ Minutes [$= 58$ minutes $+ (1.96 \times 8$ minutes)]

Unfavorable Variance

$\bar{L} = 58$ Minutes

Favorable Variance

$\bar{L} - 1.96SD_L = 42.3$ Minutes [$= 58$ minutes $- (1.96 \times 8$ minutes)]

95% Confidence Interval

Friday   Monday   Tuesday   Wednesday   Thursday

[a]$\bar{L}$ = expected labor time per unit of output; SD_L = standard deviation of labor time per unit of output.
95 percent of the area in a normal distribution lies between $\bar{L} - 1.96SD_L$ and $\bar{L} + 1.96D_L$, according to tables available in statistics texts.

Example   Electromagnet, Inc., uses a stamping machine to make a product in 10,000-unit batches. An employee adjusts this machine at the beginning of a batch. During the production run, another employee calculates and reports the materials efficiency variances. If the machine is out of adjustment, it will use considerably more materials than needed. Hence, adjusting the machine during a production run could save materials costs. Sometimes the machine uses more materials than needed because of lower-quality materials, variance reporting errors, or other factors that adjusting the machine would not correct. Experience has shown that materials efficiency variances are approximately normally distributed.

Midway through a particular production batch, the stamping department manager receives a report indicating a large negative materials efficiency variance. Based on past experience, the manager estimates a 70 percent chance of the machine's running out of adjustment when the system reports a large negative materials efficiency variance.[1]

The manager faces the decision of whether to investigate. Shutting down the machine would result in idle worker time, loss of materials, and lost managerial time. After computing the opportunity cost of lost time and the cost of lost materials, the department manager estimates the cost of variance investigation, C, to be $1,000. If the machine needs adjustment, making the adjustment will cost $1,200 but the firm will save $3,200 in materials cost. Given the costs, C, and the benefits, B, from investigation, and the probability, P, that the benefits can be obtained, the decision rule is to investigate when expected benefits exceed expected costs:[2] $P \times B > C$.

Expected benefits equal the materials cost savings, $3,200, minus the cost of machine adjustments, $1,200, in this case. Investigating is worthwhile because

$$P \times B > C$$
$$.70 \times (\$3,200 - \$1,200) > \$1,000$$
$$.70 \times \$2,000 > \$1,000$$
$$\$1,400 > \$1,000.$$

This simple example shows how to model the variance investigation decision by applying statistical decision theory tools. In practice, accountants have difficulty applying the model, because they cannot easily estimate C, B, and P. At a minimum, managers should perform sensitivity analysis to see if the decision changes when their estimates of C, B, and P change.

Statistical analysis can provide decision aids to managers. You should not infer from our discussion, however, that managers must use these decision aids in all situations. Like other decision aids—for example, regression for estimating cost behavior—managers find these more useful in some situations than in others, and some managers are more comfortable with them than others. Also, keep in mind

---

[1] Readers who have studied statistics will recognize this as the manager's posterior probability that the machine is out of adjustment, given a variance as high as the one reported. Calculation of posterior probabilities relies on Bayes' theorem, which statistics textbooks present.

[2] We have assumed that decision makers are risk-neutral in this example.

that we have barely explored the potential use of these models. Readers interested in pursuing these ideas further should consult advanced cost and managerial accounting textbooks.[3]

■ Summary ■

The most common fixed manufacturing overhead variance for performance evaluation is the *price variance* (also called a spending or budget variance), which measures the difference between budgeted and actual fixed costs. If the firm budgets rent costs at $10,000 but actually spends $12,000, the price variance is $2,000 unfavorable. This straightforward calculation has a clear meaning—the firm paid $2,000 more for rent than budgeted. The *production volume variance* occurs only when the analyst unitizes fixed costs, such as when the accountant uses full absorption costing to value inventory and to calculate the cost of goods sold. The production volume variance occurs when the estimate of activity in the denominator of the following equation does not equal actual activity.

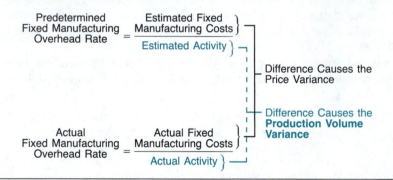

If inventory levels change, companies must decide whether to expense all of the current period purchase and production variances or to prorate them. If prorated, the company expenses variances attributable to goods sold, but the variances attributable to goods still in inventory do not become expensed until the firm sells the inventory. If materials purchased do not equal materials used, modify the cost variance model as shown in Exhibit 14.9.

Managers calculate mix variances when the various inputs (or outputs) can substitute for one another. Inputs do not substitute for outputs (or vice versa). Mix

[3]See R. Magee, *Advanced Managerial Accounting* (New York: Harper and Row, 1986), chap. 9; N. Dopuch, J. Birnberg, and J. Demski, *Cost Accounting* (New York: Harcourt Brace Jovanovich, 1982), chap. 8; R. Kaplan, "The Significance and Investigation of Cost Variances: Survey and Extensions," *Journal of Accounting Research* 13 (Autumn 1975), pp. 311–337; R. Magee, "A Simulation Analysis of Alternative Cost Variance Investigation Models," *The Accounting Review* 51 (July 1976), pp. 529–544; and Stanley Baiman and Joel Demski, "Variance Analysis Procedures as Motivational Devices," *Management Science* 26 (August 1980), pp. 840–848.

variances measure the cost of using more expensive material or labor in place of less expensive material or labor, for example.

Managers usually investigate and correct only a small fraction of the variances computed, because investigation and correction is costly—it consumes both managerial and worker time. How do managers select the variances to investigate? Often they use rules of thumb, such as "investigate if the variance is greater than 10 percent of the standard." If the accountant can estimate properties of frequency distributions, managers can base variance tolerance limits on confidence intervals, as shown in Exhibit 14.11. You may model the variance investigation using statistical decision theory and the following rule:

$$\text{Investigate if } P \times B > C,$$

where B = benefits from investigation
C = costs of investigation
P = probability of achieving benefits if variance is investigated.

Whether you use a rule of thumb or a statistical model, you should apply the simple cost-benefit criterion that forms the foundation of all managerial activity: Take action only if the benefits exceed the costs.

Appendix 14.1:
Standard Costs

Many organizations use standard costs, but only some use the standards to value inventory and product costs in the accounting records. Manufacturing companies with process systems—for example, steel, chemical, or calculator manufacturers—most commonly use standard costs to value inventory. (See Chapter 4 for a discussion of process costing systems.) The use of standard costs can save significant record-keeping costs, particularly in process manufacturing, where units are homogeneous and not easily identifiable separately.

You may wonder why users of accounting information should study standard cost flows through accounts. First, study of this system will help solidify your understanding of variance measurement and analysis. Our goal is to make your understanding of variances intuitive rather than mechanical. Looking at the way variances emerge from cost flows through the accounting system should help achieve that goal. Second, the better users understand accounting systems, the more input they can have in designing and modifying them.

Standard Cost Flows

The general model for the flow of costs in standard cost accounting systems appears in Exhibit 14.12.

A standard cost system transfers costs through the production process at standard. Process costing values units transferred between departments at standard cost; whereas job costing charges standard costs to the job for its components. Actual costs accumulate in the accounts which initially recorded transactions on the books

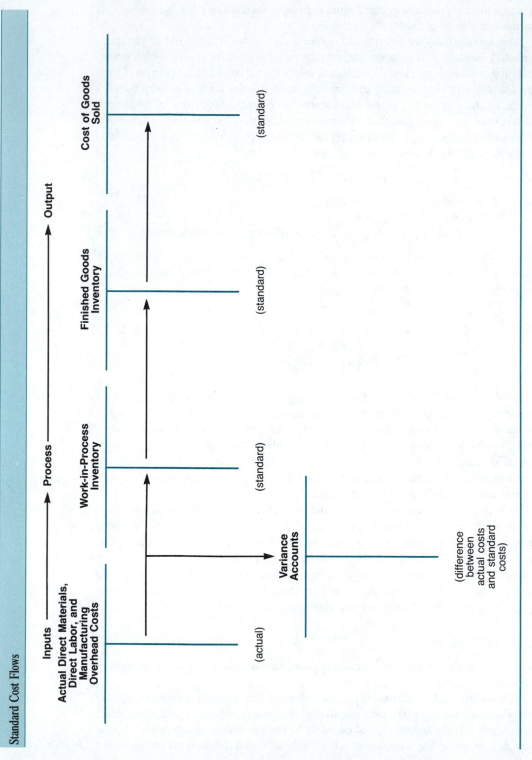

Exhibit 14.12

Standard Cost Flows

Inputs → Process → Output

Actual Direct Materials, Direct Labor, and Manufacturing Overhead Costs

Work-in-Process Inventory

Finished Goods Inventory

Cost of Goods Sold

(actual)

(standard)

(standard)

(standard)

Variance Accounts

(difference between actual costs and standard costs)

(for example, Accounts Payable, Wages Payable). The difference between the actual cost assigned to a department and the standard cost of the work done is the variance for the department.

The following sections discuss the flow of costs and demonstrate how the accounting system isolates the variances. These variances will be the same as those calculated in the chapter for Victoria Corporation, when the actual production volume was 80,000 units. Refer to the cost variance analysis in Exhibit 14.1 as you work through the following entries. Exhibit 14.1 presents all the data necessary to record the direct materials, direct labor, and variable manufacturing overhead variances. Recognize that standard cost systems vary from company to company. We present a typical model, but you may need to modify it to meet the specific needs of a particular company.

Direct Materials

Materials, whatever their actual cost, usually appear in materials inventory at the standard price per unit of material. The entry for Victoria Corporation for materials purchased follows (numbers in parentheses are the journal entry numbers):

(1) Materials Inventory	81,000	
Materials Price Variance	4,050	
Accounts Payable		85,050
To record the purchase of 81,000 pounds of material at the actual cost of $1.05 per pound, and to record the purchase in Materials Inventory at the standard cost of $1.00 per pound.		

Note that unfavorable cost variances are always debits and favorable cost variances are always credits. Exhibit 14.13 presents the flow of standard costs through T-accounts. Note that *actual costs* generally appear in the accounts on the left side of Exhibit 14.13 (for example, in Accounts Payable). The costs entered in Work-in-Process are *standard costs*.

The materials price variance appears in the accounting records when the firm purchases materials. As noted in the text, managers may wish to know the materials price variances at the time of purchase so that they can take corrective action if necessary.

We say that direct materials appear at standard cost because the $1.00 per pound is the standard allowed per unit of input. But a word of caution: The standard cost recorded is the standard cost per unit of *input* (that is, pounds), *not* standard cost per unit of *output*.

When direct materials enter production, the system assigns each operating department the *actual quantity* of input used at the *standard cost* per input unit. Thus the system assigns the production department at Victoria Corporation the standard cost of $1.00 per pound for the actual quantity of 81,000 pounds of materials. Managers do not normally hold production departments responsible for the materials price variances, which are the responsibility of the purchasing department. Managers do hold production departments responsible for materials efficiency variances, however.

Exhibit 14.13

VICTORIA CORPORATION
Flow of Costs[a]—Full Absorption Costing with Standard Costs

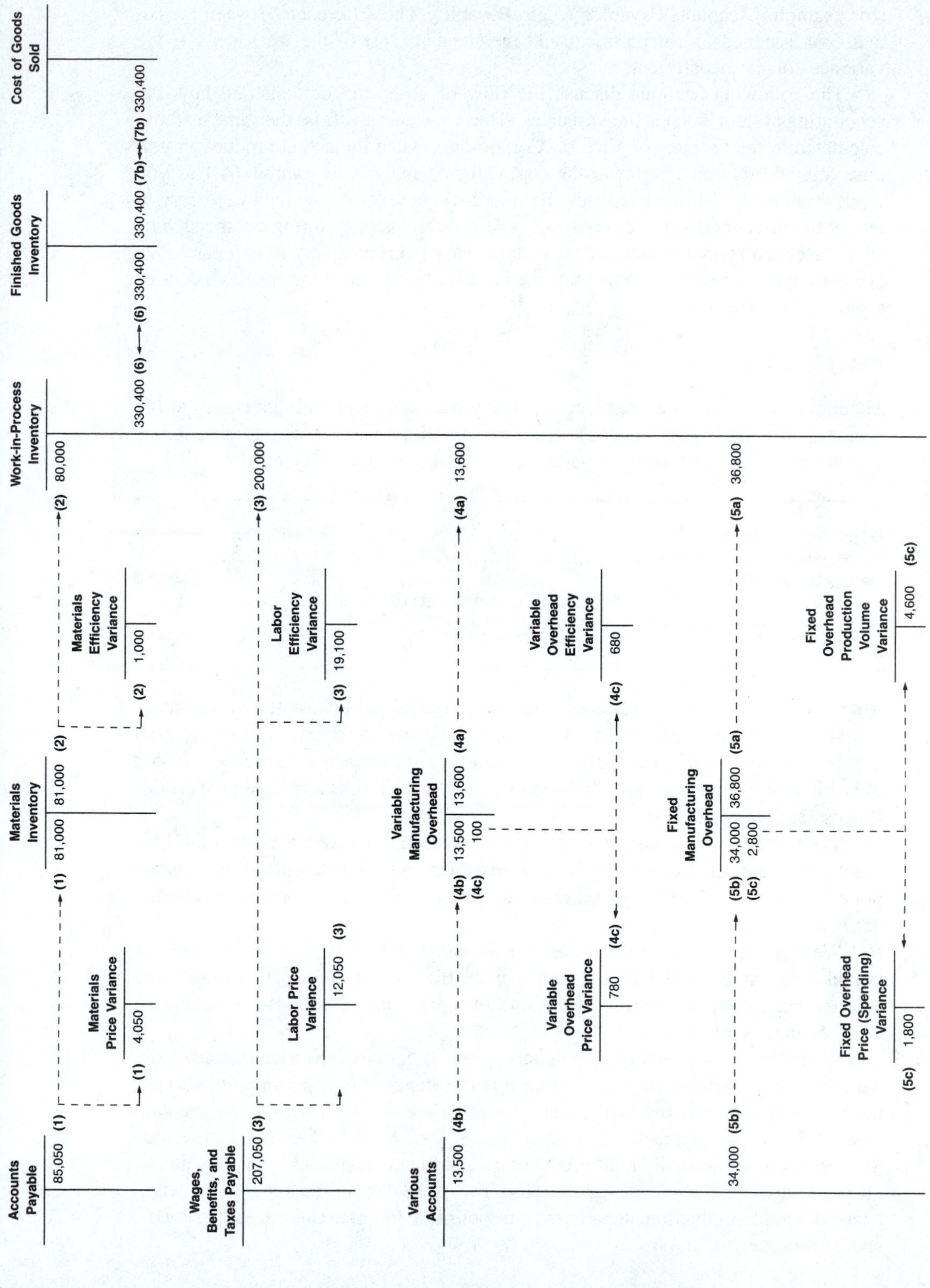

Accounts Payable
85,050 (1)

Materials Inventory
(1) 81,000 | 81,000 (2)

Materials Price Variance
(1) 4,050

Materials Efficiency Variance
(2) 1,000

Wages, Benefits, and Taxes Payable
207,050 (3)

Labor Price Variance
(3) 12,050

Labor Efficiency Variance
(3) 19,100

Various Accounts
13,500 (4b)

Variable Manufacturing Overhead
(4b) 13,500 | 13,600 (4a)
(4c) 100

Variable Overhead Price Variance
(4c) 780

Variable Overhead Efficiency Variance
(4c) 680

Fixed Manufacturing Overhead
(5b) 34,000 | 36,800 (5a)
(5c) 2,800

Fixed Overhead Price (Spending) Variance
(5c) 1,800

Fixed Overhead Production Volume Variance
(5c) 4,600

Work-in-Process Inventory
(2) 80,000
(3) 200,000
(4a) 13,600
(5a) 36,800
330,400 (6)

Finished Goods Inventory
(6) 330,400 | 330,400 (7b)

Cost of Goods Sold
(7b) 330,400

[a]Numbers in parentheses are the journal entry numbers.

The entry charging production for the standard cost of materials used follows:

---

(2) Work-in-Process Inventory   80,000
    Materials Efficiency Variance   1,000
        Materials Inventory   81,000
To record the requisition of 81,000 pounds of material at the
standard cost of $1.00 per pound to make 80,000 units of output.

(Exhibit 14.13 presents this entry in T-accounts.)

Direct Labor

The standard cost system credits the actual direct labor, including fringe benefits
and taxes, to various payable accounts. To simplify the presentation, we assume
that the credit is just to Wages Payable. The system charges direct labor to Work-in-
Process Inventory at the standard direct labor cost allowed for the output produced.
This entry for Victoria Corporation follows:

---

(3) Work-in-Process Inventory   200,000
    Labor Efficiency Variance   19,100
        Labor Price Variance   12,050
        Wages Payable   207,050
To charge Production for the standard cost of direct labor at $20
per hour times 10,000 hours allowed (that is, $\frac{1}{8}$ hour per unit of
output allowed), to record the actual direct labor cost, and to
record direct labor variances.

Variable Manufacturing Overhead

The standard cost system charges standard overhead costs to production based on
standard machine hours allowed at the rate of $6.80 per machine hour. This entry
can occur before the accountant knows the actual costs as the following sequence of
entries demonstrates:

1. The system charges standard overhead costs to production during the period.
    Debit Work-in-Process Inventory and credit Variable Manufacturing Overhead.

2. The accountant records actual costs in various accounts, then transfers them to
    Variable Manufacturing Overhead by crediting the various accounts and debit-
    ing Variable Manufacturing Overhead. Examples of the accounts credited in-
    clude Accounts Payable for costs of utilities and Wages Payable for indirect
    labor costs. The accountant cannot complete this step until after the end of the
    period.

3. Variances are the difference between the standard costs charged to production
    and actual costs incurred.

This approach is essentially the same as that used in Chapter 4 for charging production with overhead costs using normal costing. However, variance accounts replace
the Under- or Overapplied Overhead accounts used in Chapter 4.

The three entries for Victoria Corporation follow:

(4a) Work-in-Process Inventory   13,600
          Variable Manufacturing Overhead   13,600
          To charge Production for the standard variable overhead cost at
          $6.80 per machine hour times 2,000 machine hours allowed to
          make 80,000 units actually produced.
(4b) Variable Manufacturing Overhead   13,500
          Various Accounts   13,500
          To record actual variable manufacturing overhead costs incurred.
(4c) Variable Manufacturing Overhead   100
          Variable Overhead Efficiency Variance   680
               Variable Overhead Price Variance   780
          To record the variable overhead variances and to close the Variable
          Manufacturing Overhead account.

The sequence of events necessitates recording the flow of variable manufacturing overhead costs in the three entries shown. However, if such sequencing is not important, only one entry would be necessary:

Work-in-Process Inventory at Standard   13,600
Variable Overhead Efficiency Variance   680
     Various Accounts at Actual   13,500
     Variable Overhead Price Variance   780

Fixed Manufacturing Overhead

Generally accepted accounting principles require accountants to treat fixed manufacturing overhead as a product cost. That is, financial reporting requires full absorption costing. In this book, we treat fixed costs as period costs for managerial decision making, planning, and performance evaluation; that is, we use variable costing. The accountant can design standard cost systems for either full absorption or variable costing. Standard costing systems using variable costing have no special procedures for fixed overhead.

Under full absorption costing, the system unitizes fixed manufacturing overhead costs. Each unit produced receives a share of fixed manufacturing overhead.

For Victoria Corporation, we compute the fixed manufacturing overhead rate per machine hour as follows:

$$\begin{matrix} \text{Fixed} \\ \text{Manufacturing} \\ \text{Rate} \end{matrix} = \frac{\text{Estimated Fixed Manufacturing Cost}}{\text{Estimated Production Volume}}$$

$$= \frac{\$32,200}{70,000 \text{ Units Planned} \times \frac{1}{40} \text{ Hour per Unit}}$$

$$= \frac{\$32,200}{1,750 \text{ Hours}}$$

$$= \$18.40 \text{ per Hour.}$$

We compute the amount charged to production (that is, debited to Work-in-Process Inventory) as follows:

$$\begin{array}{c}\text{Amount} \\ \text{Charged} \\ \text{to Production}\end{array} = \begin{array}{c}\text{Fixed} \\ \text{Manufacturing} \\ \text{Rate}\end{array} \times \begin{array}{c}\text{Standard Hours} \\ \text{Allowed to Produce} \\ \text{the Actual Output}\end{array}$$

$$= \begin{array}{c}\$18.40 \times 2{,}000 \text{ Hours Allowed} \\ \text{to Produce } 80{,}000 \text{ Units}\end{array}$$

$$= \$36{,}800.$$

(Note that $36,800 also equals $.46 per unit times 80,000 units.)

Production Volume Variance In Chapter 13, we showed that the fixed manufacturing price variance is the difference between the actual and budgeted cost. However, the budgeted cost is not the amount charged to production, unless the actual and estimated production volumes are equal. In short, the amount applied, or charged, to production does not equal the budget if the estimated and actual activity levels used in the denominator of the calculation differ.

The following diagram summarizes the relations among actual, budget, and applied fixed manufacturing cost for Victoria Corporation (taken from Exhibit 14.12):

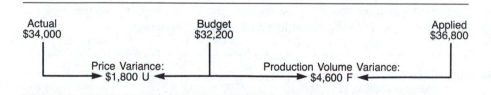

Journal Entries The method of charging fixed manufacturing standard overhead costs to production is similar to the one we used for variable manufacturing costs. For the preceding sequence of events, the three entries for Victoria Corporation follow:

(5a) Work-in-Process Inventory	36,800	
Fixed Manufacturing Overhead		36,800
To charge production with standard fixed manufacturing overhead costs at $18.40 per unit times 2,000 hours.		
(5b) Fixed Manufacturing Overhead	34,000	
Various Accounts		34,000
To record actual fixed manufacturing overhead costs incurred.		
(5c) Fixed Manufacturing Overhead	2,800	
Fixed Overhead Budget Variance	1,800	
Fixed Overhead Volume Variance.		4,600
To record fixed manufacturing overhead variances and to close the Fixed Manufacturing Overhead account.		

If the firm does not follow this sequence, only one entry would be necessary:

Work-in-Process Inventory at Standard...........................	36,800	
Fixed Overhead Budget Variance.................................	1,800	
Various Accounts at Actual		34,000
Fixed Overhead Production Volume Variance		4,600

Note that both actual and applied fixed overhead show up in the accounts, but budgeted overhead does not.

Transfer Out of Production

The total standard cost per unit follows:

Direct Materials	$1.00
Direct Labor	2.50
Variable Manufacturing Overhead	.17
Fixed Manufacturing Overhead..	.46
	$4.13

After manufacturing completes production, the accounting system transfers the standard cost of units completed to Finished Goods Inventory.

(6) Finished Goods Inventory..................................	330,400	
Work-in-Process Inventory		330,400
To transfer 80,000 completed units from Work-in-Process to Finished Goods at a standard cost of $4.13 per unit.		

The following entries record the sale of 80,000 units (selling price = $6.10 per unit):

(7a) Accounts Receivable	488,000	
Sales..		488,000
(7b) Cost of Goods Sold......................................	330,400	
Finished Goods Inventory............................		330,400
To record the sale of 80,000 units at an actual selling price of $6.10 per unit and a standard cost of $4.13 per unit.		

Closing the Variance Accounts

To complete the accounting cycle, the accountant closes variance accounts to In-come Summary or some expense account as appears on the following page:

Income Summary...	9,200	
Labor Price Variance...	12,050	
Fixed Overhead Production Volume Variance.....................	4,600	
Variable Overhead Price Variance.............................	780	
Materials Price Variance...............................		4,050
Materials Efficiency Variance...........................		1,000
Labor Efficiency Variance..............................		19,100
Variable Overhead Efficiency Variance....................		680
Fixed Overhead Price Variance		1,800

The amount debited or credited to Income Summary is a plug.

Debiting the income summary means that the net variance was unfavorable.

Prorating Variances   If the accountant has prorated the variance inventories, the amount of the variances shown in the closing entry above would change, but the method of closing variance amounts to the Income Summary would not.

Summary

Exhibit 14.13 shows the complete flow of standard costs through T-accounts. (You should find it helpful to trace each entry in this appendix to the flow of costs in Exhibit 14.13.)

Problem 1 for Self-Study[4]

During the past month, the following events took place at Computer Supply, Inc.

(1)   The company produces 50,000 computer cases. Actual fixed manufacturing cost was $83,000.

(2)   Budgeted fixed manufacturing cost was $80,000. Budgeted direct labor hours worked were 4,000 hours for budgeted production of 40,000 cases. Full absorption costing, if used, applies fixed manufacturing costs to units produced on the basis of direct labor hours.

Compute the fixed manufacturing price and production volume variances.

Suggested Solution

	Actual	Price Variance	Budget	Efficiency Variance	Budget	Production Volume Variance	Applied
Fixed Overhead	$83,000		$80,000		$80,000		$100,000[a]
		$3,000 U		Not Applicable		$20,000 F	

[a]Fixed overhead rate = $80,000/40,000 = $2 per case, or $20 per standard labor hour.

50,000 cases actually produced × $2 = $100,000 fixed overhead applied (or 5,000 standard labor hours allowed × $20 = $100,000).

---

[4]This is a continuation of Problem 1 for Self-Study in Chapters 12 and 13.

Problem 2 for Self-Study

Alexis Company makes a product, AL, from two materials, ST and EE. The standard prices and quantities follow:

	ST	EE
Price per Pound	$2	$3
Pounds per Unit of AL	10	5

In May, Alexis Company produced 7,000 units of AL, with the following actual prices and quantities of materials used:

	ST	EE
Price per Pound	$1.90	$2.80
Pounds Used	7,2000	38,000

Compute materials price, mix, and efficiency variances.

Suggested Solution

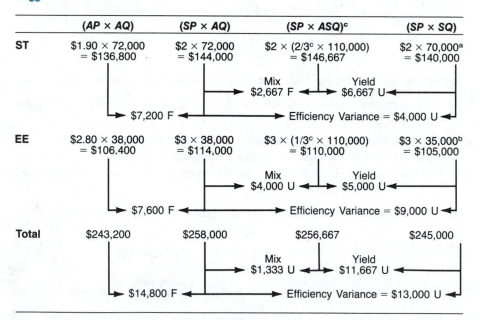

	(AP × AQ)	(SP × AQ)	(SP × ASQ)ᶜ	(SP × SQ)
ST	$1.90 × 72,000 = $136,800	$2 × 72,000 = $144,000	$2 × (2/3ᶜ × 110,000) = $146,667	$2 × 70,000ᵃ = $140,000
			Mix $2,667 F ◄──► Yield $6,667 U ◄──	
	──► $7,200 F ◄───────────────────	─► Efficiency Variance = $4,000 U ◄──		
EE	$2.80 × 38,000 = $106,400	$3 × 38,000 = $114,000	$3 × (1/3ᶜ × 110,000) = $110,000	$3 × 35,000ᵇ = $105,000
			Mix $4,000 U ◄──► Yield $5,000 U ◄──	
	──► $7,600 F ◄───────────────────	─► Efficiency Variance = $9,000 U ◄──		
Total	$243,200	$258,000	$256,667	$245,000
			Mix $1,333 U ◄──► Yield $11,667 U ◄──	
	──► $14,800 F ◄───────────────────	─► Efficiency Variance = $13,000 U ◄──		

ᵃ70,000 Pounds = 7,000 Units × 10 Pounds per Unit.

ᵇ35,000 Pounds = 7,000 Units × 5 Pounds per Unit.

ᶜMix percentage ratio of ST pounds to total and EE pounds to total. For ST, $\dfrac{10}{10+5} = \dfrac{2}{3}$. For EE, $\dfrac{5}{10+5} = \dfrac{1}{3}$. ASQ = Actual amount of the input used at the standard mix. 110,000 total = 72,000 ST plus 38,000 EE.

Problem 3 for Self-Study *(Appendix 14.1)*

Refer to Problem 1 for Self-Study in Chapters 13 and 14, but assume the purchase of 200,000 pounds of direct material (instead of 110,000 pounds) at $1.20 per pound. Assume that the accountant has recorded the information in those problems using full absorption, standard costing and that Work-in-Process Inventory has no beginning or ending inventories. After reading Appendix 14.1, show how the information would be recorded using

a. Journal entries.

b. T-accounts.

Suggested Solution

a. Journal entries:

(1) Direct Materials Inventory	200,000	
Materials Price Variance	40,000	
Accounts Payable		240,000

To record the purchase of 200,000 pounds of materials at an actual cost of $1.20 per pound and to record the transfer to Direct Materials Inventory at the standard cost of $1 per pound.

(2) Work-in-Process Inventory	100,000	
Materials Efficiency Variance	10,000	
Direct Materials Inventory		110,000

To record the requisition of 110,000 pounds of materials at the standard cost of $1 per pound and to charge Work-in-Process Inventory with the standard usage of 100,000 pounds of materials at the standard price.

(3) Work-in-Process Inventory	75,000	
Labor Efficiency Variance	15,000	
Labor Price Variance		6,000
Wages Payable		84,000

To charge Work-in-Process Inventory for the standard cost of direct labor at $15 per hour times 5,000 standard hours allowed and to record the actual cost of $14 per hour times the 6,000 hours actually worked.

(4) Work-in-Process Inventory	25,000	
Variable Overhead		25,000

To apply overhead to production at $5 per standard direct labor hour times the 5,000 hours allowed.

(5) Variable Overhead (actual)	28,000	
Various Accounts (Cash, Accounts Payable, etc.)		28,000

To record actual variable overhead.

(6) Variable Overhead Efficiency Variance	5,000	
Variable Overhead Price Variance		2,000
Variable Overhead		3,000

To record variable overhead variances and to close the Variable Overhead account.

(7) Work-in-Process Inventory	100,000	
Fixed Overhead (applied)		100,000

To record fixed overhead at a standard cost of $20 per direct labor hour times 5,000 standard hours ($80,000/4,000 hours = $20 per hour).

continued on page 646

continued from page 645

(8)	Fixed Overhead (actual)	83,000	
	Various Accounts (Cash, Accounts Payable, etc.)		83,000
	To record actual fixed overhead.		
(9)	Fixed Overhead.	17,000	
	Fixed Overhead Price Variance	3,000	
	Fixed Overhead Production Volume Variance		20,000
	To record fixed overhead variances and to close the Fixed Overhead account.		
(10)	Finished Goods Inventory	300,000	
	Work-in-Process Inventory		300,000
	To record the transfer of 50,000 units of finished goods at the standard cost of $6 per unit.		
(11)	Cost of Goods Sold	240,000	
	Finished Goods Inventory		240,000
	To record the sale of 40,000 units at a standard cost of $6 per unit.		

b. T-accounts: See Exhibit 14.14.

Key Terms and Concepts

Fixed manufacturing price (spending) variance	Mix variance
Fixed manufacturing production volume variance	Yield variance
	Variance investigation

Questions, Exercises, Problems, and Cases

Questions

1. Review the meaning of the concepts or terms given above in the Key Terms and Concepts.

2. What are the two options with respect to treating cost variances as product costs or as period expenses in companies in which production does not equal sales volume?

3. A firm incurred fixed manufacturing overhead costs of $500,000 for the year. Fixed overhead applied to units produced during the year totaled $600,000. What are some of the reasons for this difference?

4. Why doesn't management investigate all unfavorable variances?

5. Describe the basic decision that management must make when considering whether to investigate a variance.

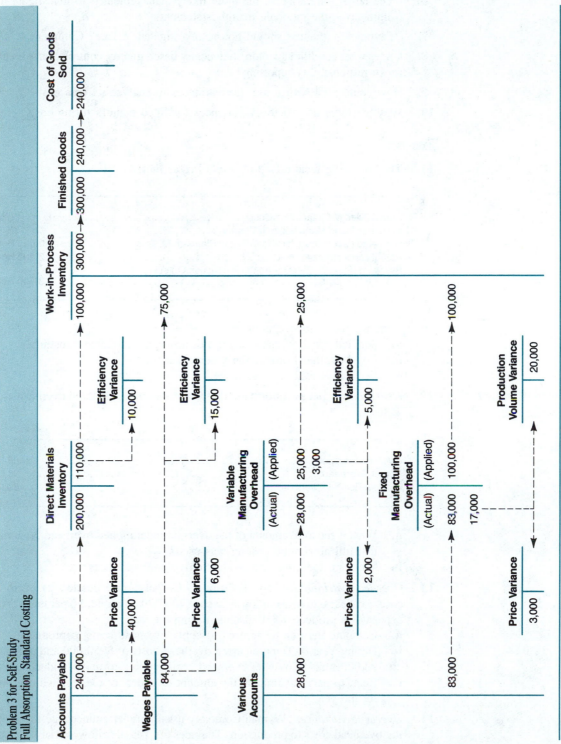

6. "The larger the variance, the more likely management is to investigate it." Comment on the rationale for this statement.

7. "Favorable variances should not be investigated." True? Comment.

8. Under what conditions would statistically based quality control charts be useful in responsibility reporting?

9. How could a CPA firm use mix variances to analyze its firm costs?

10. Why are there no efficiency variances for fixed manufacturing costs?

Exercises

11. The following facts refer to Steve's Pizza, Inc.:

Actual Fixed Manufacturing Costs	$3,500
Budgeted Fixed Manufacturing Costs	$3,300
Budgeted Labor Hours for 6,000 Pizzas Planned	3,000 Hours
Actual Labor Hours Worked	3,200 Hours
Standard Hours Allowed for Actual Production Output of 7,000 Pizzas	3,500 Hours

Compute the following amounts:
a. Applied fixed overhead using full absorption, standard costing.
b. Fixed overhead production volume variance.
c. Fixed overhead price variance.

12. *Overhead variances.* Information on Omaha Company's fixed overhead costs follows:

Overhead Applied	$80,000
Actual Overhead	86,000
Flexible Budget Overhead	83,000

a. What is the total amount of the over- or underapplied overhead, assuming that full absorption costing was used?
b. What are the price and production volume variances?

13. *Overhead variances.* Trapp Electronics Corporation estimated its overhead costs for Year 0 to be as follows: fixed, $400,000; variable, $6 per unit. Trapp expected to produce 100,000 units during the year.
a. Compute the rate to be used to apply overhead costs to products.
b. During Year 0, Trapp incurred overhead costs of $950,000 and produced 90,000 units. Compute overhead costs applied to units produced.
c. Refer to part b. Compute the amount of under- or overapplied overhead for the year.

14. *Overhead variances.* Wyman Company uses a predetermined rate for applying overhead costs to production. The rates for Year 0 follow: variable, $2 per

unit; fixed, $1 per unit. Actual overhead costs incurred follow: variable, $95,000; fixed, $45,000. Wyman expected to produce 45,000 units during the year but produced only 40,000 units.

a. What was the amount of budgeted fixed overhead costs for the year?

b. What was the amount of under- or overapplied overhead for the year?

c. Compute all possible overhead variances.

15. *Graphing overhead variances*. Refer to the data in Exercise 14. Graph the actual, budget, and applied fixed overhead costs as in the graph in Exhibit 14.3.

16. *Hospital supply variances*. Refer to Problem 21 in Chapter 13. Compute mix and yield variances for the surgical supplies.

17. *Labor variances*. Refer to Problem 22 in Chapter 13. Compute mix and yield variances for the labor costs.

18. *Variance investigation*. Manhatten Company's production manager is considering whether or not to investigate a computer-integrated manufacturing process. The investigation costs $7,000. If the manager finds that the process is out of control, correcting it costs $20,000. If the process is out of control and is corrected, the company saves $45,000 until the next scheduled investigation. The probability of the process being in control is .65, and the probability of the process being out of control is .35, given recent variance reports.

Should management investigate the process? Why or why not?

19. *Variance investigation*. The accounting system has reported a large unfavorable variance for Portland Company's food process. Conducting an investigation costs $2,000. If the process is actually out of control, the benefit of correction will be $9,000. The probability is .20 that the large negative variance indicates the process is out of control.

Should management investigate the process?

20. *Recording overhead costs* (Appendix 14.1; adapted from CPA exam). Union Company uses a standard cost accounting system. The following overhead costs and production data are available for August:

Standard Fixed Overhead Rate per Direct Labor Hour	$1
Standard Variable Overhead Rate per Direct Labor Hour	$4
Budgeted Monthly Direct Labor Hours	40,000
Actual Direct Labor Hours Worked	39,500
Standard Direct Labor Hours Allowed for Actual Production	39,000
Overall Overhead Variance—Favorable	$2,000
Actual Variable Overhead	$159,500

Show the flow of these overhead costs in T-account form.

21. *Recording overhead costs* (Appendix 14.1; adapted from CMA exam). Standard Company has developed standard overhead costs based on a capacity of 180,000 direct labor hours as appears on the following page:

Standard Costs per Unit:		
Variable Portion: 2 Hours at $3		$ 6
Fixed Portion: 2 Hours at $5		10
		$16

During April, the company scheduled 90,000 units for production, but produced only 80,000 units. The following data relate to April:

(1) Actual direct labor cost incurred was $644,000 for 165,000 actual hours of work.

(2) Actual overhead incurred totaled $1,378,000—$518,000 variable and $860,000 fixed.

(3) All inventories are carried at standard cost.

Use T-accounts to show the recording of these overhead costs in Work-in-Process Inventory together with the related variances.

Problems

22. *Comprehensive variance computations*. The following information will assist you in evaluating the performance of the manufacturing operations of the Dartmouth Company:

Units Produced (actual)	21,000
Estimated Units Produced	20,000
Budgeted Fixed Overhead	$80,000
Standard Costs per Unit:	
Direct Materials	$1.65 × 5 Pounds per Unit of Output
Direct Labor	$14 per Hour × ½ Hour per Unit
Variable Overhead	$11.90 per Direct Labor Hour
Actual Costs:	
Direct Materials Purchased and Used....	$188,700 (102,000 Pounds)
Direct Labor	$140,000 (10,700 Hours)
Overhead	$204,000 (61% Is Variable)

The company applies variable overhead on the basis of direct labor hours.
Prepare a cost variance analysis to show all variable manufacturing cost price and efficiency variances and fixed manufacturing cost price and production volume variances.

23. *Standard cost flows* (Appendix 14.1). Refer to Problem 22. Prepare journal entries for the transactions and show cost flows through T-accounts, assuming full absorption, standard costing is used.

24. *Comprehensive variance computations*. Lawrence Lawncare fertilizes and applies weed killer to lawns. The company prepared its budgets on the basis of standard costs. Accountants prepare a responsibility report monthly showing the differences between flexible budget and actual. The report analyzes variances separately. The accountants compute materials price variances at the time of purchase.

The following information relates to the current period.

Standard Costs (per average lawn):
Direct Material (fertilizer and weed killer), 1 kilogram
    @ $1 per kilogram... $ 1
Direct Labor, 2 hours @ $4 per hour 8
Overhead:
    Variable (25% of direct labor cost).................................... 2
    Fixed (master budget, 3,600 labor hours) 1
      Total Standard Cost per Average Lawn Serviced $12

Actual Costs for the Month:
Materials Purchased ....   3,000 Kilograms at $.90 per Kilogram
Output..............................   1,900 Lawns Serviced Using
                                      2,100 Kilograms of Material
Actual Labor Costs ....   3,200 Hours at $5 per Hour
Actual Overhead:
    Variable $4,500
    Fixed...............................   1,800

Prepare a cost variance analysis showing price, efficiency, and fixed overhead production volume variances.

25. *Standard cost flows* (Appendix 14.1). Refer to Problem 24. Prepare journal entries for the transactions and show cost flows through T-accounts, assuming full absorption, standard costing.

26. *Variance computations with missing data.* Merriweather Manufacturing Company engages in a chemical blending operation to produce certain industrial solvents. Merriweather manufactures one solvent, Interno, as a blend of three products: Alpha-28, Beta-32, and Gamma-07 (A, B, and G, for short). This solvent is very active and must be shipped in special containers. In addition to the materials, the blending process requires three direct labor hours per liter of solvent. The costing system applies factory overhead at the rate of 150 percent of direct labor costs.

You have been working for the Merriweather Manufacturing Company as a new management trainee in the controller's office. Today you had an opportunity to tell the controller about your background and your education. The controller handed you some information on last month's production of industrial solvents and asked you to analyze the variances for the product Interno. Confident in your abilities, you carried the computer printout with you as you left the office. Unfortunately, on the way home a gust of wind blew some of your papers away. You were able to retrieve some of the information, but a good deal of it was torn or shredded.

At home, you have pieced together fragments that appear on the following page from the computer printouts:

d costs per un

.500	1 Alpha	28 @ 5.00/1
.200	1 Beta	32 @ 10.00/
.400	1 Gamma	07 @

tal $8.30/lit

Expect

12,000 direct la
$80,000 fixed over
$71,500 variable ove
$4,000 container costs

ual costs

2,200	1 Alpha	28 @ 5.0
800	1 Beta	32 @ $11.20/1
1,000	1 Gamma	07 @ $ 9.10/1
4,010	containers	@ $ .95
Total materials		$ 32,979.50
	direct labor	97,200.
	variable ovh	61,700.
	fixed overhead	80,960.

Varia

$927 Fav. Eff

You also recall that the new actual direct labor rate is $9 per hour.

Defend your reputation with the controller and compute as many variances as possible. (*Hint:* Separating the chemical inputs from the containers will make the solution more manageable.) If you cannot compute any of the variances, state why.

27. *Prorating variances* (adapted from CMA exam). Nashville Company uses a standard cost system for all its products. Nashville carries all inventories at standard during the year. The firm adjusts the inventories and cost of goods sold for all variances at the end of the fiscal year for external financial reporting purposes. The accounting system uses a FIFO cost flow assumption for all products moving through the manufacturing process to finished goods and ultimate sale.

The standard cost of one of Nashville's products manufactured in the Dixon Plant, unchanged from the previous year, follows:

Direct Materials	$2
Direct Labor (.5 direct labor hour at $8)	4
Manufacturing Overhead	3
Total Standard Cost	$9

This product has no work-in-process inventory.

The following schedule reports the manufacturing activity and cost of goods sold measured at standard cost for the current fiscal year.

	Units	Dollars
Product Manufactured..................................	95,000	$855,000
Beginning Finished Goods Inventory (produced last year) ..	15,000	135,000
Goods Available for Sale	110,000	$990,000
Ending Finished Goods Inventory	19,000	171,000
Cost of Goods Sold....................................	91,000	$819,000

The manufacturing performance relative to standard costs was not good, both this year and last year. The balance of the finished goods inventory, $140,800, reported on the balance sheet at the beginning of the year included a $5,800 adjustment for variances from standard cost. The unfavorable standard cost variances for labor for the current fiscal year consisted of a wage rate variance of $32,000 and a labor efficiency variance of $20,000 (2,500 hours at $8). No other variances from standard cost occurred in the company for this year.

Adjust the inventories and cost of goods sold to reflect the actual costs of this year's production.

28. *Variance investigation* (adapted from CMA exam). The Bilco Oil Company currently sells three grades of gasoline: regular, premium, and regular plus— a mixture of regular and premium. Bilco advertises regular plus as being "at least 50 percent premium." Although the firm can sell any mixture containing 50 percent or more premium gas as regular plus, using exactly 50 percent costs less. A valve in the blending machine governs the percentage of premium in the mixture. If the valve works properly, the machine provides a mixture of 50 percent premium and 50 percent regular. If the valve is out of adjustment, the machine provides a mixture of 60 percent premium and 40 percent regular.

Once the machine starts, it must continue until it mixes 100,000 liters of regular plus. Available cost data follow:

Cost per Liter: Premium	$ .32
Regular	.30
Cost of Checking the Valve	80.00
Cost of Adjusting the Valve	40.00

The cost of adjusting the valve reduces the benefits of investigation. The probabilities of the valve's condition are estimated to be in adjustment, .7; out of adjustment, .3.

a. Should Bilco check the valve?
b. At what probability would Bilco be indifferent about whether or not to check the valve.

29. *Variance investigation: multiple choice* (adapted from CPA exam). The folding department manager must decide each week whether the department will operate normally the following week. The manager may order a corrective action if she believes the department will operate inefficiently; otherwise she does nothing. The manager receives a weekly folding department efficiency variance report from the accounting department. A large efficiency variance usually precedes a week in which the department operates inefficiently. The graph gives the probability that the folding department will operate normally in the following week as a function of the magnitude of the current week's efficiency variance reported to the manager. The graph appears on the following page.

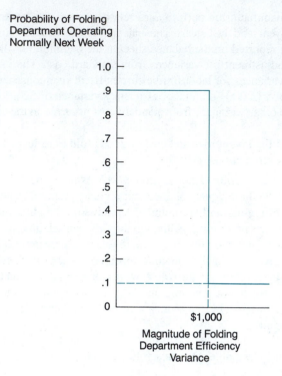

a. An efficiency variance of $1,500 this week means that the probability of operating normally the following week is (choose one)
   (1) 0.0.
   (2) 0.1.
   (3) 0.9.
   (4) 1.0.
b. What are the possible relations between the current efficiency variance and next week's operations (choose one)?
   (1) Large variance followed by normal operation, large variance followed by inefficient operation, small variance followed by normal operation, and small variance followed by inefficient operation.
   (2) Large variance followed by normal operation, small variance followed by inefficient operation, and small variance followed by normal operation.
   (3) Large variance followed by inefficient operation, small variance followed by normal operation, and small variance followed by inefficient operation.
   (4) Large variance followed by 90 percent of normal operation, small variance followed by 10 percent of normal operation, large variance followed by inefficient operation, and small variance followed by inefficient operation.
c. If the manager can determine for certain whether the folding department will operate normally next week, and if the corrective action costs less than operating the folding department inefficiently, then the best decision rule for the manager to follow is (choose one)

(1) If normal operations are predicted, do not take corrective action; if inefficient operations are predicted, take corrective action.

(2) Regardless of the current variance, do not take corrective action.

(3) If normal operations are predicted, take corrective action; if inefficient operations are predicted, do not take corrective action.

(4) Regardless of the current variance, take corrective action.

d. The following cost information should help the folding department manager decide whether corrective action is warranted that will assure normal operation of the folding department for the following week; $3,000 = excess cost of operating folding department inefficiently for one week.

The manager receives a report that the folding department efficiency variance is $600. The expected benefit of taking corrective action is (choose one)

(1) $0.

(2) $300.

(3) $2,700.

(4) $3,000.

Integrative Problems and Cases

30. *Cost and profit analysis; reconciling with full absorption costing.* "I just don't understand these financial statements at all!" exclaimed Mr. Elmo Knapp. Mr. Knapp explained that he had turned over management of Racketeer, Inc., division of American Recreation Equipment, Inc., to his son, Otto, the previous month. Racketeer, Inc., manufactures tennis rackets.

"I was really proud of Otto," he beamed. "He was showing us all the tricks he learned in business school and, if I say so myself, I think he was doing a rather good job for us. For example, he put together this budget for Racketeer, which makes it real easy to see how much profit we'll make at any sales volume (Exhibit 14.15). As best as I can figure it, in March we expected to have a volume of 8,000 units and a profit of $14,500 on our rackets. But we did much better than that! We sold 10,000 rackets, so we should have made almost $21,000 on them."

"Another one of Otto's innovations is this standard cost system," said Mr. Knapp proudly. "He sat down with our production people and came up with a standard production cost per unit (see Exhibit 14.16). He tells me this will tell us how well our production people are performing. Also, he claims it will cut down on our clerical work."

Mr. Knapp continued, "But one thing puzzles me. My calculations show that we should have shown a profit of nearly $21,000 in March. However, our accountants came up with less than $19,000 in the monthly income statement (Exhibit 14.17). This discrepancy bothers me a great deal. Now I'm not sure our accountants are doing their job properly. It appears to be that they're about $2,200 short."

"As you can probably guess," Mr. Knapp concluded, "we are one big happy family around here. I just wish I knew what those accountants are up to—coming in with a low net income like that."

Exhibit 14.15

Racketeer, Inc.
Profit Graph, Rackets

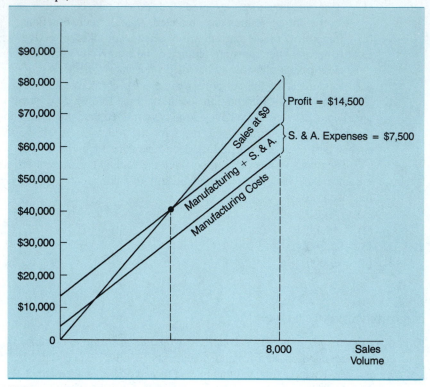

ªSelling and administrative expenses.

Exhibit 14.16

RACKETEER, INC.
Standard Costsª

	Per Racket
Raw Material:	
Frame	$3.15
Stringing Materials: 20 Feet at $.03 per Foot	.60
Direct Labor:	
Skilled ⅛ Hour at $9.60 per Hour	1.20
Unskilled ⅛ Hour at $5.60 per Hour	.70
Plant Overhead:	
Indirect Labor	.10
Power	.03
Supervision	.12ᵇ
Depreciation	.20ᵇ
Other	.15ᵇ
Total Standard Cost per Racket	$6.25

ªStandard costs are calculated for an estimated volume of 8,000 rackets each month.
ᵇFixed costs.

Exhibit 14.17

RACKETEER, INC.
Income Statement for March
Actual

Sales: 10,000 Rackets at $9	$90,000
Standard Cost of Goods Sold: 10,000 Rackets at $6.25	62,500
Gross Profit after Standard Costs	$27,500
Variances:	
Materials Variance	(490)
Labor Variance	(392)
Overhead Variance	(660)
Gross Profit	$25,958
Selling and Administrative Expense	7,200
Operating Profit.	$18,758

Exhibit 14.18

RACKETEER, INC.
Actual Production Data for March

Production	7,000 Rackets
Costs of Production:	
Direct Materials Purchased and Used:	
Stringing Materials	175,000 Feet at $.025 per Foot
Frames	7,100 at $3.15 per Frame
Labor:	
Skilled ($9.80 per hour)	900 Hours
Unskilled ($8.50 per hour)	840 Hours
Overhead:	
Indirect Labor	$800
Power	$250
Depreciation	$1,600
Supervision	$960
Other.	$1.250

Prepare a report for Mr. Elmo Knapp and Mr. Otto Knapp that reconciles the profit graph with the actual results for March. Show the source of each variance from the original plan (8,000 rackets) in as much detail as you can, and evaluate Racketeer's performance in March. (Actual production data for March appear in Exhibit 14.18.) Recommend improvements in Racketeer's profit planning and control methods.

31. *Standard cost flows* (Appendix 14.1). Refer to Problem 30. Present the flow of costs in T-account form.

32. *Cost and profit variance analysis, variable costing.* The following data are for Tondamakers, which makes Tonda riding lawnmowers. The company has no inventories of any kind at the beginning of Year 2.

Year 2

Tondamakers produced 1,500 Tondas and sold 1,200 Tondas. Actual costs of production follow:

Direct Materials: 14,000 Pounds at $21...........................	$ 294,000
Direct Labor: 3,000 Hours at $29	87,000
Manufacturing Overhead..	270,000
Actual Marketing and Administrative Costs........................	440,000
Total Revenue: 1,200 Tondas at $980..........................	1,176,000
Actual Machine Hours Worked..................................	700 Hours

Year 3

Tondamakers produced 1,200 Tondas and sold 1,500 Tondas. Actual costs of production follow:

Direct Materials: 11,000 Pounds at $22...........................	$ 242,000
Direct Labor: 2,300 Hours at $31	71,300
Manufacturing Overhead..	261,000
Actual Marketing and Administrative Costs........................	460,000
Total Revenue: 1,500 Tondas at $1,050	1,575,000
Actual Machine Hours Worked..................................	600 Hours

Additional information follows.

(1) Partition of actual overhead and marketing and administrative costs into variable and fixed components:

	Year 2	Year 3
Overhead:		
Fixed..	$190,000	$195,000
Variable	80,000	66,000
Total	$270,000	$261,000
Marketing and Administrative:		
Fixed..	$360,000	$360,000
Variable	80,000	100,000
Total	$440,000	$460,000

(2) Predetermined overhead rates for machine hours (assume an estimated .5 machine hour per Tonda): Estimated overhead = $200,000 + $80 per hour. Machine hours are used to apply overhead to products. Estimated machine hours were 625 hours per year.

(3) Standard costs per Tonda:

Materials	$200 (= 10 Pounds at $20 per Pound)
Labor	60 (= 2 Hours at $30 per Hour)
Variable Overhead	40
	$300
Fixed Overhead	160 (= $200,000/625 Hours × .5 Hours per Tonda)
	$460

(4) Budgeted sales were 1,300 Tondas each year at $1,000 budgeted price per Tonda.

(5) Budgeted marketing and administrative cost was $350,000 + $50 per Tonda.

(6) Tonda has no beginning nor ending materials inventories.

Prepare a profit variance analysis and cost variance analysis like the one in Exhibit 14.6. (Do not present the fixed cost production volume variance.)

33. *Reconciling profit variance analysis with full absorption costing.* Reconcile the amounts achieved for Tondamakers (see Problem 32) with the amounts that would be achieved using full absorption costing. (See Exhibit 14.8 on page 626.)

34. *Cost and profit variance analysis; reconciling with full absorption costing.* John Holden, president and general manager of Solartronics, Inc., was confused. Lisa Blocker, the firm's recently hired controller and financial manager, had recently instituted the preparation of a new, summarized income statement. Ms. Blocker was to issue this statement on a monthly basis. Mr. Holden had just received a copy of the statement for January, Year 7 (see Exhibit 14.19).

Solartronics, Inc., a small, Texas-based manufacturer of solar energy panels, had been in business since Year 2. By the end of Year 6, it had survived some bad years and positioned itself as a reasonably large firm within the industry. As part of a conscious effort to professionalize the firm, Mr. Holden had added Ms. Blocker to the staff in the autumn of Year 6. Previous to that time, Solartronics had employed a full-time, full-charge bookkeeper.

Exhibit 14.19

SOLARTRONICS, INC.
Income Statement
January, Year 7

Sales...			$130,000[a]
Less Cost of Goods Sold (at standard)			82,500[a]
Gross Margin..........................			$ 47,500
Less: Selling Expenses ($13,500 fixed) ...		$26,500	
General Corporate Administrative (all fixed)		18,000	
Operating Variances:			
Direct Labor.......................	$ 3,500 U		
Direct Materials....................	500 F		
Variable Factory Overhead	1,500 U		
Fixed Factory Overhead— Spending	2,000 F		
Fixed Factory Overhead— Volume.......................	17,500 U	20,000 U	64,500
Profit (loss) before Tax.................			$ (17,000)

[a]Production and sales volume are equal.

Exhibit 14.20

SOLARTRONICS, INC.
Budgeted Income Statement
Calendar Year, Year 7

Sales...		$3,000,000[a]
Less Cost of Goods Sold (at standard)		1,980,000[b]
Gross Margin.....................................		$1,020,000
Less: Selling Expenses	$420,000[c]	
General Corporate Administrative (all fixed)	240,000	660,000
Profit before Tax		$ 360,000

[a]Sales and production volume are budgeted to be equal. Inventories are budgeted to be zero.

[b]The standard cost of goods sold consisted of $420,000 direct labor, $780,000 direct materials, $360,000 variable factory overhead, and $420,000 fixed factory overhead. Ms. Blocker treated direct labor and direct materials as variable costs.

[c]Of this amount, $120,000 was considered to be fixed. The remaining $300,000 represented the 10 percent commission paid on sales.

Mr. Holden's confusion arose because he had not expected the firm to report a loss for January. Although he knew that sales had been down, primarily because of the normal seasonal downturn, and that production had been scaled back to maintain zero levels of inventory, he was still surprised. He wondered if the first month's results were a bad omen in terms of meeting the budgeted results for the year. (See Exhibit 14.20.) Even though the current year's budget represented only a 10 percent increase in sales volume over the previous year, Mr. Holden was concerned that such a poor start to the year might make it difficult to get "back on stream."

Prepare a complete analysis of Solartronics' actual performance compared to budgeted performance. Compute variances in as much detail as possible, using both profit variance and cost variance analyses. In addition, Mr. Holden (a "one-minute manager") would like an explanation for the key factors leading to the loss in 50 words or less. What is it?

35. *Cost and profit analysis; reconciling with full absorption costing and solving for missing data*. The president of Profound Analysts, Inc., called Karen Levine into her office one morning in early February. Ms. Levine was a newly hired analyst from an MBA program. "Karen," the president began, "I've just received financial data for last year for Hi-Tech, Inc. (see Exhibit 14.21). Someone else has started the analysis (see Exhibit 14.22) but was called away for an important business meeting in Bermuda. Could you complete the analysis? I am particularly interested in knowing why pretax income was virtually unchanged even though revenues were up by more than $175,000. I'd like a detailed explanation of the $1,950 profit increase based on these data (Exhibit 14.21). I recommend that you convert everything to variable costing for the variance computations, then reconcile your variable costing numbers with the amounts shown in Exhibit 14.21, if necessary."

Exhibit 14.21

HI-TECH, INC.
Operating Results for the Years Ended December 31

	Last Year	Current Year
Sales Revenues	$3,525,000	$3,701,250
Cost of Goods Sold	2,115,000	2,310,450
Gross Margin...	1,410,000	1,390,800
Marketing and Administrative	902,400	881,250
Income before Taxes	$ 507,600	$ 509,550

Other Data for Last Year
1. Sales = 88,125 units @ $40.
2. Cost of goods sold = 88,125 units @ $24.
3. Marketing and administrative (M & A) costs were $1.84 per unit variable selling cost plus $740,250 fixed M & A.
4. Production volume and sales volume were equal.
5. Production costs per unit follow for units produced and in ending inventory:

Materials........................	$ 9.60 (8 pounds at $1.20)
Direct Labor	4.80 (.50 hour at $9.60)
Variable Overhead	1.60 (per unit, 33⅓% times direct labor dollars)
Fixed Overhead..................	8.00 (based on estimated production volume of 88,125 units, also 166⅔% times direct labor dollars)
	$24.00

Other Data for Current Year
1. Sales = 78,750 units @ $47.
2. Cost of goods sold includes the current year's production cost variances. Variances are not prorated between inventories and cost of goods sold.
3. Marketing and administrative (M & A) costs were $2 per unit variable selling cost plus $723,750 fixed M & A.
4. Actual production volume was 80,750 units; estimated volume was 88,125 units.
5. 629,000 pounds of material at $1.30 were purchased and used in production.
6. 45,000 direct labor hours were worked at $10.00 per hour.
7. Actual variable overhead costs were $152,000.
8. Overhead is applied to production as a percent of direct labor dollars.

Prepare the detailed analysis of the $1,950 profit increase by completing Exhibit 14.22. Assume that the costing system valued finished goods inventory at $24 per unit (using full absorption, standard costing) at the end of the current year, no beginning finished goods inventory and no beginning or ending materials and work-in-process inventories. Be sure to indicate whether variances are favorable or unfavorable.

Exhibit 14.22

Partial Variance Analysis								
	Current Year (full absorption costing)	Inventory Adjustment	Current Year (variable costing)	Cost Variance (excluding production volume variance)	Sales Price Variance	Current Year's Volumes at Last Year's Prices and Costs	Sales Volume (activity) Variance	Last Year (actual)
Revenue......	$3,701,250		$3,701,250		$551,250 F	$3,150,000		$3,525,000
Variable Cost of Goods Sold........								
Variable M & A......	_____	_____	_____	_____		_____	_____	_____
Contribution Margin	$		$			$		$
Fixed Manu-facturing						705,000		705,000
Fixed M & A ..		_____	_____	_____		740,250		740,250
	$ 509,550	_____	_____	_____	$551,250 F	$	$	$ 507,600

Manufacturing Cost Variances:

	Actual	Price Variance	Efficiency Variance	Flexible Production Budget
Materials		$____	$____	
Labor		$____	$____	
Variable Overhead........		$____	$____	

	Actual	Price Variance	Budget	Production Volume Variance	Applied
Fixed Overhead		$____		$____	

Suggested Solutions to Even-Numbered Exercises

12.   *Overhead variances*

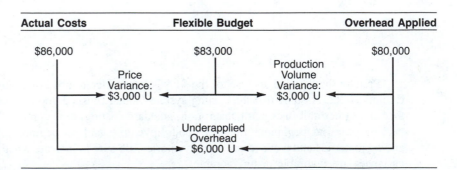

14. *Overhead variances*

    a. Budgeted Fixed Costs = \$1.00 per Unit × 45,000 Units

                                  = \$45,000.

    b.   Applied Overhead = (\$1.00 × 40,000) + (\$2.00 × 40,000)

                                    = \$120,000.

        \$140,000 − \$120,000 = \$20,000 Underapplied.

    c. $\dfrac{\text{Total Variable}}{\text{Overhead Variance}} = \text{Actual Costs} - \dfrac{\text{Flexible Production}}{\text{Budget Costs}}$

                      = \$95,000 − (40,000 × \$2.00)

                      = \$15,000 U.

Fixed overhead variance analysis:

Actual	Price Variance	Budget	Production Volume Variance	Applied
\$45,000		\$45,000		40,000
	0		\$5,000 U	

16. *Hospital supply variances.* Review price and efficiency variances as given below. Now extend the analysis to compute mix and yield variances as on page 664.

18. *Variance investigation.* Is $P \times B > C$? $P = .35$, $B = (\$45,000 - \$20,000)$, and $C = \$7,000$. We find that $.35 \times (\$45,000 - \$20,000) = .35 \times (\$25,000) = \$8,750$. \$8,750 > \$7,000; therefore, investigate.

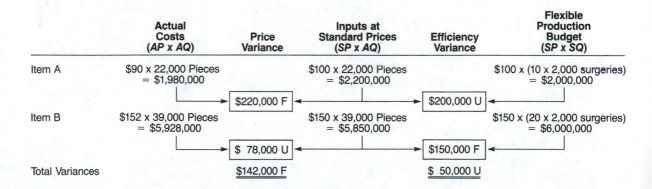

	Actual Costs (AP x AQ)	Price Variance	Inputs at Standard Prices (SP x AQ)	Efficiency Variance	Flexible Production Budget (SP x SQ)
Item A	\$90 x 22,000 Pieces = \$1,980,000		\$100 x 22,000 Pieces = \$2,200,000		\$100 x (10 x 2,000 surgeries) = \$2,000,000
		\$220,000 F		\$200,000 U	
Item B	\$152 x 39,000 Pieces = \$5,928,000		\$150 x 39,000 Pieces = \$5,850,000		\$150 x (20 x 2,000 surgeries) = \$6,000,000
		\$ 78,000 U		\$150,000 F	
Total Variances		\$142,000 F		\$ 50,000 U	

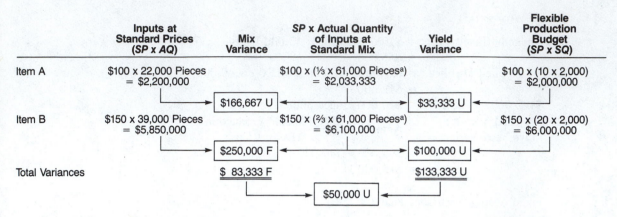

	Inputs at Standard Prices (*SP x AQ*)	Mix Variance	*SP* x Actual Quantity of Inputs at Standard Mix	Yield Variance	Flexible Production Budget (*SP x SQ*)
Item A	$100 x 22,000 Pieces = $2,200,000		$100 x (⅓ x 61,000 Pieces[a]) = $2,033,333		$100 x (10 x 2,000) = $2,000,000
		$166,667 U		$33,333 U	
Item B	$150 x 39,000 Pieces = $5,850,000		$150 x (⅔ x 61,000 Pieces[a]) = $6,100,000		$150 x (20 x 2,000) = $6,000,000
		$250,000 F		$100,000 U	
Total Variances		$ 83,333 F		$133,333 U	
			$50,000 U		

[a]61,000 = Total Prices Used = 22,000 + 39,000.

20. *Recording overhead costs* (Appendix 14.1)

Variable Overhead		Variable Overhead Price Variance		Variable Overhead Efficiency Variance		Work-in-Process	
159,500	156,000[a] 3,500	1,500[d]		2,000[b]		156,000	

Fixed Overhead		Fixed Overhead Price Variance		Fixed Overhead Production Variance			
33,500[g] 5,500	39,000[f]		6,500[e]	1,000[c]		39,000	

[a]39,000 Direct Labor Hours at $4.00 = $156,000.

[b]$(39,500 \times \$4) - (39,000 \times \$4) = \$2,000$.

[c]$(40,000 \times \$1) - (39,000 \times \$1) = \$1,000$.

[d]$159,500 - (39,500 \times \$4) = \$1,500$.

[e]$2,000 F - $1,500 U - $2,000 U - $1,000 U = $6,500 F.

[f]39,000 Direct Labor Hours at $1.00 = $39,000.

[g]Actual − Applied = $(2,000).

$159,500 + X - (\$156,000 + \$39,000) = \$(2,000)$.

$$X = \$33,500 \text{ Actual Fixed Overhead.}$$

... Chapter 15 ...

Divisional Performance Measurement and Incentives

Chapter Outline

- Divisional Organization and Performance
- Return on Investment as the Performance Measure
- Transfer Pricing: Measuring Division Revenue
- Measuring Division Operating Costs
- Measuring the Investment in Divisions
- Contribution Approach to Division Reporting
- Components of Return on Investment
- Residual Income

Companies like General Electric, McDonald's, and IBM have multiple divisions. Central corporate management sets broad corporate policies, establishes long-range plans, raises capital, and conducts other coordinating activities. But corporate management must oversee hundreds of corporate affiliates and divisions. How do companies like these measure and control the performance of their divisions in such widely diverse and geographically dispersed operating environments? Such firms rely heavily on their accounting systems to measure performance and to help control and coordinate their activities. This chapter discusses concepts and methods of measuring performance and controlling activities in multidivision companies. These concepts and methods apply equally in both manufacturing and nonmanufacturing organizations.

Divisional Organization and Performance

The term *division* means different things in different companies. Some companies use the term when referring to segments organized according to product groupings, whereas other companies use it when referring to geographic areas served. We use the term **division** to refer to a segment that conducts both production and marketing activities.

As Chapter 11 discusses, a division may be either a **profit center,** responsible for both revenues and operating costs, or an **investment center,** responsible for assets in addition to revenues and operating costs. Many companies treat the division almost as an autonomous company. Headquarters provides funds for its divisions, much as shareholders and bondholders provide funds for the company.

A partial organization chart for Honeywell, Incorporated, appears in Exhibit 15.1 showing how divisions fit into the entire organization. The organization chart in Exhibit 15.1 presents only a small part of this complex organization. Corporate executives hold managers of divisions responsible for revenues, costs, and assets invested in the divisions and groups. Corporate management holds most operating units below the division level responsible for either revenues or costs alone.

The Nature of Divisionalized Organizations

Organizations base divisionalization on the delegation, or **decentralization, of decision-making** authority and responsibility. All but very small organizations delegate managerial duties. The major advantages of delegation follow:

1. Delegation allows local personnel to respond quickly to a changing environment.
2. Delegation frees top management from detailed operating decisions.
3. Delegation divides large, complex problems into manageable pieces.
4. Delegation helps train managers and provides a basis for evaluating their decision-making performance.
5. Delegation motivates: Ambitious managers will be frustrated if they implement only the decisions of others. Delegation allows managers to make their own decisions.

Delegation has disadvantages, however. Local managers may not act congruent to the overall goals of the organization. For example, a division manager may decide to purchase materials from an outside supplier even though another division of the firm could produce the materials at a lower incremental cost using currently idle facilities. Top management must be alert to situations where the benefits of decentralized authority and the possible conflicts between the goals of a division

Exhibit 15.1

HONEYWELL, INCORPORATED
Partial Organization Chart

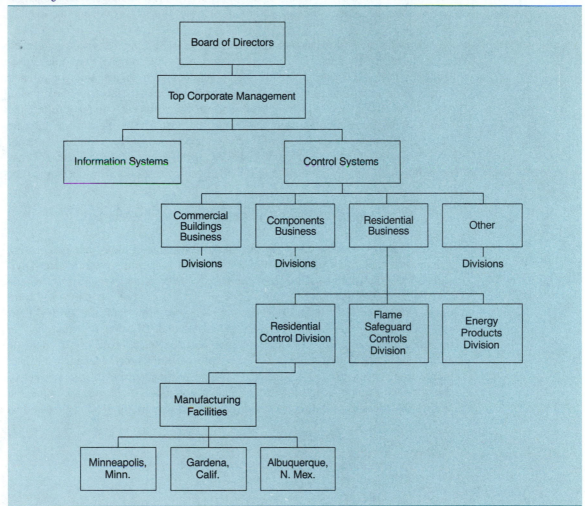

Source: Honeywell annual report.

and those of the organization as a whole require trade-offs. Thus, divisional planning and control systems attempt to create **behavioral congruence** (or **goal congruence**) to encourage division managers to act in ways consistent with organizational goals.[1]

Delegation occurs in many employee-employer relationships. Divisionalized organizations give divisional managers responsibility for nearly everything that occurs in their division.

[1]For an expanded discussion, see the classic book by David Solomons, *Divisional Performance Measurement and Control* (Homewood, Ill.: Irwin, 1968).

Separating a Manager's Performance from Divisional Performance

In general, you should distinguish between the measure of an organizational unit's performance and that of the unit manager's performance. Managers often perform well despite the division's poor performance because of factors outside the manager's control.

Consider the following interdivisional conflict. Assume a division purchased materials externally rather than from a division inside the company with idle capacity. By purchasing from an outside source, the company earned lower combined profits from the two divisions than if they purchased the materials from the division inside the company. Should the performance measure for each division reflect the results of its actual transactions? Or should the cost of idle capacity in the one division be charged against the profits of the other division? These questions are not easy to answer. The accounting system needs to inform top management of situations in which actions of individual divisions hurt overall company performance.

Return on Investment as the Performance Measure

Because management expects each division to contribute to the company's profits, managers commonly use divisional operating profit to measure performance. Divisional operating profit by itself, however, does not provide a basis for measuring a division's performance in generating a return on the funds invested in the division. For example, the fact that Division A reported an operating profit of $50,000 does not necessarily mean that it was more successful than Division B, which had an operating profit of $40,000. The difference between these profit levels could be entirely attributable to a difference in the size of the divisions. Management must therefore use some means to scale the division profit measure for the amount of capital invested in the division. Management commonly achieves a comparable statistic by measuring the **division return on investment,** or **ROI,** calculated as follows:

$$
\begin{aligned}
\text{Division Return on Investment (ROI)} &= \frac{\text{Division Operating Profit}}{\text{Division Investment}} \\[2mm]
&= \frac{\text{Division Revenue} - \text{Division Operating Costs}}{\text{Division Investment}}.
\end{aligned}
$$

In the preceding example if management invested $500,000 and $250,000 in Division A and Division B respectively, the ROIs would be 10 percent (= $50,000/$500,000) and 16 percent (= $40,000/$250,000). Thus Division B earned a higher profit given its investment base than Division A, even though Division A generated a larger absolute amount of profit.

The manager must answer several important questions before applying ROI as a control measure:

1. How does the firm measure revenues, particularly when it transfers part of a division's output to another division rather than selling it externally?

2. Which costs does the firm deduct in measuring divisional operating costs—only those that the division can control, or also a portion of allocated central corporate administration and staff costs?

3. How does the firm measure investment—total assets or net assets, at historical cost or some measure of current cost?

We consider these questions in the following sections.

Transfer Pricing: Measuring Division Revenue

In cases where, because of the nature of the product, a division cannot sell its output to another division and therefore sells all of the output externally, few unique revenue measurement problems will occur beyond those encountered in financial accounting. In other words, accounting policy will question whether the firm will recognize revenue as production takes place, at the point of sale, or as it collects cash. It may be of interest to top management to have all divisions follow the same accounting methods, thereby enhancing the comparability of the measures of ROI.

In cases where one division can potentially sell its output to another division, we confront the **transfer pricing problem.** The price accounting assigns to the interdivisional transfer of goods or services represents a revenue for the selling division and a cost to the buying division.[2] Should management set the transfer price equal to the manufacturing cost of the selling division? Or should the transfer price equal the amount at which the selling (buying) division could sell (purchase) the good or service externally? Or should the transfer price equal a negotiated amount somewhere between the selling division's cost of manufacturing and the external market price?

A superficial consideration of the transfer pricing problem may suggest that the selection of a transfer price is inconsequential. After all, what comes out of one corporate pocket goes into another. This simplistic viewpoint ignores the fact that the amount of the transfer price may affect certain divisional decisions, which in turn may affect the overall profitability of the company. For example, suppose that management sets a transfer price at $10 per unit and the product has no external market. If the buying division believes this price is too high, it may take less than it would at a lower price. In this case the buying division may be acting in its own best interests, but the actions of the two divisions together may not optimize the company's interests.

The simplistic view of the transfer pricing problem also ignores the real possibility that a transfer price central corporate headquarters sets arbitrarily may undermine the entire divisional organizational structure. Division managers should, within limits, make decisions freely, as if the divisions were separate companies. If

---

[2]Only rarely will cash equal to the transfer price actually change hands. Transfer prices are set at the time of the transfer, so performance of the selling division can be assessed as of the time of the transfer rather than waiting several periods until all manufacturing is completed and the good is sold to someone outside the company.

top management imposes a transfer price that determines the return, or profit, from a significant portion of the division's operations, divisional managers will lose some motivational and other benefits of decentralized decision making. The selection of an appropriate transfer price can therefore affect decision making significantly.

We discuss several solutions to the transfer pricing problem in the following sections.

Direct Intervention

Top management could intervene directly and order a supplying division of the company to produce and transfer products to a buying division. Top management would specify a transfer price that would be incidental to the transaction. In other words, the transfer price would not bear on the decision; rather, management would set it *after* the transaction. For an extraordinarily large order or rare internal product transfers, direct intervention could be the optimal solution because it would virtually ensure that division managers took the "right" actions.

However, when this type of transaction occurs often, direct intervention reduces the value of decentralization.[3] Further, direct intervention uses top management's time that may be better spent elsewhere. To avoid using management's time, the company may set up a transfer pricing *policy* encouraging decentralized managers to make the right decisions without reducing their autonomy.

Management-Established Transfer Pricing Policy

Rather than intervene directly and force a transaction, top management may establish rules for setting transfer prices that encourage division managers to optimize company goals. If division managers establish the transfer price incorrectly, they will not make decisions that are in the best interest of the company. We will discuss some bases for setting these transfer prices. In each case, we assume that one division of the company—the selling division—produces a product that another division of the company—the buying division—could purchase.

Market Prices as Transfer Prices   *Market price* refers to a price in an intermediate market, not the price for the end product the buying division produces. When the transferred product has a competitive external market, market prices work well as transfer prices.[4] Both the selling and buying divisions can sell and buy as much as they want at the market price. Managers of both selling and buying divisions will trade with each other or with outsiders. From a company-wide perspective, using market prices optimizes profits as long as the selling division operates at capacity. Use of a market price also helps assure profit independence of the divisions. Any gains or losses in the selling division's efficiency do not get passed on to the buying

---

[3]For an expanded discussion, see Joshua Ronen and George McKinney, "Transfer Pricing for Divisional Autonomy," *Journal of Accounting Research* (Spring 1970).

[4]You can find classic work on the economic theory of transfer pricing in Jack Hirschleifer, "On the Economics of Transfer Pricing," *Journal of Business* (July 1956), pp. 172–184. Also see Jack Hirschleifer, "Economics of the Divisionalized Firm," *Journal of Business* (April 1957), pp. 96–108 and David Solomons, *Divisional Performance: Measurement and Control* (Homewood, Ill.: Irwin, 1965), appendix A to chap. 6.

division. Use of competitive market prices also frees managers from arguing over price, thereby saving administrative costs.

A major problem with using market prices can occur when a selling division operates below capacity, as the following example demonstrates.

Example The Systems Division of Magna-Products, Incorporated, builds a navigational system that is standard equipment in many commercial and military airplanes. This division—the *selling* division—can make 300 systems per year. Its variable cost per system is $1 million. (Assume differential costs equal variable costs in this example.) The Aircraft Division of Magna-Products, Incorporated—the *buying* division—builds airplanes and uses the selling division's navigational system in those airplanes. The Systems (selling) Division can sell to outside airplane manufacturers, and the Aircraft (buying) Division can buy the system from outside suppliers.

The market for airplanes has temporarily declined so that the selling division can sell only 100 systems per year to outside buyers at a price of $2.5 million per system. The Aircraft (buying) Division of Magna-Products could use 50 systems per year in the airplane models it builds. (The Aircraft Division also operates below capacity.)

If the market price of $2.5 million per navigational system is the transfer price, the Aircraft (buying) Division treats the cost of the system as $2.5 million. Assume that the *other* variable costs of making an airplane are $16 million. From the Aircraft Division's perspective, its variable costs per airplane equal $18.5 million (= $16 million + $2.5 million). Suppose a foreign government has offered to purchase six airplanes for a price of $18 million each.

Given the soft market for airplanes, Magna-Products' company policy is to sell airplanes for any price greater than variable cost. Thus the company serves its best interests if the Aircraft Division sells the airplanes, because the price of $18 million exceeds the variable cost to the company of $17 million (= $16 million + $1 million variable cost of making the system). The Aircraft Division turns down the order, however, because *its* variable costs are $18.5 million. Exhibit 15.2 summarizes this analysis.

Exhibit 15.2

Comparison of Total Company Perspective with Buying and Selling Divisions' Perspectives[a]

	Magna-Products: Company Perspective	Aircraft Division: Buying Division Perspective	Systems Division: Selling Division Perspective
Price per Airplane	$18,000,000	$18,000,000	—
Differential (Variable) Cost of Navigational System	(1,000,000)	—	$(1,000,000)
Transfer Price	—	(2,500,000)	2,500,000
Differential (Variable) Cost of Remainder of Airplane	(16,000,000)	(16,000,000)	—
Profit (Loss)......................................	$ 1,000,000	$ (500,000)	$ 1,500,000
Decision	Although the company would make a profit of $1 million per airplane, the buying (Aircraft) division rejects the order because it incurs a loss.		

[a]Costs are in parentheses. The buying division makes airplanes; the selling division makes navigational systems.

Discussion   When products transferred between divisions have a competitive market and when the selling division operates at capacity, **market-based transfer prices** are ideal. Division managers who make decisions in response to such transfer prices to maximize division profits also maximize company-wide profits.

Competitive markets for a product being transferred between divisions rarely exist, however. The fact that two responsibility centers belong to one company indicates that they gain some advantages as opposed to dealing with each other as two separate companies in the market. For example, they have more certainty about the internal supplier's product quality or delivery reliability. Or the selling division may make a specialized product with no substitutes in the market. Hence, using market prices may be impossible.

In the following section, we show that management uses market prices when selling divisions operate at capacity as part of a general rule for transfer prices that induces division managers to make decisions in the company's best interests.

Differential Cost Plus Opportunity Cost: A General Rule

To set transfer prices so that the buying division makes the optimal economic decisions from the viewpoint of the total company, management follows the general rule of transferring at[5]

$$\begin{array}{c} \text{Differential Cost} \\ \text{to the Selling} \\ \text{Division} \end{array} + \begin{array}{c} \text{Implicit Opportunity} \\ \text{Cost to Company If} \\ \text{It Transfers Goods} \\ \text{Internally.} \end{array}$$

In the Magna-Products example, the differential cost to the selling division (that is, the Systems Division) was $1 million per unit. What was the implicit opportunity cost to the company if the Systems Division made the systems and transferred them to the buyer (that is, the Aircraft Division)? Recall that both the Systems and Aircraft divisions were operating below capacity. *If the company has no alternative uses for the idle capacity, the implicit opportunity cost to the company is zero.* Thus the transfer price should have been $1 million, and the Aircraft Division's costs would have been the total differential costs of producing an airplane—$17 million.

Selling Division Operates at Capacity   If the Systems Division had been operating at capacity, then transferring internally would have created an implicit opportunity cost. The Systems Division would have forgone a sale of a system in the intermediate market to make the internal transfer. The implicit opportunity cost to the company is the lost contribution margin (for example, $2.5 million − $1.0 million = $1.5 million) from not selling the system in the intermediate market.

---

[5]Accountants sometimes use *marginal cost, outlay cost,* or *variable cost* instead of differential cost. We use *differential cost* to be consistent with our terminology throughout this book.

Economists will sometimes refer to the general rule as ''transfer at marginal opportunity cost.'' We find it useful to distinguish between the differential cost, which can usually be derived from the accounting records, and implicit opportunity cost, which requires an ''off-the-books'' calculation.

Thus, if the selling division had sufficient sales in the intermediate market to force it to forgo those sales to transfer internally, the transfer price should have been as follows:

$$
\begin{array}{ccc}
\begin{array}{c}\text{Differential Cost}\\ \text{to the Selling}\\ \text{Division}\end{array} & + & \begin{array}{c}\text{Implicit Opportunity}\\ \text{Cost to Company If}\\ \text{Goods Are Transferred}\\ \text{Internally}\end{array}\\
\\
= \quad \$1,000,000 & + & \$1,500,000\\
\\
= \quad \$2,500,000.
\end{array}
$$

(Note that this rule is the same as the market price–based transfer price *when the selling division operates at capacity.*)

The buying division would have appropriately treated the $2.5 million as part of *its* differential cost of making and selling airplanes. Now compare how this rule affects each division and the company, both when the selling division operates below and at capacity, as Exhibit 15.3 shows. Note that when the selling division operates at capacity and the transfer price equals $2.5 million, the buying division manager decides not to sell the airplane. The selling division therefore sells the system in the external market for $2.5 million, and the company makes a profit of $1.5 million.

The rule that the transfer price should include the opportunity cost of the transfer applies to any forgone alternative use of resources because the division makes the transfer. For example, suppose that the Systems Division currently operates below capacity, but could rent the idle capacity to an outsider. The opportunity cost of an internal transfer would be the forgone profit or contribution margin from the outsider. In short, the general transfer pricing rule includes any type of opportunity cost.

Use of Full Costs and Standard Costs

Measurement Problems   When market prices are the appropriate transfer prices and management has information about them readily available, implementing a transfer price policy is not costly. But measurement problems, and costs of implementing a transfer pricing policy, can be substantial when market prices are unknown. Measuring differential costs is often difficult, and measuring implicit opportunity costs may be impossible. Consequently, many companies transfer at full cost, or full cost plus a markup, an example of **cost-based transfer prices.**

Use of Standard Costs   Whether transferring at differential cost or full cost, firms often use standard costs (where available) as the basis for the transfer. This practice encourages efficiency in the selling division because they do not pass on inefficiencies or transfer variances to the buying division. Use of standard costs reduces risk to the buyer, because the buyer knows that the seller will transfer at standard costs and the buyer avoids being charged with the supplier's cost overruns.

Exhibit 15.3

MAGNA-PRODUCTS, INCORPORATED
Applying the General Transfer Price Rule
(all dollar amounts in thousands)

	Company	Buying (Aircraft) Division	Selling (Systems) Division
Facts			
Price per Airplane	$18.0	$18.0	—
Differential Cost of the System	(1.0)	—	$(1.0)
Differential Cost of the Remainder of the Airplane . . .	(16.0)	(16.0)	—
Case 1: Selling (Systems) Division Operates below Capacity			
Transfer Price	—	(1.0)	1.0
Profit (Loss) to the Company If:			
Airplane Sold and System Purchased Internally . . .	1.0[a]	1.0	0.0
Airplane Sold and System Purchased Externally			
for $2.5 million	(0.5)[b]	(0.5)	0.0
Airplane Not Sold	0.0	0.0	0.0
Optimal Decision: Sell Airplane and Purchase System Internally.			
Case 2: Selling (Systems) Division Operates at Capacity			
Transfer Price	—	(2.5)	2.5
Profit (Loss) to the Company If:			
Airplane Sold and System Purchased Internally . . .	1.0[c]	(0.5)	1.5
Airplane Sold and System Purchased Externally . .	1.0[d]	(0.5)	1.5
Airplane Not Sold	1.5[e]	0.0	1.5
Optimal Decision: Do Not Sell Airplane, Continue Selling Systems in Outside Market.			

[a]Sales price = $18 million; variable costs = $1 million for the system plus $16 million for the rest of the airplane.

[b]Sales price = $18 million; variable costs = $2.5 million for the system and $16.0 million for the rest of the airplane.

[c]Sales price = $18 million; variable costs = $1 million for the system plus $16 million for the rest of the airplane; forgo the opportunity to sell one system in the external market.

[d]Sales price = $18 million for airplane plus $2.5 million for system sold to external market; variable costs = $1 million for system sold to external market plus $2.5 million for system purchased from external market plus $16 million for rest of airplane. To summarize, $18 + 2.5 − 1 − 2.5 − 16 = $1.

[e]Sales price of system = $2.5 million; variable cost of system = $1 million.

Motivational Problems When the Selling Division Receives No Profits

The transfer pricing rule may not give the selling division a profit on the transaction when transfers are made at actual differential cost. For example, when the selling division operates below capacity and has no opportunity for the use of idle facilities, the selling division receives only a price that equals differential cost. (Note Case 1 in Exhibit 15.3.) Under these circumstances, some criticize the transfer price rule because it does not provide incentives for the selling division to transfer internally, because the selling division can seldom, if ever, expect to profit from internal transfers. Firms deal with this situation in several ways.

Use Cost Centers   If nearly all of the selling division's transfers are internal, the seller's responsibility center is probably a cost center. As such, management would normally hold the division (if it could be called a division under these circumstances) responsible for costs but not for revenues.

Use Hybrid Centers: Cost and Profit   Suppose that the selling division does business with both internal and external customers. Management could set it up as a profit center for the external business, where the manager has some responsibility for setting prices, and as a cost center for the internal business, where the manager does not. Accountants could measure performance for external business as if it were a profit center but measure performance for internal business as if it were a cost center.

Use Dual Transfer Prices   The price paid to the selling division does not *have to* equal the price the buying division pays on an internal transaction. With **dual transfer prices,** the accounting system charges the buying division differential costs while crediting the selling division with differential costs plus a markup. Referring to the Magna-Products example, suppose that top management decides to charge the Aircraft (buying) Division with a differential cost (which was $1 million) but to credit the selling division with the intermediate market price of $2.5 million *when the selling division operated below capacity*. This practice retains the transfer pricing rule, so the Aircraft Division manager makes the correct decision to acquire the system internally and manufacture the airplane. Yet the System Division profits on the internal transfer.

Design Incentive Systems to Recognize the Benefits of Internal Transfers   We have assumed that firms reward selling division managers based only on their division's profit performance. Selling division managers will have incentives to transfer internally, even if their division earns no profits on the transaction, *if* management also rewards them for internal transfers. Thus many companies recognize internal transfers and incorporate them into the reward system. Other companies base part of the selling managers' rewards on the buying division's performance or the total company's performance. In short, management creates many incentives for managers to trade internally without losing the benefit of the transfer pricing rule.

Negotiated Transfer Prices

Transfer prices based on differential cost represent a lower limit on the price that selling divisions will accept. Transfer prices based on market prices represent an upper limit on the price that buying divisions will pay. The difference between these two prices is the total margin on the transfer. Many firms permit divisional managers to negotiate among themselves about how to split the margin. If both divisions may deal freely either with each other or in the external market, the negotiated price will be close to the external market price. If a selling division cannot sell its total

Exhibit 15.4

Transfer Pricing Practices

	Respondents Specifying Method Used	
	Number of Companies	Percent
Market Price:		
Competitor's Price	28	
Market Price—List	41	
Market Price—Bid	5	
Total Market Price Based	74	31.0%
Cost:		
Variable Cost: Actual	4	
Variable Cost: Standard	7	
Full Cost: Actual	31	
Full Cost: Standard	30	
Total Cost Based	72	30.1
Cost Plus	40	16.7
Negotiation	53	22.2
Total	239	100.0%

Source: Richard F. Vancil, *Decentralization* (Homewood, Ill.: Dow Jones–Irwin, 1978), p. 180.

Note: Questionnaires were mailed to 1,010 companies, 404 were returned, of which 357 were usable. Of these 357 companies, 249 reported that they transfer goods between profit centers; 239 of these reported their transfer pricing policy.

output on the external market (that is, they must sell a portion to the buying division), the negotiated price will be less than the market price and the divisions will share the total margin. The use of **negotiated transfer prices** corresponds with the concept of decentralized decision making in divisionalized firms.

One of the principal disadvantages of negotiated transfer prices is that the divisions may require significant time to carry out the negotiating process. Also, interdivision hostility may result, which could hurt overall company performance.

As we mentioned previously, no particular transfer pricing scheme works best in all circumstances. The choice involves such factors as the extent of external markets, the extent top management chooses to intervene in divisional decisions, the amount of trading among divisions, and other factors.

Business Practices

Some results of a survey of transfer pricing practices appear in Exhibit 15.4.[6] As shown, nearly half of the companies responding used a cost basis for setting transfer prices. Thirty-one percent used market prices and the remainder used negotiated prices. Other research shows that use of negotiated prices often means that buyers and sellers negotiate the amount of discount from the market price.

***

[6]Richard F. Vancil, *Decentralization* (Homewood, Ill.: Dow Jones–Irwin, 1978).

Measuring Division Operating Costs

In measuring divisional operating costs, management must decide how to treat the following costs: (1) controllable, direct operating costs; (2) noncontrollable, direct operating costs; (3) controllable, indirect operating costs; and (4) noncontrollable, indirect operating costs. Direct versus indirect refers to whether the cost associates directly with the division; controllable versus noncontrollable refers to whether the division manager can affect the cost. Exhibit 15.5 shows examples of each.

Direct Costs

Management virtually always deducts a division's direct operating costs, whether or not the division manager controls them, from divisional revenues in measuring divisional operating profits. From top management's perspective, any cost necessary for that division to operate is a direct cost, even if the division manager cannot control the cost. If top management believes that division managers should not be held responsible for things outside their control, it can separate the measure of costs assigned to a *division* from the costs assigned to a division *manager*—the latter measure could exclude direct costs of the division that the division manager cannot control (for example, the division manager's salary).

Indirect, Controllable Operating Costs[7]

Divisions can at least partially control indirect, controllable costs. Firms usually centralize these services because of economies of scale in doing so. In some companies, costs would exceed benefits if each division had its own legal staff, research department, data-processing department, and so forth.

For example, many companies have centralized employee training departments. Should management charge divisions for sending their people to these centralized departments? As you may expect, the experiences in most companies follow fundamental laws of economics: The use of centralized services and the price

Exhibit 15.5

Examples of Direct (Indirect) and Controllable (Noncontrollable) Costs	
Direct	**Indirect**
Controllable	
Labor Used in the Division's Production	Costs of Providing Centralized Services, Such as Data Processing and Employee Training, Which the Division's Use Partially Affects
Noncontrollable	
Salary of the Division Manager (controlled by top management)	Company President's Salary

---

[7]Assigning central headquarters' costs to divisions is part of a more general cost allocation problem discussed in Chapter 5.

charged for those services are inversely related. When companies charge a high price for employee training, people's attendance from the divisions drops, and vice versa. Top management can use this experience to decide on the desired usage and set the price accordingly. Some companies treat centralized service departments as profit or investment centers; if so, the transfer pricing issues discussed earlier are relevant.

Indirect, Noncontrollable Operating Costs

Indirect, noncontrollable operating costs may be necessary costs to the company (for example, the salaries and staff support of corporate top management). The most frequent arguments against allocating these costs are based on the divisions' inability to control the amount of costs incurred as well as the arbitrary allocation bases that the accountant must use. For example, on what basis should the accountant allocate the president's salary to the divisions—sales, number of employees, square footage of space used? Any allocation base is likely to be meaningless.

One argument advanced for allocation is that, unless the company allocates these costs to the divisions, the divisions will underprice their products and cause the company as a whole to operate at a loss. In other words, the revenues the divisions generate would be insufficient to cover both the direct operating costs of the divisions and the indirect operating costs incurred at central headquarters.

This argument is not particularly convincing in the short run. Competitive market conditions will determine prices. These prices will be the same whether or not the cost system allocates central corporate operating costs. As a basis for evaluating the month-to-month performance of divisional managers, top management should pay attention to the divisional operating profits before allocation of central corporate operating costs. If divisions seek to optimize this divisional contribution amount, they will also optimize divisional operating profits after allocation of central corporate operating costs, however allocated.

Others argue that allocation keeps division managers aware of the existence of central headquarters costs and the need for the company as a whole to cover those costs. In addition, allocation may stimulate managers to monitor those costs and put pressure on top management if the costs become too great. A top manager of a retail company told us that central headquarters costs were allocated to the stores to keep them aware of these costs. "We want our store managers to recognize that it's not enough for stores to make a profit for the company to be profitable." The corporate manager went on to say that part of a store manager's bonus was based on the store's profit after central headquarters costs had been allocated to stores. "This makes them very aware of central headquarters costs, and it makes us [top management] sensitive to their criticisms about administrative costs" (that is, central headquarters costs).

Financing Costs and Income Taxes

Some companies do not allocate nonoperating costs, such as interest on debt and income taxes, to divisions. Corporate headquarters nearly always makes decisions about the terms and type of financing—issuing short-term versus long-term bonds, issuing common versus preferred shares, and so forth. Consequently, many companies do not charge divisions with financing costs. Those that do often charge an implicit interest cost to cover both the opportunity cost of equity capital and interest on debt. This implicit interest indicates the minimum desired rate of return that the division should generate.

In the majority of cases, the system assesses income taxes on the taxable income of the company as a whole rather than on each division. Should the company allocate these income taxes to individual divisions?

Those favoring allocating income taxes to divisions argue that managers should be encouraged to make decisions with income tax implications in mind. For example, management should consider the tax savings from depreciation deductions and the tax consequences of selling versus trading in old equipment in capital budgeting decisions.

Those against allocation make arguments similar to those against arbitrary allocation of central headquarters expenses. Divisional managers cannot control the amount of income taxes assessed. In addition, the potential amount of income taxes paid on divisional income if it were a separate taxable entity may differ from the amount actually assessed when it is aggregated with income of other divisions. Thus the income taxes of one division depend on income other divisions generate.

Measuring the Investment in Divisions

Most companies use some measure of capital employed or invested in each division when calculating ROI. In this section we discuss (1) what assets firms include in the investment base and (2) what valuation basis firms use.

Assets Included in the Investment Base

Management obviously should include assets physically located in a division and used only in the division's operations in the investment base. More difficult problems arise with assets shared among divisions and assets that centralized services departments acquire (for example, buildings and equipment used in personnel training). For example, management may allocate the cost of a shared manufacturing plant between divisions based on square footage used. Where only highly arbitrary allocation bases are possible, wise management will not attribute common investment facilities to divisions.

Valuation of Assets in the Investment Base

Once the firm chooses the assets in the investment base, it must assign them a monetary value. Most firms use acquisition cost as the valuation basis. Management can obtain the necessary amounts directly from the company's accounts.

The use of book values of assets, particularly fixed assets, in the ROI denominator can have undesirable results. The manager of a division with old, low-cost, and almost fully depreciated assets may be reluctant to replace the assets with newer, more efficient, but more costly assets. Replacing old assets with new, more

Exhibit 15.6

Comparison of Alternative Methods of Valuing the Investment Base in ROI Computations

Facts

Operating profits before depreciation is subtracted (all in cash flows at end of year):
Year 1, $100; Year 2, $120; and Year 3, $144.
Annual rate of price changes, 20 percent. This rate applies both to asset replacement costs and annual cash flows.
Asset cost at *beginning* of Year 1, $500. The only asset is depreciable with 10-year life and no salvage value.
Straight-line depreciation is used; straight-line rate is 10 percent per year for managerial purposes. The denominator in the ROI computation is based on *end*-of-year asset value.
The numerator in the ROI computation equals operating profits (equals cash flow minus depreciation for the year).

	Historical Cost		Current Replacement Cost	
Year	Net Book Value (1)	Gross Book Value (2)	Net Book Value (3)	Gross Book Value (4)
1	$\text{ROI} = \dfrac{\$100^a - (.1 \times \$500)^b}{\$500^c - (.1^f \times \$500)^d}$ $= \dfrac{\$50}{\$450} = \underline{\underline{11.1\%}}$	$\text{ROI} = \dfrac{\$50}{\$500}$ $= \underline{\underline{10\%}}$	$\text{ROI} = \dfrac{\$100 - (.1 \times 1.2^e \times \$500)}{(1.2^e \times \$500) - (.1^f \times 1.2^e \times \$500)}$ $= \dfrac{\$100 - \$60}{\$600 - \$60} = \dfrac{\$40}{\$540} = \underline{\underline{7.4\%}}$	$\text{ROI} = \dfrac{\$100 - \$60}{(1.2 \times \$500)}$ $= \dfrac{\$40}{\$600} = \underline{\underline{6.7\%}}$
2	$\text{ROI} = \dfrac{\$120 - (.1 \times \$500)}{\$500 - (.2^f \times \$500)}$ $= \dfrac{\$70}{\$400} = \underline{\underline{17.5\%}}$	$\text{ROI} = \dfrac{\$70}{\$500}$ $= \underline{\underline{14\%}}$	$\text{ROI} = \dfrac{\$120 - (.1 \times 1.2 \times \$600)}{(1.2 \times \$600) - (.2^f \times 1.2 \times \$600)}$ $= \dfrac{\$120 - \$72}{\$720 - \$144} = \dfrac{\$48}{\$576} = \underline{\underline{8.3\%}}$	$\text{ROI} = \dfrac{\$120 - \$72}{(1.2 \times \$600)}$ $= \dfrac{\$48}{\$720} = \underline{\underline{6.7\%}}$
3	$\text{ROI} = \dfrac{\$144 - (.1 \times \$500)}{\$500 - (.3^f \times \$500)}$ $= \dfrac{\$94}{\$350} = \underline{\underline{26.9\%}}$	$\text{ROI} = \dfrac{\$94}{\$500}$ $= \underline{\underline{18.8\%}}$	$\text{ROI} = \dfrac{\$144 - (.1 \times 1.2 \times \$720)}{(1.2 \times \$720) - (.3^f \times 1.2 \times \$720)}$ $= \dfrac{\$144 - \$86.4}{\$864 - \$259.2} = \dfrac{\$57.6}{\$604.8} = \underline{\underline{9.5\%}}$	$\text{ROI} = \dfrac{\$144 - \$86.4}{(1.2 \times \$720)}$ $= \dfrac{\$57.6}{\$864} = \underline{\underline{6.7\%}}$

[a] The first term in the numerator is the annual operating profit before depreciation.
[b] The second term in the numerator is depreciation for the year.
[c] The first term in the denominator is the beginning of the first year value of the assets used in the investment base.
[d] The second term in the denominator reduces the beginning-of-first-year value of the asset by the amount of depreciation.
[e] This term (1.2) adjusts the beginning-of-year asset value to the end-of-year value (current value).
[f] This term reduces the net book value of the asset. The net book value is reduced by 10 percent for depreciation at the end of Year 1, by 20 percent at the end of Year 2, and by 30 percent at the end of Year 3.

costly ones decreases the numerator—operating profits—of the ROI calculation because of increased depreciation charges. It also increases the denominator—cost of total assets—of the ROI calculation. These two effects combine to reduce calculated ROI.

If use of book values in the investment base affects divisional investment behavior this way, management may deal with the problem in two possible ways. One, they may state all assets at gross book value rather than at net book value (that is, net of accumulated depreciation). They will therefore state assets at their full acquisition cost regardless of age. In another approach they will state assets at their current replacement cost or net realizable value. Exhibit 15.6 presents a comprehen-

Exhibit 15.7

Divisional Performance Measurement Practices:
Allocation of Common Costs and Assets to Divisions

Measuring Divisional Profit

Consistent with the Way Net Income Is Calculated for External Financial Reports to Shareholders?	Number	Percent of 594 Companies[a]
Yes	239	40%
No	351	59
No Answer	4	1
	594	100%

If No (from above) (multiple responses allowed):	Number	Percent of 351 Companies[b]
No Taxes Assessed to Divisions	249	71%
No Corporate Administrative Costs Allocated to Divisions...	173	49
No Interest Charges on Corporate Debt Allocated to Divisions.	225	64
All Other Variations.	100	28

Measuring Divisional Investment Base

Selected Items Included in the Division's Investment Base (multiple responses allowed):	Number	Percent of 459 Companies Having Investment Centers
Land and Buildings Used Solely by the Division	430	94%
Prorated Share of Land and Buildings Used by Two or More Divisions.	207	45
Equipment Used Solely by the Division.	380	83
Prorated Share of Equipment Used by Two or More Divisions.	188	41

[a]*Source:* James S. Reece and William R. Cool, "Measuring Investment Center Performance," *Harvard Business Review* (May–June 1978). Questionnaires were sent to 1,000 companies; 620 companies responded; 594 of these had profit centers (135 companies) or investment centers (459 companies).

[b]Companies could respond to more than one reason for the measures of profit for internal reporting and measures of net income for external reporting.

Exhibit 15.8

The Contribution Approach to Division Reporting
(all dollar amounts in thousands)

	Company as a Whole	Company Breakdown into Two Divisions		Further Breakdown of Division A into Two Product Lines		
		Division A	Division B	Product 1	Product 2	Not Allocated to Products
Revenues	$6,500	$2,500	$4,000	$1,300	$1,200	
Variable Manufacturing Cost of Goods Sold	2,300	800	1,500	500	300	
Manufacturing Contribution Margin	4,200	1,700	2,500	800	900	
Variable Selling and Administrative Costs	600	200	400	100	100	
Contribution Margin	3,600	1,500	2,100	700	800	
Fixed Costs Directly Attributable to the Division	2,400	900	1,500	275	200	425[a]
Division Contribution to Unallocated Costs and Profit	$1,200	$ 600	$ 600	$ 425	$ 600	$(425)
Unallocated Costs	800[a]					
Operating Profit	$ 400					

[a]These costs are not direct costs of the division or product line and could be allocated only by an arbitrary allocation method.

sive example of ROI computations using different valuation bases. Note that the older the assets (compare Year 3 to Year 1, for example), the higher the ROI under net book value compared to gross book value. Also, ROI is relatively higher under historical cost compared to current replacement cost as the assets get older.

Divisional Performance Measurement Practices

Exhibit 15.7 summarizes current divisional performance measurement practices based on a survey of the *Fortune* 1000 industrial companies.[8] As the top of Exhibit 15.7 shows, 59 percent of the companies use measures of divisional operating profits that differ from the measures of net income they use in external financial reports to their shareholders. These variations between external and internal reporting practices relate almost entirely to items over which division managers have little control—central corporate administration costs, income taxes, and interest. Nearly half of the companies allocate common assets to divisions, as the bottom of Exhibit 15.7 shows. In addition, this survey found that about 84 percent of the companies surveyed use historical cost, net book value in the investment base.

Contribution Approach to Division Reporting

In previous sections, we discussed some of the factors you should consider in calculating ROI. In this section, we discuss several additional considerations in using and interpreting ROI as a basis for evaluating divisional performance.

We suggested that a firm should decide how it is going to calculate ROI and then use it consistently. Firms tend, however, to overemphasize this single statistic. Exhibit 15.8 presents a divisional performance report in a format that facilitates a variety of uses. For example, management could use the report to evaluate the division and its manager's performance without regard to costs arbitrarily allocated to divisions or to product lines. Further, the report provides data about the division's performance after the firm allocates all central administrative costs. Some corporate managers like to see a bottom line which takes into account all costs, even indirect costs that accounting has arbitrarily allocated to divisions.

Allocation of Headquarters' Costs

We suggested earlier that allocating central headquarters' costs to divisions may not be desirable if the firm wants to obtain a measure for evaluating divisional performance. Divisions do not have control over these costs and, therefore, the firm should not hold them accountable. However, divisional personnel must be conscious of the need to provide a positive contribution margin to the coverage of central corporate expenses and to profits. Top management may communicate this need to divisional personnel by showing on the performance report the relation between the division's contribution and the amount that top management thinks the division should share of central headquarters' costs.

---

[8] James S. Reece and William R. Cool, "Measuring Investment Center Performance," *Harvard Business Review* (May–June 1978).

Many divisional performance reports end with "Income before Income Taxes." Some management accountants argue that income taxes are part of controllable costs if they are derived from controllable revenues and controllable costs. Placing income taxes at the bottom of the report compromises between the two positions. This placement recognizes that allocation of income taxes to divisions may be as difficult as allocating central headquarters' costs. However, it emphasizes to division managers the importance of income taxes in decisions and the need to cover them before the division can generate profits for the company's owners.

Components of Return on Investment

The rate of return on investment has two components: profit margin and investment (or asset) turnover.

$$\frac{\text{Return on}}{\text{Investment}} = \frac{\text{Profit Margin}}{\text{Percentage}} \times \frac{\text{Investment}}{\text{Turnover Ratio}}$$

$$\frac{\text{Profit Margin}}{\text{Divisional Investment}} = \frac{\text{Profit Margin}}{\text{Divisional Revenues}} \times \frac{\text{Divisional Revenues}}{\text{Divisional Investment}}.$$

To illustrate the usefulness of dividing ROI into its components, assume the following information about Division A:

Year	Sales	Profit	Investment
1	$1,000,000	$100,000	$ 500,000
2	2,000,000	160,000	1,000,000
3	4,000,000	400,000	2,500,000

The following table shows the ROI for each of the 3 years and the associated profit margin percentages and investment turnover ratios.

Year	ROI =	Profit Margin Percentage	×	Investment Turnover Ratio
1	20% =	10%	×	2.0
2	16 =	8	×	2.0
3	16 =	10	×	1.6

The **profit margin percentage** provides information for assessing divisional management's ability to combine inputs to generate outputs; that is, the accounting system has combined various cost inputs (materials, labor, depreciation) to generate revenue outputs (sales of goods and services). The profit margin percentage indicates the portion of each dollar of revenue that exceeds the costs incurred. Management often uses it as a measure for assessing efficiency in producing and selling goods and services. The profit margin percentage for Division A in this example decreased from 10 percent to 8 percent between Year 1 and Year 2. Because the investment turnover ratio remained the same between the 2 years, it appears that an inability to control costs or an inability to raise selling prices as costs have increased, or both, caused the decrease in ROI.

We indicated earlier that we can divide divisional profits by the amount invested as a means of scaling divisions of different size so that we can compare their performance measures more easily. When we disaggregate ROI, however, we can obtain potentially useful information on how effectively the management used the capital invested in the division. The **investment turnover ratio** indicates the dollars of revenue that the division generated for each dollar of invested capital. Returning to the preceding example, Division A could not increase its ROI between Year 2 and Year 3, despite an increase in its profit margin percentage, because its investment turnover ratio decreased. The division could not generate $2 of revenue for each dollar invested in Year 3, as it had done in previous years.

Studying profit margin percentages and investment turnover ratios for a given division over several periods will provide more useful information than by looking at these ratios for all divisions in a particular period. Some divisions, due to the nature of their activities, require more capital than others. For example, a division involved in manufacturing and selling heavy equipment requires more capital than one selling management consulting or advertising and promotion services. The investment turnover ratios of these two divisions differ inherently and should not cause concern for top management. A significant change in the ratio of either division between two periods, however, may signal the need for corrective action. For example, a significant decrease in investment turnover for the manufacturing division may indicate excess capacity and suggest disposal of some facilities.

Setting Minimum Desired ROIs

If the ROI is to measure divisional performance effectively, management must set a standard or desired rate each period. Management usually specifies a minimum desired ROI for each division, given its particular operating characteristics. Some divisions are in more risky businesses than others, hence management may have higher expectations for them. Some divisions have a very low investment base (for example, professional services, consulting), thus ROI is sometimes quite high. In short, management should recognize the particular characteristics of a division in setting minimum ROIs.

Residual Income

Critics of return on investment (ROI) argue that managers may turn down investment opportunities that are above the minimum acceptable rate but below the ROI currently being earned. For example, suppose that the division currently earns

$$\text{ROI} = \frac{\$1,000,000}{\$4,000,000} = 25\%.$$

Managerial Application

Relative Performance Evaluation

A major issue in divisional performance evaluation is the process companies use to separate performance results that division managers can control from those outside environmental factors cause. For instance, firms could hold division managers accountable for achieving a fixed target, independent of the performance of other divisions operating in similar product markets, or evaluate their performance relative to the performance of other divisions. The latter approach, known as *relative performance evaluation,* is analogous to "grading on the curve."

The Aerospace and Defense Business at Honeywell, Inc., has been experimenting with relative performance evaluation.[a] Honeywell is a technology-oriented company, particularly in the Aerospace and Defense Business. They historically emphasize growth, customer satisfaction, and new product development. As the aerospace and defense business has become more cost competitive, with less cost-plus contracting, in recent years top management has become more interested in providing incentives to reduce costs. Honeywell has also increased its emphasis on financial measures of performance. The firm changed incentive contracts for top management and division managers to emphasize return on investment. Aerospace and Defense, in particular, experienced a "peer company analysis" to create a self-reassessment of the status quo.

The strategic planning group that performed the peer group analysis first identified the business segments of 22 competitors in the aerospace and defense industry. Of these 22 competitors, 9 are prime contractors (e.g., Boeing and Lockheed), who are in aerospace and defense but do not face the same market environment. Of the remaining 13 competitors, public data were not available for two competitors, Hughes and Ford Aerospace, leaving 11 competitors that Aerospace and Defense believes face the same market environment.

Based on line-of-business reporting, the company used a five-year average of return-on-assets, operating profit margin, and revenue growth for the comparable aerospace and defense business segments in other companies, and found the division ranked below average, but above the bottom quartile.

Honeywell used these results initially to identify highly ranked competitors and to examine their characteristics to see what Aerospace and Defense could do to improve its financial performance. Over time, the firm will incorporate these comparisons with peer companies into the evaluation of division managers' performance.

[a]Based on M. Maher, "The Use of Relative Performance Evaluation in Organizations," in W. Bruns and R. Kaplan, eds., *Accounting and Management in Organizations: A Field Study Perspective* (Harvard Business School, 1987).

Suppose the manager has an opportunity to make an additional investment. This investment would return $400,000 per year for 5 years for a $2 million investment. At the end of 5 years, the $2 million investment would be returned. Assume that there is no inflation. The ROI each year is

$$\text{ROI} = \frac{\$400,000}{\$2,000,000} = 20\%.$$

The company requires a minimum return of 15 percent for this type of investment. This investment clearly qualifies, but it would lower the investment center ROI to 23.3 percent:

$$\text{ROI} = \frac{\$1,000,000 + \$400,000}{\$4,000,000 + \$2,000,000} = 23.3\%.$$

A comparison of the old (25 percent) and new (23.3 percent) returns would imply performance has worsened; consequently a manager might decide not to make such an investment.

An alternative to ROI is **residual income (RI).** Residual income is defined as

$$\begin{matrix} \text{Residual} \\ \text{Income} \end{matrix} = \begin{matrix} \text{Division} \\ \text{Operating} \\ \text{Profits} \end{matrix} - \left(\begin{matrix} \text{Percent} \\ \text{Capital} \\ \text{Charge} \end{matrix} \times \begin{matrix} \text{Division} \\ \text{Investment} \end{matrix} \right),$$

where the percent capital charge is the minimum acceptable rate of return. The terms *division operating profits* and *division investment* are defined as for ROI. Residual income is similar in concept to economists' definition of profits. If the firm encourages managers to maximize RI, they have incentives to accept all projects above the minimum acceptable rate of return.

Using data from the example just discussed to see the impact of the investment on residual income, we find the following:

Before the investment, the residual income is $400,000.

$$\begin{aligned} \text{RI} &= \$1,000,000 - (.15 \times \$4,000,000) \\ &= \$1,000,000 - \$600,000 \\ &= \$400,000. \end{aligned}$$

The residual income from the additional investment is $100,000.

$$\begin{aligned} \text{RI} &= \$400,000 - (.15 \times \$2,000,000) \\ &= \$400,000 - \$300,000 \\ &= \$100,000. \end{aligned}$$

Hence, *after the additional investment,* the residual income of the division increases to $500,000.

$$\begin{aligned} \text{RI} &= (\$1,000,000 + \$400,000) - [.15 \times (\$4,000,000 + \$2,000,000)] \\ &= \$1,400,000 - (.15 \times \$6,000,000) \\ &= \$1,400,000 - \$900,000 \\ &= \$500,000. \end{aligned}$$

The additional investment *increases* residual income, appropriately improving the measure of performance, whereas the use of ROI worsened the measure of performance.

Managers generally recognize this problem with ROI, and they may take it into account when a new investment lowers the ROI. This practice may explain why residual income does not dominate ROI in practice as a performance measure. Most of the companies Reece and Cool studied use ROI. Two percent used residual income only, and 28 percent used both ROI and residual income.[9] Further, ROI is expressed as a percentage that managers can intuitively compare with related percentages—like the cost of capital, the prime interest rate, and the Treasury Bill rate.

■ Summary ■

Top management must design and implement division performance measures that encourage division managers to act in the best interests of the company as a whole. Fundamentally, top management seeks answers to the following questions: (1) What behavior does the incentive system motivate? (2) What behavior do we *want* the incentive system to motivate? At a minimum, performance measurement methods should show that when division managers take actions in the company's best interests, the managers' performance looks good.

The key issues in divisional performance measurement deal with measuring revenues, costs, and investment in the division. For profit centers, the most important measure is

$$\text{Division Operating Profits} = \text{Division Revenues} - \text{Division Costs};$$

for investment centers it is

$$\text{ROI} = \frac{\text{Division Revenues} - \text{Division Costs}}{\text{Division Investment}}.$$

(We assume that divisions are investment centers unless otherwise stated.)

When one division can sell its output to another division, management sets a *transfer price* that becomes a revenue to the selling division and a cost to the buying division. Selecting the transfer price can affect decision making significantly. Ideally, management will set the transfer price so that when divisions internally optimize their buy and sell decisions, they also optimize from a company-wide viewpoint.

Transfer pricing choices have numerous alternatives, including direct top management intervention in buy and sell decisions, top management-established transfer pricing policy, and transfer prices negotiated among division managers. You could expect top management's direct intervention to induce managers to make the right decision for the company for a particular transaction. However, direct inter-

---

[9]Reece and Cool, ''Measuring Investment Center Performance,'' *Harvard Business Review* (May–June 1978).

vention reduces some of the advantages of decentralization because it overrides delegation of responsibility.

The optimal transfer pricing policy sets the price at the differential cost to the selling division plus the implicit opportunity cost to the company if it transfers the goods internally. When competitive external markets exist for the product being exchanged between divisions and the selling division operates at capacity, the product's external market price satisfies the general rule. The optimal rule requires difficult measures of differential costs and opportunity costs. Consequently, many companies transfer at some measure of cost found in the accounting records—for example, standard full cost or standard variable cost—plus a markup. Many companies carry decentralization to the limit by allowing division managers to set their own prices—so-called negotiated prices.

Top management faces the major transfer pricing problem of the trade-off between intervening to ensure that a transaction optimizes a company's interests and delegating decisions to division managers. Delegation requires top management to tolerate occasional decisions at the division level that do not optimize the company's interests.

In measuring divisional operating costs, management must ascertain which costs to allocate to divisions. Should the system allocate central headquarters costs, such as top management's salaries, to divisions, for example? Those who argue against allocation to divisions usually base their argument on the divisions' inability to affect these costs and the arbitrary allocation bases that the firm must use. Those who argue in favor of allocation point out the need to make divisions aware of central headquarters costs. The costs and benefits of allocation differ in various situations, which makes it impossible to generalize about the optimal amount of cost allocation to divisions.

The issues in measuring the investment of capital in divisions are (1) what assets should the firm include in the investment base and (2) what valuation basis should the firm use. Assets physically located in a division should be included in the investment bases. Firms usually assign assets that divisions or central headquarters share to divisions if the firm can use reasonable allocation bases. Management generally develops a reasonable policy for including assets in the investment base and tries to follow it consistently. Some criticize the use of historical cost and net book value on the grounds that managers of divisions with old, low-cost, and almost fully depreciated assets may be reluctant to replace these with newer, more costly assets that reduce calculated ROI. The majority of companies in the Reece and Cool study use historical cost and net book value, however.

Some criticize ROI because if firms encourage managers to have a high ROI, they may turn down investment opportunities that are above the minimum acceptable rate but below the ROI currently being earned. The equation for residual income (RI), an alternative measure that is not lowered by projects earning less than the current ROI but more than the minimum acceptable rate of return, follows:

$$\begin{matrix} \text{Residual} \\ \text{Income} \end{matrix} = \begin{matrix} \text{Division} \\ \text{Operating} \\ \text{Profits} \end{matrix} - \left(\begin{matrix} \text{Percent} \\ \text{Capital} \\ \text{Charge} \end{matrix} \times \begin{matrix} \text{Division} \\ \text{Investment} \end{matrix} \right).$$

Any project accepted with a return above the minimum acceptable rate (that is, the percent capital charge) will increase residual income. Hence, projects that will profit the company also improve the division manager's performance measure.

Problem 1 for Self-Study

The Venus Division of Hyperspace Company has assets of $2.4 billion, operating profits of $.60 billion, and a cost of capital of 20 percent.
    Compute return on investment and residual income.

Suggested Solution

$$\text{ROI} = \frac{\$.60 \text{ Billion}}{2.4 \text{ Billion}} = \underline{\underline{25\%}}.$$

$$\text{Residual Income} = .\$.60 \text{ Billion} - (.20 \times \$2.4 \text{ Billion})$$

$$= \$.60 \text{ Billion} - \$.48 \text{ Billion}$$

$$= \underline{\$.12 \text{ Billion}} \text{ (that is, residual income of \$120 million).}$$

Problem 2 for Self-Study

The T Division of A.T. Enterprises has depreciable assets costing $2 million. The cash flows from these assets for 3 years follow:

Year	Cash Flow
1	$600,000
2	700,000
3	810,000

The firm expected the replacement costs of these assets to increase 25 percent per year. Depreciation of these assets for managerial purposes was 10 percent per year; the assets have no salvage value. The denominator in the ROI calculation is based on *end-of-year* asset valuations.
    Compute the ROI for each year under each of the following methods:

a. Historical cost, net book value.

b. Historical cost, gross book value.

c. Replacement cost, net book value.

d. Replacement cost, gross book value.

Suggested Solution

a, b. Historical cost:

Year	Net Book Value	Gross Book Value
1	$\text{ROI} = \dfrac{\$600,000 - (.10 \times \$2,000,000)^a}{\$2,000,000 - (.10 \times \$2,000,000)}$ $= \dfrac{\$400,000}{\$1,800,000} = 22.22\%.$	$\text{ROI} = \dfrac{\$400,000}{\$2,000,000}$ $= 20\%.$
2	$\text{ROI} = \dfrac{\$700,000 - (.10 \times \$2,000,000)}{\$1,800,000 - (.10 \times \$2,000,000)}$ $= \dfrac{\$500,000}{\$1,600,000} = 31.25\%.$	$\text{ROI} = \dfrac{\$500,000}{\$2,000,000}$ $= 25\%.$
3	$\text{ROI} = \dfrac{\$810,000 - (.10 \times \$2,000,000)}{\$1,600,000 - (.10 \times \$2,000,000)}$ $= \dfrac{\$610,000}{\$1,400,000} = 43.57\%.$	$\text{ROI} = \dfrac{\$610,000}{\$2,000,000}$ $= 30.5\%.$

[a]The first term in the numerator is annual cash flow; the second term in the numerator is annual depreciation; the first term in the denominator is the beginning-of-year net book value of the asset; the second term in the denominator reduces the beginning-of-year value by the amount of the current year's depreciation.

c, d. Replacement cost:

Year	Net Book Value	Gross Book Value
1	$\text{ROI} = \dfrac{\$600,000 - (.10 \times 1.25^a \times \$2,000,000)}{(1.25 \times \$2,000,000) - (.10^b \times 1.25 \times \$2,000,000)}$ $= \dfrac{\$600,000 - \$250,000}{\$2,500,000 - \$250,000} = 15.6\%.$	$\text{ROI} = \dfrac{\$350,000}{\$2,500,000}$ $= 14\%.$
2	$\text{ROI} = \dfrac{\$700,000 - (.10 \times 1.25 \times \$2,500,000)}{(1.25 \times \$2,500,000) - (.20^b \times 1.25 \times \$2,500,000)}$ $= \dfrac{\$700,000 - \$312,500}{\$3,125,000 - \$625,000} = 15.5\%.$	$\text{ROI} = \dfrac{\$387,500}{\$3,125,000}$ $= 12.4\%.$
3	$\text{ROI} = \dfrac{\$810,000 - (.10 \times 1.25 \times \$3,125,000)}{(1.25 \times \$3,125,000) - (.30^b \times 1.25 \times \$3,125,000)}$ $= \dfrac{\$810,000 - \$390,625}{\$3,906,250 - \$1,171,875}$ $= \dfrac{\$419,375}{\$2,734,375} = 15.3\%.$	$\text{ROI} = \dfrac{\$419,375}{\$3,906,250}$ $= 10.7\%.$

[a]This term increases asset value to replacement cost.

[b]This term reduces the net book value of the asset by 10 percent after 1 year, by 20 percent after 2 years, and by 30 percent after 3 years.

Problem 3 for Self-Study

The Lee Lewis Company has two divisions, Production and Marketing. Production manufactures designer pants, which it sells to both the Marketing Division and to other retailers (to the latter under a different brand name). Marketing operates numerous pants stores, and it sells both Lee Lewis pants and other brands. The following facts also pertain to the Lee Lewis Company:

- Sales price to retailers if sold by Production: $38 per pair.
- Variable cost to produce: $19 per pair.
- Fixed costs: $200,000 per month.
- Production currently operates far below its capacity.
- Sales price to customers if sold by Marketing: $50 per pair.
- Variable marketing costs: 5 percent of sales price.

Marketing has decided to reduce the sales price of Lee Lewis pants. The company's variable manufacturing and marketing costs are differential to this decision, whereas fixed manufacturing and marketing costs are not.

a. What is the *minimum* price that Marketing can charge for the pants and still cover differential manufacturing and marketing costs?

b. What is the appropriate transfer price for this decision?

c. What if the transfer price were set at $38? What effect would this have on the minimum price set by the marketing manager?

Suggested Solution

a. From the company's perspective, the minimum price would be the variable cost of producing and marketing the goods. It would solve for this minimum price, P_C (the subscript C means that the minimum price in the *company's* best interest), follow:

$$P_C = \$19 + .05 \, P_C$$
$$P_C - .05 P_C = \$19$$
$$.95 P_C = \$19$$
$$P_C = \underline{\underline{\$20}}.$$

The *minimum* price the company should accept is $20. If the company were centralized, we would expect the information system to convey this information to the manager of Marketing, who would be instructed not to set a price below $20.

b. The transfer price that correctly informs the marketing manager about the differential costs of manufacturing is $19. Since Production operates below capacity, the opportunity cost of transferring internally equals zero.

c. If the production manager set the price at $38, the marketing manager would solve for the minimum price (which we call P_M for *Marketing's* solution):

$$P_M = \$38 + .05P_M$$
$$P_M - .05P_M = \$38$$
$$.95P_M = \$38$$
$$P_M = \underline{\underline{\$40}}.$$

So the marketing manager sets the price in excess of $40 per pair, when, in fact, prices exceeding $20 would have generated a positive contribution margin from the production and sale of pants.

Problem 4 for Self-Study

How would your answer to Problem 3 for Self-Study change if the Production Division had been operating at full capacity?

Suggested Solution

If the Production Division had been operating at capacity, an internal transfer would have had an implicit opportunity cost. Production would have forgone a sale in the wholesale market to make the internal transfer. The implicit opportunity cost to the company is the lost contribution margin ($38 − $19 = $19) from not selling in the wholesale market.

Thus, if Production had sufficient sales in the wholesale market to force it to forego those sales to transfer internally, the transfer price should have been

$$\begin{array}{l}\text{Differential Cost} \\ \text{to Production}\end{array} + \begin{array}{c}\text{Implicit Opportunity Cost} \\ \text{to Company If Goods Are} \\ \text{Transferred Internally}\end{array} = \$19 + \$19$$
$$= \underline{\underline{\$38}}.$$

Marketing would have appropriately treated the $38 as part of *its* differential cost of buying and selling the pants. When Production was operating below full capacity (hence, the implicit opportunity cost of transferring to marketing was zero), management derived the minimum price for the pants as follows:

$$P_M = \$19 + .05P_M$$
$$.95P_M = \$19$$
$$P_M = \underline{\underline{\$20}}.$$

However, if Production operates at full capacity, the minimum price is

$$P_M = \$38 + .05P_M$$
$$.95P_M = \$38$$
$$P_M = \underline{\underline{\$40}}.$$

Key Terms and Concepts

Division
Profit center
Investment center
Decentralized decision making
Behavioral or goal congruence
Division return on investment
  (ROI)
Transfer pricing problem

Market-based transfer price
Cost-based transfer price
Dual transfer price
Negotiated transfer price
Profit margin percentage
Investment turnover ratio
Residual income (RI)

Questions, Exercises, Problems, and Cases

Questions

1. Review the meaning of the concepts or terms given above in Key Terms and Concepts.

2. "It may be desirable to use a different ROI measure for evaluating the performance of a division and the performance of the division's manager." Explain.

3. "An action that is optimal for a division may not be optimal for the company as a whole." Explain.

4. Why are transfer prices necessary?

5. In what sense is the term *transfer price* a misnomer?

6. "The case for allocating central service department costs is stronger than the case for allocating central administration costs to divisions." Explain.

7. "The return on investment measure may be biased in favor of divisions with older plant and equipment." Explain.

8. What are the advantages of using the ROI measure rather than the value of division profits as a performance evaluation technique?

9. Under what conditions would the use of ROI measures inhibit goal-congruent decision making by a division manager?

10. What are the advantages of using residual income instead of ROI?

11. Why may gross book value and/or replacement cost be used instead of net book value and/or historical cost to measure the denominator (investment) in the ROI computation?

12. Describe the bases for establishing transfer prices.

13. Why may transfer prices exist even in highly centralized organizations?

14. Why do some consider market-based transfer prices optimal under many circumstances?

15. What are the limitations to market-based transfer prices?

16. What are the advantages of a centrally administered transfer price (that is, direct intervention)? What are the disadvantages of such a transfer price?

17. Why do companies often use prices other than market prices for interdivisional transfers?

18. Division A has no external markets. It produces a product that Division B uses. Division B cannot purchase this product from any other source. What transfer pricing system would you recommend for the interdivisional sale of the product? Why?

19. What are the disadvantages of a negotiated transfer price system?

20. Describe the economic basis for transfer pricing systems.

Exercises

21. *Transfer pricing.* Fizz-it, Inc., produces bottled drinks. The New England Division acquires the water, adds carbonation, and sells it in bulk quantities to the California Division of Fizz-it and to outside buyers. The California Division buys carbonated water in bulk, adds flavoring, bottles it, and sells it.

Last year, New England Division produced 1,200,000 gallons, of which it sold 1,000,000 gallons to the California Division and the remaining 200,000 gallons to outsiders for $.20 per gallon. The California Division processed the 1,000,000 gallons which it sold for $500,000. New England's variable costs were $180,000 and its fixed costs were $40,000. The California Division incurred an additional variable cost of $120,000 and $80,000 fixed costs. Both divisions operated below capacity.

a. Prepare division income statements assuming the transfer price is at the external market price of $.20 per gallon.

b. Repeat part **a** assuming a negotiated transfer price of $.15 per gallon is used.

c. Respond to the statement: "The choice of a particular transfer price is immaterial to the company as a whole."

22. *Return on investment computations.* The following information relates to the operating performance of three divisions of Langston Retail Corporation for 19X0.

	New York Division	Philadelphia Division	Los Angeles Division
Divisional Contribution to Central Corporate Expenses	$500,000	$500,000	$500,000
Divisional Investment	$4,000,000	$5,000,000	$6,000,000
Divisional Sales	$24,000,000	$20,000,000	$16,000,000
Divisional Employees	22,500	12,000	10,500

Langston evaluates divisional performance using rate of return on investment (ROI) after allocating a portion of the central corporate expenses to each division. Central corporate expenses for 19X0 were $900,000.

a. Compute the ROI of each division before allocation of central corporate expenses.

b. Compute the ROI of each division assuming central corporate expenses are allocated based on divisional investments (that is, allocate 4/15 to the New York Division, 5/15 to the Philadelphia Division, and 6/15 to the Los Angeles Division).

c. Repeat part **b,** allocating central corporate expenses based on divisional sales.

d. Repeat part **b,** assuming that management allocates central corporate expenses based on the number of employees.

23. *ROI computations with a capital charge.* The following information relates to the operating performance of three divisions of We-Haul Van Lines for 19X0.

	Local Moving Division	Intercity Division	Interstate Division
Operating Profit	$ 640,000	$ 3,000,000	$ 6,000,000
Investment....................	8,000,000	15,000,000	37,500,000

a. Compute the rate of return on investment (ROI) of each division for 19X0.

b. Assume that the firm levies a charge on each division for the use of capital. The charge is 10 percent on investment, and the accounting system deducts it in measuring divisional net income. Recalculate ROI using divisional net income after deduction of the use-of-capital charge in the numerator.

c. Which of these two measures do you think gives the better indication of operating performance? Explain your reasoning.

24. *ROI computations with replacement costs.* The following information relates to the operating performance of two divisions of Pratt Electronics Corporation for 19X0.

	Boston Division	Mexico City Division
Operating Profit	$ 400,000	$ 600,000
Total Assets (based on acquisition cost)	4,000,000	7,500,000
Total Assets (based on current replacement costs) ..	6,000,000	8,000,000

a. Compute the return on investment (ROI) of each division, using total assets stated at acquisition cost as the investment base.

b. Compute the ROI of each division, using total assets based on current replacement cost as the investment base.

c. Which of the two measures do you think gives the better indication of operating performance? Explain your reasoning.

25. *ROI computations comparing net and gross book value.* The following information relates to the operating performance of two divisions of the Hardrock Travel Agency for last year.

	Domestic Division	International Division
Operating Profit	$ 500,000	$ 800,000
Total Assets (at gross acquisition cost)	6,250,000	20,000,000
Total Assets (net of accumulated depreciation)	5,000,000	5,000,000

a. Compute the return on investment (ROI) of each division, using total assets at gross book value as the investment base.

b. Compute the ROI of each division, using total assets net of accumulated depreciation (net book value) as the investment base.

c. Which of the two measures do you think gives the better indication of operating performance? Explain your reasoning.

26. *Comparing profit margin and ROI as performance measures.* Cafe Italia operates coffeehouses on college campuses in three districts. The operating performance for each district follows.

	District		
	New Hampshire	Illinois	California
Sales...........................	$3,800,000	$17,000,000	$20,000,000
Operating Profit	200,000	500,000	1,000,000
Investment......................	2,000,000	6,250,000	8,000,000

a. Using the operating profit margin percentage as the criterion, which is the most profitable district?

b. Using the rate of return on investment as the criterion, which is the most profitable district?

c. Which of the two measures better indicates operating performance? Explain your reasoning.

27. *Profit margin and investment turnover ratio computations.* The Bears Division of the Soldier Field Company had a rate of return on investment (ROI) of 10 percent (= $200,000/$2,000,000) during 19X0, based on sales of $4,000,000. In an effort to improve its performance during 19X1, the company instituted several cost-saving programs, including the substitution of automatic equipment for work previously done by workers and the purchase of raw materials in large quantities to obtain quantity discounts. Despite these cost-saving programs, the company's ROI for 19X1 was 8 percent (= $220,000/$2,750,000), based on sales of $4,000,000.

a. Break down the ROI for 19X0 and 19X1 into profit margin and investment turnover ratios.

b. Explain the reason for the decrease in ROI between the 2 years, using results from part **a.**

28. *ROI computations with net and gross book values.* The Raiders Division of Coliseum Company has just started operations. It purchased depreciable

assets costing $1,000,000 that have an expected life of 4 years, after which the assets can be salvaged for $200,000. In addition, the division has $1,000,000 in nondepreciable assets. After 4 years, the division will have $1,000,000 available from these assets. In short, the division has invested $2,000,000 in assets that will last 4 years, after which it will salvage $1,200,000. Assume that annual cash operating profits are $400,000. In computing ROI, this division uses *end-of-year* asset values in the denominator.
   a. Compute ROI using net book value.
   b. Compute ROI using gross book value.

29. *ROI computations using replacement costs*. Assume the same facts as in exercise **28,** except that all cash flows increase 10 percent at the end of the year. This has the following effect on the assets' replacement cost and annual cash flows:

End of Year	Replacement Cost	Annual Cash Flow
1	$2,000,000 × 1.1 = $2,200,000	$400,000 × 1.1 = $440,000
2	$2,200,000 × 1.1 = $2,420,000	$440,000 × 1.1 = $484,000
⋮	Etc.	Etc.

   a. Compute ROI using replacement cost gross book value.
   b. Compute ROI using replacement cost net book value.

30. *ROI and residual income computations*. A bank considers acquiring new computer equipment. The computer will cost $160,000 and result in a cash savings of $70,000 per year (excluding depreciation) for each of the 5 years of the asset life. It will have no salvage value after 5 years.
   a. What is the ROI for each year of the asset's life if the division uses beginning-of-year asset balances for the computation?
   b. What is the residual income each year if the capital costs 25 percent?

31. *Transfer pricing (adapted from CPA exam)*. Spoke Company has two decentralized divisions, Frames and Bikes. Bikes has always purchased certain units from Frames at $75 per unit. Because Frames plans to raise the price to $100 per unit, Bikes desires to purchase these units from outside suppliers for $75 per unit. Frames' costs follow: variable costs per unit, $70; annual fixed costs, $15,000. Annual production of these units for Bikes is 1,000 units.
   If Bikes buys from an outside supplier, the facilities Frames uses to manufacture these units would remain idle. What would be the result if Spoke Company management enforces a transfer price of $100 per unit between Frames and Bikes?

32. *Transfer pricing*. The consulting group in an accounting firm offers its products to outside clients at a price of $200 per hour. Last month, the consultants billed 10,000 hours to outside clients, incurred variable costs of $70 per hour billed to outside clients and incurred $500,000 in fixed costs.

The firm's auditing group can acquire consulting services from outsiders or from the firm's own consultants. If it acquires the services from outsiders, it must pay $180 per hour. It would pay $200 for consulting services from the internal group.

a. What are the costs and benefits of the alternatives available to these two groups, the consultants and the auditors, and to the accounting firm as a whole, with respect to consulting services? Assume the consulting group operates at capacity.

b. How would your answer change if the accounting firm's consulting group had sufficient idle capacity to handle all of the auditors' needs?

Problems

33. *Transfer pricing.* Technology Plus Company produces computers and computer components. The company is organized into several divisions that operate essentially as autonomous companies. The firm permits division managers to make capital investment and production-level decisions. The division managers can also decide whether to sell to other divisions or to outside customers.

Networks Division produces a critical component for computers manufactured by Computers Division. It has been selling this component to Computers for $1,500 per unit. Networks recently purchased new equipment for producing the component. To offset its higher depreciation charges, Networks increased its price to $1,600 per unit. The manager of Networks has asked the president to instruct Computers to purchase the component for the $1,600 price rather than to permit Computers to purchase externally for $1,500 per unit. The company's records provide the following information: Computers' annual purchases of the component, 100 units; Networks' variable costs per unit, $1,200; Networks' fixed costs per unit, $300.

a. Assume that the firm has no alternative uses for Networks' idle capacity. Will the company as a whole benefit if Computers purchases the component externally for $1,500? Explain.

b. Assume that the firm can use the idle capacity of Networks for other purposes, resulting in cash operating savings of $20,000. Will the company as a whole benefit if Computers purchases the component externally for $1,500? Explain.

c. Assume the same facts as in part **b** except that the outside market price drops to $1,350 per unit. Will the company as a whole benefit if Computers purchases the component externally for $1,350? Explain.

d. As president, how would you respond to the manager of Networks? Discuss each scenario described in parts **a**, **b**, and **c**.

34. *Biases in ROI computations.* Champion Sports Products uses rate of return on investment (ROI) as a basis for determining the annual bonus of divisional managers. Before calculating ROI at year-end, the accounting system assigns all manufacturing cost variances to units produced, whether sold or in ending inventory, so that standard costs become actual costs. The firm allocates central corporate expenses to the divisions based on total sales. The calculation of ROI for 19X0 for two of its divisions follows:

	Tennis Products Division	Golf Products Division
Division Contribution to Central Corporate Expenses and Operating Profit..................	$100,000	$ 500,000
Share of Central Corporate Expenses	(10,000)	(25,000)
Divisional Operating Profit	$ 90,000	$ 475,000
Divisional Investment (assets).....................	$600,000	$4,750,000
ROI	15 Percent	10 Percent

Indicate several factors that, if present, would bias the ROI measure as Champion has calculated and lead to possible inequities in calculating the annual bonus.

35. *Issues in designing ROI measures.* The Domestic Corporation manufactures and sells a patented electronic device for detecting burglaries. The firm uses return on investment as a measure for the control of operations for each of its sixteen U.S. divisions.

Recently the firm has organized a new division in Brazil. Domestic contributed the necessary capital for the construction of manufacturing and sales facilities in Brazil, whereas it obtained debt financing locally for working capital requirements. The new division will remit annually the following amounts to the U.S. central corporate office: (1) a royalty of $10 for each burglary device sold in Brazil, (2) a fee of $40 per hour plus traveling expenses for central corporate engineering services used by the division, and (3) a dividend equal to 10 percent of the capital Domestic committed. The division will retain for its own use the remaining funds that operation generates. The division will receive the right to produce and market in Brazil any future electronic devices the central corporate research and development staff develops.

List some of the questions that the firm must address in designing a ROI measure for this division.

36. *Issues in designing ROI measures.* Durham Industries is one of the largest textile companies in the world. It manufactures and sells products through 25 individual divisions, which operate much like autonomous companies. Each division has its own manufacturing plants for making the division's products, a sales staff to market them, and an administrative staff to provide financial assistance and control. Each division receives broad policy and financial guidance from corporate management and technical assistance from the corporate staff. The latter includes treasurer, legal, personnel, advertising, engineering, and purchasing groups.

Although the firm uses several measures of divisional performance, the most significant yardstick is return on investment. The firm calculates the numerator of ROI as follows:

- Divisional Revenues (sales to outsiders plus sales to other divisions based on negotiated transfer price)

- Minus Direct Divisional Costs (excluding income taxes)

- Minus Charge for Central Corporate Costs (the costs of central administration and service departments are allocated to the divisions according to each division's investment as a percentage of the total of all of the division's investments)

- Equals Divisional Operating Profit.

The firms bases investment measure in the denominator of ROI on the book value of the following assets: (1) accounts receivable net of accounts payable; (2) inventories, including supplies, raw materials, work in process, and finished goods; and (3) long-term depreciable assets (net of accumulated depreciation). The central corporate controller's staff sets the accounting methods and all divisions use them uniformly.

The firm calculates the actual ROI monthly for each division. In evaluating ROI, corporate management uses two bases. First, management pays a great deal of attention to trends rather than absolute goals or standards. Maximum interest centers on divisions whose performance is either improving or declining. Second, management sets a minimum satisfactory ROI for each division. This standard represents a lower limit below which the division manager's job is in jeopardy. Management sets the minimum rather loosely and divisions can easily attain it in almost all cases. Management measures the minimum ROI by applying different weights to the three investment components: 20 percent for depreciable assets, 12 percent for inventories, and 6 percent for accounts receivable net of accounts payable.

Discuss the strengths and weaknesses of the return on investment measure as Durham uses it as a basis for controlling divisional performance.

37. *Evaluating profit impact of alternative transfer decisions* (adapted from CMA exam). A. R. Oma, Inc., manufactures a line of men's colognes and aftershave lotions. The firm manufactures the products through a series of mixing operations with the addition of certain aromatic and coloring ingredients; the firm packages the finished product in a company-produced glass bottle and packs it in cases containing six bottles.

Management of A. R. Oma believes appearance of the bottle heavily influences the sale of its product. Management has developed a unique bottle of which it is quite proud.

Cologne production and bottle manufacture have evolved over the years in an almost independent manner; in fact, a rivalry has developed between management personnel as to which division is the more important to A. R. Oma. This attitude is probably intensified because the bottle manufacturing plant was purchased intact 10 years ago, and no real interchange of management personnel or ideas (except at the top corporate level) has taken place.

Since the acquisition, the cologne manufacturing plant has absorbed all bottle production. Management considers each area a separate profit center and evaluated as such. As the new corporate controller, you are responsible for the definition of a proper transfer value to use in crediting the bottle production profit center and in debiting the packaging profit center.

At your request, the bottle division general manager has asked certain other bottle manufacturers to quote a price for the quantity and sizes the cologne division demands. These competitive prices follow:

Volume	Total Price	Price per Case
2,000,000 Cases[a]	$ 4,000,000	$2.00
4,000,000 Cases	7,000,000	1.75
6,000,000 Cases	10,000,000	1.67

[a]A case has six bottles each.

A cost analysis of the internal bottle plant indicates that it can produce bottles at these costs:

Volume	Total Price	Cost per Case
2,000,000 Cases	$3,200,000	$1.60
4,000,000 Cases	5,200,000	1.30
6,000,000 Cases	7,200,000	1.20

These costs include fixed costs of $1,200,000 and variable costs of $1 per case.

These figures resulted in discussion about the proper value to use in the transfer of bottles to the cologne division. Corporate executives are interested because a significant portion of a division manager's income is an incentive bonus based on profit center results.

The cologne production division incurred the following costs in addition to the bottle costs:

Volume	Total Cost	Cost per Case
2,000,000 Cases	$16,400,000	$8.20
4,000,000 Cases	32,400,000	8.10
6,000,000 Cases	48,400,000	8.07

After considerable analysis, the marketing research department furnishes you with the following price-demand relation for the finished product:

Sales Volume	Total Sales Revenue	Sales Price per Case
2,000,000 Cases	$25,000,000	$12.50
4,000,000 Cases	45,600,000	11.40
6,000,000 Cases	63,900,000	10.65

a. The A. R. Oma Company has used market price transfer prices in the past. Using the current market prices and costs, and assuming a volume of 6,000,000 cases, calculate the income for
   (1) The bottle division.
   (2) The cologne division.
   (3) The corporation.
b. Is this production and sales level the most profitable volume for
   (1) The bottle division?
   (2) The cologne division?
   (3) The corporation?
Explain your answer.

Integrative Problems and Cases

38. *Analyzing transfer pricing policy* (adapted from CMA exam). PortCo Products, a furniture manufacturer, has divisions that are autonomous segments. The firm holds each division responsible for its own sales, costs of operations, working capital management, and equipment acquisitions. Each division serves a different market in the furniture industry. Because the markets and products of the divisions differ greatly, no transfers between divisions have ever occurred.

The Commercial Division manufactures equipment and furniture that the restaurant industry purchases. The division plans to introduce a new line of counter and chair units that feature a cushioned seat for the counter chairs. John Kline, the division manager, has discussed the manufacturing of the cushioned seat with Russ Fiegel of the Office Division. They both believe that a cushioned seat the Office Division currently makes for use on its deluxe office stool could be modified for use on the new counter chair. Consequently, Kline has asked Russ Fiegel for a price for 100-unit lots of the cushioned seat. The following conversation occurred over the price Office Division would charge for the cushioned seats.

Feigel: John, we can make the necessary modifications to the cushioned seat easily. The direct materials your seat uses are slightly different and should cost about 10 percent more than those used in our deluxe office stool. However, the labor time should be less. I would sell the seat to you at our regular rate—full cost plus 30 percent markup.

Kline: That's higher than I expected, Russ. I was thinking that a good price would be your variable manufacturing costs. After all, your capacity costs will be incurred regardless of this job.

Fiegel: John, I'm at capacity. By making the cushion seats for you, I'll have to cut my production of deluxe office stools. Of course, I can increase my production of economy office stools. I can shift the labor time freed by not having to fabricate the frame or assemble the deluxe stool to the frame fabrication and assembly of the economy office stool. Fortunately, I can switch my labor force between these two models of stools without any loss of efficiency. As you know, overtime is not a feasible alternative in our community. I'd like to sell it to you at variable cost, but I have excess demand for both products. I don't mind changing my product mix to the economy model if I get a good return on the seats I make for you. Here are my standard costs for the two stools and a schedule of my manufacturing overhead. (See Exhibit 15.9 for standard costs, and see Exhibit 15.10 for the overhead schedule.)

Kline: I guess I see your point, Russ, but I don't want to price myself out of the market. Maybe we should talk to corporate to see if they can give us any guidance.

a.   John Kline and Russ Fiegel did ask PortCo corporate management for guidance on an appropriate transfer price. Corporate management suggested they consider using a transfer price based on variable manufacturing cost plus opportunity cost. Calculate a transfer price for the cushioned seat based on variable manufacturing cost plus opportunity cost.

b.   Which alternative transfer price system—full cost, variable manufacturing cost, or variable manufacturing cost plus opportunity cost—would be

Exhibit 15.9

PORTCO PRODUCTS
Office Division Standard Costs and Prices

	Deluxe Office Stool	Economy Office Stool
Direct Materials:		
Framing	$ 8.15	$ 9.76
Cushioned Seat:		
Padding	2.40	—
Vinyl	4.00	—
Molded Seat (purchased)	—	6.00
Direct Labor:		
Frame Fabrication	3.75[a]	3.75[a]
Cushion Fabrication	3.75[a]	—
Assembly	3.75[a]	2.25[b]
Manufacturing:		
Overhead...	19.20[c]	10.24[d]
Total Standard Cost	$45.00	$32.00
Selling Price (30 percent markup)	$58.50	$41.60

[a].5 × $7.50 per direct labor hour.

[b].3 × $7.50 per direct labor hour.

[c]1.5 direct labor hours × $12.80 per direct labor hour.

[d].8 direct labor hour × $12.80 per direct labor hour.

Exhibit 15.10

PORTCO PRODUCTS
Office Division Manufacturing Overhead Budget

Overhead Item	Nature	Amount
Supplies	Variable—at Current Market Prices	$ 420,000
Indirect Labor	Variable.	375,000
Supervision	Nonvariable	250,000
Power	Use Varies with Activity; Rates are Fixed.	180,000
Heat and Light	Nonvariable—Light Is Fixed Regardless of Production; Heat/Air Conditioning Varies with Fuel Charges	140,000
Property Taxes and Insurance	Nonvariable—Any Change in Amounts/Rates Is Independent of Production.	200,000
Depreciation	Fixed-Dollar Total	1,700,000
Employee Benefits	20 Percent of Supervision, Direct and Indirect Labor. . . .	575,000
Total Overhead		$3,840,000
	Capacity in Direct Labor Hours	300,000
	Overhead Rate per Direct Labor Hour	$12.80

better as the underlying concept for an intracompany transfer price policy? Explain your answer.

39. *Transfer pricing and differential analysis* (adapted from CMA exam). National Industries is a diversified corporation with separate and distinct operating divisions. Management evaluates each division's performance on the basis of total dollar profits and return on division investment.

The WindAir Division manufactures and sells air conditioner units. The coming year's budgeted income statement, based on a sales volume of 15,000 units, appears in Exhibit 15.11.

WindAir's division manager believes the division can increase sales if they reduce the unit selling price of the air conditioners. An independent firm conducted a market study at the request of the manager that indicates a 5 percent reduction in the selling price ($20) would increase sales volume by 16 percent, or 2,400 units. WindAir has sufficient production capacity to manage this increased volume with no increase in fixed costs.

At the present time, WindAir uses a compressor in its units that it purchases from an outside supplier at a cost of $70 per compressor. The division manager of WindAir has approached the manager of the Compressor Division regarding the sale of a compressor unit to WindAir. The Compressor Division currently manufactures and sells exclusively to outside firms a unit that is similar to the unit WindAir uses. The specifications of the WindAir compressor differ slightly, which would reduce the Compressor Division's direct material cost by $1.50 per unit. In addition, the Compressor Division would not incur any variable selling costs in the units sold to WindAir. The manager of WindAir wants all of the compressors it uses to come from one supplier and has offered to pay $50 for each compressor unit.

The Compressor Division has the capacity to produce 75,000 units. Exhibit 15.12 shows the coming fiscal year's budgeted income statement for

Exhibit 15.11

NATIONAL INDUSTRIES
WindAir Division
Budgeted Income Statement for the Fiscal Year

	Per Unit	Total (in thousands)
Sales Revenue	$400	$6,000
Manufacturing Costs:		
Compressor	70	1,050
Other Direct Materials	37	555
Direct Labor	30	450
Variable Overhead	45	675
Fixed Overhead	32	480
Total Manufacturing Costs	$214	$3,210
Gross Margin	$186	$2,790
Marketing and Administrative Costs:		
Variable Marketing	$ 18	270
Fixed Marketing	19	285
Fixed Administrative	38	570
Total Marketing and Administrative Costs	$ 75	$1,125
Operating Profit before Taxes	$111	$1,665

Exhibit 15.12

NATIONAL INDUSTRIES
Compressor Division
Budgeted Income Statement for the Fiscal Year

	Per Unit	Total (in thousands)
Sales Revenues	$100	$6,400
Manufacturing Costs:		
Direct Materials	12	768
Direct Labor	8	512
Variable Overhead	10	640
Fixed Overhead	11	704
Total Manufacturing Costs	$ 41	$2,624
Gross Margin	$ 59	$3,776
Marketing and Administrative Costs:		
Variable Marketing	$ 6	$ 384
Fixed Marketing	4	256
Fixed Administrative	7	448
Total Marketing and Administrative Costs	17	$1,088
Operating Profit before Taxes	$ 42	$2,688

the Compressor Division. The statement is based on a sales volume of 64,000 units without considering WindAir's proposal.

a. Should WindAir Division institute the 5 percent price reduction on its air conditioner units even if it cannot acquire the compressors internally for $50 each? Support your conclusion with appropriate calculations.

b. Without prejudice to your answer to part **a,** assume that WindAir needs 17,400 units. Should the Compressor Division be willing to supply the compressor units for $50 each? Support your conclusions with appropriate calculations.

c. Without prejudice to your answer to part **a,** assume that WindAir needs 17,400 units. Would it be in the best interest of National Industries for the Compressor Division to supply the compressor units at $50 each to the WindAir Division? Support your conclusions with appropriate calculations.

40. *Transfer pricing and organizational structure.*[10] "If I were to price these boxes any lower than $480 a thousand," said Mr. Brunner, manager of Birch Paper Company's Thompson division, "I'd be countermanding my order of last month for our salespeople to stop shaving their bids and to bid full cost quotations. I've been trying for weeks to improve the quality of our business, and if I turn around now and accept this job at $430 or $450 or something less than $480, I'll be tearing down this program I've been working so hard to build up. The division can't very well show a profit by putting in bids that don't even cover a fair share of overhead costs, let alone give us a profit."

Birch Paper Company was a medium-sized, partly integrated paper company, producing white and kraft papers and paperboard. A portion of its paperboard output was converted into corrugated boxes by the Thompson division, which also printed and colored the outside surface of the boxes. Including Thompson, the company had four producing divisions and a timberland division, which supplied part of the company's pulp requirements.

For several years management judged each division independently on the basis of its profit and return on investment. Top management had been working to gain effective results from a policy of decentralizing responsibility and authority for all decisions except those relating to overall company policy. The company's top officials believed that in the past few years they had applied the concept of decentralization successfully and that the company's profits and competitive position had definitely improved.

Early in 19X0 the Northern division designed a special display box for one of its papers in conjunction with the Thompson division, which was equipped to make the box. Thompson's package design and development staff spent several months perfecting the design, production methods, and materials needed; because of the unusual color and shape, these were far from

---

[10]Copyright © 1957, 1985 by the President and Fellows of Harvard College. Harvard Business School case 158-001. W. Rotch prepared this case under the direction of Neil E. Harlan as the basis for class discussion rather than to illustrate either effective or ineffective handling of an administrative situation. Reprinted by permission of Harvard Business School.

standard. According to an agreement between the two divisions, the Northern division reimbursed the Thompson division for the cost of its design and development work.

After the Northern division prepared the specifications, it asked for bids on the box from the Thompson division and from two outside companies, West Paper Company and Erie Papers, Ltd. Each division manager normally was free to buy from whichever supplier he or she wished, and even on sales within the company divisions were expected to meet the going market price if they wanted the business.

Early in 19X0 market competition began to squeeze the profit margins of converters such as the Thompson division. Thompson, as did many other similar converters, bought its board, liner, or paper, and its function was to print, cut, and shape it into boxes. Though it bought most of its materials from other Birch divisions, Thompson made most of its sales to outside customers. If Thompson got the order from Northern, it probably would buy its liner board and corrugating medium from the Southern division of Birch. The walls of a corrugated box consist of outside and inside sheets of linerboard sandwiching the corrugating medium.

About 70 percent of Thompson's out-of-pocket cost of $400 a thousand for the order represented the cost of linerboard and corrugating medium. Though Southern division had been running below capacity and had excess inventory, it quoted the market price, which had not noticeably weakened as a result of the oversupply. Its out-of-pocket costs on both liner and corrugating medium were about 60 percent of the selling price.

The Northern division received bids on the boxes of $480 a thousand from the Thompson division, $430 a thousand from West Paper Company, and $432 a thousand from Erie Papers, Ltd. Erie Papers offered to buy from Birch the outside linerboard with the special printing already on it, but it would supply its own liner and corrugating medium. The Southern division would supply the outsider liner at a price equivalent to $90 a thousand boxes, and the Thompson division would print it for $30 a thousand. Of the $30, about $25 would be out-of-pocket costs.

Since this situation appeared to be a little unusual, Ms. Kenton, manager of the Northern division, discussed the wide discrepancy of bids with Birch's commercial vice president. She told the commercial vice president, "We sell in a very competitive market, where higher costs cannot be passed on. How can we be expected to show a decent profit and return on investment if we have to buy our supplies at more than 10 percent over the going market?"

Knowing that Mr. Brunner had occasionally in the past few months been unable to operate the Thompson division at capacity, the commercial vice president thought it odd that Mr. Brunner would add the full 20 percent overhead and profit charge to his out-of-pocket costs. When he asked Mr. Brunner about this over the telephone, his answer was the statement that appears at the beginning of the case. Mr. Brunner continued saying that since they did the developmental work on the box and received no profit on that, he felt entitled to a good markup on the production of the box itself.

The vice president explored further the cost structures of the various divisions. He remembered a comment the controller had made at a meeting the week before to the effect that costs that for one division were variable could be largely fixed for the company as a whole. He knew that in the absence of specific orders from top management, Mr. Kenton would accept the lowest bid, namely that of the West Paper Company, for $430. However, it would be possible for top management to order the acceptance of another bid if the situation warranted such action. And though the transactions in question represent less than 5 percent of the volume of any of the divisions involved, other transactions could conceivably raise similar problems later.

  a. Does the system motivate Mr. Brunner in such a way that actions he takes in the best interest of the Thompson division are also in the best interest of the Birch Paper Company? If your answer is no, give some specific instances related as closely as possible to the type of situation described in the case. Would the system correctly motivate managers of *other* divisions?

  b. What should the vice president do?

41. *Impact of division performance measures on management incentives.* The home office staff of The Nomram Group evaluates managers of the Nomram divisions by keeping track of the rate of return each division earns on the average level of assets invested at the division. The home office staff considers 20 percent, which is The Nomram Group's after-tax cost of capital, to be the minimum acceptable annual rate of return on average investment. When a division's rate of return drops below 20 percent, division management can expect an unpleasant investigation by the home office and perhaps some firings. When the rate of return exceeds 20 percent and grows through time, the home office staff is invariably pleased and rewards division management. When the rate of return exceeds 20 percent but declines over time, the home office staff sends out unpleasant memorandums and cuts the profit-sharing bonuses of the division managers.

In Division A, average assets employed during the year amount to $60,000. Division A has been earning 40 percent per year on its average investment for several years. Management of Division A is proud of its extraordinary record—earning a steady 40 percent per year.

In Division B, average assets employed during the year also amount to $60,000. Division B has been earning 25 percent per year on its average investment. In the preceding 3 years, the rate of return on investment was 20 percent, 22 percent, and 23 percent, respectively. Management of Division B is proud of its record of steadily boosting earnings.

New investment opportunities have arisen at both Division A and Division B. In both cases, the new investment opportunity will require a cash outlay today of $30,000 and will provide a rate of return on investment of 30 percent for each of the next 8 years. The average amount of assets invested in the project will be $30,000 for each of the next 8 years. Both new investment opportunities have positive net present value when the discount rate is 20 percent per year (the after-tax cost of capital of The Nomram Group).

When word of the new opportunities reached the home office staff, the prospects of the two new investments pleased the staff, because both investments would yield a better-than-average return for The Nomram Group.

Management of Division A computed its rate of return on investment both with and without the new investment project and decided not to undertake the project. Management of Division B computed its rate of return on investment both with and without the new investment project and decided to undertake it.

When word of the two divisions' actions reached the home office staff, it was perplexed. Why did Division A's management turn down such a good opportunity? What in the behavior of the home office staff induced Division A's management to reject the new project? Is management of Division B doing a better job than management of Division A? What may the home office do to give Division A an incentive to act in a way more consistent with the well-being of The Nomram Group?

42. *Capital investment analysis and decentralized performance measurement—a comprehensive case.*[11] The following exchange occurred just after Diversified Electronics rejected a capital investment proposal.

> *Ralph Browning (Product Development):* I just don't understand why you have rejected my proposal. This new investment is going to be a sure money maker for the Residential Products division. No matter how we price this new product, we can expect to make $230,000 on it before tax.
>
> *Sue Gold (Finance):* I am sorry that you are upset with our decision, but this product proposal just does not meet our short-term ROI target of 15 percent after tax.
>
> *Browning:* I'm not so sure about the ROI target, but it goes a long way toward meeting our earnings-per-share growth target of 20 cents per share after tax.
>
> *Phil Carlson (Executive Vice President):* Ralph, you are right, of course, about the importance of earnings per share. However, we view our three divisions as investment centers. Proposals like yours must meet our ROI targets. It is not enough that you show an earnings-per-share increase.
>
> *Gold:* We believe that a company like Diversified Electronics should have a return on investment of 12 percent after tax, especially given the interest rates we have had to pay recently. This is why we have targeted 12 percent as the appropriate minimum ROI for each division to earn next year.
>
> *Carlson:* If it were not for the high interest rates and poor current economic outlook, Ralph, we would not be taking such a conservative position in evaluating new projects. This past year has been particularly rough for our industry. Our two major competitors had ROIs of 10.8 and 12.3 percent. Though our ROI of 10.9 percent after tax was reasonable (see Exhibit 15.15), performance varied from division to division. Professional Services did very well with 15 percent ROI, while the Residential Products division managed just 11 percent. The performance of the Aerospace Products division was

---

[11]J. M. Lim, M. W. Maher, and J. S. Reece, copyright © 1990. This case requires knowledge of discounted cash flow methods (see Chapter 9).

especially dismal, with an ROI of only 7 percent. We expect divisions in the future to carry their share of the load.

Chris McGregor (Aerospace Products): My division would be showing much higher ROI if we had a lot of old equipment like the Residential Products or relied heavily on human labor like Professional Services.

Carlson: I don't really see the point you are trying to make, Chris.

Diversified Electronics, a growing company in the electronics industry, had grown to its present size of more than $140 million in sales. (See Exhibits 15.13, 15.14, and 15.15 for financial data.) Diversified Electronics has three divisions, Residential Products, Aerospace Products, and Professional Services, each of which accounts for about one-third of Diversified Electronics' sales. Residential Products, the oldest division, produces furnace thermostats and similar products. The Aerospace Products division is a large job shop that builds electronic devices to customer specifications. A typical job or batch takes several months to complete. About one-half of Aerospace Products' sales are to the U.S. Defense Department. The newest of the three divisions, Professional Services, provides consulting engineering services. This division has grown tremendously since Diversified Electronics acquired it 7 years ago.

Each division operates independently of the others and corporate management treats each as a separate entity. Division managers make many of the operating decisions. Corporate management coordinates the activities of the various divisions, which includes review of all investment proposals over $400,000.

Diversified Electronic's measures return on investment as the division's adjusted net income: [Profit before Taxes and Interest $\times$ (1 − Income Tax Rate)]/(Interest-Bearing Debt + Owners' Equity). Each division's expenses

Exhibit 15.13

DIVERSIFIED ELECTRONICS
Income Statement for 1989 and 1990
(all dollar amounts in thousands, except earnings-per-share figures)

	Year Ended December 31	
	1989	1990
Sales	$141,462	$148,220
Cost of Goods Sold	108,118	113,115
Gross Margin	$ 33,344	$ 35,105
Selling and General	13,014	13,692
Profit before Taxes and Interest	$ 20,330	$ 21,413
Interest Expense	1,190	1,952
Profit before Taxes	$ 19,140	$ 19,461
Income Tax Expense	7,886	7,454
Net Income	$ 11,254	$ 12,007
Earnings per Share (2,000 shares outstanding in 1989 and 1990)	$5.63	$6.00

Exhibit 15.14

DIVERSIFIED ELECTRONICS
Balance Sheets for 1989 and 1990
(all dollar amounts in thousands)

	December 31	
	1989	**1990**
Assets		
Cash and Temporary Investments	$ 1,404	$ 1,469
Accounts Receivable	13,688	15,607
Inventories	42,162	45,467
Total Current Assets	$ 57,254	$ 62,543
Plant and Equipment:		
Original Cost	107,326	115,736
Accumulated Depreciation	42,691	45,979
Net	$ 64,635	$ 69,757
Investments and Other Assets	3,143	3,119
Total Assets	$125,032	$135,419
Liabilities and Owners' Equity		
Accounts Payable	$ 10,720	$ 12,286
Taxes Payable	1,210	1,045
Current Portion of Long-Term Debt	—	1,634
Total Current Liabilities	$ 11,930	$ 14,965
Deferred Income Taxes	559	985
Long-Term Debt	12,622	15,448
Total Liabilities	$ 25,111	$ 31,398
Common Stock	47,368	47,368
Retained Earnings	52,553	56,653
Total Owners' Equity	$ 99,921	$104,021
Total Liabilities and Owners' Equity	$125,032	$135,419

Exhibit 15.15

DIVERSIFIED ELECTRONICS
Ratio Analysis

	1989	1990
Net Income/Total Assets:	$\dfrac{\$11,254}{\$125,032} = 9.0\%$	$\dfrac{\$12,007}{\$135,419} = 8.9\%$
Return on Investment Computations:	Average Tax Rate $= \dfrac{\$7,886}{\$19,140}$ $= .412.$	Average Tax Rate $= \dfrac{\$7,454}{\$19,461}$ $= .383.$
	ROI $= \dfrac{\$20,330(1 - 0.412)}{\$12,622 + \$99,921}$ $= \dfrac{\$11,954}{\$112,543}$ $= 10.6$ Percent.	ROI $= \dfrac{\$21,413(1 - 0.383)}{\$1,634 + \$15,448 + \$104,021}$ $= \dfrac{\$13,212}{\$121,103}$ $= 10.9$ Percent.

includes the allocated portion of corporate administrative expenses. (See Exhibit 15.15.)

Since each of Diversified Electronics' divisions is located in a separate facility, management can easily attribute most assets, including receivables, to specific divisions. Management allocates the corporate office assets, including the centrally controlled cash account, to the divisions on the basis of divisional revenues.

Exhibit 15.16 shows the details of Ralph Browning's rejected product proposal.

a. Why did corporate headquarters reject Ralph Browning's product proposal? Was their decision the right one? If top management used the discounted cash flow (DCF) method instead, what would the results be? The company uses a 15 percent cost of capital (i.e., hurdle rate) in evaluating projects such as these.

b. Evaluate the manner in which Diversified Electronics has implemented the investment center concept. What pitfalls did they apparently not anticipate? What, if anything, should be done with regard to the investment center approach and the use of ROI as a measure of performance?

c. What conflicting incentives for managers can occur between the use of a yearly ROI performance measure and DCF for capital budgeting?

Exhibit 15.16

DIVERSIFIED ELECTRONICS
Financial Data for New Product Proposal

1. Projected Asset Investment:[a]

Land Purchase	$200,000
Plant and Equipment[b]	800,000
Total	$1,000,000

2. Cost Data, before Taxes (first year):

Variable Cost per Unit	$3.00
Differential Fixed Costs[c]	$170,000

3. Price/Market Estimate (first year):

Unit Price	$7.00
Sales	100,000 Units

4. Taxes: The company assumes a 40 percent tax rate for investment analyses. Depreciation of plant and equipment according to tax law is as follows: Year 1, 20 percent; Year 2, 32 percent; Year 3, 19 percent; Year 4, 14.5 percent; Year 5, 14.5 percent. Taxes are paid for taxable income in Year 1 at the end of Year 1, taxes for Year 2 at the end of Year 2, etc.

5. Inflation is assumed to be 10 percent per year and applies to revenues and all costs except depreciation.

6. The project has an 8 year life. Land will be sold at the end of Year 8. The nominal land price is expected to increase with inflation.

[a]Assumes sales of 100,000 units.

[b]Annual capacity of 120,000 units.

[c]Includes straight-line depreciation on new plant and equipment, depreciated for 8 years with no net salvage value at the end of 8 years.

Suggested Solutions to Even-Numbered Exercises

22. *Return on investment computations*

a. New York Division: $\dfrac{\$500,000}{\$4,000,000} = 12.5\%$

Philadelphia Division: $\dfrac{\$500,000}{\$5,000,000} = 10\%$

Los Angeles Division: $\dfrac{\$500,000}{\$6,000,000} = 8.33\%$

b. New York Division:

$$\frac{\$500,000 - (\$4,000,000/\$15,000,000)(\$900,000)}{\$4,000,000} = 6.5\%$$

Philadelphia Division:

$$\frac{\$500,000 - (\$5,000,000/\$15,000,000)(\$900,000)}{\$5,000,000} = 4.0\%$$

Los Angeles Division:

$$\frac{\$500,000 - (\$6,000,000/\$15,000,000)(\$900,000)}{\$6,000,000} = 2.33\%$$

c. New York Division:

$$\frac{\$500,000 - (\$24,000,000/\$60,000,000)(\$900,000)}{\$4,000,000} = 3.5\%$$

Philadelphia Division:

$$\frac{\$500,000 - (\$20,000,000/\$60,000,000)(\$900,000)}{\$5,000,000} = 4.0\%$$

Los Angeles Division:

$$\frac{\$500,000 - (\$16,000,000/\$60,000,000)(\$900,000)}{\$6,000,000} = 4.33\%.$$

d. New York Division:

$$\frac{\$500,000 - (22,500/45,000)(\$900,000)}{\$4,000,000} = 1.25\%$$

Philadelphia Division:

$$\frac{\$500,000 - (12,000/45,000)(\$900,000)}{\$5,000,000} = 5.2\%$$

Los Angeles Division:

$$\frac{\$500,000 - (10,500/45,000)(\$900,000)}{\$6,000,000} = 4.83\%.$$

24. *ROI computations with replacement costs*

a. Boston Division: $\dfrac{\$400,000}{\$4,000,000} = 10\%$;   Mexico City Division: $\dfrac{\$600,000}{\$7,500,000} = 8\%.$

b. Boston Division: $\dfrac{\$400,000}{\$6,000,000} = 6.67\%$;   Mexico City Division: $\dfrac{\$600,000}{\$8,000,000} = 7.5\%.$

c. Analysts make two principal arguments for using acquisition cost in the denominator as in part **a.** First, firms can easily obtain it from their records and it does not require estimates of current replacement costs. Second, it is consistent with the measurement of net income in the numerator (that is, depreciation expense is based on acquisition cost, and unrealized holding gains are excluded). Analysts also make two principal arguments for using current replacement cost in the denominator as in part **b.** First, it eliminates the effects of price changes and permits the division that can use the depreciable assets most efficiently to show a better ROI. Second, as discussed in the chapter, it may lead division managers to make better equipment-replacement decisions. If firms use acquisition cost as the valuation basis in calculating ROI, divisions with older, more fully depreciated assets may be reluctant to replace them and thereby introduce higher, current amounts in the denominator. If firms use current replacement cost in the denominator, the asset base will be the same regardless of whether or not the assets are replaced. Thus the replacement decision can be made properly (that is, based on net present value), independent of any effects on ROI.

26. *Comparing profit margin and ROI as performance measures.* The return on investment (ROI), profit margin percentage, and asset turnover ratio of the three divisions follow.

	Return on Investment	=	Profit Margin Percentage	×	Asset Turnover Ratio
New Hampshire District:	$\dfrac{\$200,000}{\$2,000,000}$	=	$\dfrac{\$200,000}{\$3,800,000}$	×	$\dfrac{\$3,800,000}{\$2,000,000}$
	10%	=	5.26%	×	1.9.
Illinois District:	$\dfrac{\$500,000}{\$6,250,000}$	=	$\dfrac{\$500,000}{\$17,000,000}$	×	$\dfrac{\$17,000,000}{\$6,250,000}$
	8%	=	2.94%	×	2.72.
California District	$\dfrac{\$1,000,000}{\$8,000,000}$	=	$\dfrac{\$1,000,000}{\$20,000,000}$	×	$\dfrac{\$20,000,000}{\$8,000,000}$
	12.5%	=	5%	×	2.5.

a. Using the profit margin percentage, the ranking of the divisions is (1) New Hampshire, (2) California, and (3) Illinois.

b. Using ROI, the ranking of divisions is (1) California, (2) New Hampshire, and (3) Illinois.

c. The ROI is a better measure of overall performance because it relates profits to the investment, or capital, required to generate those profits. New Hampshire had the largest profit margin percentage. It required more capital to generate a dollar of sales than did California. Thus its overall profitability is less. Illinois had the largest asset turnover ratio.

However, it generated the smallest amount of net income per dollar of sales, resulting in the lowest ROI of the three divisions.

28. *ROI computations with net and gross book values*

	a. Net Book Value	b. Gross Book Value
Year 1	$\dfrac{(\$400,000 - \$200,000)}{(\$2,000,000 - \$200,000)}$ $= \dfrac{\$200,000}{\$1,800,000} = 11.1$ Percent.	$\dfrac{(\$400,000 - \$200,000)}{\$2,000,000}$ $= \dfrac{\$200,000}{\$2,000,000} = 10$ Percent.
Year 2	$\dfrac{(\$400,000 - \$200,000)}{[(\$2,000,000 - (2 \times \$200,000)]}$ $= \dfrac{\$200,000}{\$1,600,000} = 12.5$ Percent.	$\dfrac{(\$400,000 - \$200,000)}{\$2,000,000}$ $= \dfrac{\$200,000}{\$2,000,000} = 10$ Percent.
Year 3	$\dfrac{(\$400,000 - \$200,000)}{[(\$2,000,000 - (3 \times \$200,000)]}$ $= \dfrac{\$200,000}{\$1,400,000} = 14.3$ Percent.	$\dfrac{(\$400,000 - \$200,000)}{\$2,000,000}$ $= \dfrac{\$200,000}{\$2,000,000} = 10$ Percent.
Year 4	$\dfrac{(\$400,000 - \$200,000)}{[\$2,000,000 - (4 \times \$200,000)]}$ $= \dfrac{\$200,000}{\$1,200,000} = 16.7$ Percent.	$\dfrac{(\$400,000 - \$200,000)}{\$2,000,000}$ $= \dfrac{\$200,000}{\$2,000,000} = 10$ Percent.

30. *ROI and residual income computations*

$$\text{Annual Income} = \$70,000 - \frac{\$160,000}{5} = \$38,000.$$

Year	Investment Base	a. ROI $38,000/Base	b. Residual Income $38,000 − 25 Percent × Base
1	$160,000	23.8 Percent	$ (2,000)
2	128,000[a]	29.7	6,000
3	96,000	39.6	14,000
4	64,000	59.4	22,000
5	32,000	118.8	30,000

[a]Base decreases by annual depreciation of $32,000.

32. *Transfer pricing*

a.	Auditors	Consultants		Accounting Firm	
Transfer Internally	Pay $200	Receive $200	Pays	$ 70	
		Pay 70	Pays	$ 70	
Transfer Externally	Pay $180	Receive $200	Receives	$ 20 (net)	
		Pay 70	Pays	$ 70	
			Pays	$ 50	

It is advantageous to transfer externally.

b.

	Auditors	Consultants	Accounting Firm
Transfer Internally	Pay $200	Receive $200	Pays $ 70
		Pay 70	Pays $ 70
Transfer Externally	Pays $180	Receives and	Pays $180
		Pays 0	

It is advantageous to transfer internally.

. . . PART FIVE . . .

Special Topics

. . .

... CHAPTER 16 ...

Synthesis: Managerial Accounting and External Reporting

Chapter Outline

- Illustration
- Different Data for Different Purposes
- Review and Integration

T his book focuses on three principal uses of accounting information: (1) decision making; (2) planning, control, and internal performance evaluation; and (3) external financial reporting. Data appropriate for one of these purposes may be inappropriate for another. Many managers view external reporting as unproductive—a needless cost the securities market regulators impose. In other cases, in an effort to get more output per dollar of accounting input, managers will sometimes try to use data designed for external reporting to do double duty and serve in decision-making or planning and control functions. This chapter reviews the data needed for each of these purposes and provides examples of how errors can result when managers use data designed for one purpose for a different purpose.

We present the material in this chapter in a different format than in previous chapters. This chapter synthesizes concepts discussed in previous chapters. We use case studies, both in the chapter and in the end-of-chapter materials, to bring out the key issues. We intend to raise these issues here so that you will be aware of them and be prepared to deal with them in your career.

Illustration   721

Illustration

This section contains an illustration based on discussions between a firm's president (John Presley), its controller (Jill Contreras), and the manager of a division (Tom Divito). The initial setting takes place during January, Year 2, at a meeting of the three.

Presley (President): Tom, I have just received a report on the first year of operations for your division (Exhibit 16.1), and the results look bad. You show a loss of $2,000 for the year. Our shareholders want to see increasing net income and earnings per share each year. We can't afford to have one division pulling down the rest of the company.

Divito (Division Manager): But Mr. Presley, we operated exactly according to plan during Year 1. We anticipated producing 12,000 units, and we were right on the mark. At this production level, we projected a unit production cost of $4.50, and that's right where we came out.

Presley: I'm still not happy. I've received an offer from a competitor to purchase your inventory and plant assets for $17,000, and I'm inclined to accept.

Contreras (Controller): I think such a decision would be unwise until we analyze the situation further. Basing such a decision on the divisional profit report for Year 1 could lead to a bad decision. For one thing, Exhibit 16.1 reports the results for last year. That's history now; we can't do anything about the loss incurred. What's important for decision making is what we expect to happen in the future.

Presley: Okay, Jill. You've just finished the budget for Year 2. What do you show for Tom's division this year?

Contreras: Exhibit 16.2 presents the expected results for Year 2. We expect sales to increase to 12,000 units, which should improve things a bit. Tom expects to

Exhibit 16.1

Divisional Performance Report for Year 1

Sales (10,000 × $5)..		$50,000
Cost of Goods Sold:		
Beginning Inventory.......................................	$ 0	
Direct Materials (12,000 × $2.00)	24,000	
Direct Labor (12,000 × $1.50)	18,000	
Overhead:		
Variable (12,000 units × $.75 per unit)	9,000	
Fixed (12,000 units × $.25[a] per unit)	3,000	
Total	$54,000	
Less Ending Inventory (2,000 × $4.50)	(9,000)	
Cost of Goods Sold		(45,000)
Gross Margin...		$ 5,000
Selling Expenses (.04 × $50,000).............................		(2,000)
Share of Corporate Administrative Costs (.10 × $50,000)..........		(5,000)
Divisional Net Loss...		$ (2,000)

[a] $\dfrac{\text{Budgeted and Actual Fixed Overhead Costs}}{\text{Budgeted and Actual Production in Units}} = \dfrac{\$3,000}{12,000} = \$.25$ per unit.

Exhibit 16.2

Divisional Budget for Year 2		

Sales (12,000 × $5)...		$60,000
Cost of Goods Sold:		
Beginning Inventory (2,000 × $4.50)	$ 9,000	
Direct Materials (12,000 × $2.00)............................	24,000	
Direct Labor (12,000 × $1.50)..............................	18,000	
Overhead:		
Variable (12,000 units × $.75 per unit)	9,000	
Fixed (12,000 units × $.25[a] per unit)	3,000	
Total	$63,000	
Less Ending Inventory (2,000 × $4.50)	(9,000)	
Cost of Goods Sold		(54,000)
Gross Margin...		$ 6,000
Selling Expenses (.04 × $60,000).............................		(2,400)
Share of Corporate Administrative Costs (.10 × $60,000)...........		(6,000)
Divisional Net Loss..		$ (2,400)

[a] $\dfrac{\text{Budgeted Fixed Overhead Costs}}{\text{Budgeted Production}} = \dfrac{\$3,000}{12,000} = \$.25$ per unit.

produce 12,000 units again at a unit cost of $4.50. The higher sales level, however, will mean that Tom's division must absorb a higher portion of central corporate costs. Thus we project a loss of $2,400 for next year.

Presley: You mean with an increase in sales of $10,000, we expect an even *bigger* loss next year? That about does it for me. How much loss will I report to shareholders if I sell the division for $17,000?

Contreras: The inventory on hand at the beginning of Year 2 costs us $9,000 (= 2,000 × $4.50) to produce. We acquired the plant assets at the beginning of Year 1 for $10,000. Based on straight-line depreciation and a 10-year life, they now have a book value of $9,000. Thus we would lose $1,000 (= $17,000 − $9,000 − $9,000) on the sale before taxes.

Presley: I am inclined to cut my losses and get rid of the division. I'll report a loss of $1,000 instead of $2,400 for Year 2, and I won't have to worry about the division dragging down my profits in future years.

Contreras: That may be the correct decision, but I think we should think this thing through more clearly. Exhibit 16.2 does show the expected divisional profit for Year 2 instead of actual for Year 1, but you should not base your decision on this analysis alone.

First, we prepared Exhibit 16.2 using generally accepted accounting principles (GAAP). Although we must follow GAAP for external reporting, we're not constrained to do so for internal managerial purposes. We should be looking at the future cash flows under each of our alternatives, not accounting profits.

Presley: Because we sell most of our products for cash or on short-term credit and pay most of our expenses soon after purchase, can't we assume that the revenues and expenses in Exhibit 16.2 are essentially the same as cash receipts and disbursements?

Illustration   **723**

Contreras: That's okay for most items, but not for all. For example, fixed manufacturing overhead includes a $1,000 depreciation charge, which is not a cash flow. Furthermore, we should focus primarily on those future cash flows that differ between alternatives.

Presley: Jill, why don't you show me what Exhibit 16.2 would look like if it focused just on those cash flows for Year 2 that would differ between alternatives?

Contreras: I thought you might want such analysis. Exhibit 16.3 shows what I came up with. As you can see, cash outflows for fixed manufacturing overhead will equal $2,000 if we operate the division; depreciation of $1,000 does not require a cash outflow. The $2,000 includes property taxes and insurance on the division's inventory and plant assets. Also, I have left out the $6,000 share of central corporate expenses.

Presley: Wait a minute! Your salary and my salary will require cash next year. I don't intend to work for nothing. The division's fair share of central corporate expenses is $6,000. Thus you must change the net cash inflow from operating the division of $4,600 in your analysis to a net cash outflow of $1,400.

Contreras: Mr. Presley, I don't intend to work for nothing any more than you do. I left the $6,000 out of the analysis because the firm will incur that cost whether we continue to operate the division or whether we sell it off. We can safely ignore future cash flows that will not differ between alternatives because they are the same in either case.

Presley: I'm not totally convinced yet, but let's see where we stand. If I sell the division outright, I will get $17,000 in cash. If I operate the division next year, I will receive $4,600. I am inclined to stick by my earlier inclination to sell the division for the $12,400 differential cash flow. Jill, is this right, or am I missing some other point?

Contreras: Possibly. You have compared the two alternatives over different time periods. The plant assets in the division have a remaining useful life of 9 years, not just 1 year. We have to look at the cash flows that the division would generate over the next 9 years to see the benefit of keeping the division.

Exhibit 16.3

Cash Flows Comparison: Keep Division versus Sell Divison			
	Keep Division (1)	Sell Division (2)	Keep − Sell Differential Cash Flows = (1) − (2) (3)
Sales Revenue (12,000 × $5.00)	$60,000	$ —	$ 60,000
Direct Materials (12,000 × $2.00)	(24,000)	—	(24,000)
Direct Labor (12,000 × $1.50)	(18,000)	—	(18,000)
Variable Overhead (12,000 × $.75)..............	(9,000)	—	(9,000)
Fixed Overhead ($3,000 − $1,000)..............	(2,000)	—	(2,000)
Selling Expense ($60,000 × .04)...............	(2,400)	—	(2,400)
Selling Price of Division	—	17,000	(17,000)
Net Cash Flows..............................	$ 4,600	$17,000	$(12,400)

Exhibit 16.4

After-Tax Cash Flow Comparison: Keep Division versus Sell Division

	Present Value at 12 Percent	End of Period								
		2	3	4	5	6	7	8	9	10
Keep Division										
Cash Receipts from Sales	$319,695[a]	$60,000	$60,000	$60,000	$60,000	$60,000	$60,000	$60,000	$60,000	$60,000
Cash Expenditures for Variable Manufacturing Costs	(271,741)[a]	(51,000)	(51,000)	(51,000)	(51,000)	(51,000)	(51,000)	(51,000)	(51,000)	(51,000)
Cash Expenditures for Fixed Manufacturing Costs	(10,657)[a]	(2,000)	(2,000)	(2,000)	(2,000)	(2,000)	(2,000)	(2,000)	(2,000)	(2,000)
Cash Expenditures for Selling Expenses	(12,788)[a]	(2,400)	(2,400)	(2,400)	(2,400)	(2,400)	(2,400)	(2,400)	(2,400)	(2,400)
Depreciation for Tax Purposes		(2,200)	(2,100)	(2,100)	(2,100)	—	—	—	—	—
Taxable Income		$ 2,400	$ 2,500	$ 2,500	$ 2,500	$ 4,600	$ 4,600	$ 4,600	$ 4,600	$ 4,600
Cash Expenditures for Income Taxes at 40 Percent	(7,217)	(960)	(1,000)	(1,000)	(1,000)	(1,840)	(1,840)	(1,840)	(1,840)	(1,840)
Net Present Value	$ 17,292									
Sell Division										
Selling Price	$ 17,000									
Tax Effect of Loss on Sale	200[b]									
Net Present Value	$ 17,200									

[a]Based on a factor of 5.32825, the present value of an annuity in arrears for nine periods at twelve percent.

[b]Cash inflow is 40 percent of loss at $500 = $17,000 − $9,000 − $8,500; .40 × $500 loss is $200.

Illustration   **725**

Presley: Assuming that the division will generate a net cash inflow of $4,600 each year during the next 9 years, we will generate $41,000 of cash flow. But I know that we cannot compare the $41,400 to the $17,000 cash we would get from selling the division, because the $41,400 inflows are spread out more. To make the two sets of cash flows comparable, I must discount the annual $4,600 cash flows back for 9 years at our cost of capital of 12 percent. That results in a net present value of $24,510.[1] The present value of selling the division is, of course, $17,000. Maybe we shouldn't sell the division.

Divito: That's what I like to hear. I was beginning to wonder where I would be working next year.

Presley: Jill, as I understand it, we've calculated the present value of the future cash flows that will differ between the alternatives. I think I understand now why this is the correct basis for making managerial decisions. Before bringing important nonquantitative factors into the decision, have we left out anything?

Contreras: Unfortunately, yes. We have not considered income taxes. Because 12 percent is the after-tax cost of capital, we must compute the income tax ramifications of this decision.

Presley: But Jill, you know that we have centralized our income tax planning and strategy function in central corporate headquarters. We don't hold the divisions responsible for the impact of income taxes on their decisions. We report divisional profit performance on a before-tax basis.

Contreras: Our treatment of income taxes may or may not be appropriate for internal performance reporting. But for decision making, income taxes affect cash flows and we must consider them. At our tax rate of 40 percent, income taxes can affect the decision greatly.

Presley: Well, Jill, let's see the analysis.

Contreras: Exhibit 16.4 gives the figures. The top panel shows the present value of the cash inflows and outflows along with the related tax effects, assuming that we continue to operate the division. While depreciation is itself not a cash flow, we can subtract depreciation in calculating taxable income. Thus it indirectly affects cash flows. The amounts reported as depreciation for tax purposes are the accelerated cost recovery amounts. Depreciation for tax purposes follows: Year 1, $1,500; Year 2, $2,200; Year 3, $2,100; Year 4, $2,100; Year 5, $2,100. The net present value if the division continues to operate is $17,292.

If we sell the division, we'll lose on the disposal of the inventory and equipment. As I indicated earlier, the inventory has a book value of $9,000 for both tax and financial reporting. We depreciated the plant assets, however, during Year 1 at $1,000 for financial reporting and $1,500 for tax reporting. In calculating the tax consequences of the sale, the *tax* basis of the plant assets of $8,500 (= $10,000 − $1,500) is relevant. The loss on the sale for tax purposes is $500 (= $17,000 − $9,000 − $8,500) and the tax savings are $200 (= .40 × $500).

Presley: As I see it, the net present value of the after-tax cash flows favors keeping the division, but it's so close that I think selling is more prudent—"a bird in the hand," you know.

---

[1]$24,510 = $4,600 × 5.32825, the factor for the present value of an annuity in arrears for nine periods at twelve percent.

Divito: Before you make up your mind, Mr. Presley, I would like to put in my two cents about delaying such a sale for a while. The market for our products is expanding. With aggressive promotion, I believe that we can increase our market share. Given this potential for growth, I think that we can cover not only our own costs but provide for coverage of central corporate costs as well. We also anticipate that through more efficient purchasing of raw materials and better training of our workers, we can reduce our direct manufacturing costs.

Presley: OK, Tom, I'll let you have a go at it for another year. Perhaps one year of operation is not enough to form a judgment on the profit-generating ability of your division. Good luck.

One Year Later

John Presley, Jill Contreras, and Tom Divito meet to review the performance of Tom's division for Year 2.

Presley: Well, Tom, now you face the time of reckoning. I've kept a copy of the budget for your division for Year 2 (Exhibit 16.2) in my desk for the last year. I have asked Jill to show your actual results for Year 2 side by side with your budget so that I can see clearly how you've done. Jill, have you prepared the analysis?

Contreras: Yes; Exhibit 16.5 presents the results.

Presley: Well, I like your actual bottom line for Year 2—a profit of $1,400 instead of a loss of $2,400. I'm not happy, though, with the large production cost variances. In contrast to the promises made a year ago, your production costs have

Exhibit 16.5

Comparison of Budgeted and Actual Performance for Year 2

	Budget	Actual	Variance
Sales....................................	$ 60,000	$ 61,200	$ 1,200
Cost of Goods Sold:			
Beginning Inventory	$ 9,000	$ 9,000	—
Direct Materials.............................	24,000	28,500	$ (4,500)
Direct Labor................................	18,000	21,750	(3,750)
Overhead:			
Variable	9,000	10,500	(1,500)
Fixed.....................................	3,000	3,750	(750)
Total	$ 63,000	$ 73,500	$(10,500)
Less Ending Inventory	(9,000)	(21,500)	12,500
Cost of Goods Sold	$ 54,000	$ 52,000	$ 2,000
Gross Margin...................................	$ 6,000	$ 9,200	$ 3,200
Fixed Overhead Variance	—	750	750
Selling Expenses	(2,400)	(2,520)	(120)
Share of Corporate Administrative Costs	(6,000)	(6,030)	(30)
Division Net Profit (Loss).......................	$ (2,400)	$ 1,400	$ 3,800

Illustration   727

been much larger than expected. It looks to me like you have been grossly inefficient. I don't understand two things about this performance report. What do the $12,500 variance relating to ending inventory and the $750 fixed overhead variance mean?

Contreras: In Exhibit 16.5, we base the budget amounts on a production level of 12,000 units. But the division actually produced 15,000 units. The unfavorable manufacturing cost variances and the ending inventory variance result from the fact you are comparing the manufactured costs expected to be incurred in producing 12,000 units with the actual costs of producing 15,000 units.

Presley: I read the other day about something called a "flexible budget." It seemed to apply when you produced or sold a different number of units than you expected.

Contreras: That's right. We know what the manufacturing costs should have been to produce 12,000 units. We can now see what they should have been to produce the 15,000 units actually produced. Exhibit 16.6 presents the analysis. As you can see, the actual manufacturing costs for direct material, direct labor, and variable manufacturing overhead were less than they should have been for 15,000 units. Thus the firm realized the efficiencies that Tom promised you.

Divito: I'm glad to see that they show up in my performance report. I increased production this year because I anticipate that we will capture a larger market share in Year 3. I was concerned, though, about how the increase in costs required for these additional units would show up in my performance report, because the budgeted costs based on 12,000 units were so much less. I like this flexible budget report.

Exhibit 16.6

Comparison of Flexible Budget and Actual Performance for Year 2

	Flexible Budget	Actual	Variance
Sales......................................	$ 60,000	$ 61,200	$ 1,200
Costs of Goods Sold:			
Beginning Inventory	$ 9,000	$ 9,000	$ —
Direct Materials...............................	30,000	28,500	1,500
Direct Labor..................................	22,500	21,750	750
Overhead:			
Variable	11,250	10,500	750
Fixed..	3,000	3,750	(750)
Total	$ 75,750	$ 73,500	$ 2,250
Less Ending Inventory	(21,500)	(21,500)	—
Cost of Goods Sold	$ 54,250	$ 52,000	$ 2,250
Gross Margin...................................	$ 5,750	$ 9,200	$ 3,450
Fixed Overhead Variance	—	750	750
Selling Expenses	(2,400)	(2,520)	(120)
Share of Corporate Administrative Costs	(6,000)	(6,030)	(30)
Division Net Profit.............................	$ (2,650)	$ 1,400	$ 4,050

Presley: You have answered my question about the large variable manufacturing cost variances and about the ending inventory variance. I can see now that they relate to the larger production volume achieved. But what about the $750 fixed overhead variance? What's that?

Contreras: That variance results from producing more units than anticipated. We budgeted fixed overhead costs for Year 2 to be $3,000. With anticipated production of 12,000 units, we set the fixed overhead rate at $.25 per unit. By producing 15,000 units, the division applied $3,750 (= 15,000 × $.25) to units produced. The difference of $750 is not really a variance at all. We should not give the division manager any credits for such a variance.

Divito: Now wait a minute. I used my plant assets more efficiently this year, producing 15,000 units instead of 12,000 units. The $750 fixed overhead variance measures the benefits of this more efficient utilization, and I should get credit for it.

Contreras: The practice under full absorption costing of treating fixed costs like variable costs caused the variance. We prepared Exhibit 16.6 in accordance with full absorption costing as required under GAAP for financial reporting. We divided fixed manufacturing costs for the year by the expected level of production to obtain a rate per unit, $.25 in this case. We allocated each unit produced a share of the fixed cost using this rate. Because you produced 3,000 more units than anticipated, you applied $750 (= 3,000 × $.25) more fixed overhead to production than you would have *had you anticipated that you would produce 15,000 units during Year 2*. Note that the $750 favorable variance in the lower portion offsets the unfavorable variance of $750 for fixed overhead in the upper portion of Exhibit 16.6. Full absorption costing can do some crazy things to your performance report when expected and actual production differ.

Presley: What you say makes sense, but we've little choice. We must use full absorption costing in our external financial statements.

Contreras: Yes, but GAAP do not constrain our internal reports. With some modifications, we can adapt our accounting system to generate data both on a full absorption costing basis for external reporting and on another basis for internal performance evaluation.

Presley: What do you suggest we should do?

Contreras: We should classify our costs according to their behavior, either variable or fixed. Raw materials and direct labor are variable. Except for a few easily identifiable overhead items (depreciation, insurance, property taxes), our overhead costs are essentially variable as well. Selling costs are also variable. The performance report would then distinguish costs by their behavior rather than by their nature (that is, production, selling). Exhibit 16.7 shows what I mean. Product costs include only variable material, labor, and overhead costs. Fixed costs are treated as an expense of the period. I prepared this report on a variable costing, instead of absorption costing, basis. The report shows no overapplied fixed overhead nor a favorable overhead variance resulting from producing more than expected. This format has the added advantage of classifying data in a form useful for decisions. For many decisions, incremental costs will be the variable costs. If the time horizon is short enough, fixed costs often do not change. Of course, in the long run decisions can alter even the fixed costs.

Illustration   **729**

Exhibit 16.7

Comparison of Flexible Budget and Actual Performance for Year 2 Using Variable Costing

	Flexible Budget		Actual		
	Per Unit	Total	Per Unit	Total	Variance
Sales.........................	$5.00	$60,000	$5.10	$61,200	$1,200
Variable Costs:					
Manufacturing:					
Beginning Inventory		$ 8,500		$ 8,500	
Direct Materials...........	$2.00	30,000	$1.90	28,500	$1,500
Direct Labor..............	1.50	22,500	1.45	21,750	750
Variable Overhead	.75	11,250	.70	10,500	750
Total	$4.25	$72,250	$4.05	$69,250	$3,000
Less Ending Inventory		(21,250)		(20,250)	(1,000)
Goods Sold		$51,000		$49,000	$2,000
Selling.....................	.20	2,400	.21	2,520	(120)
Total Variable Costs	$4.45	$53,400	$4.26	$51,520	$1,880
Contribution Margin	$ .55	$ 6,600	$ .84	$ 9,680	$3,080
Fixed Costs:					
Manufacturing..............	—	(3,000)	—	(3,000)	—
Contribution to Corporate Administrative Costs and Corporate Profits		$ 3,600		$ 6,680	

Presley: The only thing that bothers me with the performance report you have prepared in Exhibit 16.7 is that you have deleted the division's share of central costs. I can buy the fact that our decision to continue running the division or to sell it does not affect these costs and, therefore, they are irrelevant to that decision. However, someone must cover these costs if the company is to survive in the long run.

Divito: This is a good place for me to sound off. It really bothers me that my division can operate at a positive divisional profit before allocation of central corporate costs, but my bottom line really gets hit by costs over which I have no control. Not only can't I control these costs, but I get penalized when my sales go up. Central corporate headquarters provides us with little or no marketing support. So why should they get a bigger piece of the action when my division increases its sales?

Contreras: You have both made legitimate points. Mr. Presley, you are correct that revenues from the operating divisions must cover these costs if the firm is to survive. Tom, you have grounds for complaining that these costs are not under your control. The decentralized, divisional corporate structure makes each operating unit feel that it is running its own separate company. If the allocation of central corporate costs to the division motivates you to hold back on sales increases, we must do something about the allocation. We either have to stop allocating or else find a more appropriate allocation method. Placing your share of central corporate costs at the bottom of your divisional performance report should make you aware that you are part of the larger company and must do your share to cover costs of running the company. Yet we will judge your performance primarily on your division's contribution to central corporate expenses and net income.

Divito: This seems reasonable to me.

Presley: Good, then we have developed a new basis for internal performance evaluation. We will break out costs by responsibility center according to their behavior (variable or fixed). We will design the performance report in a variable costing format. Jill, at the end of each year, you can make the necessary adjustments to convert to an absorption costing basis for external reporting.

Contreras: Now we see the three different uses of accounting data and the appropriate model for each one. In managerial decision making, we are concerned with the differential future cash flows between alternatives. The three key words are (1) future, (2) cash flows, and (3) differential. In many cases, variable costs will differ and fixed costs will not. However, some fixed costs may also differ if we can eliminate or alter them even in the short run. In the long run, we can change all costs, which makes all costs differential. If the decision horizon extends beyond 1 year, we should discount the differential cash flows to their present value when comparing alternatives.

In planning, control, and internal performance evaluation, we focus on individual responsibility centers. We want to attribute revenues and costs to those units within a firm that control the amounts. Because unitizing fixed manufacturing overhead under absorption costing can lead to confusing results, the firm should prepare the performance report on a variable costing basis. Each division should subtract variable costs from revenue to obtain the contribution margin. Then it should subtract fixed costs of the responsibility center to obtain the center's contribution to coverage of central corporate expenses and to corporate profits.

For external reporting, we are required to follow generally accepted accounting principles. The main point to keep in mind is that we do not and, in general, should not use these same reports for managerial decision making, planning, and control. While GAAP theoretically should also be concerned primarily with economic effects, standard setters set accounting for financial reporting based on objectivity, practicability, and political pressure.

Different Data for Different Purposes

We use accounting data for several different purposes: decision making, managerial planning, control, internal performance evaluation, external financial reporting, income tax reporting, and reporting to various regulatory agencies. Data appropriate for one of these purposes is sometimes inappropriate for another.

Exhibit 16.8 summarizes some of the uses of accounting information and contrasts the data necessary for different uses. If you read across the exhibit from left to right, you will see how accounting requirements change as you move from decision making to planning to performance evaluation. The remainder of this section elaborates on particular cases where different purposes require different data.

Exhibit 16.8

Different Data for Different Purposes

	Purpose			
	Internal			External
	Decision Making	**Planning (budgeting)**	**Control and Performance Evaluation**	**External Financial Reporting**
Activity	Differential Analysis; Selecting from Alternatives for Action	Expressing Expectations for Alternatives Selected	Comparing Actual Results with Expectations	Reporting Actual Results to Owners and Other External Entities
Accounting Reports	Differential Cash Flows	Static Budgets; Profit Plans and Capital Budgets	Flexible Budgets; Performance Reports; Variances	Financial Statements
Time Orientation	Future	Future	Past and Current (input to future)	Past and Current
Focus of Accounting	Decision Specifics	Responsibility Centers	Responsibility Centers	Company-Wide plus Segments
Model	Short Run: Differential Cash Flows; Long Run: Net Present Value	Short Run: Profit; Long Run: Capital Budgets	ROI Residual Income	Earnings, ROI, EPS
Variables in the Model . .	Differential Future Cash Flows	Revenues, Variable Costs, Fixed Costs	Revenues, Variable Costs, Fixed Costs, Investment in Division	Revenues Matched with Expenses in Compliance with GAAP

Consistent with Variable Costing

Full-Absorption Costing

Review and Integration

The Projected Future versus the Actual Past

In making decisions, the manager asks: What will happen? No task in business is more difficult than trying to forecast the future. Chapter 6 discussed the techniques for cost estimation and forecasts of market demands. Good management requires skillful guessing about the future and how to adapt to it. Accounting provides a structure for gathering and analyzing data on managers' expectations that firms use for making decisions.

Once managers make a decision, they construct a plan or budget to implement the decision. As Chapters 12 and 13 pointed out, budgets are either static (fixed) or flexible. A **static (or fixed) budget** assumes a particular level of output and projects costs based on that level. A **flexible budget,** based on fixed and variable cost components, shows expected costs for various levels of output.

While plans are implemented, management wants to know if processes are in control. For these purposes, accounting needs both projections originally made and actual outcomes. Comparison of projections and outcomes helps management pinpoint the causes of deviations from expectations. This comparison serves both as a basis for evaluating past performance and for testing actions that will help assure that future performance will coincide with expectations.

Current Costs versus Historical Costs

In evaluating a lower-level manager or a division, top management compares profits generated with the investment necessary in that division to generate those profits (for example, plant, inventory, and working capital). Typically (and misleadingly), management uses the historical cost of the assets (adjusted downward for accumulated depression) as the denominator in a rate-of-return calculation or in deriving the capital charge in a residual income analysis. Some firms recognize that the current exit value (opportunity cost) of the assets may be more appropriate. If, for example, the firm could sell a plant for $10 million, the cost of using the asset is $10 million even if its depreciated historical cost is only $4 million and its replacement cost is $13 million.

Throughout accounting, reduced objectivity and verifiability may offset the benefits of the added relevance obtained from using current cost data. The benefit-cost ratio is most favorable in internally evaluating management. Although management may be tempted to use historical cost data, as required for external financial reporting, in making internal evaluations, resulting comparisons can mislead. The objection to current cost data—reduced precision—is less severe when management uses the data internally and does not subject it to official scrutiny through securities regulation or tax reporting.

Interest on Funds: Explicit, Implicit, or Ignored

Other things being equal, cash received sooner is more valuable than cash received later; cash paid later is less costly than cash paid sooner. Effective decision making requires that the firm take the time value of money explicitly into account. Chapter 9 explained and illustrated the techniques. In planning and control, the time horizon—usually a single accounting period—is so short that ignoring the time value of money is cost effective. In internal evaluations, the firm typically does not use net present value analysis, but it recognizes the cost of capital tied up while it carries out operations. A rate-of-return computation (such as return on investment, ROI) charges for capital when it divides the profit by the average amount of assets employed during the period: The larger the amount of assets employed, the larger the denominator and the smaller the computed rate of return. The firm compares the resulting rate to some norm. That norm is at least in part a function of the cost of funds.

Chapter 15 pointed out the problems of using the rate of return for project evaluation. Management compares the ROI of projects to an average, rather than a marginal, cost of funds; managers will have incentives to dispose of assets (or not undertake new projects) whenever the return on them is less than the average the division earns, even though the assets can earn a rate larger than the cost of capital. Chapter 15 suggested that management should measure residual income as an alternative method for making internal evaluations. Rather than divide earnings by average assets to get an average rate of return, subtract an explicit charge from income for capital used.

Economics and Accounting Define Costs and Profits Differently

To economists, the cost of capital is a cost of doing business. In economics, a firm realizes no profits until funds employed in a business have been paid a market wage, just as the firm realizes no profit until labor has been paid its market wage. Whereas the economist will subtract from revenues both interest on borrowed funds and the opportunity cost of owners' funds invested, accounting net income results from subtracting only the cost of borrowed funds from revenues. Thus, whereas economic analysis (for decision making and internal evaluation) explicitly takes into account the cost of all funds used, externally reported net income does not.

Similarly, external financial reporting and internal accounting sometimes ignore the time value of money. In external financial reporting and income tax reporting, the firm realizes a positive income as long as revenues (measured by amounts of cash eventually collected) exceed expenses (measured over sufficiently long time periods in amounts equal to cash expenditures). Economic analysis will report losses for the same transactions if the firm delays the cash collections so long that assets do not earn the opportunity cost of the funds invested in them.

Allocations and Unit Costs

External financial reporting and income tax accounting require the allocation of fixed costs to individual units of inventory produced. This book emphasizes that using unit costs that include an allocation of fixed costs often leads managers to incorrect internal decisions. Chapter 5 pointed out, however, that allocating the costs of service departments to production departments may affect incentives positively and, hence, total costs. The firm's charging managers of production departments with an allocated portion of service department costs gives those managers an incentive to press the service departments to operate more efficiently. Such pressure may help in reducing costs in the service departments.

Illustrations of Contrasting Uses

Static versus Flexible Budgeting   A budgeted plan usually forecasts an expected level of activity, such as sales, and projects total costs based on that level of activity. In assessing whether operations are in control, top management can understand variances from plan better if the report separates them into variances from the forecast of activity and variances from budget adjusted to the actual level of activity.

Variable Costs versus Fully Absorbed Costs   For decision making and control, accounting treats variable costs per unit separately from fixed costs per period. In external financial and income tax reporting, accounting computes the fully absorbed costs for ending inventories and cost of goods sold.

ROI or Residual Income versus Earnings per Share   Effective internal evaluation measures performance against the cost of generating that performance. Thus, for internal purposes, managers look at ROI, or better yet, at residual income. Externally, security analysts focus on earnings per share, which generally is net income divided by average shares outstanding during the period. If managers focus on earnings per share, they must inevitably focus on earnings, computed from generally accepted accounting principles. Conflicts between effective decisions and reported earnings arise here as well.

Revenues versus Receipts   In external financial reporting, accounting measures income as revenues less expenses. **Revenue** is the present value of cash the firm collects from rendering services. A firm can recognize revenue, such as from credit sales, in a period before it receives the cash. For external reporting, the firm will recognize the revenues in the period of sale. For income taxes, the firm need not report the income from the sale until the later period when it collects the cash. Because wise managers generally delay tax payments as long as possible (assuming that tax rates do not change over time), the manager will want to focus on **receipts** in tax reporting while reporting revenues in external financial statements.

Accounting for Inventories: Variable versus Full Absorption Costing

Could a business report increasing profits year after year and still be approaching bankruptcy? Yes. If production exceeds sales period after period, a manufacturing business can report increasing profits while it becomes insolvent. Effective management requires a good understanding of how the methods of accounting for inventories may cause such a misleading picture of operating performance.

Chapters 3 and 4 discussed two approaches to measuring manufacturing costs to be included in product cost: full absorption costing and variable costing. Under **full absorption costing,** a firm includes all manufacturing costs, whether direct or indirect and whether fixed or variable, in a product's cost. External financial reporting and income tax reporting require full absorption costing. Many businesses use it for managerial purposes as well. Herein lies a potential problem: Managers can make incorrect decisions based on full absorption costing, because full absorption costing does not reflect differential cost behavior. In other words, full absorption costing treats fixed manufacturing costs as if they were unit costs and, therefore, variable. Under **variable costing,** accounting considers only the variable manufacturing costs to be unit product costs. Variable costing treats fixed costs as expenses of the period when the firm incurs the costs.

Full Absorption versus Variable Costing: Reporting Effects   Consider a simplified situation in which a firm may produce one, two, or three units of a product each period. Variable costs of production are $30 per *unit* produced, and fixed costs are $120 per *period*. Thus the total cost per unit under full absorption costing will be $150, $90, or $70 per unit, depending on whether the firm produces one, two, or three units during the period. Each unit sells for $100. Exhibit 16.9 shows the income and the balance sheet amounts for ending inventory under both full absorption and variable costing for each of five cases. In each case, production and sales over the two periods total four units. Only the timing of production and sales changes. Total income over the two periods is $40 for each case. This equality over the two periods stems from both beginning and ending inventory equaling zero. Under these conditions, total expenses must equal cash expenditures.

All else being equal, the larger the long-run revenues, the larger the costs of producing those revenues. Thus, assuming that costs are under control and are as expected, accurate reporting to management will show increased operating profit and cost in periods when revenue increases. Notice in cases IV and V that under full absorption costing, reported income varies more strongly with production than with sales, whereas under variable costing, reported income varies with sales. Even in case II, the relation between income and sales, though positive for both full absorption and variable costing, is stronger under variable costing than under full absorption costing.

Justification for Variable Costing Fixed manufacturing costs provide the capacity to produce this period and the firm incurs them even if for some reason (such as a shutdown of the production line) it manufactures no products. Consider the rent on a factory. A company pays that rent even when its factory lies idle, producing nothing. Factory rent is a cost of being a going concern. Under full absorption costing, factory rent is part of inventory produced. If rent for the month is $500 and the firm produces 100 parts, each part will carry $5 (= $500/100 units) of costs for rent; but if the firm produces 200 units, each part will probably carry $2.50 (= $500/200 units) of costs for rent. Under full absorption costing, the cost of each unit produced varies inversely with the total number of units produced. Management that wants to know short-run costs of units produced needs to know the incremental costs of production—direct labor, direct materials, and variable overhead. In variable costing, accounting includes only the variable costs of production as product costs. Accounting treats all fixed costs as period expenses.

All costs are variable if the time horizon is long enough. The firm is not required to renew leases, replace salaried workers as they retire, purchase new equipment, and so on. But management wants to assess performance over shorter time horizons. Variable costing often provides information that management uses in the short run. Management asks this basic question of each cost incurred in variable costing: "Does incurring this cost today avoid having to incur this cost in the future?" If the answer is yes, the cost in question is an incremental cost and is included in product cost. If the answer is no, variable costing treats the cost as an expense of the period. Because using raw materials today in producing a particular unit eliminates the need to use raw materials tomorrow for that unit, raw materials are incremental product costs under variable costing. But the firm must pay factory rent whether or not it makes any product, so variable costing treats factory rent as a period expense rather than as a production cost. Many factory overhead costs— salaries of factory supervisors and guards, depreciation, and property taxes, for example—will not decrease next period for having been incurred this period. These costs are, therefore, period expenses in variable costing.

Exhibit 16.9

Full Absorption versus Variable Costing
(variable costs are $30 per unit; fixed costs are $120 per period; units sell for $100 each)

	Case I		Case II		Case III		Case IV		Case V	
	Period 1	Period 2	Period 1	Period 2	Period 1	Period 2	Period 1	Period 2	Period 1	Period 2
Production in Units	2	2	2	2	3	1	3	1	3	1
Sales in Units (at $100)	2	2	1	3	3	1	2	2	1	3
Full Absorption Costing										
Average Unit Cost of Production[a]	$ 90	$ 90	$ 90	$ 90	$ 70	$150	$ 70	$150	$ 70	$150
Sales	$200	$200	$100	$300	$300	$100	$200	$200	$100	$300
Cost of Goods Sold	(180)	(180)	(90)	(270)	(210)	(150)	(140)	(220)	(70)	(290)
Income (Loss)	$ 20	$ 20	$ 10	$ 30	$ 90	$(50)	$ 60	$(20)	$ 30	$ 10
Ending Inventory	$ 0	$ 0	$ 90	$ 0	$ 0	$ 0	$ 70	$ 0	$140	$ 0
Variable Costing										
Sales	$200	$200	$100	$300	$300	$100	$200	$200	$100	$300
Variable Cost of Goods Sold	(60)	(60)	(30)	(90)	(90)	(30)	(60)	(60)	(30)	(90)
Fixed Expenses	(120)	(120)	(120)	(120)	(120)	(120)	(120)	(120)	(120)	(120)
Income (Loss)	$ 20	$ 20	$(50)	$ 90	$ 90	$(50)	$ 20	$ 20	$(50)	$ 90
Ending Inventory	$ 0	$ 0	$ 30	$ 0	$ 0	$ 0	$ 30	$ 0	$ 60	$ 0

[a] Equal to $30 + $120/n, where n is the number of units produced that period.

Selling Profits to Inventory   Earlier, we pointed out that a firm could report increasing profits year after year, all the while approaching bankruptcy. We can now see how this paradox might occur. As long as production exceeds sales, full absorption costing will transfer fixed costs into ending inventory, increasing reported profits. Even if sales decline, income under full absorption costing can continue to increase as long as production exceeds sales. Eventually, a large amount of inventory will accumulate, and a firm will become insolvent or bankrupt in spite of its increasing reported income. Full absorption costing ''sells profits'' to inventory. A firm would not, of course, normally continue to increase production in the face of stable or declining sales.

Therefore, the decision about the amount of fixed costs allocated to inventory and the amount allocated to expenses for the period affects inventory valuation, cost of goods sold, and income.

■ Summary ■

This chapter illustrates the importance of using appropriate data for the particular task at hand. It also indicates areas where sound management decisions and financial reporting may conflict. Managerial decisions must rely on estimates of current and future cash flows. Financial reporting focuses on past cash flows and the allocation of those cash flows to periods in accordance with generally accepted accounting principles. Considerations of conservatism and objectivity more often guide these principles than the present value of future cash flows.

The potential uses of accounting data lead to some important implications for accounting system design. In designing a home, ideally we start with the major uses and activities, then design the structure. Similarly, in accounting we start with uses of data and work back to the appropriate system. We make the decisions keeping both the costs and benefits in mind.

Key Terms and Concepts

Static (fixed) versus flexible
   budgeting
Receipts versus revenues

Full absorption versus variable
   costing

Questions, Problems, and Cases

Questions

Note: Because of the unique nature of this chapter, we have not included self-study problems or exercises. The questions and the problems and cases are intended to synthesize concepts discussed in prior chapters or to illustrate potential conflicts between managerial decision making and accounting reporting.

1. Review the meaning of the concepts or terms discussed above in Key Terms and Concepts.

2. Each of the following terms contains the word *cost*. Accounting, business, and economics use these terms in various ways. We explain the terms in the glossary at the back of the book under the heading *cost terminology*. Review the meaning and usage of each of these terms.

   a. Avoidable cost.   k. Marginal cost.
   b. Common cost.   l. Opportunity cost.
   c. Controllable cost.   m. Out-of-pocket cost.
   d. Current cost.   n. Product cost.
   e. Differential cost.   o. Standard cost.
   f. Direct cost.   p. Sunk cost.
   g. Fixed cost.   q. Traceable cost.
   h. Historical cost.   r. Unavoidable cost.
   i. Incremental cost.   s. Variable cost.
   j. Indirect cost.

3. Assume 2 years of constant production quantities, decreasing sales, and, hence, rising end-of-year inventory quantities. In Year 2, fixed costs are substantially higher than in Year 1. Compare the differences in reported income resulting from using full absorption costing on the one hand and variable costing on the other in Years 1 and 2.

4. Under what circumstances would the shift from full absorption costing to variable costing negligibly affect the balance sheet and income statement?

5. Inventory valuations appear only on the balance sheet. How, then, do inventory valuations affect net income for the period?

6. How does the economist's view of profit differ from the accountant's?

7. Meals in restaurants are not inventoriable (usually); that is, once it's prepared, a restaurant cannot save a meal until the next accounting period. Yet some restaurants compute the cost of meals using full absorption, whereas others use variable costing methods—generally only for inventoriable items.

   Explain how the full absorption costing versus variable costing accounting methods could be relevant for analysis of such noninventoriable items.

8. Over sufficiently long time periods, income is cash in minus cash out. Eventually the entire book value of an owned asset will be written off through depreciation or on disposal of the asset, regardless of the depreciation method accountants use.

   What difference could it possibly make whether accountants use straight-line or accelerated depreciation methods for external financial reporting?

9. "Because the FASB generally does not allow a firm to capitalize its research and development (R&D) costs, internal financial statements will not be consistent with external financial reports unless the firm expenses R&D costs internally. Therefore, accounting should expense R&D costs for internal evaluation of managerial performance."

   Comment.

10. Explain how interest costs that enter into managerial decision making are often ignored in financial reporting.

Exhibit 16.10

ALL FIXED COSTS COMPANY		
	Month 1	**Month 2**
Production	20,000 Tons	0 Tons
Sales...	10,000 Tons	10,000 Tons
Selling Price per Ton	$30	$30
Costs (all fixed):		
Production	$280,000	$280,000
General and Administrative...........................	$40,000	$40,000

Integrative Problems and Cases

11. *Inventory costing.*[2] The All Fixed Costs Company is so named because it has no variable costs—all of its costs are fixed and vary with time rather than with output. The All Fixed Costs Company is located on the bank of a river and has its own hydroelectric plant to supply power, light, and heat. The company manufactures a synthetic material from air and river water, and it sells its product on a long-term, fixed-price contract. It has a small staff of employees, all hired on an annual salary basis. The output of the plant can be increased or decreased by adjusting a few dials on the control panel. Exhibit 16.10 presents data on production, sales, and cost information for the first 2 months of operations.

    a. Prepare income statements for each of the 2 months, using full absorption costing.

    b. Prepare income statements for each of the 2 months, using variable costing.

    c. Which costing method is management likely to prefer? Why?

12. *Inventory costing.* The Semi-Fixed Cost Company is just like the All Fixed Cost Company (see the preceding problem) except that its fixed production costs are $210,000 per month and variable production costs are $7 per ton. The production, sales, and general and administrative cost data for Months 1 and 2 for the All Fixed Cost Company apply to the Semi-Fixed Cost Company as well.

    a. Prepare income statements for each of the 2 months, using full absorption costing.

    b. Prepare income statements for each of the 2 months, using direct costing.

    c. Which costing method is management likely to prefer? Why?

13. *Divisional performance reports.* A company that assembles and sells cordless telephones has operations in two divisions for internal performance evaluation. The Anselmo Division assembles the firm's product, and the Ramos Division conducts the finishing, packing, and selling activities. Management expects quarterly sales during the first year of operations to be seasonal in the following percentages: 20 percent, 30 percent, 30 percent, 20 percent.

---

[2]Problems 11 and 12 are adapted from Raymond P. Marple, "Try This on Your Class, Professor," *The Accounting Review*, vol. 31.

The Anselmo Division plans to produce units at a reasonably uniform rate throughout the year. Anselmo immediately transfers its completed units to Ramos on the basis of cost of manufacturing plus a 25 percent markup on cost. A representative market price for the product at this stage is $22. The firm allocates divisional fixed selling and administrative expenses equally to each quarter during the year. It also allocates central corporate expenses to divisions on the basis of total sales.

A performance report for the first quarter appears in Exhibit 16.11.

a. What strengths and weaknesses do you see in this divisional performance report?

b. Making whatever changes you believe are appropriate, prepare a divisional performance report for these two divisions for the first quarter. Describe briefly the justification for your treatment of the transfer price, fixed manufacturing expenses, fixed selling and administrative expenses, and central corporate expenses.

14. *Financial accounting and decision making.* Biogenetics, Inc., uses a cost of capital rate of 12 percent in making investment decisions. It currently is considering two mutually exclusive projects, each requiring an initial investment of $10 million. The first project has a net present value of $21 million and an internal rate of return of 20 percent. The firm will complete this project within 1 year. It will raise accounting income and earnings per share almost immediately thereafter. The second project has a net present value of $51 million and an internal rate of return of 30 percent. The second project requires incurring large, noncapitalizable expenses over the next few years before net cash inflows from sales revenue result. Thus accounting income and earnings per share for the next few years will not only be lower than if the first project is accepted but will also be lower than earnings currently reported.

Exhibit 16.11

Performance Report for Critique in Problem 13

	Anselmo Division	Ramos Division
Annual Budgeted Production (units)	48,000	40,000
Budgeted Production—First Quarter (units)	12,000	8,000
Units Produced	10,000	8,000
Units Sold	10,000	5,000
Sales	$250,000	$500,000
Cost of Goods Sold:		
Variable Expenses	(150,000)	(375,000)
Fixed Expenses[a]	(50,000)	(50,000)
Gross Profit	$ 50,000	$ 75,000
Divisional Fixed Selling and Administrative Expenses	(12,000)	(50,000)
Central Corporate Expenses	(25,000)	(50,000)
Divisional Income (Loss)	$ 13,000	$ (25,000)

[a]Exclusive of any adjustment for under- or overapplied expenses.

a. Should the short-run effects on accounting income and earnings per share influence the decision about the choice of projects? Explain.

b. Should either of the projects be accepted? If so, which one? Why?

15. *Accounting for advertising.* Equilibrium Company spends $30,000 advertising the company's brand names and trademarks. Gross margin on sales after taxes is up $33,000 each year because of these advertising expenditures. For the purposes of this problem, assume that the firm makes all advertising expenditures on the first day of each year and that the $33,000 extra after-tax gross margin on sales occurs on the first day of the next year. Excluding any advertising assets or profits, Equilibrium Company has $100,000 of other assets that have produced an after-tax income of $10,000 per year. Equilibrium Company follows a policy of declaring dividends each year equal to net income, and it has a cost of capital of 10 percent per year.

a. Is the advertising policy a sensible one? Explain.

b. How should accounting report the expenditures for advertising in Equilibrium Company's financial statements to reflect accurately the managerial decision of advertising at the rate of $30,000 per year? In other words, how can the firm account for the advertising expenditures in such a way that the accounting rate of return for the advertising project and the rate of return on assets for the firm reflect the 10 percent return from advertising?

16. *Management incentives and financial accounting for research and development.* Many companies evaluate managerial effectiveness by examining the accounting rate of return of a given manager's division or product lines. If managers think that the firm will evaluate them using an accounting rate of return criterion, they may make decisions in order to increase (or not to decrease) the accounting rate of return. *Statement of Financial Accounting Standards No. 2* requires the immediate expensing of R&D expenditures, whereas capitalization of those expenditures is a reasonable theoretical alternative. Assume that a manager is contemplating making R&D expenditures with a positive net present value when accounting discounts cash flows at the firm's cost of capital.

Indicate how generally accepted accounting principles for R&D expenditures will affect the decision making of managers whose firms use the accounting rate of return to evaluate them.

17. *Management incentives and accounting for research and development.* The Eager Division has $300,000 of total assets, earns $45,000 per year, and generates $45,000 per year of cash flow. The cost of capital is 15 percent. Each year, Eager pays cash of $45,000 to its parent company, Greed Enterprises. Eager's management has discovered a project requiring research and development costs now that will lead to new products. The anticipated cash flows for this project follow: beginning of Year 1, outflow of $24,000; beginning of years 2, 3, and 4, inflows of $10,000 each.

Assume that Greed undertakes the project, that cash flows are as planned, and that Eager pays $45,000 to Greed at the end of the first year and $47,000 at the end of each of the next 3 years.

a. Compute Eager's rate of return on assets for each year of the project, assuming that accounting expenses R&D expenditures as they occur. Use the year-end balance of total assets in the denominator.

b. Compute Eager's rate of return on assets for each year of the project, assuming that accounting capitalizes and then amortizes R&D costs on a straight-line basis over the last 3 years of the project. Use the year-end balance of total assets in the denominator.

c. Compute the new project's accounting rate of return, independent of the other assets and of the income of Eager assuming that accounting capitalizes and then amortizes R&D costs on a straight-line basis over the entire 4 years of the project.

d. How well has the management of the Eager Division carried out its responsibility to its owners? On what basis do you make this judgment?

18. *Management incentives and financial accounting.* This chapter states that accounting can report economically sound managerial decisions as poor ones and vice versa, at least in the short run. This case provides an opportunity to explore certain areas where financial accounting rules may impede effective managerial decisions. We have not discussed all the financial accounting issues involved in the following situations in this book. The instructor can provide the student with suitable background, or students may do their own research in identifying the issues.

For each of the FASB *Statements* that follow, describe the required accounting treatment and reasonable alternatives to it. Then describe how the required treatment may alter the behavior of a manager evaluated by the accounting statements. Assume that although the manager wishes to make decisions that serve the long-run best interests of the firm by maximizing the present value of future cash flows, the firm evaluates the manager currently using reported net income.

a. FASB *Statement No. 2,* "Accounting for Research and Development Costs." This statement requires the immediate expensing of research and development costs.

b. FASB *Statement No. 5,* "Accounting for Contingencies." In the past, firms often did not carry casualty insurance on some of their assets but instead spoke of themselves as being "self-insured." They used the following accounting. Each year the firm would charge to income an amount for insurance expense while setting up an estimated liability for losses. Under that practice, firms would later charge catastrophic losses against the estimated liability rather than against income in the period when the loss occurred. This method smooths income more than when the firm charged losses to income in the period of the loss. *Statement No. 5* forbids this practice; it requires that the firm recognize such expense or loss only in the period when an actual loss occurs.

c. FASB *Statement No. 7,* "Accounting and Reporting by Development Stage Enterprises." This statement, in effect, requires expensing of (rather than capitalization of, followed by amortization of) preoperating costs new businesses incur. Preoperating costs are those costs a business incurs before it begins its intended operations.

19. *Puzzling accounting reports including inventory costing*. Lucius Green runs a
distillery under the corporate name Green's Distillery. Each year Green distills 10,000 barrels of whiskey, puts the product in barrels, and stores the
barrels for 4 years. Each year Green sells 10,000 barrels of 4-year-old whiskey to a retail chain, which bottles the whiskey and puts its own label on the
product. The retailer has a long-term, fixed-price contract with Green. The
retailer is so pleased with Green's product that it is willing to buy the whiskey
at any age. The contract specifies that the retailer will buy a barrel of newly
distilled whiskey for $100, a barrel of 1-year-old whiskey for $118, a barrel of
2-year-old whiskey for $140, a barrel of 3-year-old whiskey for $168, and a
barrel of 4-year-old whiskey for $200. In the past, Green has always sold only
4-year-old whiskey. Prices and costs have been stable for several years and
are expected to remain so. An income statement for Green's Distillery for a
typical year, when it distills 10,000 barrels and sells 10,000 barrels of 4-year-
old whiskey, appears in Exhibit 16.12.

   During Year 0, the retailer suggested to Lucius Green that he double the
capacity of the distillery and that they rewrite the contract so that the retailer
could promise to buy as much as Green wanted to produce.

   Assume that Green doubled capacity and, starting in Year 1, distilled
20,000 barrels of whiskey each year to be aged. All costs shown on the
income statement for 10,000 barrels doubled (that is, *unit costs* including
depreciation remained constant) except for general and administrative expenses, which increased $100,000 a year to $300,000 a year. By Year 5, the
first batch of extra product was fully aged, and, starting in Year 5, Green sold
20,000 barrels of 4-year-old whiskey to the retail chain. During Year 1
through Year 4, he sold 10,000 barrels.

   a. Prepare income statements for each of the Years 1 through 5, using full
   absorption costing.

   b. Prepare income statements for each of the Years 1 through 5, using variable costing.

   c. Which of the costing methods appears to give a better picture of the
   results of Green's Distillery for Years 2 through 4?

Exhibit 16.12

GREEN'S DISTILLERY Income Statement for Typical Year When 10,000 Barrels Are Produced and 10,000 Barrels Are Sold		
Sales (10,000 barrels at $200)		$2,000,000
Cost of Goods Sold:		
Variable Costs ($50 per barrel, 10,000 barrels)	$500,000	
Depreciation of Distilling Equipment	100,000	
Storage Costs of Aging Whiskey ($20 per barrel per year, 40,000 barrels)	800,000	(1,400,000)
General and Administrative Expenses		(200,000)
Income before Taxes		$ 400,000

d. You will probably judge in part **c** that full absorption costing better reflects the situation. Why does variable costing appear to fail in this case, and what should we conclude from this result?

20. *Incremental analysis and decisions involving patents.* Southeast Industries is a conglomerate firm. During the past several years, the management has analyzed two matters involving its patents. This case illustrates one use of incremental analysis and cost allocations in decision making.

Plywood Division   In its plywood division, Southeast Industries manufactures striated (decorative) plywood that sells in the marketplace for a premium over ordinary plywood. Southeast Industries owns the patent, called the Deskey patent, on the striation process, and currently is the sole producer of striated plywood. The machinery required for the striation process (in addition to the machinery usually required to make plywood) costs $15,000 and lasts 5 years. Southeast Industries currently operates its plywood manufacturing operation at 80 percent of normal capacity. It operates the specialized machinery currently used for striation also at only 80 percent of normal capacity. The variable cost of producing 1,000 board feet of striated plywood is $100. The total fixed cost for producing 1,000 board feet of striated plywood at present levels of output is $10. The selling price of 1,000 board feet of striated plywood is $160.

The market demand for striated plywood appears to be increasing. Industry experts forecast that the demand for striated plywood will increase by about 25 percent next year and remain at that level for the next 5 years. Southeast Industries can acquire additional striating machinery, if necessary, and produce more striated plywood in a plant in South Carolina that currently produces only ordinary plywood. The costs in the South Carolina plant will be comparable to current costs.

A competitor in the ordinary plywood business, Alabama Atlantic Company, has approached Southeast and asked to purchase nonexclusive rights to use the Deskey patent. Alabama Atlantic Company has calculated that, aside from the cost of the patent license to use the Deskey patent, it can make a net incremental profit (after taxes) of $50 per 1,000 board feet of striated plywood produced. Alabama Atlantic has sufficient capacity to match Southeast's production of striated plywood.

a. What is the maximum price that Alabama Atlantic should be willing to pay, per 1,000 board feet, as a royalty for the right to use the Deskey patent?

b. What is the minimum price that Southeast Industries should be willing to accept from Alabama Atlantic as a royalty to use the Deskey patent?

c. Explain why the two companies are, or are not, likely to reach a mutually agreeable price. In your opinion, what is that price likely to be?

Chemical Division   In its chemical division, Southeast Industries manufactures several kinds of flux used in welding. In particular, it owns the patent for flux no. 660; the patent on flux no. 660 expires in 4 years. At the end of that time, anyone else can manufacture the no. 660 flux without paying a royalty to Southeast Industries.

The Jefferson Electric Company requires a flux in its manufacturing of electric motors. Currently, Jefferson Electric Company owns the right to use both the no. 620 and the no. 650 fluxes, but it does not own the right to use the no. 660 flux. Engineers at Jefferson Electric Company state that neither the no. 620 nor the no. 650 flux is suitable for the line of electric motors that Jefferson wishes to build over the next decade. The no. 660 flux is suitable. The engineers also state that the series 700 fluxes, just developed at Jefferson Electric Company, will be ideal for these motors. Unfortunately, Jefferson cannot produce the series 700 fluxes in large quantities until 2 years from now. Jefferson estimates that the series 700 fluxes will be substantially cheaper to manufacture than any of the series 600 fluxes (nos. 620, 650, and 660).

If Jefferson Electric Company purchased all of its no. 660 fluxes from Southeast Industries at Southeast's normal selling prices, Southeast would add $300,000 per year to its after-tax profit.

The two companies are attempting to negotiate an agreement whereby Jefferson Electric Company pays Southeast Industries for the right to manufacture the no. 660 flux. Assume that the companies consider each year separately in the negotiations.

d. Explain why the two companies are, or are not, likely to reach a mutually agreeable royalty for each of the next 10 years. In your opinion, what payment is likely to be agreed to for each of the years? Why? What other factors, if any, would you want to consider?

21. *Management analysis of standard cost variances; full absorption and variable costing* (contributed by J. M. Patell). As a member of the board of directors of Advanced Resource Technology, you have been attempting to track down rumors of cost overruns at the BioTech Division, which produces a single product (a liquid protein supplement). You have just returned from a brief inspection of the production facilities. While there, you picked up various pieces of possibly relevant information. The first is the published version of the division's income statement from the preceding year based on standard, full absorption costing, and the second is an internal reconstruction of the same statement based on variable costing. Both appear in Exhibit 16.13. On both statements the division has carried all production variances to the cost of goods sold. Actual production output for the year exceeded originally forecast production output by 10,000 units. Information about unit costs appears in Exhibit 16.14.

a. Compute price and efficiency variances for variable manufacturing costs and price (spending) and production volume variances for fixed manufacturing costs. (Biotech had no raw materials inventories.)

b. Another member of the board of directors is impressed that the external report shows higher net income than the internal report. This person wonders, "Why are costs lower on one report than the other?" How would you respond?

Exhibit 16.13

ADVANCED RESOURCE TECHNOLOGY

Income Statement—Published Version
Standard Absorption Costing

Sales.......................................		$2,240,000
Cost of Goods Sold:		
Beginning Inventory	$ 0	
+ Goods Produced	2,200,000	
− Ending Inventory	440,000	
= Standard Cost of Goods Sold.........................	$1,760,000	
+ Correction for *All* Variances	44,500	
= Cost of Goods Sold		1,804,500
Gross Margin.......................................		$ 435,500
Selling and Administrative Expenses		150,000
Net Income		$ 285,500

Income Statement—for Internal Use Only
Variable Costing

Sales.......................................		$2,240,000
Cost of Goods Sold:		
Beginning Inventory	$ 0	
+ Goods Produced	1,900,500	
− Ending Inventory	380,100	
= Cost of Goods Sold	$1,520,400	
− Correction for Overapplied Overhead[a]	21,000	
= Cost of Goods Sold		1,499,400
Selling Expenses		80,000
Contribution Margin		$ 660,600
Factory Overhead..		365,000
Selling and Administrative Expenses		70,000
Operating Profit.......................................		$ 225,600

[a]Overhead was applied based on actual hours times overhead application rate.

Exhibit 16.14

ADVANCED RESOURCE TECHNOLOGY
Cost per Unit of Protein Supplement

	Standard		Actual	
	Quantity	Cost	Quantity	Cost
Materials	2 Quarts	$2.00 per Quart	1.9 Quarts	$2.10 per Quart
Labor	2 Hours	$6.00 per Hour	2.1 Hours	$6.15 per Hour
Total Overhead	2 Hours	$3.00 per Hour		

22. *Measuring managerial performance: new challenges.*[3] Many commentators about North American business have argued that the relative deterioration in manufacturing productivity compared to Japanese manufacturers results from a preoccupation with short-term financial performance measures. Many firms base bonus plans for senior executives on annual accounting income. This method provides incentives to take actions that enhance short-term earnings performance that may not serve the best long-term interests of the firm. By contrast, Japanese firms give executives incentives to ensure the long-run viability of their companies. Consequently, they are more concerned than their North American counterparts with long-run productivity, quality control, and managing the company's physical assets.

Not everyone agrees with the observation that North American business executives are preoccupied with short-term financial performance to the extent that they would take actions contrary to the best long-run economic interests of the organization just to make themselves look good on the performance measures. But suppose that an executive faces a choice between an action with a positive short-run effect on performance measures and one with better long-run consequences for the organization but will not affect short-run performance measures positively. We cannot fault a rational executive for taking the action that looks good in the short run. As the saying goes, "you have to look good in the short run to be around in the long run."

How would you design a control system that encourages top-level managers to be concerned about long-run productivity, quality of products, and long-run economic well being of the company? Assume that these managers have previously focused on maximizing quarterly and annual earnings numbers to the detriment of these other factors.

23. *Accounting for partial obsolescence—conflict between historical costs and opportunity costs.* The chief financial executive of a firm made the following statement:

> Production methods change. Robotics, nuclear power, and computers are only eye-catching examples of technological changes that take place. Financial accounting has done little to adapt to and report specifically on the effects of technological obsolescence, which can render already-owned assets significantly less valuable than before.
>
> As new equipment and processes become available, capable management discovers and evaluates them. If the analysis calls for the disposition of old equipment and the firm disposes of the equipment, financial accounting, using generally accepted accounting principles (GAAP), writes off the old equipment and, in doing so, recognizes the complete obsolescence of the old equipment.
>
> In other cases, the net present value analysis may indicate the operating cost savings of the new equipment does not justify its substitution for the old, because the firm does not recognize the reduced

[3]This case was influenced by Robert S. Kaplan, "Measuring Manufacturing Performance: A New Challenge for Managerial Accounting Research," *The Accounting Review* vol. 58, pp. 686–705.

economic value of the old equipment. So long as the firm holds the older, partially obsolete equipment, financial accounting, using GAAP, does not report the loss in economic value from partial obsolescence.

A machine the firm now owns has a book value of $200,000. (That is, the original cost of the machine less the depreciation recognized to date, as shown in the accounting records, is $200,000.) The machine has no current resale value because the costs of removal equal the salvage proceeds. The machine will be able to produce 1,000 units of product during each of the next 5 years if $50,000 cash is spent each year for materials and labor. A supplier has developed a new machine that costs $200,000, that will also last for 5 years, and that will also produce 1,000 units of product each year. The yearly costs of materials and labor to use the modern machine, however, are only $20,000.

What should be done?

24. *Management decisions and external financial reports.* "Squeezing oranges in your idle time is not a by-product," said the Big Six partner in charge of the audit of Regent Company, disapprovingly.

"But," replied the president of Regent, "squeezing oranges is not our usual business, and your accounting plan will make us show a substantial decline in income. We all know that our decision this year to squeeze oranges was a good one that is paying off handsomely."

The argument concerned the accounting for income during the year 1983 by Regent Company.

Background   In 1976, the Alcoholic Control Board (ACB) of Georgia, a state not known for its production of grapes and wines, wanted to encourage the production of wine within the state. The executives formed the Regent Company in response to the encouragement of the ACB. The production process for wine involves aging the product. The company commenced production in 1977, but did not sell its first batch of wine until 1979. At the start of 1977, Regent made a cash investment of $4,400,000 in grape-pressing equipment and a facility to house that equipment. The ACB has promised to buy Regent Company's output for 10 years, starting with the first batch in 1979. Regent Company decided to account for its operations by including in the cost of the wine all depreciation on the grape-pressing equipment and on the facility to house it. The firm judged the economic life of the equipment to be 10 years, the life of the contract with the ACB. Regent Company reported general and administrative expenses of $100,000 per year in external financial reports for both 1977 and 1978.

Regent Company's contract with the ACB promised payments of $1.8 million per year. The direct costs of labor and materials for each year's batch of wine were $130,000 each year. Accounting charges depreciation on a straight-line basis over a 10-year life. The income taxes were 40 percent of pretax income.

The wine sales began in 1979 and operations proceeded as planned. The income statements for the years 1979 through 1982 appear in Exhibit 16.15.

Management of Regent Company was delighted with the offer from a manufacturer of frozen orange juice to put its idle capacity to work. It con-

Exhibit 16.15

REGENT COMPANY
Income Statements
(all dollar amounts in thousands)

	1979 to 1982 Each Year, Actual	For 1983	
		Management's View	Auditor's View
Revenues:			
From Wine Put into Production 2 Years Previously	$1,800	$1,800	$1,800
From Orange Juice Squeezed in Current Year	—	100[a]	100[a]
Total Revenues	$1,800	$1,900	$1,900
Cost of Goods Sold:			
Direct Costs of Wine Put into Production 2 Years Previously	$ 300	$ 300	$ 300
Depreciation of Buildings and Equipment:			
From 2 Years Prior, Carried in Inventory until Wine Is Sold	440	440	440
From Current Year, Allocated to Orange Juice	—	100	352
Selling, General, and Administrative Expenses	130	130[a]	130[a]
Income Taxes at 40 Percent	372	372	271
Total Expenses	$1,242	$1,342	$1,493
Net Income	$ 558	$ 558	$ 407

[a]Manufacturer of orange juice pays out-of-pocket costs directly. These items are not shown here.

tracted with the manufacturer to perform the services. At the end of 1983, it compiled the income statement shown in Exhibit 16.15 as "Management's View."

The Accounting Issue   Management of Regent Company suggested that the revenues from squeezing oranges are an incremental by-product of owning the wine-making machinery. The wine-making process was undertaken on its own merits and has paid off according to schedule. The revenues from squeezing oranges are a by-product of the main purpose of the business. Ordinarily, the accounting for by-products assigns to them costs equal to their net realizable value; that is, accounting assigns costs in exactly the amount that will make the sale of the by-products show neither gain nor loss. In this case, because the incremental revenue of squeezing oranges was $100,000, Regent Company assigned $100,000 of the overhead to this process, reducing from $440,000 to $340,000 the overhead assigned to the main product. This will make the main product appear more profitable when it is sold.

Management of Regent Company was aware that its income for 1983 would appear no different from that of the preceding year. Management knew that the benefits from squeezing oranges began to occur in 1983 but allowed the benefits to appear on the financial statements later.

The Big Six auditor who saw management's proposed income statement disapproved. The partner in charge of the audit spoke as quoted at the beginning of this case.

The auditor argued that squeezing oranges under these circumstances was not a by-product and that by-product accounting was inappropriate. Regent company must allocate the overhead costs between the two processes of grape pressing and orange squeezing according to some reasonable basis. The most reasonable basis, the auditor thought, was the time devoted to each of the processes. Because grape pressing used about 20 percent of the year, whereas orange squeezing used 80 percent of the year, the auditor assigned $352,000, or 80 percent, of the overhead costs to orange squeezing and $88,000, or 20 percent, to the wine production. Exhibit 16.15 shows the auditor's income statement.

This statement upset the president of Regent Company. Reported net income in 1983 is down almost 30 percent from 1982, yet things have improved. The president fears the reaction of the board of directors and the shareholders. The president wonders what has happened and what to do.

a.   Assuming that the Regent Company faces an after-tax cost of capital of 10 percent, did the company in fact make a good decision in 1976 to enter into an agreement with the state to produce wine? Explain.

b.   Did the company in fact make a good decision in 1982 to enter into the agreement with the manufacturer of frozen orange juice?

c.   Using management's view of the proper accounting practices, construct financial statements for the years 1984, 1985, and 1986, assuming that events occur as planned and in the same way as in 1983. Generalize these statements to later years.

d.   Are management's statements correct given its interpretation of by-product accounting? If not, construct an income statement for 1983 that is consistent with by-product accounting.

e.   Is management correct in its interpretation that the orange juice is a by-product?

f.   Using the auditor's view of the situation and assuming the same facts as in part **c,** construct income statements for the years 1984, 1985, and 1986. Generalize these statements to later years.

g.   Assuming that the auditor is right, what may management of Regent Company do to solve its problem?

25.   *Managing earnings.* Champion Clothiers, Inc., owns and operates 80 retailing establishments throughout New England, specializing in quality men's and women's clothing. James Champion established the company in 1908 and a member of the Champion family has run the business since that time. Currently, Ronald Champion, grandson of the founder, is president and chief executive officer. Members of the Champion family hold the company's shares.

The setting for this case is March 1987. The following conversation takes place between Ronald Champion and Tom Morrissey, who is the company's accountant.

Champion (President): Tom, you said on the telephone that you had completed the financial statements for 1986. How much did we earn last year?

Morrissey (Accountant): Net income was $800,000, with earnings per share at $1.60. With the $1.20 per share earned in 1984 and $1.38 earned in 1985, we have maintained our 15 percent growth rate in profits.

Champion: That sounds great! Tom, at our board meeting next week I am going to announce that the Champion family has decided to take the company public. We will be issuing shares equal to a 30 percent stake in the company early in 1988. I want our earnings for 1987 to reflect the growth rate we have been experiencing. By my calculations, we need an earnings per share for 1987 in the neighborhood of $1.84. Does this seem likely?

Morrissey: I'm afraid not. Our current projections indicate an earnings per share around $1.65 for this year. Major unexpected style changes earlier this year have left us with obsolete inventory that we will have write off. In addition, increased competition in several of our major markets is putting a squeeze on margins. Even the acquisition of Green Trucking Company in June of this year will not help earnings that much.

Champion: I know that you accountants have all kinds of games you can play to doctor up the numbers. We must be able to do something to increase earnings to the desired level. What about our use of LIFO for inventories?

Morrissey: We have been using LIFO in the past because it reduces income and saves taxes during a period of rising prices. We use the more recent, higher acquisition costs of inventory items in computing cost of goods sold in the income statement. We use the older, lower acquisition prices in the valuation of inventory on the balance sheet. We could switch to FIFO for 1987. That would add about $.21 to earnings per share. However, we would probably have to use FIFO for tax purposes as well, increasing our taxes for the year by about $50,000.

Champion: I don't like paying more taxes, but FIFO certainly more closely approximates the physical flow of our goods. If we decide to stay on LIFO, can we do anything to apply the LIFO method to prop up earnings?

Morrissey: We now classify our inventory very broadly into two LIFO groups or pools, one for men's clothing and one for women's clothing. We do this to minimize the possibility of dipping into an old LIFO layer. As you will recall, if we sell more than we purchase during a given period, we dip into an old LIFO layer. We valued these LIFO layers using acquisition costs of the year we added the layer. Some of these layers reflect costs of the mid-1950s. When we dip into one of these layers, we have to use these old, lower costs in figuring cost of goods sold and net income. By defining our LIFO pools broadly to include our dollar investment in men's clothing and our dollar investment in women's clothing, we minimize the probability of liquidating an old LIFO layer. We would define our LIFO pools more narrowly to increase the possibility of dipping. We could then let the inventory of particular items run down at the end of the year, dip into the LIFO layer to increase earnings, and then rebuild the inventory early in the next year. I suspect that we could add about $.02 a share to 1987 earnings if we went with narrower pools.

Champion: We own all of our store buildings and display counters. Can we do anything with depreciation expense?

Morrissey: We now depreciate these items using the shortest lives allowed and the fastest write-off tax law permits. However, unlike LIFO, we do not have to calculate depreciation for financial reporting the same as we do for tax reporting. We could depreciate these items over the expected economic life of each asset, which would exceed the tax life. That should add about $.04 to earnings per share for 1987. We could also use the straight-line depreciation method for financial reporting. Although our depreciable assets probably decrease in value faster than the straight-line method would indicate, we would be using the depreciation method that most of our competitors use for financial reporting. The use of straight-line depreciation would add another $.08.

Champion: Now you're talking. What else can we do?

Morrissey: We have some possibilities with respect to the acquisition of Green Trucking later this year. We currently plan to account for this acquisition using the purchase method. Under the purchase method, we will record the assets (and liabilities) of Green Trucking on our books at their market value on the date of acquisition. Since we expect to pay a price higher than the market value of Green Trucking's identifiable assets, we will also record some goodwill.

Champion: How does the acquisition affect earnings for 1987?

Morrissey: On the plus side, we will include the earnings of Green Trucking from the date of acquisition in June until the end of the year. However, we must base the cost of goods sold and depreciation expense on the higher current market values recorded on our books for Champion's assets rather than the lower recorded amounts on Green's books. In addition, we will have to amortize the goodwill. I expect to pick up $.08 per share in earnings for 1987 from the Green acquisition, but I already reflect this increase in my $1.65 estimate for the year.

Champion: Can we account for the acquisition any differently?

Morrissey: If we can qualify, we may be able to use the pooling-of-interests method. Under the pooling method, we would record Green's assets (and liabilities) on our books at the amounts at which they are stated on Green's books; that is, we would carry over the older, lower book values. Then, cost of goods sold and depreciation expense will decrease this year and in the future relative to the purchase method. In addition, we would recognize no goodwill, and therefore would not have to amortize it. Also, we would reflect in our earnings for 1987 the earnings of Green Trucking for all of 1987, not just that portion after June. Using the pooling method, earnings per share should increase $.10 more than the purchase method.

Champion: That sounds great, but what do we have to do to qualify?

Morrissey: To justify carrying over the old book values of Green Trucking, we have to show that we are merely combining the predecessor companies *and their shareholders*. The shareholders of Green Trucking must receive common stock of Champion Clothiers in exchange for their shares in Green Trucking. The shareholders in each of the predecessor companies then become shareholders in the new combined company (which will carry the Champion name). The Green shareholders would own 10 percent of Champion after the acquisition. Accountants view such a transaction as a change in form rather than in substance and permit the carryover of the old book values of Green.

Champion: My family may not be too happy about this arrangement, but let's move on.

Morrissey: Well, we can do one thing very easily with our pension plan to improve earnings. When we adopted the pension plan 2 years ago, we gave all employees credit for their service prior to adoption. This policy created an immediate obligation for past service. We amortize this obligation as a charge against earnings over a 10-year period, which is the average remaining work life of our employees. Generally accepted accounting principles permit us to use 15 years instead of 10 years as the amortization period; that switch would increase earnings per share by $.05 for 1987.

Champion: All of the things you have suggested deal with the selection or application of accounting methods. Can we do anything with the timing of expenditures to help 1987's earnings?

Morrissey: Well, we could postpone the painting and other maintenance of our stores scheduled for the last quarter of this year until the first quarter of next year. That would add $.02 to earnings per share. In addition, we anticipate running a major advertising campaign just after Christmas. Although we will pay for the advertising in 1987 and it will reduce earnings per share by $.03, we realize all of the benefits of the campaign in greater sales early in 1988. Finally, we could move back capital expenditures scheduled for the first quarter of 1988 to the fourth quarter of this year. We realize a special tax saving from an investment tax credit on these expenditures. By realizing these credits this year, we could increase earnings per share by $.04.

Champion: I hadn't realized how much flexibility we had in managing our earnings. Before we decide which choices to make, can you think of any other avenues open to us?

Morrissey: We could always sell off assets on which we have potential gain. For example, we hold some marketable securities that we purchased last year. Selling those securities would net us an additional $.02 in earnings per share. In addition, we own two parcels of land that we hope to use some day for new stores. These parcels could be sold at a gain of $.04 per share.

Champion: It strikes me that these alternatives could increase earnings per share for 1987 to the $2.00-plus range. This level appeals to me more than the $1.65 per share anticipated for the year. Will we have to do anything to earnings per share for prior years, if we adopt any of these alternatives?

Morrissey: I shall prepare a summary of the impact of each of the choices on earnings per share for 1987 as well as any retroactive adjustment required for prior years. This summary should be helpful as we decide our strategy.

Exhibit 16.16 presents Morrissey's summary.

How much do you think Champion Clothiers should report as earnings per share for 1987?

Exhibit 16.16

Alternative Strategies for Managing Earnings per Share

Alternative	Impact on Earnings per Share			
	1984	1985	1986	1987
Actual or Anticipated	$1.20	$1.38	$1.60	$1.65
Adoption of FIFO	+.15	+.17	+.20	+.21
Use of Narrower LIFO Pools	+.02	+.03	+.02	+.02
Use of Longer Depreciable Lives	—	—	—	+.04
Adoption of Straight-line Depreciation	+.05	+.06	+.07	+.08
Adoption of Pooling of Interests	+.02	+.04	+.06	+.10
Amortization of Pension Obligation over 15 Years	—	—	—	+.05
Deferral of Maintenance	—	—	—	+.02
Deferral of Advertising	—	—	—	+.03
Acceleration of Capital Expenditures................	—	—	—	+.04
Sale of Marketable Securities	—	—	—	+.02
Sale of Land	—	—	—	+.04

26. *Pricing decisions and accounting data.*[4] In July 1977, John Marmon, founder of Marmon Metals Corporation, said to his son Frank, "We have held the price line for 3 years, and since we have driven one major competitor almost out of the grinding and plating business, I think our strategy paid off in getting productivity and product quality up while maintaining constant prices to keep competition out."

"I agree, Dad," said Frank Marmon. "It's been a great year, but a couple of things bother me. With steel prices going up some 7 percent next month, it could be the time to change our pricing strategy."

"I'll listen," said John, "but we are doing pretty well. I'd hate to see us either price ourselves out of the market or hold a profit umbrella over the heads of our competitors—and potential competitors as well. We didn't get 40 percent of the market by raising prices."

History   In 1951, John Marmon founded Marmon Metals to clean steel castings used in large generators. In 1954, Marmon bought two multiple-spindle drill presses, which looked like a real bargain. Later, General Telephone approached Marmon Metals and suggested that it tool up to make mounting bars for direct dialing systems. At that time Marmon was the only company in the country with any surplus drilling equipment suitable for the job. Marmon accepted.

Gradually, John Marmon embarked on a planned program of buying grinding machines on the used machine market and from war surplus. He financed his purchases largely by selling time on his machines to other com-

---

[4]Adapted from Olson Metals case that Professor Neil C. Churchill and Research Associate Ashis Gupta prepared.

panies and partly from expanding grinding and plating operations. By 1977, in the Chicago plant alone, Marmon Metals employed seven people manufacturing tooling full time. In addition, it carried between $250,000 and $300,000 worth of consumable supplies.

In 1966, Marmon Metals realized it had neither the plant capacity nor the people in Chicago to handle all the business available. The company expanded to a small town in central Indiana, which put up $25,000 as a down payment on the new plant and helped Marmon Metals borrow the rest through local banks.

Early in 1970, Frank Marmon got out of the army and decided to expand Marmon Metals into an emerging California market. In May, Frank Marmon went to California to find a site. He found it, broke ground in July, and the company ground and plated the first piece of bar in November 1970. From May 1971, the California plant made a profit under Frank's management, and within 1 year built a second bay, which doubled the size of the plant.

With the start of the California venture, Marmon moved, in all its locations, toward selling the "total product" to its customers rather than merely providing a grinding and plating service. This move permitted Marmon Metals, in John Marmon's words, "to go along without price increases and to maintain profit margins by selling steel. Increasingly, we have been buying, grinding and plating, and selling as a package instead of processing other people's steel." By 1977, John estimated that Marmon Metals held between 40 and 50 percent of the piston rod market other than the substantial captive market of original equipment manufacturers such as Caterpillar. The size of the noncaptive market was approximately $20 million per year.

Financial and Accounting Procedures By 1977, Frank Marmon was concerned that Marmon Metals had not been "managing its margins" in the face of inflation. Exhibit 16.17 shows gross margin on a product-line basis. Frank calculated that whereas the margin on material sales had remained at 11 percent from 1976 to 1977, the margin on grinding had decreased from 23.5 percent to 13.4 percent on a historical cost basis. Thus, although profits had increased substantially, the increase had come from operating leverage—increased sales without proportional increases in administrative expenses. Frank recognized the basically conservative nature of Marmon's accounting system. The system ran on a cash basis until 1973, and followed the underlying philosophy of "an expenditure is an expense." The company had consistently "expensed" the costs of refurbishing and improving old grinding machines and producing new plating tools. This practice had increased expenses in recent years, when the firm refurbished many of the old grinding machines as the business expanded and the company purchased and expensed new plating fixtures. Where the firm had capitalized and then depreciated machinery, the depreciable life was 10 years. Frank estimated that the company had written off some $1,060,500 of machinery over the 7 years from 1971 to 1977. From a public reporting point of view, this machinery would have been capitalized. For public reporting, the firm would have depreciated all machinery over 15 years.

Exhibit 16.17

MARMON METALS
Income Statements

	Year Ended June 30, 1976		Year Ended June 30, 1977	
	Historical Cost (1)	Replacement Cost (2)	Historical Cost (3)	Replacement Cost (4)
Material Sales	$3,055,217	$3,055,217	$5,928,705	$5,928,705
Total Cost of Material	2,716,652	2,716,652	5,260,211	5,260,211
Margin on Material Sales. . . . . (1)	$ 338,565	$ 338,565	$ 668,494	$ 668,494
Grinding and Plating Sales . . .	$3,832,850	$3,832,850	$5,066,196	$5,066,196
Inventory Reduction	—	—	39,523	39,523
Total Factory Compensation.	1,187,032	1,187,032	2,047,039	2,047,039
Depreciation on Machinery	90,300	367,100[a]	118,300	373,400[a]
Depreciation on Buildings	100,500	225,000[b]	100,500	236,800[b]
Other Operating Expenses.	1,447,040	1,447,040	1,982,606	1,982,606
Margin on Grinding and Plating. . . . . (2)	$1,007,978	$ 606,678	$ 778,228	$ 386,828
Total Margin = (1) + (2)	$1,346,543	$ 945,243	$1,446,722	$1,055,322
Administrative Expenses	822,322	822,322	529,614	529,614
Income before Taxes	$ 524,221	$ 122,921	$ 917,108	$ 525,708
Provision for Taxes	251,626	59,002	440,212	252,340
Net Income from Operations.	$ 272,595	$ 63,919	$ 476,896	$ 273,368

[a]See Exhibit 16.20.
[b]See Exhibit 16.21.

Replacement Cost Analysis   Frank knew that since 1976, the Securities and Exchange Commission required large corporations to show how inflation affects on their assets and profits by calculating the replacement cost of inventories, assets, cost of goods sold, and depreciation. Frank thought that this approach might help his father and him in their pricing decisions, so he compiled additional data. Exhibits 16.17 and 16.18 present income statements and balance sheets using historical cost and replacement cost. Exhibits 16.19 through 16.21 present computations.

Inventories   To adjust inventories, Frank constructed an index of steel prices and applied them to the LIFO layers of inventory beginning in 1970, the year Marmon Metals went on LIFO (see Exhibit 16.19). Because LIFO costs closely approximated replacement costs on the income statement,[5] Frank made no adjustment to the cost of purchased materials sold.

---

[5]Inventory turned over more than four times a year.

Exhibit 16.18

MARMON METALS Balance Sheets				
	June 30, 1976		June 30, 1977	
	Historical Cost (1)	Replacement Cost (2)	Historical Cost (3)	Replacement Cost (4)
Assets				
Current Assets				
Cash	$ 88,472	$ 88,472	$ 183,634	$ · 183,634
Accounts Receivable	1,184,109	1,184,109	1,164,987	1,164,987
Inventory	887,910	1,051,800ª	1,527,071	1,764,500ª
Total Current Assets........	$2,160,491	$ 2,324,381	$2,875,692	$ 3,113,121
Plant Assets				
Land	$ 92,894	$ 92,894	$ 92,894	$ 92,894
Buildings (net)	457,241	4,195,000	391,041	4,286,000
Machinery (net)	648,630	5,506,000ᵇ	590,568	5,601,000ᵇ
Cars and Trucks (net).....	55,092	55,092	78,008	78,008
Total Plant Assets..........	$1,253,857	$ 9,848,986	$1,152,511	$10,057,902
Other Assets	80,714	80,714	138,893	138,893
Total Assets	$3,495,062	$12,254,081	$4,167,096	$13,309,916
Liabilities and Equities				
Current Liabilities				
Accounts Payable........	$ 445,500	$ 445,500	$ 167,642	$ 167,642
Wages and Payroll Taxes Payable	4,907	4,907	36,916	36,916
Corporate Income Taxes ..	63,766	18,850	372,992	239,474
Other....................	27,582	27,582	31,315	31,315
Total Current Liabilities	$ 541,755	$ 496,839	$ 608,865	$ 475,347
Long-Term Liabilities	1,238,315	1,238,315	1,384,776	1,384,776
Owners' Equity				
Capital Stock	56,048	56,048	56,048	56,046
Retained Earnings (historical cost)	1,658,944	1,658,944	2,117,407ᶜ	2,117,407
Additional Owners' Equity from Revaluation to Current Cost	—	8,803,935	—	9,276,340
Total Equities..............	$3,495,062	$12,254,081	$4,167,096	$13,309,916

ªSee Exhibit 16.19.

ᵇSee Exhibit 16.20.

ᶜDividends for the year ended June 30, 1977, were $18,433.

Machinery and Equipment For the machinery, Frank prepared a list of all items still in use, mostly used machines the firm had extensively reengineered and refurbished. John Marmon estimated the cost to Marmon Metals of acquiring these machines in their present condition as of June 30, 1977. The results of the calculations appear in Exhibit 16.20. Because the firm estimated the

Exhibit 16.19

MARMON METALS
Replacement Cost of Inventory
(convert LIFO cost to replacement cost)

Year	LIFO Layer	Index[a]	Replacement Cost on June 30, 1977 (rounded to nearest $100)
1970	$ 44,400	1.70	$ 75,500
1971	99,500	1.56	155,200
1972	174,700	1.42	248,100
1973	6,800	1.28	8,700
1974	—	1.21	—
1975	514,600	1.14	586,600
1976	47,900	1.07	51,300
1977	639,100	1.00	639,100
	$1,527,000		$1,764,500

Replacement Cost on June 30, 1976 = ($1,764,500 − $639,100) ÷ 1.07
= $1,051,800.

[a]Index developed from Marmon Metals purchasing records.

Exhibit 16.20

MARMON METALS
Schedule of Machinery

Purchase Year	Cost	Book Value Using 10-Year Life on June 30		Estimated Market Value (used) as of June 30, 1977
		1976	1977	
1960	$ 7,965	—	—	$ 261,000
1961	2,445	—	—	7,000
1962	45,086	—	—	182,000
1963	70,871	—	—	473,000
1964	41,835	—	—	371,000
1965	12,150	—	—	183,000
1966	9,113	—	—	173,000
1967	12,957	—	—	11,000
1968	73,919	$ 10,885	—	293,000
1969	37,109	7,398	$ 4,388	183,000
1970	54,749	14,548	9,072	309,000
1971	159,255	67,774	51,848	1,100,000
1972	106,789	53,155	42,475	419,000
1973	48,256	31,460	26,060	81,000
1974	398,678	278,906	236,412	1,009,000
1975	59,415	49,860	42,823	184,000
1976	164,002	134,644	131,778	267,000
		$648,630		$5,506,000
1977	52,140		45,711	95,000
Total			$590,567	$5,601,000

continued

Exhibit 16.20 *continued*

	1976	1977
Replacement Cost of Used Machinery at Year End	$5,506,000[a]	$5,601,000
Annual Depreciation over 15 Years	$ 367,100	$ 373,400
Less Depreciation over 10 Years Included in Historical Cost Income Statement	(90,300)	(118,300)
Additional Depreciation Expense for Income Statement	$ 276,800	$ 255,100

[a]Note probable misstatement in June 30, 1976, balance sheet of using used asset values from June 30, 1977; actual amount might be somewhat larger or smaller.

values as those at June 30, 1977, it showed no accumulated depreciation on the balance sheet, although it took 1/15 of the reported cost as depreciation on the 1976 and 1977 income statements.

Buildings   For the buildings in California and Indiana, John and Frank estimated the cost of constructing the same facilities today. For Chicago, John estimated the plant's present market value. See Exhibit 16.21.

Income Taxes   Calculating the income tax on replacement cost–based income puzzled Frank. On the one hand, the company owed $440,212 for 1977—the

Exhibit 16.21

MARMON METALS
Schedule of Buildings
(depreciable life of 25 years)

Site of Buildings	Approximate Construction Year of Buildings	Estimated Value as of June 30, 1977	Accumulated Depreciation	
			6/30/76	6/30/77
Chicago	1951	$ 800,000	$ —[a]	$ —[a]
Indiana	1967	1,670,000	601,000	668,000
California	1970	3,450,000	828,000	966,000
		$5,920,000	$1,429,000	$1,634,000

	1976	1977
Replacement Cost of Buildings..........	$5,624,000[b]	$5,920,000
Annual Depreciation over 25 Years	$ 225,000	$ 236,800
Less Depreciation Accounted for in Historical Cost Figures	(100,500)	(100,500)
Additional Depreciation Expense for Income Statement	$ 124,500	$ 136,300

[a]Zero because current market value is being used.
[b]1976 value estimated at 95 percent of 1977 values.

amount it would pay even if it kept the books on a replacement cost basis. On the other hand, a new company coming into the industry would find its actual costs equal to Marmon's replacement costs. Taxes at 48 percent would be paid on lower actual profits. Thus Frank chose this second alternative. Frank estimated the after-tax cost of capital for such a new entrant to be about 10 percent.

The Pricing Decision   Frank and John Marmon met in early August 1977 to discuss the results of the replacement cost analysis. They had confirmed the news that steel prices would increase 7 percent later in the month and that, if Marmon was to change its prices, this time would be appropriate.

John Marmon believed that if Marmon Metals raised prices 6 percent their competition would follow. Lincoln Steel, a $300 million steel company, was their major competitor—although in John's opinion, Lincoln did plating and grinding primarily to sell more steel. John also believed that Lincoln probably sold the service side of the product at or below cost, because they didn't have the equipment edge that Marmon had. The other competitor, Geiger Machinery, had dropped from a 40 percent to a 10 percent market share due to Marmon Metals pricing policies and was not, in John's eyes, a factor in the market any more. John was hesitant, however, to raise prices more than 6 percent. "We have a fascinating business here," he told Frank, "I don't know if we've priced our products properly or not, according to your new theories, but we're making profits, increasing our market share, and getting rid of some of our competition. And that I like. I also think that keeping prices low has expanded the market—people won't do it themselves if they can get it done cheaply enough."

"I know it, Dad," Frank replied, "but look at the numbers. Our after-tax return on assets was 7.8 percent in 1976 and 11.4 percent in 1977—if you believe our accounting figures. Now, a competitor who comes in with the same equipment and facilities as we have would have to invest $13 million, and the after-tax rate of return on the assets would be 2.1 percent. I still think the figures show that we can raise our prices by at least 9 percent, get our margins under control and our return on investment up to where it should be, and still not be too fat a target for others to shoot at."

"Well, I don't know, Frank," said John. "It sounds logical, and your figures show what I always said, 'we need a dollar of investment to produce a dollar of sales.' But you've put in a lot of assumptions. I would sure hate to raise prices and lose our competitive edge. We have kept our prices down and still made profits, and not only kept competition away but driven one of our competitors out. So what if we have a little inflation—our business is fundamentally sound. I'm inclined toward 6 percent and no more, but you can convince me otherwise."

a.   Reproduce Frank's analysis to derive the rates of return in the next-to-last paragraph.
b.   What income tax data should be used in the analysis? Why?
c.   What would you do about prices and why?

Exhibit 16.22

DISCTECH, INC.
Income Statements for Fiscal Years Ending September 30
(all dollar amounts in thousands, except per-share amounts)

	1978	1979	1980	1981	1982	1983	1984	1985
Revenue	$ 5,997	$30,003	$42,004	$59,646	$81,119	$107,076	$134,916	$164,598
Cost of Sales	6,531	21,288	29,403	41,752	55,161	72,812	91,743	111,927
Gross Margin	$ (534)	$ 8,715	$12,601	$17,894	$25,958	$ 34,264	$ 43,173	$ 52,671
R&D Expense	1,354	2,528	3,760	3,772	4,056	4,283	4,722	4,938
SG&A Expense	1,990	4,138	5,220	6,561	10,545	13,920	17,539	21,398
Operating Profit	$(3,878)	$ 2,049	$ 3,621	$ 7,561	$11,357	$ 16,061	$ 20,912	$ 26,335
Interest Income	131	(517)	84	119	162	214	(104)	(541)
Profit before Tax	$(3,747)	$ 1,532	$ 3,705	$ 7,680	$11,519	$ 16,275	$ 20,808	$ 25,794
Income Tax	0	767	1,704	3,533	5,299	7,487	9,572	11,866
Profit after Tax	$(3,747)	$ 765	$ 2,001	$ 4,147	$ 6,220	$ 8,788	$ 11,236	$ 13,928
Tax Loss Forward	0	685	1,400	0	0	0	0	0
Net Income	$(3,747)	$ 1,450	$ 3,401	$ 4,147	$ 6,220	$ 8,788	$ 11,236	$ 13,928
Earnings per Share	(1.06)	0.21	0.50	0.60	0.90	1.27	1.61	1.99

Source: Annual reports.

27. *Case study in fraudulent financial reporting: Disctech, Inc.*[6] On a gray December day in 1985 Mr. William Winslow, the newly appointed president of Disctech, Inc., sat at his desk contemplating the future of the company. Disctech had been the rising star of the computer disk memory industry. After going public in 1979, sales had grown at a compound rate of 33 percent and earnings had grown at 47 percent. Earnings per share (EPS) had risen every quarter, and the stock price had increased from $3.00 a share in 1979 to $67.50 a share in October 1985. (See Exhibits 16.22 and 16.23 for financial data.)

In just the last week the entire fortune of the company had changed for the worse as reports of fraudulent sales, inflated inventory values, and possible insider stock trading rocked the company. The board of directors had stepped in and asked the chief executive officer (CEO), chief financial officer (CFO), and executive vice president for sales and marketing to take leave without pay until the board completed their investigation of the matter, and they abruptly resigned. The board also selected a new president/CEO, Mr. Winslow, and retained an outside law firm to conduct an investigation of possible improprieties.

Bill Winslow viewed his job for the next few months as reorganizing the firm to get it through this difficult period. Reorganization required identifying

Exhibit 16.23

DISCTECH, INC.
Consolidated Balance Sheets at September 30
(all dollar amounts in thousands)

	1979	1980	1981	1982	1983	1984	1985
Assets							
Cash and Marketable Securities...........	$10,020	$ 3,654	$ 3,778	$ 3,273	$ 2,947	$ 2,808	$ 3,920
Accounts Receivable (net)...............	8,752	9,801	11,921	15,508	22,091	30,843	39,300
Inventories (net)........................	12,221	8,601	11,241	15,122	22,046	27,557	36,682
Prepaid Expenses	142	375	525	746	730	750	809
Total Current Assets	$31,135	$22,431	$27,465	$34,649	$47,814	$61,958	$ 80,711
Property, Plant, and Equipment (net)	2,110	6,901	9,661	13,719	18,657	24,628	31,031
Other..................................	929	120	169	239	284	321	364
Total Assets	$34,174	$29,452	$37,295	$48,607	$66,755	$86,907	$112,106
Liabilities							
Notes Payable	$ 4,050	$ 0	$ 0	$ 0	$ 0	$ 0	$ 0
Accounts Payable	5,664	3,600	5,041	9,158	12,734	16,849	23,190
Accrued Liabilities	1,179	1,500	2,100	2,982	4,056	5,354	6,746
Total Current Liabilities	$10,893	$ 5,100	$ 7,141	$12,140	$16,790	$22,203	$ 29,936
Bank Debt	0	0	0	0	0	2,000	0
Capital Leases	1,363	4,485	6,820	8,917	12,127	16,008	18,170
Bonds.................................	3,570	0	0	0	4,000	4,000	10,000
Owners' Equity							
Common Stock.........................	3,651	3,677	3,703	3,729	3,755	3,782	3,807
Other Capital..........................	20,978	21,020	21,062	21,104	21,146	21,188	21,231
Retained Earnings......................	(6,281)	(4,831)	(1,431)	2,717	8,937	17,726	28,962
Total Liabilities and Equities	$34,174	$29,452	$37,295	$48,607	$66,755	$86,907	$112,106

Source: Annual reports.

and relieving the stresses that generated this crisis and restoring employee, consumer, and investor confidence in the company.

The Hard Disk Industry   Disctech manufactured and sold disk drives. Disks are circular platters covered with magnetic material which record data in concentric circles. Disks access data more slowly than true random access devices like semiconductors or magnetic cores but faster than magnetic tape. Since the mid-1960s, disks had dominated the rapid access portion of the data storage market.

Although disk technology was well-established, the market was fast-growing and dynamic. Data capacity doubled every 3 years, and market experts expected this trend to continue. Market positions changed rapidly, and disk-drive manufacturers had to keep up with technological advances in order to survive.

The market for disk drives has two distinct submarkets; one for disks installed as part of large computer systems and one for those installed as part of minicomputer systems. IBM dominated the market for large computer disk drives, although other large mainframe manufacturers such as Control Data also made disk drives for their own use. Independent disk-drive manufacturers served this market by supplying IBM plug–compatible systems directly to end users. Independent disk-drive manufacturers concentrated on replacing IBM drives because the sales volume for non-IBM models was considered too small. Market experts expected the mainframe disk-drive market to grow about 5 percent per year.

The market for minicomputer disk drives, in which Disctech participated, was highly competitive. Some leading minicomputer manufacturers made some of their own disk drives, but most minicomputer manufacturers were part of the Original Equipment Manufacturer (OEM) market that a large number of small independent disk-drive manufacturers serviced. Market experts expected this market to grow 25 to 30 percent per year.

Disctech Mr. John Garvey founded Disctech in 1977, a former executive of a large manufacturer of minicomputers and computer disk memories. John had trained as an electrical engineer, but was better known for his organizational skills. The staid corporate environment had constrained John and he wanted to venture out on his own. He thought that with a good product, good marketing, and the right pitch to the capital markets a "killing could be made." Three other talented executives left the large company to join John in his new endeavor: Ed Steinborn (controller for the large manufacturer) became Disctech's chief financial officer, Peter Farrell (director of manufacturing) became the vice president for Design and Operations, and Mary Foley (manager of Minicomputer Marketing) became the executive vice president for Sales and Marketing. (See Exhibit 16.24 for an organization chart.)

The team of executives spent the period from 1977 to 1978 organizing the corporation and building prototypes of the advanced 14- and 8-inch disk drives that the company would market. Early in 1979 the corporation went public with 3.3 million shares offered at $3.00 a share. At a large party for shareholders and analysts, John announced that the corporation already had significant amounts of guaranteed sales for its new drives and that he expected Disctech products to become an industry standard. John also stated that the company expected to increase revenues and earnings per share (EPS) by a minimum of 30 percent per year.

Since the inception of the company, the planning cycle had been a very simple, top-down process. During the summer of each year, John met with Mary and Ed and set sales growth for the next year. They would then roll this sales figure to the bottom line using expected margins and estimates of fixed expenses to get a net income figure and a tentative EPS. Prior to the beginning of the fiscal year in October, they would pass down these goals for net income and EPS through the Finance and Marketing organizations where they became "law." The Design and Operations division planned production from the

Exhibit 16.24

DISCTECH, INC.
Organizational Chart

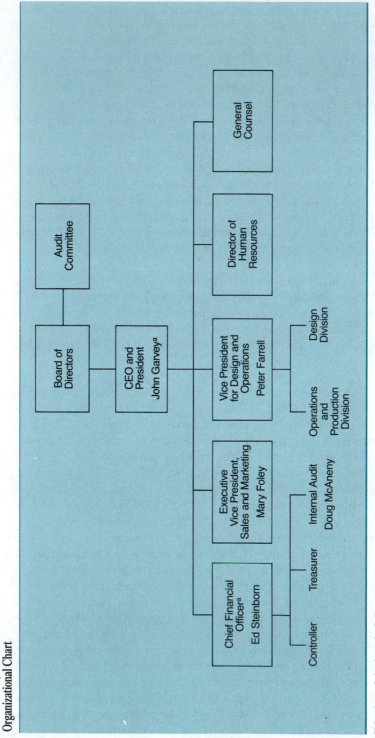

[a]Member of the board of directors.

expected revenue and gross margin figures, while John and Peter negotiated the R&D budget separately.

John, Ed, Mary, and the senior people of the marketing and sales staff conceived and implemented strategies to reach the annual plan at regularly scheduled "revenue meetings." These meetings primarily sought the means of identifying and generating potential revenues.

Disctech derived revenues from the sale and service of the company's equipment. The firm recorded revenues at the time of shipment of products or performance of services. Disctech initiated customer orders on receipt of an Equipment Order Form (EOF); either the customer completed the order or Disctech personnel prepared it pursuant to a Master Sales Agreement signed by the customer. The EOF included a description of the equipment, the price of the equipment, and the earliest equipment delivery date acceptable to the customer.

Board of Directors and Audit Committee   Since the company's inception Disctech's board of directors comprised seven members: two inside directors (the CEO and the CFO) and five outside directors. The board usually met four times a year to review the corporation's progress and plans for the future. The meetings were generally short and standardized, with John in control of the agenda. The company's performance and the dedication the top officers displayed impressed all of the outside directors.

The Audit Committee of the board comprised three outside directors. The members of the Audit Committee served three-year terms on a rotating basis, although the chair of the committee usually served for a longer period. The Audit Committee generally met twice a year, before and after the annual audit.

A number of changes came about in 1982 after the firm named Richard (Rich) O'Donnell, an outside director, as chairman of the Audit Committee. Rich firmly believed that an audit committee "could not be effective without being active." He increased the committee's schedule to at least four meetings a year and set up private meetings between the committee and the outside auditors. Rich tried to get the committee to look at the company's exposures and to question discretionary items in the financial statements. He suggested that the inside and outside auditors make some unannounced inspections and audits, and he wanted to strengthen the internal audit function through training and improved hiring practices.

Rich admitted in 1983 that he had some concerns about serving on a board of directors and, particularly, on an Audit Committee.

> A member of an Audit Committee is always a potential victim of management and the outside auditors since you depend on them so much. To a great extent you have to trust them. However, I try to set a tone of watchfulness by asking a lot of questions at all of our meetings; but I need to get other board members to do it or I will just look like an old crank.

I may be too cautious, however, because the top officers have talent, and John Garvey is dedicated. He wants to make good disk drives and sell a lot of them.

Internal and External Audit   The Internal Audit division, consisting of the head auditor, Doug McAneny, and two staff members, reported to Ed Steinborn (CFO). Internal Audit primarily ensured that the firm followed corporate accounting policies and that safeguards existed to protect the company's assets. Internal Audit was also alert to opportunities for cost-cutting and efficiency.

At the request of Rich O'Donnell, Doug McAneny had attended some meetings of the Audit Committee. Rich tried to establish a rapport with Doug and assured him that any misgivings that he had about anything, or anyone, in the company would be brought to the attention of the Audit Committee.

Disctech's external audit firm was Touche, Young, and Andersen (TYA), a Big Eight firm. Each year in July, the auditors met with top management and the Audit Committee to lay out the schedule of the annual audit and to review changes in the company since the previous year.

1979 to 1982   The years 1979 to 1982 were exciting at Disctech; sales revenues grew at a compound rate of 39 percent. Every quarter the company announced record earnings, and the stock market reacted as John predicted, with the trading price continually reaching new highs. John made regular announcements about the company, stating how earnings would to continue to grow at above-industry rates. The total market in 1979 for minicomputer disk memories at OEM prices was $2.1 billion, so Disctech had plenty of room to grow.

Disctech continued to make modest R&D expenditures, but by the middle of 1982 its once "head of the pack" products began to fall behind the latest technology. In response, John applied pressure to the Product Design division to come out with new products, even if they improved only slightly on existing products.

1983   The sales platform in 1983 proved to be a little erratic. John Garvey and Mary Foley (Executive Vice President, Sales and Marketing) agreed that quarterly sales (and earnings) must continue to grow to keep the glowing image of Disctech alive. To maintain this growth record, they sometimes found it necessary to work the shipping department round-the-clock during the last few days of each quarter in order to push as many orders as possible out the door to recognize the revenue for those transactions.

Mary also decided to take advantage of the way some OEMs ordered disk drives. Many OEMs would place a large order for 100 to 200 disks, get a discount, and then ask for delivery at a date 2 to 3 months in the future. This procedure assured them of a supply of the disks and a delivery date that supported their computer construction and shipment schedules. Many times the firm would schedule an order placed in one quarter for delivery in the next quarter. To recognize these sales in the present period, Mary directed that as many orders as possible receive early shipment to the OEM, with the understanding that the OEM's would not be liable for payment until the previously agreed-upon delivery dates.

The auditors from TYA questioned this early shipment program but Ed Steinborn convinced them that the sales met the requirements of "sales" as defined under generally accepted accounting principles: Title to the disks did transfer to the OEM upon shipment; under the contract the OEM was obliged to pay Disctech for the disks; and Disctech did contact the OEM prior to shipment to get their authorization. Some of these authorizations were, however, verbal: the salesperson responsible for an account would get the authorization and call it back to the home office.

This early shipment policy suited some OEMs, but many other OEMs did not have extra storage room and would not accept early delivery. The salespeople were told to "use their imaginations" and either find storage at the local Disctech distributor or another convenient location. The company needed the sales and the salespeople were told to "get as many authorizations as possible."

These two policies resulted in end of 1983 revenues that had grown from $81.1 million to $107.1 million, but $5.9 million of the 1983 sales were for disks originally scheduled for delivery in 1984. (Of the $5.9 million, the firm shipped $3.7 million without a valid authorization.)

1984   The only major change Disctech made in 1984 was in marketing policy. John Garvey had long thought that the minicomputer memory industry would slowly evolve to become more like the mainframe business, with fewer sales to computer manufacturers and more sales directly to end users. This evolution accelerated as the economy slowed, as many companies held onto the systems they already had installed. John believed that a truism of computers—"information to be stored quickly grows to fill all available memory"—would save Disctech. The firm hired more salespeople and directed the sales force to start approaching all current users of minicomputers compatible with Disctech disk memories to generate sales in this potentially large market.

After the firm announced the results of the second quarter (another record high), John called Mary, Ed, and Peter together for a private meeting. John indicated that he was proud of their results and that he knew they would continue to outperform the industry. He pointed out, however, that each quarter's goals were more difficult to reach, and that delays in the completion of new disk designs and prototype construction and the growing obsolescence of their inventory might level or even decrease the company's short-term earnings.

John went on to say that with his children nearing college age, he needed a lot of money set aside, not tied up in risky investments. As a result he had begun quietly to sell some of his Disctech stock, which had appreciated so much since 1979. He told them he was still optimistic about the company's future but they might be wise to examine their own financial needs. If they were to sell stock, he reminded them that they must inform the Securities and Exchange Commission of the sales, but he urged them to go about the sales discreetly in all other ways.

The marketing shift toward memory end users was a big success and significantly contributed to another record year, and early shipments continued to increase as the marketing department pressured OEMs and salespeople for early authorization. Total sales for the year were $134.9 million. Early-shipment revenues were $12.4 million, of which the firm shipped $9.8 million without a valid authorization.

Inventory Control and Allowances for Obsolescence   Disctech broke down its inventory into three categories: raw materials, work in progress (WIP), and finished goods inventory (FGI). In 1981, over 85 percent of total inventory consisted of FGI, and this percentage increased in later years. This unusual inventory mix resulted from a general shortage of raw materials in the industry, and Disctech and other manufacturers responded by sending raw materials directly to the production line. In addition, Disctech wanted as little work-in-process inventory as possible because partially assembled disk drives were highly susceptible to damage; even the slightest dirt or dent rendered the disk or its drive unit inoperable.

The firm tested and then stored assembled units until sale and shipment. The company's first-year production capacity was limited, so the firm shipped out units as soon as they were assembled. Efforts to improve efficiency and cleanliness raised production yields, and by 1980 production began to produce drives for inventory.

In 1982 the Design Division began to improve the disk drives to ensure that the product remained competitive. These improvements affected inventory levels. Disassembling the finished disk drive often caused complete disk failure, and therefore, very little rework on FGI drives resulted. Instead, the firm would modify new drives in production and then assemble them. Thus each change or alteration created another layer of FGI slightly different from the last.

Disctech's policy for creating allowances for obsolescence of inventory follows:

> Any equipment over 2 years old would have an allowance at 5 percent per quarter for 5 years so that at the end of 7 years the allowance would be a 100 percent.
> Any equipment declared unmarketable would have a 100 percent allowance taken against it.

These rules resulted in small allowances. Little technically obsolete equipment was actually old. Moreover, Disctech had no corporate standards or guidelines for ascertaining when disk drives became unmarketable. The corporate attitude that Disctech equipment was not subject to obsolescence intensified the problem.

At the end of 1982 a production controller forwarded a memo via Peter Farrell to the CFO and the executive vice president for Sales and Marketing that summarized a study he had done on the growing inventory problem. It listed three recommendations:

1. A study to produce a new allowance policy, since it appeared that the product life cycle was far shorter than 5 years.
2. An intensive effort by the Marketing department to sell the older inventory as soon as possible.

3. An increase in the allowance for obsolescence from $800,000 to $1.4 million.

The senior corporate officers discussed this memo. They all believed that the problem was not serious; they were unwilling to increase the allowance by any amount. Marketing, however, attempted to stimulate sales of the older disk drives with various specials, discounts, and promotions. The CFO also stated that he would ''watch the inventory problem.''

In 1983 the amount of obsolete inventory grew faster than the increase in allowances, and by the end of the fiscal year the production controller estimated the deficit to be almost $2.4 million. The outside auditors did not see the total extent of the problem but they did question the obsolescence allowance policy in their management letter.

> Top management should continually monitor Disctech's allowance policy and should implement procedures to develop historical experience to measure the propriety of the formula adopted. Management should also extend the policy to recognize sooner obsolescence of products no longer in production.

Disctech's management acknowledged the auditors' report but also informed the Audit Committee that they already had done an internal study in 1982 and were working actively to fix all problems with inventory control.

During 1984, Disctech management was aware that the exposure for FGI obsolescence was increasing, but did little other than continuing the marketing promotions and taking allowances as the formula calculated. Disctech's management maintained that allowing for or writing off inventory made it less likely that the firm would sell it. They stressed that they were obligated to the stockholders to find uses for the inventory rather than write it off.

By the time of the 1984 year-end audit, the inventory situation (in addition to the aggressive revenue recognition practices) agitated the auditors who sought written assurance from Disctech's management that a formal program existed to ''significantly affect the obsolescence exposure.'' The CFO, Ed Steinborn, wrote to the auditors:

> We respond to the problems in the inventory area by outlining the programs we have underway to reduce inventory levels. We will agree to study policy alternatives in the area of providing allowances for excess equipment; however, affordability considerations really preclude our ability to make any meaningful change in this area this year.

Management informed the board and the Audit Committee that a problem with inventory control still existed and that they were making ongoing efforts to rectify the situation. They also informed the board and Audit Committee that ''they might have to increase reserves for obsolescence next year as the product life cycle for disk memories shortens.'' They did not show the board and the committee the 1984 auditors' management letter containing the following sentence:

> This policy results in full valuation of excess inventory, overstates inventory, and may lead to serious future financial adjustments.

They did not tell the board that the exposure on inventory had grown to an estimated $3.9 million.

The Audit Committee asked questions about inventory valuation, but John and Ed gave quick answers and were confident that they would soon have the inventory situation under control. Nevertheless, the Audit Committee in a private session with the outside auditors admitted that some things, including inventory obsolescence, worried them. They also told the engagement partner that they intended to meet more often in 1985 and they wanted a senior representative from the outside auditors and Doug McAneny, the head of internal auditing, at their meetings.

1985   The year 1985 was difficult for Disctech, and the firm placed tremendous pressure on the sales force to achieve the planned sales goal. A combination of a soft market for the 14-inch disk drives and unexpected delays in production of the advanced 8-inch and the new 5¼-inch drives made sales difficult.

Some salespeople came up with some ingenious ideas to stimulate sales that were often designed to take advantage of the company's aggressive revenue policies. For example, one such scheme could occur when a customer filled out an EOF with a delivery date far in the future and submitted it to Disctech for processing. Within a week or two the responsible salesperson would contact the Marketing department and inform them that he or she had convinced the customer to accept an early delivery in the current quarter—with the understanding that payment would not be due until the date on the EOF. From the salesperson's view this made everyone happy: Disctech booked a sale, the salesperson got a commission, and the customer received a disk memory at a reasonable price with delayed payments and no finance charges.

At the same time sales were becoming more difficult, the firm had a growing problem with order cancellations. As Disctech's competitors came out with new products, many OEM's switched disk memory suppliers; new products also affected direct end-user sales because people wanted more memory and shorter access time for their dollars.

Near the end of the first quarter of 1985, the Marketing department met to discuss the order cancellation problem. Mary chose this opportunity to announce a new policy: the firm would ship any order cancelled within six weeks of expected delivery and record the revenue. Her staff told her that most customers would just refuse to accept delivery. She responded that on each of these deliveries the responsible salesperson would go along and ensure that "the sale stuck." All of these problems caused a lot of consternation in the sales force but they all knew better than to argue with Mary when she made up her mind.

A Midyear Meeting   At midyear John Garvey called a meeting of the top officers to review some pressing problems. The first problem was financing. As receivables grew, cash grew short. Consequently the firm would issue $10 million in bonds for public sale early in the fourth quarter; the firm would use $4 million of the cash raised to retire the bonds currently outstanding, and the rest of the proceeds would go to operations.

Second, inventory problems were getting worse. An internally generated estimate of the current obsolescence exposure was $6.8 million, and the firm expected this figure to grow to over $8 million by the end of the year. The outside auditors worried about the obsolescence exposure, but John explained he had placated them by informing them that the company was internally studying obsolescence policies and that he expected a writedown probably as early as the first quarter of 1986.

Third, the new disk memory designs still had development problems, but John expected them to be available before the end of the calendar year. Finally, the problem of returned equipment continued to grow. This problem would probably cause a significant reversal in revenues in future periods.

John admitted that all of these factors together would probably break the record string of growth and profits. John wanted the company to take all its "lumps" in the first quarter of 1986, and he wanted to take the inventory writedown at the same time as the new product announcement. He also stated that strong quarterly and annual results in 1985 would help the bond issue and would likely mitigate the impact of a loss in the first quarter of 1986. Everyone came away from the meeting clearly understanding that they had to make the 1985 budget—no matter what they had to do.

Despite heroic efforts by the sales force, fourth quarter predictions indicated that without further action Disctech would come up short of the 1985 budget. The Marketing department worked out a plan to make a large shipment to a warehouse Disctech rented under another name; the firm booked this shipment (for $4.2 million) as revenue in 1985. The firm planned to use the equipment to help fill early 1986 orders.

In the end, the firm achieved the 1985 goal of $162 million in sales; annual sales totaled $164.6 million. Early shipment revenues totaled $15.8 million, of which the firm shipped $10.6 million of equipment without authorization. This $15.8 million did not include the $4.2 million shipped to the new warehouse.

1986   The board of directors met in late October to review the results of 1985. John first went over the high points of the year and the records achieved. He next turned to the inventory problem and gave a quick summary of the events of the last few years. John then told them that to bring inventory back in line, a one-time writedown of $8.2 million would be required.

Unfortunately for John, this writedown did not surprise the outside directors. Prompted by knowledge of a large number of customer complaints, increasing levels of returned equipment, and the possible inventory obsolescence problem, they had asked the external and internal auditors to conduct some additional investigations in the last two quarters. The outside directors proceeded to ask John some difficult questions about the company's policies and practices and also questioned him on his personal finances and his recent stock dealings.

Receiving nothing but evasive answers, they told John they were retaining an outside law firm to conduct an investigation to be reported directly to the Audit Committee. The board also informed John that it would be best if he, Ed, and Mary went on leave until the investigation was complete.

With feelings of anger and humiliation, all three resigned immediately rather than accept the forced leave of absence. Disctech hired an interim president, Bill Winslow, and informed the SEC that the company was conducting an internal investigation that could affect their reported financial statements for the last three years.

a.   Describe the financial fraud that occurred at Disctech.

b.   Why did the fraud occur? What factors gave management an incentive to commit fraud?

c.   How could the fraud be prevented?

... CHAPTER 17 ...

Overview of Financial Statements

Chapter Outline

- Overview of Business Activities
- Overview of Principal Financial Statements
- The Balance Sheet—Measuring Financial Position
- The Income Statement—Measuring Operating Performance
- Accounting Methods for Measuring Performance
- Measurement Principles of Accrual Accounting
- Format and Classification within the Income Statement
- Statement of Cash Flows
- Other Items in Annual Reports

Accounting *measures* the results of business activities and *communicates* those measurements to interested users. Previous chapters explored the measurements made to assist managers in making decisions, planning operations, and evaluating performance. We also considered the appropriate formats of various managerial accounting reports (for example, income statement in contribution format). In designing accounting systems for internal, or managerial, uses, accountants have considerable flexibility in the manner in which they measure and report business activities.

A firm also reports the results of its business activities to individuals and entities outside the firm: owners, creditors, governmental agencies, labor unions, and others. This variety of users and the uses they make of financial accounting reports generate a need for some standardization in both measurement methods and reporting formats. This chapter and the next explore the content of the principal financial statements prepared for external users and the techniques used to analyze and interpret them. An understanding of the external reporting process helps the manager to see how the principal financial statements communicate the results of various financing, investing, and operating decisions to owners, creditors, and others. It also provides insights about how a firm "manages" the external reporting process.

This chapter examines the purpose and content of the principal financial statements included in annual reports to owners and other external users. Chapter 18 explores techniques for analyzing these financial statements.

Overview of Business Activities

Financial statements for external users attempt to present in a meaningful way the results of a firm's business activities. Understanding these financial statements requires an understanding of the business activities they attempt to portray.

Example 1 Bill Marsh and Janet Nelson, while working toward degrees in engineering, develop a computerized mechanism for monitoring automobile engine performance. They receive a patent on the device and want to set up their own firm to manufacture and sell it. They will call the firm Marnel Corporation.

The firm will need either to construct or to purchase a manufacturing facility. Once the facility is ready for production, the firm will need to purchase raw materials and hire factory workers. It will also need to pursue advertising and other marketing efforts.

Before the firm engages in purchasing, hiring, and other activities, Marnel Corporation will need funds, or capital. Two primary sources of capital are a firm's creditors and its owners. Creditors provide funds but require that the firm repay the funds, usually with interest, at some date in the future. Owners also provide funds. In return, they receive some evidence of their ownership in the firm. When a firm organizes as a corporation, shares of capital stock evidence the ownership. Unlike the demands creditors make in return for lending funds, owners generally do not require repayment at a particular future date. All firms must decide the amount of capital to obtain from creditors and the amount from owners. Chapter 18 explores some of the more important factors in such financing decisions.

Once a firm obtains capital, it must invest it. The firm will invest some of the capital in land, buildings, and equipment. Chapters 9 and 10 discussed techniques for making these capital budgeting, or capacity investment decisions. The firm will also invest in raw materials, employee training, and other goods and services required to carry out operating activities. A firm's business activities thus comprise three components:

Exhibit 17.1

Overview of Business Activities

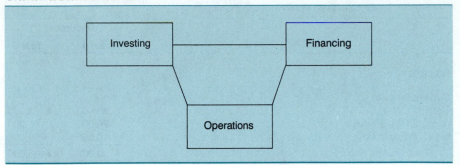

1. Financing activities: Obtaining capital.
2. Investing activities: Acquiring particular types of resources with the capital.
3. Operating activities: Using the resources to generate income.

Exhibit 17.1 depicts these three dimensions of business activity.

Overview of Principal Financial Statements

Periodic reports to external users include three principal financial statements:

1. Balance sheet.
2. Income statement.
3. Statement of cash flows.

The remainder of this chapter discusses the purpose and content of each of these three financial statements.

The Balance Sheet—Measuring Financial Position

The **balance sheet** presents a snapshot of the investments of a firm (assets) and financing on those investments (liabilities and shareholders' equity, or total equities) as of a specific time. Exhibit 17.2 presents a balance sheet for Marnel Corporation as of December 31, Year 1, and December 31, Year 2. The assets portion of the balance sheet reports as of a specific time the effects of all of a firm's past investment decisions. In this case, Marnel Corporation has invested in accounts receivable, merchandise inventory, land, buildings, and equipment. The equities portion of the balance sheet reports as of a specific time the effects of all of a firm's past financing decisions. Both short- and long-term creditors and owners have provided capital.

The balance sheet shows the following balance, or equality:

$$\text{Assets} = \text{Liabilities} + \text{Shareholders' Equity}.$$

Exhibit 17.2

MARNEL CORPORATION
Comparative Balance Sheets for December 31, Year 1 and Year 2

	December 31	
	Year 1	Year 2
Assets		
Current Assets		
Cash	$ 30,000	$ 3,000
Accounts Receivable	20,000	55,000
Merchandise Inventory	40,000	50,000
Total Current Assets.....................................	$ 90,000	$108,000
Noncurrent Assets		
Buildings and Equipment (cost)	$100,000	$225,000
Accumulated Depreciation	(30,000)	(40,000)
Total Noncurrent Assets	$ 70,000	$185,000
Total Assets...	$160,000	$293,000
Equities		
Current Liabilities		
Accounts Payable—Merchandise Suppliers	$ 30,000	$ 50,000
Accounts Payable—Other Suppliers.........................	10,000	12,000
Salaries Payable..	5,000	6,000
Total Current Liabilities	$ 45,000	$ 68,000
Noncurrent Liabilities		
Bonds Payable	0	100,000
Total Liabilities	$ 45,000	$168,000
Shareholders' Equity		
Capital Stock ($10 par value)	$100,000	$100,000
Retained Earnings	15,000	25,000
Total Shareholders' Equity	$115,000	$125,000
Total Equities..	$160,000	$293,000

This equation shows that a firm's assets balance with, or equal, the financing of those assets by creditors and owners. In the balance sheet, we view resources from two angles: a listing of the specific forms in which the firm holds them (for example, cash, inventory, equipment) and a listing of the persons or interests that provided the financing and therefore have a claim on them (for example, suppliers, employees, governments, shareholders).

We now address several questions regarding the balance sheet:

1. Which resources does a firm recognize as assets?

2. What valuations does it place on these assets?

3. How does it classify, or group, assets within the balance sheet?

4. Which claims against a firm's assets appear on the balance sheet as liabilities?

5. What valuations does a firm place on these liabilities?

6. How does a firm classify liabilities within the balance sheet?

7. What valuation does a firm place on shareholders' equity, and how does it disclose the shareholders' equity within the balance sheet?

To answer these questions, one must consider several accounting concepts underlying the balance sheet. This discussion not only provides a background for understanding the statement as currently prepared, but also permits the reader to assess alternative methods of measuring financial position.

Asset Recognition

Assets are resources with the potential for providing a firm with a future economic benefit. That benefit is the ability to generate future cash inflows or to reduce future cash outflows. Accounting recognizes the resources as assets when (1) the firm has acquired rights to their use in the future as a result of a past transaction or exchange and (2) the firm can measure or quantify the future benefits with a reasonable degree of precision.[1]

Example 1   Miller Corporation sold merchandise and received a note from the customer, who agreed to pay $2,000 within 4 months. This note receivable is an asset of Miller Corporation because it has a right to receive a definite amount of cash in the future as a result of the previous sale of merchandise.

Example 2   Miller Corporation acquired manufacturing equipment costing $40,000 and agreed to pay the seller over 3 years. After the final payment, legal title to the equipment will transfer to Miller Corporation. Even though Miller Corporation does not possess legal title, the equipment is Miller's asset because it has obtained the rights and responsibilities of ownership and can maintain those rights as long as it makes payments on schedule.

Example 3   Miller Corporation has developed a good reputation with its employees, customers, and citizens of the community. The firm expects this good reputation to provide benefits in future business activities. A good reputation, however, is generally *not* an accounting asset. Although Miller Corporation has made various expenditures in the past to develop the reputation, the future benefits are too difficult to quantify with a sufficient degree of precision to warrant recognition of an asset.

Example 4   Miller Corporation plans to acquire a fleet of new trucks next year to replace those wearing out. These new trucks are not assets now because Miller

---

[1]Financial Accounting Standards Board, *Statement of Financial Accounting Concepts No. 6,* ''Elements of Financial Statements,'' 1985, par. 25. See the Glossary for the Board's definition of an asset.

Corporation has made no exchange with a supplier, and, therefore, has not established a right to the future use of the trucks.

Most of the difficulties in deciding which items to recognize as assets relate to unexecuted or partially executed contracts. In Example 4, suppose that Miller Corporation entered into a contract with a local truck dealer to acquire the trucks next year at a cash price of $60,000. Miller Corporation had acquired rights to future benefits, but the contract remains unexecuted. Accounting does not generally recognize unexecuted contracts of this nature, sometimes called executory contracts. Miller Corporation will recognize an asset for the trucks when it receives them next year.

To take the illustration one step further, assume that Miller Corporation advances the truck dealer $15,000 of the purchase price upon signing the contract. Miller Corporation has acquired rights to future benefits and has exchanged cash. Current accounting practice treats the $15,000 as an advance on the purchase of equipment and reports it as an asset under a title such as Advances to Suppliers. The trucks are not assets at this time, however, because Miller Corporation has not received sufficient future rights to justify their inclusion in the balance sheet. Similar asset recognition questions arise when a firm leases buildings and equipment for its own use under long-term leases or manufactures custom-designed products for particular customers.

Asset Valuation Bases

Accounting must assign an amount to each asset in the balance sheet. Accountants might use several methods of computing this amount.

Acquisition or Historical Cost   The amount of cash payment (or cash equivalent value of other forms of payment) made in acquiring an asset is the acquisition, or historical, cost of the asset. The accountant can typically find this amount by referring to contracts, invoices, and canceled checks. Because a firm need not acquire a given asset, the firm must expect the future benefits from that asset to be at least as large as its acquisition cost. Historical cost, then, is a lower limit on the amount that a firm considered the future benefits of the asset to be worth at the time of acquisition.

Current Replacement Cost   Each asset might appear on the balance sheet at the current cost of replacing it. Current replacement cost is often referred to as an entry value, because it represents the amount currently required to acquire, or enter into, the rights to receive future benefits from the asset.

For assets purchased frequently, such as merchandise inventory, the accountant can often calculate current replacement cost by consulting suppliers' catalogs or price lists. The replacement cost of assets purchased less frequently, such as land, buildings, and equipment, is more difficult to ascertain. A major obstacle to using current replacement cost values is the absence of well-organized secondhand markets for many used assets. Ascertaining current replacement cost in these cases requires finding the cost of a similar new asset and then adjusting that amount downward somehow for the services of the asset already used. Difficulties can arise, however, in finding a similar asset. With technological improvements and other quality changes, equipment purchased currently will likely differ from equipment still being used but acquired 10 years previously. Thus the accountant may be unable to find similar equipment on the market to measure replacement cost. Alternatively, the accountant might substitute the current replacement cost of an asset capable of rendering equivalent services when the replacement cost of the specific asset is not readily available. This approach, however, requires subjectivity in identifying assets with equivalent service potential.

Current Net Realizable Value   The net amount of cash (selling price less selling costs) that the firm would receive currently if it sold each asset separately is the current net realizable value. This amount is an exit value, because it reflects the amount obtainable if the firm currently disposed of the asset, or exited ownership. In measuring net realizable value, one generally assumes that the firm sells the asset in an orderly fashion rather than through a forced sale at some distress price.

Measuring net realizable value entails difficulties similar to those in measuring current replacement cost. A well-organized secondhand market may not exist for used equipment, particularly equipment specially designed for a firm's needs. In this case, the current selling price of the asset (value in exchange) may be substantially less than the value of the future benefits to the firm from using the asset (value in use).

Present Value of Future Net Cash Flows   Another possible valuation basis is the present value of future net cash flows. An asset is a resource that provides a future benefit. This future benefit is the ability of an asset either to generate future net cash receipts or to reduce future cash expenditures. For example, accounts receivable from customers will lead directly to future cash receipts. The firm can sell merchandise inventory for cash or promises to pay cash. The firm can use equipment to manufacture products that it can sell for cash. A building that the firm owns reduces future cash outflows for rental payments. Because these cash flows represent the future services, or benefits, of assets, the accountant might base asset valuations on them.

Because cash can earn interest over time, today's value of a stream of future cash flows, called the present value, is worth less than the sum of the cash amounts to be received or saved over time. The accountant prepares the balance sheet as of a current date. If future cash flows are to measure an asset's value, then accountants might discount the future net cash flows to find their present value as of the date of the balance sheet.

Using discounted cash flows in the valuation of individual assets requires solving several problems. The uncertainty of the amounts of future cash flows is one. The amounts to be received can depend on whether competitors introduce new products, the rate of inflation, and other factors. A second problem is allocating the cash receipts from the sale of a single item of merchandise inventory to all of the assets involved in its production and distribution (for example, equipment, buildings, sales staff's automobiles). A third problem is selecting the appropriate rate to use in discounting the future cash flows to the present. Is the interest rate at which the firm could borrow the appropriate one? Or is the rate at which the firm could invest excess cash the one that should be used? Or is the appropriate rate the firm's cost of capital?

Selecting the Appropriate Valuation Basis

The valuation basis selected depends on the financial report being prepared.

Example 5   Miller Corporation prepares its income tax return for the current year. The Internal Revenue Code and Regulations specify that firms must use acquisition or adjusted acquisition cost valuation in most instances.

Example 6   A fire recently destroyed the manufacturing plant, equipment, and inventory of Miller Corporation. The firm's fire insurance policy provides coverage in an amount equal to the cost of replacing the assets that were destroyed. Current replacement cost at the time of the fire is appropriate for supporting the insurance claim.

Example 7   Miller Corporation plans to sell off one of its manufacturing divisions because it has been operating unprofitably. In deciding on the lowest price to accept for the division, the firm considers the net realizable value of each asset.

Example 8   Brown Corporation considers purchasing Miller Corporation. In deciding on the highest price it can pay, Brown Corporation would be interested in the present value of the future net cash flows to be realized from owning Miller Corporation.

Generally Accepted Accounting Asset Valuation Bases

The asset valuation basis appropriate for financial statements issued to shareholders and other investors is perhaps less obvious. The financial statements currently prepared by publicly held firms use one of two valuation bases—one for monetary assets and one for nonmonetary assets.

Monetary assets, such as cash and accounts receivable, generally appear on the balance sheet at their net present value—their current cash, or cash equivalent, value. Cash appears at the amount of cash on hand or in the bank. Accounts receivable from customers appear at the amount of cash the firm expects to collect in the future. If the time until a firm collects a receivable spans more than 1 year, the firm discounts the expected future cash to a present value. Most firms collect their accounts receivable within 1 to 3 months. The amount of future cash flows is approximately equal to the present value of these flows, and accounting ignores the discounting process.

Nonmonetary assets, such as merchandise inventory, land, buildings, and equipment, appear at acquisition cost, in some cases adjusted downward to reflect the services of the assets that the firm has consumed.

The acquisition cost of an asset includes more than its invoice price. Cost includes all expenditures made or obligations incurred in order to put the asset into usable condition. Transportation cost, costs of installation, handling charges, and any other necessary and reasonable costs incurred until the firm puts the asset into service are part of the total cost assigned to the asset. For example, the accountant might calculate the cost of an item of equipment as follows:

Invoice Price of Equipment	$12,000
Less: 2 Percent Discount for Prompt Cash Payment	(240)
Net Invoice Price	$11,760
Transportation Cost	326
Installation Costs	735
Total Cost of Equipment	$12,821

The acquisition cost of this equipment recorded in the accounting records is $12,821.

Instead of disbursing cash or incurring a liability, the firm might give other forms of consideration (for example, common stock, merchandise inventory, land) in acquiring an asset. In these cases, the accountant measures acquisition cost by the market value of the consideration given or the market value of the asset received, whichever market value the accountant can more reliably measure.

Foundations for Acquisition Cost   Accounting's use of acquisition cost valuations for nonmonetary assets rests on three important concepts or conventions. First, accounting assumes that a firm is a going concern. In other words, accounting assumes a firm will remain in operation long enough to carry out all of its current plans. The firm will realize any increases in the market value of assets in the normal course of business when the firm receives higher prices for its products. Second, acquisition cost valuations are more objective than the other valuations. Objectivity in accounting refers to the ability of several independent measurers to come to the same conclusion about the valuation of an asset. Obtaining consensus on the acquisition cost of an asset is relatively easy. Differences among measurers can arise in ascertaining an asset's current replacement cost, current net realizable value, or present value of future cash flows. Objectivity is necessary if independent accountants are to audit the financial statements. Third, acquisition cost generally provides more conservative valuations of assets (and measures of earnings) relative to the other valuation methods. Many accountants believe that financial statements will less likely mislead users if balance sheets report assets at lower rather than higher amounts. Thus, conservatism has evolved as a convention to justify acquisition cost valuations.

The general acceptance of these valuation bases does not justify them. The valuation basis most relevant to users—acquisition cost, current replacement cost, current net realizable value, or present value of future cash flows—is an empirical issue for which research has not yet provided convincing evidence.

Asset Classification

The classification of assets within the balance sheet varies widely in published annual reports. The following discussion gives the principal asset categories.

Current Assets   Cash and other assets a firm expects to realize in cash or sell or consume during the normal operating cycle of the business, usually 1 year, are

current assets. The operating cycle refers to the period of time that elapses for a given firm during which it converts cash into salable goods and services, sells goods and services to customers, and customers pay for their purchases with cash. Current assets include cash, marketable securities held for the short term, accounts and notes receivable, inventories of merchandise, raw materials, supplies, work in process, and finished goods and prepaid operating costs, such as prepaid insurance and prepaid rent. Prepaid costs, or prepayments, are current assets because if the firm had not paid in advance, it would use current assets within the next operating cycle to acquire those services.

Investments   A second section of the balance sheet, investments, includes long-term investments in securities of other firms. For example, a firm might purchase shares of common stock of a supplier to help assure continued availability of raw materials. Or it might acquire shares of common stock of a firm in another area of business activity to permit the acquiring firm to diversify its operations. When one corporation (the parent) owns more than 50 percent of the voting stock in another corporation (the subsidiary), it usually prepares a single set of consolidated financial statements. That is, the accounting merges, or consolidates, the specific assets, liabilities, revenues, and expenses of the subsidiary with those of the parent corporation. The investments section of the balance sheet therefore shows investments where the parent or investor has not consolidated the subsidiary's assets and liabilities.

Property, Plant, and Equipment   Property, plant, and equipment (sometimes called plant assets or fixed assets) designates the tangible, long-lived assets a firm uses in its operations over a period of years and which the firm generally does not acquire for resale. This category includes land, buildings, machinery, automobiles, furniture, fixtures, computers, and other equipment. The balance sheet shows these items at acquisition cost less accumulated depreciation, if any, since the firm acquired the asset. Frequently, only the net balance, or book value, appears on the balance sheet. Land appears at acquisition cost.

Intangible Assets   Such items as patents, trademarks, franchises, and goodwill are intangible assets. Accountants generally do not recognize expenditures a firm makes in developing intangibles as assets because they cannot objectively ascertain the existence of future benefits. Only specifically identifiable intangible assets acquired in market exchanges from other entities, such as a patent acquired from its holder, are accounting assets.

Liability Recognition

A **liability** arises when a firm receives benefits or services and in exchange promises to pay the provider of those goods or services a reasonably definite amount at a reasonably definite future time. The firm usually promises to pay cash but may promise goods or services.[2]

---

[2]Financial Accounting Standards Board, *Statement of Financial Accounting Concepts No. 6,* ''Elements of Financial Statements,'' 1985, par. 35. See the glossary for the Board's definition of a liability.

Example 9   Miller Corporation purchased merchandise inventory and agreed to pay the supplier $8,000 within 30 days. This obligation is a liability because Miller Corporation received the goods and must pay a definite amount at a reasonably definite future time.

Example 10   Miller Corporation borrowed $4 million by issuing long-term bonds. It must make annual interest payments of 10 percent on December 31 of each year, and must repay the $4 million principal in 20 years. This obligation is a liability because Miller Corporation received the cash and must repay the debt in a definite amount at a definite future time.

Example 11   Miller Corporation provides a 3-year warranty on its products. The obligation to maintain the products under warranty plans creates a liability. The selling price for its products implicitly includes a charge for future warranty services. As customers pay the selling price, Miller Corporation receives a benefit (that is, the cash collected). Past experience provides a basis for estimating the amount of the liability. Miller Corporation can estimate the proportion of customers who will seek services under the warranty agreement and the expected cost of providing warranty services. Thus, Miller Corporation can measure the amount of the obligation with a reasonable degree of accuracy and will show it as a liability.

Example 12   Miller Corporation signed an agreement with its employees' labor union, promising to increase wages by 6 percent and to provide for medical and life insurance. Although this agreement creates an obligation, it does *not* immediately create a liability. Employees have not yet provided services that require payments for wages and insurance. As employees work, a liability arises.

The most troublesome questions of liability recognition relate to obligations under unexecuted contracts. The labor union agreement in Example 12 is an unexecuted contract. Other examples include some leases, purchase order commitments, and employment contracts. Accounting does not currently recognize the obligations created by unexecuted contracts as liabilities, but the issue continues to be controversial.

Liability Valuation

Most liabilities are monetary, requiring payments of specific amounts of cash. Those due within 1 year or less appear at the amount of cash the firm expects to pay to discharge the obligation. If the payment dates extend more than 1 year into the future (for example, as in the case of the bonds in Example 10), the liability appears at the present value of the future cash outflows. The discount rate in the present value calculations throughout the life of the liability is the borrower's interest rate at the time it incurs the obligation.

A liability that requires delivering goods or rendering services, rather than paying cash, is nonmonetary. For example, magazine publishers typically collect cash for subscriptions, promising delivery of magazines over many months. The firm receives cash currently, whereas it discharges the obligation under the subscription by delivering magazines in the future. Theaters and football teams receive cash for season tickets and promise to admit the ticket holder to future events.

Landlords receive cash payment in advance and promise to let the tenant use the property. Such nonmonetary obligations are liabilities. The amount at which they appear, however, is the amount of cash received, rather than at the expected cost of publishing the magazines or of providing the theatrical or sporting entertainment. The title frequently used for nonmonetary liabilities is Advances from Customers.

Liability Classification

The balance sheet typically classifies liabilities in one of the following categories.

Current Liabilities   Obligations that a firm expects to pay during the normal operating cycle of the firm, usually 1 year, are **current liabilities.** In general, the firm uses current assets to pay current liabilities. This category includes liabilities to merchandise suppliers, employees, and governmental units. It also includes notes and bonds payable to the extent that they will require the use of current assets within the next year.

Long-Term Debt   Obligations having due dates, or maturities, more than 1 year after the balance sheet date appear as long-term debt. Long-term debt includes bonds, mortgages, and similar debts, as well as some obligations under long-term leases.

Other Long-Term Liabilities   Obligations not properly considered as current liabilities or long-term debt appear as other long-term liabilities, which include such items as deferred income taxes and some pension obligations, and advances from customers for goods to be delivered more than one year from the balance sheet date.

Shareholders' Equity Valuation and Disclosure

The **shareholders' equity** in a firm is a residual interest.[3] That is, the owners have a claim on all assets not required to meet the claims of creditors.[4] The valuation of the assets and liabilities included in the balance sheet therefore determines the valuation of total shareholders' equity.

The remaining question concerns the manner of disclosing this total shareholders' equity. Accounting distinguishes between contributed capital and earnings retained by a firm. The balance sheet for a corporation generally separates the amount shareholders contribute directly for an interest in the firm (that is, common stock) from earnings the firm subsequently realizes in excess of dividends declared (that is, retained earnings).

In addition, the balance sheet usually further separates the amount received from shareholders into the par or stated value of the shares and amounts contributed in excess of par value or stated value. A corporation's charter assigns the par or stated value of a share of stock to comply with corporation laws of each state. The

[3]Although shareholders' equity is equal to assets minus liabilities, accounting record keeping procedures provide an independent method for computing the amount.

[4]Financial Accounting Standards Board, *Statement of Financial Accounting Concepts No. 6*, "Elements of Financial Statements," 1985, par. 49.

amount will rarely equal the market price of the shares at the time the firm issues them. As a result, the distinction between par or stated value and amounts contributed in excess of par or stated value contains little information.

Example 13 Stephens Corporation legally incorporated on January 1, Year 1. It issued 15,000 shares of $10 par value common stock for $10 cash per share. During Year 1, Stephens Corporation generated net income of $30,000 and paid dividends of $10,000 to shareholders. The shareholders' equity section of the balance sheet of Stephens Corporation on December 31, Year 1, is as follows:

Common Stock (par value of $10 per share, 15,000 shares issued and outstanding)	$150,000
Retained Earnings	20,000
Total Shareholders' Equity	$170,000

Example 14 Instead of issuing $10 par value common stock as in Example 13, assume that Stephens Corporation issued 15,000 shares of $1 par value common stock for $10 cash per share. (The market price of a share of common stock depends on the economic value of the firm, not on the par value of the shares.) The shareholders' equity section of the balance sheet of Stephens Corporation on December 31, Year 1, is as follows:

Common Stock (par value of $1 per share, 15,000 shares issued and outstanding)	$ 15,000
Capital Contributed in Excess of Par Value	135,000
Retained Earnings	20,000
Total Shareholders' Equity	$170,000

Balance Sheet Account Titles

The following list shows balance sheet account titles commonly used. The descriptions should help you understand the nature of various assets, liabilities, and shareholders' equities as well as to select appropriate account names when solving problems. One can use alternative account titles. The list does not show all the account titles used in this book or in the financial statements of publicly held firms.

Assets

Cash Coins and currency and items such as bank checks and money orders. (The latter items are merely claims against individuals or institutions but by custom are called cash.) Bank deposits against which the firm can draw checks, and time deposits, usually savings accounts and certificates of deposit.

Marketable Securities   Government bonds, or stocks and bonds of corporations, which the firm plans to hold for a relatively short time. The word *marketable* implies that their owner can buy and sell them readily through a security exchange such as the New York Stock Exchange.

Accounts Receivable   Amounts due from customers of a business from the sale of goods or services. The collection of cash occurs some time after the sale. These accounts are also known as charge accounts or open accounts. The general term Accounts Receivable used in financial statements describes the figure representing the total amount the firm expects to receive from all customers. The firm, of course, keeps a separate record for each customer.

Notes Receivable   Amounts due from customers or from others to whom the firm has made loans or extended credit, when the borrower has put the claim into writing in the form of a formal note (which distinguishes it from an open account receivable).

Interest Receivable   Interest on assets such as promissory notes or bonds that has accrued (or come into existence) through the passing of time but that the firm has not yet collected as of the date of the balance sheet.

Merchandise Inventory   Goods on hand purchased for resale, such as canned goods on the shelves of a grocery store or suits on the racks of a clothing store.

Raw Materials Inventory   Unused materials for manufacturing products.

Supplies Inventory   Lubricants, abrasives, and other incidental materials used in manufacturing operations. Stationery, computer disks, pens, and other office supplies. Bags, tape, boxes, and other store supplies. Gasoline, oil, spare parts, and other delivery supplies.

Work-in-Process Inventory   Partially completed manufactured products.

Finished Goods Inventory   Completed but unsold manufactured products.

Prepaid Insurance   Insurance premiums paid for future coverage.

Prepaid Rent   Rent paid in advance for future use of land, buildings, or equipment.

Advances to Suppliers   The general name used to indicate payments made in advance for goods or services the firm will receive at a later date. If the firm does not pay when it places an order, it does not recognize an asset.

Investment in Securities   Bonds or shares of common or preferred stock in other companies where the firm plans to hold the securities for a relatively long time.

Land   Land occupied by buildings or used in operations.

Buildings   Factory buildings, store buildings, garages, warehouses, and so forth.

Equipment   Lathes, ovens, tools, boilers, computers, bins, cranes, conveyors, automobiles, and so forth.

Furniture and Fixtures   Desks, tables, chairs, counters, showcases, scales, and other store and office equipment.

Accumulated Depreciation   The cumulative amount of the cost of long-term assets (such as buildings and equipment) allocated to the costs of production or to current and prior periods in measuring net income. The amount in this account reduces the acquisition cost of the long-term asset to which it relates when measuring the net book value of the asset shown in the balance sheet.

Leasehold   The right to use property owned by someone else.

Organization Costs   Amounts paid for legal and incorporation fees, for printing the certificates for shares of stock, and for accounting and other costs incurred in organizing a business so that it can function.

Patents   Rights granted for up to 17 years by the federal government to exclude others from manufacturing, using, or selling certain processes or devices. Generally accepted accounting principles require the firm to expense research and development costs in the year incurred rather than recognize them as assets with future benefits.[5] As a result, a firm that develops a patent will not normally show it as an asset. On the other hand, a firm that purchases a patent from another will recognize the patent as an asset.

Goodwill   An amount paid by one firm in acquiring another business enterprise that exceeds the sum of the then-current values assignable to individual identifiable assets and liabilities. A good reputation and other desirable attributes are generally not accounting assets for the firm that creates or develops them. However, when one firm acquires another firm, these desirable attributes become recognized as assets insofar as they cause the value of the acquired firm to exceed the values assigned to the individual identifiable assets and liabilities.

Liabilities

Accounts Payable   Amounts owed for goods or services acquired under an informal credit agreement. The firm must pay these accounts usually within 1 or 2 months. The same items appear as Accounts Receivable on the creditor's books.

---

[5]Financial Accounting Standards Board, *Statement of Financial Accounting Standards No. 2,* "Accounting for Research and Development Costs," 1974.

Notes Payable   The face amount of promissory notes given in connection with loans from a bank or the purchase of goods or services. The same item appear as Notes Receivable on the creditor's (lender's) books.

Interest Payable   Interest on obligations that has accrued or accumulated with the passage of time but that the firm has not yet paid as of the date of the balance sheet. The liability for interest customarily appears separately from the face amount of the obligation.

Income Taxes Payable   The estimated liability for income taxes, accumulated and unpaid, based on the taxable income of the business from the beginning of the taxable year to the date of the balance sheet.

Advances from Customers   The general name used to indicate payments received in advance for goods or services to be furnished to customers in the future; a nonmonetary liability. If the firm does not receive cash when a customer places an order, it does not record a liability.

Advances from Tenants or Rent Received in Advance   Another example of a nonmonetary liability. For example, the business owns a building that it rents to a tenant. The tenant has prepaid the rental charge for several months in advance. The amount applicable to future months does not become a component of income until the landlord renders a service with the passage of time. Meanwhile the advance payment results in a liability payable in services (that is, in the use of the building). On the records of the tenant, the same amount appears as an asset, Prepaid Rent or Advances to Landlord.

Mortgage Payable   Long-term promissory notes that the borrower has protected by pledging specific pieces of property as security for payment. If the borrower does not pay the loan or interest according to the agreement, the lender can require the sale of the property to generate funds to repay the loan.

Bonds Payable   Amounts borrowed by a business for a relatively long period of time under a formal written contract or indenture. The borrower usually obtains the loan from a number of lenders, all of whom receive written evidence of the share of the loan.

Convertible Bonds Payable   Bonds that the holder can convert into, or trade in, for shares of common stock. The bond indenture specifies the number of shares the lenders will receive when they convert their bonds into stock, the date when conversion can occur, and other details.

Capitalized Lease Obligations   The present value of future commitments for cash payments to be made in return for the right to use property owned by someone else.

Deferred Income Taxes   Certain income tax obligations that are delayed beyond the current accounting period.

Shareholders' Equity

Common Stock   Amounts received for the par or stated value of a firm's principal class of voting stock.

Preferred Stock   Amounts received for the par value of a class of a firm's stock that has some preference relative to the common stock. This preference is usually with respect to dividends and to assets in the event of corporate liquidation. Sometimes the holder of preferred stock may convert it into common stock.

Capital Contributed in Excess of Par or Stated Value   Amounts received from the issuance of common or preferred stock in excess of such shares' par value or stated value. Other titles for this account are Additional Paid-in Capital and Premium on Preferred (or Common) Stock.

Retained Earnings   The increase in net assets since a business began operations, which results from its generating earnings in excess of dividend declarations. When a firm declares dividends, the accounting decreases net assets and retained earnings by equal amounts.

Treasury Shares   The cost of shares of stock originally issued but subsequently reacquired by a corporation. Treasury shares do not receive dividends and accounting does not identify them as outstanding shares. The cost of treasury shares is almost always shown on the balance sheet as a deduction from the total of the other shareholders' equity accounts.

Summary of Balance Sheet Concepts

The balance sheet comprises three major classes of items—assets, liabilities, and shareholders' equity.

Resources become accounting assets when a firm has acquired rights to their future use as a result of a past transaction or exchange and when it can measure the value of the future benefits with reasonable precision. Monetary assets appear, in general, at their current cash, or cash equivalent, values. Nonmonetary assets appear at acquisition cost, in some cases adjusted downward for the cost of services that the firm has consumed. Liabilities represent obligations of a firm to make payments of a reasonably definite amount at a reasonably definite future time for benefits already received. Shareholders' equity, the difference between total assets and total liabilities, is typically split for corporations into contributed capital and retained earnings.

The Income Statement—Measuring Operating Performance

The total assets of a firm may change over time because of financing and investment activities. For example, a firm may issue common stock for cash or acquire a building and assume a mortgage for part or all of the purchase price. Holders of

Exhibit 17.3

MARNEL CORPORATION
Income Statement for Year 2

Sales Revenue	$125,000
Less Expenses:	
Cost of Goods Sold	$ 60,000
Salaries	19,667
Depreciation	10,000
Interest	2,000
Income Taxes	13,333
Total Expenses	$105,000
Net Income	$ 20,000

convertible bonds may exchange them for shares for common stock. These financing and investment activities affect the amount and structure of a firm's assets and equities.

The total assets of a firm may also change over time because of operating activities. Firms sell goods or services to customers for an amount that the firm hopes is larger than the cost of acquiring or producing the goods and services. Creditors and owners provide capital to a firm with the expectation that the firm will use the capital to generate a profit and provide an adequate return to the suppliers of the capital. The second principal financial statement, the **income statement,** provides information about the operating performance of a firm for some particular period of time.

Exhibit 17.3 presents an income statement for Marnel Corporation for Year 2. **Net income** equals revenues minus expenses. **Revenues** measure the net assets (assets less liabilities) that flow into a firm when it sells goods or renders services. **Expenses** measure the net assets used up in the process of generating revenues. As a measure of operating performance, revenues reflect the services rendered by a firm, and expenses indicate the efforts required.

Accounting Methods for Measuring Performance

Some operating activities both start and finish within a given accounting period. For example, a firm may purchase merchandise from a supplier, sell it to a customer on account, and collect the cash, all within a particular accounting period. These cases present few difficulties in measuring performance. The difference between the cash received from customers and the cash disbursed to acquire, sell, and deliver the merchandise represents earnings from this series of transactions.

Many operating activities, however, start in one accounting period and finish in another. A firm uses buildings and equipment acquired in one period over several years. Firms purchase merchandise in one accounting period and sell it during the next period, collecting cash from customers during a third period. The major problem in measuring performance for a specific accounting period is to measure the amount of revenues and expenses from operating activities that are in process at the beginning or end of the period. Two approaches to measuring operating performance are (1) the cash basis of accounting and (2) the accrual basis of accounting.

Cash Basis of Accounting

Under the **cash basis of accounting,** a firm recognizes revenues from selling goods and providing services in the period when it receives cash from customers. It reports expenses in the period when it makes cash expenditures for merchandise, salaries, insurance, taxes, and similar items. To illustrate the measurement of performance under the cash basis of accounting, consider the following example.

Donald and Joanne Ace open a hardware store on January 1, Year 1. The firm receives $20,000 in cash from the Aces and borrows $12,000 from a local bank. The firm must repay the loan on June 30, Year 1, with interest at the rate of 12 percent per year. The firm rents a store building on January 1, and pays 2 months' rent of $4,000 in advance. On January 1, it also pays the premium of $2,400 for property and liability insurance coverage for the year ending December 31, Year 1. During January it acquires merchandise costing $40,000, of which it purchases $26,000 for cash and $14,000 on account. Sales to customers during January total $50,000, of which $34,000 is for cash and $16,000 is on account. The acquisition cost of the merchandise sold during January is $32,000, and various employees receive $5,000 in salaries.

Exhibit 17.4 presents a performance report for Ace Hardware Store for the month of January Year 1, using the cash basis of accounting. Cash receipts from sales of merchandise of $34,000 represent the portion of the total sales of $50,000 made during January that the firm collects in cash. Whereas the firm acquires merchandise costing $40,000 during January, it disburses only $26,000 cash to suppliers, and therefore subtracts only this amount in measuring performance under the cash basis. The firm also subtracts the amounts of cash expenditures made during January for salaries, rent, and insurance in measuring performance, without regard to whether the services acquired are fully consumed by the end of the month. Cash expenditures for merchandise and services exceeded cash receipts from customers during January by $3,400.[6]

As a basis for measuring performance for a particular accounting period (for example, January, Year 1, for Ace Hardware Store), the cash basis of accounting has two weaknesses. First, it does not adequately match the cost of the efforts required in generating revenues with those revenues. The performance of one period mixes with the performance of preceding and succeeding periods. The store rental payment of $4,000 provides rental services for both January and February, but the cash basis subtracts the full amount in measuring performance during January. Likewise, the annual insurance premium provides coverage for the full year, whereas the cash basis of accounting subtracts none of this insurance cost in measuring performance during February through December.

---

[6]Note that, under the cash basis, the performance report does not include cash received from owners and through borrowing (financing transactions).

Exhibit 17.4

ACE HARDWARE STORE
Performance Measurement on a Cash Basis for the Month of January, Year 1

Cash Receipts from Sales of Merchandise......................		$34,000
Less Cash Expenditures for Merchandise and Services:		
Merchandise	$26,000	
Salaries	5,000	
Rental..	4,000	
Insurance...	2,400	
Total Cash Expenditures		37,400
Excess of Cash Expenditures over Cash Receipts		$ (3,400)

The longer the period over which a firm receives future benefits, the more serious is this criticism of the cash basis of accounting. Consider, for example, the investments of a capital-intensive firm in buildings and equipment to be used for 10 or more years. The length of time between the purchase of these assets and the collection of cash for goods produced and sold can span many years.

Second, the cash basis of accounting postpones unnecessarily the time when firms recognize revenue. In most cases, the sale (delivery) of goods or rendering of services is the important event in generating revenue. Collecting cash is relatively routine or at least highly predictable. In these cases, recognizing revenue at the time of cash collection may result in reporting the effects of operating activities one or more periods after the critical revenue-generating activity has occurred. For example, sales to customers during January by Ace Hardware Store totaled $50,000. Under the cash basis of accounting, the firm will not recognize $16,000 of this amount until it collects the cash, during February or even later. If the firm checks the creditworthiness of customers prior to making the sales on account, it will probably collect a predictable amount of cash and will have little reason to postpone recognition of the revenue.

Lawyers, accountants, and other professionals are the principal users of the cash basis of accounting. These professionals have relatively small investments in multiperiod assets such as buildings and equipment, and usually collect cash from clients soon after they render services. Most of these firms actually use a modified cash basis of accounting, under which they treat the costs of buildings, equipment, and similar items as assets when purchased. They then recognize a portion of the acquisition cost as an expense when they consume services of these assets. Except for the treatment of these long-lived assets, such firms recognize revenues at the time they receive cash and recognize expenses when they disburse cash.

Most individuals use the cash basis of accounting for the purpose of computing personal income and personal income taxes. Where inventories are an important factor in generating revenues, such as for a merchandising or manufacturing firm, the Internal Revenue Code prohibits a firm from using the cash basis of accounting in its income tax returns.

Exhibit 17.5

ACE HARDWARE STORE Income Statement for January, Year 1 (accrual basis of accounting)		

Sales Revenue		$50,000
Less Expenses:		
Cost of Goods Sold	$32,000	
Salaries Expense	5,000	
Rent Expense	2,000	
Insurance Expense	200	
Interest Expense	120	
Total Expenses		39,320
Net Income		$10,680

Accrual Basis of Accounting

The **accrual basis of accounting** typically recognizes revenue when a firm sells goods or renders services. Costs incurred lead to expenses in the period when the firm recognizes the revenues that the costs helped produce. Thus accrual accounting attempts to match expenses with associated revenues. Costs incurred that a firm cannot closely identify with specific revenue streams become expenses of the period in which the firm consumes the services of an asset and the future benefits of the asset disappear.

Exhibit 17.5 presents an income statement for Ace Hardware Store for January of Year 1 using the accrual basis of accounting. The firm recognizes the entire $50,000 of sales during January as revenue, even though it has not yet received cash in that amount. Because the firm will probably collect the outstanding accounts receivable, the sale of the goods, rather than the collection of cash from customers, triggers the recognition of revenue. The merchandise sold during January costs $32,000. Recognizing this amount as an expense (cost of goods sold) matches the cost of the merchandise sold with revenue from sales. Of the advance rental payment of $4,000, only $2,000 applies to the cost of services consumed during January. The remaining rental of $2,000 applies to the month of February. Likewise, only $200 of the $2,400 insurance premium represents coverage used up during January. The remaining $2,200 of the insurance premium provides coverage for February through December and will become an expense during those months. The interest expense of $120 represents 1 month's interest on the $12,000 bank loan at an annual rate of 12 percent (= $12,000 \times .12 \times 1/12$). Although the firm will not pay this interest until the loan comes due on June 30, Year 1, the firm benefited from having the funds available for its use during January; it should therefore recognize an appropriate portion of the total interest cost on the loan as an expense of January. The salaries, rental, insurance, and interest expenses, unlike the cost of merchandise sold, do not associate directly with revenues recognized during the period. These costs therefore become expenses of January to the extent that the firm consumed services during the month.

The accrual basis of accounting provides a better measure of operating performance for Ace Hardware Store for the month of January than does the cash basis for two reasons:

1. Revenues more accurately reflect the results of sales activity during January.
2. Expenses more closely match reported revenues.

Likewise, the accrual basis will provide a superior measure of performance for future periods, because activities of those periods will bear their share of the costs of rental, insurance, and other services the firm will consume. Thus the accrual basis focuses on inflows of net assets from operations (revenues) and the use of net assets in operations (expenses), regardless of whether those inflows and outflows currently produce or use cash.

Most business firms, particularly those involved in merchandising and manufacturing activities, use the accrual basis of accounting. The next section examines the measurement principles of accrual accounting.

Measurement Principles of Accrual Accounting

Under the accrual basis of accounting, one must consider *when* a firm recognizes revenues and expenses (timing questions) and *how much* it recognizes (measurement questions).

Timing of Revenue Recognition

Exhibit 17.6 depicts the operating process for the acquisition and sale of merchandise. A firm could recognize revenue, a measure of the increase in net assets from selling goods or providing services, at the time of purchase, sale, or cash collection, at some point between these events, or even continually. Answering the timing question requires a set of criteria for revenue recognition.

Criteria for Revenue Recognition   The accrual basis of accounting recognizes revenue when both of the following have occurred:

1. A firm has performed all, or a substantial portion, of the services to be provided.
2. It has received either cash, a receivable, or some other asset susceptible to reasonably precise measurement.

Exhibit 17.6

Operating Process for a Firm's Acquisition and Sale of Merchandise

Purchase of Merchandise	Sale of Merchandise	Collection of Cash

The majority of firms involved in selling goods and services recognizes revenue at the time of sale (delivery). The firm has transferred the goods to a buyer or has performed the services. Future services, such as for warranties, are either insignificant, or, if significant, the firm can estimate them with reasonable precision. An exchange between an independent buyer and seller provides an objective measure of the amount of revenue. If the firm sells on account, past experience and an assessment of credit standings of customers provide a basis for predicting the amount of cash that the firm will collect. Thus the time of sale usually meets the criteria for revenue recognition.

Measurement of Revenue

A firm measures the amount of revenue by the cash or cash-equivalent value of other assets received from customers. As a starting point, this amount is the agreed-upon price between buyer and seller at the time of sale. Some adjustments to this amount may be necessary, however, if a firm recognizes revenue in a period before the collection of cash.

Uncollectible Accounts   If a firm does not expect to collect some portion of the sales for a period, it must adjust the amount of revenue recognized for that period for estimated uncollectible accounts arising from those sales. This adjustment of revenue occurs in the period when the firm recognizes revenue, not in a later period when it identifies specific customers' accounts as uncollectible. If the firm postpones the adjustment, the earlier decision to extend credit to customers will affect income of subsequent periods. Not to recognize anticipated uncollectibles at the time of sale incorrectly measures the performance of the firm for both the period of sale and the period when the firm judges the account uncollectible.

Sales Discounts and Allowances   Customers may take advantage of discounts for prompt payment, and the seller may grant allowances for unsatisfactory merchandise. In these cases, the stated selling price will exceed the amount of cash a firm eventually receives. It must make appropriate reductions at the time of sale in measuring the amount of revenue it recognizes.

Delayed Payments   Firms sometimes permit customers to delay payment for purchases of goods or services, but make no provision for explicit interest payments. In such cases, accountants assume the selling price includes an implicit interest charge for the right to delay payment. The accrual basis of accounting should recognize this interest element as interest revenue during the periods between sale and collection. Recognizing all revenue entirely in the period of sale results in recognizing too soon the return for services rendered over time in lending money. When a firm delays cash collection beyond 1 year, generally accepted accounting principles require it to report revenue for the current period at an amount less than the selling price. The reduction accounts for interest between sale and cash collection. At the time of sale, the firm recognizes as revenue only the present value of the amount it expects to receive.

For most accounts receivable, the period between sale and collection spans only 2 to 3 months. The interest element is usually insignificant in these cases. As a result, accounting practice makes no reduction for interest on delayed payments for receivables to be collected within 1 year. This procedure is a practical expedient rather than following strictly the underlying accounting theory.

Timing of Expense Recognition   Assets provide future benefits to the firm. Expenses measure the assets consumed in generating revenue. Assets are unexpired costs, and expenses are expired costs or "gone assets." Our attention focuses on *when* the asset expiration takes place. The critical question is "When do asset benefits expire (leaving the balance sheet) and become expenses (entering the income statement as reductions in shareholders' equity)?" Thus:

Balance Sheet	**Income Statement**
Assets or Unexpired Costs $\longrightarrow$	Expenses or Expired Costs

---

Expense Recognition Criteria   Asset expirations become expenses as follows:

1. Asset expirations associated directly with particular types of revenues are expenses in the period when a firm recognizes revenues. This treatment, called the matching convention, matches cost expirations with revenues.

2. Asset expirations not clearly associated with revenues become expenses of the period when a firm consumes services in operations.

Product Costs   The expense for the cost of goods or merchandise sold most easily associates with revenue. At the time of sale, the asset physically changes hands. The firm recognizes revenue, and the cost of the merchandise becomes an expense.

A merchandising firm purchases inventory and later sells it without changing its physical form. The inventory appears as an asset stated at acquisition cost on the balance sheet. Later, when the firm sells the inventory, the same amount of acquisition cost appears as an expense (cost of goods sold) on the income statement.

A manufacturing firm, on the other hand, incurs various costs in changing the physical form of the goods it produces. Three types of costs are (1) direct material, (2) direct labor, and (3) manufacturing overhead (sometimes called indirect manufacturing costs). Direct material and direct labor costs associate with particular products manufactured. Manufacturing overhead includes a mixture of costs that provide a firm with a capacity to produce. Examples of manufacturing overhead costs are expenditures for supervisors' salaries, utilities, property taxes, and insurance on the factory, as well as depreciation on the manufacturing plant and equipment. The firm uses the services of each of these items during a period when it creates new assets—the inventory of goods it works on or holds for sale.

Benefits from direct material, direct labor, and manufacturing overhead transfer to, or become embodied in, the asset represented by units of inventory. Because the inventory items are assets until the firm sells to customers, the various direct material, direct labor, and manufacturing overhead costs incurred in producing the goods remain in the manufacturing inventory under the titles Work-in-Process Inventory and Finished Goods Inventory. Such costs, called **product costs,** are assets transformed from one form to another. Product costs are assets; they become expenses only when the firm sells the produced goods.

Selling Costs   In most cases, the costs incurred in selling or marketing a firm's products relate to the units sold during the period. For example, a firm incurs costs for salaries and commissions of the sales staff, sales literature used, and advertising in generating revenue. Because these selling costs associate with the revenues of the period, accounting reports them as expenses in the period when the firm uses their services. One might argue that some selling costs, such as advertising and other sales promotions, provide future-period benefits for a firm and the firm should continue to treat them as assets. However, distinguishing the portion of the cost relating to the current period (an expense) from the portion relating to future periods (an asset) can be difficult. Accountants, therefore, treat most selling and other marketing activity costs as expenses of the period when the firm uses the services. Even though such costs may enhance the future marketability of a firm's products, these selling costs are **period expenses** rather than assets.

Administrative Costs   The costs incurred in administering the activities of a firm do not closely associate with units produced or sold and, like selling costs, are period expenses. Examples include the president's salary, accounting and data processing costs, and the costs of conducting various supportive activities, such as legal services, employee training, and corporate planning.

Measurement of Expenses

Expenses represent assets consumed during the period. The amount of an expense is therefore the cost of the expired asset. Thus the basis for expense measurement is the same as for asset valuation. Because accounting reports assets primarily at acquisition cost on the balance sheet, it measures expenses by the acquisition cost of the assets sold or used during the period.

Format and Classification within the Income Statement

Income Statement Format

Firms use different reporting formats in their income statements. Most firms use a multiple-step format that presents several subtotals before reporting the amount of net income for the period. One common multiple-step format separates income from operating activities and revenues and expenses relating to investment and financing activities. The upper panel of Exhibit 17.7 presents an income statement for May Department Stores in this multiple-step format. Note that this format nets revenues from sales of merchandise and expenses related to generating these revenues to obtain operating income. Then it adds interest revenues from investments and subtracts interest expenses on debt to derive income before income taxes. This

Exhibit 17.7

MAY DEPARTMENT STORES
Income Statement for Year 6, Year 7, and Year 8
(amounts in millions)

	Year 6	Year 7	Year 8
Multiple-Step Format			
Sales..	$10,376	$10,581	$11,742
Cost of Goods Sold	(7,533)	(7,706)	(8,453)
Selling and Administrative Expenses	(2,048)	(2,019)	(2,279)
Operating Income.............................	$ 795	$ 856	$ 1,010
Interest Revenue	26	22	18
Interest Expense.............................	(153)	(135)	(247)
Income before Income Taxes	$ 668	$ 743	$ 781
Income Tax Expense	(287)	(299)	(278)
Net Income	$ 381	$ 444	$ 503
Earnings per Common Share			

	Year 6	Year 7	Year 8
Single-Step Format			
Sales..	$10,376	$10,581	$11,742
Interest Revenue	26	22	18
Total Revenues............................	$10,402	$10,603	$11,760
Cost of Goods Sold	$ 7,533	$ 7,706	$ 8,453
Selling and Administrative Expenses	2,048	2,019	2,279
Interest Expense.............................	153	135	247
Income Tax Expense	287	299	278
Total Expenses............................	$10,021	$10,159	$11,257
Net Income	$ 381	$ 444	$ 503
Earnings per Common Share			

reporting format attempts to capture in the income statement the distinction made earlier in this chapter between operating, investing, and financing activities. Other multiple-step income statement formats are common.

The lower panel of Exhibit 17.7 presents an income statement for May Department Stores in a single-step format. The format presents and totals all revenue items followed by all expense items. The computation of net income results from a "single arithmetic step"—a subtraction of total expenses from total revenues. This income statement format classifies neither revenues nor expenses as operating, investing, and financing activities.

Income Statement Classification

Income statements provide information used both for evaluating the past operating performance of a firm and for projecting the amount of future net income. The income statement can help the statement user achieve these purposes when the income statement distinguishes between (1) revenues and expenses that comprise the ongoing operating activities that the firm expects to recur, and (2) unusual, nonrecurring revenues and expenses. To provide such information, income statements contain some or all of the following sections or categories, depending on the nature of the firm's income for the period:

1. Income from continuing operations.
2. Income, gains, and losses from discontinued operations.
3. Extraordinary gains and losses.
4. Adjustments for changes in accounting principles.

Most income statements include only the first section (see for example, the income statements for May Department Stores in Exhibit 17.7). The other sections appear only if necessary.

Income from Continuing Operations Revenues, gains, expenses, and losses from the continuing areas of business activity of a firm appear in the first section of the income statement, titled **Income from Continuing Operations.** Firms without nonrecurring categories of income need not use the title Income from Continuing Operations in their income statements. In this case, absence of nonrecurring types of income implies that all reported revenues and expenses relate to continuing operations.

Income, Gains, and Losses from Discontinued Operations Sometimes a firm sells a major division or segment of its business during the year or expects to sell it within a short time after the end of the accounting period. If so, the income statement must disclose separately any income, gains, and losses related to that segment. The separate disclosure appears in a section titled **Income, Gains, and Losses from Discontinued Operations.**[7] This section follows the section presenting Income from Continuing Operations.

Extraordinary Gains and Losses A separate section of the income statement presents **extraordinary gains and losses.** For an item to be extraordinary, it must generally meet both of the following criteria:

1. It is unusual in nature.
2. It is infrequent in occurrence.[8]

An example of an item likely to be extraordinary for most firms would be a loss from an earthquake or confiscation of assets by a foreign government. Such items are likely to be rare. Since 1973, when the Accounting Principles Board issued *Opinion No. 30*, extraordinary items seldom appear in published annual reports (except for gains or losses on bond retirements).[9]

Adjustments for Changes in Accounting Principles A firm that changes its principles (or methods) of accounting during the period must in some cases disclose the effects of

---

[7]Accounting Principles Board, *Opinion No. 30*, "Reporting the Results of Operations," 1973.

[8]Accounting Principles Board, *Opinion No. 30*.

[9]Financial Accounting Standards Board, *Statement of Financial Accounting Standards No. 4*, "Reporting Gains and Losses from Extinguishment of Debt," 1975.

the change on current and previous years' net income.[10] This information appears in a separate section, titled Adjustments for Changes in Accounting Principles, after Extraordinary Gains and Losses.

Earnings per Share   Publicly held firms must show earnings-per-share data in the income statement.[11] Earnings per common share results from dividing net income minus preferred stock dividends by the average number of outstanding common shares during the accounting period. For example, assume that a firm had net income of $500,000 during the year. It declared and paid dividends on outstanding preferred stock of $100,000. The average number of shares of outstanding common stock during the year was 1 million shares. The firm would report earnings per common share of $.40 [= ($500,000 − $100,000)/1,000,000].

If a firm has securities outstanding that the holder can convert into common stock (for example, convertible bonds) or exchange for common stock (for example, stock options), it may need to present two sets of earnings-per-share amounts— primary earnings per share and fully diluted earnings per share.[12]

Summary of Income Statement Concepts

Over sufficiently long time periods, income equals cash in less cash out; that is, the *amount* of income from operating activities equals the difference between the cash received from customers and the amount of cash paid to suppliers, employees, and other providers of goods and services.[13] Cash receipts from customers do not, however, always occur in the same accounting period as the related cash expenditures to the providers of goods and services. The accrual basis of accounting provides a measure of operating performance in which outflows more closely match inflows than is the case under the cash basis.

The accrual basis determines the *timing* of income recognition. The accrual basis typically recognizes revenue at the time of sale (delivery). Costs that associate directly with particular revenues become expenses in the period when a firm recognizes the revenues. A firm treats the cost of acquiring or manufacturing inventory items in this manner. Costs that do not closely associate with particular revenue streams become expenses of the period when a firm consumes the goods or services in operations. Most selling and administrative costs receive this treatment.

Statement of Cash Flows

The third principal financial statement is the **statement of cash flows.** This statement reports the net **cash flows** relating to operating, investing, and financing activities for a period of time. Exhibit 17.8 presents a statement of cash flows for

---

[10]Accounting Principles Board, *Opinion No. 20*, "Accounting Changes," 1971.

[11]Accounting Principles Board, *Opinion No. 15*, "Earnings per Share," 1969.

[12]Accounting Principles Board, *Opinion No. 15*.

[13]The general rule that over sufficiently long time periods income equals cash in minus cash out excludes cash transactions with owners, such as capital contributions and dividends.

Exhibit 17.8

MARNEL CORPORATION Statement of Cash Flows for Year 2		
Operations:		
Net Income	$ 20,000	
Plus Expenses Not Using Cash:		
Depreciation	10,000	
Plus Increases in Current Liabilities:		
Accounts Payable—Merchandise Suppliers	20,000	
Accounts Payable—Other Suppliers.....................	2,000	
Salaries Payable......................................	1,000	
Less Increases in Current Assets Other Than Cash:		
Accounts Receivable	(35,000)	
Merchandise Inventory	(10,000)	
Cash Flow from Operations		$ 8,000
Investing:		
Acquisition of Equipment................................		(125,000)
Financing:		
Issue of Long-Term Bonds	$100,000	
Dividends...	(10,000)	
Cash Flow from Financing...............................		90,000
Net Change in Cash		$ (27,000)

Marnel Corporation for Year 1. Operations lead to an increase in cash of $8,000. (Recall that not all revenues result in an immediate increase in cash and that not all expenses result in an immediate decrease in cash.) Acquiring noncurrent assets used cash of $125,000. Financing activities led to a $90,000 net increase in cash. Of what significance is a statement explaining or analyzing the change in cash during a period of time? Consider the following example.

Example 2   Diversified Technologies Corporation began business 4 years ago. In its first 4 years of operations, net income was $100,000, $300,000, $800,000, and $1,500,000, respectively. The company retained all of its earnings for growth. Early in the fifth year, the company learned that despite the retention of all of its earnings, it was running out of cash. A careful study of the problem revealed the company was expanding accounts receivable, inventories, buildings, and equipment so fast that operations and external financing were not generating funds quickly enough to keep pace with the growth.

This example illustrates a common phenomenon for business firms. Cash may not be generated in sufficient amounts or at the proper times to finance all ongoing or growing operations. If a firm is to continue operating successfully, it must generate more funds than it spends. In some cases the firm can borrow from creditors to replenish its cash, but future operations must generate funds to repay these loans.

Classification of Items in the Statement of Cash Flows   Exhibit 17.8 classifies the inflows and outflows of cash in parallel with the three principal business activities described earlier in the chapter. Exhibit 17.9 depicts these various sources and uses graphically.

Exhibit 17.9

Inflows and Outflows of Cash

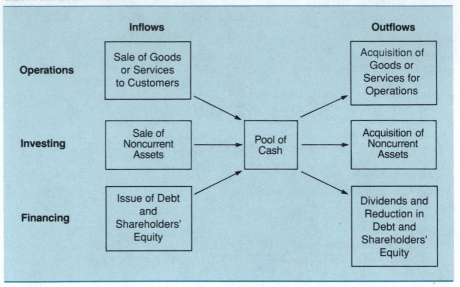

1. Operations: The excess of cash received from customers over the amount of cash paid to suppliers, employees, and others in carrying out a firm's operating activities is a primary source of cash for most firms.

2. Investing: Firms that expect either to maintain current operating levels or to grow must continually acquire buildings, equipment, and other noncurrent assets. Firms obtain some of the cash needed from selling existing land, buildings, and equipment. The cash proceeds, however, are seldom sufficient to replace the assets sold.

3. Financing: Firms obtain additional financing to support operating and investing activities by issuing bonds or common stock. The firm uses cash for dividends and retiring old financing.

Relation to Balance Sheet and Income Statement   The statement of cash flows explains the change in cash from the beginning to the end of the period. The statement also sets forth the major investing and financing activities of the period. Thus, the statement of cash flows helps explain changes in various items on the comparative balance sheet. The statement of cash flows also relates to the income statement in that it shows how operations affected cash for the period.

Other Items in Annual Reports

Supporting Schedules and Notes

The balance sheet, income statement, and statement of cash flows condense information for easy comprehension by the average reader. Some readers desire details omitted from these condensed versions. For other readers, the annual report typically includes schedules that provide more detail for some of the items reported in the three main statements. For example, the annual report presents separate schedules to explain the change in contributed capital and retained earnings.

Every set of published financial statements also contains explanatory notes that are an integral part of the statements. In preparing their financial statements, firms select accounting methods from a set of generally accepted methods. The notes indicate the actual accounting methods used by the firm and also disclose additional information that elaborates on items presented in the three principal statements. To understand fully a firm's balance sheet, income statement, and statement of cash flows requires a careful reading of the notes.

Auditor's Opinion

The annual report to the shareholders contains the opinion of the independent auditor, or certified public accountant, on the financial statements, supporting schedules, and notes.

The **auditor's opinion** generally follows a standard format, with some variations to meet specific circumstances. An auditor's opinion on the financial statements of Marnel Corporation might be as follows:

> We have audited the accompanying balance sheet of Marnel Company as of January 1 and December 31, Year 1, and the related statements of income, retained earnings, and cash flows for the year then ended. These financial statements are the responsibility of the Company's management. Our responsibility is to express an opinion on these financial statements based on our audits.
>
> We conducted our audits in accordance with generally accepted auditing standards. Those standards require that we plan and perform the audit to obtain reasonable assurance about whether the financial statements are free of material misstatement. An audit includes examining, on a test basis, evidence supporting the amounts and disclosures in the financial statements. An audit also includes assessing the accounting principles used and significant estimates made by management, as well as evaluating the overall financial statement presentation. We believe that our audits provide a reasonable basis for our opinion.
>
> In our opinion, the financial statements referred to above present fairly, in all material respects, the financial position of Marnel Company as of January 1 and December 31, Year 1, and the results of its operations and its cash flows for the years then ended in conformity with generally accepted accounting principles.

The opinion usually contains three paragraphs. The first paragraph indicates the financial presentations covered by the opinion and indicates that the responsibility for the financial statements rests with management. The second paragraph affirms that the auditor has followed auditing standards and practices generally accepted by the accounting profession unless it notes otherwise. Exceptions to the statement that the auditor's examination was conducted ''in accordance with generally accepted auditing standards'' are rare. The auditor may make occasional reference to having relied on financial statements examined by other auditors, particularly for subsidiaries or for data from prior periods.

The opinion expressed by the auditor in the third paragraph is the heart of the report. It may be an **unqualified** or **qualified opinion.** Most opinions are unqualified; that is, there are no exceptions or qualifications to the auditor's opinion that the statements "present fairly the financial position . . . and the results of operations and cash flows . . . in conformity with generally accepted accounting principles." Qualifications to the opinion result primarily from material uncertainties regarding realization or valuation of assets, outstanding litigation or tax liabilities, or accounting inconsistencies between periods caused by changes in the application of accounting principles.

A qualification so material that the auditor cannot express an opinion on the fairness of the financial statements as a whole must result in either a disclaimer of opinion or an adverse opinion. Adverse opinions and disclaimers of opinion rarely appear in published reports.

Management's Discussion and Analysis of Operations and Financial Position

The annual report to shareholders must include a discussion by management of the reasons for important changes in a firm's profitability, liquidity, and capital structure. Management must also comment on the impact of inflation on the firm.[14]

■ Summary ■

This chapter describes how accounting measures and discloses the results of a firm's activities in published accounting reports. The relation among the three principal financial statements may be depicted as follows:

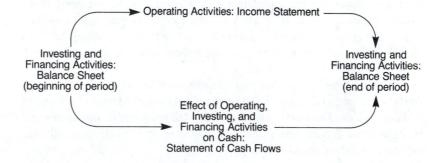

Perhaps the most effective overview of external financial reporting results from reading and studying the annual reports of several publicly held corporations.

---

[14]Securities and Exchange Commission, *Accounting Series Release No. 279,* 1980.

Problem for Self-Study

The accounting records of Digital Electronics Corporation reveal the following:

	December 31	
	Year 1	Year 2
Balance Sheet Items		
Accounts Payable to Suppliers	$250,000	$ 295,000
Accounts Receivable from Customers......................	240,000	320,000
Bonds Payable	100,000	120,000
Buildings (net of accumulated depreciation)	150,000	140,000
Cash..	30,000	50,000
Common Stock..	100,000	100,000
Equipment (net of accumulated depreciation)	140,000	220,000
Income Taxes Payable	40,000	70,000
Land	60,000	70,000
Merchandise Inventory	380,000	400,000
Retained Earnings	500,000	600,000
Salaries Payable	10,000	15,000
Income Statement Items for Year 2		
Cost of Merchandise Sold		$ 620,000
Depreciation Expense.....................................		40,000
Income Tax Expense		100,000
Insurance Expense		3,000
Interest Expense		10,000
Property Tax Expense		2,000
Rental Revenue (rental of part of building)		30,000
Salary Expense		135,000
Sales Revenue...		1,000,000
Dividend Information for Year 2		
Dividends Declared and Paid		$ 20,000

a. Prepare a comparative balance sheet for Digital Electronics Corporation as of December 31, Year 1 and Year 2. Classify the balance sheet items into the following categories: current assets, noncurrent assets, current liabilities, noncurrent liabilities, or shareholders' equity.

b. Prepare an income statement for Digital Electronics Corporation for Year 2. Separate income statement items into revenues and expenses.

c. Prepare a schedule explaining or accounting for the changes in retained earnings between the beginning and end of Year 2.

Suggested Solution

Exhibit 17.10 presents a comparative balance sheet, Exhibit 17.11 presents an income statement, and Exhibit 17.12 analyzes the change in retained earnings for Digital Electronics Corporation for Year 2.

Exhibit 17.10

DIGITAL ELECTRONICS CORPORATION Comparative Balance Sheet December 31, Year 1 and Year 2		
	December 31	
	Year 1	**Year 2**

Assets

Current Assets

Cash	$ 30,000	$ 50,000
Accounts Receivable from Customers	240,000	320,000
Merchandise Inventory	380,000	400,000
Total Current Assets..................................	$ 650,000	$ 770,000

Noncurrent Assets

Land	$ 60,000	$ 70,000
Equipment (net of accumulated depreciation)	140,000	220,000
Buildings (net of accumulated depreciation)	150,000	140,000
Total Noncurrent Assets	$ 350,000	$ 430,000
Total Assets	$1,000,000	$1,200,000

Liabilities and Shareholders' Equity

Current Liabilities

Accounts Payable to Suppliers............................	$ 250,000	$ 295,000
Salaries Payable..	10,000	15,000
Income Taxes Payable	40,000	70,000
Total Current Liabilities	$ 300,000	$ 380,000

Noncurrent Liabilities

Bonds Payable	100,000	120,000
Total Liabilities	$ 400,000	$ 500,000

Shareholders' Equity

Common Stock	$ 100,000	$ 100,000
Retained Earnings	500,000	600,000
Total Shareholders' Equity	$ 600,000	$ 700,000
Total Liabilities and Shareholders' Equity	$1,000,000	$1,200,000

Exhibit 17.11

DIGITAL ELECTRONICS CORPORATION Income Statement for Year 2	

Revenues

Sales Revenue	$1,000,000	
Rental Revenue	30,000	
Total Revenues.......................................		$1,030,000

Expenses

Cost of Merchandise Sold	$ 620,000
Salary Expense..	135,000
Property Tax Expense	2,000

continued

Exhibit 17.11 *continued*

Insurance Expense	3,000	
Depreciation Expense	40,000	
Interest Expense..	10,000	
Income Tax Expense	100,000	
Total Expenses		910,000
Net Income		$ 120,000

Exhibit 17.12

DIGITAL ELECTRONICS CORPORATION
Analysis of Change in Retained Earnings for Year 2

Retained Earnings, January 1, Year 2......................................	$500,000
Plus Net Income	120,000
Less Dividends Declared and Paid	(20,000)
Retained Earnings, December 31, Year 2	$600,000

Key Terms and Concepts

Balance sheet	Cash basis of accounting
Assets	Accrual basis of accounting
Monetary and nonmonetary assets	Product costs
Current assets	Period expenses
Liability	Income from continuing operations
Monetary and nonmonetary liabilities	Income, gains, and losses from
Current liability	discontinued operations
Shareholders' equity	Extraordinary gains and losses
Income statement	Statement of cash flows
Net income	Cash flows
Revenues	Auditor's opinion
Expenses	Unqualified or qualified opinion

Questions, Exercises, Problems, and Cases

Questions

1. Review the meaning of the concepts or terms given above in Key Terms and Concepts.

2. The *book* value of shareholders' equity equals assets minus liabilities. The *market* value of shareholders' equity equals market price per share times the number of shares outstanding. Dividing the market value by the book value yields an index of market to book. When the index exceeds 1.0, market value exceeds book value. When the index is less than 1.0, market value is less than book value.

The indexes of market to book value for several firms at the end of a recent year follow. Indicate the likely reasons for a difference between market value and book value in each case.

Company	Index
a. Eli Lilly (drug company)..	2.78
b. Boeing...	1.84
c. Texaco	1.66
d. Union Pacific Railroad	1.34
e. Citicorp (bank holding company)....................................	.76

3. A group of investors owns an office building, which it rents unfurnished to tenants. It purchased the building 5 years previously from a construction company. At that time the firm expected the building to have a useful life of 40 years. Indicate the procedures you might follow to ascertain the valuation amount for this building under each of the following valuation methods.
   a. Acquisition cost.
   b. Adjusted acquisition cost.
   c. Current replacement cost.
   d. Current net realizable value.
   e. Present value of future cash flows.

4. "Accrual accounting focuses on the use, rather than the financing, of assets." Explain.

5. If the total net income from a particular business activity equals the difference between cash inflows and cash outflows, why don't accountants use the cash basis of accounting rather than the accrual basis?

6. "The use of the accrual basis of accounting for measuring operating performance gives rise to the need for a statement of cash flows." Explain.

7. "Over sufficiently long time periods, cumulative net income equals cumulative cash provided by operations." Do you agree? Why or why not?

Exercises

8. *Preparation of personal balance sheet.* Prepare a balance sheet of your personal assets, liabilities, and owner's equity. How does the presentation of owner's equity on your balance sheet differ from that in Exhibit 17.2?

9. *Balance sheet relations.* Selected balance sheet amounts for The Limited (specialty retailer) for four recent years appear below (amounts in millions):

	Year 6	Year 7	Year 8	Year 9
Current Assets	$ 786	?a	$1,010	$1,024
Noncurrent Assets	?	?	966	?
Total Assets	?	$1,738	?	?
Current Liabilities	353	335	330	?c
Noncurrent Liabilities.....................	749	?	917	?

continued

continued from page 808

Contributed Capital	?	294	?	67
Retained Earnings	319	488	?b	?d
Total Liabilities and Shareholders' Equity	1,506	?	?	2,146

[a]Current assets − current liabilities = $600.

[b]Net income for Year 8 is $235 and dividends are $54.

[c]Current assets − current liabilities = $568.

[d]Net income for Year 9 is $245 and dividends are $35.

a. Compute the missing balance sheet amounts for each of the 4 years.

b. How did the structure of total assets (that is, the proportion of current versus noncurrent assets) change over the 4-year period? What might account for such a change?

c. What transactions might explain the changes in noncurrent liabilities and contributed capital between Year 6 and Year 7?

d. What transactions might explain the changes in noncurrent liabilities between Year 7 and Year 8?

e. What transactions might explain the changes in noncurrent liabilities and contributed capital between Year 8 and Year 9?

10. *Concept of an accounting asset.* Indicate whether or not accountants recognize each of the following items as assets under generally accepted accounting principles.

a. A patent on a new invention purchased from its creator.

b. A firm's chief scientist, who has twice won the Nobel prize.

c. The right to use a building during the coming year. The rent for the period has already been paid.

d. An automobile acquired with the issue of a note payable. Because the firm has not yet paid the note, legal title to the automobile has not yet passed to the firm.

e. A degree in engineering from a reputable university, awarded to the firm's chief executive.

f. A contract signed by a customer to purchase $1,000 worth of goods next year.

g. A favorable reputation.

11. *Asset recognition and valuation.* The transactions listed below relate to the Coca Cola Company. Indicate whether or not each transaction immediately gives rise to an asset of the Company under generally accepted accounting principles. If accounting recognizes an asset, state the account title and the amount.

a. The Company spends $10 million to develop a new soft drink. No commercially feasible product has yet evolved, but the Company hopes that such a product will evolve in the near future.

b. The Company signs a contract with United Can Corporation for the purchase of $4 million of soft drink cans. It makes a deposit of $400,000 upon signing the contract.

    c.   The Company spends $2 million for advertisements that appeared during the past month: $500,000 to advertise the Coca Cola name and $1,500,000 for specific brand advertisements, such as for Diet Coke.

    d.   The Company issues 50,000 shares of its common stock valued on the market at $2.5 million in the acquisition of all of the outstanding stock of Corning Glass Company, a supplier of soft drink bottles.

    e.   The Company spends $800,000 on educational assistance programs for its middle-level managers to obtain MBAs. Historically, 80 percent of the employees involved in the program receive their MBAs and remain with the Company for ten years or more thereafter.

    f.   The Company acquires land and a building by signing a mortgage payable for $150 million. Because the Company has not yet paid the mortgage, the title document for the land and building remains in the vault of the holder of the mortgage note.

12. *Concept of an accounting liability.* Indicate whether or not accountants recognize each of the following items as liabilities under generally accepted accounting principles.

    a.   An obligation to provide magazines next year to subscribers who have paid 1 year's subscription fees in advance (consider from the standpoint of the magazine publisher).

    b.   The reputation for poor quality control on products manufactured.

    c.   An obligation to provide warranty services for 3 years after customers purchase the firm's products.

    d.   The outstanding common stock of a corporation.

    e.   Unpaid property taxes for the preceding year.

    f.   The amount payable by a firm for a television advertisement that has appeared but for which payment is not due for 30 days.

    g.   A tenant's obligation to maintain a rented warehouse in good repair.

    h.   The incompetent son of the firm's president, who works for the family business.

13. *Liability recognition.* The transactions listed below relate to the New York Times Company. Indicate whether or not each transaction immediately gives rise to a liability of the Company under generally accepted accounting principles. If the Company recognizes a liability, state the account title and amount.

    a.   The Company receives $10 million for newspaper subscriptions covering the 1-year period beginning next month.

    b.   The Company receives an invoice for $4 million from its advertising agency for television advertisements that appeared last month.

    c.   The Company signs a 1-year lease for rental of new delivery vehicles. It pays $40,000 of the annual rental of $80,000 upon signing.

    d.   Attorneys have notified the Company that a New York city resident, seriously injured by one of the Company's delivery vehicles, has sued the Company for $10 million. Although the court is likely to find the Company guilty in the lawsuit, the Company carries sufficient insurance to cover any losses.

    e.   Refer to part **d** above. Assume now that the Company carries no insurance against such losses.

f. A 2-week strike by employees has closed down newspaper publishing operations. As a result, subscriptions totaling $2 million could not be delivered.

14. *Income statement relations*. Selected income statement information for Boise Cascade Corporation (forest products company) for 3 recent years appear below (amounts in millions):

	Year 4	Year 5	Year 6
Sales...	3,742	?	4,103
Cost of Goods Sold............................	3,117	3,067	?
Selling and Administrative			
Expenses.....................................	338	340	363
Interest Expense	114	105	100
Income Tax Expense	71	135	189
Net Income	?	183	289

a. Compute the missing amounts for each of the 3 years.

b. Prepare a common size income statement for each year where sales are equal to 100 percent and each expense and net income is expressed as a percentage of sales. What factors appear to explain the change in the ratio of net income to sales?

15. *Revenue recognition*. Indicate which of the following transactions or events immediately gives rise to the recognition of revenue under the accrual basis of accounting.

a. The receipt of an order by Mattel Toys from Toys ''R'' Us for children's toys.

b. The shipment of magazines by Time that subscribers have paid for in advance.

c. The issue of additional shares of common stock by General Motors.

d. The completion of a batch of men's suits by Hart, Schaffner & Marx.

e. The sale of tickets by the Boston Red Sox for a game in 2 weeks.

f. Same as part **e**, except the sale is made by Ticketron, a ticket agency.

g. The earning of interest by IBM on a certificate of deposit prior to maturity of CD.

h. The collection of cash by J. C. Penney from its customers for sales made on account last month.

i. The rendering of audit services by Ernst and Young to a client on account.

16. *Expense recognition*. Assume that Hewlett Packard (HP) uses the accrual basis of accounting and recognizes revenue at the time it sells goods or renders services. Indicate the amount of expense recognized during March (if any) from each of the following transactions or events.

a. HP pays an insurance premium of $1,800 on March 1 for 1 year's coverage beginning on that date.

b. On April 3, HP receives a utilities bill totaling $460 for services during March.

    c. HP purchases on account supplies costing $700 during March. It makes payment for $500 of these purchases on account in March, and pays the remainder in April. On March 1, supplies were on hand that cost $300. On March 31, supplies that cost $350 were still on hand.

    d. Data in **c,** except that $200 of supplies were on hand March 1.

    e. In January, HP paid property taxes of $4,800 on an office building for the year.

    f. On March 29, HP paid an advance of $250 on the April salary to an employee.

17. *Statement of cash flows relations.* Selected data from the statement of cash flows for Humana, Inc., a hospital management company, for Year 2, Year 3, and Year 4 appear below (amounts in millions):

	Year 2	Year 3	Year 4
Inflows of Cash			
Sale of Property, Plant, and Equipment	$ 13	$ 73	$ 36
Issue of Long-Term Debt	131	188	182
Revenues from Operations Increasing Cash	2,653	2,903	3,260
Issue of Common Stock	0	0	0
Outflows of Cash			
Dividends	$ 72	$ 75	$ 81
Repurchase of Common Stock	0	0	0
Expenses for Operations Decreasing Cash	2,188	?	2,780
Acquisition of Property, Plant, and Equipment	?	398	295
Redemption of Long-Term Debt	87	170	?
Change in Cash	−22	27	66

    a. Compute the amount of each of the missing items above. Prepare a statement of cash flows for Humana, Inc., for each of the 3 years using the format in Exhibit 17.8.

    b. What major changes do you observe in the pattern of cash flows from operating, investing, and financing activities over the 3 years? Net income for the 3 years was Year 2, $54; Year 3, $183; Year 4, $227.

Problems

18. *Cash versus accrual basis of accounting.* Thompson Hardware Store commences operations on January 1, Year 5. J. Thompson invests $10,000 and the firm borrows $8,000 from a local bank. Thompson must repay the loan on June 30, Year 5, with interest at the rate of 9 percent per year.

    The firm rents a building on January 1 and pays 2 months' rent in advance in the amount of $2,000. On January 1, it also pays the $1,200 premium for property and liability insurance coverage for the year ending December 31, Year 5.

The firm purchases $28,000 of merchandise inventory on account on January 2 and pays $10,000 of this amount on January 25. A physical inventory indicates that the cost of merchandise on hand on January 31 is $15,000.

During January, the firm makes cash sales to customers totaling $20,000 and sales on account totaling $9,000. The firm collects $2,000 from these credit sales by the end of January.

The firm pays other costs during January as follows: utilities, $400; salaries, $650; and taxes, $350.

a. Prepare an income statement for January, assuming that Thompson uses the accrual basis of accounting and recognizes revenue at the time it sells (delivers) goods.

b. Prepare an income statement for January, assuming that Thompson uses the cash basis of accounting.

c. Which basis of accounting do you believe provides a better indication of the operating performance of the firm during January? Why?

19. *Cash versus accrual basis of accounting.* Management Consultants, Inc., opens a consulting business on July 1, Year 2. Roy Bean and Sarah Bower each contribute $7,000 cash for shares of the firm's common stock. The corporation borrows $8,000 from a local bank on August 1, Year 2. The firm must repay the loan on July 31, Year 3, with interest at the rate of 9 percent per year.

The firm rents office space on August 1, paying 2 months' rent in advance. It pays the remaining monthly rental fees of $900 per month on the first of each month, beginning October 1. The firm purchases office equipment with a 4-year life for cash on August 1 for $4,800.

The firm renders consulting services for clients between August 1 and December 31, Year 2, totaling $15,000. It collects $9,000 of this amount by year-end.

It incurs and pays other costs by the end of the year as follows: utilities, $450; salary of secretary, $7,500; supplies, $450. It has unpaid bills at year-end as follows: utilities, $80; salary of secretary, $900; supplies, $70. The firm used all the supplies it had acquired.

a. Prepare an income statement for the 5 months ended December 31, Year 2, assuming that the corporation uses the accrual basis of accounting and recognizes revenue at the time it renders services.

b. Prepare an income statement for the 5 months ended December 31, Year 2, assuming that the corporation uses the cash basis of accounting.

c. Which basis of accounting do you believe provides a better indication of operating performance of the consulting firm for the period? Why?

20. *Preparation of balance sheet and income statement.* B. Stephens, L. Harris, and G. Winkle, recent graduates, set up a management consulting practice on December 31, Year 1, by issuing common stock for $750,000. The accounting records of the S, H, & W Corporation as of December 31, Year 2, reveal the following.

Balance Sheet Items:

Cash	$ 50,000
Accounts Receivable from Clients	165,000
Supplies Inventory	5,000
Office Equipment (net of depreciation)	85,000
Office Building (net of depreciation).............................	500,000
Accounts Payable to Suppliers	10,000
Payroll Taxes Payable	12,000
Income Taxes Payable	13,000
Common Stock...	750,000

Income Statement Items:

Revenue from Consulting Services	$300,000
Rental Revenue (from renting part of building)	30,000
Salaries Expense	222,000
Property Taxes and Insurance Expense	30,000
Supplies Expense	10,000
Depreciation Expense	25,000
Income Tax Expense	13,000

Dividend Information:

Dividends Declared and Paid	$ 10,000

a. Prepare an income statement for S, H, & W Corporation for the year ending December 31, Year 2. Refer to Exhibit 17.3 for help in designing the format of the statement.

b. Prepare a comparative balance sheet for S, H, & W Corporation on December 31, Year 1, and December 31, Year 2. Refer to Exhibit 17.2 for help in designing the format of the statement.

c. Prepare an analysis of the change in retained earnings during Year 2.

21. *Preparation of balance sheet and income statement.* The accounting records of Wal-Mart Stores, Inc., reveal the following (amounts in millions):

	December 31	
	Year 1	Year 2
Balance Sheet Items:		
Accounts Payable	$1,100	$ 1,430
Accounts Receivable....................................	242	267
Bank Loan Payable (due April 10, Year 2)	104	—
Bonds Payable (due Year 16).............................	1,131	1,286
Building (net of accumulated depreciation)	1,070	1,330
Cash	11	13
Common Stock...	227	231
Equipment (net of accumulated depreciation)	810	992
Income Taxes Payable	120	125
Land	265	340
Merchandise Inventory	2,652	3,351
Other Current Liabilities	420	511
Other Noncurrent Assets	82	67
Retained Earnings	2,030	2,777

continued

continued from page 814

Income Statement Items for Year 2

Cost of Merchandise Sold	$16,057
Depreciation Expense	214
Income Tax Expense	488
Interest Expense	136
Other Operating Expenses	162
Salary Expense	2,892
Sales	20,786

Dividend Information:

Dividends Declared and Paid during Year 2	$ 90

a. Prepare a comparative balance sheet for Wal-Mart Stores, Inc., as of December 31, Year 1 and Year 2. Classify each balance sheet item into one of the following categories: current assets, noncurrent assets, current liabilities, noncurrent liabilities, or shareholders' equity.

b. Prepare an income statement for Wal-Mart Stores, Inc., for Year 2. Separate income items into revenues and expenses.

c. Prepare a schedule explaining, or accounting for, the change in retained earnings between the beginning and end of Year 2.

22. *Relations among principal financial statements.* This problem illustrates the relations among the three principal financial statements. Exhibit 17.13 presents a comparative balance sheet for Articulation Corporation as of December 31, Year 1 and Year 2. Exhibit 17.14 presents an income statement and

Exhibit 17.13

ARTICULATION CORPORATION
Comparative Balance Sheets
December 31, Year 1 and Year 2

	December 31	
	Year 1	**Year 2**
Assets		
Current Assets:		
Cash	$ 80	$180
Accounts Receivable from Customers	300	340
Merchandise Inventory	150	160
Total Current Assets	$530	$680
Noncurrent Assets:		
Land	$ 40	$ 55
Buildings and Equipment (net of accumulated depreciation)	130	165
Total Noncurrent Assets	$170	$220
Total Assets	$700	$900

continued

Exhibit 17.13 *continued*

Liabilities and Shareholders' Equity

Current Liabilities:

Accounts Payable	$310	$350
Income Taxes Payable	40	60
Total Current Liabilities	$350	$410

Noncurrent Liabilities:

Bonds Payable	20	25
Total Liabilities	$370	$435

Shareholders' Equity:

Common Stock	$200	$245
Retained Earnings	130	220
Total Shareholders' Equity	$330	$465
Total Liabilities and Shareholders' Equity	$700	$900

Exhibit 17.15 presents a statement of cash flows for Articulation Corporation for Year 2.

Using amounts from these three financial statements, demonstrate that the following relations are correct:

a. Retained earnings at the end of Year 1 plus net income for Year 2 minus dividends declared and paid for Year 2 equals retained earnings at the end of Year 2.

b. Change in total assets equals change in total liabilities plus change in common stock plus net income minus dividends.

c. Accounts receivable at the end of Year 1 plus sales to customers (all on account) less cash collections from customers (see statement of cash flows) equals accounts receivable at the end of Year 2.

d. Buildings and equipment at the end of Year 1 plus acquisitions of buildings and equipment minus dispositions of buildings and equipment minus

Exhibit 17.14

ARTICULATION CORPORATION
Income Statement for Year 2

Sales Revenue		$1,000
Expenses:		
Cost of Merchandise Sold	$600	
Salary Expense	100	
Depreciation Expense	50	
Interest Expense	20	
Income Tax Expense	120	
Total Expenses		$ 890
Net Income		$ 110

Exhibit 17.15

ARTICULATION CORPORATION
Statement of Cash Flows for Year 2

Operations:

Revenues Increasing Cash	$960	
Expenses Decreasing Cash	790	
Cash Flow from Operations		$170

Investing:

Land Acquired	$(15)	
Buildings and Equipment Acquired	(85)	
Cash Flow from Investing		(100)

Financing:

Issue of Bonds	$ 5	
Issue of Common Stock	45	
Dividends Declared and Paid	(20)	
Cash Flow from Financing		30
Net Change in Cash		$100

depreciation for Year 2 equals buildings and equipment at the end of Year 2.

e.   Bonds payable at the end of Year 1 plus new bonds issued during Year 2 minus outstanding bonds redeemed during Year 2 equals bonds payable at the end of Year 2.

f.   Common stock at the end of Year 1 plus common stock issued during Year 2 minus outstanding common stock repurchased during Year 2 equals common stock at the end of Year 2.

23.   *Relations between net income and cash flows.* The ABC Company starts the year in fine shape. The firm makes widgets—just what the customer wants. It makes them for $0.75 each and sells them for $1.00. The ABC Company keeps an inventory equal to shipments of the past 30 days, pays its bills promptly, and collects cash from customers within 30 days after the sale. The sales manager predicts a steady increase of 500 widgets each month beginning in February. It looks like a great year, and it begins that way.

January 1	Cash, $875; receivables, $1,000; inventory, $750.
January	In January, the firm sells on account for $1,000, 1,000 widgets costing $750. The firm collects receivables outstanding at the beginning of the month. Production equals 1,000 units at a total cost of $750. Net income for the month is $250. The books at the end of January show:
February 1	Cash, $1,125; receivables, $1,000; inventory, $750.
February	This month's sales jump, as predicted, to 1,500 units. With a corresponding step-up in production to maintain the 30-day inventory, ABC Company makes 2,000 units at a cost of $1,500. All receivables from January sales are collected. Net income so far, $625. Now the books look like this:
March 1	Cash, $625; receivables, $1,500; inventory, $1,125.

continued

continued from page 817

March	March sales are even better—2,000 units. Collections, on time; Production, to adhere to the inventory policy, 2,500 units; Operating results for the month, net income of $500; Net income to date, $1,125. The books:
April 1	Cash, $250; receivables, $2,000; inventory, $1,500.
April	In April, sales jump another 500 units to 2,500, and the manager of ABC Company pats the sales manager on the back. Customers are paying right on time. Production increases to 3,000 units, and the month's business nets $625 for a net income to date of $1,750. The manager of ABC Company takes off for Miami before the accountant issues a report. Suddenly a phone call comes from the treasurer: "Come home! We need money!"
May 1	Cash, $0; receivables, $2,500; inventory, $1,875.

a. Prepare an analysis that explains what happened to ABC Company. (*Hint:* Compute the amount of cash receipts and cash disbursements for each month during the period January 1 to May 1.)

b. How can a firm show increasing net income but a decreasing amount of cash?

c. What insights are provided by the problem about the need for all three financial statements—balance sheet, income statement, and statement cash flows?

24. *Relation between income and cash flows* (adapted from a problem by Professor Leonard Morrissey). RV Suppliers, Incorporated, founded in July, Year 1, manufactures "Kaps." A Kap is a relatively low-cost camping unit attached to a pickup truck. Most units consist of an extruded aluminum frame and a fiberglass skin.

   After a loss in Years 1 through 2, the company was barely profitable in fiscal Year 3 and Year 4. It realized more substantial profits in fiscal Year 5 and Year 6, as indicated in the financial statements shown in Exhibit 17.16 and 17.17.

Exhibit 17.16

RV SUPPLIERS, INCORPORATED
Income Statements
(all dollar amounts in thousands)

	Fiscal Years Ended June 30		
	Year 5	Year 6	Year 7
Net Sales	$266.4	$424.0	$247.4
Cost of Goods Sold	191.4	314.6	210.6
Gross Margin.................................	$ 75.0	$109.4	$ 36.8
Operating Expenses[a]	35.5	58.4	55.2
Income (Loss) before Income Taxes	$ 39.5	$ 51.0	$ (18.4)
Income Taxes	12.3	16.4	(5.0)
Net Income (Loss)	$ 27.2	$ 34.6	$ (13.4)

[a]Includes depreciation expense of $1.7 in Year 5, $4.8 in Year 6, and $7.6 in Year 7.

Exhibit 17.17

RV SUPPLIERS, INCORPORATED Balance Sheet (all dollars amounts in thousands)			
		June 30	
	Year 5	Year 6	Year 7

Assets

Current Assets

	Year 5	Year 6	Year 7
Cash	$ 14.0	$ 12.0	$ 5.2
Accounts Receivable	28.8	55.6	24.2
Inventories	54.0	85.6	81.0
Tax Refund Receivable	0	0	5.0
Prepayments	4.8	7.4	5.6
Total Current Assets	$101.6	$160.6	$121.0
Property, Plant, Equipment—Net[a]	30.2	73.4	72.2
Total Assets	$131.8	$234.0	$193.2

Liabilities and Shareholders' Equity

Current Liabilities

	Year 5	Year 6	Year 7
Bank Notes Payable	$ 10.0	$ 52.0	$ 70.0
Accounts Payable	31.6	53.4	17.4
Income Taxes Payable	5.8	7.0	0
Other Current Liabilities	4.2	6.8	4.4
Total Current Liabilities	$ 51.6	$119.2	$ 91.8

Shareholders' Equity

	Year 5	Year 6	Year 7
Capital Stock	$ 44.6	$ 44.6	$ 44.6
Retained Earnings	35.6	70.2	56.8
Total Shareholders' Equity	$ 80.2	$114.8	$101.4
Total Liabilities and Shareholders' Equity	$131.8	$234.0	$193.2

	Year 5	Year 6	Year 7
[a]Acquisitions	$ 13.4	$ 48.4	$ 11.8
Depreciation Expense	(1.7)	(4.8)	(7.6)
Book Value and Sales Proceeds from Retirements	(.4)	(.4)	(5.4)
Net Change in Property, Plant, and Equipment	$ 11.3	$ 43.2	$ (1.2)

However, in fiscal Year 7, ended just last month, the company suffered a loss of $13,400. Sales dropped from $424,000 in fiscal Year 6 to $247,400 in fiscal Year 7. The outlook for fiscal Year 8 is not encouraging. Potential buyers continue to shun pickup trucks in preference to more energy-efficient small foreign and domestic automobiles.

How did the company finance its rapid growth during the year ended June 30, Year 6? What were the inflows and outflows of cash during the year?

Similarly, how did the company manage its financial affairs during the abrupt contraction in business during the year just ended last month?

Suggested Solutions to Even-Numbered Exercises

8. *Preparation of personal balance sheet*
No distinction is made between contributed capital and retained earnings, because an individual does not issue capital stock. The excess of assets over liabilities is called an individual's *net worth*. The methods used in valuing an individual's assets and liabilities are critical variables in determining net worth. Possibilities include acquisition cost, current replacement cost, current selling price, and others.

10. *Concept of an accounting asset*
   a. Yes. The patent will provide future benefits. Its acquisition resulted from a past exchange.
   b. No. The employment of the scientist might lead to future benefits but those benefits are considered too difficult to quantify to justify recognition as an asset.
   c. Yes. The firm has established the right to use the building in the signing of the rental contract and payment of the rental amount.
   d. Yes. The firm has established the right to use the automobile and will sustain that right as long as it makes payments on the note on time.
   e. No, for reasons similar to those in part **b** above.
   f. No, because of the lack of mutual performance.
   g. No, for reasons similar to those in part **b** above.

12. *Concept of an accounting liability*
   a. Yes. The firm has received cash and must provide future goods or services.
   b. No, because it is difficult to measure the amount and timing of future cash flows, if any, from such a reputation.
   c. Yes. In contrast to part **b,** a warranty agreement specifies the conditions when the firm will provide warranty services and over what period. Past experience under the warranty plan should provide an adequate basis for estimating the amount and timing of future cash flows.
   d. No. Common stock has no maturity date or amount under the assumption that the firm is a going concern.
   e. Yes. The firm has received benefits (governmental services) for which it owes a known amount.
   f. Yes. The firm has received benefits that create a legal obligation to make payment. The due date merely indicates the latest time before the obligation is considered past due.
   g. Probably not, unless specific damage has occurred that the firm must repair.
   h. No, because it is questionable whether benefits the firm has received in the past or if it must make future cash payments.

14. *Boise Cascade Corporation; income statement relations*
   a.   The missing items now appear in bold type.

	Year 4	Year 5	Year 6
Sales......................................	$3,742	**$3,830**	$4,103
Cost of Goods Sold........................	(3,117)	(3,067)	**(3,162)**
Selling and Administrative Expenses...........	(338)	(340)	(363)
Interest Expense	(114)	(105)	(100)
Income Tax Expense	(71)	(135)	(189)
Net Income	$ 102	$ 183	$ 289

   b.   The common size income statement is as follows:

	Year 4	Year 5	Year 6
Sales......................................	100.0%	100.0%	100.0%
Cost of Goods Sold........................	(83.3)	(80.1)	(77.1)
Selling and Administrative Expenses...........	(9.0)	(8.9)	(8.9)
Interest Expense	(3.1)	(2.7)	(2.4)
Income Tax Expense	(1.9)	(3.5)	(4.6)
Net Income	2.7%	4.8%	7.0%

The ratio of net income to sales increased over the 3 years as a result of a reduction in the ratio of cost of goods sold to sales and in the ratio of interest expense to sales. A more favorable pricing environment or a reduction in cost of goods sold might explain the reduced cost of goods sold percentage. Paper processing plants are highly capital intensive so the cost of goods sold percentage decreases as the accountant spreads depreciation expense over a higher sales base. A decrease in the level of long-term debt explains the reduced interest expense percentage. A higher percentage of net income before income taxes to sales explains the increase in the income tax percentage.

16. *Expense recognition*
   a. $150.
   b. $460.
   c. $650 (= $300 + $700 − $350).
   d. $550 (= $200 + $700 − $350).
   e. $400 (= $4,800/12).
   f.   Zero (an expense of April).

... CHAPTER 18 ...

Introduction to Financial Statement Analysis

Chapter Outline

- Objectives of Financial Statement Analysis
- Usefulness of Ratios
- Analysis of Profitability
- Analysis of Risk
- Limitations of Ratio Analysis

Investors, bankers, and others analyze the financial statements firms prepare for external users in making investment, credit, and similar decisions. Management also analyzes these financial statements, either for a firm as a whole or for segments thereof, in evaluating the performance of the firm and its various operating units. This chapter describes some of the techniques commonly used by investors and other external users in analyzing financial statements. Management can use many of the same techniques in evaluating performance internally.

Objectives of Financial Statement Analysis

The first question the analyst asks in analyzing a set of financial statements is "What do I look for?" The response to this question requires an understanding of investment decisions.

To illustrate, assume that you recently inherited $25,000 and must decide what to do with the bequest. You narrow the investment decision to purchasing either a certificate of deposit at a local bank or shares of common stock of Horrigan Corporation, currently selling for $40 per share. You will base your decision on the **return** you anticipate from each investment and the **risk** associated with that return.

The bank currently pays interest at the rate of 8 percent annually on certificates of deposit. Because the bank is unlikely to go out of business, you are virtually certain of earning 8 percent each year.

The return from investing in the shares of Horrigan Corporation's common stock has two components. First, the firm paid a cash dividend in its most recent year of $.625 per share, and you anticipate that it will continue paying this dividend in the future. Also, the market price of the stock will likely change between the date you purchase the shares and the date in the future when you sell them. The difference between the eventual selling price and the purchase price, often called a holding gain (or loss), is a second component of the return from buying the stock.

The return from the common stock investment is riskier than the interest on the certificate of deposit. Future dividends and market price changes are likely to be associated, at least partially, with the profitability of the firm. Future income might be less than you currently anticipate if competitors introduce new products that erode Horrigan Corporation's share of its sales market. Future income might be greater than you currently anticipate if Horrigan Corporation makes important discoveries or introduces successful new products.

Economy-wide factors such as inflation and changes in international tensions will also affect the market price of Horrigan Corporation's shares. Also, specific industry factors, such as raw materials shortages or government regulatory actions, may influence the market price of the shares. Because most individuals prefer less risk to more risk, you will probably demand a higher expected return if you purchase the Horrigan Corporation's shares than if you invest in a certificate of deposit.

Theoretical and empirical research has shown that the expected return from investing in a firm relates, in part, to the expected profitability of the firm.[1] The analyst studies a firm's past operating, or earnings, performance to help forecast its future profitability.

Investment decisions also require that the analyst assess the risk associated with the expected return.[2] A firm may find itself short of cash and unable to repay a short-term loan coming due. Or the amount of long-term debt in the capital structure may be so large that the firm has difficulty meeting the required interest and principal payments. The financial statements provide information for assessing how these and other elements of risk affect expected return.

Most financial statement analysis, therefore, explores some aspect of a firm's profitability or its risk, or both.

---

[1]Ray Ball and Phillip Brown, "An Empirical Evaluation of Accounting Income Numbers," *Journal of Accounting Research* (Autumn 1968): 159–178.

[2]Modern finance makes a distinction between systematic (market) risk and nonsystematic (firm-specific) risk. The discussion in this chapter makes no distinction between these two dimensions of risk.

Usefulness of Ratios

The reader may have difficulty interpreting the various items in financial statements in the form presented. For example, assessing the profitability of a firm by looking at the amount of net income alone may be difficult. Comparing earnings with the assets or capital required to generate those earnings can help. The analyst can express this relation, and other important ones between various items in the financial statements, in the form of ratios. Some ratios compare items within the income statement; some use only balance sheet data; others relate items from more than one of the three principal financial statements. Ratios are useful tools of financial statement analysis because they conveniently summarize data in a form easy to understand, interpret, and compare.

Ratios are, by themselves, difficult to interpret. For example, does a rate of return on common shareholders' equity of 8.6 percent reflect a good performance? Once calculated, the analyst must compare the ratios with some standard. Several possible standards are

1. The planned ratio for the period being analyzed.
2. The corresponding ratio during the preceding period for the same firm.
3. The corresponding ratio for a similar firm in the same industry.
4. The average ratio for other firms in the same industry.

Later sections of this chapter discuss difficulties encountered in using each of these bases for comparison.

The sections that follow describe several ratios useful for assessing profitability and various dimensions of risk. To demonstrate the calculation of various ratios, we use data for Horrigan Corporation for Years 2 through 4 appearing in Exhibit 18.1

Exhibit 18.1

HORRIGAN CORPORATION
Comparative Balance Sheets
(all dollar amounts in millions)

	December 31			
	Year 1	Year 2	Year 3	Year 4
Assets				
Cash....................................	$ 10	$ 14	$ 8	$ 12
Accounts Receivable (net)	26	36	46	76
Inventories................................	14	30	46	83
Total Current Assets......................	$ 50	$ 80	$100	$171
Land	$ 20	$ 30	$ 60	$ 60
Building	150	150	150	190
Equipment	70	192	276	313
Less Accumulated Depreciation..............	(40)	(52)	(66)	(84)
Total Noncurrent Assets	$200	$320	$420	$479
Total Assets.............................	$250	$400	$520	$650

continued

Exhibit 18.1 *continued*

Liabilities and Shareholders' Equity

Accounts Payable............................	$ 25	$ 30	$ 35	$ 50
Salaries Payable............................	10	13	15	20
Income Taxes Payable	5	7	10	20
Total Current Liabilities	$ 40	$ 50	$ 60	$ 90
Bonds Payable	50	50	100	150
Total Liabilities	$ 90	$100	$160	$240
Common Stock ($10 par value)	$100	$150	$160	$160
Additional Paid-in Capital	20	100	120	120
Retained Earnings	40	50	80	130
Total Shareholders' Equity	$160	$300	$360	$410
Total Liabilities and Shareholders' Equity	$250	$400	$520	$650

(comparative balance sheets), Exhibit 18.2 (comparative income statements), and Exhibit 18.3 (comparative statements of cash flows). Our analysis for Horrigan Corporation studies changes in its various ratios over the 3-year period. We refer to such an analysis as a **time-series analysis. Cross-section analysis** involves comparing a given firm's ratios with those of other firms for a particular period. Several problems at the end of the chapter involve cross-section analysis (problems **11, 12, 13, 34,** and **35**).

Exhibit 18.2

HORRIGAN CORPORATION
Comparative Income Statements
(all dollar amounts in millions)

	Years Ended December 31		
	Year 2	Year 3	Year 4
Sales Revenue	$210	$310	$475
Less Expenses:			
Cost of Goods Sold	$119	$179	$280
Selling...	36	42	53
Administrative	15	17	22
Depreciation	12	14	18
Interest	5	10	16
Total	$187	$262	$389
Net Income before Taxes	$ 23	$ 48	$ 86
Income Tax Expense	7	14	26
Net Income	$ 16	$ 34	$ 60

Exhibit 18.3

HORRIGAN CORPORATION
Comparative Statements of Cash Flows
(all dollar amounts in millions)

	For the Year Ended December 31		
	Year 2	Year 3	Year 4
Operations:			
Net Income	$ 16	$ 34	$ 60
Additions:			
Depreciation Expense	12	14	18
Increase in Accounts Payable	5	5	15
Increase in Salaries Payable	3	2	5
Increase in Income Taxes Payable	2	3	10
Subtractions:			
Increase in Accounts Receivable	(10)	(10)	(30)
Increase in Inventories............................	(16)	(16)	(37)
Cash Flow from Operations	$ 12	$ 32	$ 41
Investing:			
Purchase of Land	$ (10)	$ (30)	—
Purchase of Building	—	—	$(40)
Purchase of Equipment	(122)	(84)	(37)
Cash Flow from Investing	$(132)	$(114)	$(77)
Financing:			
Issuance of Bonds	—	$ 50	$ 50
Issuance of Common Stock	$ 130	30	—
Dividends..	(6)	(4)	(10)
Cash Flow from Financing...........................	$ 124	$ 76	$ 40
Net Change in Cash.................................	$ 4	$ (6)	$ 4

Analysis of Profitability

A firm engages in operations to generate net income. This section discusses three measures of **profitability:**

1. Rate of return on assets.
2. Rate of return on common shareholders' equity.
3. Earnings per common share.

Rate of Return on Assets

The **rate of return on assets** measures a firm's performance in using assets to generate earnings independent of the financing of those assets. We described earlier three principal business activities: investing, financing, and operating. The rate of return on assets relates the results of *operating* performance to the *investments* of a firm without regard to how the firm *financed* the acquisition of those investments.

The calculation of the rate of return on assets is

$$\frac{\text{Net Income plus Interest Expense Net of Income Tax Savings}}{\text{Average Total Assets}}.$$

The earnings figure used in calculating the rate of return on assets is income before deducting any payments or distributions to the providers of capital. Because the firm pays interest to suppliers of capital, the analyst does not deduct interest expense in measuring the return on total assets. To derive income before interest charges, start with net income and increase that amount. Do not add to net income the full amount of interest expense shown on the income statement, however. Because interest expense is deductible in calculating taxable income, it does not reduce *after-tax* net income by the full amount of interest expense. The amount added back to net income is interest expense reduced by the income taxes that interest deductions save.

For example, interest expense for Horrigan for Year 4, as Exhibit 18.2 shows, is $16 million. The income tax rate is 30 percent of pretax income. The income taxes saved, because Horrigan can deduct interest in computing taxable income, equals $4.8 million ($= .30 \times$ $16 million). The amount of interest expense net of income tax savings added back to net income is therefore $11.2 million ($= $16 million $-$ $4.8 million). The analyst should not add back dividends paid to shareholders, because the firm does not deduct them as an expense in calculating net income.

Because we are computing the earnings rate *for a year,* the measure of investment should reflect the average amount of assets in use during the year. A crude but usually satisfactory figure for average total assets is one-half the sum of total assets at the beginning and at the end of the year.[3]

The calculation of rate of return on assets for Horrigan Corporation for Year 4 is as follows:[4]

$$\frac{\substack{\text{Net Income plus} \\ \text{Interest Expense} \\ \text{Net of Income Tax} \\ \text{Savings}}}{\text{Average Total Assets}} = \frac{\$60 + (\$16 - \$4.8)}{\frac{1}{2}(\$520 + \$650)} = 12.2 \text{ percent.}$$

Thus, for each dollar of assets used, the management of Horrigan Corporation earned $.122 during Year 4 before payments to the suppliers of capital. The rate of return on assets was 8.9 percent in Year 3 and 6.0 percent in Year 2. Thus the rate of return increased steadily during this 3-year period.

---

[3]Most financial economists would subtract average noninterest-bearing liabilities (for example, accounts payable, salaries payable) from average total assets in the denominator. Economists realize that when liabilities do not provide for explicit interest charges, the creditor adjusts the terms of the contract, such as setting a higher selling price or lower discount, for those who do not pay cash immediately. This ratio requires in the numerator the income amount before a firm accrues any charges to suppliers of funds. We cannot measure the interest charges implicit in the noninterest-bearing liabilities; items such as cost of goods sold and salary expense are somewhat larger because of these charges. Thus, implicit interest charges reduce the measure of operating income in the numerator. Subtracting average noninterest-bearing liabilities from average total assets likewise reduces the denominator for assets financed with such liabilities. The examples and problems in this book use average total assets in the denominator of the rate of return on assets, making no adjustment for noninterest-bearing liabilities.

[4]Throughout the remainder of this chapter, we omit reference to the fact that the amounts for Horrigan Corporation are in millions of dollars.

One might question the rationale of measuring return independently of the means of financing. After all, the firm must finance the assets and must cover the cost of the financing if it is to be profitable.

The rate of return on assets has particular relevance for lenders, or creditors, of a firm. These creditors have a senior claim on earnings and assets relative to common shareholders. Creditors receive their return in the form of interest. This return typically comes from earnings generated from assets before any other suppliers of capital receive a return (for example, dividends). When extending credit or providing debt capital to a firm, creditors want to be sure that the return generated by the firm on that capital (assets) exceeds its cost.

Common shareholders find the rate of return on assets useful in assessing financial leverage. A later section of this chapter discusses financial leverage.

Disaggregating the Rate of Return on Assets

To study changes in the rate of return on assets, the analyst can disaggregate the ratio into two other ratios, as follows:

$$
\begin{matrix} \text{Rate of} \\ \text{Return} \\ \text{on Assets} \end{matrix} = \begin{matrix} \text{Profit Margin Ratio} \\ \text{(before interest expense} \\ \text{and related income tax effects)} \end{matrix} \times \begin{matrix} \text{Total Assets} \\ \text{Turnover} \\ \text{Ratio,} \end{matrix}
$$

or

$$
\frac{\begin{matrix}\text{Net Income plus}\\\text{Interest Expense}\\\text{Net of Income}\\\text{Tax Savings}\end{matrix}}{\begin{matrix}\text{Average Total}\\\text{Assets}\end{matrix}} = \frac{\begin{matrix}\text{Net Income plus}\\\text{Interest Expense}\\\text{Net of Income}\\\text{Tax Savings}\end{matrix}}{\text{Revenues}} \times \frac{\text{Revenues}}{\begin{matrix}\text{Average Total}\\\text{Assets}\end{matrix}}.
$$

The **profit margin ratio** measures a firm's ability to control the level of expenses relative to revenues generated. By holding down costs, a firm can increase the profits from a given amount of revenue and thereby improve its profit margin ratio. The **total assets turnover ratio** measures a firm's ability to generate revenues from a particular level of investment in assets. To put it another way, the total assets turnover measures a firm's ability to control the level of investment in assets for a particular level of revenues.

Exhibit 18.4 disaggregates the rate of return on assets for Horrigan Corporation into profit margin and total assets turnover ratios for Year 2, Year 3, and Year 4. Much of the improvement in the rate of return on assets between Year 2 and Year 3 resulted from an increase in the profit margin ratio from 9.3 percent to 13.2 percent. The total assets turnover ratio remained relatively stable between these two years. On the other hand, one can attribute most of the improvement in the rate of return on assets between Year 3 and Year 4 to the increased total assets turnover. The firm generated $.81 of sales from each dollar invested in assets during Year 4 as compared to $.67 of sales per dollar of assets in Year 3. The increased total assets turnover, coupled with an improvement in the profit margin ratio, permitted Horrigan Corporation to increase its rate of return on assets during Year 4. We must analyze the changes in the profit margin ratio and total assets turnover ratio in

Exhibit 18.4

HORRIGAN CORPORATION
Disaggregation of Rate of Return on Assets for Year 2, Year 3, and Year 4

$$\frac{\text{Net Income plus Interest Expense Net of Income Tax Savings}}{\text{Average Total Assets}} = \frac{\text{Net Income plus Interest Expense Net of Income Tax Savings}}{\text{Revenues}} \times \frac{\text{Revenues}}{\text{Average Total Assets}}$$

Year 2:
$$\frac{\$16 + (\$5 - \$1.5)}{\frac{1}{2}(\$250 + \$400)} = \frac{\$16 + (\$5 - \$1.5)}{\$210} \times \frac{\$210}{\frac{1}{2}(\$250 + \$400)}$$

$$6.0\% = 9.3\% \times .65$$

Year 3:
$$\frac{\$34 + (\$10 - \$3)}{\frac{1}{2}(\$400 + \$520)} = \frac{\$34 + (\$10 - \$3)}{\$310} \times \frac{\$310}{\frac{1}{2}(\$400 + \$520)}$$

$$8.9\% = 13.2\% \times .67$$

Year 4:
$$\frac{\$60 + (\$16 - \$4.8)}{\frac{1}{2}(\$520 + \$650)} = \frac{\$60 + (\$16 - \$4.8)}{\$475} \times \frac{\$475}{\frac{1}{2}(\$520 + \$650)}$$

$$12.2\% = 15.0\% \times .81$$

greater depth to pinpoint the causes of the changes in Horrigan Corporation's profitability over this 3-year period. We return to this analysis shortly.

Firms improve their rate of return on assets by increasing the profit margin ratio, the rate of asset turnover, or both. Some firms, however, have limited flexibility to alter one or the other of these components. For example, a firm committed under a 3-year labor union contract has little control over wage rates paid. Or, a firm operating under market- or government-imposed price controls may be unable to increase the prices of its products. These situations limit the opportunities for improving the profit margin ratio. To increase the rate of return on assets, the firm must reduce the level of investment in assets such as inventory, plant, and equipment, or, to put it another way, it must increase revenues per dollar of assets.

Analyzing Changes in the Profit Margin Ratio

The analyst studies changes in the profit margin ratio by examining changes in a firm's expenses relative to revenues. One approach expresses individual expenses and net income as a percentage of revenues. Exhibit 18.5 presents such an analysis for Horrigan Corporation. Note that this analysis alters somewhat the conventional income statement format by subtracting interest expense (net of its related income tax effects) as the last expense item. The percentages on the line titled Income before Interest and Related Income Tax Effect correspond to the profit margin ratios (before interest and related tax effects) in Exhibit 18.4.

The analysis in Exhibit 18.5 indicates that the improvement in Horrigan Corporation's profit margin ratio over the 3 years relates primarily to decreased selling,

Exhibit 18.5

HORRIGAN CORPORATION
Net Income and Expenses as a Percentage of Revenues for Year 2, Year 3, and Year 4

	Years Ended December 31		
	Year 2	Year 3	Year 4
Sales Revenue	100.0%	100.0%	100.0%
Less Operating Expenses:			
Cost of Goods Sold	56.7%	57.7%	58.9%
Selling..	17.1	13.6	11.2
Administrative	7.1	5.5	4.6
Depreciation	5.7	4.5	3.8
Total	86.6%	81.3%	78.5%
Income before Income Taxes and Interest	13.4%	18.7%	21.5%
Income Taxes at 30 Percent	4.1	5.5	6.5
Income before Interest and Related Income			
Tax Effect.......................................	9.3%	13.2%	15.0%
Interest Expense Net of Income Tax Effect..............	1.7	2.2	2.4
Net Income	7.6%	11.0%	12.6%

administrative, and depreciation expenses as a percentage of sales. The analyst should explore further with management the reasons for these decreasing percentages. Does the decrease in selling expenses as a percentage of sales reflect a reduction in advertising expenditures that could hurt future sales? Does the decrease in depreciation expense as a percentage of sales reflect a failure to expand plant and equipment as sales increased? On the other hand, do these decreasing percentages merely reflect the realization of economies of scale as the firm spreads fixed selling, administrative, and depreciation expenses over a larger number of units?[5] Neither the amount nor the trend in a particular ratio can, by itself, inform the reader whether to invest in a firm. Ratios indicate areas requiring additional analysis. For example, the analyst should explore further the increasing percentage of cost of goods sold to sales. The increase may reflect a successful, planned pricing policy of reducing gross margin (selling price less cost of goods sold) to increase the volume of sales. On the other hand, the replacement cost of inventory items may be increasing without corresponding increases being made in selling prices. Or the firm may be accumulating excess inventories that are physically deteriorating or becoming obsolete.

Analyzing Changes in the Total Assets Turnover Ratio

The total assets turnover ratio depends on the turnover ratios for its individual asset components. The analyst generally calculates three turnover ratios: accounts receivable turnover, inventory turnover, and fixed asset turnover.

---

[5]*Operating leverage* is the term used to describe this phenomenon, which managerial economics textbooks discuss more fully.

Accounts Receivable Turnover   The rate at which accounts receivable turn over indicates how soon the firm will collect cash. **Accounts receivable turnover** equals net sales on account divided by average accounts receivable. For Horrigan Corporation, the accounts receivable turnover for Year 4, assuming that all sales are on account (that is, none are for immediate cash), is as follows:

$$\frac{\text{Net Sales on Account}}{\text{Average Accounts Receivable}} = \frac{\$475}{\frac{1}{2}(\$46 + \$76)} = 7.8 \text{ times per year.}$$

The analyst often expresses the accounts receivable turnover in terms of the average number of days that receivables are outstanding before the firm collects cash. To calculate the ratio, divide 365 days by the accounts receivable turnover ratio. The average number of days that accounts receivable are outstanding for Horrigan Corporation for Year 4 is 46.8 days (= 365 days/7.8 times per year). Thus, on average, it collects accounts receivable approximately $1\frac{1}{2}$ months after the date of sale. Interpreting this average collection period depends on the terms of sale. If the terms of sale are "net 30 days," the accounts receivable turnover indicates that collections do not accord with the stated terms. Such a ratio would warrant a review of the credit and collection activity for an explanation and for possible corrective action. If the firm offers terms of "net 45 days," the results indicate that the firm handles accounts receivable better.

Inventory Turnover   The **inventory turnover ratio** indicates the efficiency of operations for many businesses. Inventory turnover equals cost of goods sold divided by the average inventory during the period. The inventory turnover for Horrigan Corporation for Year 4 is as follows:

$$\frac{\text{Cost of Goods Sold}}{\text{Average Inventory}} = \frac{\$280}{\frac{1}{2}(\$46 + \$83)} = 4.3 \text{ times per year.}$$

Thus inventory is typically on hand an average of 84.9 days (= 365 days/4.3 times per year) before sale.

Interpreting the inventory turnover figure involves two opposing considerations. Firms prefer to sell as many goods as possible with a minimum of capital tied up in inventories. An increase in the rate of inventory turnover between periods may indicate more profitable use of the investment in inventory. On the other hand, management does not want to have so little inventory on hand that shortages result. An increase in the rate of inventory turnover in this case may mean a loss of customers, thereby offsetting any advantage gained by decreased investment in inventory. Firms must make trade-offs in deciding the optimum level of inventory and, thus, the desirable rate of inventory turnover.

Some analysts calculate the inventory turnover ratio by dividing sales, rather than cost of goods sold, by the average inventory. As long as selling prices have a relatively constant relation with cost of goods sold, either measure will identify changes in the trend of the inventory. Using sales in the numerator is inappropriate if the analyst wishes to use the inventory turnover ratio to calculate the average number of days inventory is on hand until sale.

Plant Asset Turnover   The **plant asset turnover ratio** measures the relation between sales and the investment in plant assets such as property, plant, and equipment. The plant assets turnover ratio for Horrigan Corporation for Year 4 is

$$\frac{\text{Revenues}}{\text{Average Plant Assets}} = \frac{\$475}{\frac{1}{2}(\$420 + \$479)} = 1.1 \text{ times per year.}$$

Thus each dollar invested in plant assets during Year 4 generated $1.10 in revenues.

The analyst must interpret changes in the plant asset turnover ratio carefully. Firms often invest in plant assets (for example, production facilities) several periods before they generate sales from products manufactured in their plants. Thus a low or decreasing rate of plant asset turnover may indicate an expanding firm preparing for future growth. On the other hand, a firm may cut back its capital expenditures if it foresees a poor near-term outlook for its products. Such an action could lead to an increase in the plant asset turnover ratio.

We noted earlier that the total assets turnover for Horrigan Corporation was relatively stable between Year 2 and Year 3 but increased dramatically in Year 4. Exhibit 18.6 presents the four turnover ratios discussed for Horrigan Corporation over this 3-year period. The accounts receivable turnover ratio increased steadily over the 3 years, indicating either more careful screening of credit applications or more effective collection efforts. The inventory turnover ratio decreased during the 3 years. Coupling this result with the increasing percentage of cost of goods sold to sales shown in Exhibit 18.5 indicates that there may be excessive investments in inventories that are physically deteriorating or becoming obsolete.

Most of the increase in the total assets turnover between Year 3 and Year 4 relates to an increase in the plant assets turnover. We note in the statement of cash flows for Horrigan Corporation in Exhibit 18.3 that total capital expenditures on land, buildings, and equipment decreased over the 3-year period, possibly accounting for the increase in the plant assets turnover. The analyst should investigate more fully the reasons for this decrease.

Summary of the Analysis of the Rate of Return on Assets

This section began by stating that the rate of return on assets helps assess a firm's performance in using assets to generate earnings. We then disaggregated the rate of return on assets into profit margin and total assets turnover components. We

Exhibit 18.6

HORRIGAN CORPORATION Asset Turnover Ratios for Year 2, Year 3, and Year 4			
	Year 2	Year 3	Year 4
Total Assets Turnover	.65	.67	.81
Accounts Receivable Turnover...........................	6.8	7.6	7.8
Inventory Turnover	5.4	4.7	4.3
Plant Asset Turnover	.8	.8	1.1

analyzed the profit margin ratio further by relating various expenses and net income to sales. We tried to understand better the total assets turnover by calculating turnover ratios for accounts receivable, inventory, and plant assets.

The analysis for Horrigan Corporation revealed the following:

1. The rate of return on assets increased steadily over the 3-year period from Year 2 to Year 4.

2. An increasing profit margin over all 3 years and an improved total asset turnover during Year 4 help to explain the improved rate of return on assets.

3. Decreases in the percentages of selling and administrative expenses to sales largely explain the improved profit margin. The analyst should explore further the reasons for these decreases to ascertain whether the firm is curtailing selling and administrative efforts that might unfavorably affect future sales and operations.

4. The changes in the total assets turnover reflect the effects of increasing accounts receivable and plant asset turnover ratios and a decreasing inventory turnover. The increasing plant asset turnover might relate to a reduced level of investment in new property, plant, and equipment that could hurt future productive capacity. The decreasing rate of inventory turnover coupled with the increasing percentage of cost of goods sold to sales may indicate inventory control problems (build-up of obsolete inventory). The analyst should explore further to understand the reasons for these changes.

Rate of Return on Common Shareholders' Equity

The **rate of return on common shareholders' equity** measures a firm's performance in using assets to generate earnings. Unlike the rate of return on assets, the rate of return on common shareholders' equity explicitly considers the financing of those assets. Thus this measure of profitability incorporates the results of operating, investing, and financing decisions. It primarily interests investors in a firm's common stock. Calculate the rate of return on common shareholders' equity as follows:

$$\frac{\text{Net Income} - \text{Dividends on Preferred Stock}}{\text{Average Common Shareholders' Equity}}.$$

To calculate the amount of earnings assignable to common shareholders' equity, the analyst subtracts from net income any earnings allocable to preferred stock equity, usually the dividends on preferred stock declared during the period. The capital provided by common shareholders during the period equals the average par value of common stock, capital contributed in excess of par value on common stock and retained earnings for the period. (Alternatively, subtract average preferred shareholders' equity from average total shareholders' equity.)

The rate of return on common shareholders' equity of Horrigan Corporation for Year 4 is as follows:

$$\frac{\text{Net Income} - \text{Dividends on Preferred Stock}}{\text{Average Common Shareholders' Equity}} = \frac{\$60 - \$0}{\frac{1}{2}(\$360 + \$410)} = 15.6 \text{ percent.}$$

The rate of return on common shareholders' equity was 7.0 percent in Year 2 and 10.3 percent in Year 3. Thus, like the rate of return on assets, the rate of return on common shareholders' equity increased dramatically over the 3 years.

Relation between Return on Assets and Return on Common Shareholders' Equity

Exhibit 18.7 graphs the two measures of rate of return discussed thus far for Horrigan Corporation for Year 2, Year 3, and Year 4. In each year, the rate of return on common shareholders' equity exceeded the rate of return on assets. What accounts for this relation?

Recall that the rate of return on assets measures the profitability of a firm before any payments to the suppliers of capital. Each of the various providers of capital receives an allocated share of this return on assets. The allocated share for creditors equals any contractual interest to which they have a claim. The allocated share for preferred shareholders, if any, equals the stated dividend rate on the preferred stock. Any remaining return belongs to the common shareholders; that is, common shareholders have a residual claim on all earnings after creditors and preferred shareholders receive amounts contractually owed them. Thus

$$\begin{array}{c} \text{Rate of Return} \\ \text{on Assets} \end{array} \rightarrow \begin{array}{c} \text{Return to} \\ \text{Creditors} \\ \text{(interest)} \end{array} + \begin{array}{c} \text{Return to} \\ \text{Preferred} \\ \text{Shareholders} \\ \text{(dividends)} \end{array} + \begin{array}{c} \text{Return to} \\ \text{Common} \\ \text{Shareholders} \\ \text{(residual)}. \end{array}$$

We can now see how the rate of return on common shareholders' equity can exceed the rate of return on assets: the rate of return on assets must exceed the after-tax cost of debt (Horrigan Corporation has no preferred stock outstanding). For Year 4, the rate of return on assets was 12.2 percent and the after-tax cost of

Exhibit 18.7

Rates of Return for Horrigan Corporation

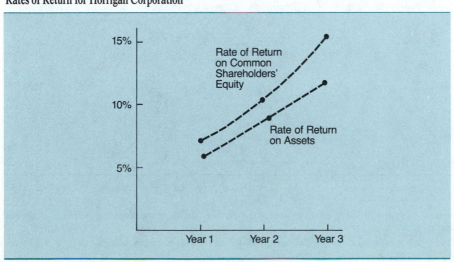

liabilities was 5.6 percent [= $(1 - .3)(\$16)/.5(\$160 + \$240)$; see Exhibits 18.1 and 18.2]. This excess return belongs to the common shareholders.

The common shareholders earned a higher return only because they undertook more risk in their investment. The riskier position results from the firm's incurring debt obligations with fixed payment dates. The phenomenon of common shareholders trading extra risk for a potentially higher return is called *financial leverage*.

Financial Leverage: Trading on the Equity

Financing with debt and preferred stock to increase the potential return to the residual common shareholders' equity is referred to as **financial leverage** or trading on the equity. As long as a firm earns a higher rate of return on assets than it paid for the capital used to acquire those assets, the rate of return to common shareholders will increase.

Exhibit 18.8 explores this phenomenon. Leveraged Company and No-Debt Company both have $100,000 in assets. Leveraged Company borrows $40,000 at a 10 percent annual rate. No-Debt Company raises all its capital from common shareholders. Both companies pay income taxes at the rate of 30 percent.

Consider first a good earnings year. Both companies earn $10,000 before interest charges (but after taxes, except for tax effects of interest charges).[6] This repre-

---

[6]Income before taxes and before interest charges is $14,286; $10,000 = (1 - .30) \times $14,286.

Exhibit 18.8

Effects of Financial Leverage on Rate of Return of Shareholders' Equity
(Income tax rate is 30 percent of pretax income.)

	Long-Term Equities		Income after Taxes but before Interest Charges[a]	After-Tax Interest Charges[b]	Net Income	Rate of Return on Total Assets[c] (percent)	Rate of Return on Common Shareholders' Equity (percent)
	Long-Term Borrowing at 10 Percent per Year	Shareholders' Equity					
Good Earnings Year							
Leveraged Company ..	$40,000	$ 60,000	$10,000	$2,800	$ 7,200	10.0%	12.0%
No-Debt Company	—	100,000	10,000	—	10,000	10.0	10.0
Neutral Earnings Year							
Leveraged Company ..	40,000	60,000	7,000	2,800	4,200	7.0	7.0
No-Debt Company	—	100,000	7,000	—	7,000	7.0	7.0
Bad Earnings Year							
Leveraged Company ..	40,000	60,000	4,000	2,800	1,200	4.0	2.0
No-Debt Company	—	100,000	4,000	—	4,000	4.0	4.0

[a]Not including any income tax savings caused by interest charges. Income before taxes and interest for *good* year is $14,286; for *neutral* year is $10,000; for *bad* year is $5,714.

[b]$40,000 (borrowed) × .10 (interest rate) × [1 − .30 (income tax rate)]. The numbers shown in the preceding column for after-tax income do not include the effects of interest charges on taxes.

[c]In each year, the rate of return on assets is the same for both companies as the rate of return on common shareholders' equity for No-Debt Company: 10 percent, 7 percent, and 4 percent, respectively.

sents a rate of return on assets for both companies of 10 percent (= $10,000/ $100,000). Leveraged Company's net income is $7,200 [= $10,000 − (1 − .30 tax rate) × (.10 interest rate × $40,000 borrowed)], representing a rate of return on common shareholders' equity of 12.0 percent (= $7,200/$60,000). Net income of No-Debt Company is $10,000, representing a rate of return on shareholders' equity of 10 percent. Leverage increased the rate of return to shareholders of Leveraged Company, because the capital contributed by the long-term debtors earned 10 percent but required an after-tax interest payment of only 7 percent [= (1 − .30 tax rate) × (.10 interest rate)]. This additional 3 percent return on each dollar of assets increased the return to the common shareholders.

Although leverage increased the return to common stock equity during the good earnings year, the increase would be larger if a greater proportion of the assets were financed with long-term borrowing and the firm's risk level increased. For example, assume that the firm financed its assets of $100,000 with $50,000 of long-term borrowing and $50,000 of shareholders' equity. Net income of Leveraged Company in this case would be $6,500 [= $10,000 − (1 − .30 tax rate) × (.10 × $50,000 borrowed)]. The rate of return on common stock equity would be 13 percent (= $6,500/$50,000). This compares with a rate of return on common stock equity of 12 percent when long-term debt was only 40 percent of the total capital provided.

Financial leverage increases the rate of return on common stock equity when the rate of return on assets is higher than the after-tax cost of debt. The greater the proportion of debt in the capital structure, however, the greater the risk the common shareholders bear. Of course, a firm cannot increase debt without limit; as it adds more debt to the capital structure, the risk of default or insolvency becomes greater. Lenders, including investors in a firm's bonds, require a higher and higher return (interest rate) to compensate for this additional risk. At some point, the after-tax cost of debt will exceed the rate of return earned on assets. At this point, leverage no longer increases the potential rate of return to common stock equity. For most large manufacturing firms, liabilities represent between 30 percent and 60 percent of total capital.

Exhibit 18.8 also demonstrates the effect of leverage in a neutral earnings year and in a bad earnings year. In the neutral earnings year, leverage neither increases nor decreases the rate of return to common shareholders, because the return on assets is 7 percent and the after-tax cost of long-term debt is also 7 percent. In the bad earnings year, the return on assets of 4 percent is less than the after-tax cost of debt of 7 percent. The return on common stock equity therefore drops below the rate of return on assets to only 2 percent. Clearly, financial leverage can work in two ways. It can enhance owners' rate of return in good years, but owners also run the risk that bad earnings years will be even worse than they would be without the borrowing.

Disaggregating the Rate of Return on Common Shareholders' Equity

The analyst can disaggregate the rate of return on common shareholders' equity into several components (in a manner similar to the disaggregation of the rate of return on assets) as the following equation shows:

$$\begin{array}{c} \text{Rate of Return} \\ \text{on Common} \\ \text{Shareholders'} \\ \text{Equity} \end{array} = \begin{array}{c} \text{Profit Margin Ratio} \\ \text{(after interest} \\ \text{expense and} \\ \text{preferred dividends)} \end{array} \times \begin{array}{c} \text{Total} \\ \text{Assets} \\ \text{Turnover} \\ \text{Ratio} \end{array} \times \begin{array}{c} \text{Leverage} \\ \text{Ratio.} \end{array}$$

The profit margin percentage indicates the portion of the revenue dollar left over for the common shareholders after covering all operating costs and subtracting all claims of creditors and preferred shareholders. The total assets turnover, as discussed earlier, indicates the revenues generated from each dollar of assets. The **leverage ratio** indicates the extent to which common shareholders provide capital. The larger the leverage ratio, the smaller the portion of capital common shareholders provide and the larger the proportion creditors and preferred shareholders provide. Thus, the larger the leverage ratio, the greater the extent of financial leverage.

The disaggregation of the rate of return on common shareholders' equity ratio for Horrigan Corporation for Year 4 is as follows:

$$\frac{\$60}{\frac{1}{2}(\$360 + \$410)} = \frac{\$ 60}{\$475} \times \frac{\$475}{\frac{1}{2}(\$520 + \$650)} \times \frac{\frac{1}{2}(\$520 + \$650)}{\frac{1}{2}(\$360 + \$410)}$$

$$15.6 \text{ percent} = 12.6 \text{ percent} \times .81 \times 1.5.$$

Exhibit 18.9 shows the disaggregation of the rate of return on common shareholders' equity for Horrigan Corporation for Year 2, Year 3, and Year 4. Just as with the rate of return on assets, most of the increase in the rate of return on common shareholders' equity relates to an increasing profit margin over the 3-year period plus an increase in total assets turnover in Year 4. The leverage ratio remained reasonably stable over this period.

Earnings per Share of Common Stock

A third measure of profitability is **earnings per share** of common stock. Earnings per share equals net income attributable to common stock divided by the average number of common shares outstanding during the period.

Earnings per share for Horrigan Corporation for Year 4 is calculated as follows:

$$\frac{\begin{array}{c}\text{Net} \\ \text{Income}\end{array} - \begin{array}{c}\text{Preferred Stock} \\ \text{Dividend}\end{array}}{\begin{array}{c}\text{Weighted Average} \\ \text{Number of Common Shares} \\ \text{Outstanding} \\ \text{during the Period}^7\end{array}} = \frac{\$60 - \$0}{16 \text{ shares}} = \$3.75 \text{ per share.}$$

Earnings per share were $1.28 (= $16/12.5) for Year 2 and $2.19 (= $34/15.5) for Year 3.

---

[7]Exhibit 18.1 indicates that the par value of a common share is $10 and that the common stock account has a balance of $160 million throughout Year 4. The shares outstanding were therefore 16 million.

Exhibit 18.9

HORRIGAN CORPORATION				
Disaggregation of Rate of Return on Common Shareholders' Equity				
	Rate of Return on Common Shareholders' Equity =	Profit Margin ×	Total Assets Turnover ×	Leverage Ratio
Year 2	7.0%	= 7.6% ×	.65 ×	1.4
Year 3	10.3	= 11.0 ×	.67 ×	1.4
Year 4	15.6	= 12.6 ×	.81 ×	1.5

If a firm has securities outstanding that holders can convert into or exchange for shares of common stock, the firm might report two earnings-per-share amounts: **primary earnings per share and fully diluted earnings per share.** Convertible bonds and convertible preferred stock permit their holders to exchange these securities directly for shares of common stock. Many firms have employee stock option plans that allow employees to acquire shares of the company's common stock. Assuming holders convert their securities or employees exercise their options, the firm will issue additional shares of common stock. Then, the amount otherwise shown as earnings per share will probably decrease, or become diluted. When a firm has securities outstanding that, if exchanged for shares of common stock, would decrease earnings per share by 3 percent or more, generally accepted accounting principles require a dual presentation of primary and fully diluted earnings per share.[8]

Primary Earnings per Share   Calculations of earnings per share adjust the denominator for securities that are nearly the same as common stock. The principal value of these common stock equivalents arises from their owners' right to exchange them for, or convert them into, common stock, rather than from the securities' own periodic cash yields. Stock options and warrants are always common stock equivalents. Convertible bonds and convertible preferred stock may or may not be common stock equivalents. If the return from these convertible securities at the date of their issue is substantially below the return available from other debt or preferred stock investments, generally accepted accounting principles presume that the securities derive their value primarily from their conversion privileges and are therefore common stock equivalents. Calculations of primary earnings per share adjust for the dilutive effects of these securities.

Fully Diluted Earnings per Share   As the name implies, fully diluted earnings per share indicates the maximum possible dilution that would occur if the owners of all options, warrants, and convertible securities outstanding at the end of the accounting period exchanged them for common stock. Therefore, this amount represents the maximum limit of possible dilution that could take place on the date of the

---

[8]Accounting Principles Board, *Opinion No. 15*, "Earnings per Share," 1969.

balance sheet. All securities convertible into or exchangeable for common stock, whether or not classified as common stock equivalents, enter into the calculation of fully diluted earnings per share if they dilute earnings per share.

Firms that do not have convertible or other potentially dilutive securities outstanding compute earnings per share in the conventional manner. Firms with outstanding securities that have the potential for materially diluting earnings per share as conventionally computed must present dual earnings-per-share amounts. Problem **33** at the end of this chapter explores more fully the calculation of earnings per share.

Interpreting Earnings per Share   Some accountants and financial analysts criticize earnings per share as a measure of profitability because it does not consider the amount of assets or capital required to generate that level of earnings. Two firms with the same earnings and earnings per share will not be equally profitable if one of the firms requires twice the amount of assets or capital to generate those earnings as does the other firm.

In comparing firms, earnings-per-share amounts are of limited use. For example, assume that two firms have identical earnings, common shareholders' equity, and rates of return on common shareholders' equity. One firm may have a lower earnings per share simply because it has a larger number of shares outstanding (perhaps due to the use of a lower par value for its shares or to different earnings retention policies; see Problem **21** at the end of this chapter).

Price-Earnings Ratio   Financial analysts often compare earnings-per-share amounts with the market price of the stock. They usually express this comparison as a **price–earnings ratio** (= market price per share/earnings per share). For example, the common stock of Horrigan Corporation sells for $40 per share at the end of Year 4. The price–earnings ratio, often called the P/E ratio, is 10.67 to 1 (= $40/ $3.75). The analyst often expresses the relation by saying that "the stock sells at 10.7 times earnings."

Tables of stock prices and financial periodicals often present price-earnings ratios. The analyst must interpret these published P/E ratios cautiously, however. In cases in which a firm has discontinued operations or has extraordinary gains and losses, the reader must ascertain whether the published ratio uses only income from continuing operations or final net income in the numerator. Also, the published P/E ratios for firms operating at a net loss for the most recent year are sometimes reported as positive numbers. This occurs because the publisher (for example, Value Line) converts the net loss for the year to a longer-run expected profit amount to calculate the P/E ratio. To serve their intended purpose, P/E ratios should use normal, ongoing earnings data in the denominator.

Summary of Profitability Analysis

This chapter has discussed three broad measures for assessing a firm's profitability. Because the rate of return on assets and rate of return on common shareholders' equity relate earnings to some measure of the capital required to generate those earnings, we have focused most of our attention on these two profitability measures.

Exhibit 18.10

Profitability Ratios

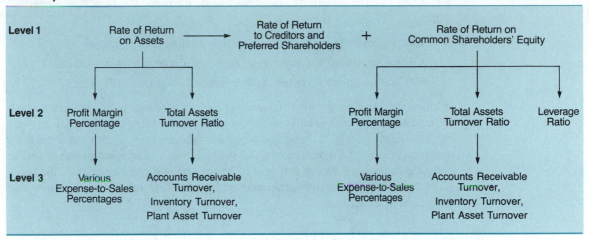

Exhibit 18.10 summarizes the analysis discussed. On the most general level (Level 1), the concern is with overall measures of profitability and the effectiveness of financial leverage. On the next level (Level 2), we disaggregate the overall measures of profitability into profit margin, asset turnover, and leverage components. On the third level (Level 3), we further disaggregate the profit margin and asset turnover ratios to gain additional insights into reasons for changes in profitability. The depth of analysis required in any particular case depends on the relative size of the observed differences or changes in profitability.

Analysis of Risk

The second parameter in investment decision making is risk. Various factors affect the risk of business firms:

1. Economy-wide factors, such as increased inflation or interest rates, unemployment, or recessions.

2. Industry-wide factors, such as increased competition, lack of availability of raw materials, changes in technology, or increased government antitrust actions.

3. Firm-specific factors, such as labor strikes, loss of facilities due to fire or other casualty, or poor health of key managerial personnel.

The ultimate risk is that a firm will become bankrupt; then, creditors and investors may lose the capital they provided to the firm.

Analysts assessing risk generally focus on the relative liquidity of a firm. Cash and near-cash assets provide a firm with the resources needed to adapt to the various types of risk; that is, liquid resources provide a firm with financial flexibility. Cash is also the connecting link that permits the operating, investing, and financing activities of a firm to run smoothly and effectively.

When assessing liquidity, time is critical. Consider the three questions that follow:

1. Does a firm have sufficient cash to repay a loan due tomorrow?
2. Will the firm have sufficient cash to repay a note due in 6 months?
3. Will the firm have sufficient cash to repay bonds due in 5 years?

In answering the first question, the analyst probably focuses on the amount of cash on hand and in the bank relative to the obligation coming due tomorrow. In answering the second question, the analyst compares the amount of cash expected from operations during the next 6 months, as well as from any new borrowing, with the obligations maturing during that period. In answering the third question, the focus shifts to the longer-run cash-generating ability of a firm relative to the amount of long-term debt maturing.

Measures of Short-Term Liquidity Risk

This section discusses four measures for assessing **short-term liquidity risk:** (1) the current ratio, (2) the quick ratio, (3) the operating cash flow to current liabilities ratio, and (4) the working capital turnover ratio.

Current Ratio

The **current ratio** equals current assets divided by current liabilities. The current ratio of Horrigan on December 31, Year 1, Year 2, Year 3, and Year 4, is

	$\text{Current Ratio} = \dfrac{\text{Current Assets}}{\text{Current Liabilities}}$	
December 31, Year 1	$\dfrac{\$\ 50}{\$\ 40} =$	1.25 to 1.0
December 31, Year 2	$\dfrac{\$\ 80}{\$\ 50} =$	1.60 to 1.0
December 31, Year 3	$\dfrac{\$100}{\$\ 60} =$	1.67 to 1.0
December 31, Year 4	$\dfrac{\$171}{\$\ 90} =$	1.90 to 1.0

The current ratio indicates the ability of the firm to meet its current obligations and, therefore, interests short-term creditors. Although the analyst generally prefers an excess of current assets over current liabilities, changes in the trend of the ratio can mislead. For example, when the current ratio is larger than 1 to 1, an increase of equal amount in both current assets and current liabilities (acquiring inventory on account) results in a decline in the ratio, whereas equal decreases (paying an accounts payable) result in an increased current ratio.

In a recession period, a business contracts, pays its current liabilities, and even though current assets may be at a low point, the current ratio may go to high levels. In a boom period, just the reverse effect may occur. In other words, a high current ratio may accompany unsatisfactory business conditions, whereas a falling ratio may accompany profitable operations.

Furthermore, firms can manipulate the current ratio. Management can take deliberate steps to produce a financial statement that presents a better current ratio at the balance sheet date than the average or normal current ratio. For example, a firm might delay normal purchases on account toward the close of a fiscal year. Or it might collect loans to officers, classified as noncurrent assets, and use the proceeds to reduce current liabilities. These actions produce a current ratio that is as favorable as possible in the annual financial statements at the balance sheet date. Such manipulation is sometimes known as "window dressing."

The current ratio, although commonly presented in statement analysis, has limited use. Its trends may not indicate substantial changes and management can easily manipulate it.

Quick Ratio

A variation of the current ratio is the **quick ratio** (sometimes called the **acid-test ratio**). The quick ratio includes in the numerator only those current assets that a firm could convert quickly into cash. The numerator customarily includes cash, marketable securities, and receivables. Some businesses can convert their inventory of merchandise into cash more quickly than other businesses can convert their receivables. The facts in each case will indicate whether the analyst should include receivables or exclude inventories.

Assuming that the quick ratios of Horrigan Corporation include accounts receivable but exclude inventory, the quick ratio on December 31, Year 1, Year 2, Year 3, and Year 4, is as follows:

	Quick Ratio $=$	Cash, Marketable Securities, Accounts Receivable / Current Liabilities
December 31, Year 1	$\dfrac{\$36}{\$40} =$	.90 to 1.0
December 31, Year 2	$\dfrac{\$50}{\$50} =$	1.0 to 1.0
December 31, Year 3	$\dfrac{\$54}{\$60} =$	.90 to 1.0
December 31, Year 4	$\dfrac{\$88}{\$90} =$	.98 to 1.0

Whereas the current ratio increased steadily over the period, the quick ratio remained relatively constant. The increase in the current ratio resulted primarily from a build-up of inventories.

Operating Cash Flow to Current Liabilities Ratio

One might criticize the current ratio and quick ratio because they use amounts at a specific point in time. If financial statement amounts at that particular time are unusually large or small, the resulting ratios will not reflect more normal conditions.

The **operating cash flow to current liabilities ratio** overcomes these deficiencies. The numerator of this ratio is cash flows from operations for the year. The denominator is average current liabilities for the year. The operating cash flow to current liabilities ratios for Horrigan Corporation for Year 2, Year 3, and Year 4 are as follows:

	$\dfrac{\text{Operating Cash Flow}}{\text{to Current Liabilities}} =$	$\dfrac{\text{Cash Flow from Operations}}{\text{Average Current Liabilities}}$
Year 2	$\dfrac{\$12}{\frac{1}{2}(\$40 + \$50)}$ =	26.7 percent
Year 3	$\dfrac{\$32}{\frac{1}{2}(\$50 + \$60)}$ =	58.2 percent
Year 4	$\dfrac{\$41}{\frac{1}{2}(\$60 + \$90)}$ =	54.7 percent

A healthy firm commonly has a ratio of 40 percent or more.[9] Thus the liquidity of Horrigan Corporation improved dramatically between Year 2 and Year 3. The decrease between Year 3 and Year 4 relates primarily to a build-up in current liabilities (which, in turn, probably relates to the build-up in inventories noted previously).

Working Capital Turnover Ratio

During the operating cycle of a firm, it

1. Purchases inventory on account from suppliers.
2. Sells inventory on account to customers.
3. Collects amounts due from customers.
4. Pays amounts due to suppliers.

This cycle occurs continually for most business firms. The longer the cycle, the longer the time that a firm ties up its funds in receivables and inventories. The interest cost on funds required to carry receivables and inventory also has negative effects on the short-run liquidity of a firm. The more quickly that a firm turns inventory and receivables into cash, the more liquid the firm is.

The **working capital turnover ratio** measures the length of the operating cycle. The working capital turnover ratio equals sales divided by the average work-

---

[9]Cornelius Casey and Norman Bartczak, "Using Operating Cash Flow Data to Predict Financial Distress: Some Extensions," *Journal of Accounting Research* (Spring 1985): 384–401.

ing capital for the year. Working capital equals current assets minus current liabilities. The working capital turnover ratio for Horrigan Corporation is as follows:

	$\dfrac{\text{Working Capital}}{\text{Turnover Ratio}} = \dfrac{\text{Sales}}{\text{Average Working Capital}}$		
Year 2...............................	$\dfrac{\$210}{\frac{1}{2}(\$10 + \$30)}$	=	10.5 times
Year 3...............................	$\dfrac{\$310}{\frac{1}{2}(\$30 + \$40)}$	=	8.9 Times
Year 4...............................	$\dfrac{\$475}{\frac{1}{2}(\$40 + \$81)}$	=	7.9 times

The turnover rate decreased over the 3-year period, primarily because inventories net of current liabilities increased faster than sales.

The analyst often converts the working capital turnover ratio into the number of days required for one revolution of the operating cycle. Dividing the turnover ratio into 365 days, working capital turned over on average every 34.8 days (= 365/10.5) during Year 2. The corresponding amounts for Year 3 and Year 4 were 41.0 days and 46.2 days, respectively.

The working capital turnover ratio varies significantly across firms depending on the nature of their business. Grocery stores turn over their working capital approximately 12 times per year, whereas a construction company turns over its working capital less than once per year. The analyst using the working capital turnover ratio to evaluate short-term liquidity must be sensitive to the type of business of the firm being analyzed.

Summary of Short-Term Liquidity Analysis

The current and quick ratios give snapshot measures of liquidity at particular times. These ratios for Horrigan Corporation indicate satisfactory conditions at the end of each year, although they indicate a build-up of inventories in Year 4.

The cash flow from operations to current liabilities and the working capital turnover ratios provide measures of short-term liquidity for a period of time. Both ratios indicate a significant improvement in liquidity between Year 2 and Year 3, primarily due to increased cash flow from operations. Both ratios decreased during Year 4 because of the build-up of inventory. However, the levels of the ratios during Year 4 do not yet indicate serious short-term liquidity problems for Horrigan Corporation. The growth rate in sales during the past 2 years (approximately 50 percent per year) would justify some build-up of inventories.

Measures of Long-Term Liquidity Risk

Analysts use measures of **long-term liquidity risk** to evaluate a firm's ability to meet interest and principal payments on long-term debt and similar obligations as they come due. If a firm cannot make the payments on time, it becomes insolvent and may have to reorganize or liquidate.

Perhaps the best indicator of a firm's long-term liquidity risk is its ability to generate profits over a period of years. If a firm is profitable, it will either generate sufficient cash from operations or obtain needed capital from creditors and owners. The measures of profitability discussed previously apply for this purpose as well. Three other measures of long-term liquidity risk are debt ratios, the cash flow from operations to total liabilities ratio, and the interest coverage ratio.

Debt Ratios

The debt ratio has several variations, but one most commonly encounters the **long-term debt ratio** in financial analysis. It reports the portion of the firm's long-term capital that is furnished by debt holders. To calculate this ratio, divide total long-term debt by the sum of total long-term debt and total shareholders' equity.

Another form of the debt ratio is the **debt-equity ratio.** To calculate the debt-equity ratio, divide total liabilities (current and noncurrent) by total equities (= liabilities plus shareholders' equity = total assets).

Exhibit 18.11 shows the two forms of the debt ratio for Horrigan Corporation on December 31, Year 1, Year 2, Year 3, and Year 4. In general, the higher these ratios, the higher the likelihood that the firm may be unable to meet fixed interest and principal payments in the future. The decision for most firms is how much financial leverage, with its attendant risk, they can afford to take on. Funds obtained from issuing bonds or borrowing from a bank have a relatively low interest cost but require fixed, periodic payments that increase the likelihood of bankruptcy.

In assessing the debt ratios, analysts customarily vary the standard in relation to the stability of the firm's earnings and cash flows from operations. The more stable the earnings and cash flows, the higher the debt ratio considered acceptable or safe. The debt ratios of public utilities are customarily high, frequently on the order of 60 to 70 percent. The stability of public utility earnings and cash flows makes these ratios acceptable to many investors. These investors might find such high leverage

Exhibit 18.11

HORRIGAN CORPORATION
Debt Ratios

$\text{Long-Term Debt Ratio} = \dfrac{\text{Total Long-Term Debt}}{\text{Total Long-Term Debt plus Shareholders' Equity}}$		$\text{Debt-Equity Ratio} = \dfrac{\text{Total Liabilities}}{\text{Total Liabilities plus Shareholders' Equity}}$	
Dec. 31, Year 1	$\dfrac{\$50}{\$210} = 24$ percent	Dec. 31, Year 1	$\dfrac{\$90}{\$250} = 36$ percent
Dec. 31, Year 2	$\dfrac{\$50}{\$350} = 14$ percent	Dec. 31, Year 2	$\dfrac{\$100}{\$400} = 25$ percent
Dec. 31, Year 3	$\dfrac{\$100}{\$460} = 22$ percent	Dec. 31, Year 3	$\dfrac{\$160}{\$520} = 31$ percent
Dec. 31, Year 4	$\dfrac{\$150}{\$560} = 27$ percent	Dec. 31, Year 4	$\dfrac{\$240}{\$650} = 37$ percent

unacceptable for firms with less stable earnings and cash flows, such as a computer software developer or biotechnology firm. The debt ratios of Horrigan Corporation are about average for an industrial firm.

Because several variations of the debt ratio appear in corporate annual reports, take care in comparing debt ratios among firms.

Cash Flow from Operations to Total Liabilities Ratio

The debt ratios do not consider the availability of liquid assets to cover various levels of debt. The **cash flow from operations to total liabilities ratio** overcomes this deficiency. This cash flow ratio resembles the one for assessing short-term liquidity risk, but here the denominator includes *all* liabilities (both current and noncurrent). The cash flow from operations to debt ratios for Horrigan Corporation follow:

	Cash Flow from Operations to Debt Ratio	=	Cash Flow from Operations / Average Total Liabilities	
Year 2..............	$\dfrac{\$12}{\frac{1}{2}(\$90 + \$100)}$	=	12.6 percent	
Year 3..............	$\dfrac{\$32}{\frac{1}{2}(\$100 + \$160)}$	=	24.6 percent	
Year 4..............	$\dfrac{\$41}{\frac{1}{2}(\$160 + \$240)}$	=	20.5 percent	

A financially healthy company normally has a ratio of 20 percent or more. Thus the long-term liquidity risk decreased significantly between Year 2 and Year 3 but increased again in Year 4.

Interest Coverage Ratio

Another measure of long-term liquidity risk is the number of times that earnings cover interest charges. The **interest coverage ratio** equals net income before interest and income tax expenses divided by interest expense. For Horrigan Corporation, the interest coverage ratios for Year 2, Year 3, and Year 4 are as follows:

	Interest Coverage Ratio	=	Net Income before Interest and Income Taxes / Interest Expense
Year 2.........	$\dfrac{\$16 + \$5 + \$7}{\$5}$ =		5.6 times
Year 3.........	$\dfrac{\$34 + \$10 + \$14}{\$10}$ =		5.8 times
Year 4.........	$\dfrac{\$60 + \$16 + \$26}{\$16}$ =		6.4 times

Thus, whereas the bonded indebtedness increased sharply during the 3-year period, the growth in net income before interest and income taxes provided increasing coverage of the fixed interest charges.

This ratio attempts to indicate the relative protection of bondholders and to assess the probability of a firm's failing to meet required interest payments. If bond indentures require periodic repayments of principal on long-term liabilities, the denominator of the ratio might include such repayments. The ratio would then be described as the fixed charges coverage ratio.

One can criticize the interest or fixed charges coverage ratios as measures for assessing long-term liquidity risk because they use earnings rather than cash flows in the numerator. Firms pay interest and other fixed payment obligations with cash, not with earnings. When the value of the ratio is relatively low (for example, two to three times), the analyst should use some measure of cash flows, such as cash flow from operations, in the numerator.

Summary of Long-Term Liquidity Analysis

Long-term liquidity analysis focuses on the amount of debt (particularly long-term debt) in the capital structure and the adequacy of earnings and cash flows to service debt (that is, to provide interest and principal payments as they mature). Although both short- and long-term debt of Horrigan Corporation increased over the 3-year period, increases in sales, earnings, and cash flows from operations all appear to be increasing sufficiently to cover the current levels of debt.

For convenient reference, Exhibit 18.12 summarizes the calculation of the ratios discussed in this chapter.

Exhibit 18.12

Summary of Financial Statement Ratios

Ratio	Numerator	Denominator
Profitability Ratios		
Rate of Return on Assets	Net Income + Interest Expense (net of tax effects)[a]	Average Total Assets during the Period[b]
Profit Margin Ratio (before interest effects)	Net Income + Interest Expense (net of tax effects)[a]	Revenues
Various Expense Ratios	Various Expenses	Revenues
Total Assets Turnover Ratio	Revenues	Average Total Assets during the Period
Accounts Receivable Turnover Ratio	Net Sales on Account	Average Accounts Receivable during the Period
Inventory Turnover Ratio	Cost of Goods Sold	Average Inventory during the Period
Plant Asset Turnover Ratio	Revenues	Average Plant Assets during the Period

continued

Exhibit 18.12 *continued*

Rate of Return on Common Shareholders' Equity	Net Income − Preferred Stock Dividends	Average Common Shareholders' Equity during the Period
Profit Margin Ratio (after interest expense and preferred dividends)	Net Income − Preferred Stock Dividends	Revenues
Leverage Ratio	Average Total Assets during the Period	Average Common Shareholders' Equity during the Period
Earnings per Share of Stock[c]	Net Income − Preferred Stock Dividends	Weighted-Average Number of Common Shares Outstanding during the Period

Short-Term Liquidity Ratios

Current Ratio	Current Assets	Current Liabilities
Quick or Acid-Test Ratio	Highly Liquid Assets (ordinarily cash, marketable securities, and receivables)[d]	Current Liabilities
Cash Flow from Operations to Current Liabilities Ratio	Cash Flow from Operations	Average Current Liabilities during the Period
Working Capital Turnover Ratio	Revenues	Average Working Capital during the Period

Long-Term Liquidity Ratios

Long-Term Debt Ratio	Total Long-Term Debt	Total Long-Term Debt Plus Shareholders' Equity
Debt-Equity Ratio	Total Liabilities	Total Equities (total liabilities plus shareholders' equity)
Cash Flow from Operations to Total Liabilities Ratio	Cash Flow from Operations	Average Total Liabilities during the Period
Times Interest Charges Earned	Net Income before Interest and Income Taxes	Interest Expense

[a]If a consolidated subsidiary is not owned entirely by the parent corporation, the minority interest share of earnings is also added back to net income.

[b]See footnote 3 on page 828.

[c]This calculation is more complicated when convertible securities, options, or warrants are outstanding.

[d]The calculation could conceivably exclude receivables for some firms and include inventories for others.

Limitations of Ratio Analysis

The analytical computations discussed in this chapter have a number of limitations that the analyst should keep in mind when preparing or using them. Several of the more important limitations are the following:

1. Because ratios use financial statement data as inputs, the ratios have shortcomings similar to the financial statements (for example, use of acquisition cost for assets rather than current replacement cost or net realizable value; the latitude permitted firms in selecting from among various generally accepted accounting principles).
2. Changes in many ratios strongly correlate with each other. For example, the changes in the current ratio and quick ratio between different times are often in the same direction and approximately proportional. The analyst need not compute all the ratios to assess a particular dimension of profitability or risk.
3. When comparing the size of a ratio between periods for the same firm, one must recognize conditions that have changed between the periods being compared (for example, different product lines or geographic markets served, changes in economic conditions, changes in prices, changes in accounting principles, corporate acquisitions).
4. When comparing ratios of a particular firm with those of similar firms, one must recognize differences between the firms (for example, use of different methods of accounting, differences in the method of operations, type of financing, and so on).

The analyst cannot use financial statement ratios as direct indicators of good or poor management. Such ratios indicate areas that the analyst should investigate further. For example, a decrease in the turnover of raw materials inventory, ordinarily considered an undesirable trend, may reflect the accumulation of scarce materials to keep the plant operating at full capacity during shortages. Such shortages may force competitors to restrict operations or to close down. The analyst must combine ratios derived from financial statements with an investigation of other facts before drawing valid conclusions.

■ Summary ■

This chapter began with the question, "Should you invest your inheritance in a certificate of deposit or in the shares of common stock of Horrigan Corporation?" Analysis of Horrigan Corporation's financial statements indicates that it has been a growing, profitable company with few indications of either short-term or long-term liquidity problems. You need at least three additional inputs before making the investment decision. First, you should consult sources of information other than the financial statements (for example, articles in the financial press, capital spending, and new product introduction plans by competitors) to improve projections of a

Exhibit 18.13

COX CORPORATION
Income and Retained Earnings Statement for Year 2

Sales Revenue		$30,000
Less Expenses:		
Cost of Goods Sold	$18,000	
Selling.	4,500	
Administrative	2,500	
Interest	700	
Income Taxes	1,300	
Total Expenses		27,000
Net Income		$ 3,000
Less Dividends:		
Preferred	$ 100	
Common	700	800
Increase in Retained Earnings for Year 2		$ 2,200
Retained Earnings, December 31, Year 1		4,500
Retained Earnings, December 31, Year 2		$ 6,700

firm's future profitability and risk. Second, you must decide your attitude toward, or willingness to assume, risk. Third, you must decide if you think the stock market price of the shares makes them an attractive current purchase.[10] At this stage in the investment decision the analysis becomes particularly subjective.

Problem 1 for Self-Study

Exhibit 18.13 presents an income statement for Year 2, and Exhibit 18.14 presents a comparative balance sheet for Cox Corporation as of December 31, Year 1 and Year 2. Using information from these financial statements, compute the following ratios. The income tax rate is 30 percent. Cash flow from operations totals $3,300.

a. Rate of return on assets.

b. Profit margin ratio (before interest and related tax effects).

c. Cost of goods sold to sales percentage.

d. Selling expense to sales percentage.

e. Total assets turnover.

f. Accounts receivable turnover.

---

[10]Finance texts discuss other important factors in the investment decision. Perhaps the most important question of all is how a particular investment fits in with the investor's entire portfolio. Modern research suggests that the suitability of a potential investment depends more on the attributes of the other components of an investment portfolio and the risk attitude of the investor than it does on the attributes of the potential investment itself.

Exhibit 18.14

COX CORPORATION
Comparative Balance Sheet
December 31, Year 1 and Year 2

	December 31	
	Year 1	Year 2
Assets		
Current Assets:		
Cash	$ 600	$ 750
Accounts Receivable	3,600	4,300
Merchandise Inventories	5,600	7,900
Prepayments	300	380
Total Current Assets..	$10,100	$13,330
Property, Plant, and Equipment:		
Land	$ 500	$ 600
Buildings and Equipment (net)	9,400	10,070
Total Property, Plant, and Equipment	$ 9,900	$10,670
Total Assets..	$20,000	$24,000
Liabilities and Shareholders' Equity		
Current Liabilities:		
Notes Payable..	$ 2,000	$ 4,000
Accounts Payable..	3,500	3,300
Other Current Liabilities....................................	1,500	1,900
Total Current Liabilities	$ 7,000	$ 9,200
Noncurrent Liabilities:		
Bonds Payable	4,000	2,800
Total Liabilities	$11,000	$12,000
Shareholders' Equity:		
Preferred Stock..	$ 1,000	$ 1,000
Common Stock	2,000	2,500
Additional Paid-in Capital	1,500	1,800
Retained Earnings	4,500	6,700
Total Shareholders' Equity	$ 9,000	$12,000
Total Liabilities and Shareholders' Equity	$20,000	$24,000

g. Inventory turnover.

h. Plant asset turnover.

i. Rate of return on common shareholders' equity.

j. Profit margin (after interest).

k. Leverage ratio.

l. Current ratio (both dates).

m. Quick ratio (both dates).

n. Cash flow from operations to current liabilities.

o. Working capital turnover.

p. Long-term debt ratio (both dates).

q. Debt-equity ratio (both dates).

r. Cash flow from operations to total liabilities.

s. Interest coverage ratio.

Suggested Solution

a. Rate of return on assets $= \dfrac{\$3,000 + (1 - .30)(\$700)}{.5(\$20,000 + \$24,000)} = 15.9$ percent.

b. Profit margin ratio $= \dfrac{\$3,000 + (1 - .30)(\$700)}{\$30,000} = 11.6$ percent.

c. Cost of goods sold to sales percentage $= \dfrac{\$18,000}{\$30,000} = 60.0$ percent.

d. Selling expense to sales percentage $= \dfrac{\$4,500}{\$30,000} = 15.0$ percent.

e. Total assets turnover $= \dfrac{\$30,000}{.5(\$20,000 + \$24,000)} = 1.4$ times per year.

f. Accounts receivable turnover $= \dfrac{\$30,000}{.5(\$3,500 + \$4,300)} = 7.6$ times per year.

g. Inventory turnover $= \dfrac{\$18,000}{.5(\$5,600 + \$7,900)} = 2.7$ times per year.

h. Plant asset turnover $= \dfrac{\$30,000}{.5(\$9,900 + \$10,670)} = 2.9$ times per year.

i. Rate of return on common shareholders' equity $= \dfrac{\$3,000 - \$100}{.5(\$8,000 + \$11,000)} = $ 30.5 percent.

j. Profit margin (after interest) $= \dfrac{\$3,000 - \$100}{\$30,000} = 9.7$ percent.

k. Leverage ratio $= \dfrac{.5(\$20,000 + \$24,000)}{.5(\$8,000 + \$11,000)} = 2.3.$

l. Current ratio

December 31, Year 1: $\dfrac{\$10,100}{\$7,000} = 1.4:1.$

December 31, Year 2: $\dfrac{\$13,330}{\$9,200} = 1.4:1.$

m. Quick ratio

December 31, Year 1: $\dfrac{\$4,200}{\$7,000} = .6:1.$

December 31, Year 2: $\dfrac{\$5,050}{\$9,200} = .5:1.$

n. Cash flow from operations to current liabilities $= \dfrac{\$3,300}{.5(\$7,000 + \$9,200)} =$

40.7 percent.

o. Working capital turnover $= \dfrac{\$30,000}{.5(\$3,100 + \$4,130)} = 8.3$ times per year.

p. Long-term debt ratio

December 31, Year 1: $\dfrac{\$4,000}{\$13,000} = 30.8$ percent.

December 31, Year 2: $\dfrac{\$2,800}{\$14,800} = 18.9$ percent.

q. Debt-equity ratio

December 31, Year 1: $\dfrac{\$11,000}{\$20,000} = 55.0$ percent.

December 31, Year 2: $\dfrac{\$12,000}{\$24,000} = 50.0$ percent.

r. Cash flow from operations to total liabilities $= \dfrac{\$3,300}{.5(\$11,000 + \$12,000)} =$

28.7 percent.

s. Interest coverage ratio $= \dfrac{\$3,000 + \$1,300 + \$700}{\$700} = 7.1$ times.

Problem 2 for Self-Study

Exhibit 18.15 presents a ratio analysis for Abbott Corporation for Year 1 to Year 3.

a. What is the likely explanation for the decreasing rate of return on assets?

b. What is the likely explanation for the increasing rate of return on common shareholders' equity?

c. What is the likely explanation for the behavior of the current and quick ratios?

d. What is the likely explanation for the decreases in the two cash flow from operations to liabilities ratios?

Suggested Solution

a. Because the profit margin (before interest expense and related tax effects) is stable over the 3 years, the decreasing rate of return on assets is attributable to a decreasing total assets turnover, which in turn relates primarily to a decreas-

Exhibit 18.15

ABBOTT CORPORATION
Ratio Analysis

	Year 1	Year 2	Year 3
Rate of Return on Assets	10.0%	9.6%	9.2%
Profit Margin (before interest and related tax effects)	6.0%	6.1%	6.1%
Total Assets Turnover	1.7	1.6	1.5
Cost of Goods Sold/Revenues	79.7%	79.6%	79.4%
Selling Expenses/Revenues	10.3%	10.2%	10.4%
Interest Expense/Revenues	1.5%	2.0%	2.5%
Accounts Receivable Turnover	4.3	4.3	4.2
Inventory Turnover	3.2	3.4	3.6
Plant Asset Turnover	.8	.7	.6
Rate of Return on Common Shareholders' Equity	14.0%	14.2%	14.5%
Profit Margin (after interest)	5.1%	4.9%	4.6%
Leverage Ratio	1.6	1.8	2.1
Current Ratio	1.4	1.3	1.2
Quick Ratio	1.0	.9	1.0
Cash Flow from Operations to Current Liabilities	38.2%	37.3%	36.4%
Working Capital Turnover	4.8	5.0	5.2
Long-Term Debt Ratio	37.5%	33.8%	43.3%
Debt-Equity Ratio	37.5%	44.4%	52.4%
Cash Flow from Operations to Total Liabilities	16.3%	13.4%	11.1%
Interest Coverage Ratio	6.7	5.1	4.1

ing plant asset turnover (the accounts receivable turnover is stable while the inventory turnover increases). Explanations for a decreasing plant asset turnover include (1) acceleration of capital expenditures in anticipation of higher sales in the future and (2) decreasing use of plant capacity so that fewer sales dollars are generated from the available level of capacity.

b. Because the rate of return on assets is decreasing, the increasing rate of return on common shareholders' equity results from increased financial leverage. The increased financial leverage is evident from the leverage ratio, the percentage of interest expense to sales, and the difference between the profit margin measures before and after interest expense.

c. Because the primary difference between the current and quick ratios relates to inventories, the decreasing current ratio coupled with a stable quick ratio must relate to more efficient inventory management. The increasing inventory turnover supports this explanation.

d. Given the stability of the profit margin (before interest expense and related tax effects) and the accounts receivable turnover and given the increased inventory turnover, the explanation lies in the impact of interest expense on operating cash flows. The increasing debt load decreased the profit margin (after interest) and drained ever greater amounts of cash for interest payments. These drains on operating cash flows, coupled with increasing amounts of debt (particularly long-term debt), drove the cash flow ratios down.

Key Terms and Concepts

Return and risk

Time-series analysis

Cross-section analysis

Profitability

Rate of return on assets

Profit margin ratio

Total assets turnover ratio

Accounts receivable turnover ratio

Inventory turnover ratio

Plant asset turnover ratio

Rate of return on common
shareholders' equity

Financial leverage

Leverage ratio

Earnings per share

Primary and fully diluted earnings
per share

Price-earnings ratio

Short-term liquidity risk

Current ratio

Quick or acid-test ratio

Operating cash flow to current
liabilities ratio

Working capital turnover ratio

Long-term liquidity risk

Long-term debt ratio

Debt-equity ratio

Cash flow from operations to total
liabilities ratio

Interest coverage ratio

Questions, Exercises, Problems, and Cases

Questions

1. Review the meaning of the concepts or terms given above in Key Terms and Concepts.

2. Describe several factors that might limit the comparability of a firm's financial statement ratios over several periods.

3. Describe several factors that might limit the comparability of one firm's financial statement ratios with those of another firm in the same industry.

4. "I can understand why the analyst adds back interest expense to net income in the numerator of the rate of return on assets, but I don't see why an adjustment is made for income taxes." Provide an explanation.

5. One company president stated, "The operations of our company are such that we must turn inventory over once every 4 weeks." Another company president in a similar industry stated, "The operations of our company are such that we can live comfortably with a turnover of four times each year." Explain what these two company presidents probably had in mind.

6. Some have argued that for any given firm at a particular time there is an optimal inventory turnover ratio. Explain.

7. Under what circumstances will the rate of return on common shareholders' equity exceed the rate of return on assets? Under what circumstances will it be less?

8. A company president stated, "The operations of our company are such that we can effectively use only a small amount of financial leverage." Explain.

9. Define financial leverage. As long as a firm's rate of return on assets exceeds its aftertax cost of borrowing, why doesn't the firm increase borrowing to as close to 100 percent of financing as possible?

10. Illustrate with amounts how a decrease in working capital can accompany an increase in the current ratio.

Exercises

11. *Calculate and disaggregate rate of return on assets*. Recent annual reports of The Coca-Cola Company and PepsiCo, Inc., reveal the following for Year 8 (in millions):

	Coca-Cola	PepsiCo
Revenues..	$8,338	$13,007
Interest Expense	199	345
Net Income	1,045	762
Average Total Assets	8,028	10,079
The income tax rate for Year 8 is 34 percent.		

a. Calculate the rate of return on assets for each company.
b. Disaggregate the rate of return on assets in part **a** into profit margin and total assets turnover components.
c. Comment on the relative profitability of the two companies for Year 8.

12. *Profitability analysis for two types of retailers*. Information taken from recent annual reports of two retailers appears below (amounts in millions). One of these companies is Wal-Mart, a discount store chain, and the other is The Limited, a speciality retailer of women's clothing. The income tax rate is 34 percent. Indicate which of these companies is Wal-Mart and which is The Limited. Explain.

	Company A	Company B
Sales.......................................	$4,071	$20,649
Interest Expense	64	136
Net Income	245	837
Average Total Assets	2,061	5,746

13. *Analyzing accounts receivable for two companies*. The annual reports of Kellogg's and Quaker Oats reveal the following for the current year (amounts in millions):

	Kellogg's	Quaker Oats
Sales.......................................	$3,793	$3,671
Accounts Receivable, January 1	218	505
Accounts Receivable, December 31	275	537

a. Compute the accounts receivable turnover for each company.

b. Compute the average number of days that accounts receivable are outstanding for each company.

c. Which company is managing its accounts receivable more efficiently.

14. *Analyzing inventories over 4 years.* The following information relates to the activities of Eli Lilly, a pharmaceutical company (amounts in millions):

	Year 5	Year 6	Year 7	Year 8
Sales...............................	$3,271	$3,720	$3,644	$4,070
Cost of Goods Sold..................	1,175	1,346	1,303	1,337
Average Inventory	662	694	655	645

a. Compute the inventory turnover for each year.

b. Compute the average number of days that inventories are held each year.

c. Compute the cost of goods sold to sales percentage for each year.

d. How well has Eli Lilly managed its inventories over the 4 years?

15. *Analyzing plant asset turnover over 3 years.* The following information relates to Sun Microsystems, a computer manufacturer (amounts in millions):

	Year 2	Year 3	Year 4
Sales...	$210	$538	$1,051
Average Plant Assets	70	145	256
Expenditures on Plant Assets	36	87	137

a. Compute the plant asset turnover for each year.

b. How well has Sun Microsystems managed its investment in plant assets over the 3 years?

16. *Calculating and disaggregating rate of return on common shareholders' equity.* Information taken from the annual reports of National Medical Enterprises for 3 recent years appears below (amounts in millions):

	Year 4	Year 5	Year 6
Revenues......................................	$2,962	$2,881	$3,202
Net Income	118	140	170
Average Total Assets	3,069	3,365	3,471
Average Common Shareholders' Equity	974	968	944

a. Compute the rate of return on common shareholders' equity for each year.

b. Disaggregate the rate of return on common shareholders' equity into profit margin, total assets turnover, and leverage ratio components.

c.   How has the profitability of National Medical Enterprises changed over the 3 years?

17. *Profitability analyses for three companies.* The following data show five items from the financial statements of three companies for a recent year (amounts in millions):

	Company A	Company B	Company C
For Year			
Revenues......................	$8,824	$9,000	$11,742
Income before Interest and Related Taxes[a]	615	1,043	611
Net Income to Common Shareholders[b]	477	974	503
Average during Year			
Total Assets	9,073	6,833	7,163
Common Shareholders' Equity	2,915	3,494	2,888

[a]Net Income + Interest Expense × (1 − Tax Rate).

[b]Net Income − Preferred Stock Dividends.

a.   Compute the rate of return on assets for each company. Disaggregate the rate of return on assets into profit margin and total assets turnover components.

b.   Compute the rate of return on common shareholders' equity for each company. Disaggregate the rate of return on common shareholders' equity into profit margin, total assets turnover, and leverage ratio components.

c.   The three companies are American Airlines, Johnson & Johnson, and May Department Stores. Which of the companies corresponds to A, B, and C? What clues did you use in reaching your conclusions?

18. *Relation of profitability to financial leverage.*

a.   Compute the ratio of return on common shareholders' equity in each of the following independent cases.

Case	Total Assets	Interest-Bearing Debt	Common Share-holders' Equity	Rate of Return on Assets	After-Tax Cost of Interest-Bearing Debt
A	$200	$100	$100	6%	6%
B	200	100	100	8	6
C	200	120	80	8	6
D	200	100	100	4	6
E	200	50	100	6	6
F	200	50	100	5	6

b. In which cases is leverage working to the advantage of the common shareholders?

19. *Analyzing financial leverage.* The Borrowing Company has total assets of $100,000 during the year. The firm's borrowings total $20,000 at a 10 percent annual rate and it pays income taxes at a rate of 30 percent of pretax income. Shareholders' equity is $80,000.

   a. Calculate the amount of net income needed for the rate of return on shareholders' equity to equal the rate of return on assets.

   b. Compute the rate of return on common shareholders' equity for the net income determined in part **a.**

   c. Calculate the amount of income before interest and income taxes needed to achieve this net income.

   d. Repeat parts **a, b,** and **c,** assuming borrowing of $80,000 and common shareholders' equity of $20,000.

   e. Compare the results from the two different debt-equity relations, making generalizations where possible.

20. *Ratio analysis of profitability and risk.* Refer to the following data for the Adelsman Company.

	Year 1	Year 2	Year 3
Rate of Return on Common Shareholders' Equity	8%	10%	11%
Earnings per Share	$3.00	$4.00	$4.40
Net Income/Total Interest Expense[a]	10	5	4
Debt-Equity Ratio (liabilities/all equities)	20%	50%	60%

[a]Note that this computation does not represent "times interest earned" as defined in the chapter.

The income tax rate was 30 percent in each year, and 100,000 common shares were outstanding throughout the period.

   a. Did the company's profitability increase over the 3-year period? How can you tell? (*Hint:* Compute the rates of return on assets.)

   b. Did risk increase? How can you tell?

   c. Are shareholders better off in Year 3 than in Year 1?

21. *Interpreting changes in earnings per share.* Company A and Company B both start Year 1 with $1 million of shareholders' equity and 100,000 shares of common stock outstanding. During Year 1, both companies earn net income of $100,000, a rate of return of 10 percent on common shareholders' equity at the beginning of the year. Company A declares and pays $100,000 of dividends to common shareholders at the end of Year 1, whereas Company B retains all its earnings and declares no dividends. During Year 2, both companies earn net income equal to 10 percent of shareholders' equity at the beginning of Year 2.

   a. Compute earnings per share for Company A and for Company B for Year 1 and for Year 2.

   b. Compute the rate of growth in earnings per share for both companies, comparing earnings per share in Year 2 with those of Year 1.

c.   Using the rate of growth in earnings per share as the criterion, which company's management appears to be doing a better job for its shareholders? Comment on this result.

22.   *Working backwards from profitability ratios to financial statement data.* The revenues of Lev Company were $1,000 for the year. A financial analyst computed the following ratios for Lev Company, using the year-end balances for balance sheet amounts. In addition, the Lev Company has no preferred shares outstanding.

Debt-Equity Ratio (all liabilities/all equities)	75 percent
Income Tax Expense as a Percentage of Pretax Income.............	30 percent
Net Income as a Percentage of Revenue	14 percent
Rate of Return on Common Shareholders' Equity	10 percent
Rate of Return on Assets	6 percent

From this information, compute each of the following items:
a.   Interest expense.
b.   Income tax expense.
c.   Total expenses.
d.   Net income.
e.   Total assets.
f.   Total liabilities.

23.   *Effect of financing strategy on earnings per share (CMA adapted).* The Virgil Company is planning to invest $10 million in an expansion program that it expects will increase income before interest and taxes by $2.5 million. Currently, Virgil Company has total equities of $40 million, 25 percent of which is debt and 75 percent of which is shareholders' equity, represented by 1 million shares. It can finance the expansion by issuing 200,000 new shares at $50 each or by issuing long-term debt at an annual interest rate of 10 percent. The following is an excerpt from the most recent income statement.

Earnings before Interest and Taxes.............................	$10,500,000
Less: Interest Charges	500,000
Earnings before Income Taxes	$10,000,000
Income Taxes (at 30 percent)...................................	3,000,000
Net Income	$ 7,000,000

Assume that Virgil Company maintains its current earnings on its present assets, achieves the planned earnings from the new program, and that the tax rate remains at 30 percent.
a.   Compute earnings per share assuming Virgil finances the expansion with debt.
b.   Compute earnings per share assuming Virgil finances the expansion by issuing new shares.

    c.   Compute the level of earnings before interest and taxes at which earnings per share will be the same, regardless of which of the two financing programs the firm uses.

    d.   Compute the level of earnings before interest and taxes at which the rate of return on shareholders' equity is the same, independent of the financing plan the firm uses.

24.   *Relation between book and market rates of return.* Net income attributable to common shareholders' equity of Florida Corporation during the current year was $250,000. Earnings per share were $.50 during the period. The average common shareholders' equity during the year was $2,500,000. The market price at year-end was $6.00.

    a.   Calculate the rate of return on common shareholders' equity for the year.

    b.   Calculate the rate of return currently being earned on the market price of the stock (the ratio of earnings per common share to market price per common share).

    c.   Why is there a difference between the rates of return calculated in parts **a** and **b?**

25.   *Calculating and interpreting short-term liquidity ratios.* Data taken from the financial statements of Boise Cascade Corporation, a forest products company, appear as follows (amounts in millions):

For the Year	Year 6	Year 7	Year 8
Revenues......................................	$3,740	$3,821	$4,095
Cash Flow from Operations......................	263	395	571

On December 31	Year 5	Year 6	Year 7	Year 8
Quick Assets.........................	$352	$395	$381	$417
Current Assets	789	861	825	867
Current Liabilities	545	548	563	681

    a.   Compute the current and quick ratios as of December 31 of each year.

    b.   Compute the cash flow from operations to current liabilities ratio and the working capital turnover ratios for each year.

    c.   How has the short-term liquidity risk of Boise Cascade Corporation changed over the 3-year period?

26.   *Calculating changes in current ratio and working capital.* A firm purchases merchandise inventory costing $30,000 on account. Indicate the effect (increase, decrease, no effect) of this transaction on (1) working capital and (2) the current ratio, assuming that current assets and current liabilities immediately before the transaction were as follows:

    a.   Current assets, $120,000; current liabilities, $120,000.

    b.   Current assets, $120,000; current liabilities, $150,000.

    c.   Current assets, $120,000; current liabilities, $80,000.

27.   *Relating profitability to short-term liquidity.* Following is a schedule of the current assets and current liabilities of the Lewis Company.

	December 31	
	Year 2	**Year 1**
Current Assets:		
Cash...	$ 355,890	$ 212,790
Accounts Receivable.............................	389,210	646,010
Inventories......................................	799,100	1,118,200
Prepayments....................................	21,600	30,000
Total Current Assets	$1,565,800	$2,007,000
Current Liabilities:		
Accounts Payable	$ 152,760	$ 217,240
Accrued Payroll, Taxes, etc.	126,340	318,760
Notes Payable	69,500	330,000
Total Current Liabilities...........................	$ 348,600	$ 866,000

During Year 2, the Lewis Company operated at a loss of $100,000. Depreciation expense during year 2 was $30,000.

a. Calculate the current ratio for each date.

b. Calculate the amount of cash provided by operations for Year 2.

c. Explain how the improved current ratio is possible under the Year 2 operating conditions.

28. *Calculating and interpreting long-term liquidity ratios.* Data taken from the financial statement of Humana, Inc., appear below (amounts in millions):

For the Year	Year 2	Year 3	Year 4
Net Income before Interest and Income Taxes	$475	$484	$499
Cash Flow from Operations......................	365	409	480
Interest Expense	164	154	146

On December 31	Year 1	Year 2	Year 3	Year 4
Long-Term Debt......................	$1,206	$1,216	$1,237	$1,211
Total Liabilities	1,817	2,020	2,197	2,268
Total Shareholders' Equity.............	902	896	1,012	1,154

a. Compute the long-term debt ratio and the debt-equity ratio at the end of Year 2, Year 3, and Year 4.

b. Compute the cash flow from operations to total liabilities ratio and the interest coverage ratio for Year 2 through Year 4.

c. How has the long-term liquidity risk of Humana, Inc., changed over this 3-year period?

29. *Effect of various transactions on financial statement ratios.* Indicate the immediate effects (increase, decrease, no effect) of each of the following independent transactions on (1) the rate of return on common shareholders' equity, (2) the current ratio, and (3) the debt-equity ratio. State any necessary assumptions.

    a. A firm purchases merchandise inventory costing $205,000 on account.

    b. A firm sells for $150,000 on account merchandise inventory costing $120,000.

    c. A firm collects $100,000 from customers on accounts receivable.

    d. A firm pays $160,000 to suppliers on accounts payable.

    e. A firm sells for $100,000 a machine costing $40,000 and with accumulated depreciation of $30,000.

    f. A firm declares dividends of $80,000. It will pay the dividends during the next accounting period.

    g. A firm issues common stock for $75,000.

    h. A firm acquires a machine costing $60,000. It gives $10,000 cash and signs a note for $50,000 payable 5 years from now for the balance of the purchase price.

30. *Effect of various transactions on financial statement ratios.* Indicate the effects (increase, decrease, no effect) of the following independent transactions on (1) earnings per share, (2) working capital, and (3) the quick ratio, where accounts receivable are *included* but merchandise inventory is *excluded* from quick assets. State any necessary assumptions.

    a. A firm sells on account for $300,000 merchandise inventory costing $240,000.

    b. A firm declares dividends of $160,000. It will pay the dividends during the next accounting period.

    c. A firm purchases merchandise inventory costing $410,000 on account.

    d. A firm sells for $20,000 a machine costing $80,000 and with accumulated depreciation of $60,000.

    e. Because of defects, a firm returns to the supplier merchandise inventory purchased for $7,000 cash. The firm receives a cash reimbursement.

    f. A firm issues 10,000 shares of $10 par value common stock on the last day of the accounting period for $15 per share. It uses the proceeds to acquire the assets of another firm composed of the following: accounts receivable, $30,000; merchandise inventory, $60,000; plant and equipment, $100,000. The acquiring firm also agrees to assume current liabilities of $40,000 of the acquired company.

Problems and Cases

31. *Calculating profitability and risk ratios.* The financial statements of the Press Company reveal the following:

	January 1	December 31
Current Assets	$180,000	$210,000
Noncurrent Assets	255,000	275,000
Current Liabilities	85,000	78,000
Long-Term Liabilities	30,000	75,000
Common Stock (10,000 shares)	300,000	300,000
Retained Earnings	20,000	32,000

continued

continued from page 864

	Operations for Year
Net Income	84,000
Interest Expense	3,000
Income Taxes (30 percent rate)	36,000
Cash Provided by Operations	30,970
Dividend Declared	72,000

Calculate the following ratios:

a. Rate of return on assets.
b. Rate of return on common shareholders' equity.
c. Earnings per share of common stock.
d. Current ratio (both dates).
e. Cash flow from operations to current liabilities.
f. Debt-equity ratio (both dates).
g. Cash flow from operations to total liabilities.
h. Interest coverage.

32. *Calculating profitability and risk ratios.* The comparative balance sheets, income statement, and statement of cash flows of Solinger Electric Corporation for the current year appear in Exhibits 18.16, 18.17, and 18.18.

a. Calculate the ratios listed in Exhibit 18.12 for Solinger Electric Corporation for the current year. You may omit expense ratios. Compute balance sheet ratios at both the beginning and end of the year. The income tax rate is 30 percent.

Exhibit 18.16

SOLINGER ELECTRIC CORPORATION
Comparative Balance Sheets
(Problem 32)

	January 1	December 31
Assets		
Current Assets:		
Cash	$ 30,000	$ 3,000
Accounts Receivable	20,000	55,000
Merchandise Inventory	40,000	50,000
Total Current Assets..........................	$ 90,000	$108,000
Noncurrent Assets:		
Buildings and Equipment (cost)	$100,000	$225,000
Accumulated Depreciation	(30,000)	(40,000)
Total Noncurrent Assets	$ 70,000	$185,000
Total Assets..................................	$160,000	$293,000

continued

Exhibit 18.16 *continued*

Liabilities and Shareholders' Equity

Current Liabilities:

Accounts Payable—Merchandise Suppliers	$ 30,000	$ 50,000
Accounts Payable—Other Suppliers...............	10,000	12,000
Salaries Payable.................................	5,000	6,000
Total Current Liabilities	$ 45,000	$ 68,000

Noncurrent Liabilities:

Bonds Payable	0	100,000
Total Liabilities	$ 45,000	$168,000

Shareholders' Equity:

Common Stock ($10 par value)	$100,000	$100,000
Retained Earnings	15,000	25,000
Total Shareholders' Equity	$115,000	$125,000
Total Liabilities plus Shareholders' Equity	$160,000	$293,000

b. Was Solinger Electric Corporation successfully leveraged during the current year?

c. Assume that the firm issued the bonds on November 1. Compute the annual interest rate at which Solinger Electric Corporation apparently issued the bonds.

d. If Solinger Electric Corporation earns the same rate of return on assets next year as it realized this year, and if it issues no more debt, will the firm be successfully leveraged next year?

Exhibit 18.17

SOLINGER ELECTRIC CORPORATION
Income Statement for the Current Year
(Problem 32)

Sales Revenue	$125,000
Less Expenses:	
Cost of Goods Sold	$ 60,000
Salaries	24,428
Depreciation	10,000
Interest..	2,000
Income Taxes	8,572
Total Expenses	$105,000
Net Income	$ 20,000

Exhibit 18.18

SOLINGER ELECTRIC CORPORATION
Statement of Cash Flows for the Current Year
(Problem 32)

Operations:		
Net Income	$ 20,000	
Additions:		
Depreciation Expense	10,000	
Increase in Accounts Payable:		
Merchandise Suppliers	20,000	
Other Suppliers....................................	2,000	
Increase in Salaries Payable	1,000	
Subtractions:		
Increase in Accounts Receivable....................	(35,000)	
Increase in Merchandise Inventory	(10,000)	
Cash Flow from Operations		$ 8,000
Investing:		
Acquisition of Buildings and Equipment		(125,000)
Financing:		
Issuance of Bonds	$100,000	
Dividends...	(10,000)	
Cash Flow from Financing............................		90,000
Net Change in Cash.................................		$(27,000)

33. *Case introducing earnings-per-share calculations for a complex capital structure.* The Layton Ball Corporation has a relatively complicated capital structure. In addition to common shares, it has issued stock options, warrants, and
convertible bonds. Exhibit 18.19 summarizes some pertinent information
about these items. Net income for the year is $9,500, and the income tax rate
used in computing income tax expense is 40 percent of pretax income.

   a. First, ignore all items of capital except for the common shares. Calculate
   earnings per common share.

   b. In past years, employees have been issued options to purchase shares of
   stock. Exhibit 18.19 indicates that the price of the common stock
   throughout the year was $25 but that the stock options could be exercised
   at any time for $15 each. The option allows the holder to surrender it
   along with $15 cash and receive one share in return. Thus the number of
   shares would increase, which would decrease the earnings-per-share figure. The company would, however, have more cash. Assume that the
   holders of options tender them, along with $15 each, to purchase shares.
   Assume that the company uses the cash to purchase shares for the treasury at a price of $25 each. Compute a new earnings-per-share figure.
   (Treasury shares are *not* counted in the denominator of the earnings-per-
   share calculation.)

   c. Exhibit 18.19 indicates that warrants were also outstanding in the hands
   of the public. The warrant allows the holder to turn in that warrant, along

Exhibit 18.19

LAYTON BALL CORPORATION
Information on Capital Structure for Earnings-per-Share Calculation
(Problem 33)

Assume the following data about the capital structure and earnings
for the Layton Ball Corporation for the year:

Number of Common Shares Outstanding throughout the Year	2,500 shares
Market Price per Common Share throughout the Year	$25
Options Outstanding during the Year:	
Number of Shares Issuable on Exercise of Options.............	1,000 shares
Exercise Price per Share	$15
Warrants Outstanding during the Year:	
Number of Shares Issuable on Exercise of Warrants...........	2,000 shares
Exercise Price per Share	$30
Convertible Bonds Outstanding:	
Number (issued 15 years ago)	100 bonds
Proceeds per Bond at Time of Issue (= par value)	$1,000
Shares of Common Issuable on Conversion (per bond)	10 shares
Coupon Rate (per year)	$4\frac{1}{8}$ percent

with $30 cash, to purchase one share of stock. If holders exercised the
warrants, the number of outstanding shares would increase, which would
reduce earnings per share. However, the company would have more
cash, which it could use to purchase shares for the treasury, reducing the
number of shares outstanding. Assume that all holders of warrants exercise them. Assume that the company uses the cash to purchase outstanding shares for the treasury. Compute a new earnings-per-share figure.
(Ignore the information about options and the calculations in part **b** at this
point.) Note that a rational warrant holder would *not* exercise his or her
warrants for $30 when a share could be purchased for $25.

d. Convertible bonds were also outstanding. The convertible bond entitles
the holder to trade in that bond for 10 shares. If holders convert the
bonds, the number of shares would increase, which would tend to reduce
earnings per share. On the other hand, the company would not have to
pay interest and thus would have no interest expense on the bond, because it would no longer be outstanding. This would tend to increase
income and earnings per share. Assume that all holders of convertible
bonds convert their bonds into shares. Compute a new net income figure
(do not forget income tax effects on income of the interest saved) and a
new earnings-per-share figure. (Ignore the information about options and
warrants and the calculations in parts **b** and **c** at this point.)

e. Now consider all the previous calculations. Which sets of assumptions
from parts **b, c,** and **d** lead to the lowest possible earnings per share when
they are all made simultaneously? Compute a new earnings per share
under the most restrictive set of assumptions about reductions in earnings
per share.

Exhibit 18.20

Income Statements for the Current Year (Problem 34)	Illinois Corp.	Ohio Corp.
Sales...	$4,300,000	$3,000,000
Less Expenses:		
Cost of Goods Sold	$2,800,000	$1,400,000
Selling and Administrative Expenses	482,860	697,140
Interest Expense.............................	100,000	200,000
Income Tax Expense	275,140	210,860
Total Expenses	$3,658,000	$2,508,000
Net Income	$ 642,000	$ 492,000

f. Accountants publish several earnings-per-share figures for companies with complicated capital structures and complicated events during the year. *The Wall Street Journal,* however, publishes only one figure in its daily columns (where it reports the price–earnings ratio—the price of a share of stock divided by its earnings per share). Which of the figures computed previously for earnings per share do you think *The Wall Street Journal* should report as *the* earnings-per-share figure? Why?

34. *Analyzing profitability and risk for two companies.* Exhibits 18.20 and 18.21 present the income statements and balance sheets of Illinois Corporation and Ohio Corporation.

Cash flow provided by operations was $600,000 for Illinois Corporation and $550,000 for Ohio Corporation.

Exhibit 18.21

Balance Sheets, December 31 (Problem 34)	Illinois Corp.	Ohio Corp.
Assets		
Cash..	$ 100,000	$ 50,000
Accounts Receivable (net)	700,000	400,000
Merchandise Inventory	1,200,000	750,000
Plant and Equipment (net).......................	4,000,000	4,800,000
Total Assets	$6,000,000	$6,000,000
Liabilities and Shareholders' Equity		
Accounts Payable..............................	$ 725,000	$ 289,000
Income Taxes Payable	275,000	211,000
Long-Term Bonds Payable (10 percent)	1,000,000	2,000,000
Common Stock	2,000,000	2,000,000
Retained Earnings	2,000,000	1,500,000
Total Liabilities and Shareholders' Equity	$6,000,000	$6,000,000

Exhibit 18.22

Data for Ratio Detective Exercise (Problem 35)

	Company Numbers						
	(1)	(2)	(3)	(4)	(5)	(6)	(7)
Balance Sheet at End of Year							
Current Receivables	0.31%	29.11%	6.81%	25.25%	3.45%	38.78%	17.64%
Inventories.....................	7.80	0.00	3.14	0.00	6.45	14.94	20.57
Net Plant and Equipment*	8.50	9.63	11.13	19.88	49.87	15.59	37.60
All Other Assets	2.16	7.02	25.59	32.93	24.05	15.54	30.07
Total Assets	18.77%	45.76%	46.67%	78.06%	83.82%	84.85%	105.88%
*Cost of Plant and Equipment (gross)	14.64%	14.80%	19.57%	29.03%	79.03%	24.80%	59.73%
Current Liabilities	6.08%	9.82%	6.41%	17.49%	14.83%	35.28%	27.68%
Long-Term Liabilities	2.12	7.96	0.00	0.00	0.00	8.33	1.33
Owners' Equity	10.57	27.98	40.26	60.57	68.99	41.24	76.87
Total Equities	18.77%	45.76%	46.67%	78.06%	83.82%	84.85%	105.88%
Income Statement for Year							
Revenues.....................	100.00%	100.00%	100.00%	100.00%	100.00%	100.00%	100.00%
Cost of Goods Sold (excluding depreciation) or Operating Expenses[a]	78.97	53.77	48.21	59.07	68.62	60.88	33.29
Depreciation	1.04	1.39	1.72	2.07	4.07	1.09	3.02
Interest Expense	0.16	0.52	0.00	0.08	0.02	1.35	0.73
Advertising Expense	3.72	0.00	11.43	0.06	4.39	2.93	2.28
Research and Development Expense.....................	0.00	1.00	0.00	0.00	0.15	0.00	9.06
Income Taxes	1.28	0.53	9.59	6.52	7.87	3.78	8.55
All Other Items (net)	13.34	18.88	18.58	24.52	6.40	24.39	27.66
Total Expenses...............	98.51%	76.09%	89.53%	92.32%	91.52%	94.42%	84.59%
Net Income	1.50%	23.92%	10.47%	7.68%	8.49%	5.59%	15.41%

continued

Assume that the balances in asset and equity accounts at year-end approximate the average balances during the period. The income tax rate is 30 percent. On the basis of this information, which company is

a. More profitable?
b. Less risky in terms of short-term liquidity?
c. Less risky in terms of long-term liquidity?
Use financial ratios, as appropriate, in doing your analysis.

35. *Detective analysis—identify company.* In this problem, you become a financial analyst/detective. Exhibit 18.22 expresses condensed financial statements for 13 companies on a percentage basis. In all cases, total sales revenues appear as 100.00%. All other numbers were divided by sales revenue for the year. The 13 companies (all corporations except for the accounting firm) shown on the next page represent the following industries:

Exhibit 18.22 *continued*

	Company Numbers					
	(8)	**(9)**	**(10)**	**(11)**	**(12)**	**(13)**
Balance Sheet at End of Year						
Current Receivables	12.94%	9.16%	25.18%	27.07%	13.10%	653.94%
Inventories	15.47	56.89	79.53	0.00	1.62	0.00
Net Plant and Equipment*	70.29	28.36	19.22	2.64	251.62	2.88
All Other Assets	18.37	26.42	24.72	223.91	23.68	200.37
Total Assets	117.07%	120.83%	148.65%	253.62%	290.02%	857.19%
*Cost of Plant and Equipment (gross)	167.16%	42.40%	35.08%	4.45%	320.90%	3.81%
Current Liabilities	19.37%	33.01%	20.42%	161.37%	28.01%	377.56%
Long-Term Liabilities	20.62	34.07	36.09	10.62	115.50	280.79
Owners' Equity	77.08	53.75	92.14	81.63	146.51	198.84
Total Equities	117.07%	120.83%	148.65%	253.62%	290.02%	857.19%
Income Statement for Year						
Revenues	100.00%	100.00%	100.00%	100.00%	100.00%	100.00%
Cost of Goods Sold (excluding depreciation) or Operating Expenses[a]	81.92	57.35	42.92	82.61	45.23	47.69
Depreciation	5.81	1.90	1.97	0.05	14.55	0.00
Interest Expense	1.23	2.69	3.11	1.07	7.15	24.33
Advertising Expense	0.00	6.93	13.04	0.00	0.00	0.00
Research and Development Expense	0.76	0.00	0.00	0.00	0.71	0.00
Income Taxes	2.15	7.47	10.63	3.92	8.73	12.89
All Other Items (net)	3.81	14.82	17.99	2.97	11.51	−5.57
Total Expenses	95.68%	91.16%	89.66%	90.62%	87.88%	79.34%
Net Income	4.32%	8.84%	10.34%	9.38%	12.11%	20.65%

[a]Represents operating expenses for the following companies: Advertising/public opinion survey firm, insurance company, finance company, and the public accounting partnership.

(1) Advertising and public opinion survey firm.
(2) Beer brewery.
(3) Department store chain (that carries its own receivables).
(4) Distiller of hard liquor.
(5) Drug manufacturer.
(6) Finance company (lends money to consumers).
(7) Grocery store chain.
(8) Insurance company.
(9) Manufacturer of tobacco products, mainly cigarettes.
(10) Public accounting (CPA) partnership.
(11) Soft drink bottler.
(12) Steel manufacturer.
(13) Utility company.

Exhibit 18.23

SARWARK COMPANY
Ratio Analysis
(Problem 36)

	Year 1	Year 2	Year 3
Rate of Return on Assets	10.1%	10.2%	9.9%
Profit Margin (before interest and related tax effects)	11.9%	10.0%	9.6%
Total Assets Turnover	0.85	1.02	1.03
Cost of Goods Sold/Revenues	72.4%	73.9%	73.8%
Selling and Administrative Expenses/Revenues	10.5%	10.4%	10.5%
Interest Expense/Revenues	2.1%	3.5%	4.0%
Income Tax Expense/Revenues	4.2%	4.1%	3.8%
Accounts Receivable Turnover...................	4.6	4.7	4.6
Inventory Turnover	3.7	3.6	3.7
Plant Asset Turnover	1.2	1.5	1.7
Rate of Return on Common Shareholders' Equity	15.5%	15.2%	14.7%
Current Ratio.................................	1.6:1	1.4:1	1.2:1
Quick Ratio	.9:1	.7:1	.5:1
Total Liabilities/Total Liabilities and Shareholders' Equity	42.0%	48.0%	60.0%
Long-Term Liabilities/Total Liabilities and Shareholders' Equity	25.0%	26.0%	25.0%
Revenues as Percentage of Year 1 Revenues.................................	100%	115%	130%
Assets as Percentage of Year 1 Assets	100%	113%	125%
Capital Expenditures as Percentage of Year 1 Capital Expenditures	100%	112%	120%

Use whatever clues you can to match the companies in Exhibit 18.22 with the industries listed above. You may find it useful to refer to average industry ratios compiled by Dun & Bradstreet, Prentice-Hall, Robert Morris Associates, and the Federal Trade Commission. Most libraries carry copies of these documents.

36. *Interpretation of ratio analysis.* Exhibit 18.23 presents a ratio analysis for Sarwark Company.
   a. What is the likely explanation for the stable rate of return on assets coupled with the decreasing rate of return on common shareholders' equity?
   b. What is the likely reason for the increasing plant asset turnover?

37. *Interpretation of ratio analysis.* Exhibit 18.24 presents a ratio analysis for Widdicombe Corporation for Year 1 through Year 3.
   a. What is the likely explanation for the increasing rate of return on assets coupled with the decreasing rate of return on shareholders' equity?

Exhibit 18.24

WIDDICOMBE CORPORATION Ratio Analysis (Problem 37)			
	Year 1	Year 2	Year 3
Rate of Return on Assets	10%	11%	12%
Profit Margin (before interest and related taxes)	18%	16%	14%
Total Assets Turnover	.56	.69	.86
Cost of Goods Sold/Revenues	62%	63%	65%
Selling and Administrative Expenses/Revenues	8%	10%	10%
Interest Expense/Revenues	16%	12%	8%
Income Tax Expense/Revenues	4%	5%	7%
Accounts Receivable Turnover....................	2.6	2.5	2.4
Inventory Turnover	3.2	2.8	2.5
Plant Asset Turnover	.3	.5	.7
Rate of Return on Common Shareholders Equity	18%	16%	14%
Profit Margin (after interest)	10%	10%	10%
Asset Turnover	.56	.69	.86
Leverage Ratio	3.2	2.3	1.6
Revenues as Percentage of Year 1 Revenues	100%	102%	99%
Assets as Percentage of Year 1 Assets	100%	104%	105%
Net Income as Percentage of Year 1 Net Income	100%	102%	99%
Capital Expenditures as Percentage of Year 1 Capital Expenditures	100%	90%	85%

   b.   How effectively has the firm managed its inventories?

   c.   What is the likely explanation for the increasing total assets turnover?

38. *Case analysis of bankruptcy.* On October 2, 1975, W. T. Grant Company filed for bankruptcy protection under Chapter XI of the Bankruptcy Act. At that time, assets totaled $1.02 billion and liabilities totaled $1.03 billion. The company operated at a profit for most years prior to 1974, but reported an operating loss of $177 million for its fiscal year January 31, 1974, to January 31, 1975.

   The accompanying Exhibits 18.25 through 18.28 contain:

   a.   Balance sheets, income statements, and statements of cash flows for W. T. Grant Company for the 1971 through 1975 fiscal periods.

   b.   Additional financial information about W. T. Grant Company, the retail industry, and the economy for the same period.

Prepare an analysis that explains the major causes of Grant's collapse. You may find it useful to refer to financial and nonfinancial data presented in other sources, such as *The Wall Street Journal,* in addition to that presented here. Assume an income tax rate of 48 percent.

Exhibit 18.25

W. T. GRANT COMPANY
Comparative Balance Sheets
(Problem 38)

	January 31				
	1971	1972	1973	1974	1975
Assets					
Cash and Marketable Securities..............	$ 34,009	$ 49,851	$ 30,943	$ 45,951	$ 79,642
Accounts Receivable........................	419,731	477,324	542,751	598,799	431,201
Inventories.................................	260,492	298,676	399,533	450,637	407,357
Other Current Assets	5,246	5,378	6,649	7,299	6,581
Total Current Assets	$719,478	$831,229	$ 979,876	$1,102,686	$ 924,781
Investments................................	23,936	32,367	35,581	45,451	49,764
Property, Plant, and Equipment (net)	61,832	77,173	91,420	100,984	101,932
Other Assets...............................	2,382	3,901	3,821	3,862	5,790
Total Assets	$807,628	$944,670	$1,110,698	$1,252,983	$1,082,267
Equities					
Short-Term Debt............................	$246,420	$237,741	$ 390,034	$ 453,097	$ 600,695
Accounts Payable	118,091	124,990	112,896	103,910	147,211
Current Deferred Taxes	94,489	112,846	130,137	133,057	2,000
Total Current Liabilities	$459,000	$475,577	$ 633,067	$ 690,064	$ 749,906
Long-Term Debt	32,301	128,432	126,672	220,336	216,341
Noncurrent Deferred Taxes	8,518	9,664	11,926	14,649	—
Other Long-Term Liabilities	5,773	5,252	4,694	4,195	2,183
Total Liabilities	$505,592	$618,925	$ 776,359	$ 929,244	$ 968,430
Preferred Stock	$ 9,600	$ 9,053	$ 8,600	$ 7,465	$ 7,465
Common Stock.............................	18,180	18,529	18,588	18,599	18,599
Additional Paid-in Capital...................	78,116	85,195	86,146	85,910	83,914
Retained Earnings	230,435	244,508	261,154	248,461	37,674
Total	$336,331	$357,285	$ 374,488	$ 360,435	$ 147,652
Less Cost of Treasury Stock.................	(34,295)	(31,540)	(40,149)	(36,696)	(33,815)
Total Shareholders' Equity	$302,036	$325,745	$ 334,339	$ 323,739	$ 113,837
Total Equities	$807,628	$944,670	$1,110,698	$1,252,983	$1,082,267

Exhibit 18.26

W. T. GRANT COMPANY
Statement of Income and Retained Earnings
(Problem 38)

	Years Ended January 31				
	1971	**1972**	**1973**	**1974**	**1975**
Sales......................................	$1,254,131	$1,374,811	$1,644,747	$1,849,802	$1,761,952
Concessions	4,986	3,439	3,753	3,971	4,238
Equity in Earnings	2,777	2,383	5,116	4,651	3,086
Other Income	2,874	3,102	1,188	3,063	3,376
Total Revenues	$1,264,768	$1,383,735	$1,654,804	$1,861,487	$1,772,652
Cost of Goods Sold.....................	$ 843,192	$ 931,237	$1,125,261	$1,282,945	$1,303,267
Selling, General, and Administration	329,768	373,816	444,377	518,280	540,953
Interest................................	18,874	16,452	21,127	51,047	199,238
Taxes: Current	21,140	13,487	9,588	(6,021)	(19,439)
Deferred	11,660	13,013	16,162	6,807	(98,027)
Other Expenses	557	518	502	—	24,000
Total Expenses......................	$1,225,191	$1,348,523	$1,617,017	$1,853,058	$1,949,992
Net Income	$ 39,577	$ 35,212	$ 37,787	$ 8,429	$ (177,340)
Dividends.............................	(20,821)	(21,139)	(21,141)	(21,122)	(4,457)
Other..................................	—	—	—	—	(28,990)
Change in Retained Earnings	$ 18,765	$ 14,073	$ 16,646	$ (12,693)	$ (210,787)
Retained Earnings— Beginning of Period..................	211,679	230,435	244,508	261,154	248,461
Retained Earnings— End of Period	$ 230,435	$ 244,508	$ 261,154	$ 248,461	$ 37,674

Exhibit 18.27

W. T. GRANT COMPANY
Statement of Cash Flows
(Problem 38)

	Years Ended January 31				
	1971	**1972**	**1973**	**1974**	**1975**
Operations					
Net Income	$39,577	$ 35,212	$ 37,787	$ 8,429	$(177,340)
Additions:					
Depreciation and Other	9,619	10,577	12,004	13,579	14,587
Decrease in Accounts Receivable	—	—	—	—	121,351
Decrease in Inventories	—	—	—	—	43,280
Increase in Accounts Payable................	13,947	6,900	—	—	42,028
Increase in Deferred Taxes	14,046	18,357	17,291	2,920	—
Subtractions:					
Equity in Earnings and Other	(2,470)	(1,758)	(1,699)	(1,344)	(16,993)
Increase in Accounts Receivable	(51,464)	(57,593)	(65,427)	(56,047)	—
Increase in Inventories	(38,365)	(38,184)	(100,857)	(51,104)	—
Increase in Prepayments	(209)	(428)	(1,271)	(651)	(11,032)
Decrease in Accounts Payable...............	—	—	(12,093)	(8,987)	—
Decrease in Deferred Taxes	—	—	—	—	(101,078)
Cash Flow from Operations....................	($15,319)	($ 26,917)	($114,265)	($ 93,205)	($ 85,197)
Investing					
Acquisitions:					
Property, Plant, and Equipment	($16,141)	($ 25,918)	($ 26,250)	($ 23,143)	($ 15,535)
Investments in Securities	(436)	(5,951)	(2,040)	(5,700)	(5,182)
Cash Flow from Investing	($16,577)	($ 31,869)	($ 28,290)	($ 28,843)	($ 20,717)
Financing					
New Financing:					
Short-Term Bank Borrowing	$64,288	—	$152,293	$ 63,063	$147,898
Issue of Long-Term Debt	—	$100,000	—	100,000	—
Sale of Common Stock:					
To Employees...........................	5,218	7,715	3,492	2,584	886
On Open Market	—	2,229	174	260	—
Reduction in Financing:					
Repayment of Short-Term Borrowing (net)	—	($ 8,680)	—	—	—
Retirement of Long-Term Debt	($ 1,538)	(5,143)	($ 1,760)	($ 6,336)	($ 3,995)
Reacquisition of Preferred Stock	(948)	(308)	(252)	(618)	—
Reacquisition of Common Stock...............	(13,224)	—	(11,466)	(133)	—
Dividends.....................................	(20,821)	(21,138)	(21,141)	(21,122)	(4,457)
Cash Flow from Financing......................	$32,975	$ 74,675	$121,340	$137,698	$140,332
Other...	(47)	(47)	2,307	(642)	(727)
Net Change in Cash	$ 1,032	$ 15,842	$(18,908)	$ 15,008	$ 33,691

Exhibit 18.28

**Additional Information
(Problem 38)**

	Fiscal Years Ending January 31				
	1971	1972	1973	1974	1975
W. T. Grant Company					
Range of Stock Price, Dollar per Share[a]	$41\frac{7}{8}$–$70\frac{5}{8}$	$34\frac{3}{4}$–$48\frac{3}{4}$	$9\frac{7}{8}$–$44\frac{3}{8}$	$9\frac{5}{8}$–41	$1\frac{1}{2}$–12
Earnings per Share in Dollars...........................	$2.64	$2.25	$2.49	$0.76	$(12.74)
Dividends per Share in Dollars........................	$1.50	$1.50	$1.50	$1.50	$ 0.30
Number of Stores	1,116	1,168	1,208	1,189	1,152
Total Store Area, Thousands of Square Feet	38,157	44,718	50,619	53,719	54,770

	Calendar Year Ending December 31				
	1970	1971	1972	1973	1974
Retail Industry[b]					
Total Chain Store Industry Sales in Millions of Dollars..	$6,969	$6,972	$7,498	$8,212	$8,714

	Calendar Year Ending December 31				
	1970	1971	1972	1973	1974
Aggregate Economy[c]					
Gross National Product in Billions of Dollars..............	$1,075.3	$1,107.5	$1,171.1	$1,233.4	$1,210
Bank Short-Term Lending Rate	8.48%	6.32%	5.82%	8.30%	11.28%

[a]Source: *Standard and Poor's Stock Reports.*

[b]Source: *Standard Industry Surveys.*

[c]Source: *Survey of Current Business.*

... APPENDIX ...

Compound Interest Examples and Applications

Managerial accountants and managers deal with interest calculations because expenditures for an asset most often precede the receipts for services that asset produces. Money received sooner is more valuable than money received later. The difference in timing can affect whether or not acquiring an asset is profitable. Amounts of money received at different times are different commodities. Managers use interest calculations to make valid comparisons among amounts of money their firm will pay or receive at different times.

Managers evaluate a series of money payments over time, such as from an investment project, by finding the present value of the series of payments. The *present value* of a series of payments is a single amount of money at the present time that is the economic equivalent of the entire series.

This appendix illustrates the use of compound interest techniques with a comprehensive series of examples.

Future Value

If you invest $1 today at 10 percent compounded annually, it will grow to $1.10000 at the end of 1 year, $1.21000 at the end of 2 years, $1.33100 at the end of 3 years, and so on, according to the formula

$$F_n = P(1 + r)^n,$$

where

F_n = accumulation or future value
P = one-time investment today

$$r = \text{interest rate per period}$$
$$n = \text{number of periods from today.}$$

The amount F_n is the future value of the present payment, P, compounded at r percent per period for n periods. Table 1, at the end of this appendix, shows the future values of $P = \$1$ for various periods and for various interest rates.

Example 1   How much will $1,000 deposited today at 8 percent compounded annually be worth 10 years from now?

One dollar deposited today at 8 percent will grow to $2.15892; therefore $1,000 will grow to $1,000(1.08)^{10} = \$1,000 \times 2.15892 = \$2,158.92$.

Present Value

This section deals with the problems of calculating how much principal, P, you must invest today to have a specified amount, F_n, at the end of n periods. You know the future amount, F_n, the interest rate, r, and the number of periods, n; you want to find P. To have $1 one year from today when deposits earn 8 percent, you must invest P of $.92593 today. That is, $F_1 = P(1.08)^1$ or $\$1 = \$.92593 \times 1.08$. Because $F_n = P(1 + r)^n$, dividing both sides of the equation by $(1 + r)^n$ yields

$$\frac{F_n}{(1 + r)^n} = P,$$

or

$$P = \frac{F_n}{(1 + r)^n} = F_n(1 + r)^{-n}.$$

Table 2 at the end of this appendix shows discount factors or, equivalently, present values of $1 for various interest (or discount) rates for various periods.

Example 2   What is the present value of $1 due 10 years from now if the interest rate (or, equivalently, the discount rate) r is 12 percent per year?

From Table 2, 12-percent column, 10-period row, the present value of $1 to be received 10 periods hence at 12 percent is $.32197.

Example 3   You project that an investment will generate cash of $13,500 three years from today. What is the net present value of this cash receipt today if the discount rate is 8 percent per year?

One dollar received 3 years hence discounted at 8 percent has a present value of $.79383. See Table 2, 3-period row, 8-percent column. Thus the project has present value $13,500 \times .79383 = \$10,717$. Exhibit A.1 shows how $10,717 grows to $13,500 in 3 years.

Exhibit A.1

Verification of Net Present Value of $10,717
Single Cash Flow of $13,500 at the End of Year 3
Discounted at 8 Percent per Year

Year	Beginning Amount	+ Interest at 8 Percent	= Ending Amount
1	$10,717	$ 857	$11,574
2	11,574	926	12,500
3	12,500	1,000	13,500

Changing the Compounding Period: Nominal and Effective Rates

"Twelve percent, compounded annually" is the price for a loan; this price means interest increases, or converts to, principal once a year at the rate of 12 percent. Often, however, the price for a loan states that compounding will take place more than once a year. A savings bank may advertise that it pays interest of 6 percent, compounded quarterly. This kind of payment means that at the end of each quarter the bank credits savings accounts with interest calculated at the rate 1.5 percent (= 6 percent/4). The investor can withdraw the interest payment or leave it on deposit to earn more interest.

If you invest $10,000 today at 12 percent compounded annually, it will grow to a future value 1 year later of $11,200. If the rate of interest is 12 percent compounded semiannually, the bank adds 6 percent interest to the principal every 6 months. At the end of the first 6 months, $10,000 will have grown to $10,600; that amount will grow to $10,600 × 1.06 = $11,236 by the end of the year. Notice that 12 percent compounded semiannually is equivalent to 12.36 percent compounded annually.

Suppose that the bank quotes interest as 12 percent, compounded quarterly. It will add an additional 3 percent of the principal every 3 months. By the end of the year, $10,000 will grow to $10,000 × $(1.03)^4$ = $10,000 × 1.12551 = $11,255. Twelve percent compounded quarterly is equivalent to 12.55 percent compounded annually. At 12 percent compounded monthly, $1 will grow to $1 × $(1.01)^{12}$ = $1.12683 and $10,000 will grow to $11,268. Thus, 12 percent compounded monthly is equivalent to 12.68 percent compounded annually.

For a given *nominal* rate, such as the 12 percent in the examples above, the more often interest compounds, the higher the *effective* rate of interest paid. If a nominal rate, r, compounds m times per year, the effective rate is equal to $(1 + r/m)^m - 1$.

In practice, to solve problems that require computation of interest quoted at a nominal rate r percent per period compounded m times per period for n periods, use the tables for rate r/m and $m \times n$ periods. For example, 12 percent compounded quarterly for 5 years is equivalent to the rate found in the interest tables for r = 12/4 = 3 percent for $m \times n$ = 4 × 5 = 20 periods.

Example 4   What is the future value 5 years hence of $600 invested at 8 percent compounded quarterly?

Eight percent compounded four times per year for 5 years is equivalent to 2 percent per period compounded for 20 periods. Table 1 shows the value of $F_{20} = (1.02)^{20}$ to be 1.48595. Six hundred dollars, then, would grow to $600 $\times$ 1.48595 = $891.57.

Example 5   How much money must you invest today at 12 percent compounded semiannually to have $1,000 four years from today?

Twelve percent compounded two times a year for 4 years is equivalent to 6 percent per period compounded for 8 periods. The *present value,* Table 2, of $1 received 8 periods hence at 6 percent per period is $.62741; that is, $.62741 invested today for 8 periods at an interest rate of 6 percent per period will grow to $1. To have $1,000 in 8 periods (4 years), you must invest $627.41 (= $1,000 $\times$ $.62741) today.

Example 6   A local department store offers its customers credit and advertises its interest rate at 18 percent per year, compounded monthly at the rate of 1½ percent per month. What is the effective annual interest rate?

One and one-half percent per month for 12 months is equivalent to $(1.015)^{12} - 1 = 19.562$ percent per year. See Table 1, 12-period row, 1½-percent column, where the factor is 1.19562.

Example 7   If prices increased at the rate of 6 percent during each of two consecutive 6-month periods, how much did prices increase during the entire year?

If a price index is 100.00 at the start of the year, it will be 100.00 $\times$ $(1.06)^2 = 112.36$ at the end of the year. The price change for the entire year is $(112.36/100.00) - 1 = 12.36$ percent.

Annuities

An *annuity* is a series of equal payments, one per equally spaced periods of time. Examples of annuities include monthly rental payments, semiannual corporate bond coupon (or interest) payments, and annual payments to a lessor under a lease contract. Armed with an understanding of the tables for future and present values, you can solve any annuity problem. Annuities arise so often, however, and their solution is so tedious without special tables that annuity problems merit special study and the use of special tables.

Terminology for Annuities

Annuity terminology can confuse you because not all writers use the same terms.

An annuity with payments occurring at the end of each period is an *ordinary annuity* or an *annuity in arrears*. Semiannual corporate bonds usually promise coupon payments paid in arrears or, equivalently, the first payment does not occur until after the bond has been outstanding for 6 months.

An annuity with payments occurring at the beginning of each period is an *annuity due* or an *annuity in advance*. Rent paid at the beginning of each month is an annuity due.

In a *deferred annuity,* the first payment occurs some time later than the end of the first period.

Annuities payments can go on forever. Such annuities are *perpetuities*. Bonds that promise payments forever are *consols*. The British and Canadian governments have issued consols from time to time. A perpetuity can be in arrears or in advance. The two differ only in the timing of the first payment.

Annuities may confuse you. Studying them is easier with a time line such as the one shown below.

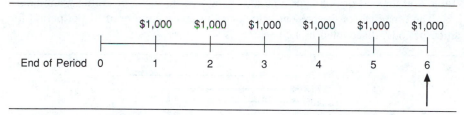

A time line marks the end of each period, numbers the period, shows the payments the investor receives or pays, and shows the time in which the accountant wants to value the annuity. The time line above represents an ordinary annuity (in arrears) for six periods of $100 to be valued at the end of period 6. The end of period 0 is "now." The first payment occurs one period from now.

Ordinary Annuities (Annuities in Arrears)

The future values of ordinary annuities appear in Table 3 at the end of this appendix.

Consider an ordinary annuity for three periods at 12 percent. The time line for the future value of such an annuity is

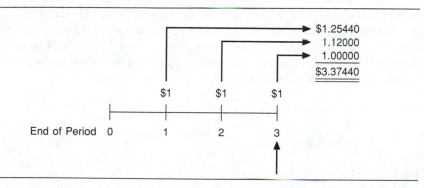

The $1 received at the end of the first period earns interest for two periods, so it is worth $1.25440 at the end of period 3. (See Table 1.) The $1 received at the end of the second period grows to $1.12000 by the end of period 3, and the $1 received at the end of period 3 is, of course, worth $1.00000 at the end of period 3. The entire annuity is worth $3.37440 at the end of period 3. This amount appears in Table 3 for the future value of an ordinary annuity for three periods at 12 percent. Factors for the future value of an annuity for a particular number of periods sum the factors for the future value of $1 for each of the periods. The future value of an ordinary annuity is

$$\text{Future Value of Ordinary Annuity} = \text{Periodic Payment} \times \text{Factor for the Future Value of an Ordinary Annuity.}$$

Thus,

$$\$3.37440 \quad = \quad \$1 \quad \times \quad 3.37440.$$

Table 4 at the end of this appendix shows the present value of ordinary annuities.

The time line for the present value of an ordinary annuity of $1 per period for three periods, discounted at 12 percent, is

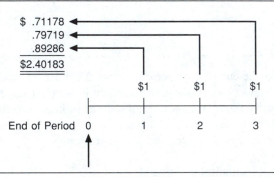

The $1 the investor receives at the end of period 1 has a present value of $.89286, the $1 the investor receives at the end of period 2 has a present value of $.79719, and the dollar the investor receives at the end of the third period has a present value of $.71178. Each of these numbers comes from Table 2. The present value of the annuity is the sum of these individual present values, $2.40183, shown in Table 4.

The present value of an ordinary annuity for n periods is the sum of the present value of $1 received one period from now plus the present value of $1 received two periods from now, and so on until we add on the present value of $1 received n periods from now. The present value of an ordinary annuity is

$$\text{Present Value of an Ordinary Annuity} = \text{Periodic Payment} \times \text{Factor for the Present Value of an Ordinary Annuity.}$$

Thus,

$$\$2.40183 \quad = \quad \$1 \quad \times \quad \$2.40183.$$

Example 8   Accountants project an investment to generate $1,000 at the end of each of the next 20 years. If the interest rate is 8 percent compounded annually, what will the future value of these flows be at the end of 20 years?

The time line for this problem is

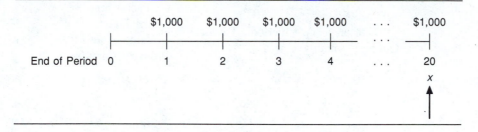

The symbol x denotes the amount you must calculate. Table 3 indicates that the factor for the future value of an annuity at 8 percent for 20 periods is 45.76196. Thus,

$$
\begin{array}{ccc}
\text{Future Value} & & \text{Factor for} \\
\text{of an} & = \text{Periodic Payment} \times & \text{the Future} \\
\text{Ordinary Annuity} & & \text{Value of an} \\
& & \text{Ordinary Annuity}
\end{array}
$$

$$
\begin{aligned}
x &= \quad \$1,000 \quad \times \quad 45.76196 \\
x &= \quad \$45,762.
\end{aligned}
$$

The cash flows have future value of $45,762.

Example 9   Parents want to accumulate a fund to send their child to college. The parents will invest a fixed amount at the end of each calendar quarter for the next 10 years. The funds will accumulate in a savings certificate that promises to pay 8 percent interest compounded quarterly. What amount must the parents invest to accumulate a fund of $50,000?

The time line for this problem is

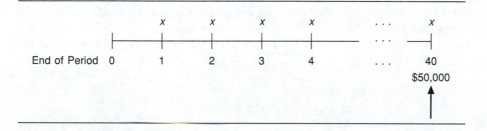

This problem is similar to Example 8 because both involve periodic investments of cash that accumulate interest over time until a specific time in the future. In Example 8, you know the periodic investment and compute the future value. In Example 9, you know the future value and compute the periodic investment. Table 3 indicates that the future value of an annuity at 2 percent (= 8 percent per year/4 quarters per year) per period for 40 (= 4 quarters per year × 10 years) periods is 60.40198. Thus,

$$\begin{array}{ccc} \text{Future Value} & & \text{Factor for} \\ \text{of an} & = \text{Periodic Payment} \times & \text{the Future} \\ \text{Ordinary Annuity} & & \text{Value of an} \\ & & \text{Ordinary Annuity} \end{array}$$

$$\$50{,}000 = x \times 60.40198$$

$$x = \frac{\$50{,}000}{60.40198}$$

$$x = \$828.$$

Because you want to find the periodic payment, you divide the future value amount of $50,000 by the future value factor.

Example 10   A firm borrows $30,000 from an insurance company. The interest rate on the loan is 8 percent compounded semiannually. The firm agrees to repay the loan in equal semiannual installments over the next 5 years and make the first payment 6 months from now. What is the amount of the required semiannual payment?

The time line is

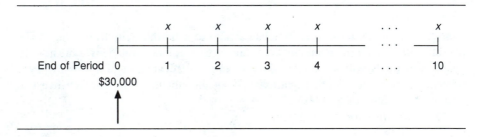

You know the present value and must compute the period payment. Table 4 indicates that the present value of an annuity at 4 percent (= 8 percent per year/2 semiannual periods per year) for 10 periods (= 2 periods per year × 5 years) is 8.11090. Thus,

$$\begin{array}{ccc} \text{Present Value} & & \text{Factor for} \\ \text{of an} & = \text{Periodic Payment} \times & \text{the Present} \\ \text{Ordinary Annuity} & & \text{Value of an} \\ & & \text{Ordinary Annuity} \end{array}$$

$$\$30{,}000 = x \times 8.11090$$

$$x = \frac{\$30{,}000}{8.11090}$$

$$x = \$3{,}699.$$

Exhibit A.2

Amortization Schedule for $30,000 Mortgage, Repaid in
10 Semiannual Installments of $3,700, Interest Rate of
8 Percent, Compounded Semiannually

6-Month Period (1)	Mortgage Principal Start of Period (2)	Interest Expense for Period (3)	Payment (4)	Portion of Payment Reducing Principal (5)	Mortgage Principal End of Period (6)
0					$30,000
1	$30,000	$1,200	$3,700	$2,500	27,500
2	27,500	1,100	3,700	2,600	24,900
3	24,900	996	3,700	2,704	22,196
4	22,196	888	3,700	2,812	19,384
5	19,384	775	3,700	2,925	16,459
6	16,459	658	3,700	3,042	13,417
7	13,417	537	3,700	3,163	10,254
8	10,254	410	3,700	3,290	6,964
9	6,964	279	3,700	3,421	3,543
10	3,543	142	3,685	3,543	0

Column (2) = column (6) from previous period.

Column (3) = .04 × column (2).

Column (4) is given, except row 10, where it is the amount such that column (4) = column (2) + column (3).

Column (5) = column (4) − column (3).

Column (6) = column (2) − column (5).

Because you are finding the periodic payment, you divide the present value amount of $30,000 by the present value factor. Exhibit A.2 shows how periodic payments of $3,700 amortize the loan. We call such a schedule an *amortization schedule*. If the periodic payments were $3,699, not $3,700, the "error" in the final payment would be even smaller.

Example 11   A company signs a lease acquiring the right to use property for 3 years. The company promises to make lease payments of $19,709 annually at the end of this and the next 2 years. The discount, or interest, rate is 15 percent per year. What is the present value of the lease payments, which is the equivalent cash purchase price for this property?

The time line is

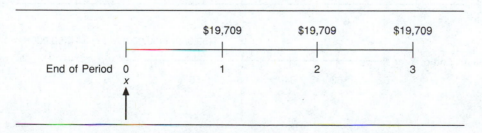

The factor from Table 4 for the present value of an annuity at 15 percent for 3 periods is 2.28323. Thus,

<table>
<tr><td>Present Value
of an
Ordinary Annuity</td><td>= Periodic Payment ×</td><td>Factor for
the Present
Value of an
Ordinary Annuity</td></tr>
<tr><td>x =</td><td>$19,709 ×</td><td>2.28323</td></tr>
<tr><td>x =</td><td>$45,000.</td><td></td></tr>
</table>

Example 12   Mr. Mason is 62 years old. He wishes to invest equal amounts on his sixty-third, sixty-fourth, and sixty-fifth birthdays so that starting on his sixty-sixth birthday he can withdraw $50,000 on each birthday for 10 years. His investments will earn 8 percent per year. How much should he invest on the sixty-third through sixty-fifth birthdays?

The time line for this problem is

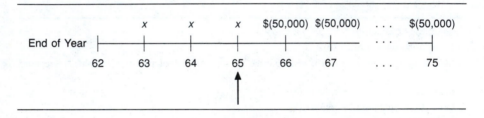

At 65, Mr. Mason needs to have accumulated a fund equal to the present value of an annuity of $50,000 per period for 10 periods, discounted at 8 percent per period. The factor from Table 4 for 8 percent and 10 periods is 6.71008. Thus,

<table>
<tr><td>Present Value
of an
Ordinary Annuity</td><td>= Periodic Payment ×</td><td>Factor for
the Present
Value of an
Ordinary Annuity</td></tr>
<tr><td>x =</td><td>$50,000 ×</td><td>6.71008</td></tr>
<tr><td>x =</td><td>$335,504.</td><td></td></tr>
</table>

The time line now appears as follows:

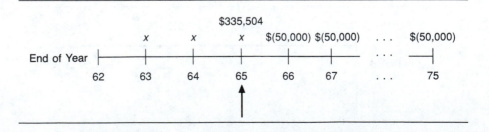

The question now becomes: How much must Mr. Mason invest on his sixty-third, sixty-fourth, and sixty-fifth birthdays to accumulate a fund of $335,504 on his sixty-fifth birthday? The factor for the future value of an annuity for three periods at 8 percent is 3.24640. Thus,

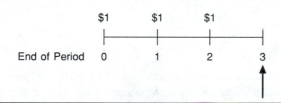

Future Value
of an = Periodic Payment ×
Ordinary Annuity

Factor for
the Future
Value of an
Ordinary Annuity

$$\$335,504 \quad = \quad x \quad \times \quad 3.24640$$

$$x \quad = \quad \frac{\$335,504}{3.24640}$$

$$x \quad = \quad \$103,346.$$

Annuities in Advance (Annuities Due)

The time line for the future value of a three-period annuity in advance is

Notice that we calculated the future value for the *end* of the period in which the last payment occurs. When you have tables of ordinary annuities, tables for annuities due are unnecessary.

To see this, compare the time line for the future value of an annuity in advance for three periods with the time axis relabeled to show the start of the period and the time line for the future value of an ordinary annuity (in arrears) for four periods.

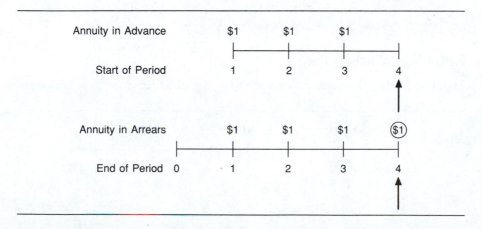

A $1 annuity in advance for *n* periods has a future value equal to the future value of a $1 annuity in arrears for *n* + 1 periods *minus* $1. The $1 circled in the time line for the annuity in arrears is the $1 that you must subtract to calculate the future value of an annuity in advance. Note that no annuity payment occurs at the end of period 3. The note at the foot of Table 3 states: "To convert from this table to values of an annuity in advance, find the annuity in arrears above for one more period and subtract 1.00000."

Example Problem Involving Future Value of Annuity Due

Example 13   A student plans to invest $1,000 a year at the beginning of each of the next 10 years in certificates of deposit paying interest of 12 percent per year, making the first payment today. What will be the amount of the certificates at the end of the tenth year?

   The time line is

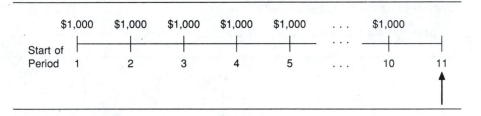

The factor for the future value of an annuity for 11 (= 10 + 1) periods is 20.65458. Because a $1,000 investment does not occur at the end of the tenth year, you subtract 1.000000 from 20.65458 to obtain the factor for the annuity in advance of 19.65458. The future value of the annuity in advance is

$$\begin{array}{c}\text{Future Value} \\ \text{of an} \\ \text{Annuity} \\ \text{in Advance}\end{array} = \text{Periodic Payment} \times \begin{array}{c}\text{Factor for} \\ \text{the Future Value} \\ \text{of an} \\ \text{Annuity} \\ \text{in Advance}\end{array}$$

$$x = \$1,000 \times 19.65458$$
$$x = \$19,655.$$

Present Value of Annuity Due

The time line for the present value of an annuity in advance for three periods is

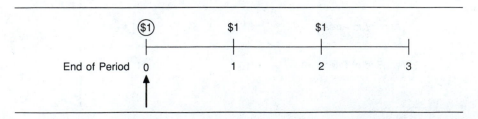

Notice that except for the first, circled payment, it looks just like the present value of an ordinary annuity for two periods. A $1 annuity in advance for n periods has a present value equal to the present value of a $1 annuity in arrears for $n - 1$ periods *plus* $1. The note at the foot of Table 4 states: "To convert from this table to values of an annuity in advance, find the annuity in arrears above for one fewer period and add 1.00000."

Example 14   What is the present value of rents of $350 paid monthly, in advance, for 1 year when the discount rate is 1 percent per month?

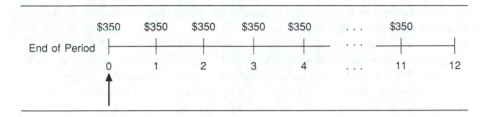

The present value of $1 per period *in arrears* for 11 periods at 1 percent per period is $10.36763; the present value of $1 per period in advance for 12 periods is $10.36763 + $1.00 = $11.36763, and the present value of this year's rent is $350 \times 11.36763 = $3,979.

Deferred Annuities

When the first payment of an annuity occurs some time after the end of the first period, the annuity is *deferred*. The time line for an ordinary annuity of $1 per period for four periods deferred for two periods is

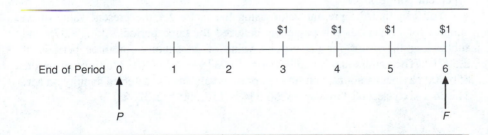

The arrow marked P shows the time of which the present value calculation; the arrow marked F shows the future value calculation. The deferral does not affect the future value, which equals the future value of an ordinary annuity for four periods.

Notice that the time line for the present value looks like one for an ordinary annuity for six periods *minus* an ordinary annuity for two periods:

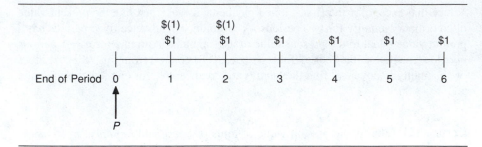

Calculate the present value of an annuity of n payments deferred for d periods by subtracting the present value of an annuity for d periods from the present value of an annuity for $n + d$ periods.

Example 15   Refer to the data in Example 12. Recall that Mr. Mason wants to withdraw $50,000 per year on his sixty-sixth through his seventy-fifth birthdays. He wishes to invest a sufficient amount on his sixty-third, sixty-fourth, and sixty-fifth birthdays to provide a fund for the later withdrawals.

The time line is

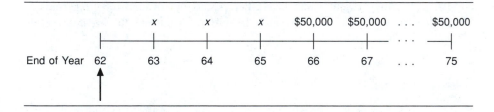

As of his sixty-second birthday, the $50,000 series of payments on Mr. Mason's sixty-sixth through seventy-fifth birthdays is a deferred annuity. The interest rate is 8 percent per year.

You can find the present value using the factor for the present value of an annuity for 13 periods (10 payments deferred for three periods) of 7.90378 and subtracting the factor for the present value of an annuity for three periods of 2.57710. The net amount is 5.32668 (= 7.90378 − 2.57710). Multiplying by the $50,000 payment amount, you find the present value of the deferred annuity on Mr. Mason's sixty-second birthday ($266,334 = $50,000 × 5.32668).

Perpetuities

A periodic payment to be received forever is a *perpetuity*. Future values of perpetuities are undefined. One dollar to be received at the end of every period discounted at rate r percent has present value of $1/r$. Observe what happens in the expression for the present value of an ordinary annuity of $A per payment as n, the number of payments, approaches infinity:

$$P_A = \frac{A[1 - (1 + r)^{-n}]}{r}.$$

As n approaches infinity, $(1 + r)^{-n}$ approaches zero, so P_A approaches $A(1/r)$. If the first payment of the perpetuity occurs now, the present value is $A[1 + (1/r)]$.

Example 16   The Canadian government offers to pay $30 every 6 months forever in the form of a perpetual bond. What is that bond worth if the discount rate is 10 percent compounded semiannually?

Ten percent compounded semiannually is equivalent to 5 percent per 6-month period. If the first payment occurs 6 months from now, the present value is $30/.05 = $600. If the first payment occurs today, the present value is $30 + $600 = $630.

Implicit Interest Rates: Finding Internal Rates of Return

The preceding examples computed a future value or a present value given the interest rate and stated cash payments. Or, they computed the required payments given their known future value or their known present value. In some calculations, we know the present or future value and the periodic payments; we must find the implicit interest rate. Assume, for example, a case in which we know that a cash investment of $10,500 will grow to $13,500 in 3 years. What is the implicit interest rate, or market rate of return, on this investment? The time line for this problem is

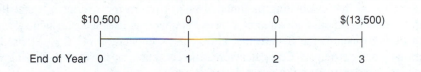

The implicit interest rate is r, such that

(A.1) $$\$10,500 = \frac{\$13,500}{(1 + r)^3}.$$

(A.2) $$0 = \$10,500 - \frac{\$13,500}{(1 + r)^3}.$$

In other words, the present value of $13,500 discounted three periods at r percent per period is $10,500. The present value of all current and future cash flows nets to zero when future flows are discounted at r percent per period. In general, the only way to find such an r is a trial-and-error procedure.[1] The procedure is finding the internal rate of return of a series of cash flows. The *internal rate of return* of a series of cash flows is the discount rate that equates the net present value of that series of cash flows to zero. Follow these steps to find the internal rate of return:

1. Make an educated guess, called the "trial rate," at the internal rate of return. If you have no idea what to guess, try zero.

2. Calculate the present value of all the cash flows (including the one at the end of year 0).

3. If the present value of the cash flows is zero, stop. The current trial rate is the internal rate of return.

4. If the amount found in step 2 is less than zero, try a larger interest rate as the trial rate and go back to step 2.

5. If the amount found in step 2 is greater than zero, try a smaller interest rate as the new trial rate and go back to step 2.

The following iterations illustrate the process for the example in Equation A.1.

Iteration Number	Trial Rate = r	Net Present Values: Right-Hand Side of A.2
1	0.00%	$(3,000)
2	10.00	357
3	5.00	(1,162)
4	7.50	(367)
5	8.75	3

With a trial rate of 8.75 percent, the right-hand side is close enough to zero so that you can use 8.75 percent as the implicit interest rate. Continued iterations would find trial rates even closer to the true rate, which is about 8.7380 percent.

You may find calculating the internal rate of return for a series of cash flows tedious and you should not attempt it unless you have at least a desk calculator. An exponential feature, the feature that allows the computation of $(1 + r)$ raised to various powers, helps.[2] Computer spreadsheets, such as LOTUS 1-2-3, have a built-in function to find the internal rate of return.

Example 17 The Alexis Company acquires a machine with a cash price of $10,500. It pays for the machine by giving a note for $12,000 promising to make payments equal to 7 percent of the face value, $840 (= .07 × $12,000), at the end of each of the next 3 years and a single payment of $12,000 in 3 years. What is the implicit interest rate in the loan?

---

[1] In cases where r appears in only one term, as here, you can find r analytically. Here, $r = (\$13,500/\$10,500)^{1/3} - 1 = .087380$.

[2] You may use other methods to guess the trial rate that will approximate the true rate in fewer iterations than the method described here. If you want to find internal rates of return efficiently with successive trial rates, refer to a mathematical reference book to learn about the "Newton search" method, sometimes called the "method of false position."

The time line for this problem is

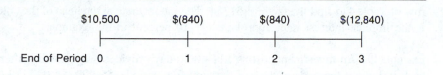

	$10,500	$(840)	$(840)	$(12,840)
End of Period	0	1	2	3

The implicit interest rate is r, such that[3]

$$(A.3) \qquad \$10,500 = \frac{\$840}{(1 + r)} + \frac{\$840}{(1 + r)^2} + \frac{\$12,840}{(1 + r)^3}.$$

The iteration process finds internal rate of return of 12.2 percent to the nearest tenth of 1 percent:

Iteration Number	Trial Rate	Right-Hand Side of A.3
1	7.0%	$12,000
2	15.0	9,808
3	11.0	10,827
4	13.0	10,300
5	12.0	10,559
6	12.5	10,428
7	12.3	10,480
8	12.2	10,506
9	12.1	10,533

Example 18   In some contexts, such as mortgages or leases, one knows the amount of a series of future periodic payments, which are identical in all periods, and the present value of those future payments. For example, a firm may borrow $100,000 and agree to repay the loan, in 20 payments of $11,746 each, at the end of each of the next 20 years. To calculate interest expense each period, you must find the interest rate implicit in the loan.

You have the following information:

$$\begin{array}{ccc}
\text{Present Value} \\
\text{of an} & = \text{Periodic Payment} \times & \text{Factor for} \\
\text{Ordinary Annuity} & & \text{the Present} \\
& & \text{Value of an} \\
& & \text{Ordinary Annuity}
\end{array}$$

$100,000	=	$11,746	×	x
x	=	$\dfrac{\$100,000}{\$11,746}$		
x	=	8.51354.		

---

[3]Compare this formulation to that in Equation A.2. Note that the left-hand side is zero in one case but not in the other. The left-hand side can be either nonzero or zero, depending on what seems convenient for the particular context.

The factor to discount 20 payments of $11,746 to a present value of $100,000 is 8.51354. To find the interest rate implicit in the discounting, scan the 20-payment row of Table 4 to find the factor 8.51354. The interest rate at the head of the column is the implicit interest rate, approximately 10 percent in the example.

Example 19   An investment costing $11,400 today provides the following after-tax cash inflows at the ends of each of the next five periods: $5,000, $4,000, $3,000, $2,000, $1,000. What is the internal rate of return on these flows? That is, find r such that

$$(A.4) \ 0 = \$(11,400) + \frac{\$5,000}{(1 + r)} + \frac{\$4,000}{(1 + r)^2} + \frac{\$3,000}{(1 + r)^3} + \frac{\$2,000}{(1 + r)^4} + \frac{\$1,000}{(1 + r)^5}.$$

Trial rates r produced the following sequence of estimates of the internal rate of return:

Iteration Number	Trial Rate	Right-Hand Side of A.4
1	0.00%	$3,600
2	10.00	692
3	15.00	(414)
4	12.50	115
5	13.50	(102)
6	13.00	6
7	13.10	(16)
8	13.01	4
9	13.02	2
10	13.03	(1)

The estimating process proceeds several steps further than necessary. To the nearest whole percentage point, the internal rate of return is 13 percent.

To the nearest one-hundredth of a percent, the internal rate of return is 13.03 percent. Futher trials find an even more precise answer, $r = 13.027$ percent. Physical scientists learn early in their training not to use more significant digits in calculations than the accuracy of the measuring devices merits. Accountants, too, should not carry calculations beyond the point of accuracy. Given the likely uncertainty in the estimates of cash flows, an estimate of the internal rate of return accurate to the nearest whole percentage point will serve its intended purpose.

Compound Interest and Annuity Tables

Table 1

Future Value of $1

$F_n = P(1 + r)^n$

r = interest rate; n = number of periods until valuation; $P = \$1$

Periods = n	½%	1%	1½%	2%	3%	4%	5%	6%	7%	8%	10%	12%	15%	20%	25%
1	1.00500	1.01000	1.01500	1.02000	1.03000	1.04000	1.05000	1.06000	1.07000	1.08000	1.10000	1.12000	1.15000	1.20000	1.25000
2	1.01003	1.02010	1.03023	1.04040	1.06090	1.08160	1.10250	1.12360	1.14490	1.16640	1.21000	1.25440	1.32250	1.44000	1.56250
3	1.01508	1.03030	1.04568	1.06121	1.09273	1.12486	1.15763	1.19102	1.22504	1.25971	1.33100	1.40493	1.52088	1.72800	1.95313
4	1.02015	1.04060	1.06136	1.08243	1.12551	1.16986	1.21551	1.26248	1.31080	1.36049	1.46410	1.57352	1.74901	2.07360	2.44141
5	1.02525	1.05101	1.07728	1.10408	1.15927	1.21665	1.27628	1.33823	1.40255	1.46933	1.61051	1.76234	2.01136	2.48832	3.05176
6	1.03038	1.06152	1.09344	1.12616	1.19405	1.26532	1.34010	1.41852	1.50073	1.58687	1.77156	1.97382	2.31306	2.98598	3.81470
7	1.03553	1.07214	1.10984	1.14869	1.22987	1.31593	1.40710	1.50363	1.60578	1.71382	1.94872	2.21068	2.66002	3.58318	4.76637
8	1.04071	1.08286	1.12649	1.17166	1.26677	1.36857	1.47746	1.59385	1.71819	1.85093	2.14359	2.47596	3.05902	4.29982	5.96046
9	1.04591	1.09369	1.14339	1.19509	1.30477	1.42331	1.55133	1.68948	1.83846	1.99900	2.35795	2.77308	3.51788	5.15978	7.45058
10	1.05114	1.10462	1.16054	1.21899	1.34392	1.48024	1.62889	1.79085	1.96715	2.15892	2.59374	3.10585	4.04556	6.19174	9.31323
11	1.05640	1.11567	1.17795	1.24337	1.38423	1.53945	1.71034	1.89830	2.10485	2.33164	2.85312	3.47855	4.65239	7.43008	11.64153
12	1.06168	1.12683	1.19562	1.26824	1.42576	1.60103	1.79586	2.01220	2.25219	2.51817	3.13843	3.89598	5.35025	8.91610	14.55192
13	1.06699	1.13809	1.21355	1.29361	1.46853	1.66507	1.88565	2.13293	2.40985	2.71962	3.45227	4.36349	6.15279	10.69932	18.18989
14	1.07232	1.14947	1.23176	1.31948	1.51259	1.73168	1.97993	2.26090	2.57853	2.93719	3.79750	4.88711	7.07571	12.83918	22.73737
15	1.07768	1.16097	1.25023	1.34587	1.55797	1.80094	2.07893	2.39656	2.75903	3.17217	4.17725	5.47357	8.13706	15.40702	28.42171
16	1.08307	1.17258	1.26899	1.37279	1.60471	1.87298	2.18287	2.54035	2.95216	3.42594	4.59497	6.13039	9.35762	18.48843	35.52714
17	1.08849	1.18430	1.28802	1.40024	1.65285	1.94790	2.29202	2.69277	3.15882	3.70002	5.05447	6.86604	10.76126	22.18611	44.40892
18	1.09393	1.19615	1.30734	1.42825	1.70243	2.02582	2.40662	2.85434	3.37993	3.99602	5.55992	7.68997	12.37545	26.62333	55.51115
19	1.09940	1.20811	1.32695	1.45681	1.75351	2.10685	2.52695	3.02560	3.61653	4.31570	6.11591	8.61276	14.23177	31.94800	69.38894
20	1.10490	1.22019	1.34686	1.48595	1.80611	2.19112	2.65330	3.20714	3.86968	4.66096	6.72750	9.64629	16.36654	38.33760	86.73617
22	1.11597	1.24472	1.38756	1.54598	1.91610	2.36992	2.92526	3.60354	4.43040	5.43654	8.14027	12.10031	21.64475	55.20614	135.5253
24	1.12716	1.26973	1.42950	1.60844	2.03279	2.56330	3.22510	4.04893	5.07237	6.34118	9.84973	15.17863	28.62518	79.49685	211.7582
26	1.13846	1.29526	1.47271	1.67342	2.15659	2.77247	3.55567	4.54938	5.80735	7.39635	11.91818	19.04007	37.85680	114.4755	330.8722
28	1.14987	1.32129	1.51722	1.74102	2.28793	2.99870	3.92013	5.11169	6.64884	8.62711	14.42099	23.88387	50.06561	164.8447	516.9879
30	1.16140	1.34785	1.56308	1.81136	2.42726	3.24340	4.32194	5.74349	7.61226	10.06266	17.44940	29.95992	66.21177	237.3763	807.7936
32	1.17304	1.37494	1.61032	1.88454	2.57508	3.50806	4.76494	6.45339	8.71527	11.73708	21.11378	37.58173	87.56507	341.8219	1262.177
34	1.18480	1.40258	1.65900	1.96068	2.73191	3.79432	5.25335	7.25103	9.97811	13.69013	25.54767	47.14252	115.80480	492.2235	1972.152
36	1.19668	1.43077	1.70914	2.03989	2.89828	4.10393	5.79182	8.14725	11.42394	15.96817	30.91268	59.13557	153.15185	708.8019	3081.488
38	1.20868	1.45953	1.76080	2.12230	3.07478	4.43881	6.38548	9.15425	13.07927	18.62528	37.40434	74.17966	202.54332	1020.675	4814.825
40	1.22079	1.48886	1.81402	2.20804	3.26204	4.80102	7.03999	10.28572	14.97446	21.72452	45.25926	93.05097	267.86355	1469.772	7523.164
45	1.25162	1.56481	1.95421	2.43785	3.78160	5.84118	8.98501	13.76461	21.00245	31.92045	72.89048	163.9876	538.76927	3657.262	22958.87
50	1.28323	1.64463	2.10524	2.69159	4.38391	7.10668	11.46740	18.42015	29.45703	46.90161	117.3909	289.0022	1083.65744	9100.438	70064.92
100	1.64667	2.70481	4.43205	7.24465	19.21863	50.50495	131.5013	339.3021	867.7163	2199.761	13780.61	83522.27	117×10^4	828×10^5	491×10^7

Table 2

Present Value of $1

$$P = F_n(1+r)^{-n}$$

r = discount rate; n = number of periods until payment; F = 1

Periods = n	½%	1%	1½%	2%	3%	4%	5%	6%	7%	8%	10%	12%	15%	20%	25%
1	.99502	.99010	.98522	.98039	.97087	.96154	.95238	.94340	.93458	.92593	.90909	.89286	.86957	.83333	.80000
2	.99007	.98030	.97066	.96117	.94260	.92456	.90703	.89000	.87344	.85734	.82645	.79719	.75614	.69444	.64000
3	.98515	.97059	.95632	.94232	.91514	.88900	.86384	.83962	.81630	.79383	.75131	.71178	.65752	.57870	.51200
4	.98025	.96098	.94218	.92385	.88849	.85480	.82270	.79209	.76290	.73503	.68301	.63552	.57175	.48225	.40960
5	.97537	.95147	.92826	.90573	.86261	.82193	.78353	.74726	.71299	.68058	.62092	.56743	.49718	.40188	.32768
6	.97052	.94205	.91454	.88797	.83748	.79031	.74622	.70496	.66634	.63017	.56447	.50663	.43233	.33490	.26214
7	.96569	.93272	.90103	.87056	.81309	.75992	.71068	.66506	.62275	.58349	.51316	.45235	.37594	.27908	.20972
8	.96089	.92348	.88771	.85349	.78941	.73069	.67684	.62741	.58201	.54027	.46651	.40388	.32690	.23257	.16777
9	.95610	.91434	.87459	.83676	.76642	.70259	.64461	.59190	.54393	.50025	.42410	.36061	.28426	.19381	.13422
10	.95135	.90529	.86167	.82035	.74409	.67556	.61391	.55839	.50835	.46319	.38554	.32197	.24718	.16151	.10737
11	.94661	.89632	.84893	.80426	.72242	.64958	.58468	.52679	.47509	.42888	.35049	.28748	.21494	.13459	.08590
12	.94191	.88745	.83639	.78849	.70138	.62460	.55684	.49697	.44401	.39711	.31863	.25668	.18691	.11216	.06872
13	.93722	.87866	.82403	.77303	.68095	.60057	.53032	.46884	.41496	.36770	.28966	.22917	.16253	.09346	.05498
14	.93256	.86996	.81185	.75788	.66112	.57748	.50507	.44230	.38782	.34046	.26333	.20462	.14133	.07789	.04398
15	.92792	.86135	.79985	.74301	.64186	.55526	.48102	.41727	.36245	.31524	.23939	.18270	.12289	.06491	.03518
16	.92330	.85282	.78803	.72845	.62317	.53391	.45811	.39365	.33873	.29189	.21763	.16312	.10686	.05409	.02815
17	.91871	.84438	.77639	.71416	.60502	.51337	.43630	.37136	.31657	.27027	.19784	.14564	.09293	.04507	.02252
18	.91414	.83602	.76491	.70016	.58739	.49363	.41552	.35034	.29586	.25025	.17986	.13004	.08081	.03756	.01801
19	.90959	.82774	.75361	.68643	.57029	.47464	.39573	.33051	.27651	.23171	.16351	.11611	.07027	.03130	.01441
20	.90506	.81954	.74247	.67297	.55368	.45639	.37689	.31180	.25842	.21455	.14864	.10367	.06110	.02608	.01153
22	.89608	.80340	.72069	.64684	.52189	.42196	.34185	.27751	.22571	.18394	.12285	.08264	.04620	.01811	.00738
24	.88719	.78757	.69954	.62172	.49193	.39012	.31007	.24698	.19715	.15770	.10153	.06588	.03493	.01258	.00472
26	.87838	.77205	.67902	.59758	.46369	.36069	.28124	.21981	.17220	.13520	.08391	.05252	.02642	.00874	.00302
28	.86966	.75684	.65910	.57437	.43708	.33348	.25509	.19563	.15040	.11591	.06934	.04187	.01997	.00607	.00193
30	.86103	.74192	.63976	.55207	.41199	.30832	.23138	.17411	.13137	.09938	.05731	.03338	.01510	.00421	.00124
32	.85248	.72730	.62099	.53063	.38834	.28506	.20987	.15496	.11474	.08520	.04736	.02661	.01142	.00293	.00079
34	.84402	.71297	.60277	.51003	.36604	.26355	.19035	.13791	.10022	.07305	.03914	.02121	.00864	.00203	.00051
36	.83564	.69892	.58509	.49022	.34503	.24367	.17266	.12274	.08754	.06262	.03235	.01691	.00653	.00141	.00032
38	.82735	.68515	.56792	.47119	.32523	.22529	.15661	.10924	.07646	.05369	.02673	.01348	.00494	.00098	.00021
40	.81914	.67165	.55126	.45289	.30656	.20829	.14205	.09722	.06678	.04603	.02209	.01075	.00373	.00068	.00013
45	.79896	.63905	.51171	.41020	.26444	.17120	.11130	.07265	.04761	.03133	.01372	.00610	.00186	.00027	.00004
50	.77929	.60804	.47500	.37153	.22811	.14071	.08720	.05429	.03395	.02132	.00852	.00346	.00092	.00011	.00001
100	.60729	.36971	.22563	.13803	.05203	.01980	.00760	.00295	.00115	.00045	.00007	.00001	.00000	.00000	.00000

Table 3

Future Value of Annuity of $1 in Arrears

$$F = \frac{(1+r)^n - 1}{r}$$

r = interest rate; n = number of payments

No. of Payments = n	½%	1%	1½%	2%	3%	4%	5%	6%	7%	8%	10%	12%	15%	20%	25%
1	1.00000	1.00000	1.00000	1.00000	1.00000	1.00000	1.00000	1.00000	1.00000	1.00000	1.00000	1.00000	1.00000	1.00000	1.00000
2	2.00500	2.01000	2.01500	2.02000	2.03000	2.04000	2.05000	2.06000	2.07000	2.08000	2.10000	2.12000	2.15000	2.20000	2.25000
3	3.01503	3.03010	3.04523	3.06040	3.09090	3.12160	3.15250	3.18360	3.21490	3.24640	3.31000	3.37440	3.47250	3.64000	3.81250
4	4.03010	4.06040	4.09090	4.12161	4.18363	4.24646	4.31013	4.37462	4.43994	4.50611	4.64100	4.77933	4.99338	5.36800	5.76563
5	5.05025	5.10101	5.15227	5.20404	5.30914	5.41632	5.52563	5.63709	5.75074	5.86660	6.10510	6.35285	6.74238	7.44160	8.20703
6	6.07550	6.15202	6.22955	6.30812	6.46841	6.63298	6.80191	6.97532	7.15329	7.33593	7.71561	8.11519	8.75374	9.92992	11.25879
7	7.10588	7.21354	7.32299	7.43428	7.66246	7.89829	8.14201	8.39384	8.65402	8.92280	9.48717	10.08901	11.06680	12.91590	15.07349
8	8.14141	8.28567	8.43284	8.58297	8.89234	9.21423	9.54911	9.89747	10.25980	10.63663	11.43589	12.29969	13.72682	16.49908	19.84186
9	9.18212	9.36853	9.55933	9.75463	10.15911	10.58280	11.02656	11.49132	11.97799	12.48756	13.57948	14.77566	16.78584	20.79890	25.80232
10	10.22803	10.46221	10.70272	10.94972	11.46388	12.00611	12.57789	13.18079	13.81645	14.48656	15.93742	17.54874	20.30372	25.95868	33.25290
11	11.27917	11.56683	11.86326	12.16872	12.80780	13.48635	14.20679	14.97164	15.78360	16.64549	18.53117	20.65458	24.34928	32.15042	42.56613
12	12.33556	12.68250	13.04121	13.41209	14.19203	15.02581	15.91713	16.86994	17.88845	18.97713	21.38428	24.13313	29.00167	39.58050	54.20766
13	13.39724	13.80933	14.23683	14.68033	15.61779	16.62684	17.71298	18.88214	20.14064	21.49530	24.52271	28.02911	34.35192	48.49660	68.75958
14	14.46423	14.94742	15.45038	15.97394	17.08632	18.29191	19.59863	21.01507	22.55049	24.21492	27.97498	32.39260	40.50471	59.19592	86.94947
15	15.53655	16.09690	16.68214	17.29342	18.59891	20.02359	21.57856	23.27597	25.12902	27.15211	31.72248	37.27971	47.58041	72.03511	109.6868
16	16.61423	17.25786	17.93237	18.63929	20.15688	21.82453	23.65749	25.67253	27.88805	30.32428	35.94973	42.75328	55.71747	87.44213	138.1085
17	17.69730	18.43044	19.20136	20.01207	21.76159	23.69751	25.84037	28.21288	30.84022	33.75023	40.54470	48.88367	65.07509	105.9306	173.6357
18	18.78579	19.61475	20.48938	21.41231	23.41444	25.64541	28.13238	30.90565	33.99903	37.45024	45.59917	55.74971	75.83636	128.1167	218.0446
19	19.87972	20.81090	21.79672	22.84056	25.11687	27.67123	30.53900	33.75999	37.37896	41.44626	51.15909	63.43968	88.21181	154.7400	273.5558
20	20.97912	22.01900	23.12367	24.29737	26.87037	29.77808	33.06595	36.78559	40.99549	45.76196	57.27500	72.05244	102.44358	186.6880	342.9447
22	23.19443	24.47159	25.83758	27.29898	30.53678	34.24797	38.50521	43.39229	49.00574	55.45676	71.40275	92.50258	137.63164	271.0307	538.1011
24	25.43196	26.97346	28.63352	30.42186	34.42647	39.08260	44.50200	50.81558	58.17667	66.76476	88.49733	118.1552	184.16784	392.4842	843.0329
26	27.69191	29.52563	31.51397	33.67091	38.55304	44.31174	51.11345	59.15638	68.67647	79.95442	109.1818	150.3339	245.71197	567.3773	1319.489
28	29.97452	32.12910	34.48148	37.05121	42.93092	49.96758	58.40258	68.52811	80.69769	95.33883	134.2099	190.6989	327.10408	819.2233	2063.952
30	32.28002	34.78489	37.53868	40.56808	47.57542	56.08494	66.43885	79.05819	94.46079	113.2832	164.4940	241.3327	434.74515	1181.881	3227.174
32	34.60862	37.49407	40.68829	44.22703	52.50276	62.70147	75.29883	90.88978	110.2181	134.2135	201.1378	304.8477	577.10046	1704.109	5044.710
34	36.96058	40.25770	43.93309	48.03380	57.73018	69.85791	85.06696	104.1838	128.2588	158.6267	245.4767	384.5210	765.36535	2456.118	7884.609
36	39.33610	43.07688	47.27597	51.99437	63.27594	77.59831	95.83632	119.1209	148.9135	187.1022	299.1268	484.4631	1014.34568	3539.009	12321.95
38	41.73545	45.95272	50.71989	56.11494	69.15945	85.97034	107.7095	135.9042	172.5610	220.3159	364.0434	609.8305	1343.62216	5098.373	19255.30
40	44.15885	48.88637	54.26789	60.40198	75.40126	95.02552	120.7998	154.7620	199.6351	259.0565	442.5926	767.0914	1779.09031	7343.858	30088.66
45	50.32416	56.48107	63.61420	71.89271	92.71986	121.0294	159.7002	212.7435	285.7493	386.5056	718.9048	1358.230	3585.12846	18281.31	91831.50
50	56.64516	64.46318	73.68283	84.57940	112.7969	152.6671	209.3480	290.3359	406.5289	573.7702	1163.909	2400.018	7217.71628	45497.19	280255.7
100	129.33370	170.4814	228.8030	312.2323	607.2877	1237.624	2610.025	5638.368	12381.66	27484.52	137796.1	696010.5	783×10^4	414×10^6	196×10^8

Note: To convert from this table to values of an annuity in advance, find the annuity in arrears above for one more period and subtract 1.00000.

Table 4

Present Value of an Annuity of $1 in Arrears

$$P_A = \frac{1 - (1 + r)^{-n}}{r}$$

r = discount rate; n = number of payments

No. of Payments = n	½%	1%	1½%	2%	3%	4%	5%	6%	7%	8%	10%	12%	15%	20%	25%
1	.99502	.99010	.98522	.98039	.97087	.96154	.95238	.94340	.93458	.92593	.90909	.89286	.86957	.83333	.80000
2	1.98510	1.97040	1.95588	1.94156	1.91347	1.88609	1.85941	1.83339	1.80802	1.78326	1.73554	1.69005	1.62571	1.52778	1.44000
3	2.97025	2.94099	2.91220	2.88388	2.82861	2.77509	2.72325	2.67301	2.62432	2.57710	2.48685	2.40183	2.28323	2.10648	1.95200
4	3.95050	3.90197	3.85438	3.80773	3.71710	3.62990	3.54595	3.46511	3.38721	3.31213	3.16987	3.03735	2.85498	2.58873	2.36160
5	4.92587	4.85343	4.78264	4.71346	4.57971	4.45182	4.32948	4.21236	4.10020	3.99271	3.79079	3.60478	3.35216	2.99061	2.68928
6	5.89638	5.79548	5.69719	5.60143	5.41719	5.24212	5.07569	4.91732	4.76654	4.62288	4.35526	4.11141	3.78448	3.32551	2.95142
7	6.86207	6.72819	6.59821	6.47199	6.23028	6.00205	5.78637	5.58238	5.38929	5.20637	4.86842	4.56376	4.16042	3.60459	3.16114
8	7.82296	7.65168	7.48593	7.32548	7.01969	6.73274	6.46321	6.20979	5.97130	5.74664	5.33493	4.96764	4.48732	3.83716	3.32891
9	8.77906	8.56602	8.36052	8.16224	7.78611	7.43533	7.10782	6.80169	6.51523	6.24689	5.75902	5.32825	4.77158	4.03097	3.46313
10	9.73041	9.47130	9.22218	8.98259	8.53020	8.11090	7.72173	7.36009	7.02358	6.71008	6.14457	5.65022	5.01877	4.19247	3.57050
11	10.67703	10.36763	10.07112	9.78685	9.25262	8.76048	8.30641	7.88687	7.49867	7.13896	6.49506	5.93770	5.23371	4.32706	3.65640
12	11.61893	11.25508	10.90751	10.57534	9.95400	9.38507	8.86325	8.38384	7.94269	7.53608	6.81369	6.19437	5.42062	4.43922	3.72512
13	12.55615	12.13374	11.73153	11.34837	10.63496	9.98565	9.39357	8.85268	8.35765	7.90378	7.10336	6.42355	5.58315	4.53268	3.78010
14	13.48871	13.00370	12.54338	12.10625	11.29607	10.56312	9.89864	9.29498	8.74547	8.24424	7.36669	6.62817	5.72448	4.61057	3.82408
15	14.41662	13.86505	13.34323	12.84926	11.93794	11.11839	10.37966	9.71225	9.10791	8.55948	7.60608	6.81086	5.84737	4.67547	3.85926
16	15.33993	14.71787	14.13126	13.57771	12.56110	11.65230	10.83777	10.10590	9.44665	8.85137	7.82371	6.97399	5.95423	4.72956	3.88741
17	16.25863	15.56225	14.90765	14.29187	13.16612	12.16567	11.27407	10.47726	9.76322	9.12164	8.02155	7.11963	6.04716	4.77463	3.90993
18	17.17277	16.39827	15.67256	14.99203	13.75351	12.65930	11.68959	10.82760	10.05909	9.37189	8.20141	7.24967	6.12797	4.81219	3.92794
19	18.08236	17.22601	16.42617	15.67846	14.32380	13.13394	12.08532	11.15812	10.33560	9.60360	8.36492	7.36578	6.19823	4.84350	3.94235
20	18.98742	18.04555	17.16864	16.35143	14.87747	13.59033	12.46221	11.46992	10.59401	9.81815	8.51356	7.46944	6.25933	4.86958	3.95388
22	20.78406	19.66038	18.62082	17.65805	15.93692	14.45112	13.16300	12.04158	11.06124	10.20074	8.77154	7.64465	6.35866	4.90943	3.97049
24	22.56287	21.24339	20.03041	18.91393	16.93554	15.24696	13.79864	12.55036	11.46933	10.52876	8.98474	7.78432	6.43377	4.93710	3.98111
26	24.32402	22.79520	21.39863	20.12104	17.87684	15.98277	14.37519	13.00317	11.82578	10.80998	9.16095	7.89566	6.49056	4.95632	3.98791
28	26.06769	24.31644	22.72672	21.28127	18.76411	16.66306	14.89813	13.40616	12.13711	11.05108	9.30657	7.98442	6.53351	4.96967	3.99226
30	27.79405	25.80771	24.01584	22.39646	19.60044	17.29203	15.37245	13.76483	12.40904	11.25778	9.42691	8.05518	6.56598	4.97894	3.99505
32	29.50328	27.26959	25.26714	23.46833	20.38877	17.87355	15.80268	14.08404	12.64656	11.43500	9.52638	8.11159	6.59053	4.98537	3.99683
34	31.19555	28.70267	26.48173	24.49859	21.13184	18.41120	16.19290	14.36814	12.85401	11.58693	9.60857	8.15656	6.60910	4.98984	3.99797
36	32.87102	30.10751	27.66068	25.48884	21.83225	18.90828	16.54685	14.62099	13.03521	11.71719	9.67651	8.19241	6.62314	4.99295	3.99870
38	34.52985	31.48466	28.80505	26.44064	22.49246	19.36786	16.86789	14.84602	13.19347	11.82887	9.73265	8.22099	6.63375	4.99510	3.99917
40	36.17223	32.83469	29.91585	27.35548	23.11477	19.79277	17.15909	15.04630	13.33171	11.92461	9.77905	8.24378	6.64178	4.99660	3.99947
45	40.20720	36.09451	32.55234	29.49016	24.51871	20.72004	17.77407	15.45583	13.60552	12.10840	9.86281	8.28252	6.65429	4.99863	3.99983
50	44.14279	39.19612	34.99969	31.42361	25.72976	21.48218	18.25593	15.76186	13.80075	12.23348	9.91481	8.30450	6.66051	4.99945	3.99994
100	78.54264	63.02888	51.62470	43.09835	31.59891	24.50500	19.84791	16.61755	14.26925	12.49432	9.99927	8.33323	6.66666	5.00000	4.00000

Note: To convert from this table to values of an annuity in advance, find the annuity in arrears above for one less period and add 1.00000.

Glossary

The definitions of many words and phrases in the glossary use other words and phrases. We *italicize* terms in a given definition (definiens) that themselves (or variants thereof) appear elsewhere under their own listings (as definienda). The cross references generally take one of two forms:

[1] **absorption costing.** See *full absorption costing*.
[2] **ABC.** *Activity-based costing*.

Form [1] refers you to another term for discussion of this **boldfaced** term (definiendum). Form [2] tells you that this **boldfaced** term (definiendum) is synonymous with the *italicized* term, which you can consult for discussion if necessary.

A

ABC. *Activity-based costing*.

abnormal spoilage. Actual spoilage exceeding that expected when operations are normally efficient. Usual practice treats this cost as an *expense* of the period rather than as a *product cost*. Contrast with *normal spoilage*.

absorbed overhead. *Overhead costs* allocated to individual products at some *overhead rate*. Also called *applied overhead*.

absorption costing. See *full absorption costing*.

Accelerated Cost Recovery System. ACRS. A form of *accelerated depreciation* that Congress enacted in 1981 and amended in 1986. The system provides percentages of the asset's cost that a firm depreciates each year for tax purposes. ACRS ignores *salvage value*. We do not generally use these amounts for *financial accounting*.

accelerated depreciation. Any method of calculating *depreciation* charges where the charges become progressively smaller each period. Examples are double-declining-balance and sum-of-the-years'-digits methods.

account. Any device for accumulating additions and subtractions relating to a single *asset, liability, owners' equity* item, including *revenues* and *expenses*.

account analysis method. A method of separating *fixed* from *variable costs* involving the classification of the various *product cost accounts*. For example, we classify *direct labor* and *direct material* as variable and *depreciation* on a factory building as fixed.

account receivable. A claim against a debtor usually arising from sales or services rendered, not necessarily due or past due. Normally, a *current asset*.

accounting. A system conveying information about a specific *entity*. The information is in financial terms and appears only if it is reasonably precise. The American Institute of Certified Public Accountants defines accounting as a service activity whose "function is to provide quantitative information, primarily financial in nature, about economic entities that is intended to be useful in making economic decisions."

accounting cycle. The sequence of accounting procedures starting with journal entries for various transactions and events and ending with the financial statements or, perhaps, the post-closing trial balance.

accounting equation. *Assets = Equities. Assets = Liabilities + Owners' Equity.*

accounting principles. The methods or procedures used in accounting for events reported in the financial statements. We tend to use this term when the method or procedure has received official authoritative sanction from a pronouncement of a group such as the *FASB* or *SEC*.

accounting rate of return. Income for a period divided by average investment during the period. Based on income, rather than discounted cash flows and, hence, is a poor decision making aid or tool. See *ratio*.

accounting system. The procedures for collecting and summarizing financial data in a firm.

accrual basis of accounting. The method of recognizing *revenues* as a firm sells goods (or delivers them) and as it renders services, independent of the time when it receives cash. This systems recognizes *expenses* in the period when it recognizes the related revenue independent of the time when it pays out cash. *SFAC No. 1* says "accrual accounting attempts to record the financial effects on an enterprise of transactions and other events and circumstances that have cash consequences for the enterprise in the periods in which those transactions, events, and circumstances occur rather than only in the periods in which cash is received or paid by the enterprise." Contrast with the *cash basis of accounting*. We could more correctly call the basis "accrual/deferral" accounting.

ACRS. *Accelerated Cost Recovery System.*

activity accounting. *Responsibility accounting.*

activity-based costing. ABC. Method of assigning *indirect costs,* including non-manufacturing *overhead*, to products and services. ABC assumes that almost all overhead costs associate with activities within the firm and vary with respect to the *drivers* of those activities. Some practitioners suggest that ABC attempts to find the drivers for all indirect costs; these people note that in the long run, all costs are *variable*, so *fixed* indirect costs do not occur.

activity basis. *Costs* are *variable* or *fixed* (*incremental* or *unavoidable*) with respect to some activity, such as production of units (or the undertaking of some new project). We refer to this activity as the "activity basis."

activity variance. *Sales volume variance.*

actual costing (system). Method of allocating costs to products using actual *direct materials*, actual *direct labor*, and actual *factory overhead*. Contrast with *normal costing* and *standard costing system*.

additional processing cost. *Costs* incurred in processing *joint products* after the *splitoff point*.

agency theory. A branch of economics relating the behavior of *principals* (such as owner non-managers or bosses) and their *agents* (such as non-owner managers or subordinates). The principal assigns responsibility and authority to the agent but the agent's own risks and preferences differ from those of the principal. The principal cannot observe all activities of the agent. Both the principal and the agent must consider the differing risks and preferences in designing incentive contracts.

agent. One authorized to transact business, including executing contracts, for another.

allocate. To spread a *cost* from one *account* to several accounts, to several products, or activities, or to several periods.

allocation base. Accounting often assigns *joint costs* to *cost objectives* with some systematic method. The allocation base specifies the method. For example, a firm might assign the cost of a truck to periods based on miles driven during the period; the allocation base is miles. Or, the firm might assign the cost of a factory supervisor to a product based on *direct labor* hours; the allocation base is direct labor hours.

analysis of variances. See *variance analysis*.

annuity. A series of payments, usually made at equally spaced time intervals.

annuity due. An *annuity* whose first payment is made at the start of period 1 (or at the end of period 0). Contrast with *annuity in arrears*.

annuity in advance. An *annuity due*.

annuity in arrears. An *ordinary annuity* whose first payment occurs at the end of the first period.

applied cost. A *cost* that a firm has *allocated* to a department, product, or activity; it is not necessarily based on actual costs incurred.

applied overhead. *Overhead costs* charged to departments, products or activities. Also called *absorbed overhead*.

approximate net realizable value method. A method of assigning joint costs to *joint products* based on revenues minus *additional processing costs* of the end products.

asset. *SFAC No. 6* defines assets as "probable future economic benefits obtained or controlled by a particular entity as a result of past transactions.... An asset has three essential characteristics: (a) it embodies a probable future benefit that involves a capacity, singly or in combination with other assets, to contribute directly or indirectly to future net cash inflows; (b) a particular entity can obtain the benefit and control others' access to it; and (c) the transaction or other event giving rise to the entity's right to or control of the benefit has already occurred." A footnote points out that "probable" means that which we can reasonably expect or believe but that is not certain or proved. May be tangible or *intangible, short term* (current) or *long term* (noncurrent).

audit. Systematic inspection of accounting records involving analyses, tests, and confirmations. See *internal audit.*

audit committee. A committee of the board of directors of a *corporation* usually consisting of outside directors who nominate the independent auditors and discuss the auditors' work with them. If the auditors believe the shareholders should know about certain matters, the auditors first bring these matters to the attention of the audit committee.

auditor's opinion. *Auditor's report.*

auditor's report. The auditor's statement of the work done and an opinion of the financial statements. The auditor usually gives unqualified ("clean") opinions, but may qualify them, or the auditor may disclaim an opinion in the report. Often called the "accountant's report."

average-cost flow assumption. An inventory flow assumption where the cost of units equals the *weighted average* cost of the *beginning inventory* and purchases.

avoidable cost. A *cost* that ceases if a firm discontinues an activity. An *incremental* or *variable* cost. See *programmed cost.*

B

backlog. Orders for which a firm has insufficient *inventory* on hand for current delivery and will fill in a later period.

balance. As a noun, the sum of debit entries minus the sum of credit entries in an *account.* If positive, we call the difference a debit balance; if negative, a credit balance. As a verb, to find the difference described above.

basic accounting equation. *Accounting equation.*

basic cost-flow equation. *Cost flow equation.*

beginning inventory. Valuation of *inventory* on hand at the beginning of the accounting period.

bill of materials. A specification of the quantities of *direct materials* a firm expects to use to produce a given job or quantity of output.

book. As a verb, to record a transaction. As a noun, usually plural, the journals and ledgers. As an adjective, see *book value.*

book inventory. An inventory amount that results, not from physical count, but from the amount of beginning inventory plus invoice amounts of net purchases less invoice amounts of requisitions or withdrawals; implies a perpetual method.

book value. The amount shown in the books or in the *accounts* for an *asset, liability,* or *owners' equity* item. Generally used to refer to the *net* amount of an *asset* or group of assets shown in the account that records the asset and reductions, such as for *amortization,* in its cost. Of a firm, the excess of total assets over total liabilities.

breakeven point. The volume of sales required so that total *revenues* and total *costs* are equal. May be expressed in units *(fixed costs/contribution per unit)* or in sales dollars [selling price per unit x (fixed costs/contribution per unit)].

budget. A financial plan that a firm uses to estimate the results of future operations. Frequently used to help control future operations. In governmental operations, budgets often become the law.

budgetary control. Management of governmental (nongovernmental) unit in accordance with an official (approved) *budget* in order to keep total expenditures within authorized (planned) limits.

budgeted cost. See *standard cost* for definition and contrast.

budgeted statements. *Pro forma statements* prepared before the event or period occurs.

burden. See *overhead costs.*

by-product. A *joint product* whose sales value is so small relative to the sales value of the other joint product(s) that it does not receive normal accounting treatment. The costs assigned to by-products reduce the costs of the main product(s). Accounting allocates by-products a share of joint costs such that the expected gain or loss upon their sale is zero. Thus, by-products appear in the *accounts* at *net realizable value.*

C

cancelable lease. See *lease.*

capacity. Stated in units of product, the amount that a firm can produce per unit of time. Stated in units of input, such as *direct labor* hours, the amount of input that a firm can use in production per unit of time. A firm uses this measure of output or input in allocating *fixed costs* if the amounts producible are normal, rather than maximum, amounts.

capacity cost. A *fixed cost* incurred to provide a firm with the capacity to produce or to sell. Consists of *standby costs* and *enabling costs.* Contrast with *programmed costs.*

capacity variance. *Production volume variance.*

capital budget. Plan of proposed outlays for acquiring long-term *assets* and the means of financing the acquisition.

capital budgeting. The process of choosing *investment* projects for an enterprise by considering the *present value* of cash flows and deciding how to raise the funds the investment requires.

capital rationing. In a *capital budgeting* context, the imposing of constraints on the amounts of total capital expenditures in each period.

carrying cost. Costs (such as property taxes and insurance) of holding, or storing, *inventory* from the time of purchase until the time of sale or use.

CASB. Cost Accounting Standards Board. A board of five members authorized by the U.S. Congress to "promulgate cost-accounting standards designed to achieve uniformity and consistency in the cost-accounting principles followed by defense contractors and subcontractors under federal contracts." The principles the CASB promulgated since 1970 have considerable weight in practice where the *FASB* has not established a standard. Congress allowed the CASB to go out of existence in 1980 but reinstated it in 1990.

cash basis of accounting. In contrast to the *accrual basis of accounting*, a system of accounting in which a firm recognizes *revenues* when it receives *cash* and recognizes *expenses* as it makes *disbursements*. The firm makes no attempt to match revenues and expenses in measuring income.

cash budget. A schedule of expected cash receipts and disbursements.

cash flow. Cash receipts minus disbursements from a given *asset*, or group of assets, for a given period. Financial analysts sometimes use this term to mean *net income + depreciation*. See also *operating cash flow*.

central corporate expenses. General *overhead expenses* incurred in running the corporate headquarters and related supporting activities of a corporation. Accounting treats these expenses as *period expenses*. Contrast with *manufacturing overhead*.

certified management accountant. *CMA.*

certified public accountant. CPA. An accountant who has satisfied the statutory and administrative requirements of his or her jurisdiction to be registered or licensed as a public accountant. In addition to passing the Uniform CPA Examination administered by the *AICPA*, the CPA must meet certain educational, experience, and moral requirements that differ from jurisdiction to jurisdiction. The jurisdictions are the 50 states, the District of Columbia, Guam, Puerto Rico, and the Virgin Islands.

CMA. Certified Management Accountant certificate. Awarded by the *Institute of Certified Management Accountants* of the *National Association of Accountants* to those who pass a set of examinations and meet certain experience and continuing education requirements.

common cost. *Cost* resulting from use of *raw materials*, a facility (for example, plant or machines), or a service (for example, fire insurance) that benefits several products or departments and that a firm must allocate to those products or departments. Common costs result when two or more departments produce multiple products together although the departments could produce them separately; *joint costs* occur when two or more departments must produce multiple products together. Many writers use common costs and joint costs synonymously. See *joint costs, indirect costs, and overhead.*

company-wide control. See *control system.*

compound interest. *Interest* calculated on *principal* plus previously undistributed interest.

compounding period. The time period for which a firm calculates *interest*. At the end of the period, the borrower may pay interest to the lender or may add the interest (that is, convert it) to principal for the next interest-earning period, which is usually a year or some portion of a year.

comptroller. Same meaning and pronunciation as *controller.*

contribution approach. Method of preparing *income statements* that separates *variable costs* from *fixed costs* in order to emphasize the importance of cost behavior patterns for purposes of planning and control.

contribution margin. *Revenue* from sales less all variable *expenses*. Contrast with *gross margin.*

contribution margin ratio. *Contribution margin* divided by net sales; usually measured from the price and cost of a single unit.

contribution per unit. Selling price less *variable costs* per unit.

control system. A device top management uses to ensure that lower-level management carries out its plans or to safeguard assets. Control designed for a single function within the firm is "operational control;" control designed for autonomous segments within the firm that generally have responsibility for both revenues and costs is "divisional control;" control designed for activities of the firm as a whole is "company-wide control." Systems designed for safeguarding *assets* are "internal control" systems.

controllable cost. A cost influenced by the way a firm carries out operations. For example, marketing executives control advertising costs. These costs are *fixed* or *variable*. See *programmed costs.*

controller. The title often used for the chief accountant of an organization. Often spelled *comptroller*.

conversion cost. *Direct labor* costs plus factory *overhead* costs incurred in producing a product. That is, the cost to convert raw materials to finished products. *Manufacturing cost*.

co-product. A product sharing production facilities with another product. For example, if an apparel manufacturer produces shirts and jeans on the same line, these are co-products. Distinguish co-products from *joint products* and *by-products* that, by their very nature a firm must produce together, such as the various grades of wood a lumber factory produces

cost. The sacrifice, measured by the price paid or required to be paid, to acquire goods or services. We often use the term "cost" when referring to the valuation of a good or service acquired. When used in this sense, a cost is an *asset*. When the benefits of the acquisition (the goods or services acquired) expire, the cost becomes an *expense* or loss. Some writers, however, use cost and expense as synonyms. Contrast with *expense*.

cost accounting. Classifying, summarizing, recording, reporting, and allocating current or predicted *costs*. A subset of *managerial accounting*.

Cost Accounting Standards Board. See *CASB*.

cost accumulation. Bringing together, usually in a single *account*, all *costs* of a specified activity. Contrast with *cost allocation*.

cost allocation. Assigning *costs* to individual products or time periods. Contrast with *cost accumulation*.

cost-based transfer price. A *transfer price* based on *historical costs*.

cost behavior. The functional relation between changes in activity and changes in *cost*. For example, *fixed* versus *variable costs;* linear versus *curvilinear cost*.

cost/benefit criterion. Some measure of *costs* compared to some measure of benefits for a proposed undertaking. If the costs exceed the benefits, then the analyst judges undertaking not worthwhile. This criterion will not yield good decisions unless the analyst estimates all costs and benefits flowing from the undertaking.

cost center. A unit of activity for which a firm accumulates expenditures and *expenses*.

cost driver. *Driver*.

cost effective. Among alternatives, the one whose benefit, or payoff, per unit of cost is highest. Sometimes said of an action whose expected benefits exceed expected costs whether or not other alternatives exist with larger benefit/cost ratios.

cost estimation. The process of measuring the functional relation between changes in activity levels and changes in cost.

cost flow equation. Beginning Balance + Transfers In = Transfers Out + Ending Balance; BB + TI = TO + EB.

cost flows. Costs passing through various classifications within an entity. See *flow of costs* for a diagram.

cost objective. Any activity for which management desires a separate measurement of *costs*. Examples include departments, products, and territories.

cost of capital. *Opportunity cost* of funds invested in a business. The rate of return rational owners require an asset to earn before they will devote that asset to a particular purpose. Sometimes measured as the average rate per year a company must pay for its *equities*. In efficient capital markets, the discount rate that equates the expected *present value* of all future cash flows to common shareholders with the market value of common stock at a given time.

Analysts often measure the cost of capital by taking a *weighted average* of the firm's debt and various equity securities. We sometimes call the measurement so derived the "composite cost of capital," and some analysts confuse this measurement of the cost of capital with the cost of capital itself. For example, if the equities of a firm include substantial amounts for the deferred income tax liability, the composite cost of capital will underestimate the true cost of capital, the required rate of return on a firm's assets, because the deferred income tax liability has no explicit cost.

cost of goods manufactured. The sum of all costs allocated to products completed during a period, including materials, labor, and *overhead*.

cost of goods sold. Inventoriable *costs* that firms *expense* because they sold the units; equals *beginning inventory* plus cost of goods purchased or manufactured minus *ending inventory*.

cost pool. *Indirect cost pool*.

cost sheet. Statement that shows all the elements comprising the total cost of an item.

cost terminology. The word "cost" appears in many accounting terms. The accompanying exhibit classifies some of these terms according to the distinctions between the terms in accounting usage. Joel Dean was, to our knowledge, the first to attempt such distinctions; we have used some of his ideas here. We discuss some of the terms in more detail under their own listings.

cost-volume-profit analysis. A study of the sensitivity of profits to changes in units sold (or produced), assuming some *semivariable costs* in the cost structure.

cost-volume-profit graph (chart). A graph that shows the relation between *fixed costs, contribution per unit, breakeven point,* and sales.

Cost Terminology Chart: Distinctions among Terms Containing the Word "Cost"

Terms (Synonyms Given in Parentheses)		Distinctions and Comments
		1. The following pairs of terms distinguish the basis measured in accounting.
Historical (Acquisition Cost)	v. Current Cost	A distinction used in financial accounting. Current cost can be used more specifically to mean replacement cost, net realizable value, or present value of cash flows. "Current cost" is often used narrowly to mean replacement cost.
Historical Cost (Actual Cost)	v. Standard Cost	The distinction between historical and standard costs arises in product costing for inventory valuation. Some systems record actual costs while others record the standard costs.
		2. The following pairs of terms denote various distinctions among historical costs. For each pair of terms, the sum of the two kinds of costs equals total historical cost used in financial reporting.
Variable Cost	v. Fixed Cost (Constant Cost)	Distinction used in breakeven analysis and in designing cost accounting systems, particularly for product costing. See (4), below, for a further subdivision of fixed costs and (5), below, for an economic distinction closely paralleling this one.
Traceable Cost	v. Common Cost (Joint Cost)	Distinction arises in allocating manufacturing costs to product. Common costs are allocated to product, but the allocations are more-or-less arbitrary. The distinction also arises in segment reporting and in separating manufacturing from nonmanufacturing costs.
Direct Cost	v. Indirect Cost	Distinction arises in designing cost accounting systems and in product costing. Direct costs can be traced directly to a cost object, (e.g., a product, a responsibility center) whereas indirect costs cannot.
Out-of-Pocket Cost (Outlay Cost; Cash Cost)	v. Book Cost	Virtually all costs recorded in financial statements require a cash outlay at one time or another. The distinction here separates expenditures to occur in the future from those already made and is used in making decisions. Book costs, such as for depreciation, reduce income without requiring a future outlay of cash. The cash has already been spent. See future v. past costs in (5), below.
Incremental Cost (Marginal Cost; Differential Cost)	v. Unavoidable Cost (Inescapable Cost; Sunk Cost)	Distinction used in making decisions. Incremental costs will be incurred (or saved) if a decision is made to go ahead (or to stop) some activity, but not otherwise. Unavoidable costs will be reported in financial statements whether the decision is made to go ahead or not, because cash has already been spent or committed. Not all unavoidable costs are book costs, as, for example, a salary promised but not yet earned, that will be paid even if a no-go decision is made.
		The economist restricts the term marginal cost to the cost of producing one more unit. Thus the next unit has a marginal cost; the next week's output has an incremental cost. If a firm produces and sells a new product, the related new costs would properly be called incremental, not marginal. If a factory is closed, the costs saved are incremental, not marginal.
Escapable Cost	v. Inescapable Cost (Unavoidable Cost)	Same distinction as incremental v. sunk costs, but this pair is used only when the decision maker is considering stopping something—ceasing to produce a product, closing a factory, or the like. See next pair.
Avoidable Cost	v. Unavoidable Cost	A distinction sometimes used in discussing the merits of variable and absorption costing. Avoidable costs are treated as product cost and unavoidable costs are treated as period expenses under variable costing.

Terms (Synonyms Given in Parentheses)			Distinctions and Comments
Controllable Cost	v.	Uncontrollable Cost	The distinction here is used in assigning responsibility and in setting bonus or incentive plans. All costs can be affected by someone in the entity; those who design incentive schemes attempt to hold a person responsible for a cost only if that person can influence the amount of the cost.

3. In each of the following pairs, used in historical cost accounting, the word "cost" appears in one of the terms where "expense" is meant.

Expired Cost	v.	Unexpired Cost	The distinction is between *expense* and *asset*.
Product Cost	v.	Period Cost	The terms distinguish product cost from period expense. When a given asset is used, is its cost converted into work in process and then into finished goods on the balance sheet until the goods are sold, or is it an expense shown on this period's income statement? Product costs appear on the income statement as part of cost of goods sold in the period when the goods are sold. Period expenses appear on the income statement with an appropriate caption for the item in the period when the cost is incurred or recognized.

4. The following subdivisions of fixed (historical) costs are used in analyzing operations. The relation between the components of fixed costs is:

$$\underbrace{\text{Fixed Costs}}_{\substack{\text{Semifixed Costs} \\ + \\ \text{"Pure" Fixed Costs}} \; + \; \substack{\text{Fixed Portions of Semi-variable Costs}} } = \underbrace{\text{Capacity Costs}}_{\text{Standby Costs} \; + \; \text{Enabling Costs}} + \text{Programmed Costs}$$

Capacity Cost (Committed Cost)	v.	Programmed Cost (Managed Cost; Discretionary Cost)	Capacity costs give a firm the capability to produce or to sell. Programmed costs, such as for advertising or research and development, may not be essential, but once a decision to incur them is made, they become fixed costs.
Standby Cost	v.	Enabling Cost	Standby costs will be incurred whether capacity, once acquired, is used or not, such as property taxes and depreciation on a factory. Enabling costs, such as for security force, can be avoided if the capacity is unused.
Semifixed Cost	v.	Semivariable Cost	A cost fixed over a wide range but that can change at various levels is a semifixed cost or "step cost." An example is the cost of rail lines from the factory to the main rail line where fixed cost depends on whether there are one or two parallel lines, but are independent of the number of trains run per day. Semivariable costs combine a strictly fixed component cost plus a variable component. Telephone charges usually have a fixed monthly component plus a charge related to usage.

5. The following pairs of terms distinguish among economic uses or decision making uses or regulatory uses of cost terms.

Fully Absorbed Cost	v.	Variable Cost (Direct Cost)	Fully absorbed costs refer to costs where fixed costs have been allocated to units or departments as required by generally accepted accounting principles. Variable costs, in contrast, may be more relevant for making decisions, such as in setting prices.

Terms (Synonyms Given in Parentheses)			Distinctions and Comments
Fully Absorbed Cost	v.	Full Cost	In full costing, all costs, manufacturing costs as well as central corporate express (including financing expenses) are allocated to product or divisions. In full absorption costing, only manufacturing costs are allocated to product. Only in full costing will revenues, expenses, and income summed over all products or divisions equal corporate revenues, expenses, and income.
Opportunity Cost	v.	Outlay Cost (Out-of-Pocket Cost)	Opportunity cost refers to the economic benefit foregone by using a resource for one purpose instead of for another. The outlay cost of the resource will be recorded in financial records. The distinction arises because a resource is already in the possession of the entity with a recorded historical cost. Its economic value to the firm, opportunity cost, generally differs from the historical cost; it can be either larger or smaller.
Future Cost	v.	Past Cost	Effective decision making analyzes only present and future outlay costs, or out-of-pocket costs. Opportunity costs are relevant for profit maximizing; past costs are used in financial reporting.
Short-Run Cost	v.	Long-Run Cost	Short-run costs vary as output is varied for a given configuration of plant and equipment. Long-run costs can be incurred to change that configuration. This pair of terms is the economic analog of the accounting pair, see (2) above, variable and fixed costs. The analogy is not perfect because some short-run costs are fixed, such as property taxes on the factory, from the point of view of breakeven analysis.
Imputed Cost	v.	Book Cost	In a regulatory setting some costs, for example the cost of owners' equity capital, are calculated and used for various purposes; these are imputed costs. Imputed costs are not recorded in the historical costs accounting records for financial reporting. Book costs are recorded.
Average Cost	v.	Marginal Cost	The economic distinction equivalent to fully absorbed cost of product and variable cost of product. Average cost is total cost divided by number of units. Marginal cost is the cost to produce the next unit (or the last unit).
Differential Cost (Incremental Cost)	v.	Variable Cost	Whether a cost changes or remains fixed depends on the activity basis being considered. Typically, but not invariably, costs are said to be variable or fixed with respect to an activity basis such as changes in production levels. Typically, but not invariably, costs are said to be differential or not with respect to an activity basis such as the undertaking of some new venture. For example, consider the decision to undertake the production of food processors, rather than food blenders, which the manufacturer has been making. To produce processors requires the acquisition of a new machine tool. The cost of the new machine tool is incremental with respect to a decision to produce food processors instead of food blenders, but, once acquired, becomes a fixed cost of producing food processors. If costs of direct labor hours are going to be incurred for the production of food processors or food blenders, whichever is produced (in a scenario when not both are to be produced), such costs are variable with respect to production measured in units, but not incremental with respect to the decision to produce processors rather than blenders. This distinction is often blurred in practice, so a careful understanding of the activity basis being considered is necessary for understanding of the concepts being used in a particular application.

costing. The process of calculating the cost of activities, products, or services. The British word for *cost accounting*.

cross-section analysis. Analysis of financial statements of various firms for a single period of time; contrast with *time-series analysis* where accountants analyze statements of a given firm for several periods of time.

current asset. Cash and other *assets* that a firm expects to turn into cash, sell, or exchange within the normal operating cycle of the firm or one year, whichever is longer. One year is the usual period for classifying asset balances on the balance sheet. Current assets include cash, marketable securities, receivables, *inventory*, and current prepayments.

current cost. Cost stated in terms of current values (of productive capacity) rather than in terms of acquisition cost. See *net realizable value*.

current liability. A debt or other obligation that a firm must discharge within a short time, usually the earnings cycle or one year, normally by expending *current assets*.

current ratio. Sum of *current assets* divided by sum of *current liabilities*. See *ratio*.

curvilinear (variable) cost. A continuous, but not necessarily linear (straight-line), functional relation between activity levels and *costs*.

D

DCF. *Discounted cash flow*.

debt-equity ratio. Total *liabilities* divided by total equities. See *ratio*. Sometimes the denominator is merely total shareholders' equity. Sometimes the numerator is restricted to *long-term debt*.

decentralized decision making. A firm gives a manager of a business unit responsibility for that unit's *revenues* and *costs*, freeing the manager to make decisions about prices, sources of supply, and the like, as though the unit were a separate business that the manager owns. See *responsibility accounting* and *transfer price*.

deferred annuity. An *annuity* whose first payment is made sometime after the end of the first period.

denominator volume. Capacity measured in the number of units the firm expects to produce this period; divided into budgeted fixed costs to obtain fixed costs applied per unit of product.

depreciation. Amortization of *plant assets;* the process of allocating the cost of an asset to the periods of benefit—the depreciable life. Classified as a *production cost* or a *period expense*, depending on the asset and whether the firm uses *absorption* or *variable costing*.

Descartes' rule of signs. In a *capital budgeting* context, the rule says that a series of cash flows will have a nonnegative number of *internal rates of return*. The number equals the number of variations in the sign of the cash flow series or is less than that number by an even integer. Consider the following series of cash flows, the first occurring now and the others at subsequent yearly intervals: $-100, -100, +50, +175, -50, +100$. The internal rates of return are the numbers for r that satisfy the equation

$$-100 - \frac{100}{(1 + r)} + \frac{50}{(1 + r)^2} + \frac{175}{(1 + r)^3} - \frac{50}{(1 + r)^4} + \frac{100}{(1 + r)^5} = 0.$$

The series of cash flows has three variations in sign: a change from minus to plus, a change from plus to minus, and a change from minus to plus. The rule says that this series must have either one or three internal rates of return; in fact, it has only one, about 12 percent.

differentiable cost. If a total cost curve is smooth (in mathematical terms, differentiable), then we say that the curve graphing the derivative of the total cost curve shows differentiable costs, the cost increments associated with infinitesimal changes in volume.

differential. An adjective used to describe the change (increase or decrease) in a *cost, expense,* investment, *cash flow, revenue,* profit, and the like as the firm produces or sells one or more additional (or fewer) units or undertakes (or ceases) an activity.

differential analysis. Analysis of *differential costs, revenues,* profits, investment, *cash flow,* and the like.

differential cost. See *differential.*

direct cost. Cost of *direct material* and *direct labor* incurred in producing a product. See *prime cost*. In some accounting literature, writers use this term to mean the same thing as *variable cost*.

direct costing. Another, less-preferred, term for *variable costing*.

direct labor (material) cost. Cost of labor (material) applied and assigned directly to a product; contrast with *indirect labor (material)*.

direct labor variance. *Price* and *quantity variances* for direct labor in standard costs systems.

discount factor. The reciprocal of one plus the discount rate. If the discount rate is 10 percent per period, the discount factor for three periods is $1/(1.10)^3 = (1.10)^{-3} = 0.75131$.

discounted cash flow. DCF. Using either the *net present value* or the *internal rate of return* in an analysis to measure the value of future expected cash expenditures and receipts at a common date. In discounted cash flow analysis, choosing the alternative with the largest *internal rate of return* may yield wrong answers given *mutually exclusive projects* with differing amounts of initial investment for two of the projects. Consider, to take an unrealistic example to illustrate the point, a project involving an initial investment of $1, with an *IRR* of 60 percent and another project involving an initial investment of $1 million with an IRR of 40 percent. Under most conditions, most firms will prefer the second project to the first, but choosing the project with the larger IRR will lead to undertaking the first, not the second. We call this shortcoming of choosing between alternatives based on the magnitude of the internal rate or return, rather than based on the magnitude of the *net present value* of the cash flows, the "scale effect."

discounted payback period.   The shortest amount of time which must elapse before the discounted present value of cash inflows from a project, excluding potential salvage value equals the discounted *present value* of the cash outflows.

discretionary costs.   *Programmed costs.*

division.   A more or less self-contained business unit which is part of a larger family of business units under common control.

divisional control.   See *control system.*

driver.   A determinant of costs incurred. Examples include order processing, issuing an engineering change order, changing the production schedule, and stopping production to change machine settings. The notion arises primarily in product costing, particularly *activity-based costing.*

dual transfer prices.   The *transfer price* charged to the buying *division* differs from that *credited* to the selling division. Such prices make sense when the selling division has excess capacity and, as usual, the fair market value exceeds the *incremental cost* to produce the goods or services being transferred.

E

earnings per share (of common stock).   *Net income* to common shareholders (net income minus preferred dividends) divided by the average number of common shares outstanding. See *ratio.*

economic depreciation.   Decline in *current cost* of an *asset* during a period.

economic order quantity.   In mathematical *inventory* analysis, the optimal amount of stock to order when demand reduces inventory to a level called the "reorder point." If A represents the *incremental cost* of placing a single order, D represents the total demand for a period of time in units, and H represents the incremental hold-

ing cost during the period per unit of inventory, then the economic order quantity $Q = \sqrt{2AD/H}$. We sometimes call Q the "optimal lot size."

efficiency variance.   A term used for the *quantity variance* for labor or *variable overhead* in a *standard costing system.*

enabling costs.   A type of *capacity cost* that a firm will stop incurring if it shuts down operations completely but will incur in full if it carries out operations at any level. Costs of a security force or of a quality control inspector for an assembly line might be examples. Contrast with *standby costs.*

ending inventory.   The *cost* of *inventory* on hand at the end of the *accounting period*, often called "closing inventory." The dollar amount of inventory is carried to the subsequent period.

engineering method (of cost estimation).   Estimates of unit costs of product built up from study of the materials, labor, and *overhead* components of the production process.

EOQ.   *Economic order quantity.*

EPVI.   *Excess present value index.*

equities.   *Liabilities* plus *owners' equity.*

equivalent production.   *Equivalent units.*

equivalent units (of work).   The number of units of completed output that would require the same costs as a firm would actually incur for production of completed and partially completed units during a period. Used primarily in *process costing* calculations to measure in uniform terms the output of a continuous process.

escapable cost.   *Avoidable costs.*

excess present value.   In a *capital budgeting* context, *present value* of (anticipated net cash inflows minus cash outflows including initial cash outflow) for a project.

excess present value index.   *Present value* of future *cash* inflows divided by initial cash outlay.

expected value.   The mean or arithmetic average of a statistical distribution or series of numbers.

expected value of (perfect) information.   Expected net benefits from an undertaking with (perfect) information minus expected net benefits of the undertaking without (perfect) information.

expense.   As a noun, a decrease in *owners' equity* caused by using up *assets* in producing *revenue* or carrying out other activities that comprise a part of the entity's operations. A "gone" asset or *net asset*; an expired cost. The amount is the *cost* of the assets used. Do not confuse with expenditure or disbursement, which may occur before, when, or after the firm recognizes the related expense. Use the word ''cost'' to refer to an item that still has service potential and is an asset. Use the word ''expense'' after the firm has used the asset's service potential. As a verb, to designate a past or current expenditure as a current expense.

extraordinary item.   A material expense or *revenue* item characterized both by its unusual nature and infrequency of occurrence that appears along with its income tax effects separately from ordinary income and *income from discontinued operations* on the *income statement*. Accountants would probably classify a loss from an earthquake as an extraordinary item. Accountants treat gain (or loss) on retirement of *bonds* as an extraordinary item under the terms of *SFAS No. 4*.

F

factory.   Used synonymously with *manufacturing* as an adjective.

factory burden.   *Manufacturing overhead.*

factory cost.   *Manufacturing cost.*

factory expense.   *Manufacturing overhead. Expense* is a poor term in this context because the item is a *product cost.*

factory overhead.   Usually an item of *manufacturing cost* other than *direct labor* or *direct materials.*

FASB.   Financial Accounting Standards Board. An independent board responsible, since 1973, for establishing *generally accepted accounting principles*. Its official pronouncements are called ''Statements of Financial Accounting Concepts'' (''SFAC''), ''Statements of Financial Accounting Standards'' (''SFAS''), and ''Interpretations.'' See also *Discussion Memorandum* and *Technical Bulletin.*

favorable variance.   An excess of actual *revenues* over expected revenues. An excess of *standard cost* over actual cost.

feedback.   The process of informing employees about how their actual performance compares with the expected or desired level of performance in the hope that the information will reinforce desired behavior and reduce unproductive behavior.

FIFO.   *First-in, first-out*; the inventory flow assumption which firms use to compute *ending inventory* cost from most recent purchases and *cost of goods sold* from oldest purchases including *beginning* inventory. Contrast with *LIFO.*

financial accounting.   The accounting for *assets, equities, revenues,* and *expenses* of a business. Primarily concerned with the historical reporting of the financial position and operations of an *entity* to external users on a regular, periodic basis. Contrast with *managerial accounting.*

financial leverage.   See *leverage.*

fixed budget.   A plan that provides for specified amounts of expenditures and receipts that do not vary with activity levels. Sometimes called a ''static budget.'' Contrast with *flexible budget.*

fixed cost (expense).   An expenditure or *expense* that does not vary with volume of activity, at least in the short run. See *capacity costs*, which include *enabling costs* and *standby costs*, and *programmed costs* for various subdivisions of fixed costs. See *cost terminology.*

fixed manufacturing overhead applied.   The portion of fixed manufacturing overhead cost allocated to units produced during a period.

fixed overhead variance.   Difference between actual fixed manufacturing costs and fixed manufacturing costs applied to production in a *standard costing system.*

flexible budget.   *Budget* that projects receipts and expenditures as a function of activity levels. Contrast with *fixed budget.*

flexible budget allowance.   With respect to manufacturing overhead, the total cost that a firm should have incurred at the level of activity actually experienced during the period.

flow of costs.   *Costs* passing through various classifications within an *entity*. See the diagram on the following page for a summary of *product* and *period cost* flows.

full absorption costing.   The method of *costing* which assigns all types of manufacturing costs (*direct material, direct labor, fixed* and *variable overhead*) to units produced; required by *GAAP*. Also called ''absorption costing.'' Contrast with *variable costing.*

full costing, full costs.   The total cost of producing and selling a unit. Full cost per unit equals *full absorption cost* per unit plus *marketing,* administrative, *interest,* and other *central corporate expenses,* per unit. The sum of full costs for all units equals total costs of the firm. Often used in *long-term* profitability and pricing decisions.

G

GAAP.   *Generally accepted accounting principles.* A plural noun.

GASB.   **Governmental Accounting Standards Board.**   An independent body responsible, since 1982, for establishing accounting standards for state and local government units. It is part of the *Financial Accounting Foundation,* parallel to the *FASB,* and currently consists of five members.

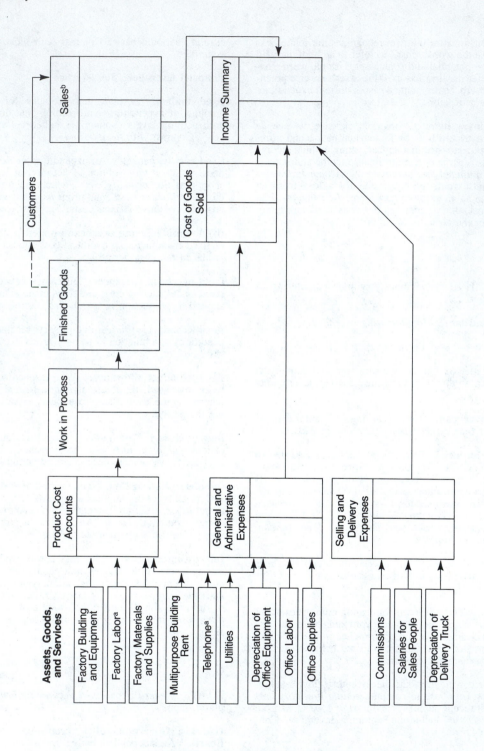

Assets, Goods, and Services

generally accepted accounting principles. GAAP. As previously defined by the *APB* and now by the *FASB*, the conventions, rules, and procedures necessary to define accepted accounting practice at a particular time; includes both broad guidelines and relatively detailed practices and procedures.

goal congruence. All members of an organization have incentives to perform for a common interest, such as shareholder wealth maximization for a corporation.

going-concern assumption. For accounting purposes, accountants assume a business will remain in operation long enough to carry out all its current plans. This assumption partially justifies the acquisition cost basis, rather than a liquidation or exit value basis, of accounting.

goods available for sale. The sum of *beginning inventory* plus all acquisitions of merchandise or finished goods during an accounting period.

Governmental Accounting Standards Advisory Council. A group that consults with the *GASB* on agenda, technical issues, and the assignment of priorities to projects. It comprises more than a dozen members representing various areas of expertise.

Governmental Accounting Standards Board. *GASB.*

gross margin. Net sales minus *cost of goods sold.*

H

historical cost. Acquisition cost; original cost; a *sunk cost.*

hurdle rate. Required rate of return in a *discounted cash flow* analysis.

I

I. *Identity matrix.*

ICMA. *Institute of Certified Management Accountants.* See *CMA* and *National Association of Accountants.*

ideal standard costs. *Standard costs* set equal to those that a firm would incur under the best possible conditions.

identity matrix. A square *matrix* with ones on the main diagonal and zeros elsewhere; a matrix **I** such that for any other matrix **A**, **IA = AI = A**. The matrix equivalent to the number one.

incentive compatible compensation. Said of a compensation plan for managers that induces them to act for the interests of owners while acting in their own interests. For example, consider a time of rising prices and increasing inventories when using a *LIFO* cost flow assumption implies paying lower income taxes than using *FIFO*. A bonus scheme for managers based on accounting *net income* would not be incentive compatible, because the owners benefit more under LIFO, while managers benefit more if they report using FIFO. (See *LIFO conformity rule.*) See *goal congruence.*

income from continuing operations. As defined by *APB Opinion No. 30*, all *revenues* less all *expenses* except for the following: results of operations (including income tax effects) that a firm has discontinued or will discontinue; gains or losses, including income tax effects, on disposal of segments of the business; gains or losses, including income tax effects, from *extraordinary items;* and the cumulative effect of accounting changes.

income from discontinued operations. Income, net of tax effects, from parts of the business that it has discontinued during the period or will discontinue in the near future. Accountants report such items on separate line of the *income statement* after *income from continuing operations* but before *extraordinary items.*

income statement. The statement of *revenues, expenses,* gains, and losses for the period ending with *net income* for the period. Accountants usually show the *earnings-per-share* amount on the income statement; the reconciliation of beginning and ending balances of retained earnings may also appear in a combined statement of income and retained earnings. See *income from continuing operations, income from discontinued operations, extraordinary items.*

incremental. See *differential.* An adjective used to describe the increase in *cost, expense,* investment, *cash flow, revenue,* profit, and the like if the firm produces or sells one or more units or if it undertakes an activity.

incremental cost. See *incremental.*

indirect cost pool. Any grouping of individual costs that a firm does not identify with a *cost objective.*

indirect costs. Costs of production not easily associated with the production of specific goods and services; *overhead costs.* Accountants may *allocate* them on some arbitrary basis to specific products or departments.

indirect labor (material) cost. An *indirect cost* for labor (material) such as for supervisors (supplies).

Institute of Certified Management Accountants. See *ICMA.*

intangible asset. A nonphysical, *noncurrent* right that gives a firm an exclusive or preferred position in the marketplace. Examples are a copyright, patent, trademark, goodwill, organization costs, capitalized advertising cost, computer programs, licenses for any of the preceding, government licenses (e.g., broadcasting or the right to sell liquor), *leases*, franchises, mailing lists, exploration permits, import and export permits, construction permits, and marketing quotas.

interest.   The charge or cost for using money; expressed as a rate per period, usually one year, the "interest rate."

internal audit.   An *audit* conducted by employees to ascertain whether *internal control* procedures are working, as opposed to an external audit conducted by a *certified public accountant*.

internal control.   See *control system*.

internal rate of return. IRR.   The discount rate that equates the net *present value* of a stream of cash outflows and inflows to zero.

inventory.   As a noun, the *balance* in an asset *account* such as raw materials, supplies, work in process, and finished goods. As a verb, to calculate the *cost* of goods on hand at a given time or to count items on hand physically.

investment center.   A *responsibility center*, with control over *revenues, costs*, and *assets*.

investment credit.   A reduction in income tax liability sometimes granted by the federal government to firms that buy new equipment. This item is a credit, in that it is deducted from the tax bill, not from pretax income. The tax credit has been a given percentage of the purchase price of certain assets purchased. The government has changed the actual rules and rates over the years. As of 1991, there is no investment credit.

investment decision.   The decision whether to undertake an action involving production of goods or services; contrast with the financing decision of how to raise cash to pay for the undertaking.

investment tax credit.   *Investment credit*.

investment turnover ratio.   This term means the same thing as *total assets turnover ratio*, but we sometimes use it for a *division*.

IRR.   *Internal rate of return*.

isoprofit line.   On a graph delimiting feasible production possibilities of two products that require the use of the same, limited resources, a line showing all feasible production possibility combinations with the same profit or, perhaps, *contribution margin*.

J

JIT.   See *just-in-time inventory*.

job cost sheet.   A schedule showing actual or budgeted inputs for a special order.

job (-order) costing.   Accumulation of *costs* for a particular identifiable batch of product, known as a job, as it moves through production.

joint cost.   Cost of simultaneously producing or otherwise acquiring two or more products, called joint products, that a firm must, by the nature of the process, produce or acquire together, such as the cost of beef and hides of cattle. Generally, accounting allocates the joint costs of production to the individual products in proportion to their respective sales value at the *splitoff* point. Other examples include central corporate expenses, overhead of a department when it manufactures several products, and basket purchases. See *common cost*.

joint cost allocation.   See *joint cost*.

joint product.   One of two or more outputs with significant value produced by a process that a firm must produce or acquire simultaneously. See *by-product* and *joint cost*.

just-in-time inventory (production). JIT.   System of managing *inventory* for manufacturing where a firm purchases or manufactures each component just before the firm uses it. Contrast with systems where firms acquire or manufacture many parts in advance of needs. JIT systems have much smaller, ideally no, carrying costs for inventory, but run higher risks of incurring *stockout* costs.

K

know-how.   Technical or business information of the type defined under *trade secret*, but that a firm does not maintain as a secret. The rules of accounting for this *asset* are the same as for other *intangibles*.

L

labor variances.   The *price* (or rate) and *quantity* (or usage) *variances* for *direct labor* inputs in a *standard costing system*.

last-in, first-out.   See *LIFO*.

lead time.   The time that elapses between placing an order and receipt of the goods or services ordered.

learning curve.   A mathematical expression of the phenomenon that incremental unit costs to produce decrease as managers and labor gain experience from practice.

lease.   A contract calling for the lessee (user) to pay the lessor (owner) for the use of an asset. A cancelable lease allows the lessee to cancel at any time. A noncancelable lease requires payments from the lessee for the life of the lease and usually shares many of the economic characteristics of debt financing. Most long-term noncancelable leases meet the usual criteria classifying them as *liabilities* but the firm need not show some leases entered into before 1977 as liabilities. *SFAS No. 13* and the *SEC* require disclosure in notes to the financial statements of the commitments for long-term noncancelable leases.

leverage. "Operating leverage" refers to the tendency of *net income* to rise at a faster rate than sales when *fixed costs* are present. A doubling of sales, for example, usually implies a more than doubling of net income. "Financial leverage" (or "capital leverage") refers to the increased rate of return on *owners' equity* (see *ratio*) when an *investment* earns a return larger than the after-tax interest rate paid for debt financing. Because the interest charges on debt are usually fixed, any *incremental* income benefits owners and none benefits debtors. When writers use the term "leverage" without a qualifying adjective, the term usually refers to financial leverage, the use of *long-term* debt in securing funds for the entity.

liability. An obligation to pay a definite (or reasonably definite) amount at a definite (or reasonably definite) time in return for a past or current benefit. That is, the obligation arises from other than a mere exchange of promises (an executory contract). A probable future sacrifice of economic benefits arising from present obligations of a particular entity to transfer assets or to provide services to other entities in the future as a result of past transactions or events. *SFAC No. 6* says that "probable" refers to that which we can reasonably expect or believe but that is neither certain nor proved. A liability has three essential characteristics: (1) an obligation to transfer assets or services at a specified or knowable date, (2) the entity has little or no discretion to avoid the transfer, and (3) the event causing the obligation has already happened; that is, it is not executory.

LIFO. *Last-in, first-out.* An *inventory* flow assumption where the *cost of goods sold* equals the cost of the most recently acquired units and a firm computes the ending inventory cost from costs of the oldest units; contrast with *FIFO*. In periods of rising prices and increasing inventories, LIFO leads to higher reported expenses and therefore lower reported income and lower balance sheet inventories than does FIFO.

linear programming. A mathematical tool for finding profit maximizing (or cost minimizing) combinations of products to produce when a firm has several products that it can produce but faces linear constraints on the resources available in the production processes or on maximum and minimum production requirements.

long run. long term. A term denoting a time or time periods in the future. How far in the future depends on context. For some securities traders, "long term" can mean anything beyond the next hour or two. For most managers, it means anything beyond the next year or two. For government policy makers, it can mean anything beyond the next decade or two. For geologists, it can mean millions of years.

long-term debt ratio. Noncurrent liabilities divided by total *assets*.

long-term solvency risk. The risk that a firm will not have sufficient cash to pay its debts sometime in the *long run*.

M

make-or-buy decision. A managerial decision about whether the firm should produce a product internally or purchase it from others. Proper make-or-buy decisions in the short run result when a firm considers only *incremental costs* in decision making.

management. Executive authority that operates a business.

management accounting. See *managerial accounting*.

management audit. An audit conducted to ascertain whether a firm or one of its operating units properly carries out its objectives, policies, and procedures. Generally applies only to activities for which accountants can specify qualitative standards. See *audit* and *internal audit*.

management by exception. A principle of management where managers focus attention on performance only if it differs significantly from that expected.

management by objective. A management approach designed to focus on the definition and attainment of overall and individual objectives with the participation of all levels of management.

managerial (management) accounting. Reporting designed to enhance the ability of management to do its job of decision making, planning, and control; contrast with *financial accounting*.

manufacturing cost. Cost of producing goods, usually in a factory.

manufacturing expense. An imprecise, and generally incorrect, alternative title for *manufacturing overhead*.

manufacturing overhead. General manufacturing *costs* incurred in providing a capacity to carry on productive activities not directly associated with identifiable units of product. Accounting treats *fixed* manufacturing overhead costs as a *product cost* under *absorption costing* but as an *expense* of the period under *variable costing*.

margin of safety.   Excess of actual, or budgeted, sales over *breakeven* sales. Usually expressed in dollars; may be expressed in units of product.

marginal cost.   The *incremental cost* or *differential cost* of the last unit added to production or the first unit subtracted from production. See *cost terminology*.

marginal costing.   *Direct costing*.

market-based transfer price.   A *transfer price* based on external market data, rather than internal company data.

marketing costs.   Costs incurred to sell; includes locating customers, persuading them to buy, delivering the goods or services, and collecting the sales proceeds.

master budget.   A *budget* projecting all financial statements and their components.

material variances.   *Price* and *quantity variances* for direct materials in *standard costing systems*. Sometimes used to mean significant variances.

matrix.   A rectangular array of numbers or mathematical symbols.

matrix inverse.   For a given square *matrix* $\mathbf{A}$, the square matrix inverse is the matrix, $\mathbf{A}^{-1}$, such that $\mathbf{A}\mathbf{A}^{-1} = \mathbf{A}^{-1}\mathbf{A} = \mathbf{I}$, the *identity matrix*. Not all square matrices have inverses. Those that do not we call "singular"; those that do are nonsingular.

mix variance.   Many *standard cost* systems specify combinations of inputs, for example, labor of a certain skill and materials of a certain quality grade. Sometimes combinations of inputs used differ from those contemplated by the standard. The mix variance attempts to report the cost difference that changing the combination of inputs causes.

mixed cost.   A *semifixed* or a *semivariable* cost.

monetary assets and liabilities.   See *monetary items*.

monetary items.   Amounts fixed in terms of dollars by statute or contract. Cash, accounts receivable, accounts payable, and debt. The distinction between monetary and nonmonetary items is important for constant dollar accounting and for foreign exchange gain or loss computations. In the foreign exchange context, account amounts denominated in dollars are not monetary items, whereas amounts denominated in any other currency are monetary.

moving average.   An *average* computed on observations over time. As a new observation becomes available, analysts drop the oldest one so that they always compute the average for the same number of observations and only the most recent ones. Some, however, use this term synonymously with *weighted average*.

mutually exclusive projects.   Competing investment projects, where accepting one project eliminates the possibility of undertaking the remaining projects.

N

National Association of Accountants. NAA.   A national society generally open to all engaged in activities closely associated with *managerial accounting*. Oversees the administration of the *CMA* Examinations through the Institute of Certified Management Accountants.

negotiated transfer price.   A *transfer price* set jointly by the buying and selling divisions.

net.   Reduced by all relevant deductions.

net income.   The excess of all *revenues* and gains for a period over all *expenses* and losses of the period.

net present value.   Discounted or *present value* of all cash inflows and outflows of a project or from an *investment* at a given discount rate.

net realizable (sales) value.   A method for allocating joint costs in proportion to realizable values of the joint products. For example, joint products A and B together cost $100 and A sells for $60 whereas B sells for $90. Then a firm would allocate to A ($60/$150) × $100 = .40 × $100 = $40 of cost while it would allocate to B ($90/$150) × $100 = $60 of cost.

noncancelable.   See *lease*.

noncontrollable cost.   A cost that a particular manager cannot *control*.

nonmanufacturing costs.   All *costs* incurred other than those to produce goods.

normal costing.   Method of charging costs to products using actual *direct materials*, actual *direct labor*, and predetermined *factory overhead* rates.

normal costing system.   *Costing* based on actual material and labor costs, but using *predetermined overhead rates* per unit of some *activity basis* (such as direct labor hours or machine hours) to apply overhead to production. Management decides the rate to charge to production for overhead at the start of the period. At the end of the period the accounting multiplies this rate by the actual number of units of the base activity (such as actual direct labor hours worked or actual machine hours used during the period) to apply overhead to production.

normal spoilage.   Costs incurred because of ordinary amounts of spoilage; accounting prorates such costs to units produced as *product costs;* contrast with *abnormal spoilage*.

normal standard cost. normal standards. The *cost* a firm expects to incur under reasonably efficient operating conditions with adequate provision for an average amount of rework, spoilage, and the like.

normal volume. The level of production over a time span, usually 1 year, that will satisfy purchasers' demands and provide for reasonable *inventory* levels.

O

objective function. In *linear programming*, the name of the profit or cost criterion the analyst wants to optimize.

operating budget. A formal *budget* for the operating cycle or for a year.

operating cash flow. Financial statement analysts use this term to mean *cash flow* − capital expenditures − dividends.

operating leverage. Usually said of a firm with a large proportion of *fixed costs* in its total costs. Consider a book publisher or a railroad: the *incremental costs* of producing another book or transporting another freight car are much less than average cost, so the *gross margin* upon sale of the unit is relatively large. Contrast, for example, a grocery store, where the *contribution margin* is usually less than 5 percent of the selling price. For firms with equal profitability, however defined, we say the one with the larger percentage increase in income from a given percentage increase in unit sales has the larger operating leverage. See *leverage* for contrast of this term with "financial leverage." See *cost terminology* for definition of terms involving the word "cost."

operational control. See *control system*.

opportunity cost. The *present value* of the income (or *costs*) that a firm could earn (or save) from using an *asset* in its best alternative use to the one under consideration.

opportunity cost of capital. *Cost of capital*.

ordinary annuity. An *annuity in arrears*.

outlier. Said of an observation (or data point) which appears to differ significantly in some regard from other observations (or data points) of supposedly the same phenomenon. Often used in describing the results of a *regression analysis* when an observation is not "near" the fitted regression equation.

out-of-stock cost. The estimated decrease in future profit as a result of losing customers because a firm has insufficient quantities of *inventory* currently on hand to meet customers' demands.

output. Physical quantity or monetary measurement of goods and services produced.

overapplied (overabsorbed) overhead. An excess of costs applied, or charged, to product for a period over actual *overhead costs* during the period. A credit balance in an overhead account after overhead is assigned to product.

overhead costs. Any cost not directly associated with the production or sale of identifiable goods and services. Sometimes called "burden" or "indirect costs" and, in Britain, "oncosts." Frequently limited to manufacturing overhead. See *manufacturing overhead*.

overhead rate. Standard, or other predetermined rate, at which a firm applies *overhead costs* to products or to services.

owners' equity. Proprietorship; *assets* minus *liabilities;* paid-in capital plus *retained earnings* of a corporation; partners' capital accounts in a partnership; owner's capital account in a sole proprietorship.

P

payback period. Amount of time that must elapse before the cash inflows from a project equal the cash outflows.

payback reciprocal. One divided by the *payback period*. This number approximates the *internal rate of return* on a project when the project life exceeds twice the payback period and the cash inflows are identical in every period after the initial period.

percent. Any number, expressed as a decimal, multiplied by 100.

period cost. An inferior term for *period expense*.

period expense (charge). Expenditure, usually based upon the passage of time, charged to operations of the accounting period rather than capitalized as an asset; contrast with *product cost*.

perpetuity. An *annuity* whose payments continue forever. The *present value* of a perpetuity in *arrears* is p/r where p is the periodic payment and r is the *interest rate* per period. If $100 is promised each year, in arrears, forever and the interest rate is 8 percent per year, then the value of the perpetuity is $1,250 = $100/.08.

physical units method. A method of allocating a *joint cost* to the *joint products* based on a physical measure of the joint products. For example, allocating the cost of a cow to sirloin steak and to hamburger, based on the weight of the meat. This method usually provides nonsensical results unless the physical units of the joint products tend to have the same value.

planning and control process. General name for the techniques of management comprising the setting of organizational goals and strategic plans, *capital budget-*

ing, operations budgeting, comparison of plans with actual results, performance evaluation and corrective action, and revisions of goals, plans, and budgets.

plant asset turnover.   Number of dollars of sales generated per dollar of plant assets. Equal to sales divided by average plant assets.

practical capacity.   Maximum level at which the plant or department can operate efficiently.

predetermined (factory) overhead rate.   Rate used in applying *overhead* to products or departments developed at the start of a period by dividing estimated overhead cost by the estimated number of units of the overhead allocation base (or *denominator volume*) activity. See *normal costing.*

present value.   Value today (or at some specific date) of an amount or amounts a firm will pay or receive later (or at other, different dates), discounted at some *interest* or *discount rate.*

price-earnings ratio.   At a given time, the market value of a company's common stock, per share, divided by the *earnings per* common *share* for the past year. Analysts usually base the denominator on *income from continuing operations* or, if they think the current figure for that amount does not represent earnings, such as when the number is negative, on some estimate of the number. See *ratio.*

price variance.   In accounting for *standard costs,* (actual cost per unit − standard cost per unit) times quantity purchased.

prime cost.   Sum of *direct materials* plus *direct labor* costs assigned to product.

principal.   An amount on which a lender (or investor) charges (or earns) *interest.* The face amount of a loan. Also, the absent owner (principal) who hires the manager (agent) in a "principal-agent" relationship.

process costing.   A method of *cost accounting* based on average costs (total cost divided by the *equivalent units* of work done in a period). Firms typically use this method for assembly lines or for products produced in a series of steps that are more continuous than discrete.

product.   Goods or services produced.

product cost.   Any *manufacturing cost* that a firm can inventory. See *flow of costs* for example and contrast with *period expenses.*

production cost.   *Manufacturing cost.*

production cost account.   A temporary account for accumulating *manufacturing costs* during a period.

production department.   A department producing salable goods or services; contrast with *service department.*

production volume variance.   Standard fixed *overhead rate* per unit of normal *capacity* (or base activity) times (units of base activity budgeted or planned for a period minus actual units of base activity worked or assigned to product during the period). Often called a "volume variance."

profit center.   A unit of activity for which a firm accumulates both *revenue* and *expenses;* contrast with *cost center.*

profit margin.   Sales minus all expenses as a single amount. Frequently used to mean ratio of sales minus all operating expenses divided by sales.

profit margin percentage.   *Profit margin* divided by net sales.

profit variance analysis.   Analysis of the causes of the difference between budgeted profit in the *master budget* and the profits earned.

profit-volume equation.   See *breakeven chart.*

pro forma statements.   Hypothetical statements. Financial statements as they would appear if some event, such as a merger or increased production and sales had occurred or were to occur. Pro forma is often spelled as one word.

programmed costs.   A *fixed cost* not essential for carrying out operations. A firm can control research and development and advertising designed to generate new business, but once it commits to incur them, they become fixed costs. Sometimes called managed costs or *discretionary costs;* contrast with *capacity costs.*

prorate.   To *allocate* in proportion to some base; for example, allocate *service department* costs in proportion to hours of service used by the benefitted department. Or, to allocate manufacturing variances to product sold and to product added to *ending inventory.*

prorating variances.   See *prorate.*

Q

quantity variance.   *Efficiency variance.* In *standard cost* systems, the standard price per unit times (actual quantity used minus standard quantity that should be used).

quick ratio.   Sum of (*cash,* current marketable securities, and receivables) divided by *current liabilities.* The analyst may exclude some nonliquid receivables from the numerator. Often called the "acid-test ratio." See *ratio.*

R

R^2.   The proportion of the statistical variance of a dependent variable explained by the equation fit to independent variable(s) in a *regression analysis.*

rate of return on assets.   *Return on assets.*

rate of return on shareholders' (owners') equity. See *ratio.*

ratio.   The number resulting when one number is divided by another. We generally use ratios to assess aspects of profitability, solvency, and liquidity. The commonly used financial ratios fall in three categories: (1) those that summarize some aspect of operations for a period, usually a year; (2) those that summarize some aspect of financial position at a given moment—the moment for which a balance sheet has been prepared; and (3) those that relate some aspect of operations to some aspect of financial position.

Exhibit 18.12 lists the most common financial ratios and shows separately both the numerator and denominator used to calculate each ratio.

For all ratios that require an average balance during the period, the analyst often derives the average as one half the sum of the beginning and ending balances. Sophisticated analysts recognize, however, that particularly when companies use a fiscal year different from the calendar year, this averaging of beginning and ending balances may mislead. Consider, for example, the rate of *return on assets* of Sears, Roebuck & Company whose fiscal year ends on January 31. Sears chooses a January 31 closing date at least in part because inventories are low and are therefore easy to count—it has sold the Christmas merchandise and the Easter merchandise has not yet all arrived. Furthermore, by January 31, Sears has collected for most Christmas sales, so receivable amounts are not unusually large. Thus at January 31, the amount of total assets is lower than at many other times during the year. Consequently, the denominator of the rate of return on assets, total assets, for Sears most likely represents the smallest amount of total assets on hand during the year, not the average amount. The return on assets rate for Sears and other companies who choose a fiscal year-end to coincide with low points in the inventory cycle usually exceeds the rate they would estimate if they used a more accurate estimate of the average amounts of total assets.

raw material.   Goods purchased for use in manufacturing a product.

reciprocal holdings.   Company A owns stock of Company B and Company B owns stock of Company A.

regression analysis.   A method of *cost estimation* based on statistical techniques for fitting a line (or its equivalent in higher mathematical dimensions) to an observed series of data points, usually by minimizing the sum of squared deviations of the observed data from the fitted line. We call the cost the analysis explains the "dependent variable"; we call the variable(s) we use to estimate cost behavior the "independent variable(s)." If we use more than one independent variable, we call the analysis "multiple regression analysis." See R^2, *standard error, t-value.*

relevant cost.   *Incremental cost. Opportunity cost.*

relevant range.   Activity levels over which costs are linear or for which *flexible budget* estimates and break-even charts will remain valid.

required rate of return.   *Cost of capital.*

research and development.   Firms engage in research in hopes of discovering new knowledge that will create a new product, process, or service or improve a present product, process, or service. Development translates research findings or other knowledge into a new or improved product, process, or service. *SFAS No.2* requires that firms expense costs of such activities as incurred on the grounds that the future benefits are too uncertain to warrant capitalization as an asset. This treatment seems questionable to us because we wonder why firms would continue to undertake R&D if they expected no future benefit; if future benefits exist, then its *costs* should be assets.

residual income.   In an external reporting context, this term refers to *net income* to common shares (= net income less preferred stock dividends). In *managerial accounting*, this term refers to the excess of income for a *division* or segment of a company over the product of the *cost of capital* for the company multiplied by the average amount of capital invested in the division during the period over which the firm earned the income.

responsibility accounting.   Accounting for a business by considering various units as separate entities, or *profit centers*, giving management of each unit responsibility for the unit's *revenues* and *expenses*. Sometimes called "activity accounting." See *transfer price.*

responsibility center.   Part or segment of an organization that top management holds accountable for a specified set of activities. Also called "accountability center." See *cost center, investment center, profit center, revenue center.*

return.   A schedule of information required by governmental bodies, such as the tax return required by the Internal Revenue Service. Also the physical return of merchandise. See also *ROI.*

return on assets.   *Net income* plus after-tax interest charges plus minority interest in income divided by average total *assets.* Perhaps the single most useful ratio for assessing management's overall operating performance. Most financial economists would subtract average non-interest bearing *liabilities* from the denominator. Economists realize that when liabilities do not provide for explicit interest charges, the creditor adjusts the terms of contract, such as setting a higher selling price or lower discount, to those who do not pay cash immediately. (To take an extreme example, consider how much higher salary a worker who receives salary once per year, rather than once per month, would demand.) This ratio requires in the numerator the income amount before the firm accrues any charges to suppliers of funds. We cannot measure the interest charges implicit in the non-interest bearing liabilities, because items such as cost of goods sold and salary expense are somewhat larger because of these charges. Subtracting their amount from the denominator adjusts for their implicit cost. Such subtraction assumes that assets financed with non-interest bearing liabilities have the same rate of return as all the other assets.

revenue.   The increase in *owners' equity* caused by a service rendered or the sale of goods. The monetary measure of a service rendered. Sales of products, merchandise, and services, and earnings from *interest*, dividends, rents, and the like. The amount of revenue is the expected *net present value* of the net assets received. Do not confuse with receipt of funds, which may occur before, when, or after revenue is recognized. Some writers use the term gross income synonymously with *revenue;* avoid such usage.

revenue center.   A *responsibility center* within a firm that controls only revenues generated; contrast with *cost center*. See *profit center*.

risk.   A measure of the variability of the return on investment (*ROI*). For a given expected amount of return, most people prefer less risk to more risk. Therefore, in rational markets, investments with more risk usually promise, or investors expect them to yield, a higher rate of return than investments with lower risk. Most people use ''risk'' and ''uncertainty'' as synonyms. In technical language, however, the meaning of these terms differ. We use ''risk'' when we know the probabilities attached to the various outcomes, such as the probabilities of heads or tails in the flip of a fair coin. ''Uncertainty'' refers to an event where we can only estimate the probabilities of the outcomes, such as winning or losing a lawsuit.

ROI.   Return on investment, but usually used to refer to a single project and expressed as a ratio: income divided by average *cost* of *assets* devoted to the project.

S

safety stock.   Extra items of *inventory* kept on hand to protect against running out.

sales activity variance.   *Sales volume variance*.

sales volume variance.   Budgeted contribution margin per unit times (planned sales volume minus actual sales volume).

scale effect.   See *discounted cash flow*.

SEC.   Securities and Exchange Commission, an agency authorized by the U.S. Congress to regulate, among other things, the financial reporting practices of most public corporations. The SEC has indicated that it will usually allow the *FASB* to set accounting principles but it often requires more disclosure than the FASB requires. The SEC states its accounting requirements in its

Accounting Series Releases (ASR), Financial Reporting Releases (FRR), Accounting and Auditing Enforcement Releases, *Staff Accounting Bulletins*, and *Regulation S-X*. See also *registration statement* and *10-K*.

Securities and Exchange Commission.   *SEC*.

semifixed costs.   *Costs* that increase with activity as a step function.

semivariable costs.   *Costs* that increase strictly linearly with activity but that are positive at zero activity level. Royalty fees of 2 percent of sales are variable; royalty fees of $1,000 per year plus 2 percent of sales are semivariable.

sensitivity analysis.   Most decision making requires the use of assumptions. Sensitivity analysis is the study of how the outcome of a decision making process changes as one or more of the assumptions change.

service cost. (current) service cost.   Pension plan expenses incurred during an accounting period for employment services performed during that period.

service department.   A department, such as the personnel or computer department, that provides services to other departments, rather than direct work on a salable product; contrast with *production department*. A firm must allocate costs of service departments whose services benefit manufacturing operations to *product costs* under *absorption costing*.

setup.   The time or costs required to prepare production equipment for doing a job.

shadow price.   One output of a *linear programming* analysis estimates the potential value of having available more of the scarce resources that constrain the production process; for example, the value of having more time available on a machine tool critical to the production of two products. We call this value a ''shadow price'' or the ''dual value'' of the scarce resource.

short-term.   Current; ordinarily, due within one year.

short-term liquidity risk.   The risk that an entity will not have enough cash in the short run to pay its *debts*.

spending variance.   In *standard costing systems*, the *rate* or *price variance* for *overhead costs*.

splitoff point.   The point where all costs are no longer *joint costs* but an analyst can identify costs associated with individual products or perhaps with a smaller number of *joint products*.

spoilage.   See *abnormal spoilage* and *normal spoilage*.

standard cost.   Anticipated *cost* of producing a unit of output; a predetermined cost a firm assigns to products it produces. Standard cost implies a norm: what costs should be. Budgeted cost implies a forecast, something likely, but not necessarily a "should," as implied by a norm. Firms use standard costs as the benchmark for gauging good and bad performance. While a firm may similarly use a budget, it need not. A firm may simply use a budget as a planning document, subject to changes whenever plans change, whereas a firm would usually change standard costs annually or when technology significantly changes or costs of labor and materials significantly change.

standard costing.   *Costing* based on *standard costs*.

standard costing system.   *Product costing* using *standard costs* rather than actual costs. May be based on either *absorption* or *variable costing* principles.

standard error (of regression coefficients).   A measure of the uncertainty about the magnitude of the estimated parameters of an equation fit with a *regression analysis*.

standard manufacturing overhead.   *Overhead costs* a firm expects to incur per unit of time and per unit produced.

standard quantity allowed.   The quantity of direct material or direct labor (inputs) that production should have used if it produced the units of output in accordance with preset standards.

standby costs.   A type of *capacity cost*, such as property taxes, incurred even if a firm shuts down operations completely. Contrast with *enabling costs*.

statement of cash flows.   The *FASB* requires that all for-profit companies present a schedule of cash receipts and payments, classified by investing, financing, and operating activities. Companies may report operating activities with either the direct method (where only receipts and payments of cash appear) or the indirect method (which starts with *net income* and shows adjustments for *revenues* not currently producing cash and for *expenses* not currently using cash). "Cash" includes cash equivalents such as Treasury bills, commercial paper, and marketable securities held as *current assets*. Sometimes called the "funds statement." Before 1987, the FASB required the presentation of a similar statement called the statement of changes in financial position, which tended to emphasize *working capital*, not cash.

static budget.   *Fixed budget*.

status quo.   Events or costs incurrences that will happen or a firm expects to happen in the absence of taking some contemplated action.

step allocation method.   *Step-down method*.

step cost.   *Semifixed cost*.

step-down method.   The method for allocating service department costs that starts by allocating one service department's costs to *production departments* and to all other service departments. Then the firm allocates a second service department's costs, including costs allocated from the first, to production departments and to all other service departments except the first one. In this fashion, a firm may allocate the costs of all service departments, including previous allocations, to production departments and to those service departments whose costs it has not yet allocated.

stepped cost.   *Semifixed cost*.

stockout.   A firm needs a unit of *inventory* in production or to sell to a customer but it is unavailable.

stockout costs.   *Contribution margin* or other measure of profits not earned because a seller runs out of *inventory* and cannot fill a customer's order. A firm may incur an extra cost because of delay in filling an order.

summary of significant accounting principles.   *APB Opinion No. 22* requires that every annual report summarize the significant *accounting principles* used in compiling the annual report. A firm may present this summary as a separate exhibit or as the first note to the financial statements.

sunk cost.   *Cost* incurred in the past that current and future decisions cannot affect, and hence are irrelevant for decision making aside from income tax effects; contrast with *incremental costs* and imputed costs. For example, the acquisition cost of machinery is irrelevant to a decision of whether or not to scrap the machinery. The current exit value of the machine is the opportunity cost of continuing to own it and the cost of, say, electricity to run the machine is an incremental cost of its operation. Sunk costs become relevant for decision making when income taxes (gain or loss on disposal of asset) are taken into account because the cash payment for income taxes depends on the tax basis of the asset. Avoid the term in careful writing because it is ambiguous. Consider, for example, a machine costing $100,000 with current salvage value of $20,000. Some (including us) would say that $100,000 is "sunk"; others would say that only $80,000 is "sunk."

T

t-statistic.   For an estimated *regression* coefficient, the estimated coefficient divided by the *standard error* of the estimate.

t-value.   In *regression analysis*, the ratio of an estimated regression coefficient divided by its *standard error*.

time-series analysis.   See *cross-section analysis* for definition and contrast.

times-interest (charges) earned.   Ratio of pretax income plus *interest* charges to interest charges. See *ratio*.

total assets turnover.   Sales divided by average total *assets*.

traceable cost.   A *cost* that a firm can identify with or assign to a specific product; contrast with a *joint cost*.

trade secret.   Technical or business information such as formulas, recipes, computer programs, and marketing data not generally known by competitors and maintained by the firm as a secret. A famous example is the secret formula for Coca-Cola (a registered trademark of the company). Compare with *know-how*. Theoretically capable of having an infinite life, this intangible asset is capitalized only if purchased and then amortized over a period not to exceed 40 years. If the firm develops it internally, then it shows no asset.

transfer price.   A substitute for a market, or arm's length, price used in profit, or *responsibility center, accounting* when one segment of the business "sells" to another segment. Incentives of profit center managers will not coincide with the best interests of the entire business unless a firm sets transfer prices properly.

transfer pricing problem.   The problem of setting *transfer prices* so that both buyer and seller have *goal congruence* with respect to the parent organization's goals.

treasurer.   The name sometimes given to the chief financial officer of a business.

U

unavoidable cost.   A *cost* that is not an *avoidable cost*.

uncontrollable cost.   The opposite of *controllable cost*.

underapplied (underabsorbed) overhead.   An excess of actual *overhead costs* for a period over costs applied, or charged, to products produced during the period. A debit balance remaining in an overhead account after accounting assigns overhead to product.

unfavorable variance.   In *standard cost* accounting, an excess of expected revenue over actual revenue or an excess of actual cost over standard cost.

unqualified opinion.   See *auditor's report*.

usage variance.   *Efficiency variance*.

V

value.   Monetary worth; the term is usually so subjective that you should not use it without a modifying adjective unless most people would agree on the amount; do not confuse with cost.

value added.   *Cost* of a product or *work in process*, minus the cost of the material purchased for the product or work in process.

value variance.   *Price variance*.

variable annuity.   An *annuity* whose periodic payments depend on some uncertain outcome, such as stock market prices.

variable budget.   *Flexible budget*.

variable costing.   This method of allocating costs assigns only variable manufacturing costs to products and treats fixed manufacturing costs as *period expenses*. Contrast with *full absorption costing*.

variable overhead variance.   Difference between actual and standard variable overhead costs.

variance.   Difference between actual and *standard costs* or between *budgeted* and actual expenditures or, sometimes, *expenses*. The word's meaning differs completely in accounting and statistics, where it means a measure of dispersion of a distribution.

variance analysis (investigation).   The investigation of the causes of *variances* in a *standard costing system*. This term's meaning differs in statistics.

variance investigation.   *Standard costing systems* produce *variance* numbers of various sorts. These numbers seldom exactly equal zero. Management must decide when a variance differs sufficiently from zero to study its cause. This terms refers to deciding when to study the cause and the study itself.

visual curve fitting method.   Sometimes, when a firm needs only rough approximations to the amounts of *fixed* and *variable costs*, management need not perform a formal *regression analysis*, but merely plot the data and draw in a line by hand that seems to fit the data, using the parameters of that line for the rough approximations.

volume variance.   *Production volume variance*. Less often, used to mean sales volume variance.

W

waste.   Residue of material from manufacturing operations with no sale value. Frequently, it has negative value because a firm must incur additional costs for disposal.

weighted average.   An average computed by counting each occurrence of each value, not merely a single occurrence of each value. For example, if a firm purchases one unit for $1 and two units for $2 each, then the simple average of the purchase prices is $1.50 but the weighted average price per unit is $5/3 = $1.67. Contrast with *moving average*.

work in process (inventory account). Partially completed product; appears on the balance sheet as *inventory*.

working capital.   *Current assets* minus *current liabilities*.

Y

yield.   *Internal rate of return* of a stream of cash flows. Cash yield is cash flow divided by book value.

yield variance.   Measures the input-output relation holding the standard mix of inputs constant. It is the part of the *efficiency variance* not called the *mix variance*. It is (standard price multiplied by actual amount of input used in the standard mix) − (standard price multiplied by standard quantity allowed for the actual output).

Z

zero-base(d) budgeting. ZBB.   In preparing an ordinary *budget* for the next period, a manager starts with the budget for the current period and makes adjustments as seem necessary, because of changed conditions for the next period. Because most managers like to increase the scope of the activities managed and since most prices increase most of the time, amounts in budgets prepared in the ordinary, incremental way seem to increase period after period. The authority approving the budget assumes the firm will carry out operations in the same way as in the past and that next period's expenditures will be at least as large as the current period's. Thus, this authority tends to study only the increments to the current period's budget. In ZBB, the authority questions the process for carrying out a program and the entire budget for next period. The authority studies every dollar in the budget, not just the dollars incremental to the previous period's amounts. The advocates of ZBB claim that in this way (1) management will more likely delete programs or divisions of marginal benefit to the business or governmental unit from the program, rather than continuing with costs at least as large as the present ones, and (2) management may discover and implement alternative, more cost-effective ways of carrying out programs. ZBB implies questioning the existence of programs, and the fundamental nature of the way firms carry them out, not merely the amounts used to fund them. Experts appear to be evenly divided as to whether the middle word should be ''base'' or ''based.''

Index